The
Church
of England

Year Book

2000

The
Church
of England

Year Book

116th Edition

2000

Church House Publishing
Church House
Great Smith Street
London SW1P 3NZ

ISBN 0 7151 8108 4
ISSN 0069 3987

The Church of England Year Book

The Official Year Book of the General Synod of the Church of England

Editor: Jo Linzey

116th edition 2000 copyright © The Archbishops' Council 2000

Cover design by Visible Edge Ltd

Typeset by RefineCatch Ltd, Bungay, Suffolk
Printed and bound by Biddles Ltd, Guildford and King's Lynn

Contents

INDEX TO ADVERTISEMENTS

The inclusion of an advertisement is for purposes of information and is not to be taken as implying acceptance of the objects of the advertiser by the publisher.

The Book of Common Prayer

contains some of the most majestic and beautiful prose into the English language. Over the centuries it has been the repository of doctrine from which Anglican beliefs could be learned. A devotional power-house, the Book of Common Prayer is a deeply valued means of communication with our Maker.

The Prayer Book Society

★ seeks to defend and uphold that doctrine and to promote the worship enshrined in the Book of Common Prayer

★ does NOT propagate Prayer Book fundamentalism but believes a modest amount of flexibility in usage is both sensible and to be desired

The Prayer Book Society aims

★ to encourage the use of the Book of Common Prayer for the training of Ordinands and Confirmands

★ to spread knowledge of the Book of Common Prayer and the doctrine contained therein

★ to encourage use of the Book of Common Prayer for private and public worship in the new Millennium.

ARE YOU A REGULAR READER OF THE SOCIETY'S TWO MAGAZINES?

**ISSUES OF *'FAITH AND HERITAGE'* ALTERNATE WITH
*'FAITH AND WORSHIP'***

Please support

THE PRAYER BOOK SOCIETY

write now to:
PBS OFFICE, ST JAMES GARLICKHYTHE
GARLICK HILL, LONDON EC4V 2AF

"If only we could get away - just for a few days!"

HOW OFTEN we hear clergy say that. Living 'over the shop' is one of the main causes of clergy stress and breakdown. Just getting out of the house is a break. A proper holiday – which is what hard-pressed clergy really need – is beyond the reach of many of them.

The Friends of the Clergy Corporation gives holiday grants to clergy and their families in time of need. It also provides grants for general welfare, for school clothing, at times of retirement, resettlement, and bereavement, and during the trauma of marriage breakdown.

Grants of money cannot in themselves solve all the problems, but they can remove some of the causes of stress. And occupational stress affects the clergy probably more than anyone else in the community.

Please help us to continue this work – with a donation or covenant – and by remembering the Corporation in your Will. And if you, or someone you know, needs our help, do get in touch with the Secretary.

THE FRIENDS OF THE CLERGY CORPORATION

27 Medway Street, Westminster, London SW1P 2BD. *Tel.* 020 7222 2288.
e-mail: focc@btinternet.com Registered Charity 264724.

Symbols of Success

Royal College of Surgeons of Edinburgh

Christ Church Cathedral

Royal Free Hospital School of Medicine

UMIST

Belfast Cathedrals' Partnership

PolioPlus

The Nottingham Trent University

The University of Liverpool

Church House Bookshop

Church House Bookshop is one of the largest religious booksellers in the UK. Its stock has been carefully chosen to meet the needs of ordained and lay members of the Anglican Church including:

- Complete range of books, reports, disks and other items produced by Church House Publishing;

- Over 15,000 books, newspapers and magazines produced by other publishers;

- Comprehensive range of software, stationery items, candles, advent calendars, crib sets, posters, gifts, wafers and greeting cards;

- Christian Bookseller of the Year 1998.

Based at the Church of England's administrative headquarters in London, **Church House Bookshop** is fully equipped to provide you with a fast, efficient mail order service whatever your requirements, and wherever you live.

SEE ALSO OUR ONLINE BOOKSHOP:
www.chbookshop.co.uk

Church House Bookshop
31 Great Smith Street, London SW1P 3BN
Tel: 020 7898 1300 Fax: 020 7898 1305
Email: bookshop@c-of-e.org.uk
Web: www.chbookshop.co.uk

CHURCH HOUSE
BOOKSHOP

COMMON WORSHIP

As the new millennium begins, the Church of England is unveiling a new generation of liturgy that brings together many diverse styles. Known as *Common Worship*, the material is a mixture of old and new that promises much for the collective worship and life of the Church. The material will replace *The Alternative Service Book 1980*, which ceases to be authorized after 31 December 2000.

email: common.worship@c-of-e.org.uk
web site: www.cofe.anglican.org/commonworship/

Information Online
You can visit the Church of England web site and get the latest information on *Common Worship* as well as resources for your church and the full text of all material published so far.

November 2000
All of the official *Common Worship* publications are being published by **Church House Publishing**.

Publications available
The material for *Calendar, Lectionary and Collects* and *Initiation Services* has already been authorized and published in interim editions. Please contact your local bookshop or in case of difficulty, Church House Bookshop on 020 7898 1300 or by email to bookshop@c-of-e.org.uk.

Church House Publishing, Church House, Great Smith Street, London, SW1P 3NZ
Phone 020 7898 1451 Fax 020 7898 1449
Email publishing@c-of-e.org.uk Web www.chpublishing.co.uk

CHURCH HOUSE
PUBLISHING

For the nation-wide work of the Church of England

The Central Church Fund is unique. It is the *only* fund available for the general purposes of the Church of England as a whole.

It helps parishes and dioceses with imaginative and innovative projects of all kinds – and especially those that meet the needs of local communities.

It provides for training for ministry in the Church (donations and bequests can be directed specifically for this purpose).

It makes money available for those unexpected and urgent needs which cannot be budgeted for.

As a general purpose Fund, its flexibility allows it to provide, without delay, for a host of needs that no other fund is geared to cope with, and its value in this way to the Church of England is incalculable.

There are inevitably many calls upon it and funds are always urgently needed. Please help with your donation, covenanted subscription or bequest – or find out more from the Secretary.

The Central Church Fund

The Central Board of Finance of the Church of England, Church House, Great Smith Street, Westminster, London SW1P 3NZ. *Tel.* 020 7898 1000. *Registered Charity 248711*

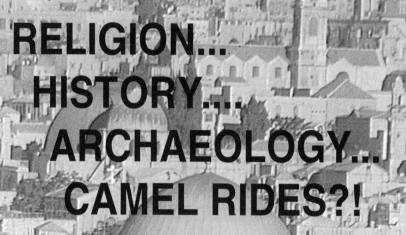

REVIEW OF THE YEAR 1999

A Personal View by Michael Perham

WHERE IS THE CHURCH OF ENGLAND?

'Good morning – the Church of England,' says the switchboard operator cheerily before trying to put the caller through to the appropriate department or official in Church House, Westminster, or at the Church Commissioners or Pensions Board. On the other end of the line the response may be less than friendly. For the Bishop of X or the Vicar of Y believes strongly that the Church of England is not located (at least not most of it) in Westminster, but in parishes and dioceses up and down the land. One may sympathize with both parties. Of course the switchboard operator is using a kind of shorthand; she is not claiming that her switchboard has lines to every part of the Church of England. Yet she is claiming for the central organization a vital part in the life of the Church. The truth is that the centre needs the dioceses and the parishes (indeed at a certain level it exists simply to service them), but also that the dioceses and parishes need the central organization. It is too easy to knock the centre, to blame it for the Church's failures and to accuse it of extravagance, even though its staff carry immense burdens, not least because financial constraints mean that they are under-resourced for the tasks we ask of them.

The ideal world in which local churches see virtue and merit in the central organization and are inspired by its leadership is probably not attainable. There will always be a local scepticism about those who develop a national vision and strategy for the Church. 'Them' and 'us' is not entirely avoidable. But in 1999 the Church of England put into place a new structure designed at least in part to usher in a new partnership between the national and the local and to provide a more focused leadership that could make things happen in a Church where decisive decision-making has for so long seemed difficult.

THE ARCHBISHOPS' COUNCIL

The Archbishops' Council came into existence on 1 January 1999. Its membership (which includes the present reviewer) is a good mixture of experience and new blood, the latter provided particularly through the six members nominated by the Archbishops after a process designed to find a membership that would bring breadth and new perceptions to the Council.

The Council has the task of providing strategic leadership for the Church. In so doing it has to face two basic challenges. The first is that its inherited management role – the responsibilities it has taken over from other bodies – could absorb all its time and energy. There is evidence that it is approaching this management task with a freshness and a concern for 'joined up thinking' that is already beginning to benefit the Church. But the management requirements could easily squeeze out the strategic leadership that is needed. Meanwhile the other challenge is that any talk of leadership has to be articulated with immense sensitivity. For leadership in the Church is properly exercised also by the House of Bishops collectively, by the General Synod, by the individual bishop in his diocese. How does the Archbishops' Council exercise a leadership that does give the Church a sharper strategy and which does not take to itself powers and responsibilities that belong elsewhere?

The Council's approach has laid particular emphasis on the concept of 'servant leadership' and tried to explore what that means in practical terms. Canon Hugh

Wilcox warned in last year's *Review of the Year* that 'those who are called on to become the Council and to serve as its officers will need to beware of the temptations to arrogance which come with power.' 'Power' is not a word one hears used in the Council and it would be surprising if the Council had earned a reputation for arrogance in its early months. There has been some scorn poured on its 'listening programme' to discover through focus groups what people inside and outside worshipping congregations say about the Church, but listening, more than exercising power, has been the Council's style. Those who knew the old Synod Standing Committee and other bodies say that the Archbishops' Council has a quite different atmosphere. For the listening begins with listening to one another and some of the factional rivalries of the past seem genuinely to have disappeared, not least because the Council spends a significant part of its time in prayer, Bible study and reflection, which gives a particular character to the business sessions that follow.

That style has been established through the personal contribution of the two archbishops. The decision during the Turnbull process to have an 'Archbishops' Council', rather than a 'National Council', was a wise one; not only because it affirms the episcopal leadership of the Church, but because it provides the archbishops with a creative setting to exercise their leadership and to take counsel. The fact that both archbishops have found that the Council has not added to their work-load, but has provided support and encouragement for their ministry, is one of the most pleasing results to have emerged from the Council's early months.

But the jury is, rightly, still out on the work of the Council. In July the General Synod gave a warm and encouraging response to the presentation of the Council's first report. But that report could not at that stage present big and brave decisions. It could only indicate a new style, present a vision of a united, confident and outward-looking Church, indicate its purposes and values and spell out twelve priority areas. The report represented a careful and thoughtful start. For most of the members there has also been the mastering of a very broad and demanding brief. But early in 2000 the Church will rightly look for challenges faced and decisions made. The Council is well on the way to having a complete overview of the Church's finance. But what policy decisions will need to emerge from that in terms of priorities and human resources? And what new areas of work may need to open up (and others close down) in response to real strategic thinking? Longer term a fascinating question is whether the Council, with its emphasis on 'servant leadership', can model a better way of engaging, living with disagreement and deciding policy that will begin to change the way the General Synod works. That ought to work its way through in time, for the officers of all three Houses of the Synod are key members of the Council. Can 'servant leadership' become a mark of the General Synod too?

THE GENERAL SYNOD

The General Synod did not meet in February 1999. This was almost certainly a mistake, for the weight of liturgical business in preparation for *Common Worship* revealed a need for a February Group of Sessions if the business were to be done with proper debate of important issues and without hurry. If the Synod is to meet less often, there needs to be a slimmer agenda and this can only be achieved by finding a different way of doing some of the detailed legislative and liturgical business that at present has to be done in a full session of the Synod. The Synod did meet for the maximum time in July at York and in November in London. There were high points that caught the attention of the national media, but not many. The television lights were rarely on. The Synod ploughed its way through its detailed agenda. The question arises – indeed it arises in the debate on the agenda at every Synod – whether it can be right for the Church to be addressing issues that seem strangely irrelevant to the secular press and the wider world in general. Certainly the synodical agenda is usually more concerned with Church issues than 'kingdom' issues. 'Is it worth me coming to York?' asked a radio reporter at a party for the press given by the Archbishops' Council. The truth is that the Synod is often at its best when quietly and unspectacularly getting on with painstaking legislation that needs to be done if the Church is to be equipped for its mission. People work at the detail that needs to be right. It doesn't thrill them any more than it does the press or the public, but there is a proper sense of duty in trying to get it right. There will be moments when the Synod engages naturally and passionately with a national or international issue because the time is ripe and the media will cover the debate fully. Such moments are important, but we need to be wary both of creating debates simply to present a relevant Church and also of undervaluing the careful 'house-keeping' role the Synod needs to exercise without commanding attention.

One area of crucial national importance where the Synod needs to speak with a clear voice is in relation to racism, and to the Church's own racism. The subject has been on the Church's agenda through the year, not least in response to Sir William Macpherson's report on the death of Stephen Lawrence. The key part played by John Sentamu, Bishop of Stepney, has been a matter of pride for the Church, but Bishop Sentamu himself has taken every opportunity to challenge the Church to engage with the issue seriously. He spoke passionately and critically to the Archbishops' Council and to the July Synod. The Synod and the Council are committed to returning to the issue with a determination to see the matter thoroughly addressed.

COMMON WORSHIP

The General Synod and its Revision Committees have spent much time during 1999 on the services that will replace *The Alternative Service Book 1980.* It is important to say that it is the General Synod that has done this, for the time when the Liturgical Commission was in the driving seat is well past. The Commission's work is several stages earlier, and the most creative period in the Commission was in the mid, not the late, 1990s. Once drafted, the new services reach their final shape through moulding and modification in the House of Bishops, in the Revision Committees (composed entirely of members of the Synod, with the liturgists very much in the minority) and even on the floor of the General Synod itself. The General Synod, though it complains (understandably) at the sheer paper weight of draft material, takes its liturgical role seriously, recognizing that much more than good services are at stake. There is always an eye to the mission potential of the texts. Perhaps even more crucially for some there is a concern to avoid any subtle doctrinal shift.

Almost inevitably the result of the synodical process is that, although the service probably emerges with an overall improvement, it will have grown more wordy and more optional material will have been made mandatory, all in the interests of preserving balanced doctrine. In 1999 the Synod has wrestled with the new eucharistic rites, with eucharistic prayers and with marriage and funeral liturgies, besides such detailed provisions as weekday lectionaries and 'rules to order the service'. In relation to the eucharistic rites, it has allowed through a fairly modest revision without too much synodical reworking. With the eucharistic prayers, doctrinal differences, such as the existence of, or position of, the *epiclesis* (the prayer that articulates the Holy Spirit's action in relation to the elements and the people) have been worked through with an openness that would have been surprising in earlier Synods. The sticking points have been much more about the style, language and length of the prayers. The marriage rite emerged richer and better than that in 1980, but without any radical departure from the intention then, and the funeral rites, which represent a much more radical rethinking of structure and text, came through their synodical stages with agreement in an area that in the past has been one of real doctrinal division. It is difficult in a Church where the majority believes prayer for the departed to be the most natural thing, but a significant minority believes it contrary to scripture and to sound doctrine, to find texts which have weight and which all can accept with integrity. The fact that it has happened is an encouragement to those who have to resolve those areas where that sort of consensus has yet to be achieved.

THE BISHOPS: LITURGY, DOCTRINE AND MARRIAGE

Two areas of disagreement have been the contemporary translations of the Lord's Prayer, where the Synod declined to go with the international 'time of trial', and of the Nicene Creed, where the translation 'of the Holy Spirit and the Virgin Mary' provoked a series of debates of high theological calibre, but where entrenched positions seemed unassailable. Neither were at heart liturgical issues, though they arose in the course of approving liturgical texts. The Lord's Prayer was essentially about the meaning of scripture, the Creed the interpretation of doctrine. The particular issues in each case are not properly part of this review, but more broadly they revealed again (especially in relation to the debate on the Creed) the tension surrounding the role of the House of Bishops in relation to doctrine. The House of Bishops, increasingly collegial in its approach, and prepared to spend more time wrestling with doctrinal issues together in a way it did not in the past, is prepared to be seen exercising the special role in relation to doctrine that the Synod constitution recognizes and gave a clear and all but unanimous lead in commending the ELLC (English Language Liturgical Consultation) text of the Creed to the Synod. The Synod, or more particularly a significant minority of the House of Laity, was either unconvinced by the bishops' line of argument or else suspicious of their attempt to lead in this area of synodical decision making. Although it is probably an overgeneralization, we seem to be a Church where the clergy are willing to allow the bishops a special place in the defining of doctrine, but where a substantial number of the laity – at least in the Synod – do not recognize the particular responsibility of the bishops to be the 'guardians of the faith'. This is an area that needs to be explored. It is in itself a theological question. The bishops' higher profile in doctrinal debate is much to be welcomed and sometimes earlier intervention would be helpful, long before things have begun to go wrong and the Synod needs to be rescued. Many would welcome a clear theological lead from the bishops at every stage of a wide range of debates.

One area into which the bishops have entered with real seriousness is the question of Christian understanding of marriage in our contemporary society. The publication in September of their teaching document on marriage,[1] timed to present Christian theology and ethics in a clear principled way, before entering into a particular issue in the report on marriage in church after divorce (by a Working Party chaired by the Bishop of Winchester), was welcome for at least three reasons. First it is an impressive document – well written, concise without being over-simple, principled with a pastoral heart and addressing with relevance areas where the Church is often thought to be hopelessly out of touch. Secondly its launch was well handled. Despite a poor headline or two, what the bishops were saying was widely and accurately reported and given a sympathetic reception. Thirdly the document provides a model. Here is a document that will serve equally well in a Synod debate, in a marriage preparation class, in a school PSE (Personal and Social Education) lesson, and that speaks authoritatively, yet with sensitivity and humility. It is a new style of presentation and

1. *Marriage*, A Teaching Document from the House of Bishops of the Church of England (Church House Publishing, 1999).

lessons can be learnt from it for those areas where the Church's message needs to be presented afresh.

CHURCHWARDENS, COMMONS AND LORDS

One area of Church life that was clearly not as well handled was the Church-wardens Measure. The parliamentary Ecclesiastical Committee indicated that it would not be able to find the Measure as it stood 'expedient'. The controversy was entirely around Clause 9, which would have granted the bishops the right to suspend a churchwarden 'for any cause which appears to [the Bishop] to be good and reason-able' and allow them to appoint someone else to take over the warden's duties. The Ecclesiastical Committee wanted the circumstances under which a church-warden could be suspended to be defined much more precisely. The General Synod reconsidered the matter in July. It would have been possible to set up a confrontation with Parliament. But the truth was that the majority perceived that the Ecclesiastical Committee was right in relation to this clause. The Synod had allowed an inadequate draft to go through and was ready to modify its proposal. The lesson to be learnt is that the role of Parliament, though sometimes tiresome, may on occasions help the Church to refine its legislation.

1999 also saw the publication of the Church's submission in relation to the place of the bishops in a revised second chamber.[2] That the government's own proposals should envisage a continuing place for the Church of England in such a chamber, alongside some representation of other Churches and faith communities if that is achievable, is welcome: both for the wisdom that bishops will continue to bring as they reflect the insights of their dioceses, and also for its affirmation of a Church/State partnership which, only a few years ago, seemed to be crumbling.

CATHEDRALS AND CHURCH BUILDINGS

Whereas the Churchwardens Measure ran into trouble, the Cathedrals Measure, des-pite a rough ride, received the Royal Assent in June. The Measure requires each cathedral to draw up a new constitution and set of statutes within a framework defined by the Measure that increases accountability, places executive power within a Chapter that will include lay people as well as the dean and canons, and ought to provide structures that will enable cathedrals to fulfil more effectively their calling to be 'the seat of the bishop and a centre of worship and mission'. A few highly publi-cized confrontations sometimes give cathedrals a bad name. The reality is that many of our cathedrals are more alive to their potential for mission than at any previous point in their history and cathedrals defy all the statistics of church decline. Although a few regret some of the changes the Measure will impose, most have seen the exercise of rewriting the constitution as the opportunity to create a structure for growth and service. About the beginning of 2000 the first of these new constitutions and statutes will come into force and cathedrals will enter a new and exciting era.

The rough ride before the Royal Assent was entirely because the 'royal peculiars' did not fall within the terms of the Measure. In the light of the troubles at Westmin-ster Abbey, mainly in relation to the dismissal of the organist, and the extraordinary vilification of the Dean of Westminster in the press, it is clearly desirable that there be an opportunity for the royal peculiars also to have the opportunity to review their way of working. A commission, chaired by Professor Averil Cameron, the Warden of Keble College, Oxford, has been appointed and is looking into the organization, management and accountability of the royal foundations.

If this is an area where confidence needs rebuilding, the care of more than twelve thousand listed buildings is a responsibility about which the Church has every

2. *The Role of Bishops in the Second Chamber: A Submission by the Church of England* (GS Misc 558), May 1999.

reason to be confident and proud. The Church Heritage Forum, chaired by the Bishop of London, bringing together those organizations and agencies that are concerned with the Church's responsibility for a major part of the nation's 'built heritage', is sounding a confident note, for we have much of which to be proud. We are, in a sense, a second 'National Trust', caring for buildings with real commitment of time, financial resources and dedication, with good opening hours in many cases and free or almost free entry. As such we need to assert our place and see that we are taken seriously nationally and regionally where heritage issues are under review and decisions made about funding.

ECUMENISM

Partnership with other Churches has continued to be on the Church's agenda. The death in June of Cardinal Basil Hume touched many Christians outside his own Church. The chief memory Anglicans will have of him is of a man of real holiness, with a Benedictine spirituality that resonated with Anglicanism, who was always gracious in his dealings with other Christians, and who was pastorally wise in the way he received those in the Church of England who could not accept the ordination of women to the priesthood. Relationships between Roman Catholics and other Christians in England had been transformed during his time as Archbishop of Westminster and his own part in that change had been crucial.

The Archbishop of Canterbury visited Rome and the Pope in February. This visit did not attract as much media interest as some in the past, and the very naturalness of such visits is a sign of how ecumenism has moved forward. The visit paved the way for a May 2000 meeting of Anglican and Roman Catholic leaders to plan future joint work. Meanwhile *The Gift of Authority*, the report of ARCIC II, the Anglican-Roman Catholic International Commission, was published in May. Engaging as it does with the issue of 'universal primacy', it will need to be explored by the churches with immense sensitivity and a willingness to work, as the report does, at getting behind the language that divides.

Meanwhile, those conducting the Formal Conversations between the Church of England and the Methodist Church began their work in 1999. They are mandated by the General Synod and the Methodist Conference to work out a new relationship on the way to full visible unity, which remains the Church of England's ultimate ecumenical goal.

GOOD NEWS

In a church that has sometimes seemed determined to do itself down, there has been much good news during the year. Much was rightly made of the increase of ordinands that was clearly not simply a 'blip', and of the fact that the increase included a growth in the number accepted for full-time training in colleges and stipendiary ministry after ordination. We may still need to develop a clearer national policy for the ministry of the whole people of God, laity and clergy in the right kind of partnerships, but the increases indicate a Church with growing confidence.

There was good news in the tremendous enthusiasm for the Archbishop of Canterbury's initiative, 'The Time of Our Lives', when between three and four thousand young Anglicans joined the bishops and a host of youth leaders and volunteers for what clearly was an unforgettable weekend in London. Occasions like these always raise the spirits and increase the faith of those who participate in them, but the good can easily fizzle out. New diocesan initiatives late in the year were designed to ensure that 'The Time of Our Lives' will not be a one-off fun weekend, but the beginning of a change of culture that will see the Church of England taking young people more seriously. The Archbishops' Council is also committed to youth evangelism and will be seeking ways to support and encourage it.

The Anglican Conference on Evangelism at Swanwick in March was also an important turning point. It looked back as the Decade of Evangelism comes to an end. It has always been possible to be dismissive of the decade and there are statistics that offer little encouragement. But there has been an important shift during this period. Expressed most simply, it is the move from where, at the beginning of the decade, evangelism was a word little heard in the majority of parishes, to the present day, where even when people are uncertain how best to evangelize, churches recognize it as a key priority. Alpha, Emmaus, Credo, Springboard all have their part to play. The Board of Mission has its strategies. But, most important, as we enter the third Christian millennium, the 'e-word' is back on the lips of ordinary Church people.

Last but not least when it comes to good news is the emphasis on more effective communications. We have knowledgeable groups of 'lead bishops' ready and trained to speak for the Church on major issues and diocesan communications officers are now a significant part of a national communications strategy. Another more dramatic example is the Church of England web site: www.cofe.anglican.org. The site receives more than half a million hits a month. And now the Council is inviting everyone of our 16,000 churches to put up details about themselves and their services on the web, via *ChurchSearch*. So alongside all the old ways of telling the good news, most of which still have a lot of life in them, there are new ones that every parish needs to take on board.

COMINGS AND GOINGS
The creation of the Archbishops' Council coincided with a number of changes among the key lay people on whom the Church of England relies. Last year's review noted the retirement of Alan McLintock as Chairman of the Central Board of Finance, and his service there was rightly recognized in the conferring of a knighthood. Early in 1999, this was followed by the retirement of Sir Michael Colman and of Mrs Margaret Laird as the First and Third Estates Commissioners respectively. Although Sir Michael was never entirely relaxed at the dispatch box, the Synod soon recognized that it had in him exactly the right man to help the Commissioners recover from their difficulties early in the decade and to establish new working practices. His seven years turned the Commissioners round in a way that has won admiration and praise. Margaret Laird served for ten years as Third Estates Commissioner, taking the Synod through detailed business associated with the various aspects of the Pastoral Measure with immense patience and courtesy.

Another retirement, this one not so much in the public eye, has been that of Viscount Churchill. Victor Churchill served for 25 years as Investment Manager for the CBF Church of England Funds and gave of his time and expertise very generously to the Church of England, instilling confidence in all who met him that Church of England investments were in safe hands and performing well through some difficult times. John Holroyd also retired. He had served for six years as the Prime Minister's Appointments Secretary. Thus he was not employed by the Church, but worked with it, taking immense care with his part in the appointment of bishops and deans. During his period of office there was a recognition that there was a greater openness in appointments and a genuine desire to hear what sort of appointment was needed in each case.

A number of diocesan bishops also retired: Patrick Harris from Southwell, Peter Nott from Norwich, Hewlett Thompson from Exeter and David Young from Ripon. David Young, the second-longest serving diocesan (22 years Bishop of Ripon), has spearheaded the Church's involvement in education with quiet skill through many years. Stephen Sykes' move cannot be regarded as a retirement, but he leaves the see of Ely for the principalship of St John's College Durham, where it is much to be hoped that his duties will leave him time to continue contributing to Anglican theological thinking, where his contribution has been crucial in recent years. He will remain Chairman of the Doctrine Commission. George Austin has also retired – not a bishop, though sometimes thought by the press to be the Arch*bishop* of York. George Austin, in reality the Arch*deacon* of York, has been a high profile commentator on Church of England affairs for more than a decade. Suspecting a liberal plot in almost everything, he has been a staunch, and sometimes humorous, defender of things conservative and catholic. Always willing to produce a quotable quote for the media, he has sworn to be quiet in retirement. We shall miss his sound-bites.

1999 saw the death of a number of loyal servants of the Church of England in their retirement. Four prominent lay people from an earlier generation of leadership – Valerie Pitt, one of the most devoted and theologically alert lay people throughout her life, but especially active in the Church Assembly in the 1960s; Christian Howard, who was a giant figure of the early days of synodical government and played a crucial role in the move towards the ordination of women to the priesthood; Sir James Cobban, with a speaking voice never to be forgotten, who was also one of the stars of the Synod in its early days and a columnist of great perception; and Sir William van Straubenzee MBE, for some years Second Estates Commissioner, who served the Church of England with distinction in Parliament, Synod and the Dioceses' Commission. Kenneth Riches died, aged 90, 25 years after his retirement as a distinguished Bishop of Lincoln, and Cyril Bowles 12 years after his retirement from the see of Derby. Both had been theological college principals (Riches at Cuddesdon in the forties, Bowles at Ridley Hall in the sixties) with a profound influence on the men they had trained. Bill Westwood enjoyed only a short retirement after his years as Bishop of Peterborough, 'Margaret Thatcher's bishop' as he became known, an independent commentator with a passion for good communications, a radio bishop if ever there was one. W.H. (Bill) Vanstone also died, probably the most academically able priest of his generation (so Robert Runcie reckoned him), who eschewed academic life and ecclesiastical preferment for the life of a parish priest and gave the Church in *Love's Endeavour Love's Expense* one of the theological classics of the twentieth century.

In 1999 Tim Stevens was appointed Bishop of Leicester, George Cassidy of Southwell, Graham James of Norwich, Michael Langrish of Exeter, and Stephen Venner as 'Bishop in Canterbury' to carry most of the Archbishop's diocesan workload. John Sclater, banker and landowner, became First Estates Commissioner, Gill (Viscountess) Brentford the latest in a long line of distinguished women Third Estates Commissioners.

THIS IS THE CHURCH OF ENGLAND

Yet the people who thought the switchboard operator's shorthand was wide of the mark have a point. The Church of England is at its most authentic, its most infuriating, its most lovable, and its most faithful in thousands of parishes up and down the land. Here priest and people are intent on saying their prayers, responding to appeals, such as those in 1999 to welcome Kosovo refugees suddenly on their doorstep, maintaining their church building, searching for new ways to commend the gospel and planning to use the millennium to make some fresh impact in the community. There's plenty of good news there too, as well as some new servant leadership at the centre.

The Very Reverend Michael Perham is Provost of Derby, has been a member of General Synod from 1989–92 and since 1993, and is a member of the Liturgical Commission and the Cathedrals Fabric Commission. From 1 January 1999 he has been a member of the Archbishops' Council.

The views expressed in the review are personal ones and should not be construed as expressing the policy of the Church of England.

CALENDAR 2000–2001

According to the Calendar, Lectionary and Collects authorized pursuant to Canon B 2 of the Canons of the Church of England for use from 30 November 1997 until further resolution of the General Synod of the Church of England.

Key

BOLD UPPER CASE – Principal Feasts and other Principal Holy Days
Bold Roman – Sundays and Festivals
Roman – Lesser Festivals
Small Italic – Commemorations
Italic – Other Observances

JANUARY

1 **The Naming and Circumcision of Jesus**
2 **The Second Sunday of Christmas**
   (*or* **THE EPIPHANY** *if transferred from 6 January*)
6 **THE EPIPHANY**
9 **The Baptism of Christ** – *The First Sunday of Epiphany*
10 *William Laud, Archbishop of Canterbury, 1645*
11 *Mary Slessor, Missionary in West Africa, 1915*
12 Aelred of Hexham, Abbot of Rievaulx, 1167
   Benedict Biscop, Abbot of Wearmouth, Scholar, 689
13 Hilary, Bishop of Poitiers, Teacher of the Faith, 367
   Kentigern (Mungo), Missionary Bishop in Strathclyde and Cumbria, 603
   George Fox, Founder of the Society of Friends (the Quakers), 1691
16 **The Second Sunday of Epiphany**
17 Antony of Egypt, Hermit, Abbot, 356
   Charles Gore, Bishop, Founder of the Community of the Resurrection, 1932
18 *Week of Prayer for Christian Unity until 25th*
19 Wulfstan, Bishop of Worcester, 1095
20 *Richard Rolle of Hampole, Spiritual Writer, 1349*
21 Agnes, Child-Martyr at Rome, 304
22 *Vincent of Saragossa, Deacon, first Martyr of Spain, 304*
23 **The Third Sunday of Epiphany**
24 Francis de Sales, Bishop of Geneva, Teacher of the Faith, 1622
25 **The Conversion of Paul**
26 Timothy and Titus, Companions of Paul
28 Thomas Aquinas, Priest, Philosopher, Teacher of the Faith, 1274
30 **The Fourth Sunday of Epiphany**
   (*or* **THE PRESENTATION OF CHRIST IN THE TEMPLE** *if transferred from 2 February*)
31 *John Bosco, Priest, Founder of the Salesian Teaching Order, 1888*

FEBRUARY

1 *Brigid, Abbess of Kildare, c.525*
2 **THE PRESENTATION OF CHRIST IN THE TEMPLE — CANDLEMAS**
3 Anskar, Archbishop of Hamburg, Missionary in Denmark and Sweden, 865
4 *Gilbert of Sempringham, Founder of the Gilbertine Order, 1189*
6 **The Fifth Sunday before Lent**
10 *Scholastica, sister of Benedict, Abbess of Plombariola, c.543*
13 **The Fourth Sunday before Lent**
14 Cyril and Methodius, Missionaries to the Slavs, 869 and 885
   Valentine, Martyr at Rome, c.269
15 *Sigfrid, Bishop, Apostle of Sweden, 1045*
   Thomas Bray, Priest, Founder of the SPCK and the SPG, 1730
17 Janani Luwum, Archbishop of Uganda, Martyr, 1977
20 **The Third Sunday before Lent**
23 Polycarp, Bishop of Smyrna, Martyr, c.155
27 **The Second Sunday before Lent**

MARCH

1 David, Bishop of Menevia, Patron of Wales, c.601
2 Chad, Bishop of Lichfield, Missionary, 672
5 **The Sunday next before Lent**
7 Perpetua, Felicity and their Companions, Martyrs at Carthage, 203
8 **ASH WEDNESDAY**
12 **The First Sunday of Lent**
17 Patrick, Bishop, Missionary, Patron of Ireland, c.460
18 *Cyril, Bishop of Jerusalem, Teacher of the Faith, 386*
19 **The Second Sunday of Lent**
20 **Joseph of Nazareth** (*transferred from 19 March*)
21 Thomas Cranmer, Archbishop of Canterbury, Reformation Martyr, 1556
24 *Walter Hilton of Thurgarton, Augustinian Canon, Mystic, 1396*
   Oscar Romero, Archbishop of San Salvador, Martyr, 1980
25 **THE ANNUNCIATION OF OUR LORD TO THE BLESSED VIRGIN MARY**
26 **The Third Sunday of Lent**
31 *John Donne, Priest, Poet, 1631*

APRIL

1 *Frederick Denison Maurice, Priest, Teacher of the Faith, 1872*

2 **The Fourth Sunday of Lent**
Mothering Sunday
9 **The Fifth Sunday of Lent**
10 William Law, Priest, Spiritual Writer, 1761
William of Ockham, Friar, Philosopher, Teacher of the Faith, 1347
11 *George Augustus Selwyn, First Bishop of New Zealand, 1878*
16 **Palm Sunday**
17 Monday in Holy Week
18 Tuesday in Holy Week
19 Wednesday in Holy Week
20 **MAUNDY THURSDAY**
21 **GOOD FRIDAY**
22 Easter Eve
23 **EASTER DAY**
24 Monday in Easter Week
25 Tuesday in Easter Week
26 Wednesday in Easter Week
27 Thursday in Easter Week
28 Friday in Easter Week
29 Saturday in Easter Week
30 **The Second Sunday of Easter**

MAY
1 **Philip and James, Apostles**
2 **George, Martyr, Patron of England, c.304** (*transferred from 23 April*)
3 **Mark the Evangelist** (*transferred from 25 April*)
4 **English Saints and Martyrs of the Reformation Era**
7 **The Third Sunday of Easter**
8 Julian of Norwich, Sprirutal Writer, c.1417
14 **The Fourth Sunday of Easter**
15 **Matthias the Apostle** (*transferred from 14 May*)
16 *Caroline Chisholm, Social Reformer, 1877*
19 Dunstan, Archbishop of Canterbury, Restorer of Monastic Life, 988
20 Alcuin of York, Deacon, Abbot of Tours, 804
21 **The Fifth Sunday of Easter**
23 *Petroc, Abbot of Padstow, 6th century*
24 John and Charles Wesley, Evangelists, Hymn Writers, 1791 and 1788
25 The Venerable Bede, Monk at Jarrow, Scholar, Historian, 735
Aldhelm, Bishop of Sherborne, 709
26 Augustine, first Archbishop of Canterbury, 605
John Calvin, Reformer, 1564
Philip Neri, Founder of the Oratorians, Spiritual Guide, 1595
28 **The Sixth Sunday of Easter**
30 Josephine Butler, Social Reformer, 1906
Joan of Arc, Visionary, 1431
Apolo Kivebulaya, Priest, Evangelist in Central Africa, 1933
31 **The Visit of the Blessed Virgin Mary to Elizabeth**

JUNE
1 **ASCENSION DAY**

2 *From Friday after Ascension Day begin the nine days of prayer before Pentecost*
3 *The Martyrs of Uganda, 1886 and 1978*
4 **The Seventh Sunday of Easter** — *Sunday after Ascension Day*
5 Boniface (Wynfrith) of Crediton, Bishop, Apostle of Germany, Martyr, 754
6 *Ini Kopuria, Founder of the Melanesian Brotherhood, 1945*
8 Thomas Ken, Bishop of Bath and Wells, Non-Juror, Hymn Writer, 1711
9 Columba, Abbot of Iona, Missionary, 597
Ephrem of Syria, Deacon, Hymn Writer, Teacher of the Faith, 373
11 **PENTECOST**
12 **Barnabas the Apostle** (*transferred from 11 June*)
14 *Richard Baxter, Puritan Divine, 1691*
15 *Evelyn Underhill, Spiritual Writer, 1941*
16 Richard, Bishop of Chichester, 1253
Joseph Butler, Bishop of Durham, Philosopher, 1752
17 *Samuel and Henrietta Barnett, Social Reformers, 1913 and 1936*
18 **TRINITY SUNDAY**
19 *Sundar Singh of India, Sadhu (Holy Man), Evangelist, Teacher of the Faith, 1929*
22 **The Day of Thanksgiving for the Initiation of Holy Communion (Corpus Christi)** or Alban, first Martyr of Britain, c.250
23 Etheldreda, Abbess of Ely, c.678
24 **The Birth of John the Baptist**
25 **The First Sunday after Trinity**
27 *Cyril, Bishop of Alexandriaa, Teacher of the Faith, 444*
28 Irenæus, Bishop of Lyons, Teacher of the Faith, c.200
29 **Peter and Paul, Apostles** *or* **Peter the Apostle**

JULY
1 *John and Henry Venn, Priests, Evangelical Divines, 1813 and 1873*
2 **The Second Sunday after Trinity**
3 **Thomas the Apostle**
6 *Thomas More, Scholar, and John Fisher, Bishop of Rochester, Reformation Martyrs, 1535*
9 **The Third Sunday after Trinity**
11 Benedict of Nursia, Abbot of Monte Cassino, Father of Western Monasticism, c.550
14 John Keble, Priest, Tractarian, Poet, 1866
15 Swithun, Bishop of Winchester, c.862
Bonaventure, Friar, Bishop, Teacher of the Faith, 1274
16 **The Fourth Sunday after Trinity**
18 *Elizabeth Ferard, First Deaconess of the Church of England, 1883*
19 Gregory, Bishop of Nyssa, and his sister Macrina, Deaconess, Teachers of the Faith, 394 and 379
20 *Margaret of Antioch, Martyr, 4th Century*
Bartolomé de las Casas, Apostle to the Indies, 1566
22 **Mary Magdalene**
23 **The Fifth Sunday after Trinity**
25 **James the Apostle**
26 Anne and Joachim, Parents of the Blessed Virgin Mary

27 *Brooke Foss Westcott, Bishop of Durham, Teacher of the Faith, 1901*

29 Mary, Martha and Lazarus, Companions of our Lord

30 **The Sixth Sunday after Trinity**

31 *Ignatius of Loyola, Founder of the Society of Jesus, 1556*

AUGUST

4 *Jean-Baptist Vianney, Curé d'Ars, Spiritual Guide*

5 Oswald, King of Northumbria, Martyr, 642

6 **The Transfiguration of Our Lord — The Seventh Sunday after Trinity**

7 **The Transfiguration of Our Lord** (*if transferred from 6 August*)
John Mason Neale, Priest, Hymn Writer, 1866

8 Dominic, Priest, Founder of the Order of Preachers, 1221

9 Mary Sumner, Founder of the Mothers' Union, 1921

10 Laurence, Deacon at Rome, Martyr, 258

11 Clare of Assisi, Founder of the Minoresses (Poor Clares), 1253
John Henry Newman, Priest, Tractarian, 1890

13 **The Eighth Sunday after Trinity**

14 *Maximilian Kolbe, Friar, Martyr, 1941*

15 **The Blessed Virgin Mary**

20 **The Ninth Sunday after Trinity**

24 **Bartholomew the Apostle**

27 **The Tenth Sunday after Trinity**

28 Augustine, Bishop of Hippo, Teacher of the Faith, 430

29 The Beheading of John the Baptist

30 John Bunyan, Spiritual Writer, 1688

31 Aidan, Bishop of Lindisfarne, Missionary, 651

SEPTEMBER

1 *Giles of Provence, Hermit, c.710*

2 *The Martyrs of Papua New Guinea, 1901 and 1942*

3 **The Eleventh Sunday after Trinity**

4 *Birinus, Bishop of Dorchester (Oxon), Apostle of Wessex, 650*

6 *Allen Gardiner, Missionary, Founder of the South American Mission Society, 1851*

8 The Birth of Blessed Virgin Mary

9 *Charles Fuge Lowder, Priest, 1880*

10 **The Twelfth Sunday after Trinity**

13 John Chrysostom, Bishop of Constantinople, Teacher of the Faith, 407

14 **Holy Cross Day**

15 Cyprian, Bishop of Carthage, Martyr, 258

16 Ninian, Bishop of Galloway, Apostle of the Picts, c.432
Edward Bouverie Pusey, Priest, Tractarian, 1882

17 **The Thirteenth Sunday after Trinity**

19 *Theodore of Tarsus, Archbishop of Canterbury, 690*

20 John Coleridge Patteson, First Bishop of Melanesia, and his Companions, Martyrs, 1871

21 **Matthew, Apostle and Evangelist**

24 **The Fourteenth Sunday after Trinity**

25 Lancelot Andrewes, Bishop of Winchester, Spiritual Writer, 1626
Sergei of Radonezh, Russian Monastic Reformer, Teacher of the Faith, 1392

26 *Wilson Carlile, Founder of the Church Army, 1942*

27 Vincent de Paul, Founder of the Congregation of the Mission (Lazarists), 1660

29 **Michael and All Angels**

30 *Jerome, Translator of the Scriptures, Teacher of the Faith, 420*

OCTOBER

1 **The Fifteenth Sunday after Trinity** (*or* **Feast of Dedication**)

4 Francis of Assisi, Friar, Deacon, Founder of the Friars Minor, 1226

6 William Tyndale, Translator of the Scriptures, Reformation Martyr, 1536

8 **The Sixteenth Sunday after Trinity**

9 *Denys, Bishop of Paris, and his Companions, Martyrs, c.250*
Robert Grosseteste, Bishop of Lincoln, Philosopher, Scientist, 1253

10 Paulinus, Bishop of York, Missionary, 644
Thomas Traherne, Poet, Spiritual Writer, 1674

11 *Ethelburga, Abbess of Barking, 675*
James the Deacon, companion of Paulinus, 7th century

12 Wilfrid of Ripon, Bishop, Missionary, 709
Elizabeth Fry, Prison Reformer, 1845
Edith Cavell, Nurse, 1915

13 Edward the Confessor, King of England, 1066

15 **The Seventeenth Sunday after Trinity**

16 *Nicholas Ridley, Bishop of London, and Hugh Latimer, Bishop of Worcester, Reformation Martyrs, 1555*

17 Ignatius, Bishop of Antioch, Martyr, c.107

18 **Luke the Evangelist**

19 Henry Martyn, Translator of the Scriptures, Missionary, 1812

22 **The Eighteenth Sunday after Trinity**

25 *Crispin and Crispinian, Martyrs at Rome, c.287*

26 Alfred the Great, King of the West Saxons, Scholar, 899
Cedd, Abbot of Lastingham, Bishop of the East Saxons, 664

28 **Simon and Jude, Apostles**

29 **The Last Sunday After Trinity —** *Bible Sunday*

31 *Martin Luther, Reformer, 1546*

NOVEMBER

1 **ALL SAINTS' DAY**

2 Commemoration of the Faithful Departed (All Souls' Day)

3 Richard Hooker, Priest, Anglican Apologist, Teacher of the Faith, 1600
Martin of Porres, Friar, 1639

5 **The Fourth Sunday before Advent —** *All Saints' Sunday*
(or **ALL SAINTS' DAY** if transferred from 1 November)

6 *Leonard, Hermit, 6th century*
  William Temple, Archbishop of Canterbury, Teacher of the Faith, 1944
7 Willibrord of York, Bishop, Apostle of Frisia, 739
8 The Saints and Martyrs of England
9 *Margery Kempe, Mystic, c.1440*
10 Leo the Great, Bishop of Rome, Teacher of the Faith, 461
11 Martin, Bishop of Tours, c.397
12 **The Third Sunday before Advent** — *Remembrance Sunday*
13 Charles Simeon, Priest, Evangelical Divine, 1836
14 *Samuel Seabury, First Anglican Bishop of North America, 1796*
16 Margaret, Queen of Scotland, Philanthropist, Reformer of the Church, 1093
   Edmund Rich of Abingdon, Archbishop of Canterbury, 1240
17 Hugh, Bishop of Lincoln, 1200
18 Elizabeth of Hungary, Princess of Thuringia, Philanthropist, 1231
19 **The Second Sunday before Advent**
20 Edmund, King of the East Angles, Martyr, 870
   Priscilla Lydia Sellon, a Restorer of the Religious Life in the Church of England, 1876
22 *Cecilia, Martyr at Rome, c.230*
23 Clement, Bishop of Rome, Martyr, c.100
25 *Catherine of Alexandria, Martyr, 4th century*
   Isaac Watts, Hymn Writer, 1748
26 **Christ the King** – *The Sunday next before Advent*
29 *Day of Intercession and Thanksgiving for the Missionary Work of the Church*
30 **Andrew the Apostle**

DECEMBER
1 *Charles de Foucauld, Hermit in the Sahara, 1916*
3 **The First Sunday of Advent**
4 *John of Damascus, Monk, Teacher of the Faith, c.749*
  Nicholas Ferrar, Deacon, Founder of the Little Gidding Community, 1637
6 Nicholas, Bishop of Myra, c.326
7 Ambrose, Bishop of Milan, Teacher of the Faith, 397
8 Conception of the Blessed Virgin Mary
10 **The Second Sunday of Advent**
13 Lucy, Martyr at Syracuse, 304
   Samuel Johnson, Moralist, 1784
14 John of the Cross, Poet, Teacher of the Faith, 1591
17 **The Third Sunday of Advent** – *O Sapientia*
24 **The Fourth Sunday of Advent** – *Christmas Eve*
25 **CHRISTMAS DAY**
26 **Stephen, Deacon, First Martyr**
27 **John, Apostle and Evangelist**
28 **The Holy Innocents**

29 Thomas Becket, Archbishop of Canterbury, Martyr, 1170
31 **The First Sunday of Christmas**

JANUARY
1 **The Naming and Circumcision of Jesus**
2 Basil the Great and Gregory of Nazianzus, Bishops, Teachers of the Faith, 379 and 389
6 **THE EPIPHANY**
7 **The Baptism of Christ** – *The First Sunday of Epiphany*
10 *William Laud, Archbishop of Canterbury, 1645*
11 *Mary Slessor, Missionary in West Africa, 1915*
12 Aelred of Hexham, Abbot of Rievaulx, 1167
   Benedict Biscop, Abbot of Wearmouth, Scholar, 689
13 Hilary, Bishop of Poitiers, Teacher of the Faith, 367
   Kentigern (Mungo), Missionary Bishop in Strathclyde and Cumbria, 603
   George Fox, Founder of the Society of Friends (the Quakers), 1691
14 **The Second Sunday of Epiphany**
17 Antony of Egypt, Hermit, Abbot, 356
   Charles Gore, Bishop, Founder of the Community of the Resurrection, 1932
18 *Week of Prayer for Christian Unity until 25th*
19 Wulfstan, Bishop of Worcester, 1095
20 *Richard Rolle of Hampole, Spiritual Writer, 1349*
21 **The Third Sunday of Epiphany**
22 *Vincent of Saragossa, Deacon, first Martyr of Spain, 304*
24 Francis de Sales, Bishop of Geneva, Teacher of the Faith, 1622
25 **The Conversion of Paul**
26 Timothy and Titus, Companions of Paul
28 **The Fourth Sunday of Epiphany**
   (*or* **THE PRESENTATION OF CHRIST IN THE TEMPLE** *if transferred from 2 February*)
30 Charles, King and Martyr, 1649
31 *John Bosco, Priest, Founder of the Salesian Teaching Order, 1888*

Other dates

16 January	Anglican Communion Sunday
30 January	Education Sunday
6 February	Accession Day
28 February	General Synod meets until 1 March
5 March	Unemployment Sunday
9 May	Christian Aid Week until 16th
30 May	Day of Prayer for Vocations to Rel Life
7 July	General Synod meets in York until
9 July	Sea Sunday
10 September	Racial Justice Sunday
4 October	World Day for Animals
15 October	Hospital Sunday
15 October	One World Week until 24th
24 October	United Nations Day
12 November	General Synod meets this week
19 November	Prisoners Sunday
1 December	World AIDS Day
8 December	Human Rights Day

Central Structures

PART 1

PART 1 CONTENTS

All details are fully accurate at the time of going to press.

THE GENERAL SYNOD OF THE CHURCH OF ENGLAND

Office

Church House, Great Smith St, London SW1P 3NZ
Tel: 020–7898 1000 *Fax:* 020–7898 1369
email: synod@c-of-e.org.uk
Web: http://www.cofe.anglican.org

Dates of Sessions

The following periods have been set aside for Groups of Sessions of the General Synod:

2000: Monday 28 February – Wednesday 1 March
Friday 7 July – Tuesday 11 July (at York)
Week beginning 12 November

2001: Monday 19 February – Wednesday 21 February if necessary
Friday 6 July – Tuesday 10 July (at York)
Week beginning 11 November

Composition of the General Synod

	Canterbury	York	Either	Totals
House of Bishops				
Diocesan Bishops	30	14		44
Suffragan Bishops ...	6	3		9
	36	17		53
House of Clergy				
Deans or Provosts ...	10	5		15
Archdeacons	29	14		43
Service Chaplains and Chaplain-General of Prisons	4			4
Elected Proctors and the Dean of Guernsey or Jersey	126	58		184
University Proctors ..	4	2		6
Religious Communities	1	1		2
Co-opted places (only one filled at present)	3	2		5
	177	82		259

	Canterbury	York	Either	Totals
House of Laity				
Elected Laity*	168	79		247
Religious Communities	2	1		3
Co-opted places (none filled at present)			5	5
Ex officio (First and Second Church Estates Commissioners) ..			2	2
	170	80	7	257
Either House of Bishops, House of Clergy or House of Laity				
Ex officio (Dean of the Arches, the two Vicars General, the Third Church Estates Commissioner, the Chairman of the Pensions Board and Appointed Members of the Archbishops' Council)			11	11
	383	179	18	580

Eight representatives of other churches have been appointed to the Synod under its Standing Orders with speaking but not voting rights.
* The representatives of laity of the Provinces of Canterbury and York are elected by lay members of Deanery Synods.

OFFICERS OF THE GENERAL SYNOD
Presidents
The Archbishop of Canterbury
The Archbishop of York

Prolocutor of the Lower House of the Convocation of Canterbury Canon Hugh Wilcox

Prolocutor of the Lower House of the Convocation of York Canon John Stanley

Chairman of the House of Laity Dr Christina Baxter

Vice-Chairman of the House of Laity Dr Philip Giddings

Secretary General Mr Philip Mawer

Clerk to the Synod Mr David Williams

Legal Adviser and *Joint Registrar of the Provinces of Canterbury and York (Registrar of the General Synod)* Mr Brian Hanson

Assistant Legal Adviser Miss Ingrid Slaughter

Standing Counsel Mr John Pakenham-Walsh

OFFICERS OF THE CONVOCATIONS
Synodical Secretary of the Convocation of Canterbury
Canon Michael Hodge, Braxton Cottage, Halletts Shute, Norton, Yarmouth, Isle of Wight PO41 0RH   *Tel* and *Fax:* (01983) 761121
          email: michael@braxton.ndo.co.uk

Synodal Secretary of the Convocation of York
Ven David Jenkins, Irvings House, Sleagill, Penrith, Cumbria CA10 3HD   *Tel:* (01931) 714400

NON-DIOCESAN MEMBERS
The following are non-diocesan members of General Synod:

Suffragan Bishops in Convocation
CANTERBURY
The Bishop of Barking
The Bishop of Grimsby
The Bishop of Maidstone
The Bishop of Woolwich
(Two vacancies)

YORK
The Bishop of Penrith
The Bishop of Selby
(Two vacancies)

Deans or Provosts in Convocation
CANTERBURY
The Provost of Southwark
The Dean of Ely
The Dean of Exeter
The Dean of Hereford
The Dean of Norwich
The Dean of Rochester
The Dean of St Albans
The Dean of St Paul's

The Dean of Wells
The Dean of Westminster

YORK
The Provost of Bradford
The Provost of Newcastle
The Dean of Durham
The Dean of Manchester
The Dean of York

Service Representatives in Convocation
Chaplain of the Fleet and Archdeacon for the Royal Navy Ven Simon Golding

Deputy Chaplain-General and Archdeacon to the Army Ven John Blackburn

Chaplain-in-Chief, Royal Air Force Ven Anthony Bishop

Chaplain-General of Prisons and Archdeacon of Prisons Ven David Fleming

University Representatives in Convocation
CANTERBURY
Oxford
Canon Trevor Williams

Cambridge
Canon John Polkinghorne

London
Revd Dr Richard Burridge

Other Universities (Southern)
Revd Dr Gavin Ashenden

YORK
Durham and Newcastle
Revd Dr Joseph Cassidy

Other Universities (Northern)
Canon Prof Anthony Thiselton

Representatives of Religious Communities in Convocation
CANTERBURY
Revd Sister Teresa Joan White CSA

YORK
Fr Aidan Mayoss CR

Lay Representatives of Religious Communities
CANTERBURY
Sister Hilary CSMV
Brother Tristam SSF

YORK
Sister Margaret Shirley OHP

Ecumenical Representatives
Revd Hugh Davidson (Church of Scotland)

Rt Revd Mgr Michael Jackson (Roman Catholic Church)
Very Revd Archimandrite Ephrem Lash (Orthodox Church)
Revd Murdoch MacKenzie (United Reformed Church)
Revd David Newman (Moravian Church)
Revd Keith Reed (Methodist Church)
Revd David Staple (Baptist Union)
Revd Nezlin Sterling (Black Christian Concerns Group)

Ex-officio **Members of the House of Laity**
Dean of the Arches Rt Worshipful Sir John Owen

Vicar-General of the Province of Canterbury
Chancellor Sheila Cameron

Vicar-General of the Province of York
His Honour Judge Thomas Coningsby

First Church Estates Commissioner Mr John Sclater

Second Church Estates Commissioner Mr Stuart Bell MP

Third Church Estates Commissioner Lady Gill Brentford

Chairman of the Church of England Pensions Board
Mr Allan Bridgewater

Appointed Members of the Archbishops' Council

Mr Stephen Bampfylde
Mr Michael Chamberlain
Mr David Lammy

Ms Jayne Ozanne
Mrs Elizabeth Paver
Prof Peter Toyne

House of Bishops

Chairman The Archbishop of Canterbury

Vice-Chairman The Archbishop of York

Acting Secretary Mr Jonathan Neil-Smith
        Tel: 020–7898 1373
    email: jonathan.neil-smith@c-of-e.org.uk

Theological Consultant Vacancy *Tel:* 020–7898 1488

The Standing Committee of the House of Bishops consists of those members of the House who are members of the Archbishops' Council, the Business Committee, and the Appointments Committee and such other members of the House as it shall from time to time determine.

Chairman of the Inspections Working Party (reporting to the Bishops' Committee for Ministry)
The Dean of St Albans

Secretary to the Inspectorate Miss Jane Melrose
        Tel: 020–7898 1379
    email: jane.melrose@c-of-e.org.uk

House of Clergy

Joint Chairmen The Prolocutors of the Convocations

Secretary Mr David Hebblethwaite
        Tel: 020–7898 1364
    email: david.hebblethwaite@c-of-e.org.uk

The Standing Committee of the House of Clergy consists of the Prolocutors of the Convocations, the two persons elected by the House to serve on the Archbishops' Council, six persons elected by and from the Lower House of the Convocation of Canterbury and four persons elected by and from the Convocation of York.

House of Laity

Chairman Dr Christina Baxter

Vice-Chairman Dr Philip Giddings

Secretary Mr Malcolm Taylor   *Tel:* 020–7898 1375
    email: malcolm.taylor@c-of-e.org.uk

The Standing Committee of the House of Laity consists of the Chairman and Vice-Chairman, the members of the Business and Appointments Committees elected by the House and the members of the Archbishops' Council elected by the House.

Principal Committees

THE BUSINESS COMMITTEE
Appointed Members
Ven Pete Broadbent (*Archdeacon of Northolt*)
Mr Brian McHenry
Canon Hugh Wilcox

Elected Members
Mrs Janet Atkinson
Canon Richard Atkinson
Revd Richard Hanford
Mr Frank Knaggs
Preb Sam Philpott
Rt Revd Gavin Reid (*Bishop of Maidstone*)
Mr Mike Tyrrell

Secretary Mr David Williams (*Clerk to the Synod*)
Tel: 020–7898 1559
email: david.williams@c-of-e.org.uk

Assistant Secretary Mr Malcolm Taylor
Tel: 020–7898 1375
email: malcolm.taylor@c-of-e.org.uk

The Committee is responsible for organizing the business of the Synod, enabling it to fulfil its role as a legislative and deliberative body.

THE LEGISLATIVE COMMITTEE
Ex-officio Members
The Archbishop of Canterbury
The Archbishop of York
The Prolocutors of the Convocations
The Chairman and Vice-Chairman of the House of Laity

The Dean of the Arches
(Rt Worshipful Sir John Owen)
The Second Church Estates Commissioner
(Mr Stuart Bell MP)

Elected Members
Mr Ian Garden
Prof David McClean
Revd Stephen Trott
Rt Revd Michael Turnbull (*Bishop of Durham*)
Mr David Wright
Revd Jonathan Young

Appointed Members (Three vacancies)

Secretary Mr Robert Wellen   Tel: 020–7898 1371
email: robert.wellen@c-of-e.org.uk

THE STANDING ORDERS COMMITTEE
Chairman Mr Geoffrey Tattersall

Ex-officio Members
The Prolocutors of the Convocations
The Chairman of the House of Laity
The Vice-Chairman of the House of Laity

Appointed Members
Mr David Ashton
Mr James Cheeseman
Mrs Joanna Ingram
Revd John Rees
Mr Trevor Stevenson
(One vacancy)

Secretary Mr Malcolm Taylor   Tel: 020–7898 1375
email: malcolm.taylor@c-of-e.org.uk

General Synod Support

Under the overall direction of the Secretary General, staff of the Archbishops' Council provide the secretariat for the General Synod, its three Houses, and its Business and Legislative Committees. Members of staff of the Council serve as secretaries of a number of the Synod's permanent Committees and Commissions, and also as secretaries of ad hoc committees as circumstances require. The Clerk to the Synod acts as Secretary to the Business Committee, and provides advice and assistance as necessary to synodical bodies and members.

Secretary General Mr Philip Mawer
Tel: 020–7898 1360
email: philip.mawer@c-of-e.org.uk

Deputy Secretary General and Director of Policy Mr Richard Hopgood   Tel: 020–7898 1787
email: richard.hopgood@c-of-e.org.uk

Clerk to the Synod Mr David Williams
Tel: 020–7898 1559
email: david.williams@c-of-e.org.uk

Legal Adviser (and Joint Provincial Registrar)
Mr Brian Hanson   Tel: 020–7898 1366
email: brian.hanson@c-of-e.org.uk

Assistant Legal Adviser Miss Ingrid Slaughter
Tel: 020–7898 1368
email: ingrid.slaughter@c-of-e.org.uk
(*Secretary* Legal Advisory Commission; Legal Aid Commission)

Standing Counsel Mr John Pakenham-Walsh

Administrative Staff
Mr David Hebblethwaite
(*Secretary* House of Clergy; Standing Committee of the House of Clergy; Dioceses Commission; Liturgical Commission)   Tel: 020–7898 1364
email: david.hebblethwaite@c-of-e.org.uk

Miss Judith Egar
(*Solicitor seconded part time to the Legal Division from the Church Commissioners*) *Tel:* 020–7898 1389
email: judith.egar@c-of-e.org.uk

Mr Jonathan Neil-Smith
(*Acting Secretary* House of Bishops; Standing Committee of the House of Bishops)
Tel: 020–7898 1373
email: jonathan.neil-smith@c-of-e.org.uk

Mr Christopher Ball
(*Assistant Secretary* Archbishops' Council; Policy and Resource Coordinating Committee; *Secretary* Appointments Committee)   *Tel:* 020–7898 1362
email: christopher.ball@c-of-e.org.uk

Dr Colin Podmore
(*Secretary* Liturgical Publishing Group and its sub-groups; Review of the Crown Appointments Commission)   *Tel:* 020–7898 1385
email: colin.podmore@c-of-e.org.uk

Mr Malcolm Taylor
(*Assistant Secretary* Business Committee; *Secretary* House of Laity; Standing Committee of the House of Laity; Standing Orders Committee; Elections Review Group)   *Tel:* 020–7898 1375
email: malcolm.taylor@c-of-e.org.uk

Miss Jane Melrose
(*Assistant Secretary* House of Bishops; *Secretary* House of Bishops Inspectorate of Theological Colleges and Courses)   *Tel:* 020–7898 1379
email: jane.melrose@c-of-e.org.uk

Mr Andrew Roberts
Private Secretary to the Secretary General
Tel: 020–7898 1386
email: andrew.roberts@c-of-e.org.uk

Mr Robert Wellen
(*Secretary* Legislative Committee; Fees Advisory Commission; Ecclesiastical Rule Committee; Appeals Tribunals under the Ordination of Women (Financial Provisions) Measure 1993; Synodical Elections Appeals Panel, *Assistant to Mr Hanson*)   *Tel:* 020–7898 1371
email: robert.wellen@c-of-e.org.uk

Mr Francis Bassett
(*Secretary* Church Working for Women Group; *Assistant to Dr Podmore*)   *Tel:* 020–7898 1363
email: francis.bassett@c-of-e.org.uk

Mrs Angela Cann
(*Registry*)   *Tel:* 020–7898 1377
email: angela.cann@c-of-e.org.uk

Mr David Pite
(*Assistant to Mr Taylor and Miss Slaughter*)
Tel: 020–7898 1374
email: david.pite@c-of-e.org.uk

Mrs Sue Score
(*Secretary* Anglican Voluntary Societies Forum; *Assistant to Mr Hebblethwaite*)   *Tel:* 020–7898 1376
email: sue.score@c-of-e.org.uk

Legislation passed 1994–99 together with dates of commencement

The date in brackets is the date when the legislation came into operation. Items of legislation no longer in force are omitted.

MEASURES
Pastoral (Amendment) Measure 1994 (1 April 1994)
Care of Cathedrals (Supplementary Provisions) Measure 1994 (1 October 1994)
Church of England (Legal Aid) Measure 1994 (1 September 1994)
Team and Group Ministries Measure 1995 (Section 2, 28 June 1995, Section 13, 12 February 1996, remainder 1 May 1996)
Church of England (Miscellaneous Provisions) Measure 1995 (1 September 1995 – except Section 6)
Pensions Measure 1997 (1 January 1998)
National Institutions Measure 1998 (1 January 1999)

Cathedrals Measure 1999 (30 June 1999, part, remainder on dates to be appointed by the Archbishops of Canterbury and York in relation to individual cathedrals)
Care of Places of Worship Measure 1999 (to be announced)

STATUTORY INSTRUMENTS
Incumbents (Vacation of Benefices) Rules 1994 SI 1994 No 703 (1 September 1994)
Church Representation Rules (Amendment) Resolution 1994 SI 1995 No 2034 (1 October 1995)
Church of England (Legal Aid) Rules 1995 SI 1995 No 2034 (1 October 1995)
Church Representation Rules (Amendment) Resolution 1995 SI 1995 No 3243 (1 January 1996 – part; 1 May 1996 – further part; 1 May 1997 – remainder)
Payments to the Churches Conservation Trust Order 1996 SI 1996 No 3086 (1 April 1997)

Church Accounting Regulations 1997 (1 August 1997)

Church of England Pensions Regulations 1997 SI 1997 No 1929 (1 January 1998)

Church Representation Rules (Amendment) Resolution 1998 SI 1998 No 319 (1 March 1998)

Faculty Jurisdiction (Appeals) Rules 1998 SI 1998 No 1713 (1 August 1998)

National Institutions of the Church of England (Transfer of Functions) Order 1998 SI 1998 No 1715 (1 January 1999)

Church Representation Rules (Amendment) Resolution 1999 SI 1999 No 2112 (1 January 2000)

Parochial Fees Order 1999 SI 1999 No 2113 (1 January 2000)

Legal Officers (Annual Fees) Order 1999 SI 1999 No 2108 (1 January 2000)

Ecclesiastical Judges, Legal Officers and Others (Fees) Order 1999 SI 1999 No 2110 (1 January 1999 – part, remainder – to be announced)

Care of Places of Worship Rules 1999 SI 1999 No 2111 (to be announced)

Copies of the above legislation may be obtained from the Stationery Office or Church House Bookshop.

The continuous and consolidated text of the Church Representation Rules is published by Church House Publishing (£4.95)

Summary of Measures and Statutory Instruments

A photocopied list of General Synod Measures which received the Royal Assent from 1920 and Statutory Instruments to date which are still in operation, is available from the Legal Adviser, General Synod Office, Church House, Great Smith St, London SW1P 3NZ. Any request should be accompanied by a stamped self-addressed envelope (at least 10" by 7") please.

Notes

Measures and most Rules made pursuant to Measures are sold by the Stationery Office; they are also obtainable from Church House Bookshop, London SW1P 3BN. Anyone wishing to obtain a Measure which is out of print should write to the Stationery Office, PO Box 276, London SW8 5DT asking for a photocopy, or copies, which will be supplied via the British Library Lending Division at the current rate of £5.50 per publication to be copied. All requests should quote as a reference the number and year of the Measure.

General Synod publications may be obtained from Church House Bookshop. These publications include the *Report of Proceedings* (price on application).

Constitution

1 The General Synod shall consist of the Convocations of Canterbury and York joined together in a House of Bishops and a House of Clergy and having added to them a House of Laity.

2 The House of Bishops and the House of Clergy shall accordingly comprise the Upper and the Lower Houses respectively of the said Convocations, and the House of Laity shall be elected and otherwise constituted in accordance with the Church Representation Rules.

3 (1) The General Synod shall meet in sessions at least twice a year, and at such times and places as it may provide, or, in the absence of such provision, as the Joint Presidents of the Synod may direct.

(2) The General Synod shall, on the dissolution of the Convocations, itself be automatically dissolved, and shall come into being on the calling together of the new Convocations.

(3) Business pending at the dissolution of the General Synod shall not abate, but may be resumed by the new Synod at the stage reached before the dissolution, and any Boards, Commissions, Committees or other bodies of the Synod may, so far as may be appropriate and subject to any Standing Orders or any directions of the

Synod or of the Archbishops of Canterbury and York, continue their proceedings during the period of the dissolution, and all things may be done by the Archbishops or any such bodies or any officers of the General Synod as may be necessary or expedient for conducting the affairs of the Synod during the period of dissolution and for making arrangements for the resumption of business by the new Synod.

(4) A member of the General Synod may continue to act during the period of the dissolution as a member of any such Board, Commission, Committee or body:

Provided that, if a member of the Synod who is an elected Proctor of the clergy or an elected member of the House of Laity does not stand for re-election or is not re-elected, this paragraph shall cease to apply to him with effect from the date on which the election of his successor is announced by the presiding officer.

4 (1) The Archbishops of Canterbury and York shall be joint Presidents of the General Synod, and they shall determine the occasions on which it is desirable that one of the Presidents shall be the chairman of a meeting of the General Synod, and shall arrange between them which of them is to take the chair on any such occasion:

Provided that one of the Presidents shall be the chairman when any motion is taken for the final approval of a provision to which Article 7 of this Constitution applies and in such other cases as may be provided in Standing Orders.

(2) The Presidents shall, after consultation with the Appointments Committee of the Church of England, appoint from among the members of the Synod a panel of no fewer than three or more than eight chairmen, who shall be chosen for their experience and ability as chairmen of meetings and may be members of any House; and it shall be the duty of one of the chairmen on the panel, in accordance with arrangements approved by the Presidents and subject to any special directions of the Presidents, to take the chair at meetings of the General Synod at which neither of the Presidents takes the chair.

[(3) Under the Synodical Government Measure the Provincial Registrars are Joint Registrars of the General Synod but since 1980 the responsibility has been exercised by the Legal Adviser to the General Synod whom each Archbishop appointed as his Joint Registrar for this purpose.]

5 (1) A motion for the final approval of any Measure or Canon shall not be deemed to be carried unless, on a division by Houses, it receives the assent of the majority of the members of each House present and voting:

Provided that by permission of the chairman and with the leave of the General Synod given in accordance with Standing Orders this requirement may be dispensed with.

(2) All other motions of the General Synod shall, subject as hereinafter provided, be determined by a majority of the members of the Synod present and voting, and the vote may be taken by a show of hands or a division:

Provided that, except in the case of a motion relating solely to the course of business or procedure, any 25 members present may demand a division by Houses and in that case the motion shall not be deemed to be carried unless, on such a division, it receives the assent of the majority of the members of each House present and voting.

(3) This Article shall be subject to any provision of this Constitution or of any Measure with respect to special majorities of the Synod or of each House thereof, and where a special majority of each House is required the vote shall be taken on a division by Houses, and where a special majority of the whole Synod is required, the motion shall, for the purposes of this Article, be one relating solely to procedure.

(4) Where a vote is to be taken on a division by Houses, it may be taken by an actual division or in such other manner as Standing Orders may provide.

6 The functions of the General Synod shall be as follows:

(*a*) to consider matters concerning the Church of England and to make provision in respect thereof –

(i) by Measure intended to be given, in the manner prescribed by the Church of England Assembly (Powers) Act 1919, the force and effect of an Act of Parliament, or

(ii) by Canon made, promulged and executed in accordance with the like provisions and subject to the like restrictions and having the like legislative force as Canons heretofore made, promulged and executed by the Convocations of Canterbury and York, or

(iii) by such order, regulation or other subordinate instrument as may be authorized by Measure or Canon, or

(iv) by such Act of Synod, regulation or other instrument or proceeding as may be appropriate in cases where provision by or under a Measure or Canon is not required;

(*b*) to consider and express their opinion on any other matters of religious or public interest.

7 (1) A provision touching doctrinal formulae or the services or ceremonies of the Church of England or the administration of the Sacraments or sacred rites thereof shall, before it is finally approved by the General Synod, be referred to the House of Bishops, and shall be submitted for such final approval in terms proposed by the House of Bishops and not otherwise.

(2) A provision touching any of the matters aforesaid shall, if the Convocations or either of them or the House of Laity so require, be referred, in the terms proposed by the House of Bishops for final approval by the General Synod, to the two Convocations sitting separately for their provinces and to the House of Laity; and no provision so referred shall be submitted for final approval by the General Synod unless it has been approved, in the terms so proposed, by each House of the two Convocations sitting as aforesaid and by the House of Laity.

(3) The question whether such a reference is required by a Convocation shall be decided by the President and Prolocutor of the Houses of that Convocation, and the Prolocutor shall consult the Standing Committee of the Lower House of Canterbury or, as the case may be, the Assessors of the Lower House of York, and the decision of the President and Prolocutor shall be conclusive:

Provided that if, before such a decision is taken, either House of a Convocation resolves that the provision concerned shall be so referred or both Houses resolve that it shall not be so referred, the resolution or resolutions shall be a conclusive decision that the reference is or is not required by that Convocation.

(4) The question whether such a reference is required by the House of Laity shall be decided by the Prolocutor and Pro-Prolocutor of that House who shall consult the Standing Committee of that House, and the decision of the Prolocutor and the Pro-Prolocutor shall be conclusive:

Provided that if, before such a decision is taken, the House of Laity resolves that the reference is or is not required, the resolution shall be a conclusive decision of that question.

(5) Standing Orders of the General Synod shall provide for ensuring that a provision which fails to secure approval on a reference under this Article by each of the four Houses of the Convocations or by the House of Laity of the General Synod is not proposed again in the same or a similar form until a new General Synod comes into being, except that, in the case of objection by one House of one Convocation only, provision may be made for a second reference to the Convocations and, in the case of a second objection by one House only, for reference to the Houses of Bishops and Clergy of the General Synod for approval by a two-thirds majority of the members of each House present and voting, in lieu of such approval by the four Houses aforesaid.

(6) If any question arises whether the requirements of this Article or Standing Orders made thereunder apply to any provision, or whether those requirements have been complied with, it shall be conclusively determined by the Presidents and Prolocutors of the Houses of the Convocations and the Prolocutor and Pro-Prolocutor of the House of Laity of the General Synod.

8 (1) A Measure or Canon providing for permanent changes in the Services of Baptism or Holy Communion or in the Ordinal, or a scheme for a constitutional union or a permanent and substantial change of relationship between the Church of England and another Christian body, being a body a substantial number of whose members reside in Great Britain, shall not be finally approved by the General Synod unless, at a stage determined by the Archbishops, the Measure or Canon or scheme, or the substance of the proposals embodied therein, has been approved by a majority of the dioceses at meetings of their Diocesan Synods, or, in the case of the Diocese in Europe, of the bishop's council and Standing Committee of that diocese.

(1A) If the Archbishops consider that this Article should apply to a scheme which affects the Church of England and another Christian body but does not fall within paragraph (1) of this Article, they may direct that this Article shall apply to that scheme, and where such a direction is given this Article shall apply accordingly.

(1B) The General Synod may by resolution provide that final approval of any such scheme as aforesaid, being a scheme specified in the resolution, shall require the assent of such special majorities of the members present and voting as may be specified in the resolution, and the resolution may specify a special majority of each House or of the whole Synod or of both, and in the latter case the majorities may be different.

(1c) A motion for the final approval of a Measure providing for permanent changes in any such Service or in the Ordinal shall not be deemed to be carried unless it receives the assent of a majority in each House of the General Synod of not less than two-thirds of those present and voting.

(2) Any question whether this Article applies to any Measure or Canon or scheme, or whether its requirements have been complied with, shall be conclusively determined by the Archbishops, the Prolocutors of the Lower Houses of the Convocations and the Prolocutor and Pro-Prolocutor of the House of Laity of the General Synod.

9 (1) Standing Orders of the General Synod may provide for separate sittings of any of the three Houses or joint sittings of any two Houses and as to who is to take the chair at any such separate or joint sitting.

(2) The House of Laity shall elect a Chairman and Vice-Chairman of that House who shall also discharge the functions assigned by this Constitution and the Standing Orders and by or under any Measure or Canon to the Prolocutor and Pro-Prolocutor of that House.

10 (1) The General Synod shall appoint a Legislative Committee from members of all three Houses, to whom shall be referred all Measures passed by the General Synod which it is desired should be given, in accordance with the procedure prescribed by the Church of England Assembly (Powers) Act 1919, the force of an Act of Parliament; and it shall be the duty of the Legislative Committee to take such steps with respect to any such Measure as may be so prescribed.

(2) The General Synod may appoint or provide by their Standing Orders for the appointment of such Committees, Commissions and bodies (in addition to the Committees mentioned in Section 10 of the National Institutions Measure 1998), which may include persons who are not members of the Synod, and such officers as they think fit.

(3) Each House may appoint or provide by their Standing Orders for the appointment of such Committees of their members as they think fit.

11 (1) The General Synod may make, amend and revoke Standing Orders providing for any of the matters for which such provision is required or

authorized by this Constitution to be made, and consistently with this Constitution, for the meetings, business and procedure of the General Synod.

(1A) Provision may be made by Standing Order that the exercise of any power of the General Synod to suspend the Standing Orders or any of them shall require the assent of such a majority of the members of the whole Synod present and voting as may be specified in the Standing Order.

(2) Each House may make, amend and revoke Standing Orders for the matter referred to in Article 10 (3) hereof and consistently with this Constitution and with any Standing Orders of the General Synod, for the separate sittings, business and procedure of that House.

(3) Subject to this Constitution and to any Standing Orders, the business and procedure at any meeting of the General Synod or any House or Houses thereof shall be regulated by the chairman of the meeting.

12 (1) References to final approval shall, in relation to a Canon or Act of Synod, be construed as referring to the final approval by the General Synod of the contents of the Canon or Act, and not to the formal promulgation thereof:

Provided that the proviso to Article 4 (1) shall apply both to the final approval and to the formal promulgation of a Canon or Act of Synod.

(2) Any question concerning the interpretation of this Constitution, other than questions for the determination of which express provision is otherwise made, shall be referred to and determined by the Archbishops of Canterbury and York.

(3) No proceedings of the General Synod or any House or Houses thereof, or any Board, Commission, Committee or body thereof, shall be invalidated by any vacancy in the membership of the body concerned or by any defect in the qualification, election or appointment of any member thereof.

13 Any functions exercisable under this Constitution by the Archbishops of Canterbury and York, whether described as such or as Presidents of the General Synod, may, during the absence abroad or incapacity through illness of one Archbishop or a vacancy in one of the Sees, be exercised by the other Archbishop alone.

General Synod Business

JULY 1999
Friday 9 July–Tuesday 13 July

LEGISLATIVE BUSINESS
The Synod
Received a report of the Legislative Committee on the draft Churchwardens Measure (GS 1165C), reintroduced the Measure for debate, and gave final approval to the draft Measure as amended. The voting at final approval of the Measure was as follows: Bishops *Ayes* 22, *Noes* 0; Clergy *Ayes* 161, *Noes* 1; Laity *Ayes* 177, *Noes* 21.

Received a report of the Revision Committee on the draft Church of England (Miscellaneous Provisions) Measure (GS 1320A) and gave final approval to the draft Measure. The voting at final approval of the Measure was as follows: Bishops *Ayes* 22, *Noes* 0; Clergy *Ayes* 176, *Noes* 0; Laity *Ayes* 177, *Noes* 2. The draft Amending Canon was referred to the House of Bishops.

Gave approval to the draft Parochial Fees Order 1999 (GS 1340), the Ecclesiastical Judges, Legal Officers and Others (Fees) Order 1999 (GS 1349) and the Legal Officers (Annual Fees) Order 1999 (1350).

Gave approval to the draft Care of Places of Worship Rules (GS 1344).

Received a report of the Steering Committee on the draft Amending Canon No 22 (GS 1278B) and completed the final drafting stage. The Canon (as amended) was referred to the House of Bishops under Article 7 of the Constitution.

Received a report of the Steering Committee on the Church Representation Rules (Amendment) Resolutions (GS 1307B) and Clergy Representation (Amendment) Rules (GS 1308B), and gave final approval to these. The Instrument for the Clergy Representation (Amendment) Rules would come into force on 1 January 2000.

Gave general approval to the Ecclesiastical Jurisdiction (Discipline) Measure (GS 1347) and the Amending Canon No 24 (GS 1348), and referred them to a Revision Committee.

LITURGICAL BUSINESS
The Synod
Received a report by the Revision Committee on *Pastoral Rites – Marriage* (GS 1298F) and re-committed the Liturgical Business entitled *Pastoral Rites – Marriage* to the Revision Committee for revision of the words 'forsaking all others' in the Declaration.

Received a report by the Revision Committee on *Eucharistic Prayers* (GS 1299A) and re-committed this business to the Revision Committee for further revision.

Approved the draft *Rules to Order the Service and Miscellaneous Liturgical Provisions* (GS 1342) and committed this business to a Revision Committee.

Received a report by the Revision Committee on *Pastoral Rites – Funerals* (GS 1298G) and committed the business to the House of Bishops.

Gave general approval to the Liturgical Business entitled *Weekday Lectionaries* (GS 1341), and committed this business to a Revision Committee.

Received a report by the Revision Committee on *Pastoral Rites – Thanksgiving for the Gift of a Child* (GS 1298H) and committed this business to the House of Bishops.

Gave final approval that the Liturgical Business entitled *The Ordinal in the Alternative Service Book 1980* (GS 1319A) be given an extended period of authorization from 1 January 2001 until 31 December 2005. The voting was as follows: Bishops *Ayes* 22, *Noes* 0; Clergy *Ayes* 133, *Noes* 1; Laity *Ayes* 137, *Noes* 3.

FINANCIAL BUSINESS

The Synod

Received an annual report of the Central Board of Finance for the year 1998 (GS 1337), approved the Draft Budget for 2000 for the general purposes of the General Synod; and approved supplementary votes for Training and Ministry; National Church Responsibilities; grants and provisions; Inter-Diocesan Support/Mission Agencies Clergy Pension Contributions.

OTHER BUSINESS

The Synod

Received a report on *Financing the Churches Conservation Trust in the Triennium 2000 to 2003* (GS 1345) and approved the recommendations.

Approved the appointment of the Venerable Pete Broadbent as Chairman of the Business Committee and the Revd Canon John Stanley as Chairman of the Appointments Committee until 31 December 2000; and the appointment of Mr Ian Robert McNeil as Chairman of the Audit Committee of the Archbishop' Council until 30 June 2000.

Received a presentation of a report on *A Learning Church for a Learning Age* (GS 1339), and carried the motion (as amended) that this Synod:

(a) affirm the importance of developing a learning culture in the Church and welcome GS 1339 as a first step towards this;

(b) request the Archbishops' Council to initiate action to follow up the specific proposals set out in GS 1339, including also partnership with existing providers of education and learning such as universities, Church colleges, theological colleges and courses, extension studies, and so forth;

(c) affirm the significance of the discipleship of lay people and clergy in daily life and occupation, and encourage dioceses and parishes to implement the proposals outlined in GS Misc. 546;

(d) congratulate those dioceses, parishes and other Church bodies that are working towards the standards of excellence embodied in Investors in People, and encourage the Church at all levels to make use of the framework and resources offered in GS Misc. 545.

Received a report by the House of Bishops on the *Nicene Creed* (GS 1346). The voting was as follows: Bishops *Ayes* 37, *Noes* 1; Clergy *Ayes* 164, *Noes* 21; Laity *Ayes* 107, *Noes* 82.

Received a presentation and report on the World Council of Churches Assembly in Harare, and carried the motion that this Synod:

(a) take note of the report of the Church of England's delegates on the Eighth Assembly of the World Council of Churches;

(b) endorse the report's recommendations that the Church of England should continue to play a role of 'critical solidarity' within the World Council of Churches;

(c) give thanks for the first 50 years of the WCC and for the contributions of the founding movements: the International Missionary Council, Life and Work, and Faith and Order;

(d) affirm Resolution IV.7(e)(iii) and (g) of the 1998 Lambeth Conference, which called for 'a radical reassessment of . . . what changes in the WCC would be required to make it possible for the Roman Catholic Church to be a full member', and invited the Joint Working Group between the WCC and the Roman Catholic Church to address this issue;

(e) welcome the establishment of the Special Commission to consider the particular concerns of the Orthodox Churches with regard to the WCC; and

(f) note with appreciation the changes made to the Constitution at the Harare Assembly which now states that 'The primary purpose of the Fellowship of the Churches in the World Council of Churches is to call one another to visible unity in one faith and in one eucharistic fellowship . . .' and urge the newly elected Central Committee of the WCC vigorously to pursue this vision.

Received the first report of the Archbishops' Council (GS 1346) and a report by the Ethical Investment Working Group (GS 1335).

Received presentations on Kosovo and on the current work of the Doctrine Commission.

Considered the Thirty-Seventh Report of the Standing Orders Committee (GS 1336) and proceeded to carry a number of motions amending its standing orders. One notable amendment was to change the words 'general approval' in its application to legislative and liturgical business to 'first consideration'.

Listened to addresses from the Rt Revd Dr John Sentamu (*Bishop of Stepney*) and Dr Giddings in response to the Stephen Lawrence Inquiry.

Debated a Private Member's Motion on Changes in Tax Policy and carried the motion:

That this Synod note the extent to which changes in tax policy over the last 20 years have adversely affected the Church; and call on Her Majesty's Government to allow churches to reclaim Value Added Tax on their expenditure.

Debated a Diocesan Synod Motion on the Approval of Changes Affecting Parishes and carried the motion (as amended):

That this Synod decide to ensure appropriate consultation with dioceses about any Measure, Canon or other provision which, if enacted, would materially affect Annual Meetings of Parishioners to elect Churchwardens, Annual Parochial Church Meetings or the Constitution of Parochial Church Councils and commends the practice of wider consultation on draft legislation and regulations before their consideration by this Synod.

NOVEMBER 1999 GROUP OF SESSIONS

LEGISLATIVE BUSINESS
The Synod
Gave Final Approval to draft Amending Canon No 22 (GS 1278C). The voting was as follows: Bishops *Ayes* 26, *Noes* 0; Clergy *Ayes* 129, *Noes* 0; Laity *Ayes* 151, *Noes* 9

Gave Final Approval to draft Amending Canon No 23 (GS 1323B). The voting was as follows: Bishops *Ayes* 32, *Noes* 1; Clergy *Ayes* 156, *Noes* 0; Laity *Ayes* 169, *Noes* 13

Gave deemed first consideration to the draft Synodical Government (Amendment) Measure (GS 1364) and referred this to a revision committee.

Revised in full Synod draft Amending Canon No

25 (Bishop of Dover's membership of Upper House)(GS 1365)

Gave deemed approval to the Payment to the Churches Conservation Trust Order (GS 1358), the Convocations (Elections to Upper House) (Amendment) Rules (GS 1366) and the Religious Communities (Lay Representatives)(Amendment) Rules (GS 1359).

LITURGICAL BUSINESS
The Synod
Gave Final Approval to the Liturgical Business entitled *Thanksgiving for the Gift of a Child* (GS 1298H), the voting at Final Approval was as follows: Bishops *Ayes* 27, *Noes* 0; Clergy *Ayes* 151, *Noes* 0; Laity *Ayes* 160, *Noes* 0.

Gave Final Approval to the Liturgical Business entitled *Funeral Services* (GS 1298 I), the voting at Final Approval was as follows: Bishops *Ayes* 29, *Noes* 0; Clergy *Ayes* 162, *Noes* 0; Laity *Ayes* 161, *Noes* 0.

Gave Final Approval to the Liturgical Business entitled *The Lord's Prayer* (GS 1271C), the voting at Final Approval was as follows: Bishops *Ayes* 34, *Noes* 1; Clergy *Ayes* 180, *Noes* 5; Laity *Ayes* 158, *Noes* 35.

Took note of a fourth report by the Revision Committee on the Liturgical Business entitled *Wholeness and Healing* (GS 1152 E). The Liturgical Business then automatically stood referred to the House of Bishops.

Took note of a second report by the Revision Committee on the Liturgical Business entitled *Eucharistic Prayers* (GS 1299B). The Liturgical Business (as amended) partly stood referred to the House of Bishops; the remainder would be further considered at the next Group of Sessions.

Took note of a report of the Revision Committee on the Liturgical Business entitled *Weekday Lectionaries* (GS 1341A). The Liturgical Business then automatically stood referred to the House of Bishops.

Took note of a report of the Revision Committee on the Liturgical Business entitled *Rules to order the Service and other Miscellaneous Liturgical Provisions* (GS 1342A). The Liturgical Business (as amended) then automatically stood referred to the House of Bishops.

Took note of a second report by the Revision Committee on the Liturgical Business entitled *Marriage Services* (GS 1298F). The Liturgical Business then automatically stood referred to the House of Bishops.

Took note of a second report by the Revision Committee on the Liturgical Business entitled *Public Worship with Communion by Extension* (formerly *Extended Communion and Sunday Worship with Holy Communion in the Absence of a Priest*) (GS 1230B). The Liturgical Business then automatically stood referred to the House of Bishops.

FINANCIAL BUSINESS
The Synod
Approved a supplementary vote for Training for Ministry.

OTHER BUSINESS
The Synod
Took note of a report by the Business Committee entitled *Report on numbers to be elected to Synod in 2000* (GS 1360) and gave approval to its recommendations.

Took note of a report by the House of Bishops entitled *The Nicene Creed* (GS 1371) and gave approval to the form of the *Nicene Creed* to be published in the Eucharistic Rites. The voting was as follows: Bishops *Ayes* 38, *Noes* 1; Clergy *Ayes* 179, *Noes* 22; Laity *Ayes* 131, *Noes* 76.

Took note of a report by the Liturgical Publishing Group entitled *Publishing Common Worship* (GS 1355) and approved the plans for publishing *Common Worship* as set out in the report.

Took note of a report by the Liturgical Commission entitled *Liturgical Material for Commendation* (GS 1370).

Took note of a report by the Liturgical Commission entitled *A Psalter for Common Worship* (GS1363) and carried the motion:

That this Synod support the proposal in paragraph 7.1 of GS 1363 that the Psalter contained in GS Misc 582 be the version of the Psalter published in *Common Worship*.

Took note of the first report by the Follow Up Group entitled the *Review of Synodical Government* (GS 1354)

Took note of a report by the Board of Mission entitled *Setting the Agenda* (GS 1368) and carried the motion (as amended) that this Synod:

(a) welcome the Board of Mission's initiative in organizing the first Church of England Conference on Evangelism known as ACE '99;
(b) commend to the Dioceses for discussion and consideration the Report of the Conference *Setting the Agenda* (GS Misc 579) together with the Report of the Working Party on Diocesan Evangelists *Good News People* (GS Misc 565) and strongly endorse the recommendations in paragraph 7:1-3 of *Good News People*,

(c) call upon every bishop, diocese and congregation to see their primary task is to share the love of God in Jesus Christ and to continue the work of evangelism beyond the Decade of Evangelism;
(d) request the Archbishops' Council to report on the follow-up to the Decade of Evangelism and the resolution from ACE '99 that a Fund for Youth Evangelism should be established; and
(e) welcome the further resolution from ACE '99 that a research project be established to assess the effectiveness of evangelism during the Decade with a view to giving direction for the future.'

Took note of a report entitled *Called to Witness and Service: The Reuilly Common Statement with Essays on Church, Eucharist and Ministry* (GS 1329) and carried the motion that this Synod:

(a) welcome the vision of visible unity and the theological agreements set out in the Reuilly Common Statement;
(b) approve the Joint declaration, consisting of mutual Acknowledgement and Commitments, in paragraph 46 of the Reuilly Common Statement;
(c) request the Council for Christian Unity to oversee the implementation of the Commitments contained in the Joint Declaration, including theological discussion of the outstanding issues that hinder fuller communion.

Heard an address by Mr Martin Narey, the Director General of the Prison service, and took noted of the a report by the Board for Social Responsibility entitled *Life in Prison* (GS 1369). They carried the motion that this Synod:

(a) welcome Her Majesty's Government to the development of restorative justice programmes which enshrine the biblical principles of holding offenders responsible for their crimes, addressing the needs of victims, and enhancing the protection of the public;
(b) welcome efforts to prevent 15 and 15 year olds being remanded into prison custody by offering constructive alternatives in the community;
(c) note the continuing public concern about the effect of crime in our communities;
(d) record the unease at the disproportionate number of black offenders in our prisons, and welcome initiatives to eradicate racism throughout the judicial and penal system;
(e) request Her Majesty's Government to reassess the situation whereby mentally ill people are often held in prison when they would be better treated in a secure hospital environment;

(f) recognize the need to reintegrate offenders into the community through prison and community based programmes and in partnership with employment and accommodation schemes;

(g) affirm the role of prison staff, chaplains, Boards of Visitors and volunteers and the part they play in supporting the families of people in prison; and

(h) urge dioceses, deaneries and parishes to promote the study of *Prisons: A Study in Vulnerability* (GS Misc 557) through criminal justice groups and other means.

Debated a Diocesan Synod Motion on *Statistics on the Ethnic Origin of Members of the Church of England* and carried the motion (as amended): That this Synod:

(a) recognize the advantages of showing that the Church of England is a multi-ethnic church with multi-ethnic leadership at all levels; and

(b) call upon the Archbishops' Council to organize the collection of statistics at the time of the next general revision of church electoral rolls (2002) on the ethnic origin of members on electoral rolls, members of church councils, churchwardens, deanery synod representatives and clergy throughout all the dioceses of the Church of England; and

(c) call further upon the Archbishops' Council to arrange the collection of the statistics by the procedure suggested in the Background Paper from the Diocese of Southwark.

Debated a Private Members motion on *The Religious Life* and carried the motion: That this Synod recognizing the contribution that the Religious Communities in the Church of England have made to the life of the Church and noting the decreasing number in those Communities, encourage clergy and parishes to pray for more vocations to the Religious Life and, in order to do this effectively, to inform themselves and others about the Religious Orders and especially those in their own neighbourhood.

Debated a Private Members Motion on *Training Courses for Strengthening Family Life* and carried the motion: That this Synod, following the lead given by the House of Bishops at its meeting in June 1997, affirm the value of courses in Marriage Preparation, Marriage Care, Baptism Preparation and Parenting in strengthening family life and furthering the mission of the Church and therefore recommend that every diocese should:

(a) develop appropriate resources and training strategies for such courses; and

(b) encourage its parishes to run such courses.

The voting was as follows: *Ayes* 235; *Noes* 0.

General Synod

15

THE ARCHBISHOPS' COUNCIL
(and Central Board of Finance of the Church of England)

Central Board of Finance of the Church of England
Company registration no: 136413
Charity registration no: 248711

Tel: 020–7898 1000
Fax: 020–7898 1369

Joint Presidents
The Archbishop of Canterbury
The Archbishop of York

Ex-officio Members
The Prolocutor of the Lower House of the Convocation of Canterbury
The Prolocutor of the Lower House of the Convocation of York
The Chairman of the House of Laity
The Vice-Chairman of the House of Laity
A Church Estates Commissioner (currently the First Church Estates Commissioner)

Elected by the House of Bishops
Rt Revd Michael Turnbull (*Bishop of Durham*)
Rt Revd John Gladwin (*Bishop of Guildford*)

Elected by the House of Clergy
Very Revd Michael Perham (*Provost of Derby*)
Ven Pete Broadbent (*Archdeacon of Northolt*)

Elected by the House of Laity
Mr Brian McHenry
Mrs Christina Rees

Appointed by the Archbishops with the approval of the General Synod
Mr Stephen Bampfylde
Mr Michael Chamberlain
Mr David Lammy
Ms Jayne Ozanne
Mrs Elizabeth Paver
Prof Peter Toyne

(The membership of the Archbishops' Council is co-terminous with that of the Central Board of Finance of the Church of England.)

STAFF
Secretary General Mr Philip Mawer
Tel: 020–7898 1360
email: philip.mawer@c-of-e.org.uk

Deputy Secretary General and Director of Policy Mr Richard Hopgood
Tel: 020–7898 1787
email: richard.hopgood@c-of-e.org.uk

Director of Central Services Mr David Williams
Tel: 020–7898 1559
email: david.williams@c-of-e.org.uk

Director of Communications Revd Dr William Beaver
Tel: 020–7898 1462
email: bill.beaver@c-of-e.org.uk

Financial Secretary and Company Secretary Mr Shaun Farrell
Tel: 020–7898 1795
email: shaun.farrell@c-of-e.org.uk

Director of Human Resources Mrs Susan Morgan
Tel: 020–7898 1565
email: su.morgan@c-of-e.org.uk

Director of Legal Services Mr Brian Hanson
Tel: 020–7898 1366
email: brian.hanson@c-of-e.org.uk

Director of Ministry Ven Gordon Kuhrt
Tel: 020–7898 1390
email: gordon.kuhrt@c-of-e.org.uk

Assistant Secretary to the Council Mr Christopher Ball
Tel: 020–7898 1362
email: christopher.ball@c-of-e.org.uk

INTRODUCTION
A key outcome of the reform of the central Church structures proposed by the Archbishops' Commission on the Organization of the Church of England (in its report *Working As One Body*) was the establishment of the Archbishops' Council on 1 January 1999. The National Institutions Measure 1998, which brought the Council into being, defined the Council's purpose as being: 'To coordinate, promote, aid and further the work and mission of the Church of England.' The Council, for the first time, brings together at a national level executive policy and resource decision-making in a single body.

The Council published its first report to the Synod in June 1999 (GS 1346), in which it set out for comment statements of vision and purpose:

Extract from the Council's first report
Vision
In drawing up a statement of purpose and values, we [the Council] have consciously echoed the three priorities set by the Archbishop of Canterbury and have framed a vision of a Church of England which is:
United — growing together in the love of God
Confident — living and proclaiming the good news of Jesus Christ

Outward-looking — sharing in the mission of God
for the world;
— working for God's justice and
peace for all.

Purpose
Building on the work of the Archbishops' Commission on the Organization of the Church of England (the 'Turnbull Commission') and the provisions of the National Institutions Measure, we offer the following statement of the Council's purpose:

Working as one body, to serve the Church of England through the power of the Holy Spirit, by supporting, promoting and extending the mission, ministry and witness of the Church to the nation.

To that end, the Council will seek to:

give a clear strategic sense of direction to the national work of the Church, informed by an understanding of the Church's opportunities, needs and resources;

encourage and resource the Church in parishes and dioceses to work as one body in witness, worship and service in today's world;

ensure the Church's national bodies work together with clarity, coherence and a strong sense of purpose;

engage confidently with the world, with a deep understanding of people's needs and perceptions;

support the Archbishops with their diverse ministries and responsibilities;

be a servant leader seeking to encourage all within the Church.

Structure
The supporting structure of the Council comprises a number of divisions with responsibility for specific areas of work (*see* diagram overleaf).

Responsibilities of the Council
The Council's main responsibilities are as listed in the table below.

Areas of responsibility	*Examples*
Ministry-related functions formerly carried out by the Advisory Board of Ministry (and now carried out by the Ministry Division).	Selection, training and deployment of clergy and (lay) Readers (functions where the Council works particularly closely with the House of Bishops).
Ministry-related functions formerly carried out by the Church Commissioners as Central Stipends Authority and the Pensions Board.	Remuneration policy, including the setting of recommended stipend levels for clergy, and pensions policy.
Functions formerly undertaken by the Church Commissioners relating to parochial fees.	Preparation of the annual Parochial Fees Order for approval by the General Synod.
Functions related to its role as the Financial Executive of the General Synod (the Council is also the Central Board of Finance).	Bringing to the General Synod a draft budget in respect of training for ministry, national Church responsibilities, etc.
Certain financial functions formerly undertaken by the Church Commissioners.	Distribution of stipends support selectively to the needier dioceses.
Oversight – through the Church and the World division – of the range of work carried out by the Boards and Councils. (These bodies are accountable to the Synod through the Council.)	The work of the Boards and Councils is detailed elsewhere in the Yearbook.
Developing human resource policies for the staff of the National Church Institutions which reflect best practice and help bring together the staffs of those bodies.	The development of joint employment policies, e.g. on equal opportunities and recruitment and selection; and the production of common training and development plans.
Developing and executing an integrated communications strategy.	The development of the lead bishops for the media programme.

ARCHBISHOPS' COUNCIL: KEY WORKING RELATIONSHIPS

HOUSE OF BISHOPS

CHURCH COMMISSIONERS

PENSIONS BOARD

CORPORATION OF THE CHURCH HOUSE

Bishoprics and Cathedrals Committee

Allocations Group

Executive Management Board (Common Services and Human Resource policies)

Audit Committee of the Archbishops' Council

GENERAL SYNOD

Appointments Committee of the Church of England

Finance Committee of the Archbishops' Council

ARCHBISHOPS' COUNCIL

INTER-DIOCESAN FINANCE FORUM

CHURCH HERITAGE FORUM

COMMITTEE FOR MINORITY ETHNIC ANGLICAN CONCERNS

CHURCH AND WORLD DIVISION

*Board of Education
Board of Mission
Board for Social Responsibility
Council for Christian Unity
Hospital Chaplaincies Council

Cathedrals Fabric Commission for England
Council for the Care of Churches

MINISTRY DIVISION♦

**Vocation, Recruitment and Selection Committee
Theological Education and Training Committee
Deployment, Remuneration and Conditions of Service Committee
Committee for Ministry Among Deaf People**

* The National Society (Church of England) for Promoting Religious Education works closely with the Board of Education and maintains a close association with the Archbishops' Council through its integrated publishing programme with Church House Publishing.

♦ The Central Readers' Council is also part of this division.

CHURCH AND WORLD

The Church and World division brings together the Boards and Councils and other national Church bodies concerned in one way or another with the external face of the Church of England. The Boards relate within the division to each other and to the Archbishops' Council, and through the Archbishops' Council, to the Synod.

This grouping together of the Boards provides a new opportunity for: developing a strategic overview (for consideration by the Council); helping the Council to assess priorities within a coherent framework; tackling cross-Board issues and working; developing the ecumenical dimension in the working of the Boards; considering resource allocation among the Boards; and addressing work priority questions. The main focus of work in this area will continue to be carried out by the individual Boards, with the Board Chairman continuing to be the Church's principal spokesman in each of the areas covered.

Lambeth Palace, the Anglican Voluntary Societies Forum and the Partnership for World Mission are also represented in this arrangement.

The Council for Christian Unity

Chairman Rt Revd Ian Cundy (*Bishop of Peterborough*)

General Secretary Prebendary Paul Avis
Tel: 020–7898 1470
email: paul.avis@c-of-e.org.uk

European Secretary Revd Dr Charles Hill
Tel: 020–7898 1474

Secretary for Local Unity Revd Flora Winfield
Tel: 020–7898 1479
email: flora.winfield@c-of-e.org.uk

Administrator Miss Linda Foster
Tel: 020–7898 1472
email: linda.foster@ccu.c-of-e.org.uk

Theological Secretary Vacancy   *Tel:* 020–7898 1488

Office Church House, Great Smith St, London SW1P 3NZ
Tel: 020–7898 1470
Fax: 020–7898 1483
email: hazel.agar@ccu.c-of-e.org.uk

The Council was established as an advisory committee of the General Synod on 1 April 1991 to continue and develop the ecumenical work formerly undertaken by the Board for Mission and Unity. That Board, set up on 1 January 1972, had inherited the responsibilities of the Missionary and Ecumenical Council of the Church Assembly (MECCA) and the Church of England Council on Foreign Relations (CFR).

FUNCTIONS OF THE COUNCIL
(*Extract from the Constitution*)

(a) To stimulate and encourage theological reflection in consultation with the Doctrine Commission and the Faith and Order Advisory Group and to advise the Archbishops' Council and through it the General Synod on unity issues and proposals in the light of the Christian understanding of God's purposes for the world.

(b) To foster ecumenical work in the Church nationally and in the dioceses.

(c) In conjunction with the Archbishops' Council to promote unity and ecumenical concerns in the work of all Boards and Councils.

(d) In ecumenical concerns on the Archbishops' Council's behalf to be the principal link between the General Synod and

  (i)   The Anglican Consultative Council;
  (ii) individual provinces and dioceses of the Anglican Communion and the United Churches incorporating former Anglican dioceses.

(e) On behalf of the Archbishops' Council to be the principal channel of communication between the General Synod and

  (i)   The World Council of Churches;
  (ii)   The Conference of European Churches;
  (iii) Churches Together in Britain and Ireland;
  (iv)   Churches Together in England;
  (v)   all other Christian Churches in the British Isles and abroad.

(f) To service committees and commissions engaged in ecumenical discussions with other Churches.

COUNCIL MEMBERS
Chairman Rt Revd Ian Cundy (*Bishop of Peterborough*)

Six members elected by the General Synod
Very Revd John Arnold (*Dean of Durham*), Rt Revd Colin Buchanan (*Bishop of Woolwich*), Canon Chad Coussmaker, Dr Carole Cull, Mrs Elizabeth Fisher, Mr Frank Knaggs

Four members appointed by the former Standing Committee
Revd Dr Gavin Ashenden, Revd Dr John Fenwick, Canon David Lickess, Mrs Rachel Moriarty

Four members chosen for expertise
Revd Mark Bratton, Revd Bill Croft, Mrs Terry Garley, Revd Dr Brian Leathard

Consultants
Rt Revd Michael Doe (*Bishop of Swindon*), Rt Revd John Hind (*Bishop of Gibraltar in Europe*), Rt Revd Bill Ind (*Bishop of Truro*), Rt Revd Barry Rogerson (*Bishop of Bristol*), Canon Richard Marsh (*Lambeth Palace*)

THE FAITH AND ORDER ADVISORY GROUP
Chairman Rt Revd John Hind (*Bishop of Gibraltar in Europe*)

The Faith and Order Advisory Group consists of not more than fifteen persons appointed by the Archbishops after consultation with the Council. The Group advises the House of Bishops or the Council on matters of ecumenical or theological concern referred to it by the House of Bishops or the Council.

COMMITTEE ON ROMAN CATHOLIC RELATIONS
Chairman Rt Revd Bill Ind (*Bishop of Truro*)

The Committee on Roman Catholic Relations consists of not more than fifteen persons appointed by the Archbishops after consultation with the Council. The Committee promotes relations between the Church of England and the Roman Catholic Church in this country. Regular meetings are held each year, of which two are joint meetings with the equivalent Roman Catholic body in the English Anglican–Roman Catholic Committee.

MEISSEN COMMISSION – ANGLICAN COMMITTEE
Chairman Rt Revd Michael Bourke (*Bishop of Wolverhampton*)

The Meissen Commission (the Sponsoring Body for Church of England–EKD Relations) was established in 1991 to oversee the implementation of the Meissen Declaration and encourage relationships with the Evangelical Church in Germany. It comprises Anglican and German Committees.

CHURCH OF ENGLAND–MORAVIAN CONTACT GROUP
Chairman Rt Revd David James (*Bishop of Pontefract*)

The Church of England–Moravian Contact Group consists of four representatives, ordained and lay, from each Church, together with ecumenical observers and staff. The Church of England representatives are appointed by the Archbishops. The Contact Group works to make real in the lives of the two Churches the commitments of the Fetter Lane Declaration – overseeing the implementation of those developments which are already possible, ensuring that further consideration is given to those areas where convergence is still required and nurturing growth in communion.

ECUMENICAL AFFAIRS
Contact is maintained with the World Council of Churches, the Conference of European Churches, Churches Together in Britain and Ireland, and Churches Together in England, where members and staff represent the Church of England at various levels. The Council is particularly concerned with helping the Church of England to relate effectively at every level to the ecumenical bodies.

The Board of Education

Chairman Rt Revd Alan Chesters (*Bishop of Blackburn*)

General Secretary Canon John Hall
Tel: 020–7898 1500
email: john.hall@c-of-e.org.uk

Adult Learning and Lay Training Mrs Hilary Ineson (*also Deputy Secretary*) Tel: 020–7898 1511
email: hilary.ineson@c-of-e.org.uk

Adult and Lifelong Learning Revd Ian Stubbs
Tel: 020–7898 1510
email: ian.stubbs@c-of-e.org.uk

Higher Education and Chaplaincy Revd Paul Brice
Tel: 020–7898 1513
email: paul.brice@c-of-e.org.uk

Children's Work Mrs Diana Murrie
Tel: 020–7898 1504
email: diana.murrie@c-of-e.org.uk

Further Education Mrs Anthea Turner
Tel: 020–7898 1517
email: anthea.turner@c-of-e.org.uk

Education and Administration Finance Officer Ms Daphne Griffith   Tel: 020–7898 1515
email: daphne.griffith@c-of-e.org.uk

Schools (*Curriculum*) Mr Alan Brown
Tel: 020–7898 1494
email: alan.brown@c-of-e.org.uk

Schools (*Governance and Management*) Mr David
Lankshear
Tel: 020–7898 1490
email: david.lankshear@c-of-e.org.uk

Youth Work
Mr Peter Ball
Tel: 020–7898 1506
email: peter.ball@c-of-e.org.uk

Ms Maxine Green
Tel: 020–7898 1507
email: maxine.green@c-of-e.org.uk

Office Church House, Great Smith St, London
SW1P 3NZ
Tel: 020–7898 1501
Fax: 020–7898 1520

BOARD MEMBERS
Rt Revd Alan Chesters (*Bishop of Blackburn,
Chairman*), Mrs Katy Blake, Mr Peter Bruinvels,
Mr Andrew Collier, Mrs Margaret Dean, Prof
Evelyn Ebsworth, Mr Nigel Greenwood, Prof
Walter James, Mr Peter LeRoy, Mr Geoff Locke,
Mr Peter Middlemiss, Mrs Heather Morgan, Mrs
Elizabeth Paver, Prof Arthur Pollard, Ven Robert
Reiss (*Archdeacon of Surrey*), Rt Revd Stephen
Venner (*Bishop of Dover*), Ven Paul Wheatley
(*Archdeacon of Sherborne*), Mr Peter Williams
(*Church in Wales*). Observers: Prof John Dickinson
(*Principal, King Alfred's College, Winchester*), Mr
Henry Head (*Salisbury DDE*).

The Board's constitution (as laid down by General Synod) sets out three functions: to advise the
General Synod through the Archbishops' Council
on all matters relating to education; to advise the
dioceses similarly; to take action in the field of
education (in the name of the Church of England
and the General Synod) on such occasion as is
required. The work of the Board is divided into
three areas, each under the general oversight of a
committee responsible to the Board.

COMMITTEES OF THE BOARD
Schools
The work of the Board in connection with schools
is carried out in close association with the
National Society (Church of England) for Promoting Religious Education (*see* page 54). The
two bodies have the same Chairman, General
Secretary, Schools Officers, and other members of
the staff of the Society and its RE centres are also
available to assist the Board in its work.

The Schools Committee reflects and serves the
Church's general involvement in the whole statutory system of schooling, with a particular interest in Church schools. It also maintains a link
with independent schools of Church of England
foundation. It seeks to be concerned with developments affecting the whole curriculum, within
which it has a special interest in religious education and school worship in both county and
Church schools.

Through its officers, the Committee communicates with the Department for Education and
Employment and other national agencies on
questions relating to schools, and maintains close
links both with professional and educational
bodies including the education departments of
other Churches (particularly through the
Churches' Joint Education Policy Committee).

It is responsible to the Board for administering
a Loan Scheme for aiding capital works at
Church schools.

Information about Church schools is available
on the National Society's web site at http://
www.churchschools.co.uk.

Further and Higher Education
The current concerns of this Committee are:

1 The development of the Church's presence and
witness in Further and Higher Education in the
light of careful study of the shifts of emphasis
and direction occurring within the national education system (involving mutual consultation
with the DfEE and with the FE/HE institutions,
attendance at conferences, and the making of
time for joint reflection).

2 The making of a particular contribution within
the Church's general activity in Further and
Higher Education by:
(1) working for the extension of Church contacts in, and impact on, the field of Further
Education;
(2) stimulating and developing the Church's
practical concern in student affairs;
(3) helping the Church to build up its ministry
in Higher Education by means of the
advisory, liaison, and representative services to chaplaincy work in HE already
established;
(4) maintaining and strengthening links with
Church Colleges of HE in the light of *An
Excellent Enterprise* (GS 1134).

Voluntary and Continuing Education
The Committee is concerned with the involvement of the Church in voluntary education. Its
task is to explore, identify and communicate how
those of differing age and circumstance can grow
into fullness of life in Christ.

The Committee is responsible:
(1) for servicing the diocesan agencies concerned with voluntary and continuing
education including parish development;
(2) for cooperating with the committees and
staffs of other Churches and educational
bodies. The purpose of such ecumenical
endeavour is to work on behalf of both
those within the membership of the
Church and those outside it.

The Committee considers and advises on work with children, young people and adults.

Adult Learning and Lay Training

The department exists to encourage adult Christian formation. For a minority this will mean training for a specific ministry in the Church but for most it involves working out the implications of Christian faith in daily life in the world.

The department has the following key functions:

(1) servicing diocesan and other networks of people working in adult learning and lay training in the Church;

(2) cooperating with other Churches and Christian training agencies;

(3) collecting and disseminating information about resources in a diverse and expanding field through *Newsboard* and other means;

(4) providing a National Training Programme in adult education and training;

(5) developing the Church's presence and witness in secular adult education;

(6) encouraging an ongoing critique of current practice through evaluation and research;

(7) being a 'centre of excellence' in the theory and practice of experiential learning and lifelong learning.

Youth Work

The department works to promote the educational, spiritual and social development of young people between the ages of 11 and 25. This work is for those outside the Church as well as those active within.

The National Youth Officers advise on appropriate training and resourcing of both voluntary and paid youth workers, and provide a Continuing Professional Development Scheme for Diocesan Youth Officers. Action is being taken to enable the better participation of young people in church life with continuing development of a Young Adult Network which includes the Observer Group at General Synod's July meeting. The National Youth Office is managing initiatives to develop youth work in rural areas and among minority ethnic young people.

The National Youth Officers consult regularly and work collaboratively with the Diocesan Youth Officers Network in responding to local, regional and national needs.

The Church's youth work also involves collaboration and partnership with a number of Anglican voluntary societies as well as with a variety of other Christian and secular agencies, including the Department for Education and Employment, the National Youth Agency, the National Council for Voluntary Youth Services, Churches Together in England, and the Centre for Youth Ministry. Receipt of a grant from the DfEE under their scheme for National Voluntary Youth Organizations has enabled youth work initiatives to be taken at local, diocesan and national level.

Youth A Part (GS 1203), a major report for General Synod on the Church's work with young people, has been, and continues to be, a great stimulus to discussion and action in youth work at every level. Last year the book *Accompanying* was published as a resource for parishes. Training, support and recognition of youth workers continues to be a focus with national and diocesan youth officers supporting developments in this area.

The Time of Our Lives in 1999 proved to be a unique and special occasion, attracting over 3,000 young Anglicans to London for a weekend with bishops and archbishops; initial follow-up to this event is being undertaken in dioceses.

Children's Work

1 The National Children's Officer is concerned primarily with the advocacy of the role and value of children in the Church, particularly:

(1) the Church as a worshipping community;

(2) the Church as a place of learning for all.

2 The National Officer works primarily with the network of diocesan Children's Advisers, organizing the National Conference, implementing induction and in-service training where appropriate, in order to provide laity and clergy at all levels with the necessary resources and training to nurture the faith of children and their families.

3 The Officer instigates and implements reflection and discussion on issues within the Church. Much of this is done in consultation with ecumenical partners and national bodies. Current major issues are:

(1) the challenge to the Church of reaching children and their families who have no church contact;

(2) Christian initiation and Communion before Confirmation;

(3) Child Protection.

4 The Officer works collaboratively with:

Church House Publishing

The National Society

Other Boards and Councils

Lambeth Palace

Other agencies including the Children's Society

The Consultative Group on Ministry among Children (an ecumenical network of CTBI)

For **Chaplains in Higher Education** *see* page 209.
For **Church Colleges of Higher Education** *see* page 215.

The Board of Mission

Chairman Rt Revd Tom Butler (*Bishop of Southwark*)

General Secretary Canon Philip King
Tel: 020–7898 1468
email: philip.king@c-of-e.org.uk

Administrative Secretary Mr Alan Tuddenham
Tel: 020–7898 1467
email: alan.tuddenham@c-of-e.org.uk

Partnership Secretary Mr John Clark
Tel: 020–7928 8681
email: john.clark@c-of-e.org.uk

Mission Theology Secretary Dr Anne Richards
Tel: 020–7898 1444
email: anne.richards@c-of-e.org.uk

National Adviser for Evangelism Canon Robert Freeman
Tel: 020–7898 1328
email: robert.freeman@c-of-e.org.uk

Mission and Evangelism Adviser Vacancy
Tel: 020–7898 1476

Interfaith Relations Adviser Canon Michael Ipgrave
Tel: 020–7898 1477
email: michael.ipgrave@c-of-e.org.uk

Church of England National Rural Officer Revd Jeremy Martineau
Tel: (01203) 696460
email: j.martineau@ruralnet.org.uk

Archbishops' Officer for the Millennium Revd Stephen Lynas
Tel: 020–7898 1436
email: stephen.lynas@c-of-e.org.uk

Millennium Administrator Ms Karen Little
Tel: 020–7898 1434
email: karen.little@c-of-e.org.uk

Office Church House, Great Smith St, London SW1P 3NZ
Tel: 020–7898 1469
Fax: 020–7898 1431

BOARD MEMBERS

Eight members elected by General Synod
Rt Revd Richard Garrard (*Bishop of Penrith*), Canon Christopher Hall, Prebendary Robert Horsfield, Mrs Christine McMullen, Dr Peter May, Canon John Moore, Very Revd John Richardson (*Provost of Bradford*), Mr Ian Smith

Three members of the General Synod appointed by the former Standing Committee, having regard to representation of persons representing the Church of England on national and international bodies concerned with mission
Mrs Pat Harris, Mr Nigel Holmes, Rt Revd Michael Nazir-Ali (*Bishop of Rochester*)

Five representatives of mission agencies appointed by the former Standing Committee on the nomination of the Partnership for World Mission
Revd Roger Bowen, Mr Paul Chandler, Rt Revd David Evans, Rt Revd Munawar Rumalshah, Miss Diana Witts

Five persons appointed by the former Standing Committee on the nomination of the Board, chosen for their knowledge of home mission concerns or interfaith relations, or for other relevant expertise
Revd Dr Brian Castle, Mrs Anne Davison, Mr Pradip Sudra, Revd Alison White, Canon Mavis Wilson

Functions of the Board

(*Extract from the Constitution*)

(a) To promote and encourage action, theological reflection and study in the area of mission.

(b) To stimulate and encourage theological reflection, in consultation with the Doctrine Commission, on issues and proposals concerning mission, evangelism, renewal and inter-faith relations in contemporary society, and to advise the General Synod and the dioceses.

(c) To be a channel of communication between the dioceses and the General Synod on the matters referred to in paragraph (b) of this clause.

(d) In conjunction with the Archbishops' Council to promote mission concerns in the work of all Boards.

(e) To bring together the General Synod and the voluntary mission agencies.

(f) In all matters related to the mission of the Church, to be a channel of communication between the General Synod, the Anglican Consultative Council, individual provinces and dioceses of the Anglican Communion, United Churches incorporating former Anglican dioceses, and other Churches.

PARTNERSHIP FOR WORLD MISSION COMMITTEE (PWM)

Partnership for World Mission (PWM) was set up in 1978 as a partnership between the General Synod and the World Mission Agencies of the Church of England. In April 1991 it changed from being an organization independent of General Synod (but with synodical representation) to a constituent committee of the Board of Mission.

The Committee draws its members from the Board, including General Synod members, from those concerned with World Mission issues, and from the eleven main World Mission Agencies of the Church of England, which are: Church Army, Church's Ministry among Jewish People, Church Mission Society, Crosslinks, Intercontinental Church Society, Mid-Africa Ministry (CMS), the Missions to Seamen, Mothers' Union, South American Mission Society, the Society for Promoting Christian Knowledge and the United Society for the Propagation of the Gospel. There are also 25 Associate Members.

Its main tasks are concerned with the Church of England's role in the Partnership in Mission process in the Anglican Communion; with Diocesan Companion Links; and with coordinating the policies and selected tasks of the Church of England's World Mission Agencies. It has an advisory role in enabling English dioceses and General Synod to see their way more clearly towards their participation in World Mission as members of the Anglican Communion and ecumenically.

Chairman Rt Revd Colin Bennetts (*Bishop of Coventry*)

Secretary Mr John Clark
email: john.clark@c-of-e.org.uk

Office Partnership House, 157 Waterloo Rd, London SE1 8XA   *Tel:* 020–7928 8681
Fax: 020–7633 0185

INTERFAITH CONSULTATIVE GROUP (IFCG)
The Interfaith Consultative Group advises the Board on Christian relations with Buddhists, Hindus, Jews, Muslims, Sikhs and other faith communities. It has published material on interfaith dialogue and such topics as multi-faith worship, mixed faith marriage and the use of church buildings by other faith communities. It provides a forum for information exchange and coordination between Church of England agencies concerned with these and related issues, and acts as a link between the Board and the ecumenical Churches' Commission for Interfaith Relations (CCIFR), of which Canon Michael Ipgrave is also Secretary.

Chairman Rt Revd John Austin (*Bishop of Aston*)

Secretary Canon Michael Ipgrave
Tel: 020–7898 1477
email: michael.ipgrave@c-of-e.org.uk

MISSION, EVANGELISM AND RENEWAL IN ENGLAND COMMITTEE
The main tasks of the Mission, Evangelism and Renewal in England Committee are to review and evaluate what is happening in evangelism and renewal, and to stimulate action accordingly. The Committee also seeks to work with the dio-

ceses to identify and promote good practice in mission, evangelism and renewal. Working with ecumenical partners, the voluntary societies, Partnership for World Mission and within the Anglican Communion forms a vital part of the work of this Committee.

Chairman Rt Revd Michael Colclough (*Bishop of Kensington*)

Secretary Vacancy   *Tel:* 020–7898 1476

MISSION THEOLOGICAL ADVISORY GROUP
The Mission Theological Advisory Group is concerned with the theology of mission and deals with theological issues referred to it by the Board and the Churches' Commission on Mission of the Churches Together in Britain and Ireland.

Chairman Rt Revd Michael Nazir-Ali (*Bishop of Rochester*)

Secretary Dr Anne Richards   *Tel:* 020–7898 1444
email: anne.richards@c-of-e.org.uk

RURAL AFFAIRS COMMITTEE
The Rural Affairs Committee is concerned to reflect to the Church structures and policy-makers the special needs and opportunities of rural churches, and to support the work of the National Rural Officer in his practical initiatives in developing rural mission and ministry.

Chairman Rt Revd Paul Barber (*Bishop of Brixworth*)

Secretary Revd Jeremy Martineau

Office The Arthur Rank Centre, National Agricultural Centre, Stoneleigh Park, Warwickshire CV8 2LZ   *Tel:* (01203) 696969
Fax: (01203) 696460
email: j.martineau@ruralnet.org.uk

ARCHBISHOPS' MILLENNIUM ADVISORY GROUP (AMAG)
The Archbishops' Millennium Advisory Group works to further plans for the year 2000 within the Church of England. It acts in close cooperation with the Churches Together in England Millennium Group to:

1 encourage Government and other official bodies to recognize that the Millennium is a Christian anniversary, and to reflect that as part of their programme;

2 encourage the Churches nationally and at local level to mark the year with suitable events and activities.

The Group also liaises with the Churches of other parts of the United Kingdom. A quarterly newsletter, *Millennium News*, is published by the Millennium Officer.

Chairman Rt Revd Gavin Reid (*Bishop of Maidstone*)

Secretary Revd Stephen Lynas *Tel:* 020–7898 1436
email: stephen.lynas@c-of-e.org.uk

The Board for Social Responsibility

Chairman Rt Revd Richard Harries (*Bishop of Oxford*)

Secretary Mr David Skidmore *Tel:* 020–7898 1521
email: david.skidmore@c-of-e.org.uk

Deputy Secretary (*Social, Economic and Industrial Affairs*) Mrs Ruth Badger *Tel:* 020–7898 1529
email: ruth.badger@c-of-e.org.uk

Assistant Secretary (*Science, Technology, Medicine and Environmental Issues*) Mrs Claire Foster
Tel: 020–7898 1523
email: claire.foster@c-of-e.org.uk

Assistant Secretary (*International and Development Affairs*) Dr Charles Reed *Tel:* 020–7898 1533
email: charles.reed@c-of-e.org.uk

Assistant Secretary (*Home Affairs*) Revd Dr Peter Sedgwick *Tel:* 020–7898 1531
email: peter.sedgwick@c-of-e.org.uk

Assistant Secretary (*Community and Urban Affairs*) Revd Dr Andrew Davey *Tel:* 020–7898 1446
email: andrew.davey@c-of-e.org.uk

Office Church House, Great Smith St, London SW1P 3NZ *Tel:* 020–7898 1521
Fax: 020–7898 1536

BOARD MEMBERS

Six members of the General Synod elected by the General Synod
Mrs Elaine Appelbee, Prof Raman Bedi, Canon Paul Brett, Mr Philip Gore, Dr Sheila Grieve, Very Revd George Nairn-Briggs (*Provost of Wakefield*)

Nine members appointed by the former Standing Committee
Prof Michael Banner, Rt Revd Robert Hardy (*Bishop of Lincoln*), Mr Dominick Harrod, Rt Revd Richard Lewis (*Bishop of St Edmundsbury and Ipswich*), Canon John Polkinghorne, Mrs Hilary Russell, Rt Revd Humphrey Taylor (*Bishop of Selby*), Revd Dr Mary Seller, Dr Alan Suggate

Up to three members co-opted by the Board Mrs Julia Flack, Rt Revd Roger Sainsbury (*Bishop of Barking*)

The Board was set up by resolution of the Church Assembly on 1 January 1958. It became an Advisory Committee of the General Synod in 1971. Its constitution requires it to 'promote and co-ordinate the thought and action of the Church in matters affecting the life of all in society'.

The Board acts on behalf of the Synod and the Church in its work on a wide range of social issues affecting both domestic and international affairs. Some of this work appears in the Board's publications and reports to Synod, but most of the work is done by staff with the help of ad hoc working parties, advisory groups, or standing committees, and through the Board's quarterly journal, *Crucible* (*see* page 26).

STANDING COMMITTEES OF THE BOARD

HOME AFFAIRS COMMITTEE
Chairman Rt Revd Robert Hardy (*Bishop of Lincoln*)

Secretary Revd Dr Peter Sedgwick
Tel: 020–7898 1531
email: peter.sedgwick@c-of-e.org.uk

The Committee has a representative membership of ten. Its terms of reference are:

1 to promote Christian theological reflection and appropriate action on criminal justice, substance abuse and mental health;

2 to monitor relevant changes in the light of Christian ethical principles;

3 to liaise with diocesan and ecumenical partners and appropriate statutory, professional and voluntary agencies;

4 to advise the Board on ways in which issues might be drawn to the attention of the wider Church.

INTERNATIONAL AND DEVELOPMENT AFFAIRS COMMITTEE
Chairman Rt Revd Humphrey Taylor (*Bishop of Selby*)

Secretary Dr Charles Reed *Tel:* 020–7898 1533
email: charles.reed@c-of-e.org.uk

The Committee has a representative membership of ten. Its terms of reference are:

1 to promote Christian theological reflection and action on international affairs and world development;

2 to monitor in particular those areas of the world in which the influence of the British Government is or has been significant, or from which requests for action have been received from member churches of the Anglican Communion or ecumenical partners;

3 to liaise with diocesan and ecumenical partners and appropriate statutory, professional and voluntary agencies;

4 to advise the Board on ways in which issues might be drawn to the attention of the wider Church;

5 to continue the commendation work of Overseas Settlement.

COMMUNITY AND URBAN AFFAIRS COMMITTEE
Co-Chairmen Rt Revd Roger Sainsbury (*Bishop of Barking*) and Prof Raman Bedi

Secretary Revd Dr Andrew Davey
Tel: 020–7898 1446
email: andrew.davey@c-of-e.org.uk

The Committee has a representative membership of up to 13 members. Its terms of reference are:

1 to maintain the Church of England's capacity to speak with authority about racism, poverty, social exclusion and social disintegration in society;

2 to promote Christian theological reflection and appropriate action on questions of poverty, racism, social exclusion and social disintegration in society;

3 to monitor developments on those issues and encourage responses to them from Church and Government;

4 to liaise with diocesan and ecumenical partners and appropriate statutory, professional and voluntary agencies;

5 to advise the Board on ways in which issues might be drawn to the attention of the wider Church.

SCIENCE, MEDICINE AND TECHNOLOGY COMMITTEE
Chairman Canon John Polkinghorne

Secretary Mrs Claire Foster   *Tel:* 020–7898 1523
email: claire.foster@c-of-e.org.uk

The Committee is made up of ten members. Its terms of reference are:

1 to promote Christian theological and ethical reflection on the exercise of human power over the natural world;

2 to monitor developments in science, medicine and technology in the light of Christian ethical principles;

3 to advise the Board on ways in which issues might be drawn to the attention of the wider Church.

SOCIAL, ECONOMIC AND INDUSTRIAL AFFAIRS COMMITTEE
Chairman Rt Revd Richard Lewis (*Bishop of St Edmundsbury and Ipswich*)

Secretary Mrs Ruth Badger   *Tel:* 020–7898 1529
email: ruth.badger@c-of-e.org.uk

The Committee has a representative membership of ten. Its terms of reference are:

1 to promote Christian theological reflection and appropriate action on contemporary social, economic and industrial issues;

2 to monitor relevant social and economic trends in the light of Christian ethical principles;

3 to liaise with diocesan and ecumenical partners and appropriate statutory, professional and voluntary agencies;

4 to advise the Board on ways in which the issues might be drawn to the attention of the wider Church.

PUBLICATIONS
The Board is responsible for the quarterly journal *Crucible* (*Editor* Revd Dr Peter Sedgwick). *Crucible* provides Christian comment on contemporary social, economic and political issues. Details about subscription to *Crucible* are available from the Board's office.

The Board also publishes from time to time reports, papers and pamphlets which give perspectives on matters of public concern and the current thinking of the Board on major social questions. These are available from Church House Bookshop.

The Hospital Chaplaincies Council

Chairman Rt Revd Christopher Herbert (*Bishop of St Albans*)

Secretary Revd Robert Clarke   *Tel:* 020–7898 1894
email: robert.clarke@c-of-e.org.uk

Hospital/Health Care Chaplaincy Training and Development Officer Revd Malcolm Masterman
Tel: 020–7898 1895
email: malcolm.masterman@c-of-e.org.uk

Administrator Mrs Liz Paffey   *Tel:* 020–7898 1894
email: liz.paffey@c-of-e.org.uk

Business Manager (Training) Miss Elspeth Dawson   *Tel:* 020–7898 1895
email: elspeth.dawson@c-of-e.org.uk

Office Fielden House, 13 Little College St, London SW1P 3SH   *Tel:* 020–7898 1894
Fax: 020–7898 1891

MEMBERS

Five members appointed by the former Standing Committee who shall have knowledge of the Health Service, the medical and nursing professions
Dr John Beal, Canon Eddie Burns, Miss Jacquie Flindall, Mrs Alison Ruoff, Ven Frank White (*Archdeacon of Sunderland*)

Three members appointed by the former Standing Committee on the nomination of the College of Health Care Chaplains from its Church of England membership
Revd Sandy Borthwick, Canon David Equeall, Revd Michael Stevens

Up to two co-opted members
Mr Tim Battle

Two observers from the Church in Wales, appointed by the Archbishop of Wales
Revd Berw Hughes, Revd Martyn Davies

Functions of the Council

1 To consider questions of policy and practice relating to spiritual ministrations to patients and staff in medical establishments and community care programmes referred to it by the General Synod.

2 To provide information and advice to the dioceses in their negotiations with Health Authorities and Trusts on the appointment of Hospital Chaplains and on other National Health Service (NHS) matters; to visit and support dioceses involved in such negotiations; and to provide similar services to Hospital Chaplains in their relations with NHS management.

3 To respond promptly to enquiries from Chief Executives and Trusts regarding chaplaincy issues and the best practice for employment of Anglican clergy in the NHS.

4 To monitor and authorize, on behalf of the Church of England, the standards and content of training provided for Hospital Chaplaincy in cooperation with other Churches and chaplaincy organizations.

5 To work jointly with the Ministry Division in providing the personnel and expertise input from qualified chaplains in preparing theological students for their ministry to the sick in hospital and in the community.

6 To monitor matters affecting spiritual ministrations in all medical establishments and community care programmes, reporting to the General Synod as and when required.

7 To act as a liaison between the Department of Health and the Church of England on all questions relating to spiritual ministrations in medical establishments and community care programmes.

8 To contribute, in cooperation with the Board for Social Responsibility, to the ongoing theological reflections on contemporary medical, ethical and social issues.

9 To exchange information and advice in matters relating to Hospital Chaplaincy with other Christian Churches in the British Isles and abroad.

10 To use its contacts to encourage, facilitate, coordinate and generally support all opportunities for learning about hospital ministry. To further this role it has, with effect from 1 January 1996, jointly funded, with the College of Health Care Chaplains, the post of Hospital/Health Care Chaplaincy Training and Development Officer. His role is to implement and monitor the work of training. The Roman Catholic Bishops' Conference of England and Wales together with the Free Churches' Council also provide financial support for this joint initiative. The Chaplaincy (Health Care) Education and Development Group, made up of equal numbers from the sponsoring bodies, provide a resource group to support the work of the Training Officer.

THE CHURCHES' COMMITTEE FOR HOSPITAL CHAPLAINCY

In management relationships with the Department of Health and the NHS Executive the council works cooperatively with the Free Churches and the Roman Catholic Church in this committee. The Secretary of the CCHC also acts as the spokesperson and link with Churches Together in England.

HERITAGE

This area of the Archbishops' Council's responsibilities relates to the Church's concern with buildings and related matters. The development of closer working relationships between all the Church heritage bodies while recognizing their separate (often statutory) responsibilities is a high priority.

The Council for the Care of Churches

Chairman Very Revd Raymond Furnell (*Dean of York*)

Vice-Chairmen Mr Tony Redman
Very Revd Graeme Knowles (*Dean of Carlisle*)

Secretary Dr Thomas Cocke   *Tel:* 020–7898 1882
     email: thomas.cocke@c-of-e.org.uk

Support and Development Officer Mr Stephen Bowler   *Tel:* 020–7898 1860
     email: stephen.bowler@c-of-e.org.uk

Casework and Law Officer Mr Jonathan Goodchild
     Tel: 020–7898 1883
     email: jonathan.goodchild@c-of-e.org.uk

Conservation Officer Mr Andrew Argyrakis
     Tel: 020–7898 1885
     email: andrew.argyrakis@c-of-e.org.uk

Conservation Assistant Mr Steven Sleight
     Tel: 020–7898 1886
     email: steven.sleight@c-of-e.org.uk

Archaeology Officer Dr Joseph Elders
     Tel: 020–7898 1875
     email: joseph.elders@c-of-e.org.uk

Librarian Miss Janet Seeley   *Tel:* 020–7898 1884
     email: janet.seeley@c-of-e.org.uk

Research Assistant Mr Simon Kemp
     Tel: 020–7898 1865
     email: simon.kemp@c-of-e.org.uk

Office Fielden House, 13 Little College St, London SW1P 3SH   *Tel:* 020–7898 1886
     Fax: 020–7898 1881

MEMBERS

Revd Michael Ainsworth, Revd Peter Cavanagh, Revd Dr Allan Doig, Revd Dr Timothy Ellis, Dr Jennifer Freeman, Ven John Gathercole (*Archdeacon of Dudley*), Mrs Philippa Glanville, Mr William Hawkes, Mr Thomas Hornsby, Miss Jane Kennedy, Mrs Judith Leigh, Ven Trevor Lloyd (*Archdeacon of Barnstaple*), Mr Huon Mallalieu, Mr John McArdell, Mr Jeremy Musson, Mr Nicholas Rank, Mr Tony Redman, Mr William Sanders, Mrs Mary Saunders, Mr Tim Tatton-Brown, Miss Fay Wilson-Rudd

The Council for the Care of Churches (CCC) was formed in 1921 to coordinate the work of the Diocesan Advisory Committees for the Care of Churches, which advise diocesan chancellors on faculty applications. The CCC originally consisted of representatives of all the Committees, but in 1958 it was reconstituted as a Council appointed by the Church Assembly. In 1972, it became a permanent Commission of the General Synod.

The CCC advises the Archbishops' Council on all matters relating to the use, care and planning or design of places of worship, their curtilages and contents; acts on the Council's behalf in contacts with Government departments and other bodies and in negotiations with professional bodies over church inspection and repair; and assists in the review or revision of legislation relating to church buildings and their contents.

The Council provides Diocesan Pastoral Committees with detailed reports about the architectural and historic qualities of churches likely to be declared redundant. It also submits specialist advice to diocesan chancellors and Diocesan Advisory Committees on proposals which are the subject of faculty applications, e.g. the construction of church extensions, re-ordering schemes, the sale of church furnishings, partial demolition of churches, etc.

The CCC maintains contact with Diocesan Advisory Committees through regular circulation of newsletters, by an annual meeting of members and by personal visits. The membership of DACs is varied: it includes both clergy and lay, some with professional expertise in architecture, art history and archaeology and others of no specialist knowledge but of sound judgement and experience, or representing the views of English Heritage, the local planning authority and the amenity societies. Every diocese has specialist advisers on organs, bells, clocks, archaeology and so on.

The CCC administers funds (generously provided by charitable bodies) for the conservation of furnishings and works of art in churches, and collaborates closely with English Heritage, the National Heritage Memorial Fund (and its Heritage Lottery Fund) and other grant-making bodies. Advice is available from the Council on specific conservation problems.

The CCC is not only concerned with the care and conservation of ancient buildings and objects, but also with the development of places of worship and the encouragement of good new furnishings and works of art. Advice is available and parishes are encouraged to consult the Council's register of artists and craftsmen and to examine photographs of their work.

PUBLICATIONS

The basic title in the Council's programme of publications is *How to Look After Your Church*; other booklets in the series (regularly revised) include *A Guide to Church Inspection and Repair*, *Church Floors and Floor Coverings*, *Heating Your Church*, *Church Organs*, *Redecorating Your Church*, and *The Repair and Maintenance of Glass in Churches*. The most recent publications are *A Guide to the Photography of Church Furnishings* and *Widening the Eye of the Needle*. There is also a 20-minute video called *Looking After Your Church*.

The CCC publishes a standard form of *Church Log Book* and a *Church Property Register*, to assist parishes in record-keeping. In addition it has produced technical leaflets and codes of practice, dealing with subjects such as lightning protection, the care of clocks and historic bells and bell-frames. The CCC publishes three light-hearted guides to the care and presentation of churches, with cartoons by Graham Jeffery: *The Church-warden's Year: A Calendar of Church Maintenance*, *Handle with Prayer: A Church Cleaner's Notebook* and *Safe and Sound? A Guide to Church Security*. *The Protection of Our English Churches* traces the history and development of the CCC from its foundation in 1921. The CCC's annual journal *Churchscape* includes articles on everyday care of churches and on their history and design, as well as reviews of books and events of current interest.

A complete list of titles and prices is available on request from the CCC or Church House Bookshop.

The Cathedrals Fabric Commission for England

Chairman Prof Averil Cameron

Vice-Chairman Sir Michael Llewellyn Smith

Secretary Dr Richard Gem   *Tel:* 020–7898 1887
                email: richard.gem@c-of-e.org.uk

Cathedrals Officer Miss Linda Monckton
                Tel: 020–7898 1888
        email: linda.monckton@c-of-e.org.uk

Office Fielden House, 13 Little College St, London SW1P 3SH
        Tel: 020–7898 1866; 029–7898 1863
                Fax: 020–7898 1881
        email: enquiries@cfce.c-of-e.org.uk

MEMBERS

Mr Robert Aagaard, Mr Michael Archer, Mrs Corinne Bennett, Mr John Burton, Mr Philip Cooper, Dr Philip Dixon, Revd Richard Hanford, Professor Jacques Heyman, Revd Paul Jenkins, Mr Julian Litten, Mr John Maine, Canon Paul Mellor, Mr John Norman, Mrs Diane Nutting, Very Revd Michael Perham (*Provost of Derby*), Mrs Sarah Quail, Mr Michael Reardon, Mr Tony Redman, Very Revd Michael Sadgrove (*Provost of Sheffield*), Rt Revd David Stancliffe (*Bishop of Salisbury*), Mr Martin Stancliffe, Very Revd Robert Willis (*Dean of Hereford*)

In 1949, at the request of Deans and Chapters, the Cathedrals Advisory Committee was set up to give help and advice on plans and problems affecting the fabric, furnishings, fittings and precincts of cathedrals.

In 1981, the Committee was reconstituted as a permanent Commission of the General Synod, under the title of The Cathedrals Advisory Commission for England.

In 1991, the Commission was further reconstituted as a statutory body under the Care of Cathedrals Measure and renamed The Cathedrals Fabric Commission. In addition to advisory functions in relation to the architecture, archaeology, art and history of cathedrals and their precincts, the Commission has regulatory powers. Before implementing proposals affecting the cathedral, its contents or its surroundings, the Dean and Chapter require the approval of the Commission in specific cases, or of a local Fabric Advisory Committee appointed jointly by the Commission and by the Dean and Chapter.

CHURCH HERITAGE FORUM

Chairman Rt Revd Richard Chartres (*Bishop of London*)

Vice-Chairman The Baroness Wilcox of Plymouth

Secretary Miss Andrea Mulkeen
        email: andrea.mulkeen@c-of-e.org.uk

The Church Heritage Forum, which was established in 1997, brings together representatives of national and local church interests in matters relating to the Church's built heritage. It enables the Church to take a more proactive role in anticipating developments in the built heritage field; ensures that heritage concerns are fed into the Archbishops' Council; provides a mechanism for members to reach a view on matters of common concern; provides a point of focus for contact both within the Church and with outside bodies;

promotes a wider public awareness of the Church's work in the built heritage area; and enables the exchange of information and facilitate mutual support.

Membership comprises representatives from the following: Advisory Board for Redundant Churches, Archbishops' Council, Association of English Cathedrals, Church Commissioners' Redundant Churches Committee, Cathedrals Fabric Commission for England, Churches Conservation Trust, Council for the Care of Churches, and an archdeacon.

FINANCE

The Archbishops' Council's responsibilities, as the financial executive of the General Synod and financial advisory body of the Church of England, are discharged through its Finance Committee. This Committee is the focus for the work formerly undertaken by (a) the Central Board of Finance as the financial executive of the General Synod and in relation to Christian Stewardship; and (b) the Church Commissioners, concerning financial provision for the clergy, including the allocation of available monies to support the needier dioceses. The Central Board of Finance remains in existence as a Trustee body, with the same membership as the Archbishops' Council, with ultimate responsibility for the CBF Church of England Investment, Fixed Interest Securities and Deposit Funds, and for the Central Church Fund and a number of other smaller trusts, although in practice this responsibility will be carried out through the Finance Committee.

The Council's Finance Committee is responsible for the management of the financial business of the Synod and the Archbishops' Council. This includes the raising and administration of money voted by the Synod for the Archbishops' Council and for other purposes, the apportionment of those costs between dioceses, the presentation of annual reports and accounts, and the presentation of the annual budget. It is responsible for the provision of accounting management information and financial control.

As the financial advisory body of the Church of England, the Committee is charged with responsibility for advice and coordination on financial matters over the Church as a whole and will periodically produce, in conjunction with the other national Church institutions, reports on the Church's general financial position.

Existing consultative arrangements with dioceses have been enhanced by the creation of the Inter-Diocesan Finance Forum, a non-statutory body. It provides a formal mechanism for the views of Diocesan Boards of Finance to be obtained on clergy remuneration, conditions of service, and other financial matters (including on the budget for national Church responsibilities before it is presented to Synod).

INTER-DIOCESAN FINANCE FORUM
Chairman Mr Michael Chamberlain

Members Three members from each diocese chosen by the Bishop's Council of each diocese.

The scope of the Forum includes consultation on remuneration policy and conditions of service; pensions policy; the national Church budget and apportionments; and allocations to dioceses for the support of ministry in poorer areas.

THE GENERAL SYNOD FUND
The revenues of the General Synod, except for a small income from legacies, donations and other sources, are furnished by the dioceses in accordance with a system of apportionment approved annually by the Synod. The Finance Committee is responsible for the preparation of an annual budget, which is produced a year in advance, and a preview of expenditure for subsequent years. As part of this process the Committee takes account of diocesan views through the Inter-Diocesan Finance Forum. The budget is agreed with the Archbishops' Council and submitted to the Synod at the July Group of Sessions for approval.

ARCHBISHOPS' COUNCIL BUDGET
The budget traditionally covers three main areas: *training for ministry, national Church responsibilities* – this latter element covers the cost of the Church's national work through the Archbishops' Council, and a variety of *grants and provisions* which enable the Church of England to play its part in the wider world through the Anglican Consultative Council and ecumenical bodies both in this country and abroad. A further item of expenditure, known as Inter-diocesan support – Mission Agencies clergy pensions contributions, has been included since the 1999 budget. This will allow the dioceses to reimburse the Church Commissioners, through the General Synod budget, for the cost of meeting the pension contributions of clergy employed by specified Mission Agencies.

Two main themes run through the 2000 budget: the continued, and very welcome, increase in the numbers coming forward for ordination training, and the second, and most

General Synod Budget

		2000
	£	£
TRAINING FOR MINISTRY		
Ordination training grants – colleges		5,801,000
Ordination training grants – courses/Ordained Local Ministry		2,680,000
Mixed Mode		13,000
		8,494,000
Financed by:		
Apportionment on the dioceses		8,204,000
Transfer from Reserves		200,000
Income from other sources		90,000
		8,494,000
NATIONAL CHURCH RESPONSIBILITIES		
Central Secretariat and Legal		1,500,600
Communications		393,100
Human Resources		245,900
Ministry Division		1,215,900
Church and World:		
Board of Education	635,700	
Board of Mission	461,200	
Board for Social Responsibility	430,100	
Council for Christian Unity	328,000	
Hospital Chaplaincies Council	109,000	
		1,963,300
Finance Division		1,212,300
Heritage (CCC/CFC)		547,500
Common Services		585,000
Establishment Charges		1,812,900
Contingency		66,000
		9,542,500
GRANTS AND PROVISIONS		
Anglican Communion Activities		332,000
English ecumenical bodies		168,000
British ecumenical bodies		214,000
Conference of European Churches and other work in Europe		91,500
World Council of Churches		109,900
Church Urban Fund		228,000
Other grants and provisions		82,900
		1,226,300
Financed by:		
Apportionment on the dioceses		10,258,800
Grant from Central Church Fund		180,000
Income from other sources		125,000
Savings brought forward/Transfers from Reserves		205,000
Allocation from Archbishops' Council to offset transferred work		(1,989,600)
Net cost		**8,779,200**
INTER-DIOCESAN SUPPORT/MISSION AGENCIES CLERGY PENSIONS		
CONTRIBUTIONS		194,000
Financed by:		
Apportionment		**194,000**

significant, stage in the phased transfer of functions from the Church Commissioners to the Archbishops' Council.

Numbers coming forward for training have increased by 125 over the 1999 levels estimated, with a further estimated increase of 30 in the 2000/2001 academic year. The good news does bring a financial cost, however, and training expenditure is budgeted to increase 157 per cent above 1999 levels to £8,494,000, of which the dioceses will be asked to meet £8,204,000.

The 2000 budget reflects the second stage of the

new administrative structure of the Archbishops' Council, with the transfer of the work of *Crockford*, Human Resources, all the Central Services departments, and Internal Audit (a new feature in the Council's activities) from the Church Commissioners. The transfer of these functions will add £1,144,600 to the General Synod budget, but at the same time this represents a corresponding saving to the Church Commissioners. This saving will therefore increase the amount made available for allocation to the dioceses and the Council will use this sum to offset the effect of the transferred costs. This will be achieved by allocating this sum on the basis of the apportionment formula, i.e. on the same basis on which the Council's budget is funded. Apart from some transitional costs associated with the relocation of staff, the impact of which will be spread over several years, total administrative expenditure under the Council is not expected to be any greater than under the existing arrangements.

Core expenditure in *National Church Responsibilities* is budgeted to increase by 55 per cent. While ahead of inflation, these figures include some staff regrading, the new Internal Audit function mentioned above, and the transfer to the Council of certain costs, where appropriate, from other Central Church organizations.

The effect of decisions in 1998 and 1999 to make early use of the reserves to keep the apportionment increases manageable had led to a depletion of the reserves. This factor, together with the expected Training overexpenditure in 1999, and the continued increase in the training numbers, has meant that increases in expenditure must feed directly into the apportionment with only a small cushion from the reserves. The overall picture is therefore an increase in the apportionment of 154 per cent over the 1999 figure. Of this figure two-thirds is attributable to the increase in the Training apportionment.

Finance Committee

Chairman Mr Michael Chamberlain

Secretary Mr Shaun Farrell   *Tel:* 020–7898 1795
          email: shaun.farrell@c-of-e.org.uk

Elected Members Mr John Booth, Mr Alan Cooper, Mr Philip Hamlyn Williams, Mr Alan King, Revd Christopher Lilley, Mr Peter Lowater, Mr Bryan Sandford, Revd Dr Richard Turnbull

Appointed Members Dr Christina Baxter, Rt Revd John Packer (*Bishop of Warrington*), (two vacancies)

Ex Officio Mr Allan Bridgewater (*Chairman of the Pensions Board*), Mr John Sclater (*First Church Estates Commissioner*)

Terms of reference

1 To advise the Archbishops' Council and the dioceses on all financial aspects of the Council's work, including its investment and trustee responsibilities, and on the overall financial needs and resources of the Church.

2 To make recommendations to the Archbishops' Council as to its annual budget and on mechanisms for monitoring and controlling the expenditure of the Council.

3 To consult with dioceses on financial matters, and to make recommendations thereon as appropriate to the Archbishops' Council and the dioceses.

4 To assess and seek to rationalize and simplify the systems for cash flow within the Church.

5 To provide a central forum for the development and promotion of Christian stewardship and fund-raising.

6 To provide and coordinate research and guidance on financial, accounting and related matters.

7 To provide a channel for communicating on financial matters with Her Majesty's Government, financial regulators and other appropriate enforcement bodies, both directly and through the Churches Main Committee.

8 To work in collaboration with ecumenical partners on matters within the Committee's terms of reference.

9 To carry out such other work as may be entrusted to it by the Archbishops' Council.

OFFICERS
Financial Secretary Mr Shaun Farrell
          Tel: 020–7898 1795
          email: shaun.farrell@c-of-e.org.uk

Head of Financial Planning and Administration Mr Jeremy Elloy   *Tel:* 020–7898 1562
          email: jerry.elloy@c-of-e.org.uk

National Stewardship Officer Mr Robin Stevens
          Tel: 020–7898 1540
          email: robin.stevens@c-of-e.org.uk

Senior Accountant Mr Stephen Rider
          Tel: 020–7898 1568
          email: stephen.rider@c-of-e.org.uk

Head of Internal Audit Mrs Mary Ball
Tel: 020–7898 1658
email: mary.ball@c-of-e.org.uk

Office Church House, Great Smith St, London SW1P 3NZ
Tel: 020–7898 1000
Fax: 020–7898 1558

CHRISTIAN STEWARDSHIP

Through its Christian Stewardship Committee, the Archbishops' Council plays an active part in affirming the principles of Christian stewardship in the discovery and use of human and financial resources available to the Church. Initiatives are promoted, support given and ideas exchanged between the diocesan members of the Christian Stewardship network. In particular, conferences, training courses and publications are used to supplement the personal contact between the National Stewardship Officer and diocesan staff.

Stewardship advisers encourage church people to respond to God's love and generosity and resource their vision by giving their time, their skills and their money – the latter regularly, tax-effectively and in proportion to their income. The challenge to Church members is to aim at a level of giving to and through the Church of not less than 5 per cent of net income and to review their giving annually.

In 1999 a major report was published for General Synod. *First to the Lord – Funding the Church's Mission* provides an overview of the financial position of the Church and looks at the Church's finances through the eyes of Christian stewardship and in the light of the imperative to mission. The report has been made available through dioceses to parishes and church people for consideration and action. It is planned that General Synod will debate the report in 2000. Copies may be obtained through Church House Bookshop at £2.50 each or 50p for 20 copies or more.

Other publications are also available:

(1) a legacy strategy for the whole Church, *Your Legacy Will Help*, which raises awareness of the additional need for giving by legacies;

(2) a booklet, *Tax-Efficient Giving*, for officers of PCCs with guidance on the best ways to give and then obtain tax relief;

(3) a leaflet, *Tax Recovery*, which explains how individuals can make their giving tax-efficient;

(4) *The Charities Act 1993 and the PCC*, which complements the *Church Accounting Regulations 1997* and provides guidance on the preparation of annual PCC accounts, their scrutiny and their reporting. This relates the requirements of the Charities Act 1993 to the particular circumstances of PCCs. It has been published as part of the corporate stewardship of the Church's financial resources, in response to the regulations for accounting, reporting and scrutiny contained in Part VI of the Charities Act 1993.

CCLA INVESTMENT MANAGEMENT LIMITED

Registered Office St Alphage House, 2 Fore St, London EC2Y 5AQ
Company Registration No 218308
Regulated by IMRO
Tel: 020–7588 1815
Fax: 020–7588 6291
Telex: 8954509

Managing Director Mr Andrew Gibbs

Investment Director Mr Tim Lavis

Director (Fixed Interest and Cash) Mr Colin Peters

Finance and Admin Director Mrs Belinda Sprigg

CCLA Investment Management Limited (CCLA) is a leading specialist investment management company serving charities, churches and local authorities. It provides investment, property and cash management, administration and registration services for the CBF Church of England Funds of which the Central Board of Finance of the Church of England is the trustee. CCLA is owned 60 per cent by the CBF Church of England Investment Fund, 25 per cent by the COIF Charities Investment Fund and 15 per cent by the Local Authorities Mutual Investment Trust. It is regulated by IMRO in the conduct of its investment business and is authorized to give investment advice to churches, charities and local authorities.

The CBF Church of England Funds

Established under the Church Funds Investment Measure 1958, these open-ended funds aim to meet most of the investment needs of a church trust and are used by diocesan boards of finance and trusts, cathedrals, diocesan boards of education, theological colleges, Church schools and educational endowments, church societies, the Church Commissioners and many PCCs.

Investment Fund
The main CBF Church of England Fund for capital that can be invested for the long term. A widely spread portfolio mainly of UK and overseas equities. Aims at steady income and capital growth. Weekly share dealings.

31 May 1999	Investment Fund	Fixed Interest Securities Fund	Deposit Fund	Property Fund
Value of Fund	£855 million	£145 million	£535 million	£39 million
Net Asset Value per Share	1108.77p	171.08p	–	102.33p
Income Yield %	3.15	7.48	5.00	5.96

Fixed Interest Securities Fund
Invested only in fixed interest stocks. Intended to supplement where necessary the initial lower income yield on the Investment Fund. Recommended only for a small proportion of long-term capital as it offers no protection from inflation. Weekly share dealings.

Deposit Fund
This money Fund is for cash balances which should be available at short notice and with minimal risk of capital loss. Accounts in the Fund obtain a rate of interest close to money market rates even on small sums. Daily deposit and withdrawal facilities. The Fund is rated Aaa (Triple A) by Moody's Investors Services.

Property Fund
Invests directly in UK commercial property. Fund is intended primarily for long-term investment by large church trusts only. Month-end share dealings but periods of notice may be imposed.

Risk Warnings: The value of the Funds and their income can fall as well as rise and you may not get back the amount invested. Past performance is no guarantee of future returns. Guarantees regarding repayment of deposits cannot be given. For full risk warnings refer to Funds' brochures.

Brochures and Reports and Accounts are available from CCLA Investment Management Limited at the address above.

THE CENTRAL CHURCH FUND
This Fund was established in 1915 and is administered by the Central Board of Finance separately from money raised on the authority of the General Synod. All money received by the Central Board for its general purposes is placed in this Fund, and also money earmarked or appropriated for special purposes, as shown in the accounts.

Grants amounting to £681,896 (1997 £587,169) were paid during the year to 31 December 1997.

The Central Board of Finance welcomes legacies, subscriptions and donations (including covenanted subscriptions) to the Central Church Fund which can be used either for the general purposes of the Church of England at the discretion of the Central Board, or for any special purposes connected therewith specified by the donor.

The Fund helps parishes and dioceses with imaginative and innovative projects of all kinds, especially those that meet the need of local communities. It assists with the cost of training for the ministry, and it makes an annual grant to the General Synod from its unappropriated funds. It is also used to meet unexpected and urgent needs which cannot be budgeted for.

During 1998 the Fund received legacies and donations totalling £105,570.

Further information and application forms are available from:
Mr Jeremy Elloy
Secretary to the Central Church Fund
Church House
Great Smith St
London SW1P 3NZ   *Tel:* 020–7898 1562
                          Fax: 020–7898 1558
              email: jerry.elloy@c-of-e.org.uk

AUDIT COMMITTEE
Chairman Mr Ian McNeil

Secretary Mr Shaun Farrell   *Tel:* 020–7898 1795
              email: shaun.farrell@c-of-e.org.uk

Members Ms Jane Bisson, Mr Anthony Hesselwood, Mrs Elizabeth Paver, Mr Mike Tyrrell

This Committee ensures an independent oversight of the Council's finances. Its duties are to oversee the discharge of the Archbishops' Council's responsibilities relating to financial statements, internal control systems and internal and external audit, and to report to the Archbishops' Council thereon with recommendations as appropriate.

MINISTRY

The provision of a properly trained and supported ministry is critical to the Church's mission. The Council brings together policy on the selection, training, deployment and remuneration of the Church of England's ministry – responsibilities that were formerly scattered at national level between different bodies – thus enabling decisions on ministry policy and strategy to be taken in the round.

The Council's responsibilities in this area are handled by four committees, each charged with a specific area of work: Vocation, Recruitment and Selection; Theological Education and Training; Deployment, Remuneration and Conditions of Service; and Ministry Among Deaf People. While the Central Readers' Council continues to fulfil its role in enhancing the contribution of Readers to the overall ministry of the Church, its work is fully integrated into the work of these committees.

The Archbishops' Council's functions as the Central Stipends Authority are discharged under the auspices of the Deployment, Remuneration and Conditions of Service Committee.

STAFF

Director of Ministry Ven Gordon Kuhrt
Tel: 020–7898 1390
email: gordon.kuhrt@c-of-e.org.uk

Vocation, Recruitment and Selection Committee Revd Roy Screech (*Secretary*)   Tel: 020–7898 1402
email: roy.screech@c-of-e.org.uk

Theological Education and Training Committee Revd Dr David Way (*Secretary*)   Tel: 020–7898 1405
email: david.way@c-of-e.org.uk

Deployment, Remuneration and Conditions of Service Committee Margaret Jeffery (*Secretary*)
Tel: 020–7898 1411
email: margaret.jeffery@c-of-e.org.uk

Committee for Ministry Among Deaf People Canon James Clarke (*Secretary*)   Tel: 020–7898 1429
email: james.clarke@c-of-e.org.uk

SELECTION SECRETARIES

Revd Roy Screech (*Senior Selection Secretary*)
Tel: 020–7898 1402
email: roy.screech@c-of-e.org.uk
Revd Ferial Etherington (*OLM Coordinator*)
Tel: 020–7898 1395
email: ferial.etherington@c-of-e.org.uk
Revd Margaret Jackson (*Secretary, Continuing Ministerial Education Panel*)   Tel: 020–7898 1408
email: margaret.jackson@c-of-e.org.uk

Revd Marilyn Parry (*Secretary, Pre-Theological Education Panel*)   Tel: 020–7898 1401
email: marilyn.parry@c-of-e.org.uk
Mrs Margaret Sentamu   Tel: 020–7898 1406
email: margaret.sentamu@c-of-e.org.uk
Revd Mark Sowerby (*Secretary, Vocations Advisory Panel*)   Tel: 020–7898 1399
email: mark.sowerby@c-of-e.org.uk

Finance and Administrative Secretary Mr David Morris (*Secretary to Bishops' Committee for Ministry and Finance Panel*)   Tel: 020–7898 1392
email: david.morris@c-of-e.org.uk

Grants Officer Dr Mark Hodge   Tel: 020–7898 1396
email: mark.hodge@c-of-e.org.uk

Honorary Secretary of the Readers' Council Miss Pat Nappin   Tel: 020–7898 1415
email: pat.nappin@c-of-e.org.uk

Honorary National Moderator for Reader Training and Honorary Acting National Moderator for the Archbishops' Diploma for Readers Mrs Wendy Thorpe   Tel: 020–7898 1414
email: wendy.thorpe@c-of-e.org.uk

Office Church House, Great Smith St, London SW1P 3NZ   Tel: 020–7898 1412
Fax: 020–7898 1421

VOCATION, RECRUITMENT AND SELECTION COMMITTEE

Chairman Rt Revd David Conner (*Dean of Windsor*)

Members Ms Sallie Bassham, Mr Ron Black, Ven Michael Bowering (*Archdeacon of Lindisfarne*), Revd Dr Francis Bridger, Revd John Cook, Canon Penny Driver, Ven Michael Fox (*Archdeacon of West Ham*), Mrs Peggy Gray, Canon David Lowman, Father Aidan Mayoss CR, Ven Bob Metcalf (*Archdeacon of Liverpool*), Ms Josile Munro, Mrs Beverley Ruddock, Ven Jeffery Watson (*Archdeacon of Ely*)

Terms of reference

1 To advise the Archbishops' Council and the House of Bishops on a strategy for the development of vocation to ministry.

2 To encourage those in education and careers work throughout the Church in the provision of sustained programmes of vocational development and recruitment for the accredited ministry, both lay and ordained.

3 To advise the House of Bishops on policy for the selection of candidates for the accredited ministry, ordained and lay.

4 To oversee and advise the work of staff in the arrangement of and participation in selection conferences.

5 To oversee the training of bishops' selectors.

6 To report regularly through the Ministry Coordinating Group to the Archbishops' Council on the work of the Committee.

7 To work in collaboration with Diocesan Directors of Ordinands and others as appropriate on policy and practice related to the selection and care of candidates for ministry.

8 To work in collaboration with ecumenical partners on matters within the Committee's terms of reference.

THEOLOGICAL EDUCATION AND TRAINING COMMITTEE
Chairman Revd Dr John Muddiman

Members Rt Revd Jonathan Bailey (*Bishop of Derby*), Mrs Margaret Baxter, Revd Dr Richard Burridge, Mrs Jennie Cappleman, Canon Christine Farrington, Revd Kenneth Howcroft, Canon Jeffrey John, Very Revd Christopher Lewis (*Dean of St Albans*), Revd Prof Gareth Lloyd Jones, Mrs Sue Page, Revd Dr Jeremy Sheehy, Canon Prof Anthony Thiselton, Revd David Thurburn-Huelin, (one vacancy)

Terms of reference

1 To advise the House of Bishops and the Archbishops' Council on a strategy for theological education and training.

2 To scrutinize and validate programmes for those training under Bishops' Regulations and to keep under review all forms of training for authorized ministry, ordained and lay, including Reader training.

3 To advise the House of Bishops and the Archbishops' Council on policy concerning theological colleges and courses.

4 To advise the Archbishops' Council and the House of Bishops on the financial aspects of theological education and training.

5 To work in collaboration with ecumenical partners on matters within the Committee's terms of reference.

6 To report regularly through the Ministry Coordinating Group to the Archbishops' Council on the work of the Committee.

DEPLOYMENT, REMUNERATION AND CONDITIONS OF SERVICE COMMITTEE
Chairman Rt Revd David Bentley (*Bishop of Gloucester*)

Members Revd Lesley Bentley, Mr Peter Bowes, Lady Gill Brentford, Mr Keith Cawdron, Mr Nicholas Dennison, Mr Tim Hind, Mrs Sarah James, Mr Alan King, Mr Robert Leach, Ven Dr John Marsh (*Archdeacon of Blackburn*), Mrs Caroline Pascoe, Mr David Philips, Revd Simon Pothen, Mr Bryan Sandford, Mr Keith Stevens, Revd Stephen Trott

Terms of Reference

1 To advise the House of Bishops and the Archbishops' Council on a strategy for ministry, with particular reference to the deployment, remuneration and conditions of service of those in authorized ministry, working in collaboration with dioceses, the Church Commissioners and the Church of England Pensions Board and with ecumenical partners.

2 To produce, in partnership with dioceses, a framework of national policy for stipends and other related matters, and to advise dioceses as appropriate on such matters.

3 To produce, in partnership with dioceses, a framework of national policy for the deployment of all ministerial resources, ordained and lay, available to the Church.

4 To monitor and advise in consultation with interested parties on sector and chaplaincy ministries within the total ministry of the Church.

5 To work in collaboration with the dioceses and, as far as possible, with ecumenical partners in the provision and development of continuing ministerial education for and review of accredited ministers, ordained and lay.

6 To report regularly through the Ministry Coordinating Group to the Archbishops' Council on the work of the Committee.

COMMITTEE FOR MINISTRY AMONG DEAF PEOPLE
Chairman Rt Revd John Perry (*Bishop of Chelmsford*)

Appointed Members Revd Gill Behenna, Mr Ken Dyson, Mr Tom Fenton, Mrs Pam Gallagher, Revd Vera Hunt, Mrs Sarah James, Canon Peter Larkin, Revd Philip Maddock, Mrs Elizabeth Metcalfe, Mrs Janice Palmer, Revd Mike Sabell.

Terms of reference

1 To monitor and advise on the progress of sector and chaplaincy ministries within the total ministry of the Church, in consultation with those responsible for specific areas.

2 To encourage and strengthen the participation of deaf people in the life and witness of the Church, to represent the views of deaf people to the Church and of the Church to deaf people, and to support the work of the chaplains.

3 To report regularly through the Ministry Coordinating Group to the Archbishops' Council on the work of the Committee.

BISHOPS' REGULATIONS FOR TRAINING
SELECTION
1 Candidates should be commended in the first place by someone who has pastoral responsibility for them to the Diocesan Director of Ordinands or Diocesan Lay Ministry Adviser. Before being accepted for training, they are required:
(1) to have the necessary educational qualifications or show that they have the potential to benefit from a formal course of training;
(2) to satisfy medical requirements;
(3) to be sponsored by their bishop for attendance at a Bishops' Selection Conference according to the following categories:
    Ordained Local Ministry;
    Ordained Ministry (Permanent Non-Stipendiary Ministry);
    Ordained Ministry (Stipendiary Ministry and Non-Stipendiary Ministry);
    Accredited Lay Ministry (Permanent Non-Stipendiary Ministry);
    Accredited Lay Ministry (Stipendiary Ministry and Non-Stipendiary Ministry).

2 Where it is envisaged that a candidate will exercise a non-stipendiary ministry from the time of ordination, such a candidate should normally be at least 30 and well established in a secular occupation before entering training.

EDUCATIONAL QUALIFICATIONS
Candidates are required to have the following qualifications:

1 *Under 25.* Five passes in academic subjects in GCSE, Grade C or above, one of which must be English Language, and two at 'A' level: or equivalent qualifications. The only exceptions to this rule are for candidates who are recommended to complete a formal programme of pre-theological education, approved by the Vocation, Recruitment and Selection Committee, to prepare them for training. Bishops' Selectors will need to be assured that candidates are capable of participating in such a course satisfactorily.

2 *Aged 25 and over.* The academic standard is not laid down in terms of GCSE or in any other absolute form, but individuals are considered and assessed in accordance with their existing qualifications and the type of training which they should do, if accepted as candidates. All who are not graduates will be seen by the bishop's examining chaplain, or other person appointed by the bishop. He may ask them to do a course of reading or to take certain examinations before attending a Bishops' Selection Conference.

TRAINING
1 *Pre-theological training.* Candidates may be required to undertake a formal programme of part-time pre-theological education of up to two years, approved by the Vocation, Recruitment and Selection Committee, to the satisfaction of the Assessors. On completion of such a programme, candidates undertake theological training in compliance with the regulations set out below.

2 *Theological training.* Candidates should always consult their bishop or Diocesan Director of Ordinands (DDO) or Diocesan Lay Ministry Adviser (DLMA) before applying to a theological college or course for admission. A recommendation to train for ordination from the Bishops' Selectors does not carry with it the right of acceptance by any particular theological college or course.

A candidate wishing to undertake a course of training varying from the Regulations approved by the Bishops (including study for a higher degree) should inform the DDO or DLMA in order that the advice of the Vocation, Recruitment and Selection Committee may be sought.

(1) *Candidates under* 30
(a) *Graduates in theology* (where at least half of the degree consists of theology) spend two years on a full-time course at a theological college and have to fulfil the Bishops' requirements by satisfactorily completing a course of education approved on behalf of the House of Bishops by the Theological Education and Training Committee.
(b) *Graduates in subjects other than theology* are required to spend three years on a full-time course at a theological college and have to fulfil the Bishops' requirements by satisfactorily completing a course of education approved on behalf of the House of Bishops by the Theological Education and Training Committee. Only those candidates with an upper second or first class degree may read for a degree in theology or post-graduate diploma in theology, unless the degree course is specially designed as a training course for the professional ministry, is approved by the Theological Education and Training Committee, and involves no additional expense or lengthening of the normal course of training.
    Certain special courses and professional qualifications may be regarded as conferring graduate status.
(c) *Non-graduates* are required to spend three

years on a full-time course at a theological college and to fulfil the Bishops' requirements by satisfactorily completing a course of education approved on behalf of the House of Bishops by the Theological Education and Training Committee.

(2) *Candidates aged 30 and over*
(a) Candidates over 30 sponsored for the *ordained ministry* (*stipendiary and non-stipendiary ministry*) are required to undertake either two years' full-time training at a theological college, or three years' part-time training on a theological course. In some instances the recommendations for training will indicate a preferred form. Candidates are required to fulfil the Bishops' requirements by satisfactorily completing a course of education approved on behalf of the House of Bishops by the Theological Education and Training Committee.
(b) Candidates for *ordained ministry* (*permanent non-stipendiary ministry*) are required to undertake three years' part-time training on a theological course and to fulfil the Bishops' requirements by satisfactorily completing a course of education approved on behalf of the House of Bishops by the Theological Education and Training Committee.

(3) *Candidates aged 50 and over*
Candidates for *ordained ministry* (*permanent non-stipendiary ministry*) usually undertake three years' part-time training on a theological course.

The exact nature of the training is decided by the sponsoring bishop.

NOTES
1 In the above regulations the age refers to the candidate's age at the start of training where the regulation concerns training; and to the candidate's age at time of sponsorship where the regulation concerns category of sponsorship.

2 The above regulations, in terms of age, sponsorship and training, also apply to Accredited Lay Ministry.

3 Exceptions to the above regulations will be considered by the Vocation, Recruitment and Selection Committee.

GRANTS
Candidates who have been recommended for training are eligible for financial help from Church funds, but should always obtain as much assistance as possible from other sources before applying for such grants. Local Education Authorities almost invariably make awards to candidates who will be undertaking a first degree course during training and who have not previously received LEA assistance. Details about grants can be obtained from the Grants Secretary, Ministry Division, Church House, Great Smith St, London SW1P 3NZ.

For **Theological Colleges** *and* **Regional Courses** *see also* pages 228–30.

The Central Readers' Council

Patron HRH The Duke of Edinburgh

Presidents The Archbishops of Canterbury and York

Chair Rt Revd Christopher Mayfield (*Bishop of Manchester*)

Vice-Chair Mrs Sarah James

Hon Secretary Miss Pat Nappin *Tel:* 020–7898 1417
email: pat.nappin@c-of-e.org.uk

Editor of 'The Reader' Vacancy
Tel: 020–7898 1415/6

Hon National Moderator for Reader Training Mrs Wendy Thorpe   *Tel:* 020–7898 1414
email: wendy.thorpe@c-of-e.org.uk

Administrative Officer Mrs Sandra Fleming
Tel: 020–7898 1416
email: sandra.fleming@c-of-e.org.uk

Office Church House, Great Smith St, London SW1P 3NZ   *Tel:* 020–7898 1415/6
Fax: 020–7898 1421

The Central Readers' Council (CRC) works to enhance the contribution of Readers to the overall ministry of the Church, particularly to encourage the most effective integration with other forms of ministry, ordained and lay. It works in cooperation with the Ministry division which moderates and coordinates the training of Reader candidates and the Archbishops' Diploma for Readers. CRC arranges national conferences for Readers, provides a forum for the exchange of ideas between dioceses on Reader matters and publishes a quarterly magazine, *The Reader*. The annual Summer Course at Selwyn College, Cambridge began in 1881 and is probably the longest established Summer School held in any university. CRC has ecumenical links through the annual Joint Readers' and Preachers' Conference at St Andrew's Hall, Selly Oak, Birmingham.

CRC is a registered charity which derives its

income mostly from capitation grants made by diocesan Readers' boards. It has its origins in the revival of Reader ministry in the Church of England in 1866 and particularly in the Central Readers' Board, which was granted a constitution by the Archbishops in 1921. CRC today is the immediate successor to the Central Readers' Conference, under a new constitution adopted in 1994.

CRC has three representatives, including the Warden and Secretary of Readers, from each diocese, and one representative from each of the Armed Forces. Any Reader elected or appointed to the Ministry division and its committees is *ex*

officio a member of CRC. A non-voting observer is invited from the Deaf Readers and Pastoral Assistants Association, the Church of Ireland, the Scottish Episcopal Church and each of the dioceses of the Church in Wales. The annual general meeting is held in March/April each year.

The CRC Executive Committee is elected for a five-year term co-terminous with General Synod. In addition to the Chair and Vice-Chair, the Committee consists of: Mr Ron Black, Revd Paul Conder, Mrs Julie Francis, Mr Cliff Harris, Mrs Gloria Helson, Miss Catherine Martineau, Mrs Gillian Newton, Mrs Wendy Plant, Revd Peter Sutton and Canon Alex Whitehead.

CENTRAL SERVICES

One of the objectives of the *Working As One Body* reforms was to secure common service arrangements across the central Church bodies in key areas such as legal advice, communications, personnel and office services. An important step towards this has been achieved through the establishment of a common services division to ensure the development of best practice and the more efficient use of resources.

Among the units located within the division are those responsible for: providing services of appropriate quality to the Archbishops' Council, the national Church institutions and, where appropriate, to the wider Church, ensuring their cost-effectiveness; assisting in the collation, analysis, publication and storage of information relating to the Church; providing advice, facilities and goods necessary to enable the day-to-day running of the Council and the other bodies; and providing strategic direction and focus for IT provisions throughout the national Church institutions.

The Director of Central Services also acts as Clerk to the Synod (*see* page 4)

The Corporation of the Church House, as landlord, is primarily responsible for the building and utilities at Church House, while the Council's Office Services Unit will be responsible for the building and utilities at Millbank, Cowley House and Fielden House. The Council works closely with the Corporation.

INFORMATION TECHNOLOGY AND OFFICE SERVICES
Head of Information Technology and Office Services
Mr John Ferguson   *Tel:* 020–7898 1666
                    email: john.ferguson@c-of-e.org.uk

The Information Technology and Office Services department provides common services for the central Church bodies, including IT systems, computer support, mapping, reprographics, telephone and central buying facilities.

Church House Publishing

Publishing Manager Mr Alan Mitchell
                    Tel: 020–7898 1450
                    email: alan.mitchell@c-of-e.org.uk

Liturgy Editor Ms Rachel Boulding
                    Tel: 020–7898 1485
                    email: rachel.boulding@c-of-e.org.uk

NS Publications Officer Mr Hamish Bruce
                    Tel: 020–7898 1453
                    email: hamish.bruce@c-of-e.org.uk

Editorial and Copyright Manager Miss Sarah Roberts   *Tel:* 020–7898 1578
                    email: copyright@c-of-e.org.uk

Production Manager Mrs Katharine Allenby
                    Tel: 020–7898 1452
                    email: katharine.allenby@c-of-e.org.uk

Sales and Marketing Manager Mr Matthew Tickle
                    Tel: 020–7898 1454
                    email: matthew.tickle@c-of-e.org.uk

Office Church House, Great Smith St, London SW1P 3NZ   *Tel:* 020–7898 1451; 020–7898 1000
                    Fax: 020–7898 1449
                    email: publishing@c-of-e.org.uk
                    Web: http://www.chpublishing.co.uk

Church of England Year Book Editor Mrs Jo Linzey
                    Tel: (01865) 201565
                    email: jolinzey@aol.com

The Department is jointly funded by the Archbishops' Council and the National Society for Promoting Religious Education and is the official publisher for the Church of England's new generation of liturgy, *Common Worship*. The imprint Church House Publishing is used for titles available through the book trade published on behalf of the Synod and its Boards and Councils. Educational material for churches and schools is co-published with the National Society.

The Department publishes *Crockford's Clerical Directory* and *The Church of England Year Book*. Around 40 new titles are published for the trade in an average year including reports commissioned by General Synod, liturgical material and books on church care and conservation.

Many low-priced, short-lived or highly specialized titles are issued by Boards and Councils under their own name and the Department is involved to a varying degree in producing and promoting them. These, together with most Synod papers, are available only from Church House Bookshop (*see below*).

The Church House Publishing catalogue, supplied on request, contains details of all publications currently available, and can also be found online at http://www.chpublishing.co.uk

Church House Bookshop

31 Great Smith Street, London SW1P 3BN

Retail Coordinator Mr Mark Clifford
Tel: 020–7898 1300
Bookshop (direct line) *Tel:* 020–7898 1304
Mail Order *Tel:* 020–7898 1301/2/6
Fax: 020–7898 1305
email: bookshop@c-of-e.org.uk
Web: http://www.chbookshop.co.uk

The Bookshop, refurbished in 1994, stocks a wide range of Christian literature as well as providing the principal retail outlet for material issued by Church House. Recorded music on cassette and compact disc, greetings cards, parochial forms and registers and other items are also carried. All the above items can be obtained to special order if not stocked, and the Mail Order department – posting to anywhere in the world – will accept orders by post, fax, telephone or email, which can either be paid for in advance or charged to most major credit cards. Details of book signings and special events are advertised in the church press – please write for further details. Shop hours: 9.00 a.m. to 5.00 p.m. Monday, Tuesday, Wednesday, Friday; 9.30 a.m. to 6.00 p.m. Thursday.

Statistics Unit

Head of Statistics Unit Vacancy

Having been responsible for the collection and tabulation of parochial statistics since 1920, the Central Board of Finance established a separate statistics division in 1955. While the gathering of parochial statistics remains at the heart of its work, the Statistics Unit has broadened the range of statistics it maintains and diversified so that it is now providing a service to a number of Boards and Councils. The Unit's role as a central resource has developed with the advent of the Archbishops' Council where it forms part of the Central Services Division.

The Unit is responsible for the collection, collation and analysis of parochial finance and membership statistics. In recent years the Unit has been able to reduce the time taken to complete the processing of these statistics, so that it is now able to devote more of its resources to researching underlying trends and evaluating the merits of the statistics collected. Working closely with the Board of Mission, the Unit has embarked on a major review of the membership statistics that are collected annually with the aim of providing a range of statistics which will be a tool for mission. The publication in 1998 of *The Church of England Today*, which presented in pamphlet form basic facts about the Church of England and which was distributed to all parishes, represented a first step in improving the way in which statistical information is communicated within church circles.

The Unit maintains a churches database which it is currently enlarging to include details of church location and facilities. Part of the information presently held on the Unit's database concerns urban deprivation, and the Unit is responsible for the maintenance of the Oxlip Index which is used for the identification of Urban Priority Areas. The Unit maintains strong links with the Ministry Division in the preparation and production of *Statistics of Licensed Ministers*, and with the Church Commissioners in the development of the *Crockford* database.

The Unit maintains links with other denominations on statistical matters and has been involved with discussions on the development of an ecumenical database and participation in the organization of the next church census.

Records Centre

Director Mr Christopher Pickford
Tel: 020–7898 1034
email: chris.pickford@c-of-e.org.uk

Address Church of England Record Centre, 15 Galleywall Rd, South Bermondsey, London SE16 3PB
Tel: 020–7898 1030
Fax: 020–7394 7018
email: archivist@c-of-e.org.uk

The Centre, which is a central service operated by the Archbishops' Council, houses the non-current records of the Church Commissioners, the General Synod and the National Society, together with those of some ecumenical bodies. The Centre serves as an advisory point for queries concerning the archives of the Church of England. Enquirers welcome by appointment, Monday to Friday, 10.00 a.m. to 5.00 p.m. A small reference library is maintained.

CENTRAL SECRETARIAT

The Secretariat of the Archbishops' Council provides administrative support both to the General Synod and the Council and to their committees; the House of Bishops; the Church of England's Appointments Committee; the Liturgical Commission; and other bodies.

THE APPOINTMENTS COMMITTEE OF THE CHURCH OF ENGLAND
Chairman Canon John Stanley

Members appointed by the Archbishops' Council Ms Jayne Ozanne, Mrs Christina Rees, Prof Peter Toyne

Elected Members Mr Anthony Archer, Ven Robin Ellis (*Archdeacon of Plymouth*), Ven John Marsh (*Archdeacon of Blackburn*), Mr Gerald O'Brien, Rt Revd John Oliver (*Bishop of Hereford*), Canon Glyn Webster, Mrs Shirley-Ann Williams

Secretary Mr Christopher Ball   *Tel:* 020–7898 1362
email: christopher.ball@c-of-e.org.uk

The Committee, a joint committee of the General Synod and the Archbishops' Council, is responsible for making appointments and/or recommendations on appointments to synodical and other bodies as the Synod or the Archbishops' Council requires.

COMMITTEE FOR MINORITY ETHNIC ANGLICAN CONCERNS
Chairman Revd Rose Hudson-Wilkin

Secretary Mrs Glynne Gordon-Carter
email: glynne.gordon-carter@c-of-e.org.uk

Members Rt Revd Colin Buchanan (*Bishop of Woolwich*), Mrs Julia Flack, Mr Frank Knaggs, Revd George Kovoor, Revd Charles Lawrence, Mr Geoffrey Locke, Mrs Christine McMullen, Revd Jonas Mdumulla, Mr Deo Meghan, Revd Ivor Morris, Ms Smitha Prasadam, Mrs Christina Rees, Mrs Beverley Ruddock, Preb Theo Samuel, Mrs Dorothy Stewart, Canon Hugh Wilcox

Co-opted Members Revd Clarry Hendrickse, Mrs Gloria Rich, (one vacancy)

Consultant Rt Revd Wilfred Wood (*Bishop of Croydon*)

The principal tasks of the Committee are to monitor and make recommendations about issues which arise or which ought to arise in the context of the work of the Archbishops' Council, its committees, and Boards and Councils, and of the General Synod itself, as far as they have policy implications for minority ethnic groups within the Church and the wider community; and to assist the dioceses in developing strategies for combating racial bias within the Church, encouraging them to make the problem of racism a priority concern in their programmes.

THE INNER CITIES RELIGIOUS COUNCIL
Secretary Revd David Rayner, Floor 4/K10, Eland House, Bressenden Place, London SW1E 5DU
Tel: 020–7890 3704
Fax: 020–7890 3709

The Council comprises participants from the Christian, Hindu, Jewish, Muslim and Sikh communities. It sponsors a programme of regional conferences and is engaged in development work. It is a forum for Government to meet with the faith communities. The Secretariat is a source of advice to faith communities and Government with a particular emphasis on urban regeneration.

LITURGICAL SUPPORT AND PUBLISHING
The Archbishops' Council also provides administrative support for the Liturgical Commission (*see* page 45), the administration of liturgical business in the House of Bishops and Synod, and the Liturgical Publishing Group.

COMMUNICATIONS

Communication is at the very heart of the operation of the Council. Through the development and implementation of an overarching communications and promotional strategy it supports the Church in its mission to communicate the gospel to the nation and beyond. A new web site has been established and has proved to be a highly useful tool in accessing information about the Church. *(Web:* http://www.cofe.anglican.org).

Director of Communications Revd Dr William Beaver　　　　　　*Tel:* 020–7898 1462
　　　　　　　　　　　　Fax: 020–7222 6672
　　　　email: bill.beaver@c-of-e.org.uk

Communications Officer Church Commissioners Mr Arun Kataria　　　　*Tel:* 020–7898 4622
　　　email: arun.kataria@c-of-e.org

Head of Media Relations Mr Steve Jenkins
　　　　　　　　　Tel: 020–7898 1457
　　email: steve.jenkins@c-of-e.org.uk

Head of Signal Logistics Revd Jonathan Jennings
　　　　　　　　　Tel: 020–7898 1456
　email: jonathan.jennings@c-of-e.org.uk

Head of Media Training Revd Martin Short
　　　　　　　　　Tel: 020–7898 1458
　　email: martin.short@c-of-e.org.uk

Head of Internal Communications Mr Alexander Nicoll　　　　　*Tel:* 020–7898 1459
　email: alexander.nicoll@c-of-e.org.uk

Office Church House, Great Smith St, London SW1P 3NZ　　　　*Tel:* 020–7898 1463
　　　　　　　　　Fax: 020–7222 6672

Enquiry Centre

Enquiries Officer Mr Stephen Empson
　　　　　　　　　Tel: 020–7898 1445
　　　　　　　　　Fax: 020–7222 6672
　　email: steve.empson@c-of-e.org.uk

The Enquiry Centre was established to deal with questions referred to it by post, by telephone or in person by members of the public on a wide variety of matters relating to Church affairs. There is a constant flow of enquiries which come from all over the world. The centre also handles a large number of calls concerning clergy movements and biographical information.

Diocesan Communications Officers Panel

Chairman Rt Revd Graham James (*Bishop of Norwich*)

Secretary Miss Andrina Barnden
　　　　　　　　　Tel: 020–7898 1463
　email: drina.barnden@c-of-e.org.uk

Members Revd John Carter, Canon Brian Chave, Mr Jeremy Dowling, Revd David Marshall, Revd Richard Thomas, Canon Simon Pettitt

HUMAN RESOURCES

A key objective of the reform of the national Church institutions was the creation of a unified staff capability to serve the Church at national level under a joint Management Board and with a single personnel department. The Human Resources Division links personnel policies to the employers' overall strategies; provides a comprehensive personnel service to the national Church institutions and to other Church bodies that request it; and aims to encourage best practice in all areas.

STAFF
Director of Human Resources Mrs Susan Morgan
　　　　　　　　　Tel: 020–7898 1565
　　email: su.morgan@c of-e.org.uk

HR Policy and Planning Manager Ms Julia Hudson
　　　　　　　　　Tel: 020–7898 1589
　　email: julia.hudson@c-of-e.org.uk

HR Project Manager Mr Fiske Warren
　　　　　　　　　Tel: 020–7898 1561
　　email: fiske.warren@c-of-e.org.uk

Organizational Development and Training Miss Liz Lowe　　　　　*Tel:* 020–7898 1751
　　　email: liz.lowe@c-of-e.org.uk

Recruitment and Deployment Ms Francesca Eridani　　　　　*Tel:* 020–7898 1171
　email: francesca.eridani@c-of-e.org.uk

Employee Resourcing Miss Mary Carroll
Tel: 020–7898 1747
email: mary.carroll@c-of-e.org.uk

Office Church House, Great Smith St, London
SW1P 3NZ
Tel: 020–7898 1566
Fax: 020–7898 1072

Advisory Committees and Permanent Commissions

The Synod's subordinate bodies, other than the Business Committee and the Legislative Committee, fall into two main groups – Advisory Committees and Permanent Commissions – usually made up of a majority of Synod members. Each of the Advisory Committees has responsibility to the Synod through the Archbishops' Council for a major area of synodical business. The Permanent Commissions are concerned with specialized areas of the Synod's business.

ADVISORY COMMITTEES
See main entries on pages 19–26.
The Board of Education (*Chairman* The Bishop of Blackburn; *Secretary* Canon John Hall)
The Board of Mission (*Chairman* The Bishop of Southwark; *Secretary* Canon Philip King)

The Council for Christian Unity (*Chairman* The Bishop of Peterborough; *Secretary* Prebendary Paul Avis)
The Board for Social Responsibility (*Chairman* The Bishop of Oxford; *Secretary* Mr David Skidmore)

PERMANENT COMMISSIONS
See main entries on pages 27–30.
The Hospital Chaplaincies Council (*Chairman* The Bishop of St Albans; *Secretary* Revd Robert Clarke)
The Cathedrals Fabric Commission (*Chairman* Dr Averil Cameron; *Secretary* Dr Richard Gem)
The Council for the Care of Churches (*Chairman* The Dean of York; *Secretary* Dr Thomas Cocke)

The Cathedral Statutes Commission

Chairman Prof David McClean

Secretary Mr Robert Wellen

Office Church House, Great Smith St, London
SW1P 3NZ
Tel: 020–7898 1371
email: robert.wellen@c-of-e.org.uk

MEMBERS
Very Revd Peter Berry, Ven John Duncan (*Archdeacon of Birmingham*), Very Revd Michael Higgins (*Dean of Ely*), Dr Kathryn Morfey, Rt Revd John Saxbee (*Bishop and Archdeacon of Ludlow*)

The Cathedral Statutes Commission, on the application of the consenting body of any Cathedral Church in England (with the single exception of Christ Church, Oxford), has the duty of preparing a scheme under the provisions of the Cathedrals Measure 1976 for revising, or for renewing, the constitution and statutes of that church.

The procedure under the 1976 Measure has in effect been superseded by the Cathedrals Measure 1999. This requires a Transitional Council to be appointed for each cathedral with the duty of framing a new constitution and statutes. Once the Archbishops of Canterbury and York are satisfied that the new constitution and statutes have been produced in accordance with the 1999 Measure, the 1976 Measure will cease to apply to the cathedral concerned, and any further amendments will be made under procedures introduced by the new legislation.

The Crown Appointments Commission

Office Fielden House, 13 Little College St, London SW1P 3SH
Tel: 020–7898 1876; 020–7233 0393 (Direct line) or 020–7222 7010 Ext 4033
email: anthony.sadler@c-of-e.org.uk

MEMBERS
Ex officio
The Archbishop of Canterbury
The Archbishop of York

Elected Members

Three members of the House of Clergy
Revd Hugh Broad
Ven Judith Rose (*Archdeacon of Tonbridge*)
Canon John Stanley

Three members of the House of Laity
The Viscountess Brentford
Mr Ian Garden
Mr Brian McHenry

Four members of the Vacancy-in-See Committee of the diocese whose bishopric is to become, or has become, vacant

Ex officio non-voting members
Mr Tony Sadler *(The Archbishops' Appointments Secretary)* Secretary to the Commission

Mr William Chapman *(The Prime Minister's Appointments Secretary)*

The Commission was established by the General Synod in February 1977. Its function is to consider vacancies in diocesan bishoprics in the Provinces of Canterbury and York, and candidates for appointments to them. At each meeting the Chair is taken by the Archbishop in whose Province the vacancy has arisen. The Commission agrees upon two names for nomination to the Prime Minister by the appropriate Archbishop or, in the case of the Archbishopric of Canterbury or York, by the chairman appointed by the Prime Minister. The names submitted may be given in an order of preference decided upon by the Commission. In accordance with the terms of the Prime Minister's statement to the House of Commons on 8 June 1976, the Prime Minister selects one of the names or may ask for others to submit to Her Majesty the Queen for approval.

The Dioceses Commission

Chairman Mr Bryan Sandford

Secretary Mr David Hebblethwaite

Office Church House, Great Smith St, London SW1P 3NZ   *Tel:* 020–7898 1364
          email: david.hebblethwaite@c-of-e.org.uk

MEMBERS
Mrs Janet Atkinson, Rt Revd George Cassidy *(Bishop of Southwell)*, Rt Revd Ian Harland *(Bishop of Carlisle)*, Dr John Holden, Mr David Kemp, Mr Peter Robottom, Chancellor June Rodgers, Mrs Marion Simpson, Very Revd Colin Slee *(Provost of Southwark)*, Rt Revd Martin Wharton *(Bishop of Newcastle)*

The Dioceses Commission was set up in 1978 under Section 1(1) of the Dioceses Measure. That Measure makes provision for such matters as the reorganization of diocesan boundaries, the creation of Area Bishops and Area Synods, the creation and revival of Suffragan Sees, and the delegation of episcopal functions to a Suffragan Bishop by a Diocesan Bishop. The Commission works only within the framework of the Measure, and has two roles. In the first place the Commission is required to consider proposals prepared under the Measure, to report upon them and to make its report available to the diocesan synod of the diocese concerned and to the General Synod. Secondly, it has an advisory role, which is set out in Section 2 of the Measure as follows:

(1) It shall be the duty of the Commission, on the instructions of the General Synod, the Archbishops' Council, or the House of Bishops of the General Synod, to advise on matters affecting the diocesan structure of the Provinces of Canterbury and York or on the action which might be taken under this Measure to improve the episcopal oversight of any diocese therein or the administration of its affairs.

(2) Where it appears to the Commission that there is any such matter as is mentioned in subsection (1) above on which it might usefully advise, it may bring that matter to the attention of the General Synod or the Archbishops' Council with a view to receiving instructions under that subsection.

(3) The Commission shall be available to be consulted by any diocesan synod or the bishop of any diocese on any action which might be taken under this Measure in relation to the diocese.

The Doctrine Commission

Chairman Rt Revd Stephen Sykes

Secretary Vacancy

Office Church House, Great Smith St, London SW1P 3NZ   *Tel:* 020–7898 1488

MEMBERS
Revd Prof Michael Banner, Prof Richard Bauckham, Dr Christina Baxter, Revd Jeremy Begbie, Dr Grace Davie, Prof David Ford, Prof Ann Loades, Rt Revd Geoffrey Rowell *(Bishop of Basingstoke)*, Rt Revd Peter Selby *(Bishop of Worcester)*, Rt Revd Kenneth Stevenson *(Bishop of Portsmouth)*, Canon Prof Anthony Thiselton, Revd Prof John Webster, Dr Linda Woodhead, (one vacancy)

Consultants Rt Revd Geoffrey Rowell *(Bishop of Basingstoke)*, Dr Fraser Watts

The functions of the Doctrine Commission are to

consider and advise the House of Bishops of the General Synod upon doctrinal questions referred to it by the House of Bishops as well as to make suggestions to that House as to what in its judgement are doctrinal issues of concern to the Church of England.

The Legal Advisory Commission

Chairman Prof David McClean

Secretary Miss Ingrid Slaughter

Office Church House, Great Smith St, London SW1P 3NZ   *Tel:* 020–7898 1368
                                        Fax: 020–7898 1369
        email: ingrid.slaughter@c-of-e.org.uk

MEMBERS
Mr Roger Arden, Mr Peter Beesley, Chancellor Timothy Briden, Ven Michael Brotherton (*Archdeacon of Chichester*), Chancellor Rupert Bursell, The Worshipful Sheila Cameron (*Vicar-General of Canterbury*), Mr David Cheetham, Chancellor Christopher Clark, His Honour Judge Thomas Coningsby (*Vicar-General of York*), Mr Quentin Edwards, Chancellor Michael Goodman, Mr Brian Hanson, Rt Revd Christopher Hill (*Bishop of Stafford*), Mr Nigel Johnson, Mr Lionel Lennox, Professor David McClean, Mrs Heather Morgan, The Rt Hon Lord Justice Mummery, Mr John Pakenham-Walsh, Dr Frank Robson, Revd Stephen Trott, Mr Edward (Ted) Wills

The Legal Advisory Commission gives advice on legal matters of general interest to the Church which are referred to it by the Archbishops' Council and its Divisions, Board, Councils and Commissions, by the General Synod and its Houses and Commissions, by the Church Commissioners and the Church of England Pensions Board, and by diocesan clerical authorities and lay officials. The Commission cannot accept requests for advice from private individuals or secular bodies. In addition, the Commission cannot normally give opinions on contentious matters, but it may be able to do so (depending on the circumstances) if the facts are agreed by all parties to the dispute, all parties join in referring the matter to the Commission for an opinion and it is not (and is not expected to become) the subject-matter of proceedings in the courts.

The opinions of the Commission and its predecessor, the Legal Board, on matters of general interest are published by Church House Publishing in a loose-leaf form under the title *Legal Opinions Concerning the Church of England*. A first supplement was published in 1997 and it is intended that a further supplement will be issued in the near future.

The Legal Aid Commission

Chairman Mr Richard Bowman

Secretary Miss Ingrid Slaughter

Office Church House, Great Smith St, London SW1P 3NZ   *Tel:* 020–7898 1368
                                        Fax: 020–7898 1369
        email: ingrid.slaughter@c-of-e.org.uk

MEMBERS
Canon Robert Baker, Mr Barry Barnes, Ven Michael Bowering (*Archdeacon of Lindisfarne*), Preb John Brownsell, Revd Helen Chantry, Mr Mark Hill, Rt Revd Edward Holland (*Bishop of Colchester*), Mrs Shirley Jackson, Revd Clive Mansell, Mr John Underwood

The Legal Aid Commission operates under the Church of England (Legal Aid) Measure 1994, and administers the Legal Aid Fund which was originally set up under the Ecclesiastical Jurisdiction Measure 1963 and is continued by the 1994 Measure.

Legal aid under the 1994 Measure may be granted, subject to various conditions, for certain types of proceedings before Ecclesiastical Courts and tribunals; details of eligibility for legal aid and the Commission's procedures, together with an application form for legal aid, are obtainable from the Secretary, on request.

The Liturgical Commission

Chairman Rt Revd David Stancliffe (*Bishop of Salisbury*)

Secretary Mr David Hebblethwaite

Office Church House, Great Smith St, London SW1P 3NZ   *Tel:* 020–7898 1364
        email: david.hebblethwaite@c-of-e.org.uk

MEMBERS

Revd Andrew Burnham, Revd Dr Christopher Cocksworth, Dr Carole Cull, Canon Jeremy Haselock, Revd Susan Hope, The Baroness James of Holland Park, Rt Revd James Jones (*Bishop of Liverpool*), Mrs Anna de Lange, Canon Stephen Oliver, Very Revd Michael Perham, Canon Jane Sinclair, Mr Timothy Slater, Revd Angela Tilby, Brother Tristam ssf, (one vacancy)

Co-opted members Revd Jeremy Fletcher, Ven Trevor Lloyd (*Archdeacon of Barnstaple*)

Consultants Revd Dr Anders Bergquist, Revd Dr Paul Bradshaw, Prof Bryan Spinks, Rt Revd Kenneth Stevenson (*Bishop of Portsmouth*)

In response to resolutions by the Convocations in October 1954, the Archbishops of Canterbury and York appointed a standing Liturgical Commission 'to consider questions of a liturgical character submitted to them from time to time by the Archbishops of Canterbury and York and to report thereon to the Archbishops'. In 1971 the Commission became a permanent Commission of the General Synod. Its functions are:

1 to prepare forms of service at the request of the House of Bishops for submission to that House in the first instance;

2 to advise on the experimental use of forms of service and the development of liturgy;

3 to exchange information and advice on liturgical matters with other Churches both in the Anglican Communion and elsewhere;

4 to promote the development and understanding of liturgy and its use in the Church.

OTHER COMMITTEES

The Elections Review Group (*Chairman* Ven Pete Broadbent (*Archdeacon of Northolt*); *Secretary* Mr Malcolm Taylor)
Church Working for Women Group (*Chairman* Mrs Shirley-Ann Williams; *Secretary* Mr Francis Bassett)
The Liturgical Publishing Group (*Chairman* Rt Revd John Gladwin (*Bishop of Guildford*); *Secretary* Dr Colin Podmore)

THE CHURCH COMMISSIONERS FOR ENGLAND

Office 1 Millbank, London SW1P 3JZ

Tel: 020–7898 1000
Fax: 020–7898 1002
email: corporate.affairs@c-of-e.org.uk

Chairman The Archbishop of Canterbury

MEMBERS
The Archbishops of Canterbury and York

The Three Church Estates Commissioners
Mr John Sclater
Mr Stuart Bell MP
The Viscountess Brentford

Four bishops elected by the House of Bishops of the General Synod Rt Revd and Rt Hon Richard Chartres (*Bishop of London*), Rt Revd Dr Peter Forster (*Bishop of Chester*), Rt Revd Peter Selby (*Bishop of Worcester*), Rt Revd David Smith (*Bishop of Bradford*)

Two deans or provosts elected by all the deans and provosts Very Revd John Methuen (*Dean of Ripon*), Very Revd John Moses (*Dean of St Paul's*)

Three clergy elected by the House of Clergy of the General Synod Canon Robert Baker, Revd Clive Mansell, Revd Stephen Trott

Four lay persons elected by the House of Laity of the General Synod Mr Peter Bruinvels, Mr Alan Cooper, Mr Gavin Oldham, Mr David Webster

Three persons nominated by Her Majesty the Queen Sir Richard Baker Wilbraham, Mr Robert Heskett, Mr Jeremy Newsum

Three persons nominated by the Archbishops of Canterbury and of York acting jointly Mr Derek Fellows, Mr Edward Nugee, Mr Robert Shaw

Three persons nominated by the Archbishops acting jointly after consultation with others including the Lord Mayors of the cities of London and York and the Vice-Chancellors of Oxford and Cambridge Mr Oliver Dawson, (two vacancies)

Six State Office Holders The First Lord of the Treasury; the Lord President of the Council; the Secretary of State for the Home Department; the Lord Chancellor; the Secretary of State for the Department for Culture, Media and Sport; and the Speaker of the House of Commons

BOARD OF GOVERNORS
All Commissioners are Board Members except for Officers of State.

ASSETS COMMITTEE
First Church Estates Commissioner (*Chairman*), Sir Richard Baker Wilbraham (*Deputy Chairman*), Mr Oliver Dawson, Mr Robert Heskett, Mr Jeremy Newsum, Mr Gavin Oldham, Rt Revd Peter Selby (*Bishop of Worcester*), Mr Martin Shaw

AUDIT COMMITTEE
Mr Alan McLintock* (*Chairman*), Canon Robert Baker, Mr Derek Fellows, Mr Miles Roberts*, Mr Trevor Stevenson

BISHOPRICS AND CATHEDRALS COMMITTEE
Third Church Estates Commissioner (*Ex officio Chairman*), Rt Revd David Smith (*Bishop of Bradford, Deputy Chairman*), Revd Canon Bob Baker, Rt Revd Richard Llewellin*, Revd Dr John Mantle*, Very Revd John Methuen (*Dean of Ripon*), Mrs Lou Scott-Joynt* (*representative of bishops' wives*), Mr David Webster, Rt Revd Stephen Lowe* (*Bishop of Hulme*), Mrs Sallie Bassham, Very Revd Peter Marshall* (*Dean of Worcester*), Revd Christopher Lilley*

MANAGEMENT ADVISORY COMMITTEE
First Church Estates Commissioner (*Chairman*), Third Church Estates Commissioner, Mr Peter Bruinvels, Rt Revd and Rt Hon Richard Chartres (*Bishop of London*), Mr Alan Cooper, Revd Clive Mansell, Very Revd John Moses (*Dean of St Paul's*), Mr David Webster

PASTORAL COMMITTEE
Third Church Estates Commissioner (*Chairman*), Rt Revd Ian Harland* (*Bishop of Carlisle, Deputy Chairman*), Mrs Janet Atkinson*, Mr Peter Bruinvels, Rt Revd Dr Peter Forster (*Bishop of Chester*), Ven David Gerrard* (*Archdeacon of Wandsworth*), Very Revd John Methuen (*Dean of Ripon*), Revd Stephen Trott, Canon David Williams*, Mrs R Harrison, Mr D Webster, Mrs S James* (*nominee of Deployment Remuneration and Conditions of Service Committee of the Archbishops' Council*)

REDUNDANT CHURCHES COMMITTEE
Third Church Estates Commissioner (*Chairman*), Mr John Burton*, Mr Alan Cooper, Very Revd David Frayne* (*Provost of Blackburn*), Ven Brian Harris*, Revd Clive Mansell, Mrs Jane Sharman*, Revd Stephen Trott, (one vacancy)

(**Non-Commissioner*)

Church Commissioners

OFFICERS
Secretary Mr Howell Harris Hughes
Tel: 020–7898 1785
email: howell.hughes@c-of-e.org.uk

Deputy Secretary (Finance and Investment) Mr Christopher Daws   *Tel:* 020–7898 1786
email: christopher.daws@c-of-e.org.uk

Accountant Mrs Marian Adams
(Head of Cash and Accounts Divisions; Financial reporting and control)   *Tel:* 020–7898 1677
email: marian.adams@c-of-e.org.uk

Chief Surveyor Mr Andrew Brown
(Head of Commercial Property Department, Agricultural, Residential and Mineral portfolios)
Tel: 020–7898 1634
email: andrew.brown@c-of-e.org.uk

Pastoral and Redundant Churches Secretary Mr Martin Elengorn
(Pastoral reorganization, redundant churches, clergy housing and glebe)   *Tel:* 020–7898 1741
email: martin.elengorn@c-of-e.org.uk

Stock Exchange Investments Manager Mr Antony Hardy
(Commissioners' Stock Exchange portfolio; Secretary to the Ethical Investment Working Group and ethical policy monitoring)
Tel: 020–7898 1122
email: tony.hardy@c-of-e.org.uk

Management Accountant Mr Brian Hardy
(Financial analysis and forecasting)
Tel: 020–7898 1667
email: brian.hardy@c-of-e.org.uk

Policy Unit Mr Philip James
(Commissioners' overall policy development, communication and implementation)
Tel: 020–7898 1671
email: philip.james@c-of-e.org.uk

Bishoprics Officer Mr Edward Peacock
(Financial and administrative support for bishops)   *Tel:* 020–7898 1062
email: ed.peacock@ c-of-e.org.uk

Chief Architect Mr John Taylor
(Head of Architects Department, *See* House maintenance)   *Tel:* 020–7898 1026
email: john.taylor@c-of-e.org.uk

LEGAL DEPARTMENT
Official Solicitor Mr Nigel Johnson
Tel: 020–7898 1712
email: nigel.johnson@c-of-e.org.uk

Deputy Official Solicitor Miss Susan Jones
Tel: 020–7898 1704
email: sue.jones@c-of-e.org.uk

Solicitors Mr Timothy Crow, Miss Judith Egar, Mr Michael Fahy, Mrs Alison Usher, Mrs Ruma Verma

CONSTITUTION
The Church Commissioners were formed on 1 April 1948, when Queen Anne's Bounty (1704) and the Ecclesiastical Commissioners (1836) were united.

The full body of Commissioners meets once a year to consider the Report and Accounts and the allocation of available money. The management of the Commissioners' affairs is shared between the Board of Governors, the Assets Committee and the Audit Committee (which are statutory), the Bishoprics and Cathedrals Committee, the Management Advisory Committee, the Pastoral Committee, and the Redundant Churches Committee.

The Church Commissioners' main tasks are to manage their assets, and make money available (for distribution by the Archbishops' Council) in accordance with the duties laid upon them by Acts of Parliament and Measures of the General Synod and former Church Assembly, and to discharge other administrative duties entrusted to them.

MANAGEMENT OF ASSETS
The Commissioners' income in the year ended 31 December 1997 was:

	£ million
Investments	76.2
Property	45.9
Mortgages and loans	9.3
Other interest receivable	8.5
Income before interest payable ...	139.9
Interest payable	(4.1)
Asset management costs	(4.3)
Total income	£131.5

The Commissioners draw no income from the State.

EXPENDITURE IN 1998
The Commissioners' income was distributed in two main ways:

1 Payment of clergy stipends. The Commissioners' investment income provides around 12 per cent of the stipends of the clergy.

2 Payment of clergy pensions and pensions to their widows. The Church of England Pensions Board authorizes pensions, but the majority of the money is provided and paid by the Church Commissioners. New arrangements to share the cost of pensions with the dioceses in the future came into being on 1 January 1998, with the Commissioners being responsible for service prior to 1 January 1998 and dioceses and parishes for pensions earned after that date. The Commissioners are also making transitional payments to help dioceses with the transfer of the pensions liability. They also provide finance for the Clergy Retirement Housing Scheme through the Pensions Board.

The Commissioners used their total income for the year ended 31 December 1998 as follows:

	£ million
Parochial Ministry Support	(20.0)
Clergy and widows' pensions.....	(85.0)
Transitional support for pension contributions..............................	(23.2)
Bishops and cathedral clergy stipends	(6.3)
Bishops' housing	(3.0)
Episcopal administration and payments to cathedrals	(11.2)
Financial provision for resigning clergy	(1.8)
Church buildings	(1.1)
Administration of central Church functions and Commissioners' own administration	(5.3)
Other Church bodies' working costs...	(2.0)
Total expenditure	(158.9)

CENTRAL STIPENDS AUTHORITY
This function and its powers were transferred to the Archbishops' Council on 1 January 1999.

ADMINISTRATIVE DUTIES
The Commissioners are responsible for dealing with schemes for pastoral reorganization proposed by diocesan authorities under the Pastoral Measure 1983. The union of benefices and parishes, the holding of one or more benefices in plurality, the formation of new benefices and parishes, the alteration of ecclesiastical boundaries and the formation of team and group ministries are some of the matters dealt with.

The Commissioners' administrative duties also include considering all proposals for the provision and sale of parsonage houses, cathedral clergy houses and certain transactions affecting diocesan glebe.

REDUNDANT CHURCHES
The Pastoral Measure 1983 provides the procedure for declaring a church pastorally redundant and then settling its future. A Diocesan Pastoral Committee may, after consultation with all the 'interested parties', and with the bishop's approval, ask the Church Commissioners to prepare a draft pastoral scheme for declaring redundant a church which is not required for parochial worship.

If, following the consideration of any representations, a scheme comes into operation, without providing for the future of the church, the redundant building will temporarily vest in the Diocesan Board of Finance for care and maintenance. The Diocesan Redundant Churches Uses Committee then has the duty of making every endeavour to find a suitable alternative use for it and of reporting to the Commissioners. The Commissioners are advised as to the historic and archaeological interest and architectural quality of redundant churches by an independent body, the Advisory Board for Redundant Churches. In the light of the Uses Committee's report and the advice of the Advisory Board, the Commissioners must prepare and publish, normally within a period of three years, a draft redundancy scheme providing for the building in one of four ways: appropriation to another suitable use; retention by the Diocesan Board of Finance; preservation by the Churches Conservation Trust; or demolition. Having carefully considered any representations, the Commissioners decide whether to make any such scheme.

The Churches Conservation Trust, an independent body whose function is the care and maintenance of redundant churches of historic and archaeological interest or architectural quality vested in it by redundancy schemes, is largely financed by Church and State. In 1998, two churches (seven in 1997) of particular merit for which no suitable alternative use could be found were passed to the Churches Conservation Trust, bringing the total number in its care to 317. The Trust requires adequate money to meet the cost of initial repairs and subsequent maintenance to buildings vested in it. For the triennium 2000–2003 the Department for Culture, Media and Sport has agreed to contribute up to a maximum of £8.8 million representing 70 per cent of the total budgeted expenditure of the Fund. The

Church's 30 per cent maximum contribution of £38 million will be made available partly from the net proceeds of sales of redundant churches and sites and partly from the Commissioners' own resources.

RECORDS CENTRE
Director Mr Christopher Pickford

Tel: 020–7898 1034
Fax: 020–7231 5243
email: chris.pickford@c-of-e.org.uk

For further details *see* page 41.

FURTHER INFORMATION
Further information is available in the Commissioners' Annual Report and Accounts which, together with other information leaflets, is available free of charge from the Corporate Affairs Department at 1 Millbank, London SW1P 3JZ. Requests for speakers to give talks about the Commissioners' work are welcomed.

THE CHURCH OF ENGLAND PENSIONS BOARD

Chairman Mr Allan Bridgewater

Vice-Chairman Ven Ian Russell (*Archdeacon of Coventry*)

Deputy Vice-Chairman Mr David Wright

Secretary Mr Roger Radford

Chief Accountant Mr Stephen Eagleton

Pensions Manager Miss Yvonne de la Praudière

Housing Manager Mr Ian Gibbins

AUDIT COMMITTEE
Chairman Mr Keith Dodgson

HON MEDICAL ADVISER
Dr Trevor Hudson

Office 7 Little College St, London SW1P 3SF

Tel: 020–7898 1800
Fax: 020–7898 1801
email: roger.radford@cepb.c-of-e.org.uk

MEMBERS
The constitution of the Board was reviewed by the General Synod in the light of both the Pensions Act 1995 and the changes made with effect from 1 January 1998 to the financial arrangements for providing pensions for those in the stipendiary ministry. It now consists of 20 members.

Appointed Chairman by the General Synod
Mr Allan Bridgewater

Nominated by the Archbishops of Canterbury and York
Mr Philip Hamlyn-Williams, Mr Nigel Sherlock

Elected by the House of Bishops
Rt Revd John Yates

Elected by the House of Clergy
Revd Richard Billinghurst, Ven Christopher Hawthorn (*Archdeacon of Cleveland*), Ven Ian Russell (*Archdeacon of Coventry*), Canon David Williams

Elected by members of the Church Workers Pension Fund
Revd Karen Curnock, Mr Colin Peters

Elected by members of the Church Administrators Pension Fund
Mr Robin Stevens

Elected by the House of Laity
Mr Keith Dodgson, Mr Tim Hind, Mr Geoffrey Hine, Mr Trevor Stevenson, Mr William Taylor, Mr David Wright

Elected by the employers participating in the Church Workers Pension Fund and Church Administrators Pension Fund
Mr Paul Chandler, Mr Philip Couse

Nominated by the Church Commissioners
Mr Derek Fellows

RESPONSIBILITIES
The Pensions Board was constituted by the Church Assembly in 1926 to serve as the pensions authority for the Church of England, and was made the administrator of a comprehensive pension scheme for the clergy. Subsequently the Board has been given wider responsibilities and powers for securing the welfare of all who retire from the stipendiary ministry, and of their widows and widowers, through the provision of pensions and retirement accommodation.

Operating as a trustee both of pension funds and of charitable funds for many different classes of beneficiary, the Board is directly accountable to the General Synod. While the Church has drawn together under the Board its central responsibilities for retirement welfare, the Board works in close cooperation with the Archbishops' Council and also with the Church Commissioners. There is a partnership between the Board and dioceses in financial commitments towards discretionary grants and housing, and at the level of personal pastoral service through Widows Officers, Archdeacons and Retirement Officers.

PENSIONS
The Board is administrator of the pension arrangements for clergy, deaconesses and licensed lay workers, and for their widows and widowers, keeping records of pensionable service and corresponding about pensions matters both with pensioners and with those not yet retired. It is corporate trustee of the Church of England Funded Pensions Scheme, to which contributions are currently being paid at the rate of some £335 million a year to provide for pensions and associated benefits arising from service after the end of 1997. The Church Commissioners continue to meet the cost of benefits arising from service prior to 1 January 1998.

The Clergy (Widows and Dependants) Pensions Fund was closed to new entrants after widows' pensions were introduced under the main scheme. It has assets of £26 million and provides an additional benefit to widows and other dependants of those who made contributions to it. As a result of favourable investment performance, the benefits were increased by 45 per cent in January 1999, following the latest triennial actuarial valuation.

The Board is also corporate trustee of the Church Workers Pension Fund, under which some 170 Church organizations make pension provision for their lay employees, and the Church Administrators Pension Fund. It is responsible for all the activities of these funds including the administration and keeping of records, payment of benefits, collection of contributions and investment of monies currently held in the funds; these now total over £155 million.

RETIREMENT HOUSING SCHEMES

The current retirement housing arrangements were presented to the General Synod by the Board and the Commissioners in July 1982 and were brought into operation by the Board in January 1983. The mortgage scheme is based on loans linked to the value of the properties and an initial low rate of interest. The Board owned approximately 400 rental properties, which it had acquired over time by outright gift or had purchased or built out of gifts in trust for that purpose. To these were added another 400 properties in which the entire equity interest had been charged to the Church Commissioners as security for loan finance. The Commissioners undertook to lend to the Board the funds necessary to finance all future mortgage loans and rental property purchases, subject of course to satisfactory terms as to interest and repayment of capital. The Board does however continue to add further properties acquired by gift. The Board now owns about 1,550 properties and there are nearly 1,700 outstanding mortgage loans.

RESIDENTIAL AND NURSING HOMES

There are eight residential homes and one nursing home which are owned and managed by the Board. Five of these were purpose-designed and another was refurbished and extended a few years ago. Modernization and extension of the nursing home was completed during 1998. The Board has identified a suitable site on which to build a replacement for another of the older homes, and consideration is also being given to modernizing the remaining one. The Board's charitable resources provide the capital for purchasing or building the homes and for their subsequent maintenance.

Each home is run by a professional staff, supported by a local committee. The resident manager of each home reports to the Board's Housing Manager. Residents and patients are charged fees which, with available State support, are affordable having regard to their financial resources. As the fee income is insufficient to cover the operating costs, the shortfall is met from the Board's charitable funds.

In addition, support may be given with fees payable by the Board's pensioners in privately run homes, if an individual cannot meet the full cost even with the maximum possible assistance available from the State.

THE BOARD AS A CHARITY

The care of the more elderly of its pensioners is an activity of the Board which attracts considerable regular support, voluntarily from within the Church at parochial and diocesan level, and from churchgoers and other people of goodwill everywhere. Money and other property given or bequeathed to the Board has averaged over £1.5 million per annum in recent years. The Pensions Board is registered as a charity. The charitable funds currently have a total net value of some £88 million (including the Board's own stake in the retirement housing scheme).

PUBLICATIONS AVAILABLE FROM THE BOARD

Your Pension Questions Answered
Information about the Pension Scheme for clergy, deaconesses and licensed lay workers.

Arrangements of the Church of England Pensions Scheme
Explains the retirement benefits available to clergy, deaconesses and licensed lay workers in return for voluntary pension contributions.

Retirement Housing
Explains the assistance which the Board is able to make (with financial support from the Church Commissioners) to clergy, their wives and widowers, and also to deaconesses and licensed lay workers for their retirement housing.

Pensions Administration for Church of England Employers
A guide to the services and schemes offered by the Board.

Christian Care in Retirement
Information about the Board's residential and nursing homes.

The Church Workers Pension Fund
An explanation of the retirement benefits available to church workers whose employers participate in the Fund.

The Church of England Pensions Board – Our Work is Caring . . .
Describes the discretionary assistance made available to its beneficiaries through the Board's charitable funds and explains how contributions may be made to support that work.

OTHER BOARDS, COUNCILS, COMMISSIONS, ETC. OF THE CHURCH OF ENGLAND

The Advisory Board for Redundant Churches

Vacancy (*Chairman*), His Honour Francis Aglionby, Dr John Blair, Mr Peter Cormack, Mr Ian Curry, Prof Roberta Gilchrist, Rt Revd David Lunn, Mr John Newman, Canon Nicholas Thistlethwaite, Mr Nicholas Thompson

Secretary Dr Jeffrey West, Fielden House, 13 Little College St, London SW1P 3SH
Tel: 020–7898 1872
Fax: 020–7898 1001
email: jeffrey.west@c-of-e.org.uk

The Churches Conservation Trust
(formerly the Redundant Churches Fund)

Ms Liz Forgan (*Chairman*), Mr Richard Butt, Canon Robert Gage, Ms Janet Gough, Mr Richard Griffiths, Rt Revd Edward Holland (*Bishop of Colchester*)

Director Miss Catherine Cullis, 89 Fleet St, London EC4Y 1DH
Tel: 020–7936 2285
Fax: 020–7936 2284

Chief Caseworker Miss Sarah Robinson

The Trust was set up in 1969 to preserve pastorally redundant churches of historic, architectural or archaeological importance. Many are in areas of urban or rural depopulation with no financial resources of their own. They may still be used for occasional services, or for concerts, exhibitions or other events considered by the Trust to be suitable.

The Corporation of the Church House

President The Archbishop of Canterbury

Chairman of Council Sir Alan McLintock

Treasurer The Hon Nicholas Assheton

Secretary Mr Colin Menzies   *Tel:* 020–7898 1310
email: colin.menzies@c-of-e.org.uk

Office Church House, Great Smith St, London SW1P 3NZ
Tel: 020–7898 1320
Fax: 020–7898 1321

The original Church House was built in the early 1890s as the Church's memorial of Queen Victoria's Jubilee, to be the administrative headquarters of the Church of England, and was replaced by the present building to a design by Sir Herbert Baker. The foundation stone was laid in 1937 by Queen Mary and on 10 June 1940 King George VI, accompanied by the Queen, formally opened the new House and attended the first Session of the Church Assembly in the great circular hall. The building was almost immediately requisitioned by the Government and for the rest of the war became the alternative meeting place of both Houses of Parliament; the Lords sat in the Convocation Hall and the Commons in the Hoare Memorial Hall. Oak panels in these halls commemorate this use.

By October 1946 some administrative offices of the Church Assembly returned to Church House and the Church Assembly was able to return for its Autumn Session in 1950. The building is now the headquarters of the new Archbishops' Council as well as being the venue for the General Synod in spring (if it meets) and in the autumn.

Following an extensive refurbishment of the whole building, Church House has also become an important national centre for conferences and meetings.

The business of the Corporation is vested in its Council of 30 members: 10 *ex officio*, 9 elected, 6 nominated by the General Synod and 5 co-opted by the Council.

The National Society (Church of England) for Promoting Religious Education

Patron Her Majesty the Queen

President The Archbishop of Canterbury

Chairman of the Council Rt Revd Alan Chesters (*Bishop of Blackburn*)

General Secretary Canon John Hall
Tel: 020–7898 1500
email: john.hall@natsec.c-of-e.org.uk

Treasurer Mr David Lambert

Deputy Secretaries
Mr Alan Brown
Tel: 020–7898 1494
email: alan.brown@natsoc.c-of-e.org.uk

Mr David Lankshear
Tel: 020–7898 1490
email: david.lankshear@c-of-e.org.uk

Finance and Administrative Officer Mr David Grimes
Tel: 020–7898 1492
email: david.grimes@natsoc.c-of-e.org.uk

Publishing Manager Mr Alan Mitchell
Tel: 020–7898 1450
email: alan.mitchell@natsoc.c-of-e.org.uk

Publications Officer Mr Hamish Bruce
Tel: 020–7898 1453
email: hamish.bruce@c-of-e.org.uk

Membership and Promotions Officer Miss Katie Lowe
Tel: 020–7898 1497
email: katie.lowe@natsoc.c-of-e.org.uk

Office Church House, Great Smith St, London SW1P 3NZ
Tel: 020–7898 1518
Fax: 020–7898 1493
email: info@natsoc.c-of-e.org.uk
web: http://www.natsoc.org.uk

Archivist Ms Sarah Duffield
Tel: 020–7898 1033
Fax: 020–7394 7018
email: sarah.duffield@natsoc.c-of-e.org

The Society's archives are held at the Church of England Record Centre (*Director* Mr Christopher Pickford) – for further details *see* page 41.

London RE Centre
Director Mrs Alison Seaman

Address 36 Causton St, London SW1P 4AU
Tel: 020–7932 1190/1191
Fax: 020–7932 1199
email: nsrec@dial.pipex.com
web: http://dspace.dial.pipex.com/nsrec/

York RE Centre
Head of Religious Studies Mrs Eileen Bellett

Centre Tutor Mrs Carrie Mercier

Address The College, Lord Mayor's Walk, York YO31 7EX
Tel: (01904) 716858
Fax: (01904) 612512
email: c.mercier@ucrysj.ac.uk

The National Society exists 'for the promotion, encouragement and support of religious education in accordance with the principles of the Church of England'. It works in close association with the Board of Education (and the Division for Education of the Church in Wales), but values its status as a voluntary body which enables it to take initiatives in developing new work. The Society has a particular concern for the support of Christian education and Christians in education.

Founded in 1811, the Society was chiefly responsible for setting up, in cooperation with local clergy and others, the nationwide network of Church schools in England and Wales; it was also, through the Church colleges, a pioneer in teacher education. A concern for Church schools is still at the heart of the Society's work; it provides a legal and advisory service for dioceses and schools as well as a range of publications for the guidance of teachers and governors. It trains and accredits inspectors for Church schools under Section 23 of the School Inspection Act 1996. In cooperation with the Board of Education the Society expresses its views on educational matters to the Department for Education and Employment, the LEAs and other bodies.

While supporting the Church's partnership with the State in statutory education, the National Society has a broader range: those responsible for RE and worship in any school, lecturers and students in colleges, and clergy and lay people in diocesan and parish education can all benefit from the resources of the Society's RE Centres, courses, conferences, archives and publications.

The London RE Centre is in London Diocesan House in Pimlico. It houses thousands of books and journals currently available for religious education and a comprehensive collection of videos, audio cassettes, slides, posters and artefacts. It is open from Monday to Friday, 9.30 a.m. to 4.30 p.m. (and at other times by arrangement), when staff are always pleased to assist visitors besides answering telephone and written enquiries. The Centre provides facilities for workshops and runs a variety of courses in RE, worship and pastoral and social education. It also works closely with the London Diocesan Board for Schools.

The York RE Centre is an integral part of the

College of Ripon and York St John. The National Society supports its work financially and through representation on the Centre's Advisory Board. The Centre offers a similarly wide range of resources and a full programme of training opportunities. It is open from 8.45 a.m. to 9.30 p.m. on Monday to Thursday, 8.45 a.m. to 7.00 p.m. Friday, and 9.00 a.m. to 1.00 p.m. on Saturday in term-time; and 9.00 a.m. to 5.00 p.m. Monday to Friday during college vacations. Visitors are always welcome but are advised to telephone beforehand if travelling from a distance.

The National Society has created a Fellowship in Special Educational Needs. Each Fellow is appointed for one year, with the results of their work being published. The fellowship covers the areas of religious education, Christian education, Church schools, spiritual, moral, social and cultural development. The Society is developing a number of new initiatives including a web site to provide support for collective worship and Church school management.

After nearly two centuries of close association with Church schools and colleges the National Society has built up an impressive collection of documents and books in its archives and library. These include about 15,000 files of correspondence with the various National Schools in England and Wales and many published works, including the Society's own. Access is available to *bona fide* researchers by appointment at the Church of England Record Centre.

In support of Christian education in schools, colleges, parishes and the home, the National Society produces a range of books and other publications, including the magazine *Together with Children*. Its publishing programme is integrated with Church House Publishing (*see* page 39), where staff salaries and other costs are part funded by the Society. A catalogue giving full details is available from the Society at the address above. Applications for membership from individuals, schools and other bodies wishing to support the Society's work and share its resources are welcomed.

REVIEWS

Archbishops' Review of Bishops' Needs and Resources

Prof Anthony Mellows (*Chairman*), Mr Richard Agutter, Canon Robert Baker, Ven Richard Inwood (*Archdeacon of Halifax*), Mr Alan King, Mr Luke March, Rt Revd Peter Nott, Mr Peter Parker, Mrs Lou Scott-Joynt

Secretary Mr Stuart Deacon, 1 Millbank, London SW1P 3JZ   *Tel:* 020–7898 1133
Fax: 020–7898 1131
email: stuart.deacon@c-of-e.org.uk

An independent review commissioned by the Archbishops of Canterbury and York. It will be considering the work and role of bishops, both diocesan and suffragan, at the present time; how that is likely to evolve during the next decade; the resources which bishops will need for the support of their ministry during that period; and the funding implications for the Church Commissioners and the wider Church.

Review of Clergy Stipends

Ven Dr John Marsh (*Archdeacon of Blackburn*) (*Chairman*), Revd Lesley Bentley, Mr Alan King, Mr David Phillips, Ven Robert Reiss (*Archdeacon of Surrey*), Mr Bryan Sandford, Mr Keith Stevens, Revd Dr Richard Turnbull

Secretary Margaret Jeffery, Church House, Great Smith St, London SW1P 3NZ
Tel: 020–7898 1411
Fax: 020–7898 1421
email: margaret.jeffery@c-of-e.org.uk

The Archbishops' Council has set up a Working Group to carry out a review of clergy stipends, under the chairmanship of the Archdeacon of Blackburn. The Working Group's terms of reference include considering the concept and definition of the stipend, examining the content of the clergy remuneration package (including retirement provision) and its comparability with remuneration for other groups, and evaluating the affordability and long-term financial sustainability of the present arrangements and any proposals for change. There will be extensive consultation with, among others, the Church Commissioners, the Pensions Board and dioceses. It is intended to carry out a large-scale survey of clergy, and make a report to the General Synod in November 2000. Further details are contained in GS Misc 573.

Church Urban Fund Review

Rt Revd David Smith (*Bishop of Bradford*) (*Chairman*), Mr Richard Best, Revd Philippa Boardman, Mr Paul Goggins, Mr Richard Leyton, Mr Justin McKenzie, Ms Josile Munro, Preb Sam Philpott, Ms Robina Rafferty, Mr John Routledge, Ms Hilary Russell, Revd Nezlin Sterling, Mr Bryan Sandford, Ms Betty Thayer, Mr Richard Wheeler

Secretary Mrs Gill Moody, Rectory, Rectory Lane, Market Harborough LE16 8AS

Tel: (01858) 462798
Fax: (01858) 466251
email: gillmoody@hotmail.com

Assessors Mr Jeremy Harris, Mr David Skidmore

An independent review commissioned by General Synod, through the Archbishops' Council.

Terms of reference
To review the experience of the Church Urban Fund with particular reference to its purpose, impact and effectiveness; the changing context in which it operates; its grant-making procedures and policies; its relationship with parishes, dioceses, the General Synod, the Archbishops' Council and others; to make recommendations for its future.

The review body plans to report through the Archbishops' Council to General Synod in July 2000.

Royal Peculiars Review Group

Prof Averil Cameron (*Chairman*), Rt Hon Lord Berwick, Very Revd Raymond Furnell (*Dean of York*), Sir Brian Jenkins

Administrative Secretary Mr David Long, Epwell Mill, Banbury, Oxon OX15 6HG

Tel and *Fax:* (01295) 788242

Terms of reference
To review and report to Her Majesty the Queen, through the Lord Chancellor, with recommendations, on the organization, management and accountability of each of Westminster Abbey, St George's Chapel, Windsor and the Chapels Royal responsible to the Dean of the Chapels Royal, but without prejudice to their status as Royal Peculiars.

THE CONVOCATIONS OF CANTERBURY AND YORK

CONSTITUTION

Each of the Convocations consists of two Houses, an Upper House and a Lower House. The Upper House consists of all the diocesan bishops in the Province and certain elected suffragan bishops, and the Archbishop presides. The Lower House comprises *ex officio* and elected members of the clergy. These are known as Proctors in Convocation. The University and Service representatives are given on page 4.

MEMBERS OF CONVOCATIONS

	Canterbury	York
Upper House		
Diocesan Bishops...........	30	14
Suffragan Bishops	6	3
	36	17
Lower House		
Deans or Provosts	10	5
Dean of Jersey or Guernsey	1	
Archdeacons	29	14
Service Chaplains	3	
Chaplain-General of Prisons	1	
Elected Proctors	125	58
University Proctors.........	4	2
Religious	1	1
Co-opted Clergy	0	1
	174	81

OFFICERS

Convocation of Canterbury
President The Archbishop of Canterbury

Prolocutor of the Lower House Canon Hugh Wilcox (St Albans)

Pro-Prolocutors
Revd David Houlding (London)
Ven Trevor Lloyd (*Archdeacon of Barnstaple*)

Standing Committee of the Upper House
Rt Revd and Rt Hon Richard Chartres (*Bishop of London*)
Rt Revd John Gladwin (*Bishop of Guildford*)
Rt Revd Michael Scott-Joynt (*Bishop of Winchester*)

Standing Committee of the Lower House
The Prolocutor
The Pro-Prolocutors

Ven Pete Broadbent (*Archdeacon of Northolt*)
Revd Andrew Burnham (Oxford)
Preb Horace Harper (Lichfield)
Very Revd Michael Perham (*Provost of Derby*)
Ven Judith Rose (*Archdeacon of Tonbridge*)
Canon Trevor Williams (Universities, Oxford)

Registrar Mr Brian Hanson

Synodical Secretary, Actuary, and Editor of the Chronicle of Convocation
Canon Michael Hodge, Braxton Cottage, Halletts Shute, Norton, Yarmouth, Isle of Wight PO41 0RH   *Tel* and *Fax:* (01983) 761121   *email:* michaelh@braxton.ndo.co.uk

Ostiarius Mr Clive McCleester, Head Virger of Winchester Cathedral

Convocation of York
President The Archbishop of York

Prolocutor of the Lower House Canon John Stanley (Liverpool)

Deputy Prolocutors of the Lower House
Revd Benjamin Hopkinson (York)
Very Revd George Nairn-Briggs (*Provost of Wakefield*)

Assessors of the Upper House
(Two vacancies)

Assessors of the Lower House
The Prolocutor
The Deputy Prolocutors
Ven David Turnbull (*Archdeacon of Carlisle*)
Canon Max Wigley (Bradford)
(Seven vacancies)

Registrar Mr Lionel Lennox

Registrar (*Provincial Elections*) Mr Brian Hanson

Synodal Secretary and Treasurer and Editor of the Journal of Convocation
Ven David Jenkins, Irvings House, Sleagill, Penrith, Cumbria CA10 3HD   *Tel:* (01931) 714400

Apparitor P. Gibson

ACTS AND PROCEEDINGS

For the Acts and Proceedings of the Convocations, readers are referred to *The Chronicle of the Convocation of Canterbury* and to the *York Journal of Convocation* available from Church House Bookshop. Back numbers are available from Wm. Dawson & Sons Ltd, Cannon House, Folkestone, Kent.

THE ECCLESIASTICAL COURTS

The Ecclesiastical Courts consist of (1) the Diocesan or Consistory Courts, (2) the Provincial Courts, and for both Provinces (3) the Court of Ecclesiastical Causes Reserved and, when required, (4) a Commission of Review. In certain faculty cases an appeal lies from the Provincial Courts to the Judicial Committee of the Privy Council. The jurisdiction of the Archdeacons' Courts is now confined to the visitations of Archdeacons. The Ecclesiastical Courts are in the main now regulated by the Ecclesiastical Jurisdiction Measure 1963. The Court of Faculties is the Court of the Archbishop of Canterbury through which the legatine powers transferred to the Archbishop of Canterbury by the Ecclesiastical Licences Act 1533 are exercised.

The personnel of the Diocesan Courts is given in the diocesan lists. The personnel of the Court of Faculties and of the Provincial and some of the other Courts is as follows:

THE COURT OF ARCHES
Dean of the Arches The Rt Worshipful Sir John Owen

Registrar Dr Frank Robson
16 Beaumont St, Oxford OX1 2LZ
Tel: (01865) 24111974

THE COURT OF THE VICAR-GENERAL OF THE PROVINCE OF CANTERBURY
Vicar-General The Worshipful Sheila Cameron

Joint Registrars
Dr Frank Robson (*as above*)
Mr Brian Hanson
Church House, Great Smith St, London SW1P 3NZ *Tel:* 020–7898 1366
email: brian.hanson@c-of-e.org.uk

THE CHANCERY COURT OF YORK
Auditor The Rt Worshipful Sir John Owen

Registrar Mr Lionel Lennox
The Registry, Stamford House, Piccadilly, York YO1 1PP *Tel:* (01904) 623487
Fax: (01904) 611458
email: denison.till@dial.pipex.com

THE COURT OF THE VICAR-GENERAL OF THE PROVINCE OF YORK
Vicar-General His Honour Judge Thomas Coningsby

Registrar Mr Lionel Lennox (*as above*)

THE COURT OF ECCLESIASTICAL CAUSES RESERVED
Judges
The Rt Hon Ralph Gibson
Rt Revd Eric Kemp (*Bishop of Chichester*)
The Rt Hon Lord Justice Lloyd
Rt Revd Ronald Gordon (*formerly Bishop of Portsmouth*)
Rt Revd Alexander Graham (*formerly Bishop of Newcastle*)

Registrar Dr Frank Robson (*as above*)

THE COURT OF FACULTIES
Master of the Faculties The Rt Worshipful Sir John Owen

Registrar Mr Peter Beesley
1 The Sanctuary, Westminster SW1P 3JT
Tel: 020–7222 5381

APPEAL PANEL CONSTITUTED UNDER THE PASTORAL MEASURE 1983 SCHEDULE 4
Chairman The Dean of the Arches

Deputy Chairmen
The Vicar-General of Canterbury
The Vicar-General of York

In addition to the Chairman, a tribunal comprises four members of the House of Clergy and two members of the House of Laity drawn from the following panels:

Convocation of Canterbury, Lower House
Canon Ray Adams (Worcester)
Canon Robert Baker (Norwich)
Revd Dr Anne Barton (Winchester)
Canon Christine Farrington (Ely)
Ven David Goldie (*Archdeacon of Buckingham*)
Canon Jeremy Haselock (Chichester)
Revd Stephen Holdaway (Lincoln)
Ven Malcolm Lesiter (*Archdeacon of Bedford*)
Preb Sam Philpott (Exeter)
Preb Terry Thake (Lichfield)
Revd Jonathan Young (Ely)

Convocation of York, Lower House
Canon Edward Burns (Blackburn)
Revd Helen Chantry (Chester)
Canon Frank Dexter (Newcastle)
Very Revd Raymond Furnell (*Dean of York*)
Ven Granville Gibson (*Archdeacon of Auckland*)
Revd Peter Hill (Southwell)
Very Revd George Nairn-Briggs (*Provost of Wakefield*)

Canon John Stanley (Liverpool)
Canon Max Wigley (Bradford)
(Two vacancies)

House of Laity of the General Synod
Mr Anthony Archer (St Albans)
Mr Roger Atkinson (Lincoln)
Mr Stewart Darlow (Chester)
Mr Keith Davidson (Peterborough)
Mr Ian Garden (Blackburn)
Dr Sheila Grieve (Chester)
Dr John Holden (Southwell)
Mr James Humpherey (Salisbury)
Dr Kathryn Morfey (Winchester)
Miss Pat Nappin (Chelmsford)
Miss Diane Parker (Blackburn)
Mr David Wright (Oxford)

Secretary Mr Robert Wellen, General Synod Office, Church House, Great Smith St, London SW1P 3NZ   *Tel:* 020–7340 0214
          email: robert.wellen@c-of-e.org.uk

APPEAL PANEL CONSTITUTED UNDER THE ORDINATION OF WOMEN (FINANCIAL PROVISIONS) MEASURE 1993
Revd Hugh Broad (Gloucester)
Canon Rex Chapman (Carlisle)
Ven Robin Ellis (*Archdeacon of Plymouth*)
Mr Ian Garden (Blackburn)
Mrs Shirley Jackson (St Albans)
Canon David Lickess (York)
Dr Kathryn Morfey (Winchester)
Miss Diane Parker (Blackburn)
Mrs Elizabeth Paver (Sheffield)
Mr Mike Tyrell (Coventry)
Revd Colin Williams (Blackburn)
(One vacancy)

Secretary Mr Robert Wellen, General Synod Office, Church House, Great Smith St, London SW1P 3NZ   *Tel:* 020–7340 0214
          email: robert.wellen@c-of-e.org.uk

APPEAL PANEL CONSTITUTED UNDER STANDING ORDER 120(d)(i)
House of Bishops
Rt Revd Peter Forster (*Bishop of Chester*)
Rt Revd Graham James (*Bishop of Norwich*)
Rt Revd Noel Jones (*Bishop of Sodor and Man*)
Rt Revd Michael Langrish (*Bishop of Exeter*)
Rt Revd Nigel McCulloch (*Bishop of Wakefield*)
Rt Revd Mark Santer (*Bishop of Birmingham*)

House of Clergy
Ven Pete Broadbent (*Archdeacon of Northolt*)
Revd Roger Combes (Chichester)
Ven Alan Hawker (*Archdeacon of Malmesbury*)
Canon Jeffery John (Southwark)
Revd George Kovoor (Birmingham)
Ven Trevor Lloyd (*Archdeacon of Barnstaple*)
Revd Clive Mansell (Ripon)

Revd Penny Martin (Durham)
Prebendary Sam Philpott (Exeter)
Canon Patience Purchas (St Albans)
Revd John Rees (Oxford)
Revd Colin Williams (Blackburn)

House of Laity
Mr Anthony Archer (St Albans)
Mrs Janet Atkinson (Durham)
Mr Frank Knaggs (Newcastle)
Mr David Lammy (*ex officio*)
Mr Brian McHenry (Southwark)
Dr Kathleen Morfey (Winchester)
Mrs Heather Morgan (Exeter)
Mr Gerald O'Brien (Rochester)
Mrs Christina Rees (St Albans)
Mr Geoffrey Tattersall (Manchester)
Mr Mike Tyrrell (Coventry)
Mrs Shirley-Ann Williams (Exeter)

Secretary Mr Robert Wellen, General Synod Office, Church House, Great Smith St, London SW1P 3NZ   *Tel:* 020–7340 0214
          email: robert.wellen@c-of-e.org.uk

APPEAL PANEL APPOINTED PURSUANT TO RULE 44(8) OF THE CHURCH REPRESENTATION RULES AS AMENDED BY THE NATIONAL INSTITUTIONS MEASURE 1998 (SCHEDULE 5, PARAGRAPH 2(c))

The Dean of the Arches
The Vicar-General of Canterbury
The Vicar-General of York
Mr Anthony Archer (St Albans)
Mrs Janet Atkinson (Durham)
Mr Frank Knaggs (Newcastle)
Mr David Lammy (*ex officio*)
Mr Brian McHenry (Southwark)
Dr Kathleen Morfey (Winchester)
Mrs Heather Morgan (Exeter)
Mr Gerald O'Brien (Rochester)
Mrs Christina Rees (St Albans)
Mr Geoffrey Tattersall (Manchester)
Mr Mike Tyrrell (Coventry)
Mrs Shirley-Ann Williams (Exeter)

Secretary Mr Robert Wellen, General Synod Office, Church House, Great Smith St, London SW1P 3NZ   *Tel:* 020–7340 0214
          email: robert.wellen@c-of-e.org.uk

APPEAL PANEL APPOINTED PURSUANT TO RULE 25(5) OF THE CLERGY REPRESENTATION RULES 1975 TO 1999
The Dean of the Arches
The Vicar-General of Canterbury
The Vicar-General of York

Ven Pete Broadbent (*Archdeacon of Northolt*)
Revd Roger Combes (Chichester)
Ven Alan Hawker (*Archdeacon of Malmesbury*)
Canon Jeffery John (Southwark)
Revd George Kovoor (Birmingham)

Ven Trevor Lloyd (*Archdeacon of Barnstaple*)
Revd Clive Mansell (Ripon)
Revd Penny Martin (Durham)
Prebendary Sam Philpott (Exeter)
Canon Patience Purchas (St Albans)
Revd John Rees (Oxford)
Revd Roger Williams (Blackburn)

Secretary Mr Robert Wellen, General Synod Office, Church House, Great Smith St, London SW1P 3NZ   *Tel:* 020–7340 0214
email: robert.wellen@c-of-e.org.uk

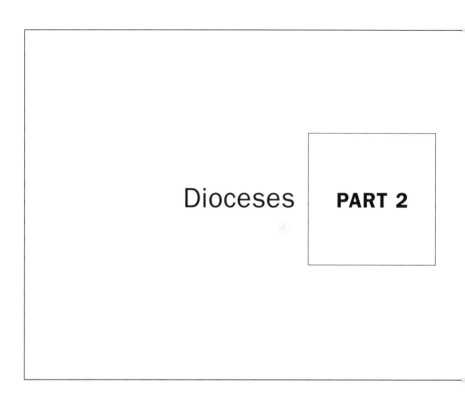

Dioceses **PART 2**

Provinces of Canterbury and York

The dioceses in the respective Provinces of Canterbury and York are as below:

The Province of Canterbury Bath and Wells, Birmingham, Bristol, Canterbury, Chelmsford, Chichester, Coventry, Derby, Ely, Europe, Exeter, Gloucester, Guildford, Hereford, Leicester, Lichfield, Lincoln, London, Norwich, Oxford, Peterborough, Portsmouth, Rochester, St Albans, St Edmundsbury and Ipswich, Salisbury, Southwark, Truro, Winchester, Worcester.

The Province of York Blackburn, Bradford, Carlisle, Chester, Durham, Liverpool, Manchester, Newcastle, Ripon and Leeds, Sheffield, Sodor and Man, Southwell, Wakefield, York.

The entry for each diocese is preceded by a territorial description and a few vital statistics:

Population Derived from the final mid-year estimates of normally resident population for 1997 published by the Office for National Statistics. Calculations are based on diocesan proportions of Ward and Civil Parish populations as at the 1991 Census.

Area in square miles, as calculated from material supplied by the Office of National Statistics and the Church Commissioners.

Stipendiary clergy Full-time clergy, men and women, working within the diocesan framework as at 31 December 1998 and counted under the current deployment formula.

Benefices Figures as at June 1997, compiled from information provided by the Church Commissioners. The figure does not include cathedrals or conventional districts.

Parishes ⎫ as listed at June 1997 (with later additions) in the Parish Register maintained by the Statistics Unit of
Churches ⎭ the Central Board of Finance.

In most cases, the Diocesan Secretary is also the Secretary of the Diocesan Synod.

PROVINCIAL LAY OFFICERS

Canterbury
Dean of the Court of Arches Rt Worshipful Sir John Owen, Bickerstaff House, Idlicote, Shipston-on-Stour, War. CV36 5DT

Vicar-General The Worshipful Sheila Cameron, 2 Harcourt Buildings, Temple, London EC4 9DB
Tel: 020–7353 8415

Joint Registrars Dr Frank Robson, 16 Beaumont St, Oxford OX1 2LZ   *Tel:* (01865) 241974

Mr Brian Hanson, Church House, Great Smith St, London SW1P 3NZ   *Tel:* 020–7898 1366

York
Official Principal and Auditor of Chancery Court (York) Rt Worshipful Sir John Owen, Bickerstaff House, Idlicote, Shipston-on-Stour, War. CV36 5DT

Vicar-General of the Province and Official Principal of the Consistory Court His Honour Judge Thomas Coningsby, 3 Dr Johnson's Buildings, Temple, London EC4Y 7BA   *Tel:* 020–7353 4854

Registrar of Province Mr Lionel Lennox, The Registry, Stamford House, Piccadilly, York YO1 9PP   *Tel:* (01904) 623487
Fax: (01904) 611458
email: denison.till@dial.pipex.com

Registrar (Provincial Elections) Mr Brian Hanson, Church House, Great Smith St, London SW1P 3NZ   *Tel:* 020–7898 1366

Archbishop of Canterbury's Personal Staff

Lambeth Palace, London SE1 7JU
Tel: 020–7898 1200   *Fax:* 020–7261 9836
Web: http//www.archbishopofcanterbury.org

BISHOP AT LAMBETH (Head of Staff)
Rt Revd Richard Llewellin

Secretary for Public Affairs and Deputy Head of Staff
Mr Jeremy Harris

Public Affairs Officer
Vacancy

Secretary for Ecumenical Affairs
Canon Richard Marsh PH D

Assistant Secretary for Ecumenical and Anglican Communion Affairs
Revd Dr Herman Browne

Secretary for Anglican Communion Affairs
Canon Andrew Deuchar

Archbishop's Domestic Chaplain (Lambeth Palace)
Canon Colin Fletcher

Archbishop's Canterbury Chaplain (and Diocesan Missioner)
Revd Stewart Jones

Secretary for Broadcasting, Press and Communications
Revd Lesley Perry

Archbishop's Private Secretary
Ms Mary Eaton

Administrative Secretary
Mr Derek Fullarton

Archbishop's Lay Assistant
Mr Andrew Nunn

Research Officer
Mrs Claire Shirley

Steward
Mr John Dean

Bursar
Mrs Anne Lindley

Archbishop of York's Personal Staff

Bishopthorpe Palace, Bishopthorpe, York YO23 2GE
Tel: (01904) 707021   *Fax:* (01904) 709204
email: office@bishopthorpe.u-net.com

Chaplain to the Archbishop
Revd Michael Kavanagh

Archbishop's Private Secretary
Mrs Mary Murray

Archbishop's Special Adviser
Ven Alan Dean

DIOCESE OF BATH AND WELLS

Founded in 909. Somerset; north Somerset; Bath; north-east Somerset; a few parishes in Dorset.

Population 841,000   Area 1,614 sq m
Stipendiary Clergy 250   Benefices 216
Parishes 482   Churches 571

BISHOP (77th)

Rt Revd James Lawton Thompson, The Palace, Wells, Som. BA5 2PD [1991]   *Tel:* (01749) 672341
Fax: (01749) 679355
email: bishop@bathwells.anglican.org
[James Bath and Wells]
Chaplain/Pastoral Assistant Preb Martin Wright (*same address*)

SUFFRAGAN BISHOP

TAUNTON Rt Revd Andrew Radford, Bishop's Lodge, Monkton Heights, West Monkton, Taunton TA2 8LU   *Tel:* (01823) 413526
Fax: (01823) 412805
email: BishopTaunton@compuserve.com

HONORARY ASSISTANT BISHOPS

Rt Revd John Waller, 102 Harnham Rd, Salisbury SP2 8JW   *Tel:* (01722) 329739
Rt Revd Alexander Hamilton, 3 Ash Tree Rd, Burnham on Sea, Som. TA8 2LB
Tel: (01278) 783823
Rt Revd Roger Wilson, Kingsett, Roper's Lane, Wrington, Bristol BS18 7NH   *Tel:* (01934) 862464
Rt Revd John Neale, 26 Prospect, Corsham, Wilts SN13 9AF   *Tel:* (01249) 712557
Rt Revd Richard Third, 25 Church Close, Martock, Yeovil, Som. TA12 6DA   *Tel:* (01935) 825519
Rt Revd William Persson, Ryalls Cottage, Burton St, Marnhull, Sturminster Newton DT10 1PS
Tel: (01258) 820452
Rt Revd Colin James, 5 Hermitage Rd, Landsdown, Bath BA1 5SN   *Tel:* (01225) 312720
Rt Revd Peter Coleman, Boxenwood Cottage, Westwood, Weir Bagborough, Bishop's Lydeard TA4 3HQ   *Tel:* (01984) 618607
Rt Revd Michael Houghton, 8 Goldney Ave, Clifton, Bristol BS8 4RA   *Tel:* 0117–973 1752

CATHEDRAL CHURCH OF ST ANDREW IN WELLS

Dean of Wells Very Revd Richard Lewis, The Dean's Lodging, 25 The Liberty, Wells, Som. BA5 2SZ [1990]   *Tel:* (01749) 670278
email: deanwels@welscathedra.u-net.com
Canons Residentiary
Precentor Revd Patrick Woodhouse, 4 The Liberty, Wells, Som. BA5 2SU   *Tel:* (01749) 673188
Archdeacon Ven Richard (Dick) Acworth, Old

Rectory, The Crescent, Croscombe, Wells, Som. BA5 3QN [1993]   *Tel:* (01749) 342242
Treasurer Canon Geoffrey Walker, 6 The Liberty, Wells, Som. BA5 2SU [1994]   *Tel:* (01749) 672224
Chancellor Canon Melvyn Matthews, 8 The Liberty, Wells, Som. BA5 2SU [1997]
Tel: (01749) 678763
Registrar Mr Tim Berry, Diocesan Registry, 14 Market Place, Wells, Som. BA5 2RE
Tel: (01749) 674747
Administrator and Chapter Clerk Mr John Roberts, Chain Gate, Cathedral Green, Wells, Som. BA5 2UE   *Tel:* (01749) 674483
Fax: (01749) 677360
Cathedral Organist Mr Malcolm Archer (*same address*)

ARCHDEACONS

WELLS Ven Richard (Dick) Acworth, Old Rectory, The Crescent, Croscombe, Wells, Som. BA5 3QN [1993]   *Tel:* (01749) 342242
Fax: (01749) 330060
BATH Ven Robert (Bob) Evens, 56 Grange Rd, Saltford, Bristol BS31 3AG [1995]   *Tel:* (01225) 873609
Fax: (01225) 874110
email: 113145.1175@compuserve.com
TAUNTON Ven John Reed, 4 Westerkirk Gate, Staplegrove, Taunton, Som. TA2 6BQ [1999]
Tel: (01823) 323838
Fax: (01823) 325420
email: 113022.235@compuserve.com

CONVOCATION (MEMBERS OF THE HOUSE OF CLERGY OF THE GENERAL SYNOD)

Dignitaries in Convocation
The Dean of Wells
The Archdeacon of Wells
Proctors for Clergy
Preb Richard Askew
Revd Michael Norman
Preb Rodney Schofield
Preb Penny West

MEMBERS OF THE HOUSE OF LAITY OF THE GENERAL SYNOD

Mrs Ann Clarke
Mr Michael Gillingham

Mr Timothy Hind
Mr Alan King
Mr Peter LeRoy
Dr Irene Riding
Mrs Diana Taylor
Miss Fay Wilson-Rudd

DIOCESAN OFFICERS
Dioc Secretary Mr Nicholas Denison, Dioc Office, The Old Deanery, Wells, Som. BA5 2UG
Tel: (01749) 670777
Fax: (01749) 674240
Chancellor of Diocese The Worshipful Timothy Briden, 1 Temple Gardens, Temple, London EC4Y 9BB
Registrar of Diocese and Bishop's Legal Secretary Mr Tim Berry, Diocesan Registry, 14 Market Place, Wells, Som. BA5 2RE   *Tel:* (01749) 674747
Fax: (01749) 676585

DIOCESAN ORGANIZATIONS
Diocesan Office The Old Deanery, Wells, Som. BA5 2UG   *Tel:* (01749) 670777
Fax: (01749) 674240
email: general@bathwells.anglican.org

ADMINISTRATION
Dioc Synod (Chairman, House of Clergy) Preb Penny West, Vicarage, 35 Kewstoke Rd, Weston Super Mare BS22 9YE *Tel:* (01934) 416162; *(Chairman, House of Laity)* Mrs Diana Taylor, Volis Farm, Hestercombe, Taunton TA2 8HS *Tel:* (01823) 451545, *Fax:* (01823) 451701; *(Secretary)* Mr Nicholas Denison, Dioc Office
Board of Finance (Chairman) Mr Alan King, 97 St Ladoc Rd, Keynsham, Bristol BS18 2EN; *(Secretary)* Mr Nicholas Denison *(as above)*
Finance and General Purposes Committee Mr Nicholas Denison *(as above)*
Houses and Glebe Committee Miss Susan George, Dioc Office
Board of Patronage Mr Philip Nokes, Dioc Office
Pastoral Committee Mr Philip Nokes *(as above)*
Redundant Churches Uses Committee Mr Philip Nokes *(as above)*
Designated Officer Mr Philip Nokes *(as above)*
Deputy Dioc Secretary Mr Philip Nokes *(as above)*
Accountant Mr Jonathan Cox
Property Officer Mrs Penny Cooke, Dioc Office
Dioc Surveyor Mr Paul Toseland, Dioc Office

CHURCHES
Advisory Committee for the Care of Churches (Chairman) Mr Hugh Playfair, Blackford House, Blackford, Yeovil BA22 7EE *Tel:* (01963) 440611; *(Secretary)* Mr Tim Berry, Dioc Registry, 14 Market Place, Wells BA5 2RE *Tel:* (01749) 674747
Association of Change Ringers Preb Christopher Marshall, Tap Cottage, High St, Milverton, Taunton TA4 1LL   *Tel:* (01823) 400419

Choral Association Mr D. B. Chandler, 69 Grenville Court, Waverley Wharf, Bridgwater, Som. TA6 3TY   *Tel:* (01278) 427574

EDUCATION
Board of Education Diocesan Education Office, The Old Deanery, Wells BA5 2UG
Tel: (01749) 670777
Dioc Director of Education Mr Mark Evans
Advisers in Religious Education Mrs Maureen Bollard and Mr Mike Brownbill *(same address)*
Senior Youth and Children's Officer Revd David Williamson, Dioc Office
Youth Officers Miss Yvonne Criddle, Mr Tony Cook, Dioc Office

COUNCIL FOR MINISTRY
Chairman The Bishop of Taunton
Director of Training Preb Russell Bowman-Eadie, Dioc Office
Lay Training Adviser Revd Graham Dodds, Dioc Office
Director of Ordinands Revd Vaughan Roberts, Rectory, Lower St, Chewton Mendip, Bath BA3 4PD   *Tel:* (01761) 332199
Dean of Women Clergy Revd Susan Trickett, The Vicarage, Church Hill, High Littleton, Bristol BS39 6HE   *Tel:* (01761) 472097
Vocations Adviser Vacancy
Warden of Readers Ven John Reed, 4 Westerkirk Gate, Staplegrove, Taunton TA2 6BQ
Tel: (01823) 323838

COUNCIL FOR MISSION
Chairman The Archdeacon of Taunton
Dioc Missioner Canon Geoffrey Walker, 6 The Liberty, Wells, Som. BA5 2SU *Tel:* (01749) 670777
Ecumenical Officer Revd Robert Shorter, Rectory, Church Lane, East Harptree, Bristol BS18 6BD
Tel: (01761) 221239
Dioc Adviser for the Ministry of Health and Healing Revd David Howell, 60 Andrew Allan Rd, Rockwell Green, Wellington, Som TA21 9DY
Tel: (01823) 664529
Bishop's Renewal Adviser Revd Christian Merivale, Quarry Welham, Castle Cary, Som. BA7 7NE   *Tel:* (01963) 350191
World Mission Adviser and Exec Secretary Zambia Link Mrs Jenny Humphries, Dioc Office

COUNCIL FOR SOCIAL RESPONSIBILITY
Chairman The Archdeacon of Wells
Social Responsibility Officer Ms Helen Stanton, Dioc Office
Chaplain to the Deaf Sister Susan Bloomfield, St Nicholas Cottage, Newtown Lane, West Pennard BA6 8NW   *Tel:* (01458) 834171
Fax: (01458) 835136

STEWARDSHIP

Resources Adviser Miss Fay Wilson-Rudd, Dioc Office

LITURGICAL GROUP

Chairman Revd Julian Smith, St Andrew's Vicarage, 118 Kingston Rd, Taunton TA2 7SR
Tel: (01823) 332544

PRESS AND PUBLICATIONS

Communications Officer Revd John Andrews, Rectory, Fosse Rd, Oakhill, Bath
Tel: (01749) 841341
Fax: (01749) 841098
Editor of 'The Grapevine' (*Dioc Newspaper*) Mrs Celia Andrews (*same address*)
Editor of Directory and Database Manager Mrs Julienne Jones, Dioc Office

WIDOWS' OFFICER

Preb Patrick Blake, 47 Lower St, Merriott, Som. TA16 5NN
Tel: (01460) 78932

RETREAT HOUSE

Abbey House, Glastonbury (*Warden* David Hill)
Tel: (01458) 831112

DIOCESAN RECORD OFFICE

Somerset County Record Office, Obridge Rd, Taunton, Som. TA2 7PU *County and Diocesan Archivist* Mr Adam Green
Tel: (01823) 278805

DIOCESAN RESOURCE CENTRE

Old Deanery, Wells BA5 2UG *Tel:* (01749) 670777
Warden Mrs Joanne Chillington

RURAL DEANS
ARCHDEACONRY OF WELLS

Axbridge Preb Victor Daley, Vicarage, Cheddar BS27 3RF
Tel: (01934) 742535
Bruton Revd John Thorogood, Vicarage, Church Lane, Evercreech BA4 6HV
Tel: (01749) 830222
Fax: (01749) 830870
Cary Revd John Thorogood (*as above*)

Frome Revd John Pescod, Vicarage, Vicarage St, Frome BA11 1PU
Tel: (01373) 462325
Glastonbury Revd Gillian Weymont, Vicarage, Othery, Bridgwater TA7 0QG *Tel:* (01823) 698073
Ivelchester Preb Trevor Farmiloe, Vicarage, 10 Water St, Martock TA12 6JN
Tel: (01935) 826113
Merston Preb Mark Ellis, St Michael's Vicarage, Yeovil BA21 4LH
Tel: (01935) 75752
Shepton Mallet Revd Bindon Plowman, Vicarage, Vicarage Lane, Wookey, Wells BA5 1JT
Tel: (01749) 677244

ARCHDEACONRY OF BATH

Bath Revd David Perryman, St Luke's Vicarage, Hatfield Rd, Bath BA2 2BD *Tel:* (01225) 311904
Chew Magna Revd Richard Hall, Rectory, 12 Beech Rd, Saltford, Bristol BS18 3BE
Tel: (01225) 872275
Locking Revd Nick Williams, St Peter's Vicarage, Bay Tree Rd, Weston-super-Mare BS22 8HG
Tel: (01934) 624247
Midsomer Norton Revd James Balliston Thicke, Westfield Vicarage, Midsomer Norton BA3 4BJ
Tel: (01761) 412105
Portishead Revd Alastair Wheeler, Vicarage, Christchurch Close, Nailsea, Bristol BS19 2DL
Tel: (01275) 853187

ARCHDEACONRY OF TAUNTON

Bridgwater Preb Roger Packer, Vicarage, 7 Durleigh Rd, Bridgwater TA6 7HU
Tel: (01278) 422437
Crewkerne and Ilminster Revd Philip Lambert, Rectory, Curry Rivel, Langport TA10 0HQ
Tel: (01458) 251375
Exmoor Revd Barry Priory, Rectory, Parsons St, Porlock, Minehead TA24 8QL *Tel:* (01643) 863172
Quantock Revd Andrew Stevens, Rectory, Kilve, Bridgwater TA5 1DZ
Tel: (01278) 741501
Taunton Revd Nigel Venning, Rectory, Rectory Drive, Staplegrove, Taunton TA2 6AP
Tel: (01823) 272787
Tone Revd Kevin Tingay, Rectory, Bradford-on-Tone, Taunton TA4 1HG *Tel:* (01823) 461423

DIOCESE OF BIRMINGHAM

Founded in 1905. Birmingham; Sandwell, except for areas in
the north (LICHFIELD) and in the west (WORCESTER); Solihull,
except for an area in the east (COVENTRY); an area of
Warwickshire; a few parishes in Worcestershire.

Population 1,433,000   Area 292 sq m
Stipendiary Clergy 223   Benefices 157
Parishes 169   Churches 194

BISHOP (7th)
Rt Revd Mark Santer, Bishop's Croft, Harborne,
Birmingham, B17 0BG [1987]   *Tel:* 0121–427 1163
Fax: 0121–426 1322
[Mark Birmingham]
Domestic Chaplain Revd James Langstaff, East
Wing, Bishop's Croft, Old Church Rd,
Birmingham B17 0BG *Tel:* 0121–427 2295 (Home)

SUFFRAGAN BISHOP
ASTON Rt Revd John Austin, Strensham House, 8
Strensham Hill, Moseley, Birmingham B13 8AG
[1992]   *Tel:* 0121–449 0675 (Home)
0121–428 2228 *or* 0121–427 5141 (Office)
Fax: 0121–428 1114

HONORARY ASSISTANT BISHOPS
Rt Revd Anthony Charles Dumper, 117 Berberry
Close, Bournville, Birmingham B30 1TB [1993]
Tel: 0121–458 3011 (Home)
Rt Revd Michael Humphrey Dickens Whinney, 3
Moor Green Lane, Moseley, Birmingham B13
8NE [1989]   *Tel:* 0121–249 2856
Rt Revd David Evans, 12 Fox Hill, Birmingham
B29 4AG [1998]   *Tel:* 0121–472 2616
Fax: 0121–472 7977
email: SAMSGB@compuserve.com
Rt Revd Peter Hall, 27 Jacey Rd, Edgbaston,
Birmingham B16 0LL [1998]   *Tel:* 0121–455 9240

CATHEDRAL CHURCH OF ST PHILIP
Provost Very Revd Gordon Mursell, The
Provost's House, 16 Pebble Mill Rd, Edgbaston,
Birmingham B5 7SA [1999]   *Tel:* 0121–472 0709

Cathedral Office Birmingham Cathedral, Colmore
Row, Birmingham B3 2QB
Tel: 0121–236 4333/6323
Fax: 0121–212 0868
Canons Residentiary
Ven John Barton, 26 George Rd, Edgbaston,
Birmingham B15 1PJ [1990]
Tel: 0121–454 5525 (Home)
0121–427 5141 (Office)
Fax: 0121–455 6085
Canon Gary O'Neill, 119 Selly Park Rd, Selly
Oak, Birmingham B29 7HY [1997]
Tel: 0121–472 0146

Canon David Lee, Dioc Office, 175 Harborne
Park Rd, Harborne, Birmingham B17 0BH [1996]
Tel: 0121–426 0422
Fax: 0121–428 1114
Chaplain Vacancy, Cathedral Office
Lay Administrator and Chapter Clerk Dr Andrew
Page, Cathedral Office
Cathedral Organist Mr Marcus Huxley, Cathedral
Office

ARCHDEACONS
ASTON Ven John Barton, 26 George Rd,
Edgbaston, Birmingham B15 1PJ [1990]
Tel: 0121–454 5525 (Home)
0121–426 0436 (Office)
Fax: 0121–455 6085
email: venjb@globalnet.co.uk
BIRMINGHAM Ven John Duncan, 122 Westfield Rd,
Edgbaston, Birmingham B15 3JQ [1985]
Tel: 0121–454 3402
Fax: 0121–455 6178

**CONVOCATION (MEMBERS OF THE
HOUSE OF CLERGY OF THE GENERAL
SYNOD)**
The Archdeacon of Birmingham
Proctors for Clergy
Revd Eve Pitts
Revd George Kovoor
Revd Hayward Osborne

**MEMBERS OF THE HOUSE OF LAITY OF
THE GENERAL SYNOD**
Dr Raman Bedi
Mrs Elizabeth Fisher
Mrs Bridget Langstaff

DIOCESAN OFFICERS
Dioc Secretary Mr Jim Drennan, 175 Harborne
Park Rd, Harborne, Birmingham B17 0BH
Tel: 0121–426 0402
Fax: 0121–428 1114
Chancellor of Diocese His Honour Judge Francis
Aglionby, The Croft, Houghton, Carlisle,
Cumbria CA3 0LP
Registrar of Diocese and Bishop's Legal Secretary Mr

Hugh Carslake, Martineau Johnson, St Philip's House, St Philip's Place, Birmingham B3 2PP
Tel: 0121–678 1483
Fax: 0121–625 3326
Dioc Surveyor Mr Alan Broadway, Dioc Office

DIOCESAN ORGANIZATIONS
Diocesan Office 175 Harborne Park Rd, Harborne, Birmingham B17 0BH   *Tel:* 0121–427 5141
Fax: 0121–428 1114

ADMINISTRATION
Dioc Synod (Chairman, House of Clergy) Revd John Hughes, 99 Wentworth Rd, Harborne, Birmingham B17 9ST *Tel:* 0121–427 4601; *(Chairman, House of Laity)* Dr Terry Slater, 5 Windermere Rd, Moseley, Birmingham B13 8HS; *(Secretary)* Mr Jim Drennan, Dioc Office
Board of Finance (Chairman) Mr Philip Couse, 23 Frederick Rd, Edgbaston, Birmingham B15 1JN
Tel: 0121–455 9930
Fax: 0121–455 7254
(Secretary) Mr Jim Drennan *(as above)*
Deputy Secretary (Finance) Mr Paul Wilson, Dioc Office
Parsonages Committee Mr Jim Drennan *(as above)*
Dioc Trustees (Secretary) Mr Paul Wilson *(as above)*
Pastoral Committee Ms Sheila Jones, Dioc Office
Designated Officer Mr Hugh Carslake, Martineau Johnson, St Philip's House, St Philip's Place, Birmingham B3 2PP   *Tel:* 0121–678 1483
Fax: 0121–625 3326

CHURCHES
Advisory Committee for the Care of Churches (Chairman) Mr William Wood, c/o Dioc Office; *(Secretary)* Mr Tim Clayton, Dioc Office

EDUCATION
Dioc Director of Education Vacancy, Dioc Office
Deputy Director of Education Mrs Betty Richmond, Dioc Office

MINISTRY
Director of Ordinands and Women's Ministry Canon Marlene Parsons, Dioc Office
Director of Post-Ordination Training The Bishop of Aston *(as above)*

Board for Ministries
Director for Ministries Canon Brian Russell PH D, Dioc Office
Bishop's Adviser for Lay Adult Education and Training Dr Pam de Wit, Dioc Office
Bishop's Adviser for Black and Asian Ministry Dr Mukti Barton, Dioc Office
Bishop's Adviser for Children's Work Revd Ruth Yeoman, Dioc Office
Bishop's Adviser for Youth Work Vacancy, Dioc Office
Parish Resource Worker Ms Gaby Melchior, Dioc Office

Dioc Music Adviser Mr Mick Perrier, Dioc Office
Readers' Board (Secretary) Mr Philip Bellingham, Tythe Cottage, Bakers Lane, Knowle, Solihull B93 0EA   *Tel:* (01564) 774529

LITURGICAL
Bishop's Liturgical Advisory Committee Chairman Revd Brian Hall, Handsworth Rectory, 288 Hamstead Rd, Handsworth Wood B20 2RB
Tel: 0121–554 3407

BOARD FOR MISSION
Chairman The Bishop of Aston *(as above)*
Director for Mission Canon David Lee PH D, Dioc Office
Bishop's Ecumenical Adviser Canon Richard Bollard, Vicarage, High St, Coleshill B46 3BP
Tel: (01675) 462188
Bishop's Ecumenical Theological Adviser Revd Tom Pyke, 27 World's End Rd, Handsworth Wood, Birmingham B20 2NP *Tel:* 0121–507 0247
Fax: 0121–233 0332
email: t.f.pyke@virgin.net
Bishop's Adviser for Stewardship Canon Jim Pendorf, 120 Stanhope St, Highgate, Birmingham B12 0XB   *Tel:* (0973) 265037

HEALTHCARE CHAPLAINCIES
Bishop's Adviser Revd Frank Longbottom, 46 Sunnybank Rd, Sutton Coldfield B73 5RE
Tel and *Fax:* 0121–350 5823
0973 838581 (Mobile)

PRESS AND PUBLICATIONS
Communications Officer Ms Sue Primmer, Dioc Office   *Tel:* 0121–507 0247 (Home)
Editor of Dioc Leaflet Ms Sue Primmer *(as above)*
Editor of Dioc Directory Ms Sue Primmer *(as above)*

INDUSTRIAL RELATIONS
Industrial Chaplain Miss Melanie King, Dioc Office   *Tel:* 0121–426 0425
email: mjk-cigb@hotmail.com
CIGB Coordinator Revd Trevor Lockwood (Methodist), Dioc Office *Tel:* 0121–426 0426

DIOCESAN RECORD OFFICES
Birmingham Reference Library, Birmingham B3 3HQ, Archives Dept Central Library, *City Archivist* Mr Nicholas Kingsley, *Tel:* 0121–303 4217 *(For parish records in the City and Diocese of Birmingham)*
Warwick County Record Office, Priory Park, Cape Rd, Warwick CV34 4JS, *County Archivist* Ms Caroline Sampson, *Tel:* (01926) 410410, Ext 2506 *(For parish records in the Metropolitan Borough of Solihull, together with those still in the County of Warwick)*
Sandwell Community History and Archives Service, Smethwick Library, High St, Smethwick, Warley, W Midlands B66 1AB *Borough Archivist and Local History Manager* Ms Claire Harrington,

Tel: 0121–558 2561 (*For parish records in the Metro-politan Borough of Sandwell*)

BOARD FOR SOCIAL RESPONSIBILITY
Community Projects and Development Officer
Canon David Collyer, Dioc Office
Bishop's Adviser for Health and Social Policy Revd Jim Woodward, The Master's House, Temple Balsall, Solihull B91 0BH   *Tel:* (01564) 730249

CHRISTIAN STEWARDSHIP
see Board for Mission

ACTION IN THE CITY PROJECTS
Chairman The Archdeacon of Aston (*as above*)
Secretary Canon David Collyer (*as above*)

AREA DEANS
ARCHDEACONRY OF ASTON
Aston Revd David Newsome, All Saints Vicarage, Broomfield Rd, Erdington, Birmingham B23 7QA   *Tel* and *Fax:* 0121–373 0730
Bordesley Vacancy
Coleshill Revd Stephen Mayes, Vicarage, Vicarage Lane, Water Orton, War. B46 1RX
          Tel and *Fax:* 0121–747 2751
Polesworth Revd Maxine Marsh, Vicarage, Church Lane, Kingsbury, Staffs B78 2LR
          Tel and *Fax:* (01827) 873500

Solihull Revd Adrian Leahy, St Mary's House, Hob's Meadow, Solihull B92 8PN
          Tel and *Fax:* 0121–743 4955
Sutton Coldfield Revd Roger Hindley, 61 Mere Green Rd, Sutton Coldfield B75 5BW
          Tel and *Fax:* 0121–308 0074
Yardley Vacancy

ARCHDEACONRY OF BIRMINGHAM
Birmingham City Centre Canon Jim Pendorf, St Alban's Vicarage, 120 Stanhope St, Highgate, Birmingham B12 0XB   *Tel:* 0121–440 4605
          Fax: 0121–446 6867
          0973 265037 (Mobile)
Edgbaston Revd John Barnett, Rectory, 773 Hagley Rd West, Quinton, Birmingham B32 1AJ
          Tel and *Fax:* 0121–422 2031
Handsworth Revd Brian Hall, Handsworth Rectory, 288 Hamstead Road, Birmingham B20 2RB   *Tel* and *Fax:* 0121–554 3407
King's Norton Vacancy
Moseley Revd Hayward Osborne, Vicarage, 18 Oxford Rd, Moseley, Birmingham B13 9EH
          Tel and *Fax:* 0121–449 1459/2243
Shirley Canon Michael Caddy, Vicarage, 2 Bishopton Close, Shirley, Solihull B90 4AH
          Tel: 0121–744 3123
          Tel and *Fax:* 0121–745 8896
Warley Revd Martin Gorick, Vicarage, Church Rd, Smethwick, Warley B67 6EE
          Tel: 0121–558 1763

DIOCESE OF BLACKBURN

Founded in 1926. Lancashire, except for areas in the east (BRADFORD) and in the south (LIVERPOOL, MANCHESTER); a few parishes in Wigan.

Population 1,283,000   Area 878 sq m
Stipendiary Clergy 245   Benefices 213
Parishes 239   Churches 286

BISHOP (7th)
Rt Revd Alan David Chesters, Bishop's House, Ribchester Rd, Clayton-le-Dale, Blackburn, Lancs. BB1 9EF [1989]   *Tel:* (01254) 248234
Fax: (01254) 246668
email: bishop.blackburn@ukonline.co.uk
[Alan Blackburn]
Domestic Chaplain Revd Stephen Ferns, Bishop's House

SUFFRAGAN BISHOPS
LANCASTER Rt Revd (Geoffrey) Stephen Pedley, Shireshead Vicarage, Forton, Preston PR3 0AE [1998]   *Tel:* (01524) 799900
Fax: (01524) 799901
email: bishop.lancaster@ukonline.co.uk
BURNLEY Rt Revd Martyn William Jarrett, Dean House, 449 Padiham Rd, Burnley, Lancs. BB12 6TE [1994]   *Tel:* (01282) 423564
Fax: (01282) 835496

CATHEDRAL CHURCH OF ST MARY THE VIRGIN
Provost Very Revd David Frayne, Provost's House, Preston New Rd, Blackburn, Lancs. BB2 6PS [1992]   *Tel:* (01254) 52502
email: provost@blackburn.anglican.org
Cathedral Office Cathedral Close, Blackburn BB1 5AA   *Tel:* (01254) 51491
Fax: (01254) 689666
email: cathedral@blackburn.anglican.org
Canons Residentiary
Sacrist Canon Andrew Hindley, 22 Billinge Ave, Blackburn, Lancs. BB2 6SD [1996]
Tel: (01254) 261152
email: andrew.hindley@blackburn.anglican.org
Chancellor Canon David Galilee, 25 Ryburn Ave, Blackburn BB2 7AU [1995]   *Tel:* (01254) 671540
Canon Peter Ballard, Wheatfield, 7 Dallas Rd, Lancaster LA1 1TN [1998]   *Tel:* (01524) 54421
email: peter.j.ballard@btinternet.com
Chapter Clerk Mr Thomas Hoyle, Dioc Registry, Cathedral Close, Blackburn, Lancs. BB1 5AB
Tel: (01254) 51491
Director of Music Mr Richard Tanner, 8 West Park Rd, Blackburn BB2 6DG
Tel: (01254) 56752 (Home)
(01254) 51491 (Office)
email: richard@westparkroad.freeserve.co.uk

ARCHDEACONS
BLACKBURN Ven Dr John Marsh, 19 Clarence Park, Blackburn BB2 7FA [1996]   *Tel:* (01254) 262571
Fax: (01254) 263394
email: vendocjon@aol.com
LANCASTER Ven Colin Williams, St Michael's House, Hall Lane, St Michael's on Wyre, Preston PR3 0TQ [1999]   *Tel:* (01995) 679242
Fax: (01995) 679747
email: archdeacon.lancaster@ukonline.co.uk

CONVOCATION (MEMBERS OF THE HOUSE OF CLERGY OF THE GENERAL SYNOD)
The Archdeacon of Blackburn
Proctors for Clergy
Canon Eddie Burns
Revd Dr John Fenwick
Revd Brian Pithers
Canon Paul Warren
Ven Colin Williams

MEMBERS OF THE HOUSE OF LAITY OF THE GENERAL SYNOD
Mrs Margaret Baxter
Mr Gerald Burrows
Mr James Garbett
Mr Ian Garden
Mr John Hudson
Mrs Roberta Ladds
Mr John Leigh
Miss Diana Parker
Mr George Phythian

DIOCESAN OFFICERS
Dioc Secretary Revd Michael Wedgeworth, Church House, Cathedral Close, Blackburn, Lancs. BB1 5AA   *Tel:* (01254) 54421
Fax: (01254) 699963
email: mike.wedgeworth@blackburn.anglican.org
Chancellor of Diocese His Honour Judge John Bullimore, Rectory, 14 Grange Drive, Emley, Huddersfield HD8 9SF   *Tel:* (01924) 463911
Registrar of Diocese and Bishop's Legal Secretary Mr Thomas Hoyle, Diocesan Registry, Cathedral Close, Blackburn, Lancs. BB1 5AB
Tel: (01254) 54421
Fax: (01254) 699963
email: registry@blackburn.anglican.org

DIOCESAN ORGANIZATIONS

Diocesan Office Church House, Cathedral Close, Blackburn, Lancs. BB1 5AA   *Tel:* (01254) 54421
Fax: (01254) 699963
email: diocese@blackburn.anglican.org

ADMINISTRATION

Dioc Synod (*Chairman, House of Clergy*) Canon Edward Burns, Christ Church Vicarage, 19 Vicarage Close, Fulwood, Preston PR2 4EG *Tel:* (01772) 719210; (*Chairman, House of Laity*) Mr Derrick Walkden, 2 Butterlands, Preston PR1 5TJ *Tel:* (01772) 792224; (*Secretary*) Revd Michael Wedgeworth, Church House
Board of Finance (*Chairman*) Mr R. M. Edwards, Sunnyfield, West Bradford Rd, Waddington, Clitheroe BB7 3JD *Tel:* (01200) 426625; (*Secretary*) Revd Michael Wedgeworth (*as above*)
Property Committee (*Chairman*) Canon J. Duxbury; (*Secretary*) Revd Michael Wedgeworth (*as above*)
Pastoral Committee Revd Michael Wedgeworth (*as above*)
Designated Officer Mr Thomas Hoyle, Dioc Registry, Cathedral Close, Blackburn, Lancs. BB1 5AB   *Tel:* (01254) 54421/52821

CHURCHES

Advisory Committee for the Care of Churches (*Chairman*) Canon Roy McCullough, Vicarage, Church Brow, Walton-le-Dale, Preston PR5 4BH *Tel:* (01772) 880233; (*Secretary*) Revd Michael Wedgeworth (*as above*)

EDUCATION

Education Council (*Dioc Director*) Canon Peter Ballard, Church House
email: education@blackburn.anglican.org
Principal Adviser Lisa Fenton, Church House
Youth Officer Revd Brian McConkey, Church House
email: brian.mcconkey@blackburn.anglican.org
Children's Work Adviser Mrs Mary Binks, Church House
email: mary.binks@blackburn.anglican.org

MINISTRY

Director of Ordinands Revd Geoffrey Connor, Vicarage, Church Lane, Whitechapel, Preston PR3 2EP   *Tel:* (01995) 640282
Director of Training Vacancy
Post-Ordination Training Revd John Priestley, Vicarage, Keighley Rd, Colne BB8 7HF
Tel: (01282) 863511
Adviser in Women's Ministry Canon Ann Wood, St Nicholas Vicarage, 187 Common Edge Rd, Marton Moss, Blackpool FY4 5DL
Tel: (01253) 762658
Mothers' Union Mrs P. Rothwell, 7 Aldon Grove, Longton, Preston PR4 5PJ   *Tel:* (01772) 614045

Readers' Board Mr William McKend, 7 Wolverton Ave, Blackpool FY2 9NT   *Tel:* (01253) 51054
Warden of Pastoral Auxiliaries Canon James Burns, St Mary's Rectory, 17 Church Rd, Rutford, Ormskirk L40 1TA   *Tel:* (01704) 821261
Resources Officer Vacancy

LITURGICAL

Chairman The Bishop of Lancaster (*as above*)
Secretary Revd Iain Rennie, Vicarage, Hornby, Lancaster LA2 8JY   *Tel:* (01524) 221238

MISSIONARY AND ECUMENICAL

Board for Mission and Unity (*Chairman*) The Bishop of Lancaster (*as above*)
Director for Mission and Evangelism Revd Simon Bessant, 1 Swallowfields, Pleckgate, Blackburn BB1 8NR   *Tel and Fax:* (01254) 580176
email: s.d.bessant@dial.pipex.com
Ecumenical Officer Vacancy

PRESS AND PUBLICATIONS

Dioc Communications Officer Mr Martyn Halsall, 42 Knowsley Rd, Ainsworth, Bolton BL2 5PU
Tel and Fax: (01204) 384996
email: martyn.halsall@ukonline.co.uk

DIOCESAN RECORD OFFICES

Diocesan Registry, Cathedral Close, Blackburn, Lancs. BB1 5AB   *Tel:* (01254) 54421
Lancashire Record Office, Bow Lane, Preston PR1 8ND *County Archivist* Mr Bruce Jackson
Tel: (01772) 254868

SOCIAL RESPONSIBILITY

Social Responsibility Officer Revd Chris Rich, St Mary's House, Cathedral Close, Blackburn BB1 5AA   *Tel:* (01254) 54421
Principal Diocesan Adoption Agency Mr Brian Williams, St Mary's House   *Tel:* (01254) 57759
Chaplain with the Deaf Revd Stephen Locke, 30 Swallowfields, Pleckgate, Blackburn BB1 8NE
Tel: (01254) 583790
Interfaith Adviser Vacancy
Rural Areas Officer The Archdeacon of Lancaster (*as above*)

RURAL DEANS
ARCHDEACONRY OF BLACKBURN

Accrington Revd Michael Ratcliffe, St Paul's Vicarage, 71 Union Rd, Oswaldtwistle, Accrington BB5 3DD   *Tel:* (01254) 231038
Blackburn with Darwen Revd Kevin Arkell, Rectory, St Peter's Close, Darwen, Lancs. BB3 2EA   *Tel:* (01254) 702411
Burnley Revd Brian Swallow, St Stephen's Vicarage, 154 Todmorden Rd, Burnley BB11 3ER
Tel: (01282) 424733
Chorley Revd David Morgan, St Paul's Vicarage, Railway Rd, Adlington, Chorley PR6 9QZ
Tel: (01257) 480253

Leyland Revd Arthur Ranson, St Ambrose Vicarage, 61 Moss Lane, Leyland PR5 2SH
Tel: (01772) 462204

Pendle Revd Edward Saville, Brierfield Vicarage, 22 Reedley Rd, Reedley, Burnley BB10 2LU
Tel and *Fax:* (01282) 613235
email: vicar@saville02.surfaid.org

Whalley Revd Paul Smith, Vicarage, Somerset Rd, Rishton, Blackburn BB1 4BP
Tel: (01254) 886191

ARCHDEACONRY OF LANCASTER

Blackpool Revd Michael Wood, St Mary's Vicarage, 59 Stony Hill Ave, Blackpool FY4 1PR
Tel: (01253) 342713

Garstang Revd Edward Angus, St Oswald's Vicarage, Lancaster Rd, Knott End-on-Sea, Poulton-le-Fylde FY6 0DU   *Tel:* (01253) 810297

Kirkham Canon Godfrey Hirst, Vicarage, Church Rd, Lytham St Annes FY8 5PX
Tel and *Fax:* (01253) 736168
email: ghirst@compuserve.com

Lancaster Revd Gary Ingram, Rectory, Church Walk, Morecambe LA4 5PR
Tel and *Fax:* (01524) 410941 (Home)
Tel: (01524) 833267 (Office)

Poulton Revd David Reeves, Vicarage, Rough Lea Rd, Thornton-Cleveleys, Blackpool FY5 1DP
Tel: (01253) 852153

Preston Revd John Powell, Vicarage, 240 Tulketh Rd, Ashton-on-Ribble, Preston PR2 1ES
Tel: (01772) 726848

Tunstall Revd Tom Maidment, Vicarage, 5 Ancliffe Lane, Bolton le Sands, Carnforth LA5 8DS   *Tel:* (01524) 822335

DIOCESE OF BRADFORD

Founded in 1919. Bradford; the western quarter of North Yorkshire; areas of east Lancashire, south-east Cumbria and Leeds.

Population 656,000   Area 920 sq m
Stipendiary Clergy 124   Benefices 112
Parishes 132   Churches 167

BISHOP (8th)
Rt Revd David James Smith, Bishopscroft, Ashwell Rd, Bradford, W Yorks. BD9 4AU [1992]
Tel: (01274) 545414
Fax: (01274) 544831
email: bishbrad@nildram.co.uk
[David Bradford]
Personal Executive Assistant Mr Michael Leeming (*same address*)

HONORARY ASSISTANT BISHOP
Rt Revd Peter St George Vaughan, 1 Dawson Lane, Tong Village, Bradford, W Yorks. BD4 0ST
Tel and *Fax:* 0113–285 3924

CATHEDRAL CHURCH OF ST PETER
Provost Very Revd John Stephen Richardson, Provost's House, 1 Cathedral Close, Bradford, W Yorks. BD1 4EG [1990]   *Tel:* (01274) 777722
Fax: (01274) 777730
Canons Residentiary
Canon Christopher Lewis, 2 Cathedral Close, Bradford, W Yorks. BD1 4EG [1993]
Tel: (01274) 727806
Fax: (01274) 777736
Canon Geoffrey Smith, 3 Cathedral Close, Bradford, W Yorks. BD1 4EG   *Tel:* (01274) 777729
Cathedral Adviser in Development and Education
Mrs Caroline Moore, Bradford Cathedral, 1 Stott Hill, Bradford, W Yorks. BD1 4EH
Tel: (01274) 777734
Fax: (01274) 777730
Cathedral Administrator Mrs Sheila Holmes (*same address*)   *Tel:* (01274) 777723
Cathedral Organist Mr Alan Horsey, 1 Stott Hill, Bradford, W Yorks. BD1 4EH   *Tel:* (01274) 777725
Fax: (01274) 777730

ARCHDEACONS
craven Ven Malcolm Grundy, Vicarage, Gisburn, Clitheroe, Lancs. BB7 4HR [1994]
Tel: (01200) 445214
Fax: (01200) 445816
email: adcraven@gisburn.u-net.com
bradford Ven Guy Wilkinson, St Michael's Vicarage, Littlelands, Cottingley, Bingley BD6 1RR
Tel: (07932) 652315
Fax: (01274) 562278

CONVOCATION (MEMBERS OF THE HOUSE OF CLERGY OF THE GENERAL SYNOD)
Dignitaries in Convocation
The Provost of Bradford
The Archdeacon of Craven
Proctors for Clergy
Revd Paul Ayers
Canon Alan Fell
Canon Max Wigley

MEMBERS OF THE HOUSE OF LAITY OF THE GENERAL SYNOD
Mrs Elaine Appelbee
Ms Sallie Bassham
Mr Tony Hesselwood

DIOCESAN OFFICERS
Dioc Secretary Mr Malcolm Halliday, Cathedral Hall, Stott Hill, Bradford, W Yorks. BD1 4ET
Tel: (01274) 725958
Fax: (01274) 726343
Chancellor of Diocese His Honour John de G. Walford, Ingerthorpe Cottage, Thwaites Lane, Markington, N Yorks. HG3 3PF
Tel: (01765) 677449
Registrar of Diocese and Bishop's Legal Secretary Mr Jeremy Mackrell, Diocesan Registry, 6/14 Devonshire St, Keighley, W Yorks. BD21 2AY
Tel: (01535) 218336
Fax: (01535) 609748
Dioc Surveyors Mr Barry Rawson, The Gatehouse, Skipton Castle, Skipton, N Yorks. BD23 1AL *Tel:* (01756) 794881; Mr Michael Greaves, Dacre, Son & Hartley, 24 Devonshire St, Keighley, W Yorks. BD21 2BD *Tel:* (01535) 605646
Fax: (01535) 610056
Dioc Insurance Adviser Mr John Watts, Hainsworth Watts, Greengates Lodge, 830a Harrogate Rd, Bradford, W Yorks. BD10 0RA
Tel: (01274) 619002
Fax: (01274) 619084

DIOCESAN ORGANIZATIONS
Diocesan Office Cathedral Hall, Stott Hill, Bradford, W Yorks. BD1 4ET   *Tel:* (01274) 725958
Fax: (01274) 726343

ADMINISTRATION

Dioc Synod (Chairman, House of Clergy) Canon Max Wigley, St John's Vicarage, Barcroft Rd, Yeadon, Leeds LS19 7XZ *Tel:* 0113–250 2274; *(Chairman, House of Laity)* Mr Chris Wright, 15 Walker Close, Glusburn, Keighley, W Yorks. BD20 8PW *Tel:* (01535) 634526; *(Secretary)* Mr Malcolm Halliday, Dioc Office
Board of Finance (Chairman) Mr Tony Hesselwood, 38 Bromley Rd, Shipley, Bradford BD18 4DT *Tel:* (01274) 586613 *(Secretary)* Mr Malcolm Halliday *(as above)*
Property Committee (Secretary) Mr Malcolm Halliday *(as above)*
Pastoral Committee Mr Malcolm Halliday *(as above)*
Ecumenical Officer Canon Bruce Grainger, Vicarage, Oxenhope, Keighley, W Yorks. BD22 9SA *Tel:* (01535) 42529
Designated Officer Mr Jeremy Mackrell, Diocesan Registry, 6/14 Devonshire St, Keighley, W Yorks. BD21 2AY *Tel:* (01535) 667731
Fax: (01535) 609748
Resources Centres Administrator Vacancy, Dioc Office *Tel:* (01274) 725958
Fax: (01274) 726343

CHURCHES

Diocesan Advisory Committee (Chairman) Mr Leonard Darley, Beck Dale, 11 Briery Close, Ilkley LS29 9DL *Tel:* (01943) 609184
(Secretary) Mr Alex McLelland, Dioc Office

CHURCH IN SOCIETY

Bishop's Officer Mrs Elaine Appelbee, 168 Highfield Lane, Keighley, W Yorks. BD21 3HH
Tel: (01535) 671377
Fax: (01535) 690709
Chaplain to Students Revd Andii Bowsher, Anglican Chaplaincy, 2 Ashgrove, Bradford BD7 1BN *Tel:* (01274) 727034 (Office)
(01274) 727976 (Home)
Interfaith Adviser Dr Philip Lewis, 9 Garden Lane, Heaton, Bradford BD9 5QJ
Tel: (01274) 543891
Rural Affairs Revd Leslie Foster, The Lune Vicarage, 5 Highfield Rd, Sedbergh, Cumbria LA10 5DH *Tel:* (015396) 20670
Social Responsibility see Bishop's Officer
Urban Adviser see Bishop's Officer

EDUCATION

Director of Education Mr Malcolm Halliday *(as above)*
Senior Executive Officer for Schools Mrs Debbie Child, Dioc Office
Strategic Education Adviser Miss Rachel Barker, Dioc Office

MINISTRY AND TRAINING

Bishop's Officer Canon Christopher Lewis, 2 Cathedral Close, Bradford, W Yorks. BD1 4EG
Tel: (01274) 727806
Fax: (01274) 722898
Director of In-Service Training see Bishop's Officer
Director of Post-Ordination Training see Bishop's Officer
Directors of Ordinands Revd Richard Hoyal, 14 Queen's Rd, Ilkley LS29 9QJ
Tel and *Fax:* (01943) 607015
Associate Director of Ordinands Revd Dr Susan Penfold, Rectory, 47 Kirkgate, Shipley BD18 3EH
Tel and *Fax:* (01274) 583652
Adult Education Officer Dr Stephen Carr, Flat 3, Clergy House, 1 Barkerend Rd, Bradford, W Yorks. BD3 9AF *Tel:* (01274) 734723
Registrar for Readers Mr Jeremy Mackrell, Dioc Registry
Warden of Readers Revd Dr Paul Moore, Vicarage, Kildwick, Keighley BD20 9BB *Tel:* (01535) 633307
Retired Clergy and Widows Officer Canon Donald Brown, 3 Northfield Gardens, Wibsey, Bradford BD6 1LQ *Tel:* (01274) 671869

WORLD CHURCH LINKS

Chairman The Bishop of Bradford *(as above)*
Officer Revd Pauline Ballaman, 12 Laburnum Grove, Cross Roads, Keighley BD22 9EP
Tel: (01535) 646205

PARISH MISSION AND DEVELOPMENT

Bishop's Officer Vacancy
Children's Work Adviser Revd Elizabeth Thomas, Vicarage, Denholme, W Yorks. BD13 4EN
Tel and *Fax:* (01274) 832813
Adviser in Evangelism Revd Robin Gamble, 6 Glenhurst Rd, Shipley BD18 4DZ
Tel: (01274) 586414
Healing Revd David Swales, 18 Sunhurst Drive, Oakworth, Keighley BD22 7RG
Tel: (01535) 647335
Liturgy Vacancy
Millennium Adviser Mrs Helen Agarwal, Dixon Hill Cottage, Oldfield, Keighley BD22 0HY
Tel: (01535) 643731
Mission Audit see Bishop's Officer
Stewardship see Bishop's Officer
Tourism Adviser Mrs Helen Agarwal *(as above)*
Youth Adviser (Rural) Revd Viv Ashworth, Vicarage, Ingleton, Carnforth, Lancs. LA6 3HG
Tel: (015242) 41440
(Urban) Ms Ruth Ward, 138 Rowantree Drive, Thorpe Edge, Bradford BD10 8DH
Tel: (01274) 619768

PRESS AND PUBLICATIONS

Communications and Press Officer Ms Alison

Bogle, 2 Springfield Terrace, Guiseley, Leeds LS20 9AW *Tel:* (01943) 870367 0468 110175 (Mobile)
Dioc News Ms Alison Bogle (*as above*)
Newsround Mr David Markham, 29 Ashley Rd, Bingley, W Yorks. BD16 1DZ
Tel: (01274) 567180

DIOCESAN RECORD OFFICES
West Yorkshire Archives Service, 15 Canal Rd, Bradford BD1 4AT, *Archivist* Mr Andrew George, *Tel:* (01274) 731931 (*For parishes in Bradford Metropolitan District*)
Archives Dept, Central Library, Northgate House, Halifax HX1 5LA *Archivist* Mr A. Bettridge, *Tel:* (01422) 357257 (*For parishes in Calderdale Metropolitan District*)
Record Office, County Offices, Kendal LA9 4RQ *County Archivist* Mr Jim Gristenthwaite, County Record Office, The Castle, Carlisle CA3 8UR, *Tel:* (01228) 23455 (*For parishes in the County of Cumbria*)
County Record Office, Bow Lane, Preston PR1 2RE *County Archivist* Mr B. Jackson, *Tel:* (01772) 254868 (*For parishes in the County of Lancashire*)
Archives Dept, Leeds District Archives, Chapeltown Rd, Sheepscar, Leeds LS7 3AP *Archivist* Mr W. J. Connor, *Tel:* 0113–262 8339 (*For parishes in Leeds Metropolitan District*)
County Record Office, County Hall, Northallerton DL7 8SG *County Archivist* Mr M. Y. Ashcroft, *Tel:* (01609) 3123, Ext. 455 (*For parishes in the County of North Yorkshire*)

RURAL DEANS
ARCHDEACONRY OF BRADFORD
Airedale Canon Ralph Crowe, Vicarage, St Chad's Rd, Toller Lane, Bradford BD8 9DE
Tel: (01274) 543957
Bowling and Horton Revd Steve Allen, Vicarage, 30 Bartle Close, Bradford BD7 4QH
Tel: (01274) 521456
Calverley Revd Simon Bailey, Vicarage, Galloway Lane, Pudsey, Leeds LS28 8JR *Tel:* (01274) 662735
Otley Revd Peter Sutcliffe, Vicarage, Cornmill Lane, Burley-in-Wharfedale, Ilkley LS29 7DR
Tel: (01943) 863216

ARCHDEACONRY OF CRAVEN
Bowland Revd David Mewis, Rectory, Sawley Rd, Grindleton, Clitheroe, Lancs. BB7 4QS
Tel: (01200) 41154
Ewecross Canon John Bearpark, St Margaret's Vicarage, 27 Station Rd, High Bentham, Lancs. LA2 7LH *Tel:* (0152 42) 61321
Skipton Revd John Ward, The Beeches, Bolton Abbey, Skipton BD23 6EX
Tel: (01756) 710326 (Home)
(01756) 710238 (Office)
South Craven Revd Peter Endall, St Barnabas Vicarage, Spring Ave, Thwaites Brow, Keighley BD21 4TA *Tel:* (01535) 602830

DIOCESE OF BRISTOL

Founded in 1542. Bristol; the southern two-thirds of South Gloucestershire; the northern quarter of Wiltshire, except for two parishes in the north (GLOUCESTER); Swindon, except for a few parishes in the north (GLOUCESTER) and in the south (SALISBURY); a few parishes in Gloucestershire.

Population 875,000   Area 474 sq m
Stipendiary Clergy 158   Benefices 118
Parishes 165   Churches 206

BISHOP (54th)
Rt Revd Barry Rogerson, Bishop's House, Clifton Hill, Bristol BS8 1BW [1985]   *Tel:* 0117–973 0222
Fax: 0117–923 9670
email: 106430.1040@compuserve.com
[Barry Bristol]

SUFFRAGAN BISHOP
SWINDON Rt Revd Michael Doe, Mark House, Field Rise, Swindon SN1 4HP [1994] *Tel* and *Fax:* (01793) 538654
email: 106064.431@compuserve.com

CATHEDRAL CHURCH OF THE HOLY AND UNDIVIDED TRINITY
Dean Very Revd Robert Grimley, The Deanery, 20 Charlotte St, Bristol BS1 5PZ [1997]
Tel: 0117–926 2443
Cathedral Office Bristol Cathedral, Abbey Gatehouse, College Green, Bristol BS1 5TJ
Tel: 0117–926 4879
Fax: 0117–925 3678
Canons Residentiary
Treasurer Canon Peter Johnson, 41 Salisbury Rd, Redland, Bristol BS6 7AR [1991]
Tel: 0117–944 4464
Theologian Canon Douglas Holt, 9 Leigh Rd, Clifton, Bristol BS8 2DA [1998]
Tel: 0117–973 7427
Precentor Canon Brendan Clover, 55 Salisbury Rd, Redland, Bristol BS6 7AS [1999]
Tel: 0117–942 1452
Administrator Mrs Joy Coupe, Cathedral Office
Cathedral Organist Mr Mark Lee, Cathedral Office
Tel: 0117–926 4879

ARCHDEACONS
BRISTOL Ven Timothy McClure, 10 Great Brockeridge, WestburyonTrym, Bristol BS9 3TY [1999]
Tel: 0117–962 2438
MALMESBURY Ven Alan Hawker, The Paddock, Church Lane, Kington Langley, Chippenham, Wilts. SN15 5NR [1999]   *Tel:* (01249) 750085
Fax: (01249) 750086

CONVOCATION (MEMBERS OF THE HOUSE OF CLERGY OF THE GENERAL SYNOD)
The Archdeacon of Malmesbury
Proctors for Clergy
Canon George Mitchell
Revd Rosie Nixson
Revd John Risdon

MEMBERS OF THE HOUSE OF LAITY OF THE GENERAL SYNOD
Mrs Katy Blake
Mr David Bone
Ms Jill Dickinson
Mr Ian Henderson

DIOCESAN OFFICERS
Dioc Secretary Mrs Lesley Farrall, Diocesan Church House, 23 Great George St, Bristol BS1 5QZ   *Tel:* 0117–906 0100
Fax: 0117–925 0460
Chancellor of Diocese Chanc Sir David Calcutt, 35 Essex St, Temple, London WC2R 3AR
Tel: 020–7353 6381
Registrar of Diocese and Bishop's Legal Secretary Mr Tim Berry, Harris and Harris, 14 Market Place, Wells BA5 2RE   *Tel:* (01749) 674747
Fax: (01749) 676585

DIOCESAN ORGANIZATIONS
Diocesan Office Diocesan Church House, 23 Great George St, Bristol BS1 5QZ   *Tel:* 0117–906 0100
Fax: 0117–925 0460

ADMINISTRATION
Assistant Dioc Secretary Mrs Sally Moody, Dioc Church House
Dioc Synod (*Chairman, House of Clergy*) Canon George Mitchell, Vicarage, Church Ave, Warmley, Bristol BS30 5JJ Tel: 0117–967 3965; (*Chairman, House of Laity*) Mrs Margaret Williams, Springfield, Stoppers Hill, Brinkworth, Chippenham, Wilts SN15 5AW
Tel: (01666) 510444
Board of Finance (*Chairman*) Mr Neil Porter, c/o Dioc Church House; (*Secretary*) Mrs Lesley Farrall, Dioc Church House

Finance Manager Mr Graham Ash, Dioc Church House
Pastoral Committee (Secretary) Mrs Lesley Farrall (as above)
Dioc Electoral Registration Officer Mrs Lesley Farrall (as above)
Designated Officer Mr Tim Berry, Harris and Harris, 14 Market Place, Wells BA5 2RE
Tel: (01749) 674747
Fax: (01749) 676585

CHURCHES

Advisory Committee for the Care of Churches (Chairman) Canon Peter Johnson, 41 Salisbury Rd, Redland, Bristol BS6 7AS   Tel: 0117–944 4464 (Secretary) Mrs Celia Gibbons, c/o Dioc Church House

EDUCATION

Board of Education (Director and Schools Adviser) Miss Caroline Barker Bennett, All Saints RE Centre, 1 All Saints Court, Bristol BS1 1JN
Tel: 0117–927 7454

BOARD OF READERS

Board of Readers (Secretary) Mr David Bone, 3 Hardy Lane, Tockington, Bristol BS32 4LJ
Tel: (01454) 614601

LITURGICAL

Chairman Revd Dr Paul Roberts, 12 Belgrave Rd, Clifton, Bristol BS8 2AB   Tel: 0117–930 3030

PARISH RESOURCES TEAM

Director of Parish Resources Canon Douglas Holt, Dioc Church House
Children and Youth Officer Revd Mark Pilgrim, Dioc Church House
Parish Development Adviser (Bristol Archdeaconry) Revd Stuart Taylor, Dioc Church House
Parish Development Adviser (Malmesbury Archdeaconry) Mr Alun Brookfield, 16 Fairholm Way, Swindon SN2 6JZ   Tel: (01793) 825658
Fax: (01793) 821554
Dioc Director of Ordinands Revd Paul Denyer, Vicarage, Kington Langley, Chippenham, Wilts. SN15 5NJ   Tel: (01249) 750231
Fax: (01249) 750784
Adviser for Women's Ministry Revd Janet Bromley, 21 Anthony Rd, Wroughton, Swindon SN4 9HN Tel: (01793) 813929
Ecumenical Officers (Bristol Archdeaconry) Vacancy
(Malmesbury Archdeaconry) Revd Brian Fessey, Vicarage, 4 Church St, Purton, Swindon, Wilts. SN5 9DS   Tel: (01793) 770210
Uganda Link Officer Revd David Lloyd, St Dunstan's Vicarage, 66 Bedminster Down Rd, Bristol BS13 7AA   Tel and Fax: 0117–963 5977
Personal Review of Ministry Revd David James, St Ambrose Vicarage, Stretford Ave, Bristol BS5 7AN   Tel: 0117–951 7299

Adviser in Pastoral Care for Clergy and their Families Revd Judith Thompson, St Barnabas Vicarage, Daventry Rd, Knowle, Bristol BS4 1DQ
Tel: 0117–966 4139

PRESS, PUBLICITY AND PUBLICATIONS

Communications Officer Vacancy
Press Officers (Bristol Archdeaconry) Vacancy
(Malmesbury Archdeaconry) Revd Stephen Oram, 3 Ockwells, Cricklade, Swindon SN6 6ED
Tel: (01793) 750300
Editor of 'Three Crowns' Mr John Hudson, Dioc Church House
Editor of Dioc Directory Mrs Sally Moody, Dioc Church House

DIOCESAN RECORD OFFICES

Bristol Record Office, 'B' Bond, Smeaton Rd, Bristol BS1 6XN County Archivist Mr J. S. Williams, Tel: 0117–922 5692 (For parish records in the Archdeaconry of Bristol)
Wiltshire Record Office, County Hall, Trowbridge, Wilts. County Archivist Mr John Darcy, Tel: (01225) 713134 (For parish records in the Archdeaconry of Malmesbury)

DIOCESAN RESOURCE CENTRE

All Saints Centre, 1 All Saints Court, Bristol BS1 1JN   Tel: 0117–927 7454
Fax: 0117–925 0404
Administrator Mrs Joanna Bailey

THE CHURCHES' COUNCIL FOR INDUSTRY AND SOCIAL RESPONSIBILITY

Director Revd Harold Clarke, St Nicholas House, Lawford's Gate, Bristol BS5 0RE
Tel: 0117–955 7430
Fax: 0117–941 3252
email: isrbristol@gn.apc.org
Administrator Miss Gillian Hiles, St Nicholas House
Industrial Chaplains Revd Heather Pencavel, Revd Gordon Wilson, Revd Michael Massey (Bristol); Revd Christine Gilbert (Swindon)
Social Responsibility Officer (Wiltshire) Mrs Kathleen Ben Rabha
Church and Society Officer Mr David Maggs
Inter-Religious Affairs Adviser Vacancy
Church Urban Fund Projects Officer Revd John Harrison
World Development Adviser Revd Gordon Holmes

AREA AND RURAL DEANS
ARCHDEACONRY OF BRISTOL

Bristol South Canon Keith Newton, Holy Nativity Vicarage, 41 Lilymead Ave, Knowle, Bristol BS4 2BY   Tel: 0117–977 4260
Bristol West Revd David Harrex, Vicarage, The Glebe, Pilning, Bristol BS35 4LE
Tel: (01454) 633409

City Revd David Self, St Paul's Rectory, 131 Ashley Rd, St Paul's, Bristol BS6 5NU
Tel: 0117–955 0150

ARCHDEACONRY OF MALMESBURY

Chippenham Revd Wendy Sanders, Vicarage, 3 Garth Close, Chippenham, Wilts. SN14 6XF
Tel: (01249) 650787

Kingswood and South Gloucestershire Revd Stephen Cook, Vicarage, Church Rd, Hanham, Bristol BS15 3AF
Tel: 0117–967 3580

North Wiltshire Revd Barry Raven, Rectory, 1 Days Court, Crudwel, Malmesbury, Wilts. SN16 9HG
Tel: (01666) 577118

Wroughton Revd Michael Johnson, Vicarage, Church Hill, Wroughton, Swindon, Wilts. SN4 9JS
Tel: (01793) 812301

DIOCESE OF CANTERBURY

Founded in 597. Kent east of the Medway, excluding the Medway Towns (ROCHESTER).

Population 825,000   Area 970 sq m
Stipendiary Clergy 185   Benefices 159
Parishes 272   Churches 329

ARCHBISHOP (103rd)
Most Revd and Rt Hon George Leonard Carey PH D, *Primate of all England and Metropolitan,* Lambeth Palace, London SE1 7JU *Tel:* 020–7928 8282 and Old Palace, Canterbury, Kent CT1 2EE [1991]   *Fax:* 020–7261 9836
[George Cantuar:]
Dioc Chaplain Revd Stewart Jones, The Old Palace, Canterbury, Kent CT1 2EE (*Archbishop's Canterbury Chaplain and Dioc Missioner*)

Matters relating to the Diocese of Canterbury should in the first instance be referred to the **Bishop of Dover** *(see below)*
For the **Archbishop of Canterbury's Personal Staff** *see page 64*

SUFFRAGAN BISHOPS
DOVER Rt Revd Stephen Squires Venner, Upway, 52 St Martin's Hill, Canterbury, Kent CT1 1PR [1999]
Office Old Palace, The Precincts, Canterbury CT1 2EE   *Tel:* (01227) 459382
                         Fax: (01227) 784985
Hon Chaplain Canon Ronald Diss

MAIDSTONE Rt Revd Gavin Hunter Reid, Bishop's House, Pett Lane, Charing, Ashford, Kent TN27 0DL [1992]   *Tel:* (01233) 712950
                         Fax: (01233) 713543
Chaplain Revd Roger Martin
                         Tel and *Fax:* (01227) 738177

PROVINCIAL EPISCOPAL VISITORS
EBBSFLEET Rt Revd Michael Houghton, 8 Goldney Ave, Clifton, Bristol BS8 4RA [1998]
                         Tel: 0117–973 1752
                         Fax: 0117–973 1762

RICHBOROUGH Rt Revd Edwin Barnes, 14 Hall Place Gardens, St Albans, Herts. AL1 3SP
                         Tel: (01727) 857764
                         Fax: (01727) 763025

HONORARY ASSISTANT BISHOP
Rt Revd Richard David Say, 23 Chequers Park, Wye, Ashford, Kent TN25 5BB *Tel:* (01233) 812720

CATHEDRAL AND METROPOLITICAL CHURCH OF CHRIST
Dean Very Revd John Simpson, The Deanery, The Precincts, Canterbury, Kent CT1 2EP [1986]
                         Tel: (01227) 765983 (Home)
                         (01227) 762862 (Office)
Cathedral Office Cathedral House, 11 The Precincts, Canterbury CT1 2EH
                         Tel: (01227) 762862
                         Fax: (01227) 865222
Canons Residentiary
Canon Peter Brett, 22 The Precincts, Canterbury, Kent CT1 2EP [1983]   *Tel:* (01227) 459757
Canon Roger Symon, 19 The Precincts, Canterbury, Kent CT1 2EP [1994]   *Tel:* (01227) 459918
Canon Treasurer Canon Michael Chandler PH D, 15 The Precincts, Canterbury, Kent CT1 2EL [1995]   *Tel:* (01227) 463056
Ven John Pritchard, 29 The Precincts, Canterbury, Kent CT1 2EP [1996]   *Tel:* (01227) 463036
                         Fax: (01227) 785209
Precentor and Sacrist Revd Kevin Goss, Cathedral Office [1998]
Receiver General Brigadier M. J. Meardon, Cathedral Office
Cathedral Organist Mr David Flood, 6 The Precincts, Canterbury CT1 2EE
                         Tel: (01227) 765219

ARCHDEACONS
CANTERBURY Ven John Pritchard, 29 The Precincts, Canterbury, Kent CT1 2EP [1996]
                         Tel: (01227) 463036
                         Fax: (01227) 785209

MAIDSTONE Ven Patrick Evans, The Old Rectory, The Street, Pluckley, Kent TN27 0QT [1989]
                         Tel: (01233) 840291
                         Fax: (01233) 840759

CONVOCATION (MEMBERS OF THE HOUSE OF CLERGY OF THE GENERAL SYNOD)
Dignitaries in Convocation
The Bishop of Maidstone
The Archdeacon of Canterbury
Proctors for Clergy
Canon Brian Chalmers PH D

Revd Bill Hopkinson
Canon Geoffrey Sidaway

MEMBERS OF THE HOUSE OF LAITY OF THE GENERAL SYNOD
Dr David Bowen
Mrs Caroline Spencer
(One vacancy)

DIOCESAN OFFICERS
Dioc Secretary Mr David Kemp, Diocesan House, Lady Wootton's Green, Canterbury, Kent CT1 1NQ *Tel:* (01227) 459401 *Fax:* (01227) 787073 *email:* dkemp@diocant.clara.co.uk
Commissary General His Honour Judge Richard Walker, 34 & 36 Castle St, Dover, Kent CT16 1PN *Tel:* (01304) 240250 *Fax:* (01304) 240040
Dioc Registrar and Legal Adviser to the Diocese Mr Richard Sturt (*same address*)

DIOCESAN ORGANIZATIONS
Diocesan Office Diocesan House, Lady Wootton's Green, Canterbury, Kent CT1 1NQ *Tel:* (01227) 459401 *Fax:* (01227) 450964 *email:* reception@diocant.clara.co.uk

ADMINISTRATION
Dioc Synod (*Chairman, House of Clergy*) Canon Brian Chalmers, Vicarage, Pett Lane, Charing, Ashford, Kent TN27 0DL *Tel:* (01233) 712598; (*Chairman, House of Laity*) Mr Raymond Harris; (*Secretary*) Mr David Kemp, Dioc House
Board of Finance (*Chairman*) Mr Richard Finlinson, Forge Hill House, Pluckley, Ashford, Kent TN27 0SL *Tel:* (01233) 840318; (*Secretary*) Mr David Kemp (*as above*)
Designated Officer Mrs Gillian Marsh, Dioc House
Dioc Accountant Miss Rosemary Collins, Dioc House
Director of Property Services Mr Philip Bell, 9 The Precincts, Canterbury, Kent CT1 2EE *Tel:* (01227) 478390

CHURCHES
Advisory Committee for the Care of Churches Mr Ross Anderson, Cullings Hill, Elham, Canterbury CT4 6TE *Tel:* (01303) 840638 (*Secretary*) Mr Ian Dodd, 9 The Precincts, Canterbury, Kent CT1 2EE *Tel:* (01227) 478390

EDUCATION
Education Committee (*Director*) Mr Rupert Bristow, Dioc House
Education Field Officer Miss Judy Bainbridge, Dioc House
Schools Executive Officer Mrs Pat Gibson, Dioc House

MINISTRY
Director of Ministry and Training Revd Bill Hopkinson, Dioc House

Director of Ordinands Revd Ian Aveyard, Dioc House
Assistant Director of Ordinands Revd Anthea Williams, Vicarage, Rolvenden, Cranbrook TN17 4ND *Tel:* (01580) 241235
Bishop's Officer for NSM Revd Michael Gooch, Vicarage, 76 Station Rd, Teynham, Kent ME9 9SN *Tel:* (01795) 522510
Adviser for Women's Ministry Vacancy
Ordained Local Ministry Principal Revd Alan Dodds, Dioc House
Local Ministry Adviser Revd Barbara Way, Dioc House
Youth Officer Mr David Brown, Dioc House
Children's Ministry Adviser Mr Ted Hurst, Dioc House
Association of Readers (*Warden*) Revd Christopher Morgan-Jones, Vicarage, Priory Rd, Maidstone ME15 6NL *Tel:* (01622) 756002; (*Hon Secretary*) Dr James Gibson, 27 Pine Grove, Maidstone, Kent ME14 2AJ *Tel:* (01622) 673050
Clergy Retirement Officers Canon Ferdie Phillips, 6 South Close, The Precincts, Canterbury CT1 2EJ *Tel:* (01227) 450891
Revd Patrick Amos, 20 Fauchons Close, Bearsted ME14 4BB *Tel:* (01622) 736725

LITURGICAL
Chairman Revd Fredrik Arvidsson, Rectory, Upper St, Kingsdown, Deal CT14 8BJ *Tel:* (01304) 373951
Secretary Miss Mary Ambrose, Zawadi, 15 The Street, Kingston, Canterbury CT4 6JB

MISSION AND ECUMENICAL
Board of Mission (*Chairman*) The Bishop of Maidstone (*as above*)
Dioc Missioner Revd Stewart Jones, The Old Palace, Canterbury CT1 2EE

PRESS AND PUBLICATIONS
Communications Officer Revd Don Witts, Dioc House *Tel* and *Fax:* (01227) 763373 0411 410079 (Mobile) *email:* don.witts@ukonline.co.uk
Editor of Dioc Directory Mrs Gill Marsh, Dioc House

DIOCESAN RECORD OFFICES
Cathedral Archives and Library, The Precincts, Canterbury CT1 2EH *Archivist* Dr Michael Stansfield *Tel:* (01227) 463510 (*For parish records in the Archdeaconry of Canterbury*)
Centre for Kentish Studies, County Hall, Maidstone, Kent ME14 1XQ *County Archivist* Ms Patricia Rowsby *Tel:* (01622) 754321 (*For parish records in the Archdeaconry of Maidstone*)

SOCIAL RESPONSIBILITY
Canterbury and Rochester Joint Council for Social Responsibility/ Senior Adviser Canon David Grimwood, 60 Marsham St, Maidstone, Kent ME14 1EW *Tel:* (01622) 755014 *Fax:* (01622) 693531

Advisers Revd Pearl Anderson, Mr Adrian Speller (*same address*)
Association for the Deaf Revd Tony Old, Dioc House

STEWARDSHIP
Adviser Mr David Noakes, Dioc House

RURAL DEANS
ARCHDEACONRY OF CANTERBURY
East Bridge Revd David Barnes, Vicarage, Queens Rd, Ash, Canterbury, Kent CT3 2BG
Tel: (01304) 812296
West Bridge Revd Clive Barlow, Rectory, The Green, Chartham, Canterbury, Kent CT4 7JW
Tel: (01227) 738256
Canterbury Revd Philip Down, Rectory, St Stephen's Green, Canterbury CT2 7JU
Tel: (01227) 765391
Reculver Canon Dick Cotton, Christ Church Vicarage, 38 Beltinge Rd, Herne Bay, Kent CT6 6BU
Tel: (01227) 366640
Dover Revd Peter Bowers, Vicarage, 23 Lewisham Rd, River, Dover, Kent CT17 0QG
Tel: (01304) 822037
Elham Canon Reg Humphriss, Rectory, Saltwood, Hythe, Kent CT21 4QA
Tel: (01303) 266932
Ospringe Revd William Mowll, Vicarage, 101 The Street, Boughton-under-Blean, Faversham, Kent ME13 9BG
Tel: (01227) 751410

Sandwich Revd Bruce Hawkins, Vicarage, St Mary's Rd, Deal, Kent CT14 7NQ
Tel: (01304) 374645
Thanet Revd Mark Hayton, Rectory, Nelson Place, Broadstairs, Kent CT10 1HQ
Tel: (01843) 862921

ARCHDEACONRY OF MAIDSTONE
Cranbrook Revd Brian Barnes, Rectory, Frittenden Lane, Staplehurst, Kent TN12 0DH
Tel: (01580) 891258
East Charing Canon Brian Chalmers, Vicarage, Pett Lane, Charing, Kent TN27 0PL
Tel: (01233) 712598
Maidstone Revd Eric Delve, Vicarage, 24 Park Avenue, Maidstone, Kent ME14 5HN
Tel: (01622) 754856
North Downs Revd Geoff Davis, Vicarage, Church Hill, Boughton Monchelsea, Kent ME17 4BU
Tel: (01622) 743321
North Lympne Revd John Tipping, Rectory, Bower Rd, Mersham, Ashford, Kent TN25 6NN
Tel: (01233) 502138
South Lympne Revd Lindsay Hammond, Vicarage, Appledore, Kent TN26 2DB
Tel: (01233) 758250
Sittingbourne Revd Gilbert Spencer, Vicarage, Vicarage Rd, Minster-in-Sheppey ME12 2HE
Tel: (01795) 873185
Tenterden Canon David Trustam, Vicarage, Church Rd, Tenterden, Kent TN30 6AT
Tel: (01580) 763118

DIOCESE OF CARLISLE

Founded in 1133. Cumbria, except for small areas in the east (NEWCASTLE, BRADFORD).

Population 487,000   Area 2,477 sq m
Stipendiary Clergy 153   Benefices 168
Parishes 270   Churches 349

BISHOP (65th)
Rt Revd Ian Harland, Rose Castle, Dalston, Carlisle, Cumbria CA5 7BZ [1989]
Tel: (01697) 476274
Fax: (01697) 476550
[Ian Carliol:]
Bishop's Chaplain Canon Keith Wood

SUFFRAGAN BISHOP
PENRITH Rt Revd Richard Garrard, Holm Croft, Castle Rd, Kendal, Cumbria LA9 7AU [1994]
Tel: (01539) 727836
Fax: (01539) 734380

HONORARY ASSISTANT BISHOPS
Rt Revd Ian Macdonald Griggs, Rookings, Patterdale, Penrith, Cumbria CA11 0NP [1994]
Tel: (01768) 482064
Rt Revd George Lanyon Hacker, Keld House, Milburn, Penrith, Cumbria CA10 1TW [1994]
Tel: (01768) 361506
Rt Revd John Richard Satterthwaite, 25 Spencer House, St Paul's Square, Carlisle CA1 1DG [1994]
Tel: (01228) 594055
Rt Revd Andrew Alexander Kenny Graham, Fell End, Butterwick, Penrith, Cumbria CA10 1QQ [1997]
Tel: (01931) 713147

CATHEDRAL CHURCH OF THE HOLY AND UNDIVIDED TRINITY
Dean Very Revd Graeme Knowles, The Deanery, Carlisle, Cumbria CA3 8TZ [1998]
Tel: (01228) 523335
Cathedral Office 7 The Abbey, Carlisle, Cumbria CA3 8TZ
Tel: (01228) 548151
Fax: (01228) 547049
Canons Residentiary
Canon Rex Chapman, 1 The Abbey, Carlisle, Cumbria CA3 8TZ [1978]
Tel: (01228) 597614
Ven David Turnbull, 2 The Abbey, Carlisle, Cumbria CA3 8TZ [1993]
Tel: (01228) 523026
Canon David Weston PH D, 3 The Abbey, Carlisle, Cumbria CA3 8TZ [1994]
Tel: (01228) 521834
Canon Colin Hill PH D, 4 The Abbey, Carlisle CA3 8TZ [1996]
Tel: (01228) 590778
Bursar and Chapter Clerk Mr Ellis Amos, Cathedral Office

Administrative Officer Mrs Carolyne Baines, Cathedral Office
Cathedral Organist Mr Jeremy Suter, 6 The Abbey, Carlisle, Cumbria CA3 8TZ   *Tel:* (01228) 526646

ARCHDEACONS
CARLISLE Ven David Turnbull, 2 The Abbey, Carlisle CA3 8TZ [1993]
Tel: (01228) 23026
Fax: (01228) 594899
email: adncarlisle-c-of-e.org

WEST CUMBERLAND Ven Alan Davis, 50 Stainburn Rd, Workington, Cumbria CA14 1SN [1996]
Tel: (01900) 66190
Fax: (01900) 873021

WESTMORLAND AND FURNESS Ven George Howe, Vicarage, Lindale, Grange over Sands, Cumbria, LA11 6LB [2000]
Tel: (01539) 534717

CONVOCATION (MEMBERS OF THE HOUSE OF CLERGY OF THE GENERAL SYNOD)
Dignitaries in Convocation
The Bishop of Penrith
The Archdeacon of Carlisle
Proctors for Clergy
Canon Rex Chapman
Canon Myrtle Langley
Revd Angus MacLeay

MEMBERS OF THE HOUSE OF LAITY OF THE GENERAL SYNOD
Mrs Dorothy Chatterley
Dr Arnold Currall
Mr Nigel Holmes
Mrs Elizabeth Metcalfe
Mr David Mills

DIOCESAN OFFICERS
Dioc Secretary Canon Colin Hill, Church House, West Walls, Carlisle, Cumbria CA3 8UE
Tel: (01228) 522573
Fax: (01228) 815400
email: chrchhse@carlisle-c-of-e.org
Chancellor of Diocese His Hon Judge Francis Aglionby, The Croft, Houghton, Carlisle, Cumbria CA3 0LD
Registrar of Diocese and Bishop's Legal Secretary

Mrs Susan Holmes, Woodside, Great Corby, Carlisle, Cumbria CA4 8LL   *Tel:* (01228) 560617   *Fax:* (01228) 562372   *email:* susan@gt-corby.demon.co.uk

DIOCESAN ORGANIZATIONS

Diocesan Office Church House, West Walls, Carlisle, Cumbria CA3 8UE   *Tel:* (01228) 522573   *Fax:* (01228) 815400   *email:* chrchhse@carlisle-c-of-e.org

ADMINISTRATION

Dioc Synod (Chairman, House of Clergy) Canon Rex Chapman, 1 The Abbey, Carlisle CA3 8TZ *Tel:* (01228) 597614; *(Chairman, House of Laity)* Mr Nigel Holmes, Woodside, Great Corby, Carlisle CA4 8LL *Tel:* (01228) 560617; *(Secretary)* Canon Colin Hill, Dioc Office
Board of Finance (Chairman) Mr Hugh Ellison, 21 Arthur St, Penrith, Cumbria CA11 7TU *Tel:* (01768) 862069; *(Secretary)* Canon Colin Hill *(as above)*
Parsonages Committees (North, South and West): Mr Stephen Mansbridge, Dioc Office
Pastoral Committee Canon Campbell Matthews, Dioc Office
Designated Officer Mrs Susan Holmes, Woodside, Great Corby, Carlisle CA4 8LL
Tel: (01228) 560617
Fax: (01228) 562372

CHURCHES

Advisory Committee for the Care of Churches (Chairman) Mr Peter Browning, Park Fell, Skelwith, Ambleside, Cumbria LA22 9NP
Tel: (01539) 433978
(Secretary) Canon Colin Hill, Dioc Office
(Administrative Secretary) Mr Stephen Mansbridge *(as above)*

EDUCATION

Board of Education, Church Centre, West Walls, Carlisle CA3 8UE   *Tel:* (01228) 538086   *Fax:* (01228) 815409
Director of Education Canon Rex Chapman, Church Centre
Adviser for RE (North) Revd Bert Thomas, Church Centre
Adviser for RE (South) Vacancy, Vicarage, Beetham Milnthorpe, Cumbria LA7 7AS
Tel: (01539) 562216
Diocesan Youth Officers (North) Revd Gill Hart, Vicarage, Irthington, Carlisle CA6 4NJ
Tel: (01697) 72379
(South) Miss Fiona Gilmour, West Lynn, Boon Walks, Burton-in-Kendal, Carnforth, Lancs LA6 1NB
Resources Centre Revd Bert Thomas, Church Centre

BOARD FOR MINISTRY AND TRAINING

Principal Carlisle and Blackburn Dioc Training
Institute and Adviser for Ministry and Training Revd Tim Herbert, Vicarage, Cotehill, Carlisle CA4 0DY   *Tel:* (01228) 561745
Adviser for Clergy Training Revd Bob Dew, Vicarage, Skelsmergh, Kendal, Cumbria LA9 6PU   *Tel:* (01539) 724498   *Fax:* (01539) 734655
Director of Ordinands Revd Nick Ash, Vicarage, Dalston, Carlisle CA5 7JF   *Tel:* (01228) 710215
Adviser for Women's Ministry Revd Carol Farrer, 18 Skirsgill Close, Penrith, Cumbria CA11 8QF   *Tel:* (01768) 899540   *email:* cfarrer@enterprise.net

BOARD FOR SOCIAL RESPONSIBILITY

Officer for Social Responsibility Canon John Higgins, Dioc Office
Council for Agriculture and Rural Life (Team Leader) Revd Jonathan Falkner, Vicarage, Lancrigg, Aspatria, Carlisle CA5 3NA   *Tel:* (01697) 781345
Industrial Mission Revd Ian Davies, St John's Vicarage, James Watt Terrace, Barrow-in-Furness, Cumbria LA14 2TS   *Tel:* (01229) 821101   *Fax:* (01229) 871505

ECUMENICAL AFFAIRS

Dioc Canon Keith Wood, Rose Castle, Dalston, Carlisle CA5 7BZ   *Tel:* (0169 74) 76274   *Fax:* (0169 74) 76550
Churches Together in Cumbria (Secretary) Revd Andrew Dodd, Dioc Office

PARISH MISSION AND DEVELOPMENT

Team Leader Responsible for Lay Training Revd Peter Wilson, Dioc Office
Council for Stewardship (Secretary and Dioc Officer) Vacancy
Council for Evangelism (Secretary and Dioc Officer) Revd David Ella, Vicarage, Loweswater, Cockermouth, Cumbria CA13 9RU
Tel: (01900) 85237
Partnership in World Mission Mrs Lynne Tembey, 2 High St, Whitehaven, Cumbria CA28 7PZ
Tel: (01946) 64738
Fax: (01946) 599931

WORSHIP ADVISER

Ven David Turnbull, 2 The Abbey, Carlisle, CA3 8TZ   *Tel:* (01228) 523026   *Fax:* (01228) 594399

PRESS AND PUBLICATIONS

Communications Officer Revd Richard Pratt, Dioc Office   *Tel:* (01228) 521982 (Home)
Editor of Dioc News Revd Nigel Davies, St Oswald's Vicarage, Burneside, Kendal, Cumbria LA9 6QX   *Tel:* (01539) 722015
Dioc Directory Canon Colin Hill, Dioc Office

DIOCESAN RECORD OFFICES

Cumbria Record Office, The Castle, Carlisle CA3 8UR *Tel:* (01228) 607282
Cumbria Record Office, County Offices, Kendal *Tel:* (01539) 773540
Cumbria Record Office, 140 Duke St, Barrow *Tel:* (01229) 894363 *County Archivist* Mr Jim Grisenthwaite *Tel:* (01228) 607282

RURAL DEANS

ARCHDEACONRY OF CARLISLE

Appleby Canon Colin Levey, Vicarage, Orton, Penrith, Cumbria CA10 3RQ *Tel:* (01539) 624532
Brampton Canon Christopher Morris, Vicarage, Lanercost, Brampton, Carlisle CA8 2HQ *Tel:* (01697) 72478
Carlisle Canon Geoffrey Ravalde, Vicarage, Longthwaite Rd, Wigton, Cumbria CA7 9JR *Tel:* (01697) 342337

Penrith Revd David Fowler, Vicarage, Kirkoswald, Penrith, Cumbria CA10 1DQ *Tel:* (01768) 898176

ARCHDEACONRY OF WESTMORLAND AND FURNESS

Furness Canon Peter Mann, Rectory, 98 Roose Rd, Barrow-in-Furness, Cumbria LA13 9RL *Tel:* (01229) 821641
Kendal Vacancy
Windermere Canon Derek Jackson, St Mary's Vicarage, Ambleside Rd, Windermere, Cumbria LA23 1BA *Tel:* (01539) 443032

ARCHDEACONRY OF WEST CUMBERLAND

Calder Canon James Baker, Vicarage, Oakbank, Whitehaven, Cumbria CA28 6HY *Tel:* (01946) 692630
Derwent Canon Brian Smith, St John's Vicarage, Ambleside Rd, Keswick, Cumbria CA12 4DD *Tel:* (01768) 772130
Solway Canon Bryan Rowe, Vicarage, King St, Aspatria, Carlisle CA5 3AL *Tel:* (01673) 20398

DIOCESE OF CHELMSFORD

Founded in 1914. Essex, except for a few parishes in the north (ELY, ST EDMUNDSBURY AND IPSWICH); five East London boroughs north of the Thames; three parishes in south Cambridgeshire.

Population 2,659,000   Area 1,531 sq m
Stipendiary Clergy 414   Benefices 359
Parishes 484   Churches 608

BISHOP (8th)
Rt Revd John Freeman Perry, Bishopscourt, Margaretting, Ingatestone, Essex CM4 0HD [1996]
Tel: (01277) 352001
Fax: (01277) 355374
email: bishopjohn@chelmsford.anglican.org
[John Chelmsford]
Bishop's Senior Assistant Canon Richard More, Willowdene, Maldon Rd, Margaretting, Ingatestone CM4 9JW   *Tel:* (01277) 352472

AREA BISHOPS
BARKING Rt Revd Roger Frederick Sainsbury, Barking Lodge, 110 Capel Rd, Forest Gate, London E7 0JS [1991]   *Tel:* 020–8478 2456
Office Suite 1B, Cranbrook House, 61 Cranbrook Rd, Ilford IG1 4PG   *Tel:* 020–8514 6044
Fax: 020–8514 6049
email: bishoproger@chelmsford.anglican.org
BRADWELL Rt Revd Laurence Alexander Green, Bishop's House, Orsett Rd, Horndon-on-the-Hill, Stanford-le-Hope, Essex SS17 8NS [1993]
Tel: (01375) 673806
Fax: (01375) 674222
email: lauriegr@globalnet.co.uk
COLCHESTER Rt Revd Edward Holland, 1 Fitzwalter Rd, Lexden, Colchester, Essex CO3 3SS [1994]
Tel: (01206) 576648
Fax: (01206) 763868
email: bishopedward@chelmsford.anglican.org

HONORARY ASSISTANT BISHOP
Rt Revd James Johnson, St Helena, 249 Woodgrange Drive, Southend-on-Sea, Essex SS1 2SQ   *Tel:* (01702) 613429

CATHEDRAL CHURCH OF ST MARY THE VIRGIN, ST PETER AND ST CEDD
Provost Very Revd Peter Judd, The Provost's House, 3 Harlings Grove, Chelmsford, Essex CM1 1YQ [1997]   *Tel:* (01245) 354318 (Home)
(01245) 294492 (Office)
email: provost@chelmsford.anglican.org
Cathedral Office 53 New St, Chelmsford CM1 1TY
Tel: (01245) 294480
Fax: (01245) 294499
Canons Residentiary
Vice-Provost Canon Timothy Thompson, 115

Rainsford Rd, Chelmsford, Essex CM1 2PF [1988]   *Tel:* (01245) 267773 (Home)
(01245) 294493 (Office)
Canon Theologian Canon Andrew Knowles, 2 Harlings Grove, Chelmsford CM1 1YQ [1998]
Tel: (01245) 355041 Home)
(01245) 294484 (Office)
Canon Precentor Canon David Knight, The Precentor's House, 1B Rainsford Ave, Chelmsford CM1 2PJ [1991]   *Tel:* (01245) 257306 (Home)
(01245) 294482 (Office)
email: precentor@chelmsford.anglican.org
Chaplain Revd Katy Hacker Hughes, 7 Rainsford Ave, Chelmsford CM1 2PJ
Tel: (01245) 350362 (Home)
(01245) 294483 (Office)
Hon Associate Chaplain Revd Ivor Moody, 4 Bishopscourt Gardens, Springfield, Chelmsford CM2 6AZ   *Tel:* (01245) 261700 (Home)
(01245) 493131 (Office)
Chapter Clerk and Administrator Mr Terry Mobbs, Cathedral Office   *Tel:* (01245) 294488
Master of Music Dr Graham Elliott, 1 Harlings Grove, Chelmsford CM1 1YQ
Tel: (01245) 262006 (Home)
(01245) 294485 (Office)
email: music@chelmsford.anglican.org
Assistant Master of Music Mr Neil Weston, Cathedral Office   *Tel:* (01245) 294486

ARCHDEACONS
COLCHESTER Ven Martin Wallace, 63 Powers Hall End, Witham, Essex CM8 1NH [1997]
Tel: (01376) 513130
Fax: (01376) 500789
email: a.colchester@chelmsford.anglican.org
HARLOW Ven Peter Taylor, Glebe House, Church Lane, Sheering, Essex CM22 7NR [1996]
Tel: (01279) 734524
Fax: (01279) 734426
email: a.harlow@chelmsford.anglican.org
SOUTHEND Ven David Jennings, 136 Broomfield Rd, Chelmsford CM1 1RN [1992]
Tel: (01245) 258257
Fax: (01245) 250845
email: a.southend@chelmsford.anglican.org

WEST HAM Ven Michael Fox, 86 Aldersbrook Rd, Manor Park, London E12 5DH [1996]
Tel: 020–8989 8557
Fax: 020–8530 1311
email: a.westham@chelmsford.anglican.org

CONVOCATION (MEMBERS OF THE HOUSE OF CLERGY OF THE GENERAL SYNOD)
Dignitaries in Convocation
The Bishop of Barking
The Archdeacon of Southend
Proctors for Clergy
Canon Paul Brett
Revd Julie Eaton
Canon John Howden
Canon David Lowman
Revd Christopher Newlands
Revd Peter Walker

MEMBERS OF THE HOUSE OF LAITY OF THE GENERAL SYNOD
Dr Susan Atkin
Mrs Joy Halstead
Mr Julian Litten
Mr Harry Marsh
Mr Vijay Menon
Mr David Morgan
Miss Pat Nappin
Dr James Rawes
Mr William Walker

DIOCESAN OFFICERS
Dioc Secretary Mr David Phillips, Diocesan Office, 53 New St, Chelmsford, Essex CM1 1AT
Tel: (01245) 294400
email: mail@chelmsford.anglican.org
Chancellor of Diocese Chanc Sheila Cameron, Diocesan Registry, 53A New St, Chelmsford, Essex CM1 1NG
Tel: (01245) 259470
Registrar of Diocese and Bishop's Legal Secretary Mr Brian Hood, Diocesan Registry, 53A New St, Chelmsford, Essex CM1 1NG *Tel:* (01245) 259470
Legal Advisers to the Board of Finance Winckworth Sherwood, 53A New St, Chelmsford CM1 1NG
Tel: (01245) 262212

DIOCESAN ORGANIZATIONS
Diocesan Office 53 New St, Chelmsford, Essex CM1 1AT
Tel: (01245) 294400
Fax: (01245) 294477
email: mail@chelmsford.anglican.org

ADMINISTRATION
Dioc Synod (*Chairman, House of Clergy*) Revd Tim Potter, Vicarage, Broomfields, Hatfield Heath, Bishops Stortford CM22 7DH *Tel:* (01279) 730288; (*Chairman, House of Laity*) Mr Gordon Simmons, 'Cartref', 2A Castle Drive, Rayleigh, Essex SS6 7HT; (*Secretary*) Mr David Phillips, Dioc Office
Board of Finance (*Chairman*) Mr Philip Hawkes,

Greenfields, Dunmow Rd, Felstead, Essex CM6 3LF
Tel: (01371) 856480
Fax: (01371) 856872
(*Secretary*) Mr David Phillips (*as above*)
Asst Dioc Secretary Mr Peter Hobbs, Dioc Office
Dioc Accountant Mr Mac Mackay, Dioc Office
Director of Property Services Mr Alan McCarthy, Dioc Office
Designated Officer Mr Brian Hood, Dioc Registry, 53A New St, Chelmsford CM1 1NG
Tel: (01245) 259470
Dioc Pastoral Committee (*Chairman*) Mr Mark Cole, 4 Achnacone Drive, Braiswick, Colchester CO4 4RL; (*Secretary*) Mr David Brown, Dioc Office

CHURCHES
Advisory Committee for the Care of Churches (*Chairman*) Mr Peter Richards, 139 Liftsan Way, Thorpe Bay SS1 2XG *Tel:* (01702) 468252; (*Asst Secretary*) Mr Peter Hobbs (*as above*); (*Administrator*) Mrs Jenny Fry, Dioc Office
Redundant Churches Committee (*Secretary*) Mr David Brown, Dioc Office
Ringers Association Mr Michael Bishop, 56 Edinburgh Gardens, Braintree, Essex CM7 6LH
Tel: (01376) 325281

DIOCESAN RESOURCE TEAM
Resource Team Leader Ven Peter Taylor, Dioc Office
Director of Education Canon Peter Hartley, Dioc Office
School and RE Advisers Chris Firth, Mark Plater, Dioc Office
Ministry Development Officer Canon Robin Greenwood, Dioc Office
Dioc Director of Ordinands Canon David Lowman, 25 Roxwell Rd, Chelmsford CM1 2LY
Tel: (01245) 264187
Adviser for Women's Ministry Vacancy
Lay Training Officer Revd Chris Burdon, Dioc Office
Lay Development Officer Revd Veronica Hydon, Dioc Office
Interfaith Adviser Mrs Ann Davison, Dioc Office
Youth Officer Mrs Lynn Money, Dioc Office
Asst Adviser for Continuing Ministerial Education Revd Julia Mourant, Dioc Office
Barking Area Continuing Ministerial Education Officer Mr Peter Harding, 26 Station Rd, Walthamstow, London E17 8AA
Tel: 020–8521 2026
Mission Officer Revd Roger Matthews, Dioc Office
Social Responsibility Officer Mrs Alison Davies, Dioc Office
Stewardship Adviser Mr Brian Pepper, Dioc Office

PRESS AND COMMUNICATIONS

Communications Manager Mrs Jenny Robinson, Dioc Office *Tel:* (01245) 294400 (Office)
07747 108606 (Mobile)
Fax: (01245) 294468
email: jrobinson@chelmsford.anglican.org
Press Officer Revd Philip Banks
Tel: (01277) 352456 (Office)
(01206) 822431 (Home)
0498 681886 (Mobile)
Fax: (01206) 822155
email: pbanks@chelmsford.anglican.org

OTHER COMMITTEES

Committee for Clergy Aid and Officer for Widows and Dependants of Clergymen Vacancy
Readers' Committee Mr John Woods, Low Roofs, Parsons Hill, Lexden, Colchester, Essex CO3 4DT
Tel: (01206) 573735
Liturgical Committee (*Chairman*) The Provost
Secretary Canon David Knight, The Precentor's House, Rainsford Ave, Chelmsford CM1 2PJ
Tel: (01245) 257306

DIOCESAN RECORD OFFICE

The County Archivist, County Hall, Chelmsford, Essex CM1 1LX *County Archivist* Mr Ken Hall
Tel: (01245) 267222, Ext. 2100

DIOCESAN HOUSE OF RETREAT

Pleshey, Chelmsford, Essex CM3 1HA (*Warden* Canon John Howden) *Tel:* (01245) 237251
Fax: (01245) 237594

RURAL DEANS
ARCHDEACONRY OF WEST HAM

Barking and Dagenham Revd John Fletcher, Vicarage, 10 St Chad's Rd, Chadwell Heath, Romford, Essex RM6 6JB *Tel:* 020–8590 2054
Fax: 020–8503 8982
Havering Revd Hugh Dibbens, 222 High St, Hornchurch, Essex RM12 6QP *Tel:* (01708) 441571
Newham Revd Ann Easter, NCRPL, 170 Harold Rd, London E13 0SE *Tel:* 020–8472 2785
Redbridge Canon Michael Cole, All Saints Vicarage, 4 Inmans Row, Woodford Green, Essex IG8 0NH *Tel:* 020–8504 0266
Waltham Forest Canon David Ainge, St Mary's Vicarage, 4 Vicarage Rd, London E10 5EA
Tel: 020–8539 7882

ARCHDEACONRY OF HARLOW

Epping Forest Revd David Driscoll, Vicarage, 2 Piercing Hill, Theydon Bois, Essex CM16 7JN
Tel: (01992) 814725
Harlow Revd Albert Watson, Rectory, Tawneys Rd, Harlow, Essex CM18 6QR *Tel:* (01279) 425138
Ongar Revd Charles Masheder, Lavers Rectory, Magdalen Laver, Ongar, Essex CM5 0ES
Tel: (01279) 426774

ARCHDEACONRY OF SOUTHEND

Brentwood Canon Robert White, St Thomas Vicarage, 91 Queens Rd, Brentwood, Essex CM14 4EY *Tel:* (01277) 225700 (Home)
Tel and *Fax:* (01277) 201094 (Office)
Basildon Revd Esther McCafferty, Rectory, Rectory Rd, Pitsea, Basildon, Essex SS13 2AA
Tel and *Fax:* (01268) 553240
Chelmsford North Revd John Mann, 18 Humber Rd, Chelmsford, Essex CM1 7PE
Tel: (01245) 259596
Chelmsford South Revd David Atkins, Rectory, Castledon Rd, Downham, Billericay, Essex CM11 1LD *Tel:* (01268) 710370
Hadleigh Revd Peter Sandberg, Rectory, Church Rd, Thundersley, Benfleet, Essex SS7 3HG
Tel: (01268) 566206
Maldon and Dengie Canon Peter Mason, All Saints' Vicarage, Church Walk, Maldon CM9 4PY *Tel:* (01621) 854179
Rochford Revd David Williams, Rectory, 36 Millview Meadows, Rochford, Essex SS4 1EF
Tel: (01702) 530621
Southend Canon Michael Ballard, Rectory, 8 Pilgrim's Close, Southend-on-Sea, Essex SS2 4XF
Tel: (01702) 466423
Thurrock Revd Robert Springett, Vicarage, 121 Foyle Drive, South Ockenden, Essex RM15 5HF
Tel: (01708) 853246

ARCHDEACONRY OF COLCHESTER

Braintree Revd John Shead, Vicarage, Finchingfield, Braintree, Essex CM7 4JR
Tel: (01371) 810309
Colchester Revd Anthony Rose, Rectory, 21 Cambridge Rd, Colchester CO3 3NS
Tel: (01206) 560175
Dedham and Tey Revd Gerard Moate, Vicarage, High St, Dedham, Colchester, Essex CO7 6DE
Tel: (01206) 322136
Dunmow Revd Tim Pigrem, Rectory, Stortford Rd, Leaden Roding, Dunmow, Essex CM6 1QZ
Tel: (01279) 876387
Harwich Revd Stephen Hardie, Rectory, 51 Highfield Ave, Dovercourt, Harwich, Essex CO12 4DR *Tel:* (01255) 502033
Hinckford Revd John Suddards, Rectory, Church Rd, Great Yeldham, Halstead, Essex CO9 4PT
Tel: (01787) 237358
Newport and Stansted Canon Christopher Bishop, 24 Mallows Green Rd, Manuden, Bishop's Stortford, Herts CM22 1DG *Tel:* (01279) 812228
Saffron Walden Revd Jeremy Saville, Ashdon Rectory, Saffron Walden, Essex CB10 2HP
Tel: (01799) 584897
St Osyth Revd Norman Issberner, Vicarage, 7 St Alban's Rd, Clacton-on-Sea, Essex CO15 6BA
Tel: (01255) 424760
Witham Revd Michael Hatchett, Vicarage, 1 Hall Road, Great Totham, Maldon CM9 8NN
Tel: (01621) 893150

Dioceses

DIOCESE OF CHESTER

Founded in 1541. Cheshire; Wirral; Halton, south of the Mersey; Warrington, south of the Mersey; Trafford, except for an area in the north (MANCHESTER); Stockport, except for a few parishes in the north (MANCHESTER) and in the east (DERBY); the eastern half of Tameside; a few parishes in Derbyshire; a few parishes in Manchester; a few parishes in Flintshire.

Population 1,573,000   Area 1,017 sq m
Stipendiary Clergy 287   Benefices 237
Parishes 278   Churches 375

BISHOP (40th)
Rt Revd Peter Robert Forster PH D, Bishop's House, Abbey Square, Chester CH1 2JD [1996]
Tel: (01244) 350864
Fax: (01244) 314187
[Peter Cestr:]
Bishop's Chaplain Revd Brian Perkes (*same address*)   *Tel:* (01829) 751265 (Home)

SUFFRAGAN BISHOPS
BIRKENHEAD Vacancy, Bishop's Lodge, 67 Bidston Rd, Oxton, Birkenhead, Merseyside CH43 6TR
Tel: 0151–652 2741
Fax: 0151–651 2330
email: bpbirkenhead@clara.net
STOCKPORT Rt Revd Geoffrey Martin Turner, Bishop's Lodge, Back Lane, Dunham Town, Altrincham, Cheshire WA14 4SG [1994]
Tel: 0161–928 5611
Fax: 0161–929 0692
email: bishop-stockport@cwcom.net

HONORARY ASSISTANT BISHOPS
Rt Revd Alan Leslie Winstanley, Vicarage, Ferry Rd, Eastham, Wirral, Merseyside CH42 0AJ
Tel: 0151–327 2182
Rt Revd Lord David Stuart Sheppard of Liverpool, Ambledown, 11 Melloncroft Drive, West Kirby, Wirral CH48 2JA

CATHEDRAL CHURCH OF CHRIST AND THE BLESSED VIRGIN MARY
Dean Very Revd Stephen Stewart Smalley PH D, Deanery, 7 Abbey St, Chester CH1 2JF [1987]
Tel: (01244) 351380
email: dean@chestercathedral.org.uk
Cathedral Office 12 Abbey Square, Chester CH1 2HU   *Tel:* (01244) 324756
Fax: (01244) 341110
email: office@chestercathedral.org.uk
Web: http://www.chestercathedral.org.uk
Vice-Dean Canon Michael Rees, 5 Abbey Green, Chester CH1 2JH [1990]   *Tel:* (01244) 347500
email: rees@chestercathedral.org.uk
Canons Residentiary
Canon Owen Conway, 9 Abbey St, Chester CH1 2JF [1991]   *Tel:* (01244) 316144
email: conway@chestercathedral.org.uk

Canon Trevor Dennis, 13 Abbey St, Chester CH1 2JF [1993]   *Tel:* (01244) 314408
email: dennis@chestercathedral.org.uk
Canon James Newcome, 5 Abbey St, Chester CH1 2JF [1994]   *Tel:* (01244) 315532
email: newcome@chestercathedral.org.uk
Chapter Clerk Mr Randal Hibbert, 20 White Friars, Chester CH1 1XS   *Tel:* (01244) 321066
Cathedral Administrator Mr David Burrows, Cathedral Office
email: burrows@chestercathedral.org.uk
Director of Music Mr David Poulter, Cathedral Office   *Tel:* (01244) 351024
email: music@chestercathedral.org.uk
Cathedral Surveyor Mr Andrew Arrol, Arrol & Snell, St Mary's Hall, St Mary's Court, Shrewsbury SY1 1EG   *Tel:* (01743) 241111

ARCHDEACONS
CHESTER Ven Christopher Hewetson, 8 Queens Park Rd, Queens Park, Chester CH4 7AD [1994]
Tel: (01244) 675417
Fax: (01244) 681959
MACCLESFIELD Ven Richard Gillings, Vicarage, Robin's Lane, Bramhall, Stockport SK7 2PE [1994]   *Tel:* 0161–439 2254
Fax: 0161–439 0878

CONVOCATION (MEMBERS OF THE HOUSE OF CLERGY OF THE GENERAL SYNOD)
The Archdeacon of Macclesfield
Proctors for Clergy
Revd Helen Chantry
Revd Dr Stephen Foster
Revd John Staley
Revd John Sutton
Revd David Walker
Canon Michael Walters

MEMBERS OF THE HOUSE OF LAITY OF THE GENERAL SYNOD
Mrs Kate Allan
Prof Tony Berry
Dr David Blackmore
Mrs Isobel Burnley

Mrs Rosalind Campbell
Mr Stewart Darlow
Dr Sheila Grieve
Mr Colin Richardson
Mr Arthur Tomlinson
Mr Paul Williams

DIOCESAN OFFICERS

Dioc Secretary Mr Stephen Marriott, Church House, Lower Lane, Aldford, Chester CH3 6HP
Tel: (01244) 620444
Fax: (01244) 620456
Chancellor of Diocese Chanc David Turner, 14 Gray's Inn Square, Gray's Inn, London WC1R 5JP
Registrar of Diocese and Bishop's Legal Secretary Mr Alan McAllester, Friars, White Friars, Chester CH1 1XS
Tel: (01244) 321066
Fax: (01244) 312582

DIOCESAN ORGANIZATIONS

Diocesan Office: Church House, Lower Lane, Aldford, Chester CH3 6HP
Tel: (01244) 620444
Fax: (01244) 620456

ADMINISTRATION

Dioc Synod (Vice-President, House of Clergy) Canon Michael Walters, Rectory, 14 Chapel St, Congleton, Cheshire CW12 4AB *Tel:* (01260) 273212;
(Vice-President, House of Laity) Dr David Blackmore, Coniston, Newton Lane, Newton, Chester CH2 2HJ *Tel:* (01244) 323494; *(Secretary)* Mr Stephen Marriott, Church House
Board of Finance (Chairman) Mr Stewart Darlow, 6 Harboro Grove, Sale, Cheshire M33 5BA *Tel:* 0161–973 4697; *(Secretary)* Mr Stephen Marriott *(as above)*
Director of Finance Mr George Colville, Church House
Houses Committee Mr George Colville *(as above)*
Dioc Surveyor Mr Michael Cram, Church House
Pastoral Committee Mr Stephen Marriott *(as above)*
Designated Officer Mr Stephen Marriott *(as above)*

CHURCHES

Advisory Committee for the Care of Churches (Chairman) Mr Derek Lawson, 1 The Serpentine, Curzon Park, Chester CH4 8AF *Tel:* (01244) 678216; *(Executive Secretary)* Mr Richard Mortimore, Church House
Redundant Churches Uses Committee Mr Stephen Marriott *(as above)*

EDUCATION

Director of Education Mr Jeff Turnbull, Church House
Children Mrs Alison Harris, Church House
Youth Revd Helen Chantry, Church House
RE Adviser Ms Gaynor Pollard, Church House

MINISTRY AND TRAINING

Director of Ministry Canon James Newcome, Bishop's House, Abbey Square, Chester, CH1 2JD
Tel: (01244) 319169
Director of Ordinands Revd Peter Robinson, Vicarage, Blackden Lane, Goostrey, Cheshire CW4 9PZ
Tel: (01477) 532109
Training Officer Revd Amiel Osmaston, Church House
Vocations Officer Revd Dr Stephen Foster, Vicarage, 99 Chatham St, Edgeley, Stockport, Cheshire SK3 9EG
Tel: 0161–480 5515
Officer for NSMs Revd Dr Roger Yates, 3 Racehorse Park, Wilmslow, Cheshire SK9 5LU
Tel: (01625) 520246
Advisers for Women in Ministry Revd Dr Judy Hunt, Rectory, Inveresk Rd, Tilston, Malpas, Cheshire SY14 7ED
Tel: (01829) 250628
email: hunt@virtual-chester.com
Revd Jane Brooke, 45 Brookfield Ave, Poynton, Stockport, Cheshire SK12 1JE *Tel:* (01625) 872822
Clergy Widows and Retirement Officers (Chester Archdeaconry) Canon Harold Aldridge, Vicarage, Vicarage Lane, Burton, Neston CH64 5TJ
Tel: 0151–336 4070
(Macclesfield Archdeaconry) Canon Peter Hunt, Rectory, Brereton, Sandbach, Cheshire CW11 1RY
Tel: (01477) 533263
Director of Reader Training Revd Simon Chesters, 225 Heath Rd South, Weston, Runcorn, Cheshire WA7 4LY
Tel: (01928) 573798
Society of Readers Mr A. Buckley, 55 Dalmorton Rd, Wallasey, Merseyside CH45 1LG
Tel: 0151–639 2407

LITURGICAL

Chairman Ven Richard Gillings *(as above)*
Secretary Mr Stephen Marriott *(as above)*

MISSIONARY AND ECUMENICAL

Dioc Missioner Canon Michael Rees, 5 Abbey Green, Chester CH1 2JH
Tel: (01244) 347500
Partners in World Mission Rt Revd Alan Winstanley, Vicarage, Ferry Rd, Eastham, Wirral, Merseyside CH62 0AJ *Tel* and *Fax:* 0151–327 2182
County Ecumenical Officer and Cheshire Church Leaders Consultation Canon Michael Rees *(as above)*
Dioc Ecumenical Officer Vacancy
Sen Industrial Missioner Vacancy

PRESS AND PUBLICATIONS

Dioc Communications Officer Revd David Marshall, Church House
Editor of Dioc News Revd David Marshall *(as above)*
Editor of Dioc Year Book Mr Stephen Marriott *(as above)*

DIOCESAN RECORD OFFICE

Cheshire Records Office, Duke St, Chester CH1 2DN *County Archivist* Mr J. Pepler

Tel: (01244) 603391

SOCIAL RESPONSIBILITY

Director of Social Responsibility Revd Bob Powley, Church House
Urban Officers Revd David Walker, Priory Rectory, 29 Park Rd West, Birkenhead, Merseyside CH43 1UR   *Tel:* 0151–652 1309
Revd Paul Robinson, St Paul's Vicarage, Huddersfield Rd, Stalybridge, Cheshire SK15 2PT

Tel: 0161–338 2514

STEWARDSHIP

Director of Parish Development (Acting) Revd Paul Reynolds, Church House

RURAL DEANS
ARCHDEACONRY OF CHESTER

Birkenhead Revd David Walker, Priory Rectory, 29 Park Rd West, Birkenhead, Merseyside CH43 1UR   *Tel:* 0151–652 1309
Chester Canon Christopher Samuels, Rectory, Handbridge, Chester CH4 7HL

Tel: (01244) 671202
Frodsham Revd Anne Samuels, Vicarage, Castle Rd, Halton, Runcorn, Cheshire WA7 2BE

Tel: (01928) 563636
Great Budworth Revd Tom Owen, St James Vicarage, Manx Rd, Warrington, Cheshire WA4 6AJ   *Tel:* (01925) 631893
Malpas Revd Tony Boyd, Vicarage, Farndon, Chester CH3 6QD   *Tel:* (01829) 270270
Middlewich Revd Michael Ridley, Vicarage, Church St, Weaverham, Northwich, Cheshire CW8 3NJ   *Tel:* (01606) 852110

Wallasey Revd Jim Florance, Vicarage, 107 Manor Rd, Wallasey, Merseyside CH45 7LU

Tel: 0151–639 1553
Wirral North Revd Paddy Benson, Vicarage, Barnston, Wirral, Merseyside CH61 1BW

Tel: 0151–648 2404
Wirral South Canon Harold Aldridge, Vicarage, Vicarage Lane, Burton, Neston CH64 5TJ

Tel: 0151–336 4070

ARCHDEACONRY OF MACCLESFIELD

Bowden Canon Brian McConnell, Vicarage, Townfield Rd, Altrincham, Cheshire WA14 4DS

Tel: 0161–928 1279
Chadkirk Revd Mike Lowe, Vicarage, 155 Church Lane, Marple, Stockport, Cheshire SK6 7LD

Tel: 0161–449 0950/427 2378
Cheadle Revd Donald Allister, 2 Massie St, Cheadle, Cheshire SK8 1BP

Tel: 0161–428 3440 (Home)
0161–428 8050 (Office)
Congleton Revd Nigel Elbourne, Odd Rode Rectory, Scholar Green, Stoke-on-Trent, Staffs ST7 3QN   *Tel:* (01270) 882195
Knutsford Canon Brian Young, Vicarage, Church Lane, Alderley Edge, Cheshire SK9 7UZ

Tel: (01625) 583249
Macclesfield Canon David Ashworth, Vicarage, Prestbury, Macclesfield, Cheshire SK10 4DG

Tel: (01625) 829288/827625
Mottram Revd Rob Watts, Vicarage, 10 Church St, Tintwistle, Glossop SK13 1JR

Tel: (01457) 852575
Nantwich Revd Bill White, Rectory, 44 Church Lane, Wistaston, Crewe CW2 8HA

Tel: (01270) 665742 (Home)
(01270) 567119 (Office)
Stockport Canon John Roff, St George's Vicarage, 28 Buxton Rd, Stockport, Cheshire SK2 6NU

Tel: 0161–480 2453

DIOCESE OF CHICHESTER

Founded in 1070, formerly called Selsey (AD 681). West Sussex, except for one parish in the north (GUILDFORD); East Sussex, except for one parish in the north (ROCHESTER); one parish in Kent.

Population 1,486,000   Area 1,459 sq m
Stipendiary Clergy 345   Benefices 299
Parishes 391   Churches 516

BISHOP (102th)
Rt Revd Eric Waldram Kemp, The Palace, Chichester, W Sussex PO19 1PY [1974]
Tel: (01243) 782161
Fax: (01243) 531332
email: bishopchi@diochi.freeserve.co.uk
[Eric Cicestr:]
Domestic Chaplain Revd Ian Chandler, The Palace (*as above*)
email: chaplain@diochi.freeserve.co.uk

AREA BISHOPS
HORSHAM Rt Revd Lindsay Goodall Urwin OGS, Bishop's House, 21 Guildford Rd, Horsham, W Sussex RH12 1LU [1993]   *Tel:* (01403) 211139
Fax: (01403) 217349
email: bishhorsham@clara.net
Chaplain Revd Christopher Smith
LEWES Rt Revd Wallace Benn, Bishop's Lodge, 16A Prideaux Rd, Eastbourne BN21 2NB [1997]
Tel: (01323) 648462
Fax: (01323) 641514
email: lewes@clara.net

HONORARY ASSISTANT BISHOPS
Rt Revd Mark Green, 27 Selwyn House, Selwyn Rd, Eastbourne, E Sussex BN21 2LF [1982]
Tel: (01323) 642707
Rt Revd Edward George Knapp-Fisher, 2 Vicars Close, Chichester, W Sussex PO19 1PT [1987]
Tel: (01243) 789219
Rt Revd Morris Henry St John Maddocks, 3 The Chantry, Canon Lane, Chichester PO19 1PZ [1987]   *Tel:* (01243) 788888
Rt Revd Simon Wilton Phipps, Sarsens, Shipley, W Sussex RH13 8PX   *Tel:* (01403) 741354
Rt Revd Christopher Charles Luxmoore, 42 Willowbed Drive, Chichester, W Sussex PO19 2JB [1991]   *Tel:* (01243) 784680
Rt Revd Michael Eric Marshall, 97A Cadogan Lane, London SW1X 9DU [1992]
Tel: 020–7235 3383
Rt Revd John William Hind, Bishop's Lodge, Church Rd, Worth, Crawley, W Sussex RH10 7RT [1993]   *Tel:* (01293) 883051
Rt Revd Michael Richard John Manktelow, 2 The Chantry, Canon Lane, Chichester, W Sussex PO19 1PX [1994]   *Tel:* (01243) 631096

Rt Revd David Peter Wilcox, 4 The Court, Hoo Gardens, Willingdon, Eastbourne, E Sussex BN20 9AX [1995]
Rt Revd Michael Edgar Adie, Greenslade, Froxfield, Petersfield, Hants GU23 1EB [1996]
Tel: (01730) 827266

CATHEDRAL CHURCH OF THE HOLY TRINITY
Dean Very Revd John Treadgold, The Deanery, Chichester, W Sussex PO19 1PX [1989]
Tel: (01243) 787337/782595 (Office)
(01243) 783286 (Home)
Fax: (01243) 536190
Cathedral Office The Royal Chantry, Cathedral Cloisters, Chichester, W Sussex PO19 1PX
Tel: (01243) 782595
Fax: (01243) 536190
Precentor Canon Roger Greenacre, 4 Vicars' Close, Chichester, W Sussex PO19 1PT [1975]
Tel: (01243) 784244
Fax: (01243) 536190
Chancellor Canon Peter Atkinson, The Residentiary, Canon Lane, Chichester, W Sussex PO19 1PX [1997]   *Tel:* (01243) 782961
Fax: (01243) 536190
Treasurer Canon Frank Hawkins, 12 St Martin's Square, Chichester, W Sussex PO19 1NR [1980]
Tel: (01243) 783509
Fax: (01243) 536190
Other members of the Administrative Chapter
Ven Michael Brotherton, 4 Canon Lane, Chichester, W Sussex PO19 1PX [1991] *Tel:* (01243) 779134
Fax: (01243) 536452
Rt Revd Michael Manktelow, 2 The Chantry, Canon Lane, Chichester, W Sussex PO19 1PX [1997]   *Tel:* (01243) 531096
Fax: (01243) 536190
Priest-Vicar Revd David Nason, 1 St Richard's Walk, Chichester, W Sussex PO19 1QA
Tel: (01243) 775615
Fax: (01243) 536190
Chapter Clerk Mr Clifford Hodgetts, Cathedral Office
Communar Capt Michael Shallow, Cathedral Office

Cathedral Organist Mr Alan Thurlow, 2 St Richard's Walk, Chichester, W Sussex PO19 1QA
Tel: (01243) 784790
Fax: (01243) 536190

ARCHDEACONS

CHICHESTER Ven Michael Brotherton, 4 Canon Lane, Chichester, W Sussex PO19 1PX [1991]
Tel: (01243) 779134
Fax: (01243) 536452
HORSHAM Ven William Filby, The Archdeaconry, Itchingfield, Horsham, W Sussex RH13 7NX [1983]
Tel: (01403) 790315
Fax: (01403) 791153
email: archhorsham@pavilion.co.uk
LEWES AND HASTINGS Ven Nicholas Reade, 27 The Avenue, Lewes, E Sussex BN7 1QT [1997]
Tel: (01273) 479530
Fax: (01273) 476529
email: archlewes@pavilion.co.uk

CONVOCATION (MEMBERS OF THE HOUSE OF CLERGY OF THE GENERAL SYNOD)

The Archdeacon of Chichester
Proctors for Clergy
Revd Roger Combes
Canon John Ford
Canon Jeremy Haselock
Revd Clay Knowles
Ven Nicholas Reade
Revd Doris Staniford

MEMBERS OF THE HOUSE OF LAITY OF THE GENERAL SYNOD

Mr John Booth
Lady Gill Brentford
Mrs Daphne Brotherton
Mrs Margaret Brown
Mrs Ruth Dunnett
Mrs Jill Loveless
Mrs Rachel Moriarty
Mrs Mary Nagel
Mr John Pope
Mr Peter Robottom
Mr Trevor Stevenson

DIOCESAN OFFICERS

Dioc Secretary Mr Jonathan Prichard, Diocesan Church House, 211 New Church Rd, Hove, E Sussex BN3 4ED
Tel: (01273) 421021
Fax: (01273) 421041
email: diocsec@diochi.org.uk
Chancellor of Diocese Chanc Mark Hill, Pump Court Chambers, 3 Pump Court, Temple, London EC4Y 7AJ
Registrar of Diocese and Bishop's Legal Secretary Mr Christopher Butcher, 5 East Pallant, Chichester, W Sussex PO19 1TS
Tel: (01243) 786111
Fax: (01243) 775640

DIOCESAN ORGANIZATIONS

Diocesan Office Diocesan Church House, 211 New Church Rd, Hove, E Sussex BN3 4ED
Tel: (01273) 421021
Fax: (01273) 421041
email: admin@diochi.org.uk

ADMINISTRATION

Dioc Synod (*Chairman, House of Clergy*) Ven Nicholas Reade, 27 The Avenue, Lewes, E Sussex BN7 1QT *Tel:* (01273) 479530; (*Chairman, House of Laity*) Vacancy (*Secretary*) Mr Jonathan Prichard, Dioc Church House
Dioc Fund and Board of Finance (*Incorporated*) (*Chairman*) Mr Hugh Wyatt
(*Secretary*) Mr Jonathan Prichard (*as above*)
Finance Committee Mr Jonathan Prichard (*as above*)
Stipends Committee (*Secretary*) Mr Jonathan Prichard (*as above*)
Parsonages Committee (*Surveyor and Property Manager*) Mr David Brown, Dioc Church House
Pastoral Committee (*Secretary*) Vacancy
Designated Officer Mr Christopher Butcher, 5 East Pallant, Chichester, PO19 1TS *Tel:* (01243) 786111
Fax: (01243) 775640

CHURCHES

Advisory Committee for the Care of Churches (*Chairman*) Mr John Ebdon, c/o Dioc Church House; (*Secretary*) Vacancy
email: buildings@diochi.org.uk

COUNCIL FOR PASTORAL CARE

Secretary Mrs R. Sewell, Folly Cottage, Duke's Rd, Fontwell, Arundel, W Sussex BN18 0SP
Tel: (01243) 542116

EDUCATION AND TRAINING
Schools
Adviser (*Director of Education*) Vacancy, Dioc Church House
email: schools@diochi.org.uk
Schools Administration Mrs Elizabeth Yates, Dioc Church House
Schools Support Mrs Chris Fitton, Dioc Church House
Children and Young People
Children's Work Adviser Miss Rachel Bennett
Youth Officers Capt Bob Carrington, Revd Stephen Gallagher, Dioc Church House
Education and Training of Adults
Adviser Miss Joy Gulliver, Dioc Church House
Readers Board (*Secretary*) Mr Derek Hansen, 7 Beach Rd, Shoreham by Sea, W Sussex BN43 5LJ
Tel: (01273) 462602

MINISTRY

Bishop's Adviser on Ministry, Lay Ministry and Director of Ordinands Canon Frank Hawkins, 12

St Martin's Square, Chichester, W Sussex PO19 1NR *Tel:* (01243) 783509
Asst DDO (Women's Ministry) Revd Doris Staniford, St Alban's Vicarage, Gossops Green, Crawley RH11 8LD *Tel:* (01293) 529848
Continuing Education of the Clergy and Fulltime Lay Workers Revd Stephen Tucker, St Wulfran's Rectory, 43 Ainsworth Ave, Ovingdean, Brighton BN2 7BG *Tel:* (01273) 303633
Post-Ordination Training Revd Stephen Tucker (*as above*)
Training for the Non-Stipendiary Ministry Vacancy
Vocations Consultants
Revd Roger Caswell, St Mary's Vicarage, 34 Fitzalan Rd, Littlehampton BN17 5ET
Tel: (01903) 724410
Revd Trevor Buxton, 24 Stanford Ave, Brighton BN1 6EA *Tel:* (01273) 561755
Revd John Edmonson, St Mark's Rectory, 11 Coverdale Ave, Bexhill-on-Sea TN39 4TY
Tel: (01424) 843733
Revd Alison Bowman, 21 Fair Meadow, Rye TN31 7NL *Tel:* (01797) 225769

MISSION AND RENEWAL
Adviser Canon John Ford, 27 Gatesmead, Haywards Heath, W Sussex RH16 1SN
Tel: (01444) 414658
Evangelist Revd Mark Payne, 12 Walsingham Rd, Hove BN3 4FF *Tel:* (01273) 326193
Resources Officer Mr Mark Forster, Dioc Church House
Overseas Council (Secretary) Canon David Pain, Vicarage, Billingshurst, W Sussex RH14 9PY
Tel: (01403) 782332

ECUMENICAL
European Ecumenical Committee (Chairman) Canon Roger Greenacre, 4 Vicars' Close, Chichester, W Sussex PO19 1PT *Tel:* (01243) 784244
Senior Ecumenical Officer Revd Terry Stratford, Staplefield Vicarage, 14 Ledgers Meadow, Cuckfield, W Sussex RH17 5EW
Tel: (01444) 456588
Archdeaconry Ecumenical Officers (Chichester) Revd Terry Stratford (*as above*)
(*Horsham*) Revd Geoffrey Driver, Vicarage, Cowfold, Horsham RH13 8AH
Tel: (01403) 864296
(*Lewes and Hastings*) Revd Simon Crittall, St Richard's Vicarage, Hailsham Rd, Heathfield TN21 8AF *Tel:* (01435) 862744

LITURGICAL
Liturgy Consultant Revd Ian Forrester, Dioc Church House
Music Consultant Revd Ian Forrester (*as above*)

SOCIAL RESPONSIBILITY
Adviser Canon Michael Butler, Dioc Church House

Association for Family Social Work (Secretary) Mr Neil Morgan, Dioc Church House

PRESS AND PUBLICATIONS
Communications Officer Canon Will Pratt, Dioc Church House *Tel:* (01273) 748756 (Home)
email: media@diochi.org.uk
Editor of Dioc Directory Canon Will Pratt (*as above*)
Editor of 'The Chichester Leaflet' and 'The Chichester Magazine' Canon Will Pratt (*as above*)

DIOCESAN RECORD OFFICES
East Sussex Mr R. Davey, *County Archivist*, The Maltings, Castle Precincts, Lewes, E Sussex BN7 1YT *Tel:* (01273) 482356
West Sussex Mr R. Childs *County Archivist*, County Records Office, County Hall, Chichester, W Sussex PO19 1RN *Tel:* (01243) 533911

RURAL DEANS
ARCHDEACONRY OF CHICHESTER
Arundel and Bognor Revd Robert Harris, Felpham Rectory, 24 Limmer Lane, Bognor Regis PO22 7ET *Tel:* (01243) 842522
Brighton Canon Douglas McKittrick, St Peter's Vicarage, 10 West Drive, Brighton BN2 2GD
Tel: (01273) 682960
Chichester Revd Victor Cassam, Rectory, St Peter's Crescent, Selsey, Chichester PO20 0NA
Tel: (01243) 602363
Hove Canon John Caldicott, Vicarage, Wilbury Ave, Hove, E Sussex BN3 3BP *Tel:* (01273) 733331
Worthing Revd Roger Russell, 63 Manor Rd, Lancing, W Sussex BN15 0EY *Tel:* (01903) 753212

ARCHDEACONRY OF HORSHAM
Cuckfield Revd Nicholas Wetherall, Vicarage, Broad St, Cuckfield, Haywards Heath RH17 5LL
Tel: (01444) 454007
East Grinstead Revd Gordon Bond, Vicarage, Windmill Lane, East Grinstead RH19 2DS
Tel: (01342) 323439
Horsham Canon David Pain, Vicarage, East St, Billingshurst RH14 9PY *Tel:* (01403) 782332
Hurst Revd Ian Prior, Vicarage, 2 Cants Lane, Burgess Hill RH15 0LG *Tel:* (01444) 232023
Midhurst Revd Michael Smith, Lynch Rectory, Fernhurst Rd, Milland, Liphook, Hants GU30 7LU *Tel:* (01428) 741285
Petworth Revd David Pollard, Rectory, Petworth, W Sussex GU28 0DB *Tel:* (01798) 342505
Storrington Revd Dr Paul Rampton, St Andrew's Vicarage, Steyning BN44 7YL *Tel:* (01903) 813256
Westbourne Revd Brian Cook, Vicarage, Chidham, Chichester, W Sussex PO18 8TA
Tel: (01243) 573147

ARCHDEACONRY OF LEWES AND HASTINGS
Battle and Bexhill Revd Dr Edward Bryant,

Rectory, Old Town, Bexhill-on-Sea, E Sussex TN40 2HE　　　　　*Tel:* (01424) 211115

Dallington Revd Roger Porthouse, St Mary's Vicarage, Vicarage Rd, Hailsham BN27 1BL
　　　　　Tel: (01323) 842381

Eastbourne Canon Gordon Rideout, All Saints Vicarage, Grange Rd, Eastbourne, BN21 4HE
　　　　　Tel: (01323) 410033

Hastings Revd Roger Combes, Rectory, St Matthews Rd, St Leonards TN38 0TN
　　　　　Tel: (01424) 423790

Lewes and Seaford Revd Hugh Atherstone, Vicarage, 46 Sutton Rd, Seaford BN25 1SH
　　　　　Tel: (01323) 893508

Rotherfield Revd Andrew Cornes, Vicarage, Chapel Green, Crowborough, E Sussex TN6 1ED
　　　　　Tel: (01892) 667384

Rye Revd Martin Sheppard, Rectory, Gun Garden, Rye, E Sussex TN31 7HH
　　　　　Tel: (01797) 222430

Uckfield Revd Geoffrey Daintree, Vicarage, Framfield, Uckfield, E Sussex TN22 5NH
　　　　　Tel: (01825) 890365

DIOCESE OF COVENTRY

Re-founded in 1918. Coventry; Warwickshire, except for small areas in the north (BIRMINGHAM) and south-west (GLOUCESTER) and one parish in the south (OXFORD); an area of Solihull.

Population 763,000   Area 686 sq m
Stipendiary Clergy 150   Benefices 139
Parishes 196   Churches 241

BISHOP (8th)
Rt Revd Colin James Bennetts, Bishop's House, 23 Davenport Rd, Coventry CV5 6PW [1998]
Tel: 024–7667 2244
Fax: 024–7671 3271
email: bishcov@clara.net
[Colin Coventry]

SUFFRAGAN BISHOP
WARWICK Rt Revd Anthony Martin Priddis, Warwick House, 139 Kenilworth Rd, Coventry CV4 7AP [1996]
Tel: 024–7641 6200
Fax: 024–7641 5254
email: bishwarwick@clara.net

CATHEDRAL CHURCH OF ST MICHAEL
Provost Very Revd John Fitzmaurice Petty, Pelham Lee House, 7 Priory Row, Coventry CV1 5ES [1987]
Tel: 024–7622 7597
Fax: 024–7663 1448
email: provost@coventrycathedral.org
Web: www.coventrycathedral.org
Canons Residentiary
Vice-Provost and Canon Pastor Canon Vivienne Faull, 35 Morningside, Coventry, W Midlands CV5 6PD [1994]
Tel: 024–7667 5446
Precentor Canon Christopher Burch, 35 Asthill Grove, Coventry CV3 6HN [1995]
Tel: 024–7650 5426
Director of International Ministry Canon Andrew White, 22 Radcliffe Rd, Earlsdon, Coventry CV5 6AA [1998]
Tel: 024–7667 5146
Canons Theologian
Canon David Mead (*Lay Canon Theologian*), Hillside House, Wood Norton, Evesham WR11 4TE [1996]
Tel: (01386) 860234
Canon Christopher Lamb PH D, Rectory, Warmington, Banbury OX17 1BT [1992]
Tel: (01295) 690213
Canon Christina Baxter PHD (*Lay Canon Theologian*), St John's College, Bramcote, Nottingham NG9 3DS
Tel: 0115–925 1114
Bursar Mr Charles Leonard, 7 Priory Row, Coventry CV1 5ES
Tel: 024–7622 7597
email: information@coventrycathedral.org
Chapter Clerk Mr John Coles, 23 Bayley Lane, Coventry CV1 5RJ
Tel: 024–7655 3311

Director of Music Mr Rupert Jeffcoat
Tel: 024–7622 7597

ARCHDEACONS
COVENTRY Ven Ian Russell, 9 Armorial Rd, Coventry CV3 6GH [1989] Tel: 024–7641 7750 (Home)
024–7667 4328 (Office)
WARWICK Ven Michael Paget Wilkes, 10 Northumberland Rd, Leamington Spa CV32 6HA [1990]
Tel: (01926) 313337 (Home)
024–7667 4328 (Office)

CONVOCATION (MEMBERS OF THE HOUSE OF CLERGY OF THE GENERAL SYNOD)
The Archdeacon of Coventry
Proctors for Clergy
Canon Mark Bryant
Canon John Moore
Revd Peter Watkins

MEMBERS OF THE HOUSE OF LAITY OF THE GENERAL SYNOD
Mr David Jones
Mrs Margaret Sedgwick
Mr Michael Tyrrell

DIOCESAN OFFICERS
Dioc Secretary Mrs Isobel Chapman, Church House, Palmerston Rd, Coventry CV5 6FJ
Tel: 024–7667 4328
Fax: 024–7669 1760
email: Isobel.Chapman@btinternet.com
Chancellor of Diocese Chanc W. M. Gage, The Royal Courts of Justice, Strand, London WC2 2LL
Registrar of Diocese and Bishop's Legal Secretary Mr David Dumbleton, Rotherham & Co, 8 The Quadrant, Coventry CV1 2EL Tel: 024–76 227331

DIOCESAN ORGANIZATIONS
Diocesan Office Church House, Palmerston Rd, Coventry CV5 6FJ
Tel: 024–7667 4328
Fax: 024–7669 1760

ADMINISTRATION
Dioc Synod (*Chairman, House of Clergy*) Ven Ian Russsell, Dioc Office; (*Chairman, House of Laity*)

Mr Julian Hall, 'Larkfield', Ashlawn Rd, Rugby CV22 5QE *Tel:* (01788) 543588; (*Secretary*) Mr Douglas Little, Church House
Board of Finance (*Chairman*) Mr J. R. Boswell, Peacock Farm, Hollywell, Shrewley CV35 7BJ
Tel: (01926) 842365
(*Secretary*) Mrs Isobel Chapman, Church House
Financial Secretary Mr Malcolm Edge, Church House
Parsonages Committee Mrs Isobel Chapman (*as above*)
Trustees Mr David Dumbleton, Rotherham & Co, 8 The Quadrant, Coventry CV1 2EL
Tel: 024–7622 7331
Pastoral Committee Mrs Isobel Chapman (*as above*)
Designated Officer Mrs Isobel Chapman (*as above*)

CHURCHES

Advisory Committee for the Care of Churches Vacancy

EDUCATION

Schools Canon John Eardley, Bubbenhall Rectory, Coventry CV8 3BD *Tel:* 024–7630 2345
and 024–7667 4328

MINISTRY

Dioc Director of Ordinands and Head of Department Revd Stuart Beake, Vicarage, Church Lane, Shottery, Stratford-upon-Avon CV37 9HQ
Tel: (01789) 293381
Dioc Adviser for Women's Ministry Revd Frances Tyler, Vicarage, 4 Farber Rd, Walsgrave, Coventry CV2 2BG *Tel:* 024–7661 5152
email: RevFTyler@aol.com
Vocations Team Leader Revd Malcolm Tyler, Vicarage, 4 Farber Rd, Walsgrave, Coventry CV2 2BG *Tel:* 024–7661 5152
Continuing Ministerial Education Adviser Revd David Tilley, 6 Church Rd, Baginton, Coventry CV8 3AR *Tel:* 024–7630 2508
Lay Training Adviser Revd Tony Bradley, Vicarage, Budbrooke, Warwick CV35 8QL
Tel: (01926) 494002
Readers (Hon Registrar and Secretary) Mr L. W. T. Sharp, 9 Evenlode Close, Stratford-upon-Avon CV37 7EL *Tel:* (01789) 293019
Ministry Amongst Deaf People Revd Richard Livingston, Wolverton Rectory, Stratford-upon-Avon CV37 0HF *Tel:* (01789) 731278

PRESS AND PUBLICATIONS

Dioc Communications Officer Revd Lawrence Mortimer, Wootton Warren Vicarage, Solihull B95 6BD *Tel:* (01564) 792659
Editor of Dioc Directory and 'Diamond' Revd Lawrence Mortimer (*as above*)

DIOCESAN RECORD OFFICE

Warwickshire County Record Office, Priory Park, Cape Rd, Warwick CV34 4JS *County Archivist* Ms Caroline Sampson *Tel:* (01926) 410410, Ext. 2508

ECUMENICAL AND SOCIAL RESPONSIBILITY

Officer Revd Liz Cowley, Cathedral Offices, 7 Priory Row, Coventry CV1 5ES
Tel: 024–7622 7597

STEWARDSHIP

Dioc Adviser Revd Michael Peatman, St James Vicarage, 171 Abbey Rd, Coventry CV3 4PG
Tel: 024–7630 1617

RURAL DEANS
ARCHDEACONRY OF COVENTRY

Coventry North Revd Barry Keeton, St John's Rectory, 9 Davenport Rd, Coventry CV5 6QA
Tel: 024–7667 3203
Coventry South Revd Charles Knowles, St Mary Magdalen's Vicarage, Craven St, Coventry CV5 8DT *Tel:* 024–7667 5838
Coventry East Canon Mark Bryant, Stoke Rectory, 365A Walsgrave Rd, Coventry CV2 4BG
Tel: 024–7663 5731
Kenilworth Revd George Baisley, Rectory, Meriden Rd, Berkswell, Coventry CV7 7BE
Tel: (01676) 533605
Nuneaton Revd John Philpott, Chilvers Coton Vicarage, Nuneaton CV11 4NJ *Tel:* 024–7638 3010
Rugby Revd Ted Lyons, Vicarage, 43 Bow Fell, Brownsover, Rugby CV21 1JF *Tel:* (01788) 573696

ARCHDEACONRY OF WARWICK

Alcester Revd Steve Burch, Rectory, Great Alne, Alcester B49 6HY *Tel:* (01789) 488344
Fosse Revd Richard Williams, Vicarage, Alveston, Stratford-upon-Avon CV37 7QB
Tel: (01789) 292777
Shipston Revd Gordon Benfield, Ivy Cottage, Butlers Marston, Warwick CV35 0NG
Tel: (01926) 640758
Southam Revd Roy Brown, Rectory, 2 Church Lane, Harbury, Leamington Spa CV33 9HA
Tel: (01926) 612377
Warwick and Leamington Revd Tim Boyns, Vicarage, Vicarage Rd, Lillington, Leamington Spa CV32 7RH *Tel:* (01926) 424674

Founded in 1927. Derbyshire, except for a small area in the north (CHESTER); a small area of Stockport; a few parishes in Staffordshire.

Population 985,000   Area 997 sq m
Stipendiary Clergy 184   Benefices 177
Parishes 252   Churches 330

BISHOP (6th)
Rt Revd Jonathan Sansbury Bailey, Derby Church House, Full St, Derby DE1 3DR [1995]
Home The Bishop's House, 6 King St, Duffield, Derby DE56 4EU
Tel: (01332) 346744 (Office)
(01332) 840132 (Home)
Fax: (01332) 295810 (Office)
(01332) 842743 (Home)
email: bishopderby@clara.net
[Jonathan Derby]

SUFFRAGAN BISHOP
REPTON Rt Revd David Christopher Hawtin, Repton House, Lea, Matlock DE4 5JP [1999]
Tel: (01629) 534644
Fax: (01629) 534003

HONORARY ASSISTANT BISHOPS
Rt Revd Kenneth John Fraser Skelton, 65 Crescent Rd, Sheffield S7 1HN [1984]
Tel: (0114) 255 1260
Rt Revd Robert Beak, Ashcroft Cottage, Butts Rd, Ashover, Chesterfield S45 0AX [1991]
Tel: (01246) 590048

CATHEDRAL CHURCH OF ALL SAINTS
Provost Very Revd Michael Perham, The Provost's House, 9 Highfield Rd, Derby DE22 1GX [1998]
Tel: (01332) 341201 (Office)
Tel and Fax: (01332) 342971 (Home)
Cathedral Office St Michael's House, Queen St, Derby DE1 3DT
Tel: (01332) 341201
Fax: (01332) 203991
email: Derby.cathedral@btinternet.com
Canons Residentiary
Sub-Provost Canon Geoffrey Marshall, 24 Kedleston Rd, Derby DE22 1GU [1993]
Tel: (01332) 343144 (Home)
(01332) 341201 (Office)
Ven Ian Gatford, Derby Church House, Full St, Derby DE1 3DR [1984]
Tel: (01332) 382233 (Office)
Canon Theologian Canon Tony Chesterman, 13 Newbridge Rd, Ambergate, Belper DE56 2GR [1989]
Tel: (01773) 852236 (Home)
(01332) 382233 (Office)

Canon Pastor Canon David Truby, 22 Kedleston Rd, Derby DE22 1GU [1998]
Tel: (01332) 341201 (Office)
NSM Canon Sheana Barby, 2 Margaret St, Derby DE1 3FE
Tel: (01332) 383301
Chapter Clerk Mr Michael Mallender, 35 St Mary's Gate, Derby DE1 3JU
Tel: (01332) 372311
Administrator Mr William Hall, Cathedral Office
Visitors' Officer Mrs Anne Johns, Cathedral Office
Master of Music and Organist Mr Peter Gould, 3 Cathedral View, Littleover, Derby DE22 3HR
Tel: (01332) 366692 (Home)
(01332) 345848 (Office)
Assistant Organist Dr Tom Corfield, 109 Palmerston St, Derby DE23 6PF
Tel: (01332) 762251 (Home)
(01332) 345848 (Office)

ARCHDEACONS
CHESTERFIELD Ven David Garnett, Vicarage, Baslow, Bakewell DE45 1RY [1996]
Tel: (01246) 583928
Fax: (01246) 583949
DERBY Ven Ian Gatford, Derby Church House, Full St, Derby DE1 3DR [1993]
Tel: (01332) 382233 (Office)
Fax: (01332) 292969 (Office)

CONVOCATION (MEMBERS OF THE HOUSE OF CLERGY OF THE GENERAL SYNOD)
The Archdeacon of Derby
Proctors for Clergy
Revd Cedric Blakey
Canon Geoffrey Marshall
Canon Timothy Yates

MEMBERS OF THE HOUSE OF LAITY OF THE GENERAL SYNOD
Mrs Joanna Ingram
Mrs Christine McMullen
Mrs Jennifer Radford
Mr David Wilkinson

DIOCESAN OFFICERS

Dioc Secretary Mr Bob Carey, Derby Church House, Full St, Derby DE1 3DR
Tel: (01332) 382233
Fax: (01332) 292969
Chancellor of Diocese His Honour Judge John Bullimore, Rectory, 14 Grange Drive, Emley, Huddersfield HD8 9SF *Tel:* (01924) 849161
Registrar of Diocese and Bishop's Legal Secretary Mr James Battie, Derby Church House

DIOCESAN ORGANIZATIONS

Diocesan Office Derby Church House, Full St, Derby DE1 3DR *Tel:* (01332) 382233
Fax: (01332) 292969

ADMINISTRATION

Dioc Synod (Chairman, House of Clergy) Canon Tony Chesterman, 13 Newbridge Rd, Ambergate, Belper DE56 2GR *Tel:* (01773) 852236; *(Chairman, House of Laity)* Mr Derek Hall, The North Pole, 3 St Peter's St, Stapenhill, Burton-on-Trent DE15 9AW *Tel:* (01283) 531744; *(Secretary)* Mr Bob Carey, Derby Church House
Board of Finance (Chairman) Mr Richard Powell, Overstones, Gorse Ridge Drive, Baslow, Bakewell DE45 1SL *Tel:* (01246) 583375; *(Secretary)* Mr Bob Carey *(as above)*
Parsonages Board Mr Jim Blackwell, Derby Church House
Dioc Surveyor Mr Ben Roper, Smith & Roper, Buxton Rd, Bakewell DE45 1BZ
Tel: (0162 981) 2722
Pastoral Committee Mr Jim Blackwell *(as above)*
Designated Officer Mr James Battie, Derby Church House

CHURCHES

Advisory Committee for the Care of Churches (Chairman) Canon Raymond Ross; *(Secretary)* Ms Belinda Bramhall, Derby Church House

EDUCATION

Dioc Education Office Derby Church House, Full St, Derby DE1 3DR *Tel:* (01332) 382233
Fax: (01332) 291988
Director Mr David Edwards
Schools Adviser Mr Andrew Burns
Children's Adviser Canon Sheana Barby
Laity Adviser Revd Michael Alexander
Youth Adviser Mr Alistair Langton
Warden, Champion House Revd Adrian Murray-Leslie, Champion House, Edale, Hope Valley S33 7ZA *Tel and Fax:* (01433) 670254

MINISTRY

Director of Ordinands Canon Geoffrey Marshall, 24 Kedleston Rd, Derby DE22 1GU
Tel: (01332) 343144 (Home)
(01332) 341201 (Office)

Bishop's Adviser on Continuing Ministerial Education Canon Tony Chesterman, Derby Church House
Bishop's Officer for NSMs Canon Tony Chesterman *(as above)*
Assistant Director of Ordinands Revd David Ashton, St Andrew's Vicarage, Broom Ave, Swanwick, Alfreton DE55 1DQ
Tel and Fax: (01773) 602684
Adviser in Women's Ministry Revd Lindsay Hughes, 214 Cromford Rd, Langley Mill, Nottingham NG16 4HB *Tel:* (01773) 712441
Readers' Board Mr Norman Stanley, 24 Ella Bank Rd, Marlpool, Heanor DE75 7HF
Tel: (01773) 714821

MISSIONARY AND ECUMENICAL

Council for Mission and Unity (Chairman) The Bishop of Repton
Ecumenical Officers Canon Richard Orchard, Vicarage, Curbar, Hope Valley S32 3YF
Tel: (01433) 630387
Revd John Henson, St John's Vicarage, 7 Onslow Rd, Mickleover, Derby DE3 5JJ *Tel:* (01332) 516545
World Development Officer Revd David Murdoch, St George's Vicarage, Church Lane, New Mills, High Peak SK22 4NP *Tel:* (01663) 743225
Dioc Missioner Vacancy
Interfaith Adviser Revd Basil Scott, 11 Harrington St, Derby DE23 8PE *Tel:* (01332) 772360

PRESS AND COMMUNICATIONS

Office Derby Church House, Derby DE1 3DR
Tel: (01332) 382233
Fax: (01332) 292969
Communications Officer Mr Bryan Harris, Derby Church House *Tel:* (01332) 553394 (Home)
Editor of Dioc News Mr Bryan Harris *(as above)*

DIOCESAN RECORD OFFICE

Derbyshire Record Office, County Offices, Matlock DE4 3AG *County Archivist* Dr Margaret O'Sullivan *Tel:* (01629) 580000, Ext. 7347

SOCIAL RESPONSIBILITY

Dioc Adviser for Social Responsibility Dr Rosemary Power, Derby Church House
Assistant for Social Responsibility Revd Stella Collishaw, Derby Church House
Industrial Mission in Derbyshire (Local Ecumenical Project) Chairman Revd Keith Orford, 27 Lums Hill Rise, Matlock DE4 3FX *Tel:* (01629) 55349

PARISH DEVELOPMENT

Parish Development Adviser Revd Barrie Gauge, Derby Church House

RURAL DEANS

ARCHDEACONRY OF DERBY

Ashbourne Revd Christopher Harrison, Vicarage, Parwich, Ashbourne, Derby DE6 1QD
Tel: (01335) 390226

Derby North Revd Gerry Reilly, St Philip's Vicarage, Taddington Rd, Chaddesden, Derby DE21 4JU
Tel: (01332) 673428

Derby South Revd David Wills, St Augustine's Rectory, 155 Almond St, Derby DE23 6LY
Tel: (01332) 766603

Duffield Revd David Perkins, Christ Church Vic, Bridge St, Belper DE56 1BA
Tel: (01773) 824974

Heanor Revd Lindsay Hughes, Vicarage, 214 Cromford Rd, Langley Mill, Nottingham NG16 4HB
Tel: (01773) 712441

Ilkeston Revd Ian Gooding, Rectory, Stanton-by-Dale, Ilkeston DE7 4QA
Tel: 0115–932 4584

Longford Revd Stewart Rayner, St Helen's Rectory, Rectory Court, Etwall, Derby DE65 6LP
Tel: (01283) 732349

Melbourne Revd Nigel Guthrie, Chellaston Vicarage, Derby DE73 1UT
Tel: (01332) 704835

Repton Revd David Horsfall, Vicarage, Church St, Swadlincote DE11 8LF
Tel: (01283) 217756

ARCHDEACONRY OF CHESTERFIELD

Alfreton Revd David Ashton, Vicarage, Broadway, Swanwick, Alfreton DE55 1DQ
Tel: (01773) 602684

Bakewell and Eyam Revd Edmund Urquhart, Bakewell Vicarage, Bakewell DE45 1FD
Tel: (01629) 812256

Bolsover and Staveley Revd Nigel Johnson, Rectory, Top Rd, Calow, Chesterfield S44 5AF
Tel: (01246) 273486

Buxton Revd James Norton, Rectory, 7 Lismore Park, Buxton SK17 9AU
Tel: (01298) 22151

Chesterfield Revd Tom Johnson, Rectory, Narrowleys Lane, Ashover, Chesterfield S45 0AU
Tel: (01246) 590246

Glossop Revd David Rowley, Vicarage, Church St South, Glossop SK13 7RU
Tel: (01457) 852146

Wirksworth Revd Dr Ian Mitchell, All Saints' Vicarage, Smedley St, Matlock DE4 3JG
Tel: (01629) 582235

DIOCESE OF DURHAM

Founded in 635. Durham, except for an area in the south-west (RIPON AND LEEDS), and two parishes in the north (NEWCASTLE); Gateshead; South Tyneside; Sunderland; Hartlepool; Darlington; Stockton-on-Tees, north of the Tees.

Population 1,484,000   Area 987 sq m
Stipendiary Clergy 237   Benefices 227
Parishes 254   Churches 299

BISHOP (70th)
Rt Revd Anthony Michael Arnold Turnbull, Auckland Castle, Bishop Auckland, Co Durham DL14 7NR [1994]   *Tel:* (01388) 602576
Fax: (01388) 605264
email: bishop.of.durham@durham.anglican.org
[Michael Dunelm:]
Bishop's Senior Chaplain Revd Stephen Conway (*same address*)

SUFFRAGAN BISHOP
JARROW Rt Revd Alan Smithson, The Old Vicarage, Hallgarth, Pittington, Durham DH6 1AB [1990]   *Tel:* 0191–372 0225
Fax: 0191–372 2326
email: bishop.of.jarrow@durham.anglican.org

HONORARY ASSISTANT BISHOP
Rt Revd Stephen Whitefield Sykes, St John's College, Durham [1999]

CATHEDRAL CHURCH OF CHRIST AND BLESSED MARY THE VIRGIN
Dean Very Revd John Robert Arnold, The Deanery, Durham DH1 3EQ [1989]
Tel: 0191–384 7500
Fax: 0191–386 4267
email: John.Arnold@durhamcathedral.co.uk
Canons Residentiary
Canon Prof David Brown, 14 The College, Durham DH1 3EQ [1990]   *Tel:* 0191–386 4657
Ven Trevor Willmott, 15 The College, Durham DH1 3EQ [1997]   *Tel:* 0191–384 7534
Fax: 0191–386 6915
email:
    Archdeacon.of.Durham@durham.anglican.org
Canon Martin Kitchen PH D, 3 The College, Durham DH1 3EQ [1997]   *Tel:* 0191–384 2415
email: martin@3college.sonnet.co.uk
Canon David Whittington, 6A The College, Durham DH1 3EQ [1998]   *Tel:* 0191–384 5489
Fax: 0191–384 7529
email:
    director.of.education@durham.anglican.org
Canon Nigel Stock, 7 The College, Durham DH1 3EQ [1998]   *Tel:* 0191–375 0242
email: nigelstock@dunelm.org.uk

Precentor Revd Michael Hampel, 16A The College, Durham DH1 3EQ
Tel: 0191–384 2481(Home)
0191–386 4266 (Office)
Fax: 0191–386 4267
email: Michael.Hampel@durhamcathedral.co.uk
Minor Canon Revd Margaret Parker, Chapter Office, The College, Durham DH1 3EH
Tel: 0191–386 4266
Chapter Clerk Mr Paul Whittaker (*same address*)
Cathedral Organist Mr James Lancelot, 6 The College, Durham DH1 3EQ   *Tel:* 0191–386 4766

ARCHDEACONS
DURHAM Ven Trevor Willmott, 15 The College, Durham DH1 3EQ [1997]   *Tel:* 0191–384 7534
Fax: 0191–346 6915
email:
    Archdeacon.of.Durham@durham.anglican.org
AUCKLAND Ven Granville Gibson, Elmside, 2 Etherley Lane, Bishop Auckland DL14 7QR [1993]   *Tel:* (01388) 451635
Fax: (01388) 607502
email:
    Archdeacon.of.Auckland@durham.anglican.org
SUNDERLAND Ven Frank White, Greenriggs, Dipe Lane, East Boldon NE36 0PH [1997]
Tel: 0191–536 2300
Fax: 0191–519 3369
email:
Archdeacon.of.Sunderland@durham.anglican.org

CONVOCATION (MEMBERS OF THE HOUSE OF CLERGY OF THE GENERAL SYNOD)
Dignitaries in Convocation
The Dean of Durham
The Archdeacon of Auckland
Proctors in Convocation
Revd Graeme Buttery
Revd Stephen Conway
Revd Penny Martin
Revd Dr Philip Thomas
Ven Frank White

MEMBERS OF THE HOUSE OF LAITY OF THE GENERAL SYNOD
Mrs Janet Atkinson
Dr James Harrison

Mr Derek Jago
Mr Paul Jefferson
Ms Anne Williams
Mrs Ioné Rippeth

DIOCESAN OFFICERS

Dioc Secretary Mr Jonathan Cryer, Dioc Office, Auckland Castle, Market Place, Bishop Auckland, Co Durham DL14 7QJ
Tel: (01388) 604515
Fax: (01388) 603695
email: Diocesan.Secretary@durham.anglican.org
Chancellor of Diocese The Worshipful the Revd Rupert Bursell, Diocesan Registry, 3 The Gate House, Auckland Castle, Bishop Auckland DL14 7NP
Tel: (01388) 450576
Fax: (01388) 604999
Deputy Chancellor His Honour Judge Thomas Coningsby (*same address*)
Registrar of Diocese and Bishop's Legal Secretary Mr A. N. Fairclough (*same address*)
Deputy Registrar Ms H. Monckton-Milnes, Dioc Registry
Dioc Surveyor Mr M. Galley, Dioc Office

DIOCESAN ORGANIZATIONS

Diocesan Office Auckland Castle, Market Place, Bishop Auckland, Co Durham DL14 7QJ
Tel: (01388) 604515
Fax: (01388) 603695
email: Diocesan.Secretary@durham.anglican.org

ADMINISTRATION

Dioc Synod (*Chairman, House of Clergy*) Canon Eric Stephenson, St George's Vicarage, 2 Ashleigh Villas, East Boldon, Tyne and Wear NE36 0LA
Tel: 0191–536 3699
email: Eric.Stephenson@btinternet.com
(*Chairman, House of Laity*) Mr Geoffrey Taylor, 14 Academy Gardens, Gainford, Darlington, Co Durham DL2 3EN
Tel: (01325) 730379
(*Secretary*) Mr Jonathan Cryer, Dioc Office
Board of Finance (*Chairman*) Ven Granville Gibson, Elmside, 2 Etherley Lane, Bishop Auckland DL14 7QR
Tel: (01388) 451635
Fax: (01388) 607502
email: Archdeacon.of.Auckland@durham.anglican.org
(*Secretary*) Mr Jonathan Cryer (*as above*)
Glebe Advisory Committee (*Chairman*) Ven Granville Gibson (*as above*); (*Secretary*) Mr Jonathan Cryer (*as above*)
Parsonages Committee (*Chairman*) Revd Jon Bell, St Cuthbert's Vicarage, 1 Aykley Court, Durham DH1 4NW
Tel: 0191–386 4526
email: jonbell.100522.45@compuserve.com
(*Secretary*) Mr G. W. Heslop, Dioc Office
Pastoral Committee (*Chairman*) Ven Granville Gibson (*as above*); (*Secretary*) Mr G. W. Heslop (*as above*)

Church Buildings Committee (*Chairman*) Ven Granville Gibson (*as above*); (*Secretary*) Mr Jonathan Cryer (*as above*)
Redundant Churches Uses Committee (*Chairman*) Ven Granville Gibson (*as above*); (*Secretary*) Mr Jonathan Cryer (*as above*)
Designated Officer Mr A. N. Fairclough, Dioc Registry (*as above*)
Tel: (01388) 450576

CHURCHES

Advisory Committee for the Care of Churches (*Chairman*) Mr Geoffrey Thrush, 9 Brierville, Durham DH1 4QE *Tel:* 0191–386 1958; (*Secretary*) Mr I. A. Richardson, Dioc Office
Tel: (01388) 450577

EDUCATION

Director of Education Canon David Whittington, Carter House, Pelaw Leazes Lane, Durham DH1 1TB
Tel: 0191–384 3692
email: director.of.education@durham.anglican.org
RE Adviser Revd Valerie Shedden (*same address*)
Children's Adviser Revd Paul Allinson (*same address*)
Youth Officer Mr Nicholas Rowark (*same address*)
Adult Education Officer Revd Colin Patterson (*same address*)

MINISTRY

Board for Ministries and Training (*Chairman*) The Bishop of Durham (*as above*); (*Secretary*) Canon Adrian Dorber, Rectory, Brancepeth, Durham DH7 8EH
Tel: 0191–378 0503
email: Adrian.Dorber@durham.anglican.org
Bishop's Adviser for Continuing Ministerial Education Revd Dr Nick Chamberlain, Rectory, Burnmoor, Houghton-le-Spring DH4 6EX
Tel: 0191–385 2695
email: Nick.Chamberlain@durham.anglican.org
Director of Post-Ordination Training Revd Dr Nick Chamberlain (*as above*)
Director of Ordinands Revd Alison White, Greenriggs, Dipe Lane, East Boldon NE36 0PH
Tel: 0191–536 2300
Fax: 0191–519 3369
email: Alison.White@durham.anglican.org
Woman Adviser in Ministry Canon Penny Jones, Rectory, Stanhope, Bishop Auckland DL13 2UE
Tel: (01388) 528308
email: Penny.Jones@durham.anglican.org
Pensions Officers Mr W. Hurworth, 34 Castlereagh, Wynard Park, Wynard, Billingham TS22 5QF
Tel: (01740) 644274
Revd Peter Welby, 21 York Villas, Tudhoe, Spennymoor DL16 6LP
Tel: (01388) 818418
Readers' Board (*Warden*) Canon Alex Whitehead, St Peter's Vicarage, 77 Yarm Rd, Stockton-on-Tees TS18 3PJ
Tel: (01642) 676625

(Registrar) Mr Philip Smithson, 2 Sea View Gardens, Roker, Sunderland SR6 9PN
Tel: 0191–548 6827

LITURGICAL

Chairman Canon Nigel Stock, 7 The College, Durham DH1 3EQ   *Tel:* 0191–375 0242
email: nigelstock@dunelm.org.uk
Secretary Revd Dr Gareth Lloyd, 6 Ruskin Rd, Birtley, Chester-le-Street DH3 1AD
Tel: 0191–410 2115
email: Gareth@dunelm.org.uk

MISSION AND UNITY

Co-Chairmen Mr A. J. Piper, 11 Briardene, Durham DH1 4UQ *Tel:* 0191–384 4040; Ven Trevor Willmott (*as above*)
Secretary Vacancy

ECUMENICAL

Ecumenical Officer Revd Sam Randall, Vicarage, Holmside Lane, Burnhope, Durham DH7 0DP
Tel: (01207) 529274
email: Sam.Randall@durham.anglican.org

PRESS AND PUBLICATIONS

Press and Communications Officer Revd Stephen Conway, Auckland Castle, Bishop Auckland DL14 7NR   *Tel:* (01388) 602576
Fax: (01388) 605264
email: Stephen.Conway@durham.anglican.org
Editor of Dioc Yearbook Mr Jonathan Cryer (*as above*)
Editor of Dioc News Revd Paul Judson, Vicarage, St Mark's Terrace, Millfield, Sunderland SR4 7BN   *Tel and Fax:* 0191–514 7872
email:
Communications.Officer@durham.anglican.org
Chaplain for Information Technology Revd Stoker Wilson, 76 Merrybent Village, Darlington DL2 2LE   *Tel:* (01325) 374510
email: IT.Adviser@durham.anglican.org

DIOCESAN RECORD OFFICE

Durham County Record Office, County Hall, Durham DH1 5UL *County Archivist* Miss J. Gill
Tel: 0191–386 4411, Ext 474

SOCIAL RESPONSIBILITY

Acting Chairman Ven Frank White, Greenriggs, Dipe Lane, East Boldon NE36 0PH
Tel: 0191–536 2300
Fax: 0191–519 3369
email:
Archdeacon.of.Sunderland@durham.anglican.org
Secretary Vacancy
BSR Development Officer Revd Caroline Dick, Vicarage, 182 Sunderland Rd, South Shields NE34 6AH   Tel: 0191–427 5538
email:
BSR.Development.Officer@durham.anglican.org

Family Welfare Council (*Chairman*) Canon Stuart Bain, St Paul's Vicarage, Horswell Gardens, Spennymoor DL16 7AA   *Tel:* (01388) 814522
Fax: (01388) 817729
(*Director*) Mrs Sue Rayner, Agriculture House, Stonebridge, Durham DH1 3RY
Tel: 0191–386 3719
Northumbrian Industrial Mission (*Chairman*) Mr J. G. Smith, The Durdans, Fellside Rd, Whickham, Newcastle-upon-Tyne NE16 4LA Tel: 0191–488 1631; (*Secretary*) Mrs C. Paul, East Thorn Farm, Kirkley, Ponteland, Newcastle-upon-Tyne NE20 0AG   *Tel:* (01661) 25950
Teesside Industrial Mission (*Chairman*) Mr J. Wills, 14 Kirk St, Stillington, Stockton-on-Tees TS21 1JR *Tel:* (01740) 630473; (*Secretary*) Mr K. Brookfield, 38 St Leonard's Rd, Guisborough TS14 8BV
Tel: (01287) 632404
Arts and Recreation Chaplaincy: (*Chairman*) Mr K. Bates, 96 Junction Rd, Norton, Stockton-on-Tees TS20 1PT *Tel:* (01642) 553794; (*Secretary*) Revd Robert Cooper, Rectory, Sadberge, Darlington, Co Durham DL2 1RP   *Tel:* (01325) 333771

STEWARDSHIP

Stewardship Development Officer Mr J. E. Roberts, Dioc Office   *Tel:* (01388) 604823
Fax: (01388) 603695

AREA DEANS
ARCHDEACONRY OF SUNDERLAND

Chester-le-Street Revd Kevin Dunne, 37 Brancepeth Rd, Oxclose, Washington NE38 0LA
Tel: 0191–416 2561
Fax: 0191–419 3182
email: revdunne@aol.com
Gateshead Revd Christopher Atkinson, Rectory, 56 Rectory Rd, Gateshead NE8 1XL
Tel: 0191–477 8522
Gateshead West Canon Hazel Ditchburn, Rectory, Shibdon Rd, Blaydon on Tyne NE21 5AE
Tel and Fax: 0191–414 2750
Houghton-le-Spring Revd Michael Beck, Rectory, Houghton Rd, Hetton-le-Hole, Houghton-le-Spring DH5 9PH   *Tel:* 0191–517 2488
Fax: 0191–526 5173
Jarrow Canon Eric Stephenson, St George's Vicarage, 2 Ashleigh Villas, East Boldon NE36 0LA   *Tel:* 0191–536 3699
Fax: 0191–536 6289
email: Eric.Stephenson@btinternet.com
Wearmouth (Acting) Revd Nigel Warner, St Nicholas' Vicarage, Queen Alexandra Rd, Sunderland SR3 1XQ   *Tel:* 0191–522 6444

ARCHDEACONRY OF DURHAM

Durham Revd Jon Bell, Vicarage, St Cuthbert's Vicarage, 1 Aykley Court, Durham DH1 4NW
Tel and Fax: 0191–386 4526
email: jonbell.100522.45@compuserve.com

Easington Revd Neville Vine, Rectory, 5 Tudor Grange, Eastington, Peterlee SR8 3DF
Tel and *Fax:* 0191–527 0287
email: neville.p.vine@lineone.net
Hartlepool Revd David Couling, Greatham Hall, Greatham, Hartlepool TS25 2HS
Tel: (01429) 871148
Lanchester Revd Peter Waterhouse, Lanchester Vicarage, 1 Lee Hill Court, Lanchester, Co Durham DH7 0QE
Tel: (01207) 521170
Sedgefield (Acting) Revd Colin Jay, 20 Haslewood Rd, Newton Aycliffe DL5 4XF
Tel: (01325) 320112

ARCHDEACONRY OF AUCKLAND
Auckland Canon Stuart Bain, St Paul's Vicarage, Horswell Gardens, Spennymoor, Co Durham DH16 7AA
Tel: (01388) 814522
Fax: (01388) 817729
email: Stuart.Bain@durham.anglican.org
Barnard Castle Canon Timothy Ollier, Gainford Vicarage, Gainford, Darlington DL2 3DS
Tel: (01325) 730261
Fax: (01325) 732078
email: timollier@onyxnet.co.uk
Darlington Revd Dr Philip Thomas, Vicarage, Heighington, Darlington, Co Durham DL5 6PP
Tel and *Fax:* (01325) 312134
email: Philip.Thomas@durham.anglican.org
Stanhope (Acting) Revd Stewart Irwin, Vicarage, Hunwick, Crook DL15 0JU
Tel: (01388) 604456
Stockton Canon Richard Smith, St Cuthbert's Vicarage, Church Rd, Billingham TS23 1BW
Tel: (01642) 553236

DIOCESE OF ELY

Founded in 1109. Cambridgeshire, except for an area in the north-west (PETERBOROUGH) and three parishes in the south (CHELMSFORD); the western quarter of Norfolk; a few parishes in Essex; one parish in Bedfordshire.

Population 635,000   Area 1,507 sq m
Stipendiary Clergy 163   Benefices 240
Parishes 311   Churches 342

BISHOP (68th)
Vacancy, The Bishop's House, Ely, Cambs. CB7 4DW
Tel: (01353) 662749
Fax: (01353) 669477
email: bishop@ely.anglican.org

SUFFRAGAN BISHOP
HUNTINGDON Rt Revd John Robert Flack, 14 Lynn Rd, Ely, Cambs. CB6 1DA [1997]
Tel: (01353) 662137
Fax: (01353) 669357
email: suffragan@ely.anglican.org

CATHEDRAL CHURCH OF THE HOLY AND UNDIVIDED TRINITY
Dean Very Revd Michael Higgins, The Deanery, The College, Ely, Cambs. CB7 4DN [1991]
Tel: (01353) 667735
Fax: (01353) 665658

Canons Residentiary
Canon John Inge, Powchers Hall, The College, Ely, Cambs. CB7 4DL   *Tel:* (01353) 663662
Precentor and Sacrist Revd Peter Moger, The Precentor's House, The College, Ely, Cambs. CB7 4JU [1995]   *Tel:* (01353) 662526
Cathedral Chaplain Vacancy
Chapter Clerk Mrs Constance Heald, Chapter House, The College, Ely, Cambs. CB7 4DN
Tel: (01353) 667735
Organist Mr Paul Trepte, The Old Sacristy, The College, Ely, Cambs. CB7 4DS

ARCHDEACONS
ELY Ven Jeffrey Watson, 1a Summerfield, Cambridge CB3 9HE [1993]   *Tel:* (01223) 515725
Fax: (01223) 571322
email: archdeacon.ely@ely.anglican.org
HUNTINGDON Ven John Stuart Beer, Rectory, Hemingford Abbots, Huntingdon, Cambs. PE18 9AN [1997]   *Tel:* (01480) 469856
Fax: (01480) 496073
email: archdeacon.huntingdon@ely.anglican.org

WISBECH Ven James (Jim) Rone, Archdeacon's House, 24 Cromwell Rd, Ely, Cambs. CB6 1AS [1995]   *Tel:* (01353) 662909
Fax: (01353) 662056
email: archdeacon.wisbech@ely.anglican.org

CONVOCATION (MEMBERS OF THE HOUSE OF CLERGY OF THE GENERAL SYNOD)
Dignitaries in Convocation
The Dean of Ely
The Archdeacon of Wisbech
Proctors for Clergy
Canon Christine Farrington
Canon Fred Kilner
Revd Jonathan Young

MEMBERS OF THE HOUSE OF LAITY OF THE GENERAL SYNOD
Mrs Penny Granger
Mr William Sanders
Mr Stephen Tooke
Mrs Ruth Whitworth

DIOCESAN OFFICERS
Dioc Secretary Dr Matthew Lavis, Bishop Woodford House, Barton Rd, Ely, Cambs. CB7 4DX   *Tel:* (01353) 663579
(01353) 652702 (Direct Line)
Fax: (01353) 652700
Chancellor of Diocese The Hon Mr Justice William Gage, The Royal Courts of Justice, The Strand, London WC2 2LL
Registrar of Diocese Mr Bill Godfrey, 18 The Broadway, St Ives, Huntingdon PE17 4BS
Tel: (01480) 464600
Joint Registrar (Legal Secretary) Mr Peter Beesley, 1 The Sanctuary, London SW1P 3JT
Tel: 020–7222 5381
Deputy Registrar Mr B. Halls, 18 The Broadway, St Ives, Huntingdon PE17 4BS *Tel:* (01480) 464600

DIOCESAN ORGANIZATIONS
Diocesan Office Bishop Woodford House, Barton Rd, Ely, Cambs. CB7 4DX   *Tel:* (01353) 652701
Fax: (01353) 652700
email: d.secretary@office.ely.anglican.org

ADMINISTRATION

Dioc Synod (Chairman, House of Clergy) Canon Michael Wadsworth D PHIL, Vicarage, 12 Church St, Great Shelford CB2 5EL *Tel:* (01223) 843274; *(Chairman, House of Laity)* Mr Stephen Tooke, Rectory, Church Rd, Christchurch, Wisbech PE14 9PQ *Tel:* (01354) 638379; *(Secretary)* Dr Matthew Lavis, Dioc Office
Finance Committee (Chairman) Mr Hugh Duberly; *(Secretary)* Dr Matthew Lavis *(as above)*
Dioc Accountant Mr Philip Wade, Dioc Office
Dioc Surveyor Vacancy, Dioc Office
Asst Secretary (Pastoral) Miss Jane Logan, Dioc Office
Board of Patronage (Secretary) Mr William Sanders, Dioc Office
Designated Officer Dr Matthew Lavis *(as above)*

CHURCHES

Advisory Committee for the Care of Churches (Secretary) Vacancy
Council of Church Music (Secretary) Mr B. E. Eaden, 64 Green End Rd, Cambridge CB4 1RY
Tel: (01223) 424363

EDUCATION

Dioc Board of Education (Secretary) Canon Tim Elbourne, Dioc Office
Director of Education Canon Tim Elbourne *(as above)*
Children's Council (RE Adviser) Mrs Gill Ambrose, Dioc Office
Dioc Youth Council (Youth Officer) Revd Anthony Chandler, Dioc Office
Adult Education Council (Adult Education and Training Officer) Revd David Cockerell, Dioc Office
RE Adviser (Schools) Dr Shirley Hall, Dioc Office

MINISTRY

Co-Director of Ordinands and Warden of Post-Ordination Training Ven John Beer, Rectory, Hemingford Abbots, Huntingdon, Cambs. PE18 9AN
Tel: (01480) 469856
Fax: (01480) 496073
Director of Women's Ministry and Co-Director of Ordinands Canon Christine Farrington, St Mark's Vicarage, Barton Rd, Cambridge CB3 9JZ
Tel: (01233) 363339
Continuing Ministerial Education Canon Tim Elbourne *(as above)*
Readers' Board (Hon Sec) Mrs Julia Jones, 39 Westlands, Comberton, Cambs. CB3 7EH
Tel: (01223) 262251
Warden The Bishop of Huntingdon

LITURGICAL

Secretary Revd Jonathan Young, Ascension Rectory, 95 Richmond Rd, Cambridge CB4 3PS
Tel: (01223) 61919

MISSIONARY AND ECUMENICAL

Council of Mission and Unity (Secretary) Mr William Sanders, Dioc Office
Ecumenical Officer Canon Frank Fisher, Stapleford Vicarage, Stapleford, Cambridge CB2 5BG
Tel: (01223) 842150

PRESS AND PUBLICATIONS

Press and Communications Officer Vacancy
Editor, 'Ely Ensign' Mr S. Levitt, 15 The Elms, Milton, Cambridge
Editor of Dioc Directory Dr Matthew Lavis, Dioc Office

DIOCESAN RECORD OFFICES

Dioc Archivist P. M. Meadows, c/o University Library
Cambridge Record Office, Shire Hall, Castle Hill, Cambridge CB3 0AP, *Archivist* Mrs Elizabeth Stazicker *Tel:* (01223) 317281 *(For parishes in the Archdeaconry of Ely)*
Cambridgeshire Record Office, Grammar School Walk, Huntingdon PE18 6LF *Tel:* (01480) 52181 *(For parishes in the Archdeaconry of Huntingdon)*
Cambridge Record Office, Shire Hall, Cambridge *(see above) (For parishes in the Deaneries of Ely and March)*
Norfolk Record Office, Central Library, Norwich NR2 1NJ *City and County Archivist* Dr John Alban *Tel:* (01603) 22233 *(For parishes in the Deaneries of Feltwell and Fincham)*
Wisbech and Fenland Museum, Museum Square, Wisbech PE13 1ES, *Tel:* (01945) 3817 *(For parishes in the deaneries of Wisbech and Lynn Marshland)*

DIOCESAN RESOURCE CENTRE

Contact Mrs Sally White and Mrs Annette Norman, Dioc Resource Centre, Dioc Office

SOCIAL RESPONSIBILITY

Board for Social Responsibility (Chairman) Canon Hugh Searle, Vicarage, Barton, Cambridge CB3 7BG
Tel: (01223) 262218
(Secretary) Dr Hilary Lavis, Dioc Office
Tel: (01353) 652720
Committee for Family and Social Welfare (Chairman) Revd Allan Viller, Vicarage, 30 Church Lane, Littleport, Cambs CB6 3TB *Tel:* (01353) 860207
Cambridgeshire Deaf Association (Ely Dioc Association for the Deaf) (Chairman) Dr G. Cumming, 8 Romsey Terrace, Cambridge
Mothers' Union (President) Mrs Della Fletcher, 12 Redhill Close, Great Shelford, Cambridge CB2 5JP
Tel: (01223) 841783

STEWARDSHIP

Stewardship Adviser Mr Rodger Sansom, Dioc Office

RURAL DEANS
ARCHDEACONRY OF ELY

Bourn Revd Jeremy Pemberton, Rectory, 2 Short St, Bourn, Cambridge CB3 7SG
Tel: (01924) 719728
Cambridge Canon Michael Diamond, St Andrew the Less Vicarage, Parsonage St, Cambridge CB5 8DN *Tel:* (01223) 353794
Fordham Revd Mark Haworth, Vicarage, Green Head Rd, Swaffham Prior, Cambridge CB5 0JT
Tel: (01638) 741409
Linton Vacancy
North Stowe Revd Hugh McCurdy, Vicarage, Church St, Histon, Cambridge CB4 4EP
Tel: (01223) 232255
email: hugh.mccurdy@dial.pipex.com
Quy Revd Brian Kerley, Rectory, Apthorpe Street, Fulbourn, Cambridge CB1 5EY
Tel: (01223) 880337
Shelford Canon Frank Fisher, Vicarage, Mingle Lane, Stapleford, Cambridge CB2 5BG
Tel: (01223) 842150
Shingay Revd Shamus Williams, Vicarage, Church St, Guilden Morden, Royston, Herts. SG8 0JP *Tel:* (01763) 853067

ARCHDEACONRY OF HUNTINGDON

Huntingdon Revd Walter King, Rectory, 1 The Walks East, Huntingdon PE18 6AP
Tel: (01480) 412674

Leightonstone Canon John Hindley, Tilbrook Rectory, Church Lane, Tilbrook, Huntingdon PE18 0JS *Tel:* (01480) 860147
St Ives Revd Stephen Leeke, Rectory, 15 Church Rd, Warboys, Huntingdon PE17 2RJ
Tel: (01487) 822237
St Neots Canon Bruce Curry, Vicarage, Everton, Sandy, Beds. SG19 3JY *Tel:* (01767) 691827
Yaxley Canon Michael Soulsby, Holy Trinity Rectory, The Village, Orton Longueville, Peterborough, Cambs. PE2 7DN
Tel: (01733) 371071

ARCHDEACONRY OF WISBECH

Ely Revd Allan Viller, Vicarage, 30 Church Lane, Littleport, Ely, Cambs. CB6 1PS
Tel: (01353) 860207
email: allan@agfv.demon.co.uk
Feltwell Revd David Kightley, Rectory, 7 Oak St, Feltwell, Thetford, Norfolk IP26 4DD
Tel: (01842) 828104
Fincham Revd David Kightley (*as above*)
Lynn Marshland Revd Tony Treen, Rectory, Walpole St Peter, Wisbech, Cambs. PE14 7NX
Tel: (01945) 780252
March Revd Peter Baxandall, St Wendreda's Rectory, 21 Wimblington Rd, March, Cambs. PE15 9QW *Tel:* (01354) 53377
Wisbech Revd Robert Bull, St Augustine's Vicarage, Lynn Rd, Wisbech, Cambs. PE13 3DL
Tel: (01945) 583724

Founded 1980 by union of the Diocese of Gibraltar (founded 1842) and the (Fulham) Jurisdiction of North and Central Europe. Area, Europe, except Great Britain and Ireland; Morocco; Turkey; the Asian countries of the former Soviet Union.

Clergy 128   Congregations 259

BISHOP OF GIBRALTAR IN EUROPE (2nd)
Rt Revd John William Hind, Bishop's Lodge, Church Rd, Worth, Crawley, W Sussex RH10 7RT [1993]   *Tel:* (01293) 883051
                                            Fax: (01293) 884479
email: bishop@eurobish.clara.co.uk
Bishop's Chaplain and Research Assistant Revd Jonathan Goodall (*same address*)
Bishop's Personal Assistant Mrs Lisa Elbourne

SUFFRAGAN BISHOP
IN EUROPE Rt Revd Henry Scriven, 14 Tufton St, London SW1P 3QZ [1995]   *Tel:* 020–7976 8001
                                    Fax: 020–7976 8002
                email: henry@dioeurope.clara.net

HONORARY ASSISTANT BISHOPS
Rt Revd Daniel de Pina Cabral, Rua Henrique Lopes de Mendonca, 253–4 Dto Hab 42, 4100 Oporto, Portugal [1976]   *Tel:* 00 351–2 617 77 72
Rt Revd Patrick Harris, Meadow Cottage, 17 Dykes End, Collingham, Newark, Notts. NG23 7LD [1999]   *Tel:* (01636) 892395
Rt Revd Eric Devenport, 32 Bishopsgate, Norwich NR1 4AA   *Tel:* (01603) 664121
Rt Revd Carlos López-Lozano, c/o Iere, Calle de Beneficencia 18, 28004 Madrid, Spain [1995]
                        Tel: 00 34–91 445 25 60
                        Fax: 00 34–91 594 45 72
Rt Revd Michael Manktelow, 2 The Chantry, Canon Lane, Chichester, W Sussex PO19 1PZ [1994]   *Tel:* (01243) 531096
Rt Revd Alan Rogers, 20 River Way, Twickenham TW2 5JP [1996]   *Tel:* 020–8894 2031
Rt Revd Jeffery Rowthorn, American Cathedral, 23 Ave George V, 75008 Paris, France [1994]
            Tel: 00 33–1 47 20 17 92 (Cathedral)
                00 33–1 47 20 02 23 (Direct)
            Fax: 00 33–1 47 23 95 30 (Cathedral)
                00 33–1 40 27 03 53 (Direct)
Rt Revd Arturo Sanchez, Calle de Beneficencia 18, 28004 Madrid, Spain [1995]
                    Tel: 00 34–1 445 25 60
Rt Revd Frank Sargeant, 32 Brotherton Drive, Trinity Gardens, Salford M3 6BH [1999]
                        Tel: 0161–839 7045

Rt Revd Fernando Soares, Rue Elias Garcia 107–1 Dto, 4400 Vila Nova de Gaia, Portugal [1995]
                        Tel: 00 351–2 304646
Rt Revd John Taylor, 22 Conduit Head Rd, Cambridge CB3 0EY [1998]   *Tel:* (01223) 313783
Rt Revd Ambrose Weekes, All Saints' Vicarage, 7 Margaret St, London W1N 8JQ [1988]
                        Tel: 020–7580 6467

CATHEDRAL CHURCH OF THE HOLY TRINITY, GIBRALTAR
Dean Very Revd Gordon Reid, The Deanery, Bomb House Lane, Gibraltar [1998]
            Tel: 00 350 78377 (Home)
                00 350 75745 (Office)
                Fax: 00 350 78463
        email: anglicangib@gibnynex.gi

PRO-CATHEDRAL OF ST PAUL, VALLETTA, MALTA
Chancellor Canon Alan Woods, Chancellor's Lodge, St Paul's Anglican Pro-Cathedral, Independence Square, Valletta VLT12, Malta [1996]   *Tel* and *Fax:* 00 356–22 57 14
            email: woods@dream.vol.net.mt

PRO-CATHEDRAL OF THE HOLY TRINITY, BRUSSELS, BELGIUM
Chancellor Canon Nigel Walker, Pro-Cathedral of the Holy Trinity, 29 rue Capitaine Crespel, 1050 Brussels [1993]   *Tel:* 00 32–2 511 71 83 (Office)
                    Fax: 00 32–2 511 10 28
        email: holy.trinity@arcadis.be

ARCHDEACONS
THE EASTERN ARCHDEACONRY Ven Jeremy Peake, Thugutstrasse 2/12, 1020 Vienna 2, Austria [1995]   *Tel* and *Fax:* 00 43–1 7 20 79 73 (Home)
                00 43–1 7 14 8900 (Office)
        email: office@christchurchvienna.org
NORTH WEST EUROPE Ven Geoffrey Allen, Ijsselsingel 86, 6991 ZT Rheden, Netherlands [1993]
                    Tel: 00 31–26 4953800
                    Fax: 00 31–26 4954922
        email: info@avadia.demon.nl
FRANCE Ven Martin Draper, 7 rue Auguste-Vacquerie, 75116 Paris, France [1994]
                    Tel: 00 33–1 47 20 22 51
                    Fax: 00 33–1 49 52 03 23

GIBRALTAR Ven Kenneth Robinson, Rua João de Deus, Lote 5, Alcoitão, 2645–128 Alcabideche, Portugal [1994]   *Tel* and *Fax:* 00 351–1 4692303
ITALY AND MALTA Ven William Edebohls, c/o All Saints' Church, Via Solferino 17, 20121 Milan, Italy [1998]   *Tel* and *Fax:* 00 39–02 655 2258
email: allsaint@tln.it
SCANDINAVIA AND GERMANY Ven David Ratcliff, Styrmansgatan 1, S-114 54, Stockholm, Sweden [1996]   *Tel:* 00 46–8 663 8248
Fax: 00 46–8 663 8911
email: anglican.church@telia.com
SWITZERLAND Ven Peter Hawker, Promenadengasse 9, 8001 Zurich, Switzerland [1986]
Tel and *Fax:* 00 41–1 252 60 24 (Office)
Tel: 00 41–1 261 22 41 (Home)
email: zurich@anglican.ch (Office)

CONVOCATION (MEMBERS OF THE HOUSE OF CLERGY OF THE GENERAL SYNOD)
Canon Chad Coussmaker
Revd Howell Sasser

MEMBERS OF THE HOUSE OF LAITY OF THE GENERAL SYNOD
Mrs Marion Jägers
Mrs Diana Webster

DIOCESAN OFFICERS
Dioc Secretary Mr Adrian Mumford, Dioc Office
Assistant Dioc Secretary Mrs Jeanne French, Dioc Office
Chancellor of Diocese Sir David Calcutt, c/o The Chambers of Alan Rawley QC, 35 Essex St, Temple, London WC2R 3AR   *Tel:* 020–7353 6381
Registrar of Diocese and Bishop's Legal Secretary Mr John Underwood, Vestry House, Laurence Pountney Hill, London EC4R 0EH
Tel: 020–7626 9236
Fax: 020–7623 6870
email: john.underwood@prpcon.demon.co.uk

DIOCESAN ORGANIZATIONS
Diocesan Office 14 Tufton St, London SW1P 3QZ
Tel: 020–7976 8001
Fax: 020–7976 8002
email: dioeurope@clara.net
Web: http://www.europe.anglican.org

ADMINISTRATION
Dioc Synod (Clerical Vice-President) Ven Ken Robinson, Rua João Deus Lote 5, Alcoitao, 2645–128 Alcabideche, Portugal *Tel* and *Fax:* 00 351–1 4692303; *(Lay Vice-President)* Mrs Maryon Jägers, Hoefbladhof 61, Post Bus 37, 3990 DA Houten, The Netherlands   *Tel:* 00 31–30 637 17 80
Fax: 00 31–30 635 10 34
(Secretary) Mr Adrian Mumford, Dioc Office

Board of Finance (Chairman) Mr Bernard Day, c/o Dioc Office
(Secretary) Mr Adrian Mumford, Dioc Office

CHURCHES
Faculty Committee (Secretary) Mr Adrian Mumford *(as above)*

MINISTRY AND TRAINING
Director of Ordinands and Warden of Readers The Suffragan Bishop, Dioc Office
Director of Training Revd Ambrose Mason, Dioc Office

LITURGY
Enquiries to the Bishop's Chaplain

MEDITERRANEAN MISSIONS TO SEAMEN
Administrator Mr Adrian Mumford *(as above)*

PRESS AND PUBLICATIONS
Press and Communications Officer Revd Rob Marshall, Dioc Office   *Tel:* 020–7584 6622
Fax: 020–7584 1960
077 85767594 (Mobile)
email: 33rpm@hotmail.com
Editor of the 'European Anglican' Revd Rob Marshall *(as above)*

DIOCESAN RECORD OFFICE
The Guildhall Library, Aldermanbury, London EC2P 2EJ   *Tel:* 020–7606 3030

ARCHBISHOP'S APOKRISARIOI AND REPRESENTATIVES
To the Holy See Vacancy, Centro Anglicano, Palazzo Dorio, Via del Corso 303, 00186 Rome, Italy   *Tel:* 00 39–06 678 0302
To the Oecumenical Patriarch Canon Ian Sherwood, British Consulate General, Tepebasi, Istanbul, c/o The Foreign and Commonwealth Office, King Charles St, London SW1A 2AH (For correspondence) *Tel* and *Fax:* 00 90–212 251 56 16
email: isherwood@turk.net
To the Patriarch of Moscow and All Russia Vacancy, British Embassy Moscow, c/o The Foreign and Commonwealth Office, King Charles St, London SW1A 2AH (For correspondence)
Tel and *Fax:* 00 7–095 229 0990
To the Catholicos-Patriarch of All Georgia Revd Phillip Storr Venter, British Embassy Yerevan, c/o The Foreign and Commonwealth Office, King Charles St, London SW1A 2AH
Tel and *Fax:* 00 37432–52 71 27
email: ArchiesDen@compuserve.com *or* ArchiesDen@hotmail.com
To the Supreme Patriarch of All Armenians Revd Phillip Storr Venter *(as above)*

To the Patriarch of Romania Revd Steve Hughes, British Embassy Bucharest, c/o The Foreign and Commonwealth Office, King Charles St, London SW1A 2AH (For correspondence)
Tel: 00 40–1 211 2550
email: steve&mandy@dnt.ro
To the Patriarch of Bulgaria Revd Steve Hughes (*as above*)
To the Patriarch of Serbia Revd Steve Hughes (*as above*)
To the Archbishop of Greece Vacancy
To the European Institutions Revd James Barnett, 16 rue Riehl, F-67100 Strasbourg-Neuhof, France
Tel: 00 33–88 40 36 15
Fax: 00 33–3 88 39 07 58
email: Anglican.Strasbourg@wanadoo.fr *or* James.Barnett@wanadoo.fr

DEANERIES

The Archdeaconry of Scandinavia and Germany has Deanery Synods rather than a single Archdeaconry Synod. The names and addresses of the officers are available from the Diocesan Office.

DIOCESE OF EXETER

Tranferred to Exeter in 1050, formerly at Crediton in 909. Devon, except for one parish in the south-east (SALISBURY) and one parish in the west (TRURO); Plymouth; Torbay.

Population 1,063,000   Area 2,575 sq m
Stipendiary Clergy 259   Benefices 236
Parishes 504   Churches 620

BISHOP (70th)
Rt Revd Michael Laurence Langrish, The Palace, Exeter EX1 1HY [2000]   *Tel:* (01392) 272362
Fax: (01392) 430923

[Michael Exon:]

SUFFRAGAN BISHOPS
CREDITON Rt Revd Richard Stephen Hawkins, 10 The Close, Exeter EX1 1EZ [1996]
Tel: (01392) 273509
Fax: (01392) 431266
PLYMOUTH Rt Revd John Garton, 31 Riverside Walk, Tamerton Foliot, Plymouth PL5 4AQ [1996]
Tel: (01752) 769836
Fax: (01752) 769818
Rt Revd John Richardson, Penberth, Stoney Rd, Lewdown, Okehampton EX20 3DQ [1994]
Tel: (01566) 783144

HONORARY ASSISTANT BISHOPS
Rt Revd Richard Fox Cartwright, 5 Old Vicarage Close, Ide, Exeter EX2 9RT [1988]
Tel: (01392) 211270
Rt Revd Ivor Colin Docker, Braemar, Bradley Rd, Bovey Tracey, Newton Abbot TQ13 9EU [1991]
Tel: (01626) 832468

CATHEDRAL CHURCH OF ST PETER
Dean Very Revd Keith Brynmor Jones, The Deanery, Exeter EX1 1HT [1996]
Tel: (01392) 252891 (Office)
(01392) 272697 (Home)
Fax: (01392) 433598
email: dean@exeter-cathedral.org.uk
Cathedral Office 1 The Cloisters, Exeter EX1 1HS
Tel: (01392) 255573
Fax: (01392) 498769
email: admin@exeter-cathedral.org.uk
Web: http://www.exeter-cathedral.org.uk
Canons Residentiary
Treasurer Canon Neil Collings, 9 The Close, Exeter EX1 1EZ [1999]   *Tel:* (01392) 279367
Precentor Canon Kenneth Parry, 6 The Close, Exeter EX1 1EZ [1991]   *Tel:* (01392) 272498
Chancellor Canon David Ison, 12 The Close, Exeter EX1 1EZ [1995]   *Tel:* (01392) 275745

Priest Vicar Revd Gregory Daxter, 6A The Close, Exeter EX1 1EZ   *Tel:* (01392) 258892
Chapter Clerk Col Michael Woodcock, Cathedral Office
Visitors' Officer Mrs Juliet Dymoke-Marr, Cathedral Office   *Tel:* (01392) 214219
Education Officer Mr David Risdon, Cathedral Office   *Tel:* (01392) 434243
Director of Music Mr Andrew Millington, 11 The Close, Exeter EX1 1EZ   *Tel:* (01392) 277521
Cathedral Organist Mr Paul Morgan, 40 Countess Wear Rd, Exeter EX2 6LR   *Tel:* (01392) 877623

ARCHDEACONS
EXETER Ven Tony Tremlett, St Matthew's House, 45 Spicer Rd, Exeter EX1 1TA [1994]
Tel: (01392) 425432
Fax: (01392) 425783
TOTNES Ven Richard Gilpin, Blue Hills, Bradley Rd, Bovey Tracey, Newton Abbot TQ13 9EU [1996]   *Tel:* (01626) 832064
Fax: (01626) 834947
BARNSTAPLE Ven Trevor Lloyd, Stage Cross, Whitemoor Hill, Bishops Tawton, Barnstaple EX32 0BE [1989]   *Tel:* (01271) 375475
Fax: (01271) 377934
PLYMOUTH Ven Robin Ellis, 33 Leat Walk, Roborough, Plymouth PL6 7AT [1982]
Tel: (01752) 793397
Fax: (01752) 774618

CONVOCATION (MEMBERS OF THE HOUSE OF CLERGY OF THE GENERAL SYNOD)
Dignitaries in Convocation
The Dean of Exeter
The Archdeacon of Plymouth
Proctors for Clergy
Ven Richard Gilpin
Revd Hilary Ison
Canon Peter Larkin
Ven Trevor Lloyd
Preb Samuel Philpott

MEMBERS OF THE HOUSE OF LAITY OF THE GENERAL SYNOD
Mr Roger Adcock
Mrs Margaret Behenna

Mrs Anne Ellis
Mrs Sheila Fletcher
Mrs Heather Morgan
Mrs ShirleyAnn Williams

DIOCESAN OFFICERS
Dioc Secretary Mr Mark Beedell, Diocesan House, Palace Gate, Exeter EX1 1HX   *Tel:* (01392) 272686
Fax: (01392) 499594
Chancellor of Diocese Chanc Sir David Calcutt, Lamb Buildings, Temple, London EC4Y 7AS
Tel: 020–7353 6381
Registrar of Diocese and Bishop's Legal Secretary Mr R. K. Wheeler, 18 Cathedral Yard, Exeter EX1 1HE   *Tel:* (01392) 421171
Fax: (01392) 215579
email: wheeler@michelmores.co.uk
Dioc Surveyors Vickery Holman, 22 Lockyer St, Plymouth PL1 2QY *Tel:* (01752) 266291; Vickery Holman, 24 Southernhay West, Exeter EX1 1PR
Tel: (01392) 203010
Barnstaple Smith & Dunn, Alliance House, Cross St, Barnstaple EX31 1BA   *Tel:* (01271) 327878

DIOCESAN ORGANIZATIONS
Diocesan Office Diocesan House, Palace Gate, Exeter, Devon EX1 1HX   *Tel:* (01392) 272686
Fax: (01392) 499594

ADMINISTRATION
Dioc Synod (Chairman, House of Clergy) Revd Bill Blakey, Rectory, Parkham, Bideford EX39 5PL *Tel:* (01237) 4511204; *(Secretary, House of Clergy)* Revd Philip Darby, Vicarage, Paternoster Lane, Ipplepen, Newton Abbot TQ12 5RY *Tel:* (01803) 812215; *(Chairman, House of Laity)* Mrs Shirley-Ann Williams, Miller's Farm, Talaton, Exeter EX5 2RE; *(Secretary, House of Laity)* Mr Charles Hodgson, Heale Moor Farm, Parracombe, Barnstaple EX31 4QE
Synod Secretary Mr Mark Beedell, Dioc House
Board of Finance (Chairman) Mr John Hutchinson, Heath Barton, Whitestone, Exeter EX4 2HJ *Tel:* (01647) 61401; *(Secretary)* Mr Mark Beedell *(as above)*
Parsonages Committee (Secretary) Mr Bob Greig, Dioc House   *Tel:* (01392) 435500
Pastoral Committee (Secretary) Miss Pru Williams, Dioc House
Board of Patronage (Chairman) Mrs Shirley-Ann Williams *(as above)*
Trusts Mr Derek Hexter, Dioc House
Designated Officer Mr Mark Beedell *(as above)*

CHURCHES
Dioc Advisory Committee (Chairman) Preb Christopher Pidsley, Dioc House
(Secretary) Miss Janet Croysdale, Dioc House
Redundant Churches Uses Committee (Secretary) Miss Pru Williams *(as above)*

EDUCATION
Director of Education Revd Christopher

Davidson, Christian Education and Resources Centre, St Mary Arches Church, St Mary Arches St, Exeter EX4 3BA   *Tel:* (01392) 432149
Fax: (01392) 436085
Asst Education Officers Mr Tony Giddings and Mrs Jennifer Pestridge *(same address)*

MINISTRY AND PARISH TRAINING
Director of Ordinands and Adviser for Team Ministries Preb Terry Nottage, 2 West Ave, Pennsylvania, Exeter EX4 4SD
Tel: (01392) 214867
Fax: (01392) 251229
Officer for Non-Stipendiary Ministry Canon David Ison PH D, Dioc House
Tel and Fax: (01392) 499710
Officer for Continuing Ministerial Education Canon David Ison PH D *(as above)*
Adviser in Women's Ministry Revd Margaret Cameron, Rectory, Hemyock, Cullompton EX15 3RQ   *Tel:* (01823) 681189
Board of Readers (Secretary) Mr Ronald Edinborough, 3 Manor Rd, Paignton TQ3 2HT
Tel: (01803) 550493
Dioc Adult Training Adviser Revd Viv Armstrong-MacDonnell, 1A The Cloisters, Exeter EX1 1JS   *Tel:* (01392) 498110
Family Life and Marriage Education Coordinator Mrs Sheila Fletcher, 11 Troarn Way, Chudleigh, Newton Abbot TQ13 0PP   *Tel:* (01626) 853607
Children's Adviser Ms Jane Whitcombe, Jasmine Cottage, Coldridge, Crediton EX17 6AY
Tel: (01636) 83415
Youth Adviser Capt Tony Williams, 22 Lawn Drive, Chudleigh, Newton Abbot TQ13 0LT
Tel: (01626) 852828
Widows and Dependants (Ottery and Honiton Deaneries) Preb John Mapson, c/o Dioc House
Tel: (01392) 272686 (Office)
(01844) 38037 (Home)
(Other Deaneries) Revd Gilbert Cowdry, 17 Hillcrest Park, Pennsylvania, Exeter EX4 4SH
Tel: (01392) 252662
Chaplain to the Deaf Revd Gill Behenna, Glenn House, 96 Old Tiverton Rd, Exeter EX4 6LD
Tel: (01392) 278875

ECUMENICAL
Ecumenical Advisers Revd Derek Newport, Rectory, Widecombe-in-the-Moor, Newton Abbot TQ13 7TF   *Tel and Fax:* (01364) 621334
Revd John Luscombe, Vicarage, 1 Hallerton Court, Hallerton Close, Plymouth PL16 8ND
Tel: (01752) 703713
Revd Martin Hunnybun, Rectory, Old Market Drive, Woolsery, Bideford EX39 5QF
Tel: (01237) 431571
Revd Keith Gale, Vicarage, Lower Town, Halberton, Tiverton EX16 7AU   *Tel:* (01884) 821149

PRESS, PUBLICITY AND PUBLICATIONS
Press and Media Liaison Officer Ms Sally Kimmis, Dioc House   *Tel:* 07654 666991

Editor of Dioc News Preb John Mapson, Dioc House Tel: (01844) 38037 (Home)
Editor of Dioc Directory Miss Janet Croysdale, Dioc House

DIOCESAN RECORD OFFICE

Devon Record Office, Castle St, Exeter EX4 3PU
County Archivist Mr John Draisey
Tel: (01392) 384253

SOCIAL RESPONSIBILITY

Board for Christian Care (Administrator) Mr Ronald Harbour, Glenn House, 96 Old Tiverton Rd, Exeter EX4 6LD Tel: (01392) 278875
Social Responsibility Officer Mr Martyn Goss (*same address*)

STEWARDSHIP

Stewardship Adviser Mr Terry Anning, Stewardship Office, 1B The Cloisters, Exeter EX1 1JS Tel: (01392) 272354
Assistant Adviser Mr John Grumett (*same address*)

RURAL DEANS
ARCHDEACONRY OF EXETER

Aylesbeare Revd John Clapham, Rectory, Lympstone, Exmouth EX8 5HP
Tel: (01395) 273343
Cadbury Revd John Hall, Rectory, Bow, Crediton EX17 6HS Tel: (01363) 82566
Christianity Revd Mark Bate, Rectory, Alphington, Exeter EX2 8XJ Tel: (01392) 437662
Cullompton Revd Margaret Cameron, Rectory, Hemyock, Cullompton EX15 3RQ
Tel: (01823) 681189
Honiton Revd Tim Schofield, Vicarage, Colyford Rd, Seaton EX12 2DF Tel: (01297) 20391
Kenn Revd Victor Standing, Rectory, 12 Church Lane, Whitestone, Exeter EX4 2JT
Tel: (01392) 811406
Ottery Revd Rik Peckham, St Francis Vicarage, Woolbrook, Sidmouth, EX10 9XH
Tel: (01395) 514522
Tiverton Revd Michael Partridge, St Paul's Vicarage, Baker's Hill, Tiverton EX16 5NE
Tel: (01884) 255705

ARCHDEACONRY OF TOTNES

Holsworthy Revd Leslie Brookhouse, Rectory, Pyworthy, Holsworthy EX22 6SU
Tel: (01409) 254769

Moreton Revd David Stanton, St John's Vicarage, Newton Rd, Bovey Tracey, Newton Abbot TQ13 9BD Tel: (01626) 833451
Newton Abbot and Ipplepen Revd Philip Darby, Vicarage, Paternoster Lane, Ipplepen, Newton Abbot TQ12 5RY Tel: (01803) 812215
Okehampton Revd Barry Wood, Vicarage, South Tawton, Okehampton EX20 2LQ
Tel: (01837) 840337
Torbay Revd Tony Macey, Vicarage, 22 Monterey Close, Livermead, Torquay TQ9 7HN
Tel: (01803) 732384
Totnes Revd Nicholas Martin, Rectory, Northgate, Castle Hill, Totnes TQ9 5NX
Tel: (01803) 862104
Woodleigh Revd Ronald White, Vicarage, Stoke Fleming, Dartmouth TQ6 0QB
Tel: (01803) 770361

ARCHDEACONRY OF BARNSTAPLE

Barnstaple Revd Michael Pearson, Rectory, Sowden Lane, Barnstaple EX32 8BU
Tel: (01271) 373837
Hartland Revd Malcolm Strange, Rectory, Abbotsham Rd, Bideford EX39 3AB
Tel: (01237) 470228
Shirwell Revd Keith Wyer, Rectory, Rectory Rd, Combe Martin, Ilfracombe EX34 0NS
Tel: (01271) 883203
South Molton Revd Stephen Girling, Vicarage, Chittlehampton, Umberleigh EX37 9QL
Tel: (01769) 540654
Torrington Revd John Carvosso, Rectory, Tawstock, Barnstaple EX31 3HZ
Tel: (01271) 374963

ARCHDEACONRY OF PLYMOUTH

Ivybridge Revd Tim Deacon, Rectory, Court Rd, Newton Ferrers, Plymouth PL8 1DL
Tel: (01752) 872530
Devonport Preb Samuel Philpott, St Peter's Vicarage, 23 Wyndham Square, Plymouth PL1 5EG Tel: (01752) 222007
Moorside Preb John Richards, St Mary's Vicarage, 58 Plymbridge Rd, Plympton, Plymouth PL7 4QG Tel: (01752) 336157
Sutton Revd Stephen Dinsmore, St Jude's Vicarage, Knighton Rd, Plymouth PL4 3BU
Tel: (01752) 661232
Tavistock Preb John Rawlings, Vicarage, 5A Plymouth Rd, Tavistock PL19 8AU
Tel: (01822) 612162

Founded in 1541. Gloucestershire except for a few parishes in the north (WORCESTER); a few parishes in the south (BRISTOL) and one parish in the east (OXFORD); the northern third of South Gloucestershire; two parishes in Wiltshire; a small area in south-west Warwickshire; a few parishes in the southern part of Worcestershire

Population 597,000   Area 1,140 sq m
Stipendiary Clergy 163   Benefices 165
Parishes 326   Churches 401

BISHOP (39th)
Rt Revd David Edward Bentley, Bishopscourt, Pitt St, Gloucester GL1 2BQ [1993]
Tel: (01452) 524598
Fax: (01452) 310025
email: bshpglos@star.co.uk
[David Gloucestr]
Personal Assistant/Chaplain Canon Roger Grey

SUFFRAGAN BISHOP
TEWKESBURY Rt Revd John Stewart Went, Green Acre, 166 Hempsted Lane, Gloucester GL2 5LG [1995]
Tel: (01452) 521824
Fax: (01452) 505554
email: bshptewk@star.co.uk

HONORARY ASSISTANT BISHOPS
Rt Revd Charles Derek Bond, Ambleside, 14 Worcester Rd, Evesham, Worcs WR11 4JU [1992]
Tel: (01386) 446156
Rt Revd John Gibbs, Farthingloe, Southfield, Minchinhampton, Stroud GL6 9DY [1985]
Tel: (01453) 886211
Rt Revd William Somers Llewellyn, Glebe House, Leighterton, Tetbury GL8 8UW [1973]
Tel: (01666) 890236
Rt Revd Michael Ashley Mann, The Cottage, Lower End Farm, Eastington, Northleach, Cheltenham GL54 3PN [1989]   *Tel:* (01451) 860767
Rt Revd John Neale, 26 Prospect, Corsham, Wilts SN13 9AF [1994]   *Tel:* (01249) 712557

CATHEDRAL CHURCH OF ST PETER AND THE HOLY AND INDIVISIBLE TRINITY
Dean Very Revd Nicholas Bury, The Deanery, Miller's Green, Gloucester GL1 2BP [1997]
Tel: (01452) 524167
Cathedral Office 2 College Green, Gloucester GL1 2LR   *Tel:* (01452) 528095
Fax: (01452) 300469
email: gloucester.cathedral@btinternet.com
Web: http://www.btinternet.com/ ~gloucester.cathedral/

Canons Residentiary
Canon Norman Chatfield, 6 College Green, Gloucester GL1 2LX [1992]   *Tel:* (01452) 521954
Precentor Canon Neil Heavisides, 7 College Green, Gloucester GL1 2LX [1993]
Tel: (01452) 523987
Diocesan Residentiary Canons
Canon Roger Grey, 4A Miller's Green, Gloucester GL1 2BN [1982]   *Tel:* (01452) 525242
Canon Christopher Morgan, 9 College Green, Gloucester GL1 2LX [1996]   *Tel:* (01452) 507002
Cathedral Chaplain and Visitors Officer Revd Judith Hubbard-Jones, 10 College Green, Gloucester GL1 2LX [1997]   *Tel:* (01452) 300655
Chapter Steward Mr Anthony Higgs, Cathedral Office
Cathedral Organist Mr David Briggs, 7 Miller's Green, Gloucester GL1 2BN   *Tel:* (01452) 524764

ARCHDEACONS
GLOUCESTER Ven Christopher Wagstaff, Glebe House, Church Lane, Maisemore, Gloucester GL2 8EY [1982]   *Tel:* (01452) 528500
Fax: (01452) 381528
CHELTENHAM Ven Hedley Ringrose, The Sanderlings, Thorncliffe Drive, Cheltenham GL51 6PY [1998]   *Tel:* (01242) 522923
Fax: (01242) 235925
email: archdchelt@star.co.uk

CONVOCATION (MEMBERS OF THE HOUSE OF CLERGY OF THE GENERAL SYNOD)
The Archdeacon of Cheltenham
Proctors for Clergy
Revd Hugh Broad
Canon Michael Page
Canon David Williams

MEMBERS OF THE HOUSE OF LAITY OF THE GENERAL SYNOD
Mr Nigel Chetwood
Mrs Pat Harris
Mrs Sarah James
Mr Timothy Royle
Mrs Elizabeth Ward

DIOCESAN OFFICERS

Dioc Secretary Mr Michael Williams, Church House, College Green, Gloucester GL1 2LY
Tel: (01452) 410022
Fax: (01452) 308324
Chancellor of Diocese Chanc June Rodgers, 2 Harcourt Buildings, The Temple, London EC4Y 9DB
Registrar of Diocese and Bishop's Legal Secretary Mr Chris Peak, Dioc Registry, 34 Brunswick Rd, Gloucester GL1 1JJ
Tel: (01452) 520224

DIOCESAN ORGANIZATIONS

Diocesan Office Church House, College Green, Gloucester GL1 2LY
Tel: (01452) 410022
Fax: (01452) 308324
email: church.house@glosdioc.org.uk

ADMINISTRATION

Dioc Synod (*Vice-President, House of Clergy*) Canon Michael Page, Vicarage, Langley Rd, Winchcombe, Cheltenham GL54 5QP *Tel:* (01242) 602368; (*Vice-President, House of Laity*) Mr John Young, Silver Birches, Water Lane, Oakridge, Stroud, Glos. GL6 7PJ *Tel:* (01452) 770537; (*Secretary*) Mr Michael Williams, Church House
Board of Finance (*Chairman*) Mr Fraser Hart, The Old Rectory, Hatherop, Cirencester, Glos. GL7 3NA *Tel:* (01285) 750200; (*Secretary*) Mr Michael Williams (*as above*)
Financial Secretary Mr Colin Albert, Church House
Houses Committee (*Secretary*) Mrs Juliet Watkins, Church House
Pastoral Committee (*Secretary*) Mr Michael Williams (*as above*)
Board of Patronage (*Secretary*) Mr Jonathan MacKechnie-Jarvis, Church House
Designated Officer Mr Michael Williams (*as above*)
Trust (*Secretary*) Mr Jonathan MacKechnie-Jarvis (*as above*)
Redundant Churches Uses Committee (*Secretary*) Mr Jonathan MacKechnie-Jarvis (*as above*)
Glebe Committee (*Secretary*) Mrs Juliet Watkins (*as above*)

CHURCHES

Advisory Committee for the Care of Churches (*Chairman*) Miss Mary Bliss, The Old Bakehouse, Beech Pike, Elkstone, Cheltenham GL53 9PL *Tel:* (01285) 821232; (*Secretary*) Mr Jonathan MacKechnie-Jarvis (*as above*)

EDUCATION

Education Committee (*Director*) Vacancy
Adviser to Schools Mr Philip Metcalf, 4 College Green, Gloucester GL1 2LB
Schools Officer Mr Rob Stephens (*same address*)
Children's Officer Sister Jacqui Hill (*same address*)

MINISTRY

Dioc Officer for Ministry Canon Christopher Morgan, 9 College Green, Gloucester GL1 2LX
Tel: (01452) 507002
Director of Ordinands Revd Dr Michael Parsons, Rectory, Hempsted, Gloucester GL2 6LW
Tel: (01452) 524550
Associate Director of Ordinands Revd David Bowers, Vicarage, The Green, Apperley, Gloucester GL19 4DQ *Tel:* (01452) 780880
Vocations Adviser Revd Pat Lyes-Wilsdon, Rectory, Cromhall, Wotton-under-Edge GL12 8AN *Tel:* (01454) 294767
Adviser for Women's Ministry Canon Eleanor Powell, Rectory, Edge, Gloucester GL6 6PF
Tel: (01452) 812319
NSM Officer Canon Michael Tucker, Rectory, Amberley, Stroud, Glos. GL5 5JG
Tel: (01453) 878515
Chaplain for Deaf and Hard of Hearing People Revd Stephen Morris, 2 High View, Hempsted, Gloucester GL2 5LN *Tel:* (01452) 416178
Readers' Board Mr W. H. Irving, 80 Melmore Gardens, Siddington, Cirencester GL7 1NS
Tel: (01285) 650012
West of England Ministerial Training Course (*Principal*) Revd Dr Richard Clutterbuck, 7c College Green, Gloucester GL1 2LX
Tel and Fax: (01452) 300494
Local Ministry and OLM Scheme Principal Mrs Caroline Pascoe, 4 College Green, Gloucester GL1 2LB
Part-time Local Ministry Officers Canon Andrew Bowden, Rectory, Coates, Cirencester, Glos. GL7 6NR *Tel:* (01285) 770235
Revd Geoffrey Neale, Vicarage, Blockley, Moreton-in-Marsh GL56 9ES *Tel:* (01386) 700283
Mrs Kathy Lawrence, Vicarage, St Anne's Way, St Briavels, Lydney, Glos. GL15 6UE
Tel: (01594) 530345

LITURGICAL

Chairman Canon Neil Heavisides, 7 College Green, Gloucester GL1 2LX *Tel:* (01452) 523987

PARISH RESOURCES

Dioc Officer for Parish Resources Revd Guy Bridgewater, 4 College Green, Gloucester GL1 2LB
Stewardship Adviser Mrs Elizabeth Ward (*same address*)
Dioc Children's Officer Sister Jacqueline Hill (*same address*)
Dioc Youth Officer Mr Justin Groves (*same address*)
Ecumenical Adviser Revd Graham Martin, Vicarage, Bibury, Cirencester GL7 5NT
Tel: (01285) 740387
County Ecumenical Officer Revd Dr David Calvert, 151 Tuffley Ave, Gloucester GL1 5NP
Tel: (01452) 301347

PRESS AND PUBLICATIONS
Communications Officer Revd Geoff Crago, Church House
Tel and Fax: (01452) 750575 (Home)
0802 367033 (Mobile)
0839 467601 (Pager)
Editor of Dioc Directory Mrs Jan Wood, Church House

DIOCESAN RECORD OFFICE
Gloucestershire Records Office, Clarence Row, Gloucester GL1 3DW *Dioc Archivist* Mr David Smith   *Tel:* (01452) 425295

DIOCESAN RESOURCE CENTRE
Warden Mrs Gill Calvert, 9 College Green, Gloucester GL1 2LX   *Tel:* (01452) 385217

SOCIAL RESPONSIBILITY
Dioc Officer for Social Responsibility Canon Adrian Slade, 38 Sydenham Villas Rd, Cheltenham GL52 6DZ   *Tel:* (01242) 253162
email: glossr@star.co.uk
Community Relations Revd Grantley Finlayson, 36 Howard St, Gloucester GL1 4US
Tel: (01452) 423986
Rural Adviser Revd David Green, Rectory, Cowley, Cheltenham GL53 9NJ
Tel: (01242) 870232
Evangelist Working with Older People Capt Colin Rudge, 10 Billingham Close, Gloucester GL4 7SS
Tel: (01452) 423988
Homeless Project Officer Sister Fiona Fisher, 3 College Yard, Gloucester GL1 2PL
Tel: (01452) 310810

RURAL DEANS
ARCHDEACONRY OF CHELTENHAM
Campden Revd Roy Wyatt, Rectory, Church Lane, Welford-on-Avon, Stratford-upon-Avon CV37 8EL   *Tel:* (01789) 750808

Cheltenham Revd Ted Crofton, Christ Church Vicarage, Malvern Rd, Cheltenham GL50 2NU
Tel: (01242) 515983
Cirencester Revd Henry Morris, Rectory, Preston, Cirencester GL7 5PR   *Tel:* (01285) 654187
Fairford Revd Tony Ross, Vicarage, Coln St Aldwyns, Cirencester GL7 5AG
Tel: (01285) 750013
Northleach Canon David Nye, Vicarage, Mill End, Northleach, Cheltenham GL54 3HL
Tel: (01451) 860293
Stow Revd Stephen Wookey, Rectory, Bourton Rd, Moreton-in-Marsh GL56 0BG
Tel: (01608) 652680
Tetbury Canon David Strong, Vicarage, Nailsworth, Stroud GL6 0PJ   *Tel:* (01453) 832181
Tewkesbury and Winchcombe Revd Peter Sibley, Holy Trinity Vicarage, 49 Barton St, Tewkesbury GL20 5PU   *Tel:* (01648) 293233

ARCHDEACONRY OF GLOUCESTER
Bisley Canon Barry Coker, Vicarage, Church St, Stroud GL5 1JL   *Tel:* (01453) 764555
Dursley Revd Simon Richards, Vicarage, Church Lane, Berkeley GL13 9BH   *Tel:* (01453) 210294
Forest North Revd Robert Sturman, St Michael's Rectory, Hawkers Hill, Mitcheldean GL17 0BS
Tel: (01594) 542434
Forest South Revd Andrew James, Vicarage, Oakland Rd, Harrow Hill, Drybrook GL17 9JX
Tel: (01594) 542232
Gloucester City Revd Ian Calder, Vicarage, Coney Hill Rd, Gloucester GL4 4LX
Tel: (01452) 523618
Gloucester North Revd Edward Mason, Vicarage, 5 Vicarage Close, Churchdown, Gloucester GL3 2NE   *Tel:* (01452) 713203
Hawkesbury Revd Pat Lyes-Wilsdon, Rectory, Cromhall, Wotton-under-Edge GL12 8AN
Tel: (01454) 294767
Stonehouse Canon Michael Tucker PH D, Rectory, Amberley, Stroud GL5 5JG   *Tel:* (01453) 878515

DIOCESE OF GUILDFORD

Founded in 1927. The western two-thirds of Surrey south of the Thames, except for a small area in the north-east (SOUTHWARK); areas of north-east Hampshire; a few parishes in Greater London; one parish in West Sussex.

Population 942,000   Area 538 sq m
Stipendiary Clergy 197   Benefices 148
Parishes 161   Churches 215

BISHOP (8th)
Rt Revd John Warren Gladwin, Willow Grange, Woking Rd, Guildford, Surrey GU4 7QS [1994]
Tel: (01483) 590500
Fax: (01483) 590501
email: bishop.john@cofeguildford.org.uk
[John Guildford]
Bishop's Chaplain Revd David Peck (*same address*)
email: david.peck@cofeguildford.org.uk

SUFFRAGAN BISHOP
DORKING Rt Revd Ian James Brackley, Dayspring, 13 Pilgrim's Way, Guildford, Surrey GU4 8AD [1996]
Tel: (01483) 570829
Fax: (01483) 567268
email: bishop.ian@cofeguildford.org.uk

CATHEDRAL CHURCH OF THE HOLY SPIRIT
Dean Very Revd Alexander Wedderspoon, The Deanery, 1 Cathedral Close, Guildford, Surrey GU2 5TL [1987]
Tel: (01483) 560328
Cathedral Office Guildford Cathedral, Stag Hill, Guildford GU2 5UP
Tel: (01483) 565287
Fax: (01483) 303350
Sub-Dean and Canon Pastor Canon Maureen Palmer PH D, 2 Cathedral Close, Guildford, Surrey GU2 5TL [1996]
Tel: (01483) 560329
Canons Residentiary Vacancy, 4 Cathedral Close, Guildford, Surrey GU2 5TL
Tel: (01483) 571826 (Office)
Precentor Canon Nicholas Thistlethwaite PH D, 3 Cathedral Close, Guildford, Surrey GU2 5TL [1999]
Cathedral Administrator Commander Bill Evershed, Cathedral Office
Treasurer Mr Roger Lilley, Cathedral Office
Chapter Clerk Mr John Brown, Triggs Turner Barton, 128 High St, Guildford, Surrey GU1 3HH
Tel: (01483) 565771
Cathedral Organist Mr Stephen Farr, 5 Cathedral Close, Guildford, Surrey GU2 5TL
Tel: (01483) 531693

ARCHDEACONS
SURREY Ven Robert Reiss, Archdeacon's House,

New Rd, Wormley, Godalming, Surrey GU8 5SU [1996]
Tel: (01428) 682563
Fax: (01428) 682993
email: bob.reiss@cofeguildford.org.uk
DORKING Ven Mark Wilson, Littlecroft, Heathside Rd, Woking, Surrey GU22 7EZ [1996]
Tel: (01483) 772713
Fax: (01483) 757353
email: mark.wilson@cofeguildford.org.uk

CONVOCATION (MEMBERS OF THE HOUSE OF CLERGY OF THE GENERAL SYNOD)
The Archdeacon of Surrey
Proctors for Clergy
Revd Richard Hanford
Canon Malcolm King
Revd Alistair Magowan
Ven Mark Wilson

MEMBERS OF THE HOUSE OF LAITY OF THE GENERAL SYNOD
Mr Peter Bruinvels
Mrs Anne Foreman
Mr David Lambert
Mr Robert Leach
Mrs Ann Warren

[handwritten: Jan Gooding tel 01932 874621]

DIOCESAN OFFICERS
Dioc Secretary Mr Stephen Marriott, Diocesan House, Quarry St, Guildford, Surrey GU1 3XG
Tel: (01483) 571826
Fax: (01483) 790333
Chancellor of Diocese His Honour Judge Michael Goodman, Parkside, Dulwich Common, London SE21 7EU
Registrar of Diocese and Bishop's Legal Secretary Mr Peter Beesley, 1 The Sanctuary, London SW1P 3JT
Tel: 020–7222 5381
Fax: 020–7222 7502
Deputy Registrar Mr Nicholas Richens

DIOCESAN ORGANIZATIONS
Diocesan Office Diocesan House, Quarry St, Guildford, Surrey GU1 3XG   *Tel:* (01483) 571826
Fax: (01483) 790333

ADMINISTRATION

Dioc Synod (Vice-President, House of Clergy) Canon Malcolm King, Vicarage, Westcott Rd, Dorking, Surrey RH4 3DP *Tel:* (01306) 882875; *(Vice-President, House of Laity)* Mr Alan Foster, Pennwood, Chiddingfold Rd, Dunsfold, Godalming, Surrey GU8 4PB *Tel:* (01483) 200960; *(Secretary)* Mr Stephen Marriott, Dioc House
Asst Secretary Mr Michael Bishop, Dioc House
  email: mike.bishop@cofeguildford.org.uk
Board of Finance (Chairman) Mr Michael Young, Dioc House
(Secretary) Mr Stephen Marriott *(as above)*
Accountant Mr Peter Smith, Dioc House
  email: peter.smith@cofeguildford.org.uk
Asst Secretaries Mr Michael Bishop, Mr John White, Mr Peter Smith, Dioc House
Parsonages and Property Committee Mr John White *(as above)*
  email: john.white@cofeguildford.org.uk
Pastoral Committee Mr Michael Bishop *(as above)*
Designated Officer Mr Peter Beesley, 1 The Sanctuary, London SW1P 3JT *Tel:* 020–7222 5381
  Fax: 020–7222 7502

CHURCHES

Advisory Committee for the Care of Churches (Chairman) Mr Hamish Donaldson, Edgecombe, Hill Rd, Haslemere, Surrey GU27 2JN; *(Secretary)* Mr Michael Bishop *(as above)*

EDUCATION

Education Centre The Cathedral, Stag Hill, Guildford, Surrey GU2 5UP *Tel:* (01483) 450423
  Fax: (01483) 450424
Director of Education and Secretary Dioc Board of Education Canon Tony Chanter
  email: tony.chanter@cofeguildford.org.uk
Children's Education Officer Mrs Margaret Dean
Assistant Children's Education Officer Mrs Alison Hendy
Youth Education Officer Vacancy
Adviser in Adult Education Mrs Joanna Walker
Further Education Adviser Mrs Kathleen Kimber
Schools' Personnel and Development Officer Mr David Ager
Schools' Administration Officer Mrs Dorothy Dellow
Resources and Training Officer Mr Roy Davey
Centre Administrator Mrs Diane Hart

MINISTRY

Director of Ministerial Training Canon Julian Hubbard, Dioc House
  email: julian.hubbard@cofeguildford.org.uk
Director of Ordinands Revd John Partington, 13 Heath Drive, Brookwood, Surrey GU24 0HG
  Tel: (01483) 799284
Director of Post-Ordination Training Canon Julian Hubbard *(as above)*

Adviser in Women's Ministry Canon Mavis Wilson, Littlecroft, Heathside Rd, Woking, Surrey GU22 7EZ *Tel:* (01483) 720057
  email: mavis.wilson@cofeguildford.org.uk
Clerical Registry (Registrar) Revd Nicholas Farbridge, 55 Curling Vale, Onslow Village, Guildford GU2 5PH *Tel:* (01483) 531140
Readers' Board (Registrar) Dr Bryan Wheeler, 40 Simons Walk, Englefield Green, Egham TW20 9SQ *Tel:* (01784) 432835

LITURGICAL

Secretary Sheila Sandison, 13 Pilgrim's Way, Guildford, Surrey GU4 8AD *Tel:* (01483) 570829

MISSIONARY AND ECUMENICAL

Director for Mission, Evangelism and Parish Development Canon Mavis Wilson *(as above)*
Dioc Ecumenical Officer Revd Stuart Thomas, 61 Ruxley Lane, Ewell, Surrey KT19 0JG
  Tel: 020–8393 5616
World Partnership Officer Revd John Burley, Rectory, Vicarage Hill, Loxwood, Billingshurst, W Sussex RH4 0RG *Tel:* (01403) 752320

PRESS AND PUBLICATIONS

Director of Communications Mrs Sally Hastings, Willow Grange, Woking Rd, Guildford, Surrey GU4 7QS *Tel:* (01483) 598400 (Office)
  (01252) 629205 (Home)
  email: sally.hastings@cofeguildford.org.uk
Publicity Officer Mr Alan Brown *(same address)*
  Tel: (01483) 598878
Editor of Dioc Newspaper Mrs Sally Hastings *(as above)*
Editor of Dioc Directory Mrs Sally Hastings *(as above)*

DIOCESAN RECORD OFFICE

Surrey History Centre, 130 Goldsworth Rd, Woking, Surrey GU2 1ND *Archivists* Dr D. B. Robinson and Miss Mary Mackey
  Tel: (01483) 594594

SOCIAL RESPONSIBILITY

Director Miss Bassi Mirzania, Dioc House
  email: bassi.mirzania@cofeguildford.org.uk

STEWARDSHIP

Dioc Adviser Vacancy

RURAL DEANS
ARCHDEACONRY OF SURREY

Aldershot Revd David Holt, Vicarage, Branksome Wood Rd, Fleet, Hants GU13 8JU
  Tel: (01252) 616361
Cranleigh Revd Nigel Nicholson, Rectory, High St, Cranleigh, Surrey GU6 8AF
  Tel: (01483) 273620
Farnham Revd Andrew Tuck, Rectory, Upper Church Lane, Farnham, Surrey GU9 7PW
  Tel: (01252) 716119

Godalming Revd John Ashe, Vicarage, Westbrook Rd, Godalming, Surrey GU7 1ET
Tel: (01483) 414135
Guildford Revd Jeremy Collingwood, Vicarage, 25 Waterden Rd, Guildford, Surrey GU1 2AX
Tel: (01483) 568886
Surrey Heath Revd Neil Turton, Rectory, Parsonage Way, Frimley, Camberley, Surrey GU16 5AG
Tel: (01276) 23309

ARCHDEACONRY OF DORKING

Dorking Revd Penelope Fleming, Rectory, Holmbury St Mary, Dorking, Surrey RH5 6NL
Tel: (01306) 730285

Emly Revd Julian Henderson, Vicarage, Church Rd, Claygate, Esher, Surrey KT10 0JP
Tel: (01372) 463603
Epsom Revd David Smethurst, Vicarage, 35 Burgh Heath Rd, Epsom, Surrey KT17 4LP
Tel: (01372) 743336
Leatherhead Revd Bryan Paradise, Rectory, Ockham Rd South, East Horsley, Leatherhead, Surrey KT24 6RL
Tel: (01483) 282359
Runnymede Revd Alistair Magowan, Vicarage, Vicarage Rd, Egham, Surrey TW20 9JN
Tel: (01784) 432066
Woking Revd Richard Cook, 8 Cardingham, Goldsworth Park, Woking, Surrey GU21 3LN
Tel: (01483) 764523

DIOCESES

DIOCESE OF HEREFORD

Founded *c* 676. Herefordshire; the southern half of
Shropshire; a few parishes in Powys and Monmouthshire.

Population 283,000   Area 1,660 sq m
Stipendiary Clergy 119   Benefices 125
Parishes 352   Churches 423

BISHOP (103rd)
Rt Revd John Oliver, The Bishop's House, The
Palace, Hereford HR4 9BN [1990]
Tel: (01432) 271355
Fax: (01432) 343047
[John Hereford]

SUFFRAGAN BISHOP
LUDLOW Rt Revd John Saxbee, The Bishop's
House, Corvedale Rd, Craven Arms, Shropshire
SY7 9BT [1994]　　　　*Tel:* (01588) 673571
Fax: (01588) 673585

**CATHEDRAL CHURCH OF THE BLESSED
VIRGIN MARY AND ST ETHELBERT**
Dean Very Revd Robert Willis, The Deanery, The
Cloisters, Hereford HR1 2NG [1992]
Tel: (01432) 359880
Cathedral Office 5 College Cloisters, Hereford
HR1 2NG　　　　*Tel:* (01432) 359880
Fax: (01432) 355929
email: office@herefordcathedral.co.uk
Canons Residentiary
Precentor Canon Paul Iles, The Canon's House,
The Close, Hereford HR1 2NG [1983]
Tel: (01432) 266193
Chancellor Canon John Tiller, The Canon's
House, 3 St John St, Hereford HR1 2NB [1984]
Tel: (01432) 265659
Treasurer Vacancy
Ven Michael Hooper, The Archdeacon's House,
The Close, Hereford HR1 2NG [1997]
Tel: (01432) 272873
email:
　　archdeacon@theclosehereford.freeserve.co.uk
Non-Residentiary Canon Canon Brian Chave, 7
College Cloisters, The Close, Hereford HR1 2NG
[1997]　　　　*Tel:* (01432) 271355
Succentor Vacancy
Cathedral Administrator and Chapter Clerk Lt Col
Andrew Eames, Cathedral Office
Cathedral Organist Dr Roy Massey, 1 College
Cloisters, Hereford HR1 2NG *Tel:* (01432) 272011
Assistant Organist Mr Peter Dyke, 14 College
Cloisters, Hereford HR1 2NG *Tel:* (01432) 264520

ARCHDEACONS
HEREFORD Ven Michael Hooper, The Archdeacon's House, The Close, Hereford HR1 2NG
[1991]　　　　*Tel:* (01432) 272873
email:
　　archdeacon@theclosehereford.freeserve.co.uk
LUDLOW Rt Revd John Saxbee, The Bishop's
House, Corvedale Rd, Craven Arms, Shropshire
SY7 9BT [1992]　　　　*Tel:* (01588) 673571

**CONVOCATION (MEMBERS OF THE
HOUSE OF CLERGY OF THE GENERAL
SYNOD)**
Dignitaries in Convocation
The Dean of Hereford
The Archdeacon of Hereford
Proctors for Clergy
Preb Kay Garlick
Preb Robert Horsfield
Preb John Reese

**MEMBERS OF THE HOUSE OF LAITY OF
THE GENERAL SYNOD**
Mr Keith Bladon
Mrs Margaret Cosh
Mrs Mary-Lou Toop

DIOCESAN OFFICERS
Dioc Secretary Miss Sylvia Green, The Palace,
Hereford HR4 9BL　　　　*Tel:* (01432) 353863
Fax: (01432) 352952
email: hereford@diooffice.freeserve.co.uk
Chancellor of Diocese Chanc Jonathan Henty,
Office of the Social Security and Child Support
Commissioners, Harp House, 83 Farringdon St,
London EC4A 4DH　　　　*Tel:* 020–7353 5145
Registrars of Diocese and Bishop's Legal Secretaries
Mr Tom Jordan, Dioc Registry, 44 Bridge St,
Hereford HR4 9DN *Tel:* (01432) 352992; Mr Peter
Beesley, 1 The Sanctuary, Westminster, London
SW1P 3JT　　　　*Tel:* 020–7222 5381
Dioc Surveyors Hook Mason Partnership, 11
Castle St, Hereford HR1 3NL *Tel:* (01432) 352299

DIOCESAN ORGANIZATIONS

Dioc Office The Palace, Hereford HR4 9BL
Tel: (01432) 353863
Fax: (01432) 352952
email: hereford@diooffice.freeserve.co.uk
Bishop's Office The Palace, Hereford HR4 9BN
Tel: (01432) 271355
Fax: (01432) 343047

ADMINISTRATION

Dioc Synod (Chairman, House of Clergy) Preb John Reese, Vicarage, 107 Church Rd, Tupsley, Hereford HR1 1RT *Tel:* (01432) 274490; *(Chairman, House of Laity)* Mr Keith Bladon, 11 Salisbury Ave, Tupsley, Hereford HR1 1QG *Tel:* (01432) 272402; *(Secretary)* Miss Sylvia Green, Dioc Office
Board of Finance (Chairman) Mr Richard Mercer, 'Tana Leas', Clee St Margaret, Craven Arms, Shropshire SY7 9DZ *Tel:* (01584) 823272; *(Secretary)* Miss Sylvia Green *(as above)*
Benefice Buildings Committee Mr Graham Horne, Dioc Office
Glebe Committee Mr Graham Horne *(as above)*
Board of Patronage Miss Sylvia Green *(as above)*
Designated Officer Mr Peter Beesley, 1 The Sanctuary, Westminster, London SW1P 3JT
Tel: 020–7222 5381
Pastoral Committee Miss Sylvia Green *(as above)*
Trusts Miss Sylvia Green *(as above)*

CHURCHES

Advisory Committee for the Care of Churches (Chairman) Mr Christopher Dalton, Upper Court, Ullingswick, Hereford HR1 3JG *Tel:* (01432) 820295; *(Secretary)* Mr Graham Horne *(as above)*

EDUCATION

Director of Education Mr Tristram Jenkins, Dioc Office
Tel: (01432) 357864
Fax: (01432) 352952
Schools Adviser (Curriculum) Mr Jonathan Rendall, Dioc Office
Dioc Youth Officer Mr Richard Betterton, The Cottage, Bishop Mascall Centre, Lower Galdeford, Ludlow, Shropshire SY8 2RU
Tel: (01584) 872334
Children's Adviser Revd Peter Privett, 165 Bargates, Leominster, Herefordshire HR6 8QT
Tel: (01568) 613176 (Home)
(01584) 872334 (Office)
Church Schools Officer Revd Michael Smith, Dioc Office

DIOCESAN CENTRE

Director Revd Graham Earney, Bishop Mascall Centre, Lower Galdeford, Ludlow, Shropshire SY8 2RU *Tel:* (01584) 873882

MINISTRY AND TRAINING

Director of Ordinands Preb Robert North, St Nicholas Rectory, 76 Breinton Rd, Hereford HR4 0JY *Tel:* (01432) 273810
email: robnorth@wbsnet.co.uk
Dioc Director of Training Canon John Tiller, The Canon's House, 3 St John St, Hereford HR1 2NB
Tel: (01432) 265659
Local Ministry Officer Preb Gill Sumner, The Cottage, Bishop Mascall Centre, Lower Galdeford, Ludlow, Shropshire SY8 2RZ
Tel: (01584) 872822
Adviser on Women in Ministry Revd Susan Strutt, Vicarage, Bosbury, Ledbury, Herefordshire HR8 1QA *Tel:* (01531) 640225
Readers' Association (Warden) Rt Revd John Saxbee, Bishop's House, Corvedale Rd, Craven Arms, Shropshire SY7 9BT *Tel:* (01588) 673571
Widows and Dependants (Hereford Archdeaconry Clerical Charities) Preb Ralph Garnett, 5 Hampton Manor, Hereford HR1 1TG *Tel:* (01432) 274985
(Ludlow Archdeaconry) Preb Robert Sharp, 62 Biddulph Way, Ledbury, Herefordshire HR8 2HN *Tel:* (01531) 631972

WORSHIP

Chairman Canon Paul Iles, The Canon's House, The Close, Hereford HR1 2NG
Tel: (01432) 266193
Secretary Revd Lesley Walker, 32 Goodwood Ave, Bridgnorth, Shropshire WV15 5BD
Tel: (01746) 765874

MISSIONARY AND ECUMENICAL

Dioc Ecumenical Officer Revd Jan Fox, Vicarage, Orleton, Ludlow, Shropshire SY8 4HN
Tel: (01568) 780863
Ecumenical Committee (Chairman) The Bishop of Ludlow; *(Secretary)* Revd Jan Fox *(as above)*
Council for World Partnership and Development (Chairman) Mrs Margaret Wickstead, Laurel Cottage, Orleton Common, Ludlow, Shropshire SY8 4JG *Tel:* (01584) 831246; *(Secretary)* Revd C. Fletcher, Rectory, Bredenbury, Bromyard, Herefordshire HR7 4TF *Tel:* (01885) 482236
Dioc Coordinator for Evangelism Revd Graham Sykes, Vicarage, Breinton, Hereford HR4 7PG
Tel: (01432) 273447
Evangelism Committee (Chairman) The Archdeacon of Hereford; *(Secretary)* Mrs Pat Rawson, 5 Crown Lea Close, Ledbury Rd, Hereford HR1 1RL *Tel:* (01432) 267846

AGRICULTURE

Chaplain Revd Nick Read, Vicarage, Lydbury North, Shropshire SY7 8AU *Tel:* (01588) 680609

PRESS, PUBLICITY AND PUBLICATIONS
Dioc Communications Officer Canon Brian Chave, The Gateway Office, The Palace, Hereford HR4 9BL   *Tel:* (01432) 271355
01523 701886 (Pager)
Fax: (01432) 343047
email: chave@hfddiocesan.freeserve.co.uk
Editor of Dioc Year Book Miss Sylvia Green (*as above*)
Editor of Dioc Newspaper Mr R. Calver, The Gateway Office (*as above*)

DIOCESAN RECORD OFFICE
Hereford Records Office, The Old Barracks, Harold St, Hereford HR1 2QX *Tel:* (01432) 265441 (*For diocesan records and parish records for Hereford Deanery*)
Shrewsbury Records and Research Centre, Castle Gates, Shrewsbury SY1 2AQ *Tel:* (01743) 255350; *Head of Records and Research* Miss R. Bagley (*For parish records for Ludlow Deanery*)

SOCIAL RESPONSIBILITY
Social Responsibility Officer Miss Jackie Boys, The Gateway Office (*as above*)   *Tel:* (01432) 355248
email: sro@hdfdio.freeserve.co.uk
Council for Social Responsibility (*Chairman*) Mrs Caroline Bond, 25 Cartway, Bridgnorth, Shropshire WV16 4SG *Tel:* (01746) 761687; (*Secretary*) Miss Jackie Boys (*as above*)

STEWARDSHIP
Christian Giving Adviser Vacancy

RURAL DEANS
ARCHDEACONRY OF HEREFORD
Abbeydore Preb Paul Barnes, Rectory, Cusop, Hay-on-Wye, Hereford HR3 5RF
Tel: (01497) 820634
Bromyard Preb Walter Gould, Vicarage, 28 Church Lane, Bromyard, Herefordshire HR7 4DZ   *Tel:* (01885) 482438
Hereford City Preb John Reese, Vicarage, Tupsley, Hereford HR1 1RT   *Tel:* (01432) 274490
Hereford Rural Preb Jeanne Summers, 99 Walkers Green, Marden, Hereford HR1 3EA
Tel: (01432) 880497
email: rsatmarden@aol.com
Kington and Weobley Revd Stephen Hollinghurst, Rectory, Pembridge, Hereford HR6 9EB
Tel: (01544) 388998
Ledbury Revd Dr Colin Beevers, Rectory, Worcester Rd, Ledbury, Herefordshire HR8 1PL
Tel: (01531) 632571
Leominster Revd P. Swain, Rectory, Church St, Leominster, Hereford HR6 8NH
Tel: (01568) 612124
Ross and Archenfield Revd Alan Jevons, Rectory, Much Birch, Hereford HR2 8HT
Tel: (01981) 540558

ARCHDEACONRY OF LUDLOW
Bridgnorth Preb Clive Williams, St Mary's Rectory, Church St, Highley, Bridgnorth, Shropshire WV16 6NA   *Tel:* (01746) 861612
Clun Forest Revd Richard Shaw, Vicarage, Clun, Craven Arms, Shropshire SY7 8JG
Tel: (01588) 640809
Condover Revd Allan Toop, Vicarage, Clun Rd, Craven Arms, Shropshire SY7 9QW
Tel: (01588) 672797
Ludlow Preb Duncan Dormor, Vicarage, Church St, Tenbury Wells, Worcs WR15 8BP
Tel: (01584) 810702
Pontesbury Revd William Rowell, Vicarage, Minsterley, Shrewsbury SY5 0AA
Tel: (01743) 791213
Telford Severn Gorge Revd Dennis Smith, Holy Trinity Vicarage, Holyhead Rd, Oakengates, Telford, Shropshire TF2 6BN   *Tel:* (01543) 262420

DIOCESE OF LEICESTER

Restored in 1926. Leicestershire, except the former county of Rutland (PETERBOROUGH); one in Northamptonshire.

Population 893,000   Area 835 sq m
Stipendiary Clergy 161   Benefices 133
Parishes 242   Churches 329

BISHOP (6th)

Rt Revd Timothy John Stevens, Bishop's Lodge, 10 Springfield Rd, Leicester LE2 3BD [1999]
Tel: 0116–270 8985
Fax: 0116–270 3288
email: bptim@leicester.anglican.org
[Timothy Leicester]
Bishop's Chaplain Revd Graham Johnson (*same address*)
Fax: 0116–270 3285

ASSISTANT BISHOP

Rt Revd William Down, St Mary's Vicarage, 56 Vicarage Lane, Humberstone, Leicester LE5 1EE [1995]
Tel: 0116–276 7281
Fax: 0116–276 4504

CATHEDRAL CHURCH OF ST MARTIN

Provost Vacancy, Provost's House, 1 St Martin's East, Leicester LE1 5FX
Tel: 0116–262 5294
Fax: 0116–262 5295
Cathedral Office 1 St Martin's East, Leicester LE1 5FX
Tel: 0116–262 5294
email: cathedral@leicester.anglican.org
Canons Residentiary
Chancellor Canon Michael Banks, 3 Morland Ave, Leicester LE2 2PF [1987]
Tel: 0116–210 9893
Fax: 0116–210 9894
Treasurer Canon Michael Wilson, 7 St Martin's East, Leicester LE1 5FX [1988] *Tel:* 0116–253 0580
Non-Residentiary Canon
Precentor Canon John Craig, 154 Barclay St, Leicester LE3 0JB [1991]
Tel: 0116–255 7327
Canons Theologian
Canon Brian Hebblethwaite, Queens' College, Cambridge; Canon Anthony Thiselton, Dept of Theology, University of Nottingham, University Park, Nottingham NG7 2RD
Chapter Clerk Mr Graham Moore, Messrs Wartnabys, Solicitors, 44 High St, Market Harborough, Leics LE16 7AH *Tel:* (01858) 463322
Cathedral Administrator Mr D. H. C. Moore, Cathedral Office
Master of Music Mr Jonathan Gregory, 27 Heron Close, Great Glen, Leicester LE8 0DZ
Tel: 0116–259 3891
Asst Master of Music Mr David Cowen, 23 Estoril Ave, Wigston, Leicester LE18 2RE
Tel: 0116–288 0054

ARCHDEACONS

LEICESTER Ven Mike Edson, 13 Stoneygate Ave, Leicester LE2 3HE [1994]
Tel: 0116–270 4441
Fax: 0116–270 1091
email: medson@leicester.anglican.org
LOUGHBOROUGH Ven Ian Stanes, The Archdeaconry, 21 Church Rd, Glenfield, Leicester LE3 8DP [1992] *Tel:* 0116–231 1632
Fax: 0116–232 1593
email: stanes@leicester.anglican.org

CONVOCATION (MEMBERS OF THE HOUSE OF CLERGY OF THE GENERAL SYNOD)

The Archdeacon of Loughborough
Proctors for Clergy
Revd Nick Baines
Revd Dr Stephen Cherry
Canon Jim Wellington

MEMBERS OF THE HOUSE OF LAITY OF THE GENERAL SYNOD

Mr John Higginbotham
Dr Hugh James
Mrs Mary Weston

DIOCESAN OFFICERS

Dioc Secretary Mr Andrew Howard, Church House, 3/5 St Martin's East, Leicester LE1 5FX
Tel: 0116–262 7445
Fax: 0116–253 2889
email: ahoward@chouse.leicester.anglican.org
Chancellor of Diocese The Worshipful Nigel Seed, 3 Paper Buildings, Temple, London EC4Y 7ED
Tel: 020–7583 8055
Registrars of Diocese and Bishop's Legal Secretaries
Mr Richard Bloor, Harvey Ingram Owston, 20 New Walk, Leicester LE1 6TX *Tel:* 0116–254 5454
Fax: 0116–255 4559
Mr Paul Morris, Winckworth Sherwood, Registry Chambers, The Old Deanery, Deans Court, London EC4V 5AA
Tel: 020–7593 5110
Fax: 020–7248 3221
email: rhb@hio.co.uk

Dioc Surveyors Martin Jones & Associates, The Reading Room, 33 Main St, Medbourne, Market Harborough, Leics LE16 8DT   Tel: (01858) 565567
Fax: (01858) 565433

DIOCESAN ORGANIZATIONS

Diocesan Office Church House, 3/5 St Martin's East, Leicester LE1 5FX   Tel: 0116–262 7445
Fax: 0116–253 2889
email: chouse@leicester.anglican.org

ADMINISTRATION

Dioc Synod (Secretary) Mr Andrew Howard, Dioc Office
Dioc Synod (Chairman, House of Clergy) Canon Jim Wellington, Rectory, Upper Church St, Syston, Leics LE7 1HR   Tel: 0116–260 8276
email: j&hwelli@leicester.anglican.org
(Chairman, House of Laity) Prof David Wilson, 56 Grangefields Drive, Rothley, Leicester LE7 7NB
Tel: 0116–230 3402
Board of Finance (Chairman) Mr William Moss, The Coach House, Mill Lane, Kegworth, Derby DE74 2EJ   Tel: (01509) 672481; (Secretary) Mr Andrew Howard (as above)
Deputy Dioc Secretary Mr Harvey Taylor, Dioc Office
email:htaylor@chouse.leicester.anglican.org
Assistant Dioc Secretary Mrs Maureen Higgins, Dioc Office
email: mhiggins@chouse.leicester.anglican.org
Financial Secretary Mr Philip Carver, Dioc Office
email: pcarver@chouse.leicester.anglican.org
Finance and General Purposes Committee Mr Andrew Howard (as above)
Property Committee Mrs Maureen Higgins, Dioc Office
Pastoral Committee Mr Harvey Taylor (as above)
Glebe Committee Mrs Maureen Higgins (as above)
Designated Officer Mr Andrew Howard (as above)
Parish Funding Directors Mr Brian Tanner, 100 Burnmill Rd, Market Harborough LE16 7JG
Tel: (01858) 432371
Mr Derek Hunt, 38 Pennine Way, Ashby-de-la-Zouch, LE65 1EW   Tel: (01530) 411966
Mr Gary Lee, 87 Maplewell Rd, Woodhouse Eaves, Loughborough LE12 8RG
Tel: (01509) 891207

CHURCHES

Advisory Committee for the Care of Churches (Chairman) Dr A. McWhirr, 37 Dovedale Rd, Stoneygate, Leicester LE2 2DN Tel: 0116–270 3031; (Secretary) Mr Harvey Taylor (as above)
Redundant Churches Uses Committee Mr Harvey Taylor (as above)

EDUCATION

Chairman Mr D. Gwynne Jones, 19 Stanton Rd, Sapcote, Leics LE9 6FQ
Director Revd Peter Taylor, Dioc Office
Tel: 0116–253 7676
Fax: 0116–251 1638
email: ptaylor@chouse.leicester.anglican.org

Youth Officer Mr Colin Udall, Dioc Office
email: cudall@chouse.leicester.anglican.org
Religious Education Adviser Miss Margaret Matthews, Dioc Office
Children's Adviser Revd Gill Dallow, Dioc Office
email: gdallow@chouse.leicester.anglican.org

MINISTRY

Advisory Board of Ministry (Chairman) Ven Ian Stanes, The Archdeaconry, 21 Church Rd, Glenfield, Leicester LE3 8DP   Tel: 0116–231 1632
Director of Lay Training Canon Anne Horton, Rectory, 157 Main St, Swithland, Loughborough LE12 8QT   Tel and Fax: (01509) 891163
Director of Ordinands Canon Peter Burrows, Rectory, Broughton Astley, Leicester LE9 6PF
Tel: (01455) 282261
email: pbddo@leicester.anglican.org
Officer for NSM Revd Geoffrey Mitchell, 36 Brick Kiln Lane, Shepshed, Loughborough LE12 9EL
Tel: (01509) 502280
Warden of Readers Revd Malcolm Lambert, Rectory, 19 Main St, South Croxton, Leicester LE7 3RJ   Tel: (01664) 840245
email: mlambert@leicester.anglican.org
Director of Continuing Ministerial Education Canon Glynn Richerby, St James the Greater Vicarage, 216 London Rd, Leicester LE2 1NE
Tel: 0116–254 211
email: glynn@leicester.anglican.org
Director of Post-Ordination Training Revd Sue Field, 134 Valley Rd, Loughborough LE11 3QA
Tel: (01509) 234472
email: s.field@leicester.anglican.org
Chaplain for Women's Ministry Revd Sue Field (as above)
Retired Clergy and Widows Officer Ven Hughie Jones, Four Trees, 68 Main St, Thorpe Satchville, Melton Mowbray, Leics LE14 2DQ
Tel: (01664) 840262

LITURGICAL

Chairman Revd Stephen Cherry, Rectory, Steeple Row, Loughborough LE11 1UX
Tel: (01509) 212780
Secretary Revd Richard Curtis, St Philip's House, 2A Stoughton Drive North, Leicester LE5 5UB
Tel: 0116–273 6204
email: lrcurtis@leicester.anglican.org

MISSION AND SOCIAL RESPONSIBILITY

Board of Mission and Social Responsibility (Adviser) Revd Martin Wilson, 278 East Park Rd, Leicester LE5 5AY   Tel: 0116–273 3893
Fax: 0116–273 7849
email: ldbmsr@leicester.anglican.org
Family Life Worker Mrs Elaine Heptonstall, (same address)
Adviser on Race and Community Relations Canon Irving Richards, Vicarage, 214 East Park Rd, Leicester LE5 5FB   Tel: 0116–273 6752

Chaplain to People Affected by HIV Canon Margaret Morris, 10 Toller Rd, Quorn, Loughborough LE12 8AH *Tel:* (01509) 412092
Rural Link Officers Revd Simon Foster, Rectory, 1 Hurds Close, Groby Rd, Anstey, Leicester LE7 7GH *Tel:* 0116–236 2176
Revd John Richardson, Rectory, Churchgate, Hallaton, Market Harborough LE16 8TY
  Tel: (01858) 555363

ECUMENICAL

Ecumenical Officer Revd Barbara Stanton, Rectory, Honeypot Lane, Husbands Bosworth, Lutterworth LE17 6LY *Tel:* (01858) 880351

PRESS AND PUBLICATIONS

Communications Officer Mrs Sue Kyriakou, Church House *Tel:* (01543) 473052
Editor of Dioc Directory Mr Andrew Howard (*as above*)
Editor of 'News and Views' Revd Jeff Hopewell, Vicarage, 5 The Stockwell, Wymeswold, Loughborough LE12 6UF *Tel:* (01509) 891163
  email: jhopewell@leicester.anglican.org

DIOCESAN RECORD OFFICE

Leicestershire Records Office, Long Street, Wigston, Leicester LE18 2AH *Tel:* 0116–257 1080
  Fax: 0116–257 1120

EVANGELISM

Dioc Evangelist Ven Mike Edson, 13 Stoneygate Ave, Leicester LE2 3HE *Tel:* 0116–270 4441

RURAL DEANS

ARCHDEACONRY OF LEICESTER

Christianity North (*Leicester*) Canon John Leonard, St Theodore's House, 4 Sandfield Close, Off Nicklaus Rd, Rushey Mead, Leicester LE4 7RE *Tel:* 0116–266 9956

Christianity South (*Leicester*) Revd Chris Oxley, Vicarage, 10 Parkside Close, Beaumont Leys, Leicester LE4 1EP *Tel:* 0116–235 2667
Framland Revd Charles Jenkin, Rectory, 67 Dalby Rd, Melton Mowbray LE13 0BQ
  Tel: (01664) 480923
Gartree I Revd Ian Gemmell, Rectory, Great Bowden, Market Harborough LE16 7ET
  Tel: (01858) 462032
Gartree II Revd Brian Glover, Vicarage, 12 Saddington Rd, Fleckney, Leicester LE8 0AW
  *Tel:*0116–240 2215
Goscote Revd Nick Baines, Rothley Vicarage, 128 Hallfields Lane, Rothley, Leicester LE7 7NG
  Tel: 0116–230 2241

ARCHDEACONRY OF LOUGHBOROUGH

Akeley East Revd David Newman, Emmanuel Rectory, 47 Forest Rd, Loughborough LE11 2NW
  Tel: (01509) 263264 (Home)
  (01509) 261773 (Office)
Akeley South Revd Kerry Emmett, Rectory, 9 Orchard Close, Ravenstone, Coalville, Leicester LE67 2JW *Tel:* (01530) 839802
Akeley West Canon Charles Dobbin, Rectory, Prior Park, Ashby-de-la-Zouch, Leicester LE6 5BH *Tel:* (01530) 412180
Guthlaxton I Canon Peter Burrows, Rectory, Broughton Astley, Leics LE9 6PF
  Tel: (01455) 282261
Guthlaxton II Vacancy
Sparkenhoe West Canon Brian Davis, St Mary's Vicarage, Hinckley, Leics LE10 1EQ
  Tel: (01455) 234241
Sparkenhoe East Canon Geoffrey Stuart, Rectory, 6 Station Rd, Kirby Muxloe, Leicester LE9 2EJ
  Tel: 0116–238 6822 (Home)
  0116–238 6811 (Office)

DIOCESE OF LICHFIELD

Founded in 664, formerly Mercia (AD 656). Staffordshire, except for a few parishes in the south-east (BIRMINGHAM, DERBY); a few parishes in the south-west (HEREFORD); the northern half of Shropshire; Wolverhampton; Walsall; the northern half of Sandwell.

Population 1,987,000   Area 1,744 sq m
Stipendiary Clergy 379   Benefices 299
Parishes 426   Churches 582

BISHOP (97th)
Rt Revd Keith Norman Sutton, Bishop's House, 22 The Close, Lichfield, Staffs. WS13 7LG [1984]
Tel: (01543) 306000
Fax: (01543) 306009
[Keith Lichfield]
Bishop's Assistant Capt David Brown (*same address*)
Bishop's Press Officer Revd Robert Ellis, St Mary's House, The Close, Lichfield, Staffs. WS13 7LD
Tel: (01543) 306030
Fax: (01543) 306039

AREA BISHOPS
SHREWSBURY Rt Revd David Hallatt, 68 London Rd, Shrewsbury SY2 6PG [1994]
Tel: (01743) 235867
Fax: (01743) 243296
email: bishop.shrewsbury@lichfield.anglican.org
STAFFORD Rt Revd Christopher Hill, Ash Garth, Broughton Crescent, Barlaston, Stoke-on-Trent, Staffs. ST12 9DD [1996]   *Tel:* (01782) 373308
Fax: (01782) 373705*email:* bishop.shrewsbury
WOLVERHAMPTON Rt Revd Michael Bourke, 61 Richmond Rd, Merridale, Wolverhampton WV3 9JH [1993]   *Tel:* (01902) 824503
Fax: (01902) 824504

CATHEDRAL CHURCH OF THE BLESSED VIRGIN MARY AND ST CHAD
Dean Very Revd Michael Yorke, The Deanery, Lichfield, Staffs. WS13 7LD [1999]
Tel: (01543) 306250
Fax: (01543) 306255
Chapter Office 19A The Close, Lichfield, Staffs. WS13 7LD   *Tel:* (01543) 306100
Fax: (01543) 306109
email: lich.cath@virgin.net
Canons Residentiary
Treasurer Ven George Frost, 24 The Close, Lichfield, Staffs. WS13 7LD [1998]
Tel: (01543) 306145
Fax: (01543) 306147
Chancellor Canon Anthony Barnard, 13 The Close, Lichfield, Staffs. WS13 7LD [1977]
Tel: (01543) 306241 (Home)
(01543) 306240 (Visitors' Study Centre)

Precentor Canon Charles Taylor, 23 The Close, Lichfield, Staffs. WS13 7LD   *Tel:* (01543) 306140
Chief Executive Officer Mr David Wallington, Chapter Office
Bursar Mr Clive Tomlinson, Chapter Office
Master of the Choristers Mr Andrew Lumsden, 11 The Close, Lichfield, Staffs. WS13 7LD
Tel: (01543) 306200
Assistant Organist Mr Robert Sharpe, 10 The Close, Lichfield, Staffs. WS13 7LD
Tel: (01543) 306201
Visits Officer Mrs Angela Bayles, Visitors' Study Centre, The Close, Lichfield, Staffs. WS13 7LD
Tel: (01543) 306240

ARCHDEACONS
LICHFIELD Ven George Frost, 24 The Close, Lichfield, Staffs. WS13 7LD [1998]
Tel: (01543) 306145
Fax: (01543) 306147
STOKE-UPON-TRENT Ven Alan Smith, 39 The Brackens, Clayton, Newcastle-under-Lyme, Staffs. ST5 4JL [1997]   *Tel:* (01782) 663066
Fax: (01782) 711165
SALOP Ven John Hall, Tong Vicarage, Shifnal, Shropshire TF11 8PW [1998]   *Tel:* (01902) 372622
Fax: (01902) 374021
WALSALL Ven Tony Sadler, 10 Paradise Lane, Pelsall, Walsall WS3 4NH [1997]   *Tel:* (01922) 445353
Fax: (01922) 445354

CONVOCATION (MEMBERS OF THE HOUSE OF CLERGY OF THE GENERAL SYNOD)
The Archdeacon of Lichfield
Proctors for Clergy
Revd David Butterfield
Revd Sally Chapman
Revd Robert Ellis
Revd Graham Fowell
Preb Horace Harper
Preb Terry Thake

MEMBERS OF THE HOUSE OF LAITY OF THE GENERAL SYNOD
Miss Sue Booth
Mr John Clark
Sir Patrick Cormack

Mr Ian Gaweda
Mrs Wendy Kinson
Mr Geoff Locke
Mr Keith Masters
Mrs Joanna Monckton
Mr Marcel Noël

DIOCESAN OFFICERS

Dioc Secretary Mr David Taylor, St Mary's House,
The Close, Lichfield, Staffs. WS13 7LD
Tel: (01543) 306030
Fax: (01543) 306039
email: (open)@ lichfield.anglican.org
Assistant Secretaries Mr Ian Gaweda (*Finance*) and
Mr Barry Toothill (*Housing*) (*same address*)
Chancellor of Diocese Judge John Shand, St Mary's
House
Registrar of Diocese and Bishop's Legal Secretary Mr
John Thorneycroft, Messrs Manby & Steward,
1 St Leonard's Close, Bridgnorth, Shropshire
WV16 4EL
Tel: (01746) 761436
Fax: (01746) 766764
Deputy Registrar Mr Niall Blackie, Messrs Manby
& Steward, Blount House, Hall Court, Hall Park
Way, Telford, Shropshire TF3 4N
Tel: (01952) 291525
Fax: (01952) 291921
Dioc Surveyors Wood, Goldstraw and Yorath,
Churchill House, Regent Rd, Hanley, Stoke-on-
Trent, Staffs. ST1 3RH
Tel: (01782) 208000

DIOCESAN ORGANIZATIONS

Diocesan Office See individual addresses below

ADMINISTRATION

Dioc Synod (*Chairman, House of Clergy*) Preb Terry
Thake, Vicarage, Little Haywood, Stafford ST18
0TS *Tel:* (01889) 881262; (*Chairman, House of Laity*)
Mr Geoff Locke, Narnia II, 88 Ravenscliffe Rd,
Kidsgrove, Stoke-on-Trent ST7 4HX *Tel:* (01782)
785544; (*Secretary*) Mr David Taylor, St Mary's
House, The Close, Lichfield, Staffs. WS13 7LD
Tel: (01543) 306030
Fax: (01543) 306039
Dioc Board of Finance (*Chairman*) Mr Glynne
Morris; (*Secretary*) Mr David Taylor (*as above*)
Benefice Buildings and Glebe Committee (*Secretary*)
Mr Barry Toothill, St Mary's House
Pastoral Committee Revd David Wright, St
Matthew's Vicarage, St George's Rd, Donnington
Wood, Telford TF2 7NJ
Tel: (01952) 604239
Trust (*Secretary*) Mr David Taylor (*as above*)
Designated Officer Mr John Thorneycroft, St
Mary's House

CHURCHES

Advisory Committee for the Care of Churches
(*Chairman*) Mr Richard Raven, Wheatlea House,
82 Upper Rd, Meole Brace, Shrewsbury,
Shropshire SY3 9JP *Tel:* (01743) 362896; (*Secretary*)
Mrs Katie Brown, St Mary's House

EDUCATION

Director of Education Revd Peter Lister, St Mary's
House
Assistant Director Mr Alan Butterworth, St
Mary's House
Youth and Children's Adviser and Team Leader
(*Salop*) Dr Leonie Wheeler, St Mary's House
Youth and Children's Adviser (*Lichfield*) Vacancy
Youth and Children's Adviser (*Stoke*) Mr Mark
Hatcher, Wetley Abbey Cottage, Wetley Rocks,
Stoke-on-Trent, Staffs. ST9 0AS
Tel and Fax: (01782) 551145
Warden – Dioc Youth Centre Mr Arthur Hack,
Dovedale House, Ilam, Ashbourne, Derby. DE6
2AZ
Tel: (01335) 350365
Fax: (01335) 350441
Warden – Shepherds Building (*self-catering youth
centre*) Vacancy, St Mary's House
Schools Advisers Mrs June Cook, 3 St Agatha's
Close, Charlton Manor, Wellington, Telford TF1
3QP
Tel and Fax: (01952) 242589
Mrs Joan Furlong, Station House, Station Rd,
Haughton, Stafford ST18 9HF
Tel and Fax: (01785) 780604

MINISTRY

Postal address and telephone Backcester Lane,
Lichfield WS13 1JJ
Tel: (01543) 411550
Fax: (01543) 411552
*Board of Ministry Team Leader and Director of
Ministry Development* Revd John Wesson (*same
address*) *email:* sue.jackson@lichfield.anglican.org
Director of Ordinands Revd Mark Geldard (*same
address*)
Director of Local Ministry Revd Robert Daborn
(*same address*)
Ordained Local Ministry Course Leader Revd
Eileen Turner (*same address*)
Adviser to Women in Ministry Revd Sally
Chapman, All Saints Vicarage, 2 Foley Church
Close, Streetly, Sutton Coldfield B74 3JX
Tel: 0121–353 3582
Dioc Vocations Adviser Revd Mark Geldard (*as
above*)
Warden of Readers Revd Ian Cardinal, Vicarage,
Wigginton, Tamworth B79 9DN
Tel: (01827) 64537
Local Vocations Advisory Service Revd Mark
Geldard (*as above*)
Readers' Association Vacancy
Local Ministry Scheme Revd Robert Daborn (*as
above*)

LITURGICAL

Secretary Canon Charles Taylor, 23 The Close,
Lichfield, Staffs WS13 7LD *Tel:* (01543) 263337

MISSION AND UNITY

Dioc Missioner Revd Mark Ireland, 14 Gorway
Gardens, Walsall WS1 3BJ
Tel: (01922) 626010
Fax: (01922) 625924

World Mission Officer Revd Dr Michael Sheard, 68 Sneyd Lane, Essington, Wolverhampton WV11 3DX   *Tel:* (01922) 445844 *Fax:* (01922) 445845
email: michael.sheard@netmatters.co.uk
Ecumenical Officer Mrs Irene Hardacre, c/o CARIS, Shallowford House, Shallowford, Norton Bridge, Stone ST15 0NZ
Tel: (01785) 761763
Fax: (01785) 761764

PRESS, PUBLICATIONS AND NEWSLETTER
Communications Officer Revd Robert Ellis, St Mary's House
Press Officer on Duty   *Tel:* (01543) 306030
(01283) 820732 (Home)
Editor of Dioc Newsletter 'Link' Revd Robert Ellis (*as above*)
Editor of Dioc Newspaper 'Spotlight' Mrs Carol Law, 19 Lincoln Croft, Shenstone, Lichfield WS14 0ND   *Tel:* (01543) 480308
Fax: (01543) 480864
email: claw@eclipse.co.uk

DIOCESAN RECORD OFFICES
Staffordshire Record Office, Eastgate St, Stafford ST16 2LZ *Tel:* (01785) 278379 *County Archivist* Mr D. V. Fowkes (*For parishes in the Archdeaconries of Lichfield and Stoke-on-Trent*)
Lichfield Record Office, The Library, The Friary, Lichfield WS13 6QG *Tel:* (01543) 256787; *Archivist in Charge* Mr M. Dorrington (*For diocesan records and parishes within the City of Lichfield*)
Shrewsbury Records and Research Centre, Castle Gates, Shrewsbury SY1 2AQ *Tel:* (01743) 255350; *Head of Records and Research* Miss R. Bagley (*For parishes in the Archdeaconry of Salop*)

CARIS (Care, Action, Responsibility and Justice in Society)
Social Responsibility Officer Ms Vanessa Geffen, Shallowford House, Norton Bridge, Stone ST15 0NZ   *Tel:* (01785) 761763
Fax: (01785) 761764
Local Development Officer Mr Malcolm Carroll (*same address*)
Association for Family Care Vanessa Geffen (as above)
Tel and *Fax:* (01902) 791100
Black Country Urban Industrial Mission (Team Leader) Revd Olwen Smith
Office St Peter's House, Exchange St, Wolverhampton WV1 1TS   *Tel:* (01902) 710407
Home Vicarage, 66 Albert Rd, Wolverhampton WV6 0AF   *Tel:* (01902) 712935
Dioc Council with Deaf People (Senior Chaplain and Secretary) Revd Philip Maddock, Rectory, 56 Uttoxeter Rd, Hill Ridware, Rugeley WS13 3QU
Tel: (01543) 402023
(*Dioc Chaplain*) Revd John Cowburn, Vicarage, Upper Belgrave Rd, Normacot, Stoke-on-Trent ST3 4QJ   *Tel:* (01782) 325832

Dioc Adviser in Pastoral Care and Counselling Revd Jeffery Leonardi, New Rectory, Bellamour Way, Colton, Rugeley WS14 3JW   *Tel:* (01889) 570897
Black Anglican Concerns Minister Vacancy

PARISH FUNDING UNIT
Team Members Mr Neil Bradley, Mr Bill Proctor, Mr Ian Law, St Mary's House

RURAL DEANS
ARCHDEACONRY OF LICHFIELD
Lichfield Revd Colin Thomas, 37 New Rd, Brownhills, Walsall WS8 6AT *Tel:* (01543) 372187
Penkridge Revd Trevor Green, Vicarage, Sandy Lane, Brewood, Stafford ST19 9ET
Tel: (01902) 850368
Rugeley Preb Terry Thake, Vicarage, Little Haywood, Stafford ST18 0TS *Tel:* (01889) 881262
Tamworth Revd Alan Barrett, Vicarage, Hospital St, Tamworth B79 7EE   *Tel:* (01827) 62446

ARCHDEACONRY OF STOKE-ON-TRENT
Alstonfield Revd Jack Nicoll, Longnor Vicarage, Buxton SK17 0PA   *Tel:* (01298) 83316
Cheadle Revd Lawrence Price, Rectory, Holt Rd, Kingsley, Stoke-on-Trent ST10 2BA
Tel: (01538) 754754
Eccleshall Revd Michael Pope, Vicarage, Gnosall, Stafford ST20 0ER   *Tel:* (01785) 822213
Leek Revd David Wilmot, Vicarage, Baddeley Green Lane, Stoke-on-Trent ST2 7EY
Tel: (01782) 534062
Newcastle-under-Lyme Revd Gerald Gardiner, St Andrew's Vicarage, 50 Kingsway West, Westlands, Newcastle ST5 3PU
Tel: (01782) 619594
Stafford Revd Geoffrey Smith, Rectory, Haughton, Stafford ST18 9HU *Tel:* (01785) 780181
Stoke (North) Revd William Slater, St James' Vicarage, 32 Pennyfield Rd, Newchapel, Stoke-on-Trent ST7 4PN   *Tel:* (01782) 782837
Stoke-on-Trent Revd Godfrey Stone, Rectory, 151 Werrington Rd, Bucknall, Stoke-on-Trent ST2 9AR   *Tel:* (01782) 214455
Trentham Revd Godfrey Simpson, Vicarage, Barlaston, Stoke-on-Trent, Staffs ST12 9AB
Tel: (0178 139) 2452
Tutbury Revd Phillip Jefferies, Horninglow Vicarage, Rolleston Rd, Burton-on-Trent DE13 0JZ   *Tel:* (01283) 568613
Uttoxeter Revd Grahame Humphries, Vicarage, Church Lane, Ashbourne, Derbys DE6 2JR
Tel: (01335) 342855

ARCHDEACONRY OF SALOP
Edgmond Revd David Butterfield, Vicarage, 25 Church Rd, Lilleshall, Newport, Shropshire TF10 9HE   *Tel:* (01952) 604281

Ellesmere Revd Trevor Thorold, Rectory, Shrewsbury Rd, Cockshutt, Ellesmere SY12 0JQ
Tel: (01939) 270211
email: trevor.thorold@lichfield.anglican.org
Hodnet Revd James Graham, Rectory, Hodnet, Market Drayton TF9 3NQ   *Tel:* (01630) 685491
Oswestry Revd David Crowhurst, St Oswald's Vicarage, Penylan Lane, Oswestry, Shropshire SY11 2AN   *Tel:* (01691) 653467
Shifnal Revd David Butterfield (*as above*)
Shrewsbury Revd Kevin Roberts, Vicarage, Vicarage Rd, Meole Brace, Shrewsbury SY3 9EZ
Tel: (01743) 231744
Telford Revd Dennis Smith, Holy Trinity Vicarage, Holyhead Rd, Oakengates, Telford, Shropshire TF2 6BN   *Tel:* (01952) 612926
Wem and Whitchurch Preb Neil MacGregor, Rectory, Ellesmere Rd, Wem, Shropshire SY4 5TU   *Tel:* (01939) 232550
Wrockwardine Revd Christopher Cooke, Rectory, Wrockwardine, Wellington, Telford, Shropshire TF6 5DD   *Tel:* (01952) 240969

ARCHDEACONRY OF WALSALL

Trysull Revd Michael Hunter, 100 Bellencroft Gardens, Merry Hill, Wolverhampton WV3 8DU
Tel: (01902) 763603
Walsall Revd David Lingwood, Rushall Vicarage, 10 Tetley Ave, Walsall WS4 2HE
Tel: (01922) 624677
Wednesbury Preb Ian Cook, Rectory, Hollies Drive, Wednesbury WS10 9EQ
Tel: 0121–556 0645
West Bromwich Revd Martin Rutter, St James' Vicarage, 151A Hill Top, West Bromwich B70 0SB   *Tel:* 0121–556 0805
Wolverhampton (Acting) Revd Robert Carter, St Jude's Vicarage, St Jude's Rd, Wolverhampton WV6 0EB   *Tel:* (01902) 753360

DIOCESES

Founded in 1072, formerly Dorchester (AD 886),
formerly Leicester (AD 680), originally Lindine (AD 678).
Lincolnshire; North East Lincolnshire; North Lincolnshire,
except for an area in the west (SHEFFIELD).

Population 930,000   Area 2,673 sq m
Stipendiary Clergy 238   Benefices 248
Parishes 512   Churches 648

BISHOP (70th)
Rt Revd Robert Maynard Hardy, Bishop's House,
Eastgate, Lincoln LN2 1QQ [1987]
Tel: (01522) 534701
Fax: (01522) 511095
email: bishlincoln@claranet.co.uk
[Robert Lincoln]
Personal Assistant Canon Raymond Rodger (*same address*)

SUFFRAGAN BISHOPS
GRANTHAM Rt Revd Alastair Llewellyn John Redfern, 243 Barrowby Rd, Grantham NG31 8NP
[1997]
Tel: (01476) 564722
Fax: (01476) 592468
GRIMSBY Rt Revd David Tustin, Bishop's House,
Church Lane, Irby-on-Humber, Grimsby DN37
7JR [1979]
Tel: (01472) 371715
Fax: (01472) 371716

HONORARY ASSISTANT BISHOPS
Rt Revd Donald Snelgrove, Kingston House, 8
Park View, Barton-on-Humber DN18 6AX [1994]
Tel: (01652) 634484
Rt Revd John Brown, 130 Oxford Rd, Cleethorpes
[1995]
Tel: (01472) 698840
Rt Revd Patrick Harris, Meadow Cottage, 17
Dykes End, Collingham, Newark NG34 7LD
[1999]

CATHEDRAL CHURCH OF THE BLESSED VIRGIN MARY
Dean Very Revd Alec Knight, The Deanery, 12
Eastgate, Lincoln LN2 1QG [1998]
Tel: (01522) 523608
Cathedral Office
Tel: (01522) 544544
Canons Residentiary
Sub-Dean Canon Rex Davis, The Sub-deanery, 18
Minster Yard, Lincoln LN2 1PX [1977]
Tel: (01522) 521932
Precentor Canon Andrew Stokes, The Precentory,
16 Minster Yard, Lincoln LN2 1PX [1992]
Tel: (01522) 523644
Chancellor Canon Vernon White, The Chancery,
11 Minster Yard, Lincoln LN2 1PJ [1993]
Tel: (01522) 525610

Chapter Clerk Mr Russell Pond, Chapter Office,
The Cathedral, Lincoln LN2 1PZ
Tel: (01522) 530320
Cathedral Organist Mr Colin Walsh, Graveley
Place, 12 Minster Yard, Lincoln LN2 1PJ
Asst Organist Vacancy

ARCHDEACONS
LINCOLN Ven Arthur Hawes, Archdeacon's
House, Northfield Rd, Quarrington, Sleaford
NG34 8RT [1995]
Tel: (01529) 304348
Fax: (01529) 304354
STOW Ven Roderick Wells, Hackthorn Vicarage,
Lincoln LN2 3PF [1989]
Tel: (01673) 860382
Fax: (01673) 863423
LINDSEY (*as Stow*)

CONVOCATION (MEMBERS OF THE HOUSE OF CLERGY OF THE GENERAL SYNOD)
Dignitaries in Convocation
The Bishop of Grimsby
The Archdeacon of Stow
Proctors for Clergy
Revd Andrew Hawes
Revd Stephen Holdaway
Revd Christopher Lilley
Revd Peter Mullins

MEMBERS OF THE HOUSE OF LAITY OF THE GENERAL SYNOD
Mr Roger Atkinson
Mrs Joy Epton
Mrs Nicolete Fisher
Mrs Sonia Marshall
Mrs Carol Ticehurst

DIOCESAN OFFICERS
Dioc Secretary Mr Philip Hamlyn Williams,
Church House, Lincoln LN2 1PU
Tel: (01522) 529241
Fax: (01522) 512717
email: lincolndio@claranet.co.uk
Chancellor of Diocese Mr Peter Collier, 12 St
Helens Rd, Dringhouses, York YO24 1HP

Registrar of Diocese and Bishop's Legal Secretary Mr Derek Wellman, 28 West Parade, Lincoln LN1 1JT *Tel:* (01522) 536161
Fax: (01522) 513007
Deputy Registrar Vacancy

DIOCESAN ORGANIZATIONS
Diocesan Office Church House, Lincoln LN2 1PU
Tel: (01522) 529241
Fax: (01522) 512717
email: lincolndio@claranet.co.uk

ADMINISTRATION
Dioc Synod (*Chairman, House of Clergy*) Canon Brian Osborne, Holy Trinity Vicarage, 64 Spilsby Rd, Boston PE21 9NS *Tel:* (01205) 363657; (*Secretary*) Mr Philip Hamlyn Williams, Dioc Office; (*Chairman, House of Laity*) Mrs Sally Smithson, Pendling, Tattershall Rd, Woodhall Spa, Lincoln LN10 6TW *Tel:* (01526) 352332
Board of Finance (*Chairman*) Mr Ian Davey, 53 Cromwell Rd, Cleethorpes *Tel:* (01472) 693133; (*Secretary*) Mr Philip Hamlyn Williams (*as above*)
Budget, Finance and Coordinating Committee Mr Philip Hamlyn Williams (*as above*)
Stipends and Clergy Conditions of Service Committee Mr Richard Wilkinson, Dioc Office
Trusts Committee Mr Philip Hamlyn Williams (*as above*)
Assets (and Glebe) Committee Mr Philip Hamlyn Williams (*as above*)
Clergy Housing and Board Property Committee Mr Philip Hamlyn Williams (*as above*)
Pastoral Committee Mr Richard Wilkinson (*as above*)
Board of Patronage Mr Richard Wilkinson (*as above*)
Designated Officer Mr Derek Wellman, 28 West Parade, Lincoln LN1 1JT *Tel:* (01522) 536161
Dioc Electoral Registration Officer Mr Philip Hamlyn Williams (*as above*)

CHURCHES
Advisory Committee for the Care of Churches (*Chairman*) Canon Raymond Rodger, Bishop's House, Eastgate, Lincoln LN2 1QQ
Tel: (01522) 534701
Fax: (01522) 511095
(*Secretary*) Mr Bryan Lilley, Dioc Office
Church Buildings Revd Neil Brunning, 11 Drover's Court, Lea Rd, Gainsborough DN21 1AN *Tel:* (01427) 732033
Church Extension Committee Mr Richard Wilkinson (*as above*)
Redundant Churches Uses Committee (*Secretary*) Mr Bryan Lilley (*as above*)

EDUCATION
Director of Education Revd John Bailey, Dioc Education Centre, Church House, Lincoln LN2 1PU *Tel:* (01522) 569600

Schools Administrator Miss Katie Read (*same address*)
Dioc RE Adviser Mrs Paulette Bissell (*same address*)

MISSION AND TRAINING
Director of Forum Canon Alan Nugent, Dioc Office *Tel:* (01522) 528886
Adviser in Continuing Ministerial Education Vacancy
Director of Ordinands Revd Angela Pavey, St Luke's Vicarage, Jasmin Rd, Birchwood, Lincoln LN6 0YR *Tel:* (01522) 683507
Adviser in Women's Ministry Revd Angela Pavey (*as above*)
Ordinands' Grants Mr Philip Hamlyn Williams (*as above*)
Mission and Training Development Forum (*Secretary*) Mr Hugh Tilney-Bassett, MTDF, Dioc Office *Tel:* (01522) 528886
Parish Programme Director Mrs Jane Chard, Dioc Office
Resources Consultant Mr Keith Bourne, Dioc Office
Adult Education Adviser Dr Joan Butterfield, Vicarage, Church Lane, Chapel St Leonards, Skegness PE24 5UJ *Tel:* (01754) 872666
Children's Work Adviser Sister Sandra Doore, Dioc Office *Tel:* (01522) 528886
Youth Work Adviser Capt Dave Rose, MTDF, Dioc Office *Tel:* (01522) 528886
Local Ministry Officer Revd Kathryn Windslow, Dioc Office *Tel:* (01522) 528886
Warden of Readers Revd Leslie Acklam, 165c Carholme Rd, Lincoln LN1 1RU
Tel: (01522) 531477
Director of Readers Revd Rosslyn Miller, 120A Station Rd, Waddington, Lincoln LN5 9QS
Tel: (01522) 720819
Readers (*Secretary*) Mr M. J. Pemberton, 23 Viceroy Drive, Pinchbeck, Spalding PE11 3TS
Tel: (01775) 760437
Clergy Widows Officers Canon and Mrs Ifor George-Jones, 42 Kelstern Rd, Doddington Park, Lincoln LN6 3NJ *Tel:* (01522) 691896
Clergy Retirement Officer Canon Edward Barlow, 8 Pynder Close, Hillcroft, Washingborough, Lincoln LN2 1EX *Tel:* (01522) 793762

LITURGICAL
Secretary Revd T. R. Barker, The Parsonage, 8 Church St, Spalding PE11 2PB *Tel:* (01775) 722772
Fax: (01775) 710273

ECUMENICAL
Ecumenical Development Officer Revd John Cole, Pelham House, Little Lane, Wrawby, Brigg DN20 8RW *Tel:* (01652) 657484
Church in Society Officer Miss Janet Ratcliffe, Dioc Office *Tel:* (01522) 528886
(01406) 540387 (Home)
Fax: (01522) 512717

DIOCESES

Rural Officer Mr Terry Miller, 120A Station Rd, Waddington, Lincoln LN5 9QS
Tel: (01522) 720819
Chaplain to Deaf Vacancy
Industrial Chaplains Revd Aileen Walker, The Manse, Old Brumby, Scunthorpe DN16 2DB
Tel: (01724) 840650
Revd Patricia McCullock, 16 Neap House Rd, Gunness, Scunthorpe DN15 8TT
Tel: (01724) 782265
Revd Andrew Vaughan, 4 Grange Close, Canwick, Lincoln LN4 2RH   *Tel:* (01522) 528266
Revd Tony Humphries, Vicarage, 4 Station Rd East, Grantham NG31 6JY   *Tel:* (01476) 575372
Revd Gareth Jones, 4 Old Brumby St, Scunthorpe DN16 2DB   *Tel:* (01724) 341618
Revd James Bolton, 1A The Avenue, Healing, Grimsby DN37 7NA   *Tel:* (01472) 883481

PRESS, PUBLICITY AND PUBLICATIONS
Press and Media Relations Officer Canon Raymond Rodger, Bishop's House (*as above*)
Editor of Dioc Directory Mr Philip Hamlyn Williams (*as above*)
Editor of Lincoln Bulletin Mr Philip Hamlyn Williams (*as above*)

DIOCESAN RECORD OFFICE
Lincolnshire Archives Office, St Rumbold St, Lincoln LN2 5AB   *Tel:* (01522) 526204

RURAL DEANS
ARCHDEACONRY OF STOW
Isle of Axholme Canon Derek Brown, Rectory, Belton Rd, Epworth, Doncaster DN9 1JL
Tel: (01427) 872471
Corringham Revd Geoffrey Richardson, Rectory, Normanby Rd, Stow, Lincoln LN1 2DF
Tel: (01427) 788251
Lawres Vacancy
Manlake Revd Michael Cooney, Vicarage, Vicarage Gardens, Scunthorpe DN15 7AZ
Tel: (01724) 842726
West Wold Revd Michael Cartwright, Vicarage, Market Rasen, Lincoln LN8 3HL
Tel: (01673) 843424
Yarborough Canon Stephen Phillips, Vicarage, Great Limber, Grimsby DN37 8JN
Tel: (01469) 560641

ARCHDEACONRY OF LINDSEY
Bolingbroke Revd Adrian Sullivan, Rectory, West Keal, Spilsby PE23 4BJ   *Tel:* (01790) 753534
Calcewaith and Candleshoe Revd Peter Coates, Rectory, Vicarage Lane, Wainfleet St Mary, Skegness PE24 4JJ   *Tel:* (01754) 880401
Grimsby and Cleethorpes Revd John Ellis, 120 Queen Mary Ave, Cleethorpes DN35 7SZ
Tel: (01472) 696521
Haverstoe Canon Peter Hall, Vicarage, 344 Pelham Rd, Immingham, Grimsby DN40 1PU
Tel: (01469) 72560
Horncastle Revd Christopher Elliott, Deanery House, 2 Millstone Close, Langton Drive, Horncastle LN9 5SU   *Tel:* (01507) 525832
Louthesk Revd Stephen Holdaway, Rectory, 49 Westgate, Louth LN11 9YE   *Tel:* (01507) 610247

ARCHDEACONRY OF LINCOLN
Aveland, Ness with Stamford Canon John Warwick, Vicarage, Bourne PE10 9LX
Tel: (01778) 422412
Beltisloe Revd Andrew Hawes, Vicarage, Church Lane, Edenham, Bourne PE10 0LS
Tel: (01778) 591272
Christianity Revd Tony Kerswill, Bracebridge Vicarage, 60 Chiltern Rd, Lincoln LN5 8SE
Tel: (01522) 532636
Elloe (East) Canon Peter Hill, Vicarage, Holbeach, Spalding PE12 7DT   *Tel:* (01406) 22185
Elloe (West) Revd Timothy Thompson, Vicarage, 11 Station Rd, Surfleet, Spalding PE11 4DA
Tel: (01775) 680906
Graffoe Revd Richard Billinghurst, St Lawrence Rectory, Vicarage Drive, Skellingthorpe, Lincoln LN6 5UY   *Tel:* (01522) 682520
Grantham Revd Richard Eyre, Saxonwell Vicarage, Church St, Long Bennington, Newark, NG23 5ES   *Tel:* (01400) 282545
Holland (East) Revd Chris Dalliston, Vicarage, Wormgate, Boston PE21 6NP   *Tel:* (01205) 362864
Holland (West) Revd Margaret Barsley, Vicarage, Church Lane, Swineshead, Boston PE20 3JA
Tel: (01205) 820271
Lafford Revd Hall Speers, Rectory, West St, Folkingham, Sleaford NG34 0SN
Tel: (01529) 497391
Loveden Revd James Hawkins, Rectory, 117 Ermine St, Ancaster, Grantham NG32 3QL
Tel: (01400) 230398

DIOCESE OF LIVERPOOL

Founded in 1880. Liverpool; Sefton; Knowsley;
St Helens; Wigan, except for areas in the north (BLACKBURN)
and in the east (MANCHESTER); Halton, north of the river
Mersey; Warrington, north of the river Mersey.

Population 1,568,000   Area 389 sq m
Stipendiary Clergy 255   Benefices 197
Parishes 210   Churches 256

BISHOP (7th)
Rt Revd James Stuart Jones, Bishop's Lodge,
Woolton Park, Woolton, Liverpool L25 6DT
[1998]   *Tel:* 0151–421 0831
[James Liverpool]
Personal Chaplain Revd Clive Gardner, 48
Babbacombe Rd, Childwall, Liverpool L16 9JW
                            Tel: 0151–421 0831 (Office)
                                 0151–722 9543 (Home)
                                 Fax: 0151–428 3055

SUFFRAGAN BISHOP
WARRINGTON Rt Revd John Richard Packer, 34
Central Ave, Eccleston Park, Prescot, Merseyside
L34 2QP [1996]   *Tel:* 0151–426 1897 (Home)
                        0151–708 9480 (Office)

HONORARY ASSISTANT BISHOP
Rt Revd James William Roxburgh, 53 Preston Rd,
Southport PR9 9EE [1991]   *Tel:* (01704) 542927
Rt Revd Ian Stuart, 55 Woolacombe Rd, Child-
wall, Liverpool L16 9JG [1999] *Tel:* 0151–722 7784

CATHEDRAL CHURCH OF CHRIST
Dean Rt Revd Rupert Hoare, The Cathedral, St
James' Mount, Liverpool L1 7AZ [1999]
                            Tel: 0151–709 6271
Canons Residentiary
Chancellor Canon David Hutton, The Cathedral
[1983]
Treasurer Canon Noel Vincent, The Cathedral
[1995]
Precentor Canon Mark Boyling, The Cathedral
[1993]
Bursar Mr Raymond Maher, The Cathedral
Chapter Clerk Mr Roger Arden, Church House, 1
Hanover St, Liverpool L1 3DW
                            Tel: 0151–709 2222
Cathedral Organist Professor Ian Tracey, The
Cathedral

ARCHDEACONS
LIVERPOOL Ven Bob Metcalf, 38 Menlove Ave,
Liverpool L18 2EF [1994]   *Tel:* 0151–724 3956
                            Fax: 0151–729 0587

WARRINGTON Ven David Woodhouse, 22 Rob
Lane, Newton-le-Willows WA12 0DR [1981]
                            Tel: (01925) 229247
                            Fax: (01925) 220423

**CONVOCATION (MEMBERS OF THE
HOUSE OF CLERGY OF THE GENERAL
SYNOD)**
The Archdeacon of Warrington
Proctors for Clergy
Canon Neville Black
Revd Peter Bradley
Revd Eric Bramhall
Canon Paul Nener
Canon John Stanley

**MEMBERS OF THE HOUSE OF LAITY OF
THE GENERAL SYNOD**
Mr Keith Cawdron
Mr Allan Jones
Mrs Lesley Michell
Dr Peter Owen
Mr Roy Pybus
Mr Christopher Pye
Mrs Margaret Swinson

DIOCESAN OFFICERS
Dioc Secretary Mr Keith Cawdron, Church
House, 1 Hanover St, Liverpool L1 3DW
                            Tel: 0151–709 9722
                            Fax: 0151–709 2885
Chancellor of Diocese His Honour Judge Richard
Hamilton, c/o Diocesan Registry, Church House
Registrar of Diocese and Bishop's Legal Secretary Mr
Roger Arden, Church House   *Tel:* 0151–709 2222

DIOCESAN ORGANIZATIONS
Diocesan Office Church House, 1 Hanover St,
Liverpool L1 3DW   *Tel:* 0151–709 9722
                            Fax: 0151–709 2885

ADMINISTRATION
Dioc Synod (Chairman, House of Clergy) Revd Eric
Bramhall, All Saints' Vicarage, Childwall Abbey
Rd, Liverpool L16 9JU *Tel:* 0151–737 2169;
(Chairman, House of Laity) Mr Christopher Pye,

140 Hinckley Rd, Blackbrook, St Helens WA11 9JY *Tel:* (01744) 36206; (*Secretary*) Mr Keith Cawdron, Church House
Board of Finance (*Chairman*) Mr Barry Moult, Cranbrook, Higher Lane, Dalton, Wigan WN8 7RP *Tel:* (01257) 462841; (*Secretary*) Mr Keith Cawdron (*as above*)
Pastoral Committee (*Chairman*) The Bishop of Warrington; (*Secretary*) Mrs Margaret Sadler, Church House; (*Bishop's Planning Adviser*) Revd Bob Lewis, Church House
Parsonages Committee (*Chairman*) Ven Bob Metcalf, Church House; (*Secretary*) Mrs Jackie Duck, Church House; (*Surveyor*) Hardcastle & Hogarth, Church House
Stipends Officer Mrs Pauline Walsh, Church House
Designated Officer Mr Roger Arden, Church House

CHURCHES

Advisory Committee for the Care of Churches (*Chairman*) Canon Malcolm Forrest, The Hall, Wigan, Lancs WN1 1HN   *Tel:* (01942) 44459
Secretary Revd Noel Michell, Church House

BOARD OF EDUCATION

Chairman The Bishop of Warrington, Church House
Director of Education Canon David Woodhouse, Church House
Youth Officer Mr Richard Turner, Church House
Children's Officer Mrs Jane Leadbetter, 11 Ryegate Rd, Grassendale, Liverpool L19 9AL
Tel: 0151–427 0413
Schools Officer Mr Graham Massey, Church House

BOARD OF MINISTRY

Chairman The Archdeacon of Warrington (*as above*)
Secretary Miss Beryl Smart, 41 Culcheth Hall Drive, Culcheth, Warrington WA3 4PT
Tel: (01925) 762655
Director of Ordinands Revd Myles Davies, St Ann's Vicarage, Derwent Square, Liverpool L13 6QT   *Tel:* 0151–228 5252
Dean of Women's Ministries Canon Lesley Bentley, St Philip's Vicarage, 89 Westbrook Crescent, Westbrook, Warrington WA5 5TC
Tel: (01925) 54400
Director of Continuing Ministerial Education Revd Peter Bradley, Rectory, 1A College Rd, Upholland, Skelmersdale WN8 0PY
Tel and Fax: (01695) 622936
Readers' Association (*Warden*) Mrs Ruth Woodward, 26 Rostron Crescent, Formby, Liverpool L37 2ET   *Tel:* (01704) 872136

LITURGICAL

Chairman Revd Myles Davies (*as above*)

BOARD OF MISSION AND UNITY

Chairman Mrs Linda Jones, St Matthew's Vicarage, 418 Stanley Rd, Bootle, Liverpool L20 5AE   *Tel:* 0151–922 3316
Secretary Revd Julian Hartley, St Paul's Vicarage, Warrington Rd, Goose Green, Wigan WN3 6QB
Tel: (01942) 42984
Director of Christian Development for Mission Mr Christopher Peck, Church House
Evangelism Adviser Mr Phil Pawley, 40 Sherdley Rd, Peasley Cross, St Helens WA9 5AB
Tel: (01744) 737291

PRESS AND PUBLICATIONS

Press and Communications Officer Mrs Katherine Miller, Church House
Editor of 'Livewire' Mrs Anne Todd, c/o Church House

DIOCESAN RECORD OFFICE

For further information apply to Registrar, Church House, 1 Hanover St, Liverpool L1 3DW *Tel:* 0151–709 9722 *or* The Lancashire Record Office, Bow Lane, Preston PR1 8ND *Archivist* Mr K. Hall
Tel: (01772) 254868

BOARD FOR SOCIAL RESPONSIBILITY

Chairman Revd Frank Kendall, Cromwell Villa, 260 Prescot Rd, St Helens WA10 3HR
Executive Officer for Social Responsibility Mr Ultan Russell, Church House   *Tel:* 0151–709 5586
Senior Industrial Chaplain c/o Church House
UPA Link Officer Revd Nicholas Anderson, St Francis' Vicarage, 42 Sherborne Rd, Kitt Green, Wigan WN5 0JA   *Tel:* (01942) 213227

MERSEYSIDE AND REGION CHURCHES ECUMENICAL ASSEMBLY

Ecumenical Officer Revd Martyn Newman, Friends Meeting House, 65 Paradise St, Liverpool L1 3BP   *Tel:* 0151–709 0125

RESOURCES

Resources Officers Mrs Kath Rogers, Mr Graeme Pollard, Church House
UPA Projects Adviser Revd Marion Boon, Church House

AREA DEANS
ARCHDEACONRY OF LIVERPOOL

Bootle Vacancy
Huyton Canon John Stanley, Vicarage, Huyton, Merseyside L36 7SA   *Tel:* 0151–489 1449
Liverpool North Revd David Lewis, Vicarage, 48 John Lennon Drive, Liverpool L6 9HT
Tel: 0151–260 3262
Liverpool South – Childwall Canon John Roberts, 67 Church Rd, Woolton, Liverpool L25 6DA
Tel: 0151–428 1853

Sefton Canon Frances Briscoe, St Stephen's Vicarage, St Stephen's Rd, Hightown, Merseyside L38 0BL   *Tel:* 0151–929 2469

Toxteth and Wavertree Revd David Kirkwood, 40 Devonshire Rd, Liverpool L8 3TZ
Tel: 0151–727 1248

Walton Canon Anthony Hawley, Rectory, Mill Lane, Kirkby, Liverpool L32 2AX
Tel: 0151–547 2155

West Derby Canon Roger Wikeley, Rectory, West Derby, Liverpool L12 5EA   *Tel:* 0151–256 6600

ARCHDEACONRY OF WARRINGTON

North Meols Revd John Burgess, St Philip's Vicarage, Scarisbrick New Rd, Southport PR8 6QF   *Tel:* (01704) 532886

Ormskirk Canon Michael Smout, Rectory, 10 Church Lane, Aughton L39 6SB
Tel: (01695) 423204

St Helens Canon Chris Byworth, 51A Rainford Rd, St Helens WA10 6BZ   *Tel:* (01744) 22067

Warrington Revd Michael Raynor, St Andrew's Vicarage, Poplars Ave, Orford, Warrington WA2 9UE *Tel:* (01925) 631903

Widnes Canon Brian Robinson, St Mary's Vicarage, St Mary's Rd, Widnes WA8 0DN
Tel: 0151–424 4233

Wigan East Canon Malcolm Forrest, The Hall, Wigan WN1 1HN   *Tel:* (01942) 44459

Wigan West Revd John Taylor, St James's Vicarage, Worsley Mesnes, Wigan WN3 5HL
Tel: (01942) 243896

Winwick Revd Bob Britton, Vicarage, 1 Barford Drive, St Mary's Park, Lowton WA3 1DD
Tel: (01942) 607705

DIOCESE OF LONDON

Founded in 314. The City of London; Greater London north of the Thames, except five East London boroughs (CHELMSFORD) and an area in the north (ST ALBANS); Surrey north of the Thames; a small area of southern Hertfordshire.

Population 3,437,000   Area 277 sq m
Stipendiary Clergy 552   Benefices 409
Parishes 410   Churches 480

BISHOP (132nd)
Rt Revd and Rt Hon Richard John Carew Chartres, The Old Deanery, Dean's Court, London EC4V 5AA [1995]   *Tel:* 020–7248 6233
Fax: 020–7248 9721
email: bishop@londin.clara.co.uk
[Richard Londin:]
Personal Jurisdiction Cities of London and Westminster (*Archdeaconries of London and Charing Cross*)
Matters relating to the other Areas should be referred to the appropriate Area Bishop
Chaplain Revd Mark Oakley
Personal Assistant Mrs Joanna Simms

AREA BISHOPS
STEPNEY Rt Revd John Sentamu PH D, 63 Coborn Rd, Bow, London E3 2DB [1996]
Tel: 020–8981 2323
Fax: 020–8981 8015
email: bishop.stepney@dlondon.org.uk
KENSINGTON Rt Revd Michael Colclough, 19 Campden Hill Square, London W8 7JY [1996]
Tel: 020–7727 9818
Fax: 020–7229 3651
email: bishop.kensington@dlondon.org.uk
EDMONTON Rt Revd Peter Wheatley, 27 Thurlow Rd, London NW3 5PP [1999]   *Tel:* 020–7435 5890
Fax: 020–7435 6049
email: bishop.edmonton@dlondon.org.uk
WILLESDEN Rt Revd Graham Dow, 173 Willesden Lane, London NW6 7YN [1992]
Tel: 020–8451 0189
Fax: 020–8451 4606
email: bishop.willesden@btinternet.com

SUFFRAGAN BISHOP
FULHAM Rt Revd John Broadhurst, 26 Canonbury Park South, London N1 2FN [1996]
Tel: 020–7354 2334
Fax: 020–7354 2335
email: bpfulham@compuserve.com
Assists the Diocesan in all matters not delegated to the Areas and pastoral care of parishes operating under the London Plan.

HONORARY ASSISTANT BISHOPS
Rt Revd Maurice Wood, 41 Fir Tree Walk, Enfield, Middx EN1 3TZ [1985]   *Tel:* 020–8363 4491
Rt Revd Michael Marshall, 97A Cadogan Lane, London SW1X 9DU [1984]
Rt Revd Roderic Coote, Friday Woods, Stoke Rd, Cobham, Surrey KT11 3AS   *Tel:* (01932) 867306
Rt Revd Donald Arden, 6 Frobisher Close, Pinner HA5 1NN   *Tel:* 020–8866 6009
Rt Revd Michael Baughen, 99 Brunswick Quay, London SE16 1PX   *Tel:* 020–7237 0167

CATHEDRAL CHURCH OF ST PAUL
Dean Very Revd John Moses PH D, 9 Amen Court, London EC4M 7BU [1996]
Tel: 020–7236 2827
Fax: 020–7332 0298
email: dean.stpauls@dial.pipex.com
Canons Residentiary
Canon John Halliburton, 1 Amen Court, EC4M 7BU [1989]   *Tel:* 020–7248 1817
email: johnhalliburton@dial.pipex.com
Canon Michael Saward, 6 Amen Court, EC4M 7BU [1991]   *Tel:* 020–7248 8572
Canon Stephen Oliver, 3 Amen Court, EC4M 7BU [1996]   *Tel:* 020–7248 2559
Canon Philip Buckler, 2 Amen Court, EC4M 7BU [1999]   *Tel:* 020–7248 3312
The College of Minor Canons
Chaplain and Warden of the College Revd Lucy Winkett, 7B Amen Court, EC4M 7BU [1997]
Tel: 020–7246 8323
email: chaplain@stpaulscathedral.org.uk
Sacrist Revd Alasdair Coles, 7A Amen Court, EC4M 7BU [1999]   *Tel:* 020–7246 8331
email: sacrist@stpaulscathedral.org.uk
Succentor Revd Gordon Giles, 8A Amen Court, EC4M 7BU [1998]   *Tel:* 020–7246 8338
email: succentor@stpaulscathedral.org.uk
Headmaster of the Choir School Mr Stephen Sides, St Paul's Cathedral Choir School, New Change, London EC4M 9AD   *Tel:* 020–7248 5156
Registrar Brigadier Robert Acworth, Chapter House, St Paul's Churchyard, EC4M 8AD
Tel: 020–7246 8311
email: registrar@stpaulscathedral.org.uk

Warden of St Paul's and Dean's Virger Mr Michael Page, 4A Amen Court, EC4M 7BU
Tel: 020–7246 8320
email: virgers@spcl.freeserve.co.uk
Chapter Clerk Mr David Faull, Winckworth & Sherwood, The Old Deanery, EC4V 5AA
Tel: 020–7593 5043
Surveyor Mr Martin Stancliffe, The Chapter House, St Paul's Churchyard, EC4M 8AD
Tel: 0171–236 4128 and (01904) 644001 (York)
Cathedral Organist Mr John Scott, 4 Amen Court, EC4M 7BU
Tel: 020–7248 6868
email: music.stpauls@dial.pipex.com
Sub Organist Mr Huw Williams, 8B Amen Court, EC4M 7BU
Tel: 020–7236 4257
Assistant Sub Organist Mr Richard Moorhouse, The Chapter House, St Paul's Churchyard, EC4M 8AD
Tel: 020–7736 0366

ARCHDEACONS

LONDON Ven Peter Delaney, Parish House, Trinity Square, London EC3N 4DJ [1999]
Tel: 020–7488 4772
Fax: 020–7488 3333
email: archdeacon.london@dlondon.org.uk
CHARING CROSS Ven William Jacob, The Old Deanery, Dean's Court, London EC4V 5AA [1996]
Tel: 020–7248 6233
Fax: 020–7248 9721
email: william.jacob@clara.co.uk
HACKNEY Ven Lyle Dennen, St Andrew's Vicarage, 5 St Andrew St, EC4A 3AB [1999]
Tel: 020–7353 3544
Fax: 020–7583 2750
email: archdeacon.hackney@dlondon.org.uk
MIDDLESEX Ven Malcolm Colmer, 59 Sutton Lane South, London W4 3JR [1996]
Tel: 020–8994 8148 (Office)
Fax: 020–8995 5374
email: archdeacon.middlesex@dlondon.org.uk
HAMPSTEAD Ven Michael Lawson, The Basement, 44 King's Henry Rd, London NW3 3RP [1999]
Tel: 020–7586 3224
Fax: 020–7586 9976
email: archdeacon.hampstead@dlondon.org.uk
NORTHOLT Ven Pete Broadbent, 247 Kenton Rd, Kenton, Harrow, Middlesex HA3 0HQ [1995]
Tel: 020–8907 5941
07957 144674 (Mobile)
Fax: 020–8909 2368
email: pete@arch-northolt.demon.co.uk

CONVOCATION (MEMBERS OF THE HOUSE OF CLERGY OF THE GENERAL SYNOD)

The Archdeacon of Charing Cross
Proctors for Clergy
Revd Philippa Boardman
Preb Kenneth Bowler
Ven Pete Broadbent
Preb John Brownsell
Revd John Cook
Revd David Houlding

Revd Malcolm Johnson
Revd Ulla Monberg
Revd David Stone
Preb Ronald Swan

MEMBERS OF THE HOUSE OF LAITY OF THE GENERAL SYNOD

Mrs Molly Dow
Sir Timothy Hoare
Mrs Mary Johnston
Ms Josile Munro
Mrs Alison Ruoff
Mr Christopher Smith
Mrs Elaine Storkey
Mr Frank Williams

DIOCESAN OFFICERS

Dioc Secretary Mr Keith Robinson, London Diocesan House, 36 Causton St, London SW1P 4AU
Tel: 020–7932 1221
Fax: 020–7932 1114
email: keith.robinson @dlondon.org.uk
Chancellor of Diocese Chanc Sheila Cameron, The Old Deanery, Dean's Court, London EC4V 5AA
Tel: 020–7593 5110
Fax: 020–7248 3221
Registrar of Diocese and Bishop's Legal Secretary Mr Paul Morris (*same address*)
Official Principal of the Archdeaconry of Hackney Mr David Smith, 3 Pump Court, Temple, London EC4Y 7AJ
Official Principal of the Archdeaconry of Hampstead Chanc Sheila Cameron, 2 Harcourt Bldgs, Temple, London EC4Y 9DB
Official of the Archdeaconry of Northolt Mr Paul Morris (*as above*)

DIOCESAN ORGANIZATIONS
CHAIRMEN

London Dioc Fund (*Dioc Board of Finance*) The Bishop of London
Deputy Chairman and Treasurer Sir Timothy Hoare
Finance Committee Sir Timothy Hoare
Dioc Synod (*House of Clergy*) Preb John Slater; (*House of Laity*) Sir Timothy Hoare
Dioc Board for Schools Ven Pete Broadbent
CARIS (*Dioc Board for Social Responsibility*) The Bishop of Edmonton

ADMINISTRATION

Diocesan Office London Diocesan House, 36 Causton St, London SW1P 4AU
Tel: 020–7932 1100
Fax: 020–7932 1112
Statutory Service Mr Roger Clayton Pearce
Financial Controller Mr Richard Walker
Office Manager and Personnel Officer Mr John Sansom
Property Finance Mrs Karen Smith
Parsonages and Glebe Revd Roger Hills
Information and Technology Mr Martin How

Dioc Advisory Committee (*Chair*) Mr Michael Gillingham; (*Secretary*) Mr Brian Cuthbertson *Designated Officer* Mr Paul Morris (*as above*)

EDUCATION

Senior Chaplain for Higher Education Revd Stephen Williams, University Chaplaincy Office, 48B Gordon Square, London WC1H 0PD
Tel: 020–7387 0670
Director, Board for Schools Mr Tom Peryer, London Dioc House

MINISTRY

Ordained Ministry
Dioc Director Revd Dr Christopher Cunliffe, London Dioc House   *Tel:* 020–7932 1236

Two Cities
Director of Ordinands Revd Ulla Monberg, 11 Ormonde Mansions, 106 Southampton Row, London WC1B 4BP   *Tel:* 020–7242 7533
Associate Director of Ordinands Revd Graham Buckle, St Peter's Vicarage, Elgin Ave, London W9 2DB   *Tel:* 020–7289 2011
0956 850089 (Mobile)
email: buckle@freeuk.com
Continuing Ministerial Education Officer Preb John Slater, St John's House, St John's Wood, London NW8 7NE   *Tel:* 020–7722 4378
Dean of Women's Ministry Revd Ulla Monberg (*as above*)

Stepney
Director of Ordinands Revd Kevin Scully, St Faith's House, Shandy St, London E1 4ST
Tel: 020–7791 0330
Director of Post-Ordination Training Revd David Paton, St Vedast's Rectory, 4 Foster Lane, London EC2V 6HH   *Tel:* 020–7606 1863
Dean of Women's Ministry Vacancy
Continuing Ministerial Education Officer Revd Rachel Montgomery, St James the Less Vicarage, St James Ave, London E2 9JD   *Tel:* 020–8979 2069
Fax: 020–8255 8095

Kensington
Director of Ordinands Revd Dr Brian Leathard, Vicarage, 46 St James Rd, Hampton Hill, Middx TW12 1DQ   *Tel:* 020–7727 5919
email: B.Leathard@btinternet.com
Director of Post-Ordination Training Revd Kevin Morris, St Michael's Vicarage, Priory Gardens, London W4 1TT   *Tel:* 020–8994 1380
Continuing Ministerial Education Officer Revd Neil Evans, All Hallows Vicarage, 138 Chertsey Rd, Twickenham, Middx TW1 1EW
Tel: 020–8892 1322
Dean of Women's Ministry Revd Madeleine Bulman, St Saviour's Vicarage, Cobbold Rd, London W12 9LQ   *Tel:* 020–8743 4769
Fax: 020–8740 1501

Willesden
Directors of Ordinands Revd Andrew Godsall, All Saints Vicarage, Ryefield Ave, Hillingdon, Middx. UB10 9BT   *Tel:* (01895) 233991
Revd Trevor Mapstone, 39 Rusland Park Rd, Harrow, Middx HA1 1UN   *Tel:* 020–8427 2616
Director of Post-Ordination Training Revd William Taylor, St Peter's Vicarage, Mount Park Rd, London W5 2RU   *Tel:* 020–8997 1620
email: tmapstone@aol.com
Continuing Ministerial Education Officer Revd David Neno, 54 Roe Green, Kingsbury, London NW9 0PJ   *Tel:* 020–8204 7531
Dean of Women's Ministry Revd Jackie Fox, 14 Cumberland Park, Acton, London W3 6SX
Tel: 020–8992 8876

Edmonton
Director of Ordinands Revd Dr Perry Butler, Rectory, 6 Gower St, London WC1E 6DP
Tel: 020–7580 4010
Director of Post-Ordination Training Revd Paul Taylor, Vicarage, Parson St, London NW4 1QR
Tel: 020–8203 2884
Assistant Director (*NSM*) Revd Tarjei Park, Vicarage, Gordon Hill, Enfield, Middx EN2 0QP
Tel: 020–8363 2483
Assistant Director Revd Nicholas Wheeler, 191 St Pancras Way, London NW1 9NH
Continuing Ministerial Education Officer Revd Richard Knowling, St John's Vicarage, 1 Bourne Hill, London N13 4DA   *Tel:* 020–8886 1348
Women's Ministry Vacancy
Secretary of Board of Women Candidates for Ordination Vacancy

MISSION
Bishop's Adviser in Evangelism Preb David Saville, London Dioc House   Tel: 020–7932 1231

LITURGICAL
Chairman Ven Malcolm Colmer (*as above*)
Secretary Dr Alan Everett, 97 Lavender Grove, London E8 3LR   *Tel:* 020–7249 2627

PRESS AND COMMUNICATIONS
Director of Communications Vacancy, London Dioc House   *Tel:* 020–7932 1240
0831 120596 (Mobile)
Fax: 020–7233 8670
Editor of Diocese Book Vacancy (*as above*)

DIOCESAN RECORD OFFICES
London Metropolitan Archive, 40 Northampton Rd, London EC1R 0HB *Head Archivist* Dr Deborah Jenkins, *Tel:* 020–7332 3824 (*All parishes except City and Westminster*)
Guildhall Library, Aldermanbury, London EC2P 2EJ *Archivist* Mr S. G. H. Freeth, *Tel:* 020–7606 3030, Ext 1862/3 (*City parishes*)
Westminster Archives Dept, 10 St Ann's St, London SW1P 2XR *Archivist* Mr Jerome Farrell *Tel:* 020–7798 2180 (*Westminster parishes*)

SOCIAL RESPONSIBILITY
CARIS (*Director*) Revd Chris Brice, London Dioc House *Tel:* 020–7932 1121

AREA DEANS
ARCHDEACONRY OF LONDON
City Preb John Oates, St Bride's Rectory, Fleet St, London EC4Y 8AU   *Tel:* 020–7353 1301

ARCHDEACONRY OF CHARING CROSS
Westminster (Paddington) Revd William Wilson, 6 Gloucester Terrace, London W2 3DD
        Tel: 020–7723 8119
Westminster (St Margaret) Revd William Scott, 30 Bourne St, London SW1W 8JJ *Tel:* 020–7730 2423
Westminster (St Marylebone) Preb John Slater, St John's House, St John's Wood, London NW8 7NE   *Tel:* 020–7586 3864

ARCHDEACONRY OF HACKNEY
Hackney Revd Elaine Jones, St Mary's House, Eastway, London E9 5JA   *Tel:* 020–7739 9823
        email: elaine.jones@dlondon.org.uk
Islington Revd Jonathan Clark, 123 Calabria Rd, London N5 1HS   *Tel:* 020–7753 7038
Tower Hamlets Revd Christopher Chessun, Stepney Rectory, Rectory Square, London E1 3NQ   *Tel:* 020–7791 3545
        email: christopher.chessun@dlondon.org.uk

ARCHDEACONRY OF MIDDLESEX
Hammersmith and Fulham Revd Jonathan Clark, 153 Blythe Rd, London W14 0HL
        Tel: 020–7602 1043
Hampton Preb David Vanstone, 40 The Avenue, Hampton, Middx TW12 3RS   *Tel:* 020–8979 2102
Hounslow Revd David Wilson, St Mary's Vicarage, Osterley Rd, Isleworth, Middx TW7 4PW   *Tel:* 020–860 3555
Kensington Revd Harold Stringer, 25 Ladbroke Rd, London W11 3PD   *Tel:* 020–7727 3439
Chelsea Revd David Stone, 20 Collingham Rd, London SW5 0LX   *Tel:* 020–7373 1693

Spelthorne Revd Christopher Swift, Rectory, Church Square, Shepperton TW17 9JY
        Tel: (01932) 220511

ARCHDEACONRY OF HAMPSTEAD
Central Barnet Revd Raymond Taylor, Vicarage, Woodland Rd, London N11 1PN
        Tel: 020–8361 1946
West Barnet Revd Dr Peter Baker, Vicarage, 3 St Alban's Close, North End Rd, London NW11 7RA   *Tel:* 020–8455 4525
North Camden (Hampstead) Revd Charles Mason, 13 Kingscroft Rd, London NW2 3QE
        Tel: 020–8452 1913
South Camden (Holborn and St Pancras) Revd Guy Pope, Vicarage, 85 Dartmouth Park Rd, London NW5 1SL   *Tel:* 020–7267 5941
Enfield Revd Richard Knowling, 1 Bourne Hill, Palmers Green, London N13 4DA
        Tel: 020–8886 1348
East Haringey Preb Roy Pearson, The Priory, Church Lane, London N17 7RA
        Tel: 020–8808 2470
West Haringey Revd Geoffrey Seabrook, Rectory, 140 Cranley Gardens, London N10 3AH
        Tel: 020–8883 6846

ARCHDEACONRY OF NORTHOLT
Brent Revd John Root, Vicarage, 34 Stanley Ave, Alperton, Middx HA0 4JB   *Tel:* 020–8902 1729
Ealing Revd Dr John Hereward, St Mellitus Vicarage, Church Rd, London W7 3BA
        Tel: 020–8563 6535
        email: 100756.2151@compuserve.com
Harrow Revd Paul Reece, Whitchurch Rectory, St Lawrence Close, Edgware, Middx HA8 6RB
        Tel: 020–8952 0019
        email: paul.reece@dlondon.org.uk
Hillingdon Revd Philip Robinson, St Giles's Rectory, 38 Swakeleys Rd, Ickenham, Middx UB10 8BE   *Tel* and *Fax:* (01895) 622970
        email: stgilesickenham@compuserve.com

Founded in 1847. Manchester, except for a few parishes in the south (CHESTER); Salford; Bolton; Bury; Rochdale; Oldham; the western half of Tameside; an area of Wigan; an area of Trafford; an area of Stockport; an area of southern Lancashire.

Population 1,960,000   Area 415 sq m
Stipendiary Clergy 299   Benefices 278
Parishes 302   Churches 365

BISHOP (10th)
Rt Revd Christopher John Mayfield, Bishops-court, Bury New Rd, Manchester M7 4LE [1993]
Tel: 0161–792 2096 (Office)
Fax: 0161–792 6826
email: +Chris@bishopscourtman.free-online.co.uk
[Christopher Manchester]
Chaplain Revd Paul Richardson, St Gabriel's Vicarage, 8 Bishop's Rd, Prestwich, Manchester M25 0HT   *Tel:* 0161–792 2096 (Office)
0161–773 8839 (Home)

SUFFRAGAN BISHOPS
BOLTON Rt Revd David Keith Gillett, Bishop's Lodge, Bolton Rd, Hawkshaw, Bury BL8 4JN [1999]   *Tel:* (01204) 882955
Fax: (01204) 882988
email: David.Gillett@ukgateway.net
MIDDLETON Rt Revd Michael Augustine Owen Lewis, The Hollies, Manchester Rd, Rochdale, Lancs. OL11 3QY [1999]   *Tel:* (01706) 358550
Fax: (01706) 354851
HULME Rt Revd Stephen Richard Lowe, 14 Moorgate Ave, Withington, Manchester M20 1HE [1999]   *Tel:* 0161–445 5922
Fax: 0161–448 9687
email: 100737.634@compuserve.com

CATHEDRAL AND COLLEGIATE CHURCH OF ST MARY, ST DENYS AND ST GEORGE
Dean Very Revd Kenneth Riley, 1 Booth Clibborn Court, Park Lane, Manchester M7 4PJ [1993]
Tel: 0161–792 2801
Cathedral Office The Cathedral, Manchester M3 1SX   *Tel:* 0161–833 2220
Fax: 0161–839 6226
email: manchester.cathedral@btinternet.com
Canons Residentiary
Canon John Atherton, 3 Booth Clibborn Court, Park Lane, Manchester M7 4PJ [1984]
Tel: 0161–792 0973
Fax: 0161–839 6226
email: drjohn.atherton@btinternet.com
Canon Albert Radcliffe, 46 Shrewsbury Road, Prestwich, Manchester, M25 8GO [1991]
Tel: 0161–798 0459
Fax: 0161–839 6226
email: albert.e.radcliffe@btinternet.com

Precentor Canon Paul Denby, 2 Booth Clibborn Court, Park Lane, Manchester M7 4PJ [1995]
Tel: 0161–792 0979
email: paul.denby@btinternet.com
Ven Alan Wolstencroft, 2 The Walled Garden, Ewhurst Ave, Swinton, Manchester M27 0FR [1998]   *Tel:* 0161–794 2401
Fax: 0161–794 2411
Chapter Clerk Mr W. A. Brock, Messrs Cobbett Leak Almond, Ship Canal House, King St, Manchester M2 4WB   *Tel:* 0161–833 3333
Cathedral Organist and Master of the Choristers Mr Christopher Stokes, c/o Cathedral Office
Sub Organist Mr Matthew Owens (*same address*)
Organ Scholar Mr Paul Walton (*same address*)

ARCHDEACONS
MANCHESTER Ven Alan Wolstencroft, 2 The Walled Gardens, Ewhurst Ave, Swinton, Manchester M27 0FR [1998]   *Tel:* 0161–794 2401
Fax: 0161–794 2411
ROCHDALE Ven Dr Mark Dalby, 21 Belmont Way, Rochdale, Lancs. OL12 6HR [1991]
Tel and Fax: (01706) 648640
BOLTON Ven Lorys Davies, 45 Rudgwick Drive, Brandlesholme, Bury, Lancs. BL8 1YA [1992]
Tel and Fax: 0161–761 6117

CONVOCATION (MEMBERS OF THE HOUSE OF CLERGY OF THE GENERAL SYNOD)
Dignitaries in Convocation
The Dean of Manchester
The Archdeacon of Bolton
Proctors for Clergy
Revd Michael Ainsworth
Canon Wendy Bracegirdle
Revd Janet Fife
Revd Simon Killwick
Canon Charles Razzall
(One vacancy)

MEMBERS OF THE HOUSE OF LAITY OF THE GENERAL SYNOD
Mrs Jessie Axtell
Dr Peter Capon
Mr Alan Cooper
Mrs Louise Da-Cocodia

Mr Stuart Emmason
Mr Philip Gore
Mr Geoffrey Tattersall
Mr Michael Winterbottom

DIOCESAN OFFICERS

Dioc Secretary Mrs Jackie Park, Diocesan Church House, 90 Deansgate, Manchester M3 2GH
Tel: 0161–833 9521
Fax: 0161–833 2751
Chancellor of Diocese Mr J. L. O. Holden, Willow Bank, 49 Brooklands Rd, Towneley, Burnley BB11 3PR
Deputy Chancellor Dr N. Doe, Dioc Registry, Dioc Church House   *Tel:* 0161–834 7545
Registrar of Diocese and Bishop's Legal Secretary Mr Michael Darlington (*same address*)
Dioc Surveyor for Parsonage Houses Mr John Prichard, The Lloyd Evans Partnership, 5 The Parsonage, Manchester M3 2HS
Tel: 0161–834 6251

DIOCESAN ORGANIZATIONS

Diocesan Office Diocesan Church House, 90 Deansgate, Manchester M3 2GH
Tel: 0161–833 9521
Fax: 0161–833 2751

ADMINISTRATION

Dioc Synod (*Chairman, House of Clergy*) Canon Anthony Durrans, Rectory, 233 Barton Rd, Stretford, Manchester M32 9RB *Tel:* 0161–865 1350; (*Chairman, House of Laity*) Mr Geoffrey Tattersall, 2 The Woodlands, Lostock, Bolton BL6 4JD
Board of Finance (*Chairman*) Mr Alan Cooper, 11 Ravensdale Gdns, Eccles, Manchester M30 9JD *Tel:* 0161–789 1514; (*General Secretary*) Mrs Jackie Park, Dioc Office; (*Deputy Secretary*) Dr Ray Hughes, Dioc Office; (*Head of Finance*) Mr Allan Molyneux, Dioc Office; (*Legal Secretary*) Mr Michael Darlington, Dioc Registry, Dioc Church House   *Tel:* 0161–834 7545
Property Committee (*Property Secretary*) Mr Geoff Hutchinson, Dioc Office
Pastoral Committee Mrs Jackie Park (*as above*)
Designated Officer Mr Michael Darlington, Dioc Registry, Dioc Church House   *Tel:* 0161–834 7545

CHURCHES

Advisory Committee for the Care of Churches (*Chairman*) Mr Adrian Golland, Peel House, 29 Higher Dunscar, Egerton, Bolton BL7 9TE; (*Administrative Secretary*) Ms Christine Hart, Dioc Office

EDUCATION

Director of Education Mrs Jan Ainsworth, Dioc Church House M3 2GJ   *Tel:* 0161–834 1022
Schools' Officer Mr David Thomas (*same address*)
Children's Work Adviser Miss Isobel Booth-Clibborn (*same address*)

Youth Work Adviser Revd Susan Howard (*same address*)
Adviser for Further and Higher Education Revd Dr Iain Bentley (*same address*)

MINISTRY

Board of Ministry (*Chairman*) The Bishop of Bolton
Director of Continuing Ministerial Education Revd Alan Tiltman, Dioc Office   *Tel:* 0161–832 5785
Director of Laity Development Ms Margaret Halsey, Dioc Office   *Tel:* 0161–832 5785
Ordained Local Ministry Governing Body (*Chairman*) Ven Dr Mark Dalby, 21 Belmont Way, Rochdale, Lancs. OL12 6HR
Tel and *Fax:* (01706) 648640
(*Director*) Canon Wendy Bracegirdle, Dioc Office
Tel: 0161–832 5785
Dioc Director of Ordinands and LNSM Officer Revd Jonathan MacGillivray, Bishopscourt, Bury New Rd, Manchester M4 4LE   *Tel:* 0161–708 9366
Fax: 0161–792 6826
Adviser in Women's Ministry Revd Averil Cunnington, Alston Londes, 629 Huddersfield Rd, Lees, Oldham OL4 3PY   *Tel:* 0161–624 9614
Readers' and Lay Assistants' Committee (*Chairman*) The Archdeacon of Bolton; (*Secretary*) Mr G. Howard, 87 Bury & Bolton Rd, Redcliffe, Manchester M26 0JY   *Tel:* 0161–797 5548

WORSHIP COMMITTEE

Chairman Revd Simon Tatton-Brown, Rectory, Market St, Westhoughton, Bolton BL5 3AZ
Tel: (01942) 813280
Secretary Mrs Sue Usher, Milnrow Vicarage, 40 Eafield Ave, Milnrow, Rochdale OL16 3UN
Tel: (01706) 42988

BOARD FOR CHURCH AND SOCIETY

Chairman The Bishop of Hulme
Dioc Executive Officer Revd Stephen Little, Dioc Office   *Tel:* 0161–832 5253
Fax: 0161–832 2869
Admin Secretary Mrs Joan Beresford (*same address*)
Ecumenical Officer Revd Ian Blay, St Andrew's Rectory, Merton Drive, Droylesden, Manchester M35 6BH   *Tel:* 0161–370 3242
Advisers on Evangelism Capt Andrew Dyer, 9 Macefin Ave, Chorlton-cum-Hardy, Manchester M21 7QQ   *Tel:* 0161–445 4063
Revd Mike Saunders, St Andrew's Vicarage, 11 Abbey Grove, Eccles, Manchester M30 9QN
Tel: 0161–707 1742

PRESS AND PUBLICATIONS

Dioc Press and Communications Officer Revd D. Johnson   *Tel:* 0161–833 9521 (Office)
(01204) 699301 (Home)
0836 224444 (Mobile)
Fax: (01204) 667924
email: dco.manchester@btinternet.com

Editor of Dioc Year Book c/o Dioc Office
Editor of Dioc Magazine Ms Jan Harney (*as above*)
Tel: (01942) 671481

DIOCESAN RECORD OFFICE
For further information apply to The Central
Library, St Peter's Square, Manchester M2 5PD
Archivist Miss D. Rayson   *Tel:* 0161–234 1980

STEWARDSHIP
Chairman The Archdeacon of Bolton
Christian Giving Officer Mr Ken Wiggans, Dioc
Office   *Tel:* 0161–833 9521

AREA DEANS
ARCHDEACONRY OF MANCHESTER
Ardwick Revd William Nelson, St Clement's
Rectory, Ashton Old Rd, Manchester M11 1HJ
Tel: 0161–370 1538
Eccles Revd Norman Jones, Rectory, 12B
Westminster Rd, Eccles, Manchester M30 9EB
Tel: 0161–281 5739
Heaton Revd Marcus Maxwell, St John's Rectory,
15 Priestnall Rd, Stockport, Cheshire SK4 3HR
Tel: 0161–432 2165
Hulme Revd Simon Gatenby, Rectory, Hartfield
Close, Brunswick, Manchester M13 9YX
Tel: 0161–273 2470
North Manchester Revd Dr Christopher Ford, St
John's Rectory, Railton Terrace, Moston,
Manchester M9 1WE   *Tel:* 0161–205 4967
Salford Revd Dr John Applegate, St John's
Rectory, 237 Great Clowes St, Higher Broughton,
Salford M7 2DZ   *Tel:* 0161–792 9161
Stretford Revd Philip Rawlings, St Bride's
Rectory, 29 Shrewsbury St, Old Trafford,
Manchester M16 9AP   *Tel:* 0161–226 6064
Withington Revd David Thomas, St Luke's
Vicarage, Brownley Rd, Benchill, Manchester
M22 4PT   *Tel:* 0161–998 2071

ARCHDEACONRY OF BOLTON
Bolton Revd Roger Oldfield, St Peter's Vicarage,
Harpers Lane, Bolton BL1 6HT
Tel: (01204) 849412
Bury Revd Ian Rogerson, St Andrew's Vicarage,
Henwick Hall Ave, Broadhey Park, Ramsbottom
BL0 9YH   *Tel:* (01706) 826482
Deane Revd Philip Brew, Lostock Vicarage, 9
Lowside Ave, Lostock, Bolton BL1 5XQ
Tel: (01204) 848631
Farnworth Revd Brian Hartley, New Bury
Rectory, 130A Highfield Rd, Farnworth, Bolton
BL4 0AJ   *Tel:* (01204) 572334
Leigh Revd Peter Leakey, Pennington Vicarage,
Schofield St, Leigh WN7 4HT *Tel:* (01942) 673619
Radcliffe and Prestwich Canon Frank Bibby,
Rectory, Church Lane, Prestwich, Manchester
M25 1LN   *Tel:* 0161–773 2912
Rossendale Revd Charles Ellis, Rectory, 539
Newchurch Rd, Rossendale BB4 9HH
Tel: (01706) 215098
Walmsley Revd David Brierley, Walmsley
Vicarage, Egerton, Bolton BL7 9RZ
Tel: (01204) 304283

ARCHDEACONRY OF ROCHDALE
Ashton-under-Lyne Revd Ronald Cassidy, Rectory,
131 Town Lane, Denton, Manchester M34 2DJ
Tel: 0161–320 4895
Heywood and Middleton Canon Nick Feist,
Middleton Rectory, Mellalieu St, Middleton,
Manchester M24 5DN   *Tel:* 0161–643 2693
Oldham Revd Richard Stephens, Holy Trinity
Rectory, 103 Oldham Rd, Failsworth,
Manchester M35 0BZ   *Tel:* 0161–682 7901
Rochdale Revd Ian Thompson, St Mary's
Vicarage, The Sett, Badger Lane, Rochdale OL16
4RQ   *Tel:* (01706) 49886
Saddleworth Revd Michael Tinker, Saddleworth
Vicarage, Station Rd, Uppermill, Oldham OL3
6HQ   *Tel:* (01457) 872412
Tandle Revd David Sharples, St Anne's Vicarage,
St Anne's Ave, Royton, Oldham OL2 5AD
Tel: 0161–624 2249

DIOCESE OF NEWCASTLE

Founded in 1882. Northumberland; Newcastle upon Tyne; North Tyneside; a small area of eastern Cumbria; two parishes in northern County Durham.

Population 784,000   Area 2,110 sq m
Stipendiary Clergy 153   Benefices 133
Parishes 175   Churches 250

BISHOP (11th)
Rt Revd (John) Martin Wharton, Bishop's House, 29 Moor Rd South, Gosforth, Newcastle upon Tyne NE3 1PA [1998]   *Tel:* 0191–285 2220
email: bishop@newcastle.anglican.org
[Martin Newcastle]
Bishop's Chaplain Canon A. S. Craig (*same addesss*)

ASSISTANT BISHOP
Rt Revd Paul Richardson, Close House, St George's Close, Jesmond, Newcastle upon Tyne NE2 2TF   *Tel:* 0191–281 2556

CATHEDRAL CHURCH OF ST NICHOLAS
Provost Very Revd Nicholas Guy Coulton, 26 Mitchell Ave, Jesmond, Newcastle upon Tyne NE2 3LA [1990]   *Tel:* 0191–281 6554
Cathedral Office The Cathedral, St Nicholas Churchyard, Newcastle upon Tyne NE1 1PF
Tel: 0191–232 1939
Fax: 0191–230 0735
Canons Residentiary
Canon Peter Strange, 55 Queens Terrace, Jesmond, Newcastle upon Tyne NE2 2PL [1986]
Tel: 0191–281 0181
Ven Peter Elliott, 80 Moorside North, Fenham, Newcastle upon Tyne NE4 9DU [1993]
Tel and Fax: 0191–273 8245
Canon Geoffrey Miller, 58 Baronswood Rd, Gosforth, Newcastle upon Tyne NE3 3UB [1999]
Tel: 0191–285 3667
Chapter Clerk Mr Derek Govier, Cathedral Office
Master of Music Mr Timothy Hone, Cathedral Office
Cathedral Secretary Mrs Lesley Wright, Cathedral Office

ARCHDEACONS
LINDISFARNE Ven Michael Bowering, 12 Rectory Park, Morpeth, Northumberland NE61 2SZ [1987]   *Tel:* (01670) 513207
NORTHUMBERLAND Ven Peter Elliott, 80 Moorside North, Fenham, Newcastle upon Tyne NE4 9DU [1993]   *Tel and Fax:* 0191–273 8245

CONVOCATION (MEMBERS OF THE HOUSE OF CLERGY OF THE GENERAL SYNOD)

Dignitaries in Convocation
The Provost of Newcastle
The Archdeacon of Lindisfarne
Proctors for Clergy
Revd Norman Banks
Canon Richard Bryant
Canon Frank Dexter

MEMBERS OF THE HOUSE OF LAITY OF THE GENERAL SYNOD
Dr John Bull
Mr Colin Keating
Mr Frank Knaggs
Mrs Hazel Simmons

DIOCESAN OFFICERS
Dioc Secretary Mr Philip Davies, Church House, Grainger Park Rd, Newcastle upon Tyne NE4 8SX   *Tel:* 0191–273 0120
Fax: 0191–256 5900
Chancellor of Diocese The Worshipful David McClean, 6 Burnt Stones Close, Sheffield S10 5TS
Tel: 0114–230 5794
Registrar of Diocese and Bishop's Legal Secretary Mrs Jane Lowdon, Crutes, 7 Osborne Terrace, Newcastle upon Tyne NE2 1PQ
Tel: 0191–281 5811
Fax: 0191–231 3608

DIOCESAN ORGANIZATIONS
Diocesan Office Church House, Grainger Park Rd, Newcastle upon Tyne NE4 8SX
Tel: 0191–273 0120
Fax: 0191–256 5900
email: church_house@newcastle.anglican.org

ADMINISTRATION
Dioc Synod (Chairman, House of Clergy) Canon Frank Dexter, St George's Vicarage, St George's Close, Jesmond, Newcastle upon Tyne NE2 2TF *Tel:* 0191–281 1628; (*Chairman, House of Laity*) Dr John Bull, 11 Glebe Mews, Bedlington, Northumberland NE22 6LJ *Tel:* 0191–222 7924 (Work); (*Secretary*) Mr Philip Davies, Church House

Finance Board (*Chairman*) Mr John Squires, Benfield Motors, Asama Court, Newcastle upon Tyne NE4 7YD *Tel:* 0191–226 1700; (*Secretary*) Mr Philip Davies (*as above*)
Accountant Mr John Hall, Church House
Parsonages Board Mr Eddie Fogg, Church House
Dioc Society (*Trusts*) Mr Philip Davies (*as above*)
Pastoral Committee Mr Nigel Foxon, Church House
Board of Patronage Mr Philip Davies (*as above*)
Designated Officer Mrs Jane Lowdon, 7 Osborne Terrace, Newcastle upon Tyne NE2 1NH
Tel: 0191–281 5811
Fax: 0191–281 3608

CHURCHES
Advisory Committee for the Care of Churches (*Chairman*) His Honour John Johnson, Kirk Fenwick, Cambo, Morpeth NE61 4BN *Tel:* (01670) 774243; (*Secretary*) Mr Nigel Foxon (*as above*)
Redundant Churches Uses Committee Mr Philip Davies (*as above*)

EDUCATION
Director of Education Mrs Margaret Nicholson, Church House
Schools Administrative Officer Mrs Valerie Foxon, Church House

MINISTRY AND TRAINING
Director of Ministry and Training Canon Robert Langley, Church Institute, Denewood, Clayton Rd, Jesmond, Newcastle upon Tyne NE2 1TL
Tel: 0191–281 9930
Fax: 0191–231 1452
Director of Ordinands Canon A. S. Craig, Bishop's House, 29 Moor Rd South, Gosforth, Newcastle upon Tyne NE3 1PA *Tel:* 0191–285 2220
Board for Ministry and Training (*Secretary*) Mrs Audrey Truman, Church Institute (*as above*)
Post-Ordination Training Canon Robert Langley (*as above*)
Adviser for Women's Ministry Revd Patricia Davies, St Hugh's Vicarage, Wansbeck Rd, Newcastle upon Tyne NE3 2LR
Tel: 0191–285 8792
Adult Education Adviser Revd Dr Peter Bryars, Church Institute (*as above*)
Youth Adviser Mr Neal Terry, Church Institute (*as above*)
Children's Work Adviser Mrs Judith Sadler, Church Institute (*as above*)
Principal of Local Ministry Scheme and Reader Training Course Canon Richard Bryant, Church Institute (*as above*)
Association of Readers Mr Ron Black, 44 Bowsden Terrace, South Gosforth, Newcastle upon Tyne NE3 1RX *Tel:* 0191–284 6718
Retreat House Mr Peter Dodgson (*Warden*),

Shepherds Dene, Riding Mill, Northumberland NE44 6AF *Tel:* (01434) 682212
Sons of Clergy Society Mrs Gwenda Gofton, 4 Crossfell, Ponteland NE20 9EA
Tel: (01661) 820344
Diocesan Widows Officer Mrs Minnie Bill, The Annexe, Etal Manor, Etal, Cornhill on Tweed TD15 2PU *Tel:* (01890) 820378

LITURGICAL
Chairman Canon Graham Revett, Rectory, Whalton, Morpeth, Northumberland NE61 3UX
Tel: (01670) 775360

MISSION, SOCIAL RESPONSIBILITY AND ECUMENISM
Adviser in Evangelism Rt Revd Paul Richardson, Close House, St George's Close, Jesmond, Newcastle upon Tyne NE2 2TF
Tel: 0191–281 2556
Social Responsibility Adviser Mr Barry Stewart, Church House
Board for Mission and Social Responsibility (*Secretary*) Vacancy, Church House
Ecumenical Officer Canon Clive Price, St Oswald's Vicarage, Wall, Hexham, Northumberland NE46 4DU *Tel:* (01434) 681354
Urban Officer Canon Geoffrey Miller, 58 Baronswood Rd, Gosforth, Newcastle upon Tyne NE3 3UB *Tel:* 0191–285 3667

PRESS, PUBLICITY AND PUBLICATIONS
Dioc Communications Officer Mrs Sue Scott, Church House
Editor of 'The New Link' Mrs Christine Henshall, Church House
Editor of Dioc Directory Mr Philip Davies (*as above*)

DIOCESAN RECORD OFFICE
For further information apply to The Northumberland County Record Office, Melton Park, North Gosforth, Newcastle upon Tyne NE3 5QX
Tel: 0191–236 2680

DIOCESAN RESOURCE CENTRE
Contact Karenza Passmore, Church Institute, Denewood, Clayton Rd, Jesmond, Newcastle upon Tyne NE2 1TL *Tel:* 0191–281 9930
Fax: 0191–231 1452

STEWARDSHIP
Dioc Funding Adviser Mrs Jane Highnam, Church House

RURAL DEANS
ARCHDEACONRY OF NORTHUMBERLAND
Bedlington Revd Brian Benison, St Mary's Vicarage, 51 Marine Terrace, Blyth, Northumberland NE24 2JP *Tel:* (01670) 353417

Bellingham Revd Paul Adamson, Falstone Rectory, Hexham, Northumberland NE48 1AE
Tel: (01434) 240213
Corbridge Revd Audrey Elkington, Vicarage, 5 Kepwell Court, Prudhoe, Northumberland NE42 5PE
Tel: (01661) 836059
Hexham Revd Vincent Ashwin, Vicarage, Station Yard, Haydon Bridge, Northumberland NE47 6LL
Tel: (01434) 684307
Newcastle Central Revd Kit Widdows, 9 Chester Crescent, Newcastle upon Tyne NE2 1DH
Tel: 0191–232 9789
Newcastle East Revd Michael Webb, St Gabriel's Vicarage, 9 Holderness Rd, Heaton, Newcastle upon Tyne NE6 5RH
Tel: 0191–276 3957
Newcastle West Revd John Clasper, St James & St Basil Vicarage, Wingrove Rd North, Newcastle upon Tyne NE4 9EJ
Tel: 0191–274 5078

Tynemouth Revd James Robertson, St Peter's Vicarage, 6 Elmwood Rd, Whitley Bay NE25 8FX
Tel: 0191–252 1991

ARCHDEACONRY OF LINDISFARNE

Alnwick Revd Brian Cowen, Lesbury Vicarage, Alnwick, Northumberland NE66 3AU
Tel: (01665) 830281
Bamburgh and Glendale Revd Adrian Hughes, Vicarage, North Bank, Belford, Northumberland NE70 7LT
Tel: (01668) 213545
Morpeth Revd Richard Ferguson, Vicarage, Kirkwhelpington, Northumberland NE29 2RT
Tel: (01830) 540260
Norham Revd Jim Shewan, St John's Vicarage, 129 Main St, Spittal, Berwick-upon-Tweed, Northumberland TD15 1RP
Tel: (01289) 307342

DIOCESE OF NORWICH

Founded in 1094, formerly Thetford (AD 1070), originally Dunwich (AD 630) and Elmham (AD 673). Norfolk, except for the western quarter (ELY); an area of north-east Suffolk.

Population 803,000   Area 1,804 sq m
Stipendiary Clergy 198   Benefices 217
Parishes 577   Churches 647

BISHOP (71st)
Rt Revd Graham Richard James, Bishop's House, Norwich, Norfolk NR3 1SB [1999]
Tel: (01603) 629001
Fax: (01603) 761613
[Graham Norvic:]
Bishop's Chaplain Revd Tom Heffer (*same address*)
Tel and *Fax:* (01603) 614172
Bishop's Secretary Mrs Brenda Goodson (*same address*)

SUFFRAGAN BISHOPS
THETFORD Rt Revd Hugo de Waal, Rectory Meadow, Bramerton, Norwich NR14 7DW [1992]
Tel: (01508) 538251
Fax: (01508) 538371
Bishop's Secretary Mrs Maggi Sprange (*same address*)
LYNN Rt Revd Anthony Foottit, The Old Vicarage, Castle Acre, King's Lynn, Norfolk PE32 2AA [1999]
Tel: (01760) 755553
Fax: (01760) 755085
Bishop's Secretary Mrs Rosie Foottit (*same address*)

CATHEDRAL CHURCH OF THE HOLY AND UNDIVIDED TRINITY
Dean Very Revd Stephen Platten, The Deanery, The Close, Norwich, Norfolk NR1 4EG [1995]
Tel: (01603) 218308
Fax: (01603) 766032
email: dean@cathedral.org.uk
Cathedral Office 12 The Close, Norwich, Norfolk NR1 4DH
Tel: (01603) 764383
Fax: (01603) 766032
Web: http://www.cathedral.org.uk
Canons Residentiary
Vice-Dean, Pastor and Custos Canon Richard Hanmer, 52 The Close, Norwich, Norfolk NR1 4EG [1994]
Tel: (01603) 665210 (Home)
(01603) 764383 (Office)
Precentor Canon Jeremy Haselock, 34 The Close, Norwich, Norfolk NR1 4DZ [1998]
Tel: (01603) 219484 (Home)
(01603) 218306 (Office)

Canon Librarian Ven Clifford Offer, 26 The Close, Norwich, Norfolk NR1 4DZ [1994]
Tel: (01603) 630525
Fax: (01603) 661104
Canon Treasurer Canon Michael Kitchener, 55 The Close, Norwich NR1 4EG [1999]
Tel: (01603) 764383 (Office)
High Steward The Rt Hon The Earl Ferrers, Ditchingham Hall, Bungay, Suffolk NR35 2LE
Tel: (01508) 482250
Steward Mr Timothy Cawkwell, 12 The Close, Norwich, Norfolk NR1 4DH   *Tel:* (01603) 764386
Chapter Clerk Mr Colin Pordham (*same address*)
Tel: (01603) 218316
Fax: (01603) 766032
Cathedral Campaign Coordinator Mr Andrew Davies (*same address*)   *Tel:* (01603) 218311
email: campaign@cathedral.org.uk
Cathedral Organist Mr David Dunnett (*same address*)   *Tel:* (01603) 218313
Sacrist Mr Peter Lugar (*same address*)
Tel: (01603) 767617

ARCHDEACONS
NORWICH Ven Clifford Offer, 26 The Close, Norwich, Norfolk NR1 4DZ [1994] *Tel:* (01603) 630525
Fax: (01603) 661104
LYNN Ven Martin Gray, Holly Tree House, Whitwell Rd, Sparham, Norwich NR9 5PW [1999]
Tel and *Fax:* (01362) 688032
email: Martin.Gray@lynnarch.freeserve.co.uk
NORFOLK Ven Michael Handley, 40 Heigham Rd, Norwich, Norfolk NR2 3AU [1993]
Tel: (01603) 611808
Fax: (01603) 618954

CONVOCATION (MEMBERS OF THE HOUSE OF CLERGY OF THE GENERAL SYNOD)
Dignitaries in Convocation
The Dean of Norwich
The Archdeacon of Norwich
Proctors for Clergy
Canon Robert Baker
Revd Catherine Milford
Very Revd Michael Perham
Revd Martin Smith

MEMBERS OF THE HOUSE OF LAITY OF THE GENERAL SYNOD
Mr Tom Gilbert
Mrs Faith Hanson
Mrs Sue Johns
Major Patrick King
Mrs Sue Page

DIOCESAN OFFICERS
Dioc Secretary Mr David Adeney, Diocesan House, 109 Dereham Rd, Easton, Norwich, Norfolk NR9 5ES   *Tel:* (01603) 880853
Fax: (01603) 881083
email: davidadeny@norwich.anglican.org
Chancellor of Diocese The Hon Mr Justice Blofeld, Hoveton House, Wroxham, Norwich NR12 8JE
Registrar of Diocese and Bishop's Legal Secretary Mr John Herring, Mills and Reeve, 3–7 Redwell St, Norwich NR2 4TJ   *Tel:* (01603) 660155
Fax: (01603) 633027

DIOCESAN ORGANIZATIONS
Diocesan Office Diocesan House, 109 Dereham Rd, Easton, Norwich, Norfolk NR9 5ES
Tel: (01603) 880853
Fax: (01603) 881083
email: diocesanhouse@norwich.anglican.org

ADMINISTRATION
Dioc Synod (*Chairman, House of Clergy*) Revd John Simpson, Vicarage, Corton, Lowestoft NR32 5HT *Tel:* (01502) 731272; (*Chairman, House of Laity*) Mr David Pearson, 16/17 North Drive, Great Yarmouth NR30 4EW *Tel:* (01493) 842623; (*Secretary*): Mr David Adeney, Dioc House; (*Assistant Secretary*) Mr Jonathan Davis, Dioc House
Board of Finance (*Chairman*) Mr David Gurney, Bawdeswell Hall, Bawdeswell, Dereham NR20 4SA *Tel:* (01362) 688308; (*Secretary*) Mr David Adeney (*as above*)
Property Committee (*Chairman*) Mr George Kendall, York Cottage, Blakeney, Holt, Norfolk NR25 7NU; (*Secretary*) Mr Ray Levett, Dioc House
Surveyor Mr Eddie Mann, Dioc House
Designated Officer Mr David Adeney (*as above*)
Dioc Electoral Registration Officer Mr Jonathan Davis (*as above*)

PASTORAL
Pastoral Committee (*Chairman*) Ven Michael Handley (*as above*); (*Secretary*) Mr David Adeney (*as above*); (*Assistant Secretary*) Mr Jonathan Davis (*as above*)
Redundant Churches Uses Committee (*Chairman*) Mr Tony Gent, The Paddocks, Little Barney, Fakenham NR21 0NL *Tel:* (01328) 838803; (*Secretary*) Mr Jonathan Davis (*as above*)
Board of Patronage (*Chairman*) Mr Neville Houseago, 159 Drayton High Rd, Drayton, Norwich NR8 6BN *Tel:* (01603) 427042; (*Secretary*) Canon P. H. Atkins, Rectory, West Runton, Cromer NR27 9QT   *Tel:* (01263) 837279

Advisory Committee for the Care of Churches (*Chairman*) Mr Donald Ray, 2 Lindford Drive, Eaton, Norwich NR4 6LT *Tel:* (01603) 457271; (*Secretary*) Mrs Lizzie Halfacre, Dioc House
Ringers' Association Mr G. R. Drew, Munsal, 6 Hall Moor Rd, Hingham NR9 4LB
Tel: (01953) 850853
Bishop's Furnishings Officer Mr P. King, 10 Bridewell St, Little Walsingham NR22 6BJ
Tel: (01328) 820709

EDUCATION
Board of Education (*Chairman*) Revd Brian Cole, Rectory, Great Dunham, King's Lynn PE32 2LQ
Tel: (01328) 701466
Director of Education Miss Cynthia Wake, Dioc House   *Tel:* (01603) 881352
Schools Administrative Officer Mr Gerald Ward, Dioc House   *Tel:* (01603) 881352
Youth Officer Mr John Reaney, Dioc House
Tel: (01603) 881352
Children's Officer Miss Stella Noons, Dioc House
Tel: (01603) 881352
Horstead Centre (*Warden*) Mrs Valerie Khambatta, Rectory Rd, Horstead, Norwich NR12 7EP
Tel: (01603) 737215
Fax: (01603) 737494
email: Horstead.Centre@Zoo.co.uk

MISSION AND MINISTRY
Advisory Board for Mission and Ministry (*Chairman*) The Bishop of Thetford (*as above*); (*Secretary*) Revd Richard Impey, Dioc House
Tel: (01603) 880722
Director of Parish Development and Training Revd Richard Impey (*as above*)
Dioc Director of Ordinands Canon Michael Kitchener, 55 The Close, Norwich NR1 4EG
Tel: (01603) 764383
Principal LNSM Scheme Canon John Goodchild, Emmaus House, 65 The Close, Norwich NR1 4DH   *Tel:* (01603) 611196
Asst Director for Lay and Reader Training Revd Clive Blackman
Continuing Ministerial Training Officer Vacancy
Dioc Officer for NSMs Revd Roger MacPhee
Readers' Committee (*Chairman*) Ven Clifford Offer (*as above*); (*Secretary*) Mr Peter Pease, 19 Woodview Rd, Easton, Norwich NR9 5EU
Tel: (01603) 880255
Bishop's Officer for Retired Clergy and Widows Canon Cedric Bradbury, 66 Grove Lane, Holt NR25 6ED   *Tel:* (01263) 712634
Clergy Pre-Retirement Adviser Ven George Marchant, 28 Greenways, Eaton, Norwich NR4 6PE   *Tel:* (01603) 58295
Officer for Evangelism Revd Christopher Collison, Rectory, Church Rd, Newton Flotman, Norwich NR15 1QB   *Tel:* (01508) 470762
Fax: (01508) 470487
email: chris@collison.freeserve.co.uk

Evangelism Committee (*Chairman*) Canon Peter Taylor, Rectory, Necton, Swaffham PE37 8HT *Tel:* (01760) 722021; (*Secretary*) Mrs Mary Brookes, Dioc House

World Mission Committee (*Chairman*) Revd Cathy Milford, Vicarage, Barnham Broom, Norwich NR9 4DB *Tel:* (01603) 759204; (*Secretary*) Mrs P. Dutton, Pevers Farm, Martin's Lane, Kirkstead Green, Brooke NR15 1ED

Tel: (01508) 550638

Ecumenical Committee (*Chairman*) Mrs Sheila Ashford, Holly Lodge, Strumpshaw, Norwich NR13 4NS *Tel:* (01603) 712324; (*Ecumenical Officer*) Revd Robin Hewetson, Rectory, Marsham, Norwich NR10 5PP

Tel: (01263) 733249
Fax: (01263) 733799

Committee for Christian Stewardship (*Chairman*) Vacancy

Secretary and Adviser Mr Christopher Hedges, Dioc House

LITURGICAL

Chairman Canon Jeremy Haselock, 34 The Close, Norwich NR21 4DZ *Tel:* (01603) 218314
Fax: (01603) 766032

Secretary Vacancy

PRESS, PUBLICITY AND PUBLICATIONS

Communications Committee (*Chairman*) The Dean of Norwich (*as above*)

Communications Officer Revd J. McFarlane, Dioc House

Editor of Dioc Directory Mrs S. A. J. Robinson, Dioc House

DIOCESAN RECORD OFFICE

Norfolk Record Office, Gildengate House, Anglia Square, Upper Green Lane, Norwich NR3 1AX
County Archivist Dr John Alban

Tel: (01603) 761349
Fax: (01603) 761885

SOCIAL RESPONSIBILITY

Board for Social Responsibility (*Chairman*) Dr Michael Green, 35 The Close, Norwich NR1 4EG (*Secretary*) Mrs Alison Howard, Dioc House
Tel: (01603) 881385

Social Responsibility Officer Mrs Alison Howard (*as above*)

Industry Committee (*Secretary*) Canon Hereward Cooke, 31 Bracondale, Norwich NR1 2AT
Tel: (01603) 624827

Honorary Tourism Officer Revd Alan Pyke, 20 Bell Meadow, Martham, Great Yarmouth NR29 4AW
Tel: (01493) 740048

Rural Chaplains Mr Gordon Reynolds, Vicarage, Easton, Norwich NR9 5ES *Tel:* (01603) 880197
Revd W. M. C. Bestelink, Rectory, High Road, Roydon, Diss IP22 3RD

Tel: (01379) 642180

Chaplain to the Deaf Revd Gordon Howells, Rectory, Stone Hill, Rackheath, Norwich NR13 6NG
Tel: (01603) 720097

RURAL DEANS
ARCHDEACONRY OF NORWICH

Norwich East Canon Hereward Cooke, 31 Bracondale, Norwich NR1 2AT
Tel: (01603) 624827
email: cookehd@paston.co.uk

Norwich North Canon Michael Stagg, Vicarage, 2 Wroxham Rd, Sprowston, Norwich NR7 8TZ
Tel: (01603) 426492

Norwich South Revd Dr Samuel Wells, St Elizabeth's Vicarage, 75 Cadge Rd, North Earlham, Norwich NR5 8DQ
Tel: (01603) 250764

ARCHDEACONRY OF NORFOLK

Blofield Revd Vivien Elphick, Rectory, Barn Close, Lingwood, Norwich NR13 4TS
Tel: (01603) 713880

Depwade Revd Selwyn Swift, Rectory, Carleton Rode, Norwich NR16 1RN *Tel:* (01953) 789218

Great Yarmouth Revd Anthony Ward, Vicarage, Duke Rd, Gorleston, Great Yarmouth NR31 6LL
Tel: (01493) 663477

Humbleyard Revd Di Lammas, Rectory, Hethersett, Norwich NR9 3AR
Tel: (01603) 810273

Loddon Revd Dr Peter Knight, Vicarage, 29 Ashby Rd, Thurton, Norwich NR14 6AX
Tel: (01508) 480738

Lothingland Revd John Simpson, St Margaret's Rectory, 147 Hollingworth Rd, Lowestoft NR32 4BW *Tel:* (01502) 573046

Redenhall Revd Des Whale, Rectory, Winfarthing, Diss IP22 2EA *Tel:* (01379) 642543

Saint Benet at Waxham and Tunstead Revd Andrew Parsons, Vicarage, Church Lane, Wroxham, Norwich NR12 8SH
Tel: (01603) 782678

Thetford and Rockland Revd Charles Hall, 6 Redcastle Rd, Thetford IP24 3NF
Tel: (01842) 762291

ARCHDEACONRY OF LYNN

Breckland Revd Richard Bowett, Vicarage, Norwich Rd, Watton, Thetford IP25 6DB
Tel: (01953) 881439

Brisley and Elmham Revd Brian Cole, Rectory, Great Dunham, King's Lynn PE32 2LQ
Tel: (01328) 701466

Burnham and Walsingham Revd Alan Bell, Rectory, Fakenham NR21 9BZ *Tel:* (01328) 862678

Dereham in Mitford Revd David Pearson, Vicarage, Back Lane, Mattishall, Dereham NR20 3PU *Tel:* (01362) 850243

Heacham and Rising Canon George Hall, Rectory, Sandringham, King's Lynn PE35 6EH
Tel: (01485) 540587

Holt Revd Peter Barnes-Clay, Rectory, Weybourne, Holt NR25 7SY *Tel:* (01263) 588268

Ingworth Revd Patrick Foreman, Rectory, Westgate Green, Hevingham, Norwich NR10 5NH *Tel:* (01603) 754643

Lynn Canon William Hurdman, St Margaret's Vicarage, St Margaret's Place, King's Lynn PE30 5DL *Tel:* (01553) 767090

Repps Canon David Hayden, Vicarage, Cromer NR27 0BE *Tel:* (01263) 512000

Sparham Revd Paul Illingworth, Rectory, Weston Longville, Norwich NR9 5JU *Tel:* (01603) 880163

Founded in 1542. Oxfordshire; Berkshire; Buckinghamshire; one parish in each of Bedfordshire, Gloucestershire, Hampshire, Hertfordshire and Warwickshire.

Population 2,096,000   Area 2,221 sq m
Stipendiary Clergy 446   Benefices 324
Parishes 630   Churches 819

BISHOP (41st)
Rt Revd Richard Douglas Harries, Diocesan Church House, North Hinksey, Oxford OX2 0NB [1987]   *Tel:* (01865) 208200 (Office)
Fax: (01865) 790470
email: bishopoxon@oxford.anglican.org
[Richard Oxon:]
Bishop's Domestic Chaplain Revd Dr Edmund Newell (*same address*)
email: bishopschaplain@oxford.anglican.org

AREA BISHOPS
READING Rt Revd Dominic Walker, Bishop's House, Tidmarsh Lane, Tidmarsh, Reading RG8 8HA [1997]   *Tel:* 0118–984 1216
Fax: 0118–984 1218
email: bishopreading@oxford.anglican.org
BUCKINGHAM Rt Revd Michael Hill, Sheridan, Grimms Hill, Gt Missenden, Bucks HP16 9BD [1998]   *Tel:* (01494) 862173
Fax: (01494) 890508
email: bishopbucks@oxford.anglican.org
DORCHESTER Rt Revd Anthony John Russell, Holmby House, Sibford Ferris, Banbury, Oxon OX15 5RG [1988]   *Tel:* (01295) 780589/3 (Home)
(01295) 780589 (Office)
Fax: (01295) 788686
email: bishopdorchester@oxford.anglican.org

HONORARY ASSISTANT BISHOPS
Rt Revd Keith Arnold, 9 Dinglederry, Olney, Bucks MK46 5ES [1997]   *Tel:* (01234) 713044
Rt Revd John Bone, 4 Grove Rd, Henley-on-Thames, Oxon RG9 1DH [1997]
Tel: (01491) 413482
Rt Revd Paul Burrough, 6 Mill Green Close, Bampton, Oxon OX18 2HE [1995]
Rt Revd Albert Kenneth Cragg, 3 Goring Lodge, White House Rd, Oxford OX1 4QE [1982]
Tel: (01865) 249895
Rt Revd Ronald Gordon, 16 East St Helen St, Abingdon, Oxon OX4 5EA [1991]
Tel: (01235) 529956
Rt Revd Michael Houghton, 8 Goldney Ave, Clifton, Bristol BS8 4RA [1998] *Tel:* 0117–973 1752
Fax: 0117–973 1762

Rt Revd Henry Richmond, 39 Hodges Court, Marlborough Rd, Oxford OX1 4NZ [1999]
Tel: (01865) 790466
Rt Revd Stephen Verney, Charity School House, Church Rd, Blewbury, Didcot, Oxon OX11 9PY
Tel: (01235) 850004

CATHEDRAL CHURCH OF CHRIST
Dean Very Revd John Drury, The Deanery, Christ Church, Oxford OX1 1DP [1991]
Tel: (01865) 276162
Fax: (01865) 276238
Dean's Secretary Mrs Jan Bolongaro (*same address*)
Tel: (01865) 276161
email: jan.bolongaro@chch.ox.ac.uk
Canons Residentiary
Canon Prof Oliver O'Donovan, Christ Church, Oxford OX1 1DP [1982]   *Tel:* (01865) 276219
Ven John Morrison, Archdeacon's Lodging, Christ Church, Oxford OX1 1DP [1998]
Tel: (01865) 204440
email: archdoxf@oxford.anglican.org
Canon Martin Peirce, 70 Yarnells Hill, Oxford OX2 9BG [1987]   *Tel:* (01865) 721330
email: ordinands@oxford.anglican.org
Very Revd Robert Jeffery (*Sub-Dean*), Christ Church, Oxford OX1 1DP [1996]
Tel: (01865) 276278
email: robert.jeffery@christ-church.oxford.ac.uk
Canon Prof Keith Ward, Christ Church, Oxford OX1 1DP [1991]   *Tel:* (01865) 276246
email: keith.ward@chch.ox.ac.uk
Canon Prof John Webster, Priory House, Christ Church, Oxford OX1 1DP [1997]
Tel: (01865) 276247
email: john.webster@christ-church.oxford.ac.uk
Lay Canon Prof H. M. R. E. Mayr-Harting, Christ Church, Oxford OX1 1DP [1997]
Tel: (01865) 286334
Precentor Revd Justin Lewis-Anthony, Christ Church, Oxford OX1 1DP [1999]
Tel: (01865) 276214
email: justin.lewis-anthony@chch.ox.ac.uk
Cathedral Registrar Mr David Burnside, Christ Church, Oxford OX1 1DP   *Tel:* (01865) 276155
email: david.burnside@christ-church.oxford.ac.uk

Cathedral Secretary Miss Sally-Ann Ford, Christ Church, Oxford OX1 1DP   *Tel:* (01865) 276155
Fax: (01865) 276277
email: sally-ann.ford@chch.ox.ac.uk
Cathedral Organist Mr Stephen Darlington, Christ Church, Oxford OX1 1DP   *Tel:* (01865) 276195
email: stephen.darlington@christ-church.oxford.ac.uk

ARCHDEACONS

OXFORD Ven John Morrison, Archdeacon's Lodging, Christ Church, Oxford OX1 1DP [1998]
Tel: (01865) 204440
Fax: (01865) 204465
email: archdoxf@oxford.anglican.org
BERKSHIRE Ven Norman Russell, Foxglove House, Love Lane, Donnington, Newbury RG13 2JG [1998]   *Tel:* (01635) 552820
email: archdber@oxford.anglican.org
BUCKINGHAM Ven David Goldie, 60 Wendover Rd, Aylesbury, Bucks HP21 9LW [1998]
Tel: (01296) 423269
email: archdbuc@oxford.anglican.org

CONVOCATION (MEMBERS OF THE HOUSE OF CLERGY OF THE GENERAL SYNOD)

The Archdeacon of Oxford
Proctors for Clergy
Revd Valerie Bonham
Canon Simon Brown
Revd Andrew Burnham
Ven David Goldie
Revd Christopher Hall
Revd Robert Key
Revd John Rees
Revd Philip Tovey

MEMBERS OF THE HOUSE OF LAITY OF THE GENERAL SYNOD

Mr John Bowen
Dr Carole Cull
Dr Philip Giddings
Mrs Viviane Hall
Mrs Penny Keens
Mr Terry Landsbert
Mr Gavin Oldham
Ms Beverley Ruddock
Dr Anna Thomas-Betts
Mr David Wright

DIOCESAN OFFICERS

Dioc Secretary Mrs Rosemary Pearce, Diocesan Church House, North Hinksey, Oxford OX2 0NB
Tel: (01865) 208200
Fax: (01865) 790470
email: diosec@oxford.anglican.org
Chancellor of Diocese Chanc P. T. S. Boydell, Diocesan Registry, 16 Beaumont St, Oxford OX1 2LZ   *Tel:* (01865) 241974
email: oxford@winckworths.co.uk

Joint Registrars of Diocese and Bishop's Legal Secretaries Dr Frank Robson and Revd John Rees (*same address*)
Registrars of the Archdeaconries Dr Frank Robson and Revd John Rees (*as above*)

DIOCESAN ORGANIZATIONS

Diocesan Office Diocesan Church House, North Hinksey, Oxford OX2 0NB   *Tel:* (01865) 208200
Fax: (01865) 790470

ADMINISTRATION

Dioc Synod (*Vice-President, House of Clergy*) Canon Simon Brown, The Precincts, Burnham, Slough SL1 7HU *Tel:* (01628) 604173; (*Vice-President, House of Laity*) Dr Philip Giddings, 5 Clifton Park Rd, Caversham, Reading, Berks RG4 7PD *Tel:* 0118–931 8207; (*Secretary*) Mrs Rosemary Pearce, Dioc Church House
Board of Finance (*Chairman*) Mr John Yaxley, Old Housing, Church St, Fifield, Milton-under-Wychwood, Chipping Norton OX7 6HF *Tel* and *Fax:* (01993) 831385; (*Secretary*) Mrs Rosemary Pearce (*as above*)
Principal Buildings Officer and Dioc Surveyor Mr Roger Harwood, Dioc Church House
Dioc Trustees (*Oxford*) *Ltd* Mrs Rosemary Pearce (*as above*)
Pastoral Committee (*Secretary*) Mrs Mary Saunders, Dioc Church House
email: dac@oxford.anglican.org
Designated Officer Dr Frank Robson (*as above*)

CHURCHES

Advisory Committee for the Care of Churches (*Chairman*) Sir Timothy Raison, Dioc Church House; (*Secretary*) Mrs Mary Saunders (*as above*)
Redundant Churches Uses Committee (*Secretary*) Mrs Mary Saunders (*as above*)

STEWARDSHIP, TRAINING, EDUCATION AND MINISTRY

Secretary Canon Keith Lamdin, Dioc Church House
email: training@oxford.anglican.org
Dioc Director of Ordinands and Post-Ordination Training Canon Martin Peirce, 70 Yarnell's Hill, Oxford OX2 9BG   *Tel:* (01865) 721330
email: ordinands@oxford.anglican.org
Dept of Training and Parish Resources Canon Keith Lamdin (*as above*)
Adviser in Women's Ministry Revd Julia Wilkinson, Vicarage, Micklefield Rd, High Wycombe HP13 7HU   *Tel:* (01494) 531141
Licensed Lay Ministers' Association (*Warden*) Revd Bob Rhodes, Dioc Church House
Dioc Youth Adviser Mr Andrew Gear, Dioc Church House
email: youthofficer@oxford.anglican.org

Dioc Children's Adviser Mrs Jenny Hyson, Dioc Church House
email: childofficer@oxford.anglican.org
Dioc Stewardship Adviser Mr David Haylett
email: steward@oxford.anglican.org

EDUCATION
Director of Education (Schools) Canon Tony Williamson, Dioc Church House
email: schools@oxford.anglican.org

MISSIONARY AND ECUMENICAL
Dioc Advisory Group for Mission Canon David Meara, Buckingham Rectory, 39 Fishers Field, Buckingham MK18 1SF   *Tel:* (01280) 813178
Bishop's Officer for Evangelism Vacancy
email: evang@oxford.anglican.org
Partnership in World Mission (Secretary) Revd Michael Sams, 13 Hound Close, Abingdon, Oxon OX14 2LU   *Tel:* (01235) 529084

COMMUNICATIONS
Director of Communications Revd Richard Thomas, Dioc Church House
Tel: (01235) 553360 (Home)
01893 703279 (Pager)
email: communications@oxford.anglican.org
Editor of Dioc Newspaper 'The Door' Mrs Christine Zwart, Dioc Church House
email: door@oxford.anglican.org

DIOCESAN RECORD OFFICES
County Archivist, Oxfordshire County Record Office, County Hall, Oxford OX1 1ND *Tel:* (01865) 815203 *Fax:* (01865) 815429 *email:* Archives@occdla@dial.pipex.com (*For records of the diocese, and parish records in the Archdeaconry of Oxford*) (*From Sept 2000* St Luke's Church, Temple Rd, Cowley, Oxford OX4 2EN)
Berkshire Record Office, Shire Hall, Shinfield Park, Reading RG2 9XD *Tel:* 0118–901 5132 (*For parish records in the Archdeaconry of Berkshire*)
Buckinghamshire Record Office, County Hall, Aylesbury, Bucks HP20 1UA *Tel:* (01296) 395000 Ext 588 (*For parish records in the Archdeaconry of Buckingham*)

SOCIAL RESPONSIBILITY
Board of Social Responsibility (Secretary) Mrs Jo Saunders, Dioc Church House
email: socresp@oxford.anglican.org
PACT (Parents and Children Together) Council for Social Work Mrs Yvette Gayford, 48 Bath Rd, Reading, Berks RG1 6PQ   *Tel:* 0118–958 1861
Council for the Deaf (Chairman) Canon David Manship, Dioc Church House

BOROUGH DEAN
MILTON KEYNES
Vacancy

AREA DEANS
ARCHDEACONRY OF OXFORD
Aston and Cuddesdon Canon John Crowe, Dorchester Rectory, Dorchester, Wallingford, Oxon OX9 8HZ   *Tel:* (01865) 340007
email: dorchesterabbey@enterprise.net
Bicester and Islip Revd Guy Chapman, Vicarage, Ambrosden, Bicester, Oxon OX6 0UJ
Tel: (01869) 247813
Chipping Norton Revd Graham Canning, 'Moredays', 36 The Slade, Charlbury, Chipping Norton, Oxon OX7 3SY   *Tel:* (01608) 810421
email: gcanning@g.canning.u-net.com
Cowley Revd Tony Price, Vicarage, Elsfield Rd, Marston, Oxford OX3 0PR   *Tel:* (01865) 247034
email: tonypr@globalnet.co.uk
Deddington Canon Timothy Wimbush, Rectory, Sibford Gower, Banbury, Oxon OX15 5RW
Tel: (01295) 750555
Henley Revd Phillip Nixon, Vicarage, Manor Rd, Goring, Reading RG8 9DR   *Tel:* (01491) 872196
Oxford Revd Anthony Gann, Rectory, Lonsdale Rd, Oxford OX2 7ES   *Tel:* (01865) 556079
Witney Revd Cameron Butland, Rectory, Station Lane, Witney, Oxon OX8 6BH *Tel:* (01993) 775003
Woodstock Revd Geoff van der Weegen, Rectory, Stonesfield, Oxon OX8 8PR   *Tel:* (01993) 891664
email: Brabo@weredi.demon.co.uk

ARCHDEACONRY OF BERKSHIRE
Abingdon Revd Leighton Thomas, Vicarage, 3 Tullis Close, Sutton Courtenay, Abingdon, Oxon OX14 4BD   *Tel:* (01235) 848297
email: leightonthomas@demon.co.uk
Bracknell Revd Sebastian Jones, Vicarage, Vicarage Rd, South Ascot, Berks SL5 9DX
Tel: (01344) 22388
email: sebjones@aol.com
Bradfield Revd Roger Howell, Rectory, 1 Westridge Ave, Purley, Reading, Berks RG8 8DE
Tel: (01734) 417727
Maidenhead Canon David Rossdale, Vicarage, Church Gate, Cookham, Berks SL6 9SP
Tel: (01628) 523969
email: rossdale@btinternet.com
Newbury Revd David Cook, Rectory, 64 Northcroft Lane, Newbury, Berks RG14 1BN
Tel: (01635) 40326
Reading Canon Brian Shenton, 39 Downshire Square, Reading, Berks RG1 6NH
Tel: 0118–957 1057
Sonning Revd Dr Alan Wilson, Rectory, 155 High St, Sandhurst, Berks GU47 8HR
Tel: (01252) 890079
email: atwilson@macline.co.uk
Vale of White Horse Revd Andrew Bailey, Vicarage, Coach Lane, Faringdon, Oxon SN7 8AB   *Tel:* (01367) 240106
Wallingford Revd Edwin Clements, Rectory, Church End, Blewbury, Didcot OX11 9QH
Tel and Fax: (01235) 850267
email: revedwin@aol.com

Wantage Revd Alan Wadge, Ridgeway Rectory, Letcombe Regis, Wantage, Oxon OX12 9LD
Tel: (01235) 763805

Amersham Revd Roger Salisbury, Rectory, Church St, Chesham, Bucks HP15 1HY
Tel: (01494) 783629

Aylesbury Revd Tim Higgins, Rectory, Parsons Fee, Aylesbury HP20 2QZ
Tel: (01296) 24276

Buckingham Canon David Meara, Rectory, 39 Fishers Field, Buckingham MK18 1SF
Tel: (01280) 813178

Burnham Canon Simon Brown, Rectory, The Precincts, Burnham, Slough SL1 7HU
Tel: (01628) 604173
email: sndbrown@compuserve.com

Claydon Revd Tom Thorp, Vicarage, White Horse Lane, Whitchurch, Aylesbury HP22 4JZ
Tel: (01296) 641768
email: recthorp@nildram.co.uk

Milton Keynes Revd Ian Pusey, Rectory, 75 Church Green Rd, Bletchley, Milton Keynes MK3 6BY
Tel: (01908) 373357
email: Ianpusey@aol.com

Mursley Revd Norman Cotton, Stewkley Vicarage, Stewkley, Leighton Buzzard, Beds LU7 0HH
Tel: (01525) 240287

Newport Revd Maurice Stanton-Saringer, Rectory, 21 School Lane, Sherington, Newport Pagnell MK16 9NF
Tel: (01908) 610521

Wendover Revd Alan Bennett, Rectory, Aston Clinton, Aylesbury, Bucks HP22 5JD
Tel: (01296) 631626

Wycombe Revd Christopher Bull, Vicarage, 9 Chapel Rd, Flackwell Heath, High Wycombe HP10 9AA
Tel: (01628) 522795
email: christopher.bull@virgin.net

Founded in 1541. Northamptonshire, except for one parish in the west (LEICESTER); Rutland; Peterborough, except for an area in the south east; one parish in Lincolnshire.

Population 761,000   Area 1,149 sq m
Stipendiary Clergy 162   Benefices 166
Parishes 356   Churches 380

BISHOP (37th)
Rt Revd Ian Patrick Martyn Cundy, Bishop's Lodgings, The Palace, Peterborough, Cambs. PE1 1YA [1996]   *Tel:* (01733) 562492
Fax: (01733) 890077
[Ian Petriburg:]
Bishop's Chaplain Canon Richard Cattle

SUFFRAGAN BISHOP
BRIXWORTH Rt Revd Paul Everard Barber, 4 The Avenue, Dallington, Northampton NN5 7AN [1989]   *Tel:* (01604) 759423
Fax: (01604) 750925

CATHEDRAL CHURCH OF ST PETER, ST PAUL AND ST ANDREW
Dean Very Revd Michael Bunker, The Deanery, Peterborough, Cambs. PE1 1XS [1992]
Tel: (01733) 562780
Fax: (01733) 897874
Canons Residentiary
Canon Thomas Christie, Prebendal House, Minster Precincts, Peterborough, Cambs. PE1 1XX [1980]   *Tel:* (01733) 569441
Canon Jack Higham, Canonry House, Minster Precincts, Peterborough, Cambs. PE1 1XX [1983]
Tel: (01733) 562125
Canon Philip Spence, Norman Hall, Minster Precincts, Peterborough, Cambs. PE1 1XX [1997]
Tel: (01733) 564899
Precentor Revd Bill Croft, 18 Minster Precincts, Peterborough, Cambs. PE1 1XX [1998]
Tel: (01733) 343389
Chapter Clerk Mr Bernard Kane, Chapter Office, Minster Precincts, Peterborough, Cambs. PE1 1XS   *Tel:* (01733) 343342
Fax: (01733) 552465
Cathedral Organist Mr Christopher Gower, Choir House, Laurel Court, Minster Precincts, Peterborough, Cambs. PE1 1XX
Tel: (01733) 891333

ARCHDEACONS
NORTHAMPTON Ven Michael Chapman, 11 The Drive, Northampton NN1 4RZ [1991]
Tel: (01604) 714015
Fax: (01604) 792016

OAKHAM Ven David Painter, 7 Minster Precincts, Peterborough, Cambs. PE1 1XS [1999]
Tel: (01733) 891360
Fax: (01733) 555271

CONVOCATION (MEMBERS OF THE HOUSE OF CLERGY OF THE GENERAL SYNOD)
The Archdeacon of Northampton
Proctors for Clergy
Revd David Bird
Canon Thomas Christie
Revd Stephen Trott

MEMBERS OF THE HOUSE OF LAITY OF THE GENERAL SYNOD
Mrs Beatrice Brandon
Mr Keith Davidson
Mrs Sheila Saunders
Mr Malcolm Tyler

DIOCESAN OFFICERS
Dioc Secretary Canon Richard Cattle, Diocesan Office, The Palace, Peterborough, Cambs. PE1 1YB   *Tel:* (01733) 564448
Fax: (01733) 555271
Chancellor of Diocese His Honour Judge Thomas Coningsby, Leyfields, Elmore Rd, Chipstead, Surrey CR3 3PG
Deputy Chancellor Mr George Pulman, c/o The Diocesan Registrar, 4 Holywell Way, Longthorpe, Peterborough, Cambs. PE3 6SS
Registrar of Diocese and Bishop's Legal Secretary Mr Raymond Hemingray, 4 Holywell Way, Longthorpe, Peterborough, Cambs. PE3 6SS
Tel: (01733) 262523

DIOCESAN ORGANIZATIONS
Diocesan Office The Palace, Peterborough, Cambs. PE1 1YB   *Tel:* (01733) 564448
Fax: (01733) 555271

ADMINISTRATION
Dioc Synod (Vice-President, Clergy) Canon Thomas Christie, Prebendal House, Minster Precincts, Peterborough, Cambs. PE1 1XX *Tel:* (01733) 569441; *(Vice-President, Laity)* Mrs Beatrice

Brandon, Clopton Manor, Clopton, Kettering NN14 3DZ *Tel:* (01832) 720346; (*Secretary*) Canon Richard Cattle, Dioc Office
Board of Finance (*Chairman*) Mr Scott Durward, The Old House, Medbourne, Market Harborough, Leics LE16 8DX *Tel:* (01858) 565207; (*Secretary*) Canon Richard Cattle (*as above*)
Deputy Dioc Secretary and Financial Controller Mrs Sue McMeekin, Dioc Office
Houses Committee (*Chairman*) Mr Alastair Stirling, 14 Redmiles Lane, Kelton, Stamford PE9 3RG *Tel:* (017880) 720320; (*Secretary*) Mrs Sandra Allen, Dioc Office
Pastoral Committee Canon Richard Cattle (*as above*)
Board of Patronage Canon Richard Cattle (*as above*)
Designated Officer Mr Raymond Hemingray, 4 Holywell Way, Longthorpe, Peterborough, Cambs. PE3 6SS *Tel:* (01733) 262523
Trust Committee Mrs Sue McMeekin (*as above*)

CHURCHES

Advisory Committee for the Care of Churches (*Chairman*) Mr Stephen Billings, DAC Office, Ecton House, Church Way, Ecton, Northampton NN6 0QE *Tel and Fax:* (01604) 416657; (*Secretary*) Mrs Diana Evans (*same address*)
Redundant Churches Uses Committee (*Chairman*) Mr Adrian Christmas, 1 Minster Precincts, Peterborough, Cambs.; (*Secretary*) Vacancy, Dioc Office

EDUCATION

Board of Education (*Schools*) (*Director of Education* (*Schools*) *and Secretary*) Dr Stephen Partridge, Dioc Office
Schools Officer Revd Philip Davies, Rectory, 3 Hall Yard, King's Cliffe, Peterborough, Cambs. PE8 6XQ *Tel:* (01780) 470314

MINISTRY

Director of Ordinands Revd Bill Croft, 18 Minster Precincts, Peterborough, Cambs. PE1 1XX
Tel: (01733) 343389
Director of Post-Ordination Training Revd Ronald Hawkes, Vicarage, 12 New St, Oundle, Peterborough, Cambs. PE8 4EA
Tel: (01832) 273595
Adviser in Women's Ministry Revd Dr Judith Rose, Rectory, Aldwincle, Kettering NN14 3EP
Tel: (01832) 720613
Continuing Ministerial Education Revd Stephen Evans, Rectory, 32 West St, Ecton, Northampton NN6 0QF *Tel:* (01604) 416322
Warden of Readers Canon John Westwood, Irthlingborough Rectory, 79 Fineden Rd, Irthlingborough, Northants NN9 5TY
Tel: (01933) 650278

Warden of Pastoral Assistants Revd Paul Paynton, Vicarage, 19 Station Rd, Irchester, Northants NN9 7EH *Tel:* (01933) 312674
Warden of Parish Evangelists Canon Timothy Partridge, Rectory, Church Lane, Bugbrooke, Northampton NN7 3PB *Tel:* (01604) 830373
Lay Training Officer Vacancy
Local Ministry Officer Revd Paul Dunthorne, Rectory, 6 Ridlington Rd, Preston, Oakham LE15 9NN *Tel:* (01572) 737287

MISSION

Children's Officer Mrs Pamela Jones, Peterborough House, 90 Harlestone Rd, Northampton NN5 7AG *Tel:* (01604) 751907
Fax: (01604) 580301
Parish Development Director Mr Tony Armitage, Dioc Office
Youth Officer Capt P. Niemiec, Peterborough House (*as above*)
Urban Priority Areas Link Officer and Church Urban Fund Canon David Staples, Vicarage, 4 West End, West Haddon, Northampton NN6 7AY
Tel: (01788) 510207
Ecumenical Officer Revd Robert Giles, Rectory, Gate Lane, Broughton, Kettering NN14 1ND
Tel: (01536) 791373
Hospital Chaplaincy Adviser Revd Leslie Turner, 4 Stratton Close, Langlands, Northampton NN3 3HQ *Tel:* (01604) 635512 (Home)
(01604) 634700 (Office)
Industrial Chaplain Canon Mostyn Davies, 16 Swanspool, Peterborough, Cambs. PE3 7LS
Tel: (01733) 262034

LITURGICAL
Officer Revd Stephen Evans (*as above*)

PRESS, PUBLICITY AND PUBLICATIONS
Dioc Publications and Communications Mrs Jackie Newman, Dioc Office
Media Officer Revd Paul Needle, 106 Wharf Rd, Higham Ferrers, Northants NN10 8BH
Tel: (01933) 312800
0802 731751 (Mobile)

DIOCESAN RECORD OFFICES
Wootton Park, Northampton NN4 9BQ *County Archivist* Miss R. Watson *Tel:* (01604) 762129 (*For all parishes in Northants and the former Soke of Peterborough*)
Leicestershire Record Office, Long St, Wigston Magna, Leicester LE18 2AH, *County Archivist* Mr Carl Harrison *Tel:* 0116–257 1080 (*For all parishes in Rutland*)

SPIRITUALITY
Ecton House (*Retreat House*) *Warden* Revd Stephen

Evans, Ecton House, Church Way, Ecton, Northampton NN6 0QE   *Tel:* (01604) 406442
Spiritual Director Canon Peter Garlick, 120 Worcester Close, Northampton NN3 9ED
Tel: (01604) 416511

RURAL DEANS
ARCHDEACONRY OF NORTHAMPTON

Brackley Revd John Roberts, Pimlico House, Pimlico, Brackley, Northants NN13 5TN
Tel: (01280) 850378
Brixworth Canon Brian Lee, Vicarage, 2 Church Rd, Spratton, Northampton NN6 8HR
Tel: (01604) 847212
Daventry Canon David Evans, Rectory, Church Lane, Nether Heyford, Northampton NN7 3LQ
Tel: (01327) 340487
Northampton Revd Kevin Ashby, Rectory, Church Walk, Great Billing, Northampton NN3 9ED   *Tel:* (01604) 784870
Towcester Canon Michael Baker, Vicarage, Towcester NN12 6AB   *Tel:* (01327) 350459
Wellingborough Revd David Witchell, St Barnabas Vicarage, St Barnabas St, Wellingborough, Northants NN8 3HB   *Tel:* (01933) 226337

Wootton Revd Richard Ormston, Rectory, Collingtree, Northampton NN4 0NF
Tel: (01604) 761895

ARCHDEACONRY OF OAKHAM

Barnack Revd Roger Watson, Rectory, Wittering, Peterborough, Cambs. PE8 6AQ
Tel: (01780) 782428
Corby Vacancy
Higham Canon William Kentigern-Fox, Vicarage High St, Raunds, Northants. NN9 6HS
Tel: (01933) 461509
Kettering Revd Bob Giles, Rectory, Gate Lane, Broughton, Kettering, Northants. NN14 1ND
Tel and *Fax:* (01536) 791373
Oundle Revd Dr Judith Rose, Rectory, Aldwincle, Kettering, Northants. NN14 3EP
Tel: (01832) 720613
Peterborough Canon Haydn Smart, Vicarage, 315 Thorpe Rd, Peterborough PE3 6LU
Tel: (01733) 263016
Rutland Revd Michael Rogers, Rectory, Cottesmore, Oakham, Rutland LE15 7DJ
Tel: (01572) 812202

DIOCESE OF PORTSMOUTH

Founded in 1927. The south-eastern third of
Hampshire; the Isle of Wight.

Population 713,000   Area 408 sq m
Stipendiary Clergy 115   Benefices 128
Parishes 142   Churches 173

BISHOP (8th)

Rt Revd Kenneth Stevenson PH D, Bishopsgrove,
26 Osborn Rd, Fareham, Hants PO16 7DQ [1995]
Tel: (01329) 280247
Fax: (01329) 231538
email: bishports@clara.co.uk
[Kenneth Portsmouth]
Bishop's Chaplain Revd Andrew Tremlett, 11
Burnham Wood, Fareham, Hants PO16 7UD
Tel: (01329) 221326 (Home)
(01329) 280247 (Office)
Fax: (01329) 231538
Secretaries Mrs Jean Maslin, Ms Julia Anderson

HONORARY ASSISTANT BISHOPS

Rt Revd Michael Adie, Greenslade, Froxfield,
Petersfield, Hants GU32 1EB   *Tel:* (01730) 827266
Rt Revd Henry David Halsey, Bramblecross,
Gully Rd, Seaview, Isle of Wight PO34 5BY
Tel: (01983) 613583
Rt Revd Edward James Keymer Roberts, The
House on the Marsh, Quay Lane, Brading, Isle of
Wight PO36 0BD   *Tel:* (01983) 407434

CATHEDRAL CHURCH OF ST THOMAS OF CANTERBURY

Provost Vacancy, Provost's House, 13 Pembroke
Rd, Old Portsmouth, Hants PO1 2NS
Tel: 023–9282 4400 (Home)
023–9234 7401 (Office)
Fax: 023–9229 5480
Cathedral Office Cathedral Office, St Thomas's St,
Old Portsmouth, Hants PO1 2HH
Tel: 023–9282 3300
Fax: 023–9229 5480
Canons Residentiary
Canon David Isaac, 1 Pembroke Close, Port-
smouth, Hants PO1 2NX [1990]
Tel: 023–9282 2053
Fax: 023–9229 5081
Pastor Canon Jane Hedges, 51 High St,
Portsmouth, Hants PO1 2LU [1993]
Tel: 023–9273 1282
Fax: 023–9236 6928

Precentor Canon Gavin Kirk, 61 St Thomas's St,
Old Portsmouth, Hants PO1 2EZ [1998]
Tel: 023–9282 4621
Fax: 023–9282 1356
Missioner Canon Ian Jagger, 50 Penny St, Old
Portsmouth, Hants PO1 2NL [1998]
Tel and Fax: 023–9273 0792
*Cathedral Administrator, Chapter Clerk and Clerk to
Cathedral Council* Mr Brandon Mudditt,
Cathedral Office
Cathedral Organist Mr David Price, 8 Lombard St,
Old Portsmouth, Hants PO1 2HX
Tel: 023–9243 0811
Fax: 023–9229 5480

ARCHDEACONS

PORTSDOWN Ven Christopher Lowson, 5 Brading
Ave, Southsea PO4 1QJ [1999]   *Tel:* 023–9243 2693
Fax: 023–9229 8788
email: lowson@surfaid.org
THE MEON Ven Peter Hancock, Victoria Lodge, 36
Osborn Rd, Fareham, Hants PO16 7DS [1999]
Tel: (01329) 280101
Fax: (01329) 281603
ISLE OF WIGHT Ven Mervyn Banting, 5 The
Boltons, Kite Hill, Wootton Bridge, Ryde, Isle
of Wight PO33 4PB [1996]
Tel and Fax: (01983) 884432
email:
mervynbanting@theboltons.freeserve.co.uk

CONVOCATION (MEMBERS OF THE HOUSE OF CLERGY OF THE GENERAL SYNOD)

The Archdeacon of the Isle of Wight
Proctors for Clergy
Canon John Byrne
Canon David Isaac
Canon Robert White

MEMBERS OF THE HOUSE OF LAITY OF THE GENERAL SYNOD

Mr Christopher Hedges
Mr Peter Lowater
Mrs Anahid Thomas

DIOCESAN OFFICERS

Dioc Secretary Mr Michael Jordan, Cathedral

House, St Thomas's St, Portsmouth, Hants PO1 2HA
Tel: 023–9282 5731
Fax: 023–9229 3423
email:
diocesansecretary@portsmouth.anglican.org
Chancellor of Diocese His Honour Judge Francis Aglionby, The Croft, Houghton, Carlisle, Cumbria CA3 0LD
Registrar of Diocese and Bishop's Legal Secretary Miss Hilary Tyler, Messrs Bruttons, 288 West St, Fareham, Hants PO16 0AJ   *Tel:* (01329) 236171
Fax: (01329) 289915
email: h.tyler@bruttons.co.uk
Parsonage and Property Committee Surveyors (Portsmouth) Mr Roger Boyce, Roger Boyce Associates, Purbrook House, Purbrook Gardens, London Rd, Purbrook, Hants PO7 5JY *Tel:* 023–9226 6620; *(Isle of Wight)* Mr Robert Biggs, A. G. Biggs Partnership, 66 Carisbrooke Rd, Newport, Isle of Wight PO30 1BW
Tel: (01983) 522190

DIOCESAN ORGANIZATIONS
Diocesan Office Cathedral House, St Thomas's St, Portsmouth, Hants PO1 2HA   *Tel:* 023–9282 5731
Fax: 023–9229 3423
email: admin@portsmouth.anglican.org

ADMINISTRATION
Dioc Synod (Chairman House of Clergy) Revd John Pinder, Rectory, 27 Farlington Ave, Cosham, Portsmouth PO6 1DF   *Tel:* 023–9237 5145
Fax: 023–9221 9670
(Chairman, House of Laity) Dr Hugh Mason, 32 Chelsea Rd, Southsea PO5 1NJ
Tel: 023–9281 6794
(Secretary) Mr Michael Jordan, Dioc Office
Board of Finance (Chairman) Mr Peter Lowater, Lower Gubbles, Hook Lane, Warsash, Southampton SO31 9HH   *Tel:* (01489) 572156
Fax: (01489) 572252
(Secretary) Mr Michael Jordan *(as above)*
Parsonages and Property Committee (Secretary) Mr Rodney Baker, Dioc Office
email: property@portsmouth.anglican.org
Dioc Board of Ministry, Pastoral Committee (Secretary) Mrs Lindie Sawtell, Dioc Office
email: dbm_dpc@portsmouth.anglican.org
Patronage Board (Secretary) Miss Hilary Tyler, Messrs Bruttons, 288 West St, Fareham, Hants PO16 0AJ   *Tel:* (01329) 236171
Fax: (01329) 289915
Designated Officer Miss Hilary Tyler *(as above)*

CHURCHES
Advisory Committee for the Care of Churches (Chairman) Mrs Sarah Quail; *(Secretary)* Mrs Lindie Sawtell, Dioc Office
email: dac@portsmouth.anglican.org
Redundant Churches Uses Committee (Secretary) Mr Rodney Baker *(as above)*

EDUCATION
Director of Education Canon David Isaac, Cathedral House, St Thomas's St, Portsmouth, Hants. PO1 2HA   *Tel:* 023–9282 2053
Fax: 023–9229 5081
Board of Education (Secretary) Canon David Isaac *(as above)*
Schools Officer Mr Brian Hay *(same address)*
Youth and Children's Work Adviser and Bishop's Representative for Child Protection Revd Karina Green *(same address)*
Further Education Chaplain Revd David Gibbons, 6 Carlton Way, Gosport, Hants. PO12 1LN
Tel: 023–9250 3921
Fax: 023–9252 8704

MINISTRY
Dioc Director of Ordinands Revd Richard Brand, Vicarage, Church Lane, Hambledon, Waterlooville PO7 4RT   *Tel and Fax:* 023–9263 2717
Dioc Director of NSM Revd Dr Trevor Reader, Rectory, Blendworth, Horndean, Waterlooville PO8 1AB   *Tel:* 023–9259 2174
Fax: 023–9259 7023
Dioc Director of Continuing Ministerial Education Canon Terry Louden, Vicarage, East Meon, Petersfield, Hants GU32 1NH *Tel:* (01730) 823221
Chaplain for Women's Ministry Canon Jane Hedges, Cathedral Office
Warden of Readers Revd Peter Sutton, Vicarage, Victoria Square, Lee-on-the-Solent, Hants. PO13 9NF   *Tel and Fax:* 023–9255 0269
Clerical Registry (Winchester and Portsmouth) Revd Dr Ronald Pugh, Church House, 9 The Close, Winchester, Hants. SO23 9LS   *Tel:* (01962) 844644
Fax: (01962) 841815
Widows Officers (Mainland) The Archdeacon of Portsdown; The Archdeacon of the Meon *(Isle of Wight)*; The Archdeacon of the Isle of Wight

BISHOP'S ADVISORY GROUP ON WORSHIP
Chairman Canon Gavin Kirk, 61 St Thomas's St, Old Portsmouth, Hants. PO1 2EZ
Tel: 023–9282 4621
Fax: 023–9282 1356

MISSIONARY AND ECUMENICAL
Dioc Ecumenical Officer Revd Peter Pimentel, St Paul's Vicarage, Staplers Rd, Barton, Newport, Isle of Wight PO30 2HZ   *Tel:* (01983) 522075
Canon Missioner Canon Ian Jagger, 50 Penny St, Old Portsmouth, Hants. PO1 2NL
Tel and Fax: 023–9273 0792
Council for Mission and Unity (Chairman) Ven Peter Hancock, Victoria Lodge, 36 Osborn Rd, Fareham, Hants PO16 7DS   *Tel:* (01329) 280101
Fax: (01329) 281603
(Secretary) Vacancy

COMMUNICATIONS
Dioc Communications Officer Vacancy
Dioc Directory All communications to Dioc Office

DIOCESAN RECORD OFFICES

Portsmouth City Records Office, 3 Museum Rd, Portsmouth PO1 2LE *Archivist* Mrs S. Quail *Tel:* 023–9282 7261 (*For Gosport, Fareham, Havant and Portsmouth Deaneries*)

Hampshire Record Office, 20 Southgate St, Winchester SO23 9EF *County Archivist* Miss R. C. Dunhill *Tel:* (01962) 846154 (*For Bishop's Waltham and Petersfield Deaneries*)

Isle of Wight County Record Office, 26 Hillside, Newport, Isle of Wight PO30 2EB *Archivist* Mr R. Smout *Tel:* (01983) 823821 (*For the Isle of Wight Deaneries*)

SOCIAL RESPONSIBILITY

Social Responsibility Adviser Canon David Tonkinson, All Saints Church, Commercial Rd, Portsmouth, Hants. PO1 4BT *Tel:* 023–9282 1137
Fax: 023–9283 8116
email: davitonk@aol.com

SPIRITUALITY

Warden Revd Dr Philip Newell, St John's House, 102 Copnor Rd, Portsmouth, Hants. PO3 5AL
Tel: 023–9266 6535

STEWARDSHIP

Parish Resources Adviser Mr Gordon Uphill, Dioc Office
email: resources@portsmouth.anglican.org

Part-time Christian Stewardship Adviser (Isle of Wight) Dr John Wibberley, Alsace, 48 High Park Rd, Ryde, Isle of Wight PO33 1BX
Tel: (01983) 564287
Fax: (01983) 566770

RURAL DEANS
ARCHDEACONRY OF PORTSMOUTH

Bishop's Waltham Revd Ian Coomber, All Saints' Rectory, Brook Lane, Botley, Southampton SO30 2ER *Tel:* (01489) 781534

Fareham Revd Michael Cooper, Vicarage, 164 Castle St, Portchester, Fareham PO16 9QH
Tel: 023–9237 6289

Gosport Revd Peter Wadsworth, Vicarage, 21 Elson Rd, Gosport, Hants. PO12 4BL
Tel: 023–9258 2824

Havant Canon Robert White, Vicarage, Riders Lane, Leigh Park, Havant, Hants. PO9 4QT
Tel: 023–9247 5276
Fax: 023–9248 1228

Petersfield Revd April Richards, Vicarage, Blackmoor, Liss GU33 6BN *Tel:* (01420) 473548

Portsmouth Revd John Pinder, Rectory, 27 Farlington Ave, Cosham, Portsmouth PO6 1DF
Tel: 023–9237 5145
Fax: 023–9221 9670

ARCHDEACONRY OF THE ISLE OF WIGHT

East Wight Revd Andrew Menniss, Vicarage, Bembridge, Isle of Wight PO35 5NA
Tel: (01983) 872175
Fax: (01983) 875255

West Wight Revd Jon Russell, Shorwell Vicarage, 5 Northcourt Close, Shorwell, Isle of Wight PO30 3LD *Tel* and *Fax:* (01983) 741044

DIOCESE OF RIPON AND LEEDS

Re-constituted in 1836. The central third of North Yorkshire; Leeds, except for an area in the west (BRADFORD), an area in the east (YORK) and an area in the south (WAKEFIELD); an area of south-western County Durham.

Population 781,000   Area 1,359 sq m
Stipendiary Clergy 160   Benefices 127
Parishes 158   Churches 262

BISHOP (12th)

Vacancy, Bishop Mount, Ripon, N Yorks HG4 5DP   *Tel:* (01765) 602045
                    Fax: (01765) 600758
Domestic Chaplain Vacancy, Bishop Mount (*as above*)

SUFFRAGAN BISHOP

KNARESBOROUGH Rt Revd Frank Valentine Weston, 16 Shaftesbury Ave, Roundhay, Leeds LS8 1DT   *Tel:* 0113–266 4800
                    Fax: 0113–266 5649
email: Knaresborough@btinternet.com

HONORARY ASSISTANT BISHOPS

Rt Revd Ralph Emmerson, 15 High St Agnesgate, Ripon, N Yorks. HG4 1QR   *Tel:* (01765) 601626
Rt Revd David Jenkins, Ashbourne, Cotherstone, Barnard Castle, DL12 9PR   *Tel:* (01833) 650804
Rt Revd John Gaisford, 3 North Lane, Roundhay, Leeds LS8 2QJ   *Tel:* 0113–273 2003
                    Fax: 0113–273 3002
email: 101740.2725@compuserve.com

CATHEDRAL CHURCH OF ST PETER AND ST WILFRID

Dean Very Revd John Methuen, The Minster House, Ripon, N Yorks. HG4 1PE [1995]
                    Tel: (01765) 603615
    email: dean.john@riponcathedral.org.uk
Cathedral Office High St Agnesgate, Ripon HG4 1QT   *Tel:* (01765) 603462
                    Fax: (01765) 690530
    email: postmaster@riponcathedral.org.uk
    Web: http://www.riponcathedral.org.uk
Canons Residentiary
Canon Michael Glanville-Smith, St Wilfrid's House, Minster Close, Ripon HG4 1QR [1990]
                    Tel: (01765) 600211
    email: canon.michael@riponcathedral.org.uk
Canon Keith Punshon, St Peter's House, Minster Close, Ripon HG4 1QR [1996]
                    Tel: (01765) 604108
    email: canon.keith@riponcathedral.org.uk
Chapter Clerk Dr Howard Crawshaw, Cathedral Office
    email: howard.crawshaw@riponcathedral.org.uk

Cathedral Bursar Mr Nigel Clay, Cathedral Office
    email: nigel.clay@riponcathedral.org.uk
Cathedral Organist Mr Kerry Beaumont, c/o The Cathedral, Ripon, N Yorks. HG4 1QT
                    Tel: (01765) 600237
    email: kerry.beaumont@riponcathedral.org.uk

ARCHDEACONS

LEEDS Ven John Oliver, 3 West Park Grove, Leeds LS8 2HQ [1992]   *Tel* and *Fax:* 0113–269 0594
email: johnanne@archdeaconleeds.freeserve.co.uk
RICHMOND Ven Kenneth Good, 62 Palace Rd, Ripon, N Yorks. HG4 1HA [1993]
                    Tel and *Fax:* (01765) 604342
    email: good.richmond@freeuk.com

CONVOCATION (MEMBERS OF THE HOUSE OF CLERGY OF THE GENERAL SYNOD)

The Archdeacon of Leeds
Proctors for Clergy
Canon Penny Driver
Revd Clive Mansell
Revd David Rhodes

MEMBERS OF THE HOUSE OF LAITY OF THE GENERAL SYNOD

Mr Robert Aagaard
Dr John Beal
Mrs Katherine Carr
Mr Nigel Greenwood
Mrs Dorothy Stewart

DIOCESAN OFFICERS

Dioc Secretary Mr Philip Arundel, Diocesan Office, St Mary's St, Leeds LS9 7DP
                    Tel: 0113–248 7487
                    Fax: 0113–249 1129
    email: philipa@riponleeds-diocese.org.uk
Chancellor of Diocese The Worshipful Simon Grenfell, St John's House, Sharow Lane, Ripon, N Yorks. HG4 5BN
Joint Registrars of Diocese and Bishop's Legal Secretaries Mr Christopher Tunnard and Mrs Nicola Harding, Ripon Diocesan Registry, Cathedral Chambers, 4 Kirkgate, Ripon HG4 1PA   *Tel:* (01765) 600755
                    Fax: (01765) 690523

Dioc Surveyor Mr Michael Lindley, Dioc Office
email: michael@riponleeds-diocese.org.uk

DIOCESAN ORGANIZATIONS

Diocesan Office Ripon Diocesan Office, St Mary's St, Leeds LS9 7DP   *Tel:* 0113–248 7487
                              Fax: 0113–249 1129

ADMINISTRATION

Dioc Synod (*Chairman, House of Clergy*) Canon Richard Cooper, Rectory, Church Wynd, Richmond DL10 7AQ *Tel:* (01748) 82339; (*Chairman, House of Laity*) Dr Alan Stanley, The Limes, 35 Potterton Lane, Barwick in Elmet, Leeds LS15 4DU *Tel:* 0113–281 2769; (*Secretary*) Mr Philip Arundel, Dioc Office
Board of Finance (*Chairman*) Dr Raymond Head, Walden Cottage, New Row, Birstwith, Harrogate HG3 2NH *Tel:* (01423) 770450; (*Secretary*) Mr Philip Arundel (*as above*); (*Administrative and Deputy Secretary*) Mr Peter Mojsa, Dioc Office email: peterm@riponleeds-diocese.org.uk; (*Financial Secretary*) Ms Ruth Debney, Dioc Office
                    email: ruthd@riponleeds-diocese.org.uk
Parsonages Board Mr Philip Arundel (*as above*); (*Parsonages Officer*) Mr Michael Lindley, Dioc Office
Pastoral Committee Mr Peter Mojsa (*as above*)
Board of Patronage Mr Peter Mojsa (*as above*)
Designated Officer Mr Philip Arundel (*as above*)
Dioc Electoral Registration Officer Mr Philip Arundel (*as above*)
Widows and Dependants (*Widows' Officer*) Mr Philip Arundel (*as above*)

CHURCHES

Advisory Committee for the Care of Churches (*Chairman*) Mr Robert Aagaard, The Manor House, High Birstwith, Harrogate HG3 2LG; (*Secretary*) Mrs D. B. Cartwright, Dioc Office
Church Buildings Committee Mr Peter Mojsa (*as above*)
Redundant Churches Uses Committee Mr Peter Mojsa (*as above*)

EDUCATION

Director of Education Mr Ian Mackenzie, The Castle CE School, Stockwell Rd, Knaresborough HG5 0JN   *Tel:* (01423) 869839
Religious Education Adviser (*Richmond, Wensley and Ripon Deaneries*) Revd Shirley Griffiths, Vicarage, East Cowton, Northallerton DL7 0BN
                              Tel: (01325) 378230
(*Leeds Archdeaconry and Harrogate Deanery*) Miss Janet Newell, High Mistels, High View, Burnt Yates, Harrogate HG3 3ET
                              Tel: (01423) 771683

Development Education Worker Mrs Sarah Fishwick, 153 Cardigan Rd, Leeds LS6 1LJ
                              Tel: 0113–278 4030

COUNCIL FOR MISSION

Chair The Bishop of Knaresborough
Director of Mission Canon James Bell, 12 Clotherholme Rd, Ripon HG4 2DA
                  Tel and *Fax:* (01765) 604835
Dioc Training Officer Mrs Liz Williams, 24 Lakeland Crescent, Alwoodley, Leeds LS17 7PR
                              Tel: 0113–267 8589
Director of Ordinands Canon Penny Driver, The School House, Berrygate Lane, Sharow, Ripon HG4 5BJ   *Tel:* (01765) 607017
Adviser for Women's Ministry Canon Penny Driver (*as above*)
Children's Work Adviser Vacancy
Youth Work Adviser Capt Nic Sheppard, 7 Loxley Grove, Wetherby LS22 7YG   *Tel:* (01937) 585440
Warden of Readers Revd Alison Montgomery, Washington House, Littlethorpe, Ripon HG4 3LJ
                              Tel: (01765) 605276
Officer for Local Ministry Revd Stephen Brown, Ripley Rectory, Harrogate HG3 3AY
                              Tel: (01423) 770147
Adviser for Non-Stipendiary Ministry Revd Dr David Peat, 12 North Grange Mews, Leeds LS6 2EW   *Tel:* 0113–275 3179
Convenor of Advisory Group on Christian Healing Canon Rachel Stowe, Preston Cottage, East Cowton, Northallerton DL7 0BD
                  Tel and *Fax:* (01325) 378173
World Mission Officer Revd Peter Roberts, Vicarage, Church Lane, Collingham, Wetherby LS22 5AU   *Tel:* (01937) 573975
Ecumenical Officer Revd Jeff King, Vicarage, Church View, Thorner, Leeds LS14 3ED
                              Tel: 0113–289 2437
ACUPA Link Officer Revd Nick Howe, Holy Trinity Vicarage, 28 Hawkswood Ave, Leeds LS5 3PN   *Tel:* 0113–259 0031
Social Responsibility Officer Mrs Maureen Browell, c/o Dioc Office   *Tel:* (01226) 249099 (Home)
Community Chaplain for People with Learning Difficulties Revd Robert Brooke, 51 St James Approach, Leeds LS14 6JJ   *Tel:* 0113–273 1396
Racial Justice Officer Revd Douglas Emmott, All Soul's Vicarage, Blackman Lane, Leeds LS2 9EY
                              Tel: 0113–245 3078
Rural Ministry Officer Canon Leslie Morley, 18 Station Rd, Brompton, Northallerton DL6 2RE
                              Tel: (01609) 780734
Urban Ministry Officer Revd Kathryn Fitzsimons, 17 Strawberry Dale Ave, Harrogate HG1 5EA
                              Tel: (01423) 563074

LITURGICAL

Chairman The Dean of Ripon (*as above*)
Secretary Revd Paul Summers, Rectory, Kirkby Overblow, Harrogate HG3 1HD
                  Tel and *Fax:* (01423) 872314

COMMUNICATIONS

Communications Committee Revd John Carter, 7 Blenheim Court, Harrogate HG2 9DT
Tel: (01423) 530369
Fax: (01423) 538557
email: jhgcarter@aol.com
Press Officer Revd John Carter (*as above*)
Editor of Dioc Directory Mr Philip Arundel (*as above*)

DIOCESAN RECORD OFFICES

County Record Office, County Hall, Northallerton DL7 8DF *County Archivist* Mr M. Y. Ashcroft
Tel: (01609) 3123
Leeds Archives Department, Chapeltown Rd, Sheepscar, Leeds LS7 3AP *Leeds City Archivist* Mr William Connor
Tel: 0113–214 5814
Fax: 0113–214 5815

STEWARDSHIP

Stewardship Adviser Mr Paul Winstanley, Dioc Office

AREA DEANS

ARCHDEACONRY OF RICHMOND

Harrogate Revd Paul Summers, Rectory, Kirkby Overblow, Harrogate HG3 1HD
Tel: (01423) 872314
Richmond Revd Peter Midwood, Rectory, Ronaldkirk, Barnard Castle DL12 9EE
Tel: (01833) 650202
Ripon Revd Simon Talbott, Vicarage, Westerns Lane, Markington, Harrogate HG3 3PB
Tel: (01765) 677123
Wensley Revd Clive Mansell, Rectory, Kirklington, Bedale DL8 2NJ *Tel:* (01845) 567429

ARCHDEACONRY OF LEEDS

Allerton Revd Stephen Jarratt, Vicarage, Wood Lane, Leeds LS7 3QF *Tel:* 0113–268 3072
Armley Revd Tim Lipscomb, Armley Vicarage, Wesley Rd, Leeds LS12 1SR *Tel:* 0113–263 8620
Headingley Revd Michael Cross, Headingley Vicarage, 16 Shire Oak Rd, Leeds LS6 2DE
Tel: 0113–275 1526
Whitkirk Revd Alan Payne, Rectory, Kippax, Leeds LS25 7HF *Tel:* 0113–286 2710

DIOCESE OF ROCHESTER

Founded in 604. Kent west of the Medway, except for one parish in the south-west (CHICHESTER); the Medway Towns; the London boroughs of Bromley and Bexley, except for a few parishes (SOUTHWARK); one parish in East Sussex.

Population 1,190,000   Area 542 sq m
Stipendiary Clergy 238   Benefices 193
Parishes 216   Churches 264

BISHOP (106th)
Rt Revd Michael Nazir-Ali PHD, Bishopscourt, Rochester, Kent ME1 1TS [1995]
Tel: (01634) 842721
Fax: (01634) 831136
[Michael Roffen:]
Chaplain Revd Paul Williams   *Tel:* (01634) 814439

SUFFRAGAN BISHOP
TONBRIDGE Rt Revd Brian Smith, Bishop's Lodge, 48 St Botolph's Rd, Sevenoaks, Kent TN13 3AG [1993]
Tel: (01732) 456070
Fax: (01732) 741449
email: sevenoaks@clara.net

HONORARY ASSISTANT BISHOP
Rt Revd Michael Gear, 10 Acott Fields, Yalding, Maidstone, Kent ME18 6DQ [1999]
Tel: (01622) 817388

CATHEDRAL CHURCH OF CHRIST AND THE BLESSED VIRGIN MARY
Dean Very Revd Edward Shotter, The Deanery, Rochester, Kent ME1 1TG [1989]
Tel: (01634) 844023 (Home and Office)
Cathedral Office Cathedral Office, Garth House, The Precinct, Rochester, Kent ME1 1SX
Tel: (01634) 843366
Fax: (01634) 401410
Canons Residentiary
Vice-Dean Canon Edward Turner, Prebendal House, King's Orchard, The Precinct, Rochester, Kent ME1 1TG [1981]   *Tel:* (01634) 848664 (Office)
Fax: (01634) 401410
Canon Pastor Canon Jonathan Meyrick, 2 King's Orchard, The Precinct, Rochester, Kent ME1 1TG [1998]   *Tel:* (01634) 841491
Canon Evangelist Ven Norman Warren, The Archdeaconry, Rochester, Kent ME1 1SX [1989]
Tel: (01634) 842527
Precentor Canon John Armson, Easter Garth, King's Orchard, The Precinct, Rochester, Kent ME1 1SX [1989]   *Tel:* (01634) 406992
Cathedral Administrator Vacancy
Cathedral Organist and Director of Music Mr Roger Sayer, 7 Minor Canon Row, Rochester, Kent ME1 1ST   *Tel:* (01634) 400723

ARCHDEACONS
ROCHESTER Ven Norman Warren, The Archdeaconry, Rochester, Kent ME1 1SX [1989]
Tel: (01634) 842527
TONBRIDGE Ven Judith Rose, 3 The Ridings, Blackhurst Lane, Tunbridge Wells, Kent TN2 4RU [1996]   *Tel:* (01892) 520660
email:
archdeacon.tonbridge@rochester.anglican.org
BROMLEY Ven Garth Norman, 6 Horton Way, Farningham, Kent DA4 0DQ [1994]
Tel: (01322) 864522

CONVOCATION (MEMBERS OF THE HOUSE OF CLERGY OF THE GENERAL SYNOD)
Dignitaries in Convocation
The Dean of Rochester
The Archdeacon of Bromley
Proctors for Clergy
Revd John Banner
Canon Peter Lock
Canon Gordon Oliver
Ven Judith Rose

MEMBERS OF THE HOUSE OF LAITY OF THE GENERAL SYNOD
Mr James Cheeseman
Dr Helen Jennings
Mr Ernie Mann
Mr Ian Myers
Mr Gerald O'Brien
Mr David Webster

DIOCESAN OFFICERS
Dioc Secretary Mr Peter Law (*until March 2000*), St Nicholas Church, Boley Hill, Rochester, Kent ME1 1SL   *Tel:* (01634) 830333
Fax: (01634) 829463
Chancellor of Diocese His Honour Judge Michael Goodman, Parkside, Dulwich Common, London SE21 7EU   *Tel:* 020–8693 3564
Registrar of Diocese and Bishop's Legal Secretary Mr Michael Thatcher, Registry Chambers, The Old Deanery, Dean's Court, London EC4V 5AA
Tel: 020–7593 5110
Fax: 020–7248 3221

DIOCESAN ORGANIZATIONS
Diocesan Office St Nicholas Church, Boley Hill, Rochester, Kent ME1 1SL   *Tel:* (01634) 830333
                         Fax: (01634) 829463
           email: dio.off@rochdiooff.co.uk

ADMINISTRATION
Assistant Secretary Mr Geoff Marsh, Dioc Office
Assistant Secretary Mrs Penny Law (*until March 2000*), Dioc Office
Dioc Synod (*Chairman, House of Clergy*) Canon Peter Lock, Vicarage, 9 St Paul's Square, Bromley, Kent BR2 0XH *Tel:* 020–8460 6275; (*Chairman, House of Laity*) Mr Ernie Mann, 39 Windyridge, Gillingham ME7 3BG *Tel:* (01634) 304893; (*Secretary*) Mr Peter Law, Dioc Office
Board of Finance (*Chairman*) Mr Ian Fawkner, 13 Lyndhurst Drive, Sevenoaks, Kent TN13 2HD; (*Secretary*) Mr Peter Law (*as above*); (*Dioc Treasurer*) Mr Dennis Barden (*until May 2000*), Dioc Office
Pastoral Committee Revd Brenda Hurd, Dioc Office
Board of Patronage Mrs Penny Law (*as above*)
Designated Officer Mr Michael Thatcher, Registry Chambers, The Old Deanery, Dean's Court, London EC4V 5AA   *Tel:* 020–7593 5110
Trusts Mrs Louise Kirby, Dioc Office

CHURCHES
Advisory Committee for the Care of Churches (*Chairman*) Canon Douglas Redman, Vicarage, 37 Kingswood Rd, Bromley BR2 0HG *Tel:* 020–8460 4989; (*Administrator*) Mrs Sue Haydock, Dioc Office
Redundant Churches Uses Committee Revd Brenda Hurd (*as above*)

EDUCATION
Education Office Deanery Gate, The Precinct, Rochester, Kent ME1 1SJ   *Tel:* (01634) 843667
                         Fax: (01634) 843674
      email: education@rochester.anglican.org
Board of Education (*Chairman*) Canon David Herbert, Vicarage, Bickley Park Rd, Bickley, Bromley BR1 2BE
Secretary, Director of Education and Bishop's Officer Revd John Smith, Educ Office
Schools Adviser Vacancy
Assistant Director of Education (*Youth Work*) Capt Neil Thomson, Educ Office
Assistant Director of Education (*Children's Work*) Mrs Margaret Withers, Educ Office
Assistant Director of Education (*Finance*) Mr John Constanti, Educ Office

MINISTRY AND TRAINING
Advisory Council for Ministry and Training (*Chairman*) The Bishop of Tonbridge (*as above*); (*Secretary, Director of Ministry and Training and Bishop's Officer*) Canon Gordon Oliver, Dioc Office

Lay Ministry Adviser Revd Dr Jeremy Ive, Dioc Office
Director of Ordinands Canon Paul Longbottom, Vicarage, Butchers Hill, Shorne, Gravesend, Kent DA12 3EB   *Tel:* (01474) 822239
Associate Director of Ordinands Revd Elizabeth Walker, Rectory, 266 Rochester Rd, Burham, Rochester, Kent ME1 3RJ   *Tel:* (01634) 666862
Ministry Development Officer Revd Anne Dyer, Dioc Office
Adviser for Women's Ministry Revd Anne Dyer (*as above*)
Director of Continuing Ministerial Education Canon Gordon Oliver (*as above*)
Readers' Association (*Warden*) Mr John Field, Dioc Office
Clerical Registry and Dioc Retirement Officer Revd Brian Pearson, St Placids, 32 Swan St, West Malling, Kent ME19 6LP   *Tel:* (01732) 848462
Chaplain for Deaf People Revd Heather Turner, Rectory, Borough Green Rd, Wrotham, Kent TN15 7RA   *Tel:* (01732) 882211
                  (01732) 887188 (Minicom)
Evangelists (*Warden*) Revd Jean Kerr, Vicarage, 1 Binnacle Rd, Rochester, Kent ME1 2XR
                     Tel: (01634) 400673
Pastoral Assistants (*Warden*) Canon Penny Avann, 21 Glanfield Rd, Beckenham BR3 3JS
                     Tel: 020–8460 0481

LITURGICAL
Chairman Canon Paul Wright, St John's Vicarage, 13 Church Ave, Sidcup DA14 6BU
                     Tel: 020–8300 0382
Secretary Revd Jonathan Watson, Vicarage, 44A Colyers Lane, Erith, Kent DA8 3NP
                     Tel: (01322) 332809

MISSION, ECUMENISM AND PARISH DEVELOPMENT
Advisory Council for Mission, Ecumenism and Parish Development (*Chairman*) The Archdeacon of Rochester; (*Secretary and Bishop's Officer for Mission, Ecumenism and Parish Development*) Canon Michael Howard, Vicarage, Church Rd, Weald, Sevenoaks, Kent TN14 6LT
                     Tel: (01732) 463291
Ecumenical Officer Revd Colin Crook, Vicarage, Eynsford Rd, Crockenhill, Swanley, Kent BR8 8JS   *Tel:* (01322) 662157
Interfaith (*Chairman*) Revd Alan Amos, 4 King's Row, St Margaret's St, Rochester, Kent ME1 1UJ
                     Tel: (01634) 814542
Local Evangelism (*Chairman*) Revd Steve Davie, Vicarage, Battle St, Cobham, Gravesend, Kent DA12 3DB   *Tel:* (01474) 814332
World Mission (*Chairman*) Canon John Saunders, Vicarage, Vicarage Rd, Gillingham, Kent ME7 5JA   *Tel:* (01634) 851818

PRESS, PUBLICITY AND COMMUNICATIONS

Advisory Council for Communications (*Chairman*) Mr David Webster, 5 Rosehill Walk, Tunbridge Wells, Kent TN1 1HL   *Tel:* (01892) 526055
(*Secretary, Director of Communications and Bishop's Officer*) Revd Christopher Stone, The Flat, Bishopscourt, Rochester, Kent ME1 1TS
Tel: (01634) 404343
07885 876729 (Mobile)
Fax: (01634) 402793
Editor of 'Link' Newspaper Mr Bryan Harris, 57 Neal Rd, West Kingsdown, Sevenoaks, Kent TN15 6DG   *Tel:* (01474) 852474

DIOCESAN RECORD OFFICES

Kent Archives Office, County Hall, Maidstone, Kent ME14 1XH *Tel:* (01622) 671411 (*For diocesan records and parish records for Tonbridge Archdeaconry*)
Archives Office, Civic Centre, Strood, Rochester, Kent *Tel:* (01634) 727777 (*For parish records for Rochester Archdeaconry*)

CHURCH IN SOCIETY (SOCIAL RESPONSIBILITY)

Advisory Council for Church in Society (*Chairman*) The Archdeacon of Bromley
(*Secretary, Director of Church in Society and Bishop's Officer*) Canon David Grimwood, 60 Marsham St, Maidstone, Kent ME14 1EW
Tel: (01622) 755014
Fax: (01622) 693531
Canterbury and Rochester Dioc Joint Council for Social Responsibility (*Senior Adviser*) Canon David Grimwood (*as above*); (*Advisers*) Revd Pearl Anderson, Mr Adrian Speller (*same address*)
Industrial Chaplaincy Revd Noel Beattie, 181 Maidstone Rd, Chatham, Kent ME4 6JG
Tel: (01634) 844867
Rural Issues Canon Michael Insley, Rectory, Goudhurst Rd, Horsmonden, Kent TN12 8JU
Tel: (01892) 836653
Urban Priorities Revd Tony Smith, Vicarage, The Hill, Northfleet, Kent DA11 9EU
Tel: (01474) 566400
Older People Mrs Dot Hooker, Kenwyn, Vicarage Rd, Yalding, Maidstone, Kent ME18 6DW
Tel: (01622) 814440
Environmental Issues (*Chairman*) Revd Dr Brian Godfrey, Rectory, Chevening Rd, Sundridge, Sevenoaks, Kent TN14 6AB   *Tel:* (01959) 563749
FLAME (*Chairman*) Mrs Ingrid Walsh, 25 Barnehurst Ave, Erith, Kent DA8 3NF
Tel: (01322) 330265
Poverty and Hope (*Director*) Mr Vivian Walton, Stansted Lodge Farm, Tumblefield Rd, Stansted, Sevenoaks, Kent TN15 7PR   *Tel:* (01732) 822530

STEWARDSHIP

Canon Brian Simmons, Vicarage, The Green, Langton Green, Tunbridge Wells, Kent TN3 0JB
Tel: (01892) 862072

RURAL DEANS

ARCHDEACONRY OF ROCHESTER

Cobham Revd James Tipp, Vicarage, St Katherine's Lane, Snodland, Kent ME6 5EH
Tel: (01634) 240232
Dartford Revd David Kitley, Vicarage, 67 Shepherds Lane, Dartford, Kent DA1 2NS
Tel: (01322) 220036
Gillingham Revd Paul Harvey, Vicarage, 27 Gillingham Green, Gillingham, Kent ME7 2RL
Tel: (01634) 850529
Gravesend Revd Clifford Goble, Rectory, Hook Green Rd, Southfleet, Kent DA13 9NQ
Tel: (01474) 833252
Rochester Canon Christopher Collins, Luton Rectory, Capstone Rd, Chatham, Kent ME5 7PN
Tel: (01634) 843780
Strood Revd David Low, Vicarage, Vicarage Lane, Hoo, Rochester, Kent ME3 9BB
Tel: (01634) 250291

ARCHDEACONRY OF BROMLEY

Beckenham Canon Douglas Redman, Vicarage, 37 Kingswood Rd, Shortlands, Bromley, Kent BR2 0HG   *Tel:* 020–8460 4989
Bromley Canon Peter Lock, Vicarage, 9 St Paul's Square, Bromley, Kent BR2 0XH
Tel: 020–8460 6275
Erith Revd David Springthorpe, Vicarage, 93 Pelham Rd, Barnehurst, Bexleyheath, Kent DA7 4LY   *Tel:* (01322) 523344
Orpington Revd Paul Miller, Vicarage, 46 World's End Lane, Green Street Green, Orpington, Kent BR6 6AG   *Tel:* (01689) 852905
Sidcup Revd Nicholas Kerr, Vicarage, 64 Days Lane, Sidcup, Kent DA15 8JR   *Tel:* 020–8300 1508

ARCHDEACONRY OF TONBRIDGE

Malling Canon Brian Stevenson, Vicarage, 138 High St, West Malling, Kent ME19 6NE
Tel: (01732) 842245
Paddock Wood Revd Michael Camp, Vicarage, Maidstone Rd, Hadlow, Tonbridge, Kent TN11 0DJ   *Tel and Fax:* (01732) 850238
Sevenoaks Revd Dr Brian Godfrey, Rectory, Chevening Rd, Sundridge, Sevenoaks, Kent TN14 6AB   *Tel:* (01959) 563749
Shoreham Revd David Francis, Vicarage, Comp Lane, Platt, Sevenoaks, Kent TN15 8NR
Tel: (01732) 885482
Tonbridge Revd Robert Bawtree, Vicarage, 194 Tonbridge Rd, Hildenborough, Kent TN11 9HR
Tel: (01732) 833596
Tunbridge Wells Vacancy

BISHOP (9th)
Rt Revd Christopher William Herbert, Abbey Gate House, St Albans, Herts. AL3 4HD [1995]
Tel: (01727) 853305
Fax: (01727) 846715
[Christopher St Albans]
Chaplain Revd Derwyn Williams
Secretaries Mrs Mary Handford, Mrs Lynn Bridger

SUFFRAGAN BISHOPS
HERTFORD Rt Revd Robin Jonathan Norman Smith, Hertford House, Abbey Mill Lane, St Albans, Herts. AL3 4HE [1990]
Tel: (01727) 866420
Fax: (01727) 811426
BEDFORD Rt Revd John Henry Richardson, 168 Kimbolton Rd, Bedford MK41 8DN [1994]
Tel: (01234) 357551
Fax: (01234) 218134

HONORARY ASSISTANT BISHOPS
Rt Revd and Rt Hon the Lord Runcie of Cuddesdon, 26A Jennings Rd, St Albans, Herts. AL1 4PD
Rt Revd David John Farmbrough, St Michael Mead, 110 Village Rd, Bromham, Beds. MK43 8HU [1993]
Tel: (01234) 825042
Rt Revd Edwin Ronald Barnes, 14 Hall Place Gardens, St Albans, Herts. AL1 3SP
Tel: (01727) 857764
Fax: (01727) 763025

CATHEDRAL AND ABBEY CHURCH OF ST ALBAN
Dean Very Revd Christopher Lewis PH D, The Deanery, Sumpter Yard, St Albans, Herts. AL1 1BY [1994]
Tel: (01727) 852120
Cathedral Office The Chapter House, Sumpter Yard, St Albans, Herts. AL1 1BY
Tel: (01727) 860780
Fax: (01727) 850944
email: cathedra@alban.u-net.com
Web: www.stalbansdioc.org.uk/cathedral/
Canons Residentiary
Canon Christopher Foster (*SubDean*), The Old Rectory, Sumpter Yard, St Albans, Herts. AL1 1BY [1994]
Tel: (01727) 854827

Canon Bill Ritson, 2 Sumpter Yard, St Albans, Herts AL1 1BY [1987]
Tel: (01727) 861744
Canon Michael Sansom PH D, 4D Harpenden Rd, St Albans, Herts. AL3 5AB [1988]
Tel: (01727) 833777
Canon Anders Bergquist PH D, 7 Corder Close, St Albans, Herts. AL3 4NH [1997]
Tel: (01727) 841116
Minor Canons
Precentor Revd David Munchin, 1 The Deanery, Sumpter Yard, St Albans, Herts. AL1 1BY [1996]
Tel: (01727) 855321
Chaplain Revd Christopher Pines, Deanery Barn, Sumpter Yard, St Albans, Herts. AL1 1BY [1997]
Tel: (01727) 854950
Cathedral Administrator Mr Nicholas Bates, Cathedral Office
Master of the Music Mr Andrew Lucas, 31 Abbey Mill Lane, St Albans, Herts. AL3 4HA
Tel: (01727) 860780
Assistant Master of the Music and Director of the St Albans Abbey Girls' Choir Mr Andrew Parnell, 16 Glenferrie Rd, St Albans, Herts. AL1 4JU
Tel: (01727) 867818
Cathedral Education Officer Susanna Ainsworth, Education Centre, Sumpter Yard, St Albans, Herts. AL1 1BY *Tel:* (01727) 836223
Archaeological Consultant Prof Martin Biddle
Architect Mr Andrew Anderson

ARCHDEACONS
ST ALBANS Ven Richard Cheetham, 6 Sopwell Lane, St Albans, Herts. AL1 1RR [1999]
Tel: (01727) 847212
Fax: (01727) 848311
BEDFORD Ven Malcolm Lesiter, 17 Lansdowne Rd, Luton, Beds. LU3 1EE [1993]   *Tel:* (01582) 730722
Fax: (01582) 877354
HERTFORD Ven Trevor Jones, St Mary's House, Church Lane, Stapleford, Hertford SG14 3NB [1997]   *Tel:* (01992) 581629
Fax: (01992) 558745
email: archdhert@stalbansdio.org.uk

CONVOCATION (MEMBERS OF THE HOUSE OF CLERGY OF THE GENERAL SYNOD)
Dignitaries in Convocation
The Dean of St Albans

The Archdeacon of Bedford
Proctors for Clergy
Canon Brian Andrews
Revd Mark Bonney
Revd Christine Hardman
Canon Les Oglesby
Canon Patience Purchas
Canon Hugh Wilcox

MEMBERS OF THE HOUSE OF LAITY OF THE GENERAL SYNOD
Mr Anthony Archer
Dr Keith Barker
Mr Michael Catty
Mrs Anna de Lange
Mr Paul Godfrey
Mrs Shirley Jackson
Mr Philip Lovegrove
Mrs Christina Rees
Mr David Warner

DIOCESAN OFFICERS
Dioc Secretary Mr Lawrence Nicholls, Holywell Lodge, 41 Holywell Hill, St Albans, Herts. AL1 1HE   *Tel:* (01727) 854532
Fax: (01727) 844469
email: mail@stalbansdioc.org.uk
Chancellor of Diocese His Honour the Worshipful Canon Rupert Bursell, Holywell Lodge, 41 Holywell Hill, St Albans, Herts. AL1 1HD
Tel: (01727) 865765
Registrar of Diocese and Bishop's Legal Secretary Mr David Cheetham (*same address*)
Surveyor Vacancy, c/o 41 Holywell Hill, St Albans, Herts. AL1 1HE   *Tel:* (01727) 854516

DIOCESAN ORGANIZATIONS
Diocesan Office Holywell Lodge, 41 Holywell Hill, St Albans, Herts. AL1 1HE
Tel: (01727) 854532
Fax: (01727) 844469
email: mail@stalbansdioc.org.uk

ADMINISTRATION
Dioc Synod (*Chairman, House of Clergy*) Canon Brian Andrews, Vicarage, High St, Abbots Langley, Herts. WD5 0AS *Tel:* (01923) 263013/261795 *Fax:* (01923) 261795; (*Chairman, House of Laity*) Mr Nicholas Alexander; (*Secretary*) Mr Lawrence Nicholls, Dioc Office
Board of Finance (*Chairman*) Mr Philip Lovegrove, Vicarage, 159 Baldwins Lane, Croxley Green, Rickmansworth, Herts. WD3 3LL *Tel:* (01923) 232387; (*Secretary*) Mr Lawrence Nicholls (*as above*)
Financial Secretary Vacancy, Dioc Office
Estates Secretary Mrs Michèle Manders, Dioc Office
Board of Patronage Mr Roger Collor, Dioc Office
Designated Officers (*Joint*) Mr David Cheetham and Mr Lawrence Nicholls, Dioc Office

Pastoral Committee Mr Roger Collor (*as above*)
Trusts Mrs Emma Critchley, Dioc Office

CHURCHES
Advisory Committee for the Care of Churches (*Chairman*) Dr Christopher Green, Dioc Office; (*Secretary*) Mr Roger Collor (*as above*)

EDUCATION
Dioc Education and Resources Centre Education Centre, Hall Grove, Welwyn Garden City, Herts. AL7 4PJ   *Tel:* (01707) 332321
Fax: (01707) 373089
Director of Education Mr Jon Reynolds, Education Centre (*as above*)
Schools Adviser Mr Richard Butcher (*same address*)
School Buildings Officer Mrs Ronnie Taylor (*same address*)

MINISTRY
Director of Ordinands Canon Michael Sansom, 4D Harpenden Rd, St Albans, Herts. AL3 5AB
Tel: (01727) 833777
Ministerial Development Officer Canon Anders Bergquist, Dioc Office   *Tel:* (01727) 830802
Continuing Ministerial Education Officer Vacancy, Dioc Office   *Tel:* (01727) 830802
Local Ministry Officer Vacancy, Dioc Office
Tel: (01727) 830802
Bishop's Officer for Women's and Non-Stipendiary Ministry Canon Patience Purchas, Rectory, Church St, Wheathampstead, Herts. AL4 8LR
Tel and *Fax:* (01582) 834285
Board of Readers' Work (*Hon Secretary*) Mr Philip McDonough, 28 Washbrook Close, Barton-le-Cley, Beds. MK45 4LF   *Tel:* (01582) 881772
Youth Officer Mr David Green, Education Centre (*as above*)
Youth Outreach Officer Mr Jo Stephens, Education Centre (*as above*)
Children's Work Adviser Revd Andrew Pattman, Education Centre (*as above*)

LITURGICAL
Chairman Canon Michael Sansom (*as above*)

MISSIONARY AND ECUMENICAL
Ecumenical Officer Vacancy
Board of Mission and Unity Mrs Carolyn Mercurio, Holy Saviour Vicarage, St Anne's Rd, Hitchin, Herts. SG5 1QB   *Tel:* (01462) 456140
Council for Partnership in World Mission Revd John Schild, Vicarage, Church Rd, Kings Walden, Hitchin, Herts. SG4 8JX   *Tel:* (01438) 871278
Workplace Ministry The Administrator, 41 Holywell Hill, St Albans, Herts. AL1 1HE
Tel: (01727) 869461

PRESS AND PUBLICATIONS
Dioc Communications Officer Capt Andrew Crooks, Dioc Office   *Tel:* (01727) 869506
(01582) 467247 (Home)

Editor of Dioc Directory Mr Lawrence Nicholls (*as above*)
Dioc Leaflet Capt Andrew Crooks (*as above*)

DIOCESAN RECORD OFFICES
County Hall, Hertford, Herts SG13 8DE *Tel:* (01992) 555105 (*For diocesan records and parish records for St Albans and Hertford Archdeaconries*) County Hall, Bedford MK42 9AP *County Archivist* Mr Kevin Ward *Tel:* (01234) 63222, Ext 277 (*For parish records for Bedford Archdeaconry*)

SOCIAL RESPONSIBILITY
Board for Social Responsibility (*Adviser and Secretary*) Revd Richard Wheeler, Dioc Office
Tel: (01727) 851748

STEWARDSHIP
Stewardship Development Officer Mr Nigel Guard, Dioc Office *Tel:* (01727) 854532

RURAL DEANS
ARCHDEACONRY OF ST ALBANS
Aldenham Revd Grant Fellows, Vicarage, Church Field, Christchurch Crescent, Radlett, Herts. WD7 8EE *Tel:* (01923) 856606
Berkhamsted Revd Richard Clarkson, Kingsmead, Gravel Path, Berkhamsted, Herts. HP4 2PH
Tel: (01442) 873014
Hemel Hempstead Revd Paul Hughes, St John's Vicarage, 10 Charles St, Boxmoor, Hemel Hempstead, Herts. HP1 1JH *Tel:* (01442) 255382
Hitchin Revd Frank Mercurio, Holy Saviour Vicarage, St Ann's Rd, Hitchin, Herts. SG5 1QR
Tel: (01462) 456140
Rickmansworth Revd John Kingsley-Smith, Christ Church Vicarage, Chorleywood Common, Rickmansworth, Herts. WD3 5SG
Tel: (01923) 282149
St Albans Revd Tony Hurle, St Paul's Vicarage, 7 Brampton Rd, St Albans, Herts. AL1 4PN
Tel: (01727) 836810
(01727) 846281 (Office)
Watford Revd John Brown, St Michael's Vicarage, 5 Mildred Ave, Watford, Herts. WD1 7DY
Tel: (01923) 232460
Wheathampstead Revd Jonathan Smith, St John's Vicarage, 5 St John's Rd, Harpenden, Herts. AL5 1DJ *Tel:* (01582) 467168

ARCHDEACONRY OF BEDFORD
Ampthill Revd Norman Jeffery, Vicarage, 30 Church Rd, Woburn Sands, Milton Keynes MK17 8TG *Tel:* (01908) 582581
Bedford Revd Trevor Maines, Vicarage, Goldington, Bedford MK41 0AP
Tel: (01234) 355024
Biggleswade Canon Robert Sibson, Vicarage, Shortmead St, Biggleswade, Beds. SG18 0AT
Tel: (01767) 312243
Dunstable Revd Graham Newton, Rectory, 8 Furness Ave, Dunstable, Beds. LU6 3BN
Tel: (01582) 664467
Elstow Revd Christopher Strong, Vicarage, Wootton, Bedford MK43 9HF *Tel:* (01234) 768391
Luton Revd Barry Etherington, Vicarage, 33 Felix Ave, Luton, Beds. LU2 7LE *Tel:* (01582) 724754
Sharnbrook Canon Ian Arthur, Rectory, 81 High St, Sharnbrook, Bedford MK44 1PE
Tel: (01234) 781444
Shefford Revd Ken Dixon, Rectory, 8 Rectory Close, Clifton, Shefford, Beds. SG17 5EL
Tel: (01462) 850150

ARCHDEACONRY OF HERTFORD
Barnet Revd Roger Huddleston, Holy Trinity Vicarage, 18 Lyonsdown Rd, New Barnet EN5 1JE *Tel:* 020–8449 0382
Bishop's Stortford Revd Clive Slaughter, Rectory, Vicerons Place, Thorley, Bishop's Stortford, Herts. CM23 4EL *Tel:* (01279) 654955
Buntingford Revd Leslie Harman, Vicarage, 31 Baldock Rd, Royston, Herts. SG8 5BJ
Tel: (01763) 246371 (Office)
(01763) 243145 (Home)
Cheshunt Revd John Springbett, Vicarage, 11 Amwell St, Hoddesdon, Herts. EN11 8TS
Tel: (01992) 462127
Hatfield Revd Jim Smith, 34 Cherry Tree Rise, Walkern, Stevenage, Herts. SG2 7JL
Tel: (01438) 861951
Hertford and Ware (Joint rural deans) Revd Graham Edwards, St Andrew's Rectory, 43 North Rd, Hertford SG14 1LZ *Tel:* (01992) 582726
Revd Roger Bowen, Little Amwell Vicarage, 17 Barclay Close, Hertford Heath, Hertford SG13 7RW *Tel:* (01992) 589140
Stevenage Revd Christine Hardman, Holy Trinity Vicarage, 18 Letchmore Rd, Stevenage, Herts. SG1 3JD *Tel:* (01438) 353229
email: chris@hardman.demon.co.uk

DIOCESE OF ST EDMUNDSBURY AND IPSWICH

Founded in 1914. Suffolk, except for a small area in the north-east (NORWICH); one parish in Essex.

Population 595,000   Area 1,439 sq m
Stipendiary Clergy 167   Benefices 177
Parishes 442   Churches 478

BISHOP (9th)
Rt Revd (John Hubert) Richard Lewis, Bishop's House, 4 Park Rd, Ipswich, Suffolk IP1 3ST [1997]
Tel: (01473) 252829
Fax: (01473) 232552
email:
bishop.richard@stedmundsbury.anglican.org
[Richard St Edm and Ipswich]
Bishop's Secretary Mrs Marion Crane (*same address*)

SUFFRAGAN BISHOP
DUNWICH Rt Revd Clive Young, 28 Westerfield Rd, Ipswich, Suffolk IP4 2UJ [1999]
Tel: (01473) 222276
Fax: (01473) 210303
email: bishop.clive@stedmundsbury.anglican.org
Bishop's Secretary Mrs Kati Wakefield (*same address*)

CATHEDRAL CHURCH OF ST JAMES, BURY ST EDMUNDS
Provost Very Revd James Edgar Atwell, Provost's House, Bury St Edmunds, Suffolk IP33 1RS [1995]
Tel: (01284) 754852
Cathedral Office Cathedral Office, Angel Hill, Bury St Edmunds, Suffolk IP33 1LS
Tel: (01284) 754933
Fax: (01284) 768655
email: cathedral@btconnect.com
Canons Residentiary
Precentor Canon Martin Shaw, 1 Abbey Precincts, Bury St Edmunds, Suffolk IP33 1RS [1989]
Tel: (01284) 761982
email: baritone@globalnet.co.uk
Canon John Parr PH D, 2 Abbey Precincts, Bury St Edmunds, Suffolk IP33 1RS [1999]
Tel and Fax: (01284) 753400
email: johnp@stedmundsbury.anglican.org
Canon Pastor Canon Marion Mingins, 54 College St, Bury St Edmunds, Suffolk IP33 1NH [1993]
Tel: (012840) 753396
Cathedral Chaplain Vacancy
Clerk to the Administrative Chapter Mr Christopher Fowler, Cathedral Office
Arts and Visitors Officer Mr Charles Borthwick, Cathedral Office
email: charlesb@btconnect.com

Director of Music Mr James Thomas, Cathedral Office
Tel: (01284) 756520
Assistant Director of Music Mr Michael Bawtree (*same address*)

ARCHDEACONS
IPSWICH Ven Terry Gibson, 99 Valley Rd, Ipswich, Suffolk IP1 4NF [1984]
Tel: (01473) 250333
Fax: (01473) 286877
email:
archdeacon.terry@stedmundsbury.anglican.org
SUDBURY Ven John Cox, 84 Southgate St, Bury St Edmunds, Suffolk IP33 2BJ
Tel: (01284) 766796
Fax: (01284) 723163
email:
archdeacon.john@stedmundsbury.anglican.org
SUFFOLK Ven Geoffrey Arrand, Glebe House, The Street, Ashfield cum Thorpe, Stowmarket, Suffolk IP14 6LX [1994]
Tel: (01728) 685497
Fax: (01728) 685969
email: archdeacon.geoffrey@stedmundsbury.anglican.org

CONVOCATION (MEMBERS OF THE HOUSE OF CLERGY OF THE GENERAL SYNOD)
The Archdeacon of Ipswich
Proctors for Clergy
Revd Jonathan Alderton-Ford
Canon Colin Bevington
Canon Cedric Catton

MEMBERS OF THE HOUSE OF LAITY OF THE GENERAL SYNOD
Mrs Jenny Freeman
Mr Richard Simmons
Mr Tony Redman
Mr Peter Smith

DIOCESAN OFFICERS
Dioc Secretary Mr Nicholas Edgell, Diocesan House, Tower St, Ipswich, Suffolk IP1 3BG
Tel: (01473) 211028
Fax: (01473) 232407
email: dbf@stedmundsbury.anglican.org
Chancellor of Diocese The Honourable Mr Justice Blofeld, 20–32 Museum St, Ipswich, Suffolk IP1 1HZ

Registrar of Diocese and Bishop's Legal Secretary Mr James Hall, 20/32 Museum St, Ipswich, Suffolk IP1 1HZ   Tel: (01473) 232300
Fax: (01473) 230524

DIOCESAN ORGANIZATIONS

Diocesan Office Diocesan House, Tower St, Ipswich, Suffolk IP1 3BG   Tel: (01473) 211028
Fax: (01473) 232407
email: dbf@stedmundsbury.anglican.org

ADMINISTRATION

Dioc Secretary Mr Nicholas Edgell, Dioc House
Dioc Synod (Chairman, House of Clergy) Canon Cedric Catton, Vicarage, Exning, Newmarket CB8 7HS Tel: (01638) 577413; (Chairman, House of Laity) Mr Peter Smith, Lusaka House, Great Glemham, Saxmundham IP17 2DH Tel: (01728) 663466; (Secretary) Mr Nicholas Edgell, Dioc House
Board of Finance (Chairman) Brigadier Adam Gurdon, Burgh House, Burgh, Woodbridge, Suffolk IP13 6PU Tel: (01473) 735273; (Secretary) Mr Nicholas Edgell (as above)
Assistants Mrs Katy Reade, Mr James Halsall, Mr Eric Brown, Mr Malcolm Green
Dioc Surveyor Mr Christopher Clarke, Clarke & Simpson, Well Close Square, Framlingham, Suffolk IP13 9DU   Tel: (01728) 724200
Board of Patronage Mr Nicholas Edgell (as above)
Pastoral Committee Mr Nicholas Edgell (as above)
Glebe and Investment Committee Mr Nicholas Edgell (as above)
Parsonages Committee Mr Eric Brown (as above)
Designated Officer Mr Nicholas Edgell (as above)

CHURCHES

Advisory Committee for the Care of Churches (Chairman) Mrs Hester Agate, The Old Rectory, Chattisham, Ipswich, Suffolk IP8 3PY Tel and Fax: (01473) 652306; (Secretary) Mr James Halsall (as above)
Church Buildings Committee (Chairman) The Hon Jill Ganzoni, Rivendell, Spring Meadow, Playford, Ipswich IP6 9ED   Tel: (01473) 624662
Secretary Mr James Halsall (as above)
Redundant Churches Uses Committee (Chairman) The Hon Jill Ganzoni; (Secretary) Mr Eric Brown (as above)

COUNSELLING

Adviser in Pastoral Care and Counselling Revd Harry Edwards, Rectory, Marlesford, Woodbridge IP13 0AT   Tel: (01728) 746747
email: Harry@psalm23.demon.co.uk
Bishop's Adviser on Exorcism and Deliverance Revd Philip Gray, Vicarage, Mendlesham, Stowmarket IP14 5RS   Tel: (01449) 766359

MINISTRY

Accredited Ministry Group (Chairman) The Bishop of Dunwich (as above)
Vocations Adviser Vacancy

Dioc Director of Ordinands Revd Mark Sanders, Rectory, The Street, Framsden, Stowmarket, Suffolk IP14 6MG   Tel: (01473) 890934
Dioc Director of Continuing Ministerial Education 1–4 Revd Mark Sanders (as above)
Continuing Ministerial Education Officer Canon John Parr PH D, 2 Abbey Precincts, Bury St Edmunds, Suffolk IP33 1RS
Tel and Fax: (01284) 753400
email: johnp@stedmundsbury.anglican.org
Principal of Dioc Ministry Scheme Canon Michael West PH D, c/o Dioc House
Director of Studies, Dioc Ministry Scheme Revd David Herrick, c/o Dioc House
Dioc Adviser for Women's Ministry Canon Sally Fogden, Rectory, Honington, Bury St Edmunds IP31 1RG   Tel: (01359) 269265
Lay Education and Training Adviser Miss Elizabeth Moore, Dioc House   Tel: (01473) 254263
Warden of Readers Revd Richard Willcock, Rectory, Framlingham, Woodbridge IP13 9BJ
Tel: (01728) 621082
Dioc Youth Adviser Ms Jane Boyce, Dioc House
Dioc Children's Adviser Vacancy
Dioc Widows Officers Canon John and Mrs Marjorie Gore, 8 De Burgh Place, Clare, Sudbury CO10 8QL   Tel: (01787) 278558
Clergy Retirement Officer Canon Dennis Pearce, 74 Hintlesham Drive, Orwell Green, Felixstowe IP11 8YL   Tel: (01394) 279189

SCHOOLS

Dioc Director of Education Revd David Underwood, Dioc House
Schools Administrator Mr Andrew Firth, Dioc House

LITURGICAL

Chairman The Bishop of St Edmundsbury and Ipswich
Secretary Canon Stuart Morris, Milestone House, 17 Gainsborough Rd, Sudbury CO10 6EU
Tel: (01787) 880487

MISSION AND SOCIAL RESPONSIBILITY

Mission and Rural Affairs Adviser c/o Dioc Secretary
Stewardship Adviser c/o Dioc House
Social Responsibility Adviser c/o Dioc Secretary
FLAME – Family Life and Marriage Education Mrs Kathy Blair, 59 Old Barrack Rd, Woodbridge IP12 4ER   Tel: (01394) 382030
Suffolk Christian Resource Library (Administrator) Mrs Shirley Nicholls, Dioc House
Tel: (01473) 213452

COMMUNICATIONS

Dioc Communications Officer Canon Simon Pettitt, Dioc House and 3 Crown St, Bury St Edmunds, Suffolk IP33 1QX   Tel and Fax: (01284) 753866
(0850) 480533 (Mobile)
email: canon@globalnet.co.uk

Editor of Dioc Directory Canon Simon Pettitt (*as above*)
Editor of 'The Church in Suffolk' Canon Simon Pettitt (*as above*)

DIOCESAN RECORD OFFICES

77 Raingate St, Bury St Edmunds, Suffolk IP33 2AR *Tel:* (01284) 352000 Ext 2352 (*For parish records for Sudbury and Hadleigh deaneries*)
Gatacre Rd, Ipswich IP1 2LQ *Tel:* (01473) 264541 (*For parish records for Ipswich and Suffolk archdeaconries*)
The Central Library, Lowestoft NR32 1DR *Tel:* (01502) 566325 Ext 3308 (*For parish records for NE Suffolk parishes*)

SPIRITUALITY

Bishop's Adviser in Spirituality Canon Martin Shaw, 1 Abbey Precincts, Bury St Edmunds IP33 1RS *Tel:* (01284) 761982
Dioc Spiritual Director for Cursillo Revd Ian Morgan, Rectory, 74 Ancaster Rd, Ipswich IP2 9AJ *Tel:* (01473) 601895
Lay Director for Cursillo Mr Craig Young, 31 Appledown Drive, Bury St Edmunds IP32 7HG *Tel:* (01284) 760293

RURAL DEANS
ARCHDEACONRY OF IPSWICH

Bosmere Revd Roger Dedman, Vicarage, Vicarage Lane, Bramford, Ipswich, Suffolk IP8 4AE *Tel:* (01473) 741105
Colneys Canon Geoffrey Grant, Rectory, Nacton, Ipswich, Suffolk IP10 0HY *Tel:* (01473) 659232
Hadleigh Canon David Stranack, Vicarage, Bear St, Nayland, Colchester CO4 4LA *Tel:* (01206) 262316
Ipswich Revd David Cutts, St Margaret's Vicarage, 32 Constable Rd, Ipswich IP4 2UW *Tel:* (01473) 253906

Samford Canon Colin Bevington, 44 Thorney Rd, Capel St Mary, Ipswich IP9 2LH *Tel:* (01473) 310069
Stowmarket Revd Deidre Parmenter, Vicarage, The Folly, Haughley, Stowmarket IP14 3NS *Tel:* (01449) 771647
Woodbridge Revd Robert Clifton, Rectory, Orford, Woodbridge, Suffolk IP12 2NN *Tel:* (01394) 450336

ARCHDEACONRY OF SUDBURY

Clare Revd Edmund Betts, Rectory, 10 Hopton Rise, Hanchett Grange, Haverhill, Suffolk CB9 9FS *Tel:* (01440) 708768
Ixworth Revd David Mathers, Thurston Vicarage, Bury St Edmunds, Suffolk IP31 3RU *Tel:* (01359) 230301
Lavenham Revd Derrick Stiff, Rectory, Lavenham, Sudbury, Suffolk CO10 9SA *Tel:* (01787) 247244
Mildenhall Canon Geoffrey Smith, St Mary's Rectory, 5A Fitzroy St, Newmarket, Suffolk CB8 0JW *Tel:* (01638) 662448
Sudbury Revd Lawrence Pizzey, Rectory, Christopher Lane, Sudbury, Suffolk CO10 6AS *Tel:* (01787) 372611
Thingoe Vacancy

ARCHDEACONRY OF SUFFOLK

Beccles and South Elmham Vacancy
Halesworth Revd Tony Norton, Vicarage, Church Lane, Spexhall, Halesworth, Suffolk IP19 0RQ *Tel and Fax:* (01986) 875453
Hartismere Revd Christopher Atkinson, Vicarage, 41 Castle St, Eye, Suffolk IP23 7AW *Tel:* (01379) 870277
Hoxne c/o The Archdeacon of Suffolk
Loes Vacancy
Saxmundham Canon Roger Smith, Rectory, Rectory Rd, Middleton, Saxmundham, Suffolk IP17 3NR *Tel:* (01728) 648421

Founded in 1075, formerly Sherborne (AD 705) and Ramsbury (AD 909). Wiltshire, except for the northern quarter (BRISTOL); Dorset, except for an area in the east (WINCHESTER); a small area of Hampshire; a parish in Devon.

Population 848,000   Area 2,046 sq m
Stipendiary Clergy 234   Benefices 182
Parishes 453   Churches 579

BISHOP (77th)
Rt Revd David Stancliffe, South Canonry, 71 The Close, Salisbury, Wilts. SP1 2ER [1993]
Tel: (01722) 334031
Fax: (01722) 413112
email: dsarum@eluk.co.uk
[David Sarum]

AREA BISHOPS
SHERBORNE Rt Revd John Dudley Galtrey Kirkham, Little Bailie, Dullar Lane, Sturminster Marshall, Wimborne, Dorset BH21 4AD [1976]
Tel: (01258) 857659
Fax: (01258) 857961
RAMSBURY Rt Revd Peter Fearnely Hullah, Ramsbury Office, Sarum House, High St, Urchfont, Devizes, Wilts. SN10 4QH [1999]
Tel: (01380) 840373
Fax: (01380) 848247
email: adsarum@compuserve.com
Home Bishop's Croft, Winterbourne Earls, Salisbury, Wilts. SP4 6HJ
email: HullahP@aol.com

HONORARY ASSISTANT BISHOP
Rt Revd John Kingsmill Cavell, 5 Constable Way, West Harnham, Salisbury, Wilts. SP2 8LN
Tel: (01722) 334782

CATHEDRAL CHURCH OF THE BLESSED VIRGIN MARY
Dean Very Revd Derek Richard Watson, The Deanery, 7 The Close, Salisbury, Wilts. SP1 2EF [1996]
Cathedral Office 6 The Close, Salisbury SP1 2EF
Tel: (01722) 555110
Fax: (01722) 555155
Canons Residentiary
Precentor Canon Jeremy Davies, Hungerford Chantry, 54 The Close, Salisbury, Wilts. SP1 2EL [1985]
Tel: (01722) 555179 (Home)
Office Dept of Liturgy and Music, Ladywell, 33 The Close, Salisbury, Wilts. SP1 2EJ
Tel: (01722) 555125
Fax: (01722) 555116
email: jeremy@mcenery.demon.co.uk

Treasurer Canon June Osborne, 23 The Close, Salisbury, Wilts. SP1 2EH [1995]
Tel: (01722) 555176
Fax: (01722) 555177
email: OSBGOULD@aol.com
Chancellor Canon David Durston, 24 The Close, Salisbury, Wilts. SP1 2EH [1992]
Tel: (01722) 555193
Fax: (01722) 323569
Chapter Clerk Brigadier Christopher (Kit) Owen, Cathedral Office
Tel: (01722) 555100
Fax: (01722) 555109
email: CHAPOFFICE@aol.com
Director of Music Mr Simon Lole, Dept of Liturgy and Music (*as above*)

ARCHDEACONS
SHERBORNE Ven Paul Wheatley, Rectory, West Stafford, Dorchester, Dorset DT2 8AB [1991]
Tel: (01305) 264637
Fax: (01305) 260640
email: 101543.3471@compuserve.com
DORSET Ven Geoffrey Walton, Vicarage, Witchampton, Wimborne, Dorset BH21 5AP [1982]
Tel: (01258) 840422
Fax: (01258) 840786
WILTSHIRE Ven Barney Hopkinson, Sarum House, High St, Urchfont, Devizes, Wilts. SN10 4QH [1986]
Tel: (01380) 840373
Fax: (01380) 848247
email: adsarum@compuserve.com
SARUM (Acting) Ven Barney Hopkinson (*as above*)

CONVOCATION (MEMBERS OF THE HOUSE OF CLERGY OF THE GENERAL SYNOD)
The Archdeacon of Wiltshire
Proctors for Clergy
Revd Christopher Brown
Revd Mary Crameri
Canon Jeremy Davies
Canon Barry Lomax

MEMBERS OF THE HOUSE OF LAITY OF THE GENERAL SYNOD
Mrs Rosemary Bassett
Mrs Mary Bordass

Mr Paul Boyd-Lee
Lt Col John Darlington
Mrs Jane Dibdin
Mrs Deirdre Ducker
Mr James Humphery
Mrs Anne Parry

DIOCESAN OFFICERS

Dioc Secretary Revd Karen Curnock, Church House, Crane St, Salisbury, Wilts. SP1 2QB
Tel: (01722) 411922
Fax: (01722) 411990
email: diosec@saldbf.freeserve.co.uk
Chancellor of Diocese His Honour Judge Samuel Wiggs, c/o Dioc Office
Registrar of Diocese and Bishop's Legal Secretary Mr Andrew Johnson, Minster Chambers, 42/44 Castle St, Salisbury, Wilts. SP1 3TX
Tel: (01722) 411141
Fax: (01722) 411566
Registrar of Dorset Archdeaconry Mr John Arkell, Palladwr House, Bleke St, Shaftesbury, Dorset SP7 8AH
Tel: (01747) 852176

DIOCESAN ORGANIZATIONS

Diocesan Office Church House, Crane St, Salisbury, Wilts. SP1 2QB   *Tel:* (01722) 411922
Fax: (01722) 411990
email: diosec@saldbf.freeserve.co.uk

ADMINISTRATION

Deputy Dioc Secretaries Mr John Voaden, Dioc Office and Mr Richard Trahair, Dioc Office
Tel: (01722) 411933
Dioc Synod (*Chairman, House of Clergy*) Canon Clive Cohen, Rectory, Winterslow, Salisbury SP5 1RE *Tel:* (01980) 862231; (*Chairman, House of Laity*) Mr Neil Whitton, Homanton Cottage, Salisbury Rd, Shrewton, Salisbury, Wilts. *Tel:* (01980) 620433; (*Secretary*) Revd Karen Curnock, Dioc Office
Board of Finance (*Chairman*) Mr Hugh Privett, The Manor House, Marston Magna, Yeovil, Som. BA22 8DW *Tel:* (01935) 850294; (*Secretary*) Revd Karen Curnock (*as above*)
Deputy Secretary: Mr John Voaden (*as above*)
Property Secretary Mr Richard Trahair (*as above*)
Diocesan Surveyor Mr John Carley, Dioc Office
Tel: (01722) 411933
Pastoral Committee (*Secretary*) Mr John Voaden (*as above*)
Designated Officer Mr Andrew Johnson, Minster Chambers, 42/44 Castle St, Salisbury, Wilts. SP1 3TX
Tel: (01722) 411141

CHURCHES

Advisory Committee for the Care of Churches (*Chairman*) The Dean, Cathedral Office (*as above*); (*Secretary*) Miss Carolann Johnson, Dioc Office
Tel: (01722) 321996

Redundant Churches Uses Committee and Furnishings Officer Mr Richard Trahair (*as above*)
Ringers' Association Mr Anthony Lovell-Wood, 11 Brook Close, Tisbury, Salisbury, Wilts.
Tel: (01747) 871121

EDUCATION

Director of Education Mr Henry Head, Audley House, Crane St, Salisbury, Wilts. SP1 2QA
Tel: (01722) 411977
Fax: (01722) 331159
Buildings and Trusts Officer Mr Simon Franklin (*same address*)
Adviser to Schools and Governors Mrs Ruth Eade (*same address*)
Youth and Children's Officer Young Sarum Team (*same address*)

MINISTRY

Director of Ministry Revd Sheila Watson, Dioc Office
Tel: (01722) 411944
email: ministry@saldbf.freeserve.co.uk
Director of Ordinands Canon Stanley Royle, South Canonry, 71 The Close, Salisbury SP1 2ER
Tel: (01722) 334031
Adviser for Women's Ministry Revd Sheila Watson (*as above*)
Principal of Ordained Local Ministry and Integrated Education Revd Anne Dawtry, Dioc Office
Vice-Principal of Ordained Local Ministry Revd Rosalind Brown, Dioc Office
Vocations Adviser Revd Sandy Railton, Dioc Office

PARISH DEVELOPMENT

Adviser for Parish Development Revd Alan Jeans, Dioc Office
Tel: (01722) 411955
Liturgical Revd Stephen Lake, Vicarage, St Aldhelm's Rd, Branksome, Poole, Dorset BH13 6BT
Tel: (01202) 764420
Christian Stewardship Adviser Mr Chris Love, Dioc Office
Tel: (01722) 411955
email: chris_love@compuserve.com

CHURCH AND SOCIETY

Adviser for Church and Society Revd Ian Woodward, Dioc Office
Tel: (01722) 411966
Social Responsibility (*Secretary*) (*Wilts.*) Mrs Kathleen Ben Rabha (*also Bristol Diocese and Ecumenical*), Dioc Office
Tel: (01722) 411966
(*Dorset*) Vacancy
Ecumenical (*Secretary*) Revd Nigel LLoyd, Rectory, 19 Springfield Rd, Parkstone, Poole, Dorset BH14 0LG
Tel: (01202) 748860
email: nigel@branksea.demon.co.uk
Family Life Project Worker Mrs Fran Tolond, White Horse Cottage, Yards Lane, Hilcott, Pewsey, Wilts. SN9 6HJ
Tel: (01672) 851546
Ecumenical Officer (*Sherborne*) Revd Nigel LLoyd (*as above*)

County Ecumenical Officer (Wiltshire) Miss Anne Doyle, 26 Sherwood Ave, Melksham, Wilts. SN12 7HJ   Tel:(01225) 704748
(Dorset) Mrs Val Potter, 22 Durbeville Close, Dorchester, Dorset DT1 2JT   Tel: (01305) 264416
Officer for Urban Priority Areas Revd Anthony Macrow-Wood, Vicarage, 58 Littlemoor Rd, Preston, Weymouth, Dorset DT3 6AA
Tel: (01305) 815366
Officers for Rural Areas (Ramsbury Episcopal Area) Revd Terry Brighton, Vicarage, White St, West Lavington, Devizes, Wilts. SN10 4LW
Tel: (01380) 818388
(Sherborne Episcopal Area) Revd Dr Jean Coates, Rectory, Main St, Broadmayne, Dorchester CT2 8EB   Tel: (01305) 852435
Officer for Minority Ethnic Concerns Revd Peter Barnett, Pilsdon Manor, Pilsdon, Bridport, Dorset DT66 5NZ   Tel: (01308) 868308
Officer for Interfaith Relations Canon John Sargant, Preshute Vicarage, 7 Golding Ave, Marlborough, Wilts. SN8 1TH   Tel: (01672) 513408
European Affairs Officer Revd Richard Franklin, Holy Trinity Vicarage, 7 Glebe Close, Weymouth, Dorset DT44 9RL   Tel: (01305) 760354

PRESS AND PUBLICATIONS

Communications (Secretary and Communications Officer) Mr Julian Hewitt, Dioc Office
Tel: (01722) 411988
0370 961629 (Mobile)
Editor of ' The Sarum Link' Mrs Jane Warner, Dioc Office   Tel: (01722) 339447
Editor of Dioc Directory Mrs Miriam Darke, Dioc Office   Tel: (01722) 411922
Editor of Dioc Handbook Dioc Secretary (as above)

DIOCESAN RECORD OFFICES

Diocesan Record Office and Wiltshire Parochial Records, Library HQ, Bythesea Rd, Trowbridge, Wilts. BA14 8BS Principal Archivist Mr John D'Arcy Tel: (01225) 713136 (For diocesan records and parishes in the archdeaconries of Wiltshire and Sarum)   .
County Record Office, Bridport Rd, Dorchester, Dorset DT1 1RP County Archivist Mr Hugh Jàcques Tel: (01305) 250550 (For parishes in the County of Dorset)
County Record Office, 20 Southgate St, Winchester, Hants. SO23 9EF County Archivist Miss Rosemary Dunhill Tel: (01962) 846154 (For the few Salisbury diocesan parishes situated in the County of Hampshire)

RURAL DEANS
ARCHDEACONRY OF SHERBORNE

Dorchester Revd Ken Scott, Rectory, Church Lane, Frampton, Dorchester, Dorset DT2 9NL
Tel: (01300) 320429

Lyme Bay Revd Robin Johnson, Rectory, 56 Prince of Wales Rd, Dorchester, Dorset DT1 1PP
Tel: (01305) 268837
Sherborne Canon Eric Woods, Vicarage, Abbey Close, Sherborne, Dorset DT9 3LQ
Tel: (01935) 812452
Weymouth Canon Keith Hugo, Wyke Regis Rectory, 1 Portland Rd, Weymouth, Dorset DT4 9ES   Tel: (01305) 784649

ARCHDEACONRY OF DORSET
Blackmore Vale Revd William Ridding, Vicarage, Kington Magna, Gillingham, Dorset SP8 5EW
Tel: (01747) 838494
Milton and Blandford Canon Gerald Squarey, Vicarage, Shaston Rd, Stourpaine, Blandford, Dorset DT11 8TA   Tel: (01258) 480580
Poole Canon Vic Barron, Rectory, 51 Millham's Rd, Kinson, Bournemouth, Dorset BH10 7LJ
Tel: (01202) 571996
Purbeck Canon Peter Hardman, Rectory, 19 Pound Lane, Wareham, Dorset BH20 4LQ
Tel: (01929) 552684
Wimborne Revd Tony Watts, Rectory, 250 New Rd, West Parley, Wimborne, Dorset BH22 8EW
Tel: (01202) 873561

ARCHDEACONRY OF SARUM
Alderbury Revd Christine Allsopp, Rectory, High St, Porton, Salisbury, Wilts. SP4 0LH
Tel: (01980) 610305
Chalke Revd Michael Ridley, Rectory, Mill End, Damerham, Fordingbridge SP6 3HU
Tel: (01725) 518642
Heytesbury Revd Michael Flight, Vicarage, Bitham Lane, Westbury, Wilts. BA13 3BU
Tel: (01373) 822209
Salisbury Revd Keith Robinson, Rectory, Tollgate Rd, Salisbury, Wilts. SP1 2JJ Tel: (01722) 335895
Stonehenge Revd Malcolm Bridger, Rectory, 10 St James St, Ludgershall, Andover, Hants. SP11 9QF   Tel: (01980) 790393

ARCHDEACONRY OF WILTSHIRE
Bradford Canon Christopher Brown, Rectory, Union St, Trowbridge, Wilts. BA14 8RU
Tel: (01225) 755121
Calne Revd Peter Giles, Old Vicarage, Honeyhill, Wootton Bassett, Swindon SN3 7DY
Tel: (01793) 852643
Devizes Canon John Record, Rectory, 39 Long St, Devizes, Wilts. SN10 1NS   Tel: (01380) 723705
Marlborough Revd Henry Pearson, Rectory, 1 Rawlingswell Lane, Marlborough, Wilts. SN8 1AU   Tel: (01672) 512357
Pewsey Revd Nicolas Leigh-Hunt, Vicarage, 5 Eastcourt, Burbage, Marlborough, Wilts. SN8 3AG   Tel: (01672) 810258

DIOCESE OF SHEFFIELD

Founded in 1914. Sheffield; Rotherham; Doncaster, except for a few parishes in the south east (SOUTHWELL); an area of North Lincolnshire; an area of south-eastern Barnsley; a small area of the East Riding of Yorkshire.

Population 1,197,000   Area 576 sq m
Stipendiary Clergy 198   Benefices 158
Parishes 178   Churches 224

BISHOP (6th)
Rt Revd John (Jack) Nicholls, Bishopscroft, Snaithing Lane, Sheffield, S Yorks. S10 3LG [1998]
Tel: 0114–230 2170
Fax: 0114–263 0110
[Jack Sheffield]
Domestic Chaplain Revd Nick Helm, 23 Hill Turrets Close, Sheffield S11 9RE
Tel: 0114–235 0191
Fax: 0114–235 2275

SUFFRAGAN BISHOP
DONCASTER Rt Revd Cyril Ashton, 3 Farrington Court, Wickersley, Rotherham [1999]
Tel: (01709) 512449
Fax: (01709) 512550

HONORARY ASSISTANT BISHOPS
Rt Revd Kenneth John Fraser Skelton, 65 Crescent Rd, Sheffield S7 1HN   *Tel:* 0114–255 1260
Rt Revd Kenneth Harold Pillar, 75 Dobcroft Rd, Millhouses, Sheffield S7 2LS   *Tel:* 0114–236 7902
Rt Revd John Gaisford, 3 North Lane, Roundhay, Leeds LS8 2QJ *Tel:* 0113–273 2003
Fax: 0113–273 3002
email: 101740,2275@compuserve.com

CATHEDRAL CHURCH OF ST PETER AND ST PAUL
Provost Very Revd Michael Sadgrove, The Cathedral, Church St, Sheffield S1 1HA [1996]
Tel: 0114–275 3434
Fax: 0114–278 0244
email: provshef@aol.com
Web: http://www.shef.ac.uk/uni/projects/shefcath
Canons Residentiary
Canon Trevor Page, The Cathedral [1982]
Ven Richard Blackburn, The Cathedral [1999]
Canon Christopher Smith, The Cathedral [1991]
Canon Jane Sinclair, The Cathedral [1993]
email: shefflit@aol.com
Cathedral Administrator Mr Brian Watson, The Cathedral   *email:* sheffexec@aol.com
Master of the Music Mr Neil Taylor, The Cathedral   *email:* sheffmusic@aol.com
Asst Master of Music Mr Mark Pybus, The Cathedral

ARCHDEACONS
SHEFFIELD Ven Richard Blackburn, 34 Wilson Rd, Sheffield S11 8RN [1999]   *Tel:* 0114–266 6099
Fax: 0114–267 9782
Office Diocesan Church House, 95–99 Effingham St, Rotherham S65 1BL   *Tel:* (01709) 512449
Fax: (01709) 512550
DONCASTER Ven Bernard Holdridge, Fairview House, 14 Armthorpe Lane, Doncaster DN2 5LZ [1994]   *Tel:* (01302) 325787
Fax: (01302) 760493
Office Diocesan Church House (*as above*)

CONVOCATION (MEMBERS OF THE HOUSE OF CLERGY OF THE GENERAL SYNOD)
The Archdeacon of Doncaster
Proctors for Clergy
Revd Richard Atkinson
Revd Michael Breen
Revd James Forrester
Canon Jane Sinclair

MEMBERS OF THE HOUSE OF LAITY OF THE GENERAL SYNOD
Prof David McClean
Mrs Elizabeth Paver
Mr Jonathan Redden
Mrs Janet Vout

DIOCESAN OFFICERS
Dioc Secretary Mr Tony Beck, Diocesan Church House, 95–99 Effingham St, Rotherham S65 1BL
Tel: (01709) 512368
Fax: (01709) 512550
email: sheffield.diocese@ukonline.co.uk
Chancellor of Diocese Prof David McClean, 6 Burnt Stones Close, Sheffield S10 5TS
Tel: 0114–230 5794
Registrar of Diocese and Bishop's Legal Secretary Mrs Miranda Myers, Old Cathedral Vicarage, St James Row, Sheffield, S Yorks S1 1XA
Tel: 0114–272 2061
Fax: 0114–270 0813 or 275 0243

DIOCESAN ORGANIZATIONS

Diocesan Office Diocesan Church House, 95–99 Effingham St, Rotherham S65 1BL
Tel: (01709) 511116
Fax: (01709) 512550
email: sheffield.diocese@ukonline.co.uk
Web: http://web.ukonline.co.uk/trafic

ADMINISTRATION

Dioc Secretary Mr Tony Beck, Dioc Office
Tel: (01709) 512368
Deputy Secretary Miss Margaret Barlow, Dioc Office
Tel: (01709) 512370
Property Manager Mr Brian Cook, Dioc Office
Tel: (01709) 512445
Finance Officer Mr Roger Pinchbeck, Dioc Office
Tel: (01709) 515877
Computer Manager Mr Jack Hudson, Dioc Office
Tel: (01709) 515881
Dioc Synod (*Chairman, House of Clergy*) Canon Gordon Taylor, Vicarage, 22 Clifton Gardens, Goole DN14 6AS *Tel:* (01405) 764259; (*Chairman, House of Laity*) Mrs Elizabeth Paver, 113 Warning Tongue Lane, Bessacarr, Doncaster DN4 6TB *Tel:* (01302) 530706; (*Secretary*) Mr Tony Beck (*as above*)
Board of Finance (*Chairman*) Mr John Biggin, 7 Ranmoor Crescent, Sheffield S10 3GU *Tel:* 0114–268 5880 *Fax:* 0114–230 4546; (*Secretary*) Mr Tony Beck (*as above*)
Pastoral Committee (*Chairman*) The Provost of Sheffield (*as above*); (*Secretary*) Miss Margaret Barlow (*as above*)
Redundant Churches Uses Committee (*Chairman*) Ven Bernard Holdridge (*as above*); (*Secretary*) Mr Brian Cook (*as above*)
Parsonages Committee (*Chairman*) Ven Bernard Holdridge (*as above*); (*Secretary*) Mr Brian Cook (*as above*)
Board of Patronage (*Secretary*) Mr David Wilson, 363 Fulwood Rd, Sheffield, S Yorks. S10 3GE
Tel: 0114–266 2066
Designated Officer Revd Nick Helm, Bishopscroft, Snaithing Lane, Sheffield S10 3LG
Tel: 0114–230 2170
Fax: 0114–263 0110

CHURCHES

Advisory Committee for the Care of Churches (*Chairman*) Rt Revd Kenneth Skelton, 65 Crescent Rd, Sheffield S7 1HN *Tel:* 0114–255 1260; (*Secretary*) Miss Margaret Barlow (*as above*)

EDUCATION

Dioc Board of Education (*Chairman*) Ven Bernard Holdridge (*as above*); (*Secretary*) Mr Malcolm Robertson, Dioc Office *Tel:* (01709) 512446
Director of Education Mr Malcolm Robertson (*as above*)
RE and Worship Adviser Revd Alan Parkinson, Dioc Office *Tel:* (01709) 512446

PARISH TRAINING

Training Committee (*Chairman*) The Bishop of Doncaster; (*Secretary*) Canon Peter Chambers, Dioc Office *Tel:* (01709) 515871
Director of Training Canon Peter Chambers (*as above*)
Lay Ministry Officer Mr John Bouch, Dioc Office
Tel: (01709) 515871
Youth Outreach Officer Capt Robert Drost, Dioc Office *Tel:* (01709) 512447
Children's and Youth Officer Mrs Bridget Fudger, Dioc Office *Tel:* (01709) 512447
Resources and Information Officer Vacancy, Dioc Office *Tel:* (01709) 512378

MINISTRY

Mission and Unity Committee (*Chairman*) The Bishop of Doncaster (*as above*); (*Secretary and Ecumenical Officer*) Revd Hilary Smart, Dioc Office *Tel:* 0114–239 8202
Adviser in Evangelism Revd David Sherwin, Dioc Office *Tel:* (01709) 515874
Director of Ordinands Canon Trevor Page, 393 Fulwood Rd, Sheffield S10 3GE
Tel: 0114–230 5707
Asst POT Officers Revd Mark Cockayne, St Polycarp's Vicarage, 33 Wisewood Lane, Sheffield S6 4WA *Tel:* 0114–266 1932
Revd Peter Hughes, St Thomas' Vicarage, 331 Kimberworth Rd, Rotherham S61 1HD
Tel: (01709) 554441
Bishop's Adviser on Women in Ministry Canon Sue Proctor, Rectory, 217 Nursery Rd, Dinnington, Sheffield S31 7QU *Tel:* (01909) 562335
email: sueproctor@dinnington.demon.co.uk
Bishop's Adviser on Non-Stipendiary Ministry Revd Bridget Brooke, 166 Tom Lane, Sheffield S10 3PG
Tel: 0114–230 2147
Bishop's Adviser on Church Army Ministry Vacancy
Warden of Readers Revd Andrew Teal, Vicarage, 2 Sunderland St, Tickhill, Doncaster DN11 9QJ
Tel: (01302) 742224
Readers' Board (*Secretary*) Mr Stuart Carey, Corben House, 3 Station Rd, Hatfield, Doncaster DN7 6PQ *Tel:* (01302) 844936

PRESS AND PUBLICATIONS

Communications Officer Revd Dr Peter Bold, 40 Renecliffe Ave, Broom Valley, Rotherham S60 2RP *Tel:* (01709) 364729
Fax: (01709) 363959
email: PEBold@aol.com
Editor of Dioc News Revd Peter Gascoigne, Bilham Vicarage, Churchfield Rd, Clayton, Doncaster DN5 7DH *Tel and Fax:* (01977) 643756
Editor of Dioc Year Book Mr Tony Beck, Dioc Office

DIOCESAN RECORD OFFICES

Sheffield City Archives, 52 Shoreham St, Sheffield S1 4SP *Tel:* 0114–273 4756 (*For parishes in the archdeaconry of Sheffield*)
Doncaster Archives, King Edward Rd, Balby,

Doncaster DN4 0NA *Tel:* (01302) 859811 (*For parishes in the archdeaconry of Doncaster*)

FAITH AND JUSTICE
Faith and Justice Committee (*Chairman*) Revd David Walker, Vicarage, 88 Main St, Bramley, Rotherham S66 2SQ   *Tel* and *Fax:* (01709) 702828
Secretary Ms Rachel Ross, Dioc Office
Tel: (01709) 512448
Social Responsibility Officer Ms Rachel Ross (*as above*)
Faith in the City Development Worker Dr Ian McCollough, Dioc Office   *Tel:* (01709) 512448
Industrial Mission (*Senior Chaplain*) Canon Michael West, 21 Endcliffe Rise Rd, Sheffield S11 8RU   *Tel:* 0114–266 1921
Office The Industrial Mission in South Yorkshire, Cemetery Rd Baptist Church, Napier St Entrance, Sheffield S11 8HA   *Tel:* 0114–275 5865
Bishop's Adviser on Black Concerns Mrs Carmen Franklin, 13 Staindrop View, Chapeltown, Sheffield S30 4YS   *Tel:* 0114–246 9650
Bishop's Representative for Child Protection Mrs Deidre Offord, Warren House, Pelham Court, Pelham Rd, Nottingham NG5 1AP
Tel: 0115–960 3010
Bishop's Rural Adviser Revd Philip Ireson, Rectory, 4A Barkers Hades Rd, Letwell, Worksop S81 8DF   *Tel:* (01909) 730346
European Link Officer Canon Bob Fitzharris

STEWARDSHIP
Christian Giving Adviser Mr Derek Lane, Dioc Office   *Tel:* (01709) 515875

AREA DEANS
ARCHDEACONRY OF SHEFFIELD
Attercliffe Revd Mike Cameron, Vicarage, 27 Tynker Ave, Beighton, Sheffield S19 6DX
Tel: 0114–248 7635

Ecclesall Revd David Williams, 51 Vicarage Lane, Dore, Sheffield S17 3GY   *Tel:* 0114–236 3335
Ecclesfield Revd James Forrester, Vicarage, 230 The Wheel, Ecclesfield, Sheffield S35 9ZB
Tel: 0114–257 0002
Hallam Revd Philip West, 214 Oldfield Rd, Stannington, Sheffield S6 6DY
Tel: 0114–232 4490
Hickleton Revd Harold Loxley, St Catherine's House, 300 Hastilar Rd South, Sheffield S13 8EJ
Tel and *Fax:* 0114–239 9598
Laughton Canon Sue Proctor, Rectory, 217 Nursery Rd, Dinnington, Sheffield S31 7QU
Tel: (01909) 562335
Rotherham Revd John Wraw, Clifton Vicarage, 10 Clifton Crescent North, Rotherham S65 2AS
Tel: (01709) 363082
Tankersley Revd Sue Hope, Vicarage, 23 Housley Park, Chapeltown, Sheffield S35 2UE
Tel: 0114–257 0966

ARCHDEACONRY OF DONCASTER
Adwick-le-Street Canon Bob Fitzharris, Vicarage, 3A High St, Bentley, Doncaster DN5 0AA
Tel and *Fax:* (01302) 876272
email: 106517.1056@compuserve.com
Doncaster Revd Norman Young, Vicarage, Barnby Dun, Doncaster DN3 1AA
Tel: (01302) 882835
Fax: (01302) 880029
Snaith and Hatfield Canon Gordon Taylor, Vicarage, 22 Clifton Gardens, Goole DN14 6AS
Tel: (01405) 764259
Wath Canon Martin Baldock, Vicarage, Christchurch Rd, Wath upon Dearne, Rotherham S63 6NW   *Tel:* (01709) 873210
West Doncaster Revd Graham Marcer, Balby Vicarage, 6 Greenfield Lane, Doncaster DN4 0PT
Tel: (01302) 853278
email: Graham.Marcer@btinternet.com

DIOCESE OF SODOR AND MAN

Founded in 447. The Isle of Man.

Population 73,000   Area 221 sq m
Stipendiary Clergy 22   Benefices 26
Parishes 27   Churches 42

BISHOP (79th)
Rt Revd Nöel Debroy Jones, The Bishop's House, Quarterbridge Rd, Douglas, Isle of Man IM2 3RF [1989]   *Tel:* (01624) 622108
                                    Fax: (01624) 672890
[Nöel Sodor and Man]
Domestic Chaplain Revd David Guest (*same address*)   *Tel:* (01624) 621547
Personal Secretary Mrs Joyce Jones (*same address*)

CATHEDRAL CHURCH OF ST GERMAN, PEEL
Dean The Bishop
Canons
Canon Brian Kelly, Cathedral Vicarage, Albany Rd, Peel, Isle of Man IM5 1JS [1980]
                                    Tel: (01624) 842608
Canon Hinton Bird PH D, Vicarage, Rushen, Port St Mary, Isle of Man IM9 5LP [1993]
                                    Tel: (01624) 832275
Canon Duncan Whitworth, St Matthew's Vicarage, Alexander Drive, Douglas, Isle of Man IM2 3QN [1996]   *Tel:* (01624) 676310
Canon Malcolm Convery, Marown Vicarage, Crosby, Isle of Man IM4 4BH [1999]
                                    Tel: (01624) 851378
Chapter Clerk The Hon Christopher Murphy, c/o 26 The Fountains, Ramsey, Isle of Man IM8 1NN   *Tel* and *Fax:* (01624) 816545

ARCHDEACON
ISLE OF MAN Ven Brian Partington, St George's Vicarage, 16 Devonshire Rd, Douglas, Isle of Man IM2 3RB [1996]   *Tel:* (01624) 675430
                                    Fax: (01624) 616136

MANX CONVOCATION
(*Secretary*) Canon Hinton Bird PH D, Vicarage, Rushen, Port St Mary, Isle of Man IM9 5LP
                                    Tel: (01624) 832275

CONVOCATION (MEMBERS OF THE HOUSE OF CLERGY OF THE GENERAL SYNOD)
The Archdeacon of Man
Proctor for the Clergy
Canon Hinton Bird PH D

MEMBER OF THE HOUSE OF LAITY OF THE GENERAL SYNOD
Dr Paul Bregazzi

DIOCESAN OFFICERS
Dioc Secretary The Hon Christopher Murphy, c/o 26 The Fountains, Ramsey, Isle of Man IM8 1NN   *Tel* and *Fax:* (01624) 816545
Vicar-General and Chancellor of Diocese The Worshipful Clare Faulds, 30 Athol St, Douglas, Isle of Man IM1 1JB   *Tel:* (01624) 676868
Registrar of Diocese and Bishop's Legal Secretary Mr Christopher Callow, 6 Hill St, Douglas, Isle of Man IM1 1EF   *Tel:* (01624) 611211
                                    Fax: (01624) 675125
Dioc Architect Mr Guy Thompson, The Old Paint Shop, Athol St, Port St Mary, Isle of Man
                                    Tel: (01624) 835510
                                    Fax: (01624) 835521

CHURCH COMMISSIONERS FOR THE ISLE OF MAN
The Lord Bishop
The Archdeacon of Man
Mrs Audrey Ainsworth
Mr H. Dawson
Revd Philip Frear
Revd Roderick Geddes
Revd Roger Harper
Mr P. Kelly
Mr Timothy Mann
Revd Michael Roberts
(*Secretary*) The Hon Christopher Murphy

DIOCESAN ORGANIZATIONS
Diocesan Office c/o 26 The Fountains, Ramsey, Isle of Man IM8 1NN *Tel* and *Fax:* (01624) 816545

ADMINISTRATION
Dioc Synod (*Chairman, House of Clergy*) Canon Hinton Bird PH D, Vicarage, Rushen, Port St Mary, Isle of Man IM9 5LP *Tel:* (01624) 832275; (*Chairman, House of Laity*) Mr J. E. Noakes, St Jude, Quarterbridge Rd, Douglas, Isle of Man *Tel:* (01624) 628548; (*Secretary*) The Hon Christopher Murphy, Dioc Office
Board of Finance (*Chairman*) Revd Roger Harper, 16–18 St George's St, Douglas, Isle of Man IM1

1PL *Tel:* (01624) 624945; (*Secretary*) The Hon Christopher Murphy (*as above*)
Designated Officer Vacancy

CHURCHES
Advisory Committee for the Care of Churches (*Secretary*) Hon Christopher Murphy (*as above*)
Council of Church Music (*Secretary*) Miss Phyllis Christian, 12 Western Ave, Douglas, Isle of Man IM1 4ER   *Tel:* (01624) 672433

EDUCATION
Council for Education (*Secretary*) Mrs Beverley Wells, St Peter's Vicarage, Onchan, Isle of Man IM3 1BF   *Tel:* (01624) 675797
Director of Diocesan Institute Canon Malcolm Convery, Vicarage, Marown, Crosby, Isle of Man IM4 4BH   *Tel:* (01624) 851378
Bishop's Youth Officer Revd Nicholas Wells, Vicarage, Onchan, Isle of Man IM3 1BF
                Tel: (01624) 675797
                email: NAW@mcb.net
Dioc Adviser for Children's Work Revd Paul Bennett, Kirk Patrick Vicarage, Peel, Isle of Man IM5 3AW   *Tel:* (01624) 842637
Adult Education Vacancy

MINISTRY
Dioc Director of Ordinands Canon John Sheen, Kentraugh Hill, Colby, Isle of Man IM9 4AU
                Tel: (01624) 832406
Council for Health and Healing (*Bishop's Adviser*) Revd David Green, Vicarage, Maughold, Isle of Man IM7 1AS   *Tel:* (01624) 812070
Bishop's Adviser for Non-Stipendiary Ministries Revd Neville Pilling, Morwenna, Athol Park, Port Erin, Isle of Man IM9 6ES
                Tel: (01624) 832382
Readers' Board (*Warden*) Revd John Gulland, Anchor House, Queen's Rd, Port St Mary, Isle of Man IM9 5ES *Tel:* (01624) 834548; (*Secretary*) Mrs Nancy Clague, The Villa Rhenny, Greeba, Marown, Isle of Man IM4 2DT
                Tel: (01624) 851877

LITURGICAL
Bishop's Adviser Canon Duncan Whitworth, St Matthew's Vicarage, Alexander Drive, Douglas, Isle of Man IM2 3QN   *Tel:* (01624) 676310

MISSIONARY AND ECUMENICAL
Council for Mission (*Secretary*) Mrs Anne Kean, 14 Barrule Park, Ramsey, Isle of Man IM8 2BN
                Tel: (01624) 813984
Ecumenical Officer Revd William Martin, Vicarage, 56 Ard Reayrt, Ramsey Rd, Laxey, Isle of Man IM4 7QQ   *Tel:* (01624) 862050
ACORA Officer Mr Alan Matthews, Crosh Yvor, Ballachrink Crossing, Ballasalla, Isle of Man IM9 2AD   *Tel:* (01624) 822432

PRESS AND PUBLICATIONS
Communications Officer Revd David Guest, 62 Ballabrooie Way, Douglas, Isle of Man IM1 4AB
                Tel: (01624) 621547
Editor of the Dioc Newspaper Mr Ian Faulds, 14 Douglas St, Peel, Isle of Man IM5 3LQ
                Tel: (01624) 843102
                Fax: (01624) 842325
Editor of Dioc Directory Mrs Anne Kean (*as above*)

DIOCESAN RECORD OFFICE
Further information can be obtained from the Manx Museum Library, Kingswood Grove, Douglas, Isle of Man IM1 3LY *Archivist* Miss Miriam Critchlow   *Tel:* (01624) 675522

BOARD OF SOCIAL RESPONSIBILITY
Representative Mrs Wendy Fitch, Vicarage, Marathon Ave, Douglas, Isle of Man IM2 4JA
                Tel: (01624) 611503

STEWARDSHIP
Christian Stewardship Adviser Revd John Guilford, Strathallan Rd, Douglas, Isle of Man IM2 4PN   *Tel:* (01624) 672001

RURAL DEANS
Castletown and Peel Canon Brian Kelly, Cathedral Vicarage, Albany Rd, Peel, Isle of Man IM5 1JS
                Tel: (01624) 842608
Douglas Canon Duncan Whitworth, St Matthew's Vicarage, Alexander Drive, Douglas, Isle of Man IM2 3QN *Tel:* (01624) 676310
Ramsey Revd David Green, Vicarage, Maughold, Isle of Man IM7 1AS *Tel:* (01624) 812070

Founded in 1905. Greater London south of the Thames, except for most of the London Boroughs of Bromley and Bexley (ROCHESTER), and a few parishes in the south-west (GUILDFORD); the eastern third of Surrey.

Population 2,369,000   Area 317 sq m
Stipendiary Clergy 382   Benefices 291
Parishes 306   Churches 379

BISHOP (9th)
Rt Revd Thomas Frederick Butler, Bishop's House, 38 Tooting Bec Gardens, London SW16 1QZ [1998]   *Tel:* 020–8769 3256
Fax: 020–8769 4126
email: bishop.tom@dswark.org.uk
[Thomas Southwark]
Chaplain and Personal Assistant Revd Dr Jane Steen (*same address*)
email: jane.steen@dswark.org.uk
Secretary Vacancy

AREA BISHOPS
CROYDON Rt Revd Dr Wilfred Wood, St Matthew's House, 100 George St, Croydon, Surrey CR0 1PE [1985]   *Tel:* 020–8681 5496
Fax: 020–8686 2074
email: bishop.wilfred@dswark.org.uk
KINGSTON Rt Revd Peter Price, Kingston Episcopal Area Office, Whitelands College, West Hill, London SW15 3SN [1997]   *Tel:* 020–8392 3742
Fax: 020–8392 3743
email: bishop.peter@dswark.org.uk
WOOLWICH Rt Revd Colin Buchanan, 37 South Rd, Forest Hill, London SE23 2UJ [1996]
Tel: 020–8699 7771
Fax: 020–8699 7949
email: bishop.colin@dswark.org.uk

HONORARY ASSISTANT BISHOPS
Rt Revd John Hughes, Hospital of the Holy Trinity, Block 6, Flat 2, North End, Croydon CR0 1UB [1987]   *Tel:* 020–8686 8313
Rt Revd Hugh Montefiore, White Lodge, 23 Bellevue Rd, London SW17 7EB [1987]
Tel: 020–8672 6697
Rt Revd Simon Phipps, Sarsens, Shipley, W Sussex RH13 8PX [1987]   *Tel:* (01403) 741354
Rt Revd Munawar Ramulshah, Partnership House, 157 Waterloo Rd, London SE1 8XA [1999]
Tel: 020–7928 8681
Fax: 020–7928 2371

CATHEDRAL AND COLLEGIATE CHURCH OF ST SAVIOUR AND ST MARY OVERIE
Provost Very Revd Colin Slee, Provost's Lodging 51 Bankside, London SE1 9JE [1994]
Tel and Fax: 020–7928 6414 (Home)
Cathedral Office Montague Chambers, Montague Close, London SE1 9DA   *Tel:* 020–7407 3708
020–7407 2939 (Vestry)
Fax: 020–7357 7389
email: cathedral@dswark.org.uk
Canons Residentiary
Vice-Provost Canon Andrew Nunn, Cathedral Office [1999]   *Tel:* 020–7735 8322 (Home)
Treasurer Vacancy, Trinity House, 4 Chapel Court, London SE1 1HW   *Tel:* 020–7403 8686
Pastor Canon Helen Cunliffe, Cathedral Office [1995]   *Tel:* 020–7587 1831 (Home)
Chancellor and Theologian Canon Jeffrey John D PHIL, Trinity House, 4 Chapel Court, London SE1 1HW [1997]   *Tel:* 020–7403 8686 (Office)
020–7820 8079 (Home)
email: jeffrey.john@dswark.org.uk
Missioner Canon Bruce Saunders, Trinity House, 4 Chapel Court, London SE1 1HW [1997]
Tel: 020–7403 8686 (Office)
020–7820 8376 (Home)
email: bruce.saunders@dswark.org.uk
Succentor Revd John Paton, Cathedral Office [1998]
Chaplain Canon Roger Royle, Cathedral Office [1993]
Administrator Mrs Sarah King, Cathedral Office
Education Officer Miss Rachel Murray, Cathedral Office
Cathedral Organist Mr Peter Wright, Cathedral Office

ARCHDEACONS
CROYDON Ven Anthony Davies, St Matthew's House, 100 George St, Croydon CR0 1PE [1994]
Tel: 020–8681 5496
Fax: 020–8686 2074
email: tony.davies@dswark.org.uk
LAMBETH Vacancy, Kingston Episcopal Area Office, Whitelands College, West Hill, London SW15 3SN   *Tel:* 020–8392 3742
Fax: 020–8392 3743
email: kingston@dswark.org.uk

LEWISHAM Ven David Atkinson, 3A Court Farm Rd, Mottingham, London SE9 4JH [1996]
Tel: 020–8857 7982
email: david.atkinson@dswark.org.uk
REIGATE Ven Martin Baddeley, St Matthew's House (*as above*) [1996]
email: martin.baddeley@dswark.org.uk
SOUTHWARK Ven Douglas Bartles-Smith, 1A Dog Kennel Hill, East Dulwich, London SE22 8AA 1985]
Tel: 020–7274 6767
email: douglas.bartles-smith@dswark.org.uk
WANDSWORTH Ven David Gerrard, Kingston Episcopal Area Office (*as above*) [1989]
email: david.gerrard@dswark.org.uk

CONVOCATION (MEMBERS OF THE HOUSE OF CLERGY OF THE GENERAL SYNOD)

Dignitaries in Convocation
The Provost of Southwark
The Archdeacon of Wandsworth
Proctors for Clergy
Revd Colin Boswell
Canon Bernice Broggio
Revd Stephen Burdett
Canon Jeffrey John D PHIL
Revd Geoffrey Kirk
Revd Peter Ronayne
Revd Jennifer Thomas

MEMBERS OF THE HOUSE OF LAITY OF THE GENERAL SYNOD

Mr Barry Barnes
Mr Mark Birchall
Miss Vasantha Gnanadoss
Mr Brian McHenry
Mrs Marion Simpson
Mr John Smallwood
Mr Tom Sutcliffe
Mr William Taylor

DIOCESAN OFFICERS

Dioc Secretary Mr Simon Parton, Trinity House, 4 Chapel Court, Borough High St, London SE1 1HW
Tel: 020–7403 8686
Fax: 020–7403 4770
email: simon.parton@dswark.org.uk
Chancellor of Diocese The Worshipful Charles George, 2 Harcourt Buildings, Temple, London EC4Y 9DB
Tel: 020–7353 8415
Registrar of Diocese and Bishop's Legal Secretary Mr Paul Morris, Registry Chambers, The Old Deanery, London EC4V 5AA
Tel: 020–7593 5119
Fax: 020–7248 3221

DIOCESAN ORGANIZATIONS

Diocesan Office Trinity House, 4 Chapel Court, Borough High St, London SE1 1HW
Tel: 020–7403 8686
Fax: 020–7403 4770
email: trinity@dswark.org.uk

ADMINISTRATION

Dioc Synod (*Chairman, House of Clergy*) Canon Graham Corneck, St Nicholas Vicarage, 41 Creek Rd, London SE8 3BU *Tel:* 020–8692 2749; (*Chairman, House of Laity*) Mrs April Alexander; (*Secretary*) Mr Simon Parton, Dioc Office
South London Church Fund and Dioc Board of Finance (*Chairman*) Mr John Smallwood, The Willows, Parkgate Rd, Newdigate, Dorking, Surrey RH5 5AH *Tel:* (01306) 631457; (*Secretary*) Mr Simon Parton (*as above*)
Parsonages Board (*Secretary*) Mr Simon Parton (*as above*)
Pastoral Committee (*Secretary*) Mr Andrew Lane, Dioc Office
email: andrew.lane@dswark.org.uk
Redundant Churches Uses Committee (*Secretary*) Mr Roger Pickett, Dioc Office
Chapter of Ministers in Secular Employment
Chapter Dean for Kingston Revd Peter King, 49 Leinster Ave, East Sheen, London SW14 7JW
Tel: 020–8876 8997
Chapter Dean for Croydon Revd Frances Plummer, 50 Park View Rd, Salfords, Redhill, Surrey RH1 5DN
Tel: (01293) 785852
Chapter Dean for Woolwich Revd Adam Scott, 19 Blackheath Park, London SE3 9RW
Tel: 020–8852 3286
Designated Officer Mr Paul Morris, Registry Chambers, The Old Deanery, London EC4V 5AA
Tel: 020–7593 5119
Fax: 020–7248 3221

CHURCHES

Advisory Committee for the Care of Churches (*Chairman*) Mr J. Michael Davies c/o Trinity House (*as above*); (*Secretary*) Mr Andrew Lane (*as above*)

ECUMENICAL

Archdeaconry Ecumenical Officers
Croydon Revd Alan Middleton, Rectory, 35 Dane Rd, Warlingham, Surrey CR6 9NP
Lambeth Revd Simon Butler, Immanuel Vicarage, 51A Guildersfield Rd, London SW16 5LS
Tel: 020–8764 5103
Lewisham Revd Christine Bainbridge, 56 Weigall Rd, Lee, London SE12 8HF *Tel:* 020–8318 2363
Reigate Revd Colin Corke, Rectory, Ticketts Hill Rd, Tatsfield, Westerham, Kent TN16 2NA
Tel: (01959) 577289
Southwark Revd Cecil Heatley, 173 Choumert Rd, London SE15 4AW *Tel:*020–7732 3435
Wandsworth Revd Jim McKinney, 7 Ponsonby Rd, London SW15 4LA *Tel:*020–8788 9460

EDUCATION

Board of Education (*Director*) Mrs Linda Borthwick, 48 Union St, London SE1 1TD
Tel: 020–7407 7911
email: info@sdbe.demon.co.uk

DIOCESES

BOARD FOR CHURCH IN SOCIETY

Chair The Bishop of Southwark
Vice Chair The Archdeacon of Southwark (*as above*)
Secretary Canon Bruce Saunders
Executive Officer Mr Paul Buxton
Office 1st Floor, Trinity House, 4 Chapel Court, London SE1 1HW

Tel: 020–7403 8686 Ext 212
Fax: 020–7403 2242
email: bcs@dswark.org.uk

Adviser in Women's Ministry Canon Helen Cunliffe, Cathedral Office (*as above*)
Canon Missioner for Church in Society Canon Bruce Saunders, Trinity House (*as above*)
Children's Officer Revd Kevin Parkes, Kingston Area Mission Team (*as above*)
Dioc Child Protection Co-ordinator Jill McKinnon, Trinity House Ext 217
Community Development Adviser Vacancy, Trinity House Ext 217
Canon Chancellor, Theologian and Bishop's Adviser for Ministry Canon Jeffrey John, Trinity House
Dioc Director of Ordinands Vacancy, Trinity House Ext 246
Faith in the City Officer Canon Grahame Shaw, St Paul's Vicarage, Lorrimore Square, London SE17 3QU

Tel: 020–7735 3506

Housing and Homelessness Adviser Dr Patrick Logan, Trinity House Ext 219
Industrial Mission Revd John Paxton (*Senior Chaplain*), SLIM, Christchurch Industrial Centre, 27 Blackfriars Rd, London SE1 8NY

Tel: 020–7928 3970
Fax: 020–7928 1148

Interfaith Group Chair Canon Bruce Saunders, Trinity House
Ordained Local Ministry Training Revd Stephen Lyon (*Principal*), St Michael's Hall, Trundle St, London SE1 1QT

Tel: 020–7378 7506
Fax: 020–7403 6497

Liturgical Committee Revd Dr John Thewlis (*Secretary*), 107 Westmount Rd, London SE9 1XX

Tel: 020–8850 3030

Ministry Development Officer Revd Geoff Mason, St Michael's Hall (*as above*)
Pastoral Care and Counselling Adviser Revd Susan Walrond-Skinner, 78 Stockwell Park Rd, London SW9 0DA

Tel: 020–7733 8676

Race Relations Commission St Michael's Hall (*as above*)
Reader Training Revd Anne Stevens, St Michael's Vicarage, 93 Bolingbroke Grove, London SW11 6HA
Warden of Readers Ven Martin Baddeley, St Matthew's House, 100 George St, Croydon CR0 1PE

Tel: 020–8681 5496
Fax: 020–8686 2074
email: martin.baddeley@dswark.org.uk

Rural Ministry Adviser Revd John Goodden, Rectory, Starrock Lane, Chipstead, Surrey CR5 3QD

Tel: (01737) 552157

Southwark Pastoral Auxiliary Training Ms Joanna Cox, Croydon Area Mission Team, St Matthew's House, 100 George St, Croydon CR0 5NS

Tel: 020–8681 5496
Fax: 020–8686 2074

Urban Ministry Adviser Mr Chris Chapman, St Michael's Hall (*as above*)
Urban Projects/CUF Adviser Ms Steph Blackwell, Trinity House Ext 215
WelCare Service for Parents and Children Mrs Anne-Marie Garton (*Director*), Trinity House Ext 224
Youth Officer Capt Rayman Khan, Croydon Area Mission Team (*as above*)

COMMUNICATIONS

Director of Communications and Resources Wendy Robins, Dioc Office   Tel: 020–7403 8686 (Office)

email: wendy.s.robins@dswark.org.uk

Communications Officer, Bishop's Press Officer and Editor of Dioc Directory Enquiries to Mr Patrick Olivier, Dioc Office   0831 694021 (Mobile)

email: patrick.olivier@dswark.org.uk

DIOCESAN RECORD OFFICES

London Metropolitan Archives, 40 Northampton Rd, London EC1R 0HB Tel: 020–7332 3820 *Fax:* 020–7833 9136 (*Parish records for Inner London Boroughs except Lewisham*)
Lewisham Local Studies and Archives Centre, Lewisham Library, 199–201 Lewisham High St, London SE13 6LG Tel: 020–8297 0682 *Fax:* 020–8297 1169 (*Parish records for East and West Lewisham deaneries*)
London Borough of Bexley Local Studies Centre, Hall Place, Bourne Rd, Bexley, Kent DA5 1PQ *Tel:* 020–8303 7777 (*Parishes in the London Borough of Bexley*)
Surrey History Centre, 130 Goldsworth Rd, Woking, Surrey GU21 1ND Tel: (01483) 594594 *Fax:* (01483) 594595 (*County of Surrey and Surrey London Boroughs*)
London Borough of Sutton Local Studies Centre, St Nicholas Way, Sutton, Surrey SM1 1JN *Tel:* 020–8770 5000 (*London Borough of Sutton*)

STEWARDSHIP

Director, Communications and Resources Wendy Robins, Dioc Office

email: wendy.s.robins@dswark.org.uk

Resources Officer Mr Kevin Hawkes, Dioc Office

email: kevin.hawkes@dswark.org.uk

RURAL DEANS
ARCHDEACONRY OF SOUTHWARK

Bermondsey Revd Stuart Wilmot, Vicarage, 10 Thorburn Square, London SE1 5QH

Tel: 020–7237 3950

Camberwell Revd Stephen Roberts, St George's Vicarage, 115 Wells Way, London SE5 7SZ

Tel: 020–7703 2895

Dulwich Revd Cecil Heatley, 173 Choumert Rd, London SE15 4AW   Tel: 0171–639 5072 (Home)
020–7732 3435 (Office)
Southwark and Newington Canon Grahame Shaw, St Paul's Vicarage, Lorrimore Square, London SE17 3QU   Tel: 020–7735 2947 (Home)
020–7735 3506 (Office)
Fax: 020–7639 7860

ARCHDEACONRY OF LAMBETH

Brixton Vacancy
Lambeth Revd Richard Truss, St John's Vicarage, 1 Secker St, London SE1 8UF
Tel: 020–7928 4470 (Home)
020–7633 9819 (Office)
Merton Revd Nigel Worn, Vicarage, Sherwood Park Rd, Mitcham, Surrey CR4 1NF
Tel: 020–8764 1258
Clapham Revd David Houghton, 15 Elms Rd, Clapham Common, London SW4 9ER
Tel: 020–7622 8703
Streatham Revd Jeffry Wilcox, 1 Becmead Ave, London SW16 1UH   Tel: 020–8769 1216

ARCHDEACONRY OF REIGATE

Caterham Revd Michael Hart, Rectory, 5 Whyteleafe Rd, Caterham, Surrey CR3 5ER
Tel: (01883) 342062
Godstone Revd Clare Edwards, Bletchingley Rectory, Outwood Lane, Bletchingley, Surrey RH1 4LR   Tel: (01883) 743252
Reigate Revd Robert McLean, Vicarage, The Avenue, Tadworth, Surrey KT20 5AS
Tel: (01737) 813152

ARCHDEACONRY OF LEWISHAM

Deptford Canon Graham Corneck, St Nicholas Vicarage, 41 Creek Rd, London SE8 3BU
Tel: 020–8692 2749
East Lewisham Vacancy

Greenwich Thameside Revd Dr Malcolm Torry, St George's Vicarage, 89 Westcombe Park Rd, London SE3 7RZ   Tel: 020–8305 2339 (Home)
020–8858 3006 (Office)
Greenwich South Revd John Neal, Vicarage, Sowerby Close, London SE9 6HB
Tel: 020–8850 2731
West Lewisham Canon John Ardley, 41 Trewsbury Rd, Sydenham, London SE26 5DP
Tel: 020–8778 3065

ARCHDEACONRY OF WANDSWORTH

Battersea Canon Peter Clark, Christ Church Vicarage, Candahar Rd, London SW11 2PU
Tel: 020–7228 1225
Kingston Revd Peter Holmes, 21 Wolsey Close, Kingston-upon-Thames, Surrey KT2 7ER
Tel: 020–8942 8330
Richmond and Barnes Revd Richard Ames-Lewis, Rectory, 25 Glebe Rd, London SW13 0DZ
Tel: 020–8878 6982
Tooting Canon Bernice Broggio, Holy Trinity Vicarage, 14 Upper Tooting Park, London SW17 7SW   Tel: 020–8672 4790
Wandsworth Revd Colin Pritchard, St Andrew's Vicarage, 22 St Andrew's Court, London SW18 3QF   Tel: 020–8946 4214

ARCHDEACONRY OF CROYDON

Croydon Addington Revd Arthur Quinn, Vicarage, 49 Shirley Church Rd, Shirley, Croydon CR0 5EF   Tel: 020–8654 1013
Croydon Central Revd Graham Derriman, 23A St Augustine's Ave, South Croydon CR2 6JN
Tel: 020–8688 2663
Croydon North Revd Andrew Studdert-Kennedy, 220 Norbury Ave, Thornton Heath CR7 8AJ
Tel: 020–8764 2853
Croydon South Revd Alan Wait, 84 Higher Drive, Purley, Surrey CR8 2HJ   Tel: 020–8660 3251
Sutton Canon David Lewis, Holy Trinity Vicarage, Maldon Rd, Wallington, Surrey SM6 8BL   Tel: 020–8647 7605

DIOCESE OF SOUTHWELL

Founded in 1884. Nottinghamshire; a few parishes in Doncaster.

Population 1,041,000   Area 847 sq m
Stipendiary Clergy 189   Benefices 184
Parishes 258   Churches 314

BISHOP (10th)

Rt Revd George Henry Cassidy, Bishop's Manor, Southwell, Notts. NG25 0JR [1999]
Tel: (01636) 812112
Fax: (01636) 815401
email: bishop@bishop-southwell.prestel.co.uk
[George Southwell]
Chaplain Revd Jeremy Fletcher (*same address*)

SUFFRAGAN BISHOP

SHERWOOD Rt Revd Alan Wyndham Morgan, Sherwood House, High Oakham Rd, Mansfield, Notts. NG18 5AJ [1989]   *Tel:* (01623) 657491
Fax: (01623) 662526
email: bishop.sherwood@john316.com

CATHEDRAL AND PARISH CHURCH OF THE BLESSED VIRGIN MARY

Provost Very Revd David Leaning, The Residence, Southwell, Notts. NG25 0HP [1991]
Tel: (01636) 812593
Fax: (01636) 812782
Office The Minster Office, Trebeck Hall, Bishop's Drive, Southwell, Notts. NG25 0JP
Tel: (01636) 812649
Fax: (01636) 815904
email: southwellminster@prestel.co.uk
Web: http://www2.prestel.co.uk/southwellminster

Canons Residentiary
Precentor Canon Ian Collins, 5 Vicars' Court, Southwell, Notts. NG25 0HP [1985]
Tel: (01636) 815056
Chancellor Canon Graham Hendy, 2 Vicars' Court, Southwell, Notts. NG25 0HP [1997]
Tel: (01636) 813188
Canon Pastor Canon Richard Davey, 3 Vicars' Court, Southwell, Notts. NG25 0HP [1999]
Tel: (01636) 813767
Cathedral Administrator Mr D. F. J. Mills, The Minster Office
Rector Chori Mr Paul Hale, 4 Vicars' Court, Southwell, Notts. NG25 0HP   *Tel:* (01636) 812228

ARCHDEACONS

NOTTINGHAM Ven Gordon Ogilvie, 2B Spencer Ave, Mapperley, Nottingham NG3 5SP [1996]
Tel: (01636) 814490 (Office)
Fax: (01636) 815882
0115–967 0875 (Home)
Fax: 0115–967 1014 (Home)
NEWARK Ven Nigel Peyton, 4 The Woodwards, Newark, Notts. NG24 3GG [1999]
Tel: (01636) 814490 (Office)
Fax: (01636) 815882
(01636) 612249 (Home)
Fax: (01636) 611952 (Home)
email: archdeacon-newark@
southwell-sdbf.prestel.co.uk

CONVOCATION (MEMBERS OF THE HOUSE OF CLERGY OF THE GENERAL SYNOD)

The Archdeacon of Nottingham
Proctors for Clergy
Revd Dr Francis Bridger
Revd Jeremy Fletcher
Revd Peter Hill
Ven Nigel Peyton

MEMBERS OF THE HOUSE OF LAITY OF THE GENERAL SYNOD

Dr Christina Baxter
Mr Andrew David
Dr John Holden
Mr Colin Slater

DIOCESAN OFFICERS

Dioc Secretary Mr Peter Prentis, Dunham House, Westgate, Southwell, Notts. NG25 0JL
Tel: (01636) 814331
Fax: (01636) 815084
Chancellor of Diocese Worshipful John Shand, Dioc Office
Deputy Chancellor The Worshipful Simon Tonking, Dioc Office
Registrar of Diocese and Bishop's Legal Secretary Mr Christopher Hodson, Dioc Office
Dioc Surveyors (Parsonages) c/o Dioc Office

DIOCESAN ORGANIZATIONS

Diocesan Office Dunham House, Westgate, Southwell, Notts. NG25 0JL
Tel: (01636) 814331 *Fax:* (01636) 815084
email: SDBF@John316.com

ADMINISTRATION

Dioc Synod (*Chairman, House of Clergy*) Revd Peter Hill, Vicarage, 18 Crookdole Lane, Calverton, Nottingham NG14 6GF *Tel:* 0115–965 2552; (*Chairman, House of Laity*) Mr Grenville Gibson, 'Westering', 6 Cresta Gardens, Mapperley Rise, Nottingham NG3 5GD; (*Secretary*) Mr Peter Prentis, Dioc Office
Board of Finance (*Hon Dioc Treas*) Mr Patrick Bailey, Dioc Office; (*Secretary*) Mr Peter Prentis (*as above*)
Parsonages Board Mr Peter Prentis (*as above*)
Parsonages Officer Mr Ian Greaves, Dioc Office
Glebe Committee Mr Michael Jeffrey (*as above*)
Pastoral Committee Mr Stephen Langford, Dioc Office
Designated Officer Mr Christopher Hodson, Dioc Office
Redundant Churches Uses Committee (*Chairman*) The Archdeacon of Nottingham; (*Secretary*) Mr Stephen Langford (*as above*)
Dioc Board of Patronage Mr Peter Prentis (*as above*)

CHURCHES

Advisory Committee for the Care of Churches (*Chairman*) Revd Keith Turner, Rectory, Main St, Linby, Nottingham NG15 8AE *Tel:* 0115–963 2346; (*Secretary*) Mr Stephen Langford (*as above*)

EDUCATION

Dioc Director Mr Nigel Ladbury, Dioc Office
Tel: (01636) 814504
Schools (*Inspector*) Revd Anthony Shaw (*same address*); (*Administration*) Mrs Brenda Greenland (*same address*)
Adult Work Adviser Revd Michael Allen (*same address*)
Youth Work Adviser Capt Denis Tully (*same address*)
Children's Work Adviser Vacancy (*same address*)

MINISTRY

Director of Ordinands and Bishop's Research Officer Revd Terence Joyce, 36 Moorgreen, Newthorpe, Nottingham NG16 2FB *Tel:* (01773) 712509
Adviser for Women's Ministry Canon Valerie Rampton, Vicarage, Baulk Lane, Kneesall, Newark, Notts. NG22 0AA *Tel:* (01623) 835820
Director of Post-Ordination Training and Bishop's Adviser on Training Revd Dr Neil Burgess, Dioc Office

Dioc Ministry Development Adviser Vacancy
Dioc Officer for Tourism Revd Anthony Tucker, Vicarage, Main St, Norwell, Notts. NG23 6JT
Tel: (01636) 636329
email: t.tucker@john316.com
Readers' Association (*Secretary*) Mr G. W. Richardson, The Limit, Sutton-cum-Lound, Retford, Notts. DN22 8PN *Tel:* (01777) 705080
Warden of Readers and Director of Studies Canon Andrew Woodsford, Gamston Rectory, Retford, Notts. DN22 0QB *Tel:* (0177 783) 706
email: woodsford@msn.com
Assistant Warden of Readers Revd Susan Spencer, 29 Marlock Close, Fiskerton, Notts. NG25 0UB
Tel: (01636) 830331
Chaplain to Retired Clergy Canon Charles Young, 9 The Paddocks, London Rd, Newark, Notts. NG24 1SS
Clergy Widows Officer Revd Reg Hoye, 1 Whiteacre, Burton Joyce, Nottingham NG14 5BU
Tel: 0115–931 2485

LITURGICAL

Liturgical Officer Revd Anthony St John Walker, St Saviour's Vicarage, 31 Richmond Rd, Retford, Notts. DN22 6SJ *Tel:* (01777) 703800

MISSION

Chairman The Archdeacon of Nottingham
Secretary Vacancy
Bishop's Adviser on Evangelism and Dioc Officer for the Millennium Revd Paul Morris, 39 Davies Rd, West Bridgford, Nottingham NG2 5JE
Tel: 0115–981 1311
Assistant Dioc Adviser in Evangelism Revd David Rowe, 13 Rolleston Drive, Lenton Abbey, Nottingham NG7 1JS *Tel:* 0115–947 2777
Bishop's Ecumenical Officer Revd David Bignell, Edwalton Vicarage, Nottingham NG12 4AB
Tel: 0115–923 2034
Ecumenical Officer for Derbyshire and Nottinghamshire Mrs Terry Garley, 64 Wyndale Drive, Ilkeston, Derby DE7 4JO
Bishop's Adviser on Overseas Relations Revd Andrew Wigram, 2 Dobbin Close, Cropwell Bishop, Nottingham NG12 3GR
Tel: 0115–989 3172

PRESS, PUBLICITY AND PUBLICATIONS

Communications Officer Mrs Rachel Farmer, Dioc Office *Tel and Fax:* (01636) 816276
07712 196381 (Mobile)
Editor of Dioc Newspaper 'See' Mrs Rachel Farmer (*as above*)

DIOCESAN RECORD OFFICE

Nottinghamshire Archives, County House, Castle Meadow Rd, Nottingham NG1 1AG *Principal Archivist* Mr A. J. M. Henstock *Tel:* 0115–950 4524

SOCIAL RESPONSIBILITY

(*Chairman*) Canon Eric Forshaw
(*Secretary and Social Responsibility Officer*) Ms Patricia Stoat, St Catharine's House, St Ann's Well Rd, Nottingham NG3 1EJ *Tel:* 0115–958 5517
Council for Family Care (*Director*) Mrs Muriel Weisz, Warren House, Pelham Court, Pelham Rd, Nottingham NG5 1AP   *Tel:* 0115–950 1805
Fax: 0115–950 4959
(*Chairman*) Mr Grenville Gibson (*same address*)
Dioc Rural Officer Revd Michael Brock, Rectory, Main St, Epperstone, Notts. NG14 6AG
Tel: 0115–996 4220

STEWARDSHIP

Funding Advisers/Directors Mrs Carole Park, Mr Anthony Yates and Mr Steve Cumberland c/o Dioc Office

For details of other Diocesan Advisers and Chaplaincies please contact the Diocesan Office

RURAL DEANS
ARCHDEACONRY OF NEWARK

Bawtry Revd John Britton, Vicarage, Tickhill Rd, Harworth, Notts. DN11 8PD   *Tel:* (01302) 744157
Mansfield Revd Angela Smythe, Vicarage, Pleasley Hill, Mansfield, Notts. NG19 7SZ
Tel: (01623) 812390
Newark Revd Alistair Conn, Rectory, 1 Vicarage Close, Collingham, Newark, Notts. NG23 7PQ
Tel: (01636) 892317
Newstead Canon Fred Green, Rectory, Annesley Rd, Hucknall, Nottingham NG15 7DE
Tel: 0115–963 2033

Retford Canon Andrew Woodsford, Gamston Rectory, Gamston, Retford, Notts. DN22 0QB
Tel: (01777) 838706
email: woodsford@msn.com
Worksop Revd Annette Cooper, Vicarage, 5 West Lane, Edwinstowe, Mansfield NG21 9QT
Tel: (01623) 822430

ARCHDEACONRY OF NOTTINGHAM

Beeston Revd Jonathan Smithurst, 46 Sandy Lane, Bramcote, Nottingham NG9 3GS
Tel: 0115–922 6588
Bingham Canon George Barrodale, Rectory, Thurman Drive, Cotgrave, Nottingham NG12 3HT   *Tel:* 0115–989 2223
Bingham South Revd Trevor Sisson, Keyworth Rectory, Keyworth, Nottingham NG12 5ED
Tel: 0115–937 2017
Bingham West Revd Graham Pigott, The Parsonage, Boundary Rd, West Bridgford, Notts. NG2 7BD   *Tel:* 0115–923 3492
Gedling Revd Gordon Calthrop-Owen, Vicarage, Lingwood Lane, Woodborough, Nottingham NG14 6DX   *Tel:* 0115–965 2250
Nottingham Central Revd Eileen McLean, 15 Hamilton Drive, The Park, Nottingham NG7 1DF   *Tel:* 0115–924 3354
Nottingham North Revd John Walker, Carrington Vicarage, 6 Watcombe Circus, Nottingham NG5 2DT   *Tel:* 0115–962 1291
Nottingham West Revd Allen Hart, St John's Vicarage, Graylands Rd, Nottingham NG8 4FD
Tel: 0115–929 3320
Southwell Revd Peter Hill, Vicarage, Crookdole Lane, Calverton, Notts. NG14 6GF
Tel: 0115–965 2552
email: peter.hill@ichthus.dircon.co.uk

DIOCESE OF TRURO

Founded in 1877. Cornwall; the Isles of Scilly; one parish in Devon.

Population 488,000   Area 1,390 sq m
Stipendiary Clergy 129   Benefices 143
Parishes 224   Churches 314

BISHOP (14th)
Rt Revd William Ind, Lis Escop, Truro, Cornwall TR3 6QQ   *Tel:* (01872) 862657
Fax: (01872) 862037
email: bishop@truro.anglican.org
[William Truro]
Domestic Chaplain Revd Robert Sellers, Vicarage, Devoran, Truro, Cornwall TR3 6PA
Tel: (01872) 863116 (Home)
(01872) 862657 (Office)

SUFFRAGAN BISHOP
ST GERMANS Vacancy, 32 Falmouth Rd, Truro, Cornwall TR1 2HX   *Tel:* (01872) 273190
Fax: (01872) 277883

CATHEDRAL CHURCH OF ST MARY
Dean Very Revd Michael Moxon, The Deanery, Lemon St, Truro, Cornwall TR1 2PE [1998]
Tel: (01872) 272661
Cathedral Office 14 St Mary's St, Truro, Cornwall TR1 2AP   *Tel:* (01872) 276782
Fax: (01872) 277788
Canons Residentiary
Chancellor Canon Perran Gay, St Michael's House, 52 Daniell Rd, Truro, Cornwall TR1 2DA [1994]   *Tel:* (01872) 276491
email: perrangay@aol.com
Treasurer Canon Paul Mellor, Lemon Lodge, Lemon St, Truro, Cornwall TR1 2PE [1994]
Tel: (01872) 272094
email: KPMellor@aol.com
Librarian Canon Peter Goodridge, 16 Crescent Rise, Truro, Cornwall TR1 3ER [1996]
Tel: (01872) 270940
Cathedral Administrator Mrs Bette Owen, Cathedral Office
Cathedral Organist Mr Andrew Nethsingha, Cathedral Office

ARCHDEACONS
BODMIN Vacancy, Archdeacon's House, Cardynham, Bodmin, Cornwall PL30 4BL
Tel: (01208) 821614
Fax: (01208) 821602
CORNWALL Ven Rodney Whiteman, c/o Diocesan House, Kenwyn, Truro, Cornwall TR1 1JQ [2000]
Tel: (01872) 274351
Fax: (01872) 222510

CONVOCATION (MEMBERS OF THE HOUSE OF CLERGY OF THE GENERAL SYNOD)
Dignitaries in Convocation
The Archdeacon of Cornwall
Proctors for Clergy
Canon Robert Law
Canon Paul Mellor
Canon Tony Neal

MEMBERS OF THE HOUSE OF LAITY OF THE GENERAL SYNOD
Mrs Pat Brown
Mr Jeremy Dowling
Mr Terence Musson

DIOCESAN OFFICERS
Dioc Secretary Mr Ben Laite, Diocesan House, Kenwyn, Truro, Cornwall TR1 1JQ
Tel: (01872) 274351
Fax: (01872) 222510
Chancellor of Diocese The Worshipful Timothy Briden, 1 Temple Gardens, Temple, London EC4Y 9BB
Registrar of Diocese and Bishop's Legal Secretary Mr Martin Follett, Follett Stock, Malpas Rd, Truro, Cornwall TR1 1QH   *Tel:* (01872) 241700
Fax: (01872) 225052
Dioc Surveyor Mr Richard Thomas, Dioc House, Kenwyn, Truro, Cornwall TR1 1JQ
Tel: (01872) 274351

DIOCESAN ORGANIZATIONS
Diocesan Office Diocesan House, Kenwyn, Truro, Cornwall TR1 1JQ   *Tel:* (01872) 274351
Fax: (01872) 222510

ADMINISTRATION
Dioc Synod and Bishop's Council (Secretary) Mr Ben Laite, Dioc Office
Dioc Synod (Chairman, House of Clergy) Canon Michael Warner, Rectory, 18 Fore St, Tregony, Truro TR2 5RN *Tel:* (01872) 530507; *(Chairman, House of Laity)* Mr Robert Foulkes, Beechwood, Lower Tremar, Liskeard, Cornwall PL14 5HF
Tel: (01579) 342821
Board of Finance (Chairman) Mr Graham Tyson, Dioc Office; *(Secretary)* Mr Ben Laite *(as above)*

Parsonages Committee Mr Ben Laite (*as above*)
Pastoral Committee Mr Ben Laite (*as above*)
Glebe Committee Mr Ben Laite (*as above*)
Board of Patronage Canon Maurice Friggens, Vicarage, St Cleer, Liskeard, Cornwall PL14 5DJ
Tel: (01579) 343240
Designated Officer Mr Ben Laite (*as above*)

CHURCHES
Advisory Committee for the Care of Churches (*Chairman*) Canon Alan Dunstan, 7 The Crescent, Truro, Cornwall TR1 3ES *Tel:* (01872) 279604; (*Secretary*) Canon Michael Warner, Dioc Office
Truro Diocesan Guild of Ringers (*President*) Revd F. M. Bowers; (*Gen Secretary*) Mr Robert Perry, 34 Cornubia Close, Truro TR1 1SA
Tel: (01872) 277117

EDUCATION AND TRAINING
Director and Secretary of Education Mr Julian Pykett, Dioc Office *Tel:* (01872) 274352
Youth Officer Mrs Jacquie Price (*same address*)
RE Adviser Revd Frank Yates (*same address*)
Children's Adviser Revd Graham Barrett (*same address*)

BOARD OF MINISTRY
Director of Ministerial Training Revd Tim Russ, Rectory, Carne Hill, St Dennis, St Austell, Cornwall PL26 8AZ *Tel and Fax:* (01726) 822317
Director of Lay Training Canon Tim Gouldstone, Rectory, Tresillian, Truro, Cornwall TR2 4AA
Tel: (01872) 520431
Director of Ordinands The Archdeacon of Cornwall (*as above*)
Director of Ordained Local Ministry Revd David Thurburn-Huelin, Dioc Office *Tel:* (01872) 276766
Adviser in Women's Ministry Revd Diane Powell, Rectory, Gerrans, Portscatho, Truro, Cornwall TR2 5EB *Tel:* (01872) 580277
email: DianePowell@email.msn.com
Dioc Readers Rear Admiral Alec Weir, Tipton, St Kew Highway, Bodmin PL30 3ET
Tel: (01208) 84289
Clergy Retirement and Widows Officer Revd Owen Blatchly, 1 Rose Cottages, East Rd, Stithians, Truro TR3 7BD *Tel:* (01209) 860845

LITURGICAL
Chairman The Bishop of Truro
Secretary Canon Perran Gay (*as above*)

COUNCIL FOR EVANGELISM AND UNITY
Chairman The Archdeacon of Cornwall (*as above*)
Officer in Evangelism Preb Brian Anderson, Rectory, 31 Trevanion Rd, Wadebridge, Cornwall PL27 7NZ *Tel:* (01208) 812460
Officer for Unity Mrs Daphne Worraker, 12 Crescent Rise, Truro, Cornwall TR1 3ER
Tel: (01872) 277134

World Church Committee (*Chairman*) Mrs Pam Miller, Chy-an-Garth, Tregowris, St Keverne Helston, Cornwall TR12 6PT *Tel:* (01326) 28027

COUNCIL FOR SOCIAL RESPONSIBILITY
Adviser Mr Allan Chesney, 1 Oaklands, The Square, Week St Mary, Holsworthy, Devon EX22 6XH *Tel and Fax:* (01288) 34129

PRESS AND PUBLICATIONS
Dioc Communications Officer Mr Jeremy Dowling, Rosecare Villa Farm, St Gennys, Bude, Cornwall E23 0BG *Tel:* (01840) 23032
Fax: (01288) 35278
Editor of Dioc News Leaflet Mr Jeremy Dowling (*as above*)
Editor of Dioc Directory Mr Ben Laite (*as above*)

DIOCESAN RECORDS
Diocesan Records Officer Mrs Christine North, County Archivist, County Hall, Truro TR1 3AY
Tel: (01872) 322000

STEWARDSHIP
Christian Stewardship Adviser Mrs Sheri Sturgess, Dioc House *Tel:* (01872) 270162

RURAL DEANS
ARCHDEACONRY OF CORNWALL
St Austell Revd Malcolm Bowers, Vicarage, Church St, St Blazey, Par, Cornwall PL24 2NG
Tel: (01726) 817665
Carnmarth North Revd Roger Bush, 53 Clinton Rd, Redruth, Cornwall TR15 2LP
Tel: (01209) 215258
Carnmarth South Canon Roger Gilbert, Rectory, Albany Rd, Falmouth, Cornwall TR11 3RR
Tel: (01326) 314176
Kerrier Revd Peter Walker, Vicarage, Pendeen Rd, Porthleven, Helston, Cornwall TR13 9AL
Tel: (01326) 562419
Penwith Revd Andrew Couch, Vicarage, St Andrew's St, St Ives, Cornwall TR26 1AH
Tel: (01736) 796404
Powder Canon Tim Gouldstone, Rectory, Tresillian, Truro, Cornwall TR2 4AA
Tel: (01872) 520431
Pydar Canon Robert Law, Rectory, St Columb Major, Cornwall TR9 6AE *Tel:* (01637) 880252

ARCHDEACONRY OF BODMIN
East Wivelshire Revd Robert Oakes, Rectory, Liskeard Rd, Callington, Cornwall PL17 7DJ
Tel: (01579) 383341
Stratton Revd John Ayling, Rectory, Boscastle, Cornwall PL35 0DJ *Tel:* (01840) 250359
Trigg Major Canon Allan Brownridge, Rectory, Werrington, Launceston, Cornwall PL17 8TP
Tel: (01566) 773932

Trigg Minor and Bodmin Preb Brian Anderson, Rectory, 31 Trevanion Rd, Wadebridge, Cornwall PL27 7NZ   *Tel:* (01208) 812460

West Wivelshire Revd Brian McQuillen, St Martin's Rectory, Barbican Rd, Looe, Cornwall PL13 1NX   *Tel:* (01503) 263070

BISHOP (11th)

Rt Revd Nigel Simeon McCulloch, Bishop's Lodge, Woodthorpe Lane, Wakefield WF2 6JL [1992]   *Tel:* (01924) 255349
Fax: (01924) 250202
email: bishopofwakefield@compuserve.com
[Nigel Wakefield]
Bishop's Chaplain Canon Roy Clements (*same address*)
email: 100612.1514@compuserve.com

SUFFRAGAN BISHOP

PONTEFRACT Rt Revd David Charles James, Pontefract House, 181A Manygates Lane, Wakefield WF2 7DR [1998]   *Tel:* (01924) 250781
Fax: (01924) 240490
email:
davidjames@bishopofpontefract.freeserve.co.uk

CATHEDRAL CHURCH OF ALL SAINTS

Provost Very Revd George Nairn-Briggs, 1 Cathedral Close, Margaret St, Wakefield WF1 2DP [1997]   *Tel:* (01924) 210005
Fax: (01924) 210009
email: provost@nairn-briggs.freeserve.co.uk
Cathedral Office Cathedral Office, Northgate, Wakefield WF1 1HG   *Tel:* (01924) 373923
Fax: (01924) 215054
Canons Residentiary
Vice-Provost Canon Richard Capper, 3 Cathedral Close, Margaret St, Wakefield WF1 2DP [1996]
Tel: (01924) 210007
email: capper@3cathedralclose.freeserve.co.uk
Canon Precentor Canon Robert Gage, 4 Cathedral Close, Margaret St, Wakefield WF1 2DP [1997]
Tel: (01924) 210008
email: gage@tromba.freeserve.co.uk
Chapter Clerk Mrs Linda Box, Bank House, Burton St, Wakefield WF1 2DA
Tel: (01924) 373467
Fax: (01924) 366234
email: box@dixon-coles-gill.co.uk
Cathedral Organist Mr Jonathan Bielby, Womack Cottage, Heath, Wakefield, WF1 5SN
Tel: (01924) 378841
Asst Organist and Director of the Cathedral Girls' Choir Miss Louise Marsh, Cathedral Office

ARCHDEACONS

HALIFAX Ven Richard Inwood, 2 Vicarage Gardens, Rastrick, Brighouse HD6 3HD [1995]
Tel: (01484) 714553
Fax: (01484) 711897
email: richard@inwood53.freeserve.co.uk
PONTEFRACT Ven Tony Robinson, 10 Arden Court, Horbury, Wakefield WF4 5AH [1997]
Tel: (01924) 276797
Fax: (01924) 261095
email: awrobinson@arden.clara.net

CONVOCATION (MEMBERS OF THE HOUSE OF CLERGY OF THE GENERAL SYNOD)

The Archdeacon of Halifax
Proctors for Clergy
Canon Margaret Bradnum
Canon John Hudson
Canon John Hawley
Very Revd George Nairn-Briggs

MEMBERS OF THE HOUSE OF LAITY OF THE GENERAL SYNOD

Mr David Ashton
His Honour Judge John Bullimore
Mrs Mary Judkins
Mr Tim Slater
Mr Andrew Waude

DIOCESAN OFFICERS

Dioc Secretary Mr Ashley Ellis, Church House, 1 South Parade, Wakefield WF1 1LP
Tel: (01924) 371802
Fax: (01924) 364834
Chancellor of Diocese Chanc Peter Collier, 12 St Helens Rd, Dringhouses, York YO2 2HP
Registrar of Diocese and Bishop's Legal Secretary Mrs Linda Box, Bank House, Burton St, Wakefield WF1 2DA   *Tel:* (01924) 373467
Fax: (01924) 366234
email: box@dixon-coles-gill.co.uk
Deputy Registrar Mr Julian Gill (*same address*)

DIOCESAN ORGANIZATIONS

Diocesan Office Church House, 1 South Parade, Wakefield WF1 1LP   *Tel:* (01924) 371802
Fax: (01924) 364834

ADMINISTRATION

Dioc Secretary Mr Ashley Ellis, Church House
Dioc Synod (*Chairman, House of Clergy*) Revd Trevor Hicks, Vicarage, Womersley, Doncaster DN6 9BG *Tel:* (01977) 620436; (*Chairman, House of Laity*) Mrs Mary Judkins, The Old Vicarage, 3 Church Lane, East Ardsley, Wakefield WF3 2LJ *Tel:* (01924) 826802; (*Secretary*) Mr Ashley Ellis (*as above*)
Board of Finance (*Chairman*) Mrs Pamela Green, Church House; (*Secretary*) Mr Ashley Ellis (*as above*)
Secretary (*Finance*) Mrs Sandra Rowland, Church House
Dioc Property Manager Mr Nick Shields, Church House
Secretary (*Houses*) Mr Peter Thomas, Church House
Pastoral Committee Mr Ashley Ellis (*as above*)
Dioc Trust Mrs Sandra Rowland (*as above*)
Board of Patronage Mrs Linda Box, Bank House, Burton St, Wakefield WF1 2DA
Tel: (01924) 373467
Fax: (01924) 366234
email: box@dixon-coles-gill.co.uk
Designated Officer Mrs Linda Box (*as above*)

CHURCHES

Advisory Committee for the Care of Churches Mrs Linda Box (*as above*)
Parish Development Officer Vacancy

EDUCATION

Director of Education Miss Anne Young, Church House
Board of Education (*Chairman*) Ven Richard Inwood; (*Secretary*) Miss Anne Young (*as above*)
Legal and Training Officer Mr David Barraclough, Church House
Statutory Education Officer Mrs Marlene Redgwick, Church House
Parish Education Adviser (*Children*) Revd Betty Pedley, Church House
Assistant Parish Education Adviser (*Children*) Mrs Judith Wigley, Church House

MINISTRY

Dioc Dean of Ministry and Director of Ordinands Revd Felicity Lawson, 24 Pledwick Lane, Sandal, Wakefield WF2 6DN
Tel: (01924) 240547
Fax: (01924) 251921
Warden of Readers Canon Margaret Bradnum, Church House
Adviser for Women's Ministry Revd Felicity Lawson (*as above*)
Bishop's Adviser for Pastoral Care and Counselling Vacancy, Church House
Bishop's Officer for NSMs Revd Stephen Bradberry, Church House

Retired Clergy and Widows Officers Canon Roland Taylor, 57 Fair View, Carleton, Pontefract
Tel: (01977) 796564
Revd Richard Bradnum, 13 Boothtown Rd, Halifax HX3 6EU
Tel: (01422) 321740

BISHOP'S COUNCIL WORKING GROUPS

Anglican Communion Officer Canon Bill Jones, 316 Huddersfield Rd, Mirfield WF14 9PY
Tel and *Fax:* (01924) 491537
Child Protection Support Coordinator Revd Richard Swindell, Church House
Church in Society Officer Canon Ian Gaskell, Church House
Clergy Education and Training Director Revd Dr John Williams, Church House
Communications Ms Pippa Allott, Church House
Tel: 0411 538863 (Mobile)
Bishop's Adviser for Ecumenical Affairs Dr Edmund Marshall (for West Yorkshire), 14 Belgravia Rd, Wakefield WF1 3JP
Tel: (01924) 378360
email: e.i.marshall@bradford.ac.uk
Ecumenical Affairs Officer Revd Philip Munby (for South Yorkshire), St George's, 100 Dodworth Rd, Barnsley S70 6HL
Tel: (01226) 203870
email: phil.munby@extra-computers.co.uk
Canon Missioner Canon John Holmes, 5 Kingfisher Grove, Pledwick, Wakefield WF2 6SD
Tel: (01924) 255832
Fax: (01924) 258761
Parish Evangelism Adviser Revd Simon Foulkes, Church House
Family Life and Marriage Education Officers Revd Richard Swindell and Mrs Lisa Senior, Church House
Higher and Further Education Officer Revd Margaret McLean, Anglican Chaplain, University of Huddersfield, Queensgate, Huddersfield HD1 3DH
Tel: (01484) 472090
Lay Education and Training Officer Canon Margaret Bradnum, 13 Boothtown Rd, Boothtown, Halifax HX3 6EU *Tel:* (01422) 321740
Liturgy and Worship Secretary Vacancy
Mara Link Officer Canon Bill Jones (*as above*)
Millennium – Bishop's Adviser for Social Responsibility Canon Ian Gaskell, Church House
Ministry among Children – Parish Education Adviser Revd Betty Pedley, Church House
Assistant Parish Education Adviser Mrs Judith Wigley, Church House
Ministry Among Deaf People Chairman Revd Felicity Lawson (*as above*)
Chaplain Among Deaf People Revd Bob Shrine, Church House
Ministry Among Young People – Youth Missioner Mr Tony Washington, Church House
Minority Ethnic Anglican Concerns Officer Canon Bill Jones (*as above*)
Order and Law – Chairman Capt Terry Bayford, Wakefield Prison, Love Lane, Wakefield WF2 9AG
Tel: (01924) 378282

Prayer and Spirituality – Chairman Canon Richard Capper, 3 Cathedral Close, Wakefield WF1 2DP *Tel:* (01924) 210007
email: capper@3cathedralclose.freeserve.co.uk
Relations with other Faiths – *Officer* Canon Bill Jones (*as above*)
Vocations Officer Revd Felicity Lawson (*as above*)
Wakefield Ministry Scheme – Principal Canon Margaret Bradnum (*as above*)
Wakefield Ministry Scheme – Officer Revd Dr John Williams (*as above*)

PRESS AND PUBLICATIONS
Communications Officer Ms Pippa Allott, Church House
Tel: 0411 538863 (Mobile)
Dioc Newspaper Revd Catherine Ogle, 3 Church St, Woolley, Wakefield WF4 2JU
Tel: (01226) 382550
Dioc Year Book (Editor) Ms Pippa Allott (*as above*)
Editor of Dioc News and Publications Adviser Revd Michael Bootes, 1 Manor Farm Close, Kellington, Goole DN14 0PF *Tel:* (01977) 662876
Fax: (01977) 663072
email: mb@theoratory.demon.co.uk

DIOCESAN RECORD OFFICE
County Archivist Mrs Ruth Harris, West Yorkshire Archive Service, Registry of Deeds, Newstead Rd, Wakefield WF1 2DE
Tel: (01924) 305980

DIOCESAN RESOURCES CENTRE
Childrens' Adviser Revd Betty Pedley, Church House

STEWARDSHIP
Christian Giving Adviser Graham Richards, Church House

RURAL DEANS
ARCHDEACONRY OF HALIFAX
Almondbury Canon Mark Thomas, 2 Westgate, Almondbury, Huddersfield HD5 8XE
Tel: (01422) 256088
Brighouse and Elland Revd Martin Wood, Rectory, 50 Victoria Rd, Elland HX5 0QA
Tel and *Fax:* (01422) 256088
email: martin@phyll.force9.co.uk
Calder Valley Canon Peter Calvert, Vicarage, Todmorden OL14 7BS *Tel:* (01706) 813180
Halifax Canon Alastair Ross, Vicarage, Kensington Rd, Halifax HX3 0HN
Tel: (01422) 365477
Huddersfield Revd Martyn Crompton, Vicarage, Golcar, Huddersfield HD7 4PX
Tel: (01484) 654647
Kirkburton Revd Graham Whitcroft, Vicarage, 138 Wakefield Rd, Lepton, Huddersfield HD8 0LU *Tel:* (01484) 602172

ARCHDEACONRY OF PONTEFRACT
Barnsley Canon John Hudson, The Clergy House, Church St, Royston, Barnsley S71 4QZ
Tel: (01226) 722410
Birstall Revd Dhoe Craig-Wild, St Andrew's Vicarage, 4 Lewisham St, Morley, Leeds LS27 0LA *Tel:* 0113–252 3783
Chevet Revd John White, Vicarage, 3 Church Lane, Chapelthorpe, Wakefield WF4 3JF
Tel: (01924) 255360
Dewsbury Revd Lindsay Dew, 51 Frank Lane, Thornhill, Dewsbury WF12 0JW
Tel: (01924) 465064
Pontefract Revd Trevor Hicks, Vicarage, Womersley, Doncaster DN6 9BG
Tel: (01977) 620436
Wakefield Revd Tony Macpherson, Vicarage, 166 Horbury Rd, Wakefield WF2 8BQ
Tel: (01924) 380689
Fax: (01924) 362551

DIOCESE OF WINCHESTER

Founded in 676. Hampshire, except for the south-eastern quarter (PORTSMOUTH), an area in the north-east (GUILDFORD), a small area in the west (SALISBURY) and one parish in the north (OXFORD); an area of eastern Dorset; the Channel Islands.

Population 1,162,000   Area 1,216 sq m
Stipendiary Clergy 245   Benefices 211
Parishes 303   Churches 406

BISHOP (96th)
Rt Revd Michael Charles Scott-Joynt, Wolvesey, Winchester, Hants. SO23 9ND [1995]
Tel: (01962) 854050
Tel and *Fax:* (01962) 842376
email: michael.scott-joynt@dial.pipex.com
[Michael Winton]
Bishop's Assistant Mr Stephen Adam (*same address*)
email: stephen.adam@dial.pipex.com

SUFFRAGAN BISHOPS
SOUTHAMPTON Rt Revd Jonathan Gledhill, Ham House, The Crescent, Romsey, Hants. SO51 7NG [1996]
Tel: (01794) 516005
Fax: (01794) 830242
email: jonathan.gledhill@dial.pipex.com
BASINGSTOKE Rt Revd Geoffrey Rowell, Bishopswood End, Kingswood Rise, Four Marks, Alton, Hants. GU34 5BD [1994]
Tel: (01420) 562925
Fax: (01420) 561251
email: geoffrey.rowell@dial.pipex.com

HONORARY ASSISTANT BISHOPS
Rt Revd Leslie Lloyd Rees, Kingfisher Lodge, 20 Arle Gardens, Alresford, Hants. SO24 9BA [1987]
Tel: (01962) 734619
Rt Revd Hassan Barnaba Dehqani-Tafti, c/o Church House, 9 The Close, Winchester, Hants. SO23 9LS
Tel: (01962) 844644
Rt Revd John Austin Baker, Norman Corner, 4 Mede Villas, Kingsgate Rd, Winchester, Hants. SO23 9QQ [1994]
Tel: (01962) 861388
Rt Revd Simon Hedley Burrows, 8 Quarry Rd, Winchester, Hants. SO23 8JF [1994]
Tel: (01962) 853332
Rt Revd John Yates, 15 Abbotts Ann Rd, Harestock, Winchester, Hants. SO22 6ND [1995]
Tel: (01962) 882854
Rt Revd John Dennis, 7 Conifer Close, Winchester SO22 6SH
Tel: (01962) 868881

CATHEDRAL CHURCH OF THE HOLY TRINITY, AND OF ST PETER, ST PAUL AND OF ST SWITHUN
Dean Very Revd Michael Till, The Deanery, The Close, Winchester, Hants. SO23 9LS [1996]
Tel: (01962) 857203
Fax: (01962) 853738
email: the.dean@winchester-cathedral.org.uk
Cathedral Office 1 The Close, Winchester, Hants. SO23 9LS
Tel: (01962) 857200
Fax: (01962) 857201
email: cathedral.office@winchester-cathedral.org.uk

Canons Residentiary
Canon Keith Walker, 11 The Close, Winchester, Hants. SO23 9LS [1987]
Tel: (01962) 857240
email: keith.walker@winchester-cathedral.org.uk
Ven John Guille, 6 The Close, Winchester, Hants. SO23 9LS [1998]
Tel and *Fax:* (01962) 857241
email: john.guille@winchester-cathedral.org.uk
Canon Philip Morgan, 8 The Close, Winchester, Hants. SO23 9LS [1994]
Tel: (01962) 857237
email: philip.morgan@winchester-cathedral.org.uk
Canon Charles Stewart, 5 The Close, Winchester, Hants. SO23 9LS [1994]
Tel: (01962) 857211
email: charles.stewart@winchester-cathedral.org.uk

Receiver General Mr Keith Bamber, Cathedral Office
Tel: (01962) 857206
email: keith.bamber@winchester-cathedral.org.uk
Chapter Clerk Mr Julian Hartwell, Godwin Bremridge & Clifton, 12 St Thomas St, Winchester, Hants. SO23 9HF
Tel: (01962) 841484
Fax: (01962) 841554
Cathedral Organist Mr David Hill, 10 The Close, Winchester, Hants. SO23 9LS *Tel:* (01962) 857218
email: david.hill@winchester-cathedral.org.uk
Sub-Organist Mr Philip Scriven, Cathedral Office
Tel: (01962) 857214

ARCHDEACONS
WINCHESTER Ven Adrian Harbidge, Glebe House, 22 Bellflower Way, Chandler's Ford, Eastleigh, Hants. SO53 4HN [1999]
Tel and *Fax:* 023–8026 0955
email: adrian.harbidge@dial.pipex.com

BASINGSTOKE Ven John Guille, 6 The Close, Winchester, Hants. SO23 9LS [1998]
Tel: (01962) 624742
Fax: (01962) 857242
email:john.guille@winchester-cathedral.org.uk

CONVOCATION (MEMBERS OF THE HOUSE OF CLERGY OF THE GENERAL SYNOD)
The Archdeacon of Winchester
Proctors for Clergy
Revd Dr Anne Barton
Revd Barry Fry
Ven John Guille
Revd Dr Richard Turnbull
Channel Islands
The Dean of Guernsey

MEMBERS OF THE HOUSE OF LAITY OF THE GENERAL SYNOD
Mr Peter Bray
Ms Christine Fry
Mr Richard Leyton
Dr Peter May
Dr Kathryn Morfey
Mrs Angela Southern
Mrs Margot Townsend
Channel Islands
Ms Jane Bisson
Mr David Robilliard

DIOCESAN OFFICERS
Dioc Secretary Mr Ray Anderton, Church House, 9 The Close, Winchester, Hants. SO23 9LS
Tel: (01962) 844644 Ext 271
Fax: (01962) 841815
Chancellor of Diocese Chanc Christopher Clark, 3 Pump Court, Temple, London EC4Y 7AJ
Tel: 020–7353 0711
Registrar of Diocese and Bishop's Legal Secretary Mr Peter White, 19 St Peter St, Winchester, Hants. SO23 8BU
Tel: (01962) 844440
Fax: (01962) 842300

DIOCESAN ORGANIZATIONS
Diocesan Office Church House, 9 The Close, Winchester, Hants. SO23 9LS   Tel: (01962) 844644
Fax: (01962) 841815
email: chsewinchester@clara.net

ADMINISTRATION
Asst Dioc Secretary (Churches and Administration) Mr Andrew Robinson, Church House
Asst Dioc Secretary (Synod and Property) Mrs Cate Hart, Church House
Finance Manager and Asst Dioc Secretary Mr Stephen Collyer, Church House
Parish Resources Adviser Mr Roger Parsons, Church House
Dioc Synod (Chairman, House of Clergy) Canon Clifford Wright, Rectory, 44 Cheriton Rd, Winchester SO22 5AY *Tel:* (01962) 854849;
(Chairman, House of Laity) Dr Katharine Morfey, 2 Royston Close, Southampton SO17 1TB *Tel:* 023–8055 4396; *(Secretary)* Mr Ray Anderton, Church House; *(Asst Secretary)* Mrs Cate Hart *(as above)*
Board of Finance (Chairman) Mr Robin Hodgson, Tara, Dean Lane, Winchester SO22 5RA *Tel:* (01962) 862119; *(Secretary)* Mr Ray Anderton *(as above)*
Property Committee Mrs Cate Hart *(as above)*
Dioc Surveyor and Property Services Manager Mr Simon Neale, Church House
Dioc Surveyor (Schools) Mr Trevor Samphier, Church House
Pastoral Steering Group Mrs Cate Hart *(as above)*
Electoral Registration Officer Mrs Cate Hart *(as above)*
Designated Officer Mr Andrew Robinson *(as above)*

CHURCHES
Advisory Committee for the Care of Churches (Chairman) Mr Nicholas Jonas, North House, St Peter's St, Bishop's Waltham, Southampton SO32 1AD   *Tel:* (01489) 892585
(Secretary) Mr Andrew Robinson *(as above)*

EDUCATION
Director of Education Revd Richard Lindley, Church House
RE Adviser Mrs Lilian Weatherley, Church House
Schools Officer Mr George McNeill, Church House

MINISTRY AND FAITH DEVELOPMENT
Ministry Development
Director of Ministry Development (inc Continuing Ministerial Education and POT) Canon John Cullen, Church House
Adviser for Women's Ministry Canon John Cullen *(as above)*
Lay Ministry Adviser and Warden of Readers Revd Simon Baker, Church House
Lay Training Officers (Basingstoke Archdeaconry) Revd Michael Kenning, Rectory, North Waltham, Basingstoke RG25 2BQ
Tel and Fax: (01256) 397256
(Winchester Archdeaconry) Mrs Margaret Hounsham, 46 Augustine Rd, Drayton, Portsmouth PO6 1HZ   *Tel:* 023–9221 4463
Director of Ordinands Revd Caroline Baston, Rectory, 19 Petersfield Rd, Winchester SO23 8JD
Tel: (01962) 853777
Fax: (01962) 841714
email: caroline.baston@ukgateway.net
Vocations Adviser (Convenor) Revd Nigel Vigers, Rectory, London Rd, Hook RG27 9EG
Tel: (01256) 762268
email: vigers@compuserve.com

Clerical Registry Revd Dr Ronald Pugh, Church House

Faith Development
Director of Faith Development and Field Officer Winchester Archdeaconry (Adults) Revd Stephen Pittis, Church House
Faith Development Field Officer Basingstoke Archdeaconry (Adults) Revd Tim Humphrey, 19 Sainfoin Lane, Oakley, Basingstoke RG23 7HZ
Tel: (01256) 782790
email: tim_humphery@netmatters.co.uk
Basingstoke Archdeaconry (Youth and Children) Mr Nigel Argall, Church House
Winchester Archdeaconry (Youth) Mrs Mel McPherson, Church House; *(Children)* Miss Diana Lester, Church House

Partnership and Ecumenical
Partnership Committee (Secretary) Mr Andrew Robinson, Church House
Ecumenical Officer Revd John Pragnell, Copythorne Vicarage, Romsey Rd, Cadnam SO40 2NN
Tel: 023–8081 4769

LITURGICAL
Secretary Canon Charles Stewart, 5 The Close, Winchester SO23 9LS
Tel: (01962) 857211
email: charles.stewart@dial.pipex.com
Development and Research Officer for Liturgical Matters Revd Dr Anne Barton, Rectory, Wolverton, Tadley RG26 5RU *Tel:* (01635) 298008
email: anne@barton.swintenet.co.uk

COMMUNICATIONS, PUBLICATIONS AND RESOURCES
Communications Officer Mr Simon Barwood, Church House
Publications (inc Dioc Directory) Mr Ian Knight, Church House
Resource Centre (Manager) Mr Ian Knight *(as above)*
Dioc Newspaper (Editor) Miss Hazel Southam, Church House

DIOCESAN RECORD OFFICES
Hants Record Office, Sussex St, Winchester, Hants SO23 8TH *Archivist* Miss Rosemary Dunhill *Tel:* (01962) 846154 *(For diocesan records and parishes in Hampshire except Southampton)*
Southampton City Record Office, Civic Centre, Southampton SO14 7LY *Archivist* Mrs Sue Woolgar *Tel:* 023–8083 2251 *(For parishes in Southampton)*
Guernsey Archive Service, 29 Victoria Rd, St Peter Port, Guernsey GY1 1HU
Tel: (01481) 724512
Fax: (01481) 715814
Jersey Archive Service, Jersey Museum, The Weighbridge, Jersey JE2 3NF *Tel:* (01534) 633303
Fax: (01534) 633301

SOCIAL RESPONSIBILITY
Director of Social Responsibility Vacancy
Housing and Homelessness Adviser Mrs Audrey Hollingbery, Church House
Social and Community Work Team (Leader) Ms Marilyn Taylor, Church House
Voluntary Care Groups Advisers Mr Kevin Fray, Revd Helen Jesty and Ms Gillian Limb, Church House
World Development Education Adviser Mr Kevin Fray *(as above)*
Hampshire, Isle of Wight and Channel Islands Association for the Deaf (Chaplain) Vacancy
Community Development Team (Leader) Mr Jeremy Coombe, Youngs Yard, Finches Lane, Twyford, Winchester SO21 1QB *Tel:* (01962) 711511
Rural Officer Canon Tony Jardine, Farringdon Rectory, Alton GU34 3EE
Tel and *Fax:* (01420) 588398

RURAL DEANS
ARCHDEACONRY OF WINCHESTER
Bournemouth Canon Godfrey Taylor, St John's Vicarage, 17 Browning Ave, Boscombe, Bournemouth BH5 1NR
Tel: (01202) 396667
Christchurch Revd John Williams, Vicarage, 33 Nea Rd, Highcliffe, Christchurch, Dorset BH23 4NB *Tel:* (01425) 272767
Eastleigh Revd Peter Vargeson, Vicarage, School Rd, Bursledon, Southampton SO31 8BW
Tel: 023–8040 2821
Lyndhurst Vacancy
Romsey Revd Bruce Kington, Rectory, Braishfield, Romsey, Hants SO51 0PR
Tel: (01794) 368335
Southampton Canon Bruce Hartnell, Vicarage, 41 Station Rd, Sholing, Southampton SO19 8FN
Tel: 023–8044 8337

ARCHDEACONRY OF BASINGSTOKE
Alresford Revd Graham Trasler, Rectory, 37 Jacklyns Lane, Alresford SO24 9LF
Tel: (01962) 732105
Alton Revd John Webb, Rectory, Bentworth, Alton, Hants GU34 5RB *Tel:* (01420) 563218
Andover Revd Errol Williams, Chilbolton Rectory, Stockbridge, Hants.
Tel: (01264) 860258
Basingstoke Canon David Picton, Vicarage, Church Lane, Old Basing, Basingstoke, Hants RG24 7DJ *Tel:* (01256) 473762
Odiham Revd Neville Beamer, Vicarage, 99 Reading Rd, Yateley, Camberley, Surrey GU46 7LR *Tel:* (01252) 873133
Fax: (01252) 878809
Whitchurch Revd Martin Coppen, Vicarage, St Mary Bourne, Andover, Hants. SP11 6AY
Tel: (01264) 738308
email: martin.coppen@dial.pipex.com

Winchester Revd Peter Seal, St Luke's Vicarage, Mildmay St, Winchester SO22 4BX
Tel: (01962) 865240

Dean of Jersey Very Revd John Seaford, The Deanery, David Place, St Helier, Jersey, CI JE2 4TE
Tel: (01534) 720001
Fax: (01534) 617488
email: deanofjersey@cinergy.co.uk
Dean of Guernsey Very Revd Marc Trickey, The Rectory, La Grande Rue, St Martin's, Guernsey, CI GY4 6RR
Tel: (01481) 238303
Fax: (01481) 237710

DIOCESE OF WORCESTER

Founded in 679. Worcestershire, except for a few parishes in the south (GLOUCESTER) and in the north (BIRMINGHAM). Dudley; a few parishes in northern Gloucestershire.

Population 831,000   Area 671 sq m
Stipendiary Clergy 163   Benefices 119
Parishes 190   Churches 281

BISHOP (112th)
Rt Revd Peter Stephen Maurice Selby PH D, The Bishop's House, Hartlebury Castle, Kidderminster, Worcs DY11 7XX [1997]
Tel: (01299) 250214
Fax: (01299) 250027
email: bishop.peter@CofE-worcester.org.uk
[Peter Wigorn]

AREA BISHOP
DUDLEY Vacancy, Bishop's House, 366 Halesowen Rd, Cradley Heath, W Midlands B64 7JF
Tel: 0121–550 3407
Fax: 0121–550 7340

HONORARY ASSISTANT BISHOPS
Rt Revd Derek Bond, Ambleside, 14 Worcester Rd, Evesham, Worcs. WR11 4JU
Tel: (01386) 446156
Rt Revd George Briggs, 1 Lygon Lodge, Newland, Malvern, Worcs. WR13 5AX
Tel: (01684) 572941
Rt Revd Kenneth Woollcombe, 19 Ashdale Ave, Pershore, Worcs. WR10 1PL   *Tel:* (01386) 556550

CATHEDRAL CHURCH OF CHRIST AND THE BLESSED VIRGIN MARY
Dean Very Revd Peter Marshall, The Deanery, 10 College Green, Worcester WR1 2LH [1997]
Tel: (01905) 27821
email: WorcesterDeanPJM@compuserve.com
Cathedral Office 10A College Green, Worcester WR1 2LH   *Tel:* (01905) 28854
Fax: (01905) 611139
email: worcestercathedral@compuserve.com
Canons Residentiary
Canon Iain MacKenzie, 2 College Green, Worcester WR1 2LH [1989]   *Tel:* (01905) 25238
Canon Bruce Ruddock, 15 College Green, Worcester WR1 2LH [1999]   *Tel:* (01905) 28854
Ven Joy Tetley, Archdeacon's House, 56 Battenhall Rd, Worcester WR5 2BQ [1999]
Tel: (01905) 764446
Precentor Revd Christine Owen, Cathedral Office
Cathedral Steward Mr Michael Lumley, Cathedral Office
Master of Choristers and Cathedral Organist Mr Adrian Lucas, Cathedral Office

ARCHDEACONS
WORCESTER Ven Joy Tetley, Archdeacon's House, 56 Battenhall Rd, Worcester WR5 2BQ [1999]
Tel: (01905) 764446
Office The Old Palace, Deansway, Worcester WR1 2JE   *Tel:* (01905) 20537
Fax: (01905) 612302
DUDLEY Ven John Gathercole, 15 Worcester Rd, Droitwich, Worcs WR9 8AA [1987]
Tel and *Fax:* (01905) 773301

CONVOCATION (MEMBERS OF THE HOUSE OF CLERGY OF THE GENERAL SYNOD)
Dignitaries in Convocation
The Bishop of Dudley
The Archdeacon of Dudley
Proctors for Clergy
Canon Ray Adams
Revd Robert Jones
Revd Melvyn Smith

MEMBERS OF THE HOUSE OF LAITY OF THE GENERAL SYNOD
Prof Michael Clarke
Mr Harry Jeffery
Mr John Layton
Mr Peter Middlemiss

DIOCESAN OFFICERS
Dioc Secretary Mr Robert Higham, The Old Palace, Deansway, Worcester WR1 2JE
Tel: (01905) 20537
Chancellor of Diocese Mr Charles Mynors, 2 Harcourt Buildings, The Temple, London EC4Y 9DB   *Tel:* 020–7353 8415
Registrar of Diocese and Bishop's Legal Secretary Mr Michael Huskinson, Messrs March & Edwards, 8 Sansome Walk, Worcester WR1 1LN
Tel: (01905) 723561
Fax: (01905) 723812
Dioc Surveyor Mr Jonathan Reeves, Fisher Hoggarth Estate Office, Dumbleton, Evesham, Worcs. WR11 6TH   *Tel:* (01386) 881214

DIOCESAN ORGANIZATIONS
Diocesan Office The Old Palace, Deansway, Worcester WR1 2JE *Tel:* (01905) 20537
Fax: (01905) 612302

ADMINISTRATION
Asst Dioc Secretary (Finance) Mr Stephen Lindner, Dioc Office
DAC Secretary Mr Stephen Bowyer, Dioc Office
Dioc Synod (Chairman, House of Clergy) Vacancy; *(Chairman, House of Laity)* Mr Alastair Findlay, Commissioner Cottage, Cowsden, Upton Snodsbury, Worcester WR7 4NX *Tel:* (01905) 381841; *(Secretary)* Mr Robert Higham, Dioc Office

RESOURCES BOARD
(Chairman) Mr Alastair Findlay; *(Secretary)* Mr Robert Higham *(as above)*
Parsonages Board (Chairman) Revd David Hassell, Rectory, Bishampton, Pershore, Worcs. WR10 2LT *Tel:* (01386) 4626648; *(Secretary)* Mr Stephen Lindner *(as above)*
Investment and Glebe Committee (Chairman) Mr Peter Seward, Lantern Cottage, Little Comberton, Worcs. WR10 3EH *Tel:* (01386) 710417; *(Secretary)* Mr Stephen Lindner *(as above)*
Glebe Agent Mr Jonathan Reeves, Fisher Hoggarth Estate Office, Dumbleton, Evesham, Worcs. WR11 6TH *Tel:* (01386) 881214
Stewardship Committee (Chairman) Mr John Jones, Cymafon, 28 Avon Green, Wyre Piddle, Pershore WR10 6NJ *Tel:* (01386) 552861
Stewardship and Resources Officer Revd Mel Smith, Dioc Office
Pastoral Committee Mr Robert Higham *(as above)*
Board of Patronage Mr Robert Higham *(as above)*
Designated Officer Mr Robert Higham *(as above)*
Trust Mr Michael Huskinson, Messrs March & Edwards, 8 Sansome Walk, Worcester WR1 1LN
Tel: (01905) 723561
Fax: (01905) 723812

CHURCHES
Advisory Committee for the Care of Churches (Chairman) Vacancy; *(Secretary)* Mr Stephen Bowyer *(as above)*
Change Ringers Association Mr M. D. Fellows, 70A Hagley Rd, Stourbridge, W Midlands DY8 1QT
Tel: (0138 43) 75320

EDUCATION
Board of Education (Chairman) Heather Haines, 33 Lyttelton Rd, Droitwich, Worcs. WR9 7AB
Tel: (01905) 774529
Director of Education Revd David Morphy, Dioc Office
Tertiary Education Officer Revd David Morphy *(as above)*
RE – Spirituality Adviser Mrs Patricia Wheeler, Dioc Office

Children's Officer Mrs Lesley Towey, Dioc Office
Youth Officer Vacancy, Dioc Office

TRAINING
Director of Development Miss Janice Price, Dioc Office
Board for Ordained and Lay Development (Chairman) Vacancy
Dioc Director of Ordinands Canon John Green, Vicarage, Cropthorne, Pershore, Worcs. WR10 3NB *Tel:* (01386) 861304
Adviser in Women's Ministry Canon Hilary Hanke, 25 Middleway Ave, Wordsley, Stourbridge DY8 5NB *Tel:* (01384) 293350
Adult Education and Ministerial Training Officer Vacancy
Associate Officer Revd John Reader, Rectory, Elmley Lovett, Droitwich, Worcs. WR9 0PU
Tel: (01905) 251798
Local Ministry Development Officer Mr Martin Murphy, Dioc Office
Chaplaincy to People who are Deaf or Hard of Hearing — Chaplain Revd Paul Harrison, Vicarage, 16 Church Rd, Astwood Bank, Redditch, Worcs. B69 6EH *Tel:* (01527) 892489
Chaplaincy to People with Learning Difficulties – Chaplain Canon Hazel Hughes, Wribbenhall Vicarage, Trimpley Lane, Bewdley, Worcs. DY12 1JJ *Tel:* (01299) 402196

MINISTRY
Dioc Director of Ordinands Canon John Green *(as above)*
Convenor for Women's Ministry Canon Hilary Hanke, Dioc Office
Association of Readers Mr Roy Peacock, 44 Whitehall Rd, Stourbridge, W Midlands DY8 2JT
Tel: (01384) 379972

LITURGICAL
Secretary Revd Doug Chaplin, St Clement's Rectory, 124 Laugherne Rd, Worcester WR2 5LT
Tel: (01905) 422675
email: doug@kairos.force9.co.uk
Web: www.kairos.force9.co.uk

MISSION AND UNITY
Board for Mission (Chairman) Revd Robert Jones, St Barnabas Rectory, Church Rd, Worcester WR3 8NX 5NJ *Tel and Fax:* (01905) 23785
World Mission Officer Miss Catherine Graham, Dioc Office
Ecumenical Officer Revd Clifford Owen, Rectory, Clifton-on-Teme, Worcester WR6 6DJ
Tel: (01886) 812483

PRESS AND PUBLICATIONS
Bishop's and Dioc Communications Officer Mrs Nicola Currie, St Stephen's Vicarage, 1 Beech Ave, Worcester WR3 8PZ *Tel:* (01905) 454768
Fax: (01905) 755405
email: nicola_currie@ecunet.org

Editor of the Dioc Directory Mr Robert Higham (*as above*)
Editor of Dioc News and Public Information Officer
Mrs Nicola Currie (*as above*)

DIOCESAN RECORD OFFICES
St Helen's Church, Fish St, Worcester WR1 2HN
County Archivist Revd Anthony Wherry *Tel:*
(01905) 765921 (*For diocesan records and most parish records*)
Dudley Archives and Local History Dept, Mount
Pleasant St, Coseley, W Midlands WV14 9JR
Archivist Mrs K. H. Atkins *Tel:* (01384) 812770 (*For parish records for the deaneries of Himley, Dudley and Stourbridge*)

SOCIAL RESPONSIBILITY
Board for Social, Economic and Local Development
Chairman Canon Stephen Hutchinson, Vicarage,
34 South Rd, Stourbridge, W Midlands DY8 3YB
Secretary Alison Webster, Dioc Office
Social Responsibility Officer Alison Webster (*as above*)
Industrial Mission: Team Leader Canon Stephen
Kendal, 15 St John's Ave, Kidderminster, Worcs.
DY11 6AT   *Tel:* (01562) 823929
Chaplaincy to Agriculture and Rural Life Canon
John Willis, Glebe House, Grafton Flyford,
Worcester WR7 4PG   *Tel:* (01905) 381460
                            Fax: (01905) 381110

RURAL DEANS
ARCHDEACONRY OF WORCESTER
Evesham Revd Harold Goddard, Rectory,
Sedgeberrow, Evesham, Worcs. WR11 6UE
                            Tel: (01386) 881291

Malvern Revd Dr Dennis Lloyd, 48 Longridge
Rd, Malvern, Worcs. WR14 3JB
                            Tel: (01684) 573912
Martley and Worcester West Canon Michael Nott,
Crown East Vicarage, Rushwick, Worcester
WR2 5TU   *Tel:* (01905) 428801
Pershore Revd Ken Boyce, Fladbury Rectory,
Pershore, Worcs. WR10 2QW *Tel:* (01386) 860356
Upton Revd Christopher Hardwick, Rectory, The
Cross, Ripple, Tewkesbury, Glos. GL20 6HA
                            Tel: (01684) 592655
Worcester East Vacancy

ARCHDEACONRY OF DUDLEY
Bromsgrove Canon David Salt, St Stephen's
Vicarage, 248 Birchfield Rd, Redditch, Worcs.
B97 4LZ   *Tel:* (01527) 61543
Droitwich Revd Sheila Banyard, Vicarage, 205
Worcester Rd, Droitwich, Worcs. WR9 8AS
                            Tel: (01905) 773134
Dudley Revd Matthew Baynham, St Luke's
Vicarage, Upper High St, Cradley Heath,
Warley, W Midlands B64 5HX *Tel:* (01384) 569940
Himley Canon Fred Trethewey, 5 Leys Rd,
Brockmoor, Brierley Hill, W Midlands DY5 3UR
                            Tel: (01384) 263327
Kidderminster Revd Geoffrey Shilvock, Vicarage,
Kidderminster, Worcs. DY11 5XD
                            Tel: (01562) 851133
Stourbridge Canon Paul Tongue, Vicarage, 4 The
Holloway, Amblecote, Stourbridge, W Midlands
DY8 4DH   *Tel:* (01384) 394057
Stourport Revd Barry Gilbert, Vicarage,
Stourport-on-Severn, Worcs. DY13 9DD
                            Tel: (01299) 822041

DIOCESE OF YORK

Founded in 627. York; East Riding of Yorkshire, except for an area in the south west (SHEFFIELD); Kingston-upon-Hull; Redcar and Cleveland; Middlesbrough; the eastern half of North Yorkshire; Stockton-on-Tees, south of the Tees; an area of Leeds.

Population 1,359,000   Area 2,661 sq m
Stipendiary Clergy 284   Benefices 278
Parishes 478   Churches 609

ARCHBISHOP (96th)

Most Revd and Rt Hon David Michael Hope, *Primate of England and Metropolitan*, Bishopthorpe Palace, Bishopthorpe, York YO23 2GE [1995]
Tel: (01904) 707021/2
Fax: (01904) 709204
email: office@bishopthorpe.u-net.com
[David Ebor]
Chaplain to the Archbishop Revd Michael Kavanagh
Private Secretary to the Archbishop Mrs Mary Murray

SUFFRAGAN BISHOPS

SELBY Rt Revd Humphrey Taylor, 10 Precentor's Court, York YO1 7EJ [1991]   *Tel:* (01904) 656492
Fax: (01904) 655671
email: bishselby@clara.net
HULL Rt Revd Richard Frith, Hullen House, Woodfield Lane, Hessle HU13 0ES [1998]
Tel: (01482) 649019
Fax: (01482) 647449
WHITBY Rt Revd Robert Ladds, 60 West Green, Stokesley, Middlesbrough TS9 5BD [1999]

PROVINCIAL EPISCOPAL VISITOR

BEVERLEY Rt Revd John Scott Gaisford, 3 North Lane, Roundhay, Leeds LS8 2QJ [1994]
Tel: 0113–273 2003
0410 887756 (Mobile)
Fax: 0113–273 3002
email: 101740.2725@compuserve.com

HONORARY ASSISTANT BISHOPS

Rt Revd Clifford Barker, 15 Oaktree Close, Strensall, York YO3 5TR [1991]   *Tel:* (01904) 490406
Rt Revd Ronald Graham Gregory Foley, Ramsey Cottage, 3 Poplar Ave, Kirkbymoorside, York YO6 6ES [1989]   *Tel:* (01751) 432439
Rt Revd David Galliford, Bishopsgarth, Maltongate, Thornton Le Dale YO18 7SA [1991]
Tel: (01751) 474605
Rt Revd Michael Henshall, Brackenfield, 28 Hermitage Way, Eskdaleside, Sleights, Whitby YO22 5HG [1996]   *Tel:* (01947) 811233
Rt Revd David Lunn, Rivendell, 28 Southfield Rd, Wetwang, Driffield YO25 9XX [1997]

CATHEDRAL CHURCH OF ST PETER

Dean Very Revd Raymond Furnell, The Deanery, York YO1 7JQ [1994]   *Tel:* (01904) 623608
Fax: (01904) 672002
Dean and Chapter Office Church House, Ogleforth, York YO1 7JN   *Tel:* (01904) 557200
Fax: (01904) 557201
Precentor and Chamberlain Canon Paul Ferguson, 2 Minster Court, York YO1 7JJ [1995]
Tel: (01904) 624965
Treasurer Canon Glyn Webster, 4 Minster Yard, York YO1 7JD [1999]   *Tel:* (01904) 620877
Chancellor Canon Edward Norman PH D, 1 Precentor's Court, York YO1 7EJ [1999]
Tel: (01904) 673097
Theologian Canon Jonathan Draper, 3 Minster Court, York YO1 7JJ [2000]   *Tel:* (01904) 625599
High Steward The Earl of Halifax
Chapter Clerk Brigadier Peter Lyddon, Church House, Ogleforth, York YO1 7JN
Tel: (01904) 557210
Bursar Mr Martin Vevers, Church House, Ogleforth, York YO1 7JN   *Tel:* (01904) 557213
Fax: (01904) 557215
Master of the Music Mr Philip Moore, 1 Minster Court, York YO1 7JJ   *Tel:* (01904) 557206

ARCHDEACONS

YORK Ven Richard Seed, Vicarage, Boston Spa, Wetherby LS23 6EA   *Tel:* (01937) 842454
EAST RIDING Ven Peter Harrison, Brimley Lodge, 27 Molescroft Rd, Beverley HU17 7DX [1998]
Tel and Fax: (01482) 881659
email: PeterRWHarrison@breathemail.net
CLEVELAND Ven Christopher Hawthorn, Park House, Rosehill, Great Ayton, Middlesbrough TS9 6BH [1991]   *Tel:* (01642) 723221
Fax: (01642) 724137

CONVOCATION (MEMBERS OF THE HOUSE OF CLERGY OF THE GENERAL SYNOD)

Dignitaries in Convocation
The Bishop of Hull
The Bishop of Selby
The Dean of York
The Archdeacon of Cleveland

Proctors for Clergy
Revd Benjamin Hopkinson
Canon David Lickess
Revd Simon Stanley
Canon Glyn Webster
Revd John Weetman
Canon John Young

MEMBERS OF THE HOUSE OF LAITY OF THE GENERAL SYNOD
Mrs Bernadette Burbridge
Mr Martin Dales
Mrs Rachel Harrison
Mr Arthur Pollard
Mr John Porter
Mr Bryan Sandford
Mrs Carole Smith
Mr Ian Smith

DIOCESAN OFFICERS
Dioc Secretary Mr Colin Sheppard, Diocesan House, Aviator Court, Clifton Moor, York YO30 4WJ   *Tel:* (01904) 699500
Fax: (01904) 620375
Chancellor of Diocese His Honour Judge Thomas Coningsby, Leyfields, Elmore Rd, Chipstead, Surrey CR3 3SG
Registrar of Diocese and Archbishop's Legal Secretary Mr Lionel Lennox, The Registry, Stamford House, Piccadilly, York YO1 9PP
Tel: (01904) 623487
Fax: (01904) 611458
email: denison.till@dial.pipex.com
Dioc Surveyors Messrs Ferrey and Mennim, 12 Minster Yard, York YO1 2HH   *Tel:* (01904) 624103
Fax: (01904) 626983

DIOCESAN ORGANIZATIONS
Diocesan Office Diocesan House, Aviator Court, Clifton Moor, York YO30 4WJ
Tel: (01904) 699500
Fax: (01904) 620375

ADMINISTRATION
Dioc Synod (*Chairman, House of Clergy*) Canon Glyn Webster, 4 Minster Yard, York YO1 7JD *Tel:* (01904) 620877; (*Chairman, House of Laity*) Mr Richard Liversedge, 1 Caledonia Park, Victoria Dock, Hull *Tel:* (01482) 588357; (*Secretary*) Mr Colin Sheppard, Dioc Office
Assistant Dioc Secretary Ms Shirley Davies, Dioc Office
Board of Finance (*Chairman*) Mr Robin Clough, Dioc Office; (*Secretary*) Mr Colin Sheppard (*as above*)
Financial Secretary Mr David Fletcher, Dioc Office
Parsonages Committee (*Secretary*) Mr Colin Sheppard (*as above*)
Pastoral Committee (*Secretary*) Mr Colin Sheppard (*as above*)
Designated Officer Mr Colin Sheppard (*as above*)
Property and Trust Committee Mr Colin Sheppard (*as above*)

CHURCHES
Advisory Committee for the Care of Churches (*Secretary*) Canon Edwin Newlyn, 'Markham', North Wing, Bishopthorpe Palace, Bishopthorpe, York YO23 2EE   *Tel:* (01904) 704477
Furnishings Officer Mrs Jean Nugent, c/o DAC Office (*same address*)
Redundant Churches Uses Committee Mr Colin Sheppard (*as above*)

EDUCATION
Board of Education (*Director*) Revd Andrew Martlew, Dioc Office
email: acm.yorkdbe@demon.co.uk
Dioc Advisers for Schools Mrs Sue Foster and Mrs Sue Holmes, Dioc Office
Adviser for Children and Youth Work (*East Riding*) Mr Justin Fielder, 106 Maplewood Ave, Hull HU5 5YF   *Tel and Fax:* (01482) 854272
Archbishop's Senior Adviser in Youth Work Vacancy
Children's Officer (*part-time*) Revd Richard Burge, Vicarage, Lythe, Whitby YO21 2RL
Tel: (01947) 893479
Young Adults and Vocations Officer (*part-time*) Revd Tim Jones, 7 Spring Hill, Welbury, Northallerton DL6 2JQ   *Tel:* (01609) 882401

MINISTRY AND MISSION
Resources Consultant Vacancy
Dean of Women's Ministry Revd Catherine Rowling, Vicarage, Ingleby Greenhow, Middlesbrough TS9 6LL   *Tel:* (01642) 723947
Director of Ordinands Revd Michael Kavanagh, Bishopthorpe Palace, Bishopthorpe, York YO23 2GE   *Tel:* (01904) 707021/2
Officer for NSMs Revd Raymond Morris, 3 Medina Gardens, Brookfield, Middlesbrough TS5 8BN   *Tel:* (01642) 593726
Readers' Association Mr Peter Bowes, Vicarage, Ings Rd, Wilberfoss, York   *Tel:* (01759) 388288
Dioc Forum for Mission and Evangelism (*Secretary*) Revd Paul Wordsworth, St Thomas's Vicarage, 157 Haxby Rd, York YO3 7JL *Tel:* (01904) 652228
Ecumenical Adviser to the Diocese Vacancy
Ecumenical Council (*Secretary*) Vacancy

LITURGICAL
York Diocesan Liturgical Group The Dean of York

PRESS AND PUBLICATIONS
Archbishop's Media Adviser (*National*) Revd Rob Marshall, 33rpm, Unit 226, 28 Old Brompton Rd, London SW7 3SS   *Tel:* 020–7584 6622
0385 767594 (Mobile)
Communications Officer (*Diocese*) Mr Martin Sheppard, Dioc Office
Editorial Committee of Dioc Handbook c/o Dioc Office
Editor of Dioc Manual c/o Dioc Office
Editor of Dioc Magazine 'SEEN' Revd Simon Stanley, c/o Down Your Way Publishing Ltd,

Windsor House, Green Park Business Centre, Sutton-on-the-Forest, York YO61 1ET
Tel: (01347) 811882
Fax: (01347) 811886

DIOCESAN RECORD OFFICES
The Borthwick Institute, St Anthony's Hall, Peasholme Green, York YO1 7PW *Director and Diocesan Archivist* Prof David Smith *Tel:* (01904) 642315 (*For parish records in the Archdeaconry of York*)
East Riding of Yorkshire Archive Office, County Hall, Beverley HU17 9BA *Archivist* Mr Ian Mason *Tel:* (01482) 885005/885044 (*For parish records in the archdeaconry of the East Riding*)
North Yorkshire County Record Office, County Hall, Racecourse Lane, Northallerton DL7 8AD *County Archivist* Mr M. Y. Ashcroft *Tel:* (01609) 780780 (*For parish records in the archdeaconry of Cleveland**)
*Parishes within the present county boundaries of Cleveland may, if they so wish, deposit their records in the Cleveland County Archives Dept, Exchange House, 6 Marton Rd, Middlesbrough TS1 1DB (*Archivist* Mr D. Tyrell)
Tel: (01642) 248321

SOCIAL RESPONSIBILITY
Secretary for Social Action Mr David Mather, SRC Resource Centre, Central Methodist Church, St Saviourgate, York YO1 2NQ *Tel:* (01904) 631715

RURAL DEANS
ARCHDEACONRY OF YORK
Buckrose, Bulmer and Malton Revd Jeremy Valentine, Vicarage, Sand Hutton, York YO4 1LB
Tel: (01904) 468443
Fax: (01904) 468670
Derwent Revd Christopher Simmons, Vicarage, York Rd, Barlby, Selby YO8 7JP
Tel: (01757) 702384
Easingwold Revd Tony Hart, Vicarage, Church Hill, Easingwold,York YO6 3JT
Tel: (01347) 821394
New Ainsty Revd Colin Cheeseman, Vicarage, Tockwith, York YO5 8PY *Tel:* (01423) 358338
South Wold Revd David Cook, Rectory, Holme-on-Spalding Moor, York YO4 4AG
Tel: (01403) 860248
Selby Revd Gwynne Richardson, Rectory, Main St, Hillam, Leeds LS25 5HH *Tel:* (01977) 682357
Fax: (01757) 703742)

York Canon Glyn Webster, 4 Minster Yard, York YO1 7JD *Tel:* (01904) 620877

ARCHDEACONRY OF THE EAST RIDING
Beverley Revd David Hoskin, St Mary's Vicarage, 15 Molescroft Rd, Beverley HU17 7DX
Tel: (01482) 881437
Bridlington Revd Stephen Cope, Rudston Vicarage, Driffield YO25 0XA *Tel:* (01262) 420313
Central and North Hull Canon John Waller, Holy Trinity Vicarage, 66 Pearson Park, Hull HU5 2TQ
Tel: (01482) 342292
Harthill (Acting) Revd Robert Jones, Vicarage, Wetwang, Driffield YO25 9XT *Tel:* (01377) 236410
Holderness North Revd Martyn Dunning, Rectory, West St, Leven HU17 5LR
Tel: (01964) 543793
Holderness South Revd Stuart Robinson, Rectory, Staithes Rd, Preston in Holderness, Hull HU12 7TB *Tel:* (01482) 898375
Howden Revd Ian Ellery, Minster Rectory, Howden, Goole DN14 7BL *Tel:* (01430) 430332
Kingston-upon-Hull Canon John Waller, Holy Trinity Vicarage, 66 Pearson Park, Hull HU5 2TQ
Tel: (01482) 342292
Scarborough Revd Christopher Humphries, Vicarage, Filey YO14 9AD *Tel:* (01723) 512745
West Hull Revd Stephen Whaley, 10 Calvert Rd, Hull HU5 5DH *Tel:* (01482) 352175

ARCHDEACONRY OF CLEVELAND
Guisborough Revd John Weetman, Vicarage, Boosbeck, Saltburn by the Sea TS12 3AY
Tel: (01287) 651728
Helmsley Canon John Purdy, Vicarage, Kirkby Moorside, York YO6 6AZ *Tel:* (01751) 431452
Middlesbrough Revd David Hodgson, Ascension Vicarage, Penrith Rd, Berwick Hills, Middlesbrough TS3 7JR *Tel:* (01642) 244857
Mowbray Revd David Biles, Vicarage, Kilburn, York YO6 4AH *Tel:* (01347) 868234
Pickering Canon Francis Hewitt, Vicarage, Whitby Rd, Pickering YO18 7HD
Tel: (01751) 472983
Stokesley Canon David Lickess, Vicarage, Hutton Rudby, Yarm TS15 0HY *Tel:* (01642) 700223
Whitby Revd Bob Lewis, Vicarage, Danby, Whitby YO21 2NQ *Tel:* (01287) 660388

Dioceses

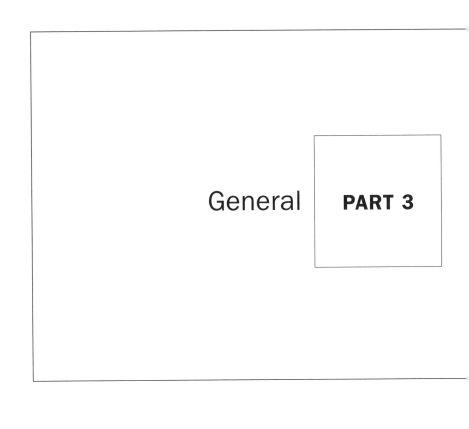

General | **PART 3**

PART 3   CONTENTS

GENERAL INFORMATION

Addressing the Clergy

Since the Lambeth Conference of 1968, at which styles of address were debated, there has been a trend towards simpler forms of address. Resolution 14 stated: 'The Conference recommends that the bishops, as leaders and representatives of a servant Church, should radically examine the honours paid to them in the course of divine worship, in titles and customary address, and in style of living, while having the necessary facilities for the efficient carrying on of their work.'

Whereas formerly a bishop would have been addressed as 'My Lord' and a dean as 'Mr Dean', it has become more usual to address a bishop in speech as 'Bishop' and a dean as 'Dean'. There is, however, a correct way to address clergy on an envelope, which is normally as follows:

Archbishop of Canterbury or York	The Most Revd and Rt Hon the Lord Archbishop of
Archbishop of another Province	The Most Revd the Lord Archbishop of
Bishop of London	The Rt Revd and Rt Hon the Lord Bishop of
Diocesan/Suffragan Bishop	*Either* The Rt Revd the Lord Bishop of
	or The Rt Revd the Bishop of
Assistant/Retired Bishop	The Rt Revd J.D. Smith (*or* John Smith)
Dean	The Very Revd the Dean of
Provost	The Very Revd the Provost of
Archdeacon	The Ven the Archdeacon of
Canon	The Revd Canon J.D. Smith (*or* John or Jane Smith)
Prebendary	The Revd Prebendary J.D. Smith (*or* John or Jane Smith)
Rural Dean	No special form of address (The Rev, the Revd Canon, etc)
Dean of Oxford/Cambridge College	No special form of address
Cleric also Professor	*Either* The Revd Professor J.D. Smith
	or Professor the Revd J.D. Smith
Canon also Professor	*Either* The Revd Canon Professor J.D. Smith
	or Professor the Revd Canon J.D. Smith
Cleric also Doctor	*Either* The Revd Dr J.D. Smith
	or The Revd J.D. Smith (degree)
Canon also Doctor	The Revd Canon J.D. Smith (degree)
Other Clergy/Priest/Deacon	The Revd J.D. Smith (*or* John or Jane Smith)

The following points should be noted particularly:

1 A diocesan or suffragan bishop has a title conferred on him by his consecration or subsequent translation, which he is entitled to hold until he resigns. He then reverts to his personal name, retaining the title 'Right Reverend'.

2 A dean, provost or archdeacon has a territorial title until he resigns. He then reverts to his personal name, and his title is 'Reverend' unless the rank of dean, provost or archdeacon emeritus has been awarded.

3 Retired archbishops properly go back to the status of a bishop but may be given as a courtesy the style of an archbishop.

4 A bishop holding office as a dean or archdeacon is addressed as The Rt Revd the Dean/Archdeacon of.

5 If a cleric's name or initials are unknown, he or she should be addressed as The Revd — Smith or the Revd Mr/Mrs/Miss/Ms Smith. It is never correct to refer to a cleric as 'The Reverend Smith' or 'Revd Smith'.

6 There is no universally accepted way of addressing an envelope to a married couple of whom both are in holy orders. We recommend the style 'The Revd A. B. and the Revd C. D. Smith'.

Archbishops of Canterbury and York

CANTERBURY

597 Augustine
604 Laurentius
619 Mellitus
624 Justus
627 Honorius
655 Deusdedit
668 Theodore
693 Beorhtweald
731 Tatwine
735 Nothelm
740 Cuthbeorht
761 Breguwine
765 Jaenbeorht
793 Æthelheard
805 Wulfred
832 Feologild
833 Ceolnoth
870 Æthelred
890 Plegmund
914 Æthelhelm
923 Wulfhelm
942 Oda
959 Æfsige
959 Beorhthelm
960 Dunstan
c988 Athelgar
990 Sigeric Serio
995 Ælfric
1005 Ælfheath
1013 Lyfing
1020 Æthelnoth
1038 Eadsige
1051 Robert of Jumièges
1052 Stigand
1070 Lanfranc
1093 Anselm
1114 Ralph d'Escures
1123 William de Corbeil
1139 Theobald
1162 Thomas Becket
1174 Richard [of Dover]
1185 Baldwin
1193 Hubert Walter
1207 Stephen Langton
1229 Richard le Grant
1234 Edmund Rich
1245 Boniface of Savoy
1273 Robert Kilwardby
1279 John Peckham
1294 Robert Winchelsey
1313 Walter Reynolds
1328 Simon Mepeham
1333 John Stratford
1349 Thomas
    Bradwardine
1349 Simon Islip
1366 Simon Langham

1368 William Whittlesey
1375 Simon Sudbury
1381 William Courtenay
1396 Thomas Arundel[†]
1398 Roger Walden
1414 Henry Chichele
1443 John Stafford
1452 John Kemp
1454 Thomas Bourchier
1486 John Morton
1501 Henry Dean
1503 William Warham
1533 Thomas Cranmer
1556 Reginald Pole
1559 Matthew Parker
1576 Edmund Grindal
1583 John Whitgift
1604 Richard Bancroft
1611 George Abbot
1633 William Laud
1660 William Juxon
1663 Gilbert Sheldon
1678 William Sancroft
1691 John Tillotson
1695 Thomas Tenison
1716 William Wake
1737 John Potter
1747 Thomas Herring
1757 Matthew Hutton
1758 Thomas Secker
1768 Frederick
    Cornwallis
1783 John Moore
1805 Charles Manners
    Sutton
1828 William Howley
1848 John Bird Sumner
1862 Charles Thomas
    Longley
1868 Archibald Campbell
    Tait
1883 Edward White
    Benson
1896 Frederick Temple
1903 Randall Thomas
    Davidson
1928 Cosmo Gordon Lang
1942 William Temple
1945 Geoffrey Francis
    Fisher
1961 Arthur Michael
    Ramsey
1974 Frederick Donald
    Coggan
1980 Robert Alexander
    Kennedy Runcie
1991 George Leonard
    Carey

YORK

BISHOPS

625 Paulinus
[vacancy for 30 years]
664 Ceadda
669 Wilfrith I
678 Bosa[‡]
705 John of Beverley
718 Wilfrith II

ARCHBISHOPS

c734 Ecgbeorht
767 Æthelbeorht
780 Eanbald I
796 Eanbald II
c812 Wulfsige
837 Wigmund
854 Wulfhere
900 Æthelbeald
c928 Hrothweard
931 Wulfstan I
958 Oscytel
971 Edwaldus
972 Oswald
992 Ealdwulf
1003 Wulfstan II
1023 Ælfric Puttoc
1041 Æthelric[§]
1051 Cynesige
1061 Ealdred
1070 Thomas I
1100 Gerard
1109 Thomas II
1119 Thurstan
1143 William Fitzherbert
1147 Henry Murdac[*]
1154 Roger of Pont
    l'Eveque
1191 Geoffrey Plantagenet
1215 Walter de Gray
1256 Sewal de Bovill
1258 Godfrey Ludham
1266 Walter Giffard
1279 William Wickwane
1286 John le Romeyn
1298 Henry Newark
1300 Thomas Corbridge
1306 William Greenfield
1317 William Melton
1342 William Zouche
1352 John Thoresby
1374 Alexander Neville
1388 Thomas Arundel
1396 Robert Waldby
1398 Richard le Scrope
1407 Henry Bowet
1426 John Kemp
1452 William Booth

1465 George Nevill
1476 Lawrence Booth
1480 Thomas Rotherham
    (or Scot)
1501 Thomas Savage
1508 Christopher
    Bainbridge
1514 Thomas Wolsey
1531 Edward Lee
1545 Robert Holgate
1555 Nicholas Heath
1561 Thomas Young
1570 Edmund Grindal
1577 Edwin Sandys
1589 John Piers
1595 Matthew Hutton
1606 Tobias Matthew
1628 George Montaigne
1629 Samuel Harsnett
1632 Richard Neile
1641 John Williams
1660 Accepted Frewen
1664 Richard Sterne
1683 John Dolben
1688 Thomas Lamplugh
1691 John Sharp
1714 William Dawes
1724 Lancelot Blackburn
1743 Thomas Herring
1747 Matthew Hutton
1757 John Gilbert
1761 Robert Hay
    Drummond
1777 William Markham
1808 Edward Venables
    Vernon Harcourt
1847 Thomas Musgrave
1860 Charles Thomas
    Longley
1863 William Thomson
1891 William Connor
    Magee
1891 William Dalrymple
    Maclagan
1909 Cosmo Gordon
    Lang
1929 William Temple
1942 Cyril Foster Garbett
1956 Arthur Michael
    Ramsey
1961 Frederick Donald
    Coggan
1975 Stuart Yarworth
    Blanch
1983 John Stapylton
    Habgood
1995 David Michael
    Hope

[†] On 19 October 1399 Boniface IX annulled Arundel's translation to St Andrews and confirmed him in the see of Canterbury.
[‡] Wilfrith was restored to office in 686 and Bosa in 691.
[§] Ælfric Puttoc was restored in 1042.
[*] William Fitzherbert was restored in 1153.

Bishops in the House of Lords

The Archbishops of Canterbury and York and the Bishops of London, Durham and Winchester always have seats in the House of Lords. The twenty-one other seats are filled by diocesan bishops in order of seniority. In the case of bishops awaiting seats, the order of seniority is shown (1), (2), (3) etc.

The Bishop of Sodor and Man and the Bishop of Gibraltar in Europe are not eligible to sit in the House of Lords.

	Election as Diocesan Bishop confirmed	Translated to present See	Entered House of Lords
Canterbury (Most Revd & Rt Hon G. L. Carey)	1987	1991	1991
York (Most Revd & Rt Hon D. M. Hope)	1985	1995	1990
London (Rt Revd & Rt Hon R. J. C. Chartres)	1995		1996
Durham (Rt Revd M. Turnbull)	1988	1994	1994
Winchester (Rt Revd M. C. Scott-Joynt)	1995		1996
Bath and Wells (Rt Revd J. L. Thompson)	1991		1997
Birmingham (Rt Revd M. Santer)	1987		1994
Blackburn (Rt Revd A. D. Chesters)	1989		1995
Bradford (Rt Revd D. J. Smith)	1992		1997
Bristol (Rt Revd B. Rogerson)	1985		1990
Carlisle (Rt Revd I. Harland)	1989		1996
Chelmsford (Rt Revd J. F. Perry)	1996		(1)
Chester (Rt Revd P. Forster)	1996		(3)
Chichester (Rt Revd E. W. Kemp)	1974		1979
Coventry (Rt Revd C. Bennetts)	1997		(9)
Derby (Rt Revd J. S. Bailey)	1995		1999
Ely (Vacancy)			
Exeter (Rt Revd M. L. Langrish)	1999		(14)
Gloucester (Rt Revd D. E. Bentley)	1993		1998
Guildford (Rt Revd J. Gladwin)	1994		1999
Hereford (Rt Revd J. K. Oliver)	1990		1997
Leicester (Rt Revd T. J. Stevens)	1999		(11)
Lichfield (Rt Revd K. N. Sutton)	1984		1989
Lincoln (Rt Revd R. M. Hardy)	1987		1993
Liverpool (Rt Revd J. S. Jones)	1998		(10)
Manchester (Rt Revd C. J. Mayfield)	1993		1998
Newcastle (Rt Revd J. M. Wharton)	1997		(7)
Norwich (Rt Revd G. R. James)	1999		(13)
Oxford (Rt Revd R. D. Harries)	1987		1993
Peterborough (Rt Revd I. P. M. Cundy)	1996		(2)
Portsmouth (Rt Revd K. Stevenson)	1995		1999
Ripon (Vacancy)			
Rochester (Rt Revd M. Nazir-Ali)	1994		1999
St Albans (Rt Revd C. W. Herbert)	1995		1999
St Edmundsbury and Ipswich (Rt Revd J. H. R. Lewis)	1996		(4)
Salisbury (Rt Revd D. S. Stancliffe)	1993		1998
Sheffield (Rt Revd J. Nicholls)	1997		(8)
Southwark (Rt Revd T. F. Butler)	1991	1998	1997
Southwell (Rt Revd G. H. Cassidy)	1999		(12)
Truro (Rt Revd W. Ind)	1997		(5)
Wakefield (Rt Revd N. S. McCulloch)	1992		1997
Worcester (Rt Revd P. S. M. Selby)	1997		(6)

Chaplains in Her Majesty's Services

ROYAL NAVY

Chaplains of all denominations are employed in many parts of the world, ashore and afloat in capital ships, squadrons of frigates and destroyers, Royal Marine Commandos, hospitals, Naval Colleges, Royal Naval Air Stations, HM Naval Bases and Training Establishments. Apart from conducting the customary services in their ships, units or establishments, for which all the necessary facilities are provided, chaplains find numerous opportunities for extending the work of the Church through pastoral contacts with families and dependants, as well as being 'friend and adviser of all on board'. They are given particular opportunity to teach the Christian faith to young people in Training Establishments. In-Service training for all Royal Naval Chaplains is carried out at the Armed Forces Chaplaincy Centre, Amport House, Andover, Hants. SP11 8BG. Christian Leadership Courses for all service personnel are provided at the centre during the year. The Anglican Church in the Royal Navy is served by 46 priests and is very much a part of the Anglican Communion with the Single Service and Tri-Service Synodical structures. The Senior Anglican Chaplain in the Royal Navy is granted the ecclesiastical dignity of Archdeacon by the Archbishop of Canterbury. The Archbishop is the Ordinary for all service chaplains and grants ecclesiastical licences to all Anglican chaplains on the Active List. The Royal Navy is an Equal Opportunities employer and applications for entry from both male and female priests under 39 are always welcome. Full particulars concerning the entry of Anglican Chaplains can be obtained from the Archdeacon for the Royal Navy, Ven Simon Golding, Room 201, Victory Building, HM Naval Base, Portsmouth PO1 3LS

Tel: (01705) 727904

ARMY

There is a definite Establishment of Chaplains, Church of England, Church of Scotland, Roman Catholic, Methodist and United Board (United Reformed Church and Baptist). This Establishment is governed by the strength of the Army. Chaplains of all denominations (except Roman Catholic) are administered by the Chaplain General assisted by the Deputy Chaplain General at the Ministry of Defence (Army), and through

Senior Chaplains at the Headquarters of Commands/Districts at home and overseas. The Chaplain General (the present holder of the office is a Church of Scotland Minister) is responsible to the 2nd Permanent Under-Secretary of State for the general well-being of the Department. The religious training of the Army is an integral part of military life. Regular periods of Religious Instruction/Discussion are provided. The Armed Forces Chaplaincy Centre is situated at Amport and the Royal Army Chaplains' Department Depot at Netheravon. These centres serve the double purpose of a spiritual home for all chaplains, and as training centres for all ranks, with different courses to develop leaders, refresh churchmen, or inform enquirers. Courses for military personnel are also held at centres overseas. *The Chaplain General* Revd Dr Victor Dobbin. *Deputy Chaplain General* Ven John Blackburn. Ministry of Defence Chaplains (Army), Trenchard Lines, Upavon, Wiltshire SN9 6BE

Tel: (01980) 615802
Fax: (01980) 615800

ROYAL AIR FORCE

From the foundation of the Royal Air Force, Chaplains have been proud to minister to the needs of servicemen and women and their families, in peace and war. The Chaplains' Branch of the Royal Air Force offers a real challenge and a rewarding ministry to young priests who have the necessary qualities, initiative and enthusiasm. The Royal Air Force is a large body of men and women drawn from every corner of Britain and from every stratum of society. There is a continuing need for clergy to minister to these men and women and the Royal Air Force understands and supports this ministry. Chaplains are commissioned by Her Majesty the Queen to provide for the moral and spiritual needs of all Service personnel and their families. This care is unlimited, and extends wherever members of the Royal Air Force are called to serve. Further details concerning Chaplaincy in the Royal Air Force can be obtained from: The Chaplain-in-Chief (RAF), Ministry of Defence, P & T Command HQ, RAF Innsworth, Gloucester GL3 1EZ

Tel: (01452) 712612 Ext 5032

For a list of **Chaplains to Her Majesty's Services** *see Crockford*

Forces Synodical Council

President The Archbishop of Canterbury

Senior Vice-President Rt Revd John Kirkham (*Bishop of Sherborne and the Archbishop of*

Canterbury's Episcopal Representative to Her Majesty's Forces)
Clergy Vice-President Vacancy
Lay Vice-President Wing Commander Chris Hill

The Forces Synodical Council was first convened in 1990. Since 1997 it has had thirty-six elected members, six clergy and six lay members from the Royal Navy, Army and the Royal Air Force, and nine *ex-officio* members. The Council carries out many of the responsibilities of a diocesan synod and is the highest tier of the synodical structure within the Armed Forces. The Council gives the clergy and laity of the Services the opportunity to contribute their ideas and opinions, and to make decisions pertinent to the life of the Church in the Armed Forces. Each Service has an elected Archdeaconry Synod, and elected representation at chaplaincy level is to Chaplaincy Councils. The three archdeacons represent the Armed Forces, as *ex-officio* members, on General Synod.

Chaplains in Higher Education

Note: Only one name is given for each institution, many of which have several chaplains.

UNIVERSITIES

Anglia Polytechnic University Revd Dr Malcolm Guite, The Chaplaincy Centre, 31 Park Rd, Chelmsford, Essex   *Tel:* (01382) 308447
email: M.Guite@anglia.ac.uk

Aston Revd Thomas Pyke, The Chaplaincy Suite, Lawrence Tower, Aston University, Aston Triange, Birmingham B4 7ET
Tel: 0121–359 6531 Ext 4059
email: t.f.pyke@aston.ac.uk

Bath Revd Jonathan Lloyd, The Chaplaincy Centre, University of Bath, Claverton Down, Bath, Avon BA2 7AY   *Tel:* (01225) 826458
email: chaplaincy@bath.ac.uk

Birmingham Revd Andrew Gorham, Anglican Chaplaincy, St Francis' Hall, Edgbaston Park Rd, Birmingham B15 2TT   *Tel:* 0121–416 7000
email: a.a.gorham@bham.ac.uk

Bournemouth Revd Dr David Hart, Bournemouth University, Wallisdown Rd, Poole, Dorset BH12 5BB   *Tel:* (01202) 595383
email: bournemouth.ac.uk

Bradford Revd Andii Bowsher, Anglican Chaplaincy, Michael Ramsey House, 2 Ashgrove, Bradford, W Yorks BD7 1BN
Tel: (01274) 727034
email: anglican-chaplain@bradford.ac.uk

Brighton Revd Colin Lawler, The Chaplaincy, Cockcroft Building, Lewes Rd, Moulsecoomb, Brighton, E Sussex BN2 4GJ   *Tel:* (01273) 643592

Bristol Revd Dr Angus Stuart, Ecumenical Chaplaincy Centre, 1 Priory Rd, Clifton, Bristol BS8 1TX   *Tel:* 0117–928 8823
email: angus.stuart@bris.ac.uk

Brunel Revd Stephen Roberts, The Meeting House, Brunel University, Uxbridge UB8 3PH
Tel: (01895) 203308
email: stephen.roberts@dlondon.org.uk

Cambridge Colleges

Christ's Revd Owen Spencer-Thomas
Tel: (01223) 334922
email: ors22@cam.ac.uk

Churchill Revd Dr John Rawlinson
Tel: (01223) 336000

Clare Revd Jo Bailey Wells (Dean)
Tel: (01223) 333240
email: jbw21@cam.ac.uk

Corpus Christi Revd Dr Mark Pryce
Tel: (01223) 338002
email: rmp31@cam.ac.uk

Downing Revd Bruce Kinsey   *Tel:* (01223) 334810
email: brlk@dow.cam.ac.uk

Emmanuel Revd Jeremy Caddick
Tel: (01223) 334264
email: jlc24@cam.ac.uk

Fitzwilliam Revd Vanessa Herrick
Tel: (01223) 332013
email: vah24@cam.ac.uk

Girton Revd Jeremy Clark-King
Tel: (01223) 338956
email: jc223@cam.ac.uk

Gonville and Caius Revd Jack McDonald
Tel: (01223) 332408
email: jdm39@cam.ac.uk

Jesus Revd Timothy Jenkins (Dean)
Tel: (01223) 339303
email: tdj22@jesus.cam.ac.uk

King's Revd Dr George Pattison (Dean)
Tel: (01223) 331248
email: Dean@kings.cam.ac.uk

Magdalene Revd Dr Hueston Finlay
Tel: (01223) 332129
email: hef21@cam.ac.uk

Newnham Revd Dr Nicholas Cranfield
Tel: (01223) 335775

Pembroke Canon Brian Watchorn
Tel: (01223) 338147

Peterhouse Revd Dr Ben Quash (Dean)
Tel: (01223) 338217
email: jbq1000@cam.ac.uk

Queens' Revd Dr Jonathan Holmes (Dean)
Tel: (01223) 335545
email: jmh38@cam.ac.uk

Robinson Revd Hugh Shilson-Thomas
Tel: (01223) 339140
email: hds21@cam.ac.uk

GENERAL

St Catharine's Revd Dr David Goodhew
Tel: (01223) 338346
email: djg27@cam.ac.uk
St Edmund's Revd Dr Michael Robson (Dean)
Tel: (01223) 336123
email: mjpr100@cam.ac.uk
St John's Revd Dr Andrew Macintosh (Dean)
Tel: (01223) 338709
email: aam1003@cus.cam.ac.uk
Selwyn Revd Ian Thompson   Tel: (01223) 335875
email: chaplain@sel.cam.ac.uk
Sidney Sussex Revd Ellen Clark-King
Tel: (01223) 338870
email: ejc35@cam.ac.uk
Trinity Revd Dr Arnold Browne (Dean)
Tel: (01223) 338563
email: asb32@cam.ac.uk
Trinity Hall Revd Dr Charles Elliott (Dean)
Tel: (01223) 332525
email: cme13@cam.ac.uk
Wolfson Canon Christine Farrington
Tel: (01223) 335900

University of Central England in Birmingham
Revd Michael Harris, The Chaplaincy, Student
Services, Baker Building, Perry Barr, Birmingham
B42 2SU   Tel: 0121-331 5345

Central Lancashire Revd Bill Turner, University
of Central Lancashire, Corporation St, Preston
PR1 2HE   Tel: (01772) 892615

City University Revd Andrew Baughen, The
City University, St John's St, London EC1V 4PB
Tel: 020-7477 8000 Ext 4057

Coventry Revd Carolyn Kennedy, The
Chaplaincy, Coventry University, Priory St,
Coventry CV1 5FB   Tel: (01203) 838315

Cranfield Revd Hugh Symes-Thompson,
Cranfield University, Cranfield, Beds MK43 0AL
Tel: (01234) 750111 Ext 3344

De Montfort Revd Jane Curtis, Chaplaincy &
Centre for Religions, Newarke Close, Leicester
LE1 9BH   Tel: 0116-255 1551 Ext 8599

Derby Revd David Hart, Spirit Zone, University
of Derby, Kedlestone Rd, Derby DE22 1GB
Tel: (01332) 622222 Ext 1878
email: d.hart@derby.ac.uk

Durham Colleges
Collingwood and Grey Revd Benedick de la Mare
Tel: 0191-374 4563
Hatfield Revd David Glover   Tel: 0191-374 3163
St Aidan's Vacancy
Tel: 0191-374 3269
St Chad's Revd Dominic Barrington
Tel: 0191-374 3362
email: dominic.barrington@durham.ac.uk

St Hild and St Bede Revd Alan Bayes
Tel: 0191-374 306(
email: f.a.bayes@durham.ac.uk
St John's Revd Mark Cartledge Tel: 0191-374 357(
email:m.j.cartledge@durham.ac.uk
St Mary's Revd Margaret Parker
Tel: 0191-384 270(
Trevelyan and Van Mildert Revd Kenneth
Anderson   Tel: 0191-374 377(
email: kenneth.anderson@durham.ac.uk
University Revd Ben Gordon-Taylor
Tel: 0191-374 386(

Durham, Stockton Campus Revd Philip
Ashdown, The Chaplaincy, University of
Durham Stockton Campus, University Boule-
vard, Thornaby, Stockton-on-Tees TS17 6BH
Tel: (01642) 33501(
email: p.d.ashdown@durham.ac.uk

East Anglia Revd Garth Barber, The Chaplaincy,
University of East Anglia, Norwich NR4 7TJ
Tel: (01603) 592166
email: g.barber@uea.ac.uk

East London Vacancy, c/o Student Services
Centre, Romford Rd, Stratford, London E15 4LZ
Tel: 020-8590 7722 Ext 4450

Essex Revd Pat Mossop, Multifaith Chaplaincy
Centre, University of Essex, Wivenhoe Park,
Colchester, Essex CO4 3SQ   Tel: (01206) 872098
email: patm@essex.ac.uk

Exeter Revd Dr Jeremy Law, Dept of Theology,
Queen's Building, University of Exeter, The
Queen's Drive, Exeter EX4 4QE
Tel: (01392) 264240
email: j.t.law@exeter.ac.uk

Goldsmith's Revd Justus Ogunleyi

Greenwich Revd Lou Gale, Greenwich
University, Wellington St, Woolwich, London
SE18 6PF   Tel: 020-8331 8150

Hertfordshire Revd George Bolt (Ecumenical),
University of Hertfordshire, Hatfield Campus,
College Lane, Hatfield, Herts AL10 9AB
Tel: (01707) 284456

Huddersfield Revd Margaret McLean, The
Chaplaincy Centre, University of Huddersfield,
Queensgate, Huddersfield HD1 3DH
Tel: (01484) 472090
email: m.a.mclean@hud.ac.uk

Hull Revd Dr Judith Bryan, Anglican Chaplaincy, 13 Salmon Grove, Hull, Humberside
HU6 7SX   Tel: (01482) 493251

Humberside Revd Rodney Ward, The
Chaplaincy, Student Services, Grimsby College,
Nun's Corner, Grimsby DN34 5BQ
Tel: (01482) 440550 Ext 5066

Keele Revd Catherine Lack, The Chapel, Keele University, Keele, Staffs ST5 5BG
Tel: (01782) 621111 Ext 7163
email: cpado@keele.ac.uk

Kent Revd Stephen Laird, Chaplaincy, Keynes College, University of Kent, Canterbury, Kent CT2 7NP
Tel: (01227) 764000 Ext 7491

Kingston Revd David Buckely (Ecumenical), Room 7, Kenry House, Kingston University, Kingston-upon-Thames KT2 7LB
Tel: 020–8547 7311
email: davidbuckley@kingston.ac.uk

Lancaster Revd Di Williams, The Chaplaincy Centre, Lancaster University, Bailrigg, Lancaster LA1 4YW
Tel: (01524) 594071
email: d.p.williams@lancaster.ac.uk

Leeds Revd Dr Simon Robinson, Emmanuel Institute, Leeds University, Leeds LS2 9JT
Tel: 0113–533 5070
email: s.j.robinson@leeds.ac.uk

Leeds Metropolitan Revd Dr Mike Benwell, Chaplaincy Centre, Leeds Metropolitan University, Calverley St, Leeds LS1 3UE
Tel: 0113–283 2600 Ext 3522
email: m.benwell@lmu.ac.uk

Leicester Revd Ian McIntosh, The Gatehouse, University Rd, Leicester LE1 7RH
Tel: 0116–285 6493
email: imm4@le.ac.uk

Lincolnshire and Humberside Revd Leslie Acklam, Chaplaincy, Lincoln University Campus, Brayford Pool, Lincoln LN6 7TS
Tel: (01522) 886079
email: lacklam@lincoln.ac.uk

Liverpool Revd Jonathan Clatworthy, Anglican Chaplaincy, Mulberry Court, Mulberry St, Liverpool L7 7EZ
Tel: 0151–794 3302/03
email: j.clatworthy@liv.ac.uk

Liverpool John Moores Revd Robert Dickinson, Ecumenical Chaplaincy, Roscoe Court, 4 Rodney St, Liverpool L1 2TP
Tel: 0151–231 3171
email: perbdick@livjm.ac.uk

London Guildhall University Revd William Taylor, The Chaplaincy, Calcutta House, Old Castle St, London E1 7NT
Tel: 020–7320 1379

London Colleges
Senior Chaplain Revd Stephen Williams, Anglican Chaplaincy, 48B Gordon Square, London WC1H 0PD
Tel: 020–7387 0670
email: chaplaincy@admin.lou.ac.uk
Guildhall School of Music Revd William Gulliford, 32B Wilton Place, London SW1X 8SH
Tel: 020–7245 0072
email: wgullifo@gsmd.ac.uk
Imperial College of Science, Technology and Medicine

Revd Alan Gyle, 10 Princes Gardens, London SW7 1NE
Tel: 020–7594 9600
King's (Dean) Revd Dr Richard Burridge, King's College, Strand, London WC2R 2LS
Tel: 020–7873 2333/2063
email: richard.burridge@kcl.ac.uk
London School of Economics Revd Neil Nicholls, Houghton St, Aldwych, London WC2A 2AE
Tel: 020–7955 7965

Medical Schools
Imperial College of Science, Technology and Medicine Revd Alastair McCollum, 10 Princes Gardens, London SW7 1NE
Tel: 020–7594 9600
Royal Free Revd Giles Legood, 15 Ormonde Mansions, 106 Southampton Row, London WC1B 4BP
Tel: 020–7242 2574
email: glegood@rvc.ac.uk
Royal London Hospital Revd Dr Jenny King, Department of Human Science and Medical Ethics, London Hospital, Turner St, London E1 2AD
Tel: 020–7377 7000 Ext 3068
Royal Veterinary Revd Giles Legood (*as above*)
St Bartholomew's Revd Dr Jenny King (*as above*)
University College Hospital Revd Giles Legood (*as above*)
Royal Academy of Music Revd Dr Julian Davies, 16 Clarence Gate Gardens, London NW1 6AY
Tel: 020–7402 6979
Royal College of Art Revd Alan Gyle (*as above*)
Queen Mary and Westfield Revd David Peebles, Queen Mary and Westfield College, Mile End Rd, London E1 4NS
Tel: 020–7775 3179
Royal Holloway and Bedford New College Revd Andrew Taylor, Royal Holloway and Bedford New College, Egham Hill, Egham, Surrey TW20 0EX
Tel: (01784) 443070/950
email: a.taylor@rhbnc.ac.uk
St Bartholomew's & Royal London School of Medicine and Dentistry Revd Dr Nick Goulding
Tel: 020–8980 1204
email: n.j.goulding@mds.qmw.ac.uk
St George's Hospital Medical School The Anglican Chaplain
Tel: 020–8672 9944 Ext 55298
School of Oriental and African Studies Revd Stephen Williams (*as above*)
West London Institute of Higher Education Revd David Wilson
Tel: 020–8568 8741 Ext 2655

Loughborough Revd Jeanette Gosney, Edward Herbert Building, Loughborough, Leics LE11 3TU
Tel: (01509) 223740
email: j.gosney@lboro.ac.uk

Luton Revd Catherine Bell, University of Luton, Park Square, Luton, Beds LU1 3JU
Tel: (01582) 453236

Manchester Revd Liz Carnelley, St Peter's House, Precinct Centre, Oxford Rd, Manchester M13 9GH
Tel: 0161–273 1465

Manchester Metropolitan Revd Ian Gomersall, Student Services, All Saints, Manchester M15 6BH
Tel: 0161–247 3496/0161–273 1465

Middlesex Revd Jan Beer (Ecumenical), Middlesex University, Student Services Area, Enfield Campus, Queensway, Enfield, Middx
Tel: 020–8362 6421
email: Jan2@nw.mdx.ac.uk

Newcastle Revd Roger Mills, The Chaplaincy, University of Newcastle, Newcastle upon Tyne NE1 7RU
Tel: 0191–222 6341
email: roger.mills@ncl.ac.uk

Nottingham Canon Ian Tarrant, 3 Wortley Hall Close, Nottingham University, University Park, Nottingham NG7 2RD
Tel: 0115–951 3927
email: ian.tarrant@nottingham.ac.uk

Nottingham Trent Revd Lakshmi Deshpande, Clifton Chaplaincy, Clifton Main Site, Clifton Lane, Nottingham NG11 8NS
Tel: 0115–848 3279
email: lakshmi.deshpande@ntu.ac.uk

North London Revd Jonathan Clark, University of North London, Holloway Rd, London N7 8DB
Tel: 020–7753 7038
email: jd.clark@unl.ac.uk

Northumbria at Newcastle Revd Andrew Shipton, Chaplaincy, Student Services, Ellison Buildings, Ellison Place, Newcastle upon Tyne NE1 8ST
Tel: 0191–222 1679
email: andrew.shipton@unn.ac.uk

Oxford Colleges
All Souls Revd John McManners
Tel: (01865) 279368
Balliol Revd Dr Douglas Dupree
Tel: (01865) 277777
Brasenose Revd Richard Smail *Tel:* (01865) 277833
Christ Church Revd Ralph Williamson
Tel: (01865) 276236
Corpus Christi Revd Dr Judith Maltby
Tel: (01865) 276722
Exeter Revd Stephen Hampton
Tel: (01865) 279610
Green Dr David Cook (Baptist)
Tel: (01865) 274785
Harris Manchester Revd Peter Hewis
Tel: (01865) 271006
Hertford Revd Michael Chantry
Tel: (01865) 279400
Jesus Revd Elisabeth Goddard *Tel:* (01865) 279757
email: elisabeth.goddard@jesus.ox.ac.uk
Keble Vacancy *Tel:* (01865) 272727
Lady Margaret Hall Revd Dr Alan Doig
Tel: (01865) 274386
Lincoln Vacancy *Tel:* (01865) 279800
Magdalen Revd Dr Michael Piret
Tel: (01865) 276027
Mansfield Revd Dale Rominger
Tel: (01865) 270999
email: dale.rominger@mansfield.oxford.uk
Merton Revd Mark Everitt *Tel:* (01865) 276365
New Revd Dr Robert Harnish *Tel:* (01865) 279541

Nuffield Revd Dr Margaret Yee (URC)
Tel: (01865) 27856
email: margaret.yee@nuf.ox.ac.u

Oriel Revd Thomas Meyrick *Tel:* (01865) 27655
Pembroke Revd Dr John Platt *Tel:* (01865) 27642
email: John.Platt@pmb.ox.ac.u
Queen's Revd Peter Southwell *Tel:* (01865) 27914
Regent's Park Revd Dr Jane Shaw
Tel: (01865) 28812
St Catherine's Revd Hugh White
Tel: (01865) 27170
St Edmund Hall Revd Duncan MacLaren
Tel: (01865) 27902
St Hilda's Canon Brian Mountford
Tel: (01865) 24380
St Hugh's Revd Jeremy Gilpin *Tel:* (01865) 27490
email: gilpin@compuserve.con
St John's Revd Dr Elizabeth Carmichael
Tel: (01865) 27735
St Peter's Revd Christopher Jones
Tel: (01865) 27890
Somerville Revd Sabine Akire *Tel:* (01865) 27060
Trinity Revd Trevor Williams *Tel:* (01865) 27988
University Revd Bill Sykes *Tel:* (01865) 27666
Wadham Revd Giles Fraser *Tel:* (01865) 27790
Westminster Revd Richard Griffiths
Tel: (01865) 24664
Worcester Revd Peter Doll *Tel:* (01865) 27837
email: peter.doll@worc.ox.ac.uk

Oxford Brookes Revd Andrew Coleby, 46 Lower Rd, Chinnor, Oxon OX9 4DO *Tel:* (01865) 354052
email: amcoleby@brookes.ac.uk

Plymouth Revd Barry Hallett (Ecumenical), University of Plymouth, Drake Circus, Plymouth PL4 8AA *Tel:* (01752) 232261

Portsmouth Revd Fiona Stewart-Darling, The Chaplaincy, Gun House, Hampshire Terrace, Portsmouth PO1 2QX *Tel:* (02392) 843161
email: fiona.stewart-darling@port.ac.uk

Reading Revd Graham Rainey, The Chaplaincy Centre, Park House Lodge, University of Reading, Whiteknights, PO Box 217, Reading, Berks RG6 2AH *Tel:* (01734) 318797
email: chaplaincy@reading.ac.uk

Salford Revd Janet Fife, University of Salford, Salford, Lancs. M5 4WT *Tel:* 0161–285 4660

Sheffield Revd Cheryl Collins, The Chaplaincy Office, The Octagon, University of Sheffield S10 2TN *Tel:* 0114–282 4956
email: c.a.collins@shef.ac.uk

Sheffield Hallam Revd Sandra Howes (Ecumenical), Sheffield Hallam University, City Campus, Pond St, Sheffield S1 1WB
Tel: 0114–253 2139
email: s.howes@shu.ac.uk

Southampton Revd David Simpson, The Chaplaincy Centre, The University, 52 University Rd, Southampton SO17 1BJ   *Tel:* (01703) 558126
email: chaplain@soton.ac.uk

South Bank Revd Frank Hung, South Bank University, Borough Rd, London SE1 0AA
Tel: 020–7815 6419
email: hungfy@sbu.ac.uk

Staffordshire Revd Ernest Pettengell, Chaplaincy, Staffordshire University, College Rd, Shelton, Stoke-on-Trent ST4 2DE
Tel: (01782) 744531 Ext 3273
email: e.t.pettengell@staffs.ac.uk

Surrey Revd Dr Robin Harvey, University of Surrey, Guildford, Surrey GU2 5XH
Tel: (01483) 300800 Ext 2754
email: r.harvey@surrey.ac.uk

Surrey Institute of Art and Design: University College Revd Mike Todd, Student Services, Chaplaincy, Farnham Campus, Falkner Rd, Farnham, Surrey GU9 7DS   *Tel:* (01252) 892614
email: mtodd@surrart.ac.uk

Sussex Revd Dr Gavin Ashenden, The Meeting House, University of Sussex, Falmer, Brighton BN1 9QN   *Tel:* (01273) 678217
email: g.ashenden@sussex.ac.uk

Teesside Revd Dian Leppington, The Chaplaincy, University of Teesside, Middlesbrough, Cleveland TS1 3BA
Tel: (01642) 342264
email: d.leppington@tees.ac.uk

Thames Valley Revd Jeremy Hurst, Chaplaincy Office, Thames Valley University at Slough, Wellington St, Slough SL1 1YG
Tel: (01753) 542068

Warwick Revd Mark Bratton, The Chaplaincy Centre, University of Warwick, Coventry CV4 7AL   *Tel:* (01203) 528158
email: cpsad@csv.warwick.ac.uk

Westminster Revd Jonathan Brewster, Staff and Student Centre, 104/108 Bolsover St, London W1P 7HF   *Tel:* 020–7911 5050
email: brewstj@wmin.ac.uk

West of England, Bristol Canon Shaun Darley, University of the West of England, The Octagon, Coldharbour Lane, Frenchay, Bristol BS16 1QY
Tel: 0117–344 2334
email: shaun.darley@uwe.ac.uk

Wolverhampton Preb Geoffrey Wynne, The Chaplaincy Centre, The University, Wolverhampton WV1 1SB   *Tel:* (01902) 25747
email: ex1170@wlv.ac.uk

York Revd John Robertson, Chaplaincy, Goodricke College, University of York, York YO1 5DD   *Tel:* (01904) 433131
email: jcr7@york.ac.uk

COLLEGES AND INSTITUTES OF HIGHER EDUCATION

Bath Spa University College Revd Richard Hall, Bath Spa University College, Newton Park, Newton St Loe, Bath BA2 9BN
Tel: (01225) 875875

Bolton Institute Revd Gary Lawson, Bolton Institute of Higher Education, Deane Rd, Bolton BL3 5AB   *Tel:* (01204) 528851 Ext 3080

Bretton Hall College Revd Catherine Ogle, Bretton Hall College, West Bretton, Wakefield BD7 1AY   *Tel:* (01924) 830261
email: ogle@woolleyvic.freeserve.com

Buckingham Chiltern University College Revd Frank Hillebrand, Queen Alexandra Road, High Wycombe, Buckinghamshire HP11 2JZ
Tel: (01494) 522141
email: chaplain@buckscol.ac.uk

Surrey Institute of Art and Design: University College Revd Mike Todd, Student Services, Chaplaincy, Farnham Campus, Falkner Rd, Farnham, Surrey GU9 7DS   *Tel:* (01252) 892614
email: mtodd@surrart.ac.uk

University College Northampton Revd Peter Moseling, Park Campus, Boughton Green Rd, Northampton NN2 7AL   *Tel:* (01604) 735500

For **Church Colleges of Higher Education** *see* page 215

Chaplains in the Prison Service

The Prison Service Chaplaincy provides chaplains for all HM Prisons in England and Wales. It works within the Prison Service part of the Home Office, and the responsibilities of the Chaplain General and his headquarters colleagues include the giving of advice to ministers and officials about policy decisions with a religious or ethical dimension. In addition chaplains are recruited, trained, deployed and supported in their work of providing for the religious needs of prisoners,

giving opportunities for worship, evangelism and instruction, and offering a pastoral ministry at times of crisis and opportunity. Chaplains are also involved in facilitating the observance of other faiths. Their ministry is always available to staff.

All prisons have an Anglican, a Roman Catholic and a Methodist chaplain; the headquarters team includes senior representatives of all three denominations.

The Bishop to Prisons
Rt Revd The Bishop of Lincoln, Bishop's House,
Eastgate, Lincoln LN2 1QQ   *Tel:* (01522) 534701

Chaplain General
Ven David Fleming, Prison Service Chaplaincy,
Room 709, Abell House, John Islip St, London
SW1P 4LH   *Tel:* 020–7217 5817

Assistants Chaplain General
Revd Thomas Johns, Prison Service Chaplaincy,
Room 715, Abell House, John Islip St, London
SW1P 4LH   *Tel:* 020–7217 2024

Revd Bob Payne, Revd Peter Taylor, Revd Bob
Wiltshire, Prison Service Chaplaincy, PO Box 349,
Gaol Square, Stafford ST16 3DL
Tel: (01785) 213456

For a list of **Prison Chaplains** *see Crockford.*

Christian Aid

In a world where 500 million people suffer from chronic malnutrition and 2.4 billion have no adequate sanitation, organizations like Christian Aid play a vital role in helping poor communities to overcome their poverty.

Christian Aid is the official agency of the British and Irish Churches – including the Church of England – and as such is one of the largest church relief agencies in Europe. But both at home and overseas it also works with people of other faiths or none who share its concerns.

The agency's income in 1997/98 was nearly £38 million. A substantial amount of its general income is received through the annual Christian Aid Week collections. It spends under 12 per cent of the money it raises on fundraising and administration. More than 80 per cent is spent on tackling poverty overseas.

It funds projects in more than 70 countries worldwide, standing by the poor whether they are digging wells or fighting famine, building homes or growing crops, learning to read or writing about human rights abuses, healing the wounds of war or preventing the spread of illness.

Money spent overseas is passed to local partner organizations which ensures that it is spent where local people need it most. Christian Aid has no permanent offices abroad, believing that poor communities are best placed to devise and run their own projects and solve their own problems. Channelling money through partners is an effective and respectful way of giving the poor the means to help themselves.

In Sri Lanka, for example, Christian Aid funds Gami Seva Sevana, a farm training centre which teaches teenage apprentices to grow a wide range of crops using only natural, organic manure and pesticides. In Uganda, it supports the Rukararwe Partnership Workshop for Rural Development, which helps farmers to earn a living from crafts without destroying their country's own dwindling forests. In Jamaica the Small Projects Assistance Team, also supported by Christian Aid, is helping farmers to reduce dependence on banana exports by growing crops such as breadfruit and plantain, and training them in livestock and poultry rearing.

Prevention of hunger is better than cure, but Christian Aid is also active in emergencies, sending money to provide food, shelter, medicine and transport when floods, famine, earthquakes or war strike.

The agency's education work in the UK and Ireland accounts for up to ten per cent of its income. This is because Christian Aid recognizes the role of richer countries in creating the conditions that keep people poor. It believes that education and campaigning can help people to understand the root causes of poverty and encourage action by politicians and the public to remove them.

Director Dr Daleep Mukarji, Inter-Church House, 35–41 Lower Marsh, London SE1 7RL
Tel: 020–7620 4444
Fax: 020–7620 0719

Church Army

Church Army Evangelists share the Christian faith through words and action and equip others to do the same. Over 400 full-time evangelists and 350 further staff are devoted to a wide range of service in Anglican churches, projects and teams throughout the British Isles.

Church Army trains and sends evangelists to work in five areas of focus.

Area Evangelism providing training and resources for groups of churches.
Children and Young People introducing the Christian message in new and fresh ways.
Church Planting providing expertise and resources to establish new congregations.
Homeless People helping churches and communities support those in need.

Older People recognizing the gifts of older people and communicating the Gospel to them in practical ways.

President The Archbishop of Canterbury.
Chief Secretary Capt Philip Johanson, Church Army Headquarters, Independents Rd, Blackheath, London SE3 9LG   *Tel:* 020–8318 1226
Fax: 020–8318 5258
email: information@churcharmy.org.uk

Principal Revd David Jeans, Wilson Carlile College of Evangelism, 50 Cavendish St, Sheffield S3 7RZ   *Tel:* 0114–278 7020
Fax: 0114–279 5863
email: trainingcollege@sheffieldcentre.org.uk

Church Colleges of Higher Education

Canterbury *Christ Church College*, North Holmes Rd, Canterbury, Kent CT1 1QU
Tel: (01227) 767700; *Principal:* Professor Michael Wright; *Dean of Chapel:* Revd Dr Brian Kelly, 1 St Martin's Cottages, St Martin's Priory, North Holmes Rd, Canterbury, Kent CT1 1QU
Tel: (01227) 782747
email: bek1@cant.ac.uk

Cheltenham *Cheltenham and Gloucester College of Higher Education*, PO Box 220, The Park Campus, The Park, Cheltenham GL50 2QF
Tel: (01242) 532701; *Principal:* Miss J. O. Trotter; *Chaplain:* Revd Keith Hitchman

Chester *University College Chester*, Cheyney Rd, Chester CH1 4BJ *Tel:* (01244) 375444 Ext 2305; *Principal:* Professor Tim Wheeler; *Chaplain:* Revd Michael French
email: m.french@chester.ac.uk

Lancaster *St Martin's College*, Bowerham, Lancaster LA1 3JD *Tel:* (01524) 384562/1; *Principal:* Prof Christopher Carr; *Chaplain:* Revd Dr John Daniels

Lincoln *Bishop Grosseteste College*, Lincoln LN1 3DY *Tel:* (01522) 527347; *Principal:* Mrs Eileen Baker; *Chaplain:* Revd Stuart Foster
email: s.j.foster@bgc.ac.uk

Liverpool **Liverpool Hope University College*, Hope Park, Liverpool L16 9JD *Tel:* 0151–291 3000;

Pro-Rector: Revd Dr R. J. Elford; *Chaplain:* Rt Revd Ian Stuart

London **Roehampton Institute*, Whitelands College, West Hill, London SW15 3SN *Tel:* 020–8392 3000; *Principal:* Revd David Peacock; *Chaplain:* Revd Richard Lane

Plymouth *The College of St Mark and St John*, Derriford Rd, Plymouth PL6 8BH *Tel:* (01752) 636829 Ext 5701; *Principal:* Dr John Rea; *Chaplain:* Revd Karl Freeman

Winchester *King Alfred's College*, Sparkford Rd, Winchester SO22 4NR *Tel:* (01962) 827222; *Principal:* Professor John Dickinson; *Chaplain:* Revd Jonathan Watkins

York *The University College of Ripon and York St John*, Lord Mayor's Walk, York YO3 7EX *Tel:* (01904) 656771; *Principal:* Professor Robin Butlin; *Chaplain:* Revd David McCoulough
email: d.mccoulough@ucrysj.ac.uk

*These colleges are constituent members of ecumenical federal Institutes of Higher Education.

College in a Special Relationship with the Church of England
Bognor/Chichester *The Chichester Institute of Higher Education*, Bishop Otter Campus, College Lane, Chichester PO19 4PE *Tel:* (01243) 816050; *Director:* Dr Philip Robinson; *Chaplain:* Revd Simon Griffiths

Church Urban Fund

Chairman
The Archbishop of Canterbury

Vice-Chairman
Mr Stephen O'Brien

Other Trustees
Mrs Elaine Appelbee, Rt Revd John Austin, Mr Patrick Coldstream, Mr Mark Cornwall-Jones, Mr Richard Farnell, Ven Granville Gibson, Revd

Eileen Lake, Mr Michael Mockridge, Canon John Stanley, Mrs Dorothy Stewart

Chief Executive Mrs Angela Sarkis

Office 2 Great Peter St, London SW1P 3LX
Tel: 020–7898 1000
Fax: 020–7898 1601

The Fund supports practical action for justice in

disadvantaged and marginalized communities by awarding grants for local projects and by working in partnership with others to inform the wider debate on urban regeneration. The Fund aims to help the Church better understand the needs and gifts of people living in urban priority areas, and develop and implement a range of sustainable responses that take full account of local resources and potential.

The Fund was born out of the landmark *Faith in the City* report, and since allocating its first grant in 1988 has awarded more than £29 million to over 1,500 projects. Grants are awarded for work in such categories as community development, social care, youth and education, housing and homelessness, evangelism and interfaith efforts, and opening up church buildings for community use.

Application to the Fund is made through the local diocese. However, the national office is happy to respond to initial enquiries and can provide details of the appropriate diocesan contact.

The Fund is grateful for the continuing support of parishes and individuals who have contributed to its work.

Clergy Appointments Adviser

The Adviser has been appointed by the Archbishops of Canterbury and York to assist clergy, both from overseas and in England, to find suitable new appointments, and also to assist patrons and others responsible for making appointments to find suitable candidates. The Adviser has the responsibility to assist beneficed and unbeneficed clergy, men and women, together with deaconesses and accredited lay workers. The Adviser produces a list of vacancies for incumbencies, team posts, assistant curates and specialized ministries. The list is available free of charge. Those seeking advice should contact: Revd John Lee, Clergy Appointments Adviser, Fielden House, Little College St, London SW1P 3SH

Tel: 020–7898 1898
Fax: 020–7898 1899
email: sue.manners@caa.cof.e.org.uk

Conference Centres and Retreat Houses

CONFERENCE CENTRES

ASHBURNHAM PLACE	Ashburnham Place, Battle, E Sussex TN33 9NF *Tel:* (01424) 892244 *Fax:* (01424) 894200 *email:* bookings@ashburnham.org.uk *Web:* http://www.ashburnham.org.uk (*Administrator:* Mrs Jennifer Oldroyd)
HAYES CONFERENCE CENTRE	Hayes Conference Centre, Swanwick, Derbyshire DE55 1AU *Tel:* (01773) 526000 *Fax:* (01773) 540841 (*Manager:* Mr Peter Anderson) *email:* peter@cct.org.uk *Web:* http://www.cct.org.uk
HENGRAVE HALL	Hengrave Hall Centre, Bury St Edmunds, Suffolk IP28 6LZ *Tel:* (01284) 701561 *Fax:* (01284) 702950 *email:* co-ordinator@hengravehallcentre.org.uk *Web:* http://hengravehallcentre.org.uk
HIGH LEIGH CONFERENCE CENTRE	High Leigh Conference Centre, Lord St, Hoddesdon, Herts. EN11 8SG *Tel:* (01992) 463016 *Fax:* (01992) 446594 *Web:* www.cct.org.uk (*Manager:* Mr Ian Andrews)
LEE ABBEY	Lee Abbey Fellowship, Lynton, Devon EX35 6JJ *Tel:* (01598) 752621 *Fax:* (01598) 752619 *email:* relax@leeabbey.org.uk *Web:* http://www.leeabbey.org.uk (*Warden:* Revd Bob Payne)
SCARGILL HOUSE	Scargill House, Kettlewell, Skipton, N Yorks. BD23 5HU *Tel:* (01756) 760234 *Fax:* (01756) 760499 *email:* Scargill.house@dial.pipex.com (*Warden:* Revd Keith Knight)

RETREAT HOUSES

The following is a list of diocesan conference centres and retreat houses including some run by religious communities. For details of accommodation for individual retreats *see* Religious Communities page 249, or contact the National Retreat Association, The Central Hall, 256 Bermondsey St, London SE1 3JJ *Tel:* 020–7357 7736 whose journal *Vision* is published annually in December.

BATH AND WELLS	Abbey House, Chilkwell St, Glastonbury, Som. BA6 8DH (*Retreat House*) *Tel:* (01458) 831112 (*Warden:* David Hill)
	Community of St Francis, Compton Durville Manor House, South Petherton TA13 5ES *Tel:* (01460) 40473
BLACKBURN	Whalley Abbey, Whalley, Clitheroe, Lancs. BB7 9SS *Tel:* (01254) 822268 *Fax:* (01254) 824227 (*Warden:* Revd Christopher Sterry; *Manager:* Mrs Dinah Critchley)
BRADFORD	Parcevall Hall, Appletreewick, Skipton, N Yorks. BD23 6DG *Tels:* (0175 672) 213 and 283 *Fax:* (01756) 720656 (*Warden:* Miss Florence Begley)
CARLISLE	Carlisle Diocesan Conference House, Rydal Hall, Ambleside, Cumbria LA22 9LX *Tel:* (0153 94) 32050 *Fax:* (0153 94) 34887 (*Warden:* Revd Peter Lippiett)
CHELMSFORD	Diocesan House of Retreat, Pleshey, Chelmsford, Essex CM3 1HA *Tel:* (01245) 237251 (*Warden:* Canon John Howden)
CHESTER	Chester Diocesan Conference Centre, Foxhill, Frodsham, Cheshire WA6 6XB *Tel:* (01928) 733777 (*Wardens:* Mr & Mrs Ian Cameron)
	The Retreat House, 11 Abbey Square, Chester CH1 2HU *Tel:* (01244) 321801 (*Warden:* Sister Margaret CHN)
CHICHESTER	Monastery of the Holy Trinity, Crawley Down, Crawley, W Sussex RH10 4LH *Tel:* (01342) 712074
	Neale House Conference Centre, Moat Rd, East Grinstead, W Sussex RH19 3LB *Tel:* (01342) 312552
	St Margaret's Convent, St John's Rd, East Grinstead, W Sussex RH19 3LE *Tel:* (01342) 323497
COVENTRY	Coventry Diocesan Retreat House, Offchurch, Leamington Spa, Warks. CV33 9AS *Tel:* (01926) 423309 (*Wardens:* Revd Michael and Revd Sharon Simpson)
DERBY/SOUTHWELL	Morley Retreat and Conference House, Morley, Derby DE7 6DE *Tel:* (01332) 831293 (*Warden:* Revd J. A. Heslop)
DURHAM	*See* entry for NEWCASTLE
ELY	Bishop Woodford House, Barton Road, Ely, Cambs. CB7 4DX *Tels:* (01353) 663039 (Office); 665065 (Warden's Residence); and 662746 (Visitors).
	The Community of the Resurrection, St Francis' House, Hemingford Grey, Huntingdon PE18 9BJ *Tel:* (01480) 462185

EXETER	Mercer House Diocesan Conference Centre, Exwick Road, Exeter EX4 2AT *Tel:* (01392) 219609 *Fax:* (01392) 218758 (*Warden:* Mr Graeme and Mrs Christine Williams)
GLOUCESTER	Glenfall House, Mill Lane, Charlton Kings, Cheltenham, Glos. GL54 4EP *Tel:* (01242) 583654 *Fax:* (01242) 251314 (*Warden:* Mrs Anne Murgatroyd)
GUILDFORD	St Columba's House, Maybury Hill, Woking, Surrey GU22 8AB *Tel:* (01483) 766498
	House of Bethany, Tilford Rd, Hindhead, Surrey GU26 6RB *Tel:* (01428) 604578
HEREFORD	Bishop Mascall Centre, Lower Galdeford, Ludlow, Shropshire SY8 2RU *Tel:* (01584) 873882. (*Director:* Revd Graham Earney)
LEICESTER	Launde Abbey, East Norton, Leicestershire LE7 9XB *Tel:* (01572) 717254 (*Warden:* Revd Graham Johnson)
LICHFIELD	Lichfield Diocesan Retreat and Conference Centre, Shallowford House, Norton Bridge, Stone, Staffs. ST15 0NZ *Tel:* (01785) 760233 *Fax:* (01785) 760390 (*Warden:* Mr David Rowlands)
LINCOLN	Edward King House, The Old Palace, Lincoln LN2 1PU *Tel:* (01522) 528778 *Fax:* (01522) 527308 (*Warden:* Revd Alex Adkins)
LONDON	The Royal Foundation of Saint Katharine, 2 Butcher Row, London E14 8DS *Tel:* 020–7790 3540 *Fax:* 020–7702 7603 (*Master:* Prebendary Ronald Swan)
NEWCASTLE/DURHAM	Shepherd's Dene, Riding Mill, Northumberland NE44 6AF *Tel:* (01434) 682212 (*Warden:* Mr P. Dodgson)
NORWICH	Horstead Centre, Norwich NR12 7EP *Tel:* (01603) 737215 (*Office*); (01603) 737674 (*Guests*) (*Warden:* Mrs Valerie Khambatta)
	All Hallows Convent, Ditchingham, Bungay NR35 2DT *Tel:* (01986) 892749
OXFORD	Priory of Our Lady, Priory Lane, Burford OX18 4SQ *Tel:* (01993) 823605/823141
	Clewer Spirituality Centre, Convent of St John Baptist, Hatch Lane, Windsor SL4 3QR *Tel:* (01753) 850618
	St Mary's Convent, Wantage OX12 9DJ *Tel:* (01235) 763141
PETERBOROUGH	Ecton House, Ecton, Northampton NN6 0QE *Tel:* (01604) 406442 (*Warden:* Revd Stephen Evans)
SALISBURY	Sarum College, 19 The Close, Salisbury SP1 2EE *Tel:* (01722) 424800 *Fax:* (01722) 338508 *email:* admin@sarum.ac.uk (*Director:* Canon Bruce Duncan)
	Society of St Francis, The Friary, Hilfield, Dorchester DT2 7BE *Tel:* (01300) 341345 *Fax:* (01300) 341293
	St Denys Retreat Centre, 2 Church St, Warminster BA12 8PG *Tel:* (01985) 214824

SHEFFIELD	Whirlow Grange Conference Centre, Ecclesall Road South, Sheffield, S Yorks. S11 9PZ *Tel:* 0114–236 3173 (*Office*) and 236 1183 (*Visitors*) (*General Manager:* Mr Jonathon Green)
SOUTHWARK	Wychcroft, Bletchingley, Redhill, Surrey RH1 4NE *Tel:* (01883) 743041 (*Bookings Secretary:* Mr Chris Archer) The Community of Sisters of the Church, St Michael's Convent, 56 Ham Common, Richmond TW10 7JH *Tel:* 020–8940 8711/8948 2502
SOUTHWELL	*See* entry for DERBY.
TRURO	Community of the Epiphany, Copeland Court, Kenwyn, Truro, Cornwall TR1 3DU *Tel:* (01872) 272249
WAKEFIELD	Community of the Resurrection, Mirfield, W Yorks. WF14 0BN *Tel:* (01924) 497596 *Fax:* (01924) 492738 Community of St Peter, Horbury, W Yorks. WF4 6BB *Tel:* (01924) 272181 *Fax:* (01924) 261225
WINCHESTER	Old Alresford Place, Old Alresford, Hants SO24 9DH *Tel:* (01962) 732518 (*Director:* Canon Terry Pinner, *Warden:* Mrs Penny Matthews) *email:* old.alresford.place@dial.pipex.com Alton Abbey, Beech, Alton, Hants GU34 4AP *Tel:* (01420) 562145/563575
WORCESTER	Holland House, Cropthorne, nr Pershore, Worcs. WR10 3NB (*Retreat House*) *Tel:* (01386) 860330 (*Warden:* Mr Peter Middlemiss) *email:* holhse@aol.com
YORK	York Diocesan House, Wydale Hall, Brompton-by-Sawdon, Scarborough, N Yorks. YO13 9DG *Tel:* (01723) 85270 (*Warden:* Mr Peter Fletcher) St Oswald's Pastoral Centre, Woodlands Drive, Sleights, Whitby, N Yorks. YO21 1RY *Tel:* (01947) 810496

Evangelism

The Lambeth Conference recommended that the closing years of this millennium should be 'a "Decade of Evangelism" during which, in cooperation with other Christians, there should be a renewed and united emphasis on making Christ known to the people of his world'. The General Synod of the Church of England endorsed this recommendation at its meeting in York in 1989. The Board of Mission (in partnership with initiatives such as 'Springboard') is working to build upon the lessons learned in the Decade.

The Board has three staff, Canon Robert Freeman (National Adviser for Evangelism), Mission and Evangelism Secretary (Vacancy), and Mr Alan Tuddenham (Administrator), who work closely with the Diocesan Missioners and Advisers on Evangelism. The Officers also work in partnership with their colleagues in other Churches, the ACC, the Missionary Societies, Churches Together in England, and other evangelistic organizations in this country. Their work and the strategy for the work of evangelism beyond the Decade of Evangelism are shaped and encouraged by the Mission, Evangelism and Renewal Committee, a subcommittee of the Board of Mission which draws its membership from a broad cross-section of the traditions within the Church of England.

SPRINGBOARD

Springboard – Lambeth Palace, London SE1 7JU
Administrative Office 4 Station Yard, Abingdon,
Oxon OX14 3LD   *Tel:* (01235) 553722
                                                 Fax: (01235) 553922
        email: springboard.UK@btinternet.com
Director Mr Martin Cavender
Administrator Mr Martin Hayward
Archbishops' Adviser in Evangelism Canon Michael
Green
Springboard Team
Revd Angela Butler (Priest-in-Charge of Chip-
perfield, Herts)
Revd Stephen Cottrell (Wakefield Adviser in
Evangelism)
Revd James Lawrence (Team Evangelist, CPAS)
Canon Robert Warren (former National Officer
for Evangelism)

Working to the vision, 'to encourage, renew and
mobilize the church for evangelism', Springboard is the joint initiative of the Archbishops of
Canterbury and York. Working alongside the
Diocesan Missioners and others, it is an additional resource for dioceses and parishes
throughout the country, and in the wider Anglican Communion. Receiving its policy from the
Archbishops, the strategy for work is set by an
18-member executive representing all the Anglican Church traditions. The core Springboard
Team works alongside others in a widening network of evangelists, missioners, teachers and
other practitioners holding to a three-stranded
cord of 'spirituality – evangelism – and apologet-
ics'. Always working ecumenically, and across
the traditions of the Church, Springboard is
available at the invitation of dioceses, deaneries
and parishes to support and encourage the existing work; to help unlock potential; and to help
increase the effectiveness of the Church in evangelism and mission. Strategic elements of the
work include Diocesan Travelling Schools, Long
Courses in evangelism, conferences, CME/POT
and other leadership training, conferences, work
in theological colleges, and parish, deanery and
area missions and consultancy.

Faculty Office and Special Marriage Licences

The Faculty Office of the Archbishop of Canterbury, otherwise known as The Court of Faculties,
exercises on behalf of the Archbishop the dis-
pensing powers that he has by virtue of the
Ecclesiastical Licences Act of 1533. These comprise the appointment of Notaries Public, the
granting of degrees, and the granting of marriage
licences. The right to grant a Special Licence for
marriage at any convenient time or place in England or Wales is unique to the Archbishop, and
this jurisdiction is sparingly exercised and good
cause must always be shown why a more normal
preliminary to Anglican marriage cannot be
used. Marriage with any other preliminary must
be solemnized between 8.00 a.m. and 6.00 p.m.,
and although a Special Licence could omit this
requirement, that will only in practice be done in
a case of serious illness.

The more common need for a Special Licence is
the parties' desire to marry in a building not
normally authorized for Anglican marriage, or in
a parish where they cannot satisfy the residence
requirements. Even in the last case cause must be
shown, normally in the form of a real connection
with the parish or church in question; the *Special*

*Licence procedure is not intended to enable parties to
choose a church building on aesthetic or sentimental
grounds.*

More detailed guidance on the grounds that
may be considered sufficient for the granting of a
Special Licence may always be sought from the
Faculty Office by letter or telephone.

Special arrangements may sometimes be made
in a genuine emergency. In such cases the clergy
or the couple concerned should first contact the
Diocesan Registrar, archdeacon, or diocesan or
area bishop. If unable to resolve the difficulty
himself he will make arrangements for the Faculty Office to be approached.

Orders made by the Master of the Faculties
prescribe from time to time fees which are to be
charged for applications for Special Licences. The
fee is currently £120.00.

The Faculty Office is open to telephone and
personal callers between 10.00 a.m. and 4.00 p.m.
Monday to Friday, except on certain days around
Easter and Christmas.
Office 1 The Sanctuary, Westminster, London
SW1P 3JT   *Tel:* 020–7222 5381 Ext 2262

Hospice Movement

The word 'Hospice' was first used from the
fourth Century onwards when Christian orders
welcomed travellers, the sick and those in need.
It was first applied to the care of dying patients
by Mme Jeanne Garnier who founded the Dames
de Calvaire in Lyon, France in 1842. The modern
hospice movement, however, with its twin
emphases on medical and psychosocial enquiry,
dates from the founding of St Christopher's Hospice by Dame Cicely Saunders in 1967. Since
1967, 'Hospice' has become a worldwide philosophy adapting to the needs of different

cultures and settings – hospital, hospice and community – and is established in six continents.

Hospice and palliative care is the active, total care of patients whose disease no longer responds to curative treatment, and for whom the goal must be the best quality of life for them and their families. Palliative medicine is now a distinct medical speciality in the UK. It focuses on controlling pain and other symptoms, easing suffering and enhancing the life that remains. It integrates the psychological and spiritual aspects of care, to enable patients to live out their lives with dignity. It also offers support to families, both during the patient's illness and their bereavement. It offers a unique combination of care in hospices and at home.

Hospice and palliative care services mostly help people with cancer although increasingly patients with other life-threatening illnesses may also be supported; this includes HIV/AIDS, Motorneurone Disease, heart failure, kidney dis-ease. Hospice and palliative care is free of charge regardless of whether it is provided by a voluntary hospice, Macmillan Service, Marie Curie Cancer Care, Sue Ryder Home or by an NHS service. The criteria for admission are based on medical, social and emotional need. Referral to a hospice or palliative care service (including inpatient and home care nursing services) is normally arranged by the patient's own GP or hospital doctor. Further information on hospice care in the UK and overseas, including a membership service and publications for health professionals, is available from the Hospice Information Service (*see below*). A *Directory of Hospice and Palliative Care Services in the UK and Ireland* is published annually and is available (on receipt of a large SAE and 70p stamp) from the Hospice Information Service, 51–59 Lawrie Park Rd, Sydenham, London SE26 6DZ   *Tel:* 020–8778 9252
Fax: 020–8776 9345

The Children's Hospice Movement

The Children's Hospice Movement grew out of a recognition that families with children with life-limiting illnesses usually want to look after their children at home once hospital no longer seems appropriate. The strain and loneliness can be very great, especially when the illness is slow and progressive. The children's hospices are small and as much like home as possible, places where children and their families can come to stay from time to time, much in the way that people have a holiday occasionally or go to stay with friends and relatives.

In other societies the existence of the close-knit extended family and the greater involvement of the local community provide a kind of support which is generally lacking in contemporary British society. Using the extended family as their model, children's hospices have a role, outside the immediate family, to be alongside, offering friendship, support and practical help, however protracted, throughout the child's illness and during the terminal phase and the months and years of bereavement that follow.

The children's hospices offer respite care, accompanied or unaccompanied, terminal care and bereavement care. In some cases, home care is also offered. New referrals are not normally accepted over the age of 16. No charge is made to families.

Details of individual hospices for adults and children can be obtained from the Hospice Information Service at the above address.

For details of the **Association of Hospice Chaplains** *see* page 272.

Marriage: Legal Aspects

A comprehensive statement of the law and information on related matters is available from the Faculty Office of the Archbishop of Canterbury. Copies of *Anglican Marriage in England and Wales – A Guide to the Law for Clergy* were sent to incumbents and licensed clergy of the Church of England and the Church in Wales in 1992. Further copies are available by post, price £2.00, from: The Faculty Office, 1 The Sanctuary, Westminster, London SW1P 3JT

For details of **Special Marriage Licences** *see* the entry for the Faculty Office, page 220.

Mothers' Union

The Mothers' Union is an Anglican organization which promotes the well-being of families worldwide. This is done through developing prayer and spiritual growth in families, studying and reflecting on family life and its place in society and resourcing members to take practical action to improve conditions for families, both nationally and in the communities in which they live. It has over 750,000 members throughout the world, and is organized locally into branches attached to a local church It works extensively overseas throughout the Anglican Communion It has a quarterly magazine *Home and Family*.
World Wide President Christine Eames
Chief Executive Mr Reg Bailey
Office Mary Sumner House, 24 Tufton St, London SW1P 3RB   *Tel:* 020–7222 5533
Fax: 020–7222 1591
email: mu@themothersunion.org
Web: http://www.the mothersunion.org

Press

CHURCH TIMES
Established 1863. An independent weekly newspaper which reports on the Anglican Church worldwide. As well as full news coverage, it includes comment and opinion on matters of the day; general features; clergy appointments and resignations; obituaries; reviews of the latest books, music and art; with classified advertisements. Goes to press on Wednesday; published on Friday; price 50p; annual subscription on application. *Editor* Mr Paul Handley. *Office* 33 Upper St, London N1 0PN   *Tel:* 020–7359 4570
Fax: 020–7226 3073/3051
Subscriptions: *Tel:* (01502) 711171
Fax: (01502) 711585

CHURCH OF ENGLAND NEWSPAPER
A weekly newspaper which aims to provide a full, objective and lively coverage of Christian news from Britain and overseas. Contents include general features, book reviews, the latest clergy appointments, a weekly theology page and comment on current issues. Goes to press on Wednesday; published Friday; price 50p (annual subscription £36.00). Now includes *Celebrate* magazine as a weekly feature section. *Editor* C. M. Blakely. *Office* The Church of England Newspaper, 10 Little College St, London SW1P 3SH
Tel: 020–7878 1545
Fax: 020–7976 0783
Subscriptions: *Tel:* 020–7878 1510
Fax: 020–7976 0783
email: cen@parlicom.com

ENGLISH CHURCHMAN
Church of England newspaper (established 1843), incorporating *St James's Chronicle* (1766). Protestant and evangelical. News, various features, diocesan round-up, book reviews, correspondence and church calendar. Published fortnightly, Fridays, price 30p. *Editor* Dr Napier Malcolm. *Office* 22 Lesley Ave, Canterbury, Kent CT1 3LF   *Tel:* (01227) 781282
Fax: (01934) 712520
email: nama@kpws.demon.co.uk

Schools, Church of England

Throughout the country there are 4,774 Church of England schools within the maintained system of education, together with a number of schools in the private sector which are able to claim strong connection with the Church. The term 'Church of England School' is at present properly applicable only to voluntary aided, controlled, special agreement and grant maintained Church of England schools, which are funded through the local Education Authority and the Department for Education as part of the national schools system, whilst still retaining their position as autonomous educational charities. New legislation in 1998 changed the nomenclature and status of controlled, special agreement and grant maintained Church of England schools.

All such schools lie within the responsibilities of the Diocesan Boards of Education. They provide education for 904,000 children and young people, and represent a major investment on the part of the Church of England in the national education system. In addition to these schools there are many independent schools, founded on trusts which provide that worship and religious teaching taking place in them shall be of a Church of England character. These include many of the well-known public schools and grammar schools of ancient foundation, some of which are associated with cathedrals or other major Churches.

In recent years, Government legislation has created and continues to create a number of changes both in the framework within which all schools are required to operate and also in the arrangements for their administration. Such changes challenge the governors and staff of Church schools to establish clear policies which indicate how they express their understanding of their role as Church of England schools in their particular circumstances. In this task the schools are supported by the staff of the Diocesan Boards of Education as stipulated by the DBE Measure and by the work of the General Synod Board of Education and the National Society, which provides a range of publications and other resources. The National Society has also established training courses for inspectors of Church schools under section 23 of the School Inspection Act 1996. Details of these courses and of the publications and support service provided by the National Society and the General Synod Board of Education can be obtained from their offices, whose address is given elsewhere in the Year Book. Details of individual schools may be obtained from the Diocesan Directors of Education in the case of maintained schools or in *The Church of England Schools and Colleges Handbook* (published by The School Government Publishing Company), and in the case of independent schools from the *Public and Preparatory Schools Year Book* (published by A & C Black).

Services Authorized and Commended

Public worship in the Church of England is a matter governed by law.

Canon B2 provides that the General Synod may approve forms of service with or without time limit. Services thus approved are alternative to those of *The Book of Common Prayer*. The power given to General Synod under Canon B2 derives from the Worship and Doctrine Measure 1974.

Canon B4 provides that the convocations, the archbishops in their provinces or the bishops in their dioceses may approve forms of service for use on occasions for which *The Book of Common Prayer* or *Authorized Alternative Services* do not provide.

Canon B5 (paragraph 2) allows discretion to any minister where no other provision has been made under Canons B1 or B4, to use other forms of service which are considered suitable. If questions are raised as to whether such forms of service are suitable the decision rests with the bishop.

Authorized Alternative Services are those approved by the General Synod under Canon B1 (for fuller details *see* page 224).

Commended Services are those which the bishops corporately have judged to be 'suitable' either for approval under Canon B4 or for use in the contexts envisaged in Canon B5 (for fuller details *see* page 225).

The forms of service currently *authorized* for use in public worship (as at 1 January 1999) are: *the Book of Common Prayer* – authorized without time limit.

The Alternative Service Book 1980 and *Ministry to the Sick* – authorized until 31 December 2000 with the exception of the Ordinal in *The Alternative Service Book 1980* which is authorized to 31 December 2005.

Series 1 Solemnization of Matrimony, Series 1 Burial Services – authorized until 31 December 2005.

Series 2 Baptism and Confirmation – authorized until 31 December 2000.

Further Alternative Rules to Order the Service together with an Additional Alternative Lectionary – authorized until 31 December 2000.

A Service of the Word – authorized until further resolution of the General Synod.

Affirmations of Faith – authorized until further resolution of the General Synod.

Common Worship, Calendar, Lectionary and Collects – authorized until further resolution of the General Synod.

Common Worship, Initiation Services – authorized until further resolution of the General Synod.

A leaflet entitled *Public Worship in the Church of England* was issued on the authority of the Standing Committee of the General Synod (sixth edition, published in 1994), taking account of the revision of the liturgical canons and the authorization of *A Service of the Word*. A new edition is envisaged in 2001.

A further leaflet entitled *A Brief Guide to Liturgical Copyright* deals with the procedures for local reproduction. It provides guidance on preparing local texts and information about copyright requirements. The current edition (October 1997) is available price £1.50 from Church House Bookshop.

a) *The Alternative Service Book 1980* containing   *Corresponding separate editions*
The Calendar and Rules to Order the
Service
General Notes
Sentences

Morning Prayer and Evening Prayer	ASB 10 Morning and Evening Prayer
Prayers for Various Occasions	ASB 12 Evening Prayer
Holy Communion Rite A	ASB 20 Holy Communion Rite A
Holy Communion Rite B	ASB 22 Holy Communion Rite B
Initiation Services	ASB 31 Baptism of Children (card)
	ASB 35 Thanksgiving for the Birth of a Child/or after Adoption (card)
	ASB 40 Confirmation
The Marriage Service	ASB 50 Marriage Service
Funeral Services	ASB 60 Funeral Services (large format)
	ASB 62 Funeral Services (standard format)

The Ordinal (authorized to 31 December
2005)

Sentences, Collects and Readings	ASB 87 Collects
Tables of Psalms, Readings and Sunday Themes	Collects (Traditional Language) for use with Rite B

b) Ministry to the Sick (1983)

ASB 70 contains Communion with the Sick (Rite A and Rite B), The Laying on of Hands with Prayer, and Anointing, A Commendation at the Time of Death, Prayers for Use with the Sick	ASB 71 Ministry to the Sick (card) (Distribution of Communion Rite A, Laying on of Hands)
	ASB 73 (Rite A) Holy Communion at Home
	ASB 74 (Rite B) (or in Hospital) (cards)

c) Series 2 Baptism and Confirmation
d) Further Alternative Rules to Order the
Service together with an Additional
Alternative Lectionary (these are for use
with the Prayer Book).

e) Series 1 Solemnization of Matrimony	AS 152 Matrimony
Series 1 Burial Services	AS 160 Burial Services (standard format)
	AS 162 Burial Services (large format)

f) A Service of the Word } published together
Affirmations of Faith
g) Common Worship – Calendar, Lectionary
and Collects
Selections of this material are also contained
in:
h) Common Worship: Collects and Post
Communion Prayers for Sundays and
Festivals
i) Common Worship: Advent 1999 to Advent
2000 (the third in a series of annual
publications)
j) Common Worship: Initiation Services

k) A Service for Remembrance Sunday
(*see also The Promise of His Glory* below)

COMMENDED SERVICES
COMMENDED BY THE HOUSE OF BISHOPS OF THE GENERAL SYNOD

Services of Prayer and Dedication after Civil Marriage (1985)

Lent, Holy Week, Easter: Services and Prayers (1986)
   Night Prayer: A Service for Late Evening (from the above, published separately (1987))

Funeral Service for a Child dying near the time of birth (1989)

Ministry at the Time of Death (1991)

The Promise of His Glory: Services and Prayers for the Season from All Saints to Candlemas (1991)
(This includes the Service for Remembrance Sunday — *see* (k) above)
NOTE The suggested Calendar and Lectionaries appended to the above are now subsumed in a revised form in the newly authorized calendar and lectionary.

Patterns for Worship (1995) (this incorporates texts commended by the House of Bishops and the authorized A Service of the Word and Affirmations of Faith)

VERSIONS OF THE BIBLE AND OF THE PSALMS

The following may be used in Book of Common Prayer services (with the permission of the PCC) instead of the Authorized Version of the Bible and the Psalter in *The Book of Common Prayer*:

Bible	*Psalters*
Revised Version	Revised Psalter
Revised Standard Version	The Liturgical Psalter (The Psalms
New English Bible	a New Translation for Worship)
Jerusalem Bible	
Good News Bible	
(Today's English Version)	

NOTE: Any version of the Bible or Psalter may be used with alternative services.

TV and Radio

BBC LOCAL RADIO
There are thirty-nine BBC local radio stations in counties and cities throughout England. Each station is responsible for its own religious broadcasting and some have religious advisory panels. Religious programmes are often presented and produced by local clergy and lay people who observe the editorial policy of the BBC. For details of stations, contact the BBC Regions' Press Office   *Tel:* 020–7765 2795

BBC RELIGIOUS BROADCASTING DEPARTMENT
Arranges a wide variety of religious broadcasts for transmission in the BBC's television service, local radio, the five domestic radio services and the World Service. The aims of religious broadcasting are (1) to seek to reflect the worship, thought and action of the principal religious traditions represented in the UK, recognizing that those traditions are mainly, though not exclusively, Christian; (2) to seek to present to viewers and listeners those beliefs, ideas, issues and experiences in the contemporary world which are evidently related to a religious interpretation or dimension of life; and (3) to seek also to meet the religious interests, concerns and needs of those on the fringe of, or outside, the organized life of the religious bodies. On matters of policy the Corporation is advised by a representative Central Religious Advisory Committee which also acts as adviser to the ITC. *Head of Religious Broadcasting* Revd Ernest Rea, BBC, Room 5038, Oxford Rd, Manchester M60 1SJ

CENTRAL RELIGIOUS ADVISORY COUNCIL
CRAC advises the BBC and the ITC on policy matters relating to religion. Its membership is drawn from the major Christian traditions and world faiths represented in the United Kingdom. CRAC can be contacted c/o the BBC or ITC.

CHURCHES' ADVISORY COUNCIL FOR LOCAL BROADCASTING

CACLB is an ecumenical body with charitable status established in 1967 for the advancement of the Christian religion through broadcasting on radio and television. It is a formal network of CTBI. Its council is drawn from the Church of England, Roman Catholic Church, Methodist, Baptist, United Reformed, Evangelical Alliance, Salvation Army, Free Churches' Council, CTBI, Churches Together in England, Church of Ireland, Churches Together in Wales, and ACTS (Scotland), with representatives of the BBC, Independent Television Commission, Radio Authority, Association of Christians in Broadcasting, Churches Media Trust, and Christian broadcast training organizations. *President* Baroness Emma Nicholson. *Chairman* Rt Revd Tom Butler, Bishop of Southwark. *Gen Secretary* Mr Jeff Bonser, PO Box 124, Westcliff-on-Sea, Essex SS0 0QU   *Tel:*(01702) 348369
Fax: (01702) 305121
email: office@caclb.org.uk
Web: http://www.caclb.org.uk

FOUNDATION FOR CHRISTIAN COMMUNICATION LTD (CTVC)

Major producer and co-producer of religious television programmes. Distributes television programmes worldwide. Training courses are held in the use of radio and television and in personal communication. Television and sound studios fitted to full broadcast standard and post-production facilities. All are available for hire. A large video distribution service is available on request. Catalogue available. *Director* Revd Barrie Allcott, Hillside Studios, Merry Hill Rd, Bushey, Watford, Herts. WD2 1DR   *Tel:* 020–8950 4426
Fax: 020–8950 1437
email: ctvc@ctvc.co.uk
web: http://www.ctvc.co.uk

INDEPENDENT RADIO

The Radio Authority licenses and regulates all commercial radio services (non-BBC). It is responsible for monitoring the obligation on its licensees required by the Broadcasting Acts 1990 and 1996. The Authority is required, after consultation, to publish Codes to which its licensees must adhere. These cover programmes (including religious broadcasts), advertising and sponsorship, and engineering. Complaints about the content of any broadcast on an Independent Radio station should be addressed to the station concerned, or to the Radio Authority, Holbrook House, 14 Great Queen St, London WC2B 5DG
Tel: 020–7430 2724
Fax: 020–7405 7062
email: info@radioauthority.org.uk
Web: http://www.radioauthority.org.uk

INDEPENDENT TELEVISION COMMISSION

The Independent Television Commission was established under the Broadcasting Act 1990 to regulate all non-BBC television services in the United Kingdom including the terrestrial channels, ITV, Channel 4, Channel 5, and services on satellite and cable television. Further details from Ms Rachel Viney, Religious Broadcasting Officer, ITC, 33 Foley St, London W1P 7LB
Tel: 020–7306 7848

INDEPENDENT TELEVISION, RELIGIOUS PROGRAMMES ON

Religious Broadcasting on Independent Television includes programmes which are carried by the entire ITV network; programmes on Channels 4 and 5; items on the breakfast service, and programmes made by individual ITV companies for their own regional audiences. Most of the ITV network religious programmes are shown on Sundays. Regional religious programmes, usually transmitted during the week, though not exclusively so, include documentary series, religious magazine programmes and short reflective slots.

Anglican Advisers to the ITV Companies:
ANGLIA TELEVISION Canon Philip Spence, Norman Hall, Minster Precincts, Peterborough PE1 1XS   *Tel:* (01733) 564899
CENTRAL INDEPENDENT TELEVISION Mrs A. M. Gatford, 72 Pastures Hill, Littleover, Derby DE3 7BB   *Tel:* (01332) 512700
Rt Revd John Saxby, Bishop's House, Corvedale Rd, Halford, Craven Arms, Shropshire SY7 9BT
Tel: (01588) 673571
BORDER TELEVISION Revd Christopher Morris, Vicarage, Lanercost, Brampton, Cumbria CA8 2HQ   *Tel:* (01697) 72478
CHANNEL TELEVISION Revd Marc Trickey, St Martin's Rectory, Grande Rue, Guernsey
Tel: (01481) 38303
GRAMPIAN TELEVISION Revd Emsley Nimmo, St Margaret's House, Gallowgate, Aberdeen AB1 1EA   *Tel:* (01224) 644969
GRANADA TELEVISION Revd David Johnston, 671 Chorley New Rd, Horwich, Bolton BL6 6HR
Tel: (01204) 699301
HTV WEST Rt Revd Peter Firth, 7 Ivywell Rd, Bristol BS9 1NX   *Tel:* (01904) 634531
LONDON WEEKEND TELEVISION Revd Dr Perry Butler, c/o LWT, Southbank Television Centre, London SE1 9TL   *Tel:* 020–7261 3434
MERIDIAN BROADCASTING c/o Revd Ray Short, 36–38 Southampton St, London SE1 9RD
TYNE TEES TELEVISION Canon Peter Strange, St Nicholas Cathedral, Newcastle upon Tyne NE1 1PF   *Tel:* 0191–232 1939
ULSTER TELEVISION Rt Revd Dr James Mehaffey, The See House, Culmore Rd, Londonderry
Tel: (01504) 51206

WESTCOUNTRY TELEVISION c/o Sue Bannister, Westcountry Television, Langage Science Park, Plymouth, Devon PL7 5BG
Mr Jeremy Dowling, Rosecare Villa Farm, St Gennys, Bude EX23 0BG　*Tel:* (01840) 230326
YORKSHIRE TELEVISION Revd Martin Short, 30 Newall Hall Park, Otley, W Yorks. LS21 2RD
Tel: (01943) 465071

SANDFORD ST MARTIN (CHURCH OF ENGLAND) TRUST

A registered charity founded 1978 to support excellence in broadcast programmes concerned with religion and spiritual values, and to encourage Christian participation and interest in radio and television. The Trust makes five awards annually for outstanding programmes concerned with religion. These awards are given to radio and television in alternate years. The Trust was initially provided from an Anglican source but its scope is ecumenical. The Trust has sponsored a number of consultations and courses including, in 1995, a seminar with the Farmington Institute for teachers of religious education and writers and producers working in religious broadcasting. As a result of this consultation, the Trust made a further series of awards in 1997 and 1999 for outstanding programmes in the specific field of religious education. *Chairman* Rt Revd Nigel McCulloch, Bishop of Wakefield. *Hon Secretary* Dr Robert Towler, Church House, Great Smith St, London SW1P 3NZ　*Tel:* 020–7898 1796
Fax: 020–7898 1797
email: SandfordSMT@c-of-e.org.uk

WORLD ASSOCIATION FOR CHRISTIAN COMMUNICATION (WACC)

WACC is an organization of corporate and personal members who wish to give high priority to Christian values in the world's communication and development needs. It is not a council or federation of churches. The majority of members are communication professionals from all walks of life. Others include partners in different communication activities, and representatives of churches and agencies. It funds communication activities that reflect regional interests, and encourages ecumenical unity among communicators. As a professional organization, WACC serves the wider ecumenical movement by offering guidance on communication policies, interpreting developments in communications worldwide, discussing the consequences that such developments have for churches and communities everywhere but especially in the Third World, and assisting the training of Christian communicators. It publishes *Action*, a newsletter, ten times a year, and the quarterly journal *Media Development*. It has 819 members in 117 countries. UK members include the Anglican Communion Office, BBC Religious Programmes Dept, The Foundation for Christian Communication, Council for World Mission, Feed the Minds, Church of England Communications Unit, Independent Television Commission, and SPCK. *Gen Secretary* Revd Carlos A. Valle, 357 Kennington Lane, London SE11 5QY　*Tel:* 020–7582 9139
Fax: 020–7735 0340
email: wacc@wacc.org.uk
web: http://www.wacc.org.uk

Women's Ministry

Women and men may be ordained priest or deacon, licensed as Accredited Lay Worker or admitted as Reader. Under the Priests (Ordination of Women) Measure 1993 and Canon C4B, women may be ordained priest and are eligible for appointment to most offices in the Church of England. There is no provision for women to become bishops. Under Canon C21 a deacon who has been ordained for more than six years may now be appointed as canon residentiary of a cathedral.

Theological Colleges and Regional Courses

THEOLOGICAL COLLEGES			Fees
Address and Telephone Number	Diocese	Principal or Warden	p.a. £
Cranmer Hall (St John's College), Durham DH1 3RJ *Tel:* 0191–374 3579 *Fax:* 0191–374 3573	Durham	Rt Revd Stephen Sykes (Principal) Revd Dr Steven Croft (Warden)	7,020
College of the Resurrection, Mirfield, W Yorks WF14 0BW *Tel:* (01924) 490441 *Fax:* (01924) 492738 *email:* CIrvine@mirfield.org.uk	Wakefield	Revd Christopher Irvine	4,407
Oak Hill Theological College, Southgate, London N14 4PS *Tel:* 020–8449 0467 *Fax:* 020–8441 5996 *email:* DavidP@Oakhill.ac.uk	London	Revd Dr David Peterson	7,299
The Queen's College, Somerset Rd, Edgbaston, Birmingham B15 2QH (Ecumenical) *Tel:* 0121–454 1527 *Fax:* 0121–454 8171 *email:* Queens-College@compuserve.com	Birmingham	Revd Peter Fisher	7,401
Ridley Hall, Cambridge CB3 9HG *Tel:* (01223) 741080 *Fax:* (01223) 741081 *email:* SMB41@cam.ac.uk	Ely	Revd Graham Cray	7,443
Ripon College, Cuddesdon, Oxford OX44 9EX *Tel:* (01865) 874404	Oxford	Revd John Clarke	7,245
St John's College, Chilwell Lane, Bramcote, Nottingham NG9 3DS *Tel:* 0115–925 1114 *Fax:* 0115–943 6438	Southwell	Dr Christina Baxter	7,320
St Stephen's House, 16 Marston St, Oxford OX4 1JX *Tel:* (01865) 247874 *Fax:* (01865) 794338 *email:* dgmoss@ermine.ox.ac.uk	Oxford	Revd Dr Jeremy Sheehy	7,020
Trinity College, Stoke Hill, Bristol BS9 1JP *Tel:* 0117–968 2803 *Fax:* 0117–968 7470 *email:* principal@trinity-bris.ac.uk	Bristol	Revd Dr Francis Bridger	7,290
Westcott House, Jesus Lane, Cambridge CB5 8BP *Tel:* (01223) 741000 *Fax:* (01223) 741002 *email:* westcott-house@lists.cam.ac.uk	Ely	Revd Michael Roberts	7,425
Wycliffe Hall, Oxford OX2 6PW *Tel:* (01865) 274200 *Fax:* (01865) 274215 *email:* enquiries@wycliffe.ox.ac.uk	Oxford	Revd Dr Alister McGrath	7,122
Theological Institute of the Scottish Episcopal Church, Old Coates House, 32 Manor Place, Edinburgh EH3 7EB *Tel:* 0131–220 2272 *Fax:* 0131–220 2294 *email:* tisec@scotland.anglican.org	Edinburgh	Revd Dr Michael Fuller	N/A
St Michael's College, Llandaff, Cardiff CF5 2YJ *Tel:* 029 2056 3379 *Fax:* 029 2057 6377 *email:* stmichaels@nildram.co.uk	Llandaff	Revd Dr John Holdsworth	N/A

REGIONAL COURSES	
Address and Telephone Number	Principal or Director

Carlisle and Blackburn Diocesan Training Institute
    Church House, West Walls, Carlisle, Cumbria CA3 8UE
    Tel: (01228) 522573
	Canon Tim Herbert

East Anglian Ministerial Training Course
    EAMTC Office, 5 Pound Hill, Cambridge CB3 0AE
    Tel: (01223) 741026 *Fax:* (01223) 741027
    email: admin@eamtc.org.uk
	Vacancy

East Midlands Ministry Training Course
    University of Nottingham, Jubilee Campus, Wollaton Rd,
    Nottingham NG8 1BB *Tel:* 0115–951 4854 *Fax:* 0115–951 4817
    email: emmtc@nottingham.ac.uk
	Revd Michael Taylor

North East Oecumenical Course
    Regional office: Ushaw College, Durham DH7 9RH *Tel:*
    0191–373 7600 *Fax:* 0191–373 7601 *email:* neocoffice@aol.com
	Canon Trevor Pitt

Northern Ordination Course
    Luther King House, Brighton Grove, Rusholme,
    Manchester M14 5JP *Tel:* 0161225 6668 *Fax:* 0161–248 9201
    email: office@noc1.u-net.com
	Revd Chris Burdon

North Thames Ministerial Training Course
    Chase Side, Southgate, London N14 4PS *Tel:* 020–8364 9442
    Fax: 020–8364 8889
	Revd David Sceats

St Albans and Oxford Ministry Course
    Diocesan Church House, North Hinksey, Oxford OX2 0NB
    Tel: (01865) 208260 *Fax:* (01865) 790470
	Revd Dr Mike Butterworth

South East Institute for Theological Education
    Ground Floor, Sun Pier House, Sun Pier, Medway St,
    Chatham, Kent ME4 4HF *Tel:* (01634) 832299
	Revd Alan Le Grys

Southern Theological Education and Training Scheme
    19 The Close, Salisbury, Wilts SP1 2EE *Tel:* (01722) 412996
    Fax: (01722) 424811 *email:* cjcocksworth@stets.ac.uk
	Revd Dr Christopher Cocksworth

South West Ministry Training Course
    SWMTC Office, Petherwin Gate, North Petherwin,
    Launceston PL15 8LW *Tel:* (01566) 785545
    Fax: (01566) 785749 *email:* swmtc@surfaid.org
	Revd Dr David Hewlett

West Midlands Ministerial Training Course
    Queen's Birmingham, Somerset Rd, Edgbaston,
    Birmingham B15 2QH *Tel:* 0121–452 2604
	Revd Dr Dennis Stamps

West of England Ministerial Training Course
    7c College Green, Gloucester GL1 2LX *Tel* and *Fax:* (01452)
    300494 *email:* betty@wemtc.freeserve.co.uk
	Revd Dr Richard Clutterbuck

GENERAL

ORDAINED LOCAL MINISTRY SCHEMES RECOGNIZED BY THE HOUSE OF BISHOPS	
Address and Telephone Number	Principal or Director
Canterbury OLM Scheme, Diocesan House, Lady Wootton's Green, Canterbury, Kent CT1 1NQ *Tel:* (01227) 459401 *Fax:* (01227) 450964	Revd Alan Dodds
Carlisle LNSM Scheme, Church House, West Walls, Carlisle, Cumbria CA3 8UE *Tel:* (01228) 522573	Canon Tim Herbert
Gloucester OLM, 4 College Green, Gloucester GL1 2LX *Tel:* (01452) 410022 *Fax:* (01452) 382905 *email:* localmin@glosdioc.org.uk	Mrs Caroline Pascoe
Guildford Diocesan Ministry Course, Vicarage, 5 Burwood Rd, Hersham, Surrey KT12 4AA *Tel:* (01932) 269343 *Fax:* (01932) 230274 *email:* hazel@nickhaze.demon.co.uk	Revd Hazel Whitehead
Hereford Local Ministry Scheme, The Cottage, Bishop Mascall Centre, Lower Galdeford, Ludlow, Shropshire SY8 1RZ *Tel:* (01584) 872822 *Fax:* (01584) 877945	Preb Gill Sumner
Lichfield OLM Scheme, Backcester Lane, Lichfield WS13 6JH *Tel:* (01543) 411550 *Fax:* (01543) 411552 *email:* rob.daborn@lichfield.anglican.org	Revd Robert Daborn
Lincoln OLM Scheme, The Forum, Church House, Lincoln LN2 1PU *Tel:* (01522) 528886 *Fax:* (01522) 512717 *email:* lincolndio@claranet.co.uk	Revd Kathryn Windslow
Liverpool OLM Scheme, Rectory, Halsall Rd, Halsall, Ormskirk, Lancs L39 8RN *Tel:* (01704) 841202	Canon Peter Goodrich
Manchester OLM Scheme, Church House, 90 Deansgate, Manchester M3 2GJ *Tel:* 0161–832 5785 *Fax:* 0161–832 1466 *email:* bom.manchesterdio@btinternet.com	Canon Wendy Bracegirdle
Newcastle LNSM Scheme, Denewood, Clayton Rd, Jesmond, Newcastle NE2 1TL *Tel:* 0191–281 9930/1452 or 0191–263 7922 *Fax:* 0191–281 1452	Canon Richard Bryant
Norwich OLM Scheme, Emmaus House, 65 The Close, Norwich NR1 4DH *Tel:* (01603) 611196 *Fax:* (01603) 766476	Canon John Goodchild
Oxford LNSM, SAOMC, Diocesan Church House, North Hinksey, Oxford OX2 0NB *Tel:* (01865) 208260	Revd Dr Mike Butterworth
St Edmundsbury and Ipswich Diocesan Ministry Course, Diocesan House, 13 Tower St, Ipswich IP1 3BG *Tel:* (01473) 211028	Canon Michael West
Southwark OLM Scheme, Diocese of Southwark Ministry Development Dept, St Michael's Church Hall, Trundle St, London SE1 1QT *Tel:* 020–7378 7506 *Fax:* 020–7403 6497 *email:* trundlest@dwark.org.uk	Revd Stephen Lyon
Truro OLM Scheme, Diocesan House, Kenwyn, Truro TR1 1JQ *Tel:* (01872) 276766/274351 *Fax:* (01872) 222510	Revd David Thurburn-Huelin

TABLES

Selected Church Statistics

The following pages contain a selection of tables reprinted from *Church Statistics* (published as General Synod Misc Paper 549) and *Statistics of Licensed Ministers* (published as General Synod Misc Paper 561).

Please note that in Tables D to I the following definitions apply:-

Income

Total planned giving — net covenants including regular Gift Aid donations and non-covenanted planned giving

Total direct giving — planned giving plus church collections and boxes.

Other voluntary income — all other voluntary income for ordinary expenditure excluding direct giving and income tax on covenants. e.g. fund-raising events, net profit on magazine/bookstall, sundry donations.

Total voluntary income — direct giving plus income tax on covenants plus other voluntary income.

Expenditure

Total charitable donations — payments by parochial church councils to:

(a) the recognized missionary societies, or other overseas missions, diocesan associations, Diocesan Mission Councils.

(b) Christian organizations primarily concerned with relief and development.

(c) payments to home missions and other Church societies and organizations (including the Church Urban Fund).

(d) payments to other charities which are secularly based.

Please also note that:

1. Many figures in these tables have been rounded, and that in general totals, percentages and averages were calculated before rounding. Hence row and column totals will not always agree exactly with the sum of the stated amounts.

2. Among the 13,000 parishes of the Church of England there are a number of Local Ecumenical Projects in some (around 300) of which there is a congregation and a ministry shared between the Church of England and certain other churches. In such circumstances it is not always possible (or indeed desirable) to isolate the Anglican component of the congregation. The parochial membership figures will therefore include a small element which may appear also in the statistics of other churches.

3. Where figures are not available for any reason, 'n.a.' appears in the tables.

A Distribution of Full-time Stipendiary Diocesan Clergy

(Actual and according to the deployment formula)

Ref. No.	Diocese	December 31st 1998 Actual	December 31st 1998 Share	Number over under (-) share	Percent over under (-) share	*
1	Bath and Wells	250	232	18	7.8%	(4)
2	Birmingham	223	209	14	6.7%	(6)
3	Blackburn	245	234	11	4.7%	(9)
4	Bradford	124	122	2	1.6%	(16)
5	Bristol	158	153	5	3.3%	(13)
6	Canterbury	185	174	11	6.3%	(7)
7	Carlisle	153	156	-3	-1.9%	(26)
8	Chelmsford	414	446	-32	-7.2%	(40)
9	Chester	287	292	-5	-1.7%	(25)
10	Chichester	344	320	24	7.5%	(5)
11	Coventry	150	148	2	1.4%	(18)
12	Derby	184	191	-7	-3.7%	(31)
13	Durham	237	243	-6	-2.5%	(27)
14	Ely	163	157	6	3.8%	(12)
15	Exeter	259	273	-14	-5.1%	(36)
16	Gloucester	162	162	0	0.0%	(22)
17	Guildford	197	178	19	10.7%	(2)
18	Hereford	119	125	-6	-4.8%	(35)
19	Leicester	161	170	-9	-5.3%	(37)
20	Lichfield	377	372	5	1.3%	(19)
21	Lincoln	238	247	-9	-3.6%	(30)
22	Liverpool	255	251	4	1.6%	(17)
23	London	550	529	21	4.0%	(11)
24	Manchester	298	312	-14	-4.5%	(32)
25	Newcastle	153	165	-12	-7.3%	(41)
26	Norwich	198	223	-25	-11.2%	(43)
27	Oxford	465	442	23	5.2%	(8)
28	Peterborough	162	173	-11	-6.4%	(39)
29	Portsmouth	115	128	-13	-10.2%	(42)
30	Ripon	160	159	1	0.6%	(21)
31	Rochester	238	212	26	12.3%	(1)
32	St. Albans	292	300	-8	-2.7%	(28)
33	St. Edms and Ipswich	167	175	-8	-4.6%	(34)
34	Salisbury	234	245	-11	-4.5%	(33)
35	Sheffield	198	192	6	3.1%	(14)
36	Sodor and Man	22	20	2	10.0%	(3)
37	Southwark	382	367	15	4.1%	(10)
38	Southwell	189	187	2	1.1%	(20)
39	Truro	129	133	-4	-3.0%	(29)
40	Wakefield	178	181	-3	-1.7%	(24)
41	Winchester	245	247	-2	-0.8%	(23)
42	Worcester	163	160	3	1.9%	(15)
43	York	284	302	-18	-6.0%	(38)
	Province of Canterbury	**6,924**	**6,891**	**33**	**0.5%**	
	Province of York	**2,783**	**2,816**	**-33**	**-1.2%**	
	CHURCH OF ENGLAND	**9,707**	**9,707**			

NOTES The 'Actual' is the number of full-time clergy plus the whole-time equivalent of the part-time clergy.

The set of figures marked * gives the magnitude, in descending order, of the figures immediately to the left. Thus Bath and Wells Diocese is the 4th highest and Birmingham is the 6th.

B   Non-Stipendiary Ministers and Church Army Evangelists 1998

Ref. No.	Diocese		Non-stipendiary Clergy			Ordained Local Ministers			Church Army		
			men	women	total	men	women	total	men	women	total
1	Bath and Wells	C	24	16	40				4	2	6
2	Birmingham	C	14	6	20				2	2	4
3	Blackburn	Y	15	9	24				5	1	6
4	Bradford	Y	7	4	11				3	2	5
5	Bristol	C	19	8	27					1	1
6	Canterbury	C	29	17	46				3	1	4
7	Carlisle	Y	20	11	31				2	1	3
8	Chelmsford	C	37	43	80				9	4	13
9	Chester	Y	22	10	32				1	1	2
10	Chichester	C	53	19	72				6	3	9
11	Coventry	C	10	11	21				5	1	6
12	Derby	C	19	13	32				2	3	5
13	Durham	Y	17	13	30				3		3
14	Ely	C	24	11	35				5	3	8
15	Exeter	C	39	22	61				9		9
16	Gloucester	C	28	13	41	5	2	7	5	5	10
17	Guildford	C	27	14	41	9	4	13	4		4
18	Hereford	C	15	10	25				1		1
19	Leicester	C	27	14	41				3	1	4
20	Lichfield	C	21	13	34	5	3	8	8	7	15
21	Lincoln	C	22	12	34	14	7	21	1	1	2
22	Liverpool	Y	25	3	28	2	7	9	6	3	9
23	London	C	78	22	100				9	6	15
24	Manchester	Y	37	12	49	20	15	35	7	2	9
25	Newcastle	Y	15	14	29						
26	Norwich	C	21	11	32	17	11	28	3	1	4
27	Oxford	C	120	40	160	6	7	13	11	6	17
28	Peterborough	C	14	7	21				2	1	3
29	Portsmouth	C	28	28	56				2		2
30	Ripon	Y	10	4	14				4	2	6
31	Rochester	C	32	13	45				3	3	6
32	St. Albans	C	51	37	88				6	4	10
33	St. Edms & Ipswich	C	21	14	35	11	5	16	3	1	4
34	Salisbury	C	32	26	58	6	4	10	3		3
35	Sheffield	Y	12	2	14				15	4	19
36	Sodor and Man	Y	12		12						
37	Southwark	C	77	27	104	18	10	28	14	4	18
38	Southwell	Y	27	25	52				1	2	3
39	Truro	C	23	5	28	4	3	7	2		2
40	Wakefield	Y	16	9	25				4	2	6
41	Winchester	C	35	24	59				2	2	4
42	Worcester	C	14	10	24				2	2	4
43	York	Y	17	10	27				8		8
Totals Province of Canterbury (C)			**954**	**506**	**1,460**	**95**	**56**	**151**	**129**	**64**	**193**
Totals Province of York (Y)			**252**	**126**	**378**	**22**	**22**	**44**	**59**	**20**	**79**
Totals CHURCH OF ENGLAND			**1,206**	**632**	**1,838**	**117**	**78**	**195**	**188**	**84**	**272**

C   Licensed Readers 1998

Ref. No.	Diocese		Admissions during year		Number licensed at 31 December 1998				Number in training at 31 December 1998	
			men	women	men		women		men	women
1	2		3	4	5		6		7	8
1	Bath and Wells	C	6	11	159	(40)	92	(13)	15	19
2	Birmingham	C	10	6	102	(21)	78	(4)	11	13
3	Blackburn	Y	14	9	121	(24)	73	(6)	15	18
4	Bradford (a)	Y	3	6	68	(17)	40	(6)	5	13
5	Bristol	C	9	10	87	(25)	68	(7)	3	8
6	Canterbury	C	2	6	81	(16)	68	(5)	10	16
7	Carlisle	Y	4	4	87	(25)	50	(6)	4	4
8	Chelmsford	C	9	8	192	(33)	133	(12)	21	20
9	Chester	Y	11	16	247	(45)	153	(8)	45	36
10	Chichester	C	4	5	140	(63)	73	(13)	26	12
11	Coventry	C	6	3	94	(24)	40	(9)	4	21
12	Derby	C	10	10	159	(5)	105	(5)	21	29
13	Durham	Y	6	4	84	(13)	41	(1)	9	28
14	Ely	C	9	9	83	(13)	57	(3)	12	25
15	Exeter	C	9	8	104	(58)	60	(15)	23	32
16	Gloucester	C	5	12	121	(41)	103	(13)	17	13
17	Guildford	C	7	6	115	(18)	60	(4)	19	13
18	Hereford	C	1	1	43	(11)	37	(6)	7	10
19	Leicester	C	5	1	108	(27)	70	(10)	7	8
20	Lichfield	C	11	11	274	(49)	150	(6)	11	11
21	Lincoln	C	5	12	88	(25)	71	(3)	15	25
22	Liverpool	Y	11	9	201	(18)	122	(4)	23	33
23	London	C	9	4	125	(28)	74	(5)	23	24
24	Manchester	Y	3	3	155	(44)	67	(10)	12	15
25	Newcastle	Y	6	3	60	(15)	44	(5)	14	12
26	Norwich	C	7	13	135	(31)	102	(21)	34	26
27	Oxford	C	12	8	203	(37)	132	(15)	23	29
28	Peterborough	C	1	6	68	(12)	40	(4)	13	9
29	Portsmouth	C	11	6	62	(15)	40	(7)	20	16
30	Ripon	Y	2	5	56	(19)	49	(2)	7	12
31	Rochester	C	13	15	188	(43)	105	(13)	25	24
32	St. Albans	C	8	9	127	(42)	87	(10)	28	42
33	St. Edms & Ipswich	C	10	10	112	(38)	74	(11)	25	25
34	Salisbury	C	4	4	115	(43)	68	(14)	11	11
35	Sheffield	Y	4	10	134	(0)	88	(0)	15	15
36	Sodor and Man	Y	-	1	14	(0)	10	(0)	6	3
37	Southwark	C	12	12	198	(39)	104	(18)	34	44
38	Southwell	Y	9	12	151	(29)	113	(10)	27	24
39	Truro	C	3	3	55	(24)	37	(8)	4	2
40	Wakefield	Y	2	9	83	(21)	75	(6)	10	22
41	Winchester	C	6	7	113	(54)	59	(12)	24	20
42	Worcester	C	4	6	83	(14)	41	(3)	11	8
43	York	Y	4	8	136	(39)	105	(12)	21	20
Totals Province of Canterbury (C)			208	222	3,534	(889)	2,228	(269)	497	555
Totals Province of York (Y)			79	99	1,597	(309)	1,030	(76)	213	255
Totals CHURCH OF ENGLAND			287	321	5,131	(1,198)	3,258	(345)	710	810

NOTE   Figures in brackets in cols 5 and 6 refer to the additional number of Readers with Permission to Officiate and active Emeriti.

Selected Financial Comparisons 1964 to 1997

D Covenanted planned giving to Parochial Church Councils:
Contributors, amounts and average weekly rates

Year	Subscribers under covenants 000s	Actual		In real terms of 1997*	
		Covenanted giving: net subscriptions £ 000s	Weekly average per subscriber £	Covenanted giving: net subscriptions £ 000s	Weekly average per subscriber £
1	2	3	4	5	6
1964	126	2,113	0.32	23,436	3.58
1970	168	3,325	0.38	28,307	3.24
1980	362	17,692	0.94	41,652	2.21
1990	405	71,130	3.38	88,842	4.22
1991	403	77,902	3.71	91,907	4.38
1992	403	86,617	4.14	98,500	4.71
1993	405	95,301	4.52	106,680	5.06
1994	405	103,745	4.93	113,393	5.39
1995	404	111,045	5.28	117,301	5.58
1996	404	118,111	5.62	121,824	5.79
1997	401	124,439	5.96	124,439	5.96

E Uncovenanted planned giving to Parochial Church Councils:
Contributors, amounts and average weekly rates

Year	Uncovenanted planned giving subscribers 000s	Actual		In real terms of 1997*	
		Uncovenanted planned giving: subscriptions £ 000s	Weekly average per subscriber £	Uncovenanted planned giving: subscriptions £ 000s	Weekly average per subscriber £
1	2	3	4	5	6
1964	1,029	7,198	0.13	79,837	1.49
1970	800	6,348	0.15	54,044	1.30
1980	529	13,748	0.50	32,366	1.18
1990	326	23,565	1.39	29,433	1.74
1991	326	26,243	1.55	30,960	1.83
1992	317	29,212	1.77	33,220	2.01
1993	311	31,257	1.93	34,990	2.16
1994	304	32,845	2.08	35,899	2.27
1995	298	34,401	2.22	36,340	2.34
1996	290	35,032	2.32	36,133	2.39
1997	283	36,490	2.48	36,490	2.48

F Direct giving to Parochial Church Councils

Year	Actual		In real terms of 1997*	
	Total direct giving £ 000s	Weekly average per electoral roll member £	Total direct giving £ 000s	Weekly average per electoral roll member £
1	2	3	4	5
1964	14,961	0.11	165,941	1.18
1970	15,847	0.12	134,914	1.03
1980	51,521	0.55	121,294	1.29
1990	141,076	1.94	176,205	2.43
1991	152,549	2.04	179,974	2.41
1992	164,854	2.17	187,469	2.47
1993	175,898	2.29	196,901	2.57
1994	187,468	2.44	204,900	2.67
1995	197,163	2.58	208,271	2.73
1996	205,417	3.06	211,875	3.16
1997	215,599	3.15	215,599	3.15

GENERAL

G Total voluntary income of Parochial Church Councils

Year	Actual		In real terms 1997*	
	Total voluntary income £ 000s	Weekly average per electoral roll member £	Total voluntary income £ 000s	Weekly average per electoral roll member £
1	2	3	4	5
1964	20,033	0.14	222,197	1.59
1970	22,110	0.17	188,234	1.44
1980	72,798	0.77	171,385	1.82
1990	195,193	2.69	243,797	3.36
1991	212,974	2.85	251,262	3.36
1992	230,005	3.03	261,558	3.45
1993	246,050	3.21	275,429	3.59
1994	262,886	3.42	287,332	3.74
1995	275,388	3.61	290,903	3.81
1996	288,358	4.30	297,423	4.43
1997	305,345	4.46	305,345	4.46

H Total ordinary income of Parochial Church Councils

Year	Total ordinary income	
	Actual £000s	In real terms of 1997* £000s
1	2	3
1964	22,108	245,212
1970	26,396	224,723
1980	85,880	202,184
1990	237,385	296,496
1991	256,796	302,962
1992	273,546	311,072
1993	287,421	321,740
1994	307,598	336,201
1995	327,531	345,983
1996	344,897	355,738
1997	374,324	374,324

I Charitable giving and total ordinary expenditure by Parochial Church Councils

Year	Actual		In real terms of 1997*	
	Total charitable donations £ 000s	Total ordinary expenditure £ 000s	Total charitable donations £ 000s	Total ordinary expenditure £ 000s
1	2	3	4	5
1964	2,173	21,711	24,102	240,809
1970	2,593	28,038	22,076	238,702
1980	8,480	77,849	19,964	183,277
1990	24,573	227,314	30,692	283,917
1991	25,945	250,704	30,609	295,774
1992	26,366	270,365	29,983	307,455
1993	24,990	289,447	27,974	324,008
1994	25,814	307,698	28,214	336,311
1995	25,154	320,197	26,571	338,237
1996	25,361	338,671	26,158	349,317
1997	26,874	365,433	26,874	365,433

NOTES ON TABLES D to I
1. Figures for cathedrals and their daughter churches are included.
2. * i.e. adjusted by the Retail Price Index to reflect 1997 purchasing power.

J Marriages in England 1981–1995

	Number of marriages solemnized			Marriages solemnized in Church of England as a proportion per 1,000 marriages	
	Church of England	With religious ceremonies	All marriages	With religious ceremonies	All marriages
1981	111,819	168,182	332,213	665	337
1982	110,511	166,305	323,137	665	342
1983	110,348	165,720	324,443	666	340
1984	111,248	167,761	330,012	663	337
1985	110,121	166,330	327,241	662	337
1986	111,476	168,417	328,411	662	339
1987	114,958	172,245	332,233	667	346
1988	112,184	168,535	329,183	666	341
1989	112,612	168,869	327,244	667	344
1990	109,369	163,634	312,712	668	350
1991	97,446	145,889	290,118	668	336
1992	96,828	145,418	294,962	666	328
1993	91,214	137,457	283,326	664	322
1994	86,143	130,500	275,531	660	313
1995	79,616	119,901	268,344	664	297

* Figures exclude Isle of Man (Sodor and Man Diocese) and Channel Islands (part of Winchester Diocese) together with a small number of Church of England parishes in Wales.

K Combinations of previous marital condition in England and Wales 1995

Marital condition	Church of England / Church in Wales	With religious ceremonies	All marriages
All	83,685	127,522	283,012
Bachelor marrying:			
Spinster	74,509	101,293	166,418
Widow	354	546	1,437
*Divorced woman	2,086	6,729	30,353
Widower marrying:			
Spinster	334	546	1,276
Widow	903	1,509	3,082
*Divorced woman	268	722	3,479
*Divorced man marrying:			
Spinster	3,556	9,589	30,909
Widow	192	618	3,021
*Divorced woman	1,483	5,970	43,037

* no record is kept of whether the previous partner is still alive.

Source: Marriage and Divorce statistics, 1995. Crown Copyright 1998. Reproduced by permission of the Controller of HMSO and the Office for National Statistics.

Note: 1995 is the latest year for which these data are available.

GENERAL

L Baptisms 1997

Ref. No.	Diocese	Live births 1997	Baptisms			
			Infants under one year of age	Infant baptism rates per 1,000 live births	Children aged 1 to 12 years	All other persons
1	2	3	4	5	6	7
1	Bath and Wells	8,900	3,000	340	710	230
2	Birmingham	20,100	2,600	127	960	160
3	Blackburn	15,200	4,000	261	900	150
4	Bradford	8,900	1,400	159	360	60
5	Bristol	11,500	2,200	192	620	130
6	Canterbury	9,700	2,700	280	1,010	190
7	Carlisle	5,200	2,500	484	410	80
8	Chelmsford	35,500	4,900	137	2,060	420
9	Chester	18,000	5,100	285	1,250	200
10	Chichester	16,100	4,200	259	1,330	370
11	Coventry	9,000	1,900	211	590	80
12	Derby	11,200	2,800	251	620	140
13	Durham	16,900	5,200	310	980	120
14	Ely	7,400	2,100	289	530	150
15	Exeter	11,200	3,100	279	930	220
16	Gloucester	6,900	2,200	323	540	160
17	Guildford	11,400	3,100	274	980	210
18	Hereford	3,100	1,400	458	310	50
19	Leicester	10,800	1,900	172	560	140
20	Lichfield	24,100	5,900	245	1,600	260
21	Lincoln	10,200	4,700	457	920	210
22	Liverpool	18,500	4,900	265	1,260	180
23	London	50,400	4,100	81	2,230	590
24	Manchester	25,600	5,100	201	1,350	210
25	Newcastle	8,500	2,500	288	530	90
26	Norwich	8,600	2,400	286	690	180
27	Oxford	27,100	6,900	255	2,030	360
28	Peterborough	9,500	2,100	217	760	180
29	Portsmouth	8,000	1,900	233	610	100
30	Ripon	9,100	2,200	241	590	100
31	Rochester	15,300	3,200	207	1,280	240
32	St. Albans	21,600	4,300	197	1,630	370
33	St. Edms & Ipswich	7,000	1,800	253	480	120
34	Salisbury	9,300	2,900	316	860	150
35	Sheffield	14,100	3,700	262	840	120
36	Sodor and Man	900	200	279	70	10
37	Southwark	35,400	4,300	121	1,970	380
38	Southwell	12,200	2,600	213	850	180
39	Truro	5,100	1,500	301	460	120
40	Wakefield	13,500	3,100	233	720	150
41	Winchester	14,000	4,400	316	1,130	230
42	Worcester	9,900	2,800	283	770	120
43	York	15,300	5,100	329	1,060	230
	Totals Province of Canterbury	**428,200**	**91,200**	**213**	**29,200**	**6,260**
	Totals Province of York	**181,800**	**47,600**	**262**	**11,180**	**1,890**
	Totals CHURCH OF ENGLAND	**610,000**	**138,900**	**228**	**40,380**	**8,150**
Comparable figures for 1996 :						
	Totals Province of Canterbury	**430,200**	**92,700**	**215**	**28,190**	**5,900**
	Totals Province of York	**186,700**	**48,700**	**261**	**11,370**	**1,840**
	Totals CHURCH OF ENGLAND	**616,900**	**141,400**	**229**	**39,560**	**7,740**

NOTES
1. Figures for cathedrals are included.
2. The information in columns 4, 6 and 7 was extracted from the 1997 parochial returns. Data in columns 3 and 5 are based on statistics obtained from the Office for National Statistics (ONS).
3. The figures in columns 6 and 7 have been rounded to the nearest 10. Other roundings in the table are to the nearest 100.

M   Confirmations 1997

Ref. No.	Diocese	Services	Males	Females	Totals
1	2	3	4	5	6
1	Bath and Wells	59	324	482	806
2	Birmingham	57	243	440	683
3	Blackburn	114	835	1,149	1,984
4	Bradford	29	186	200	386
5	Bristol	58	236	318	554
6	Canterbury	79	349	605	954
7	Carlisle	76	287	512	799
8	Chelmsford	126	604	1,002	1,606
9	Chester	114	461	755	1,216
10	Chichester	116	654	905	1,559
11	Coventry	53	246	366	612
12	Derby	59	224	393	617
13	Durham	37	309	551	860
14	Ely	30	186	285	471
15	Exeter	102	400	659	1,059
16	Gloucester	59	234	418	652
17	Guildford	146	399	519	918
18	Hereford	41	121	209	330
19	Leicester	51	214	319	533
20	Lichfield	136	656	1,120	1,776
21	Lincoln	58	278	402	680
22	Liverpool	97	569	962	1,531
23	London	207	905	1,385	2,290
24	Manchester	114	632	1,054	1,686
25	Newcastle	67	210	290	500
26	Norwich	44	198	336	534
27	Oxford	176	964	1,309	2,273
28	Peterborough	45	279	463	742
29	Portsmouth	28	186	293	479
30	Ripon	56	259	423	682
31	Rochester	80	406	679	1,085
32	St. Albans	98	534	846	1,380
33	St. Edms & Ipswich	55	165	272	437
34	Salisbury	72	414	711	1,125
35	Sheffield	80	235	419	654
36	Sodor and Man	10	23	24	47
37	Southwark	110	651	1,116	1,767
38	Southwell	32	244	323	567
39	Truro	47	127	217	344
40	Wakefield	70	212	438	650
41	Winchester	108	404	630	1,034
42	Worcester	53	230	383	613
43	York	123	430	751	1,181
44	Europe	37	93	132	225
	Province of Canterbury	**2,353**	**10,831**	**17,082**	**27,913**
	Province of York	**1,056**	**4,985**	**7,983**	**12,968**
	CHURCH OF ENGLAND	**3,409**	**15,816**	**25,065**	**40,881**

Comparative figures for 1996 (do not include Europe)

	Province of Canterbury	**2,386**	**11,427**	**17,645**	**29,072**
	Province of York	**1,100**	**5,252**	**8,444**	**13,696**
	CHURCH OF ENGLAND	**3,486**	**16,679**	**26,089**	**42,768**

NOTE   Confirmations in the Armed Forces are not included.

Church Electoral Rolls

C.B.F. ref nos	Dioceses	Numbers on Church Electoral Rolls 1989	Numbers on Church Electoral Rolls 1994	
(1)	(2)	(3)	(4)	(5)
	PROVINCE OF CANTERBURY			**1. QUALIFICATION**
1	Bath and Wells	53,777	49,082	
2	Birmingham	21,433	20,832	
5	Bristol	23,322	22,971	
6	Canterbury	23,515	21,910	
8	Chelmsford	59,082	60,111	
10	Chichester	72,247	67,101	
11	Coventry	23,308	20,718	
12	Derby	25,759	24,533	
14	Ely	26,961	24,386	
15	Exeter	42,932	39,147	
16	Gloucester	32,040	29,862	
17	Guildford	40,140	34,140	
18	Hereford	22,802	20,665	
19	Leicester	22,327	19,181	
20	Lichfield	62,306	58,961	
21	Lincoln	40,213	32,850	
23	London	49,307	47,775	
26	Norwich	34,935	32,042	
27	Oxford	66,736	64,923	
28	Peterborough	23,244	22,518	
29	Portsmouth	22,015	21,687	
31	Rochester	39,524	36,669	
32	St Albans	61,271	54,402	
33	St Edms. and Ipswich	28,614	27,808	
34	Salisbury	54,317	51,190	
37	Southwark	51,651	50,718	
39	Truro	25,028	21,254	
41	Winchester	45,195*	43,470*	
42	Worcester	22,323	24,173	
44	Europe	10,284	10,158	
	Totals, Province of Canterbury	**1,126,608**	**1,055,580**	
	PROVINCE OF YORK			
3	Blackburn	63,587	47,797	
4	Bradford	16,992	15,542	
7	Carlisle	34,015	27,980	
9	Chester	55,386	56,563	
13	Durham	39,240	32,420	
22	Liverpool	42,324	38,655	
24	Manchester	47,550	42,658	
25	Newcastle	20,978	20,802	
30	Ripon	29,358	26,814	
35	Sheffield	24,768	24,938	
36	Sodor and Man	3,923	3,359	
38	Southwell	24,053	22,341	
40	Wakefield	29,604	28,025	
43	York	42,826	42,039	
	Totals, Province of York	**474,604**	**429,933**	
	GRAND TOTALS	**1,601,212**	**1,485,513**	

* This figure excludes the Channel Islands

1. QUALIFICATION

In 1919–20 a new system of Church Government was set up. The electoral basis was the roll which had to be prepared in each parish and there have been only small changes in qualifications for entry since that time. The present rule provides that a person may apply for entry if he/she (i) is baptized; (ii) is a member of the Church of England or another Church of the Anglican Communion or Church in Communion with the Church of England; (iii) is sixteen or over and (iv) is resident in the parish or if not so resident, has habitually attended public worship in the parish during a period of six months prior to enrolment.

2. REVISION

Church electoral rolls are revised annually, the names of those no longer qualified being removed and the names of others applying being added. The system is not always effective in establishing a realistic roll as insufficient care may be taken in revision. Another important factor is that any person who is baptized and resident has a right to claim membership of the Church of England and entry on the roll regardless of whether he/she attends services or otherwise shows interest in Church affairs. The names of persons within this category cannot be removed without their consent.

3. NEW ROLLS

The Church Representation Rules attached to the Synodical Government Measure 1969 required that in 1972 for the first time existing rolls should come to an end, and that thereafter new rolls should be prepared every six years. The fourth preparation of new rolls was in 1990 and the fifth took place in 1996.

4. INTERPRETATION

It is impossible to draw any accurate conclusions from the figures on either the total membership of the Church or the practising membership for the following reasons:

(1) The roll is an electoral roll not a membership roll. No member need apply for entry unless he/she wishes to exercise certain rights.

(2) Any resident may have his/her name entered on the new roll regardless of whether he/she is a practising member.

(3) Since 1974 a person may have his/her name on any number of rolls if he/she is properly qualified. Previously he/she could be enrolled in two parishes, but not more.

(4) Persons under the age of seventeen were not eligible until the qualifying age was reduced to sixteen as from 1 May 1980.

(5) While parishes are urged to inform qualified practising Church members of their rights, it is likely that there are considerable differences in the steps taken and energy with which they are pursued.

But having mentioned these caveats the figures are of interest.

The figures for 1989 and 1994 are those certified in those years by the secretaries of diocesan synods: the numbers of members elected to the House of Laity of the General Synod are based on these figures.

TABLE OF PAROCHIAL FEES **From 1 January 2000** Prepared by the Archbishops' Council under the Ecclesiastical Fees Measure 1986 Authorized by the Parochial Fees Order 1999	Fee payable towards stipend of incumbent (See Note 2)	Fee payable to Parochial Church Council	Total fee payable
	£	£	£
BAPTISMS			
Certificate issued at time of baptism	8.00	—	8.00
Short certificate of baptism given under Section 2, Baptismal Registers Measure 1961	6.00	—	6.00
MARRIAGES			
Publication of banns of marriage	10.00	5.00	15.00
Certificate of banns issued at time of publication	8.00	—	8.00
Marriage service	60.00	72.00	132.00
(Marriage certificate – See Note 6)			
FUNERALS AND BURIALS			
Service in church			
Funeral service in church	36.00	30.00	66.00
Burial in churchyard following on from service in church	—	119.00	119.00
Burial in cemetery or cremation following on from service in church (See Note 3(ii))	—	—	NIL
Burial of body in churchyard on separate occasion (See Notes 3(iii))	24.00	119.00	143.00
Burial of cremated remains in churchyard on separate occasion	24.00	36.00	60.00
Burial in cemetery on separate occasion (See Note 3(ii))	24.00	—	24.00
No service in church			
Service in crematorium or cemetery (See Note 3(ii))	66.00	—	66.00
Burial of body in churchyard (See Note 3(iv))	24.00	119.00	143.00
Burial of cremated remains in churchyard (See Note 3(iv))	24.00	36.00	60.00
Certificate issued at time of burial (See Note 3(v))	8.00	—	8.00
MONUMENTS IN CHURCHYARDS			
Erected with consent of incumbent under Chancellor's general directions –			
Small cross of wood	4.00	8.00	12.00
Small vase not exceeding 305mm × 203mm × 203mm (12" × 8" × 8")	8.00	17.00	25.00
Tablet, erected horizontally or vertically and not exceeding 533mm × 533mm (21" × 21"), commemorating person cremated	15.00	29.00	44.00
Any other monument	34.00	68.00	102.00
(the above fees to include the original inscription)			
Additional inscription on existing monument (See Note 4)	24.00	—	24.00
SEARCHES IN CHURCH REGISTERS, ETC.			
Searching registers of marriages for period before 1 July 1837 (See Note 5)			
(for up to one hour)	8.00	5.00	13.00
(for each subsequent hour or part of an hour)	6.00	5.00	11.00
Searching registers of baptisms or burials (See Note 5) (including the provision of one copy of any entry therein) (for up to one hour)	8.00	5.00	13.00
(for each subsequent hour or part of an hour)	6.00	5.00	11.00
Each additional copy of an entry in a register of baptisms or burials	8.00	5.00	13.00
Inspection of instrument of apportionment or agreement for exchange of land for tithes deposited under the Tithe Act 1836	6.00	—	6.00
Furnishing copies of above (for every 72 words)	6.00	—	6.00

'EXTRAS'
The fees shown in this table are the statutory fees payable. It is stressed that the figures do not include any charges for extras such as music (e.g. organist, choir), bells, flowers and special heating, which are fixed by the Parochial Church Council.

Published by
The Archbishops' Council,
Ministry Division,
1 Millbank,
LONDON SW1P 3JZ

NOTES

1 Definitions
The definitions in the Order include the following:
'Burial' includes deposit in a vault and the interment or deposit of cremated remains.
'Churchyard' includes the curtilage of a church and a burial ground of a church whether or not immediately adjoining such church.
'Cemetery' means a burial ground maintained by a Burial Authority.
'Monument' includes headstone, cross, kerb, border, vase, chain, railing, tablet, flatstone, tombstone or monument or tomb of any other kind.

2 Incumbent's Fee
Incumbents declare their fees to the Diocese, which takes them into account in determining the stipend paid to the incumbent.

3 Funerals and Burials
(i) No fee is payable in respect of a burial of a still-born infant, or for the funeral or burial or an infant dying within one year after birth.
(ii) The fees prescribed by this table for a funeral service in any cemetery or crematorium are mandatory except where a cemetery or crematorium authority has itself fixed different charges for these services, in which case the authority's charges apply.
(iii) The fee for a burial in a churchyard on a *separate occasion* applies when burial does not follow on from a service in church.
(iv) If a full funeral service is held at the graveside in a churchyard the incumbent's fee is increased to that payable where the service is held in church.
(v) The certificate issued at the time of burial is a copy of the entry in the register of burials kept under the Parochial Registers and Records Measure 1978.

4 Monuments in Churchyards
The fee for an additional inscription on a small cross of wood, a small vase or a tablet not exceeding 533mm × 533mm shall not exceed the current fee payable to the incumbent for the erection of such a monument.

5 Searches in Church Registers
The search fee relates to a particular search where the approximate date of the baptism, marriage or burial is known. The fee for a more general search of a church register would be negotiable.

6 Fee for Marriage Certificate
The following fees are currently payable to the incumbent under the Registration of Births, Deaths and Marriages (Fees) Order 1998: certificate of marriage —
at registration £3.50; subsequently £6.50.
These fees may be increased from 1 April 2000.

ROYAL PECULIARS, THE CHAPELS ROYAL, ETC.

 ## Westminster Abbey

Description of Arms. Azure, a cross patonce between five martlets or; on a chief or France and England quarterly on a pale, between two roses, gules, seeded and barbed proper.

COLLEGIATE CHURCH OF ST PETER

The collegiate church of St Peter in Westminster, usually called Westminster Abbey, is a Royal Peculiar, and, as such, it is extra-provincial as well as extra-diocesan and comes directly under the personal jurisdiction of Her Majesty the Queen, who is the Visitor.

Throughout medieval times it was the Abbey Church of a great Benedictine Monastery, which was in existence at Westminster before the Norman Conquest. After the dissolution of the monastery in 1540 it became increasingly a great national shrine, where famous writers, poets, statesmen and leaders in the Church and State are buried. It is the Coronation Church, and in it also take place from time to time Royal weddings and many services on great occasions of a National or Commonwealth character. Daily, the Holy Communion is celebrated and Morning and Evening Prayers are said or sung.

DEAN
Very Revd Wesley Carr, The Deanery, Westminster [1997]   *Tel:* 020–7222 2953
     email: dean@westminster-abbey.org
     web: http://www.westminster-abbey.org

CANONS OF WESTMINSTER
Archdeacon and SubDean Canon David Hutt, 5 Little Cloister, SW1P 3PL [1995]
     Tel: 020–7222 6939
     email: david.hutt@westminster-abbey.org

Treasurer and Almoner Canon Michael Middleton, 1 Little Cloister, SW1P 3PL [1997]
     Tel: 020–7222 5791
email:
     michael.middleton@westminster-abbey.org

Lector Theologiae Canon Tom Wright, 3 Little Cloister, SW1P 3PL [1999]
     Tel: 020–7222 4174

RECTOR OF ST MARGARET'S
Revd Robert Wright, 2 Little Cloister, London SW1P 3PL [1999]   *Tel:* 020–7222 4027
     Fax: 020–7233 2131
     email: robert.wright@westminster-abbey.org

PRECENTOR
Revd Dominic Fenton, 7 Little Cloister SW1P 3PL [1995]   *Tel:* 020–7222 4023
     email: dominic.fenton@westminster-abbey.org

CHAPLAIN AND SACRIST
Revd John Townend, 4B Little Cloister, SW1P 3PL [1998]   *Tel:* 020–7222 1386
     email: john.townend@westminster-abbey.org

PRIEST VICARS
Revd John Pedlar
Revd Roger Holloway
Revd Philip Chester
Revd Peter Cowell
Revd Dr Paul Bradshaw
Revd Huw Mordecai

PASTORAL ASSISTANT
Sister Hilary Markey CSMV

LAY OFFICERS
High Steward The Lord Blake of Braydeston, Norfolk

Deputy High Steward The Rt Worshipful the Lord Mayor of Westminster

High Bailiff and Searcher of the Sanctuary The Lord Weatherill

Deputy High Bailiff Rear Admiral Kenneth Snow

Chapter Clerk and Receiver General Major-General David Burden, 2 The Cloister, SW1P 3PA
     Tel: 020–7222 5152
     email: david.burden@westminster-abbey.org

Registrar Mr S. J. Holmes (*same address*)
     email: stuart.holmes@westminster-abbey.org

Organist and Master of the Choristers Mr James O'Donnell, correspondence c/o The Chapter Office

Surveyor of the Fabric Mr John Burton, 2b Little Cloister, SW1P 3PL   *Tel:* 020–7222 5801

Legal Secretary Mr C. L. Hodgetts, Thomas Eggar & Son, East Pallant, Chichester, Sussex PO19 1TS
     Tel: (01243) 786111

Auditor Mr D. Hunt, Binder Hamlyn, 20 Old Bailey, London EC4M 7BH   *Tel:* 020–7489 9000

Librarian Dr Tony Trowles, The Library, Westminster Abbey, London SW1P 3PL
     Tel: 020–7222 5152
     email: tony.trowles@westminster-abbey.org

Headmaster of the Choir School Mr R. P. Overend, Dean's Yard, London SW1P 3NY
Tel: 020–7222 6151

Keeper of the Muniments Dr R. Mortimer, The Muniments Room and Library, Westminster Abbey, London SW1 3PL   *Tel:* 020–7222 515
email: richard.mortimer@westminster-abbey.or;

Windsor

Description of Arms. The shield of St George, argent a cross gules, encircled by the Garter

THE QUEEN'S FREE CHAPEL OF ST GEORGE WITHIN HER CASTLE OF WINDSOR

A ROYAL PECULIAR
Founded by Edward III in 1348 and exempt from diocesan and provincial jurisdictions, the College of St George is a self-governing secular community of priests and laymen, the first duty of which is to celebrate Divine Service daily on behalf of the Sovereign, the Royal House and the Order of the Garter. Its present Chapel was founded by Edward IV in honour of Our Lady, St George and St Edward in 1475 and, with the cloisters and buildings annexed, is vested in the Dean and Canons. In it the Eucharist, Mattins and Evensong are sung or said daily and are open to all.

The Order of the Garter has its stalls and insignia in the Quire, where Knights and Ladies Companions are installed by the Sovereign. Beneath the Quire — the scene of many Royal funerals — are vaults in which lie the bodies of six monarchs. Elsewhere in the Chapel are the tombs of four others.

The College has its own school, where it maintains twenty-four choristerships. It also awards an organ scholarship. A house for conferences has been established under the name of St George's House.

THE VISITOR
The Lord Chancellor

DEAN
Rt Revd David Conner, The Deanery, Windsor Castle, Windsor, Berks SL4 1NJ [1998]
Tel: (01753) 865561

CANONS
Precentor Canon John White, 8 The Cloisters, Windsor Castle [1982]   *Tel:* (01753) 860409

Treasurer Canon Barry Thompson, 4 The Cloisters, Windsor Castle [1998]
Tel: (01753) 864142

Steward Canon Laurence Gunner, 6 The Cloisters, Windsor Castle [1996]
Tel: (01753) 86631;

Chaplain in the Great Park Canon John Ovenden Chaplain's Lodge, Windsor Great Park, Windsor Berks [1998]   *Tel:* (01784) 43243

MINOR CANONS
Succentor and Dean's Vicar Vacancy
Revd Trevor Harvey, 12 The Cloisters, Windsor Castle [1987]   *Tel:* (01753) 84208(

LAY OFFICERS
Chapter Clerk Lt Col Nigel Newman, Chapter Office, The Cloisters, Windsor Castle [1990]
Tel: (01753) 86553(

Organist and Master of the Choristers Mr Jonathan Rees-Williams, 23 The Cloisters, Windsor Castle [1991]   *Tel:* (01753) 86452(

Clerk of Accounts Mr Stanford Robinson, Chapter Office, The Cloisters   *Tel:* (01753) 86141(

Clerk of Works Mr Fred Wilson, Clerk of Works Office, The Cloisters   *Tel:* (01753) 860824

Archivist and Librarian Dr Eileen Scarff, The Aerary, The Cloisters
Tel: (01753) 857942 *or* 865538

Virger Mr David Wilson, 22 Horseshoe Cloister, Windsor Castle   *Tel:* (01753) 859218

Headmaster, St George's School Mr Roger Jones, St George's School, Windsor Castle
Tel: (01753) 865553

Warden, St George's House Vacancy, St George's House, Windsor Castle   *Tel:* (01753) 861341

Domestic Chaplains to Her Majesty the Queen

Buckingham Palace Revd William Booth
Windsor Castle The Dean of Windsor

Sandringham Canon George Hall

Chapels Royal

The Chapel Royal is the body of Clergy, Singers and Vestry Officers appointed to serve the spiritual needs of the Sovereign — in medieval days on Progresses through the Realm as well as upon the battlefields of Europe, as at Agincourt. Its ancient foundation is first century with the British Church: its latter day choral headquarters have been at St James's Palace since 1702 along with the Court of St James. Since 1312 the Chapel Royal has been governed by the Dean who, as the Ordinary, also exercises, along with the Sub-Dean, jurisdiction over the daughter establishments of Chapels Royal at the Tower of London and at Hampton Court Palace. Members of the public are welcome to attend Sunday and week-day services as advertised.

The Chapel Royal conducts the Service of Remembrance at the Cenotaph in Whitehall, with Forces Chaplain in company, and combines with the choral establishment of the host abbey or cathedral on the occasion of Royal Maundy, under the governance of the Lord High Almoner and Sub-Almoner. Each Member of the College of thirty-six Chaplains to Her Majesty the Queen, headed by the Clerk and Deputy Clerk of the Closet, is required by Warrant to preach with the Chapel Royal once a year, and are visibly distinguished, along with the Chapel Royal, Forces and Mohawk Chaplains, by the wearing of red cassocks.

Dean of the Chapels Royal
The Bishop of London

Sub-Dean
Revd William Booth
Chapel Royal, St James's Palace, London SW1

CHAPEL ROYAL, ST JAMES'S AND THE QUEEN'S CHAPEL, ST JAMES'S

Priests in Ordinary
Revd Richard Bolton
Canon Paul Thomas
Revd Stephen Young

Deputy Priests
Revd Paul Abram
Revd Hugh Mead
Revd Mark Oakley
Revd Timothy Thornton

HAMPTON COURT PALACE
East Molesey, Surrey   *Tel:* 020–8977 2762

Chaplain
Vacancy

HM TOWER OF LONDON
The Chaplain's Residence, London EC3N 4AP
                                           Tel: 020–7709 0765
(includes the Chapels Royal of St John the Evangelist and St Peter ad Vincula.)

CHAPLAIN
Revd Paul Abram

THE ROYAL CHAPEL OF ALL SAINTS, WINDSOR GREAT PARK
This is a Private Chapel and the property of the Crown within the grounds of the Royal Lodge. Attendance is restricted to residents and employees of the Great Park.

Chaplain
Revd John Ovenden, Chaplain's Lodge, Windsor Great Park, Windsor, Berks   *Tel:* (01784) 432434

College of Chaplains

The position of Royal Chaplain is a very ancient one. The College of Chaplains, the members of which as such must not be confused with the Priests in Ordinary, preach according to a Rota of Waits in the Chapels Royal. The College comprises the Clerk of the Closet (who presides), the Deputy Clerk of the Closet, and thirty-six Chaplains. When a vacancy in the list of chaplains occurs, the Private Secretary to Her Majesty the Queen asks the Clerk of the Closet to suggest possible names to Her Majesty. The duties of the Clerk of the Closet include the presentation of bishops to Her Majesty when they do homage before taking possession of the revenues of their Sees; and he also examines theological books whose authors desire to present copies to Her Majesty the Queen. He preaches annually in the Chapel Royal, St James's Palace.

CLERK OF THE CLOSET
The Bishop of Derby (Rt Revd Jonathan Bailey)

DEPUTY CLERK OF THE CLOSET
Revd William Booth

CHAPLAINS TO HER MAJESTY THE QUEEN
Revd David Adams
Ven Douglas Bartles-Smith
Ven Frank Bentley
Canon Michael Benton
Canon Andrew Bowden
Canon Raymond Brazier
Canon Eric Buchanan
Revd David Burgess
Canon Peter Calvert
Canon Rex Chapman

Canon Anthony Chesterman
Revd Robert Clarke
Canon James Colling
Canon Alan Craig
Canon Christine Farrington
Ven David Fleming
Canon Roger Gilbert
Canon Donald Gray
Canon George Hall
Canon Ian Hardaker
Revd John Haslam
Canon Glyndwr Jones
Canon Marion Mingins
Canon Brian Osborne
Ven Keith Pound
Revd John Priestley

Revd John Robson
Ven Ian Russell
Canon Ivor Smith-Cameron
Canon John Stanley
Canon John Sykes
Canon Lionel Webber
Canon David Wheaton

Extra Chaplains
Canon Anthony Caesar
Canon Eric James
Canon Gerry Murphy
Revd John Stott
Preb Austen Williams
Ven Edwin Ward

Royal Almonry

The Royal Almonry dispenses the Queen's charitable gifts and is responsible for the Royal Maundy Service each year, at which Her Majesty distributes Maundy money to as many men and as many women pensioners as the years of her own age.

HIGH ALMONER
Rt Revd Nigel McCulloch (*Bishop of Wakefield*)

SUB-ALMONER
Revd William Booth
Chapel Royal, St James's Palace, London SW1

The Queen's Chapel of the Savoy

Savoy Hill, Strand, London WC2R 0DA
Tel: 020–7836 7221

CHAPEL OF THE ROYAL VICTORIAN ORDER
The Queen's Chapel of the Savoy is the Chapel of Her Majesty The Queen in right of her Duchy of Lancaster, and Her Majesty the Queen appoints the chaplain. It is, therefore, a 'free' Chapel not falling within any ecclesiastical jurisdiction.

On the occasion of his Coronation in 1937, the late King George VI commanded that the sixteenth-century Chapel of the Savoy should be placed at the disposal of the Victorian Order and be regarded by members as their Chapel. Membership of the Order is an honour in the personal gift of the Sovereign. By Her Majesty the Queen's appointment the present chaplain is also Chaplain of the Order.

In 1958, an Ante-Chapel, a Robing Room for the Queen and a Chaplain's Room were added. A new three-manual Walker organ was presented to the Chapel by Her Majesty the Queen in 1965.

Members of the public are most welcome to attend the Services on Sundays (11.00 a.m.) and weekdays with the exception of those for special or official occasions. The Chapel uses the Book of Common Prayer and has a particularly fine musical tradition with a choir of men and boys.

CHAPLAIN
Revd John Robson, Chaplain of the Royal Victorian Order [1989]
Tel and *Fax:* 020–7379 8088

MASTER OF MUSIC
Mr Philip Berg

VERGER
Mr Phillip Chancellor   *Tel:* 020–7836 7221

HONORARY WARDENS
Mr Colin Brough
Mr William Culver
Mr Randall Edwards
Dr Roy Palmer
Sir Walter Verco
Mr Stephen White

Royal Memorial Chapel Sandhurst

Camberley, Surrey GU15 4PQ
The Royal Memorial Chapel Sandhurst, the Domestic Chapel of the Royal Military Academy Sandhurst is also the Memorial Chapel of the officers of the Army.

Built in 1879 it was considerably enlarged between 1919 and 1921 (though some work was not completed until 1937) as a memorial to all Sandhurst-trained officers who gave their lives in the First World War.

Following the Second World War, the names of all officers of the Armies of the British Commonwealth who died in that conflict were inscribed on a Roll of Honour. A page of this book is turned at the commencement of the main Sunday service.

A Book of Remembrance containing the names of all former cadets who have been killed or died whilst serving since 1947 is kept in the Chapel of Remembrance, sometimes referred to as the South Africa Chapel.

All services are normally open to the public on application for a pass.

CHAPLAIN
Revd Alan Brown

CHOIRMASTER AND ORGANIST
Mr Christopher Connett

CONSTITUTION OF THE CHAPEL COUNCIL
Maj-Gen A. G. Denaro (*Chairman*); Maj-Gen T. J. Granville-Chapman; Revd Dr V. Dobbin, *Chaplain-General*; General Sir Robert Ford; Gen Sir William Jackson; Gen Sir John Mogg; Maj-Gen J. D. Stokoe; Revd A. J. Brown *Treasurer:* Maj J. C. Preston, Academy Administrative Officer; *Hon Secretary:* Brig M. C. Owen

The Royal Foundation of St Katharine in Ratcliffe

Butcher Row, London E14 8DS
Tel: 020–7790 3540
Fax: 020–7702 7603

The Royal Foundation of St Katharine was originally founded by Queen Matilda in about 1147 and was situated for nearly seven centuries adjacent to the Tower of London. One of the oldest charities in the United Kingdom, the Foundation is now located in Stepney, East London. Its purpose is to maintain a Christian centre providing prayer, conferences, retreats and counselling and also to work locally in the East London community. It is able to offer hospitality to those doing research or on sabbatical, as well as to visitors from the Church overseas.

Her Majesty Queen Elizabeth The Queen Mother is Patron of the Royal Foundation of St Katharine. The Chapter consists of a Master and a number of resident lay people.

MEMBERS OF THE COURT
The Viscount Churchill (*Chairman*)
Mr Benjamin Hanbury (*Treasurer*)
Dame Frances Campbell-Preston
Rt Revd and Rt Hon Richard Chartres (*Bishop of London*)
Mrs Alison Mayne
Lady Ailsa O'Brien
Preb Ronald Swan

CLERK TO THE COURT
Mr S. J. Northcott, 10 Great James St, London WC1N 3DQ
Tel: 020–7831 9661
Fax: 020–7405 4101

MASTER
Preb Ronald Swan

Deans of Peculiars

The few present-day Deans of Peculiars are the residue of some 300 such office-holders in the medieval period, when the granting of 'peculiar' status, fully or partially exempting a jurisdiction from episcopal control, was commonly employed by popes and others to advance the interests of a particular institution, or limit the power of the bishops. Unlike the Royal Peculiars, the deaneries had little in common, and the privileges and duties of the individual posts ranged from nominal to significant. Most of the special provisions were brought to an end in the nineteenth century. But each Peculiar has interesting light to throw on a phase of Anglican or national history.

Battle
Very Revd William Cummings, The Deanery, Battle, E Sussex TN33 0JY [1991]
Tel: (01424) 772693

Bocking
Very Revd Philip Need, The Deanery, Bocking, Braintree, Essex CM7 5SR (Bocking, Essex) [1996]
Tel: (01376) 324887
Fax: (01376) 553092
email: philip.need@virgin.net

Very Revd David Strannack, The Deanery, Hadleigh, Ipswich IP7 5DT (Hadleigh, Suffolk) [1999]
Tel: (01473) 822218

Guernsey and its Dependencies
Very Revd Marc Trickey, St Martin's Rectory, Guernsey GY4 6RR [1995]
Tel: (01481) 38303
Fax: (01481) 37710

Jersey
    Very Revd John Seaford, The Deanery, David Place, St Helier, Jersey JE2 4TE [1993]
    Tel: (01534) 720001
    Fax: (01534) 617488

Stamford
    Rt Revd Alastair Redfern, 243 Barrowby Rd, Grantham NG31 8NP [1998]
    Tel: (01476) 564722
    Fax: (01476) 592468

Preachers at The Inns of Court

THE TEMPLE
Master Revd Robin Griffiths-Jones, The Master's House, Temple, London EC4Y 7BB
    Tel: 020–7353 8559
Reader Revd A. H. Mead, 11 Dungarvan Ave, London SW15 5QU
    Tel: 020–8876 5833

LINCOLN'S INN
Canon William Norman, 37 Cloudesdale Rd, London SW17 8ET
    Tel: 020–8673 9134

GRAY'S INN
Revd Roger Holloway, Flat 6, 2 Porchester Gardens, London W2 6JL
    Tel: 020–7402 4937

RELIGIOUS COMMUNITIES

Anglican Religious Communities

The roots of the Religious Life can be traced back to the Early Church in Jerusalem, and the subsequent traditions such as the Benedictines, Franciscans, etc., were flourishing in England until the Reformation when all were suppressed.

Most Anglican Communities were founded in the last century as a result of the Oxford Movement. There are now over sixty different Communities in the British Isles and throughout the Anglican Communion. Some are very small. Some have over eighty members.

Religious Communities are formed by men and women who feel called to seek God and live out their baptismal vows in a particular way under vows. There are some 1,200 Anglican men and women living this life in the United Kingdom.

PRAYER AND WORK
Each Community has its own history and character; some follow one of the traditional Rules, and others those written by more recent founders, but all have one thing in common: their daily life based on the work of prayer and living together centred in their Daily Office and the Eucharist. The work grows from the prayer, depending on the particular Community and the gifts of its members.

Some Communities are 'enclosed'. The members do not normally go out, but remain within the convent or monastery and its grounds, seeking and serving God through silence and prayer, study and work. Other Communities share the basic life of prayer and fellowship and may also be involved in work outside the Community.

HOSPITALITY
Most Community houses offer a place where people can go for a time of Retreat, either alone or with a group, for a day, several days, or occasionally for longer periods of time. They offer a place of quiet to seek God, grow in prayer and find spiritual guidance.

THE CALLING
People who feel called to the Religious Life and who wish to apply to a Community are usually aged between 21 and 45. They normally need to be physically and psychologically robust. Academic qualifications are not essential. There is a training period of about three years before any vows are taken.

Those who are considering a vocation are advised to visit Community houses to experience their particular ethos: further information is available from the houses or general enquiries may be made to The Communities Consultative Council at the address below.

Advisory Council on the Relations of Bishops and Religious Communities

This Council, to serve the two Provinces, is responsible to the Archbishops and the House of Bishops. Its functions are: (1) to advise Bishops upon (*a*) questions arising about the charters and rule of existing Communities, (*b*) the establishment of new Communities, (*c*) matters referred to it by a diocesan bishop; (2) to advise existing Communities or their Visitors in any matters that they refer to it; (3) to give guidance to those who wish to form Communities. The Chairman and Convenor of the Council must be a diocesan bishop appointed by the Archbishops of Canterbury and York. The Council consists of at least 13 members, 3 of whom are nominated by the Bishops and 10 elected by the Communities. Up to 5 additional members may be co-opted. The present membership is: *Chairman* The Bishop of Bradford; *3 members nominated by the House of*

Bishops The Archbishop of York, the Bishop of Oxford, the Bishop of Sheffield; *10 members elected by the Communities* Abbot Basil Matthews OSB, Father Christopher Lowe CR, Brother Damian SSF, Father Gregory CSWG, Sister Margaret Angela CSJD, Sister Alison OHP, Sister Lillian CSA, Mother Mary Jean CHN, Sister Pamela CAH, Sister Tessa SLG; *one co-opted member* Sister Elizabeth Mary CSD; Father Fergus Kelly (RC Observer).

Hon Pastoral Secretary Revd David Platt, 1 Saxons Way, Didcot, Oxon OX11 9RA *Tel:* (01235) 814729 *Fax:* (01235) 811590

Administrative Secretary Miss Jane Melrose, General Synod Office, Church House, Great Smith St, London SW1P 3NZ *Tel:* 020–7898 1379

Communities Consultative Council

The Communities Consultative Council was set up in 1975. It consists of elected representatives from all Anglican Religious Communities who have houses in this country. The Council exists to promote cooperation and exchange of ideas between Religious Communities as well as providing general and vocational information about Communities and the Religious Life. To this end, the Council has produced a range of literature which is available upon receipt of an A4 SAE (31p stamp). The leaflets include a brief introduction to the Religious Life, vocation, associates etc., together with material for the annual Day of Prayer for Vocations to the Religious Life (Trinity 5). The *Anglican Religious Communities Year Book* is published by Canterbury Press (£4.99 plus 75p p&p). *Chair:* Sister Elizabeth Mary CSD, St Margaret's Church, Barking, Essex IG11 8AS
Tel: 020–8594 1736

Communities for Men

BENEDICTINE COMMUNITY OF ELMORE ABBEY
Church Lane, Speen, Newbury, Berks RG14 1SA
Tel: (01635) 33080

Abbot Dom Basil Matthews OSB

Visitor Rt Revd Rowan Williams (*Bishop of Monmouth*)

Founded 1914. 1926–87 Nashdom Abbey. From 1987 Elmore Abbey. Resident community 10 monks. Oblate confraternity over 350. Various pastoral works undertaken including retreats. Fine theological library.

BENEDICTINE COMMUNITY OF THE PRIORY OF OUR LADY, BURFORD
See **Mixed Communities** page 258.

COMMUNITY OF OUR LADY AND ST JOHN
Alton Abbey, Alton, Hants GU34 4AP
Tel: (01420) 562145/563575
Fax: (01420) 561691

Abbot Rt Revd Dom Giles Hill OSB

Visitor Rt Revd Michael Scott-Joynt (*Bishop of Winchester*)

Founded 1884. A community of Benedictine monks which undertakes retreats. Guest accommodation for 18 people. Other work includes the manufacture of altar wafers. Commissions accepted for painting of icons. The Seamen's Friendly Society of St Paul is managed from the Abbey. Day conference facilities and residential groups welcome: contact the Guestmaster.

COMMUNITY OF THE GLORIOUS ASCENSION
Lamacraft Farm, Start Point, Kingsbridge, Devon
TQ7 2NG
Tel: (01548) 511474

Prior Bro Simon CGA

Visitor Rt Revd Edward Holland (*Bishop of Colchester*)

Founded 1960, the brothers, lay and clerical, are called to unite a working life outside their Priories with a monastic community life.

COMMUNITY OF THE RESURRECTION
House of the Resurrection, Mirfield, W Yorks.
WF14 0BN
Tel: (01924) 494318
Fax: (01924) 490489
email: cr@mirfield.org.uk

Superior Fr Crispin Harrison CR

Visitor Most Revd David Hope (*Archbishop of York*)

Founded 1892, it undertakes teaching (theological college), retreats, missions and missionary works.

Theological College College of the Resurrection, Mirfield, W Yorks. WF14 0BW *Tel:* (01924) 490441
Fax: (01924) 492738

The Mirfield Centre offers a meeting place for about 50 people, small conferences, day and evening events. *Address* Mirfield Centre, College of the Resurrection, Mirfield, W Yorks. WF14 0BW
Tel: (01924) 481920
Fax: (01924) 492738
email: centre@mirfield.org.uk

Retreat House St Francis House, Hemingford Grey, Huntingdon, Cambs. PE18 9BJ
Tel: (01480) 462185.

Branch House St Michael's Priory, 14 Burleigh St, London WC2E 7PX.
Tel: 020–7379 6669
Fax: 020–7240 5294

Overseas St Peter's Priory, PO Box 991, Southdale 2135, S Africa.
Tel: 00 27–11 434 2504
Fax: 00 27–11 434 4556
email: crpriory@acunet.co.za

THE COMMUNITY OF THE SERVANTS OF THE WILL OF GOD

Monastery of the Holy Trinity, Crawley Down, Crawley, W Sussex RH10 4LH *Tel:* (01342) 712074

Father Superior Revd Fr Gregory CSWG

Visitor Rt Revd Eric Kemp (*Bishop of Chichester*)

Founded 1953 for men (clerical and lay). Women are now received also. Contemplative. Retreats and conferences.

Monastery of Christ the Saviour, 23 Cambridge Rd, Hove, E Sussex BN3 1DE *Tel:* (01273) 726698

Prior Revd Fr Brian CSWG. Contemplative: Fostering ministry and mission of urban church; providing an opportunity for men and women to live a monastic life within this urban setting.

EWELL MONASTERY

Water Lane, West Malling, Kent ME19 6HH

Prior Revd Fr Aelred Arnesen

Visitor Rt Revd Richard Llewellin

Founded 1966. An Anglican Cistercian order for men.

ORATORY OF THE GOOD SHEPHERD

See **Organizations** p. 300

THE SOCIETY OF ST FRANCIS

The Brothers of the First Order, founded in 1921, engage in active work especially in the areas of the poor and underprivileged. Three Friaries (at Hilfield, Glasshampton and Alnmouth) have a ministry with guests and retreatants. The other centres of work are principally within a city context from which the brothers engage in various active ministries. Some work with educational institutions, conducting retreats and with parishes continues.

There are four Provinces: Europe, the Pacific Islands, America and Australia/New Zealand.

Minister General Brother Daniel SSF (Brisbane)

Protector General Rt Revd Richard Appleby (*Bishop of the Northern Territory*)

Minister, European Province Brother Damian SSF, Alverna, 110 Ellesmere Rd, Gladstone Park, London NW10 1JS   *Tel:* 020–8452 7285
    Fax: 020–8452 1946
    email: Damianssf@aol.com

Asst Minister Brother Samuel SSF (Hilfield)

Bishop Protector, Europe Rt Revd Michael Scott-Joynt (*Bishop of Winchester*)

Houses Hilfield *Tel:* (01300) 341345, *email:* Hilfield@ssf.orders.anglican.org; Cambridge *Tel:* (01223) 353903; Glasshampton *Tel:* (01299) 896345; Plaistow *Tel:* 020–7476 5189; Paddington *Tel:* 020–7723 9735; 10 Halcrow St, Stepney *Tel:* 020–7247 6233; Gladstone Park *Tel:* 020–8452 7285; Alnmouth *Tel:* (01665) 830213/830660, *email:* Alnmouthfr@aol.com; Birmingham *Tel:* 0121–475 4482; Edinburgh *Tel:* 0131–228 3077; and Glasgow *Tel:* 0141–550 1202

Minister, Australia and New Zealand Province Brother Colin Wilfred SSF. *Houses:* Brisbane (QLD), Stroud (NSW), Auckland

Pacific Islands Province

Regional Minister, Papua New Guinea Brother Clifton Henry SSF. *Houses:* Goroka, Haruro, Lae, Katerada, Siomoromoro, Dogura

Regional Minister, Solomon Islands Brother Andrew Manu SSF. *Houses:* Auki, Hautambu, Honiara, Kira Kira, Santa Cruz, Vanga Point

Minister, American Province Brother Justus Richard SSF. *Houses:* Long Island, San Francisco, New York.

The Society comprises a First Order for men (*see above*) and women (Community of St Francis), called to the Franciscan life under the vows of poverty, chastity and obedience; a Second Order of enclosed sisters (Order of St Clare); and a Third Order for ordained and lay people.

SOCIETY OF ST JOHN THE EVANGELIST

St Edward's House, 22 Gt College St, Westminster, London SW1P 3QA   *Tel:* 020–7222 9234
    Fax: 020–7799 2641

Superior General Revd James Naters SSJE

Visitor Rt Revd Dominic Walker (*Bishop of Reading*)

Founded 1866, for men, clerical and lay. Engaged in retreats, missions and educational work.

Branch House The Priory, 228 Iffley Rd, Oxford OX4 1SE   *Tel:* (01865) 248116

SOCIETY OF THE SACRED MISSION

1 Linford Lane, Milton Keynes, Bucks MK15 9DL   *Tel:* (01908) 663749

Director Fr Christopher Myers SSM

Visitor Most Revd Richard Holloway (*Bishop of Edinburgh*)

Founded 1893. A religious community engaged in educational, pastoral and missionary work. The Society is divided into Provinces:

Province of Europe

Provincial Fr Douglas Brown SSM

Houses 1 Linford Lane, Milton Keynes, Bucks MK15 9DL   *Tel:* (01908) 663749

St Antony's Priory, 77 Claypath, Durham DH1 1QT   *Tel:* 0191–384 3747
Fax: 0191–384 4939

90 Vassall Rd, Kennington, London SW9 6JA
Tel: 020–7582 2040
Fax: 020–7582 6640

Southern Province

Provincial Fr Christopher Myers SSM

Houses St John's Priory, 14 St John's St, Adelaide S Australia 5000; St Michael's Priory, 75 Watsons Rd, Diggers Rest, Victoria, Australia 3427; PO Box 1579, Maseru 100, Lesotho, Southern Africa Newton Theological College, PO Box 162 Popondetta, Ora Province, Papua New Guinea

Communities for Women

BENEDICTINE COMMUNITY OF ST MARY AT THE CROSS
Convent of St Mary at the Cross, Priory Field Drive, Edgware, Middx HA8 9PZ
Tel: 020–8958 7868
Fax: 020–8958 1920

Abbess Mother Mary Thérèse Zelent OSB

Visitor Rt Revd Peter Wheatley (*Bishop of Edmonton*)

Founded in 1866; caring for disabled people throughout its history. This work, now including the care of frail elderly people, continues today in Henry Nihill House, a modern residential/nursing home. The community gives priority to prayer and worship in the Divine Office and Eucharist and its ministry of intercession. A growing number of people and parishes are united in the community's prayer through its 'Prayer Link'. Easily accessible from the M1 and A1, it offers an excellent day conference centre, guest accommodation for rest or retreat, and space for Quiet Days. The monastic experience can be shared by women wishing to take 'Time Out' for up to three months.

BENEDICTINE COMMUNITY OF ST MARY'S ABBEY
West Malling, Kent ME19 6JX   *Tel:* (01732) 843309

Abbess Sister Mary John Marshall OSB

Visitor Rt Revd John Waine

Founded 1891. Monastic community with a guest house in the grounds.

BENEDICTINE COMMUNITY OF THE PRIORY OF OUR LADY, BURFORD
See **Mixed Communities** page 258

COMMUNITY OF ALL HALLOWS
All Hallows Convent, Ditchingham, Norfolk

Postal Address Bungay, Suffolk NR35 2DT
Tel: (01986) 892749
Fax: (01986) 892731

Superior Revd Mother Sheila CAH

Visitor Vacancy

Founded 1855. Augustinian Visitation Rule. Work and Houses at Ditchingham:
The Convent (*as above*)
All Hallows House: Guests and retreats
Tel: (01986) 892840
Holy Cross House: Guests and retreats
Tel: (01986) 894092
St Mary's Lodge: Silent house for self-catering retreats   *Tel:* (01986) 892731
St Gabriel's Retreat and Conference Centre: 100 residential and 200 day visitors
Tel: (01986) 892133; 892749 (*Bookings*)
St Michael's House: Conferences and retreats
Tel: (01986) 895749
St Raphael's: available for self-catering groups who are happy with dormitory accommodation
Tel: (01986) 892133
Day Nursery – up to 20 children
Tel: (01986) 895091
All Hallows Country Hospital (accommodates 30 patients)   *Tel:* (01986) 892728
Adele House: 38-bed Nursing Home (including EMI patients)   *Tel:* (01986) 892643
Spiritual Direction and Retreat Work.

COMMUNITY OF REPARATION TO JESUS IN THE BLESSED SACRAMENT
Convent of St John Baptist, Hatch Lane, Windsor, Berks. SL4 3QR   *Tel:* (01753) 850618

Superior Revd Mother Jane Olive CSJB

Visitor Rt Revd Richard Harries (*Bishop of Oxford*)

Founded 1869. Work with the elderly.

COMMUNITY OF ST ANDREW
St Andrew's House, 2 Tavistock Rd, Westbourne Park, London W11 1BA   *Tel:* 020–7229 2662
Fax: 020–7792 5993

Superior Revd Mother Donella CSA

Visitor Rt Revd Richard Chartres (*Bishop of London*)

Founded 1861. Full membership of the Community consists of professed sisters who are ordained, or who, though not seeking ordination, serve in other forms of diaconal ministry, such as the caring professions. Present number is ten.

The fundamental ministry is the offering of prayer and worship, evangelism, pastoral work and hospitality. This is carried out through parish and specialized ministry.

COMMUNITY OF ST CLARE
St Mary's Convent, Freeland, Witney, Oxon OX8 8AJ   *Tel:* (01993) 881225
Fax: (01993) 882434

Abbess Sister Paula OSC

Bishop Protector Rt Revd Michael Scott-Joynt (*Bishop of Winchester*)

Founded 1950. Second Order of Society of St Francis. Contemplative and enclosed.

COMMUNITY OF ST DENYS
Sarum College, 19 The Close, Salisbury SP1 2EE
Tel: (01722) 339761

Superior Revd Mother Frances Anne CSD

Visitor Rt Revd David Stancliffe (*Bishop of Salisbury*)

Founded 1879. Undertakes mission work in the UK, adult teaching, parish work, retreats. Three sisters are priests.

Branches St Denys Retreat House, 2/3 Church St, Warminster BA12 8PG   *Tel:* (01985) 214824
St Margaret's Centre, The Broadway, Barking, Essex IG11 8AS   *Tel:* 020–8594 1736
Sarum College, 19 The Close, Salisbury, SP1 2EE
Tel: (01722) 339761
There are two other houses in Warminster.

COMMUNITY OF ST FRANCIS
Founded 1905, the sisters of the First Order of the Society of St Francis engage in active ministries: evangelistic, caring, conferences, retreats, spiritual direction, and hospitality. Some sisters who live in urban areas engage in paid part-time work. Some sisters live a life of contemplative solitude as hermits.

There are two provinces: European and American.

Minister General Sister Teresa CSF, Newcastle-under-Lyme   *Tel* and *Fax:* (01782) 611180

Minister Provincial, European Province Sister Joyce CSF, Brixton   *Tel* and *Fax:* 020–8674 5344
email: Joycecsf@aol.com

Visitor Rt Revd Michael Scott-Joynt (*Bishop of Winchester*)

Houses 43 Endymion Rd, Brixton, London SW2 2BU   *Tel:* 020–8671 9401
St Francis Convent, Compton Durville, South Petherton, Somerset TA13 5ES
Tel: (01460) 240473/241248
Fax: (01460) 242360
Greystones St Francis, First Ave, Porthill, Newcastle-under-Lyme, Staffs. ST5 8QX
Tel: (01782) 636839
10 Halcrow St, Stepney, London E1 2EP
Tel and *Fax:* 020–7247 6233
St Francis House, 113 Gillott Rd, Birmingham B16 0ET   *Tel:* 0121–454 8302
Fax: 0121–455 9784

Minister Provincial, American Province Sister Pamela Clare CSF, 3743 Cesar Chavez St, San Francisco CA 94110, USA

COMMUNITY OF ST JOHN BAPTIST
Convent of St John Baptist, Hatch Lane, Windsor, Berks. SL4 3QR   *Tel:* (01753) 850618
Fax: (01753) 869989
email: csjbclewer@dial.pipex.com

Superior Mother Jane Olive CSJB

Visitor Rt Revd Richard Harries (*Bishop of Oxford*)

Chaplain Revd Lister Tonge

Founded 1852 to honour and worship Almighty God and to serve him in works of charity. Runs a Retreat/Spirituality Centre and undertakes care of the aged, mission and parish work. Church Embroidery. *Tel:* (01753) 861924. Responsible for St John's Convent Home (for mentally handicapped women), *Tel:* (01753) 850618 and St Anne's House, Windsor (for elderly women) *Tel:* (01753) 865757

COMMUNITY OF ST JOHN THE DIVINE
St John's House, 652 Alum Rock Rd, Birmingham, W Midlands B8 3NS   *Tel:* 0121–327 4174

Superior Mother Christine CSJD

Visitor Rt Revd Mark Santer (*Bishop of Birmingham*)

Founded in 1848. The ethos of the Community covers all aspects of health, healing, reconciliation and wholeness in its widest context. The Community is at the beginning of an exploration, considering how religious (committed for life) and lay people (committed for a set period) could form a Christian community and share their lives together. The Community's life is based on prayer from which the different expressions of ministry flow. Within the House there is an important ministry of listening and hospitality, and larger facilities for more day-group activities are planned. Outside the House, members of the Community are involved with local ministries where they feel called.

COMMUNITY OF ST LAURENCE
Convent of St Laurence, Field Lane, Belper, Derby DE56 1DD   Tel: (01773) 822585/823390

Superior Mother Jean Mary CSL

Visitor Rt Revd Jonathan Bailey (*Bishop of Derby*)

Founded 1874. The house is available for parish weekends, teaching weekends, conferences and Quiet Days. Guests taken for limited periods, including Christmas and Easter. Parish visiting.

COMMUNITY OF ST MARY THE VIRGIN
St Mary's Convent, Challow Rd, Wantage, Oxon. OX12 9DJ   Tel: (01235) 763141

Superior Mother Barbara Claire CSMV

Visitor Rt Revd Richard Harries (*Bishop of Oxford*)

Founded 1848. The Sisters work in England, India and South Africa.

England
St Mary's Convent. (Retreats for individuals and groups; Printing Press; Studio and Workshop.)
St Peter's Bourne, 40 Oakleigh Park South, London N20 9JN (Retreats for individuals and groups.)   Tel: 020–8445 5535.
366 High St, Smethwick B66 3PD
     Tel: 0121–558 0094
St Katharine's House, Ormond Rd, Wantage OX12 8EA (Home for the Elderly.)
     Tel: (01235) 762739
St Mary's Lodge, Challow Rd, Wantage OX12 9DH   Tel: (01235) 767112

India
Christa Prema Seva Ashram, Shivajinagar, Pune 411005, Maharashtra, India (Ecumenical; interfaith dialogue.)

South Africa
3 Keurboom Ave, Omega Park, Brakpan 1541, South Africa   Tel: 00 27–11 740 9156

COMMUNITY OF ST PETER
St Peter's Convent, Maybury Hill, Woking, Surrey GU22 8AE   Tel: (01483) 761137
     Fax: (01483) 714775

Superior Mother Margaret Paul CSP

Visitor Rt Revd John Gladwin (*Bishop of Guildford*)

Founded 1861. A house for retreats and conferences was opened 1968 within the convent grounds. Guests, men and women, taken all year round.

COMMUNITY OF ST PETER, HORBURY
St Peter's Convent, Dovecote Lane, Horbury, Wakefield, W Yorks WF4 6BB Tel: (01924) 272181
     Fax: (01924) 261225

Superior Mother Robina CSPH

Visitor Rt Revd Nigel McCulloch (*Bishop of Wakefield*)

Benedictine in spirit. Undertakes a variety of pastoral ministries and retreat work.

COMMUNITY OF THE COMPANIONS OF JESUS THE GOOD SHEPHERD
Convent of St John Baptist, Hatch Lane, Windsor, Berks SL4 3QR   Tel: (01753) 850618
     Fax: (01753) 869989

Superior Mother Ann Verena CJGS

Visitor Rt Revd Richard Cartwright

Founded 1920. Undertakes work with the elderly, lay and LNSM training, quiet days and retreats, spiritual direction.

COMMUNITY OF THE EPIPHANY
Copeland Court, Kenwyn, Truro, Cornwall TR1 3DR   Tel: (01872) 722249

Administrator Delma Byrom

Visitor Rt Revd Bill Ind (*Bishop of Truro*)

Founded 1883. Thirteen single bedrooms available for retreatants. Private retreats can be arranged. Organized day retreats are held during the year. Day conferences can now be catered for. Details on application to the Administrator.

COMMUNITY OF THE GLORIOUS ASCENSION
Prasada, Quartier Subrane, 83440 Montauroux, France   Tel: 00 334–94 47 74 26

Prioress Sister Jean CGA

The Sisters are called to unite a monastic community life with work alongside other people. At Prasada they welcome visitors who seek a peaceful environment in which to find refreshment. Guests have the opportunity to use the chapel for private prayer and to join the Sisters for Eucharist and Divine Office.

COMMUNITY OF THE HOLY CROSS
Holy Cross Convent, Rempstone Hall, Rempstone, Nr Loughborough LE12 6RG

Tel: (01509) 880336
Fax: (01509) 881812

Mother Superior Revd Mother Mary Luke CHC

Visitor Rt Revd Eric Kemp (*Bishop of Chichester*)

Founded in 1857 for mission work but later adopted the Rule of St Benedict. All the work, centred on the daily celebration of the Divine Office and the Eucharist, is done within the Enclosure.

The Sisters produce and send out two series of leaflets of devotional and spiritual content, one concerning Unity between Christians, and a wider ecumenism, and the other Prayer and Faith, reflecting the mission of the Church in the world. A variety of prayer and greeting cards are also produced by the Sisters. The Community provides for Quiet Days for individuals and groups, and there is limited residential accommodation for those wishing to make longer retreats.

COMMUNITY OF THE HOLY FAMILY
The Gatehouse, St Mary's Abbey, West Malling, Kent ME19 6LP *Tel*: (01732) 849016

Superior Mother Kathleen Mary CHF

Visitor Rt Revd Eric Kemp (*Bishop of Chichester*)

Since January 1997, the Community has continued its life in the Gatehouse of Malling Abbey. It is anticipated that the spirit of the educational work begun by the Foundress, Mother Agnes Mason, at the beginning of this century, will still be continued in the eastern end of the Diocese of Chichester through the operation of the Mother Agnes Trust which undergirds the Community of the Holy Family. The charity in the future will seek to provide a theological library and an extensive educational resource centre.

COMMUNITY OF THE HOLY NAME
Convent of the Holy Name, Morley Rd, Oakwood, Derby DE21 4QZ *Tel*: (01332) 671716
Fax: (01332) 669712

Superior Revd Mother Jean Mary CHN

Visitor Rt Revd David Smith (*Bishop of Bradford*)

Founded 1865. Undertakes mission and retreat work. Guests received.

Branch Houses
Holy Name House, Ambleside Rd, Keswick, Cumbria CA12 4DD *Tel*: (01768) 772998
St Michael's House, 53 Wimborne Rd, Radford, Nottingham NG7 5PD *Tel*: 0115–978 5101
88 Braunston Rd, Oakham, Rutland LE15 6LE
Tel: (01572) 770287
6 St Peter's Court, 398 Woodborough Rd, Nottingham NG3 4JF *Tel*: 0115–960 8794
Cottage 5, Lambeth Palace, London SE1 7JU
Tel: 020–7928 5407
The Community also has charge of the Retreat House, 11 Abbey Square, Chester
Tel: (01244) 321801

Overseas

Lesotho Convent of the Holy Name, PO Box LR 43, Leribe; CHN Mission House, PO Box MS 7142, Maseru

Zululand Convent of the Holy Name, Kwa Magwaza, P/B 806, Melmoth, RSA; St Vincent's Mission, P/B 675, Nqutu 3135, RSA; St Luke's Mission, PO Box 175, 3950 Nongoma, RSA; Usuthu Mission, PO 8, via Luyengo, Swaziland; 14 Web Castle Way, Castle Hill, Marble Ray 4037, RSA.

Moçambique CP 120, Maputo, Moçambique.

COMMUNITY OF THE SACRED PASSION
Mother House: Convent of the Sacred Passion, Lower Rd, Effingham, Leatherhead, Surrey KT24 5JP *Tel*: (01372) 457091

Superior Mother Philippa CSP

Visitor Rt Revd Ian Brackley (*Bishop of Dorking*)

Founded 1911. An order which combines prayer and mission work in varying forms. A house opened in Walsall in 1981 and in the autumn of 1983 in the parish of St John the Divine, Kennington. Since 1991 three sisters have been living and working next to the Julian Shrine in Norwich. The Community withdrew from Tanzania in June 1991, leaving behind a community of more than ninety Tanzanian women known as the Community of St Mary.

COMMUNITY OF THE SERVANTS OF THE CROSS
Marriott House, Tollhouse Close, Chichester, W Sussex PO19 3EZ *Tel*: (01243) 781620

Superior Mother Angela CSC

Visitor Rt Revd Eric Kemp (*Bishop of Chichester*)

Warden Canon Keith Hobbs

Augustinian Rule.

COMMUNITY OF THE SISTERS OF THE LOVE OF GOD
Convent of the Incarnation, Fairacres, Oxford OX4 1TB   *Tel:* (01865) 721301/2

Superior Revd Mother Rosemary SLG

Visitor Rt Revd Richard Harries (*Bishop of Oxford*)

Founded 1906 and has a modern rule based on monastic principles and Carmelite spirituality. Membership, with Oblature and Associations for men and women. *Function:* The contemplative life. It offers hospitality for private retreats. The SLG Press publishes pamphlets and books on spirituality and prayer.

Other Convents Convent of St Mary and the Angels, Woodland Ave, Hemel Hempstead, Herts. HP1 1RG   *Tel:* (01442) 256989
Bede House, Staplehurst, Tonbridge, Kent TN12 0HQ (with its solitaries)   *Tel:* (01580) 891262
St Isaac's Retreat, PO Box 93, Opononi, Northland, New Zealand.

FRANCISCAN SERVANTS OF JESUS AND MARY
Posbury St Francis, Crediton, Devon EX17 3QG
                                   Tel: (01363) 772304

Superior Mother Hilary FSJM

Visitor Rt Revd John Richards

Founded 1930; its work consists of a life of prayer, work and hospitality; guests are received and retreats conducted between Easter and October.

ORDER OF THE HOLY PARACLETE
St Hilda's Priory, Sneaton Castle, Whitby, N Yorks. YO21 3QN   *Tel:* (01947) 602079
                                   Fax: (01947) 820854
email: ohppriorywhitby@btinternet.com

Superior Sister Judith OHP

Visitor Most Revd David Hope (*Archbishop of York*)

Founded 1915 and based on Rule of St Benedict. Main undertaking: prayer, pastoral work, children's hospice, retreats, conferences, missions, parish work.

Residential Centre Sneaton Castle Centre, Whitby, N Yorks. YO21 3QN   *Tel:* (01947) 600051
                                   Fax: (01947) 603490
email: sneaton@globalnet.co.uk

Accommodation and facilities for large and small groups for parish activities, conferences and educational courses.

Branch Houses
Beach Cliff, 14 North Promenade, Whitby, N Yorks. YO21 3JX   *Tel:* (01947) 601968
St Oswald's Pastoral Centre, Woodlands Drive, Sleights, Whitby, N Yorks. YO21 1RY
                                   Tel: (01947) 810496
                                   Fax: (01947) 810759
           email: ohpstos@globalnet.co.uk
The Abbey Cottage, Rievaulx, York YO62 5LB
                                   Tel: (01439) 798209
7 Minster Yard, York YO1 7JD   *Tel:* (01904) 620601
St Michael's House, 15 Portman St, Belgrave, Leicester LE4 6NZ   *Tel:* 0116–266 7805
                                   Fax: 0116–268 0374
       email: sistersohp@leicester.anglican.org
Martin House, Grove Rd, Clifford, Wetherby, W Yorks. LS23 6TX   *Tel:* (01937) 843449
           email: sisters.martinhs@onet.co.uk
St Hilda's House, 20 Criagielea Place, Dundee DD4 8HL   *Tel:* (01328) 509206

Overseas

Swaziland PO 1272, Manzini: Industrial Training Centres and other development work, diocesan youth work.

Republic of S Africa St Benedict's Retreat House, PO Box 27, Rosettenville, 2130

Ghana PO Box 594, Accra, Training for Lay Ministry.

PRIORY OF OUR LADY OF WALSINGHAM
Priory of Our Lady, Walsingham, Norfolk NR22 6ED
                                   Tel: (01328) 820340
                                   Fax: (01328) 820899
email:
   motherteresa@walsingham1439.freeserve.co.uk

Superior Mother Mary Teresa SSM

Visitor Rt Revd Michael Manktelow

Autonomous house of the Society of St Margaret. Sisters are involved in the ministry of healing and reconciliation in the Shrine, the local parishes and the wider Church and ministry to people with HIV/AIDS and their carers at Falcon House. They are also available to pilgrims and visitors and work in the education department in the Shrine. Guests are welcome for short periods of rest, relaxation and retreat.

ST MARY'S CONVENT
Burlington Lane, Chiswick, London W4 2QE
                                   Tel: 020–8994 4641
                                   Fax: 020–8995 9796

Superior Sister Jennifer Anne SSM

Visitor Rt Revd Eric Kemp (*Bishop of Chichester*)

Has a Residential Home for elderly retired ladies; and Nursing Home for those needing full-time nursing care.

See **Society of St Margaret**, East Grinstead, below.

ST SAVIOUR'S PRIORY
18 Queensbridge Rd, London E2 8NS
    Tel and *Fax:* 020–7739 6775 (Revd Mother)
               020–7739 9976 (Sisters)
                     Fax: 020–7739 1248

Superior Sister Elizabeth SSM

Visitor Rt Revd Dominic Walker (*Bishop of Reading*)

Convent of the Society of St Margaret, working as staff members in various parishes, in schools, with the homeless etc; retreats and individual spiritual direction. The Priory has a few guest rooms and facilities for individual private retreats as well as excellent facilities for small group meetings.

SISTERS OF BETHANY
7 Nelson Rd, Southsea, Hants. PO5 2AR
                     Tel: 023–9283 3498

Superior Mother Gwenyth SSB

Visitor Rt Revd Kenneth Stevenson (*Bishop of Portsmouth*)

Founded 1866 for hospitality, retreat work and praying for Christian Unity. The Sisters are available for leading quiet days and retreats, as spiritual directors, and also to give talks on prayer. People are welcome to come individually or as groups to spend time in silence and prayer. It is possible to accommodate a few residential guests or groups of up to 24 for the day.

SISTERS OF CHARITY
St Elizabeth's House, Longbrook St, Plympton St Maurice, Plymouth PL7 1NL   *Tel:* (01752) 336112

Superior Revd Mother Mary Theresa SC

Visitor Rt Revd John Garton (*Bishop of Plymouth*)

Founded 1869. The Rule is based on that of St Vincent de Paul. Undertakes care of those in need, young or old; parish work, missions, retreats.

Branch Houses St Vincent's Nursing Home, Plympton St Maurice, Plymouth PL7 3NE
                   Tel: (01752) 336205

6 North View, Castletown, Sunderland SR5 3AF
81 Fore St, Plympton St Maurice, Plymouth PL7 3NE   *Tel:* (01272) 345918

Overseas The Convent of the Sisters of Charity and Holy Spirit Retreat and Conference Center, 701 Park Place, PO Box 818, Boulder City, Nevada, 89005 USA.

SISTERS OF THE CHURCH
(Regd Charity: Church Extension Association Inc)
St Michael's Convent, Ham Common, Richmond, Surrey TW10 7JH
      Tels: 020–8940 8711 *and* 020–8948 2502
                  Fax: 020–8332 2927

Superior Sister Anita CSC

Visitor Rt Revd Peter Selby (*Bishop of Worcester*)

Founded 1870. Has a two-fold ethos of worship and active mission. Undertakes group and private retreats and workshops; chaplaincy, educational and pastoral work, hospitality.

Branch Houses
St Gabriel's, 27A Dial Hill Rd, Clevedon, Avon BS21 7HL   *Tel:* (01275) 872586
82 Ashley Rd, St Paul's, Bristol BS6 5NT
               Tel: 0117–941 3268
               Fax: 0117–908 6620
112 St Andrew's Rd North, St Annes-on-Sea, Lancs. FY8 2JQ   *Tel:* (01253) 728016
10 Furness Rd, West Harrow, Middx HA2 0RL
          Tel and *Fax:* 020–8423 3780
and in Australia, Canada, Solomon Islands.

SOCIETY OF ALL SAINTS SISTERS OF THE POOR
All Saints Convent, St Mary's Rd, Oxford OX4 1RU   *Tel:* (01865) 249127
               Fax: (01865) 726547

Superior Mother Helen ASSP

Visitor Rt Revd Robert Runcie

Founded in London 1851. Works of the Society:
St John's Home for the elderly, St Mary's Rd, Oxford OX4 1QE   *Tel:* (01865) 247725
               Fax: (01865) 247920
Helen House, a hospice for children, 37 Leopold St, Oxford OX4 1QT   *Tel:* (01865) 728251
               Fax: (01865) 247920
Church Embroidery Department
               Tel: (01865) 248627
Small Guest House. Enquiries regarding visits and private retreats welcomed.
The Porch. A drop-in centre for the homeless
               Tel: (01865) 728545
All Saints House, 82 Margaret St, London W1N 8LH   *Tel:* 020–7637 7818
               Fax: 020–7636 5364

SOCIETY OF ST MARGARET

St Margaret's Convent, St John's Rd, East Grinstead, W Sussex RH19 3LE

Tel: (01342) 323497
Fax: (01342) 328505

Superior Mother Raphael Mary ssm

Visitor Rt Revd Eric Kemp (*Bishop of Chichester*)

Founded 1855 and undertakes nursing work, runs guest and retreat houses and a home for the aged, and in Sri Lanka a retreat house and a children's home.

Neale House Conference Centre
Tel and *Fax:* (01342) 312552

Branch Houses St Mary's Convent and Nursing Home, Burlington Lane, Chiswick, London W4 2QE (guest house for elderly ladies and nursing home for geriatric and handicapped ladies)
Tel: 020–8994 4641
Fax: 020–8995 9796

Overseas St Margaret's Convent, Polwatte, Colombo 3, Sri Lanka, and St John's Home, 133 Galle Rd, Moratuwa, Sri Lanka.

Independent Convents of the Society St Margaret's Convent, 17 Spital, Aberdeen, AB24 3HT
Tel: (01224) 632648
St Saviour's Priory, Queensbridge Rd, London E2 8NS (*see* p. 257)
Tel: 020–7739 6775
Priory of Our Lady, Walsingham, Norfolk, NR22 6ED (*see* p. 256)
Tel: (01328) 820340
Fax: (01328) 820899

St Margaret's Convent, 17 Highland Park St, Roxbury, MA 02119, USA.

SOCIETY OF THE HOLY TRINITY

Ascot Priory, Ascot, Berks SL5 8RT

Superior Mother Cecilia sht

Founded 1845. Order based on Poor Clares. Contemplative. St Michael's and St Gabriel's Retreat House, self-catering. Day conference facilities available.

SOCIETY OF THE PRECIOUS BLOOD

Burnham Abbey, Lake End Rd, Taplow, Maidenhead, Berks SL6 0PW   *Tel:* (01628) 604080

Superior The Revd Mother spb

Visitor Rt Revd Richard Harries (*Bishop of Oxford*)

Founded 1905 and based on rule of St Augustine. Contemplative and exists for the purpose of perpetual intercession for the Church and for the world.

Branch House St Pega's Hermitage, Peakirk, Peterborough PE6 7NP   *Tel:* (01733) 252219

Overseas Independent Daughter House Priory of Our Lady Mother of Mercy, Masite, PO Box MS 7192, Maseru 100, Lesotho

Dependent House St Monica's House of Prayer, 46 Green St, West End, Kimberley 8301, Cape, RSA

Mixed Communities

BENEDICTINE COMMUNITY OF THE PRIORY OF OUR LADY, BURFORD

Burford Priory, Priory Lane, Burford, Oxon OX18 4SQ   *Tel:* (01993) 823605

Prior Brother Stuart Burns osb

Visitor Rt Revd James Thompson (*Bishop of Bath and Wells*)

Founded in 1941 from Wantage under its official title 'The Society of the Salutation of Mary the Virgin', this is a monastic community living under the Rule of St Benedict. In 1987 it formally opened its novitiate to men as well as women, and since then has evolved as a mixed monastery. The Community has oblates and a Friends' Association.

The nuns and monks seek to support themselves by a variety of work including printing, writing, icon mounting and retreat work. They do not normally undertake work outside the Priory but are concerned to develop a life of prayer and hospitality which is open to all. Guests are accommodated in the Guest House and are welcome to share in the life and worship of the Community. Day groups and small residential groups are also welcome.

Organizations

PART 4

Classified List of Organizations included in this Section

Animal Welfare
Anglican Society for the Welfare of Animals
Animal Christian Concern
Christian Consultative Council for the Welfare of
    Animals

Art, Architecture
Art and Christianity Enquiry
Christian Arts
Ecclesiological Society
Friends of Friendless Churches
Historic Churches Preservation Trust
York Glaziers' Trust

Bellringing
Ancient Society of College Youths
Central Council of Church Bell-Ringers
Society of Royal Cumberland Youths

Bible Study
Bible Reading Fellowship
Bible Society
Scripture Gift Mission
Scripture Union
Vacation Term for Biblical Study

Blind People
Blind, Royal National Institute
Blind, St John's Guild for
Guild of Church Braillists

Church Buildings
Friends of Friendless Churches
Greater Churches Group
Historic Churches Preservation Trust
Incorporated Church Building Society
Marshall's Charity
Vergers, Church of England Guild of

Church Societies — General
Additional Curates Society
Affirming Catholicism
Anglican Association
Anglican Evangelical Assembly
Association of English Cathedrals
Cathedral Administration and Finance
    Association
Cathedral and Church Shops Association
Catholic Group in General Synod
Catholic League
Church Pastoral Aid Society
Church Society
Church Union
Churches' Advertising Network
Modern Churchpeople's Union
Open Synod Group
Parish and People

Protestant Reformation Society
Society for the Maintenance of the Faith

Church Societies — Specific
Anglican Fellowship in Scouting and Guiding
Baptismal Reform Movement
Christian Evidence Society
Church of England Record Society
Church House Deaneries Group
Community of St Aidan and St Hilda
Ecumenical Society of the Blessed Virgin Mary
Forward in Faith
Guild of St Helena
Guild of St Leonard
Guild of Servants of the Sanctuary
Lord's Day Observance Society
Movement for the Reform of Infant Baptism
Reform
Royal Martyr Church Union
Society of King Charles the Martyr
Society of Mary
Third Province Movement

Clergy Associations
Association of Black Clergy
Association of Hospice Chaplains
Association of Ordinands and Candidates for
    Ministry
College of Health Care Chaplains
Company of Mission Priests
English Clergy Association
Federation of Catholic Priests
International Association of Civil Aviation
    Chaplains
Lesbian and Gay Clergy Consultation
MSF Clergy Section
Oratory of the Good Shepherd
Retired Clergy Association
School Chaplains' Conference
Society of the Holy Cross
Society of Ordained Scientists
See also **Professional Groups**

Consultancy
Christians Abroad
Church and Community Trust
Grubb Institute

Co-ordinating Bodies
Anglican Voluntary Societies Forum
Church of England Evangelical Council
Churches' Group on Funeral Services
Churches' Main Committee
Evangelical Alliance
Religious Education Council of England and
    Wales
Universities and Colleges Christian Fellowship
    of Evangelical Unions

Counselling
Lesbian and Gay Christian Movement
Magdalene Fellowship
Relate
True Freedom Trust

Deaf People
British Deaf Association
Deaf People, Royal Association in Aid of
Deaf, Royal National Institute
National Deaf Church Conference

Defence, Disarmament, Pacifism
Anglican Pacifist Fellowship
Commonwealth War Graves Commission
Council on Christian Approaches to Defence and
    Disarmament

Diocesan Associations *see* pages 315–16

Drama
Actors' Church Union
Radius

Ecumenism
Anglican and Eastern Churches Association
Anglican–Lutheran Society
Christians for Europe
Churches' Group on Funeral Services
Churches' Main Committee
Fellowship of St Alban and St Sergius
Fellowship of St Therese of Lisieux
Harold Buxton Trust
International Ecumenical Fellowship
Nikaean Club
Order of Christian Unity
Society of St Willibrord

Education
Archbishop's Examination in Theology
Association of Church College Trusts
Christian Education Movement
Church Schools Company
Corporation of SS Mary and Nicolas
Culham College Institute
Lincoln Theological Institute for the Study of
    Religion and Society
Mirfield Centre
North of England Institute for Christian
    Education
Religious Education Council of England and
    Wales
Royal Alexandra and Albert School
Royal Asylum of St Ann's Society

Family
Care Trust
Family Life and Marriage Education Network
Family Welfare Association
Fellowship of St Nicholas
St Michael's Fellowship

Finance
Anglican Stewardship Association

Christian Ethical Investment Group
Ecclesiastical Insurance Group
Ecumenical Council for Corporate Responsibilty
Fidelity Trust Ltd
Number One Trust Fund

Grant-Making Bodies
Church of England Clergy Stipend Trust
EFAC Bursary Scheme
Newton's Trust
Pilgrim Trust
Queen Victoria Clergy Fund
See also **Welfare**

Health, Healing and Medicine
Acorn Christian Healing Trust
Association of Hospice Chaplains
Burrswood
Christian Medical Fellowship
Churches' Council for Health and Healing
College of Health Care Chaplains
Crowhurst Christian Healing Centre
Fellowship Charitable Foundation
Guild of Health
Guild of Pastoral Psychology
Guild of St Barnabas
Guild of St Raphael
Harnhill Centre of Christian Healing
Holy Rood House
Pilsdon Community
Richmond Fellowship for Community Mental
    Health
St Luke's Hospital for the Clergy

Interfaith, Religions
Council of Christians and Jews
INFORM
Inter Faith Network for the United Kingdom
World Congress of Faiths

Libraries *see* pages 317–19

Marriage
Anglican Marriage Encounter
Broken Rites
Family Life and Marriage Education Network
Magdalene Fellowship
Relate

Ministry
Diaconal Association of the Church of England
Diakonia
Distinctive Diaconate
Edward King Institute for Ministry Development
MODEM
Royal Naval Lay Readers' Society

Ministry, Women
Anglican Group Educational Trust
Li Tim-Oi Foundation
Society for the Ministry of Women in the Church
WATCH

Organizations

Mission

Bible Society
Careforce
Christian Witness to Israel
Church Pastoral Aid Society
Church's Ministry among Jewish People
Greenbelt Festivals
London City Mission
Mersey Mission to Seamen
Message
Missions to Seamen
Romsey House
Scripture Gift Mission
Scripture Union in Schools
Society for Promoting Christian Knowledge
Soldiers' and Airmen's Scripture Readers
    Association
Student Christian Movement
Trinitarian Bible Society
United Society for Christian Literature
Universities and Colleges Christian Fellowship
    of Evangelical Unions

Mission Overseas

Africa Inland Mission International
All Nations Christian College
Bush Brotherhoods
Crosslinks
Church Mission Society
College of the Ascension
Crowther Hall
Feed the Minds
Foreign Missions Club
Intercontinental Church Society
Interserve
Korean Mission Partnership
Leprosy Mission
Melanesian Mission
Mid-Africa Ministry
New England Company
OMF International Ltd
Overseas Bishoprics Fund
Oxford Mission
Papua New Guinea Church Partnership
Reader Missionary Studentship Association
South American Mission Society
Southern Africa Church Development Trust
Tearfund
United Society for the Propagation of the Gospel
World Vision

Music

Archbishops' Certificate in Church Music
Choir Benevolent Fund
Choir Schools Association
Church Music Society
Gregorian Association
Guild of Church Musicians
Hymn Society of Great Britain and Ireland
Jubilate Hymns
Morse-Boycott Bursary Fund

Plainsong and Medieval Music Society
Royal College of Organists
Royal School of Church Music

Ordination Candidate Funds

(General)
St Aidan's College Charity

Overseas

Womenaid International
Centre for International Briefing
Christianity and the Future of Europe
Christians Abroad
Christians for Europe
Churches' Commission on Overseas Students
European Christian Industrial Movement
United Nations Association
World Vision

Patronage Trusts *see* pages 319–20

Prayer, Meditation, Retreats

Archway
Association for Promoting Retreats
Confraternity of the Blessed Sacrament
Guild of All Souls
Julian Meetings
Julian of Norwich, Shrine of Lady
National Retreat Association
St Aidan Trust
Servants of Christ the King
Society of Retreat Conductors
Women's World Day of Prayer

Professional Groups

Actors' Church Union
Anglican Association for Social Responsibility
Association of Christian Teachers
Association of Christian Writers
Association of Ordinands and Candidates for
    Ministry
Chaplains' Conference
Christian Arts
Christians at Work
Church Computer Users Group
Church House Deaneries' Group
Church Schoolmasters' and School Mistresses'
    Benevolent Institution
Deans' and Provosts' Conference
Deans' and Provosts' Vergers' Conference
Ecclesiastical Law Society
Grayswood Studio
Guild of Pastoral Psychology
Homes for Retired Clergy
Industry Churches Forum
Librarians' Christian Fellowship
MSF Clergy Section
National Association of Diocesan Advisers for
    Women's Ministry
Society of Retreat Conductors
Vergers, Church of England Guild of
See also **Clergy Associations**

Publishing, Print Media
Bray Libraries
Feed the Minds
National Christian Education Council
Rebecca Hussey's Book Charity
Scripture Union
Society for Promoting Christian Knowledge
Trinitarian Bible Society
United Society for Christian Literature

Renewal
Anglican Renewal Ministries
Keswick Convention
SOMA

Research
Arthur Rank Centre
Care Trust
Centre for the Study of Christianity and Sexuality
Christian Research
Churches' Fellowship for Psychical and Spiritual
   Studies
Keston Institute
Rural Theology Association
St George's House, Windsor
Urban Theology Unit
William Temple Foundation

Rural Affairs
Arthur Rank Centre
Rural Theology Association

Scholarship and Science
Alcuin Club
Canterbury and York Society
Henry Bradshaw Society
Latimer House
Philip Usher Memorial Fund
Public Record Office
Pusey House
Society for Liturgical Study
Society for Old Testament Study
Society of Ordained Scientists
Vacation Term for Biblical Study
Victoria Institute

Social Concern
Age Concern England
Careforce
Changing Attitude
Christian Socialist Movement
Church Action with the Unemployed
Church Housing Trust
English Churches Housing Group
Evangelical Christians for Racial Justice
Lesbian and Gay Christian Movement
Metropolitan Visiting and Relief Association
National Viewers' and Listeners' Association
Order of Christian Unity
Pilsdon Community
St Pancras Housing
Samaritans

Shaftesbury Society
Social Concern

Training
Administry
Anglican Marriage Encounter
Anglican Stewardship Association
Association of Church Fellowships
Catechumenate Network
Christians at Work
Clinical Theology Association
College of Preachers
GFS Platform for Young Women
Industrial Christian Fellowship
National Christian Education Council
Student Christian Movement
Time Ministries International
William Temple Foundation

Travel, Pilgrimage
Pilgrim Adventure
Walsingham, Shrine of Our Lady of

Welfare
Almshouses, National Association of
Becker's Charity
Bromley and Sheppard's Colleges
Came's Charity
Charterhouse
Church Moral Aid Association
Church of England Soldiers', Sailors' and Air-
   men's Clubs
Church of England Soldiers', Sailors' and Air-
   men's Housing Association
Church Schoolmasters' and School Mistresses'
   Benevolent Institution
Community Housing and Therapy
Compassionate Friends
Corporation of the Sons of the Clergy
Crosse's Charity
Diocesan Institutions of Chester, Manchester,
   Liverpool and Blackburn
DGAA
Family Welfare Association
Frances Ashton's Charity
Friends of the Clergy Corporation
Friends of the Elderly
Homes for Retired Clergy
House of St Barnabas in Soho
KeyChange
Langley House Trust
MACA – Partners in Mental Health
Mayflower Family Centre
Partis College
Pyncombe Charity
Richards Charity
RPS Rainer
St Michael's Fellowship
Samaritans
Seamen's Friendly Society of St Paul
Society for the Assistance of Ladies in Reduced
   Circumstances

Society for the Relief of Poor Clergymen
Society of Mary and Martha
Toc H
YMCA
Young Women's Christian Association

Worship
Alcuin Club
Praxis
Prayer Book Society

Youth
Barnardo's
Boys' Brigade
Campaigners

Cathedral Camps
Children's Society
Church Lads' and Church Girls' Brigade
Crusaders
Fellowship of St Nicholas
Frontier Youth Trust
Girls' Brigade
Guides Association
Lee Abbey Household Communities
Lee Abbey International Students' Club
London Union of Youth Clubs
RPS Rainer
St Christopher's Fellowship
Scout Association
Shaftesbury Homes and 'Arethusa'
William Temple House

ORGANIZATIONS

The following list of societies and organizations with importance for the Church of England includes many that are specifically Anglican, others that are inter-denominational, and others without religious affiliation.

The inclusion of an organization is for the purposes of information and is not to be taken as implying acceptance of the objects of the organization by the Editor and Publishers of the Year Book or by the General Synod.

A classified list of organizations is provided in the preceding pages. **Diocesan Associations** (in support of overseas provinces and dioceses), **Libraries**, and **Patronage Trusts** are grouped together at the end of the section. See also Part 3 General Information.

Acorn Christian Healing Trust
Founded in 1983 by Bishop Morris Maddocks and his wife Anne to see the Church and nation renewed in the service of Christ the Healer, believing that every person has the right to receive the best care and attention that will enable them to grow into wholeness. Acorn offers all Christian churches a variety of teaching and training resources in Christian healing. Many of these are conducted at Whitehill Chase, Acorn's resource centre in Hampshire, which also holds a weekly open day every Tuesday (10.30 am – 3.00 pm) in conjunction with a service of healing. Other components of the trust's ministry are the Christian Listener Project, which trains people in learning how to offer the gift of listening; the Apostolate, which is the teaming together of someone trained in professional health care with a person with pastoral skills, who together offer care to the whole person; and the training of resource advisers in healing in all major denominations, demonstrating the trust's commitment to working within the structure of the churches. *Patron:* The Archbishop of Canterbury. *Director:* Revd Russ Parker, Whitehill Chase, High St, Bordon, Hants GU35 0AP
Tel: (01420) 478121
Fax: (01420) 478122

Actors' Church Union
Founded 1899, members and associates serve those engaged in the performing arts through their interest, their action — often in association with other related bodies — and their prayers. Additionally, more than 200 honorary chaplains serve all members of the profession in theatres, studios and schools at home and overseas. As well as spiritual counsel and practical advice, material help is given when possible. Through the Children's Charity, for example, funds are available for theatrical parents facing difficulties with the costs of their children's education. *President:* Rt Revd Frank Sargeant. *Senior Chaplain:* Canon Bill Hall, St Paul's Church, Bedford St, Covent Garden, London WC2E 9ED
Tel: 020–7836 5221

Additional Curates Society
Founded in 1837 to help maintain additional curates in poor and populous parishes and especially in new areas. The society also fosters vocations to the priesthood. *Chairman:* Ven Bernard Holdridge. *Secretary:* Revd Stephen Leach, Gordon Browning House, 8 Spitfire Rd, Birmingham, W Midlands B24 9PB
Tel: 0121–382 5533
Fax: 0121–382 6999

Administry
Good management, co-ordination, organization and leadership are all necessary if the Church is to be effective in its mission. Administry serves churches by helping them organize and co-ordinate their activities. We provide a unique service: publications to give fresh ideas to PCCs and groups, training events for leaders and church members, and consultancy to help churches organize and grow. *Executive Director:* Rob Norman, PO Box 57, St Albans, Herts AL1 3DT
Tel: (01727) 856370
Fax: (01727) 843765
email: administry@ibm.net

Affirming Catholicism
A movement within the Church of England and the Anglican Communion, formed in 1990. 'The object of the Foundation shall be the advancement of education in the doctrines and the historical development of the Church of England and the Churches of the wider Anglican Communion, as held by those professing to stand within the catholic tradition' (extracted from the Trust Deed). Its purposes are to promote theological thinking about the contemporary implications of Catholic faith and order; to further the spiritual growth and development of clergy and laity; to organize or support lectures, conferences and seminars; to publish or support books, tracts, journals and other educational material; to provide resources for local groups meeting for purposes of study and discussion. *Secretary:*

Elizabeth Field, Affirming Catholicism, St Luke's Centre, 90 Central St, London EC1V 8AQ
Tel: 020–7253 1138
Fax: 020–7253 1139
email: affcath@affirmingcatholicism.org.uk
Web: http://www.affirmingcatholicism.org.uk

Africa Inland Mission International

An evangelical, inter-denominational and inter-national mission founded in 1895. It has 750 members working in 14 countries in Africa and the adjacent islands. The mission's main aims are to take the gospel to people who have so far been unevangelized and to assist churches to grow strong though it is also involved in other forms of compassionate work. It has particular interest in the training of leaders and plans to increase its work in urban areas and with children. *International Director:* Dr Fred Beam. *UK Director:* Revd John Brand, 2 Vorley Rd, Archway, London N19 5HE
Tel: 020–7281 1184
email: uk@aim-eur.org

Age Concern England

(The National Council on Ageing)
The centre of a network of over 1400 independent local Age Concern groups serving the needs of elderly people with help from over 250,000 volunteers. Age Concern England's governing body also includes representatives of over 100 national organizations and works closely with Age Concern Scotland, Cymru and Northern Ireland. Age Concern groups provide a wide range of services which can include visiting, day care, clubs and specialist services for physically and mentally frail elderly people. Age Concern England supports and advises groups through national field officers and a variety of grant schemes. Other work includes training, information, campaigning, and the provision of services such as insurance, tailored to meet the needs of older people. Activities also include innovative projects which promote healthier lifestyles, pro-vide older people with opportunities to give the experience of a lifetime back to their com-munities and encourage interaction between the young and old in order to break down stereo-types. *Director General:* Sally Greengross, Astral House, 1268 London Rd, London SW16 4ER
Tel: 020–8765 7200
Fax: 020–8765 7211
email: ace@ace.org.uk
Web: http://www.ace.org.uk/

Alcuin Club

Founded 1897 to promote liturgical studies, the club has a long record of publishing works of liturgical scholarship and more practical publica-tions. It continues to publish Liturgical Studies (jointly with Grove Books) and Collections; new series of handbooks and monographs are planned. The club organizes occasional confer-ences. Members receive some publications free, others at special rates. *President:* The Bishop of Chichester. *Chairman:* Canon Donald Gray. *Secretary:* Revd Tim Barker, Alcuin Club, The Parsonage, Church St, Spalding PE11 2PB
Tel: (01775) 722675
Fax: (01775) 710273
email: tr.barker@cwcom.net
Web: http://www.alcuin.mcmail.com

All Nations Christian College

The college came into existence in 1971 following the merger of three Bible colleges. Whilst inter-denominational in character, many of its staff and students are members of the Anglican Com-munion. Several of the staff are licensed readers and two are ordained Anglicans, including the Principal. The college exists to train students primarily for cross-cultural ministries. The 185 students are mainly post-graduates and follow a two-year theological course incorporating mis-siological and pastoral lectures. There is also practical training in church work and the devel-opment of technical skills appropriate to devel-oping countries. In addition to its own diploma and certificate, the college also offers a two-year BA in Biblical and Cross-cultural Studies and a one-year post-graduate Diploma/MA in Mis-siology, validated by the Open University. Candi-dates can be accepted for doctoral studies. Many of the students are married and about half are from overseas. A day nursery is provided whilst parents attend lectures. *For details of courses apply to:* The Admissions Secretary, ANCC, Easneye, Ware, Herts SG12 8LX
Tel: (01920) 461243
Fax: (01920) 462997
email: mailbox@allnations.ac.uk
Web: http://www/allnations.ac.uk

Almshouse Association

(National Association of Almshouses)
Is concerned with the preservation and extension of over 1,750 member Almshouse Trusts. A number of major almshouses have a resident Anglican chaplain, or appoint Anglican clergy as Master or Custos of the foundation. It advises members on any matters concerning almshouses and the welfare of the elderly and aims to pro-mote improvements in almshouses, to promote study and research into all matters affecting almshouses, and to make grants or loans to members. It also keeps under review existing and proposed legislation affecting almshouses and when necessary takes action, and encourages the provision of almshouses. *Exec Ctee Chairman:* Lady Benson. *Director:* Mr Anthony Leask, Bill-ingbear Lodge, Carters Hill, Wokingham, Berks RG11 5RU
Tel: (01344) 452922
Fax: (01344) 862062

Ancient Society of College Youths

Established 1637. The College Youths take into membership distinguished and respected bell-ringers from the British Isles and overseas, wherever English change-ringing is practised. From its headquarters in the City of London the society meets a number of obligations to provide ringers for and maintain the bells of particular churches, and runs a charitable fund that contributes to maintenance costs. *Secretary:* Mr Phil Rogers, 193 Lennard Rd, Beckenham, Kent BR3 1QN   *Tel and Fax:* 020–8778 6308

Anglican and Eastern Churches Association
Founded 1864 to promote mutual understanding of, and closer relations between, the Orthodox, Oriental and Anglican Churches. *Presidents:* Archbishop Gregorios of Thyateira and the Bishop of London. *Chairman:* Revd John Salter. *General Secretary:* Revd Philip Warner, St Mark's Vicarage, St Mark's Rd, Teddington, Middx TW11 9DE   *Tel:* 020–8977 4067
email: aeca@ssmkjb.demon.co.uk

Anglican Association
Founded in 1969, incorporating the Anglican Society founded 1924, to insist on theological integrity and to maintain the identity of the Church of England, it is traditionalist in both doctrine and liturgy. The Association publishes its own journal the *Anglican Catholic*. *President:* Canon Prof Roy Porter. *General Secretary and Treasurer:* Mr Robin Davies, 22 Tyning Rd, Winsley, Bradford on Avon, Wilts BA15 2JJ
Tel: (01225) 862965

Anglican Association for Social Responsibility
Established in 1985 as a support for its members who work in social responsibility, social work and social projects. The association, which welcomes members from other churches in related fields, provides opportunities for professional development. Regional groups meet regularly to share and support each other in their work. Among other facilities open to members are an annual conference, a national newsletter, retreats, consultations and seminars. *President:* The Bishop of Guildford. *Secretary:* Capt Terry Drummond, St Matthew's House, 100 George St, Croydon CR0 1PE   *Tel:* 020–8681 5496
Fax: 020–8686 2074
email: amtcroydon@dswark.org.uk

Anglican Association of Advisers in Pastoral Care and Counselling
Founded in 1998 to support the work of advisers already appointed; to encourage the appointment of an adviser in every diocese and to promote good practice in pastoral care and pastoral counselling through the Church of England. Full membership is open to appointed advisers, or to those who are undertaking advisers' tasks within the dioceses. Associate membership is open to those holding similar appointments in other denominations and to all who are interested in furthering the work of the association. *Chair:*

Revd Sue Walrond-Skinner. *House of Bishops' Representative:* The Bishop of Worcester. *Secretary:* Canon Ronald Smythe, 94 Wangford Rd, Reydon, Southwold, Suffolk IP18 6NY *Tel:* (01502) 723413

Anglican Evangelical Assembly
The assembly is organized each year by the Church of England Evangelical Council in pursuance of its aim to consult with the evangelical constituency within the Church of England and to foster leadership. Membership is broadly representative of evangelicalism within the dioceses of the Church of England, and of other evangelical interests in the Church such as societies and theological colleges. *President:* Vacancy. *Chairman:* Preb Richard Bewes. *Exec Officer:* Mr Frank Knaggs, PO Box 93, Heaton, Newcastle upon Tyne NE6 5WL *Tel and Fax:* 0191–240 2084
email: CEEC@cableinet.co.uk

Anglican Fellowship in Scouting and Guiding
Founded in 1983 at the request of guiders, scouters and clergy. Its aims are to support leaders and clergy in the religious aspects of the Promise and Law and the training programme in Scouting and Guiding, and to maintain links with other Guide/Scout religious guilds and fellowships in order to foster ecumenical understanding. Individual membership is open to persons aged 15 years or over who are members of the Scout and Guide movements, or others (e.g. clergy) who are sympathetic to the aims of Guiding and Scouting. Collective membership is available for Scout Groups and Guide Units (which do not have to be church sponsored), and for Anglican churches. *Chairman:* Mrs June Davies, 31 Loseley Rd, Farncombe, Godalming GU7 3RE   *Tel:* (01483) 428876

Anglican Group Educational Trust
Formed in 1973 to assist women engaged in theological studies or work within the Church of England and to carry out such other legally charitable purposes for the advancement of the ministry of women within the Church of England as the trustees shall from time to time decide. The trust currently awards scholarships for women clergy who wish to study abroad as part of their career development or sabbatical leave. Applications for the Roxburgh Scholarships for 2001 will be considered in September 2000. Application forms and details of the trust may be obtained from the *Chair:* Ven Joy Tetley, Archdeacon's House, 56 Battenhall Rd, Worcester WR5 2BQ
Tel: (01905) 20537
Fax: (01905) 612302

Anglican Marriage Encounter
Anglican Marriage Encounter is a voluntary organization which offers residential and non-residential programmes for married and engaged couples to review and deepen their relationship

by developing a compelling vision for their marriage, and providing the communication skills to support this. *Episcopal adviser:* Rt Revd Michael Scott-Joynt. *Lay Executive couple:* Peter and Janet Cox, 5 Hillside Way, Welwyn, Herts AL6 0TY

Tel and *Fax:* (01438) 715337

email: peter_janet_cox@hotmail.com

Web:

http://www.marriageencounter.freeserve.co.uk

Anglican Pacifist Fellowship

Founded 1937. Members pledge to renounce war and all preparation to wage war and to work for the construction of Christian peace in the world. Bi-monthly Newsletter *Challenge*. *Chairman:* Revd Dr Henry Jansma. *Hon Secretary:* Dr Tony Kempster, 11 Weavers End, Hanslope, Milton Keynes MK19 7PA *Tel:* (01908) 510642

email: Kempster@compuserve.com

Anglican Renewal Ministries

Established in 1980 to encourage charismatic renewal in the Church of England. Produces training courses for churches and groups and runs residential and one-day conferences in various parts of the country and a quarterly magazine *Anglicans for Renewal*. *Director:* Revd John Leach, 42 Friar Gate, Derby DE1 1DA

Tel: (01332) 200175

Fax: (01332) 200185

email: ARMDerby@aol.com

Web:

http://www.members.aol.com/ARMDerby

Anglican Society for the Welfare of Animals

Founded 1972, for the purpose of including the whole creation in the redemptive love of Christ and especially for prayer, study and action on behalf of animals. *President:* Rt Revd John Austin Baker. *Chairman:* Rt Revd Dominic Walker OGS. *Treasurer:* Revd Kenneth Hewitt. *Correspondence Secretary:* Mrs S. J. Chandler, The Old Toll Gate, Hound Green, Hook, Hants RG27 8LQ

Tel: (01189) 326586

Anglican Stewardship Association

A registered charity formed to promote the ideals of responsible ownership and giving amongst Christians and the Church. The association's aim is to assist Christians at parish, deanery and diocesan level to address issues of money and wealth-handling in order to make full use of all the latent resources of the Church so that its mission may be fully developed. *General Secretary:* Mrs Carol Sims, 71 Dee Banks, Chester CH3 5UX

Tel: (01244) 341996

Fax: (01244) 400338

email: peter@patent.u-net.com

Anglican Voluntary Societies Forum

Founded in 1980 to promote understanding and co-operation between the Voluntary Societies and the Boards and Councils of the General Synod. To be eligible for membership, societies must be Anglican, national, and involved in mission. The forum meets two or three times a year to discuss matters of mutual concern. *Chairman:* Mrs Daphne Cook (Chairman of the Trustees of Family Life and Marriage Education). *Secretary:* Mr Robert Wellen, General Synod Office, Church House, Great Smith St, London SW1P 3NZ

Tel: 020–7898 1371

Fax: 020–7898 1369

email: robert.wellen@c-of-e.org.uk

Anglican-Lutheran Society

Founded in 1984 to pray for the unity of the Church and especially the Anglican and Lutheran Communions; to encourage opportunities for common worship, study, friendship and witness; to encourage a wider interest in and knowledge of the Anglican and Lutheran traditions and contemporary developments within them. The society publishes a newsletter, *The Window*, organizes conferences, lectures and other events. *Co-Presidents:* Very Revd John Arnold and Rt Revd Erik Vikstrom. *Co-Moderators:* Revd Ronald T. Englund, (one vacancy). *Secretary:* Mrs Valerie Philips, 15 Hampden, Kimpton, Hitchin, Herts SG4 8QH

Animal Christian Concern

Founded 1985 with the following aims: (1) to express the view that cruelty of any kind is incompatible with Jesus Christ's teachings of love, that love is indivisible and that cruelty towards any sentient creature is a breach of love; (2) to hold services for animal welfare; (3) to oppose such practices as animal experimentation, intensive farming, fur trade and blood sports. *President:* Rt Revd Alwyn Rice Jones, former Archbishop of Wales. *Patrons:* Very Revd John Southgate, Monsignor Michael Buckley, Rt Revd John Austin Baker. *Co-ordinator:* Mrs May Tripp, PO Box 70, Leeds LS18 5UX

Tel: 0113–258 3517

Archbishop's Examination in Theology

(leading to the Lambeth Diploma of Student in Theology (S Th))

Founded 1905 to provide a means of scholarly theological study. Originally for women, but opened to men in 1944, it can be taken by thesis, for suitably qualified candidates, or by examination. A limited number of candidates with good theological qualifications may register for a Lambeth MA by thesis. *Hon Director:* Rt Revd Geoffrey Rowell. *Hon Secretary:* Canon Martin Kitchen, 3 The College, Durham DH1 3EQ

Tel: 0191–384 2415

email: martin@3college.sonnet.co.uk

Archbishops' (Canterbury and Westminster) Certificate in Church Music

Founded 1961 to provide a minimum qualification for church organists, choirmasters, cantors and instrumentalists. Now fully ecumenical. *General Secretary:* Mr John Ewington, Guild of Church Musicians, Hillbrow, Godstone Rd, Blechingley, Surrey RH1 4PJ   *Tel:* (01883) 741854
Fax: (01883) 740570

Archway

Anglican Retreat and Conference House Wardens' Association. Promotes the use of retreat and conference houses as a vital contribution to the life and development of Church and community. *Secretary:* Mr Peter Fletcher, Wydale Hall, Brompton by Sawdon, Scarborough, N Yorks YO13 9DG   *Tel:* (01723) 859270
Fax: (01723) 859702

Art and Christianity Enquiry (ACE)

Begun in 1991 ACE draws together all for whom the visual arts are vital in their understanding, teaching and practice of the faith. Now a charitable trust, it organizes lectures, undertakes research, energizes, encourages. Quarterly bulletin by subscription, complimentary copy on request. *Director:* Revd Tom Devonshire Jones, 4 Regent's Park Rd, London NW1 7TX
Tel and *Fax:* 020–7284 3006

Arthur Rank Centre

Established in 1972 as a collaborative venture between the Churches, the Royal Agricultural Society of England and the Rank Foundation. It is fully ecumenical and recognized as the rural focus and resource centre for churches nationally. It provides the secretariat for the Churches' Rural Group, a representative ecumenical body which is a network of the Churches Together in England and of Churches Together in Britain and Ireland. It runs clergy courses especially for those recently appointed to rural areas. Members of staff are peripatetic and are available for consultations and local conferences. The Diocesan Rural Officers meet regularly with the Church of England Rural Officer who is a member of staff. It is also concerned with rural community issues and with farming and environmental matters. Recent initiatives have been the Rural Stress Information Network, the National Churches Tourism Group, the Church and Community Fund, grants for rural youth work, study panels on the ethics of land ownership and animal welfare. It also produces material for rural churches including the magazine *Country Way*. *Director:* Revd Gordon Gatward, Arthur Rank Centre, National Agricultural Centre, Stoneleigh Park, Warws CV8 2LZ
Tel: (02476) 696969
Fax: (02476) 414808
email: arthur.rank.centre@virgin.net
Web: http://www.ruralnet.org.uk/~arc/

Association for Promoting Retreats

Founded in 1913 to foster the growth of the spiritual life in the Anglican Communion by the practice of retreats. Welcomes as members all Christians in sympathy with this aim. Membership by subscription for individuals, parishes and retreat houses. The APR is one of the six retreat groups which form the National Retreat Association (*see* separate entry). *Administrator:* Paddy Lane, The Central Hall, 256 Bermondsey St, London SE1 3UJ   *Tel:* 020–7357 7736
Fax: 020–7357 7724
email: apr@retreats.org.uk

Association of Black Clergy

Founded 1982 to provide support for each other, identification of issues of social justice and theological reflection upon them, and action in the community and church which will be a sign of the association's commitment to 'kingdom' principles. *Chairman:* Revd Charles Lawrence. *Secretary:* Mrs F. Roberts. *Facilitator:* Canon Ivor Smith-Cameron, 100 Prince of Wales Drive, London SW11 4BD   *Tel* and *Fax:* 020–7622 3809

Association of Christian Teachers

Formed in 1971 from three existing Christian teacher organizations to unite Christians in education and to work at bringing Christian insights and values into education at all levels and into every subject. ACT runs a variety of courses on educational subjects for teachers, administrators, parents and church leaders at its study centre, Stapleford House. ACT is represented on the Religious Education Council and has been actively involved in the current debate about religious education as well as wider issues in education. It publishes a magazine, *ACT NOW*, *The Journal of Education and Christian Belief*, the RE resource magazine *Digest*, and other specialist publications. It has 50 local groups and regularly organizes education conferences. It is in partnership with the Stapleford Centre for Educational Research, Training and Resources. *General Secretary:* Mr Richard Wilkins, ACT, 94A London Rd, St Albans, Herts AL1 1NX   *Tel:* (01727) 840298

Association of Christian Writers

A group of Christians who wish to serve God in the field of writing. Some members are professional writers, others part time and many are beginners in different areas of writing. Three writers' days a year are held and many local groups meet regularly. Members receive a quarterly magazine and a manuscript criticism service is available. *Administrator:* Mr Warren Crawford, 73 Lodge Hill Rd, Farnham, Surrey GU10 3RB   *Tel* and *Fax:* (01252) 715746
email: christian-writers@dial.pipex.com
Web: http://dspace.dial.pipex.com/christian

Association of Church College Trusts

In 1979 the Association of Church College Trusts was established as a loosely knit organization to facilitate an exchange of information and cooperation. It meets every six months. The Church College Trusts were formed following the closure of their respective Colleges of Education. They are autonomous, answerable only to the Charity Commission; their financial management policies are such that they are required both to sponsor present work from their income and also to ensure that their capital is maintained at a level that can finance similar levels of work in the future. In the last 20 years they have been involved in helping individual teachers, students and others, sponsoring corporate projects in part or in total, and aiding schools, colleges and Church educational activities. They also maintain certain residual college functions relating to former students and staff such as keeping records, giving references and holding reunions. The individual Trusts are:

ALL SAINTS EDUCATIONAL TRUST

Personal awards to teachers, intending teachers, students in dietetics. Not assisted-school pupils, students in counselling, engineering, law, medicine, ordination, social work. Corporate awards — imaginative new projects that will enhance the Church's contribution to higher and further education. Date for applications 31 January each year.

Correspondent Mr Alfred Bush, St Katharine Cree Church, 86 Leadenhall St, London EC3A 3DH

Tel: 020–7283 4485
Fax: 020–7283 2920

CULHAM EDUCATIONAL FOUNDATION

The Trust gives mainly personal grants not exceeding £1,000 to practising Anglicans who are pursuing personal study or undertaking projects or research primarily relating to RE in schools. Consideration is also given to similar types of work relating to parish and Church school education and, for Anglican clergy, to general school issues.

Correspondent Mrs S. Thirkettle, The Malthouse, 60 East St Helen St, Abingdon, Oxon OX14 5EB

Tel: (01235) 520458
Fax: (01235) 535421
email: cef@culham.ac.uk
Web: http://www.culham.ac.uk

HOCKERILL EDUCATIONAL FOUNDATION

Personal awards are made to teachers, intending teachers and others in further or higher education, with a priority to the teaching of RE. No awards to those training for ordination, mission, social work or counselling, or to children at school. Corporate grants to support the development of religious education, particularly in the dioceses of Chelmsford and St Albans. Applications by 1 March each year.

Correspondent Mr Colin Broomfield, 16 Hagsdell Rd, Hertford SG13 8AG   *Tel:* (01992) 303053
Fax: (01992) 425950

ST GABRIEL'S TRUST

The object of the Trust is the advancement of higher and further education in religious education. Grants are made to foster good practice in RE teaching.

Correspondent Mr P. M. Duffell, Ladykirk, 32 The Ridgeway, Enfield, Middx EN2 8QH

Tel: 020–8363 6474

KESWICK HALL CHARITY

The Trustees' spending gives priority to their own initiatives, but they also give grants in response to personal or corporate applicants for research or study in religious education. Within this field, they give priority to teachers or student teachers and to work in East Anglia.

Correspondent Mrs H. Herrington, Keswick Hall RE Centre, School of Education and Professional Development, University of East Anglia, Norwich NR4 7TJ   *Tel:* (01603) 592632
Fax: (01603) 505975
email: a.m.miller@uea.ac.uk
Web: http://www.uea.ac.uk/edu/religion.html

ST LUKE'S COLLEGE FOUNDATION

The foundation's object is the advancement of further and higher education in religious education and theology. Grants are awarded to individuals for research and taught postgraduate qualifications in these fields; and to eligible organizations for related initiatives and facilities. The foundation does not finance buildings, or provide bursaries for institutions to administer; and it is precluded from the direct support of schools (although it supports teachers who are taking eligible studies).

Correspondent Prof M. Bond, Heathayne, Colyton, Devon EX13 6RS   *Tel* and *Fax:* (01297) 552281
email: mbond@eclipse.co.uk

ST MARY'S COLLEGE TRUST

The Trust's annual income is normally committed to supporting the Welsh National Centre for Religious Education and the Anglican Chaplaincy at the University of Wales, Bangor. As a result, grants to individuals and other institutions are only awarded in very exceptional circumstances.

Correspondent Mr Gwilym T. Jones, Chwarel Plas, Llangefni, Anglesey, Gwynedd

Tel: (01248) 382934
Fax: (01248) 372187

FOUNDATION OF ST MATTHIAS

Considers applications for grants for higher and further education, priority being given to residents of Bristol, Bath and Wells, and Gloucester dioceses and to courses with a teaching/RE

element. Second degrees are not normally considered.
Correspondent Mrs V. Prater, Diocesan Church House, 23 Great George St, Bristol BS1 5QZ
Tel: 0117–921 4411
Fax: 0117–925 0460

SARUM ST MICHAEL EDUCATIONAL CHARITY
Further and higher education — preference given to those living or working in the diocese of Salisbury.
Correspondent Mrs Diana Arundale, 13 New Canal, Salisbury, Wilts. SP1 2AA
Tel: (01722) 422296

ST HILD AND ST BEDE TRUST
The Trust's annual income is restricted to the advancement of higher and further education in the dioceses of Durham and Newcastle, and is presently committed to supporting the North of England Institute for Christian Education, the North East Religious Learning Resources Centre, several lectureships, chaplaincies (in particular the chaplaincy in the College of St Hild and St Bede), scholarships, libraries and a demonstration school.
Correspondent Mrs Mary Gullick, c/o The College of St Hild and St Bede, University of Durham, Durham DH1 1SZ
Tel: 0191–374 3083

ST PETER'S SALTLEY TRUST
The Trust's annual income is committed to initiating, supporting and evaluating locally based projects in adult theological education, further education and RE development in schools. The Trust's area of benefit comprises the region covered by the Anglican dioceses of Birmingham, Coventry, Hereford, Lichfield and Worcester. The Trust does not make grants to individuals for research or continuing education purposes.
Correspondent Mrs J. E. Jones, Grays Court, 3 Nursery Rd, Edgbaston, Birmingham B15 3JX
Tel: 0121–427 6800
Fax: 0121–428 3392

ST CHRISTOPHER'S COLLEGE TRUST
Small one-off grants given to maintain or enlarge any institution or centre for religious education (Church of England) or payments towards the provision of facilities for research into theory and practice of teaching religious education.
Correspondent Mr D. Grimes, The National Society, Church House, Great Smith St, London SW1P 3NZ
Tel: 020–7898 1492
Fax: 020–7898 1493
email: david.grimes@natsoc.c-of-e.org.uk

Please note that applications have to be made to the individual Trusts concerned and not centrally through the Association.

SECRETARY TO THE ASSOCIATION OF CHURCH COLLEGE TRUSTS
Revd Dr John Gay, Director, Culham College Institute, 60 East Saint Helen St, Abingdon, Oxon OX14 5EB
Tel: (01235) 520458
Fax: (01235) 535421
email: enquiries@culham.ac.uk
Web: http://www.culham.ac.uk

Association of Church Fellowships
Founded 1963. Sponsored by clergy and laity to meet a growing need in this country and overseas to encourage and enable the laity to take their full part in the life and work of the Church in open groups and in co-operation with existing groups. *Patrons:* Archbishops of Canterbury and York. *National Chairman:* Canon Stanley Owen, Bickenhill House, 154 Lode Lane, Solihull, W Midlands B91 2HP
Tel: 0121–704 9281

Association of English Cathedrals
Established in 1990 and authorized by the Administrative Chapters of the Anglican Cathedrals as their representative organization, the AEC deals with governmental agencies, the General Synod, and their constituent bodies and the Churches' Main Committee on behalf of the English cathedrals, provided only that it cannot commit any individual cathedral chapter to a specific decision. It monitors the negotiations resulting from the Bishops' Commission on Cathedrals. In particular, the process of establishing new draft constitutions and statutes for each cathedral under the provisions of the Cathedrals Measure. Membership consists of one representative of each Administrative Chapter. *Chairman:* Very Revd Raymond Furnell, Dean of York. *Secretary:* Very Revd Edward Shotter, The Deanery, Rochester, Kent ME1 1TG
Tel: (01634) 844023
Fax: (01634) 401410

Association of Hospice Chaplains
The Association of Hospice Chaplains seeks to promote the provision of good pastoral and spiritual care in hospice and palliative care units. It offers training and support for clergy involved (whether on a full-time or part-time basis) by means of advice about appointments, induction, and training courses. St Columba's Hospice, Edinburgh and St Christopher's Hospice, Sydenham both provide courses for chaplains newly appointed, and many hospices offer placements and courses which form part of pre- and post-ordination training. The Association monitors professional developments within the constituency of palliative care, and maintains a networking relationship with the College of Health Care Chaplains. It also offers a three-day residential training course for practising chaplains each spring (usually at All Saints Pastoral Centre, London Colney). *Hon Secretary:* Revd John

Casselton, St Elizabeth's Hospice, 565 Foxhall Rd, Ipswich IP3 8LX *Tel:* (01473) 727776

Association of Ordinands and Candidates for Ministry

Founded in 1968, AOCM currently represents over 1,000 ordinands from all of the Anglican theological colleges, courses, schemes and institutes in England, Ireland, Scotland and Wales. AOCM also represents those training for accredited lay ministry including Church Army students. At three conferences each year, representatives from these institutions meet to discuss issues related to theological training. The Chair of AOCM, who is a member of the Theological Education and Training Committee of the Ministry Division of the Bishops' Council, communicates the conclusions of these conferences to those who make decisions affecting ordinands. The Association publishes *Training for Ministry*, an annual handbook for ordinands. *Chairperson:* Mrs Jennie Cappleman, 107 Dover Crescent, Bedford MK41 8QR *Tel:* (01234) 266952
email: JennieC@tesco.net
Web: http://societies.anglican.org/aocm/

Baptismal Reform Movement
See **MORIB** page 298.

Barnardo's
Founded 1866. Barnardo's works with over 30,000 children, young people, and their families. The charity finds its inspiration in the Christian faith and its work is enriched and shared by people of other faiths and philosophies. Barnardo's operates as a separate charity in the Republic of Ireland, Australia and New Zealand. Working in partnership with local authorities, parents, voluntary agencies and churches, Barnardo's runs over 285 community based services which include: fostering and adoption, day care, family support services, youth and community work and services for young people with physical and learning difficulties. *Chair of Council:* Revd D. Gamble. *Senior Director:* Mr Roger Singleton, Tanners Lane, Barkingside, Essex IG6 1QG *Tel:* 020–8550 8822

Becker's (Mrs) Charity for Clergy
Founded 1852 to provide relief, either generally or individually, to clergy of the United Church of England and Ireland retired through sickness or age and who are in conditions of need, hardship or distress. Grants of money or providing or paying for items, services or facilities, not exceeding £520 p.a. at the discretion of the Trustees. *Chairman:* Senior of the four trustees. *Secretary:* Mr A. P. Newman, 71 Eastfield Ave, Weston, Bath BA1 4HH *Tel:* (01225) 424229

Bible Reading Fellowship
Since 1922 BRF has encouraged Christian growth through devotional Bible reading and prayer. Publishes daily Bible reading notes and books for Advent and Lent, and in the areas of bible reading and study, and prayer and spirituality. BRF's *Barnabas* imprint provides resources for children up to age of 11. *Chair of Trustees:* The Bishop of Coventry. *Chief Exec:* Mr Richard Fisher, Peter's Way, Sandy Lane West, Oxford OX4 5HG
Tel: (01865) 748227
Fax: (01865) 773150
email: enquiries@brf.org.uk
Web: http://www.brf.org.uk

Bible Society
Bible Society is committed to changing attitudes, changing minds, and opening people's hearts to the Bible by developing campaigning programmes to highlight the relevance of the Bible in today's world. The Society aims to tune into twenty-first-century culture and use dynamic formats and media to communicate the Scriptures both at home and overseas. *Chief Exec:* Mr Neil Crosbie, Bible Society, Stonehill Green, Westlea, Swindon, Wilts SN5 7DG
Tel: (01793) 418100
Fax: (01793) 418118
email: info@bfbs.org.uk
Web: http://biblesociety.org.uk

Blind, Royal National Institute for the (RNIB)
RNIB is the largest organization working on behalf of blind and partially sighted people throughout the UK. It runs over 60 different services to help blind people at all stages of their lives. It aims to improve the quality of life of all visually impaired people by promoting the same opportunities and choices that sighted people enjoy — in education, training, employment, health and leisure. To achieve this RNIB provides a wide range of practical services, advice, information and special equipment. RNIB runs schools for blind children of all abilities. It equips people for work by offering training and advice on special equipment to employers and employees. RNIB designs and sells specially adapted equipment and games, and publishes a wide range of material in Braille, Moon and on tape. It runs Braille and tape libraries, including the well-known RNIB Talking Book Service. It also runs residential care homes, holiday hotels and rehabilitation centres. Research into the prevention of blindness, and into the needs of visually impaired people, is also a part of RNIB's work. *President:* His Grace the Duke of Westminster. *Chairman:* Mr John Wall. *Director-General:* Mr Ian Bruce, 224 Great Portland St, London W1N 6AA *Tel:* 020–7388 1266
0345 669999 (Helpline)
Fax: 020–7388 2034
email: helpline@rnib.org.uk
Web: http://www.rnib.org.uk

Blind, St John's Guild for the

Founded 1919 to bring blind and partially sighted people more closely into the life of the Church. There are 24 branches in the UK meeting regularly to share in worship, fellowship and friendship. A quarterly magazine *The Church Messenger* produced in Braille, Moon, and on tape is produced and a newsletter three times a year in Braille, Moon, tape, large and ordinary print. A residential home is maintained at St Albans. The guild administers the Braille Bible Reading Fellowship. *Warden and Chairman:* Revd Graeme Hands. *General Secretary:* Ms Margaret Chambers, 8 St Raphaels Court, Avenue Rd, St Albans, Herts AL1 3EH   *Tel:* (01727) 864076
Fax: (01727) 835809

Boys' Brigade

Founded 1883 for the advancement of Christ's Kingdom among boys and the promotion of habits of obedience, reverence, discipline, self-respect and all that tends towards a true Christian manliness. *Brigade Secretary:* Mr Sydney Jones, Felden Lodge, Felden, Hemel Hempstead, Herts HP3 0BL   *Tel:* (01442) 231681
email: felden@boys-brigade.org.uk
Web: http://www.boys.brigade.org.uk

Bray Libraries

A programme of SPCK which assists the establishment and refreshing of small libraries within parish, deanery or diocesan groups in the UK and overseas. There must be significant Anglican participation. Financed by subscriptions and a trust fund with substantial additional funding from SPCK. In 1999, to mark the society's tercentenary and in recognition of Thomas Bray's substantial work in the 17th century for the welfare of prisoners, a scheme for Bray Libraries in Prisons was launched in England and Wales. *Contact:* The Project Co-ordinator, SPCK Worldwide, Holy Trinity Church, Marylebone Rd, London NW1 4DU   *Tel:* 020–7387 5282
Fax: 020–7387 3411
email: spckww@spck.org.uk
Web: http://www.spck.org.uk

British Deaf Association

The British Deaf Association is a membership organization co-ordinated through its Executive Council and 12 Area Councils around the country. It supports the profoundly deaf whose first language is British Sign Language and campaigns for full and equal access for its members in all walks of life. It provides services and information on a wide range of subjects including BSL, health, education, youth issues, community advocacy and campaigning. Publishes a monthly magazine. *Patron:* HRH The Duke of York. *Chair:* Mr Austin Reeves. *Chief Exec:* Jeff McWhinney, 1–3 Worship St, London EC2A 2AB
Tel: 020–7588 3520 (Voice/text)
Fax: 020–7588 3527

Broken Rites

Formed in 1983, Broken Rites is an independen association of divorced and separated wives o Anglican clergy and ministers of Non-Anglican Churches, living in the United Kingdom. I affirms the Christian ideal of life-long marriage It welcomes the support of everyone who is in sympathy with its aims, which are to support one another with sympathy and understanding and practical help where possible; to continue to draw the attention of the Churches to the problems of ex-wives of the clergy; and to promote a more vivid awareness among Christian people of the increasing incidence of clergy marriage breakdown and the implications for the witness of the Church and its teaching on marriage. *Chairman:* Mrs Wendy Catley. *Hon Secretary:* Christine McMullen, 114 Brown Edge Rd, Buxton, Derbys SK17 7AB   *Tel:* (01298) 73997
email: christin@noc6.u-net.com

Bromley and Sheppard's Colleges

Bromley College was founded in 1666 to provide houses for clergy widows and Sheppard's College in 1840 to provide houses for unmarried daughters of clergy widows, who had lived with their mothers at Bromley College. Houses in both colleges have been converted into flats and widows/widowers of clergy, retired clergymen and their spouses, divorced and separated spouses of clergy or retired clergy of the Church of England, the Church in Wales, the Scottish Episcopal Church or the Church of Ireland may now be admitted. Unmarried daughters or step-daughters of a deceased former resident may also apply. Contact the *Chaplain/Clerk to the Trustees:* Chaplain's Office, Bromley & Sheppard's Colleges, London Rd, Bromley, Kent BR1 1PE
Tel: 020–8460 4712

Burrswood

Christian Centre for Health Care and Ministry Burrswood was founded by Dorothy Kerin who received a commission from God to 'heal the sick, comfort the sorrowing and give faith to the faithless'. The Dorothy Kerin Trust is a registered charity, administered by a board of trustees. The main buildings, set in beautiful surroundings, comprise a Christian non-surgical hospital with 35 beds for short-term inpatient care and an inter-disciplinary team of resident doctors, nurses, physiotherapists and counsellors; a church with two resident chaplains which is fully integrated with the hospital and has healing services open to the public four times a week; a guest/retreat house with single and twin rooms, sleeping 15; a physio and hydrotherapy complex for inpatients and outpatients, a medical and counselling out-patient facility and a conference centre for up to 40 delegates. *Director:* Dr Gareth Tuckwell. *Senior*

Chaplain: Revd Michael Fulljames, Burrswood, Groombridge, nr Tunbridge Wells, Kent TN3 9PY
Tel: (01892) 863637 (Enquiries)
(01892) 863818 (Admissions)
Fax: (01892) 863623

Bush Brotherhoods

Founded 1897 to preach the Gospel and administer the Sacraments to members of the Anglican Communion in the Outback of Australia. *President:* The Bishop of Rockhampton. *Secretary:* Revd C. N. Lavender, 25 Holme Cottages, The Great Hospital, Norwich, Norfolk NR1 4EL
Tel: (01603) 665524

Came's Charity for Clergymen's Widows

Founded to provide small annual grants to benefit clergy widows who are wanting. *Apply:* The Clerk, Worshipful Company of Cordwainers, Eldon Chambers, 30 Fleet St, London EC4Y 1AA
Tel: 020–7353 4309
Fax: 020–7583 4931

Campaigners

Founded 1922 this Christian youth organization is committed to providing a modern local church structured programme, catering for the mental, physical and spiritual needs of young people in an exciting relevant way. Campaigners teach the Bible and the Gospel, not only in word but also through practical activity and relationship building pursuits. Further details from the *Director General:* Revd Kenneth Argent, Campaigner House, Colney Heath, Herts AL4 0NQ
Tel: (01727) 824065

Canterbury and York Society

Founded 1904 for the printing of bishops' registers and other ecclesiastical records. *Jt Presidents:* The Archbishops of Canterbury and York. *Chairman:* Prof D. M. Smith. *Secretary:* Prof Christopher Harper-Bill, 15 Cusack Close, Twickenham, Middx TW1 4TB
Tel: 020–8892 0500

CARE Trust

CARE (Christian Action Research and Education) is a registered charity concerned to promote and defend Christian family values, particularly marriage and the sanctity of life. As an interdenominational evangelical charity, it is a resource centre for all who wish to strengthen marriage and the family, to see a strong Christian influence in national education and to create compassionate parallel programmes directed towards those who are in need. CARE Campaigns is an associated body concerned more directly with changes in the law. Other departments include Caring Services, CARE for Education, CARE for Europe, CARE for Life, and Ethics Development Initiative and an international department. *Exec Director:* Mr Charles Colchester, 53 Romney St, London SW1P 3RF
Tel: 020–7233 0455
Fax: 020–7233 0983
email: mail@care.org.uk
Web: http://www.care.org.uk

Careforce

Founded in 1980 to serve churches and Christian projects by recruiting volunteers age 18 to 25 to spend a year in the UK and Ireland engaged in youth and outreach ministries in local churches, serving homeless people, the elderly, those with difficult family situations, those with addiction difficulties, and those with learning difficulties or physical disability. *Director:* Revd Ian Prior, 35 Elm Rd, New Malden, Surrey KT3 3HB
Tel and *Fax:* 020–8942 3331
email: enquiry@careforce.co.uk
Web: http://www.careforce.co.uk

Catechumenate Network

The network promotes the use of the Catechumenate (also known as 'The Adult Way to Faith') which was a principal component of the House of Bishops' Report *On the Way*, by means of training seminars and the exchange of information and experience about the preparation of adults for baptism and confirmation. The network publishes a Starter Pack for parishes. Membership is open to individuals (lay or ordained), parishes, chaplaincies and diocesan organizations. The process emphasizes welcome, accompanied journey into faith, celebration of stages of commitment and a strong ministry for lay people with experience of Christian community. The Catechumenate Network is ecumenical in approach and is a founder member of the international network incorporating Roman Catholic, Anglican and Lutheran traditions. *Contact:* Revd Dr John Railton, Rectory, 3 Butts Rd, Chiseldon, Swindon SN4 0NN *Tel* and *Fax:* (01793) 740369
email: johnrailton@webleicester.co.uk

Cathedral and Church Shops Association

The Cathedral and Church Shops Association provides a forum for the exchange of information amongst its members. It arranges an annual conference and trade fair in November and sponsors meetings of staff from cathedral and church shops in different areas of the country each spring. It also gives advice and assistance for the setting up and running of church shops from experienced shop managers. Membership is open to the staff of any shop operating within, or associated with, a cathedral or church and which is open for trading for five or six days a week all the year or during the visitor season of the area which it serves. *Chairman:* Mr John Simmons.

Secretary: Mrs Gill Green, Cathedral Enterprises (St Albans) Ltd, St Albans Cathedral, St Albans AL1 1BY   *Tel:* (01727) 864738
Fax: (01727) 850944
email: cathedra@alban.u-net.com
Web: http://www.stalbansdioc.org.uk/
cathedral/

Cathedral Camps
Organizes working summer holidays for young people beween 16 and 30, though most are under 25, at cathedrals and large churches in Britain. Volunteers help to conserve and restore parts of these ancient buildings which might well be neglected otherwise. The sort of work available varies enormously. It is unskilled, but often demanding. It offers the privilege of close contact with magnificent buildings and with those who work full-time there. Volunteers are asked to contribute £50.00 towards the cost of the camp, though bursaries are available. Accommodation and food are basic, but the enthusiasm and comradeship generated by a week together overcomes most hardships. There are no religious expectations or restrictions, but most have had some contact with the Church in its different traditions. Volunteers come from Britain and Europe, as well as other parts of the world. There is a heavy demand for places. *Chairman:* Mr Robert Aagaard. *Administrator and Booking Secretary:* Ms Shelley Bent, 16 Glebe Ave, Flitwick, Beds MK45 1HS   *Tel:* (01525) 716237
email: Cathedralcamps@compuserve.com
Web: http://www.cathedralcamps.org.uk

Cathedral Libraries and Archives Association
The CLAA supports the work of cathedral and capitular libraries and archives in the Anglican churches of the United Kingdom and Ireland. It seeks to advance education by the promotion, preservation and protection of those collections and provides a forum for co-operation and the exchange of information among those who care for them. *Chairman:* Revd Patrick Mitchell. *Hon Secretary:* Dr Tony Trowles, Westminster Abbey Library, London SW1P 3PA   *Tel:* 020–7222 5152
Fax: 020–7222 6391
email: library@westminster-abbey.org

Cathedrals Administration and Finance Association (CAFA)
In 1975 cathedral administrators and treasurers began, as a body, to exchange information on all matters touching on best practice and the most effective administration of the English Anglican cathedrals. The association now enjoys a valued link with the Association of English Cathedrals for which organization it undertakes research as needed. There is an annual conference and regular regional meetings. *Chairman:* Canon David Mead. *Admin Secretary:* Mr Jamie Milford,

Church Commissioners, 1 Millbank, London SW1P 3JZ   *Tel:* 020–7898 1000
email: jamie.milford@c-of-e.org.uk

Catholic Group in General Synod
The Catholic Group consists of those on General Synod committed to the catholic, traditional and orthodox voice in the Church of England. It seeks to make a positive contribution to all debates and especially where Catholic faith and order are involved. It welcomes both the ARCIC discussions and dialogue with the Orthodox churches. The group maintains that ethical teaching which scripture and tradition have consistently upheld. It is not averse to change where contemporary church life demands it, but stands firm on a Gospel that is based on God's revelation of Himself as Father, Son and Holy Spirit. Members represent a variety of practice within the doctrinal framework. *Chairman:* Ven Robin Ellis. *Secretary:* Mrs Anne Williams, 30 Blackhills Terrace, Horden, Co Durham SR8 4LJ   *Tel:* 0191–586 7238

Catholic League
Founded in 1913 with the aim of promoting fellowship among Catholics in all communions. Its special objects are the union of all Christians with the Apostolic See of Rome, the spread of the Catholic Faith, and the deepening of the spiritual lives of the members. It is governed by a Priest Director, the General Secretary and a council of elected members. Further details from the *General Secretary:* Mr Geoffrey Wright, 205 Merlin House, Napier Rd, Enfield, Middx EN3 4QN
Tel: 020–8805 5107
Fax: 020–8292 4520
email: gjwright@aol.com

Central Council of Church Bell Ringers
Founded 1891. Its aims are to promote the ringing of church bells, to represent the ringing exercise to the world at large and to provide expert information and advice to ringers, church authorities and the general public on all matters relating to bells and bell ringing. *President:* Mr John Anderson. *Hon Secretary:* Mr Christopher Rogers, 50 Cramhurst Lane, Witley, Godalming, Surrey GU8 5QZ   *Tel and Fax:* (01428) 682790
Web: http://www.cccbr.org.uk

Centre for International Briefing
The centre, which occupies Farnham Castle, is an independent organization founded in 1953. Its purpose is to help men and women who have been recruited to work over seas by Government, the private sector or the Churches, to gain a deeper understanding and appreciation of the societies and aspirations of the peoples of the countries in which they are to be resident with the aim that they may live and work among them successfully. Financial assistance to cover some

art of course fees, in the form of bursaries, is available to missionary and charitable organizations. *Director:* Mr David Ellison, Farnham Castle, Farnham, Surrey GU9 0AG   *Tel:* (01252) 721194
Fax: (01252) 711283
email: cib.farnham@dial.pipex.com
Web: http://www.cibfarnham.com

Centre for the Study of Christianity and Sexuality

Launched 1996, CSCS aims to provide a safe platform to promote objective debate within the Christian churches on matters concerning human sexuality, with a view to developing the spiritual teaching and doctrines of such Christian churches. CSCS publishes, among others, the international journal *Theology and Sexuality*. *Enquiries and donations to:* Dr Andrew Yip (Chair), CSCS, Department of Social Sciences, Nottingham Trent University, Burton St, Nottingham NG1 4BU   *Tel:* 0115–848 5535
Fax: 0115–948 6826
email: a.yip@ntu.ac.uk
Web: http://www.ntu.ac.uk/soc/cscs

Changing Attitude

Working for lesbian and gay affirmation within the Anglican Communion, the group, founded in 1996 is open to all whose concern is to work for an emotionally intelligent, compassionate awareness of human sexuality within the church, recognizing that any exploration has to begin with ourselves. Members meet every two months to review developments, plan for the future and offer one another encouragement and support. Changing Attitude is working within the Anglican churches of the UK through its membership network and conversations with archbishops, bishops and other key participants in the human sexuality debate. Through its membership of ALGA, the international Alliance of Lesbian and Gay Anglicans, it is also working within the Anglican Communion, responding to the 1998 Lambeth Conference resolution. *Founder:* Revd Colin Coward, 11 Murfett Close, Wimbledon, London SW19 6QB   *Tel:* 020–8788 1384
Fax: 020–8780 1733
email: ChangingUK@aol.com
Web: http:
//www.users.aol.com/changinguk/index.htm

Charterhouse

(Sutton's Hospital)
Founded 1611. Residence and care for bachelors and widowers of limited means, retired from the services, business or the professions. *Apply to:* The Master, Charterhouse, London EC1M 6AH
Tel: 020–7253 9503

Children's Society

The Children's Society has been caring for children in the name of the Church of England and the Church in Wales since 1881. Today the society has grown into one of Britain's most innovative charities with more than 90 projects. The society has supporters in parishes throughout the country whose prayers and donations make a genuine difference to the lives of the country's most vulnerable children. The society's work includes: reaching out to child runaways, afraid and in danger on the streets; helping children and families living in some of Britain's most deprived areas to make a better life for themselves by taking an active part in regenerating their own communities; supporting children experiencing problems at school to help avoid the downward spiral into truancy or exclusion; working with 15 and 16 year olds on remand to get them out of prison and helping them face up to the consequences of their behaviour and turn away from a life of crime. *Chairman:* The Bishop of Bath and Wells. *Chaplain Missioner:* Revd David Rhodes. *Chief Exec:* Mr Ian Sparks, Edward Rudolf House, Margery St, London WC1X 0JL
Tel: 020–7841 4400 (admin)
020–7841 4436 (enquiries)
Fax: 020–7837 0211
email: info@childsoc.org.uk
Web: http://www.the-childrens-society.org.uk

Choir Benevolent Fund

Founded 1851. A registered Friendly Society for subscribing Cathedral and Collegiate Lay Clerks and Organists. *Trustees:* The Deans of St Paul's, Westminster and Windsor. *Secretary:* Mr Roland Tatnell, Foxearth Cottage, Frittenden, Cranbrook, Kent   *Tel:* (01580) 712825

Choir Schools Association

Founded 1919 to promote the welfare of cathedral, collegiate and parish church choir schools. In 1985 it set up a bursary trust to help children from low income families become choristers. *Chairman:* Mr R. White. *Administrator:* Mrs Wendy Jackson, CSA, The Minster School, Deangate, York YO1 7JA   *Tel:* (01904) 624900
Fax: (01904) 557232

Christian Aid

See page 214.

Christian Alliance

See **KeyChange** page 294.

Christian Arts

An association of artists, architects, designers, craftsmen and women and all involved in the arts who are committed Christians and wish to explore and deepen their relationship between their faith and the arts. Its activities include holding exhibitions and an annual conference. An illustrated journal is published quarterly. *Contact:* Revd Michael Day, 40 Thistlewaite Rd, London E5 0QQ   *Tel:* 020–8985 8568

Christian Education Movement

(Incorporating Student Christian Movement in Schools and Institute of Christian Education) Founded in 1965, a servicing and support agency for teachers concerned with education from a Christian perspective, especially religious education. Provides professional development for teachers of religious education, inter-school conferences to explore beliefs and values in the contemporary world, and regular mailings for primary and secondary schools, libraries and resource centres. The Professional Council For Religious Education circulates curriculum material (including examinations) ideas and information to RE specialists and non-specialists and in-service training guidelines. Publications: *The British Journal of Religious Education*, *RE Today*, and a wide variety of professional papers and class room material. *President:* Lady Margaret Parkes. *Chairman:* Revd Dr Kenneth Wilson. *General Secretary:* Revd Prof Stephen Orchard, Royal Buildings, Victoria St, Derby DE1 1GW

Tel: (01332) 296655
Fax: (01332) 343253
email: cem@cem.org.uk
Web: http://www.cem.org.uk

Christian Ethical Investment Group

Founded in 1988 as a voluntary pressure group to promote a stronger ethical investment policy in the Church of England. In April 1996 it adopted a constitution with the following objects: (1) to promote an awareness and study of ethical investment issues within the Christian Churches and organizations in Britain and Ireland. This to be both by individual church members and by congregations, parishes, dioceses, national bodies and other equivalent structures; (2) to encourage the development of clearly stated theologically based ethical investment policy by Church bodies with financial investment responsibilities; (3) to promote personal and corporate responsibility through the active and responsible use of shareholder action and other appropriate ways in order to encourage a Christian approach to business and economic activity. The CEIG does not seek to promote a specific line on any particular ethical issue and is not able to offer financial advice. The Group works closely with the Ethical Investment Research Service (EIRIS) and the Ecumenical Council for Corporate Responsibility (ECCR). Membership is open to all who can support the objects. Subscription £10 p.a. for individuals and £50 p.a. for financial institutions. *Chair:* Mr Mike Tyrrell. *Secretary:* Canon Bill Whiffen, 90 Booker Ave, Bradwell Common, Milton Keynes MK13 8EF

Tel and Fax: (01908) 677466

Christian Evidence Society

Founded 1870 for the study, proclamation and defence of the Christian faith. *President:* The Archbishop of Canterbury. *Chairman:* Canon

Donald Gray. *Administrator:* Revd Eric Britt, Hylands Close, Barnston, Great Dunmow, Essex CM6 1LG *Tel:* (01371) 87603

email: eric.b@netchannel.co.uk

Christian Medical Fellowship

Founded 1949 (1) to unite Christian doctors in seeking the highest attainable standards of Christian and professional conduct; (2) to increase in the medical profession faith in Christ and the acceptance of his ethical teaching and (3) to support the work of Christian medical missionaries throughout the world. *President:* Mr Richard Cook. *General Secretary:* Dr Andrew Fergusson 157 Waterloo Rd, London SE1 8XN

Tel: 020–7928 4694
Fax: 020–7620 2453
email: cmfuk@compuserve.com
Web: http://www.cmf.org.uk

Christian Research

Christian Research serves churches and church leaders by researching and publishing trends in today's society, such as in the *UK Christian Handbook*, *Religious Trends* and *World Churches Handbook*. Members receive *Quadrant* – 'Information to Steer By' — six times a year. Christian Research helps Christian leaders turn data into decisions by providing relevant data, running regular seminars on *Priorities, Planning and Paperwork, Know Yourself, Know Your Team*, and *Interpretation of Data*. Please ask for details. *Chairman:* Chris Radley. *Exec Director:* Dr Peter Brierley, Vision Building, 4 Footscray Rd, Eltham, London SE9 2TZ

Tel: 020–8294 1989
Fax: 020–8294 0014
email: 100616.1657@compuserve.com

Christian Socialist Movement

Formed in 1960. Encourages Christians to work for a democratic socialist order of society as the political expression of their faith, and to make Christian values a significant influence upon the socialist movement. Publications: *Christian Socialist* (quarterly) and the annual Tawney Lectures. *President:* Vacancy. *Chairman:* Revd David Haslam. *Contact:* Eric Wright, 36 Cross Flats, Leeds LS11 7BG *Tel:* 0113–270 5756

Christian Witness to Israel

(formerly Barbican Mission to the Jews and International Society for Evangelisation of the Jews) Founded in 1889 and 1842 to preach the Gospel to the Jews. *Chief Exec Officer:* Revd John Ross, 166 Main Rd, Sundridge, Sevenoaks, Kent TN14 6EL

Tel: (01959) 565955
Fax: (01959) 565966
email: cwi@cwi.org.uk
Web: http://www.cwi.org.uk

Christianity and the Future of Europe

CAFE is an independent ecumenical association set up in 1989 and registered as a charity. It is a

body in association' of Churches Together in Britain and Ireland. Its objectives are the promotion of education, research, and public reflection on the issues that arise for the Christian churches of Britain from the continuing evolution of a European identity. Its Council includes corresponding secretaries in Ireland, Scotland and Wales. It functions in association with the Lincoln Theological Institute in the University of Sheffield and has links with similar bodies and church organizations in mainland Europe. Help is offered for parish twinnings. *Director:* Revd Prof Kenneth Medhurst, Lincoln Theological Institute, University of Sheffield, 36 Wilkinson St, Sheffield S10 2GB   *Tel:* 0114–222 6399
Fax: 0114 276 3973
email: Lincoln@Sheffield.ac.uk
Web: http://www.shef.ac.uk/~lti/

Christians Abroad

An ecumenical organization for people of any faith or none seeking work overseas in development or mission. Provides an information and advice service for individuals including free booklet, a vacancy bulletin and guidance interviews, as well as a recruitment and selection programme for Christian professionals on behalf of overseas employers. *General Secretary:* Mr Colin South, Christians Abroad, 1 Stockwell Green, London SW9 9HP   *Tel:* 020–7346 5950
Fax: 020–7346 5955
email: wse@cabroad.org.uk

Christians at Work

Founded in 1942 to bring together Christians to work for the extension of Christ's kingdom in the world of business and industry. To encourage active evangelism and fellowship. To provide information, literature and other facilities. To help Christians who stand alone in their place of work and to provide a means whereby young Christians starting work may be strengthened in their faith. *Contact:* Vacancy, 148 Railway Terrace, Rugby, Warws CV21 3HN   *Tel:* (01788) 579738

Christians for Europe

An ecumenical group which aims to strengthen links with the European Community; to foster studies; to educate public opinion, especially in the Christian community and so to bring the Judeo-Christian inheritance to bear upon the problems and opportunities and structures of today; to undertake particular projects in the field of research, of publications, of local friendship links, and in other appropriate ways; to co-operate with the European Movement and with ecumenical organizations based in Brussels and Strasbourg. *Hon Secretary:* Miss Diana Garnham, Europe House, 1A Whitehall Place, London SW1A 2HA

Church Action with the Unemployed

Formed in 1981, an ecumenical organization supported by the leaders of the main Churches in Great Britain. Its objective is to help and encourage churches in their ministry with unemployed people by the promotion of Unemployment Sunday (last Sunday before Lent) and by the provision and distribution of information outlining different ways in which local churches can support and sustain unemployed people. *Chairman:* Canon Frank Scuffham. *Contact:* Ms Catherine Smyth, 45B Blythe St, London E2 6LN
Tel: 020–7729 9990
Fax: 020–7256 1072

Church and Community Trust

An independent organization that offers guidance and information to local churches concerning the more effective use of their resources — buildings, money, people — for worshipping God and serving the community. *Coordinator:* Mrs Pam Nicholls, Napier Hall, Hide Place, London SW1P 4NJ   *Tel* and *Fax:* 020–7976 6347

Church Computer Users Group

An independent, non-profit making, charity seeking to support all in the churches who are exploring the use of computers and their associated technology for the glory of God and the work of the Church. It publishes a newsletter *Church Computer* three times a year and the *Church Computer Software Directory* annually. It frequently appears at Christian Resources Exhibitions and has organized its own Church Computer Roadshows throughout the country. *Patron:* The Archbishop of Canterbury. *Membership Secretary:* Revd Mark Prevett, c/o CCUG, 15 Cricklewood Drive, Halesowen B62 8SN
Tel and *Fax:* 0121–550 9748
email: prevtherev@cix.co.uk
Web: http://www.churchcomputer.org.uk

Church House Deaneries' Group

The Church House Deaneries' Group exists to stimulate local and national consideration of the developing role of the deanery, to encourage an informal network for the exchange of information about deanery thinking and deanery initiatives, and to realize the mission opportunities of deaneries. Every two years since 1988 it has held a national conference about deaneries. It has very close links with Parish and People which resources deaneries with printed material (*see* separate entry). *Chairman:* Canon Colin Hill. *Secretary:* Canon Graham Corneck, 41 Creek Rd, London SE8 3BU   *Tel:* 020–8692 2749

Church Housing Trust

A Christian organization committed to changing the lives of homeless people, providing the help and services they would otherwise be denied.

Through fundraising we support cold weather shelters and move-on homes throughout England; turning hostels into homes; caring for all irrespective of age, sex, creed or physical and mental ability. Resettlement and rehabilitation are key priorities, and donations are put towards re-education and training in areas ranging from cooking to computer skills. With encouragement and preparation, people can return to life in the community with the knowledge that someone understands and cares and will continue to support them in their first faltering months of independence. *Chairman:* Mr David Cade. *Chief Exec:* Mrs Jan Bunstead, Sutherland House, 70–78 West Hendon Broadway, London NW9 7BT
Tel: 020–8202 3458
Fax: 020–8202 1440
email: info@cht.dircon.co.uk
Web: http://www.charitynet.org/~cht

Church Lads' and Church Girls' Brigade
This uniformed and exclusively Anglican organization has more than a century of experience of serving the Church. Parish based and with the requirement that all officers are communicants, it offers a unique and effective means of extending Christ's Kingdom among children and young people. Fun and friendship are its hallmarks so helping its members develop as balanced Christians in a modern society. *President:* The Archbishop of Canterbury. *Governor:* Major General Sir Desmond Langley. *General Secretary:* Wing Commander Stewart Cresswell, National Headquarters, 2 Barnsley Rd, Wath upon Dearne, Rotherham S63 6PY
Tel: (01709) 876535
Fax: (01709) 878089
email:
General-Secretary@Church-Brigade.syol.com
Web: http://www.Church-Brigade.syol.com

Church Mission Society
CMS, founded in 1799, is 'an association of people united in obedience to the call of God to proclaim the Gospel in all lands and to gather the people of all races into the fellowship of Christ's Church'. Today's mission partners serve in a wide range of posts in 27 countries in Africa, Asia, Eastern Europe and Britain. They go at the invitation of Churches within the Anglican Communion, of United Churches and of ecumenical interdenominational agencies. Today the society works in partnership with local churches, sharing in evangelism, leadership and theological training, church growth and community development. CMS is a voluntary membership society set within the Anglican Communion. Members affirm that they will commend the Gospel, inform themselves and pray regularly for mission, and use their time and money responsibly as God's gifts. A budget of about £6 million a year is needed to maintain and expand this work. The staff in this country includes a team of area secretaries and co-ordinators representing

CMS to the dioceses of Britain. Publications include *YES* with *Prayer Paper* published four times a year; *Christians in Contact*, a tape magazine programme with notes, published ten times a year; the *General Secretary's CMS Newsletter* and a range of audio-visual materials. CMS has sister societies in Ireland, Australia and New Zealand (*See also* Crowther Hall CMS Training College and Mid-Africa Ministry (CMS)) *President:* The Viscountess Brentford. *General Secretary:* Canon Diana Witts, Partnership House, 157 Waterloo Rd, London SE1 8UU
Tel: 020–7928 8681
Fax: 020–7401 3215
email: info@cms-uk.org
Web: http://www.cms-uk.org

Church Music Society
Founded 1906. The society is a leading publisher of all types of Church music, and has consistently served the Church of England since the beginning of the century. An annual lecture and other events for members pursue further aims of advancing knowledge of the art of Church music and its historical perspective. OUP has recently been re-appointed the society's publisher. Details of membership and activities are available from the secretary. *Chairman:* Mr Ian Curror. *Hon Secretary:* Mr Simon Lindley, 8 The Chandlers, The Calls, Leeds LS2 7EZ *Tel* and *Fax:* 0113–234 1146

Church of England Clergy Stipend Trust
Founded 1952 to augment stipends of parochial clergy, normally through Diocesan Boards of Finance. *Chairman:* Mr Anthony Trower, 6 New Square, Lincoln's Inn, London WC2A 3RP
Tel: 020–7831 6292

Church of England Evangelical Council
Founded 1960 to (1) bring together evangelical leaders of the Church of England for mutual counsel and discussion (2) seek to reach a common mind on the issues of the day and when appropriate to reveal their findings to the Church and nation (3) encourage those societies and individuals in a position to do so to increase the evangelical contribution to the Church of England (4) assist in such work throughout the Anglican Communion. It organizes an annual assembly, the Anglican Evangelical Assembly, to help further its aims. *President:* The Bishop of Southwell. *Chairman:* Preb Richard Bewes. *Exec Officer:* Mr Frank Knaggs, PO Box 93, Heaton, Newcastle upon Tyne NE6 5WL
Tel and *Fax:* 0191–240 2084
email: CEEC@cableinet.co.uk

Church of England Record Society
Founded in 1991 with the object of promoting interest in and knowledge of the history of the Church of England from the sixteenth century onwards, the society publishes primary material

of national significance for Church history. It aims to produce one volume each year, set against an annual subscription of £20 (individuals), and £30 (institutions). *Exec Secretary COERS:* Miss Melanie Barber, Lambeth Palace Library, London SE1 7JU   *Tel:* 020–7928 6222
Fax: 020–7928 7932

Church of England Soldiers', Sailors' and Airmen's Clubs (1891)
A registered charity which, since its foundation in 1891, has maintained clubs at home and abroad for HM Forces and their dependants, whatever their religious denomination. The work of the association now encompasses rented housing for elderly ex-Service people or their widows/widowers. The association also liaises with other charities to build sheltered housing for ex-service people, working in parallel with its sister organization, CESSA Housing Association. Donations always welcomed. *General Secretary:* Cdr Tom O'Rourke, Head Office, 1 Shakespeare Terrace, High St, Portsmouth, Hants PO1 2RH
Tel: 023–982 9319

Church of England Soldiers', Sailors' and Airmen's Housing Association Ltd (1972)
Registered with the Housing Corporation to provide rented sheltered accommodation for elderly ex-Service people or their widows/widowers of all denominations. Construction costs were provided partly by Government grants, but donations are always welcome to help fund further homes. *Chief Exec:* Cdr Tom O'Rourke, 1 Shakespeare Terrace, High St, Portsmouth, Hants PO1 2RH   *Tel:* 023–982 9319

Church Pastoral Aid Society
CPAS was founded in 1836 and today resources local churches in the UK and Ireland. The focus of CPAS is to resource local churches in evangelism and leadership as they develop their expression of what it means to be an all-age missionary church. CPAS's resources address a wide range of ministry needs and seek to be biblically based, culturally relevant and pioneering, using innovative ways of approaching leadership and evangelism. The most important resource they have is people. Specialists in children's and youth ministry, vocational support and home group leadership work in partnership with local churches, to provide home grown solutions which engage both with immediate issues and strategy for future mission. *President:* The Bishop of Liverpool. *General Director:* Canon Brian Pearson, CPAS, Athena Drive, Tachbrook Park, Warwick CV34 6NG   *Tel:* (01926) 458458
Fax: (01926) 458459
email: info@cpas.org.uk
Web: http://www.cpas.org

Church Schoolmasters' and School Mistresses' Benevolent Institution
Founded 1857 for the relief of financial distress among past and present members of the Church of England in the teaching profession. Provides a Dual Registered Home catering for both residential and nursing care on a 24-hour basis. *President:* The Bishop of London. *Chairman:* Mr R. G. Whitwell. *Secretary:* Mr D. J. F. Godfrey, Glen Arun, 9 Athelstan Way, Horsham, Sussex RH13 6HA
Tel: (01403) 253881

Church Schools Company
Founded as an educational charity in 1883 to create schools that offer pupils a good academic education based on Christian principles with particular reference to the Church of England. The Company's council has developed the concept of a group of individually strong schools each capable of offering a broad and challenging education. To achieve this it has invested in the provision of excellent buildings and facilities including extensive ICT at each school. This ideal of strong schools embraces not just academic learning to high standards, but also the development of skills that will be essential throughout life both at work and socially. Teamwork, leadership, an enthusiastic response to challenge and an active concern for others are all attributes which are valued. Schools at Southampton, Guildford, Surbiton, Caterham, Hull, Lincoln, and Sunderland. Clergy bursaries available. *Chairman:* Mr J. H. W. Beardwell. *Chief Exec:* Mr Ewan Harper, Church Schools House, Titchmarsh, Kettering, Northants NN14 3DA
Tel: (01832) 735105
Fax: (01832) 734760
email: admin@church-schools.com

Church Society
Formed in 1950 by the amalgamation of the Church Association and National Church League which was founded in 1835, continues to seek to maintain the evangelical and reformed faith of the Church of England, based upon the authority of Holy Scripture (see Canon A5) and the foundational doctrines of the Thirty-nine Articles and the Book of Common Prayer. Publishes a journal *Churchman* and a quarterly broadsheet *Cross+Way*. The society publishes books, booklets and leaflets on current issues and organizes conferences and public meetings. Patronage is administered through the Church Society Trust. (*See also Patronage Trusts*) *President:* The Viscount Brentford. *Chairman:* Revd Donald Allister. *Director:* Revd David Philips, Dean Wace House, 16 Rosslyn Rd, Watford, Herts WD1 7EY
Tel: (01923) 235111 (24 Hours)
Fax: (01923) 800362
email: admin@churchsociety.org
Web: http://www.churchsociety.org

Church Union

Founded in 1859, at the time of the 'Oxford Movement', to promote catholic faith and order, it continues this work today by providing support and encouragement to those lay people and priests who wish to see catholic faith, order, morals and spirituality maintained and upheld, and who wish to promote catholic unity. The union runs Faith House Bookshop (Christian books, cards and sacristry supplies), publishes books, tracts, and a biannual theological journal, *The Tufton Review* produces a quarterly magazine, the *Church Observer*, and has full-time staff who can advise on matters liturgical, legal and musical. *President:* Rt Revd Eric Kemp, Bishop of Chichester. *Chairman:* Rt Revd Lindsay Urwin, Bishop of Horsham, Faith House, 7 Tufton St, London SW1P 3QN   *Tel:* 020–7222 6952
Fax: 020–7976 7180

Church Urban Fund

See page 215.

Church Welfare Association (Incorporated)

(formerly the Church Moral Aid Association) Founded 1851. Gives financial aid to Church projects assisting and supporting women and children in need of residential care and/or moral support. *Chairman:* Mrs Coral Hallums. *Secretary:* Mr D. J. Boddington, 15 Marina Court, Alfred St, Bow, London E3 2BH

Church's Ministry Among Jewish People

Founded 1809 as London Society for Promoting Christianity among the Jews, to take the Christian Gospel to Jewish people. *President:* Rt Revd John Taylor. *Chairman:* Miss Elizabeth Hodkinson. *General Director:* Revd Tony Higton, 30c Clarence Rd, St Albans, Herts AL1 4JJ
Tel: (01727) 833114
Fax: (01727) 848312
email: enquiries@cmj.org,uk
Web: www.cmj.org.uk

Churches Commission on Overseas Students

The national ecumenical co-ordinating agency for concern towards all students from abroad. *Chair:* Dr Gwenda Thompson. *Exec Secretary:* Ms Gillian Court, 1 Stockwell Green, London SW9 9HP   *Tel:* 020–7737 1101
Fax: 020–7346 5955
email: exec@ccos.cablenet.co.uk

Churches Main Committee

Founded 1941, and registered as a charity in 1966, to advance the charitable work, whether religious or otherwise, of the Churches by furthering their common interests in secular matters relating to that work, other than education; to give advice to the Churches on these matters; to conduct negotiations and take such action as may be thought fit; to act as a liaison body between the Churches and the machinery of Government. *Chairman:*

The Bishop of London. *Secretary:* Mr Derek Taylo Thompson. *Asst Secretary:* Mrs Betty Cracknell Fielden House, Little College St, London SW1F 3SH   *Tel:* 020–7898 1878; 020–7222 498
Fax: 020–7898 189⁹

Churches' Advertising Network

A professional group of Christians from all tradi tions co-operating to develop the professiona use of advertising as part of the churches' com munication and outreach. CAN seeks free or low cost poster space and radio airtime from leading media owners, which it uses on behalf of the churches. All members give their services free *Contact:* Revd Robert Ellis, St Mary's House The Close, Lichfield WS13 7LD
Tel: (01543) 30603(
Fax: (01543) 30603⁹
email: communications@lichfield.anglican.org

Churches' Council for Health and Healing

British Churches of all denominations and the main medical bodies, including the British Medical Association and the Royal Colleges, are officially represented on the council, together with the guilds and fellowships of healing which work within the Churches' ministry of healing or a basis of mutual understanding and co-operation with the medical profession. It acts as a centre for co-ordinating activities and distributing appropriate material as part of the regular work of the churches. *President:* The Archbishop of Canterbury. *Secretary:* Vacancy, St Luke's Hospital for the Clergy, 14 Fitzroy Square, London W1P 6AH   *Tel:* 020–7388 7903

Churches' Fellowship for Psychical and Spiritual Studies

Founded 1953 to study the psychic and spiritual and their relevance to Christian faith and life. *President:* Canon Michael Perry. *Chairman:* Prebendary Michael Shrewsbury. *General Secretary:* Mr Julian Drewett, The Rural Workshop, South Rd, North Somercotes, Louth, Lincs LN11 7PT
Tel and *Fax:* (01507) 358845
email: gensec@cfpss.freeserve.co.uk
Web: http://www.cfpss.freeserve.co.uk

Churches' Group on Funeral Services at Cemeteries and Crematoria

Formed in 1980 by the mainstream Churches in England and Wales to co-ordinate their policies in connection with the pastoral and administrative aspects of funeral services at cemeteries and crematoria and to represent the Churches at national level in joint discussions with public and private organizations on any matters relating to ministry at such funerals. Publications sponsored by the group include a handbook of funeral procedures, *Funerals and Ministry to the Bereaved* (Church House Publishing, second edition 1989), intended for use by clergy, funeral directors and cemetery and crematorium staff; and two joint

uneral service books (The Canterbury Press, Norwich), one for use in England (1986 and 1994) the other for use in Wales (1987); *The Role of the Minister in Bereavement: Guidelines and Training Suggestions* (Church House Publishing, 1989); and a leaflet entitled *Questions Commonly Asked About Funerals* (1994). Reports of the Group's conferences on *The Role of a Minister at a Funeral* (1991) *Bereavement and Belief* (1993) and *Clergy and Cremation Today* (1995) are available on application from the General Synod Office, Church House, London SW1P 3NZ (price £2.75). A bibliography, *Death, Dying and Bereavement. Guidelines for Best Practice of Clergy at Funerals* (1997) (price £3.95 inc VAT) is also available. The Group keeps in close touch with the main organizations concerned with funeral provision and bereavement counselling. *Chairman:* Rt Revd Geoffrey Rowell. *Hon Secretary:* Revd Michael Bray. *Asst Secretary:* Mr David Hebblethwaite, Church House, Great Smith St, London SW1P 3NZ
Tel: 020–7898 1364
Fax: 020–7898 1369
email: david.hebblethwaite@c-of-e.org.uk

Clinical Theology Association
Founded in 1962. The core activity of the association is seminars in pastoral care and pastoral counselling which are directed by authorized tutors and widely available in the UK. Seminars are designed to promote self-awareness which is needed for effective pastoral work, and to teach the theory and practice of pastoral counselling with reference to the assumptions, values and meanings of the Christian faith. Further information about Clinical Theology education and training may be obtained from the *General Director:* Revd Peter van de Kasteele, St Mary's House, Church Westcote, Oxford OX7 6SF
Tel: (01993) 830209

College of Health Care Chaplains
Founded in 1992, the college is a multi-faith, interdenominational professional organization open to all recognized health care chaplaincy staff, full-time and part-time, voluntary and support workers, and those with an interest in health care chaplaincy. It provides peer support, advice and fellowship for its members nationally and through 19 regional branches throughout the UK. A focus for professional development, good practice standards and training activities, the college publishes the *Journal of Health Care Chaplaincy* (available on subscription to non-members) and issues regular newsletters. An autonomous section of the Manufacturing, Science and Finance Union (MSF). *President:* Canon David Equeall. *Registrar:* Mr Chris Webber, 2 Edwards College, South Cerney, Cirencester GL7 5TR
Tel: (01285) 861312
Fax: (01285) 862221

College of Preachers
Founded 1960 to help, encourage and stimulate those engaged in the ministry of preaching. Arranges training courses and conferences for preachers on an ecumenical basis. Open-Learning courses at certificate and masters levels validated by the University of Wales. *Chairman:* The Bishop of Liverpool. *Director:* Revd Dr Stephen Wright. *Administator:* Mrs Karen Atkin, 10A North St, Bourne, Lincs PE10 9AB
Tel and *Fax:* (01778) 422929
email: collpreach@mistral.co.uk
Web: http://www3.mistral.co.uk/collpreach

Commonwealth War Graves Commission
Founded 1917. Responsible for marking and maintaining in perpetuity the graves of those of Commonwealth Forces who fell in the 1914–18 and 1939–45 Wars and for commemorating by name on memorials those with no known grave. *President:* HRH The Duke of Kent. *Chairman:* The Secretary of State for Defence in the United Kingdom. *Enquiries:* Legal Adviser and Solicitor, 2 Marlow Rd, Maidenhead, Berks SL6 7DX
Tel: (01628) 634221
Fax: (01628) 771208

Community Housing and Therapy
CHT runs educational and therapeutic residential programmes for people with mental health problems. It educates in a practical and in a psychological way. Clients learn practical living skills and learn to become emotionally and intellectually articulate members of a community. Through dialogue with others, CHT's clients gain the confidence to become integrated citizens. *Director of Social Work:* Mr John Gale, Bishop Creighton House, 378 Lillie Rd, London SW6 7PH
Tel: 020–7381 5558
0800 018 1261 (Freephone)
Fax: 020–7610 0608
email: cht.charity@email-me.co.uk
Web: http://www.cht.org.uk

Community of St Aidan and St Hilda
Established 1994, the community seeks to cradle a Christian spirituality for today, inspired by the Celtic saints. Its three aims are: to restore the memory and experience of the Celtic Church in ways that relate to God's purposes today and bring healing to the land; to research the history, spirituality and relationship to cultural patterns of the Celtic mission, and how they apply to the renewal of today's church and society; to resource through provision of materials for prayer, worship and study, personal and group retreats, workshops, networking with link churches and centres. The primary resources are the Explorers and members who follow the community's Way of Life with a personal soul friend. *Community Soul Friend:* The Bishop of Carlisle. *Guardian:* Revd Ray Simpson, The Open

Gate, Marygate, Holy Island, Berwick-upon-Tweed TD15 2SD   *Tel* and *Fax:* (01289) 389249
email: theopengate@bigfoot.com
Web: http://www.ndirect.co.uk/~raysimpson

Company of Mission Priests

Founded 1940. An association of male priests of the Anglican Communion who, wishing to consecrate themselves wholly to the Church's mission, keep themselves free from the attachments of marriage and family, and endeavour to encourage and strengthen each other by mutual prayer and fellowship, sharing the vision of St Vincent de Paul of a priesthood dedicated to service. *Visitor:* The Bishop of Horsham. *Warden:* Canon Michael Shields, Flat 14, Bromley College, London Rd, Bromley, Kent BR1 1PE
Tel: 020–8464 7906
email: gregorymps@email.msn.com

Compassionate Friends

A nationwide organization of bereaved parents and their families offering friendship and understanding to others similarly bereaved. Personal and group support. Quarterly news letter, annual conferences, postal book library and a range of leaflets. *Office Administrator:* Jon Gilbody, 53 North St, Bristol BS3 1EN
Tel: 0117–953 9639 (Helpline)
Tel and *Fax:* 0117–966 5202 (Admin)

Confraternity of the Blessed Sacrament

Founded 1862 to honour Jesus Christ our Lord in the Blessed Sacrament; to make mutual eucharistic intercession and to encourage eucharistic devotion. *Superior-General:* Revd Timothy Bugby. *Secretary General:* Revd Dr Lawson Nagel, Aldwick Vicarage, 25 Gossamer Lane, Bognor Regis, W Sussex PO21 3AT   *Tel:* (01243) 262049
email: lnagel@netcomuk.co.uk
Web: http://www.netcomuk.co.uk/~lnagel/cbs.html/

Corporation of SS Mary and Nicolas (The Woodard Schools)

Founded by Canon Nathaniel Woodard in 1848 to promote education in the doctrines and principles of the Church of England. The corporation now runs some 23 schools and a further 15 schools are affiliated to the corporation. *President:* The Bishop of Dover. *Registrar:* Mr Peter Beesley, 1 The Sanctuary, London SW1P 3JT
Tel: 020–7222 5381
Fax: 020–7222 7502
email: 106102.1723@compuserve.com

Corporation of the Sons of the Clergy

(Trustees for the Clergy Orphan Corporation)
Founded 1655. Incorporated by Royal Charter 1678. For helping clergy of the Anglican Communion in the UK, Eire and Anglican missionaries abroad providing they are sponsored by a UK based missionary society. The corporation can also help widows and widowers of such clergy their separated or divorced spouses, and the dependent children of any of the above. Help can also be given to unmarried daughters of pensionable age. Grants are not made for holidays or the purchase or running of cars. *President:* The Archbishop of Canterbury. *Registrar:* Mr Christopher Leach, 1 Dean Trench St, London SW1P 3HB   *Tel:* 020–7799 3696 and 020–7222 5887
Fax: 020–7233 1913

Council of Christians and Jews

Founded 1942 to combat all forms of religious and racial intolerance, to promote mutual understanding and goodwill between Christians and Jews, and to foster co-operation in educational activities and in social and community service. 60 local branches in the UK. *Presidents:* The Archbishop of Canterbury, the Cardinal Archbishop of Westminster, the Moderator of the Church of Scotland, the Moderator of the Free Churches' Council, the Archbishop of Thyateira and Great Britain and the Chief Rabbi. *Director:* Sister Margaret Shepherd, Drayton House, 30 Gordon St, London WC1H 0AN   *Tel:* 020–7388 3322
Fax: 020–7388 3305
email: ccjuk@aol.com
Web: http://www.ccj.org.uk

Council on Christian Approaches to Defence and Disarmament

CCADD was established in 1963 by the Rt Rev Robert Stopford, then Bishop of London, to study problems relating to defence and disarmament within a Christian context. The British Group of CCADD comprises Christians of different traditions, varying vocations and specializations and political views, with a range of responsibilities, governmental and non-governmental. CCADD seeks to bring an ethical viewpoint to bear on disarmament and arms control and related issues and to this end the British Group has always stressed the importance of dialogue between official and non-official bodies. *President:* The Bishop of Oxford. *Chairman:* Mr Brian Wicker. *Admin Secretary:* Mrs Liza Hamilton, CCADD, 48 Lawrence Ave, Mill Hill, London NW7 4NN
Tel: 020–8201 0890
email: ccadd@lineone.net

Crosse's Charity

Provides small annuities for widows of clergymen of the Church of England. Preference given to those, who from age, ill-health, accident or infirmity are unable to maintain themselves by their own exertions. *For form of application please apply to:* Clerks to Trustees, Hinckley Birch & Brown, 20 Saint John St, Lichfield, Staffs WS13 6PD   *Tel:* (01543) 262491

Crosslinks

Founded 1922 as the Bible Churchmen's Missionary Society (BCMS). Crosslinks is an international evangelical Anglican mission agency with the slogan *God's Word to God's World*. It supports and encourages churches through the exchange of mission and study partners and is a full member of the Partnership for World Mission. Mission partners work in East, North and South Africa, Zimbabwe, Spain, Portugal, France and Asia as well as among those of other faiths in the UK. *President:* Revd Dr C. Wright. *General Secretary:* Revd Roger Bowen, 251 Lewisham Way, London SE4 1XF   *Tel:* 020–8691 6111
Fax: 020–8694 8023
email: crosslinks@pro-net.co.uk

Crowhurst Christian Healing Centre

Opened in 1928. Guests come for a few days or up to two weeks for rest, renewal, healing prayer and ministry in peaceful and beautiful surroundings. The daily programme revolves around Christ-centred worship, Holy Communion and twice-weekly healing services. Courses on the healing ministry and creative courses are also available. *Apply to the:* Secretary, Crowhurst Christian Healing Centre, The Old Rectory, Crowhurst, Battle, E Sussex TN33 9AD
Tel: (01424) 830204
Fax: (01424) 830053

Crowther Hall CMS Training College

Crowther Hall is one of three colleges for training in mission which, together with seven others, make up the Selly Oak Colleges at Birmingham. All CMS long-term Mission Partners spend from three to nine months in preparation for service abroad. Students from overseas (including several involved in the Centre for Anglican Communion Studies, CEFACS) spend one to three terms studying in different departments in Selly Oak. Leasow House offers facilities for Mission Partners on leave, sabbaticals, retreats and small conferences. *Principal:* Revd George Kovoor, Crowther Hall, Selly Oak, Birmingham B29 6QT
Tel: 0121–472 4228
Fax: 0121–471 2662
email: crowtherhall@sellyoak.ac.uk

Crusaders

A well-established youth movement working with churches and Christians of all main denominations to show the relevance of Jesus Christ to young people between the ages of 4 and 18. The backbone of this national organization is the regular youth group which has a mix of Bible teaching through active learning, games, outings, holidays, local and national activities. It aims to help churches with their youth outreach strategies and provides teaching resources, activity materials, an extensive Leadership Training Programme, a Leaders' magazine, short term service opportunities, over 40 adventure holidays for young people each summer, backed up by a team of area workers, a head office team and book centre in St Albans. There are three residental centres available to schools and youth groups. *Director:* Vacancy, Crusaders, 2 Romeland Hill, St Albans, Herts AL3 4ET   *Tel:* (01727) 855422
Fax: (01727) 848518
email: email@crusaders.org.uk
Web: http://www.crusaders.org.uk

Culham College Institute

This is a research, development, and information agency working in the fields of Church schools, Church colleges, and RE. It is managed by the Culham Educational Foundation and arose out of the closure of a Church of England college of education. It has established a national system of networking, collaborative activity, and project management. Current collaboration includes work with the Jerusalem Trust, the St Gabriel's Trust, the All Saints Trust, British Telecom and the school broadcasting departments of the BBC and Channel 4. The Association of Church College Trusts has its base at Culham. *Director:* Revd Dr John Gay, 60 East St Helen St, Abingdon, Oxon OX14 5EB   *Tel:* (01235) 520458
Fax: (01235) 535421
email: enquiries@culham.ac.uk
Web: http://www.culham.ac.uk

Deaf People, Royal Association in Aid of

(formerly The Royal Association in Aid of the Deaf and Dumb)
Founded 1841 to promote the spiritual, social and general welfare of deaf people. Works in the dioceses of London, Chelmsford, Guildford, Rochester and Southwark. *Patron:* HM The Queen. *President:* The Archbishop of Canterbury. *Vice-Presidents:* The Bishops of London, Rochester, Southwark, Guildford and Chelmsford. *Chief Executive:* Mr Tom Fenton. *Administrator:* Miss Tracey Barlow, RAD Head Office, Centre for Deaf People, Walsingham Rd, Colchester CO2 7BP
Tel: (01206) 509509
(01206) 577090 (Minicom)
Fax: (01206) 769755
email: info@royaldeaf.org.uk
Web: http://www.royaldeaf.org.uk/royaldeaf/

Deaf People, Royal National Institute for

The RNID is the largest charity representing the 8.7 million deaf and hard of hearing people in the UK. As a membership charity, it aims to achieve a radically better quality of life for deaf and hard of hearing people by campaigning and lobbying to change laws and government policies, by providing information and raising awareness of deafness, hearing loss and tinnitus, by running training courses and consultancy on deafness and disability, offering communication services including sign language interpreters. It trains interpreters, lipspeakers and speech-to-text operators. It seeks lasting change in education for

deaf children and young people and runs employment programmes to help deaf people into work. It provides residential and community services for deaf people with special needs. Other areas of work include the provision of equipment and products for deaf and hard of hearing people and social, medical and technical research. *Chairman:* Mr David Livermore. *Chief Exec:* Mr James Strachan, 19–23 Featherstone St, London EC1Y 8SL   *Tel:* 020–7296 8000 (Voice)
020–7296 8001 (Text)
Fax: 020–7296 8199
email: helpline@rnid.org.uk
Web: http://www.rnid.org.uk

Deans' and Provosts' Conference
The Deans' and Provosts' Conference is the meeting together (three times annually) of those who preside over their Cathedral Chapters to reflect upon Cathedral issues of particular concern to Deans and Provosts in their public and cathedral roles. *Chairman:* The Dean of Hereford. *Treasurer:* The Dean of Exeter. *Secretary:* The Provost of Blackburn, Provost's Office, Cathedral Close, Blackburn BB1 5AA   *Tel:* (01254) 51491
email: provost@blackburn.anglican.org

Deans' and Provosts' Vergers' Conference
Founded in 1989 to bring together Head Vergers who are employed in that capacity by a Dean or Provost and Chapter of the Church of England. The conference enables members to communicate with each other, exchange and discuss ideas of common interest and to have regular contact with the Deans and Provosts Conference. The Head Vergers of the 42 English Cathedrals, Westminster Abbey and St George's Windsor are eligible for membership. *Chairman:* Mr W. Ross. *Secretary:* Mr Paul Timms, Southwark Cathedral, Montague Close, London SE1 9DA
Tel: 020–7633 0433 (Home)
020–7367 6701 (Office)

DGAA
Founded 1897 as the Distressed Gentlefolk's Aid Asssociation to alleviate need and distress by giving financial help to people of professional or similar background and their families, of British or Irish nationality, irrespective of religious denomination, and to provide and maintain nursing and residential accommodation. *Chairman:* Mr Billy Carbutt. *Chief Exec:* Mr Jonathan Welfare, 1 Derry St, London W8 5HY
Tel: 020–7396 6700
Fax: 020–7396 6739

Diaconal Association of the Church of England
DACE is a professional association for Diaconal Ministers (deacons, accredited lay workers, and Church Army officers) working in the Church of England, established in 1988 to succeed the Deaconess Committee and the Anglican Accredited Lay Workers Federation. Associated membership is also open to priests, students in training for ministry, and diaconal ministers working in other provinces in the UK. DACE exists to promote the distinctive (permanent) diaconate and other diaconal ministries in the Church of England, support all nationally recognized diaconal ministers, and consider the theological and practical implications of diaconal ministry within the total ministry of the Christian church, in partnership with other agencies and denominations. *Secretary:* Capt Neil Thomson, 95 Ballens Rd, Lordswood, Chatham, Kent ME5 8PA
Tel: 07020–960520
email: secretary@dace.societies.anglican.org
Web: http://www.societies.anglican.org/dace

Diakonia
Founded in 1947 to link the various European deaconess associations, it is now a 'World Federation of Diaconal Associations'. It concerns itself with the nature and task of 'Diakonia' and encourages deaconesses, deacons, and lay people doing diaconal work. It also furthers ecumenical relations between the diaconal associations in other countries. The Diaconal Association of the Church of England is a member. There is a Diakonia *UK Liaison Group* which also includes representatives from the Methodist Diaconal Order, the Church of Scotland Diaconate and the Deaconesses of the Presbyterian Church in Ireland. *UK representative on International Exec Committee:* Miss Jane Martin, 12A Carnoustie Court, Ardler, Dundee DD2 3RB   *Tel:* (01382) 813786
email: Janimar@aol.com

Diocesan Institutions of Chester, Manchester, Liverpool and Blackburn
For the relief of widows and orphans of clergymen who have officiated in their last sphere of duty in the Archdeaconries of Chester, Macclesfield, Manchester, Rochdale, Liverpool, Warrington or Blackburn. *For further details please contact:* Revd Michael Finlay, Rectory, Warrington, Cheshire WA1 2TL   *Tel:* (01925) 635020

Distinctive Diaconate
An unofficial Church of England centre which serves to promote the diaconate as one of the historic orders of the Church's ministry with manifold potential for ministry today by sharing information about current developments through the newsletters *Distinctive Diaconate News* and *Distinctive News of Women in Ministry.* The *Mission and Ministry* report of Lambeth 1988 recommended the sharing of experiences with the diaconate within the Anglican Communion and suggested using Distinctive Diaconate. *Editor:* Revd Sr Teresa, CSA, St Andrew's House, 2 Tavistock Rd, Westbourne Park, London W11 1BA   *Tel:* 020–7229 2662 Ext 24
Fax: 020–7792 5993
email: sister.teresa@dllondon.org.uk

Distressed Gentlefolk's Aid Association
See **DGAA** page 286.

Ecclesiastical Insurance Group
Founded 1887 to offer specialist insurance for church property and personal policies for clergy and laity. Grants to English dioceses are made. The Company also provide Life insurance including Pensions, Mortgages, Free Standing AVC and Ethical Unit Trusts. (In the last five years alone grants for churches and charitable purposes have amounted to £16.5 million.) *Chairman:* Mr M. A. Cornwall-Jones. *Managing Director:* Mr Graham Doswell. *Branch Offices: Belfast:* Chamber of Commerce House, 22 Great Victoria St, Belfast BT2 7LX; *Birmingham:* Berwick House, 35 Livery St, Birmingham B3 2PB; *Bristol:* Kings Court, King St, Bristol BS1 4EE; *Cambridge:* Abbeygate House, 164/167 East Rd, Cambridge CB1 1DB; *Cardiff:* Riverside House, 31 Cathedral Rd, Cardiff CF1 9HB; *Manchester:* Lincoln House, 1 Brazennose St, Manchester M2 5FJ; *Southampton:* Adyar House, 32 Carlton Crescent, Southampton SO15 2YP; *East Grinstead:* Kings House, 13/21 Cantelupe Rd, E Grinstead, Sussex RH19 3BE; *Edinburgh:* 55 North Castle St, Edinburgh EH2 3QA; *Harrogate:* 7 Cambridge Rd, Harrogate, N Yorks HG1 1PB; *London:* 19/31 Billiter St, London EC3M 2RY. *Head Office:* Beaufort House, Brunswick Rd, Gloucester GL1 1JZ   *Tel:* (01452) 528533
Fax: (01452) 423557
email: gbeigmkg@ibmmail.com
Web: http://www.eigonline.co.uk

Ecclesiastical Law Society
Founded in 1987 to promote the study of ecclesiastical law, through the education of office bearers and practitioners in the ecclesiastical courts, the enlargement of knowledge of ecclesiastical law among clergy and laity of the Anglican Communion, and assistance in matters of ecclesiastical law to the General Synod, Convocations, Bishops and Church dignitaries. *President:* The Bishop of Chichester. *Chairman:* Dr Frank Robson. *Secretary:* Mr Peter Beesley, 1 The Sanctuary, London SW1P 3JT   *Tel:* 020–7222 5381

Ecclesiological Society
St Andrew-by-the Wardrobe, Queen Victoria St, London EC4V 5DE. Founded as the Cambridge Camden Society in 1839. Studies the arts, architecture and liturgy of the Christian Church by meetings, tours and publications. *President:* Donald Buttress. *Contact:* Paul Velluet, 9 Bridge Rd, St Margaret's, Twickenham, Middx TW1 1RE

Ecumenical Council for Corporate Responsibility
ECCR was set up in 1989 to study and research the corporate responsibility of the Churches' investments and the companies in which those investments are held, with special reference to those which are transnational corporations.

ECCR is an ecumenical body with membership from many different denominations, societies, religious orders and other Church organizations. Its membership is approaching 200 corporate bodies and individuals. It has the status of a Body in Association with Churches Together in Britain and Ireland and it is structured as a company limited by guarantee, registered in England and Wales. *Co-ordinator:* Revd Crispin White, PO Box 4317, Bishop's Stortford CM22 7GZ
Tel: (01279) 718274
Fax: (01279) 718097
email: ECCR@GEO2.poptel.org.uk

Ecumenical Society of the Blessed Virgin Mary
Founded in London in 1967, 'to advance the study at various levels of the place of the Blessed Virgin Mary in the Church under Christ and to promote ecumenical devotion'. *Patrons:* Cardinal Basil Hume, Lord Runcie, Archbishop Gregorios of Thyateira, Revd Dr John Newton. *Secretary:* Mr Joe Farrelly, 11 Belmont Rd, Wallington, Surrey SM6 8TE   *Tel:* 020–8647 5992

Edward King Institute for Ministry Development
Founded in 1986 as a forum for lay and ordained involved in ministry who have a concern to reflect together on current practice and future issues in ministry and mission. Its focus is: exploring new ways of being church; working with God in the world; and developing patterns of ministry and mission. The membership is ecumenical and international. The institute sponsors day and residential consultations and publishes a journal *Ministry*, three times a year. *Co-Directors:* Mrs Caroline Pascoe and Canon Robin Greenwood, *Hon Secretary:* Mrs Jo Cook, 4 College Green, Gloucester GL1 2LX
Tel: (01452) 410022
Fax: (01452) 382905
email: EKI@fosdike.demon.co.uk

EFAC Bursary Scheme
See **Studylink — EFAC International Training Partnership**, page 309.

English Churches Housing Group
Formed in 1991 by the merger of the Church Housing Association and the Baptist Housing Association. Manages 10,000 self-contained homes and 60 supported housing schemes with space for 2,000 people. Offers a wide range of housing from general needs to sheltered schemes for elderly people and supported housing schemes for single homeless people. ECHG's subsidiary company, Heritage Care, provides domiciliary care to enable people with daily care needs to live independently in the community. *Chairman:* Mr Tim Richmond. *Chief Exec:* Caroline White, Sutherland House, 70–78 West Hendon Broadway, London NW9 7BT   *Tel:* 020–8203 9233
Fax: 020–8203 0092

English Clergy Association
Recently revived, formerly the Parochial Clergy Association, founded 1938, sustains in fellowship all Clerks in Holy Orders in their vocation and ministry within the Church of England, promoting in every available way the good of English parish and cathedral life and the welfare of clergy. Related trustees give discretionary clergy holiday grants upon application to the Hon Almoner. The association seeks to foster the independence of the clergy whether in freehold office or not, and broadly supports the patronage system. Publishes *Parson and Parish* Journal. *Patron:* The Bishop of London. *Chairman:* Revd John Masding, The Old School, Norton Hawkfield, Bristol BS39 4HB   *Tel* and *Fax:* (01275) 830017
email: masding@breathe.co.uk

European Christian Industrial Movement (Bridgebuilders)
Founded in June 1975, firstly to remind people of the Christian Gospel and its full implications in the new technological society with its multinational groups, and secondly to help build the many bridges of trust, understanding and co-operation that are necessary, not only between the peoples of the nations but also between the many opposing sections of each community. (Associated with The Bridge Builders, Rue Gachard 35, B-1050, Brussels). *Secretary General:* Mr Tom Chapman, Barrowdale, Stainton with Adgarley, Barrow-in-Furness, Cumbria LA13 0NW   *Tel:* (01229) 63743

Evangelical Alliance
Founded 1846 as a representative body for evangelical Christians to promote evangelical unity and truth and represent evangelical concern to government and media. Co-ordinates corporate activity in evangelism, theological issues and social involvement. *President:* Sir Fred Catherwood. *General Director:* Revd Joel Edwards, Whitefield House, 186 Kennington Park Rd, London SE11 4BT   *Tel:* 020–7207 2100
Fax: 020–7207 2150
email: London@eauk.org
Web: http://www.eauk.org

Evangelical Christians for Racial Justice
Originally the Evangelical Race Relations Group, the name was changed in 1984 to reflect an increasing commitment to positive action to combat racism. ECRJ now offers a radical biblical critique of both Church and society in the area of racial justice. It is based on a nationwide, multiracial membership and aims to support its members at a local level as well as address issues on a national canvas. The journal *Racial Justice* is published three times a year. *Co-chairs of Exec Committee:* Beverley Thomas and Peter Hobson, 109 Homerton High St, London E9 6DL
Tel: 020–8985 2764

Family Life and Marriage Education Network
A church network launched in 1990. Most dioceses are now involved, and there are links with other churches and agencies. FLAME aims to co-ordinate, support and sustain the work of Family Life and Marriage Education in dioceses of the Church of England and to act as a network for the exchange of information and expertise. It also aims to encourage good practice and to initiate new projects where needed. It has developed from the work of the Family Life Education Advisory Group since 1972 and the House of Bishops' Marriage Education Panel between 1984 and 1988. Contact can be made through individual dioceses, or through FLAME. *Chairman of Trustees:* Canon David Grimwood, 60 Marsham St, Maidstone, Kent ME14 1EW
Tel: (01622) 755014
Fax: (01622) 693531
email: flame@csr.org.uk
Web: http://welcome.to/familylife

Federation of Catholic Priests
A federation of diocesan associations of priests in communion with the See of Canterbury who have undertaken to live in accordance with Catholic doctrine and practice. It exists for mutual support in propagating, maintaining and defending such doctrine and practice and for the deepening of the spiritual life of members. *Chairman:* Revd Scott Anderson. *Secretary General:* Prebendary Brian Tubbs, Vicarage, Palace Place, Paignton TQ3 3AU   *Tel:* (01803) 559059
email: FATHER_TUBBS@compuserve.com

Feed the Minds
Grant-making charity established in 1964 which supports Christian literature and communication, literacy, and theological education in developing countries and Eastern Europe. Feed the Minds is interdenominational, and 22 British and Irish missionary societies and Churches are member bodies. *President:* Dr Pauline Webb. *Chair:* Mr John Clark. *Director:* Dr Alwyn Marriage, Albany House, 67 Sydenham Rd, Guildford GU1 3RY   *Tel:* (01483) 888580
Fax: (01483) 888581
email: feedtheminds@gn.apc.org

Fellowship of St Alban and St Sergius
Founded 1928. An unofficial body which fosters understanding and friendship between Eastern Orthodox and Western Christians. *Presidents:* Lord Runcie and Archbishop Gregorios of Thyateira and Great Britain. *General Secretary:* Revd Stephen Platt, 1 Canterbury Rd, Oxford OX2 6LU
Tel: (01865) 552991
Fax: (01865) 316700
email:
stephen.platt-albanandsergius@btinternet.com
Web: http://www.btinternet.com/~sobornost

Fellowship of St Nicholas
Founded in 1939 to provide a loving Christian home for children. We now work from the St Nicholas Centre in St Leonard's providing a wide and expanding range of after school and holiday-care, a mobile playbus and a range of services for children and support for parents working in partnership with other locally based voluntary and statutory agencies. *Chairman:* Mrs Mollie Green. *Director:* Mr Tony Cox, 10 Carisbrooke Rd, St Leonards-on-Sea, E Sussex TN38 0JS
Tel: (01424) 423683
Fax: (01424) 460446
email: St@nicolas14.freeserve.co.uk

Fellowship of St Therese of Lisieux
Founded in 1997, the centenary year of St Therese's death and in anticipation of her being proclaimed a Doctor of the Church in 1998. Its purpose is to inform members of the Church of England about her teaching and its relevance to Christians of all denominations, particularly as we begin the next millennium and to gain an entry for her in the Anglican calendar of saints. Those who would like to know more about her approach to spirituality and Christian disciple-ship and share in the interest of others are wel-come to join the fellowship. Members commit themselves to learn more about St Therese through reading, study and prayer; pray for other members regularly; take opportunities to spread her message within our churches; meet together once a year for a time of retreat and teaching; and encourage one another by contact and correspondence as appropriate. *Contact:* Revds Graeme and Sue Parfitt, St Michael's Vic-arage, 78 Stockwell Park Rd, London SW9 0DA
Tel: 020–7274 6357

Fidelity Trust Limited
Founded 1908 for the holding of trusteeships of real and personal property for Church and char-itable purposes. *Chairman:* Bernard Moss. *Director and Secretary:* Revd David Maudlin, Keeley House, 22–30 Keeley Rd, Croydon, Surrey CR0 1TE
Tel: 020–8661 6081

Foreign Missions Club
Christian guesthouse on quiet private road with ample on-street parking. Reductions for missionaries/clergy. *Manager:* Mrs B. Littlehales, 26 Aberdeen Park, London N5 2BJ
Tel: 020–7226 2663
Fax: 020–7704 1853
email: fmc_gh@compuserve.com

Forward in Faith
Founded in November 1992, Forward in Faith exists to support all who in conscience are unable to accept the ordination of women to the priest-hood or the episcopate. It seeks an ecclesial struc-ture which will continue the orders of bishop and priest as the church has received them. It offers support to all who need it via a national and local network. It is governed by an elected council, drawn from the members of its National Assembly, which meets annually. It publishes the monthly journal *New Directions*, the quarterly newspaper *Forward Plus* and a variety of catech-etical material. *Chairman:* The Bishop of Fulham. *Director:* Mr Stephen Parkinson, Faith House, 7 Tufton St, London SW1P 3QN *Tel:* 020–7976 0727
Fax: 020–7976 0737
email: forwardinfaith@compuserve.com

Frances Ashton's Charity
Provides grants of variable amounts for needy clergymen of the Church of England, serving or retired, and the widows or widowers of such clergy. Completed applications are required by 1 June for the annual distribution in September. *Details from:* The Receiver, Mrs Barbara Davis, Charities Aid Foundation, Kings Hill, West Malling, Kent ME19 4TA *Tel:* (01732) 520081
email: bdavis@caf.charitynet.org

Friends of Friendless Churches
Founded 1957 to preserve churches and chapels of architectural or historic interest. Now owns 20 redundant places of worship in England and Wales. *President:* Prof R. W. Brunskill. *Chairman:* Mr Roger Evans. *Hon Secretary:* Mr John Bowles. *Hon Director:* Mr Matthew Saunders, St Ann's Vestry Hall, 2 Church Entry, London EC4V 5HB
Tel: 020–7236 3934
Fax: 020–7329 3677

Friends of the Clergy Corporation
This charity gives financial and other assistance to (1) the clergy of the Anglican Communion, and (2) any widow or other dependant of such per-sons, who may be in financial necessity or dis-tress, wherever they may be. Grants are made to cover many kinds of emergency including debts, bereavement or illness; also for removals, school clothing, holidays, etc. Administers the assets of the former Curates Augmentation Fund. *Enquir-ies to:* The Secretary, The Friends of the Clergy Corporation, 27 Medway St, London SW1P 2BD
Tel: 020–7222 2288
Fax: 020–7233 1244

Friends of the Elderly
Founded 1905. A voluntary society administering homes for elderly professional people and a wel-fare department giving general help to elderly people of any background. *President:* HRH The Princess Margaret, Countess of Snowdon. *Chief Exec:* Sally Levett, 40–42 Ebury St, London SW1W 0LZ
Tel: 020–7730 8263
Fax: 020–7259 0154

Frontier Youth Trust
Founded 1964. Provides training, resources information, support and association for Chris-tians working with disadvantaged young people

in the community, whether church based, unattached or within the youth and community service, particularly in urban/industrial areas. *Secretary:* Mr Dave Wiles, 4th Floor, 70–74 City Rd, London EC1Y 2BJ   *Tel:* 020–7336 7744
Fax: 020–7324 9900
email: frontier@fyt.org.uk

FWA (Family Welfare Association)
Founded 1869. Provides social work and social care services for families and individuals. Administers trust funds which give financial grants to individuals. Provides information to students through the Educational Grants Advisory Service. *Chief Exec:* Helen Dent, 501/505 Kingsland Rd, Dalston, London E8 4AU
Tel: 020–7254 6251

GFS Platform for Young Women
A world-wide charity committed to supporting and protecting vulnerable young women. The work in this country is increasingly directed to helping young disadvantaged women who are homeless and generally at risk. Eight inner city shared housing schemes provide over 350 secure bed-spaces. 200 voluntary support groups meet regularly. Five community projects provide education and support for young women and young unsupported mothers and their children. *Chief Exec:* Mrs Hazel Crompton, 126 Queen's Gate, London SW7 5LQ   *Tel:* 020–7589 9628
Fax: 020–7225 1458
email: platform@gfs.u-net.com
Web: hppt://www.tabor.co.uk/gfs/

Girls' Brigade
An international inter-denominational youth organization having as its aim 'to help girls to become followers of the Lord Jesus Christ and through self-control, reverence and sense of responsibility to find true enrichment of life'. *National Director:* Vacancy, Girls' Brigade House, Foxhall Rd, Didcot, Oxon OX11 7BQ
Tel: (01235) 510425
Fax: (01235) 510429
email: gb@girlsbrigadeew.org.uk
Web: http:/www.girlsbrigadeew.org.uk

Grayswood Studio
Established in 1975. Engages in video and audio production and media training. A primary purpose is to give the power of communication to people who have pressing social, medical and spiritual needs; and to those who serve them. The studio also enables Christians to communicate the Gospel for themselves by putting professional direction, training and equipment into their hands. Grayswood Studio produces and sells a range of videos including programmes for evangelism, stewardship, deaf people, and education. *President:* The Bishop of Guildford. *Chairman:* Mr Christopher Wigdor. *Director:* Canon Geoffrey Curtis, Grayswood Studio, The Vicar-

age, Clammer Hill, Grayswood, Surrey GU27 2DZ   *Tel:* (01428) 644208
Fax: (01428) 656684
email: grayswood.studio@grayswood.co.uk

Greater Churches Group
The group was founded in 1991 as an informal association of non-cathedral churches which, by virtue of their great age, size, historical, architectural or ecclesiastical importance, display many of the characteristics of a cathedral, also fulfil a role which is additional to that of a normal parish church. Its aims are to provide help and mutual support in dealing with the special problems of running a 'cathedral-like' church within the organizational and financial structure of a parish church, to enhance the quality of parish worship in such churches and to promote wider recognition of the unique position and needs of churches in this category. The group also serves as a channel of communication for other organizations wishing to have contact with churches of this type. *Hon Secretary:* Mr Marcus Ashman, 12 Colston Parade, Bristol BS1 6RA
Tel and *Fax:* 0117–929 1487

Greenbelt Festivals
Organizes an annual Christian arts festival which takes place at Cheltenham racecourse, a venue that combines the outdoor festival feel with the comfort of indoor venues. Average audience figures are between fifteen and twenty thousand, most of whom camp for the four-day event held at the end of July. There is a large open-air venue which hosts nightly concerts and the main communion service on Sunday morning. There are also tented and indoor venues for music, seminars, theatre, film, art galleries, workshops, resources, cafes and shops. The event is inter-denominational. *Chair:* Dot Reid. *General Manager:* Andy Thornton, The Greenhouse, Hillmarton Rd, London N7 9HE   *Tel:* 020–7700 6585
Fax: 020–7700 5765
email: andy.thornton@greenhouse.greenbelt.org
Web: http://www.greenbelt.org.uk

Gregorian Association
Founded 1870 to spread reliable information on Plainsong and to promote its use; to demonstrate its suitability to the English language by means of services and holding lectures and conferences; to provide expert advice and instruction on the use of Plainsong. *President:* The Archbishop of Canterbury. *General Secretary:* Mr Grey Macartney, 26 The Grove, Ealing, London W5 5LH
email: pjsw@beaufort.demon.co.uk
Web: http://www.beaufort.demon.co.uk/chant.htm

Grubb Institute
The Grubb Institute's central aim is to contribute to the well-being of society. It is committed to

explore ways in which the Christian faith and theology can be a resource for understanding society and for generating the hope that society needs. The institute pursues these aims by engaging with individuals, groups and institutions through advisory work training assignments, applied social research and evaluations. It focuses on the interaction between leadership, management, organization and vocation. Its starting point is the working experience of those in the situation, analysing this by using scientific disciplines based on a psycho-dynamic and systematic approach, in dialogue with theology. It considers that the task of the Church is to create conditions for the transformation of society and works with clergy and lay people to bring them about. Since 1969 it has worked with churches, religious orders and Christian agencies in many different parts of the world. *Director of Development:* Miss Jean Hutton, The Grubb Institute, Cloudesley St, London N1 0HU

Tel: 020–7278 8061
Fax: 020–7278 0728
email: GrubbUK@aol.com

Guides Association

Founded 1910. Open to all girls and women between 5 and 65 years regardless of race, faith or any other circumstance,who are willing to make The Promise and endeavour to keep The Guide Law. Its purpose is to enable girls to mature into confident, capable and caring women determined, as individuals, to realize their potential in their career, home and personal life, and willing as citizens to contribute to their community and the wider world. *President:* HRH The Princess Margaret, Countess of Snowdon. *Chief Guide:* Miss Bridget Towle. *Chief Exec:* Vacancy, 17/19 Buckingham Palace Rd, London SW1W 0PT

Tel: 020–7834 6242
email: chq@guides.org.uk

Guild of All Souls

Founded 1873 as an intercessory guild, caring for the dying, the dead and the bereaved. Open to members of the Church of England and Churches in communion with her. Chantry chapel at Walsingham and at St Stephen's, Gloucester Rd, London. Patron of 39 livings. *President:* The Bishop of Richborough. *General Secretary:* Charles Brown, St Katharine Cree Church, 86 Leadenhall St, London EC3A 3DH   *Tel:* 020–7621 0098

Guild of Church Braillists

The guild consists of a group of people who give their services to help blind readers by transcribing a variety of religious literature into Braille. Requests are welcome from individual readers for books, special services, etc. All other productions are sent to the National Library for the Blind or the Library of the RNIB. For further details contact the *Secretary:* Mrs Mabel Owen, 321 Feltham Hill Rd, Ashford, Middx TW15 1LP

Tel: (01784) 258040

Guild of Church Musicians

See **Archbishops' Certificate in Church Music** page 270.

Guild of Health

Founded in 1904 to further the Church's Ministry of Healing through prayer, sacrament and visiting the sick, and by co-operation with Christian doctors, nurses and other members of the healing team. It publishes a quarterly magazine *Way of Life*. *President:* Vacancy. *General Secretary:* Revd Antonia Lynn, Guild of Health, Edward Wilson House, 26 Queen Anne St, London W1M 9LB

Tel: 020–7580 2492

Guild of Pastoral Psychology

The guild offers a meeting ground for all interested in the relationship between religion and depth psychology, particularly the work of C. G. Jung and his followers. Depth psychology has contributed many new insights into the meaning of religion and its symbols and their relevance to everyday life. The guild has monthly lectures in central London, a day conference in London in the Spring and a three-day Summer conference at Oxford. Further information and details of membership available from *Administrator:* Nicola Stanley, PO Box 1107, London W3 6ZP

Tel: 020–8993 8366

Guild of Servants of the Sanctuary

Founded 1898 to raise the spiritual standard of servers, to promote friendship among them and to encourage attendance at Holy Communion in addition to times of duty. *Patrons:* The Archbishops of Canterbury, York and Wales. *Warden:* Rev David Moore, Vicarage, St Ives, Huntingdon, Cambs PE17 4DH. *Secretary General:* Mr Roy Cresswell, 20 Doe Bank Rd, Ocker Hill, Tipton, W Midlands DY4 0ES   *Tel:* 0121–556 2257

Guild of St Barnabas

Founded 1876 to be a fellowship of nurses within the Church of England. Membership is now open to all who are qualified or training in the health care professions and who are committed members of the Anglican Church, or of other churches in communion with it. The guild aims to encourage the development of the spiritual life of members who are trying to witness to their Christian commitment through their professional practice. Members, both active and retired, support one another through prayer and caring friendship. *President:* Miss B. Ashton. *Organizing Secretary:* Mrs Mary Morrow, 16 Copperwood, Ashford, Kent TN24 8PZ   *Tel:* (01233) 635334

Guild of St Helena

Founded in 1875, the guild offers Christian fellowship and charitable giving to wives, families and members of the armed forces. *President:* Lady Cowan. *Warden:* Mrs Sarah-Jane Gilchrist. *Chief Secretary:* Mrs Janice Carson, Guild of St Helena, Wellington Barracks, Birdcage Walk, London SW1E 6HQ *Tel:* 020–7414 3461
Web: http://www.army.mod.uk/army/press/family/more.htm

Guild of St Leonard

The guild, with a membership of about 750, publishes a quarterly Intercession Paper. The Annual Eucharist and General Meeting are held in the autumn, usually in a prison chapel. *Warden:* Rt Revd Lloyd Rees. *Chaplain and Secretary:* Revd Peter Walker , The Chaplain's Office, HMP/YO1 Moorland, Bawtry Rd, Hatfield Woodhouse, Doncaster DN7 6BW *Tel:* (01302) 351500

Guild of St Raphael

Founded 1915 to work for the restoration of the Ministry of Healing as part of the normal function of the Church, by preparing the sick for all ministries of healing, by teaching the need of repentance and faith, by making use of the Sacraments of Healing and by Intercession. *Organizing Secretary:* Ms Jo Parry, 2 Green Lane, Tuebrook, Liverpool L13 7EA
Tel and *Fax:* 0151–228 3193
email: straphael@enterprise.net

Harnhill Centre of Christian Healing

A resource centre for the ministry of Christian Healing through counselling, prayer, quiet days, teaching courses and Christian Healing Services. The centre provides residential accommodation. *Chairman:* Mr Angus Baillie-Hamilton. *Chaplain/Warden:* Revd Paul Springate, Harnhill Manor, Cirencester, Glos GL7 5PX *Tel:* (01285) 850283
Fax: (01285) 850519
email: harnhill@btinternet.com
Web: http://www.btinternet.com/~harnhill

Harold Buxton Trust

Founded 1919 by the Rev Harold Buxton, late Bishop of Gibralter, who had a particular concern for international ecumenism. The trust's main focus is to promote mutual understanding and interchange between the Anglican, Roman Catholic and Orthodox Churches, particularly through the support of study and exchange visits to and from churches in Eastern Europe, the former Soviet Union and the Middle East. The trustees meet twice a year (May and November) to allocate grants. Further details and application form available from the *Secretary:* Mrs Pat Phillips, c/o SPCK, Holy Trinity Church, Marylebone Rd, London NW1 4DU *Tel:* 020–7387 5282
Fax: 020–7388 2352
email: pphillips@spck.org.uk

Henry Bradshaw Society

Founded 1890 for printing liturgical texts from manuscripts and rare editions of service books, etc. For available texts, apply to the *Secretary:* Dr David Chadd, School of Music, University of East Anglia, Norwich NR4 7TJ
email: d.chadd@uea.ac.uk

Historic Churches Preservation Trust

Founded 1953 to assist with the preservation of historic churches of any Christian denomination whose parishioners are unable to commission essential repairs without outside financial help. *Patron:* HM The Queen. *Chairman of Trustees:* Lord Nicholas Gordon Lennox. *Secretary:* Wing Cdr Michael Tippen, Fulham Palace, London SW6 6EA *Tel:* 020–7736 3054

Holy Rood House, Centre for Health and Pastoral Care

Opened in 1993 the centre is a friendly house with a residential community. The house offers a gentle and holistic approach in a Christian environment where individuals or groups, of all ages and backgrounds, can work towards their own healing and explore their spiritual journey within an atmosphere of acceptance, love and openness. Professional counsellors and therapists, working closely with the medical profession, offer support at times of bereavement, abuse, addiction, relationship breakdown or illness, and creative arts and stress management play an important role in the healing process. Holy Rood House ministers within an awareness of justice and peace to daily or residential guests. *Visitor:* The Archbishop of York. *Directors:* Revds Stanley and Elizabeth Baxter, Holy Rood House, 10 Sowerby Rd, Sowerby, Thirsk YO7 1HX
Tel: (01845) 522580
Fax: (01845) 527300

Homes for Retired Clergy

BEAUCHAMP COMMUNITY, NEWLAND, MALVERN
Home for retired people, clerical or lay, either sex. Unfurnished, single and double flats available from time to time. Apply to the *Administrator to Trustees,* Beauchamp Community, Newland, Malvern, Worcs WR13 5AX *Tel:* (01684) 562100

COLLEGE OF ST BARNABAS, LINGFIELD, SURREY
Permanent homes for 40 retired clergy with limited accommodation for married couples. Sick Bay-Resident Nursing Staff, for residents falling ill. Next to Dormans Station. *Apply:* The Warden, College of St Barnabas, Blackberry Lane, Lingfield, Surrey RH7 6NJ *Tel:* (01342) 870260

House of St Barnabas in Soho

Founded 1846, provides accommodation for 38 single homeless women aged 18–55 who have low care support needs. All meals are provided and support is given to find permanent, secure accommodation. *Director:* Wendy Taylor. *Project Manager:* Madhu Patel, 1 Greek St, Soho, London W1V 6NQ   *Tel:* 020–7437 1894   *Fax:* 020–7434 1746

Hymn Society of Great Britain and Ireland

Founded in 1936 to encourage the study of hymns, both words and music; to raise the standard of hymn singing and to encourage a more discerning use of hymns. The society publishes a bulletin four times a year, and there is a three-day annual conference. Further information and details of membership from the *Secretary:* Revd Geoffrey Wrayford, 7 Paganel Rd, Minehead, Somerset TA24 5ET   *Tel* and *Fax:* (01643) 703530

Incorporated Church Building Society

Founded 1818 as the 'Incorporated Society for promoting the Enlargement, Building and Repairing of Churches and Chapels' in the Anglican dioceses of England and Wales. A charity wholly dependent on voluntary giving, which makes interest free loans to Anglican churches in need of repair. Since 1963 the society has been managed by the Historic Churches Preservation Trust. *President:* The Archbishop of Canterbury. *Secretary:* Wing Cdr Michael Tippen, Fulham Palace, London SW6 6EA   *Tel:* 020–7736 3054

Industrial Christian Fellowship

Founded 1918 as successor to the Navvy Mission (1877), and incorporating the Christian Social Union. ICF is a nationwide network which provides support for Christians who want to apply their faith in fresh and creative ways in the everyday working world, especially in industry and commerce. ICF aims to: Bring the concerns and opportunities of the world of work to the attention of clergy and congregations so that they will be alert to the scope for prayer and Christian action. Ensure that the relationship between faith, work and worship receives proper attention in Church life. Promote Christian training, counselling and prayer support for members of the congregation in their working vocations. Arrange special services of thanksgiving and prayer for industry and commerce. ICF is ecumenical and has close links with other groups and agencies involved with the Church's mission to industry and commerce. Membership is open to all. *Acting Secretary:* Terry Drummond, ICF, St Matthew House, 100 George St, Croydon CR0 1PE   *Tel:* 020–8656 1644

INFORM

(Information Network Focus on Religious Movements)

INFORM is a non-sectarian organization, started in 1988 with funding from the Home Office, the Church of England and other main-line Churches. Further support has been received from the Wates and Nuffield Foundations, Smith's Charity and the Sainsbury family trusts. Its primary aims are to collect and to disseminate accurate, up-to-date information about new religious movements (or 'cults'), and to put enquirers in touch with a network of people and organizations with specialist knowledge. It will also put people in touch with a further, complementary, network of people or organizations that can advise or counsel those who are experiencing difficulties because of their own, a friend's or a relative's involvement in one of the movements. *Chairman:* Prof Eileen Barker, Houghton St, London WC2A 2AE   *Tel:* 020–7955 7654   *Fax:* 020–7955 7679   *email:* INFORM@LSE.ac.uk

Inter Faith Network

Established in 1987 to encourage contact and dialogue at all levels between different faith communities in the United Kingdom. It aims to advance public knowledge and mutual understanding of the teaching, traditions and practices of the different faith communities in Britain, including an awareness of their distinctive features and of their common ground, and to promote good relations between persons of different faiths. *Co-chairs:* Dr Manazir Ahsan and Rt Revd Roy Williamson. *Director:* Mr Brian Pearce, 5–7 Tavistock Place, London WC1H 6SN   *Tel:* 020–7388 0008   *Fax:* 020–7387 7968   *email:* ifnet.uk@btinternet.com   *Web:* http://www.interfaith.org.uk

Intercontinental Church Society

Founded 1823. ICS is an evangelical Anglican mission society which supports the ministry of English-speaking, international congregations in Europe, North Africa, the Gulf, the South Atlantic and South America and ministers to holiday makers in European and Mediterranean resorts, including those on Thomson *Young at Heart* Holidays. ICS also publishes the *Directory of English-speaking Churches Abroad. President:* Viscount Brentford. *International Director:* Canon John Moore. *Communications Manager:* Mr David Healey, 1 Athena Drive, Tachbrook Park, Warwick CV34 6NL   *Tel:* (01926) 430347   *Fax:* (01926) 330238   *email:* enquiries@ics-uk.org

International Association of Civil Aviation Chaplains

In many airports throught the world chapels and other places of worship are provided for passengers and staff who need prayer, counselling or simply peace and quiet. Chaplains are normally appointed and supported by their own denomination and recognized by the airport authorities. The association consists of about 150 members who hold annual conferences worldwide and regional meetings once or twice a year.

In the UK and Eire there are three full-time Anglican chaplains at Heathrow, Gatwick and Manchester and the number of part-time members increases every year. Members maintain a worldwide network of prayer and support and offer services to groups or individuals on a 24 hour basis. *International Vice-President:* Revd David Smith (London Heathrow). *Secretary, UK and Eire Chaplains:* Revd Michael Banfield, London Luton Airport, Halcyon House, Percival Way, Luton LU2 9LU   *Tel:* (01582) 395516

International Ecumenical Fellowship
Founded Fribourg 1967. Its aim is to 'seek in fellowship to serve the will of God and unite the People of God, by hearing the Word of God, declaring the praise of God and breaking the Bread of God unto the Glory of God'. Regions of the IEF have been established in Britain, Holland, Germany, France, Spain, Belgium, the USA, Poland and the Czech Republic. *Chairman of British Region:* Lady Davson. *Secretary:* Miss June Foster, Dryfe View, Boreland, Lockerbie DG11 2LH

Interserve
(formerly BMMF International)
Founded 1852. An international and interdenominational mission. Evangelical in its basis, it has five hundred personnel serving the peoples of South and Central Asia, the Middle East and also among ethnic groups in Britain. Personnel are involved in many different ministries – all with the common aim of sharing Good News of Jesus Christ in word and action. Those with professional training are welcomed, both long and short-term periods of service, to fill a wide range of vacancies. *Chairman:* Mr Alastair Watson. *National Director:* Mr Richard Clark, 325 Kennington Rd, London SE11 4QH
Tel: 020–7735 8227
Fax: 020–7587 5362
email: isewi@isewi.globalnet.co.uk
Web: http://www.interserve.org/ew

Jubilate Hymns
An association of authors and musicians formed in 1974 for the purpose of publishing material for contemporary worship: *Hymns for Today's Church, Church Family Worship, Carols for Today, Carol Praise, Let's Praise! 1* and *2, Prayers for the People, Psalms for Today, Songs from the Psalms, The Dramatised Bible, The Wedding Book, Hymns for the People, World Praise 1* and *2, Sing Glory. Chairman:* Canon Michael Saward. *Secretary:* David Peacock. *Copyright Manager:* Mrs M. Williams, 4 Thorne Park Rd, Chelston, Torquay TQ2 6RX
Tel: (01803) 607754
Fax: (01803) 605682
email: JubilateMW@aol.com

Julian Meetings
A network of contemplative prayer groups, begun in Britain in 1973. There are now about four hundred groups in the UK and some in Australia, South Africa and the USA. Ecumenical. *Contact:* Yvonne Walker, 5 Fernbrook Drive, Harrow, Middx HA2 7EE

Julian of Norwich, Shrine of Lady
The cell of Julian of Norwich, a chapel attached to St Julian's Church, Norwich, stands on the site where the 14th-century anchoress wrote her book *Revelations of Divine Love*. There is accommodation in the convent of the Community of the Sacred Passion beside the Church. Quiet days and retreats can be arranged. The Julian Centre where there is a bookstall and library of spirituality, welcomes visitors and pilgrims (open weekdays 11am-4pm summer; 11am-3pm winter). Large parties and those wanting overnight accommodation must book in advance. *Booklist and mail order books:* The Julian Centre, Rouen Rd, Norwich NR1 1QT *Tel:* (01603) 767380 (hours as above) *Accommodation and visits:* Sister in Charge, All Hallows House, Rouen Rd, Norwich NR1 1QT   *Tel:* (01603) 624738

Keston Institute
The centre for the study of religion and church-state relations in the postcommunist and communist world. Founded in 1970 following a request by persecuted Ukranian Christians, Keston defends the right to believe by publishing information and research in a weekly email news bulletin *Keston News Service*, a bimonthly magazine *Frontier* and a quarterly academic journal *Religion, State & Society*. It is also producing a list of prisoners in the former Soviet Union and communist countries in Asia who are imprisoned for their religious beliefs. Keston maintains offices in Oxford and Moscow and its staff are frequently cited in the international news media. Its unique archive and library are used by believers, scholars, government departments, the news media and visitors from all over the world. *Director:* Mr Lawrence Uzzell, 4 Park Town, Oxford OX2 6SH   *Tel:* (01865) 311022
Fax: (01865) 311280
email: keston.institute@keston.org
Web: http://www.keston.org

Keswick Convention
Founded 1875 to promote personal, practical and scriptural holiness. *Chairman:* Mr Jonathan Lamb. *Convention Secretary:* Mr Mark Smith, The Keswick Convention Centre, Skiddaw St, Keswick, Cumbria CA12 4BY   *Tel:* (01768) 772589
Fax: (01768) 775276
email: kesconv@aol.com
Web: http://www.sovereign.uk.com/keswick

KeyChange
(formerly Christian Alliance)
Established 1920. Offers care, acceptance and Christian community to people in need through the provision of residential care for frail elderly

people and supported accommodation for young homeless people. *Chief Exec:* David Shafik, 5 St George's Mews, 43 Westminster Bridge Rd, London SE1 7JB   *Tel:* 020–7633 0533
Fax: 020–7928 1872
email: info@keychange.org.uk
Web: http://www.keychange.org.uk

Korean Mission Partnership
Founded 1889 to support the Anglican Church in Korea. *Hon Secretary and Treasurer:* Miss Eilene Hassall, Lewis Cottage, The Palace, Hereford HR4 9BJ   *Tel:* (01432) 274238

Langley House Trust
Founded in 1958 the Langley House Trust, a national Christian charity, provides care and rehabilitation for ex-offenders to work towards crime-free independence and integration into normal society. The trust aims to help ex-offenders to address their physical, emotional, mental and spiritual needs. It currently runs 14 residential homes and seven move-on projects scattered across the UK providing different types of accommodation for varying needs including drug rehabilitation, mental disorder and alcohol related offending. *Chairman:* Colin Honey. *Chief Exec:* John Adams. *Contact:* Paul Langley, PO Box 181, Witney, Oxon OX8 6WD   *Tel:* (01993) 774075
Fax: (01993) 772425
email: langley@housetrust.freeserve.co.uk

Latimer House
Founded 1959 to promote from an evangelical standpoint theological research and scholarly writing on current Church questions. *Chairman of the Council:* Revd Dr Mark Burkill. *Warden:* Vacancy, 131 Banbury Rd, Oxford OX2 7AJ
Tel: (01865) 513879
Fax: (01865) 556706

Lee Abbey Household Communities
There are three household communities based in Urban Priority Areas in Birmingham, Blackburn, and Bristol. Community members live under a common rule of life and seek to be involved in their local community and church. *Contact:* Ven Alan Smith, Archdeacon's House, 39 The Brackens, Clayton, Newcastle-under-Lyme, Staffs ST5 4JL   *Tel:* (01782) 663066
Fax: (01782) 711165

Lee Abbey International Students' Club
Founded in 1964 by the Lee Abbey Fellowship as a ministry to students of all nationalities, the club provides long- and short-term hostel accommodation for students of all faiths or none and is served by a Christian community, many of whom are young people. Applications are invited from anyone interested in joining the community, residing as a student or staying as a holiday-maker when students are away. *Warden:* Revd David Weekes, Lee Abbey International

Students' Club, 57/67 Lexham Gardens, London W8 6JJ   *Tel:* 020–7373 7242
Fax: 020–7244 8702
email:
studentsclub@leeabbeylondon.freeserve.co.uk

Leprosy Mission
Founded 1874 (1) to minister in the name of Jesus Christ to the physical, mental and spiritual needs of sufferers from leprosy (2) to assist in their rehabilitation and (3) to work towards the eradication of leprosy. *Exec Director:* Revd J. A. Lloyd, Goldhay Way, Orton Goldhay, Peterborough PE2 5GZ   *Tel:* (01733) 370505
Fax: (01733) 370960
email: post@tlmew.org.uk

Lesbian and Gay Christian Movement
LGCM has four principal aims: to encourage fellowship, friendship and support among lesbian and gay Christians through prayer, study and action; to help the whole Church examine its understanding of human sexuality and to work for positive acceptance of lesbian and gay relationships; to encourage members to witness to their Christian faith within the lesbian and gay community and to their convictions about human sexuality within the Church; to maintain and strengthen links with other lesbian and gay Christian groups both in Britain and elsewhere. An extensive network of local groups exists and a wide range of resources are available. *Secretary:* Revd Richard Kirker, LGCM, Oxford House, Derbyshire St, Bethnal Green, London E2 6HG
Tel: 020–7739 1249
020–7739 8134 (Counselling Helpline)
Fax: 020–7739 1249
email: lgcm@aol.com
Web: http://members.aol.com/lgcm

Lesbian and Gay Clergy Consultation
The national support organization for gay and lesbian clergy and ordinands in the Anglican Churches of Great Britain. It holds six-monthly meetings offering a safe environment for discussion and mutual support. It also seeks to act as a forum for educational dialogue and the exploration of theological issues within the Church and as a prophetic voice for gay and lesbian clergy and ordinands. It represents the concerns of gay and lesbian clergy and ordinands to the House of Bishops and the wider Church. *Convenor:* Revd Colin Coward, 11 Murfett Close, Wimbledon, London SW19 6QB   *Tel:* 020–8788 1384
Fax: 020–8780 1733
email: CCMCoward@aol.com

Li Tim-Oi Foundation
Perpetuates the name of the first Anglican woman priest. It was founded on the 50th anniversary of her priesting on 25 January 1944. It provides bursaries to help women in the majority

world of the 'South' train for Christian work, lay or ordained, in their own countries. It welcomes enquiries for help from, or on behalf of, candidates who are members of Anglican dioceses or of United Churches in communion with Canterbury, but only exceptionally for those seeking training at institutions in the 'North'. Requests for help, particularly from Africa, are already outstripping funds available. Thus all donations from parishes and individuals are put to good use. *Patrons:* Lord Coggan, Lord Runcie, Bishop Penny Jamieson of Dunedin, the Archbishop of Canterbury and Bishop K. H. Ting. *Chair:* Canon Ruth Wintle. *Secretary:* Revd Christopher Hall, The Knowle, Deddington, Banbury OX15 0TB
Tel: (01869) 338225
Fax: (01869) 337766
email: achall@mail.globalnet.co.uk

Librarians' Christian Fellowship
Constituted 1976 to provide opportunities for Christian librarians to consider issues in librarianship from a Christian standpoint, and to promote opportunities for presenting the Christian faith to people working in libraries of all kinds. *Hon Secretary:* Graham Hedges, 34 Thurlestone Ave, Ilford, Essex IG3 9DU   *Tel:* 020–8599 1310
email: fm128@viscount.org.uk
Web:
http://churchnet.ucsm.ac.uk/lcf/lcfhome.htm

Lincoln Theological Institute for the Study of Religion and Society
Inaugurated in 1997, the Institute is a research and teaching unit of the University of Sheffield, specializing in the study of religion and society. The Institute focuses on postgraduate and postdoctoral research and works on funded projects that benefit society, churches and higher education by applying theological insights to issues of common concern. Students may enrol in MA (taught), M Phil and Ph D programmes. There are also courses and lectures open to the public and resources for lay people and clergy. The Lincoln Theological Institute originated from Lincoln Theological College, founded as an ordination training college in 1874. The Institute has an extensive library, developed since the original foundation, containing approximately 20,000 volumes on theology and related subjects, as well as an extensive periodical collection and works of reference. The library has been fully computerized to allow for flexible searching and retrieval. Visitors are welcome. For further information and library subscription details contact the Administrator/Librarian. *Director:* Dr Martyn Percy. *Administrator/Librarian:* Caroline Dicker, 36 Wilkinson St, Sheffield S10 2GB   *Tel:* 0114–222 6399
Fax: 0114–276 3973
email: Lincoln@Sheffield.ac.uk
Web: http://www.shef.ac.uk/~lti/

London City Mission
Founded 1835 to extend the knowledge of the Gospel among the inhabitants of London and its vicinity. Interdenominational. *Chairman:* David Houghton. *General Secretary:* Revd James McAllen, Nasmith House, 175 Tower Bridge Rd, London SE1 2AH   *Tel:* 020–7407 7585
Fax: 020–7403 6711
email: lcm.uk@btinternet.com
Web: http://www.lcm.org.uk

London Union of Youth Clubs
A long established voluntary association of youth organizations in the Greater London area. Brings skills and resources to voluntary and statutory youth clubs and groups, and provides a London resource for work with young women. *Chief Exec:* Mark Wakefield, 64 Camberwell Rd, London SE5 0EN   *Tel:* 020–7701 6366
email: name@youthworklondon.demon.co.uk
Web: http://www.youthworklondon

Lord Wharton's Charity
Founded 1696 to distribute Bibles and other religious books to children and young people of all denominations in all counties of the United Kingdom and Northern Ireland. *Clerk to the Trustees:* Mrs B. Edwards, 30 Prentis Rd, London SW16 1QD   *Tel and Fax:* 020–8769 1924

Lord's Day Observance Society (Inc)
Founded 1831 to preserve Sunday as the national day of rest and to promote its observance as the Lord's Day for worship and Christian service. *President:* Mr Neville Knox. *Secretary:* Mr John Roberts, Unit 3, Epsom Business Park, Kiln Lane, Epsom, Surrey KT17 1JF   *Tel:* (01372) 728300
Fax: (01372) 722400
email: info@lordsday.co.uk
Web: http://www.lordsday.co.uk

MACA – (Mental After Care Association)
MACA provides a wide range of quality community-based services for people with mental health needs and their carers. Its facilities offer care which is appropriate to each individual and is designed to encourage their independence and self-respect. MACA develops new services in conjunction with Health and Social Services organizations to meet the needs of local communities. These include: supported housing and community support; day care and social clubs; employment training; carer support; services for offenders with mental health needs; and information and training services. MACA is registered to offer assessment for NVQs in Care and special needs housing. *Chairman:* Mr J. Birney. *Chief Exec:* Mr Gilbert Hitchon, 25 Bedford Square, London WC1B 3HW   *Tel:* 020–7436 6194
Fax: 020–7637 1980
email: maca-bs@maca.org.uk
Web: http://www.maca.org.uk

Magdalene Fellowship

An ecumenical and national Christian fellowship to support and pray for the divorced and separated. The fellowship aims to help people to keep in relationship with Christ through sharing together and through simple Christian discipleship. *Protector:* Rt Revd Donald Arden. *Guardians:* David and Rosemary Norwood, St Aidan's Rectory, 8 Golf Rd, Clarkston, Glasgow G76 7LZ
Tel: 0141–571 8018

Marshall's Charity

Founded 1627. Makes grants for (1) building, purchasing or modernizing parsonages of the Church of England or the Church in Wales. (2) repairs to churches in Kent, Surrey and Lincolnshire. *Clerk to the Trustees:* Mr Richard Goatcher, Marshall House, 66 Newcomen St, London SE1 1YT
Tel: 020–7407 2979
Fax: 020–7403 3969
email: grantoffice@marshalls.org.uk
Web: http://www.marshalls.org.uk

Mayflower Family Centre

A local church and community centre in Canning Town in the East End of London. Activities include groups for all ages, sports facilities, pensioners' luncheon club, advice desk, youth work, worship and Christian teaching. Three hostels, a launderette/coffee bar, charity shop and workshops. The centre offers residential facilities and ministry to those in need. The Mayflower Family Centre, Vincent St, London E16 1LZ
Tel: 020–7476 1171
Fax: 020–7511 1019
email: mayflower@teleregion.co.uk
Web: http://www.teleregion.co.uk/mayflower

Melanesian Mission

Founded in 1849 to preach the Gospel and to teach and care for the sick in the Solomon Islands and Vanuatu (then the Diocese of Melanesia). Its present function is to support by prayer, interest, alms, and staff when necessary, the Church of the Province of Melanesia formed in 1975. *Chairman:* The Bishop of Bristol. *General Secretary:* Revd Peter Fox, Harpsden Rectory, 2 Harpsden Way, Henley-on-Thames, Oxon RG9 1NL
Tel: (01491) 573401
Fax: (01491) 579871
email: CMelanesUK@aol.com

Mersey Mission to Seamen

Founded 1855 for the spiritual and temporal welfare of seafarers frequenting Merseyside. *Chairman:* Mr L. A. Holder. *Chapl Supt:* Revd John Simmons, Colonsay House, 20 Crosby Rd South, Liverpool, Merseyside L22 1RQ
Tel: 0151–920 3253
Fax: 0151–928 0244
email: liverangel@aol.com
Web: http://
netministries.org/see/charmin/CH01395

Message

Founded 1969 by Miss Norah Coggan. Message is 'the service offered by local groups of churches through the medium of two-minute recorded telephone talks explaining the Good News of Jesus Christ as revealed in the Bible'. *President:* The Archbishop of Canterbury. *Chairman:* Mr Michael Graves. *National Admin Secretary:* Mrs Rita Hatch, 6 Darnley Rd, Woodford Green, Essex IG8 9HU
Tel: 020–8504 4134

Metropolitan Visiting and Relief Association

Founded 1843 for promoting the relief of destitution in London and for improving the conditions of the poor. It aims to assist the clergy of the Church of England in the Metropolitan area (1) in giving financial help in their parishes (2) to help them in constructive social work by providing financial help for cases where permanent good results may be expected (3) to assist clergy who co-operate with other agencies engaged in social work (4) to assist some married ordinands' families. *Enquiries to the :* Grants Administrator, Family Welfare Assn, 501/505 Kingsland Rd, Dalston, London E8 4AU
Tel: 020–7249 6636

Mid-Africa Ministry (CMS)

(formerly Ruanda Mission)
Founded in 1921 and working in partnership with the Anglican Church in South West Uganda, Rwanda, Burundi and Democratic Republic of Congo through theological training, medical, educational, agricultural and technical work. *Chairman:* Revd David Applin. *Enquiries to:* General Secretary, Partnership House, 157 Waterloo Rd, London SE1 8UU
Tel: 020–7261 1370
Fax: 020–7401 2910
email: mid_africa_ministry@compuserve.com

Mirfield Centre

Offers a meeting place for about 50 people at the College of the Resurrection. Small residential conferences are possible in the summer vacation. Day and evening events are arranged by the management team comprising members of the Community of the Resurrection, the College, and the Northern Ordination Course (Eastern Wing) to stimulate Christian life and witness in the region. *Director:* Kath Hinchcliffe, The Mirfield Centre, College of the Resurrection, Mirfield, W Yorks WF14 0BW
Tel: (01924) 481920
Fax: (01924) 481921
email: center@mirfield.org.uk

Missions to Seamen

Anglican missionary society which supports and links the Anglican Church's ministry to seafarers of all races and creeds in ports throughout the world. It has full-time staff and/or seafarers' centres in over 100 ports, honorary chaplains in over 200 others. In many ports it works in close co-operation with Christian societies of other denominations, and it is a member of the

International Christian Maritime Association. *President:* HRH The Princess Royal. *Secretary General:* Canon Glyn Jones. *Justice and Welfare Secretary:* Canon Ken Peters. *Ministry Secretary:* Canon Bill Christianson, St Michael Paternoster Royal, College Hill, London EC4R 2RL

Tel: 020–7248 5202
Fax: 020–7248 4761
email: general@missionstoseamen.org
Web: http://www.missionstoseamen.org

MODEM
(Managerial and Organizational Disciplines for the Enhancement of Ministry)

MODEM aims to link good practice in churches and voluntary organizations with management experience in commercial and industrial companies. It also aims to enable dialogue between those interested in ministry and those interested in management. It aims to set the agenda for management/ministry issues so that the values and disciplines of those engaged in the management of secular and church organizations will be mutually recognized and respected. Corporate, group or congregational, and individual members of MODEM are able to share in the developing network of those offering, or needing, experience and resources. MODEM publishes a directory of members to facilitate the exchange of skills and information.

Its members are encouraged to combine to offer specialized information, courses or topical consultations. It is associated with the Edward King Institute in the publication of the journal *Ministry*, and in association with Canterbury Press has published two ground-breaking books *Management and Ministry — appreciating contemporary issues* and *Leading, Managing, Ministering — challenging questions for church and society*. *Chairman:* Revd Bryan Pettifer. *Membership information:* MODEM, Carselands, Woodmancote, Henfield, W Sussex BN5 9SS   *Tel* and *Fax:* (01273) 493172
email: peter@bateshouse.freeserve.co.uk
Web: http://churchnet.ucsm.ac.uk/modem/

Modern Churchpeople's Union
Founded 1898. A society within the Church of England and the Anglican Communion for the advancement of liberal Christian thought. MCU embraces the spirit of freedom and informed enquiry, seeks to involve the Christian faith in an ongoing search for truth by interpreting traditional doctrine in the light of present day understanding. Publishes a quarterly journal *Modern Believing*. It sponsors and encourages likeminded organizations as well as the setting up of local groups and conferences to foster dialogue and exchange views. Holds an annual conference on contemporary issues. MCU affirms a comprehensive Church of England, respects other churches and is prepared to learn from other world religions and concerned people. *President:*

Rt Revd John Saxbee. *General Secretary:* Revd Nicholas Henderson, MCU Office, 25 Birch Grove, London W3 9SP   *Tel:* 020–8932 4379
Fax: 020–8993 5812
email: modchurchunion@btinternet.com
Web: http://www.mcm.co.uk/modchurchunion

Morse-Boycott Bursary Fund
(formerly St Mary-of-the-Angels Song School Trust)

Founded 1932 originally as a parochial Choir School but from 1935 to 1970 served the Church at large and now takes the form of bursaries for boys at cathedral choir schools. *Administrator:* The Communar, Cathedral Office, Royal Chantry, Cathedral Cloisters, Chichester PO19 1PX
Tel: (01243) 782595

Mothers' Union
See page 222.

Movement for the Reform of Infant Baptism (MORIB)
MORIB has four aims: to bring an end to the practice of indiscriminate infant baptism; to demonstrate that baptism is the sacrament instituted by Christ for those becoming members of the visible Church; to seek the reform of the Canons and rules of the Church of England in line with the above stated aims; to promote within the Church of England debate and review of the biblical, theological, pastoral and evangelistic aspects of Christian initiation. *President:* Rt Revd Colin Buchanan. *Chairman:* Revd Clifford Owen. *Secretary:* Mrs Carol Snipe, 18 Taylors Lane, Lindford, Bordon, Hants GU35 0SW
Tel: (01420) 477508

MSF Clergy and Church Workers
The Clergy Section of the Manufacturing, Science and Finance union was set up in 1994 in response to the needs of clergy for a professional association with the facilities and support of a modern trade union. Membership is wholly ecumenical and open to all who work in the service of the churches and other faiths, throughout the United Kingdom and Ireland. The section's name has been changed recently to reflect its growing membership among lay workers, as well as ordained ministers. MSF itself is Britain's third largest union, with almost 500,000 members, and the clergy and church workers are part of its voluntary sector. *Chair:* Revd W. F. Ward. *Exec Chair:* Revd Hazel Barkham. *Communications:* Revd Stephen Trott. *National Secretary:* Dr Chris Ball, MSF Centre, 33–37 Moreland St, London EC1V 8BB   *Tel:* 020–7505 3000
Fax: 020–7505 3282
email: ballc@msf.org.uk

National Association of Diocesan Advisers for Women's Ministry
NADAWM is a national support network for monitoring, supporting and promoting the min-

istry of ordained women in the Church of England. It organizes an annual conference for diocesan representatives and provides consultancy and advice. *Chair:* Revd Lesley Bentley. *Secretary:* Revd Penny Driver, The School House, Berrygate Lane, Sharow, Ripon HG4 5BJ

Tel: (01765) 607017

National Christian Education Council
(Incorporating International Bible Reading Association)

An ecumenical body concerned with development and training in Christian education in the church. Publishers of books and visual aids covering all aspects of Christian education. *General Manager:* Sheila Sharman, 1020 Bristol Rd, Selly Oak, Birmingham B29 6LB   *Tel:* 0121–472 4242
Fax: 0121–472 7575
email: ncec@ncec.org,uk
Web: http://www.ncec.org.uk

National Deaf Church Conference
Founded in 1967 by the late Canon Tom Sutcliffe, who was himself deaf. It is the national forum for delegates from the Deaf Church and meets twice yearly for weekend and day conferences where the spiritual and social issues facing the Church of England are discussed. The main objective is to make the general public aware that deaf Christians are not isolated worshipping communities, but part of the whole Church. *Chair:* Revd Vera Hunt, 27 Redriff Close, Maidenhead, Berks SL6 4DJ

National Retreat Association
Comprising these Christian retreat groups — Association for Promoting Retreats, Baptist Union Retreat Group, Methodist Retreat Group, National Retreat Movement (RC), Quaker Retreat Group, United Reformed Church Silence and Retreat Network. Offers information and resources about retreats to both the would-be and the seasoned retreatant, co-ordinates training opportunities in the field of retreat giving and spiritual direction, promotes the work of retreat houses and encourages regional activity. *Retreats,* an ecumenical journal listing retreat houses in Britain and Ireland and their programmes is published annually (2000 edition £4.90 inc p&p). Other literature is also available, send for publications list. *Exec Officer:* Paddy Lane, The Central Hall, 256 Bermondsey St, London SE1 3UJ

Tel: 020–7357 7736
Fax: 020–7357 7724
email: nra@retreats.org.uk
Web: http://www.retreats.org.uk

National Viewers' and Listeners' Association
The association was founded in 1965 by Mrs Mary Whitehouse and her associates who felt that television was attacking and undermining Christian family life. National VALA, which is a non-denominational voluntary association, believes that violence on television contributes significantly to the increase of violence in society and should be curtailed in the public interest; that the use of swearing and blasphemy are destructive of our culture and our Christian faith and that the broadcasting authorities are failing to meet their statutory obligations by allowing the frequent use of offensive language; that sexual innuendo and explicit sex trivialize and cheapen human relationships whilst undermining marriage and family life; and that the media are indivisible and broadcasting standards are inevitably affected by the standards of film, theatre and publishing. Benefits of membership include regular newsletters, a list of media addresses to enable members to make their voices heard, and programme comment cards for posting back to National VALA whenever the need arises. *President:* Revd Graham Stevens. *Director:* Mr John Beyer, National VALA, All Saints House, High St, Colchester CO1 1UG

Tel: (01206) 561155
Fax: (01206) 766175
email: info@nvala.org
Web: http://www.nvala.org

New England Company
A charity founded 1649 and is the senior English missionary society. *Governor:* Mr T. C. Stephenson. *Treasurer:* Viscount Bridgeman. *Secretary:* Mrs Jenny Carter, The Bower House, Clavering, Saffron Walden, Essex CB11 4QR

Tel: (01799) 550212
Fax: (01799) 550169

Newton's Trust
Established to provide assistance to widows or unmarried daughters of deceased clergymen and to divorced or separated wives of clergymen of the Church of England. Applications are considered by the grants committee appointed by the Trustees, and one time cash grants are made at their discretion. *Chairman:* Mr Dale Bridgewater. *Secretary:* Mr C. Tomlinson, 19A The Close, Lichfield, Staffs WS13 7LD   *Tel:* (01543) 306100
Fax: (01543) 306109
email: lich.cath@virgin.net

Nikaean Club
Founded 1925 to exercise hospitality on behalf of the Archbishop of Canterbury to Christians of non-Anglican traditions. *Chairman:* Sir Peter Marshall. *Guestmaster:* Canon Richard Marsh. *Hon Secretary:* Ms Gill Harris Hogarth, Lambeth Palace, London SE1 7JU   *Tel:* 020–7898 1218
Fax: 020–7401 9886
email: gill.harris-hogarth@lampal.c-of-e.org.uk

North of England Institute for Christian Education
Founded in 1981 as an ecumenical foundation managed by a board representing the educational interests of the Churches, universities and other

educational institutions in the North East of England. Its primary objective is to create links, at both the theoretical and practical level, between Christian theology and education so as to contribute, mainly by research projects, towards the further education of those with a responsibility for teaching the Christian faith. *Director:* Revd Prof Jeff Astley, NEICE, Carter House, Pelaw Leazes Lane, Durham DH1 1TB

Tel: 0191–384 1034
0191–374 2000 Ext 7807
Fax: 0191–384 7529
email: Jeff.Astley@durham.ac.uk

Number One Trust Fund
Founded 1908 for holding property and investments for the promotion of catholic practice and teaching within the Church of England, reformed by the Fidelity Trust Act 1976, and incorporated by the Charity Commissioners in 1996. The trustees are appointed by the Abbot of Elmore, the Superior of the Community of the Resurrection, the President of the Church Union, the President of the Society for the Maintenance of the Faith, the Master of the Guardians of the Shrine at Walsingham, the Principal of Pusey House, Oxford and the Principal of St Stephen's House, Oxford. *Chairman:* Revd Dr Jeremy Sheehy. *Secretary:* Mr Tim Belben, Church Farm, Wookey, Wells, Som BA5 1JX

Tel and *Fax:* (01749) 674136

OMF International (UK)
(formerly China Inland Mission)
Founded 1865 to work in partnership with East Asia's churches through evangelism, church planting, discipling, theological training and professional services. *Contact:* Mr Guido Braschi, Station Approach, Borough Green, Sevenoaks, Kent TN15 8BG
Tel: (01732) 887299
Fax: (01732) 887224
email: Gbraschi@omf.org.uk
Web: http://www.omf.org.uk

Open Synod Group
The objects of the Group are the promotion and advancement of the Christian religion. Its particular emphasis is working through the synodical structures for the growth of unity between all the Churches and the renewal of the life and organization of the Church of England. Membership is open to all Christians but will be of particular interest to serving or one-time members of the General Synod, of any Diocesan or Deanery Synod, and of any PCC (PCCs are also eligible for corporate membership). The Group meets during each Group of Sessions of the General Synod. It publishes a magazine twice a year and holds a national conference every two or three years. There are several diocesan branches. *President:* The Bishop of Bristol. *Chairman:* Canon Richard

Atkinson. *Secretary:* Dr Carole Cull, 6 Forndon Close, Lower Earley, Reading RG6 3XR
Tel: 0118–961 7923
email: carole.cull@drl.ox.ac.uk

Oratory of the Good Shepherd
Founded in 1913 at Cambridge University. The Oratory is a society of professed priests and brothers working in five provinces, Britain, USA, Southern Africa, Canada and Australia. Oratorians are Regulars and bound together by a common Rule and discipline. They do not normally live together in community but meet for Chapter and are resident each year for the Oratory Retreat and General Chapter. Members include bishops, parish priests, lecturers, and missionaries. There is a noviciate before temporary profession after which life vows may be taken. The Rule of the Oratory requires celibacy, a regular account of spending and direction of life. In addition, 'Labour of the Mind' is a characteristic of the Oratory and members are expected to spend time in study. Attached to the Oratory are Companions, lay, ordained, married and single, who keep a Rule of Life and are part of the Oratory family. *English Provincial:* Rt Revd Lindsay Urwin OGS. *Secretary General:* Fr Michael Bootes OGS, Vicarage, 1 Manor Farm Close, Kellington, Goole DN14 0PF
Tel: (01977) 662876
Fax: (01977) 663341
email: mb@ogs.net

Order of Christian Unity
Christians from all churches who care about Christian values in the family, medical ethics, Christian education and the media, and who provide specialist back-up in the form of information and literature. *President:* Rt Revd Maurice Wood. *Chairman:* Mr James Bogle, Christian Unity House, 58 Hanover Gardens, London SE11 5TN
Tel: 020–7735 6210
Fax: 020–7582 1174

Ordination Candidate Funds (General)
ANGLO-CATHOLIC ORDINATION CANDIDATES' FUND
Secretary: Revd C. W. Danes, 31 Oakley Rd, Bocking, Braintree, Essex CM7 5QS

BRISTOL CLERICAL EDUCATION SOCIETY
Grants of up to £200 to ordinands and, occasionally, to clergy undertaking in-service training, for specific and exceptional items. *Secretary:* Revd Paul Denyer, Director of Ordinands, Vicarage, Kington Langley, Chippenham, Wilts SN15 5NJ
Tel: (01249) 750231

CHURCH PASTORAL AID SOCIETY MINISTERS IN TRAINING FUND
Grants for men and women, married or single, in training for ordained or accredited ministry, facing financial hardship; for evangelical candidates only. *Ministry and Vocation Adviser:* Revd Andy Piggott, CPAS Ministry and Vocation Unit,

Athena Drive, Tachbrook Park, Warwick CV34 6NG   *Tel:* (01926) 458458
Fax: (01926) 458459

CLEAVER ORDINATION CANDIDATES' FUND
An academic trust to assist ordinands, clergy pursuing recognized courses of post-graduate study, and parochial clergy on approved study leave. Candidates must belong to the Catholic tradition within the Anglican Communion. Preference may be given to graduates of British universities. There is no permanent office, the Clerk of the time being working from his home address. *Apply:* Revd Dr Peter Lynn, Clerk to the Cleaver Trustees, Vicarage, Firle, Lewes, E Sussex BN8 6NP   *Tel* and *Fax:* (01273) 858227

ELLAND SOCIETY ORDINATION FUND
Grants are made to applicants who are Evangelical in conviction, who are in training, and who must spend their first two years of ministry in the Province of York. Grants are usually made to help in cases of special need. *Apply:* Revd Tony Bowering, Vicarage, 2 Sunderland St, Tickhill, Doncaster DN11 9QJ   *Tel:* (01302) 742224

LADY PEEL LEGACY TRUST
A small charity making grants to ordinands of catholic tradition. *Apply:* Prebendary James Trevelyan, Rectory, Honiton, Devon EX14 8BH

Overseas Bishoprics' Fund
Founded 1841 to assist towards the endowment and maintenance of bishoprics in any part of the world and to act as trustees of episcopal endowment funds. *Chairman:* Mr John Broadley. *Hon Secretary:* Mr John Clark. *Hon Clerk:* Vacancy Church House, Great Smith St, London SW1P 3NZ   *Tel:* 020–7928 8681

Oxford Mission
Founded 1880. The Oxford Mission consists of two Religious Communities, the Brotherhood and Sisterhood of the Epiphany and the Christa Sevika Sangha. Has houses in India and Bangladesh. Their work is pastoral, medical and educational and is carried on in the Dioceses of Calcutta and Dhaka. *India:* Father James Stevens (on loan from the diocese of Calcutta) and Sister-in-Charge, Sister Florence SE; *Bangladesh:* Rev Fr Francis Pande BE and Revd Mother Susila CSS. *Secretary:* Mrs Mary Marsh, PO Box 86, Romsey, Hants SO51 8YD   *Tel:* (01794) 515004
Fax: (01794) 515004

Papua New Guinea Church Partnership
Founded 1891 as the New Guinea Mission to give support to the then Diocese of New Guinea in prayer, by sending staff and raising money. In 1977, when the Province of Papua New Guinea was inaugurated, the agency name was changed to Papua New Guinea Church Partnership in order to be more descriptive of the work. In mid-1999 ten staff, partly funded by PNGCP, served in governmentally approved teaching, health and admin training posts. An annual block grant of £12,000 goes to the provincial budget and money is raised for provincially approved projects (£66,000 in 1998); audited accounts are sent to the UK. It is hoped to maintain this level of support for the foreseeable future. *President:* The Archbishop of York. *Chairman:* Rt Revd Paul Richardson. *General Secretary:* Mrs Chris Luxton, PNG Church Partnership, Partnership House, 157 Waterloo Rd, London SE1 8XA
Tel: 020–7928 8681
Fax: 020–7928 2371
email: PNGCP@USPG.ORG

Parish and People
Founded 1949 and was instrumental in effecting a quiet revolution in popularizing the parish communion. In 1963 it merged with the Keble Conference Group and spearheaded movements towards team ministry, synodical government and church unity. It has continued to promote new life in the Anglican denomination, and publishes a range of stimulating material for parishes and deaneries in order to enable growth from the grass roots up of a lively, open, people's church in which lay ministry can blossom. In 1988 it took *Partners* under its wing, thus widening its interests to include publications on evangelism. In 1989 it set up the Deanery Resource Unit which provides a bi-annual mailing to over 200 deaneries which includes the well-established *Deanery Exchange* broadsheet, together with copies of books, pamphlets and briefings on matters of deanery concern. The unit works in cooperation with the Church House Deaneries Group. *Contact:* Revd Jimmy Hamilton-Brown, The Old Mill, Spetisbury, Blandford Forum, Dorset DT11 9DF
Tel and *Fax:* (01258) 453939
email: PandPeople@aol.com

Partis College
Founded 1825 to provide accommodation (house) for ladies who are communicant members of the Church of England with low incomes. The college was founded for the widows or daughters of clergymen, HM forces and other professions. *Chairman:* Ven John Burgess. *Bursar:* Major Max Young, 1 Partis College, Newbridge Hill, Bath BA1 3QD   *Tel:* (01225) 421532
email: partiscoll@aol.com

Philip Usher Memorial Fund
Founded 1948. Grants annual scholarships to Anglican priests, deacons or ordinands, preferably under 35 years of age, to study in a predominantly Orthodox country. Applications not later than 31 January for that year. *Chairman:* The Archbishop of Canterbury. *Hon Secretary of the*

Exec Ctee: Administrative Secretary, CCU, Church House, Great Smith St, London SW1P 3NZ   *Tel:* 020–7898 1472
email: @ccu.c-of-.org.uk

Pilgrim Adventure

Founded in 1987, Pilgrim Adventure provides a selection of *Pilgrim Journeys* for people who like to travel off the beaten track. Hill walking, island hopping and worship in out of the way places are all part of the experience. Pilgrim Adventure is Anglican based and ecumenical in outlook. *Patrons:* Rt Revd Richard Rutt, Very Revd Horace Dammers. *Chair:* David Gleed. *Enquiries:* The Secretary, Pilgrim Adventure, 120 Bromley Heath Rd, Downend, Bristol BS16 6JJ
Tel and *Fax:* 0117 957 3997
Web: http://www.yell.co.uk/sites/pilgrim-adventure-uk/

Pilgrim Trust

Founded 1930 by the late Edward S. Harkness of New York with a sum of £2 million. The Trustees give grants to charities or recognized public bodies concerned with social welfare, art and learning and preservation. Current priorities for social welfare projects include the diversion of young people away from crime and substance misuse, the support of those with mental illness living as part of the community and the housing and rehabilitation of the long-term homeless. Grants are also offered to projects which seek to widen access to the arts and for the preservation of historic buildings. Block grants are given to the Council for the Care of Churches and the Historic Churches Preservation Trust for the repair and conservation of parish churches. *Director:* Miss Georgina Nayler, Fielden House, Little College St, London SW1P 3SH   *Tel:* 020–7222 4723

Pilsdon Community

The Pilsdon Community is dedicated to the ideals of the Christian gospel in the context of community living and open hospitality. The community at any one time will comprise of six to eight community members (leadership) and their children, about 25 guests (staying from one month to several years), up to six visitors (staying one day to two weeks) and up to eight wayfarers (staying up to three days). Many of the guests have experienced a crisis in their lives (e.g. mental breakdown, alcoholism, drug addiction, marital breakdown, abuse, homelessness, prison, drop out of school or college, asylum seeking etc.). Pilsdon provides a working therapeutic environment of communal living, manual work, creative opportunities (pottery, art, crafts, music etc.) recreation, worship and pastoral care, to rebuild peoples' lives, self-respect, confidence and faith. Founded in 1958 by an Anglican priest, the community occupies an Elizabethan manor house and its outbuildings and smallholding of ten acres, six miles from the sea near Lyme Regis.

The community life is inspired by the monastic tradition and the Little Gidding Community built around families. The worship and spirituality is Anglican and sacramental, but ecumenical in membership and all faiths and none as well as all races and cultures are welcome. Membership, guest and visitor enquiries should be made to the *Warden:* Revd Peter Barnett, Pilsdon Community, Pilsdon Manor, Pilsdon, Bridport, W Dorset DT6 5NZ   *Tel:* (01308) 868308
Fax: (01308) 868161
email: pilsdon@btinternet.com
Web: http://www.btinternet.com/~pilsdon

Plainsong and Mediaeval Music Society

Formed 1888 to promote the study and appreciation of plainsong and mediaeval music; to arrange the printing, publication and sale of facsimiles, transcriptions, musical texts and studies; and to promote lectures and performances thereof. Publishes an annual scholarly journal. *Secretary:* Dr Stephen Farmer, Magdalene College, Cambridge CB3 0AG

Praxis

Founded 1990, Praxis is sponsored by the Liturgical Commission, the Alcuin Club and the Grove Group for the Renewal of Worship. Its aims are to enrich the practice and understanding of worship in the Church of England; to serve congregations and clergy in their exploration of God's call to worship; and to provide a forum in which different worshipping traditions can meet and interact. Praxis events include day meetings in London and the regions, residential conferences and national consultations. In 1997 Praxis, together with the ecumenical Institute for Liturgy and Mission at Sarum College in Salisbury, appointed a National Education Officer to help promote education in worship at every level. *Chairman:* Canon Stephen Oliver. *National Education Officer:* Revd Mark Earey. *Secretary:* Revd Gilly Myers, 20 Great Peter St, London SW1P 2BU   *Tel:* 020–7222 3704
email: praxis@stmw.globalnet.co.uk
Web: http://www.sarum.ac.uk/praxis/

Prayer Book Society

Founded in 1975 to uphold the worship and doctrine of the Church of England as enshrined in the *Book of Common Prayer.* The society has a branch in every diocese of the Church of England and affiliated branches in Ireland, Scotland and Wales. Journals are published quarterly, also a quarterly newsletter, and the society publishes other material of a critical or educational kind, related to the *Book of Common Prayer.* The society encourages the use of the *Book of Common Prayer* as a major element in the worshipping life of the Church of England and seeks to spread knowledge and love of the 1662 Prayer Book. *Patron:* The Bishop of London. *Chairman:* Anthony Kilmister. *Hon Secretary:* Mrs Elaine Bishop, St

ames Garlickhythe, Garlick Hill, London EC4V
2AF   *Tel:* (01243) 784832
  Web: http://www.churchnet.ucsm.ac.uk/
                     prayerbook/index.htm

Protestant Reformation Society
Founded 1827 to study the doctrine and theology
of the English Reformers and to promote the
religious principles of the English Reformation.
Secretary: Dr D. A. Scales, PO Box 47, Ramsgate,
Kent CT11 9XB   *Tel:* (01843) 580542

Public Record Office
Records of central government and courts of law
from the Norman Conquest (Domesday Book) to
the recent past (for example, the Suez Campaign). Ruskin Ave, Kew, Richmond, Surrey TW9
4DU   *Tel:* 020–8876 3444
                   Web: http://www.pro.gov.uk

Pusey House, Oxford
Founded 1884 to continue the work of Dr Pusey,
academic and pastoral, in Oxford. *Principal:* Revd
Philip Ursell, Pusey House, Oxford OX1 3LZ
                           Tel: (01865) 278415

Pyncombe Charity
Income about £10,000 p.a. applied to assist needy
serving clergymen in financial difficulties due to
illness or other special circumstances within
the family. Applications to be made through the
Bishop. *Secretary:* Mr Ian Billinge, The Old Rectory, Crowcombe, Taunton, Som TA4 4AA
                          Tel: (01984) 618287
                          Fax: (01984) 618416
                   email: billingeil@msn.com

Queen Victoria Clergy Fund
Founded 1897 to raise money towards the sup-
port of Church of England parochial clergy.
Apart from one particular endowment, all the
Fund's income is disbursed annually in block
grants to dioceses specifically for the help of the
clergy. *Chairman:* Mr Bryan Sandford. *Secretary:*
Mr Colin Menzies, Church House, Great Smith
St, London SW1P 3NZ   *Tel:* 020–7898 1310
              email: colin.menzies@c-of-e.org.uk

Radius
(The Religious Drama Society of Great Britain)
Founded 1929 to encourage drama which throws
light on the human condition. Assists and brings
together those who create drama as a means of
Christian understanding. Maintains an extensive
lending library, publishes a quarterly magazine,
organizes summer schools, workshops and play
writing competitions. Also publishes 'Radius
Plays'. *Patrons:* The Archbishop of Canterbury,
Dame Judi Dench. *Contact:* The Secretary, Radius
Office, Christ Church and Upton Chapel, 1A
Kennington Rd, London SE1 7QP
                           Tel: 020–7401 2422

Reader Missionary Studentship Association
Founded 1904 to offer financial assistance to
Readers training as priests for service in the
Church overseas. *Chairman:* Mr G. E. Crowley.
Hon Treasurer: Miss M. Brown. *Hon Secretary:* Mrs
Anne Ward, 3 Churchill Rd, Wells, Somerset BA5
3HZ   *Tel:* (01749) 671409

Rebecca Hussey's Book Charity
Established 1714 to give grants of religious and
useful books to institutions in the United Kingdom. *Clerk to the Trustees:* Mrs Anne Butters, 21
Erleigh Rd, Reading RG1 5LR *Tel:* 0118–987 1845

Reform
An evangelical network of clergy and laity in
churches throughout the country. It came into
being in 1993 and has campaigned for biblical
integrity. It holds regular conferences and has
over 1,600 members. It has published a number of
booklets on matters relating to biblical teaching
on doctrine and morality within the Church of
England. *Chairman:* Revd Philip Hacking. *Administrators:* Jonathan and Fiona Lockwood, Reform,
PO Box 1183, Sheffield S10 3YA
                      Tel and Fax: 0114–230 9256
             email: administrator@reform.org.uk
                   Web: http://www.reform.org.uk

Relate
(formerly National Marriage Guidance Council)
Offers counselling and psychosexual therapy to
those who seek advice with adult couple relationships, whether married or not. Relate also
publishes a wide range of helpful literature
available from its bookshop. There are 115 Relate
Centres – to contact your nearest consult the local
telephone directory. *Chief Exec:* Ms Sarah Bowler,
Herbert Gray College, Little Church St, Rugby,
Warws CV21 3AP   *Tel:* (01788) 573241
                          Fax: (01788) 535007

**Religious Education Council of England and
Wales**
The Council was formed in 1973 and is open to
national organizations which have a special
interest in the teaching of religious education in
schools and colleges. The present membership of
40 organizations includes representation from
the main Christian denominations, the World
Faiths, the British Humanist Association and the
main educational bodies with professional RE
interests. *Chair:* Mr Ian Wragg. *Secretary:* Revd
Prof Stephen Orchard, CEM, Royal Buildings,
Victoria St, Derby DE1 1GW *Tel:* (01332) 296655
                          Fax: (01332) 343253
                     email: cem@cem.org.uk
                   Web: http://www.cem.org.uk

Retired Clergy Association
Founded 1927 to act as a bond of friendship in
prayer and mutual help to retired clergy. Membership at 31 December 1998 was 3,198. There are

local branches in Bexhill, Birmingham, Blackburn, Bournemouth, Bristol, Bury St Edmunds, Cambridge, Canterbury, Cheltenham, Chester, Chichester, Eastbourne, East Devon, Ely, Harrogate, Henfield, Hereford, Huntingdonshire, Isle of Wight, Lancaster, Leamington, Ludlow, Norwich, Oxford, Portsmouth (Mainland), Ripon, Rochester, Scarborough and Filey, Shrewsbury, Southampton, Stockport, Wells, West London, Weston-super-Mare, Winchester and Alresford, Worcester, Worthing and York. *Chairman:* Rt Revd Derek Bond. *Hon Secretary:* Mr Kenneth Lightfoot, 12 Clouston Rd, Farnborough, Hants GU14 8PN   *Tel:* (01252) 546486

Rev Dr George Richards' Charity
Founded 1837 to financially assist clergy of the Church of England forced to retire early due to ill-health. Widows, widowers and other dependants can also apply for assistance. *Secretary:* Mr David Newman, 51 Pole Barn Lane, Frinton-on-Sea, Essex CO13 9NQ   *Tel:* (01255) 676509

Richmond Fellowship for Community Mental Health
Established in 1959 to provide residential care services for people with mental health problems, and to promote understanding of mental health issues and human relations in the wider community. It now operates more than 70 residential, supported housing, day care and workscheme services for people with mental health, substance misuse and/or socio-emotional problems throughout the UK. Richmond Fellowship Training and Consultancy Services run an extensive programme of short courses on mental health, group work, supervision and management, which are open to those working in the care field. In addition, Training and Consultancy Services run an RSA Diploma in Post Traumatic Stress Counselling. *For further information contact:* The Richmond Fellowship, 8 Addison Rd, Kensington, London W14 8DJ   *Tel:* 020–7603 6373   *Fax:* 020–7602 8652

Royal Alexandra and Albert School
Founded in 1758, a voluntary-aided junior and secondary school providing boarding education for boys and girls aged 8–16 who are without one or both parents or who would benefit from boarding education because of home circumstances. Only boarding fees payable and bursaries available. Exceptional facilities. *President:* HRH The Duchess of Gloucester. *Contact:* Foundation Secretary, Gatton Park, Reigate, Surrey RH2 0TW   *Tel:* (01737) 642576

Royal Asylum of St Ann's Society
The society, founded in 1702, offers grants towards the expenses of educating children, from the age of 11, at boarding or day schools. Most, but not all, of those aided are children of clergy of the Church of England, however, in the first

instance clergy should approach the Corporation of the Sons of the Clergy. The Society welcomes collections, donations and legacies towards this purpose. *President:* The Dean of Westminster. *Chairman:* Mr Hugh Baddeley. *Secretary:* Mr David Hanson, King Edward's School Witley Petworth Rd, Wormley, Surrey GU8 5SG

Royal College of Organists
Founded 1864, incorporated by Royal Charter 1893, 'to promote the art of organ-playing and choir training'. Holds lectures, recitals and master-classes nationwide. Examinations for Fellowship, Associateship, and Diploma in Choral Teaching. Membership open to all who take an interest in the work and profession of the organist and in organ music. *Patron:* HM The Queen. *President:* Mr Stephen Darlington. *Senior Exec:* Mr Alan Dear, 7 St Andrew St, Holborn, London EC4A 3LQ   *Tel:* 020–7936 3606 (Admin)
020–7936 4321 (Library)
Fax: 020–7353 8244
email: rco@rco.org.uk
Web: http://www.rco.org.uk

Royal Martyr Church Union
Founded 1906 to promote the restoration of King Charles's name to its proper place in the worldwide Church's Calendar and maintain the principles of Faith, Loyalty and Liberty for which he died and bring together descendants of cavalier officers and men, and anyone interested in Caroline history. *Chairman:* Mr Hubert Wandesford Fenwick. *Hon Secretary:* Mr Ronald Miller of Pittenweem, The Priory, Pittenweem, Fife KY10 2LJ

Royal Naval Lay Readers' Society
Founded 1860. Licensed Readers assist in the work of the Anglican Church amongst the men and women of the Royal Navy and their families. In ships at sea and in naval establishments ashore they work alongside Naval Chaplains in the furtherance of the Christian faith and the welfare of the Navy's people. The society is dependent financially on voluntary contributions for the maintenance of its work. *Treasurer:* Mrs Stella Crawford, Room 203, Victory Building, HM Naval Base, Portsmouth, Hants PO1 3LS
Tel: (01705) 727902

Royal School of Church Music
Music has a vital part to play in our worship, the RSCM is currently engaged in a series of initiatives to provide music for the new book of *Common Worship*, and to foster greater understanding of the place and effective use of music of all kinds in every style of worship. The RSCM also promotes the use of music in worship by providing the musical and educational resources to train, develop and inspire clergy, church musicians and congregations of all denominations. A particularly important part of the RSCM's work over the last sixty years has centred on young people

through holiday courses, training schemes, awards and festivals. Appointed the official music agency for the Church of England from April 1996. *President:* The Archbishop of Canterbury. *Chairman:* Sir David Harrison. *Director General:* Professor John Harper, Cleveland Lodge, Westhumble, Dorking, Surrey RH5 6BW

> *Tel:* (01306) 872800
> *Fax:* (01306) 887260
> *email:* cl@rscm.com
> *Web:* http://www.rscm.com

RPS Rainer
(The Royal Philanthropic Society, incorporating the Rainer Foundation)
A national voluntary organization, founded in 1788, working primarily with young people at risk to delinquency, homelessness and abuse, through several community-based projects, some in partnership with local authorities and other voluntary organizations. Particular services include aftercare projects and bail support schemes, youth information, accommodation and support to young people on release from young offender institutions, youth training and employment schemes. *Patron:* HRH Prince Philip The Duke of Edinburgh. *Chair:* Mr Geoff Dalby. *Chief Exec:* Mr Don Coleman, Rectory Lodge, High St, Brasted, Westerham, Kent TN16 1JF

> *Tel:* (01959) 578200
> *Fax:* (01959) 561891
> *email:* RPSCharity@aol.com

Rural Theology Association
Founded 1981 to provide a forum for the rural churches and to focus for the Church at large the distinctive ways and needs and contributions of the rural. Its aims are to study the gospel and develop theology in a rural setting, to encourage the development of patterns of ministry and mission appropriate to the countryside today, and to discover ways of living in the countryside which embody a Christian response to the world. *President:* Revd Prof Leslie Francis. *Chairman:* Revd Eric Ashby. *Secretary:* Revd Geoff Platt, Brecklands Cottage, Brecklands Green, North Pickenham, Swaffham, Norfolk PE37 8LG

> *Tel:* (01760) 441581
> *email:* rta@brecklands.demon.co.uk
Web:
http://www.brecklands.demon.co.uk/rural.htm

Samaritans
A registered charity, founded in 1953 at St Stephen, Walbrook, EC4, which provides confidential and emotional support to people in crisis. The Samaritans is available, 24 hours a day, for anyone passing through crisis and at risk of suicide. It aims to provide society with a better understanding of suicide and the value of expressing feelings that may lead to suicide. Local branches can be found in the phone book under S or call 0345 90 90 90 (local rate) or write to Chris, PO Box 9090, Stirling FK8 2SA. *Chief Exec:* Mr Simon Armson, 10 The Grove, Slough, Berks SL1 1QP

> *Tel:* (01753) 216500
> *Fax:* (01753) 819004
> *email:* jo@samaritans.org

School Chaplains' Conference
An association for anyone, ordained and lay, involved in Christian ministry in state and independent schools. *President:* Rt Revd Paul Barber, Bishop of Brixworth. *Chairman:* Revd Richard Warden. *Secretary:* Revd Stephen Burgess, The Leys School, Cambridge CB2 2AD

Scout Association
Founded 1907 to encourage the physical, intellectual, social, and spiritual development of young people so that they may take a constructive place in society. Membership 600,000 of which a third are in Scout Groups sponsored by Anglican churches. *Chief Scout:* Mr George Purdy. *Contact:* Programme and Development Dept, The Scout Association, Gilwell Park, Chingford, London E4 7QW

> *Tel:* 020–8524 5246
> *Fax:* 020–8498 5329
> *email:* ukgilscout@aol.com
> *Web:* http://www.scoutbase.org.uk/

Scripture Gift Mission International
SGM offers free Bible booklets and leaflets to help people communicate God's word to today's generation. A new, research-based range uses up-to-date Bible versions and contemporary graphics. SGM resources are available in over 450 languages, free of charge. *Internation Director:* Mr Hugh Davies. *Exec Director:* Mr Bryan Stonehouse, Radstock House, 3 Eccleston St, London SW1W 9LZ

> *Tel:* 020–7730 2155
> *Fax:* 020–7730 0240
> *email:* lon@sgm.org

Scripture Union
Scripture Union seeks to make the Christian faith known to children, young people and families and to support the Church through resources, Bible reading and training. SU's work in Britain includes schools work, Bible ministries, publishing, training, evangelism, holidays, missions and family ministry. Scripture Union is active in more than one hundred countries. *Chief Exec:* Mr Peter Kimber, 207–209 Queensway, Bletchley, Milton Keynes MK2 2EB

> *Tel:* (01908) 856000
> *Fax:* (01908) 856111
> *email:* postmaster@scriptureunion.org.uk
> *Web:* http://www.scripture.org.uk

Scripture Union in Schools
Works to establish, encourage and resource a voluntary Christian presence in primary and secondary schools through term-time work and holiday activities. *Head of Dept:* Mr Emlyn

Williams, 207–209 Queensway, Bletchley, Milton Keynes MK2 2EB   Tel: (01908) 856000
Fax: (01908) 856111
email: schools@scriptureunion.org.uk
Web: http://www.scripture.org.uk

Seamen's Friendly Society of St Paul
Trust administered by Alton Abbey, able to offer financial assistance to merchant sailors. *Contact:* The Abbot, Alton Abbey, Beech, Alton, Hants GU34 4AP   *Tel:* (01420) 562145/563575
Fax: (01420) 561691

Servants of Christ the King
Founded 1942 by Canon Roger Lloyd of Winchester. A movement of groups or 'Companies' of Christians who seek to develop a corporate life by praying together in silence, with disciplined discussion. They actively wait upon God to be led by the Holy Spirit, and undertake to do together any work which they are given by him to do. *Enquirers' Correspondent:* Mrs S. Wilsdon, Well Cottage, The Street, Kilmington, Axminster, Devon EX13 7RW   *Tel:* (01297) 34142

Shaftesbury Homes and *Arethusa*
Founded 1843 to house and educate homeless children in London, the society continues its work with 12 housing projects including residential children's homes, bedsitter projects, and a careers and education service giving the support essential in enabling young people to find their way back into society with confidence. It also provides the challenges of sail training in the ocean-going training ketch *Arethusa* and provides opportunities for children from the inner-city to swim, canoe, sail and climb at the Arethusa Venture Centre on the Medway, developing self confidence and a sense of achievement. *Chief Exec:* Alison Chesney, The Chapel, Royal Victoria Patriotic Building, Trinity Rd, London SW18 3SX   *Tel:* 020–8875 1555
Fax: 020–8875 1954

Shaftesbury Society
Shaftesbury exists to enable people in great need to achieve security, self-worth and significance and through this to show Christian care in action. It provides care and education services to people with learning and/or physical disabilities, and support for people who are poor or disadvantaged. It works with churches and Christian organizations and contracts with many different public sector organizations. *Chief Exec:* Ms F. M. Beckett, The Shaftesbury Society, 16–20 Kingston Rd, London SW19 1JZ   *Tel:* 020–8239 5555
Fax: 020–8239 5580

Social Concern
(formerly the Church of England National Council for Social Aid, Church of England Temperance Society and Police Court Missionaries) Social Concern – an independent charity raising its own funds – works to promote social justice and reconciliation and to protect the vulnerable in society. It seeks to identify unmet needs and help develop services and support to meet them. Currently it is focusing on two areas: (1) restorative justice – a process for bringing together all the parties involved in an offence to decide jointly how to deal with what has happened and how to face the future. Social Concern organizes conferences and workshops to publicize new developments in this field at home and overseas; (2) educational material for schools – on topics such as gambling, to help young people gain a greater understanding of the pressures on them. In addition, Social Concern as a campaigning organization responds to Government consultations and works with other groups in this field. It also acts as a resource and information centre for students and others. *Presidents:* The Archbishops of Canterbury and York. *Chairman:* Rt Revd Colin Docker. *Director:* Mr Peter Carlin, Montague Chambers, Montague Close, London SE1 9DA
Tel: 020–7403 0977
Fax: 020–7403 0799
email: info@social-concern.demon.co.uk

Society for Liturgical Study
Founded 1978. The society promotes liturgical study and research, and holds a conference in alternate years. Membership is interdenominational and is open by invitation to persons involved in teaching liturgy, or in research in this field, or holding official appointments with responsibility for liturgy and worship. *Secretary:* Dr Carol Wilkinson, 52 Lowick Drive, Poulton le Fylde, Lancashire FY6 8HB

Society for Old Testament Study
Founded 1917 as a society for OT Scholars in Britain and Ireland. Scholars not resident in the British Isles may also become members. Two meetings to hear and discuss papers are arranged annually. The society also publishes its annual *Book List* and is involved in other publishing activities. It maintains links with OT scholars throughout the world, particularly the Dutch-Flemish OT Society with which it holds joint meetings every three years. Candidates for membership must be proficient in Hebrew and be proposed by two existing members. *Hon Secretary:* Dr Katharine Dell, The Divinity School, St John's St, Cambridge CB2 1TW
Tel: (01223) 332586
Fax: (01223) 332582
email: kjd24@cam.ac.uk

Society for Promoting Christian Knowledge
Founded in 1698, SPCK is the oldest Anglican mission agency and seeks to support the work of the Church in every part of the world through the production and distribution of Christian literature and other communication resources. SPCK has three areas of activity: SPCK Publishing pro-

duces books to help Christians understand and deepen their faith, and provides resources for worship and evangelism. Under its five imprints — SPCK, Triangle, Azure Books, Lynx Communications and Sheldon Press — the society has numerous titles in print and international distribution, which make it one of the largest and most active Christian publishers in Britain. SPCK Bookselling is one of Britain's largest chain of Christian bookshops, with shops located throughout England and Wales. Through these shops the society sells a wide range of new and secondhand Christian books. The shops aim to encourage people to read and learn more about the Christian faith. They support local churches by providing ready access to Christian books and other church requisites. Parishes are further assisted through co-operation in book agency schemes and by the provision of bookstalls at conferences and other major church events. Special discounts are made available to those training for full time ministry. SPCK Worldwide assists the development of Christian publishing and bookselling throughout the world and provides literature and other resources for education, worship and the training of church leaders in many countries. SPCK Worldwide's activities include the making of book grants to ordinands and theological libraries, the provision of capital and equipment to enable churches to establish publishing facilities in their own countries, the translation and production of liturgical material in indigenous languages, and the development of a wide range of Christian communications projects. These projects are dependent upon the voluntary giving of parishes and individuals, all such gifts being used directly in project work, with costs carried by the society's endowment income. Projects are supported in almost 60 countries each year. All work is undertaken in partnership with local Christian churches and groups as SPCK has no staff overseas. *President:* The Archbishop of Canterbury. *Chairman of the Governing Body:* General Sir Hugh Beach. *General Secretary:* Paul Chandler, Holy Trinity Church, Marylebone Rd, London NW1 4DU

Tel: 020–7387 5282
Fax: 020–7388 2352
email: spck@spck.org.uk
Web: http://www.spck.org.uk

Society for the Assistance of Ladies in Reduced Circumstances
Founded by the late Miss Edith Smallwood in 1886. Assistance is given to ladies of British nationality living alone on low incomes domiciled in the British Isles. A registered charity, solely dependent on voluntary contributions. *Patron:* Her Majesty The Queen. *Apply:* The Secretary, Lancaster House, 25 Hornyold Rd, Malvern, Worcs WR14 1QQ   *Tel:* (01684) 574645

Society for the Maintenance of the Faith
Founded in 1873 the society presents, or shares in the presentation of, priests to over eighty benefices. As well as its work as a patronage body the society aims to promote Catholic teaching and practice in the Church of England at large. *Secretary:* Revd Paul Conrad, Christ Church Vicarage, 10 Cannon Place, London NW3 1EJ
Tel: 020–7435 6784

Society for the Ministry of Women in the Church
Founded 1929, the aim of this ecumenical society is to win support for the conviction that women as well as men should be eligible for ordination to the full ministry of word and sacrament by means of a *Newsletter* and meetings. With more churches ordaining women, it encourages the working together for the ministry of the whole people of God and fosters initiatives and exchanges experiences in the areas of women's ministry, lay and ordained. It encourages the deployment of women in a wider spectrum of ministries and keeps in touch with other organizations that have similar aims. *President:* Dr Pauline Webb. *Exec Chair:* Revd Sister Teresa CSA. *Membership Secretary and Editor:* Revd Dr Janet Wootton, 19A Compton Terrace, Islington, London N1 2UN   *Tel:* 020–7354 3631
Fax: 020–7354 3989
email: janet.wootton@ukonline.co.uk

Society for the Relief of Poor Clergymen
Founded 1788 to aid evangelical Anglican clergy and their dependants in times of financial distress due to sickness, bereavement or other difficulties. c/o CPAS, Athena Drive, Tachbrook Park, Warwick CV34 6NG   *Tel:* (01926) 458460
email: srpc@cpas.org.uk

Society of King Charles the Martyr
Founded 1894 to promote a wide observation of January 30, the day of the martyrdom of King Charles I in 1649, and work for the reinstatement of this day in the Kalendar of the Churches of the Anglican Communion. Publishes various material including the journal *Church and King.* *Chairman:* Mr Robin Davies, 22 Tyning Rd, Winsley, Bradford on Avon, Wilts BA15 2JJ
Tel: (01225) 862965

Society of Mary
Founded 1931 to promote devotion to Our Lady; mainly an Anglican society but welcomes members from other churches of a Catholic tradition. *President and Superior General:* The Bishop of Ebbsfleet. *Secretary:* Mr Richard North, 11 Larkfield Rd, Farnham, Surrey GU9 7DB
Tel: (01252) 722095

Society of Mary and Martha
An independent ecumenical charity providing support for people in Christian ministry and/or

their spouses. Sheldon is a converted farm in the Teign Valley run by a lay community. It welcomes guests taking part in programme of events such as *12,000-mile Service* weeks, family holidays, reading weeks, retreats, workshops, seminars and quiet days. It also offers hospitality and support to people needing an emergency bolthole or a safe place at a time of stress or crisis. Enquiries by letter or telephone welcome. *Warden:* Carl Lee. *Administrator:* Sarah Horsman, Sheldon, Dunsford, Exeter EX6 7LE
Tel and *Fax:* (01647) 252752

Society of Ordained Scientists
Founded 1987. A dispersed order for ordained scientists, men and women. Members aim to offer to God, in their ordained role, the work of science in the exploration and stewardship of creation, to express the commitment of the Church to the scientific enterprise and their concern for its impact on the world and to support each other in their vocation. *Visitor:* Rt Revd Rupert Hoare, Dean of Liverpool. *Warden:* Canon Maureen Palmer. *Secretary:* Revd Ursula Shone, 4 Park Rd, Brechin, Angus DD9 7AF

Society of Retreat Conductors
Founded in 1923 for the training of retreat conductors, the running of retreat houses and the conducting of retreats. *Administrator:* Revd David Rogers, Stacklands Retreat House, West Kingsdown, School Lane, nr Sevenoaks, Kent TN15 6AN
Tel: (01474) 852247

Society of Royal Cumberland Youths
Bell ringing society founded in 1747. Its headquarters are at St Martin in the Fields and the society is responsible for ringing at a number of London churches. The society has a worldwide membership, promoting high standards among proficient change ringers. *Master:* Mr Alan Regin. *Secretary:* Ms Linda Garton, Thriplow House West, Middle St, Thriplow, Royston, Herts SG8 7RD
Tel: (01763) 208171
Web:
http://www.hblock.demon.co.uk/srcy.html

Society of St Willibrord
(The Anglican and Old Catholic Society of St Willibrord)
Founded 1908 to promote friendly relations between the Anglican and Old Catholic Churches, including the fullest use of the full Communion established between them in 1931. *Presidents:* The Bishop of Gibraltar in Europe and the Bishop of Haarlem, Holland. *Exec Secretary:* Revd Ivor Morris, Vicarage, 57 Maltese Rd, Chelmsford CM1 2PB
Tel and *Fax:* (01245) 353914

Society of the Holy Cross (SSC)
Founded 1855 for priests (850 members) 'maintain and extend the Catholic faith and discipline

and to form a special bond of union between Catholic clergy'. *Provinces:* European Union, Australasia, Canada, Africa, USA. *Master General:* Canon Michael Shields. *Master:* Revd David Houlding, All Hallow's House, 52 Courthope Rd, London NW3 2LD
Tel: 020–7267 7833

Soldiers' and Airmen's Scripture Readers Association
Founded 1838 to present the claims of Christ to the men and women serving in the Army and later the RAF, to promote interdenominational Christian fellowship among them and to encourage individual serving Christians to witness to their comrades. *Chairman:* Brigadier Ian Dobbie. *General Secretary:* Lt Col Malcolm Hitchcott, Havelock House, Barrack Rd, Aldershot, Hants GU11 3NP
Tel: (01252) 310033
Fax: (01252) 350722
email: hq@sasra.org.uk
Web: http://www.sasra.org.uk

SOMA – Sharing of Ministries Abroad
Founded 1978 to serve the renewal of the Church throughout the world, particularly in the Anglican Communion. SOMA now has eight centres in different parts of the world. Its work includes the provision of teams for ministry, mainly in the Two-Thirds World; welcoming teams and individuals for ministry in parishes (in the UK or other home countries); and international leadership conferences. A newsletter *SHARING*, is published three times a year. *SOMA International Chairman:* Revd David Harper. *SOMA UK Director:* Revd Don Brewin, PO Box 6002, Heath and Reach, Leighton Buzzard LU7 0ZA
Tel: (01525) 237953
Fax: (01525) 237954
email: SOMAUK@compuserve.com

South American Mission Society
(Incorporating the Spanish and Portuguese Church Aid Society)
Founded 1844 to make known the Gospel of the Lord Jesus Christ to the people of Latin America and the Iberian Peninsula and continuing in active partnership now with their mission priorities. *General Secretary:* Rt Revd David Evans, Allen Gardiner House, 12 Fox Hill, Birmingham B29 4AG
Tel: 0121–472 2616
Fax: 0121–472 7977
email: samsgb@compuserve.com

Southern Africa Church Development Trust
Founded 1960 to inform, encourage concern for and involvement in the Church in Southern Africa. Supports projects for building village churches, education, clergy and lay training, and medical work. Publishes a quarterly bulletin of information and projects which is sent to all subscribers. *President:* Mr Martin Kenyon. *Director:* Miss Joan Antcliff, Little Court, Pound Lane, Shaldon, Devon TQ14 0HA *Tel:* (0162 687) 2726

St Aidan's College Charity

Founded in 1980 with the funds of the former St Aidan's Theological College, Birkenhead, the Charity exists to assist ordinands to meet the cost of their theological training and the support of their dependants. Limited grants may also be available towards the cost of In-Service Training for clergy. Grants to Ordinands are considered by the trustees annually in November, and applications must reach the Clerk to the Trustees by 15 September. Applications for in-service training grants must reach the Clerk by 31 March for consideration at the Trustees' April meeting. *Chairman:* Canon John Bowers. *Enquiries to:* The Clerk to the Trustees, St Aidan's College Charity, Church House, Lower Lane, Aldford, Chester CH3 6HP   *Tel:* (01244) 620444

St Christopher's Fellowship

Formed by the amalgamation of the Fellowship of St Christopher (founded 1929) and Homes for Working Boys in London (founded 1870). Provides a project for severely (including sexually) abused children aged 4–12. It also provides 24-hour care for adolescents preparing to leave the care of local authorities in three hostels in Hillingdon, Lewisham and Richmond. Accommodation and support is also provided for over 250 young single homeless people aged 16–22 in shared accommodation on assured shorthold tenancies at 21 projects throughout London. Young people living in housing tenancies receive levels of support according to individual need to help them achieve fuller independence. The fellowship also operates a 56 bedspace nightshelter in partnership with London Borough of Hammersmith and Fulham. *Chairman:* Mr Brian Blackler. *Chief Exec:* Mr Jonathan Farrow, 217 Kingston Rd, Wimbledon, London SW19 3NL
Tel: 020–8543 3619
Fax: 020–8544 1633
email: st-chris@dircon.co.uk
Web: http://www.users.dircon.co.uk/˜st˜chris

St George's House, Windsor Castle

Founded 1966. A residential study centre within Windsor Castle, and part of the fourteenth century College of St George. Apart from three mid-service clergy courses each year of two to four weeks, most consultations cover one or two days. Some are arranged by the house, others by outside groups. The range of themes is wide but all share a concern for ethical and social issues and values. Accomodation for up to 32 people. *Chairman:* The Dean of Windsor. *Vice-Chairman:* HRH The Duke of Edinburgh. *Contact:* The Warden, St George's House, Windsor Castle, Windsor, Berks SL4 1NJ   *Tel:* (01753) 861341
Fax: (01753) 832115
email: georges.house@ukonline.co.uk

St Luke's Hospital for the Clergy

A surgical and medical hospital for the clergy, their spouses, widows, and dependent children, monks and nuns, deaconesses, ordinands, Church Army staff, and overseas missionaries. Over 150 leading London consultants give their services free of charge. Treatment is entirely free. The usual referral letter from a patient's doctor should be sent to the Medical Officer at the Hospital. *President:* The Archbishop of Canterbury. *Chairman:* Ven Derek Hayward. *General Secretary:* Canon Paul Thomas, 14 Fitzroy Square, London W1P 6AH   *Tel:* 020–7388 4954

St Michael's Fellowship

Runs four residential family assessment units in South London working in partnership with parents to enable them to meet the needs of their child. Works with adolescent mothers, one or two parent families where parents may have learning disabilities, psychiatric illness, a history of abuse, domestic violence and where there are child protection concerns. Runs one supported housing scheme for families where parents have learning disabilities, with self-contained flats and day support. *Director:* Mrs Sue Pettigrew, 53ᴀ Clapham High St, London SW4 7TH
Tel: 020–7622 6322
Fax: 020–7622 6323
email: archangel@zetnet.co.uk

St Pancras Housing

Founded 1924 by Rev Basil Jellicoe, this charitable association provides housing and support for families, single people and those with special needs in nearly 4,500 flats and houses in N London and Hertfordshire. *President:* The Bishop of London. *New Business Manager:* Ms Lucy Nuttall, St Richard's House, 110 Eversholt St, London NW1 1BS   *Tel:* 020–7209 9287
Fax: 020-7209 9223

Student Christian Movement

An ecumenical movement founded in 1889, it offers an intelligent and liberal approach to the challenges and questions of the Christian faith. It also offers support and empowerment to students in nearly seventy affiliated groups and chaplaincies across Britain, holds regular national conferences, produces a variety of resources for study, worship and publishes the journal *Movement*. It is affiliated to the World Student Christian Federation. SCM, Westhill College, 14–16 Weoley Park Rd, Selly Oak, Birmingham B29 6LL   *Tel:* 0121–471 2404
Fax: 0121–414 1251
email: scm@charis.co.uk
Web: http://www.charis.co.uk/scm

Studylink – EFAC International Training Partnership

Started in 1965 as part of the work of the Evangelical Fellowship in the Anglican Communion,

and renamed Studylink in 1996. Provides bursaries to ordained nationals who are potential leaders or theological educators in Anglican churches overseas to enable them to undertake further academic study at theological colleges in the United Kingdom. Financial support comes from evangelical parishes in England, who also offer hospitality and parish experience to the partners. *Chairman:* Revd Howard Peskett. *Secretary:* Mr Peter LeRoy, 8 Brook Cottage, Lower Barton, Corston, Bath BA2 9BA   *Tel:* (01225) 873023
Fax: (01225) 873871
email: a.leroy@clara.net

Tearfund
An evangelical Christian relief and development agency founded in 1968, a registered charity. It works in partnership with local churches and Christian organizations to bring good news to the poor in over 90 countries. Work supported includes community development, primary healthcare, education and childcare, and rural development. Tearfund provides funding, training, consultancy and personnel for locally run projects. In disaster situations it sends emergency relief teams into the field. Tearcraft, Tearfund's trading arm, markets goods from developing countries in the UK and Ireland. *General Director:* Mr Doug Balfour, 100 Church Rd, Teddington, Middx TW11 8QE   *Tel:* 020–8977 9144
0845 355 8355 (Enquiries)
Fax: 020–8943 3594
email: enquiry@tearfund.dircon.co.uk
Web: http://www.tearfund.org

Third Province Movement
The object of the Third Province Movement, which was started in November 1992, is to advocate, and eventually secure, the establishment within the Church of England of an autonomous province for all those, whatever their churchmanship, who in conscience cannot accept the ordination of women to the priesthood and other liberal developments. It also advocates a realignment on the same principle within the whole Anglican Communion. *Chairman:* Mrs Margaret Brown, Luckhurst, Mayfield, E Sussex TN20 6TY   *Tel:* (01435) 873007
email: tpm@phi.cix.co.uk
Web: http://www.cix.co.uk/~phi/tpm

Time Ministries International
The Time Strategy for development of the local church stresses unity of vision leading to the formation of ministry teams for evangelism, intercession, pastoral and practical work. The foundation workbook, for leaders and members, *Called to Serve,* is used by over 1,000 churches worldwide. Time also places an emphasis on a balanced eschatology. *Directors:* Revd Tony Higton (Chairman), Mrs Patricia Higton (Executive),

Emmanuel Church, Hawkwell, Hockley, Essex SS5 4NR   *Tel:* (01702) 54351
Fax: (01702) 54355
email: hawkwell@compuserve.com

Toc H
Founded 1915, Toc H fights to break down barriers by challenging individuals' preconceptions of others and the divisions which exist in society. While its work is based on Christian principles all faiths and none are recognized and accepted. Toc H works with people from all walks of life tackling social problems such as loneliness, isolation and deprivation through an approach which focuses on self-help and taking responsibility for oneself and the local community. *Enquiries to the:* Director, Toc H Central Services, 1 Forest Close, Wendover, Bucks HP22 6BT
Tel: (01296) 623911
Fax: (01296) 696137
email: info@toch.org.uk
Web: http://www.toch.org.uk

Trinitarian Bible Society
Founded in 1831 to circulate faithful Protestant translations of the Word of God. *General Secretary:* Mr Paul Rowland, Tyndale House, Dorset Rd, London SW19 3NN   *Tel:* 020–8543 7857
Fax: 020–8543 6370
email: trinitarian.bible.society@ukonline.co.uk
Web: http://biz.ukonline.co.uk/
trinitarian.bible.society/contents

True Freedom Trust
An interdenominational counselling and teaching ministry on homosexuality and related issues, for the Church and people seeking Christian counsel. It believes that the Bible forbids homosexual acts. It supplies resources, speakers and organizes conferences to help the Church overcome fear and prejudice and act with understanding and love in a biblical and Christ-like way. *Chairman:* Mr Walter Hurst. *Director and Founder:* Mr Martin Hallett, PO Box 13, Prenton, Wirral CH43 6YB   *Tel:* 0151–653 0773
Fax: 0151–653 7036
email: martin@tftrust.u-net.com
Web: http://www.tftrust.u-net.com

United College of the Ascension
(USPG and Methodist Church)
Founded 1923 within the Selly Oak Colleges' Federation, for training missionaries, the college is a community of people from many nations, cultures and religious traditions, who are studying within the Selly Oak federation in preparation for mission, and other church-related and educational work, overseas and in the UK. The college offers short courses and sabbaticals for the church in Britain. An international Centre for Anglican Communion Studies began in September 1992 in association with the CMS College, Crowther Hall. *Responsible body:* USPG and the

Methodist Church. *Principal:* Canon Andrew Wingate, United College of the Ascension, Weoley Park Rd, Birmingham B29 6RD

Tel: 0121–472 1667
Fax: 0121–472 4320

United Nations Association of Great Britain and Northern Ireland

UNA is a grassroots membership organization, independent of the United Nations and of government, which supports the UN and its family of agencies and programmes. It lobbies, educates and informs government, members of both houses of Parliament, the media and the general public to encourage the UK to use its position as a permanent member of the UN Security Council to the best advantage of the whole world community. Though any UN issue is of interest to UNA it concentrates its energies on three main areas — sustainable development, UN and conflict, and refugees and human rights. It works with schools and universities to develop understanding of the UN and internationalism, in particular by means of Model United Nations General Assemblies (MUNGA). It has close links with UNA International Service which sends qualified volunteers to work with partners in developing countries. In addition to campaigning and educating in relation to UN issues, UNA fundraises for the vital development work of agencies such as UNICEF and the UN High Commissioner for Refugees. *Director:* Mr Malcolm Harper, 3 Whitehall Court, London SW1A 2EL

Tel: 020–7930 2931
Fax: 020–7930 5893
email: una_uk@compuserve.com
Web: http://www.oneworld.org/una_uk

United Society for Christian Literature

Founded 1799 for the production of Christian literature for home and overseas. Today through Feed the Minds it also assists churches overseas in the translation, production, selling and distribution of Christian literature. *President:* Dr Pauline Webb. *Chairman:* Mr John Clark. *Secretary:* Dr Alwyn Marriage, Albany House, 67 Sydenham Rd, Guildford GU1 3RY

Tel: (01483) 888580
Fax: (01483) 888581
email: feedtheminds@gn.apc.org

United Society for the Propagation of the Gospel

USPG is one of the oldest Anglican missionary societies, which began in 1701 as SPG, and was formed by merging with the Universities' Mission to Central Africa and the Cambridge Mission to Delhi in the 1960s. USPG's vision is to see God's reconciling love for creation, as shown in Christ, brought to life in all people and in all places. Today USPG works by serving the church in Britain and Ireland and throughout the world, including Central, Southern, East and West Africa, the West Indies, India, Pakistan, South America, East Asia and the islands of the Indian and Atlantic Oceans. USPG does not directly employ mission personnel working overseas, rather supporting the dioceses and provinces which employ them as priests, teachers, health, employment or environmental project workers. About 105 people serve in these ways, plus 30 on short term special skills placements. Additionally, the Experience Exchange Programme offers the chance to explore some part of the worldwide church for six to twelve months. Following a major review of its strategy through the millennium, USPG has adopted an option for those who are poor and/or marginalized, and allocates more than £1 million in its funding programme of grants to churches worldwide. USPG in partnership with the Methodist Church runs the United College of the Ascension, part of the Selly Oak Federation in Birmingham, which, as well as preparing people to serve abroad offers an extensive programme of theological and mission education for church leaders from overseas who come as bursars to the college. USPG also offers a bursaries scheme to enable church leaders to train in their own countries. USPG is a member of Partnership for World Mission and is committed to its principles of mission in partnership, including transparency, consultation, sharing and justice. It has a regular International Encounter programme which brings church members from different continents and countries to Britain and Ireland to share their particular expertise and experience with the church here. USPG welcomes the interest of individual church members and parishes, both in prayer and finance, and through LINKS — USPG Friends in Action is establishing a worldwide network of interested supporters to encourage a wider understanding of world mission today. USPG also welcomes enquiries from those interested in serving the world church and encourages the church to kindle vocations to such service today. Parishes can also develop strong links with mission personnel abroad through the Projects scheme. *President:* The Archbishop of Canterbury. *Chair:* Canon Helen Cunliffe. *General Secretary:* Rt Revd Mano Rumalshah, Partnership House, 157 Waterloo Rd, London SE1 8XA

Tel: 020–7928 8681
Fax: 020–7928 2371
email: enquiries@uspg.org.uk

Universities and Colleges Christian Fellowship

(formerly Inter-Varsity Fellowship of Evangelical Unions)

Is the co-ordinating body for the interdenominational evangelical student Christian Union in Britain. Founded in 1928 by 14 university CUs, there are now groups in all universities, most other HE institutions and many FE colleges in Britain. The aim is to be a Christian witness in the student world, the work being based on expressing orthodox Christian belief in the contemporary

scene. Regional staff workers support and encourage groups. The publishing arm is the Inter-Varsity Press. The academic research arms are Tyndale House in Cambridge and the Whitefield Institute in Oxford. *Office:* 38 De Montfort St, Leicester LE1 7GP   *Tel:* 0116–255 1700
Fax: 0116–255 5672
email: enquiries@uccf.org.uk

Urban Theology Unit
Founded 1969 (1) to develop new insights of theology derived from the life of the city; (2) to create a community of clergy and laity concerned to discover relevant forms of ministry and action within urban areas; (3) to help people discover their vocation in relation to Gospel calls. Conducts Urban Priority Area Ministry Courses; a Master and Doctor of Ministry programme (MMin, DMin, degree awarded by Sheffield University); courses for MA, MPhil and PhD in Contextual, Urban and Liberation theologies; a Study Year in Sheffield leading to Diploma in Theology and Mission; basic ministerial training leading to a Diploma or Bachelor degree in Ministry and Theology, (BMinTh); and two-year in-service Diploma in Community Ministry; Conferences and Consultations on Church and Urban Mission. Ecumenical. Publishes various books on urban issues. *Chairperson:* Revd Raymond Goadby. *Director:* Revd Inderjit Bhogal. *Administrator:* Mr Peter Colby, Pitsmoor Study House, 210 Abbeyfield Rd, Sheffield, S Yorks S4 7AZ
Tel and *Fax:* 0114–243 5342
email: office@utu-sheffield.demon.co.uk
Web: http://www.utu-sheffield.demon.co.uk

Vacation Term for Biblical Study
The Vacation Term for Biblical Study is a Summer School held each summer at St Anne's College, Oxford, primarily devoted to the study of the Bible and related subjects. The aim is to enable people of all ages, occupations and denominations to become acquainted with contemporary scholarship. *Chairman:* Dr Barbara Spensley. *Further details are available from:* Mrs Elizabeth Lee, 13 Oxford Rd, Dewsbury, W Yorks WF13 4LN
Tel: (01924) 467319
email: http://www.web4wise.com

Vergers, Church of England Guild of
Founded in 1932 for the spiritual and social benefit of all vergers, full or part-time. Help and advice is given on request to those seeking assistance with a problem relating to their vocation and ministry. Provides a comprehensive training scheme, which is available to all members, each student being under the guidance of an area tutor. The scheme is scrutinized by an internal and an independent external panel of assessors. The annual residential training conference takes place at a college or university which is regarded as an integral part of the training scheme. *General*

Secretary: Mr Ian Griffiths, 14 Pennington Court 245 Rotherhithe St, London SE16 1FT
Tel: 020–7231 6888
email: gensec@cegv.freeserve.co.uk
Web: http://www.societies.anglican.org/guild-of-vergers

Victoria Institute
(or Philosophical Society of Great Britain)
Founded 1865 to enquire into the relationship between the Christian revelation and advancing scientific knowledge. Publishes *Faith and Thought Bulletin* and jointly with Christians in Science, *Science and Christian Belief. President:* Dr D. J. E. Ingram. *Secretary:* Mr Brian Weller, 41 Marne Ave, Welling, Kent DA16 2EY
Tel and *Fax:* 020–8303 0465

Walsingham, Shrine of Our Lady of
Founded in 1061 in response to a vision, destroyed in 1538, restored in 1922 by Revd A. Hope Patten, vicar of Walsingham. Since 1931, when it was moved from the parish church, the shrine has contained the image of Our Lady of Walsingham together with the Holy House. The house represents the home in Nazareth where the Blessed Virgin Mary and St Joseph cared for Jesus in his formative years. Nowadays Walsingham is England's premier place of pilgrimage. It is administered by a College of Guardians. There are facilities for pilgrims to be accommodated. Special facilities are available for receiving sick and handicapped people. There is also a full-time Education Officer who will facilitate visits for schools and other young people's groups. Information is available from the *Administrator:* Revd M. Warner, The Shrine Office, Walsingham, Norfolk NR22 6EE   *Tel:* (01328) 820255
Fax: (01328) 820990

WATCH (Women and the Church)
Founded in 1996. WATCH provides a forum for promoting women's ministry in the Church of England, based on a vision of the Church as a community of God's people where, regardless of gender, justice and equality prevail. *Chair:* Ms Christina Rees, Churchfield, Pudding Lane, Barley, Royston, Herts SG8 8JX   *Tel:* (01763) 848822
Fax: (01763) 848774
email: chrisrees@xc.org
Web: http://watchwomen.com

William Temple Foundation
Founded in 1947, as a research and training centre focusing on the links between theology, the economy and urban mission practice. The foundation works with practitioners in industrial mission, community work, social responsibility etc. to deepen the social and theological analysis of contemporary society and to develop innovative responses. There is a particular concern for the perspectives of people marginalized by current economic trends. The foundation works

losely with churches and practitioners across Europe especially the Work and Economy Network in the European Churches. Foundation staff contribute to training programmes for industrial mission, community work etc. and to post-graduate teaching in the University of Manchester. It produces regular papers and the quarterly journal *Foundations* available on subscription. *Contact:* Revd Malcolm Brown, William Temple Foundation, Luther King House, Brighton Grove, Rusholme, Manchester M15 6PB

Tel: 0161–224 6404
Fax: 0161–248 9201
email: temple@wtf.org.uk

William Temple House
Residence for students from overseas and the United Kingdom, men and women of all nationalities and faiths, where they can exercise responsibility and develop spiritually in a learning by experience situation. Under the Management of International Students Club (Church of England) Ltd. Registered Charity. *Enquiries to:* The Warden, 29 Trebovir Rd, London SW5 9NQ

Tel: 020–7373 6962
Fax: 020–7341 0003

Women's World Day of Prayer
Founded in America in 1887 (Britain 1930–34) to unite Christian women in prayer by means of services held on the first Friday in March each year, by fostering local inter-denominational prayer groups meeting throughout the year and to give financial support to charitable educational projects and the Christian literature societies. *President:* Mrs Rose Rivers. *Chairperson:* Mrs Marlene Moore. *Administrator:* Mrs Lynda Lynam, WWDP, Commercial Rd, Tunbridge Wells, Kent TN1 2RR

Tel and *Fax:* (01892) 541411

Womenaid International
A humanitarian aid and development agency run by volunteers in the UK which provides relief and assistance to women and children suffering distress caused by war, disasters or poverty. It seeks to empower women through education, training, provision of credit, and also campaigns against violations of women's human rights. An implementing partner of the European Community Humanitarian Office (ECHO), the British government and several UN agencies, it has provided over 30,000 tonnes of food, medical supplies and clothing to more than 1.5 million refugees in the former Yugoslavia, the Caucasus and Central Asia. Development assistance globally has ranged from building and repairing schools, supporting rescue centres for street children, repairing hospitals and providing medical equipment/supplies, micro-credit support, and

water/sanitation projects. *Founder:* Ms Pida Ripley, 3 Whitehall Court, London SW1A 2EL

Tel: 020–7839 1790
Fax: 020–7839 2929
email: womenaid@womenaid.org
Web: http://www.womenaid.org

World Congress of Faiths
Founded 1936 to promote mutual understanding and promote a spirit of fellowship between people of different religious traditions. The current programme explores issues arising out of religious pluralism. WCF works to explain and reconcile religious conflict and the tensions between the different faith communities. Conferences and lectures are arranged, the journal *World Faiths Encounter* is published three times a year together with a newsletter *One Family. Presidents:* Professor Keith Ward and Revd Marcus Braybrooke. *Chairman:* Revd Dr Richard Boeke. *Editor:* Revd Alan Race. *Hon Secretary:* Shahin Bekhradnia, World Congress Of Faiths, 2 Market St, Oxford OX1 3EF

Tel: (01865) 202751
Fax: (01865) 202746

World Vision
Formed in London in 1979, World Vision UK is part of the international World Vision partnership and is a major UK relief and development agency. World Vision is at work in over 100 countries in Africa, Asia, Eastern Europe, Latin America, and the Middle East. It is involved in partnering churches and other non-governmental organizations in projects ranging from relief work in Rwanda to income generation projects in Bangladesh. *Exec Director:* Mr Charles Clayton, 599 Avebury Boulevard, Milton Keynes MK9 3PG

Tel: (01908) 841000
Fax: (01908) 841001
email: peter_scott@wvi.org

YMCA
Founded 1844 to promote the physical, intellectual and spiritual well-being of young people. *President:* Lord Judd. *Secretary:* Mr E. Thomas, National Council of YMCAs, 640 Forest Rd, London E17 3DZ

Tel: 020–8520 5599
email: 11352.3504@compuserve.com

York Glaziers' Trust
Established 1967 by the Dean and Chapter of York and the Pilgrim Trust (i) to conserve and restore the stained glass of York Minster; (ii) to conserve, restore and advise on all stained glass or glazing of historic or artistic importance, in any building whether religious or secular, public or private; (iii) to establish and maintain within the city of York a stained glass workshop dedicated to the training and employment of conservators and craftsmen specializing in the

preservation of glass of historic and artistic importance; and (iv) to encourage public interest in the preservation of stained glass, to collaborate with educational institutions and to assist with scientific and art historical research into stained and painted glass. Advice should always be sought when considering treatment of glass of artistic or historic value. The trust welcomes enquiries from all sources. It offers a full advisory service and will compile comprehensive condition reports. *Chairman:* The Dean of York. *Secretary:* Ms Penelope Winton, 6 Deangate, York YO1 7JB   *Tel:* (01904) 557228
email: ygt@compuserve.com

Young Women's Christian Association of Great Britain

The YWCA of Great Britain strives for social justice and equality for young women through its work as a membership movement and as a youth work organization. It aims to provide a platform for young women to be heard and to contribute to debate on issues affecting young women at local, national and international levels. *President:* Mrs Sheila Brain. *Chief Exec:* Ms Gill Tishler. YWCA Headquarters, Clarendon House, 52 Cornmarket House, Oxford OX1 3EJ
Tel: (01865) 304200
Fax: (01865) 204805

Diocesan Associations

Arctic Fellowship	Miss M. Dean 81 Kerrysdale Ave Leicester LE4 7GN *Tel:* 0116–266 8664
Association of the Dioceses of Singapore and West Malaysia	Revd Ann Bucknall 20 St Margaret's Rd Lichfield Staffs WS13 7RA *Tel:* (01543) 257382
Belize Church Association	Mrs Barbara Harris Honeysuckle Cottage 19 Whittal St Kings Sutton Banbury Oxon OX17 3RD *Tel:* (01295) 811310
Central Tanganyika Diocesan Association	Miss S. M. Horsman 15 Woodstock Ave Harold Park Romford Essex *Tel:* (01708) 345691 *email:* shorsman@ema.co.uk
Church of Burma Association	Mrs Nita Sharpley 6 Parklands Swan Lane London N20 0PW *Tel:* 020–8446 1970
Church of Ceylon Association	Canon Bob Campbell-Smith Vicarage Church Lane Modbury Ivybridge Devon PL21 0QN *Tel:* (01548) 830260
Congo Church Association	Mrs Rosemary Peirce 70 Yarnells Hill Oxford OX2 9BG *Tel:* (01865) 721330/248367 *Fax:* (01865) 721330 *email:* ordinands@oxford.anglican.org
Diocese of the North Eastern Caribbean and Aruba Association	Canon Robert Eke 77 Hangleton Way Hove E Sussex BN3 8AF *Tel* and *Fax:* (01273) 421443
Egypt Diocesan Association	Lady Morris 26 Bickerton Rd Headington Oxford OX3 7LS *Tel* and *Fax:* (01865) 761461
Fellowship of the Maple Leaf (*Supports the work of the Church in Canada*)	Canon John Williams 2 Fox Spring Rise Edinburgh EH10 6NE *Tel* and *Fax:* 0131–445 2983 *email:* canonjohn@cix.co.uk
Friends of the Church in India	Revd Barrie Scopes 12 Bedgebury Close Rochester Kent ME1 2UT *Tel:* (01634) 828491
Friends of the Diocese of Cyprus and the Gulf	Mrs Mary Banfield Garden Corner Old London Rd Mickleham Surrey RH5 6DL *Tel* and *Fax:* (01372) 373912
Friends of the Diocese of Iran	Mrs Eleanor Ashton 104 Pelham Rd Wimbledon London SW19 1PA *Tel:* 020–8543 1167
Friends of the Diocese of Uruguay	Revd Charles Bradshaw Rectory 4 Rutland Lane Bottesford NG13 0DG *Tel:* (01949) 842335 *Fax:* (01949) 842533
Guyana Diocesan Association	Mr J. R. Chee-a-tow 13E Courtleet Drive Erith Kent DA8 3NB *Tel:* (0132 24) 42897
Hong Kong Anglican Church Association	Canon Stephen Sidebotham 87 Aston Abbotts Rd Weedon Bucks HP22 4NH *Tel:* (01296) 640098

Jerusalem and the Middle East Church Association	Mrs Vanessa Wells 1 Hart House The Hart Farnham Surrey GU9 7HA *Tel:* (01252) 726994 *Fax:* (01252) 735558
Kenya Church Association	Dr Hugh Sansom 29 Holmewood Ridge Langton Green Tunbridge Wells Kent TN3 0ED *Tel:* (01892) 862430 *email:* hughwsansom@ lineone.net
Lesotho Diocesan Association	Canon Ron Tovey 86 Kings Rd Oakham Leics. LE15 6PD *Tel:* (01572) 770628
Mozambique and Angola Anglican Association	Miss Joan Antcliff Little Court Pound Lane Shaldon Devon TQ14 0HA *Tel:* (01626) 872726
Nigeria Fellowship	Dr Rena Partridge 55 Hipwell Court Olney Bucks MK46 5QB *Tel:* (01234) 240018
North Queensland Auxiliary in England	Canon Leslie Buffee 46 Stone Bridge Way Faversham Kent ME13 7SB *Tel:* (01795) 535790
Province of the Indian Ocean Support Association	Mrs Judith Hepper 61 Queens Rd Alton Hants GU34 1JG

Sierra Leone Inter-Diocesan Association	Mrs Elfreda Taylor 18 Dovedale Ave Clay Hall Ilford Essex IG5 0QF
Sudan Church Association	Mrs Sara Taffinder 69 Poynders Rd Clapham London SW4 8PL *Tel:* 020–8671 1974
Transvaal, Zimbabwe and Botswana Association	Mrs Pat Dutton Pevers Farm Clapham Martins Lane Kirkstead Green Norfolk NR15 1ED *Tel* and *Fax:* (01508) 550638
Uganda Church Association	Mr David Thomson 37 Murray Rd Northwood Middx HA6 2YP *Tel:* (01923) 827015
Willochran Association	Revd Roger Jones Vicarage Wiston Haverfordwest Pembs SA62 4PL *Tel:* (01437) 731266 *email:* rjones4330@aol.com
Windward Islands Diocesan Association	Mrs Mary Anderson 115 Broadfield Rd Catford London SE6 1TJ *Tel:* 020–8461 1775
Zululand Swaziland Association	Canon Edgar Ruddock Rectory St Peter's Close Stoke-on-Trent Staffs ST4 1LP *Tel* and *Fax:* (01782) 845287 *email:* edrud@cix.co.uk

Libraries

Canterbury

Cathedral Library
Cathedral House
The Precincts
Canterbury
Kent CT1 2EH

Cathedral Librarian Mrs Sheila Hingley

Archivist Dr Michael Stansfield

Tel: (01227) 463510 (Archives)
(01227) 865247 (Library)
Fax: (01227) 762897
email:
catlib@ukc.ac.uk(library)

50,000 volumes with large collections of manuscripts.

Durham

Dean and Chapter Library
The College
Durham
DH1 3EH

Librarian Canon Prof David Brown

Deputy Librarian Mr Roger Norris

Tel: 0191–386 2489
email:
R.C.Norris@durham.ac.uk

Open: 0900–1300; 1415–1700 hours Mon—Fri

Search room open p.m. only

40,000 printed books including 70 incunabula, 360 manuscripts 6th–16th centuries. Other MS collections include Hunter, Sharp, Raine, Surtees, Ian Ramsey, J.B. Lightfoot, early music. Meissen Library of German Theology of approx 20,000 books donated by the EKD inaugurated 1998. Archdeacon Sharp Library of modern theology in English. Published catalogues of Saxon and Medieval manuscripts (1825, 1964, etc.), printed music (1968) and manuscript music (1986).

Lambeth

Lambeth Palace Library
London
SE1 7JU

Librarian and Archivist Dr Richard Palmer

Deputy Librarian and Archivist Miss Melanie Barber

Tel: 020–7898 1400
Fax: 020–7928 7932

Open: 1000–1700 hours Mon–Fri
Closed Public Holidays and ten days at Christmas and Easter.

Main library for the history of the Church of England, open for public use since 1610. 200,000 printed books, 4,000 manuscripts 9th–20th centuries. Registers and correspondence of Archbishops of Canterbury 12th–20th centuries. Records of Province of Canterbury, Lambeth Conferences, Bishops of London, and papers of churchmen, statesmen and organizations within the Church of England. Manuscripts and printed books earlier than 1850 from Sion College Library.

Partnership House

Partnership House Mission Studies Library
157 Waterloo Rd
London
SE1 8XA

Librarian Mr Colin Rowe

Tel: 020–7928 8681
Fax: 020–7928 3627
email:
c.rowe@mailbox.ulcc.ac.uk

Open: 0930–1700 hours Mon–Fri
Closed Public Holidays

Books also lent by post

25,000 volumes, 400 periodicals. Post-1945 collections of the former Church Missionary Society and United Society for the Propagation of the Gospel missionary libraries. Pre-1945 books from the CMS Library (CMS Max Warren collection).

ORGANIZATIONS

Pusey House

Pusey House
Oxford
OX1 3LZ

Custodian Revd William Davage

Tel: (01865) 278415

Open: 0915–1245, 1400–1645
Mon–Fri; 0915–1245 Sat
During Full Term

Contact the Custodian for vacation opening times

100,000 volumes. Includes Dr Pusey's Library (a theological library specializing in patristics, Church history and liturgy) and the library from St Augustine's College, Canterbury (a theological library specializing in Church of England and the Anglican Communion).

St Deiniol's

St Deiniol's Residential Library
Hawarden
Nr Chester
Flintshire
CH5 3DF

Warden and Chief Librarian Revd Peter Francis
Tel: (01244) 532350
Fax: (01244) 520643
email: deiniol.visitors@ btinternet.com
Web: http:// www.btinternet.com/ ˜st.deiniols/homepage.htm

200,000 plus volumes, including 50,000 pamphlets. Theology, biblical studies, spirituality, liturgy, 19th–century ecclesiastical and secular history, Bishop Moorman Franciscan Library, and all areas of the arts/ humanities. Residential accommodation for 47 people. Bursaries for clergy and students. Financial assistance for sabbaticals. Scholarship grants for research and writing for higher degrees or publication, meeting the entire cost of the stay at St Deiniol's.

St Paul's

The Library
St Paul's Cathedral
London
EC4M 8AE

Librarian Mr Jo Wisdom

Tel: 020–7246 8345
Fax: 020–7246 8325

Re-established after the Great Fire of 1666, the library is strong in theology, ecclesiastical history, and sermons, especially of 17th and 18th centuries. Special collections include early printed Bibles; St Paul's Cross sermons; 19th-century theological tracts. The archive of Dean and Chapter is deposited at Guildhall Library, Aldermanbury, London EC2P 2EJ.

Sion College

The library has closed. The older books (–1850) were transferred to Lambeth Palace Library. The bulk of the balance of the collection is in the library of King's College, London.

Fifty current periodicals. Biblical studies, philosophy, Anglican theology, church history, biography and liturgy. Special collections include Sion College Port Royal Library, Industrial Christian Fellowship Library, and extensive pamphlet collections.

United Society for the Propagation of the Gospel
Rhodes House Library
South Parks Rd
Oxford
OX1 3RG

Librarian Mr John Pinfold
Tel: (01865) 270909
Fax: (01865) 270912
email: rhodes.house.library@ bodley.ox.ac.uk
Written application necessary before first visit.

The Society's library to 1944 and archival material. Extensive collections from the 19th century, back holdings of missionary journals.

Westminster Abbey

Westminster Abbey Muniment
Room and Library
London
SW1P 3PA

Librarian Dr Tony Trowles

Keeper of the Muniments Dr
Richard Mortimer

Tel: 020–7222 5152
Fax: 020–7222 6391
email: library@westminster-
abbey.org
Web: http://
www.westminster-abbey.org

Open: 1000–1300, 1400–1645
hours Mon–Fri;
appointments desirable

14,000 volumes (16th–18th
century), 70,000 archives
(monastic history 8th–16th
century, Abbey records to
present day).

York Minster

York Minster Library
Dean's Park
York
YO1 2JQ

Librarian
Mrs Deidre Mortimer

Archivist
Mrs Louise Hampson

Tel: (01904) 625308
(01904) 611118 (Archives &
MSS)
Fax: (01904) 611119
Web: http://
www.yorkminster.org
Library catalogue
Web: http://
www.york.ac.uk/services/
library/guides/minster/htm

Open: 0900–1700 hours
Mon–Thur; 0900–1200 Fri

120,000 volumes. Extensive
collections of manuscripts,
incunables, prints, music,
photographs, Civil War tracts;
archives of Dean and Chapter
from medieval times.

See also main Organizations section

ORGANIZATIONS

Patronage Trusts

**Church Pastoral Aid Society
Patronage Trust**

Secretary Revd David Field
CPAS, Athena Drive
Tachbrook Park
Warwick CV34 6NG
Tel: (01926) 458457
Fax: (01926) 458459
email: dfield@cpas.org.uk

A Trust holding Rights of
Presentation to a number of
benefices. Administered by the
Church Pastoral Aid Society.

Church Patronage Trust

Secretary Revd Kenneth
Habershon
Truckers Ghyll
Horsham Rd, Handcross
W Sussex RH17 6DT
Tel: (01444) 400274

A Trust holding the Rights of
Presentation to a number of
benefices. Evangelical tradition.

Church Society Trust

Secretary J. M. Lindeck
Dean Wace House
16 Rosslyn Rd
Watford, Herts. WD1 7EY
Tel: (01923) 235111 (24 hrs)
Fax: (01923) 800362
email:
admin@churchsociety.org

Patron of more than 100 livings.

Church Trust Fund Trust	*Secretary* Revd David Field CPAS, Athena Drive Tachbrook Park Warwick CV34 6NG *Tel:* (01926) 458457 *Fax:* (01926) 458459 *email:* dfield@cpas.org.uk	A Trust holding Rights of Presentation to a number of benefices. Administered by the Church Pastoral Aid Society.
Guild of All Souls	*General Secretary* Charles Brown Guild of All Souls St Katharine Cree Church 86 Leadenhall St London EC3A 3DH *Tel:* 020–7621 0098	Patron of 39 livings of Catholic tradition.
Hulme Trustees	*Secretary* Mr Jonathan Shelmerdine, Taylor, Kirkman and Mainprice, Solicitors, 205 Moss Lane, Bramhall, Stockport SK7 1BA *Tel:* 0161–439 8228	A Trust holding the Rights of Presentation to a number of benefices.
Hyndman's (Miss) Trustees	*Administrative Secretary* Mrs Ann Brown 6 Angerford Ave Sheffield S8 9BG *Tel* and *Fax:* 0114–255 8522	Patronage Trust. Varied churchmanship.
Martyrs Memorial and Church of England Trust	*Secretary* Revd David Field CPAS, Athena Drive Tachbrook Park Warwick CV34 6NG *Tel:* (01926) 458457 *Fax:* (01926) 458459 *email:* dfield@cpas.org.uk	A Trust holding Rights of Presentation to a number of benefices. Administered by the Church Pastoral Aid Society.
Peache Trustees	*Secretary* Revd Kenneth Habershon Truckers Ghyll Horsham Rd, Handcross W Sussex RH17 6DT *Tel:* (01444) 400274	A Trust holding the Rights of Presentation to a number of benefices. Evangelical tradition.
Simeon's Trustees	*Administrative Secretary* Mrs Ann Brown 6 Angerford Ave Sheffield S8 9BG *Tel* and *Fax:* 0114–255 8522	Holds and administers the patronage of those livings in the Church of England which belong to the Trust on the principles laid down in Charles Simeon's Charge.
Society for the Maintenance of the Faith	*Secretary* Revd Paul Conrad Christ Church Vicarage 10 Cannon Place London NW3 1EJ *Tel:* 020–7435 6784	Administers patronage and promotes Catholic teaching and practice.

Anglican and Porvoo Communions

PART 5

PART 5 CONTENTS

THE ANGLICAN COMMUNION

There are nearly 70 million members of the Anglican household of 38 self-governing churches made up of about 500 dioceses, 30,000 parishes and 64,000 individual congregations in a total of 164 countries. While the Anglican Communion does not rank among the biggest groupings of Christians it is, after the Roman Catholic Church, arguably the most widespread.

The Anglican Communion has developed in two stages. During the first stage, which began in the seventeenth century, Anglicanism was established by colonization in countries such as Australia, Canada, New Zealand, Southern Africa and the USA. In the early days of expansion a somewhat remote control was exercised by the Bishops of London. After the American War of Independence Samuel Seabury of Connecticut, USA was consecrated in Scotland as the first bishop of the Anglican Communion outside the British Isles. Soon this precedent was followed by the Church in Canada and then India, Australia, New Zealand and South Africa.

The second stage began just over a century ago. During that era Anglican churches were planted all over the world as a result of the missionary work of the churches in England, Ireland, Scotland, and Wales which were joined in this task by the churches formed in the previous two centuries. Most of these churches became constitutionally independent in the period following the Second World War, usually before attainment of political independence. In regions which are large, diverse, and the population of Anglicans is perceived as too small to support a province, a useful halfway house has been found in the development of regional councils such as the Council of the Churches of East Asia.

Anglican churches uphold and proclaim the Catholic and Apostolic faith, based on Scripture and creeds, interpreted in the light of Christian tradition, scholarship and reason. Following the teachings of Jesus Christ, the Churches are committed to the proclamation of the good news of the gospel to the whole creation.

By baptism, in the name of the Father, Son and Holy Spirit, a person is made one with Christ and received into the Church.

Central to worship for Anglicans is the celebration of the Holy Eucharist (also called the Holy Communion, the Lord's Supper, or the Mass). In this offering of prayer and praise are recalled the life, death and resurrection of Christ, through the proclamation of the Word and celebration of the sacrament.

Worship is at the very heart of Anglicanism. Its styles vary from the simple to the elaborate, from Evangelical to Catholic, from charismatic to traditional or indeed from a combination of these various traditions. *The Book of Common Prayer*, in its various revisions throughout the Communion, gives expression to the comprehensiveness found within the Church whose principles reflect, since the time of Elizabeth I, a *via media* in relation to other Christian traditions.

Other rites include Confirmation, Holy Orders, Reconciliation, Marriage and Anointing of the Sick.

Almost everywhere Anglican Churches are self-supporting. Only a small percentage of income is transferred from richer to less affluent churches. Many of the member churches of the Anglican Communion are to be found in the so-called developing or 'Third' world. It is estimated that 3,000 persons are added to membership each day through birth, baptism or conversion. The fastest-growing areas are in the global south.

For over 200 years there has been a process of decentralization which has led to flexibility and a capacity for indigenization and involvement in local ecumenical negotiations and projects. This leaves open the possibility of loss of identity. But to compensate for this the Anglican Communion has developed a number of institutions which have ensured cohesion and communication. The oldest and most important of these is the Lambeth Conference. The 1968 Lambeth Conference agreed to the formation of the Anglican Consultative Council which brings together clergy and lay as well as episcopal representatives once every two or three years. More recently there have been regular meetings of Primates – senior bishops and archbishops from each member church.

The Churches of the Anglican Communion are linked by affection and common loyalty. They are in full communion with the See of Canterbury, and thus the Archbishop of Canterbury, in his person, is a unique focus of Anglican unity. He calls the once-a-decade Lambeth Conference, is Chairman of the meeting of Primates and is President of the Anglican Consultative Council.

The Secretary General of the Anglican Communion, aided by a permanent Secretariat staff, assists the Archbishop of Canterbury in servicing the Lambeth Conference and meetings of the Primates and thereby exercises a vital co-ordinating role.

During recent years, in addition to local ecumenical negotiations and projects, the Anglican Communion has been engaged in international dialogues with a number of major churches including the Roman Catholic Church, the Lutheran World Federation, the Orthodox Churches, and the World Alliance of Reformed Churches. Through the Faith and Order Commission of the World Council of Churches it has also been engaged in a multilateral dialogue process which has resulted in the publication of the Faith and Order Document *Baptism, Eucharist and Ministry*.

Outstanding features within the Anglican Communion in the past 25 years are the constitution of many new autonomous provinces in Africa, Asia and Latin America and the emergence of the Anglican Consultative Council. These are both parts of a bigger process of transition and maturing whereby relationships within the Communion have progressed in becoming a family of varied but essentially equal members within the Body of Christ. The family is interdependent. There is still need for the small, the poor, the weak to receive help from the stronger and richer, because the responsibilities of the Communion and the mission of the whole family are one and interdependent in the Body of Christ.

OUR CHURCHES

The present list of member churches or provinces, and of councils, is:

The Church of the Province of Aotearoa, New Zealand and Polynesia
The Anglican Church of Australia
The Episcopal Anglican Church of Brazil
The Episcopal Church of Burundi
The Anglican Church of Canada
The Church of the Province of Central Africa
The Anglican Church of the Central American Region
The Church of Ceylon (Sri Lanka)
The Anglican Church of the Congo
The Church of England

Hong Kong Sheng Kung Hui
The Church of the Province of the Indian Ocean
The Church of Ireland
The Anglican Communion in Japan (Nippon Sei Ko Kai)
The Episcopal Church in Jerusalem and the Middle East
The Anglican Church of Kenya
The Anglican Church of Korea
The Church of the Province of Melanesia
The Anglican Church of Mexico
The Church of the Province of Myanmar
The Church of Nigeria (Anglican Communion)
The Anglican Church of Papua New Guinea
The Episcopal Church in the Philippines
The Lusitanian Church of Portugal
The Episcopal Church of Rwanda
The Scottish Episcopal Church
The Church of the Province of South East Asia
The Church of the Province of Southern Africa
The Anglican Church of the Southern Cone of America
The Spanish Reformed Episcopal Church
The Church of the Province of the Sudan
The Anglican Church of Tanzania
The Church of Uganda
The Episcopal Church in the United States of America
The Church in Wales
The Church of the Province of West Africa
The Church in the Province of the West Indies

In addition: The Churches of Bangladesh, Pakistan, North and South India.

The Lambeth Conference

It could be said that the Lambeth Conference has its origin in 1865 when, on 20 September, the Provincial Synod of the Church of Canada unanimously agreed to urge the Archbishop of Canterbury and the Convocation of his province to find a means by which the bishops consecrated within the Church of England and serving overseas could be brought together for a General Council to discuss issues facing them in North America, and elsewhere. Part of the background for this request was a serious dispute about the interpretation and authority of the Scriptures which had arisen in Southern Africa between Robert Gray, Archbishop of Cape Town, and Bishop Colenso, Bishop of Natal.

Notwithstanding the opposition of a significant number of the bishops in England, Archbishop Longley invited Anglican bishops to their first Conference together at Lambeth Palace on 24 September 1867 and the three following days. Seventy-six bishops finally accepted the invitation and the Conference was called to order and

met in the Chapel of Lambeth Palace. A request to use Westminster Abbey for a service was not granted.

Of the 76 bishops attending the first Lambeth Conference the distribution was the following:

England	– 18 bishops
Ireland	– 5 bishops
Scotland	– 6 bishops
Colonial and Missionary	– 28 bishops
United States	– 19 bishops

It was made clear at the outset that the Conference would have no authority of itself as it was not competent to make declarations or lay down definitions on points of doctrine. But the Conference was useful in that it explored many aspects of possible inter-Anglican co-operation and by providing common counsel it inaugurated a practical way in which the unity of the faith of the Church could be maintained. The Conference did not take any effective action regarding the ssues raised by Bishop Colenso but its far-reaching impact can be seen in the fact that it was the precursor of the Lambeth Conference which we know today.

In 1878 the second Lambeth Conference was convened by Archbishop Tait and 100 bishops attended. The heavy agenda included 'Modern forms of infidelity'. It marked another milestone in the growth of the relationship of diverse parts of the Anglican Communion and reinforced the value of the meeting of Anglican bishops to share their common experience.

One hundred and forty-five bishops attended the Lambeth Conference of 1888 called by Archbishop Benson. Meeting at Lambeth Palace in the Library, its agenda addressed such contemporary issues as intemperance, purity, divorce, care of immigrants, and socialism. More important for the ongoing life of the Church itself, the agenda concerned itself with the issues of Oecumenism. In 1886 the House of Bishops of the Episcopal Church in the United States of America, meeting in Chicago, had devised a formula which provided a basic framework of recognition of 'authentic' Christian tradition. This formula, known as the Chicago Quadrilateral, was a statement, from the Anglican standpoint, of the essentials for a reunited Christian Church. The four main elements were as follows:

1. The Holy Scriptures of the Old and New Testaments, as 'containing all things necessary to Salvation', and as being the rule and ultimate standard of faith.
2. The Apostles' creed, as the baptismal symbol; and the Nicene creed, as the sufficient statement of the Christian faith.
3. The two sacraments ordained by Christ himself – Baptism and the Supper of Our Lord ministered with unfailing use of Christ's words of institution, and of the elements ordained by him.
4. The Historic Episcopate.

The 1888 Conference, taking this statement, promulgated the first of several successive versions of what has become known as the Lambeth Quadrilateral. It is this Lambeth Quadrilateral which has been one of the major contributions of the Anglican Communion to the evolving search for unity between the churches which is at the heart of the ecumenical movement.

The 1897 Lambeth Conference was attended by 194 bishops and presided over by Archbishop Frederick Temple. There were two main matters of interest: first, the Conference warmly commended the concept of deaconesses; and, second, it asked for the establishment of a consultative committee which was to be the direct ancestor of the Anglican Consultative Council.

The Conference of 1908 with Archbishop Davidson in the chair was attended by 242 bishops and concerned itself with the issues of the Ministry of Healing, the possible revision of the Prayer Book, and the supply and training of the clergy.

The Lambeth Conference should have convened again in 1918 but this was postponed due to the outbreak of the Great War. Much had changed in the way in which many people understood the world around them when the next Conference met in 1920. This Conference, attended by 252 bishops, was dominated by the subject of Church Unity. The celebrated 'Appeal to All Christian People' which was promulgated at the 1920 Conference invited other churches to accept episcopacy as the indispensable precondition for their unity with Anglicans. Developing from the consideration of the 1897 Conference there was also greater sympathy for a more prominent role for women in the governing and in the ministry of the Church. The 1920 Conference addressed itself to the issue of contraception and rejected its use outright.

The 1930 Conference was presided over by Archbishop Cosmo Lang, 307 bishops in attendance. It proved to be a very crowded occasion in the Lambeth Palace Library. The momentum towards Church Unity in South India found support, encouraging Anglicans in the Indian subcontinent to enter seriously into discussions related to a United Church in India.

Archbishop Geoffrey Fisher presided over two Conferences – 1948 attended by 349 bishops and 1958 attended by 310 bishops. By 1948 the Church of South India was an accomplished fact. In 1958 the proposal for a United Church of North India was welcomed. Nuclear disarmament was an issue in 1958 with the majority being in favour of disarmament, and the report on the family was a milestone with its sensitive treatment of the subject of contraception within marriage. The 1958 Conference approved the appointment of the first Anglican Executive Officer, thus assisting in the evolution both of the role of the Archbishop of Canterbury and of inter-Anglican structures. This was also the first Conference in which wives of the bishops were taken into account in the planning and organization.

The Conference of 1968, under Archbishop Ramsey, was attended by 462 bishops. With this Conference it was no longer possible to meet at Lambeth Palace and the Conference was thus convened in the Church Assembly Hall at Church House, Westminster. Preparatory papers were offered to members of the Conference written by expert consultants and some 35 committees prepared the work for the final report. The issue of the ordination of women came forward and a proposed constitution for the establishment of the Anglican Consultative Council was agreed to. With the 1968 Conference the Lambeth Conferences became the modern phenomenon that we know them to be today with more extensive preparation, more committee work, and more concern for communication both between the churches and with the general public.

Another change of venue was to find the 1978 Conference meeting residentially in the University of Kent at Canterbury under Archbishop Coggan. Living and worshipping together gave a new community dynamic to the Conference. Again, preparatory work was a key element in the deliberations of the Conference and an important factor in this was the development of the work and role of the Anglican Consultative Council whose full Standing Committee was present for the Conference. Among the important and controversial issues on the agenda of the 1978 Conference were the ordination of women to the priesthood, the training of bishops, human rights, and the evolving inter-Anglican bodies.

In 1988, the Conference was again held at the University of Kent at Canterbury, under the chairmanship of Archbishop Runcie. The Conference began on Sunday 17 July with a great opening service at Canterbury Cathedral and concluded on Sunday 7 August with a great closing service, again in Canterbury Cathedral. The Conference resolved to set up several inter-Anglican bodies: a Commission on the Ordination of Women to the Episcopate and on the implications of such ordinations for relations between the Churches of the Anglican Communion; an Advisory Body on Prayer Book Revision; an Inter-Faith Committee which would offer guidelines towards establishing a common approach to people of other faiths on a Communion-wide basis; a Commission on Anglican-Oriental Orthodox relations; conversations with the World Methodist Council and the Baptist World Alliance with a view to the beginning of international dialogues with these two traditions. The report of the Lambeth Conference 1988, *The Truth Shall Make You Free*, is published by Church House Publishing, price £8.50.

The Lambeth Conference 1998 was held in Canterbury, convened by Archbishop George Carey. Nearly 800 bishops attended. Mrs Carey led a spouses programme for over 650 women and men and there were 70 communications persons, 20 monks and nuns and a host of diocesan volunteers. This was the largest Lambeth Conference yet, as all suffragan, assistant, and auxiliary bishops were included.

Much of the energy of the Conference was centred on questions relating to the developing world Church and especially international debt. The Conference spent much time on inter-faith matters as well as hearing from Cardinal Edward Cassidy from the Vatican at an Ecumenical Vespers Service.

Women who are bishops were present for the first time.

The discussion relating to homosexuality showed clearly that the Communion is not of one mind on this issue. A vast number of resolutions on a vast number of topics surfaced and were accepted by the Conference. These included Modern Technology and Ethics, the significance of Jerusalem for the world faiths, and the allowing of differing views on the ordination of women to the priesthood and episcopate.

OTHER MEANS OF CONSULTATION

A second field of communication has been the Pan-Anglican Congresses. These have been held in London in 1908, in Minneapolis, USA in 1954 and in Toronto, Canada in 1963. Normally held at a time midway between Lambeth Conferences, the Congress, though like the Conference in having no executive authority, is distinguished from it by the presence of clerical and lay representatives from all the dioceses in the Communion.

Apart from the value of persons meeting one another, these Congresses have played a lesser role than the Lambeth Conferences and have had less influence. A significant contribution, though, to Anglican self-understanding came from the 1963 Congress. This was the concept of Mutual Responsibility and Interdependence in the Body of Christ. Unfortunately it became popularly identified solely with finance and projects, whereas it describes admirably the proper relationships within a worldwide family of autonomous churches.

The third step in forwarding the process of inter-Anglican consultation and common action was taken in 1958, when the Lambeth Conference of that year recommended 'that a full time Secretary of the Advisory Council on Missionary Strategy should be appointed by the Archbishop of Canterbury with the approval of the Advisory Council' and then went on to say, 'This Officer would collect and disseminate information, keep open lines of communication and make contact when necessary with responsible authority.' This official became known as the **Anglican Executive Officer**. The appointment was first held by Bishop Stephen Bayne of the United States who established the practice of travelling widely and personally meeting the Church in many parts of the world. Bishop Ralph Dean of Canada succeeded him and also acted as Episcopal Secretary to the 1968 Lambeth Conference. In 1969 he was succeeded by Bishop John Howe.

The 1968 Lambeth Conference called for the setting up of an **Anglican Consultative Council** (*see below*). The Council would come into being if two-thirds of the provinces of the Anglican Communion gave their consent. By the end of 1969 all had expressed their approval, and so the Council, asked for by the whole Anglican Communion, came into being. Canon Samuel Van Culin of the USA served as Secretary General until retiring in 1994.

The Lambeth Conference of 1978 requested that **Primates'** meetings should be set up to enable regular consultation between the Primates of the Anglican Communion. The first meeting took place in Ely, England, in November/December 1979. The second meeting took place in Washington DC, USA, in April/May 1981, the third was in Limuru, Kenya, in October 1983, the fourth in Toronto, Canada, in March 1986, the fifth in Larnaca, Cyprus, in April/May 1989, the sixth in Ireland in April 1991, the seventh with the ACC in Cape Town, and the eighth in Windsor, England, in 1995. The 1997 meeting was held in Jerusalem. The Primates met briefly following the Lambeth Conference 1998 in Canterbury. The next formal meeting will be in Portugal in 2000.

The Anglican Communion Office

Secretary General Canon John L. Peterson

Anglican Communion Office Partnership House, 157 Waterloo Rd, London SE1 8UT
Tel: 020–7620 1110
Fax: 020–7620 1070

The Anglican Consultative Council

MEMBERSHIP
The Archbishop of Canterbury is President and the Council chooses its own Chairman and Secretary General, which appointment replaces the former one of Anglican Executive Officer.

Each province or member church chooses up to three members. There are also six co-opted members, two of whom shall be women and two under 28 years of age. The resulting membership, made up of bishops, clergy and lay people, is notable for its spread of nationalities and races.

FUNCTIONS
The Council meets every two or three years and its Standing Committee in the intervening years. Council meetings are held in different parts of the world.

True to the Anglican Communion's style of working, the Council has no legislative powers. It fills a liaison role, consulting and recommending, and at times representing the Anglican Communion. The functions of the Council are stated as follows:

1. To share information about developments in one or more provinces with the other parts of the Communion and to serve as needed as an instrument of common action.
2. To advise on inter-Anglican, provincial and diocesan relationships, including the division of provinces, the formation of new provinces and of regional councils and the problems of extra-provincial dioceses.
3. To develop as far as possible agreed Anglican policies in the world mission of the Church and to encourage national and regional churches to engage together in developing and implementing such policies by sharing their resources of manpower, money and experience to the best advantage of all.
4. To keep before national and regional churches the importance of the fullest possible Anglican collaboration with other Christian churches.
5. To encourage and guide Anglican participation in the Ecumenical Movement and the ecumenical organizations; to co-operate with the World Council of Churches and the world confessional bodies on behalf of the Anglican Communion; and to make arrangements for the conduct of Pan-Anglican conversations with the Roman Catholic Church, the Orthodox Churches and other churches.
6. To advise on matters arising out of national or regional church union negotiations or conversations and on subsequent relations with united churches.
7. To advise on problems of inter-Anglican communication and to help in the dissemination of Anglican and ecumenical information.
8. To keep in review the needs that may arise for further study and, where necessary, to promote enquiry and research.

RECORD OF MEETINGS
FIRST MEETING, LIMURU, KENYA 1971

SECOND MEETING, DUBLIN, IRELAND 1973

THIRD MEETING, TRINIDAD 1976

FOURTH MEETING LONDON, ONTARIO, CANADA 1979

FIFTH MEETING, NEWCASTLE UPON TYNE, ENGLAND 1981

SIXTH MEETING OF THE COUNCIL, BADAGRY, NIGERIA 1984
Sections:

1. Mission and Ministry: Evaluation of Mission (Mission Audit); Mission Strategy and Ministry.
2. Dogmatic and Pastoral Matters: Anglican/ Roman Catholic Marriages; Polygamy; Christian Marriage and Family Life; Relations with Islam.
3. Ecumenical Relations: Steps Towards Unity; International Dialogues; World Council of Churches; and Church of England in South Africa.

4. Christianity and the Social Order: Social Issues; Peace; Refugees; Family; and United Nations.

Sections:

1. Mission and Ministry: Mission Agencies; New Mission Issues and Strategy Advisory Group; Renewal of the Church in Mission; Ordination of Women to the Priesthood and the Episcopate.
2. Dogmatic and Pastoral Concerns: Inter-Anglican Theological and Doctrinal Commission; Inter-Faith Relations; Christian Initiation; Anglican Communion Liturgical Commission.
3. Ecumenical Relations: Emmaus Report (which refers to dialogues with other churches); Anglican-Roman Catholic International Commission (ARCIC); Baptism, Eucharist and Ministry (BEM); United Churches in Full Communion.
4. Christianity and the Social Order: Peace and Justice; The Family; South Africa; AIDS.

The report of the meeting, *Many Gifts, One Spirit*, was published by Church House Publishing for the ACC, price £4.50.

Sections:

1. Spirituality and Justice.
2. Mission, Culture and Human Development.
3. Evangelism and Communication.
4. Unity and Creation.

The report of the meeting, *Mission in a Broken World*, with an overview by the editor – a new feature – was published by Church House Publishing for the ACC, price £6.50.

Working groups:

1. Running the Family.
2. Mission and Evangelism.
3. Dynamics of Communion.

The report, *A Transforming Vision*, was published by Church House Publishing for the ACC/Primates, price £7.50, alongside a video and magazine, *Anglican World*.

Theme: Witnessing as Anglicans in the Third Millennium.
Sections:

1. Looking to the Future in Worship.
2. Looking to the Future in Ministry.
3. Looking to the Future in Relation to Society.
4. Looking to the Future in Communicating Our Beliefs.

Hearings: Human Sexuality, Jerusalem, Islam, United Nations.
The report, *Being Anglican in the Third Millennium*, was published by Morehouse Publishing.

The eleventh meeting of the Council met in Scotland, Diocese of Brechin, September 1999. A report will be published in early 2000.

PUBLICATIONS
The Anglican Cycle of Prayer
The Essential Guide to the Anglican Communion
Anglican World magazine
The Compass Rose Society Newsletter
The Virginia Report
The Official Report of the Lambeth Conference 1998

The Anglican Centre in Rome

The Metropolitans of the Anglican Communion endorsed the establishment of the Anglican Centre in Rome in April 1966. This followed consultations among representatives of the several Churches of the Anglican Communion on action for the furtherance of Christian Unity and considering the prospect for renewed fellowship and co-operation between Anglicans and Roman Catholics in particular, held out by the Second Vatican Council and by the historic visit of the Archbishop of Canterbury to Rome in March 1966.

The purposes of the Centre are:
1. To provide a meeting place and opportunities for clergy and seriously interested laity of the Anglican Communion, and those of other Christian denominations, particularly Roman Catholic, to come together for discussion, worship and prayer for the achievement of Christian Unity.
2. To provide a focal point for Anglican collaboration with the various agencies of the Roman Catholic Church and in particular its Council for Promoting Christian Unity.
3. To provide a library of Anglican history, theology and liturgy for the use of students, theologians and churchmen of all Christian denominations.

4. To give all possible help to Anglican scholars who wish to work in Rome and to aid them in meeting and working with those in Rome.
5. To sponsor various activities including lectures, seminars and discussion groups to elucidate Anglicanism and its relation to the thinking and practice of Roman Catholic and other theologians.
6. To provide information and, as appropriate, publicity concerning the Churches of the Anglican Communion, the Anglican Centre, and its objectives, programmes and activities.
7. To provide a base where the appointees of the several Anglican churches may pursue co-ordinated discussions on appropriate lines of action for promoting unity, with the Roman Catholic Church and others.

The Centre publishes a quarterly magazine *CENTRO*, and organizes seminars, including the ROMESS Summer School, open to clergy and laity with a genuine interest in ecumenism. The Centre's library is open from 9 a.m. to 12.30 p.m. Monday to Friday, except holidays.

The activities of the Centre are governed by a governing body, and a director.

Director and Archbishop of Canterbury's Representative to the Vatican Rt Revd John Baycroft, The Anglican Centre in Rome, Palazzo Doria Pamphilj, Piazza Collegio Romano 2, Int. 7, 00186 Rome, Italy. *Tel*: 39–06–678–0302 *Fax*: 39–06–678–0674 *email*: anglican.centre.rome@flashnet.it

FRIENDS OF THE ANGLICAN CENTRE IN ROME
Founded in 1984 to enlist support both through prayer and financial assistance for the work of the Centre.

President The Archbishop of Canterbury

Chairman The Bishop of Chichester

Vice-Chairman Revd Sir Derek Pattinson

Chairman, English Friends Revd Sir Derek Pattinson, 4 Strutton Court, Great Peter St, London SW1P 2HH

CHURCHES AND PROVINCES OF THE ANGLICAN COMMUNION

Anglican Church in Aotearoa, New Zealand and Polynesia

Members 220,659

Formerly known as the Church of the Province of New Zealand, the Church covers 106,000 square miles and includes the countries of New Zealand, Fiji, Tonga, Samoa and the Cook Islands. It was established as an autonomous church in 1857. A revised constitution adopted in 1992 reflects a commitment to bicultural development that allows freedom and responsibility to implement worship and mission in accordance with the culture and social conditions of the Maori, white European and Polynesian membership. The Church has a strong and effective board of missions.

Presiding Bishop and Primate Most Revd John Campbell Paterson (*Bishop of Auckland*)

Co-presiding Bishops
Rt Revd Whakahuihui Vercoe (*Bishop of Aotearoa*)
Rt Revd Jabez Leslie Bryce (*Bishop of Polynesia*)

General Secretary and *Treasurer* Mr Robin Nairn, PO Box 885, Hastings   *Fax*: 06–878 7905
          email: gensec@hb.ang.org.nz

THEOLOGICAL COLLEGES
College of the Southern Cross, 202 St John's Rd, Remuera, Auckland 5 (Serves both Anglicans and Methodists. *Administrative Manager* Ms Carol Anne Sensicle)   *Fax*: 09–521 2420

Te Rau Kahikatea College Maori Theological College, 202 St John's Rd, Auckland 5 (*Te Ahorangi/ Dean* Ms J. Te Paa)

College of the Diocese of Polynesia, 202 St John's Rd, Remuera, Auckland 5 (*Principal* Ven W. Halapua)

College House, 100 Waimairi Rd, Christchurch 4 (*Director* Revd Dr K. Booth)

Selwyn College, 560 Castle St, Dunedin

The two last named cater for pre-ordination or post-graduate studies.

AOTEAROA
Bishop Rt Revd Whakahuihui Vercoe, PO Box

146, Rotorua, New Zealand   *Fax*: 07–348 6091
          email: wvercoe@aot.org.nz

Bishop in Tai Tokerau Rt Revd Waiohau Rui Te Haara, PO Box 25, Paihia   *Fax*: 09–402 6663
          email: bishop@pih.ang.org.nz

Bishop in Tai Rawhiti Rt Revd William Brown Turei, PO Box 1128, Napier   *Fax*: 06–835 7465

Bishop in Te Upoko O Te Ika Rt Revd Muru Walters, 6 Rajputana Way, Kandallah, Wellington   *Fax*: 04–479 8513
          email: muruwalters@compuserve.com

Bishop in Te Waipounamu Rt Revd John Robert Kuru Gray, PO Box 10086, Christchurch
          Fax: 03–389 0912

AUCKLAND
Bishop Rt Revd John Campbell Paterson (*Primate and Presiding Bishop of the Anglican Church in Aotearoa, New Zealand and Polynesia and Bishop of Auckland*), PO Box 37–242, Parnell, Auckland
          Fax: 09–303 3321
          email: 100400.2636@compuserve.com

CHRISTCHURCH
Bishop Rt Revd Dr David John Coles, PO 4438, Christchurch   *Fax*: 03–372 3357
          email: bishop@chch.ang.org.nz

DUNEDIN
Bishop Rt Revd Dr Penelope Ann Bansall Jamieson, PO Box 5445, Dunedin
          Fax: 03–477 4932
          email: pennydn@dn.ang.org.nz

NELSON
Bishop Rt Revd Derek Lionel Eaton, Bishopdale, PO Box 100, Nelson   *Fax*: 03–548 2125
          email: +derek@nn.ang.org.nz

POLYNESIA
Bishop in Rt Revd Jabez Leslie Bryce, Bishop's House, Box 35 GPO, Suva, Fiji Islands
          Fax: 679 302 687

Assistant Bishop Rt Revd V. M. Hala'api'api (*same address*) Fax: 679 302 152

WAIAPU
Bishop Rt Revd Murray John Mills, 8 Cameron Terr, PO Box 227, Napier, Hawkes Bay
Fax: 06–835 0680
email: murray.waiapu@hb.ang.org.nz

Bishop in the Bay of Plenty Rt Revd George Howard Douglas Connor, 60 Judea Rd, Tauranga
Fax: 07–577 0684
email: georgebop@ang.org.nz

WAIKATO
Bishop Rt Revd David John Moxon, PO Box 21, Hamilton, Waikato Fax: 07–838 0050
email: davidm@wave.co.nz

Assistant Bishop in Taranaki Rt Revd Philip Richardson (*same address*)

WELLINGTON
Bishop Rt Revd Dr Thomas John Brown, PO Box 12–046, Wellington Fax: 04–449 1360
email: bishoptom@ibm.net

Anglican Church of Australia

Members 3,998,444
The Church came to Australia in 1788 with the 'First Fleet', which was made up primarily of convicts and military personnel. Free settlers soon followed. A General Synod held in 1872 formed the Australian Board of Missions; missionary work among the aborigines and Torres Strait Islanders was key to the growth of the Church. The Church became fully autonomous in 1962 and in 1978 published its first prayer book. A second Anglican prayer book was published in 1996. The Anglican Church of Australia is part of the Christian Conference of Asia and of the Council of the Church of East Asia. Links with churches of New Guinea, Melanesia, and Polynesia are strong especially through the Australian Board of Mission.

Primate of the Anglican Church of Australia Most Revd Keith Rayner (*Archbishop of Melbourne*)

General Secretary of the General Synod Revd Dr B. N. Kaye

Hon Treasurer Mr Adrian Scarra

General Synod Office Box Q190, QVB Post Office, New South Wales 1230 Fax: 02–9264 6552

THE ANGLICAN THEOLOGICAL COLLEGES
Anglican Institute of Theology and Religious Education, Cnr Hardy and Leura St, Nedlands, WA6009 (*Director* Revd Dr J. Dunhill)
Fax: 08–9386 8327

Institute of Theological Education, PO Box 535, Boronia, Vic 3155 (*Director* Revd Trevor Smith)
Fax: 03–9761 2344

Moore Theological College, 1 King St, Newtown, NSW 2042 (*Principal* Canon Peter Jensen)
Fax: 02–9577 9988
email: admin@moore.usyd.edu.au

Nungalinya College, PO Box 40371, Casuarina, NT 0811 (*Principal* Wali Fejo) Fax: 08–8927 2332

Ridley College, 106 The Avenue, Parkville, Vic 3052 (*Principal* Revd Dr Graham Cole)
Fax: 03–9387 5099

St Barnabas Theological College, 34 Lipsett Terrace, Brooklyn Park, SA 5032 (*Principal* Revd Dr Scott Cowdell) Fax: 08–8416 8450
email: barbara.dalton@flinders.edu.au

St Francis Theological College, 233 Milton Rd, PO Box 1261, Milton Qld 4064 (*Principal* Canon James McPherson) Fax: 07–3369 4691
email: stfrancis@docnet.org.au

St John's College Ministry Centre, PO Box 71, Morpeth, NSW 2321 (*Principal* Canon Ann McElligott) Fax: 02–4934 5170
email: annep@bigpond.com

St Mark's National Theological Centre, 15 Blackall St, Barton, ACT 2600 (*Director* Dr Stephen Pickard) Fax: 02–6273 4067
email: cdundon@csu.edu.au

Trinity College Theological School, Royal Parade, Parkville, Vic 3052 (*Director* Revd Dr David Cole)
Fax: 03–9347 1610

Wollaston Theological College, Wollaston Rd, Mt Claremont, WA 6010 (*Principal* Revd Roger Sharr)
Fax: 08–9385 3364
email: wollasto@starwon.com.aus

CHURCH PAPERS
The Adelaide Church Guardian 16-page magazine containing Archbishop's letter and wide news coverage. *Editorial Offices* PO Box 556, Glenelg, SA 5045.

The Melbourne Anglican 12-page diocesan newspaper for Melbourne, including news from Bendigo and Wangaratta. *Director* The Anglican Centre, 209 Flinders Lane, Melbourne 3000.

Anglican Encounter 8-page newspaper of Newcastle Diocese, containing diocesan and Australian news. *Editorial Offices* PO Box 817, Newcastle 2300.

Tasmanian Anglican 8-page, small newspaper format, from Tasmania Diocese, containing wide comment. *Editorial Offices* PO Box 254, Sandy Bay, TAS 7006.

Southern Cross 16-page newspaper of Sydney Diocese, containing diocesan, national and world news, letter from the Archbishop. *Editorial Offices* PO Box Q190, Queen Victoria PO, Sydney 1230.

Anglican Messenger 16-page newspaper based in Perth, containing news from North West Australia and Bunbury. *Editorial Offices* PO Box 1182, East Victoria Park, WA 6101.

Market Place a monthly independent Anglican newspaper. *Editorial Offices* PO Box 335, Orange, NSW 2800.

The Dioceses of Ballarat, Bathurst, Brisbane, Rockhampton, Gippsland, Canberra and Goulburn, Willochra and North Queensland also produce monthly magazines/Bishop's newsletters, with mainly diocesan and parochial news.

PROVINCE OF NEW SOUTH WALES

Metropolitan Most Revd Harry (Richard Henry) Goodhew (*Archbishop of Sydney*)

ARMIDALE
Bishop Rt Revd Peter Robert Brain, Bishopscourt, PO Box 198, Armidale, NSW 2350
Fax: 02–6772 9261
email: diocarm@northnet.com.au

BATHURST
Bishop Rt Revd Bruce Winston Wilson, Bishopscourt, PO Box 23, Bathurst, NSW 2795
Fax: 02–6332 2772

CANBERRA AND GOULBURN
Bishop Rt Revd George Victor Browning, The Anglican Registry, GPO Box 1981, Canberra, ACT 2601
Fax: 02–6247 6829
email:
registrar@canberragoulbourn.anglican.org.au

Assistant Bishops
Rt Revd Richard Randerson (*same address*)
email: richard.randerson@fc.accnet.net.au

Rt Revd Godfrey Fryar, Church St, Wagga Wagga, NSW 2650

GRAFTON
Bishop Rt Revd Philip James Huggins, Bishopsholme, PO Box 4, 37 Victoria St, Grafton, NSW 2460
Fax: 02–6643 1814
email: angdiog@nor.com.au

NEWCASTLE
Bishop Rt Revd Roger Adrian Herft, Bishop's

Registry, PO Box 817, 250 Darby St, Newcastle, NSW 2300
Fax: 02–4926 1968
email: roher@bigpond.com

RIVERINA
Bishop Rt Revd Bruce Quinton Clark, PO Box 10, Narrandera, NSW 2700
Fax: 02–6929 2903
email: riverina.diocese@accnet.net.au

SYDNEY
Archbishop Most Revd Harry (Richard Henry) Goodhew (*Archbishop of Sydney, Metropolitan of the Province of NSW*), PO Box Q190, QVB Post Office, NSW 2000
Fax: 02–9265 1504
email: res@glebeaust.com.au

Assistant Bishops
Rt Revd Raymond George Smith (*Bishop of Liverpool*) (*same address*)
Fax: 02–9261 4485
email: mpj@glebeaust.com.au

Rt Revd Dr Paul William Barnett (*Bishop of North Sydney*) (*same address*)
Fax: 02–9419 6761

Rt Revd Peter R. Watson (*Bishop of South Sydney*) (*same address*)
Fax: 02–9265 1543

Rt Revd Reg Piper (*Bishop of Wollongong*), 74 Church St, Wollongong 2500
Fax: 02–4228 4296

Rt Revd Dr Brian King (*Bishop of Parramatta*), PO Box 1443, Parramatta, NSW 2124
Fax: 02–9633 3636

PROVINCE OF QUEENSLAND
Metropolitan Most Revd Peter John Hollingworth (*Archbishop of Brisbane*)

BRISBANE
Archbishop Most Revd Peter John Hollingworth (*Archbishop of Brisbane, Metropolitan of Queensland*), Bishopsbourne, Box 421, GPO, Brisbane 4001, Queensland
Fax: 07–3832 5030
email: archbishops.office@docnet.org.au

Assistant Bishops
Rt Revd Ronald John Chantler Williams (*same address*)
email: bishopsoffice@docnet.org.au

Rt Revd John Ashley Noble (*same address*)
email: janoble@gil.com.au

Rt Revd Richard Franklin Appleby (*same address*)
email: rappleby@anglicanbrisbane.org.au

Rt Revd Raymond Bruce Smith, Box 2600, Toowoomba, Queensland 4350
Fax: 07–4632 6882
email: toowoomba.office@docnet.org.au

NORTH QUEENSLAND
Bishop Rt Revd Clyde Wood, Diocesan Registry, Box 1244, Townsville, Queensland 4810
Fax: 07–4721 1756
email: clyde.wood@accnet.net.au

Assistant Bishops
Rt Revd Ted Mosby (*Bishop in the Torres Strait Islands*) (*same address*)

Rt Revd Ian Campbell Stuart, PO Box 235, Char-
ers Towers, Queensland 4820   *Fax*: 07–4787 3049
email: assg@httech.com.au

Rt Revd Arthur Malcolm, 6 Loridin Drive,
Brinsmead Glen, Cairns, Queensland 4870
Fax: 089–480 585

THE NORTHERN TERRITORY
Bishop Rt Revd Philip Leslie Freier, PO Box 2950,
Darwin, NT 0801   *Fax*: 08–8941 7446
email: dio.nt@octa4.net.au

ROCKHAMPTON
Bishop Rt Revd Ronald Francis Stone, PO Box
6158, Central Queensland Mail Centre,
Rockhampton, Queensland 4702
Fax: 07–4922 4562
email: bishop@anglicanrock.org.au

PROVINCE OF SOUTH AUSTRALIA
Metropolitan Most Revd Ian Gordon Combe
George (*Archbishop of Adelaide*)

ADELAIDE
Archbishop Most Revd Ian Gordon Combe
George (*Archbishop of Adelaide, Metropolitan of the
Province of South Australia*), 26 King William Rd,
N Adelaide, S Australia 5006   *Fax*: 08–8305 9399
email: anglade@comtech.net.au

Assistant Bishop Rt Revd Phillip John Aspinall
(*same address*)

THE MURRAY
Bishop Rt Revd Graham Howard Walden, PO
Box 394, Murray Bridge, S Australia 5253
Fax: 08 8532 5760

WILLOCHRA
Bishop Rt Revd William David Hair McCall,
Bishop's House, PO Box 96, Gladstone,
S Australia 5473   *Fax*: 08–8662 2027
email: David.McCall@fc.accnet.net.au

PROVINCE OF VICTORIA
Metropolitan Vacancy

BALLARAT
Bishop Rt Revd David Silk, PO Box 89, Ballarat,
Victoria 3350   *Fax*: 03–5333 2982
email: angdio@cbl.com.au

BENDIGO
Bishop Rt Revd Raymond David Bowden, PO
Box 2, Bendigo, Victoria 3550   *Fax*: 03–5441 2173
email: bgodioc@ruralnet.net.au

GIPPSLAND
Bishop Rt Revd Arthur Jones, PO Box 28, Sale,
Victoria 3850   *Fax*: 03–5144 7183
email: registrargipps@biso.aone.net.au

MELBOURNE
Archbishop Vacancy (*Archbishop of Melbourne,
Metropolitan of the Province of Victoria and
Primate*), The Anglican Centre, 209 Flinders
Lane, Melbourne, Victoria 3000
Fax: 03–9650 2184
email: leigh.mackay@accnet.net.au

Assistant Bishops
Rt Revd Andrew St John (*Bishop in Geelong*), The
Bishop's House, 364 Shannon Ave, Newtown,
Victoria 3220   *Fax*: 03–5222 2378
email: astjohn@pipeline.com.au

Rt Revd John Warwick Wilson (*same address*)

Rt Revd Andrew William Curnow (*same address*)
email: bishop@nthregion.org.au

Rt Revd John Craig Stewart (*same address*)
email: jcstew@ozemail.com.au

WANGARATTA
Bishop Rt Revd David Farrer, PO Box 457,
Wangaratta 3676   *Fax*: 03–5722 1427
email: dwang@w140.aone.net.au

PROVINCE OF WESTERN AUSTRALIA
Metropolitan Most Revd Peter Frederick Carnley
(*Archbishop of Perth*)

BUNBURY
Bishop Vacancy, Bishopscourt, PO Box 15,
Bunbury 6231, W Australia   *Fax*: 08–9791 2300
email: bishop@diocese.altu.net.au

NORTH-WEST AUSTRALIA
Bishop Rt Revd Anthony Howard Nicholls, PO
Box 171, Geraldton, W Australia 6530
Fax: 08–9964 2200
email: dnwa@wn.com.au

(*Regional Bishop for the Kimberley*), PO Box 158,
Broome, W Australia 6725   *Fax*: 091–93 5482

PERTH
Archbishop Most Revd Peter Frederick Carnley
(*Archbishop of Perth and Metropolitan of the
Province of Western Australia*), GPO Box W2067,
Perth, W Australia 6001   *Fax*: 08–9325 6741

Assistant Bishops
Rt Revd Gerald Edward Beaumont (Goldfields
Region), PO Box 439, Kalgoorlie, W Australia
6430   *Fax*: 08–9091 2757
email: gebart@ludin.com.au

Rt Revd David Owen Murray, Anglican Church
Office, 26 Queens St, Freemantle, W Australia
6160   *Fax*: 08–9336 3374
email: srbishop@iinet.net.au

Rt Revd Brian George Farran, PO Box 42, Joonda-
lup, W Australia 6919   *Fax*: 08–9300 0893
email: plusbrian@bigpond.com

EXTRA-PROVINCIAL DIOCESE
TASMANIA
Bishop Vacancy, GPO 748H, Hobart, Tasmania
7001   *Fax*: 03–6223 8968
email: diocese.tas@anglicare-tas.org.au

ANGLICAN AND PORVOO COMMUNIONS

The Episcopal Anglican Church of Brazil

(Igreja Episcopal Anglicana Do Brasil)

Members 103,021

Expatriate Anglican chaplaincies were established in Brazil in 1810, with missionary work beginning in 1889, after the separation of Church and State. The province, which is one of the few Portuguese-speaking churches in the Communion, became autonomous in 1965. In 1990 Brazil's economic and social problems prompted the Partners in Mission Consultation to focus on three priorities: education, service, and expansion. The Church has a valued ministry with the street children and poor throughout the vast country, especially in urban centres.

Primate Most Revd Glauco Soares de Lima (*Bishop of São Paulo*)

Provincial Secretary Canon Mauricio de Andrade, Caixa Postal 11510, Cep 90841–970, Porto Alegre, RS, Brazil   *Fax*: 55–051–318 6200
     email: m_andrade@ieab.org.br

Provincial Treasurer Mr Ricardo Hallbarg Luiz (*same address*)

CHURCH PAPER

A monthly church journal in Portuguese, *Estandarte Cristão*, published since 1893, which contains general articles and news about the life of the Church at local, national and international level. This journal is the main channel of the Communication Department of the Church. *Editor/ Editorial Offices*: Claudio Simões de Oliveira, Caixa Postal 11510, Cep 90841–970, Porto Alegre, RS, Brazil
     email: comunicacao@ieab.org.br

BRASILIA

Bishop Rt Revd Almir dos Santos, Caixa Postal 00515, Cep 70359–970 Brasilia, DF, Brazil
     Fax: 55–061–443 807
     email: familia.santos@nutecnet.com.b

PELOTAS

Bishop Rt Revd Luiz Osório Pires Prado, Caixa Postal 791, Cep 96001–970, Pelotas, RS, Brazil
     Fax: 55–0532–22 134.
     email: dprado@conesul.com.b

RECIFE

Bishop Rt Revd Edward Robinson de Barros Calvalcanti, Caixa Postal 04704, Cep 51012–970 Recife, PE, Brazil   *Fax*: 55–081–325 208*

RIO DE JANEIRO

Bishop Rt Revd Sydney Alcoba Ruiz, Av Rio Branco 277/907-Centro, CEP 20047–900, Rio de Janeiro, RJ, Brazil   *Fax*: 55–021–220 270£

SÃO PAULO

Archbishop Most Revd Glauco Soares de Lima (*Primate of the Episcopal Church of Brazil*), Rua Com Elias Zarzur, 1239, CEP 04736–002 São Paulo, SP, Brazil   *Fax*: 55–011–246 0383
     email: dasp@dialdata.com.br

SOUTH WESTERN BRAZIL

Bishop Rt Revd Jubal Pereira Neves, Caixa Postal 98, CEP 97001–970, Santa Maria, RS, Brazil
     Fax: 55–055–223 1196
     email: jneves@sm.conex.com.br

SOUTHERN BRAZIL

Bishop Rt Revd Orlando Santos de Oliveira, Caixa Postal 11504, Cep 90870–970, Porto Alegre, RS, Brazil   *Fax*: 55–051–318 6199
     email: oso@hotnet.net

The Church of the Province of Burundi

Members 425,000

There are approximately 400,000 Anglicans out of a population of just over 6 million in Burundi. The Catholic White Fathers came to Burundi at the time of early exploration but met a hostile reaction. In the closing years of the last century, the Roman Catholic Church was established and is still the largest Christian church, with 62 per cent of the population baptized. A Protestant Alliance was formed in 1935 comprising Baptists, Free Methodists, and others, and there has been a healthy conversion rate, especially in the 1940s and 1950s, building on early medical and mission

school work. However, momentum in this growth has ceased and African church and youth leaders and evangelists are now looking for further training to help them build on this work.

Primate Most Revd Ndayisenga (*Archbishop of Burundi*)

Provincial Secretary Revd Pascal Bigirimana, BP 2098, Bujumbura, Burundi

THEOLOGICAL COLLEGES

Canon Warner Memorial College, Eglise Episcopale du Burundi, EEB Buye, BP 94 Ngozi, Burundi

Kosiya Shalita Interdiocesan Theological College and Bible School, EEB Matana, DS 12, Bujumbura, Burundi

BUJUMBURA
Bishop Rt Revd Pie Ntukamazina, BP 1300, Bujumbura, Burundi   *Fax*: 257 229 275

BUYE
Bishop Most Revd Samuel Ndayisenga *Archbishop of Burundi and Bishop of Buye)*, EEB Buye, BP 94, Ngozi, Burundi
                         Fax: 257 030 2317

GITEGA
Bishop Rt Revd Jean Nduwayo, BP 23, Gitega, Burundi

MAKAMBA
Bishop Rt Revd Martin Blaise Nyaboho, BP 96, Makamba, Burundi   *Fax*: 257 229 129

MATANA
Bishop Rt Revd Bernard Ntahoturi, BP 447, Bujumbura, Burundi   *Fax*: 257 22 9129

The Anglican Church of Canada

Members 740,262
The Anglican witness in Canada started in the eighteenth century with the Church Missionary Society and the United Society for the Propagation of the Gospel. The Eucharist was first celebrated in Frobisher Bay in 1578; the first church building was St Paul's, Halifax in 1750. The Church includes a large number of the original inhabitants of Canada – Indians, Inuit, and Meti and has been a strong advocate of their rights. A book of alternative services was published in 1985. The Church has a strong international role in crisis assistance through its Primate's Fund.

Primate of The Anglican Church of Canada Most Revd Michael G. Peers, 600 Jarvis St, Toronto, Ontario, M4Y 2J6   *Fax*: 416 924 0211
          email: primate@national.anglican.ca
          Web: http://www.anglican.ca

Offices of the General Synod and of its Departments Anglican Church of Canada, 600 Jarvis Street, Toronto, ON M4Y 2J6   *Fax*: 416 968 7983

UNIVERSITIES AND COLLEGES OF THE ANGLICAN CHURCH OF CANADA
British Columbia
Vancouver School of Theology*, 6000 Iona Dr, Vancouver, BC V6T 1L4 (*Principal* Revd Dr William J. Phillips)

Manitoba
Henry Budd College for Ministry, Box 2518, The Pas MB R9A IM3 (*President* Canon Fletcher Stewart)
St John's College, 92 Dysart Rd, Winnipeg MB R3T 2M5 (*Warden* Dr Janet Hoskins)

Newfoundland
Queen's College, 210 Prince Philip Dr (Q3000), St John's NF A1B 3R6 (*Principal* Revd Dr Boyd Morgan)

Northwest Territories
Arthur Turner Training School, Box 378, Pangnirtung, Nunavut X0A 0R0

Nova Scotia Atlantic School of Theology*, 640 Francklyn St, Halifax, NS B3H 3B5 (*President* Revd Dr Gordon MacDermid)

Ontario
Canterbury College, 172 Patricia Rd, Windsor ON N9B 3B9 (*Principal* Revd Dr David T. A. Symons)
Huron College, 1349 Western Rd, London, ON N6G 1H3 (*Principal* Dr David G. Bevan)
Renison College, Westmount Rd, N, Waterloo, ON N2L 3G4 (*Principal* Dr Gail Brandt)
Thorneloe College, Ramsey Lake Rd, Sudbury, ON P3E 2C6 (*Provost* Dr Donald Thompson)
Trinity College, 6 Hoskin Ave, Toronto, ON M5S 1H8 (*Dean of Divinity* Dr Donald Wiebe)
Wycliffe College, 5 Hoskin Ave, Toronto, ON M5S 1H7 (*Principal* Revd Dr George Sumner)

Quebec
Bishop's University, PO Box 5000, Lennoxville, QC J1M 1Z7
Montreal Diocesan Theological College, 3473 University St, Montreal, QC H3A 2A8 (*Principal* Revd Dr John Simons)

Saskatchewan
College of Emmanuel and St Chad, 1337 College Dr, Saskatoon, SK S7N OW6 (*Principal* Canon William Christensen)

*Ecumenical

CHURCH PAPERS
Anglican Journal/Journal anglican Tabloid format, national church paper under management of a Board of Trustees appointed by General Synod. It circulates as an insert for a number of diocesan publications. Issued monthly except July and August. *Editorial Offices*: 600 Jarvis St, Toronto, ON M4Y 2J6.
Ministry Matters Published three times a year by the Information Resources Dept of General Synod. Intended primarily for clergy and lay leaders. *Editorial Offices*: 600 Jarvis St, Toronto, ON M4Y 2J6

The dioceses of the Anglican Church of Canada are grouped in four ecclesiastical provinces, each with a metropolitan archbishop. Each province and diocese has its own synod.

The first General Synod of the Anglican Church of Canada was held in 1893. General Synod now meets every three years, comprising the archbishops, the bishops and elected clergy and lay representatives of all the dioceses.

Work of General Synod between sessions is carried out under the authority of the Council of General Synod, which meets semi-annually. National headquarters are at 600 Jarvis Street, Toronto, Ontario M4Y 2J6. Here the work of administration, planning and programming is carried out, and it is also the headquarters of the Primate.

PROVINCE OF BRITISH COLUMBIA AND YUKON

Metropolitan Most Revd David P. Crawley (*Archbishop of Kootenay*)

BRITISH COLUMBIA
Bishop Rt Revd R. Barry R. Jenks, 900 Vancouver St, Victoria, BC V8V 3V7 *Fax*: 250 386 4013
email: bishop@acts.bc.ca

CALEDONIA
Bishop Rt Revd John E. Hannen, PO Box 278, Prince Rupert, BC V8J 3P6 *Fax*: 250 624 4299
email: synodofc@citytel.net

CARIBOO
Bishop Rt Revd James D. Cruikshank, Suite #5, 618 Tranquille Rd, Kamloops, BC V2B 3H6
Fax: 250 376 1984
email: cariboo@sage.ark.com

KOOTENAY
Archbishop Most Revd David P. Crawley (*Archbishop of Kootenay and Metropolitan of the Ecclesiastical Province of British Columbia and Yukon*), 1876 Richter St, Kelowna, BC V1Y 2M9
Fax: 250 762 4150
email: diocese_of_kootenay@bc.sympatico.ca

NEW WESTMINSTER
Bishop Rt Revd Michael C. Ingham, Suite 580, 401 West Georgia St, Vancouver BC V6B 5A1
Fax: 604 684 7017
email: michael_ingham@ecunet.org

YUKON
Bishop Rt Revd Terrence O. Buckle, PO Box 4247, Whitehorse, Yukon Y1A 3T3 *Fax*: 867 667 6125
email: dioyuk@yukon.net

PROVINCE OF CANADA
Metropolitan Most Revd Arthur Peters (*Archbishop of Nova Scotia*)

CENTRAL NEWFOUNDLAND
Bishop Rt Revd Edward F. Marsh, 34 Fraser Rd, Gander, NF A1V 2E8 *Fax*: 709 256 2396
email: bishop_marsh@ecunet.org

EASTERN NEWFOUNDLAND AND LABRADOR
Bishop Rt Revd Donald F. Harvey, 19 King's Bridge Rd, St John's, NF A1C 3K4
Fax: 709 576 712
email: dharvey@anglicanenl.nf.ne

FREDERICTON
Bishop Rt Revd William J. Hockin, 115 Church St, Fredericton, NB E3B 4C8 *Fax*: 506 460 052(
email: diocfton@nbnet.ab.c

MONTREAL
Bishop Rt Revd Andrew Sandford Hutchison 1444 Union Ave, Montreal, QC H3A 2B8
Fax: 514 843 322
email: bishops.office@montreal.anglican.org

Assistant Bishop Rt Revd Russell Hatton (*same address*)

NOVA SCOTIA
Bishop Most Revd Arthur G. Peters (*Archbishop o Nova Scotia and Metropolitan of the Ecclesiastica Province of Canada*), 5732 College St, Halifax, NS B3H 1X3 *Fax*: 902 425 0717
email: diocese@fox.nstn.ca

Suffragan Bishop Rt Revd Frederick J. Hiltz (*same address*)

QUEBEC
Bishop Rt Revd A. Bruce Stavert, 31 rue des Jardins, Quebec, PQ G1R 4L6 *Fax*: 418 692 3876
email: diocese_of_quebec@sympatico.ca

WESTERN NEWFOUNDLAND
Bishop Rt Revd Leonard Whitten, 25 Main St, Corner Brook, NF A2H 1C2 *Fax*: 709 634 1636
email: dsown@nf.sympatico.ca

PROVINCE OF ONTARIO
Metropolitan Most Revd Percy R. O'Driscoll (*Archbishop of Huron*)

ALGOMA
Bishop Rt Revd Ronald C. Ferris, Box 1168, Sault Ste Marie, ON P6A 5N7 *Fax*: 705 946 1860
email: dioceseofalgoma@on.aibn.com

HURON
Archbishop Most Revd Percy R. O'Driscoll (*Archbishop of Huron and Metropolitan of the Ecclesiastical Province of Ontario*), One London Place #903-255 Queens Ave, London, ON N6A 5R8 *Fax*: 519 673 4151
email: bishops@wwdc.com

Bishop Suffragan Rt Revd C. Robert Townshend (*same address*)

MOOSONEE

Bishop Rt Revd Caleb J. Lawrence, Box 841, Schumacher, ON P0N 1G0   *Fax*: 705 360 1120
email: moosonee@ntl.sympatico.ca

NIAGARA

Bishop Rt Revd David Ralph Spence, Cathedral Place, 252 James St North, Hamilton, ON L8R 2L3   *Fax*: 905 527 1281
email: c/o adatri@niagara.anglican.ca

ONTARIO

Bishop Rt Revd Peter Ralph Mason, 90 Johnson St, Kingston, ON K7L 1X7   *Fax*: 613 547 3745

OTTAWA

Bishop Rt Revd Peter Coffin, 71 Bronson Ave, Ottawa ON K1R 6G6   *Fax*: 613 232 7088
email: c/o ann-day@ottawa.anglican.ca

TORONTO

Bishop Rt Revd Terence E. Finlay, 135 Adelaide St East, Toronto, ON M5C 1L8   *Fax*: 416 363 3683
email: diocese@toronto.anglican.ca

Bishops Suffragan
Rt Revd Douglas Charles Blackwell, 63 Glen Dhu Drive, Whitby, Ontario L1R 1K3
Fax: 905 668 8216
email: bishopb@yesic.com

Rt Revd James Taylor Pryce, 15224 Yonge St, Suite 1, Aurora, Ontario L4G 1L9
Fax: 905 727 4937
email: ysimcoe@neptune.on.ca

Rt Revd Michael Hugh Harold Bedford-Jones, St Paul's, L'Amoreaux, 3333 Finch Ave East, Scarborough, Ontario M1W 2R9   *Fax*: 416 497 4103
email: mbj@total.net

Rt Revd Ann Elizabeth Tottenham, 256 Sheldon Ave, Etobicoke, Ontario M8W 4X8
Fax: 416 503 8229
email: cvalley@tap.net

PROVINCE OF RUPERT'S LAND
Metropolitan Vacancy

THE ARCTIC

Bishop Rt Revd Christopher Williams, Box 1454, 4910 51st St, Yellowknife, NWT X1A 2P1
Fax: 867 873 8478
email: diocese@internorth.com

Suffragan Bishops
Rt Revd Paul Idlout, Box 2219, Iqaluit, NWT X0A 0H0   *Fax*: 867 979 7814
email: pidlout@nunanet.com

Rt Revd Larry Robertson, Box 1040, Inuvik, NT X0E 0T0   *Fax*: 867 777 4960
email: larryr@permafrost.com

Rt Revd Andrew Atagotaaluk, Box 119, Salluit QC, J0M 1S0   *Fax*: 819 255 8880

ATHABASCA

Bishop Rt Revd John R. Clarke, Box 6868, Peace River, AB T8S 1S6   *Fax*: 780 624 2365
email: dioath@telusplanet.net

BRANDON

Bishop Rt Revd Malcolm A. W. Harding, Box 21009 W.E. PO, Brandon, MB R7B 3W8
Fax: 204 727 4135
email: diobrandon@techplus.com

CALGARY

Bishop Rt Revd Barry Hollowell, Suite #560, 1207 11th Ave SW, Calgary, AB T3C 0M5
Fax: 403 243 2182
email: synod@calgary.anglican.ca

Assistant Bishop Rt Revd Gary F. Woolsey, St Peter's Anglican Church, 903–75th Avenue SW, Calgary, AB T2V 0S7   *Fax*: 403 255 0752

EDMONTON

Bishop Rt Revd Victoria Matthews, 10033–84 Ave, Edmonton, AB T6E 2G6
Fax: 780 439 6549
email: synod@freenet.edmonton.ab.ca

KEEWATIN

Bishop Rt Revd Gordon W. Beardy, 915 Ottawa St, Keewatin, ON P0X 1C0   *Fax*: 807 547 3356
email: keewatin@kenora.com

QU'APPELLE

Bishop Rt Revd Duncan Douglas Wallace, 1501 College Ave, Regina, SK S4P 1B8
Fax: 306 352 6808
email: quappelle@sk.sympatico.ca

RUPERT'S LAND

Bishop Vacancy, 935 Nesbitt Bay, Winnipeg, MB R3T 1W6   *Fax*: 204 452 3915
email: diocese@escape.ca

SASKATCHEWAN

Bishop Rt Revd Anthony J. Burton, 1308 5th Ave East, Prince Albert, SK S6V 2H7
Fax: 306 764 5172
email: diosask@hotmail.com

Bishop Suffragan Rt Revd Charles J. Arthurson, Box 96, Lac La Ronge, SK S0J 1L0

SASKATOON

Bishop Rt Revd Thomas Oliver Morgan, PO Box 1965, Saskatoon, SK S7K 3S5   *Fax*: 306 933 4606
email: diocese.stoon@sk.sympatico.ca

The Church of the Province of Central Africa

Members 600,000

The province includes Botswana, Malawi, Zambia and Zimbabwe. The first Anglican missionary to Malawi was Bishop Charles Mackenzie who arrived with David Livingstone in 1861. The province was inaugurated in 1955 and has a movable bishopric. The countries forming the province are very different. Zambia and Botswana suffer the difficulties of rapid industrialization, along with undeveloped, thinly populated areas. In Malawi 30 per cent of the adult males are away as migrant labourers in other countries at any given time. Zimbabwe is experiencing problems of social adjustment after independence.

Archbishop of the Province Most Revd Walter P. K. Makhulu (*Bishop of Botswana*)

Acting Provincial Secretary Revd Richard J. Chance, PO Box 769, Gaborone, Botswana
Fax: 352075

Provincial Treasurer Mr Simon Thomas, Accounting Services Pty Ltd, PO Box 1229, Gaborone, Botswana

ANGLICAN THEOLOGICAL COLLEGES
National Anglican Theological College of Zimbabwe (Ecumenical Institute of Theology), 11 Thornburg Ave, Groombridge, Mount Pleasant, Harare, Zimbabwe

Zomba Theological College, PO Box 130, Zomba, Malawi (jointly with the Presbyterian Church of Central Africa)

St John's Seminary, Mindolo, PO Box 21493, Kitwe, Zambia

CHURCH PAPERS
Link Monthly newspaper for the Dioceses of Mashonaland and Matabeleland giving news and views of the dioceses. *Editorial Offices* Link Board of Management, PO Box UA7, Harare City.

A Mpingo (previously *Ecclesia*) Monthly duplicated magazine for the Dioceses of Southern Malawi and Lake Malawi giving news and views of the dioceses. *Editor* Revd Bernard Njakare, c/o Chilema Lay Training Centre, PO Chilema, Malawi.

Epifania Triennial magazine for the province published by the Archbishop's Office. *Editor* Provincial Secretary.

BOTSWANA
Bishop Most Revd Walter Oaul Khotso Makhulu (*Bishop of Botswana and Archbishop of the Province*

of Central Africa), PO Box 769, Gaborone Botswana *Fax*: 267 313 01!
email: angli_diocese@info.bv

CENTRAL ZAMBIA
Bishop Rt Revd Clement Williard Hlanya Shaba PO Box 70172, Ndola, Zambia *Fax*: 260 2 615 95

CENTRAL ZIMBABWE
Bishop Rt Revd Ishmael Mukuwanda, PO Box 25 Gweru, Zimbabwe *Fax*: 263 54 21 09?

EASTERN ZAMBIA
Bishop Rt Revd John Osmers, PO Box 510154 Chipata, Zambia *Fax*: 260 62 21 29
email: josmers@zamnet.zm.zm

HARARE
Bishop Rt Revd Jonathan Siyachitema Bishopsmount Close, PO Box UA7, Harare, Zimbabwe *Fax*: 263 4 700 419
email: dioceschre@mango.zw

LAKE MALAWI
Bishop Rt Revd Peter Nathaniel Nyanja, PO Box 30349, Lilongwe 3, Malawi *Fax*: 265 731 966

LUSAKA
Bishop Rt Revd Leonard Jameson Mwenda, Bishop's Lodge, PO Box 30183, Lusaka, Zambia *Fax*: 260 1 262 379

MANICALAND
Bishop Rt Revd Dr Sebastian Bakare, 115 Herbert Chitepo St, Mutare, Zimbabwe *Fax*: 263 20 63 076
email: diomani@syscom.co.zw

MATABELELAND
Bishop Rt Revd Theophilus Tswere Naledi, PO Box 2422, Bulawayo, Zimbabwe *Fax*: 263 9 68353

NORTH MALAWI
Bishop Rt Revd Jackson Cunningham Biggers, Box 120, Mzuzu, Malawi
email: biggers@malawi.net

NORTHERN ZAMBIA
Bishop Rt Revd Bernard Amos Malango, PO Box 20173, Kitwe, Zambia *Fax*: 260 2 224 778
email: malango@zamnet.zm

SOUTHERN MALAWI
Bishop Rt Revd James Tengatenga, P/Bag 1, Chilema, Zomba, Malawi *Fax*: 265 531 243
email: jtengatenga@unima.wn.apc.org

The Anglican Church of the Central American Region

(Iglesia Anglicana de la Region Central de America)

Members 13,409

The newest province of the Anglican Communion is made up of the Dioceses of Guatemala, El Salvador, Nicaragua, Costa Rica and Panama. With the exception of Costa Rica, all were part of the Episcopal Church of the United States of America. The Church was introduced by the Society for the Propagation of the Gospel when England administered two colonies in Central America, Belize (1783–1982) and Miskitia (1740–1894). In the later years Afro-Antillean people brought their Anglican Christianity with them. The province is multicultural and multiracial and is committed to evangelization, social outreach, and community development.

COSTA RICA

Bishop Rt Revd Cornelius Joshua Wilson, Apartado 2773, 1000 San José, Costa Rica
Fax: 253 8331
email: amiecr@sol.racsa.co.cr.cr

EL SALVADOR

Bishop Rt Revd Martin de Jesus Barhona Pascacio, 47 Avenida Sur, 723 Col. Flor Blanca, Apartado Postal (01), 274 San Salvador, El Salvador
Fax: 223 7952
email: martinba@gbm.net

GUATEMALA

Bishop Rt Revd Armando Guerra-Soria, Apartado 58A, Guatemala City, Guatemala
Fax: 472 0764
email: diocesis@infovia.com.gt

NICARAGUA

Bishop Rt Revd Sturdie Downs, Apartado 1207, Managua, Nicaragua
Fax: 02 226 701

PANAMA

Bishop Rt Revd Clarence W. Hayes-Dewar, Box R, Balboa, Republic of Panama
Fax: 262 2097
email: furriola@sinfo.net

The Church of the Province of the Congo

Members 300,000

Ugandan evangelist Apolo Kivebulaya established an Anglican presence in Zaire in 1896. The Church reached the Shaba region in 1955, but evangelization did not progress on a large scale until the 1970s. Following independence, the Church expanded and formed dioceses as part of the Province of Uganda, Burundi, Rwanda, and Boga-Zaire. The new province was inaugurated in 1992 and changed its name in 1997.

Archbishop of the Province Most Revd Patrice Byankya Njojo, PO BOX 25586, Kampala, Uganda
email: comnet@infocom.co.ug

Provincial Secretary Revd Molanga Botola (*same address*)

Provincial Treasurer Mr Philip Bingham (*same address*)

THEOLOGICAL COLLEGE
The Anglican Theological Seminary, PO Box 25586, Kampala, Uganda

BOGA

Bishop Most Revd Patrice Byankya Njojo (*Archbishop of Congo and Bishop of Boga*), PO BOX 25586, Kampala, Uganda
email: comnet@infocom.co.ug

BUKAVU

Bishop Rt Revd Fidèle Balufuga Dirokpa, PO Box 134, Cyangugu, Rwanda

KATANGA

Bishop Rt Revd Henri Isingoma Kahwa, EAC-Lubumbashi, c/o United Methodist Church, PO Box 22037, Kitwe, Zambia
Fax: 254 154 40 557

KINDU

Bishop Rt Revd Zacharie Masimango Katanda, c/o Mr Philip Betts, ESCO Uganda, PO Box 7892, Kampala, Uganda
email: angkindu@antenna.nl

KISANGANI

Bishop Rt Revd Sylvestre Tibafa Mugera, CAC-Kisangani, PO Box 25586, Kampala, Uganda

Assistant Bishop Rt Revd Antoine Mavatikwa Kany, c/o CAC-Kinshasa, BP 16482, Kinshasa 1, Dem Rep Congo
Fax: 243 884 008

NORD KIVU

Bishop Rt Revd Methusela Musubaho Munzenda, CAZ-Butembo-Congo, PO Box 506, Bwera-Kasese, Uganda
Fax: 871 166 1121

The Church of England

Baptized Members 26,000,000

Covering all of England, the Isle of Man and the Channel Islands; Europe except Great Britain and Ireland; Morocco; Turkey; and the Asian countries of the former Soviet Union. The Church of England is the ancient national Church of the land. Its structures emerged from the missionary work of St Augustine, sent from Rome in AD 597, and from the work of Celtic missionaries in th north. Throughout the Middle Ages, the Churc was in communion with the See of Rome, but i the sixteenth century it separated from Rome an rejected the authority of the Pope. The Churc of England is the established Church, with it administration governed by a General Syno which meets twice a year.

Hong Kong Sheng Kung Hui

Members 29,000

This dynamic province was inaugurated in 1998. The history of the Church dates back to the mid-nineteenth century; missionaries were provided by the American Church, the Church of England, the Church of England in Canada, the Church of Ireland, the Churches of Australia and New Zealand. Western missionaries withdrew in 1950. All churches were closed in 1966 and did not begin to re-open until 1979. Most denominations then joined the China Christian Council.

The suppression of the pro-democracy movement in 1989 resulted in stricter regulations for religious groups. Today's members of the Chung Hua Sheng Kung Hui (the Holy Catholic Church in China) are found in the post-denominational church, the Three-Self Movement, except for Hong Kong which returned to Chinese sovereignty in 1997, and in Macao, which was to be returned to China by Portugal in 1999.

Primate and Bishop of Hong Kong Island Most Revd Peter Kwong Kong-kit, Bishop's House, 1 Lowe Albert Rd, Hong Kong   Fax: 2521 219
email: dkhi@hkskh.or

Provincial General Secretary Revd Andrew Cha
(*same address*)   *email:* office1@hkskh.or
Web: http://www.hkskh.or

Bishop of Eastern Kowloon Rt Revd Louis Tsui
Eastern Kowloon Diocesan Office, 139 Ma Tau
Chung Rd, Kowloon City, Hong Kong
Fax: 2711 160
email: ekdiocese@hknet.com

Bishop of Western Kowloon Rt Revd Thomas Soo,
Western Kowloon Diocesan Office, 15th Floor,
Ultragrace Commercial Building, 5 Jordon Rd,
Kowloon, Hong Kong   Fax: 2783 079
email: hkskhdwk@netvigator.com

The Church of the Province of the Indian Ocean

Members 90,486

The province, covering Madagascar, Mauritius and Seychelles, was founded in 1973, combining two bishoprics. The Anglican mission began in Mauritius in 1810, after the capture of the other islands from the French. Missionaries were sent to the other islands.

Archbishop of the Province Most Revd Remi Joseph Rabenirina (*Bishop of Antananarivo*)

Provincial Secretary Revd Bery Rakotoarimanana, c/o Évêché Anglican, Ambohimanoro, 101 Antananarivo, Madagascar

Chancellor/Registrar of the Province Maître Bernard Georges, PO Box 44, Victoria, Mahé, Seychelles
Fax: 248 224296

Dean of the Province Rt Revd Keith Benzies (*Bishop of Antsiranana*)

ANGLICAN THEOLOGICAL COLLEGES
St Paul's College, Ambatohararana, Merimand-roso, Ambohidratrimo, Madagascar (*Warden* Revd Vincent Rakotoarisoa)

St Paul's College, Rose Hill, Mauritius (*Warden* Vacancy)

St Philip's Theological College, La Misère, Seychelles (*Diocesan Trainer* Mr Neville Marston)

CHURCH MAGAZINES
Newsletters of Province of the Indian Ocean Support Assn. *Editor* Mrs M. Woodward, Vicarage, Old Town, Brackley, Northants NN13 7BZ

Seychelles Diocesan Magazine A quarterly newspaper covering diocesan events and containing articles of theological and other interest.

Magazine du Diocese de Maurice A quarterly newspaper covering diocesan events and containing articles of theological and ecumenical interest.

ANTANANARIVO
Bishop Most Revd Remi Rabenirina, Évêché Anglican, Lot VK57 ter, Ambohimanoro, 101 Antananarivo, Madagascar   *Fax*: 261 20 226 1331
email: eemdanta@dts.mg

ANTSIRANANA
Bishop Rt Revd Keith John Benzies, Évêché Anglican, BP 278, 201 Antsiranana, Madagascar

MAHAJANGA
Bishop Rt Revd Jean-Claude Andrianjafimanana, BP 169, Mahajanga 401, Madagascar
email: eemdmaha@dts.mg

MAURITIUS
Bishop Rt Revd Luc Rex Victor Donat, Bishop's House, Phoenix, Mauritius   *Fax*: 230 697 1096
email: diocese_mauritius@ecunet.org

SEYCHELLES
Bishop Rt Revd French Kitchener Chang-Him, PO Box 44, Victoria, Mahé, Seychelles
Fax: 248 224 296

TOAMASINA
Bishop Vacancy, Évêché Anglican, BP 531, Toamasina 501, Madagascar

The Church of Ireland

Members 410,000

Tracing its origins to St Patrick and his companions in the fifth century, the Irish Church has been marked by strong missionary efforts. In 1537 the English king was declared head of the Church, but most Irish Christians maintained loyalty to Rome. The Irish Church Act of 1869 provided that the statutory union between the Churches of England and Ireland be dissolved and that the Church of Ireland should cease to be established by law. A General Synod of the Church, established in 1890 and consisting of archbishops, bishops, and representatives of the clergy and laity, has legislative and administrative power. Irish church leaders have played a key role in the work of reconciliation in the Northern Ireland conflict.

The Primate of All Ireland and Metropolitan Most Revd Robert Henry Alexander Eames (*Archbishop of Armagh*)

Hon Secretaries of the General Synod
Clerical Very Revd Herbert Cassidy, The Library, Abbey St, Armagh, Co Armagh BT61 7DY
Tel: 028 3752 3142
Fax: 028 3752 4177

Canon Desmond Harman, Rectory, Sandford Close, Ranelagh, Dublin 6   *Tel*: 01–497 2983
Fax: 01–496 4789

Lay Lady Sheil, Oaxaca, Saintfield Rd, Killinchy, Newtownards, Co Down BT23 6RL
Tel: 028 9754 1802
Fax: 028 9754 2832

Mr S. R. Harper, Cramer's Grove, Kilkenny, Co Kilkenny   *Tel*: (056) 22842/160
Fax: (056) 63449

Assistant Secretary of the General Synod Ms Valerie Beatty

Chief Officer and Secretary of the Representative Church Body Mr Robert Sherwood

Central Office of the Church of Ireland Church of

Ireland House, Church Ave, Rathmines, Dublin 6
Tel: 01–4978422
Fax: 01–4978821

THEOLOGICAL COLLEGE
The Church of Ireland Theological College, Braemor Park, Rathgar, Dublin 14, which conducts courses in conjunction with the School of Hebrew, Biblical and Theological Studies, Trinity College, Dublin (*Principal* Canon John Bartlett)
Tel: 01–4923506/4923274
Fax: 01–4923082

CHURCH PAPER
Church of Ireland Gazette Weekly Deals with items of general interest to the Church of Ireland in a national context and also contains news from the various dioceses and parishes together with articles of a more general nature. *Editor/Editorial Offices* Canon Cecil Cooper, 36 Bachelor's Walk, Lisburn, Co Antrim BT28 1XN   *Tel*: 028 9267 5743
Fax: 028 9267 5743

The Irish Church Act 1869 provided that from 1 January 1871, the statutory union between the Churches of England and Ireland should be dissolved and that the Church of Ireland should cease to be established by law. To prepare the ground for the future government of the Church of Ireland, a General Convention was held in 1870 when it was declared 'that a General Synod of the Church of Ireland, consisting of the archbishops and bishops, and of representatives of the clergy and laity, shall have chief legislative power therein, and such administrative power as may be necessary for the Church, and consistent with its episcopal constitution'.

The General Synod consists of two Houses, the House of Bishops and the House of Representatives. The archbishops and bishops for the time being constitute the House of Bishops. The House of Representatives is composed of 216 clerical and 432 lay representatives, elected triennially by the various diocesan synods. Both Houses sit together in General Synod. While either House may sit separately, and the House of Bishops does so from time to time, there has never been a separate meeting of the House of Representatives. Legislation must be passed by both Houses, and in the House of Representatives a vote by orders may be demanded, in which case a majority of both clerical and lay representatives is required. To make any liturgical change a vote by orders must always be taken, and a two-thirds majority of each order is necessary.

Each diocesan synod consists of the clergymen of the diocese and of lay synodsmen elected triennially by the registered vestrymen of each parish in the proportion of two (or up to five) to each clergyman officiating therein. The diocesan synod, subject to the control of the General Synod, administers the temporalities of the diocese, and it makes provision for the appointment of a Diocesan Council to carry on the financial and other business of the diocese.

The Select Vestry of each parish consists of the officiating clergymen, two churchwardens (one nominated by the incumbent and one elected), two glebewardens (appointed in like manner) and not more than 20 other persons. It is the executive body, and it controls parochial funds.

An incumbent of a parish is nominated by a Board of Nomination, which consists of the bishop (chairman), four clergymen and one layman appointed by the diocesan synod, and four laymen elected by the parish.

The Archbishop of Armagh is elected by the House of Bishops from among its own number. Other episcopal elections are made by an electoral college, presided over by the Metropolitan, and comprising three representatives of the House of Bishops and representatives of all the dioceses in the province, the vacant diocese having 24 representatives (twelve clerical and twelve lay) and each other diocese having four representatives (two clerical and two lay).

Under the Irish Church Act, all church property was, subject to certain interests then existing, vested in the Commissioners of Church Temporalities, created by that Act, who carried out all the transactions which the Act required. As all the ecclesiastical corporations were dissolved by the Act, it was necessary to create a corporate body to take over from the Commissioners the property and monies transferred to the disestablished Church. Thus, the Representative Church Body was incorporated in 1870 as trustee of the property and funds then transferred or subsequently acquired. It consists of the archbishops and bishops, one clerical and two lay representatives of each of the dioceses or united dioceses, and twelve co-opted members. Its recent Reports show that its assets now amount to over IR£338m.

PROVINCE OF ARMAGH
ARMAGH
Archbishop Most Revd Robert Henry Alexander Eames, The See House, Cathedral Close Armagh, Co Armagh BT61 7EE
Tel: 028 3752 2851 (Home)
028 3752 7144 (Office)
Fax: 028 3752 7823
email: archbishop@armagh.anglican.org

Secretary of Diocesan Council Mrs Jane Montgomery, Church House, 46 Abbey St, Armagh, Co Armagh BT61 7DZ
Tel: 028 3752 2858
Fax: 028 3751 0596

CATHEDRAL CHURCH OF ST PATRICK, Armagh
Dean Very Revd Herbert Cassidy, The Library, Abbey Street, Armagh BT61 7DY
Tel: 028 3752 3142
Fax: 028 3752 4177
email: armroblib@aol.com

CLOGHER
Bishop Rt Revd Brian Desmond Anthony Hannon, The See House, Fivemiletown, Co Tyrone BT75 0QP
Tel: 028 8952 1265
Fax: 028 8952 2299

Secretary of Diocesan Council Very Revd Thomas Moore, The Deanery, 10 Augher Rd, Clogher, Co Tyrone BT76 0AD
Tel and *Fax*: 028 8554 8235

CATHEDRAL CHURCHES OF ST MACARTAN, Clogher, and ST MACARTIN, Enniskillen
Dean Very Revd Thomas Moore (*as above*)

CONNOR
Bishop Rt Revd James Edward Moore, Bishop's House, 113 Upper Rd, Greenisland, Carrickfergus, Co Antrim BT38 8RR
Tel: 028 9086 3165
Fax: 028 9036 4266

Secretary of Diocesan Council Mr Neil Wilson, Diocesan Office, Church of Ireland House, 61–67 Donegall St, Belfast BT1 2QH
Tel: 028 9032 2268/9032 3188
Fax: 028 9032 1635

CATHEDRAL CHURCH OF ST SAVIOUR, Lisburn
Dean Very Revd George Moller, St Bartholomew's Rectory, 16 Mount Pleasant, Stranmillis, Belfast BT9 5DS *Tel*: 028 9066 9995

CATHEDRAL CHURCH OF ST ANNE, Belfast
(Cathedral of the United Dioceses of Down and Dromore and the Diocese of Connor)
Dean Very Revd John Shearer, The Deanery, 5 Deramore Drive, Belfast BT9 5JQ
Tel: 028 9066 0980 (Home)
028 9032 8332 (Cathedral)
Fax: 028 9023 8855
email: belfast.cathedral@dial.pipex.com

DERRY AND RAPHOE
Bishop Rt Revd James Mehaffey, The See House, 112 Culmore Rd, Londonderry, Co Derry BT48 8JF   *Tel*: 028 7135 1206 (Home)
028 7126 2440 (Office)
Fax: 028 7135 2554

Secretary of Diocesan Council Mr G. Kelly, Diocesan Office, London St, Londonderry, Co Derry BT48 6RQ   *Tel*: 028 7126 2440
Fax: 028 7137 2100

CATHEDRAL CHURCH OF ST COLUMB, Derry
Dean Very Revd William Wright Morton, The Deanery, 30 Bishop St, Londonderry, Co Derry BT48 6PP   *Tel*: 028 7126 2746

CATHEDRAL CHURCH OF ST EUNAN, Raphoe
Dean Very Revd Stephen White, The Deanery, Raphoe, Lifford, Co Donegal   *Tel*: (074) 45226

DOWN AND DROMORE
Bishop Rt Revd Harold Creeth Miller, The See House, 32 Knockdene Park South, Belfast BT5 7AB   *Tel*: 028 9047 1973
Fax: 028 9065 0584
email: bishop@down.anglican.org

Secretary of Diocesan Council Mr Neil Wilson, Diocesan Office, Church of Ireland House, 61–67 Donegall St, Belfast BT1 2QH
Tel: 028 9032 2268/9032 3188
Fax: 028 9032 1635

CATHEDRAL CHURCH OF THE HOLY AND UNDIVIDED TRINITY, Down
Dean Very Revd John Dinnen, 17 Dromore Rd, Hillsborough, Co Down BT26 6HS
Tel and *Fax*: 028 9268 2366

CATHEDRAL CHURCH OF CHRIST THE REDEEMER, Dromore
Dean Very Revd David Chillingworth, Seagoe Rectory, 8 Upper Church Lane, Portadown, Craigavon, Co Armagh BT63 5JE
Tel: 028 3833 2538 (Home)
Tel and *Fax*: 028 3835 0583 (Office)
email: chillingworth@seagoe.source.co.uk

KILMORE, ELPHIN AND ARDAGH
Bishop Rt Revd Michael Hugh Gunton Mayes, The See House, Cavan   *Tel*: (049) 4331336
Fax: (049) 4362829
email: bishop@kilmore.anglican.org

Secretaries of Diocesan Councils
Revd Eileen O'Reilly, Rectory, Cootehill, Co Cavan (*Kilmore*)   *Tel*: (049) 5552004
Fax: (049) 5556321
email: dco@kilmore.anglican.org

Canon Ian Gallagher, Rectory, Drumcliffe, Co Sligo (*Elphin and Ardagh*)
Tel and *Fax*: (071) 63125
email: drumcliffe@elphin.anglican.org

CATHEDRAL CHURCH OF ST FETHLIMIDH, Kilmore
Dean Very Revd David Godfrey, The Deanery, Danesfort, Cavan   *Tel* and *Fax*: (049) 4331918
email: dean@kilmore.anglican.org

CATHEDRAL CHURCH OF ST MARY THE VIRGIN AND ST JOHN THE BAPTIST, Sligo
Dean Vacancy

TUAM, KILLALA AND ACHONRY
Bishop Rt Revd Richard Henderson, Bishop's House, Knockglass, Crossmolina, Co Mayo
Tel: (096) 31317
Fax: (096) 31775
email: bishop@tuam.anglican.org

Secretary of Diocesan Council Mrs Heather Sherlock, Stonehall House, Ballisodare, Co Sligo
Tel: (071) 67280
Fax: (071) 30264

CATHEDRAL CHURCH OF ST MARY, Tuam
Dean Vacancy, The Rectory, Deanery Place, Cong, Co Mayo   *Tel* and *Fax*: (092) 46017

CATHEDRAL CHURCH OF ST PATRICK, Killala
Dean Very Revd Edward Ardis, Rectory, Ballina, Co Mayo   *Tel*: (096) 21654

PROVINCE OF DUBLIN
CASHEL, WATERFORD, LISMORE, OSSORY, FERNS AND LEIGHLIN
Bishop Rt Revd John Robert Winder Neill (*Bishop of Cashel and Ossory*), The Palace, Kilkenny, Co Kilkenny   *Tel*: (056) 21 560
Fax: (056) 64 399
email: bishop@cashel.anglican.org

Secretaries of Diocesan Councils
Mrs Denise Hughes, Diocesan Office, St Canice's Library, Kilkenny (*Cashel, Ossory and Leighlin*)
Tel: (056) 61910 (Office)
(056) 27248 (Home)
Fax: (056) 51813

Mrs Joan Deacon, Garranvabbey, The Rower, Thomastown, Co Kilkenny (*Ferns*)
Tel: (051) 423637
Fax: (051) 423691

CATHEDRAL CHURCH OF ST JOHN THE BAPTIST AND ST PATRICK'S ROCK, Cashel
Dean Very Revd Phillip Knowles, The Deanery, Cashel, Co Tipperary   *Tel*: (062) 61232

CATHEDRAL CHURCH OF THE BLESSED TRINITY
(CHRIST CHURCH), Waterford
Dean Very Revd Peter Barrett, The Deanery,
41 Grange Park Rd, Waterford, Co Waterford
Tel and *Fax*: (051) 874119
email: dean@waterford.anglican.org

CATHEDRAL CHURCH OF ST CARTHAGE, Lismore
Dean Vacancy

CATHEDRAL CHURCH OF ST CANICE, Kilkenny
Dean Very Revd Norman Lynas, The Deanery,
Kilkenny   *Tel*: (056) 21516
                            Fax: (056) 51817

CATHEDRAL CHURCH OF ST EDAN, Ferns
Dean Very Revd Leslie Forrest, The Deanery,
Ferns, Co Wexford   *Tel*: (054) 66124

CATHEDRAL CHURCH OF ST LASERIAN, Leighlin
Dean Vacancy

CORK, CLOYNE AND ROSS
Bishop Rt Revd William Paul Colton, The Palace,
Bishop St, Cork, Co Cork   *Tel*: (021) 316114
                            Fax: (021) 273 437
                            email: bishop@cork.anglican.org

Secretary of Diocesan Council Mr Wilfred Baker, St
Nicholas House, 14 Cove St, Cork, Co Cork
                            Tel: (021) 272262
                            Fax: (021) 968467
                            email: office@cork.anglican.org

CATHEDRAL CHURCH OF ST FIN BARRE, Cork
Dean Very Revd Michael Jackson, The Deanery,
9 Dean St, Cork   *Tel* and *Fax*: (021) 964742

CATHEDRAL CHURCH OF ST COLMAN, Cloyne
Dean Very Revd George Hilliard, The Deanery,
Midleton, Co Cork   *Tel*: (021) 631449
                            Fax: (021) 964742

CATHEDRAL CHURCH OF ST FACHTNA, Ross
Dean Very Revd Christopher Peters, The
Deanery, Rosscarbery, Co Cork   *Tel*: (023) 48166

DUBLIN AND GLENDALOUGH
Archbishop Most Revd Walton Newcombe
Francis Empey (*Archbishop of Dublin, Bishop of
Glendalough, Primate of Ireland and Metropolitan*),
The See House, 17 Temple Rd, Milltown,
Dublin 6   *Tel*: 01–4977849
                            Fax: 01–4976355

Secretary of Diocesan Council Mr Keith Dungan,
Diocesan Office, Church of Ireland House,
Church Ave, Rathmines, Dublin 6
                            Tel: 01–4966981
                            Fax: 01–4972865

CATHEDRAL CHURCH OF THE HOLY TRINITY
(commonly called CHRIST CHURCH)
Cathedral of the United Dioceses of Dublin and
Glendalough, Metropolitan Cathedral of the
United Provinces of Dublin and Cashel
Dean Very Revd John Paterson, The Deanery, St
Werburgh St, Dublin 8   *Tel*: 01–4781797 (Home)
                            01–6778099 (Cathedral)
                            Fax: 01–6798991
email: dean@dublin.anglican.org/paterson@iol.ie

THE NATIONAL CATHEDRAL AND COLLEGIATE
CHURCH OF ST PARTICK, Dublin
(The 'National Cathedral of the Church of Ireland
having a common relation to all the dioceses of
Ireland')
Dean and Ordinary Very Revd Robert MacCarthy,
The Deanery, Upper Kevin St, Dublin 8
                            Tel: 01–4755449 (Home)
                            01–4754817 (Cathedral)
                            01–4539472 (Office)
                            Fax: 01–4546374

LIMERICK, ARDFERT, AGHADOE, KILLALOE, KILFENORA, CLONFERT, KILMACDUAGH AND EMLY
Bishop Rt Revd Edward Flewett Darling (*Bishop
of Limerick and Killaloe*), Bishop's House, North
Circular Rd, Limerick   *Tel*: (061) 451532
                            Fax: (061) 451100
                            Mobile: 087–2221700
                            email: bplimick@iol.ie

Secretary of Diocesan Council Canon Joseph
Condell, St Cronan's Rectory, Roscrea, Co
Tipperary   *Tel*: (0505) 21725
                            Fax: (0505) 21993
                            email: condell@iol.ie

Assistant Secretary Canon Robert Warren, St
John's Rectory, Ashe St, Tralee, Co Kerry
                            Tel: (066) 22245
                            Fax: (066) 29004
                            Mobile: 088–521133

CATHEDRAL CHURCH OF ST MARY, Limerick
Dean Very Revd Maurice Sirr, The Deanery,
7 Kilbane, Castletroy, Limerick *Tel*: (061) 338697
                            Fax: (061) 332158
                            Mobile: 088–541121/086–2541121

CATHEDRAL CHURCH OF ST FLANNAN, Killaloe
Dean Very Revd Nicholas Cummins, The
Deanery, Killaloe, Co Clare
                            Tel and *Fax*: (061) 376687

CATHEDRAL CHURCH OF ST BRENDAN, Clonfert
Dean Very Revd Nicholas Cummins (*as above*)

MEATH AND KILDARE

Bishop Most Revd Richard Lionel Clarke, Bishop's House, Moyglare, Maynooth, Co Kildare   *Tel*: 01–6289354
Fax: 01–6289696
email: bishop@meath.anglican.org

Secretary of Diocesan Council Mrs Karen Seaman, Rivendell, Temple Mills, Celbridge, Co Kildare
Tel: 01–6275352
Fax: 01–6270749

CATHEDRAL CHURCH OF ST PATRICK, Trim
Dean of Clonmacnoise Very Revd Andrew Furlong, St Patrick's Deanery, Loman St, Trim, Co Meath   *Tel* and *Fax*: (046) 36698

CATHEDRAL OF ST BRIGID, Kildare
Dean Very Revd Robert Townley, Dean's House, Curragh Camp, Co Kildare
Tel and *Fax*: (045) 441654

The Anglican Communion in Japan

(Nippon Sei Ko Kai)

Members 57,273

In 1859 the American Episcopal Church sent two missionaries to Japan, followed some years later by representatives of the Church of England and the Church in Canada. The first Anglican Synod took place in 1887. The first Japanese bishops were consecrated in 1923. The Church remained underground during the Second World War and assumed all church leadership after the war.

Primate Most Revd John Makoto Takeda (*Bishop of Tokyo*)

Provincial Office Nippon Sei Ko Kai, 65 Yarai-cho, Shinjuku-ku, Tokyo 162–0805, Japan (Please use this address for all correspondence)
Fax: 03 5228 3175
email: province@nskk.org

General Secretary Revd Samuel Isamu Koshiishi

THEOLOGICAL TRAINING
Central Theological College, 1–12–31 Yoga, Setagaya-ku, Tokyo 158–0097, for clergy and lay workers

Bishop Williams Theological School, Shimotachiuri-agaru, Karasuma Dori, Kamikyo-ku, Kyoto 602–8332

CHURCH NEWSPAPERS
Sei Ko Kai Shimbun Published on 20th of each month in Japanese. Usually 8 pages, tabloid format. Subscription through the Provincial Office. Each diocese also has its own monthly paper.

NSKK News English language newsletter. Usually 2 pages. Published quarterly. Available through the Provincial Office.

CHUBU
Bishop Rt Revd Francis Toshiaki Mori, 1–47 Yamawaki-cho, Showa-ku, Nagoya 466–0063
Fax: 052 731 6222

HOKKAIDO
Bishop Rt Revd Nathaniel Makoto Uematsu, Kita 15 jo, 20 Nishi 5-chome, Kita-ku, Sapporo 001–0015
Fax: 011 736 8377

KITA KANTO
Bishop Rt Revd James Toru Uno, 2–172 Sakuragi-cho, Omiya-shi, Saitama 311–0852
Fax: 048 648 0358

KOBE
Bishop Rt Revd John Jun'ichiro Furumoto, 3–10–20 Nakayamate, Chuo-ku, Kobe 650–0011
Fax: 078 382 1095
email: xpl0661@niftyserve.or.jp

KYOTO
Bishop Rt Revd Barnabas Mutsuji Muto, 380 Okakuen, Shimotachiuri-agaru, Karasumadori, Kamikyo-ku, Kyoto 602–8011   *Fax*: 075 441 4238

KYUSHU
Bishop Rt Revd Gabriel Shoji Igarashi, 2–9–22 Kusagae, Chuo-ku, Fukuoka 810–0045
Fax: 092 771 9857

OKINAWA
Bishop Rt Revd David Shoji Tani, 101 Aza Yoshihara, Chatan-cho, Nakagami-gum, Okinawa 904–0105   *Fax*: 098 936 0606

OSAKA
Bishop Rt Revd Augustine Koichi Takano, 2–1–8 Matsuzaki-cho, Abeno-ku, Osaka 545–0053
Fax: 06 621 3097

TOHOKU
Bishop Rt Revd John Tadao Sato, 2–13–15 Kokubu-cho, Aoba-ku, Sendai 980–0803
Fax: 022 223 2349

TOKYO
Bishop Most Revd John Makoto Takeda, 3–6–18 Shibakoen, Minato-ku, Tokyo 105–0011
Fax: 03 3433 8678
email: jmtakeda@nskk.org

YOKOHAMA
Bishop Rt Revd Raphael Shiro Kajiwara, 14–57 Mitsuzawa Shimo-cho, Kanagawa-ku, Yokohama 221–0852   *Fax*: 045 323 2763

The Episcopal Church in Jerusalem and the Middle East

Members 10,000

The Church covers Jerusalem, Iran, Egypt, Cyprus, and the Gulf. The Jerusalem bishopric was founded in 1841 and became an archbishopric in 1957. Reorganization in January 1976 ended the archbishopric and combined the Diocese of Jordan, Lebanon and Syria with the Jerusalem bishopric after a 19-year separation. Around the same time, the new diocese of Cyprus and the Gulf was formed and the Diocese of Egypt was revived. The Cathedral Church of St George the Martyr in Jerusalem is known for its ministry to pilgrims. St George's College, Jerusalem is in partnership with the Anglican Communion.

THE CENTRAL SYNOD

President-Bishop Most Revd Ghais Abd El-Malik (*Bishop in Egypt with North Africa, Ethiopia, Somalia, Eritrea, and Djibouti*)

Provincial Secretary Rt Revd Riah Hanna Abu El-Assal, St George's Close, PO Box 19122, Jerusalem   *Fax*: 02–627 3847
            email: ediosces@netvision.net.il

Provincial Treasurer Rt Revd Clive Handford (*Bishop of Cyprus and the Gulf*), Diocesan Office, 2 Grigori Afxentiou St, PO Box 2075, Nicosia, Cyprus

The Jerusalem and the Middle East Church

Association acts in support of the Episcopal Church in Jerusalem and the Middle East, the Central Synod and all four dioceses. *Secretary* Mrs Vanessa Wells, 1 Hart House, The Hart, Farnham, Surrey GU9 7HA   *Tel*: (0252) 726994
            Fax: (0252) 735558

CYPRUS AND THE GULF

Bishop in Rt Revd Clive Handford, Diocesan Office, 2 Grigori Afxentiou St, PO Box 2075, Nicosia, Cyprus   *Fax*: 02 466 553
            email: bishop@spidernet.com.cy

EGYPT

Bishop Elect in Revd Dr Mouneer Hanna Anis (*President-Bishop of the Episcopal Church in Jerusalem and the Middle East*), Diocesan Office, PO Box 87, Zamalek, Cairo, Egypt
            Fax: 02 340 8941
            email: diocese@intouch.com

IRAN

Bishop in Rt Revd Iraj Mottahedeh, PO Box 135, Postal Code 81465, Isfahan, Iran

JERUSALEM

Bishop in Rt Revd Riah Hanna Abu El-Assal, St George's Close, PO Box 19122, Jerusalem
            Fax: 02 627 3847
            email: ediosces@netvision.net.il

The Anglican Church of Kenya

Members 2,500,000

Mombasa saw the arrival of Anglican missionaries in 1844, with the first African ordained to the priesthood in 1885. Mass conversions occurred as early as 1910. The first Kenyan bishops were consecrated in 1955. The Church became part of the Province of East Africa, established in 1960, but by 1970 Kenya and Tanzania were divided into separate provinces.

Primate Most Revd David Gitari (*Bishop of Nairobi*), PO Box 40502, Nairobi, Kenya
            Fax: 2542 714750
            email: davidgitari@insightkenya.com

Provincial Secretary Mrs Susan Mumina (*same address*)   *email*: ackenya@insightkenya.com

Provincial Treasurer Mr William Ogara, Corat Africa, PO Box 42593, Nairobi, Kenya
            Fax: 2542 714750

THEOLOGICAL COLLEGES

St Paul's United Theological College (Ecumenical), PO Limuru, Kenya

Trinity College, PO Box 72430, Nairobi, Kenya (Centre for Theological Extension)

Carlile College for Theology and Business Studies, PO Box 72584, Nairobi, Kenya (*Principal* Revd Capt Tim Dakin)

BONDO
Bishop Vacancy

BUNGOMA
Bishop Rt Revd Eliud Wabukala, PO Box 2392, Bungoma, Kenya

BUTERE
Bishop Rt Revd Horace Etemesi, PO Box 54, Butere, Kenya   *Fax*: 254 333 20 038

ELDORET
Bishop Rt Revd Thomas Kogo, PO Box 3404, Eldoret, Kenya   *Fax*: 254 321 33 477

EMBU
Bishop Rt Revd Moses Njue, PO Box 189, Embu, Kenya   *Fax*: 254 161 30 468

KAJIADO
Bishop Rt Revd Jeremiah John Mutua Taama, PO Box 203, Kajiado, Kenya   *Fax*: 254 301 21 106

KATAKWA
Bishop Rt Revd Eliud Okiring Odera, PO Box 68, Amagoro, Kenya

KIRINYAGA
Bishop Rt Revd Daniel Munene Ngoru, PO Box 95, Kutus, Kenya   *Fax*: 254 163 44 020
        email: ACK-Kirinyaga@thorntree.com

KITALI
Bishop Rt Revd Stephen Kewasis Nyorsok, PO Box 4176, Kitali, Kenya   *Fax*: 254 325 31 387

KITUI
Bishop Rt Revd Benjamin M. P. Nzimbi, PO Box 1054, Machakos, Kenya   *Fax*: 254 141 22 119

MACHAKOS
Bishop Rt Revd Joseph Mutie Kanuku, PO Box 282, Machakos, Kenya   *Fax*: 254 145 20 178

MASENO NORTH
Bishop Rt Revd Simon Mutingole Oketch, PO Box 416, Kakamega, Kenya   *Fax*: 254 331 30 752

MASENO SOUTH
Bishop Rt Revd Francis Mwayi Abiero, PO Box 380, Kisumu, Kenya   *Fax*: 254 35 21 009

MASENO WEST
Bishop Rt Revd Joseph Otieno Wasonga, PO Box 793, Siaya, Kenya   *Fax*: 254 334 21 483

MBEERE
Bishop Rt Revd Gideon Grishon Ireri, PO Box 122, Siakago, Kenya   *Fax*: 254 2 714 750

MERU
Bishop Rt Revd Henry Paltridge, PO Box 446, Meru, Kenya

MOMBASA
Bishop Rt Revd Julius Robert Kalu Katoi, PO Box 80072, Mombasa, Kenya   *Fax*: 254 11 1131 6361

MOUNT KENYA CENTRAL
Bishop Rt Revd Julius Gatambo Gachuche, PO Box 121, Murang'a, Kenya   *Fax*: 254 156 22 642

MOUNT KENYA SOUTH
Bishop Rt Revd Peter Njenja, PO Box 886, Kiambu, Kenya   *Fax*: 254 154 22 408

MOUNT KENYA WEST
Bishop Rt Revd Alfred Chipman, PO Box 229, Nyeri, Kenya   *Fax*: 254 171 30 214

MUMIAS
Bishop Rt Revd William Wesa Shikukule, PO Box 213, Mumias, Kenya

NAIROBI
Bishop Most Revd David Gitari (*Archbishop of Kenya and Bishop of Nairobi*), PO Box 40502, Nairobi, Kenya   *Fax*: 254 2 718 442
        email: davidgitari@insightkenya.com

NAKURU
Bishop Rt Revd Stephen Njihia Mwangi, PO Box 56, Nakuru, Kenya   *Fax*: 254 37 44 379

NAMBALE
Bishop Rt Revd Josiah Were, PO Box 4, Nambale, Kenya   *Fax*: 254 33 66 2407

NYAHURURU
Bishop Rt Revd Charles Gaikia Gaita, PO Box 926, Nayahururu, Kenya   *Fax*: 254 37 44 379

SOUTHERN NYANZA
Bishop Rt Revd Haggai Nyang', PO Box 65, Homa Bay, Kenya   *Fax*: 254 385 220 56

TAITA TAVETA
Bishop Rt Revd Samson Meakitawa Mwaluda, PO Box 75, Voi, Kenya

THIKA
Bishop Rt Revd Gideon Gichuhi Githiga, PO Box 214, Thika, Kenya

The Anglican Church of Korea

Members 14,558
From the time when Bishop John Corfe arrived in Korea in 1890 until 1965, the Diocese of Korea has had English bishops. In 1993 the Archbishop of Canterbury installed the newly elected Primate and handed jurisdiction to him, making the Anglican Church of Korea a province of the Anglican Communion. There are four religious communities in the country as well as an Anglican university.

Primate Most Revd Matthew Chul Bum Chung (*Bishop of Seoul*)

Secretary General Revd Amos K. S. Kim, # 3 Chong-dong, Chung-ku, Seoul 100–120, Korea
        Fax: 82–2–737–4210
        email: anck@peacenet.or.kr
        Web: http://www.anck.peacenet.or.kr

ANGLICAN UNIVERSITY
(*Songgonghoe Daehak*) # 1 Hand-dong, Kuro-ku, Seoul 152–140, Korea (*President* Revd Dr John Lee)   *Fax*: 82–2–737–4210

Songgonghoebo This fortnightly paper of the Anglican Church of Korea is the joint concern of all three dioceses. Newspaper format. Printed in Korean. Contains regular liturgical and doctrinal features as well as local, national and international church news.

PUSAN
Bishop Rt Revd Joseph Dae Yong Lee, Anglican Diocese of Pusan, PO Box 103, Tongrae-ku, Pusan 607–600, Korea   *Fax*: 82 51–553–9643

SEOUL
Bishop Most Revd Matthew Chul Bum Chung, Anglican Church of Korea, # 3 Chong-dong, Chung-ku, Seoul 100–120, Korea
Fax: 82 2–723 264(
email: bishop100@hosanna.ne

TAEJON
Bishop Rt Revd Paul Hwan Yoon, Anglican Church, PO Box 22, Taejon 300–600, Korea
Fax: 82 42–255–891&

The Church of the Province of Melanesia

Members 163,884
After 118 years of missionary association with the Church of the Province of New Zealand, the Church of the Province of Melanesia was formed in 1975. The province encompasses the Republic of Vanuatu, Solomon Islands, and the French Trust Territory of New Caledonia, both sovereign island nations in the South Pacific.

Archbishop of the Province Most Revd Ellison L. Pogo (*Bishop of Central Melanesia*)

General Secretary Mr Nicholas Ma'aramo, Provincial Headquarters, PO Box 19, Honiara, Solomon Islands   *Fax*: (677) 21098

ANGLICAN THEOLOGICAL COLLEGE
Bishop Patteson Theological Centre, Kohimarama, PO Box 19, Honiara, Solomon Islands (trains students up to diploma standard) (*Principal* Revd Sam Ata)

BANKS AND TORRES
Bishop Rt Revd Charles W. Ling, PO Box 19, Sola, Vanualava, Torba Province, Republic of Vanuatu

CENTRAL MELANESIA
Bishop Most Revd Ellison L. Pogo (*Bishop of Central Melanesia and Archbishop of the Province*), Archbishop's House, PO Box 19, Honiara, Solomon Islands   *Fax*: 21098

CENTRAL SOLOMONS
Bishop Rt Revd Charles Koete, PO Box 52, Tulagi, Central Province, Solomon Islands   *Fax*: 32113

HANUATO'O
Bishop Rt Revd James P. Mason, c/o PO Kirakira, Makira/Ulawa Province, Solomon Islands
Fax: 50128

MALAITA
Bishop Rt Revd Dr Terry M. Brown, Bishop's House, PO Box 7, Auki Malaita, Solomon Islands
Fax: 40027

TEMOTU
Bishop Rt Revd Lazarus Munamua, Bishop's House, Luesalo, Lata, Santa Cruz, Solomon Islands   *Fax*: 53080

VANUATU
Bishop Rt Revd Michael H. Tavoa, Bishop's House, PO Box 238, Luganville, Santo, Vanuatu
Fax: 36 026
email: DIOCESE-OF-VANUATU@acunet.org

YSABEL
Bishop Rt Revd Zephaniah Legumana, Bishop's House, PO Box 6, Buala, Jejevo, Ysabel Province, Solomon Islands   *Fax*: 35071

The Anglican Church of Mexico

Members 21,000
The Mexican Episcopal Church symbolically began with Mexico's war for independence in 1810. Religious reform in 1857 secured freedom of religion, separating the Roman Catholic Church from government and politics. In 1860 the newly formed Church of Jesus contacted the Episcopal Church in the United States, seeking leadership, guidance and support. In 1958 the fourth missionary bishop of Mexico was the first of the Church's bishops to be consecrated on Mexican soil. The Church became an autonomous province of the Anglican Communion in 1995.

Primate Most Revd Samuel Espinoza-Venegas (*Bishop of Western Mexico*)

Provincial Secretary Vacancy, Calle La Otra Banda # 40, Col. San Angel, Delegación Alvaro Obregón, 01000 Mexico, D.F., Mexico
Fax: 616–4063
email: ofipam@planet.com.mx

CUERNAVACA
Bishop Most Revd Martiniano Garcia-Montiel, Minerva # 1, Fracc. Las Delicias, 62330 Cuernavaca, Morelos, Mexico   *Fax*: 073 152870
     email: diovca@giga.com.mx

MEXICO
Bishop Rt Revd Sergio Carranza-Gomez, Ave San Jeronimo # 117, Col San Angel, Deleg Alvaro Obregón 01000, Mexico DF   *Fax*: 05 616 2205
     email: diomex@planet.com.mx

NORTHERN MEXICO
Bishop Rt Revd Germán Martinez-Márquez, Simon Bolivar 2005 Nte, Colonia Mitras Centro, 64460 Monterrey, NL, Mexico   *Fax*: 08 348 7362
     email: dionte@infosel.com.mx

SOUTHEASTERN MEXICO
Bishop Rt Revd Benito Juárez-Martinez, Avenue de Las Americas # 73, Colonia Aguacatal, 91130, Xalapa, Veracruz, Mexico   *Fax*: 028 14 4387

WESTERN MEXICO
Bishop Most Revd Samuel Espinoza-Venegas (*Bishop of Western Mexico and Archbishop of the Province*), Francisco J. Gamba # 255, Sector Juárez, 44100 Guadalajara, Jalisco, Mexico
     Fax: 03 615 4413
     email: diocte@vianet.com.mx

The Church of the Province of Myanmar

Members 49,257
Anglican chaplains and missionaries worked in Burma in the early and mid-nineteenth century. The Province of Myanmar was formed in 1970, nine years after the declaration of Buddhism as the state religion and four years after all foreign missionaries were forced to leave.

Archbishop of the Province Most Revd Andrew Mya Han (*Bishop of Yangon*)

Provincial Secretary Revd Saw Kenneth, 140 Pyidaungsu Yeiktha Rd, Dagon PO (11191), Yangon, Myanmar   *Fax*: 95 1251405

Provincial Treasurer Revd Peter Thein Maung (*same address*)

Secretary and Treasurer, Yangon Diocesan Trust Association Mr Stanley Peters (*same address*)

ANGLICAN THEOLOGICAL COLLEGES
Holy Cross Theological College, 104 Inya Rd, University PO (11041), Yangon, Myanmar (*Principal* Revd Saw Maung Doe)

Emmanuel Theological College, Mohnyin, Kachin State (*Principal* Bishop John Shan Lum)

CHURCH NEWSLETTER
The province publishes a monthly 36-page *Newsletter*. *Editor and Manager* Mr Saw Peter Aye, Bishopscourt, 140 Pyidaungsu Yeiktha Rd, Dagon PO (11191), Yangon, Myanmar

HPA-AN
Bishop Rt Revd Daniel Hoi Kyin, Bishopscourt, Cathedral of St Peter, Bishop Gone, Hpa-an, Kayin State, Myanmar   *Fax*: 1 77 512

MANDALAY
Bishop Rt Revd Andrew Hla Aung, Bishopscourt, 22nd St 'C' Rd (between 85–86 Rd), Mandalay, Myanmar

MYITKYINA
Bishop Rt Revd John Shan Lum, Diocesan Office, Tha Kin Nat Pe Rd, Thida Ya, Myitkyina, Myanmar

SITTWE
Bishop Rt Revd Barnabas Theaung Hawi, St John's Church, Paletwa, Sittwe, Myanmar

Assistant Bishop Rt Revd Aung Tha Tun (*same address*)

TOUNGOO
Bishop Rt Revd Saw (John) Wilme, Diocesan Office, Nat Shin Naung Rd, Toungoo, Myanmar

YANGON
Bishop Most Revd Andrew Mya Han (*Bishop of Yangon and Archbishop of the Province*), 44 Prome Rd, Dagon PO (11191), Yangon, Myanmar
     Fax: 01 251 405

Assistant Bishop Rt Revd Joseph Than Pe
     Fax: 01–77 512

The Church of Nigeria

(Anglican Communion)

Members 17,500,000
The rebirth of Christianity began with the arrival of Christian freed slaves in Nigeria in the middle of the nineteenth century. The Church Missionary Society established an evangelistic ministry, particularly in the south. The division of the Province of West Africa in 1979 formed the Province of Nigeria and the Province of West Africa. In the 1990s nine missionary bishops consecrated themselves to evangelism in northern Nigeria.

Membership growth has dictated the need for new dioceses year by year.

Archbishop Province I Most Revd Joseph A. Adetiloye (*Bishop of Lagos*)

Archbishop Province II Most Revd Jonathan Arinzechukwu Onyemelukwe (*Bishop of the Diocese on the Niger*)

Archbishop Province III Most Revd Peter Jasper Akinola (*Bishop of Abuja*)

General Secretary Ven Samuel B. Akinola, 29 Marina, PO Box 78, Lagos, Nigeria

Provincial Treasurer Chief S. O. Adekunle, Church House, 29 Marina, PO Box 78, Lagos, Nigeria

Dean of the Province Rt Revd B. C. Nwankiti (*Bishop of Owerri*)

THEOLOGICAL COLLEGES
Immanuel College (Ecumenical), PO Box 515, Ibadan

Trinity College (Ecumenical), Umuahia, Imo State, Nigeria

Vining College, Akure, Ondo State, Nigeria

St Francis of Assisi College, Wusasa, Zaria, Nigeria

ABA (Province II)
Bishop Rt Revd Augustine Onyeyrichukwu Iwuagwu, Bishopscourt, 70/72 St Michael's Rd, PO Box 212, Aba, Nigeria

ABAKALIKI (Province II)
Bishop Rt Revd Benson C. Onyeibor, All Saints' Cathedral, PO Box 112, Abakaliki, Ebonyi State, Nigeria

ABUJA (Province III)
Bishop Most Revd Peter Jasper Akinola, Archbishop's Palace, PO Box 212, ADCP, Abuja, Nigeria   *Fax*: 234 9 523 0986
          email: abuja@anglican.skannet.com.ng

AKOKO (Province I)
Bishop Rt Revd O. O. Obijole, PO Box 572, Ikare-Akoko, Ondo State, Nigeria

AKURE (Province I)
Bishop Rt Revd Emmanuel Bolanle Gbonigi, Bishopscourt, PO Box 1622, Akure, Nigeria
                         Fax: 234 34 241 572
          email: akdangc@akure.rcl.nig.com

ASABA (Province II)
Bishop Rt Revd Dr Rowland Nwafo Nwosu, Bishopscourt, Cable Point, PO Box 216, Asaba, Delta State, Nigeria

AWKA (Province II)
Bishop Rt Revd Maxwell Samuel Chike Anikwenwa, Bishopscourt, Ifite Rd, PO Box 130, Awka, Anambra State, Nigeria
                          Fax: 234 46 550 052
          email: angawka@infoweb.abs.net

BAUCHI (Province III)
Bishop Rt Revd Laudamus Ereaku, Bishop's House, 2 Hospital Rd, PO Box 2450, Bauchi, Nigeria

BENIN (Province I)
Bishop Rt Revd Peter Imhona Onekpe, Bishopscourt, PO Box 82, Benin City, Edo State, Nigeria

BIDA (Province III)
Bishop Rt Revd Jonah Kolo

CALABAR (Province II)
Bishop The Ven Tunde Adeleye, Bishopscourt, PO Box 74, Calabar, Cross River State, Nigeria
                          Fax: 234 88 220 835

DAMATURU (Province III)
Bishop Rt Revd Daniel Abu Yisa, PO Box 312, Damaturu, Yobe State, Nigeria

DIOCESE ON THE NIGER (Province II)
Bishop Most Revd Jonathan Arinzechukwu Onyemelukwe, Bishopscourt, PO Box 42, Onitsha, Nigeria

DUTSE (Province III)
Bishop Rt Revd Yesufu Ibrahim Lumu, PO Box 15, Dutse, Jigawa State, Nigeria

EGBA (Province I)
Bishop Rt Revd Dr Matthew Oluremi Owadayo, Bishopscourt, Onikolobo, PO Box 267, Ibara, Abeokuta, Nigeria

EGBU (Province II)
Bishop Rt Revd Emmanual Uchechukwu, All Saint's Cathedral, PO Box 1967, Owerri, Imo State, Nigeria

EKITI (Province I)
Bishop Rt Revd Samuel Adedaye Abe, Bishopscourt, PO Box 12, Ado-Ekiti, Nigeria

EKITI WEST (Province I)
Bishop Rt Revd Samuel Oke

ENUGU (Province II)
Bishop Rt Revd Dr Emmanuel O. Chukwuma, Bishop's House, PO Box 418, Enugu, Nigeria

GOMBE (Province III)
Bishop Rt Revd H. Ndukube

GUSAU (Province III)
Bishop Rt Revd Simon Bala

GWAGWALADA (Province III)
Bishop Rt Revd Tanimu Samari Aduda

IBADAN (Province I)
Bishop Rt Revd Gideon I. O. Olajide, Bishopscourt, Arigidi St, Bodija Estate, PO Box 3075, Ibadan, Nigeria   *Fax*: 234 2 810 1413
          email: bishop@ibadan.skannet.com

IBADAN NORTH (Province I)
Bishop Rt Revd Dr Segun Okubadejo, Bishopscourt, Moyede, PO Box 182, Dugbe, Ibadan, Nigeria

IBADAN SOUTH (Province I)
Bishop Rt Revd Jacob Ademola Ajetunmobi, Bishopscourt, PO Box 166, St David's Compound, Kudeti, Ibadan, Nigeria
email: jacajet@aol.com

IDEATO (Province II)
Bishop Rt Revd Godson Chinyere Ejiefu, Bishopscourt, PO Box 2, Ndizuogu, Imo State, Nigeria

IFE (Province I)
Bishop Rt Revd Gabriel B. Oloniyo, Bishopscourt, PO Box 312, Ife-Ife, Osun State, Nigeria

IGBOMINA (Province I)
Bishop Rt Revd Michael Oluwakayode Akinyemi, St David's Cathedral Church Kudeil, PO Box 166, Ibadan, Nigeria

IJEBU (Province I)
Bishop Rt Revd Joseph Akinyele Omoyajowo, Bishopscourt, Ejirin Rd, PO Box 112, Ijebu-Ode, Nigeria

IKALE-ILAJE (Province I)
Bishop Rt Revd Joseph Oluwafemi Arulefela, Bishopscourt, Ikoya Rd, P M B 3, Ilutitun, Ondo State, Nigeria

ILESA (Province I)
Bishop Rt Revd Ephraim Adebola Ademowo, Bishopscourt, Oke-Oye, PO Box 237, Ilesa, Nigeria

JALINGO (Province III)
Bishop Vacancy, PO Box 4, Jalingo, Taraba State, Nigeria

JOS (Province III)
Bishop Rt Revd Benjamin Argak Kwashi, Bishopscourt, PO Box 6283, Jos, Plateau State, Nigeria   *Fax*: 234 73 612 221
email: argak.kasco@pinet.net

KABBA (Province I)
Bishop Rt Revd Solomon Olaife Oyelade, Bishopscourt, Obaro Way, PO Box 62, Kabba, Kogi State, Nigeria

KADUNA (Province III)
Bishop Rt Revd Josiah Idowu-Fearon, PO Box 72, Kaduna, Nigeria   *Fax*: 234 62 235 273
email: 106101.2127@compuserve.com

KAFANCHAN (Province III)
Bishop Rt Revd William Weh Diya, Bishopscourt, 5b Jemma'a St, PO Box 29, Kafanchan, Kaduna State, Nigeria

KANO (Province III)
Bishop Rt Revd Zakka Lalle Nyam, Bishop's Court, PO Box 362, Kano, Nigeria
Fax: 234 64 647 816
email: kano@anglican.skannetcom.nig

KATSINA (Province III)
Bishop Rt Revd James S. Sekari Kwasu, Bishop's Lodge, PO Box 904, Katsina, Nigeria

KEBBI (Province III)
Bishop Rt Revd Edmund Efoyikeye Akanya, PO Box 701, Birnin Kebbi, Kebbi State, Nigeria
Fax: 234 68 21 179

KWARA (Province I)
Bishop Rt Revd Jeremiah Olagbamigbe A. Fabuluje, Bishopscourt, Fate Rd, PO Box 1884, Ilorin, Kwara State, Nigeria

LAFIA (Province III)
Bishop Rt Revd Miller Maza

LAGOS (Province I)
Bishop Most Revd Joseph Abiodun Adetiloye, T, 29 Marina, PO Box 13, Lagos, Nigeria
Fax: 234 1 263 6026
email: bishop@rcl.nig.com

LAGOS WEST (Province I)
Bishop Rt Revd Peter A. Adebiyi

LOKOJA (Province I)
Bishop Rt Revd George Bako, PO Box 11, Lokoja, Kogi State, Nigeria   *Fax*: 234 58 220 5881

MAIDUGURI (Province III)
Bishop Rt Revd Emmanuel K. Mani, Bishopscourt, Off Lagos St, GRA PO Box 1693, Maiduguri, Borno State, Nigeria

MAKURDI (Province III)
Bishop Rt Revd Nathan Nyitar Inyom, Bishopscourt, PO Box 1, Makurdi, Nigeria
Fax: 234 44 533 349

MBAISE (Province II)
Bishop Rt Revd Bright Ogu, Bishopscourt, PO Box 10, Ife, Ezinihitte Mbaise, Imo State, Nigeria

MINNA (Province III)
Bishop Rt Revd Nathaniel Yisa, Bishopscourt, Dutsen Kura, PO Box 2469, Minna, Nigeria

THE NIGER DELTA (Province II)
Bishop Rt Revd Gabriel Pepple, Bishopscourt, PO Box 115, Port Harcourt, Rivers State, Nigeria

NIGER DELTA NORTH (Province II)
Bishop Rt Revd Samuel Onyuku Elenwo, PO Box 53, Port Harcourt, Nigeria

NNEWI (Province II)
Bishop Rt Revd Godwin Izundu Nmezinwa Okpala, c/o Bishopscourt (opposite Total Filling Station), PO Box 2630, Uruagu-Nnewi, Anambra State, Nigeria   *Fax*: 234 46 462 676

NSUKKA (Province II)
Bishop Rt Revd Jonah Iloñuba, PO Box 516, Nsukka, Enugu State, Nigeria

OFFA (Province I)
Bishop Rt Revd Gabriel Akinbolarin Akinbiyi, St George's Church, PO Box 28, Sabon-Gari, Zaria, Nigeria

OJI (Province II)
Bishop Rt Revd Amos Imado, c/o Bishop's House, PO Box 418, Enugu, Nigeria

OKE-OSUN (Province I)
Bishop Rt Revd Abraham O. Awosan, Bishopscourt, PO Box 251, Gbongan, Osun State, Nigeria

OKIGWE NORTH (Province II)
Bishop Rt Revd Alfred Iheanyichukwu Sunday Nwaizuzu, PO Box 156, Okigwe, Imo State, Nigeria

OKIGWE SOUTH (Province II)
Bishop Rt Revd Caleb Anny Maduoma, Bishopscourt, Ezeoke Nsu, PO Box 235 Nsu, Ehime Mbano L.G.A., Imo State, Nigeria

ONDO (Province I)
Bishop Rt Revd George L. Lasebikan, Bishopscourt, College Rd, PO Box 265, Ondo, Nigeria

ORLU (Province II)
Bishop Rt Revd Bennett Okoro, Bishopscourt, PO Box 260, Nkwerre, Imo State, Nigeria

OSUN (Province I)
Bishop Rt Revd Seth Oni Fagbemi, Bishopscourt, Isale-Aro, PO Box 285, Osogbo, Nigeria

OTURKPO (Province III)
Bishop Rt Revd Ityobee Ugede, St John's Cathedral, Depot Rd, PO Box 360, Oturkpo, Benue State, Nigeria

OWERRI (Province II)
Bishop Rt Revd Dr Cyril Chukwunonyerem Okorocha, Bishop's Bourne, PO Box 31, Owerri, Imo State, Nigeria   *Fax*: 2324 82 440 183
email: owerri@anglican.skannet.com.ng

OWO (Province I)
Bishop Vacancy, Bishopscourt, PO Box 472, Owo, Ondo State, Nigeria

REMO (Province I)
Bishop Rt Revd Elijah Oluremi Ige Ogundana, Bishopscourt, Ewusi St, PO Box 522, Sagamu, Ogun State, Nigeria

SABONGIDA ORA (Province I)
Bishop Rt Revd Albert Agbaje, Bishopscourt, PO Box 13, Sabongida Ora, Edo State, Nigeria

SOKOTO (Province III)
Bishop Rt Revd Joseph Akinfenwa, Bishop's Lodge, PO Box 3489, Sokoto, Nigeria

UGHELLI
Bishop Rt Revd Vincent O. Muoghereh, Bishopscourt, Ovurodawanre, PO Box 762, Ughelli, Delta State, Nigeria   *Fax*: 234 53 250 091

UKWA (Province II)
Bishop Rt Revd Uju Otuokwesiri Wachukwu Obinya, PO Box 20468, Aba, Nigeria

UMUAHIA (Province II)
Bishop Rt Revd Ugochuckwu Uwaoma Ezuoke, St Stephen's Cathedral Church Compound, PO Box 96, Umuahia, Nigeria

UYO (Province II)
Bishop Rt Revd Emmanuel E. Nglass, Bishopscourt, PO Box 70, Uyo, Akwa Ibom State, Nigeria   *Fax*: 234 85 200 451

WARRI (Province I)
Bishop Rt Revd Nathaniel Enuku, Bishopscourt, 17 Mabiaku Rd, GRA, PO Box 4571, Warri, Nigeria

WUSASA (Province III)
Bishop Rt Revd Ali Buba Lamido, Box 28, Wusasa Zaria, Nigeria

YEWA (Province I)
Bishop Rt Revd Timothy I. O. Bolaji, Bishopscourt, PO Box 484, Ilaro, Ogun State, Nigeria

YOLA (Province III)
Bishop Rt Revd Christian Ogochukwu Efobi, PO Box 601, Yola, Adamawa State, Nigeria

The Anglican Church of Papua New Guinea

Members 246,000
Organized as a missionary diocese of Australia in 1898, the Church was part of the Australian province of Queensland until 1977. The first indigenous priest was ordained in 1914. The Anglican Church functions mostly in rural areas where mountains and rainforest provide natural barriers to travel. Some 60 per cent of the funding is raised internally; the balance comes from grants from Australia, New Zealand and the UK-based Papua New Guinea Church Partnership.

Archbishop Most Revd James Ayong, PO Box 893, Mt Hagen, Western Highlands Province
Fax: 542 1181
email: achgn@global.net.pg

General Secretary Mr Howard Graham, PO Box 673, Lae, Morobe Province *Fax*: 472 1852
email: acpng@global.net.pg

Provincial Registrar Mr Martin Gardham, PO Box 893, Mt Hagen, Western Highlands Province
Fax: 542 1181

THEOLOGICAL COLLEGE
Newton Theological College, PO Box 162, Popondetta, Oro Province (*Principal* Revd Roderick MacDougall SSM) *Fax*: 3297476

CHURCH PAPER
Family. Published three times a year. *Editor* Tim Williams, PO Box 6491, Boroko, NCD
Fax: 323 2493

AIPO RONGO
Bishop Most Revd James Simon Ayong, PO Box 893, Mt Hagen, Western Highlands Province
Fax: 542 1181
email: achgn@global.net.pg

DOGURA
Bishop Rt Revd Tevita Talanoa, PO Box 19, Dogura, MBP *Fax*: 641 1129

NEW GUINEA ISLANDS
Bishop Vacancy

POPONDOTA
Bishop Rt Revd Reuben Barago Tariambari, PO Box 26, Popondetta, Oro Province *Fax*: 3297 476
email: acpop@global.net.pg

PORT MORESBY
Bishop Rt Revd Michael George Hough, PO Box 6491, Boroko, NCD *Fax*: 3232 493
email: hough@dg.com.pg

The Episcopal Church in the Philippines

Members 118,187
With its history as a Spanish colony, the Philippines was predominantly Roman Catholic. When Americans colonized the country in 1898, Anglican missionary work began in the north and among Muslim populations in the south. Four dioceses were established by 1971. The Church consecrated its first bishop in 1963 and became an autonomous province in 1990.

National Office The ECP Mission Center, 275 E Rodriguez Sr Blvd, Cathedral Heights, 1112 Quezon City, Philippines

Mail Address PO Box 10321, Broadway Centrum, 1112 Quezon City, Philippines *Fax*: 721 1923
email: ecp@phil.gn.apc.org

Prime Bishop Most Revd Ignacio Capuyan Soliba (*same address*)

CENTRAL PHILIPPINES
Bishop Rt Revd Benjamin Gayno Botengan, PO Box 655, Manila 1099, Philippines *Fax*: 724–2143

NORTH CENTRAL PHILIPPINES
Bishop Rt Revd Joel A. Pachao, PO Box 137, 2600 Baguio City, Philippines *Fax*: 74–442–3638

NORTHERN LUZON
Bishop Rt Revd Renato M. Abibico, Bulanao, Tabuk, Kalinga-Apayao 3800, Philippines
Fax: 721 1923

NORTHERN PHILIPPINES
Bishop Rt Revd Edward Pacyaya Malecdan, Diocesan Center, Bontoc, Mountain Province 0601, Philippines *Fax*: 74–602–1026

Suffragan Bishop Rt Revd Miguel Paredes Yamoyam (*same address*)

SOUTHERN PHILIPPINES
Bishop Rt Revd James Buanda Manguramas, PO Box 113, Cotabato City 9600, Philippines
Fax: 64 421 1703

The Church of the Province of Rwanda

Members 1,000,000
In just over 10,170 square miles are one million Anglicans, out of a quickly growing population of 7.7 million. The former Ruanda Mission established its first station at Gahini in 1925 and grew through the revival of the 1930s and 1940s, with the first Rwandan bishop appointed in 1965. Eight dioceses have up to 40 parishes, which in turn comprise 15 to 20 congregations. Like all strata of Rwandan society, the Church suffered, on many levels, through the genocide, and it is a major priority of the Church to replace clergy

through training. The Church has a role as a healing ministry to the many traumatized people in Rwanda and to reconciliation, restoration, and rehabilitation. The Church has also been involved in rural development, medical work, vocational training, and education.

Archbishop of the Province Most Revd Emmanuel Mbona Kolini

Dean of the Province Rt Revd Onesphore Rwaje (*Bishop of Byumba*)

Provincial Secretary Canon Josias Sendegeya, BP 2487, Kigali, Rwanda   Fax: 250 73 213
    email: byumba@rwandate11.rwanda1.com

BUTARE
Bishop Rt Revd Venuste Mutiganda, BP 225, Butare, Rwanda   Fax: 250 30 504

BYUMBA
Bishop Rt Revd Onesphore Rwaje, BP 17, Byumba, Rwanda   Fax: 250 64 242
    email: byumba@rwandate11.rwanda1.com

CYANGUGU
Bishop Rt Revd Ken Barham, BP 52, Cyangugu, Rwanda   Fax: 01424 773 073
    email: BishopKen@compuserve.com

GAHINI
Bishop Rt Revd Alexis Bilindabagado, BP 22, Kigali, Rwanda   Fax: 250 77 831

KIBUNGO
Bishop Rt Revd Prudence Ngarambe, EER Kibungo Diocese, BP 719, Kigali, Rwanda

KIGALI
Bishop Most Revd Emmanuel Mbona Kolini, BP 61, Kigali, Rwanda   Fax: 250 73 213

KIGEME
Bishop Rt Revd Norman Kayumba, BP 67, Gikongoro, Rwanda   Fax: 250 34 011
    email: dkigeme@rwandate11.rwanda1.com

SHYIRA
Bishop Rt Revd John Rucyahana Kabango, BP 26, Ruhengeri, Rwanda   Fax: 250 46 449

SHYOGWE
Bishop Rt Revd Jered Karimba, BP 27, Gitarama, Rwanda   Fax: 250 62 460

The Scottish Episcopal Church

Members 53,553
The roots of Scottish Christianity go back to St Ninian in the fourth century and St Columba in the sixth. After the Reformation, the Episcopal Church was the established church of Scotland. It was disestablished and replaced by the Presbyterian Church in 1689. Penal statutes in force from 1746 to 1792 further weakened the Church, yet bishops maintained continuity. In 1794 in Aberdeen, the Scottish Church consecrated the first bishop of the American Church. There was rapid growth in the nineteenth century influenced by the Tractarian movement.

THEOLOGICAL COLLEGE
The Theological Institute of the Scottish Episcopal Church, Old Coates House, 32 Manor Place, Edinburgh EH3 7EB (Director Revd Rosemary Nixon)   Tel: 0131–220 2272
                  Fax: 0131–220 2294
    email: tisec@scotland.anglican.org

CHURCH NEWSPAPER
The Scottish Episcopalian 8 pages, 10 issues yearly. Newspaper format. Editor Mrs Nan Macfarlane, Edrington Mains Cottage, Foulden, By Berwick on Tweed TD15 1UZ   Tel: (01289) 386288
    email: episcopalian@scotland.anglican.org

GENERAL SYNOD
President The Primus Most Revd Richard Holloway (Bishop of Edinburgh)

Convener of Standing Committee Mr Gavin Gemmell, Baillie Gifford & Co, 1 Rutland Court, Edinburgh EH3 8EY

Secretary General Mr John Stuart, 21 Grosvenor Crescent, Edinburgh EH12 5EE
                  Tel: 0131–225 6357
                  Fax: 0131–346 7247
    email: secgen@scotland.anglican.org
          office@scotland.anglican.org

Communications Officer Revd Jim Wynn-Evans (same address) email: press@scotland.anglican.org

Since 1982 the governing authority of the Episcopal Church has been the General Synod. This is an elected body of some 160 members which meets once a year.
    The General Synod operates five principal Boards: Faith and Order, Mission, Administration, Information and Communication and a Board for Ministry. These in turn have pendant committees that work in particular areas.
    The Church raises funds for social responsibility (including homes for the elderly), education, support of overseas partnership, clergy stipends, pensions, retirement housing and maintenance and development of buildings.

ABERDEEN AND ORKNEY
Bishop Rt Revd Bruce Cameron, Diocesan Centre, 39 King's Crescent, Aberdeen AB24 3HP
                  Tel: (01224) 636653
                  Fax: (01224) 636186
    email: office@aberdeen.anglican.org

Dean Very Revd Gerald Stranraer-Mull, Rectory, Ellon, Aberdeenshire AB41 9NP
                  Tel: (01358) 720366

ST ANDREW'S CATHEDRAL, Aberdeen
Provost Very Revd David Wightman, 15 Morningfield Rd, Aberdeen AB15 4AP
Tel: (01224) 314765 (Home)
(01224) 640119 (Office)

ARGYLL AND THE ISLES
Bishop Rt Revd Douglas Cameron, The Pines, Ardconnel Rd, Oban PA34 5DR
Tel and *Fax*: (01631) 566912
email: office@argyll.anglican.org

Dean Very Revd John Henry James Macleay, St Andrew's Rectory, Parade Rd, Fort William PH33 6BA
Tel: (01397) 702979

ST JOHN THE DIVINE CATHEDRAL, Oban
(the Cathedral of Argyll)
Provost Very Revd Allan Murray MacLean, Rectory, Ardconnel Terrace, Oban PA34 5DJ
Tel: (01631) 562323

COLLEGIATE CHURCH OF THE HOLY SPIRIT, Cumbrae
(The Cathedral of The Isles)
Clergy Rt Revd Douglas Cameron (*as above*)

BRECHIN
Bishop Rt Revd Neville Chamberlain, Bishop's Office, St Paul's Cathedral, 1 High St, Dundee DD1 1TD
Tel: (01382) 229230
Fax: (01382) 203446
email: office@brechin.anglican.org

Dean Very Revd Robert William Breaden, 46 Seafield Rd, Broughty Ferry DD5 3AN
Tel: (01382) 477477

ST PAUL'S CATHEDRAL, Dundee
Provost Very Revd Miriam Byrne, Cathedral Office, 1 High St, Dundee DD1 1TD
Tel: (01382) 224486

EDINBURGH
Bishop Most Revd Richard Holloway, Diocesan Centre, 21A Grosvenor Crescent, Edinburgh EH12 5EL
Tel: 0131–538 7044
Fax: 0131–538 7088
email: office@edinburgh.anglican.org

Dean Very Revd Timothy David Morris, The Rectory, Parsonage Rd, Galashiels TD1 3HS
Tel and *Fax*: (01896) 753118
email: tim@parsonage.scotborders.co.uk

ST MARY'S CATHEDRAL, Edinburgh
Provost Very Revd Graham John Thomson Forbes, 8 Lansdowne Crescent, Edinburgh EH12 5EQ
Tel: 0131–225 2978
Fax: 0131–225 3181

GLASGOW AND GALLOWAY
Bishop Rt Revd Idris Jones, Diocesan Office, 5 St Vincent Place, Glasgow G1 2DH
Tel: 0141–221 5720/2694
Fax: 0141–221 7014
email: bishop@glasgow.anglican.org

Dean Very Revd Dr Gregor Duncan, St Columba's Rectory, Aubery Crescent, Largs KA30 8PR
Tel: (01475) 673143
Fax: (01475) 676020

ST MARY THE VIRGIN CATHEDRAL, Glasgow
Provost Very Revd Griff Dines, St Mary's Cathedral, 300 Great Western Rd, Glasgow G4 9JB
Tel and *Fax*: 0141–339 6691
email: provost@glasgow.anglican.org

MORAY, ROSS AND CAITHNESS
Bishop Rt Revd John Michael Crook, Diocesan Office, 11 Kenneth St, Inverness IV3 5NR
email: office@moray.anglican.org

Dean Very Revd Michael Francis Hickford, The Parsonage, 4 Castle St, Dingwall IV15 9HU
Tel: (01349) 862204

ST ANDREW'S CATHEDRAL, Inverness
Provost Very Revd Malcolm Grant, 15 Ardross St, Inverness IV3 5NS
Tel: (01463) 233535

ST ANDREWS, DUNKELD AND DUNBLANE
Bishop Rt Revd Michael Henley, Diocesan Office, 28A Balhousie St, Perth PH1 5HJ
Tel: (01738) 443173
Fax: (01738) 443174
email: office@standrews.anglican.org

Dean Very Revd Randall MacAlister, 33 Stirling Rd, Milnathort KY13 9XS
Tel: (01577) 865711

ST NINIAN'S CATHEDRAL, Perth
Provost Very Revd Hunter Farquharson, 40 Hay St, Perth PH1 5HS
Tel: (01738) 626874

ANGLICAN AND PORVOO COMMUNIONS

Churches and Provinces: Scotland
357

The Church of the Province of South East Asia

Members 168,079

The Anglican Church in South East Asia was originally under the jurisdiction of the Bishop of Calcutta. The first chaplaincy was formed in West Malaysia in 1805; the first bishop was consecrated in 1855. The Diocese of Labuan, Sarawak and Singapore was formed in 1881, dividing in 1909, 1962, and 1970. Until the inauguration of the Church of the Province of South East Asia, the four dioceses (Kuching, Sabah, Singapore, and West Malaysia) were under the jurisdiction of the Archbishop of Canterbury. Although the province exists under the restrictions of a Muslim government, the Church has experienced spiritual renewal and has sent out its own mission partners to various parts of the world.

Primate Most Revd Moses Tay (*Bishop of Singapore*)

THEOLOGICAL COLLEGES
House of the Epiphany, PO Box No 347, 93704 Kuching, Sarawak, Malaysia (*Warden* Revd Aeries Sumping Jingan)

Trinity College, 7 Mount Sophia, Singapore 0922 (interdenominational)

St Peter's Hall, residential hostel for Anglican students (*Warden* Revd Soon Soo Kee)

Seminari Theoloji Malaysia (STM), Xavier's Hall, 133 Jalan Gasing, 46000 Petaling Jaya, Malaysia (*Principal* Revd Hwa Yung)

KUCHING
Bishop Rt Revd Made Katib, Bishop's House, PO Box 347, 93704 Kuching, Sarawak, Malaysia
Fax: 60 82 426 488
email: bkg@pc.jaring.my

Assistant Bishop Rt Revd Bolly Anak Lapok, PO Box 120, 97007 Bintulu, Sarawak
Fax: 60 86 310 693
email: blapok@tm.net.my

SABAH
Bishop Rt Revd Datuk Ping Chung Yong, Rumah Bishop, Jalan Tangki, PO Box 10811, 88809 Kota Kinabalu, Sabah, Malaysia   *Fax*: 60 88 245 942
email: pcyong@pc.jaring.my

Assistant Bishop Rt Revd Chen Fah Yong, Good Shepherd Church, WDT No 254, 90009 Sandakan, Sabah, Malaysia   *Fax*: 60 89 271 862
email: cogs@tm.net.my

SINGAPORE
Bishop Most Revd Moses Tay, Bishopsbourne, 4 Bishopsgate, Singapore 249970   *Fax*: 65 479 5482
email: province@livingstreams.org.sg

Assistant Bishop Rt Revd John Tan (*same address*)
email: johntan@livingstreams.org.sg

WEST MALAYSIA
Bishop Rt Revd Datuk Cheng Ean Lim, Rumah Bishop, 14 Pesiaran Stonor, 50450 Kuala Lumpur, Malaysia   *Fax*: 60 3 201 3225
email: diocese@tm.net.my

Assistant Bishop Rt Revd Moses Ponniah, St Christopher's Church, 5 Jalan Mustaffa, 80100 Johor Bahru, Malaysia   *Fax*: 60 7 224 3054
email: prteo@pl.jaring.my

The Church of the Province of Southern Africa

Members 2,000,000

The province is the oldest in Africa. British Anglicans met for worship in Cape Town after 1806, with the first bishop appointed in 1847. The 23 dioceses of the province extend beyond the Republic of South Africa and include the Foreign and Commonwealth Office (St Helena and Tristan da Cunha), Mozambique (Lebombo and Niassa), the Republic of Namibia, the Kingdom of Lesotho, and the Kingdom of Swaziland. This Church and its leaders played a significant role in the abolition of apartheid in South Africa and in peace-keeping in Mozambique and Angola.

Primate Most Revd Winston Njongonkulu Ndungane (*Archbishop of Cape Town*)

Provincial Executive Officer Canon Luke Pato, 16 Bishopscourt Drive, Claremont, Cape 7700
Fax: 21–761 4193

THEOLOGICAL COLLEGE
The College of the Transfiguration, PO Box 77, Grahamstown 6140 (*Warden* Vacancy)

CHURCH PAPER
Anglican New Life, PO Box 411, Bloemfontein 9300

BLOEMFONTEIN
Bishop Rt Revd Patrick Glover, PO Box 411, Bloemfontein 9300   *Fax*: 51 447–5874
email: rabdsc@global.co.za

Bishop Suffragan Vacancy

CAPE TOWN
Archbishop Most Revd Njongonkulu Winston Hugh Ndungane (*Archbishop of Cape Town and*

Metropolitan of Southern Africa), 16–20
Bishopscourt Drive, Claremont, Cape 7700
Fax: 21 761–4193
email: archbish@iafrica.com

Bishops Suffragan
Rt Revd Mervyn Edwin Castle, PO Box 2804,
Somerset West 7129   Fax: 21 852 9430
email: mcastle@cpsa.org.za

Rt Revd Edward Mackenzie, 39 Paradise Rd,
Newlands, 7700   Fax: 21 465 1571
email: emackenz@cpsa.org.za

Rt Revd John Christopher Gregorowski, PO Box
1932, Cape Town 8001   Fax: 21 465 7686
email: tablebay@cpsa.org.za

CHRIST THE KING
Bishop Rt Revd Peter John Lee, PO Box 1653,
Rosettenville 2130   Fax: 11 435 2868
email: dioctk@cpsa.org.za

GEORGE
Bishop Rt Revd Donald Frederick Harker, PO Box
227, George 6530, Cape Province Fax: 44 873 2267
email: dharker@intekom.co.za

GRAHAMSTOWN
Bishop Rt Revd David Patrick Hamilton Russell,
PO Box 162, Grahamstown 6140, Cape Province
6140   Fax: 27 46 622 5231
email: bpgtn@intekom.co.za

Bishop Suffragan Rt Revd Bethlehem Nopece, PO
Box 1772, Queenstown 5320   Fax: 45 8382874
email: bishopnopece@intekom.co.za

HIGHVELD
Bishop Rt Revd David Albert Beetge, PO Box 563,
Brakpan 1540   Fax: 11 740 9156
email: dbeetge@cpsa.org.za

JOHANNESBURG
Bishop Rt Revd Brian Charles Germond, PO Box
1131, Johannesburg 2000   Fax: 11 333–3053
email: jhbishop@cpsa.org.za

KIMBERLEY AND KURUMAN
Bishop Rt Revd Itumeleng Baldwin Moseki, PO
Box 45, Kimberley 8300   Fax: 53 831 2730
email: opswartz@cpsa.org.za

KLERKSDORP
Bishop Rt Revd David Cecil Tapi Nkwe, PO Box
11417, Klerksdorp 2570   Fax: 18 462–4939
email: dnkwe@wn.apc.org

LEBOMBO
Bishop Rt Revd Dinis Salomâo Sengulane, CP
120, Maputo, Mozambique   Fax: 92581 401093
email: libombo@zebra.uem.mz

LESOTHO
Bishop Rt Revd Joseph Mahapu Tsubella, PO Box
87, Maseru 100, Lesotho   Fax: 266 310 161
email: jandjgay@lesloff.com

NAMIBIA
Bishop Rt Revd Nehemiah Shihala Hamupembe,
PO Box 57, Windhoek, Namibia
Fax: 926461 225903

Bishop Suffragan Rt Revd Petrus Hilukiluah, PO
Box 663, Ohangwena, Namibia
Fax: 264 65 267 670

NATAL
Bishop Rt Revd Rubin Phillip, PO Box 899,
Pietermaritzburg 3200   Fax: 331 948 785
email: rphillip@cpsa.org.za

Bishop Suffragan
Rt Revd Matthew M. Makhaye, PO Box 463,
Ladysmith 3370   Fax: 36 637 4949
email: mmakhaye@interkom.co.za

NIASSA
Bishop Rt Revd Paulino Tomas Manhique, CP
264, Lichinga, Niassa, Mozambique
Fax: 9258 71–2336
email: anglican-niassa@maf.org.mz

BISHOP FOR THE ORDER OF ETHIOPIA
Rt Revd Sigqibo Dwane, PO Box 46803, Glos-
derry, Cape 7708   Fax: 21 683 0008

PORT ELIZABETH
Bishop Rt Revd Eric Pike, PO Box 7109, Newton
Park 6055   Fax: 41 365 2049
email: epike@cpsa.org.za

PRETORIA
Bishop Rt Revd Johannes Seoka, PO Box 1032,
Pretoria 0001   Fax: 12 322 9411
email: ptabish@cpsa.org.za

Bishop Suffragan Rt Revd Robin Briggs, PO Box
187, White River 1240   Fax: 13 750 0773
email: robin.briggs@cpsa.org.za

ST HELENA
Bishop Rt Revd John William Salt, PO Box 62,
Island of St Helena, South Atlantic Ocean
Fax: 290 4330

ST JOHN'S
Bishop Vacancy, PO Box 163, 1 Callaway St,
Umtata, Transkei   Fax: 471 312 474

ST MARK THE EVANGELIST
Bishop Rt Revd Martin Andre Breytenbach, PO
Box 643, Pietersburg 0700   Fax: 15 297 0408
email: stmarks@pixie.co.za

ANGLICAN AND PORVOO COMMUNIONS

SWAZILAND
Bishop Rt Revd Lawrence Bekisisa Zulu, PO Box 118, Mbabane, Swaziland   *Fax*: 268 4046759

UMZIMVUBU
Bishop Rt Revd Geoffrey Francis Davies, PO Box 644, Kokstad 4700   *Fax*: 37 727 4117
email: mzimvubu@cpsa.org.za

ZULULAND
Bishop Rt Revd Anthony Mdletshe, PO Box 147, Eshowe 3815   *Fax*: 354 42 047
email: zlddio@netactive.co.za

THE ORDER OF ETHIOPIA is a body which in August 1900 approached and petitioned the archbishop and the bishops of the Church of the Province for a share in the graces and mercies which God has bestowed upon his Catholic Church, viz. valid episcopate and priesthood. The Order is an integral part of the Church of the Province of Southern Africa and adheres to its liturgy, rites and discipline. Its priests are trained at Anglican theological colleges.

The Order is independent and manages its own affairs.

All Order churches are open to all people without distinction of race or colour.

The Order has a Constitution approved by the Provincial Synod. The annual Conference is its legislative body.The Provincial Synod of 1979 made provision for a bishop for the Order who is recognized as a bishop of the province and who also acts as Provincial of the Order. The Rt Revd Sigqibo Dwane was consecrated first bishop in April 1983. The Archbishop of Cape Town is the Visitor.

The Order works chiefly in the Dioceses of Cape Town, George, Port Elizabeth, Grahamstown, St John's (Transkei), Johannesburg, Kimberley and Kuruman and Natal.

The Anglican Church of the Southern Cone of America

Members 22,490
British immigrants brought Anglicanism to South America in the nineteenth century. The South American Missionary Society continues to work effectively among indigenous peoples. In 1974 the Archbishop of Canterbury gave over his metropolitical authority for the dioceses of the Southern Cone, and in 1981 the new province was formed. It includes Argentina, Bolivia, Chile, Paraguay, Peru and Uruguay.

Presiding Bishop Rt Revd Maurice Sinclair, Casilla de Correo 187, CP 4400, Salta, Argentina
Fax: 87–31–2622
email: sinclair@salnet.com.ar

Provincial Secretary Sr Rolando Dalmas, Reconquista 522, 11000 Montevideo, Uruguay

Provincial Treasurer Sr Teodosio Rivas, Casilla 1124, Asunción, Paraguay

THEOLOGICAL EDUCATION
Planned and carried out by a Theological Education Commission which selects candidates, applies grants and sets courses of study, some of which are led by clergy of the diocese. Some students follow courses of theological training 'by extension' and others attend ecumenical seminaries.

ARGENTINA
Bishop Rt Revd David Leake, CC. 4293, 1000 Correo Central, Argentina   *Fax*: 11 4331 0234
email: diocesisanglibue@arnet.com.ar

BOLIVIA
Bishop Rt Revd Gregory Venables, Casilla 9574, La Paz, Bolivia   *Fax*: 2 371 414
email: bpgreg@megalink.com

CHILE
Bishop Rt Revd Tito Zavala, Casilla 50675, Correo Central, Santiago, Chile   *Fax*: 2 639 4581
email: tzavala@red6.mic.cl

Assistant Bishop Rt Revd Abelino Apeleo, Casilla de Correo 26-D, Temuco, Chile   *Fax*: 45 211 130

NORTHERN ARGENTINA
Bishop Rt Revd Maurice Sinclair (*Bishop of Northern Argentina and Primate of the Province of the Southern Cone of America*), Casilla de Correo 187, CP 4400, Salta, Argentina   *Fax*: 387 4312 622
email: sinclair@salnet.com.ar

Assistant Bishops
Rt Revd Humberto Axt (*same address*)

Rt Revd Mario Lorenzo Mariño, Casilla 19, 3636 Ingeniero Juárez, Formosa, Argentina

PARAGUAY
Bishop Rt Revd John Ellison, Iglesia Anglicana Paraguya, Casilla de Correo 1124, Asunción, Paraguay   *Fax*: 21 214 328
email: butellis@pla.net.py

PERU
Bishop Rt Revd Harold William Godfrey, c/o Apartado 18–1032 Miraflores, Lima 18, Peru
Fax: 1 445 3044
email: godfrey@telematic.com.pe

URUGUAY
Bishop Rt Revd Migel Tamayo Zaldivar, CC 6108, Montevideo, CP11000, Uruguay   *Fax*: 2 916 251
email: mtamayo@netgate.com.uy

The Church of the Province of the Sudan

Members 2,000,000

The Church Missionary Society began work in 1899 in Ombudman; Christianity spread rapidly among black Africans of the southern region. Until 1974, the diocese of Sudan was part of the Jerusalem archbishopric. It reverted to the jurisdiction of the Archbishop of Canterbury until the new province, consisting of four new dioceses, was established in 1976. Civil and religious strife and a constant flow of refugees have challenged the Church. Its heroic witness to faith in Christ continues to inspire the Anglican Communion and its people.

Archbishop Vacancy, c/o PO Box 52802, Nairobi, Kenya

Provincial Secretary Revd Nelson K. Nyumbe, PO Box 110, Juba, Sudan

Acting Provincial Treasurer Mr Joel Lupin (*same address*)

THEOLOGICAL COLLEGE
Bishop Gwynne College, Juba, Equatoria (*Principal* Canon Micah Laila Dawidi)

CHURCH NEWS LETTER
News Letter of the Episcopal Church of the Sudan Monthly. Covers news of the whole province. *Editor* PO Box 47429, Nairobi, Kenya

BOR
Bishop Rt Revd Nathaniel Garang Angleth, c/o NSCC, PO Box 52802, Nairobi, Kenya

CUEIBET
Bishop Rt Revd Reuben Macir Makoi, c/o CEAS, PO Box 40870, Nairobi, Kenya *Fax*: 254 2 570 807

EL OBEID
Bishop Rt Revd Ismail Abudigin Kawo Gibreil, PO Box 65, Omdurman, Sudan

EZZO
Bishop Rt Revd Benjamin Ruati, c/o NSCC, PO Box 52802, Nairobi, Kenya *Fax*: 447 015

IBBA
Bishop Rt Revd Levi Hassan Nzakara, c/o PO Box 110, Juba, Sudan

JUBA
Bishop Vacancy, PO Box 110, Juba, Sudan

KADUGULI AND NUBA MOUNTAINS
Bishop Rt Revd Peter Kuthurdu Elbersh Kowa, c/o PO Box 65, Omdurman, Sudan

KAJO-KEJI
Bishop Rt Revd Manasseh Dawidi Binyi, c/o NSCC, PO Box 52802, Nairobi, Kenya

KHARTOUM
Bishop Rt Revd Bulus Idris Tia, PO Box 65, Omdurman, Sudan

LAINYA
Bishop Rt Revd Eliaba Ladu Menesona, c/o PO Box 110, Juba, Sudan

LUI
Bishop Rt Revd Bullen A. Dolli, PO Box 3364, Khartoum, Sudan

MALAKAL
Bishop Rt Revd Kedhekia Mabior, c/o NSCC, PO Box 52802, Nairobi, Kenya

MARIDI
Bishop Rt Revd Joseph Biringi Hassan Marona, PO Box 676, Arua, Uganda *Fax*: 447 015

MUNDRI
Bishop Rt Revd Eluzai Gima Munda, PO Box 110, Juba, Sudan

PORT SUDAN
Bishop Rt Revd Yousif Abdalla Kuku, PO Box 278, Red Sea State, Sudan

REJAF
Bishop Rt Revd Michael Sokiri Lugor, PO Box 110, Juba, Sudan

RENK
Bishop Rt Revd Daniel Deng Bul Yak, PO Box 1532, Khartoum, Sudan *Fax*: 249 11 775 742

ROKON
Bishop Rt Revd Francis Loyo, PO Box 60837, Nairobi, Kenya

RUMBEK
Bishop Rt Revd Gabriel Roric Jur, PO Box 65, Omdurman, Sudan *Fax*: 249 11 777 100

TORIT
Bishop Rt Revd Wilson Arop Ogwok Ocheng, c/o Church of Uganda, PO Box 14123, Kampala, Uganda *Fax*: 256 41 254 423

WAU
Bishop Rt Revd Henry Cuir Riak, All Saint's Cathedral, PO Box 135, Khartoum, Sudan

YAMBIO
Bishop Rt Revd Peter Munde Yacoub, ECS-Kampala Office, PO Box 7576, Kampala, Uganda *email*: ecs-kla@maf.org

YEI
Bishop Rt Revd Seme L. Solomona, c/o PO Box 370, Arua, Uganda

YIROL
Bishop Rt Revd Benjamin Mangar Mamur, c/o All Saint's Cathedral, PO Box 3364, Khartoum, Sudan

ANGLICAN AND PORVOO COMMUNIONS

The Anglican Church of Tanzania

Members 1,379,366

The Universities Mission to Central Africa and the Church Missionary Society began work in 1864 and 1878 at Mpwapa. The province was inaugurated in 1970 following the division of the Province of East Africa into the Province of Kenya and the Province of Tanzania. The 16 dioceses represent both evangelical and Anglo-Catholic Churches.

Archbishop Most Revd Donald Leo Mtetemela (*Bishop of Ruaha*), PO Box 1028, Iringa, Tanzania
Fax: 64 2479

Dean Rt Revd Gerald Mpango, PO Box 13, Kasulu, Tanzania

Provincial Secretary Canon Mkunga Mtingele, PO Box 899, Dodoma, Tanzania

Provincial Treasurer Mr John Maligana, PO Box 2, Mpwapwa, Tanzania

Provincial Registrar Mr Dominic Mbezi, PO Box 103, Dodoma, Tanzania

THEOLOGICAL COLLEGES
St Philip's Theological College, PO Box 26, Kongwa, Tanzania (*Acting Principal* Revd Boniface Kwangu)

St Mark's Theological College, PO Box 25017, Dar es Salaam, Tanzania (*Principal* Canon Lawrence Mnubi)

CHURCH NEWSPAPER
Sauti ya Jimbo Quarterly newspaper in Swahili and English containing diocesan, provincial and world church news. *Editor* c/o Provincial Secretary

CENTRAL TANGANYIKA
Bishop Rt Revd Godfrey Mdimi Mhogolo, PO Box 15, Dodoma, Tanzania   *Fax*: 255 61 320 004
email: mhogolo@maf.org

Assistant Bishop Rt Revd John Ball (*same address*)

DAR ES SALAAM
Bishop Rt Revd Basil Mattiya Sambano, PO Box 25016, Ilala, Dar es Salaam, Tanzania
Fax: 255 51 153 042

KAGERA
Bishop Rt Revd Aaron Kijanjali, PO Box 18, Ngara, Tanzania   *Fax*: 255 871 176 0266

MARA
Bishop Rt Revd Hilkiah Deya Omindo, PO Box 131, Musoma, Tanzania   *Fax*: 255 68 662 414
email: MaraCPT@maf.org

MASASI
Bishop Rt Revd Patrick Mwachiko, Private Bag, PO Masasi, Mtwara Region, Tanzania

MOROGORO
Bishop Rt Revd Dudley Mageni, PO Box 320, Morogoro, Tanzania   *email*: phunter@maf.org

MOUNT KILIMANJARO
Bishop Rt Revd Simon Elilekia Makundi, PO Box 1057, Arusha, Tanzania
email: DMK@khabari.co.tz

MPWAPWA
Bishop Rt Revd Simon Chiwanga, PO Box 2, Mpwapwa, Tanzania
email: SEChiwanga@aol.com

RIFT VALLEY
Bishop Rt Revd Alpha Francis Mohamed, PO Box 16, Manyoni, Tanzania   *Fax*: 255 61 324 565

RUAHA
Bishop Most Revd Donald Leo Mtetemela (*Bishop of Ruaha and Archbishop of the Province*), PO Box 1028, Iringa, Tanzania   *Fax*: 255 61 702 479

RUVUMA
Bishop Rt Revd Maternus Kapinga, PO Box 1, Liuli, Mbinga District, Tanzania

SOUTHERN HIGHLANDS
Bishop Rt Revd John Mwela, PO Box 198, Mbeya, Tanzania

SOUTH-WEST TANGANYIKA
Bishop Vacancy, PO Box 32, Njombe, Tanzania

TABORA
Bishop Rt Revd Francis Nzaganya Ntiruka, PO Box 1408, Tabora, Tanzania   *Fax*: 255 62 4899

VICTORIA NYANZA
Bishop Rt Revd John Paul Changae, PO Box 278, Mwanza, Tanzania

WESTERN TANGANYIKA
Bishop Rt Revd Gerard Mpango, PO Box 13, Kasulu, Tanzania   *Fax*: 255 695 3434

ZANZIBAR AND TANGA
Bishop Rt Revd John Acland Ramadhani, PO Box 35, Korogwe, Tanzania   *Fax*: 255 61 324 565

The Church of the Province of Uganda

Members 8,000,000

After its founding in 1877 by the Church Missionary Society, the Church grew through the evangelization of Africa by Africans. The first Ugandan clergy were ordained in 1893 and the Church of Uganda, Rwanda and Burundi became an independent province in 1961. The history of the Church in Uganda has been marked by civil strife and martyrdom. In May 1980 the new province of Burundi, Rwanda and Zaire was inaugurated; the Province of Uganda has since grown from 17 to 27 dioceses.

Archbishop of the Province Most Revd Livingstone Mpalanyi-Nkoyoyo (*Bishop of Kampala*)

Provincial Secretary Canon George K. Tibeesigwa

Provincial Treasurer Mr Moses Makasa

Primatial and Provincial Headquarters PO Box 14123, Kampala, Uganda
email: coups@uol.co.ug

THEOLOGICAL COLLEGES
Bishop Tucker Theological College, PO Box 4, Mukono (*Principal* Revd E. Maari)

Bishop Balya College, PO Box 368, Fort-Portal (*Principal* Revd Y. Kule)

Canon Barham Divinity College, PO Box 3, Kabale (*Principal* Canon Kamagara)

Mityana Theological Training College, PO Box 102, Mityana (*Principal* Revd Mukasa-Mutambuze)

Ngora Diocesan Training Centre, PO Box 1, Ngora (*Principal* Revd S. Amuret)

Namugongo Martyrs Seminary, PO Box 20183, Lugogo, K'la (*Principal* Revd S. Sekadde)

Aduku Diocesan Theological College, PO Aduku, Lira (*Principal* Revd S. O. Obura)

Kabwohe College, PO Kabwohe, Mbarara (*Principal* Revd Y. R. Buremu)

Ringili College, PO Box 370, Arua (*Principal* Revd P. Nigo)

CHURCH PAPER
The New Century Published monthly. Contains diocesan, provincial and world church news and items of general interest. *Editorial and business office* PO Box 6246, Kampala, Uganda

BUKEDI
Bishop Rt Revd Nicodemus Engwalas-Okille, PO Box 170, Tororo, Uganda

BUNYORO-KITARA
Bishop Rt Revd Wilson Nkuna Turumanya, PO Box 20, Hoima, Uganda   *Fax*: 256 465 40 399

BUSOGA
Bishop Vacancy, PO Box 1658, Jinja, Uganda
Fax: 256 43 20 547

CENTRAL BUGANDA
Bishop Rt Revd George Sinabulya, PO Box 1200, Karoni-Gomba, Mpigi, Uganda
Fax: 256 41 242 724

EAST ANKOLE
Bishop Rt Revd Elisha Kyamugambi, PO Box 14, Mbarara, Ankole, Uganda

KAMPALA
Bishop Most Revd Livingstone Mpalanyi-Nkoyoyo (*Archbishop of Uganda and Bishop of Kampala*), PO Box 14123, Kampala, Uganda
Fax: 256 41 251 925
email: couab@uol.co.ug

Assistant Bishop Rt Revd Eliphaz Maari, PO Box 335, Kampala, Uganda   *Fax*: 256 41 342 601

KARAMOJA
Bishop Rt Revd Peter Lomongin, c/o MAF, PO Box 1, Kampala, Uganda

KIGEZI
Bishop Rt Revd George Katwesigye, PO Box 14123, Kampala, Uganda   *Fax*: 256 486 22 447

KINKIZI
Bishop Rt Revd John Ntegyereize, PO Box 77, Karuhinda, Rukungiri, Uganda

KITGUM
Bishop Rt Revd Macleord Baker Ochola II Ameda Mollo, PO Box 187, Kitgum, Uganda

LANGO
Bishop Rt Revd Melchizedek Otim, PO Box 6, Lira, Uganda

LUWERO
Bishop Rt Revd Evans Mukasa Kisekka, PO Box 125, Luwero, Uganda   *Fax*: 256 41 610 132

MADI AND WEST NILE
Bishop Rt Revd Enock Lee Drati, PO Box 370, Arua, Uganda

MBALE
Bishop Rt Revd Samwiri Namakhetsa Khaemba Wabulakha, Bishop's House, PO Box 473, Mbale, Uganda

MITYANA
Bishop Rt Revd Wilson Mutebi, PO Box 102, Mityana, Uganda

MUHABURA
Bishop Rt Revd Ernest Shalita, Church of Uganda, PO Box 22, Kisoro, Uganda

MUKONO
Bishop Rt Revd Michael Solomon Ndawula Senyimba, PO Box 39, Mukono, Uganda

NAMIREMBE
Bishop Rt Revd Samuel Balagadde Ssekkadde, PO Box 14297, Kampala, Uganda

NEBBI
Bishop Rt Revd Henry Orombi, PO Box 27, Nebbi, Uganda

NORTH KIGEZI
Bishop Rt Revd John Kahigwa, PO Box 23, Rukungiri, Uganda

NORTH MBALE
Bishop Rt Revd Nathan Muwombi, Bishop's House, PO Box 1837, Mbale, Uganda
Fax: 256 41 254 576

NORTHERN UGANDA
Bishop Rt Revd Nelson Onono-Onweng, PO Box 232, Gulu, Uganda   *Fax*: 250 828

RUWENZORI
Bishop Rt Revd Benezeri Kisembo, Bishop's House, PO Box 37, Fort Portal, Uganda
Fax: 256 493 22 636

SEBEI
Bishop Rt Revd Augustine Joe Arapyona Salimo, PO Box 23, Kapchorwa, Uganda

SOROTI
Bishop Rt Revd Geresom Ilukor, PO Box 107, Soroti, Uganda

SOUTH RUWENZORI
Bishop Rt Revd Zebedee Masereka, PO Box 142, Kasese, Uganda   *Fax*: 256 483 44 450
email: bishopzmase@uge.healthnet

WEST ANKOLE
Bishop Rt Revd William Magambo, PO Box 140, Bushenyi, Uganda   *Fax*: 256 485 21 304

WEST BUGANDA
Bishop Rt Revd Samuel Wakuze Kamya, PO Box 242, Masaka, Uganda

The Episcopal Church in the United States of America

Members 2,400,000
Anglicanism was brought to the New World by explorers and colonists with the first celebration of the Holy Eucharist in Jamestown, Virginia in 1607. There was no resident bishop for nearly two hundred years, causing problems when many of the clergy sided with the Crown during the American Revolution. In 1784 the Scottish Episcopal Church consecrated the first American bishop. The Church maintains 98 dioceses plus 20 overseas jurisdictions. The province is a strong base of support to the Anglican Communion and has a significant crisis ministry through the Presiding Bishop's Fund for World Relief.

Presiding Bishop Most Revd Frank Tracy Griswold III

President, House of Deputies Dr Pamela Chinnis

Executive Officer, The General Convention and Secretary, The Executive Council Revd Rosemari Sullivan

Secretary, House of Bishops Rt Revd Mary Adelia McLeod

Offices of the Episcopal Church and its Departments Episcopal Church Center, 815 Second Ave, New York, NY 10017

NATIONAL SEMINARIES
California
Church Divinity School of the Pacific, 2451 Ridge Rd, Berkeley, CA 94709 (*Dean* Very Revd Dr D. F. Morgan)

Connecticut
Berkeley Divinity School at Yale University, 363 St Ronan St, New Haven, CT 06511 (*Dean* Mr William Franklin)

Illinois
Seabury-Western Theological Seminary, 2122 Sheridan Rd, Evanston, IL 60201 (*Dean* Very Revd James Lemler)

Massachusetts
Episcopal Divinity School, 99 Brattle St, Cambridge, MA 02138 (*Dean* Very Revd Steven Charleston)

New York
Bexley Hall, 1110 South Goodman St, Rochester, NY 14620 (*Dean* Very Revd John Kevern)

The General Theological Seminary of the Protestant Episcopal Church in the United States, 175 Ninth Ave, New York, NY 10011 (*Dean* Very Revd Ward Ewing)

Philadelphia
Trinity Episcopal School for Ministry, 311 Eleventh St, Ambridge, PA 15003 (*Dean* Very Revd Peter Moore)

Tennessee
School of Theology of the University of the South, Sewanee, TN 37375 (*Dean* Very Revd Guy E. Lytle, III)

Texas
The Episcopal Theological Seminary of the Southwest, PO Box 2247, Austin, TX 78768 (*Dean* Very Revd D. McDonald)

Virginia
Virginia Theological Seminary, Alexandria, VA 22304 (*Dean* Very Revd Martha Horne)

Wisconsin
Nashotah House, Nashotah, WI 53058 (*Provost* Very Revd Gary Kriss)

CHURCH PAPERS
Episcopal Life An independently edited, officially sponsored monthly newspaper published by The Domestic and Foreign Missionary Society of the Episcopal Church, 815 Second Ave, New York NY 10017, upon authority of the General Convention of the Protestant Episcopal Church in the USA.

The Living Church Weekly magazine. *Editorial and Business Offices* 407 E. Michigan St, Milwaukee, WI 53202. Contains news and features about Christianity in general and the Episcopal Church in particular.

ALABAMA (Province IV)
Bishop Rt Revd Henry Nutt Parsley Jr, Carpenter House, 521 N. 20th St, Birmingham AL 35203
Fax: 205 715 2066
email: DioAla@aol.com

ALASKA (Province VIII)
Bishop Rt Revd Mark Lawrence MacDonald, 1205 Denali Way, Fairbanks, Alaska 99701–4178
Fax: 907 456 6552
email: mark.macdonald@ecunet.org

ALBANY (Province II)
Bishop Rt Revd Daniel William Herzog, 62 So. Swan St, Albany NY 12210   *Fax*: 518 436 1182
email: dherzog@christcom.net

ARIZONA (Province VIII)
Bishop Rt Revd Robert Reed Shahan, 114 West Roosevelt St, Phoenix AZ 85003
Fax: 602 495 6603
email: ROBERT_SHAHAN@ecunet.org

ARKANSAS (Province VII)
Bishop Rt Revd Larry Earl Maze, Cathedral House, PO Box 164668, Little Rock AR 72216
Fax: 501 372 2147
email: Bishopmaze@aol.com

ATLANTA (Province IV)
Bishop Rt Revd Robert Gustave Trache, 2744 Peachtree Rd, NW Atlanta GA 30363
Fax: 404 261 2515
email: fallan@mindspring.com

BETHLEHEM (Province III)
Bishop Rt Revd Paul Victor Marshall, 333 Wyandotte St, Bethlehem PA 18015
Fax: 610 691 1683
email: Paul.Marshall@ecunet.org

CALIFORNIA (Province VIII)
Bishop Rt Revd William Edwin Swing, 1055 Taylor St, San Francisco CA 94108
Fax: 415 673 9268
email: bishop@diocal.org

Assisting Bishops
Rt Revd George Richard Millard, 1812 Sandhill Rd, 311, Palo Alta CA 14304–2136;

Rt Revd John R. Wyatt, 1204 Chelsa Way, Redwood City CA 44061

CENTRAL ECUADOR (Province IX)
Bishop Rt Revd Jose Neptali Larrea-Moreno, Av Amazonas 4430 Y Villalengua, Piso 7 Oficina 708, Edificio Banco Amazonas, Quito, Ecuador
Fax: 2 252 226

CENTRAL FLORIDA (Province IV)
Bishop Rt Revd John Howe, Diocesan Office, 1017 E Robinson St, Orlando, Florida 32801–2023
Fax: 407 872 006
email: bcf3@aol.com

Assistant Bishop Rt Revd Hugo Pina-Lopez (*same address*)   *Fax*: 407 872 0096

CENTRAL GULF COAST (Province IV)
Bishop Rt Revd Charles Farmer Duvall, Box 13330, Pensacola, Florida 32591–3330
Fax: 904 434 8577
email: staff@diocgc.org

CENTRAL NEW YORK (Province II)
Bishop Vacancy, 310 Montgomery St, Suite 200, Syracuse NY 13202–2093   *Fax*: 315 478 1632

CENTRAL PENNSYLVANIA (Province III)
Bishop Rt Revd Michael Whittington Creighton, 221 N. Front St, Box 11937, Harrisburg PA 17108–1937   *Fax*: 717 236 6448
email: bishopcpa@aol.com

CHICAGO (Province V)
Bishop Rt Revd William Persell, 65 E. Huron St, Chicago IL 60611   *Fax*: 312 787 4534

Bishop Suffragan Rt Revd William W. Wiedrich (*same address*)

COLOMBIA (Province IX)
Bishop Rt Revd Bernardo Merino-Botero, Apartado Aereo 52964, Bogota 2, Colombia SA
Fax: 1 288 3248

COLORADO (Province VI)
Bishop Rt Revd William Winterrowd, 1300 Washington St, Denver CO 80203
Fax: 303 837 1311

Assisting Bishop Rt Revd William H. Wolfrum

CONNECTICUT (Province I)
Bishop Rt Revd Andrew Donnan Smith, 1335 Asylum Ave, Hartford CT 06105–2295
Fax: 860 523 1410
email: adsmith@ctdiocese.org

DALLAS (Province VII)
Bishop Rt Revd James Monte Stanton, 1630 North Garrett Ave, Dallas TX 75206
Fax: 214 826 5968
email: jmsdallas@aol.com

Bishop Suffragan Rt Revd David Bruce MacPherson (*same address*)

DELAWARE (Province III)
Bishop Rt Revd Wayne Parker Wright, 2020 Tatnall St, Wilmington DE 19802
Fax: 302 656 7342
email: wright@delanet.com

DOMINICAN REPUBLIC (Province IX)
Bishop Rt Revd Julio Cesar Holguin Khoury, Apartado 764, Calle Santiago No 114, Santo Domingo, Dominican Republic
Fax: 809 686 6364
email: h.rkhoury@codetel.net.do

EAST CAROLINA (Province IV)
Bishop Rt Revd Clifton Daniel, PO Box 1336, Kinston NC 27803   *Fax*: 919 523 5272
email: diocese.ec@coastalnet.com

Assisting Bishop Rt Revd C. Charles Vaché

EAST TENNESSEE
Bishop Rt Revd Charles von Rosenberg, 401 Cumberland Ave, Knoxville, Tennessee 37902–2302   *Fax*: 615 521 2905

EASTERN MICHIGAN
Bishop Rt Revd Edward Max Leidel Jr, Diocesan Office, 924 N Niagara St, Saginaw, Michigan 48602   *Fax*: 517 752 6120
email: ed.leidel@ecunet.org

EASTERN OREGON (Province VIII)
Bishop Rt Revd Rustin Ray Kimsey, PO Box 620, The Dalles, Oregon 97058   *Fax*: 541 298 7875
email: edeo@gorge.net

Bishop Elect (Alexander) James Mackenzie

EASTON (Province III)
Bishop Rt Revd Martin Gough Townsend, Box 1027, Easton MD 21601   *Fax*: 410 763 8259
email: MARTIN_TOWNSEND@ecunet.org

EAU CLAIRE (Province V)
Bishop Rt Revd Keith Whitmore, 510 So. Farwell St, Eau Claire WI 54701   *Fax*: 715 835 9212
email: w750dec@aol.com

EL CAMINO REAL (Province VIII)
Bishop Rt Revd Richard L. Shimpfky, Box 1903 Monterey, CA 93940   *Fax*: 408 394 7133
email: saltig@aol.com

EUROPE, CONVOCATION OF AMERICAN CHURCHES IN
Bishop Vacancy, 23 Avenue George V, 75008 Paris, France   *Fax*: 1 4723 9530
email: rowthorn@american-cath.assoc.fr

FLORIDA (Province IV)
Bishop Rt Revd Stephen Hays Jecko, 325 Market St, Jacksonville FL 32202   *Fax*: 904 355 1934
email: bfl7@crci.net

FOND DU LAC (Province V)
Bishop Rt Revd Russell Edward Jacobus, PO Box 149, Fond du Lac WI 54936–0149
Fax: 920 921 8761
email: plusruss@vbe.com

FORMOSA
See Missionary Diocese of Taiwan

FORT WORTH (Province VII)
Bishop Rt Revd Jack Leo Iker, 6300 Ridglea Place, Suite 1100, Fort Worth, Texas 76116
Fax: 817 738 9955
email: jliker@dfw.net

GEORGIA (Province IV)
Bishop Rt Revd Henry Irving Loutitt Jr, 611 E Bay St, Savannah GA 31401–1296   *Fax*: 912 236 2007

HAITI (Province II)
Bishop Rt Revd Jean Zache Duracin, Eglise Episcopale d'Haiti, PO Box 1309, Port-au-Prince, Haiti   *Fax*: 57 3412
email: epihaiti@globalsud.net

HAWAII (Province VIII)
Bishop Rt Revd Richard Sui On Chang, Diocesan Office, 229 Queen Emma Sq, Honolulu HI 96813–2304   *Fax*: 808 538 7194
email: rsoc@aloha.net

HONDURAS (Province IX)
Bishop Rt Revd Leopold Frade, Apartado Postal 586, San Pedro Sula, Honduras CA *Fax*: 556 6467
email: episcopal@mayanet.hn

IDAHO (Province VIII)
Bishop Rt Revd Harry Bainbridge, PO Box 936, Boise ID 83701   *Fax*: 208 345 9735
email: bishopb@micron.net

INDIANAPOLIS (Province V)
Bishop Rt Revd Catherine Elizabeth Maples Waynick, 1100 W. 42nd St, Indianapolis IN 46208
Fax: 317 926 5456
email: hob929@aol.com

IOWA (Province VI)
Bishop Rt Revd Christopher Epting, 225 37th St, Des Moines IA 50312   *Fax*: 515 277 0273
email: BISHOP.EPTING@ecunet.org

ANSAS (Province VII)
Bishop Rt Revd William Smalley, Bethany Place,
33–35 Polk St, Topeka KS 66612
Fax: 913 235 2449
email: wsmalley@espicopal-ks.org

KENTUCKY (Province IV)
Bishop Rt Revd Edwin Funsten Gulick, 600 East
Main St, Louisville KY 40202   Fax: 502 587 8123
email: TGULICK@ecunet.org

LEXINGTON (Province IV)
Bishop Vacancy, PO Box 610, Lexington KY 40586
Fax: 606 231 9077

Assisting Bishop Rt Revd Rogers Harris (same
address)

**LITORAL DIOCESE OF ECUADOR (Province
X)**
Bishop Rt Revd Alfredo Morante-Arevalo, Box
901–5250, Amarilis Fuentes entre V Trusillo, y
La 'D', Guayaquil, Equador   Fax: 4 443 088

LONG ISLAND (Province II)
Bishop Rt Revd Orris Walker Jr, 36 Cathedral
Ave, Garden City, NY 11530   Fax: 516 248 4883
email: dioceseli@aol.com

Bishop Suffragan Rt Revd Rodney Rae Michel
(same address)

LOS ANGELES (Province VIII)
Bishop Rt Revd Frederick Houk Borsch, Box
2164, Los Angeles CA 90051   Fax: 213 482 5304
email: Bishop@ladiocese.org

Bishop Suffragan Rt Revd Chester L. Talton (same
address)   email: suffragan@ladiocese.org

Coadjutor Bishop Joseph Jon Bruno

LOUISIANA (Province IV)
Bishop Rt Revd Charles Edward Jenkins III, 1623
Seventh St, New Orleans LA 70115–4111
Fax: 504 895 6637
email: revchuck@worldnet.att.net

MAINE (Province I)
Bishop Rt Revd Chilton Abbie Richardson
Knudsen, Loring House, 143 State St, Portland
ME 04101   Fax: 207 773 0095
email: Chilton_knudsen@ecunet.org

MARYLAND (Province III)
Bishop Rt Revd Robert Wilkes Ihloff, 4 East
University Parkway, Baltimore MD 21218
Fax: 410 554 6387
email: rihloff@ang-md.org

Bishop Suffragan Rt Revd John Leslie Rabb (same
address)

MASSACHUSETTS (Province I)
Bishop Rt Revd Thomas Shaw SSJE, Society of St
John the Evangelist, 980 Memorial Drive,
Cambridge, MA 02138   Fax: 617 482 8431

Bishop Suffragan Rt Revd Barbara Harris, 138
Tremont St, Boston MA 02111   Fax: 617 482 8431
email: BARBARA.HARRIS@ecunet.org

MICHIGAN (Province V)
Bishop Rt Revd Stewart Wood, 4800 Woodward
Ave, Detroit MI 48201   Fax: 313 831 0259
email: stewwood@aol.com

Coadjutor Bishop Rt Revd Wendell Nathaniel
Gibbs (same address)

MILWAUKEE (Province V)
Bishop Rt Revd Roger J. White, 804 E. Juneau
Ave, Milwaukee WI 53202   Fax: 414 272 7790
email: MILWAUKEE.DIOCESE@ecunet.org

MINNESOTA (Province VI)
Bishop Rt Revd James Louis Jelinek, 1730 Clifton
Place, Suite 201, Minneapolis MN 55403
Fax: 6112 871 0552
email: JIM.JELINEK@ecunet.org

MISSISSIPPI (Province IV)
Bishop Rt Revd Alfred Clark Marble Jr, PO Box
23107, Jackson MS 39225–3107   Fax: 601 354 3401

MISSOURI (Province V)
Bishop Rt Revd Hays Rockwell, 1210 Locust St, St
Louis MO 63103   Fax: 314 231 3373
email: bishop@missouri.anglican.org

MONTANA (Province VI)
Bishop Rt Revd Charles I. Jones, 515 North Park
Ave, Helena MT 59601   Fax: 406 442 2238
email: CI_JONES@ecunet.org

**NAVAJOLAND AREA MISSION (Province
VIII)**
Bishop Rt Revd Steven Tsosie Plummer, Box 720,
Farmington, New Mexico 87499
Fax: 435 672 2369

NEBRASKA (Province VI)
Bishop Rt Revd James Edward Krotz, 200 N.
62nd St, Omaha NB 68132–6357
Fax: 402 558 0094
email: Diocese_of_Nebraska@ecunet.org

NEVADA (Province VIII)
Bishop Rt Revd Stewart C. Zabriskie, 2100 S.
Maryland Parkway, Suite 4, Las Vegas NV 89104
Fax: 702 737 6488
email: diocese.of.nevada@ecunet.org

NEW HAMPSHIRE (Province I)
Bishop Rt Revd Douglas E. Theuner, 63 Green St,
Concord NH 03301   Fax: 603 225 7884
email: DOUGLAS.THEUNER@ecunet.org

NEW JERSEY (Province II)
Bishop Vacancy, 808 W. State St, Trenton NJ 08618
Fax: 609 394 9546

Assisting Bishop Rt Revd David Joslin (same
address)

NEW YORK (Province II)
Bishop Rt Revd Richard Frank Grein, Synod House, 1047 Amsterdam Ave, Cathedral Heights, New York NY 10025 *Fax*: 212 932 7312
email: cybersexton@dioceseny.org

Coadjutor Bishop Rt Revd Mark Sean Sisk (*same address*) *email*: MarkSisk@worldnet.att.net

Assisting Bishop Rt Revd Don Taylor (*same address*) *Fax*: 212 316 7405

Suffragan Bishop Rt Revd Catherine S. Roskam, Region Two Office, 55 Cedar St, Dobbs Ferry, NY 10522 *Fax*: 914 693 0407
email: Glenregli@aol.com

NEWARK (Province II)
Bishop Rt Revd John Shelby Spong, 31 Mulberry St, Newark NJ 07102 *Fax*: 923 622 3503
email: cmsctm@aol.com

Bishop Coadjutor Rt Revd John Palmer Croneberger, Highwood Ave and Engle, Tenafly, NJ 07670

NORTH CAROLINA (Province IV)
Bishop Rt Revd Robert Carroll Johnson Jr, PO Box 17025, Raleigh NC 27619–7025 *Fax*: 919 787 0156
email: DIOCESE.OF.NC@ecunet.org

Bishop Suffragan Rt Revd James Gary Gloster (*same address*)

NORTH DAKOTA (Province VI)
Bishop Rt Revd Andrew Hedtler Fairfield, 33600 25th St (Box 10337), Fargo ND 58106–0337
Fax: 701 232 3077

NORTHERN CALIFORNIA (Province VIII)
Bishop Rt Revd Jerry Lamb, Box 161268, Sacramento CA 95816 *Fax*: 916 442 6927
email: bishopjal@aol.com

NORTHERN INDIANA (Province V)
Bishop Elect Rt Revd Edward Stuart Little, Cathedral House, 117 N. Lafayette Blvd, South Bend, Indiana 46601 *Fax*: 219 287 7914

NORTHERN MICHIGAN (Province V)
Bishop Rt Revd James Kelsey, 131 E. Ridge St, Marquette MI 49855 *Fax*: 906 228 7171

NORTHWEST TEXAS (Province VII)
Bishop Rt Revd C. Wallis Ohl Jr, The Episcopal Church Center, 1802 Broadway, Lubbock TX 79408 *Fax*: 806 472 0641
email: wallisohl@hub.ofthe.net

NORTHWESTERN PENNSYLVANIA (Province III)
Bishop Rt Revd Robert Deane Rowley, 145 W. 6th St, Erie PA 16501 *Fax*: 814 454 8703
email: ROBERT_ROWLEY@ecunet.org

OHIO (Province V)
Bishop Rt Revd J. Clark Grew II, 2230 Euclid Av Cleveland OH 44115–2499 *Fax*: 216 771 925
email: bishop@dohio.or

Bishop Suffragan Rt Revd Arthur Benjami Williams Jr (*same address*) *Fax*: 216 623 073
email: bishsuff@diohio.or

OKLAHOMA (Province VII)
Bishop Rt Revd Robert Moody, 924 N. Robinsor Oklahoma City OK 73102 *Fax*: 405 232 491

OLYMPIA (Province VIII)
Bishop Rt Revd Vincent Warner Jr, Box 1212€ Seattle WA 98102 *Fax*: 206 325 463

OREGON (Province VIII)
Bishop Rt Revd Robert Louis Ladehoff, PO Bo 467, Lake Oswego OR 97034–0467
Fax: 503 636 561
email: robertl@diocese-oregon.or

PENNSYLVANIA (Province III)
Bishop Rt Revd Charles E. Ellsworth Bennison J 240 South Fourth St, Philadelphia PA 19106
Fax: 215 627 775€
email: cbenni4455@aol.con

Bishop Suffragan Rt Revd Franklin Turner (*sam address*)

PITTSBURGH (Province III)
Bishop Rt Revd Robert William Duncan Jr, 32! Oliver Ave, Pittsburgh PA 15222–2467
Fax: 412 471 559}
email: duncan@pgh.anglican.org

QUINCY (Province V)
Bishop Rt Revd Keith Ackerman, 3601 N. Nortl St, Peoria IL 61604 *Fax*: 309 688 822€
email: quincy8@ocslink.com

RHODE ISLAND (Province I)
Bishop Rt Revd Geralyn Wolf, 275 N. Main St Providence RI 02903 *Fax*: 401 331 9430

RIO GRANDE (Province VII)
Bishop Rt Revd Terence Kelshaw, 4304 Carlisle NE, Albuquerque NM 87107–4811
Fax: 505 883 9048
email: tkelshaw@aol.com

ROCHESTER (Province II)
Bishop Rt Revd Jack McKelvey, 935 East Ave, Rochester NY 14607 *Fax*: 716 473 3195

SAN DIEGO (Province VIII)
Bishop Rt Revd Gethin Benwil Hughes, 2728 Sixth Ave, San Diego CA 92103–6397
Fax: 619 291 8362
email: SEE_SANDIEGO@ecunet.org

AN JOAQUIN (Province IV)
Bishop Rt Revd John-David Mercer Schofield, 159 E. Dakota Ave, Fresno CA 93726
Fax: 209 244 4832
email: s.joaquin@genie.geis.com

OUTH CAROLINA (Province IV)
Bishop Rt Revd Edward L. Salmon Jr, Box 20127, Charleston SC 29413–0127   *Fax*: 803 723 7628
email: elsalmon@dioceseofsc.org

Suffragan Bishop Rt Revd William J. Skilton (*same address*)   *email*: bskilton@dioceseofsc.org

SOUTH DAKOTA (Province VI)
Bishop Rt Revd Creighton Robertson, 500 S. Main St, Sioux Falls, South Dakota 57104–6814
Fax: 605 336 6243
email: CREIGHTON_ROBERTSON@ecunet.org

SOUTHEAST FLORIDA (Province IV)
Bishop Rt Revd Calvin Onderdonk Schofield Jr, 525 NE 15 St, Miami FL 33132   *Fax*: 305 375 8054
email: DioseF@aol.com

Bishop Suffragan Rt Revd John L. Said (*same address*)   *email*: BishopSaid@aol.com

SOUTHERN OHIO (Province V)
Bishop Rt Revd Herbert Thompson, 412 Sycamore St, Cincinnati OH 45202
Fax: 513 421 0315

Bishop Suffragan Rt Revd Kenneth Price Jr, 125 E. Broad St, Columbus OH 43215   *Fax*: 614 461 1015
email: BishopKen@aol.com

SOUTHERN VIRGINIA (Province III)
Bishop Rt Revd David Conner Bane Jr, 600 Talbot Hall Rd, Norfolk VA 23505   *Fax*: 804 440 5354
email: dcbjr@southernvirginia.anglican.org

Assistant Bishop Rt Revd Donald P. Hart
email: DON.HART@ecunet.org

SOUTHWEST FLORIDA (Province IV)
Bishop Rt Revd John Bailey Lipscomb, DaySpring Episcopal Center, Box 763 Ellenton, Fl 34222   *Fax*: 941 776 9811
email: jlipscom@dioceseswfla.org

Assisting Bishop Rt Revd Telesforo Alexander Isaac (*same address*)

SOUTHWESTERN VIRGINIA (Province III)
Bishop Rt Revd Frank Neff Powell, PO Box 2279, Roanoke VA 24009–2279   *Fax*: 540 343 9114
email: NEFF_POWELL@ecunet.org

SPOKANE (Province VIII)
Bishop Vacancy, 245 E. 13th Ave, Spokane WA 99202   *Fax*: 509 747 0049

SPRINGFIELD (Province V)
Bishop Rt Revd Peter Hess Beckwith, 821 S. 2nd St, Springfield IL 62704–2694   *Fax*: 217 525 1877

TAIWAN (Province VIII)
Bishop Rt Revd John Chien, 1–105–7 Hangchow, South Rd, Taipei, Taiwan 10044, Republic of China   *Fax*: 02 396 2014
email: skhtpe@msiz.hinet.net

TENNESSEE (Province IV)
Bishop Rt Revd Bertram Nelson Herlong, 1 LeFleur Bld, Suite 107, 50 Vantage Way, Nashville, TN 37228–1504   *Fax*: 615 251 8010
email: bishop@mail.episcopaldiocese-tn.org

TEXAS (Province VII)
Bishop Rt Revd Claude E. Payne, 3203 W. Alabama St, Houston TX 77098 *Fax*: 713 520 5723
email: cepayne@neosoft.com

Bishop Suffragan Rt Revd Leopoldo J. Alard (*same address*)   *email*: ebpleo@aol.com

UPPER SOUTH CAROLINA (Province IV)
Bishop Rt Revd Dorsey Felix Henderson Jr, 1115 Marion, Columbia SC 29201   *Fax*: 803 799 5119
email: dioceseusc@aol.com

UTAH (Province VIII)
Bishop Rt Revd Carolyn Tanner Irish, 80 S. 300 E. St, PO Box 3090, Salt Lake City UT 84110–3090
Fax: 801 322 5096

VERMONT (Province I)
Bishop Rt Revd Mary Adelia Rosamond McLeod, 5 Rock Point Rd, Burlington VT 05401–2735
Fax: 802 860 1562
email: vtbishop3@aol.com

VIRGIN ISLANDS (Province II)
Bishop Rt Revd Theodore Athelbert Daniels, PO Box 10437, St Thomas, VI 00801 *Fax*: 340 777 8485
email: tad@aol.com

VIRGINIA (Province III)
Bishop Rt Revd Peter James Lee, 110 W. Franklin St, Richmond VA 23220   *Fax*: 804 644 6928

Assistant Bishop Rt Revd Robert P. Atkinson (*same address*)

Bishops Suffragan
Rt Revd F. Clayton Matthews, 8100 Three Chopt Rd, Suite 102, Richmond, Virginia 23229
Fax: 804 282 6008
email: F_CLAYTON_MATTHEWS@ecunet.org

Rt Revd David Colin Jones, 6043 Burnside Landing Drive, Burke, Virginia 22015 *Fax*: 703 823 9524
email: DAVID_COLIN_JONES@ecunet.org

WASHINGTON (Province III)
Bishop Rt Revd Ronald Hayward Haines, Episcopal Church House, Mount St Alban, Washington DC 20016　　*Fax*: 202 364 6605
email: rhaines@cathedral.org

Bishop Suffragan Rt Revd Jane Holmes Dixon (*same address*)

WEST MISSOURI (Province VII)
Bishop Rt Revd John Clark Buchannan, PO Box 413227, Kansas City MO 64141–3227
Fax: 816 471 0379
email: wemy42c@prodigy.com

Bishop Coadjutor Rt Revd Barry Robert Howe (*same address*)
email: 105646.1226@compuserve.com

WEST TENNESSEE (Province IV)
Bishop Rt Revd James Coleman, 692 Poplar Ave, Memphis TN 38105　　*Fax*: 901 526 1555
email: edwt1@magibox.net

WEST TEXAS (Province VII)
Coadjutor Bishop Rt Revd James Edward Folts, PO Box 6885, San Antonio TX 78209
Fax: 210 822 8779

Bishop Suffragan Rt Revd Robert Boyd Hibbs (*same address*)　　*email*: bphibbs@aol.com

WEST VIRGINIA (Province III)
Bishop Vacancy, PO Box 5400, Charlestown WV 25361–5400　　*Fax*: 304 343 3295
email: jhswv@ecunet.org

WESTERN KANSAS (Province VII)
Bishop Rt Revd Vernon Edward Strickland, PO Box 2507, Salina KS 67402–2507
Fax: 913 825 0974

WESTERN LOUISIANA (Province IV)
Bishop Rt Revd Robert Hargrove Jr, PO Box 203⁊, Alexandria, Louisiana 71301　　*Fax*: 318 442 871

WESTERN MASSACHUSETTS (Province I)
Bishop Rt Revd Gordon P. Scruton, 37 Chestnu St, Springfield MA 01103　　*Fax*: 413 746 987
email: BishopWMA@aol.com

WESTERN MICHIGAN (Province V)
Bishop Rt Revd Edward Lee Jr, The Cathedral 2600 Vincent Ave, Portage MI 49024–5653
Fax: 616 381 706.
email: diowestmi@aol.com

WESTERN NEW YORK (Province II)
Bishop Rt Revd J. Michael Garrison, 111 Delaware Ave, Buffalo NY 14209
Fax: 716 881 172⸲
email: DAVID.BOWMAN@ecunet.org

WESTERN NORTH CAROLINA (Province IV)
Bishop Rt Revd Robert Hodges Johnson, Box 369 Vance Ave, Black Mountain NC 28711
Fax: 828 669 275€
email: bishopwnc@compuserve.com

WYOMING (Province VI)
Bishop Rt Revd Bruce Caldwell, 104 South Fourth St, Laramie WY 82070　　*Fax*: 307 742 6782

EXTRA-PROVINCIAL, PROVINCE IX PUERTO RICO
Bishop Rt Revd David Alvarez-Velazquez, PO Box 902, Saint Just Sta., St Just, PR 00978, Puerto Rico　　*Fax*: 787 761 0320

VENEZUELA
Bishop Rt Revd Orlando de Jesús Guerrero, Apartado 49–143, Avenue Caroni 100, Colinas de Bello Monte, Caracas 1042-A, Venezuela
Fax: 02 751 3180

The Church in Wales

Members 94,000
The Church in Wales was disestablished and partially disendowed in 1914 and 1919. In 1920 the new Province of Wales was created. The Anglican Church is the largest denomination in the country with its own Board of Missions and two bilingual church magazines.

THE GOVERNING BODY
President The Most Revd Rowan Douglas Williams (*Archbishop of Wales*)

Clerical Secretary Vacancy

Secretary General and Lay Secretary Mr David McIntyre, 39 Cathedral Rd, Cardiff CF11 9XF
Tel: 029–2023 1638

The Welsh Church Acts enabled the bishops, clergy and laity of the Church in Wales to appoint a legislative body with power to frame constitutions and regulations for the general management and good government of the Church and the property and affairs thereof whether as a whole or according to dioceses. The Church in Wales set up a Governing Body for the whole province consisting of the three orders of bishops, clergy and laity. The Governing Body has a membership of 356 representing the six dioceses.
　The order of bishops consists of the archbishop and the diocesan bishops; the order of clergy consists of the deans and archdeacons (*ex officio*) and 15 members elected by each of the six diocesan conferences; and the order of the laity consists of

0 lay persons elected by each of the six diocesan onferences. In addition, there are 15 clerical and 0 lay members co-opted and 14 members *ex ficio*.

Its President is the Archbishop; it has two rdinary meetings annually and such other spe-ial meetings as may be necessary. Its powers are ery wide and its decisions are binding upon all nembers of the Church. At its first session it assed the following resolution:

The Governing Body does hereby accept the Articles, Doctrinal Statements, Rites, and Ceremonies, and save in so far as they may be necessarily varied by the Welsh Church Act 1914, the formularies of the Church of England as accepted by that Church and set forth in or appended to the Book of Common Prayer of the Church of England.

THE REPRESENTATIVE BODY OF THE CHURCH IN WALES

Chairman Mr Richard Parkinson, 42 Victoria Rd, Penarth CF64 2HY

Secretary General Mr David McIntyre, 39 Cathedral Rd, Cardiff CF11 9XF
Tel: 029–2023 1638

Provision was made in the Welsh Church Acts for the setting up of a Representative Body of the Church in Wales with power, *inter alia*, to hold property for any of the uses and purposes of the bishops, clergy and laity of the Church in Wales.

The Representative Body was incorporated by Royal Charter on 24 April 1919. It bears some-what the same relation to the Governing Body as the Central Board of Finance bears to the General Synod of the Church of England. It is subject to the order and control of the Governing Body, but this does not mean that everything it does has to be confirmed by the Governing Body in order to make it effective. Its powers are mainly financial and administrative; it has certain statutory obligations; it has authority to do certain things under its charter; by Chapter III of the Constitution it is enabled to carry through sales, purchases, leases, investments, etc., and it has further powers under schemes approved from time to time by the Governing Body.

All churches, most churchyards, parsonages, and other church properties are vested in the Representative Body. It is expected to initiate financial reforms and to make recommendations accordingly for the approval of the Governing Body.

The stipends of the bishops and dignitaries are paid by the Representative Body. It also pays substantial grants towards stipends of beneficed clergy and assistant curates; it pays the pensions of retired clergy and clergy widows and makes grants for the benefit of widows, orphans and dependants of deceased clergy. It administers funds out of which parsonage houses in the prov-ince are kept in good repair.

Archbishop Vacancy, Esgobty, St Asaph, Clwyd LL17 0TW
Tel: (01745) 583503
Fax: (01745) 584301

Assistant Bishop Rt Revd David Thomas, Bodfair, 3 White's Close, Belmont Rd, Abergavenny NP7 5HZ
Tel: (01873) 858780
Fax: (01873) 858269

Secretary General and Archbishop's Registrar Mr David McIntyre, 39 Cathedral Rd, Cardiff CF11 9XF
Tel: 029–2023 1638

Archbishop's Media Officer Revd David Williams (*same address*)

THEOLOGICAL COLLEGE
St Michael's Theological College, Llandaff, Car-diff CF5 2YJ (*Warden* Revd Dr John Holdsworth)
Tel: 029–2056 3379

CHURCH PAPER
Welsh Church Life Monthly publication in English. 16 pages. Contains general items of parish interest and articles on current church matters together with a children's page, editorial and news of diocesan clergy movements. *Editor* Revd Glynne Ball, Church in Wales Centre, Woodland Place, Penarth CF64 2YQ
Tel: 029–2070 5278
Fax: 029–2071 2413

BANGOR
Bishop Rt Revd Francis James Saunders Davies, Ty'r Esgob, Bangor LL57 2SS   Tel: (01248) 362895
Fax: (01248) 254866

Chancellor His Honour Judge David Davies, 10 Dee Hills Park, Chester CH3 5AR

Registrar Vacancy, Diocesan Centre, Cathedral Close, Bangor LL57 1RL   Tel: (01248) 354999

Secretary of Diocesan Board of Finance Ms Stella Schultz, Bangor Diocesan Board of Finance, Diocesan Centre, Cathedral Close, Bangor LL57 1RL   Tel: (01248) 354999

CATHEDRAL CHURCH OF ST DEINIOL, Bangor, Gwynedd
Dean Very Revd Trevor Evans, The Deanery, Cathedral Precinct, Bangor LL57 1LH
Tel: (01248) 370693

LLANDAFF
Bishop Rt Revd Barry Cennydd Morgan, Llys Esgob, The Cathedral Green, Llandaff, Cardiff CF5 2YE   Tel: 029–2056 2400

Chancellor His Hon Norman Francis, 2 The Woodlands, Lisvane, Cardiff CF4 5SW

Registrar Mr David Lambert, Diocesan Registry, 9 The Chantry, Llandaff, Cardiff CF5 2NN
Tel: 029–2082 3510

Secretary of Diocesan Board of Finance Mr Michael Beasant, Llandaff Diocesan Board of Finance, Heol Fair, Llandaff, Cardiff CF5 2EE
Tel: 029–2057 8899

CATHEDRAL CHURCH OF ST PETER AND ST PAUL, Llandaff, Cardiff
Dean Vacancy, The Deanery, The Cathedral Green, Llandaff, Cardiff CF5 2YF
Tel: 029–2056 1545

MONMOUTH
Bishop Most Revd Rowan Douglas Williams, Bishopstow, 91A Stow Hill, Newport NP9 4EA
Tel: (01633) 263510
Fax: (01633) 259946

Chancellor His Honour Judge Philip Price, 23 Ty Draw Rd, Roath, Cardiff CF2 5HB

Registrar Mr Nigel Williams, Diocesan Registry, 7 Clytha Park Rd, Newport NP9 1SE
Tel: (01633) 244933

Secretary of Diocesan Board of Finance Mr Richard Tarran, Diocesan Office, 64 Caerau Rd, Newport NP9 4HJ   Tel: (01633) 267490

CATHEDRAL CHURCH OF ST WOOLOS, Newport
Dean Very Revd Richard Fenwick, The Deanery, Stow Hill, Newport NP9 4ED Tel: (01633) 263338

ST ASAPH
Bishop Rt Revd John Stewart Davies, Esgobty, St Asaph LL17 0TW   Tel: (01745) 583503
Fax: (01745) 584301

Chancellor John Rogers, 15 St Peter's Square, Ruthin LL15 1AA

Registrar Mr David Hooson, Diocesan Registry, High St, St Asaph LL17 0RF   Tel: (01745) 583393

Secretary of Diocesan Board of Finance Mr Christopher Seaton, St Asaph Diocesan Board of Finance, High St, St Asaph LL17 0RD
Tel: (01745) 582245

CATHEDRAL CHURCH OF ST ASAPH, St Asaph, Denbighshire
Dean Very Revd Kerry Goulstone, The Deanery, St Asaph LL17 0RL   Tel: (01745) 583597

ST DAVIDS
Bishop Rt Revd David Huw Jones, Llys Esgob, Abergwili, Carmarthen SA31 2JG
Tel: (01267) 23659
Fax: (01267) 22304

Chancellor His Hon Michael Evans, The Old Rectory, Reynoldston, Swansea SA3 1AD

Registrar Mr Basil Richards, Diocesan Registry, 4 St Mary St, Carmarthen, Dyfed SA31 1TN
Tel: (01267) 23642

Secretary of Diocesan Board of Finance Mr Vincent Lloyd, Diocesan Office, Abergwili, Carmarthen Dyfed SA31 2JG   Tel: (01267) 23614

CATHEDRAL CHURCH OF ST DAVID AND ST ANDREW, St Davids, Pembrokeshire
Dean Very Revd Wyn Evans, The Deanery, St Davids SA62 6RH   Tel: (01437) 72020?

SWANSEA AND BRECON
Bishop Rt Revd Anthony Edward Pierce, Ely Tower, Brecon LD3 9DE
Tel and Fax: (01874) 62200?

Hon Assistant Bishops
Rt Revd Benjamin Vaughan, 4 Caswell Drive Newton, Swansea SA3 4RJ

Rt Revd Eryl Stephen Thomas, 17 Orchard Close Gilwern, Abergavenny NP7 0EN

Chancellor Leolin Price, Moor Park, Llanbedr Crickhowell NP8 1SS

Registrar Mr Timothy Davenport, Diocesan Registry, 8A High St, Brecon LD3 7AL
Tel: (01874) 625151

Secretary of Diocesan Board of Finance Mr Huw Thomas, Swansea and Brecon Diocesan Centre Cathedral Close, Brecon LD3 9DP
Tel: (01874) 623716

CATHEDRAL CHURCH OF ST JOHN THE EVANGELIST, Brecon, Powys
Dean Very Revd Geraint Hughes, The Deanery, Cathedral Close, Brecon LD3 9DP
Tel: (01874) 623344

The Church of the Province of West Africa

Members 1,000,000
Church work began in Ghana as early as 1752 and in the Gambia, Guinea, Liberia and Sierra Leone in the nineteenth century. The Province of West Africa was founded in 1951 and was divided to form the Province of Nigeria and the Province of West Africa in 1979. The Church exists in an atmosphere of civil strife and Christians remain a minority.

Archbishop and Primate of the Province of West Africa Most Revd Robert Garshong Allotey Okine (Bishop of Koforidua)

ean of the Province of West Africa Rt Revd
Edward W. Neufville (*Bishop of Liberia*)

Episcopal Secretary of the Province of West Africa Rt
Revd Solomon Tilewa Johnson (*Bishop of The
Gambia*)

Provincial Secretary Mr Nat Stanley, PO Box 8,
Accra, Ghana   *Fax*: 011 233 21 669125

Provincial Treasurer Mrs S. O. Thompson, PO Box
00, Freetown, Sierra Leone

THEOLOGICAL COLLEGES
Ghana
Trinity College (Ecumenical), PO Box 48, Legon
St Nicholas Anglican Theological College, PO
Box A 162, Cape Coast, Ghana

Liberia
Cuttington University College, Suacoco, PO Box
0–0277, 1000 Monrovia 10, Liberia

Sierra Leone
Theological Hall and Church Training Centre, PO
Box 128, Freetown, Sierra Leone

ACCRA
Bishop Rt Revd Justice Ofei Akrofi, Bishopscourt,
PO Box 8, Accra, Ghana   *Fax*: 011 233 21 669125

BO
Bishop Rt Revd Samuel Sao Gbonda, PO Box 21,
Bo, Southern Province, Sierra Leone
                          Fax: 022 251 306 (via Ghana)

CAMEROON (missionary diocese)
Bishop Rt Revd Jonathan Ruhumuliza, BP 6204,
New Bell, Douala   *Fax*: 237 408 552
          email: camanglica-church@camnet.cm

CAPE COAST
Bishop Rt Revd Kobina Adduah Quashie,

Bishopscourt, PO Box A 233, Adisadel Estates,
Cape Coast, Ghana   *Fax*: 042 2637

FREETOWN
Bishop Rt Revd Julius Olotu Prince Lynch,
Bishopscourt, PO Box 537, Freetown, Sierra
Leone   *Fax*: 022 251 306 (via Ghana)

GAMBIA
Bishop Rt Revd Solomon Tilewa Johnson,
Bishopscourt, PO Box 51, Banjul, The Gambia,
West Africa   *Fax*: 373 803
          email: 106617.1404@compuserve.com

GUINEA
Bishop Vacancy, BP 105, Conakry, Guinea

KOFORIDUA
Bishop Most Revd Robert Garshong Allotey
Okine (*Archbishop and Primate of the Province of
West Africa*), PO Box 980, Koforidua, Ghana
                          Fax: 021 669 125

KUMASI
Bishop Rt Revd Daniel Yinka Sarfo, Bishop's
House, PO Box 144, Kumasi, Ghana
                          Fax: 051 24 117

LIBERIA
Bishop Rt Revd Edward W. Neufville, PO Box
10–0277, 1000 Monrovia 10, Liberia *Fax*: 227 519

SEKONDI
Bishop Vacancy, PO Box 85, Sekondi, Ghana
                          Fax: 021 669 125

SUNYANI
Bishop Rt Revd Thomas Ampah Brient, PO Box
23, Sunyani, Ghana   *Fax*: 061 7203
          email: Deegyab@IGHMail.Com

TAMALE
Bishop Rt Revd Emmanuel Arongo, PO Box 110,
Tamale NR, Ghana   *Fax*: 071 22849

The Church in the Province of the West Indies

Members 770,000
The West Indies became a self-governing province of the worldwide Anglican Communion in
1883 because of the Church of England missions
in territories that became British colonies. It is
made up of two mainland dioceses and six island
dioceses including Barbados, Belize, Guyana,
Jamaica, Nassau and the Bahamas, Tobago,
Trinidad, and the Windward Islands. Great
emphasis is being placed on training personnel
for an indigenous ministry as the island locations
and scattered settlements make pastoral care
difficult and costly.

Archbishop of the Province Most Revd Drexel
Wellington Gomez (*Bishop of Nassau and the
Bahamas*), Addington House, PO Box N-7107,
Nassau, Bahamas   *Fax*: 1242 322 7943

Administrative Assistant to the Archbishop Mr
O. W. Flax (*same address*)

Provincial Secretariat PO Box 23, St John's,
Antigua, WI   *Fax*: 462 2090

Provincial Secretary Rt Revd Drexel Gomez
(*Bishop of Nassau and the Bahamas*), PO Box N-
7107, Nassau, Bahamas   *Fax*: 242 322 7943

Codrington College, St John, Barbados (*Principal* Canon Noel Titus)

United Theological College of the West Indies, PO Box 136, Golding Ave, Kingston 7, Jamaica (*Anglican Warden* Canon Ralston (Roy) Smith)

BARBADOS
Bishop Rt Revd Rufus Theophilus Broome, Leland, Philip Drive, Pine Gardens, St Michael, Barbados   *Fax*: 1246 426 0871
                    email: mandeville@sunbeach.com

BELIZE
Bishop Rt Revd Sylvestre Donato Romero-Palma, Bishopsthorpe, PO Box 535, Southern Foreshore, Belize City, Belize   *Fax*: 501 2 76 898
                    email: bzediocese@btl.net

GUYANA
Bishop Rt Revd Randolph Oswald George, Austin House, 49 High St, Georgetown 1, Guyana   *Fax*: 592 2 64 183

JAMAICA
Bishop Rt Revd Neville Wordsworth de Souza, Church House, 2 Caledonia Ave, Kingston 5, Jamaica   *Fax*: 1876 968 0618

Bishops Suffragan
Rt Revd Herman Victor Spence (*Bishop of Kingston*) (*same address*)   *email*: sspence@toj.com

Vacancy (*Bishop of Mandeville*), PO Box 159, Mandeville, Jamaica   *Fax*: 1876 962 322

Rt Revd Alfred Charles Reid (*Bishop of Montego Bay*), PO Box 346, Montego Bay, St James, Jamaica

NASSAU AND THE BAHAMAS
Bishop Most Revd Drexel W. Gomez (*Archbishop of the West Indies and Bishop of Nassau and the Bahamas*), Addington House, PO Box N-7107, Nassau, Bahamas   *Fax*: 1242 322 794

NORTH EASTERN CARIBBEAN AND ARUBA
Bishop Rt Revd Leroy Errol Brooks, St Mary's Rectory, PO Box 180, The Valley, Anguilla
                          Fax: 1264 497 301
                    email: dioceseneca@candw.a

TRINIDAD AND TOBAGO
Bishop Rt Revd Rawle Douglin, Hayes Court, 21 Maraval Road, Port of Spain, Trinidad
                          Fax: 1868 628 131
                    email: red@trinidad.ne

WINDWARD ISLANDS
Bishop Rt Revd Sehon Goodridge, Bishop's Court, Montrose, PO Box 502, St Vincent
                          Fax: 1 809 456 259

Other Churches and Extra-Provincial Dioceses

BERMUDA
(Anglican Church of Bermuda)
Members 24,800
This extra-provincial diocese is under the metro-political jurisdiction of the Archbishop of Canterbury.

Bishop Rt Revd Ewen Ratteray, Bishop's Lodge, PO Box HM 769, Hamilton HM CX, Bermuda
                          Fax: 441 296 0592
                    email: bishopratteray@ibl.bm

Diocesan Office PO Box HM 769, Hamilton HM CX, Bermuda   *Fax*: 441 292 5421

Archdeacon Ven Dr Arnold Hollis, Sandys Rectory, 3 Middle Rd, Somerset Bridge, Sandys SB-02   *Fax*: 441 234 2723
                    email: athol@ibl.bm

EPISCOPAL CHURCH OF CUBA
(Iglesia Episcopal de Cuba)
Members 3,000
The Episcopal Church of Cuba is under a Metropolitan Council in matters of faith and order. Council members include the Primate of Canada, the Archbishop of the West Indies, and the President Bishop of Episcopal Church's newest province, the Anglican Church of the Central American Region.

Bishop Rt Revd Jorge Perera Hurtado, Calle 6, No 273 Vedado, Habana 4, 10400 Cuba
                          Fax: 07 3332 93

THEOLOGICAL COLLEGE
Seminario Evangelico de Teologica, Aptdo. 149 Matanzas (Interdenominational, run in co-operation with the Methodist and Presbyterian Churches).

CHURCH PAPER
Heraldo Episcopal Published quarterly. Contains diocesan, provincial and world news, homiletics, devotional and historical articles.

FALKLAND ISLANDS
In 1977 the Archbishop of Canterbury resumed episcopal jurisdiction over the Falkland Islands and South Georgia which had been relinquished in 1974 to the Church of the Southern Cone of America.

Rector Revd Alistair McHaffie, The Deanery, Stanley, Falkland Islands, South Atlantic
                          Fax: 010–500–21842
                    email: deanery@horizon.co.fk

LUSITANIAN CHURCH
(Portuguese Episcopal Church)
Members 5,000

The American Episcopal Church organized the Lusitanian Church, Catholic Apostolic Evangelical, in 1880. The Church consisted of Roman Catholic priests who formed congregations in and around Lisbon using a translation of the 1662 English Prayer Book. A Lusitanian bishop was consecrated in 1958 and in the early 1960s many provinces of the Anglican Communion established full communion with the Church in Portugal. Full integration occurred in 1980 when the Church became an extra-provincial diocese under the metropolitical authority of the Archbishop of Canterbury. It takes seriously its role in the emerging Europe and has a commitment to helping the elderly. It has a strong mission emphasis for the many unchurched people in the country. The Church and its leaders co-operate fully with the Diocese in Europe (Church of England) and the Convocation of American Churches in Europe, assisting in each other's congregation and being a united Anglican voice in an increasingly secular Europe. In 1998 the diocesan synod of the Lusitanian Church approved and accepted the Porvoo Declaration, expressing its desire to be involved in the life of the Porvoo Communion and to co-operate, with interchangeable ministries, with the congregations of the Porvoo Churches in Portugal.

Bishop Rt Revd Dr Fernando da Luz Soares, Secretaria Diocesana, Apartado 392, P-4430 Vila Nova de Gaia, Portugal   *Fax*: 351 2 3752016
email: ilcae@mail.telepac.pt

SPANISH REFORMED EPISCOPAL CHURCH
Members 5,000

Under the leadership of a former Roman Catholic priest, the Spanish Reformed Episcopal Church was under the pastoral care of the Bishop of Mexico starting in 1880. In 1894 the Bishop of Meath consecrated the first bishop and the Church of Ireland accepted metropolitan authority. The Church was fully integrated in 1980 as an extra-provincial diocese under the metropolitical authority of the Archbishop of Canterbury. It has a strong evangelistic and mission commitment and a new Anglican Centre is being built in the university city of Salamanca. Its history has been one of persecution and difficulties but it is firm in its co-operation with the Diocese in Europe and the Convocation of American Churches in Europe for a stronger Anglican presence throughout Europe.

Bishop Rt Revd Carlos López-Lozano, Beneficiencia 18, 28004 Madrid
Fax: 34 91 594 4572

Regional Councils

CONFERENCE OF THE ANGLICAN PROVINCES OF AFRICA

The Council of the Anglican Provinces of Africa was inaugurated at Chilema, Malawi in September 1979. CAPA meets every two years and each province (Burundi, Central Africa, Congo, the Indian Ocean, Kenya, Nigeria, Rwanda, Southern Africa, Sudan, Tanzania, Uganda, West Africa and the Diocese of Egypt) is represented by its archbishop or his episcopal representative, one clergyman and one layperson. CAPA's purposes include meeting regularly for fellowship, conferring on matters concerning the churches in the rapidly changing continent of Africa, sharing experience, and considering opportunities for joint and ecumenical action.

Chairman Most Revd Robert Okine (*Archbishop of the Province of West Africa*)

Acting Administrator Most Revd David Gitari, PO Box 20017, Nairobi, Kenya   *Fax*: 2–712512

THE COUNCIL OF THE CHURCHES OF EAST ASIA

This Council, whose history began in 1954, has gone through an evolution. With most of the dioceses forming into provinces, the Council is now a fellowship for common action. Its membership includes dioceses in the Province of South East Asia, the Church of Korea, the Philippine Episcopal Church, Hong Kong Sheng Kung Hui, the Diocese of Taiwan (which is associated with the Episcopal Church of the USA), the Province of Myanmar, the Philippine Independent Church and the Anglican Church of Australia who are members as a national church or province.

Chairman Rt Revd Datuk Yong Ping Chung, Rumah Bishop, Jalan Tangki, PO Box 10881, 88809 Kota Kinabalu, Sabah, Malaysia
Fax: 60–88 245942
email: pcyong@pc.jaring.my

THE SOUTH PACIFIC ANGLICAN COUNCIL

The Council now comprises the Province of Melanesia, the Province of Papua New Guinea, and the Diocese of Polynesia.

Chairman Rt Revd Elison Pogo (*Primate of the Church of Melanesia*), Archbishop's House, PO Box 19, Honiara, Solomon Islands   *Fax*: 21 098

Secretary Rt Revd Jabez Bryce (*Bishop of Polynesia*), PO Box 35, Suva, Fiji   *Fax*: 302 503

UNITED CHURCHES IN FULL COMMUNION

CHURCHES RESULTING FROM THE UNION OF ANGLICANS WITH CHRISTIANS OF OTHER TRADITIONS

The population of the countries of South Asia is over 1,000 million and these Churches cover the whole area. The total Christian population is around 22–23 million and Christians of many different traditions, ranging from ancient oriental to pentecostal, are to be found here.

The region is undergoing rapid social, economic and political change. There is also a resurgence of some of the great world religions. Although there is a great deal of industrialization and there have been 'green revolutions' in the agricultural sector in many countries there is still a tremendous inequality in the distribution of wealth and income.

In spite of the relatively small numbers of Christians, the Churches have grown steadily and have been responsible for many initiatives in education, medical work and community development. Their influence is out of all proportion to their size.

The Church of England continues to relate to these Churches mainly through its mission agencies: CMS, USPG, SPCK and Crosslinks. In addition, the Oxford Mission, the Dublin University

Mission to Chota Nagpur and the Religious Communities are doing valuable work. Support in money and personnel also comes from churches in Canada, from CMS in Australia and New Zealand, from the USA, Holland, Germany, Scandinavia, Japan and Singapore.

The Churches themselves are involved in the training and sending of mission personnel both inside and outside India, including the sending of mission partners to the UK.

Mission partners from the Church of England work under the authority of the local church or institution to which they have been sent.

The Church of North India, the Church of South India and Mar Thoma Syrian Church of Malenkara are in full communion with each other and are members of a joint council to further and deepen their unity.

Since 1988, these Churches have become full members of the Lambeth Conference and the Anglican Consultative Council. Their moderators also attend the meetings of Anglican Primates.

The Church of Bangladesh

Members 12,500

Bangladesh was part of the State of Pakistan which was partitioned from India in 1947. After the civil war between East and West Pakistan ended in 1971, East Pakistan became Bangladesh. The Church of Bangladesh is one of the United Churches, formed by a union of Anglicans with Christians of other traditions.

THEOLOGICAL COLLEGE

St Andrew's Theological College, St Thomas's Church Compound, 54 Johnson Rd, Dhaka 1100, Bangladesh (*Principal* Revd Bart Baak)

DHAKA

Bishop Most Revd Barnabas Dwijen Mondal (*Moderator COB*), St Thomas's Church, 54 Johnson Rd, Dhaka 1100   *Fax*: 880 2 238 218
email: cbdacdio@bangla.net

KUSHTIA

Bishop Rt Revd Michael Baroi, 94 N S Rd, Thanapara, Kushtia, Bangladesh
Fax: 880 71 54 818
email: cbdacdio@bangla.net

The Church of Sri Lanka

Members 52,500

Until 1970 the Church was part of the Church of India, Pakistan, Burma and Ceylon. The first Anglican services were held in 1796 and missionaries began their work in 1818. The Church continues as extra-provincial under the Archbishop of Canterbury. The Church gives a strong witness to human rights in the midst of conflicts in the country.

HEOLOGICAL COLLEGE
Theological College of Lanka, Pilimatalawa, nr
Kandy, Sri Lanka

COLOMBO
Bishop Rt Revd Kenneth Michael James
Fernando, Bishop's House, 358/2 Bauddhaloka

Mawatha, Colombo 7, Sri Lanka
Fax: 94 1 684 811
email: bishop@eureka.lk

KURUNAGALA
Bishop Rt Revd Andrew Kumarage, Bishop's
House, Kandy Rd, Kurunagala, Sri Lanka
Fax: 94 37 22 191

The Church of North India

Members 1,250,000
The Church was inaugurated in 1970 after many
years of preparation. It includes the Anglican
Church, the United Church of Northern
India (Congregationalist and Presbyterian), the
Methodist Church (British and Australian Conferences), the Council of Baptist Churches in
Northern India, the Church of the Brethren
in India, and the Disciples of Christ. Along with
the Church of South India, the Church of Pakistan and the Church of Bangladesh, it is one of
the four United Churches.

Moderator Most Revd Dhirendra Kumar
Mohanty (*Bishop of Cuttack*)

Deputy Moderator Rt Revd Vinod Peter (*Bishop of
Nagpur*)

General Secretary Dr Vidya Sagar Lall, CN1, 16
Pandit Pant Marg, New Delhi 110 001

Treasurer Mr Enos Das Pradhan (*same address*)

CHURCH PAPER
The North India Church Review The official
monthly magazine of the CNI. Contains articles,
reports, diocesan news, world news and letters.
Editorial Office 16 Pandit Pant Marg, New Delhi
110001.

The dioceses in the CNI are:

AGRA
Bishop Vacancy, Bishop's House, St Paul's
Church Compound, 4/116-B Church Rd, Civil
Lines, Agra 282002 UP   *Fax*: 0562 350244

AMRITSAR
Bishop Rt Revd Pradeep Kumar Samantaroy, 26
R. B. Prakash Chand Rd, Amritsar 143001
Fax: 0183 222910

ANDAMAN AND NICOBAR ISLANDS
Bishop Rt Revd Edmund Matthew, Cathedral
Church Compound, House No. 1, Staging Post,
Car Nicobar, 744 301, Andaman and Nicobar
Islands

BARRACKPORE
Bishop Rt Revd Brojen Malakar, Bishop's Lodge,
86 Middle Rd, Barrackpore 743101, W. Bengal

BHOPAL
Bishop Rt Revd Manohar Singh, 7 Old Sehore Rd,
Indore, 452001 MP

CALCUTTA
Bishop Rt Revd Dinesh Chandra Gorai, Bishop's
House, 51 Chowringhee Rd, Calcutta, WB
700071   *Fax*: 033 2426340

CHANDIGARH
Bishop Rt Revd Joel Vidyasagar Mal, Bishop's
House, Mission Compound, Brown Rd,
Ludhiana, 141008 Punjab

CHOTA NAGPUR
Bishop Rt Revd Zechariah James Terom, Bishop's
Lodge, PO Box 1, Church Rd, Ranchi, 834001
Bihar

CUTTACK
Bishop Most Revd Dhirendra Kumar Mohanty
(*Moderator CNI*), Bishop's House, Madhusudan
Rd, Cuttack 753 001, Orissa   *Fax*: 0671 602 206

DELHI
Bishop Rt Revd Karam Masih, Bishop's House, 1
Church Lane, Off North Ave, New Delhi 110 001
email: stmartin@del3.vsnl.net.in

DURGAPUR
Bishop Rt Revd Onil Kumar Tirkey, Bishop's
House, PO Box No 20, S. E. Railway, Bankura
722 101, W. Bengal   *Fax*: 0343 5123

EASTERN HIMALAYAS
Bishop Rt Revd Gerald Andrews, Diocesan
Centre, Gandhi Rd, Darjeeling 734 101, W.
Bengal   *Fax*: 0354 52 208

GUJARAT
Bishop Rt Revd Vinod Kumar Malaviya, Bishop's
House, Ellis Bridge, Ahmedabad 380 006,
Gujarat State   *Fax*: 0272 6561 950

JABALPUR
Bishop Rt Revd Sunil Cak, Bishop's House, 2131
Napier Town, Jabalpur, MP 482 001
Fax: 0761 322 109

KOLHAPUR
Bishop Rt Revd MacDonald Claudius, Bishop's House, EP School Compound, Kolhapur 416 003, Maharashtra   *Fax*: 0231 654 832

LUCKNOW
Bishop Rt Revd Anil Stephen, Bishop's House, 25 Mahatma Gandhi Marg, Allahabad, UP 211011
          Fax: 0532 623 324

MARATHWADA
Bishop Rt Revd Michael Marcus Arsud

MUMBAI
Bishop Rt Revd Baiju Gavit, St John's House, Duxbury Lane, Colaba, Mumbai 400005
          Fax: 022 206 0248

NAGPUR
Bishop Rt Revd Vinod Peter (*Deputy Moderator CNI*), Cathedral House, Civil Lines, Sadar, Nagpur 440 001, Maharashtra   *Fax*: 0712 523 089

NASIK
Bishop Rt Revd Pradeep Lemuel Kamble, Bishop's House, 1 Outram Rd, Tarakpur, Ahmednagar, 414 001 Maharashtra
          Fax: 0241 28 682

NORTH EAST INDIA
Bishop Rt Revd Purely Lyndoh, Bishop's Kuti, Shillong 1, Meghalaya 793 001   *Fax*: 0364 223 15:

PATNA
Bishop Rt Revd Philip Phembuar Marandih, Bishop's House, Christ Church Compound, Bhagalpur 812 001, Bihar   *Fax*: 0641 400 31

PHULBANI
Bishop-in-Charge Most Revd D. K. Mohanty (*Moderator CNI*), Mission Compound, POC, Udayagari, Dist Phulbani, Orissa 762 100

PUNE
Bishop Vacancy

RAJASTHAN
Bishop Rt Revd Emmanual Christopher Anthony 63/X, Savitri Girls' College Rd, Civil Lines, Ajmer 305 001, Rajasthan

SAMBALPUR
Bishop Rt Revd Lingaraj Tandy, Mission Compound, Balangir 767 001, Orissa

The Church of Pakistan

Members 800,000
One of four United Churches in the Anglican Communion, the Church of Pakistan was inaugurated in 1970. Members include the Anglican Churches of India, Pakistan, Burma, and Ceylon, two conferences of the United Methodist Church, the United Presbyterian Church in Pakistan, two Church Councils and the Pakistan Lutheran Church.

Moderator Rt Revd Samuel Azariah (*Bishop of Raiwind*)

Deputy Moderator Rt Revd John Samuel (*Bishop of Faisalabad*)

General Secretary Vacancy

Treasurer Sardar Hassan Ghauri, SAS Accountant, 26-Sarhad Colony, Ram Dass Gate, Peshawar, Pakistan

ARABIAN GULF
Bishop for Rt Revd Azad Marshall, PO Box 3192, Gulberg-1, Lahore, Punjab 54660
          Fax: 92 42 5220 591

FAISALABAD
Bishop Rt Revd John Samuel (*Deputy Moderator COP*), Bishop's House, PO Box 27, Mission Rd, Gojra Distt Toba Tek Sing, Faisalabad
          Fax: 92 411 4651 274

HYDERABAD
Bishop Rt Revd S. K. Dass, 27 Liaquat Rd, Civil Lines, Hyderabad 71000, Sind *Fax*: 92 221 28 772
          email: hays@hyd.infolink.net.pk

KARACHI
Bishop Vacancy, Bishop's House, Trinity Close, Karachi 0405

LAHORE
Bishop Rt Revd Dr Alexander John Malik, Bishopsbourne, Cathedral Close, The Mall, Lahore 54000   *Fax*: 92 42 722 1270

MULTAN
Bishop Rt Revd John Victor Mall, 113 Qasim Rd, PO Box 204, Multan Cantt

PESHAWAR
Bishop Vacancy, Diocesan Centre, 1 Sir-Syed Rd, Peshawar 25000, North West Frontier Province
          Fax: 091 277 499

RAIWIND
Bishop Rt Revd Samuel Azariah (*Moderator COP*), 17 Warris Rd, PO Box 2319, Lahore 3, Pakistan
          Fax: 042 757 7255

SIALKOT
Bishop Rt Revd Samuel Pervez Sant Masih, Lal Kothi, Barah Patthar, Sialkot 2, Punjab
          Fax: 0432 264 828

The Church of South India

Members 2,000,000
The Church was inaugurated in 1947 by the union of the South India United Church (itself a union of Congregational and Presbyterian/ Reformed traditions), the southern Anglican dioceses of the Church of India, Burma, and Ceylon, and the Methodist Church in South India. It is one of the four United Churches in the Anglican Communion.

Moderator Most Revd Vasant P. Dandin (*Bishop in Karnataka North*)   *Fax*: 044 852 3528

Deputy Moderator Rt Revd William Moses (*Bishop in Coimbatore*)

Hon Treasurer Mr Frederick William, CSI Centre, 5 Whites Rd, Royapettah, Chennai 600041, S India

General Secretary Prof George Koshy (*same address*)

CHURCH PAPERS
The South India Churchman Monthly. Contains articles, reports and news from the dioceses. *Editor* CSI Communications Dept, 1–2–288/31 Damalguda, Hyderabad, 29, AP, India; *Agent in UK* Mrs D. Elton, The Rectory, Great Ellingham, Norfolk NR17 1LD. Subscription £1.00 per annum.

Pilgrim Published by The Friends of the Church in India (London) in Feb and Aug. Subscription (minimum) 50p per annum. Contains news, letters from CSI and CNI and prayer topics.

CHENNAI
Bishop in Rt Revd Dr V. Devasahayan, Diocesan Office, PO Box 4914, 226 Cathedral Rd, Chennai 600 086, Tamil Nadu   *Fax*: 044 827 0608

COIMBATORE
Bishop in Rt Revd William Moses (*Deputy Moderator CSI*), Bishop's House, Coimbatore 641018, T N 1   *Fax*: 044 852 3528

DORNAKAL
Bishop in Rt Revd Rajarathnam Allu, Bishop's House, Cathedral Compound, Dornakal, Andhra Pradesh 506 381

EAST KERALA
Bishop in Rt Revd Joseph Samuel Kunnumpurathu, Bishop's House, Melukavu-mattom P.O. Kottayam 686 652, Kerala State
          Fax: 0482 291 044

JAFFNA
Bishop in Rt Revd Dr Subramaniam Jabanesan,
Bishop's House, 39 Fussels Lane, Colombo 6, Sri Lanka   *Fax*: 01 584 836

KANYAKUMARI
Bishop in Rt Revd Messiadhas Kesari, CSI Diocesan Office, 71A Dennis St, Nagercoil 629 001   *Fax*: 04652 31 295

KARIMNAGAR
Bishop in Rt Revd Sanki John Theodore, Bishop's House, PO Box 40, Karimnagar 505 001, Andhra Pradesh

KARNATAKA CENTRAL
Bishop in Rt Revd Vasanthkumar Suputhrappa, Diocesan Office, 20 Third Cross, CSI Compound, Bangalore 560 027, Karnataka

KARNATAKA NORTH
Bishop in Rt Revd Dr Vasant P. Dandin (*Moderator CSI*), Bishop's House, Haliyal Rd, Dharwad 508 008, Karnataka State
          Fax: 044 852 3528

KARNATAKA SOUTH
Bishop in Rt Revd Christopher Lazarus Furtado, Bishop's House, Balmatta, Mangalore 575 001
          Fax: 0824 425 042

KRISHNA-GODAVARI
Bishop in Rt Revd Prakasa Rao Babu Deva Thumaty, Bishop's House, Bishop Azariah High School Compound, Vijayawada, 520010 AP
          Fax: 0866 476 007

MADHYA KERALA
Bishop in Rt Revd Sam Mathew Valiyathottathil, Bishop's House, Cathedral Rd, Kottayam 686 001, Kerala State

MADURAI-RAMNAD
Bishop in Rt Revd Thavaraj David Eames, CSI New Mission Compound, Thirumangalam 625 706, Madurai District, Tamil Nadu

MEDAK
Bishop in Rt Revd Badda Peter Sugandhar, Bishop's Annexe, 145 MacIntyre Rd, Secunderabad 500 003, Andhra Pradesh
          Fax: 040 867297

NANDYAL
Bishop in Vacancy, Bishop's House, Nandyal RS, Kurnool Dist AP 518502   *Fax*: 08514 42 255

NORTH KERALA
Bishop in Rt Revd Dr George Isaac, Diocesan Office, PO Box 104, Shoranur 679 121 Kerala State

ANGLICAN AND PORVOO COMMUNIONS

RAYALASEEMA

Bishop in Rt Revd Chowtipalli Bellam Moses Fredrick, Bishop's House, CSI Compound, Gooty, Andhra Pradesh 515 401

SOUTH KERALA

Bishop in Rt Revd John Wilson Gladstone, Bishop's House, LMS Compound, Trivandrum 695 033, Kerala State   *Fax*: 0471 316 439

TIRUNELVELI

Bishop in Rt Revd Jason S. Dharmaraj, Bishopstowe, Box 18, Palayamkottai, Tirunelveli 627 002, Tamil Nadu   *Fax*: 0462 574 525

TRICHY-TANJORE

Bishop in Rt Revd Daniel James Srinivasan, PO Box 31, 8 V.O.C. Rd, Tiruchirapalli 620 001, Tamil Nadu

VELLORE

Bishop in Rt Revd Mahimai Rufus, Ashram Bungalow, 13 Filterbed Rd, Vellore, N Arcot D 632 001   *Fax*: 01416 2749

Bishops without diocesan charge Rt Revd C. S Sundaresan, c/o CSI Synod Office; Rt Revd Pereji Solomon, c/o The Bishop of the Dornaka Diocese; Rt Revd C. Selvamony; Rt Revd P Prabhudas; Rt Revd G. B. Devasahayam; R Revd G. S. Luke; Rt Revd W. V. Karl; Rt Revd K E. Gill; Rt Revd B. G. Prasada Rao; Rt Revd T. B. Benjamin; Rt Revd S. Daniel Abraham Rt Revd Dr Sundar Clarke; Rt Revd Dr M. C Mani; Rt Revd P. John; Rt Revd Sam Ponniah Rt Revd K.C. Seth; Rt Revd I. Jesudasan; Rt Revd K. Michael John; Rt Revd Dr P. Victo Premasagar; Rt Revd K. E. Swamidas; Rt Revd H. S. Thanaraj; Rt Revd D. Pothirajulu; Rt Revd L. V. Azariah

Note: The bishops in the Church of South India are designated as 'The Rt Revd the Bishop in – *not* 'of' and sign with their individual names.

THE HOLY CATHOLIC CHURCH IN CHINA

(Chung Hua Sheng Kung Hui)

The Chung Hua Sheng Kung Hui was an important denomination in China and its history dates back to the mid-nineteenth century. Today the CHSKU, as a separate denomination, no longer exists in the People's Republic of China, except for Hong Kong which returned to Chinese sovereignty on 1 July 1997. Under the formula 'one country – two systems' Hong Kong keeps its autonomy for 50 years, including the religious situation. The same will apply to Macao when it is returned by Portugal to China at the end of 1999.

On the Chinese mainland the Protestant churches, with few exceptions, have entered into a post-denominational phase under the China Christian Council. A united church is in the process of being created and Christians of Anglican inspiration are very much a part of this process. Bishop K. H. Ting, now in his old age, has retired from active leadership of the China Christian Council.

Although the CHSKU no longer is in existence, many former Anglicans still share a strong spiritual affinity with other Anglican Churches on matters of belief and liturgical tradition. As the Chinese Protestant Church develops its own ecclesiology and forms of worship, the Anglican traditions will no doubt contribute to a richer synthesis.

The Chung Hua Sheng Kung Hui owes its beginnings to the prayers and the men and women of six member Churches of the Anglican Communion:

1. The American Church, through its Department of Missions: work was begun in 1844, when the first bishop, Wm J. Boone, arrived in Shanghai, commissioned as 'Bishop of China'. The work extended up the valley of the Yangtze River, and three dioceses were founded: Kiangsu, Hankow and Anking.
2. The Church of England, through its missionary societies:
   (a) The CMS also began work in 1844, and in 1849 George Smith was consecrated Bishop of Victoria, Hong Kong, with jurisdiction over all British Anglican work in China and Japan. CMS did most of its work south of the Yangtze, and the Dioceses of Victoria, Hong Kong; Fukien; Chekiang; Kwangsi-Hunan; Yun-Kwei; and Szechwan were founded, the last being subsequently divided into the Dioceses of Eastern and Western Szechwan.
   (b) The Society for the Propagation of the Gospel in Foreign Parts in 1874 opened work in northern China, and the Dioceses of North China and Shantung were founded.
   (c) The Church of England Zenana Mission worked in several CMS dioceses, and the BCMS later opened work in the south and west.
   (d) The Anglican portion of the China Inland Mission worked in East Szechwan.
3. The Church of England in Canada, through its Missionary Society, founded the Diocese of Honan in 1909.
4. The Church of Ireland, through the Dublin University Mission, worked in association with the CMS in Fukien.
5. and 6. The Churches of Australia and New Zealand, through their Boards of Mission, worked in association with the Dioceses of Shantung and North China, respectively. The CMS of Australia and Tasmania also worked in a number of dioceses.

Shensi, established in 1934 as the missionary diocese of the CHSKH, later became one of the 14 regular dioceses of the Church.

In 1912 eleven dioceses were in being and in that year was held the first General Synod, with its House of Bishops and House of Delegates (clerical and lay). The Constitution was approved in 1915; and three years later came the election, confirmation and consecration of the first Chinese bishop, T. S. Sing, as Assistant Bishop of Chekiang. Additions to the Chinese episcopate followed, until by 1947 the majority of the House of Bishops were Chinese.

At the General Synod in that year the Rt Revd Lindel Tsen was elected Chairman of the House of Bishops, and after his resignation because of ill health the Rt Revd Chen Chien-tsun was elected in his place.

[Note: For the sake of continuity, the Wade-Giles romanization for Chinese localities and dioceses is retained for this historical section. The new system of pin-yin for Chinese names will be used for the period after 1949.]

In 1949 the People's Republic of China was established in Beijing and it became obvious that Western missionaries were no longer a help to the Chinese Church in the new situation. In 1950 there was a general withdrawal which included the remaining Western bishops. They were replaced by Chinese colleagues who were elected and consecrated according to the Canons of the CHSKU. The Anglican Church in China, with most of the other churches in that country, adopted the principles of the Three-Self Movement – self-support, self-government and self-propagation. The old diocese of Victoria, Hong Kong, was divided into South China and Hong Kong and Macao, which became a new province in 1998.

After the establishment of the People's Republic, contacts with the churches outside China became few and sporadic. Nevertheless, between 1955 and 1963 there were a limited number of visits in both directions. Outstanding among these were the visits of Bishop K. H. Ting of Chekiang to England in 1956; and in the same year visits to China of the Bishop of Hong Kong and subsequently of a delegation from the Australian Church led by the late Primate of Australia, the Most Revd H. W. K. Mowll.

With the outbreak of the Great Proletarian Cultural Revolution in China in 1966, contacts with churches outside China became very difficult. All the churches were closed and most church leaders were imprisoned or sent to work in factories or in the countryside. It was only after the death of Mao Zedong in 1976 and the downfall of the extreme left that organized religious activities returned to normal. In 1979 churches began to reopen and in 1980 the National Christian Conference was held. Besides the reconstituting of the Three-Self Movement, a significant new development was the creation of the China Christian Council to take charge of the internal affairs of the Church. In the mid-1980s the China Christian Council decided the time was ripe to take a new ecumenical step forward and declared that the Protestant Church in China had entered a post-denominational phase, although a few churches remained outside and the process did not involve the Roman Catholic Church.

The Church in China has gone through a period which can only be described as an experience of death and resurrection. In spite of the sufferings and difficulties the number of Christians is greater than ever before. In 1949 there were 700,000 Protestant Christians and three million Roman Catholics. The official figure today is fifteen million plus Protestants and ten to twelve million Catholics; other estimates put the figure much higher. Under the direction of the China Christian Council more than 30,000 churches and meeting points are now open for worship. More than twenty million Bibles have been printed, not only in Chinese but also in a few ethnic languages. Several thousand students have graduated from 17 theological training centres and over 1,000 are currently in ministerial training. The Nanjing Theological Seminary has a graduate school which trains teachers in theology; a new Centre for Theological Research was established in 1996, and a successful correspondence course

sends out more than 30,000 copies of a bi monthly set of training materials for the use o volunteer evangelists.

International relationships have also been established. Bishop K. H. Ting visited the US, and Canada in 1979. A Chinese Christian delega tion, composed of Catholics and Protestants, took part in the first Christian conference on China in Montreal in 1980. In 1981 Bishop Ting and others attended a conference in Hong Kong sponsored by the Christian Conference of Asia during which they were able to be present at the con secration of the new Anglican Bishop of Hong Kong, Peter Kwong.

This was followed by many mutual visits including the churches in Britain. In October 1982 a Chinese delegation visited Britain and Ireland at the invitation of the British Council o Churches. Lord Runcie, the Archbishop of Can terbury at the time, made a private visit to China in the same year, and in December 1983 he led a BCC delegation of 20 representatives of the Brit ish churches to China. The present Archbishop of Canterbury, Dr George Carey, visited China in 1994 and other bishops in 1995 and 1996. Chinese bishops were also invited to the Lambeth Conference with representatives from the China Christian Council.

Churches Together in Britain and Ireland continue to develop the relations with China Regular exchanges take place. Those worth mentioning include delegations of women's groups, youth groups, theological students as well as theological educators. The British and Irish churches also co-operate with the Amity Foundation, a church-sponsored development agency, in areas of social service, rural development and English-language teaching. Every year several Amity English teachers are sent to various colleges in China. Since 1996 a British person has been seconded to the Hong Kong office of the Amity Foundation.

The suppression of the pro-democracy movement in June 1989 has cast a shadow on this encouraging development. Other factors, such as the perceived threat from the fast growth of the Christian churches and the collapse of Marxist regimes in Eastern Europe and Russia, contribute to a tighter policy of political and ideological control. Religious freedom is generally respected but the practical implementation of religious policy is governed by a stricter set of regulations. Non-official groups are under pressure to accept the regulations.

The relations between the Church in China and the churches in Britain are facilitated by the China Department of the Churches' Commission for Mission. The latter is a section of the Churches Together in Britain and Ireland (CTBI). The China Department is a continuation of the ecumenical China Study Project which was established in 1972 by the leading missionary societies, including Anglican organizations such as the

CMS, USPG and the Archbishop's China Appeal Fund. In 1987 it was integrated into the British Council of Churches. The latter passed a resolution in 1988 and appealed to its member churches to respond ecumenically to the post-denominational challenge of the Protestant Church in China by renouncing bilateral relations with China on a denominational basis. This challenge has taken on a new dimension since the Roman Catholic Church of England, Wales and Scotland joined the CTBI in 1990.

The Friends of the Church in China, an ecu-menical association which works closely with the China Department of CTBI, takes a more grass-roots approach in relation to Christians in China. It publishes a popular news-sheet on China and organizes a yearly visit to Chinese churches.

China Department/CTBI, Inter-Church House, 35–41 Lower Marsh, London SE1 7RL. *Tel*: 020–7620 4444. The contact is Mr Edmond Tang.

Friends of the Church in China, 49 Pages Lane, Muswell Hill, London N10 1QB. Its Chairman is Dr Martin Conway and the Secretary is the Revd David Mullins.

OTHER CHURCHES IN COMMUNION WITH THE CHURCH OF ENGLAND

Old Catholic Churches of the Union of Utrecht

The Old Catholic Churches are a family of nationally organized churches which bound themselves together in the Union of Utrecht in 1889. Most of them owe their origin to Roman Catholics who were unable to accept the decrees of the First Vatican Council in 1870 and left the communion of that Church. The Archbishopric of Utrecht (from which the other Old Catholic Churches derived their episcopal orders) has been independent of Rome since the eighteenth century following a complex dispute involving papal and capitular rights of nomination and accusations of Jansenism (until 1910 in the Netherlands only). The Latin Mass continued in use, though all the Old Catholic Churches now worship in the vernacular. Their rites stand within the Western tradition, with various 'Eastern' features.

By the acceptance of the Bonn Agreement on 20 and 22 January 1932, the Convocation of Canterbury established full communion with the Old Catholic Churches by means of the following resolutions:

'That this House approves of the following statements agreed on between the representatives of the Old Catholic Churches and the Churches of the Anglican Communion at a Conference held at Bonn on 2 July 1931:

1. Each Communion recognises the catholicity and independence of the other and maintains its own.
2. Each Communion agrees to admit members of the other Communion to participate in the Sacraments.
3. Intercommunion does not require from either Communion the acceptance of all doctrinal opinion, sacramental devotion, or liturgical practice characteristic of the other, but implies that each believes the other to hold all the essentials of the Christian Faith.

'And this House agrees to the establishment of Intercommunion between the Church of England and the Old Catholics on these terms.'

An Anglican–Old Catholic International Co-ordinating Council was established in 1998.

AUSTRIA
Bishop Rt Revd Bernhard Heitz, Schottenring 17/1/3/12, A–1010 Vienna

CROATIA
(Bishopric vacant)

CZECH REPUBLIC
Bishop Rt Revd Dusan Hejbal, Cirkve Starokatolicke v CR, Hladkóv 3, CZ–169 00 Prague 6

GERMANY
Bishop Rt Revd Joachim Vobbe, Gregor Mendelstrasse 28, 53115 Bonn, Germany

NETHERLANDS
Archbishop Most Revd Antonius Jan Glazemaker (Archbishop of Utrecht and President of the International Bishops' Conference), Kon Wilhelminalaan, 3, NL–3818 HN Amersfoort

POLAND (The Polish National Catholic Church)
Prime Bishop Most Revd Wiktor Wysoczanski, ul. Balanowa 7, PL–02–635 Warsaw

SWITZERLAND
Bishop Rt Revd Hans Gerny, Willadingweg 39, CH–3006 Bern

USA (Polish National Catholic Church of America and Canada)
Prime Bishop Most Revd John Swantek, 115 Lake Scranton Rd, Scranton PA18505, USA

Philippine Independent Church

The Philippine Independent Church is in part the result of the Philippine revolution against Spain in 1896 for religious emancipation and Filipino identity. It was formally established in 1902, declaring its independence from the Roman Catholic Church but seeking to remain loyal to the Catholic Faith. It now derives its succession from the Protestant Episcopal Church in the

United States of America (and therefore from Anglican sources), with which full communion was established in September 1961.

It has a membership of approximately four million followers, 28 dioceses with 50 bishops, 600 regular church buildings and 2,000 village chapels served by about 600 priests.

Following the report of a Commission appointed by the Archbishop of Canterbury, full communion on the basis of the Bonn Agreement was established between the Church of England and the Philippine Independent Church in 1963 by the Convocations of Canterbury and York. It is in full communion with all the member Churches in the Anglican Communion.

The Philippine Independent Church is very active in its ecumenical relations. It is the most senior member in the National Council of the Churches in the Philippines, a member of the Council of Churches in East Asia, a member of the Christian Churches in Asia, and an active member of the World Council of Churches.

Supreme Bishop (*Obispo Maximo*) Most Revd Alberto Ramento, 1500 Taft Avenue, Ermita, Manila, Philippines 2801

Mar Thoma

During the latter part of the nineteenth century the Syrian Orthodox Church of Malabar divided into two over the issues of autonomy from the Patriarchate of Antioch and the removal of non-biblical features from teaching and worship, the latter issue being a result of the influence of Anglican missionaries of the Church Missionary Society who had been working in Malabar since the beginning of the century. The larger section (which itself has subsequently divided into the Indian Orthodox and Jacobite Churches) chose closer links with Antioch and remained 'unreformed'; the smaller group which eventually adopted the name of Mar Thoma Syrian Church of Malabar rejected Patriarchal authority and undertook a conservative revision of its rites, removing elements (such as the invocation of saints) which were felt not to be scriptural in origin. The general form of Mar Thoma worship remains Orthodox. Its episcopal succession derives from the Patriarchate of Antioch.

The former CIPBC (Church of India, Pakistan, Burma and Ceylon) had partial intercommunion with the Mar Thoma Church from 1937 until 1961 when a Concordat of Full Communion was established. The Mar Thoma Church is now in full communion with the united churches in India and Pakistan. With the Church of South India and the Church of North India it has formed a Joint Council to facilitate co-operation in mission and theological and social issues. The Mar Thoma Church has stated its desire to preserve its Eastern traditions and is not willing to merge with the two Western-derived united churches. Several Anglican provinces have recently entered into a relationship of full communion with the Mar Thoma Church, and others are in the process of doing so. The Church of England established communion with the Mar Thoma Church in 1974.

In 1989 the Metropolitan of the Malabar Independent Syrian Church of Thozhiyoor (a small 'unreformed' Syrian Orthodox Church in communion with the Mar Thoma Church) visited England and expressed his willingness to extend eucharistic hospitality to members of the Church of England.

THE MAR THOMA SYRIAN CHURCH
Most Revd Dr Alexander Mar Thoma
Metropolitan
Poolatheen
Tiruvalla 689 101
Kerala
South India

THE MALABAR INDEPENDENT SYRIAN CHURCH
Most Revd Joseph Mar Koorilose
Thozhiyur
680 520 Trichur (Dt)
Kerala
South India

Maps of the Churches and Provinces of the Anglican Communion

The maps of the Anglican Communion which follow have been supplied by Barbara Lawes of
The Mothers' Union. She will be happy to hear of any changes which need to be made.

ANGLICAN AND PORVOO COMMUNIONS

MAP 1

The Scottish Episcopal Church
1   Moray, Ross and Caithness
2   Argyll and the Isles
3   St Andrews, Dunkeld and Dunblane
4   Aberdeen and Orkney
5   Brechin
6   Glasgow and Galloway
7   Edinburgh

.... Diocesan Boundary

— — — Provincial Boundary

The Isles of Scilly are included
in the Diocese of Truro

The Channel Islands are annexed
to the Diocese of Winchester

The Church of Ireland
Province of Armagh
8 Derry and Raphoe
9 Connor
10 Tuam, Killala and Achonry
11 Kilmore, Elphin and Ardagh
12 Clogher
13 Armagh
14 Down and Dromore

Province of Dublin
15 Limerick and Killaloe
16 Meath and Kildare
17 Cork, Cloyne and Ross
18 Cashel and Ossory
19 Dublin and Glendalough

The Church in Wales
20 Bangor
21 St Asaph
22 St Davids
23 Swansea and Brecon
24 Llandaff
25 Monmouth

The Church of England
Province of York
26 Carlisle
27 Newcastle
28 Durham
29 Ripon
30 Bradford
31 Blackburn
32 York
33 Wakefield
34 Manchester
35 Liverpool
36 Chester
37 Sheffield
38 Southwell
39 Sodor and Man

Province of Canterbury
40 Lichfield
41 Derby
42 Lincoln
43 Hereford
44 Worcester
45 Birmingham
46 Coventry
47 Leicester
48 Peterborough
49 Ely
50 Norwich
51 St Edmundsbury and Ipswich
52 Gloucester
53 Bristol
54 Oxford
55 St Albans
56 London
57 Chelmsford
58 Truro
59 Exeter
60 Bath and Wells
61 Salisbury
62 Winchester
63 Portsmouth
64 Guildford
65 Southwark
66 Rochester
67 Chichester
68 Canterbury
Diocese in Europe

Extra-Provincial Dioceses
Bermuda
Lusitanian Church
Spanish Reformed Episcopal Church

Falkland Islands

MAP 2

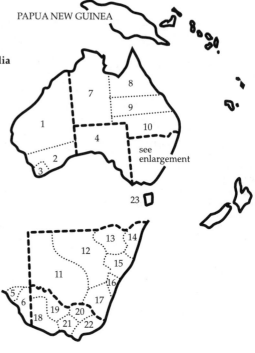

PAPUA NEW GUINEA

The Anglican Church of Australia

Province of Western Australia
1 North West Australia
2 Perth
3 Bunbury

Province of South Australia
4 Willochra
5 Adelaide
6 The Murray

Province of Queensland
7 The Northern Territory
8 North Queensland
9 Rockhampton
10 Brisbane

Province of New South Wales
11 Riverina
12 Bathurst
13 Armidale
14 Grafton
15 Newcastle
16 Sydney
17 Canberra and Goulburn

Province of Victoria
18 Ballarat
19 Bendigo
20 Wangaratta
21 Melbourne
22 Gippsland

23 Tasmania *(extra-provincial)*

The Anglican Church of Papua New Guinea
24 Aipo Rongo
25 Dogura
26 New Guinea Islands
27 Popondota
28 Port Moresby

MAP 3

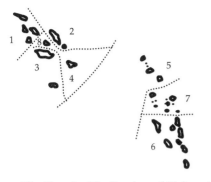

FIJI

16

TONGA

The Church of the Province of Melanesia
1 Ysabel
2 Malaita
3 Central Melanesia
4 Hanuato'o
5 Temotu
6 Vanuatu
7 Banks and Torres
8 Central Solomons

The Anglican Church in Aotearoa, New Zealand and Polynesia
9 Auckland
10 Waikato
11 Waiapu
12 Wellington
13 Nelson
14 Christchurch
15 Dunedin
16 Polynesia

Bishopric of Aotearoa
A Hui Amorangi ki te Tai Tokerau
B Hui Amorangi ki te Manawa o te Wheke
C Hui Amorangi ki te Tairawhiti
D Hui Amorangi ki te Upoko o te Ika
E Hui Amorangi ki te Waipounamu

—·—·—·—·—·— Bishopric of Aotearoa

ANGLICAN AND PORVOO COMMUNIONS

The Episcopal Church in the United States of America

Province I
1 Connecticut
2 Maine
3 Massachusetts
4 New Hampshire
5 Rhode Island
6 Vermont
7 Western Massachusetts

Province II
8 Albany
9 Central New York
10 Long Island
11 New Jersey
12 New York
13 Newark
14 Rochester
15 Western New York
Haiti *(see Map 5)*
Virgin Islands *(see Map 5)*
Convocation of American Churches
   in Europe

Province III
16 Bethlehem
17 Central Pennsylvania
18 Delaware
19 Easton
20 Maryland
21 Northwestern Pennsylvania
22 Pennsylvania
23 Pittsburgh
24 Southern Virginia
25 Southwestern Virginia
26 Virginia
27 Washington
28 West Virginia

Province IV
29 Alabama
30 Atlanta
31 Central Florida
32 Central Gulf Coast
33 East Carolina

34 East Tennessee
35 Florida
36 Georgia
37 Kentucky
38 Lexington
39 Louisiana
40 Mississippi
41 North Carolina
42 South Carolina
43 Southeast Florida
44 Southwest Florida
45 Tennessee
46 Upper South Carolina
47 West Tennessee
48 Western North Carolina

Province V
49 Chicago
50 Eau Claire
51 Fond du Lac
52 Indianapolis
53 Michigan
54 Milwaukee
55 Missouri
56 Northern Indiana
57 Northern Michigan
58 Ohio
59 Quincy
60 Southern Ohio
61 Springfield
62 Western Michigan
63 Eastern Michigan

Province VI
64 Colorado
65 Iowa
66 Minnesota
67 Montana
68 Nebraska
69 North Dakota
70 South Dakota
71 Wyoming

Province VII
72 Arkansas
73 Dallas
74 Fort Worth
75 Kansas
76 Northwest Texas
77 Oklahoma
78 Rio Grande
79 Texas
80 West Missouri
81 West Texas
82 Western Kansas
83 Western Louisiana

Province VIII
84 Arizona
85 California
86 Eastern Oregon
87 El Camino Real
88 Idaho
89 Los Angeles
90 Navajoland
91 Nevada
92 Northern California
93 Olympia
94 Oregon
95 San Diego
96 San Joaquin
97 Spokane
98 Utah
Hawaii
Alaska *(see Map 6)*
Taiwan *(see Map 13)*

MAP 4

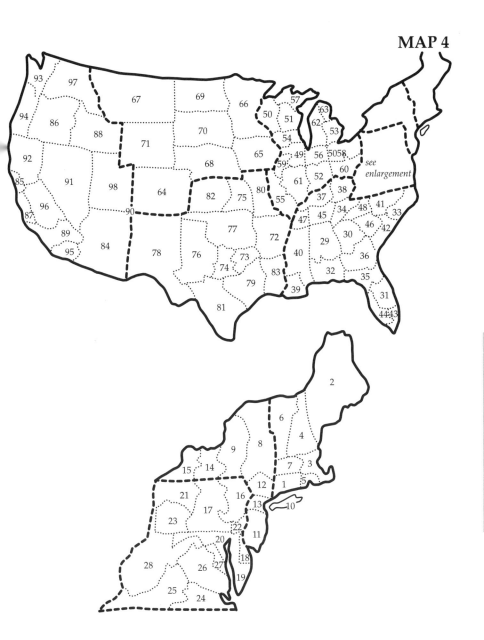

see enlargement

ANGLICAN AND PORVOO
COMMUNIONS

MAP 5

**The Church in the Province
of the West Indies**
32 Belize
33 Jamaica
34 North Eastern Caribbean
   & Aruba
35 Windward Islands
36 Barbados
37 Trinidad and Tobago
38 Guyana
39 Nassau and the Bahamas

**The Episcopal Church
of Cuba**
(Autonomous diocese)
40 Cuba

Province IX
2 Honduras
6 Litoral
7 Ecuador
8 Colombia
9 Dominican Republic
11 Puerto Rico (*extra-provincial*)
12 Venezuela (*extra-provincial*)
Europe (Convocation of American Churches)

The Anglican Church of Mexico
13 Western Mexico
14 Northern Mexico
15 Mexico
16 Cuernavaca
17 Southeastern Mexico

The Anglican Church of the Central American Region
1 Guatemala
3 El Salvador
4 Nicaragua
5 Panama
10 Costa Rica

The Episcopal Anglican Church of Brazil
18 Rio de Janeiro (formerly Central Brazil)
19 Recife (formerly Northern Brazil)
20 Southern Brazil
21 São Paulo (formerly South Central Brazil)
22 Southwestern Brazil
23 Brasilia
24 Pelotas

FALKLAND
ISLANDS

Anglican Church of the Southern Cone of America

25 Argentina	29 Peru
26 Chile	30 Uruguay
27 Northern Argentina	31 Bolivia
28 Paraguay	

41 Bermuda (*extra-provincial
   to Canterbury*)

MAP 6

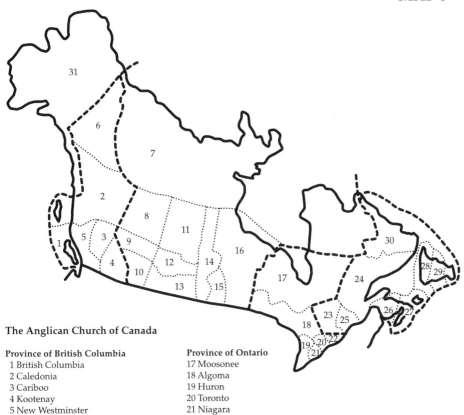

The Anglican Church of Canada

Province of British Columbia
1 British Columbia
2 Caledonia
3 Cariboo
4 Kootenay
5 New Westminster
6 Yukon

Province of Rupert's Land
7 Arctic
8 Athabasca
9 Edmonton
10 Calgary
11 Saskatchewan
12 Saskatoon
13 Qu'Appelle
14 Brandon
15 Rupert's Land
16 Keewatin

Province of Ontario
17 Moosonee
18 Algoma
19 Huron
20 Toronto
21 Niagara
22 Ontario

Province of Canada
23 Ottawa
24 Quebec
25 Montreal
26 Fredericton
27 Nova Scotia
28 Western Newfoundland
29 Central Newfoundland
30 Eastern Newfoundland and Labrador

31 Alaska *(in Province VIII of ECUSA)*

ANGLICAN AND PORVOO COMMUNIONS

MAP 7

Angola is at present an Archdeaconry of the Diocese of Lebombo

The Church of the Province of Southern Africa

1 Niassa
2 Lebombo
3 St Mark the Evangelist
4 Pretoria
5 Highveld
  (formerly South Eastern Transvaal)
6 Christ the King
7 Johannesburg
8 Klerksdorp
9 Kimberley and Kuruman
10 Namibia
11 Cape Town
12 George
13 Port Elizabeth

14 Grahamstown
15 St John's
16 Umzimvubu
17 Bloemfontein
18 Natal
19 Zululand
20 Lesotho
21 Swaziland
  St Helena
  Order of Ethiopia

The Church of the Province of Central Africa

22 Northern Zambia
23 Central Zambia
24 Lusaka
25 Eastern Zambia
26 Lake Malawi
27 Northern Malawi
28 Southern Malawi
29 Harare
30 Manicaland
31 Central Zimbabwe
32 Matabeleland
33 Botswana

The Church of the Province of the Indian Ocean

34 Antsiranana
35 Mahajanga
36 Antananarivo
37 Toamasina
38 Mauritius
39 Seychelles

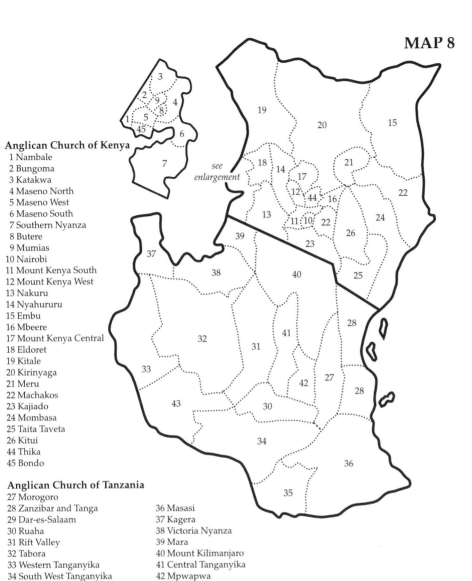

MAP 8

Anglican Church of Kenya
 1 Nambale
 2 Bungoma
 3 Katakwa
 4 Maseno North
 5 Maseno West
 6 Maseno South
 7 Southern Nyanza
 8 Butere
 9 Mumias
10 Nairobi
11 Mount Kenya South
12 Mount Kenya West
13 Nakuru
14 Nyahururu
15 Embu
16 Mbeere
17 Mount Kenya Central
18 Eldoret
19 Kitale
20 Kirinyaga
21 Meru
22 Machakos
23 Kajiado
24 Mombasa
25 Taita Taveta
26 Kitui
44 Thika
45 Bondo

Anglican Church of Tanzania
27 Morogoro
28 Zanzibar and Tanga
29 Dar-es-Salaam
30 Ruaha
31 Rift Valley
32 Tabora
33 Western Tanganyika
34 South West Tanganyika
35 Ruvuma

36 Masasi
37 Kagera
38 Victoria Nyanza
39 Mara
40 Mount Kilimanjaro
41 Central Tanganyika
42 Mpwapwa
43 Southern Highlands

see enlargement

ANGLICAN AND PORVOO
COMMUNIONS

Maps of the Anglican Communion   397

MAP 9

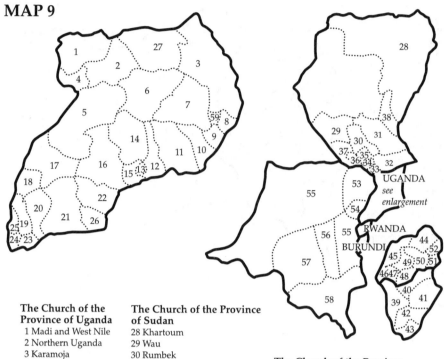

The Church of the Province of Uganda
1 Madi and West Nile
2 Northern Uganda
3 Karamoja
4 Nebbi
5 Bunyoro-Kitara
6 Lango
7 Soroti
8 North Mbale
9 Mbale
10 Bukedi
11 Busoga
12 Mukono
13 Kampala
14 Luwero
15 Namirembe
16 Mityana
17 Ruwenzori
18 South Ruwenzori
19 North Kigezi
20 West Ankole
21 East Ankole
22 West Buganda
23 Kigezi
24 Muhabura
25 Kinkizi
26 Central Buganda
27 Kitgum
59 Sebei

The Church of the Province of Sudan
28 Khartoum
29 Wau
30 Rumbek
31 Bor
32 Juba
33 Kajo-Keji
34 Yei
35 Mundri
36 Maridi
37 Yambio
38 Malakal
The following dioceses have also been created
El Obeid
Rejaf
Ezzo
Lui
Kadugli and Nubian Mountains
Yirol
Renk
Torit
Cueibit
Ibba
Rokon
Lainya
Port Sudan

The Church of the Province of Burundi
39 Bujumbura
40 Buye
41 Gitega
42 Matana
43 Makamba

The Church of the Province of Rwanda
44 Byumba
45 Shyira
46 Cyangugu
47 Kigeme
48 Butare
49 Shyogwe
50 Kigali
51 Kibungo
52 Gahini

The Church of the Province of the Congo
53 Boga
54 Nord-Kivu
55 Kisangani
56 Kindu
57 Bukavu
58 Katanga (formerly Shaba)

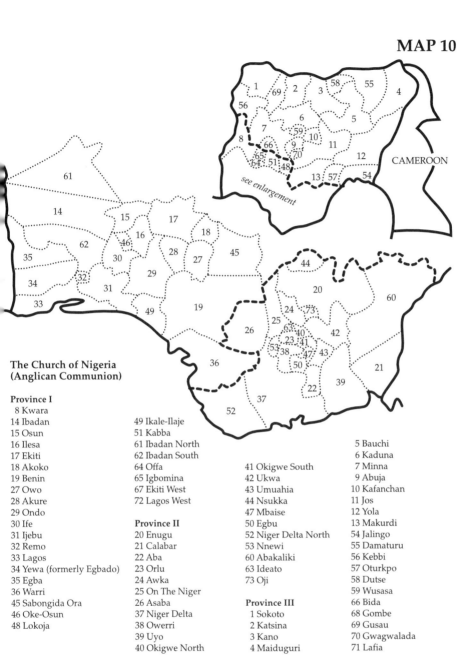

MAP 10

CAMEROON

see enlargement

The Church of Nigeria (Anglican Communion)

Province I
8 Kwara
14 Ibadan
15 Osun
16 Ilesa
17 Ekiti
18 Akoko
19 Benin
27 Owo
28 Akure
29 Ondo
30 Ife
31 Ijebu
32 Remo
33 Lagos
34 Yewa (formerly Egbado)
35 Egba
36 Warri
45 Sabongida Ora
46 Oke-Osun
48 Lokoja

49 Ikale-Ilaje
51 Kabba
61 Ibadan North
62 Ibadan South
64 Offa
65 Igbomina
67 Ekiti West
72 Lagos West

Province II
20 Enugu
21 Calabar
22 Aba
23 Orlu
24 Awka
25 On The Niger
26 Asaba
37 Niger Delta
38 Owerri
39 Uyo
40 Okigwe North

41 Okigwe South
42 Ukwa
43 Umuahia
44 Nsukka
47 Mbaise
50 Egbu
52 Niger Delta North
53 Nnewi
60 Abakaliki
63 Ideato
73 Oji

Province III
1 Sokoto
2 Katsina
3 Kano
4 Maiduguri

5 Bauchi
6 Kaduna
7 Minna
9 Abuja
10 Kafanchan
11 Jos
12 Yola
13 Makurdi
54 Jalingo
55 Damaturu
56 Kebbi
57 Oturkpo
58 Dutse
59 Wusasa
66 Bida
68 Gombe
69 Gusau
70 Gwagwalada
71 Lafia

ANGLICAN AND PORVOO COMMUNIONS

Maps of the Anglican Communion

399

MAP 11

The Episcopal Church in Jerusalem and the Middle East
1 Cyprus and the Gulf
2 Iran
3 Egypt
4 Jerusalem

Anglican Communion in Japan (Nippon Sei Ko Kai)
1 Hokkaido
2 Tohoku
3 Kita Kanto
4 Tokyo
5 Yokohama
6 Chubu (Mid Japan)
7 Kyoto
8 Osaka
9 Kobe
10 Kyushu
   Okinawa (*see Map 13*)

The Church of the Province of West Africa
1 The Gambia
2 Guinea
3 Liberia
4 Freetown
5 Bo
6 Tamale
7 Kumasi
8 Koforidua
9 Accra
10 Cape Coast
11 Sekondi
12 Sunyani
Cameroon (*see Map 7*)

MAP 12

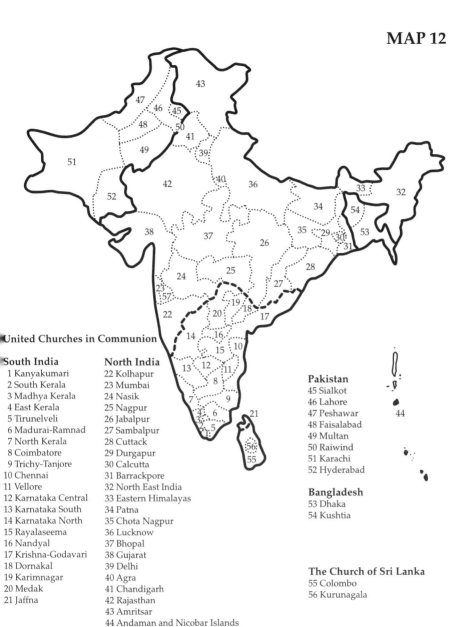

United Churches in Communion

South India
1 Kanyakumari
2 South Kerala
3 Madhya Kerala
4 East Kerala
5 Tirunelveli
6 Madurai-Ramnad
7 North Kerala
8 Coimbatore
9 Trichy-Tanjore
10 Chennai
11 Vellore
12 Karnataka Central
13 Karnataka South
14 Karnataka North
15 Rayalaseema
16 Nandyal
17 Krishna-Godavari
18 Dornakal
19 Karimnagar
20 Medak
21 Jaffna

North India
22 Kolhapur
23 Mumbai
24 Nasik
25 Nagpur
26 Jabalpur
27 Sambalpur
28 Cuttack
29 Durgapur
30 Calcutta
31 Barrackpore
32 North East India
33 Eastern Himalayas
34 Patna
35 Chota Nagpur
36 Lucknow
37 Bhopal
38 Gujarat
39 Delhi
40 Agra
41 Chandigarh
42 Rajasthan
43 Amritsar
44 Andaman and Nicobar Islands
57 Pune

Pakistan
45 Sialkot
46 Lahore
47 Peshawar
48 Faisalabad
49 Multan
50 Raiwind
51 Karachi
52 Hyderabad

Bangladesh
53 Dhaka
54 Kushtia

The Church of Sri Lanka
55 Colombo
56 Kurunagala

ANGLICAN AND PORVOO COMMUNIONS

MAP 13

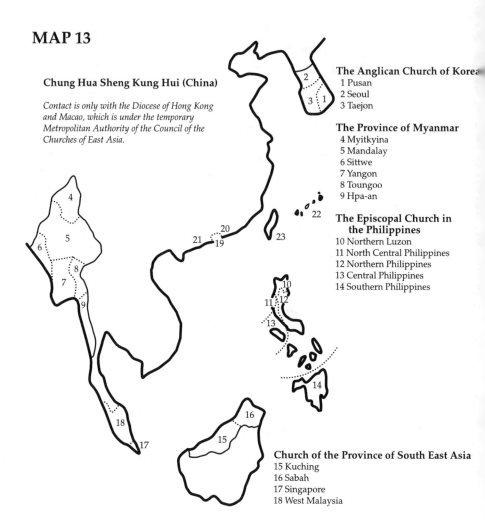

Chung Hua Sheng Kung Hui (China)

Contact is only with the Diocese of Hong Kong and Macao, which is under the temporary Metropolitan Authority of the Council of the Churches of East Asia.

The Anglican Church of Korea
1 Pusan
2 Seoul
3 Taejon

The Province of Myanmar
4 Myitkyina
5 Mandalay
6 Sittwe
7 Yangon
8 Toungoo
9 Hpa-an

The Episcopal Church in the Philippines
10 Northern Luzon
11 North Central Philippines
12 Northern Philippines
13 Central Philippines
14 Southern Philippines

Church of the Province of South East Asia
15 Kuching
16 Sabah
17 Singapore
18 West Malaysia

22 Okinawa
(Diocese in the Holy Catholic Church of Japan)

23 Taiwan
(Diocese in Province VIII of ECUSA)

Hong Kong Sheng Kung Hui
19 Hong Kong Island
20 Eastern Kowloon
21 Western Kowloon

THE PORVOO COMMUNION

n October 1992 representatives of the four British and Irish Anglican churches, the five Nordic Lutheran churches and the three Baltic Lutheran churches met in Finland for the fourth and final plenary session of their formal Conversations, which had commenced in 1989. They agreed *The Porvoo Common Statement*, named after Porvoo Cathedral, in which they had celebrated the Eucharist together.

The Common Statement recommended that the participating churches jointly make the Porvoo Declaration, bringing them into communion with each other. This involves common membership, a single, interchangeable ministry and structures to enable the churches to consult each other on significant matters of faith and order, life and work. The implementation of the commitments contained in the Declaration is co-ordinated by the Porvoo Agreement Contact Group.

In 1994 and 1995 the Declaration was approved by the four Anglican churches, four of the Nordic Lutheran churches and two of the Baltic Lutheran churches. The General Synod's final approval of the Declaration in July 1995, following a reference to the diocesan synods, was by overwhelming majorities in each House. The Danish bishops announced in August 1995 that none of them was able to approve the Declaration, and the Evangelical-Lutheran Church of Latvia has not yet reached its decision. The Declaration was signed in the autumn of 1996 at services in Trondheim (Norway), Tallinn (Estonia) and Westminster Abbey.

The Nordic Lutheran churches are the historic national churches of their respective countries. At the Reformation, when they adhered to Lutheranism, they continued to be episcopally ordered, retaining the historic sees. In Sweden and Finland the succession of the laying on of hands at episcopal consecration was unbroken, whereas in Denmark, Norway and Iceland this was not the case. The Estonian and Latvian Lutheran churches are similarly their countries' historic national churches, which became Lutheran at the Reformation. Only in the northern part of Estonia was episcopacy retained, and there only until 1710, but it was restored in both Estonia and Latvia in the twentieth century, the bishops being consecrated in the historic succession. The Lithuanian Lutheran Church, which is now a small minority church, adopted episcopacy in historic succession in 1976.

The Porvoo Agreement supersedes earlier separate agreements dating from the 1920s, 1930s and 1950s with the churches concerned (except the Lithuanian Lutheran Church). These provided for mutual eucharistic hospitality and (with the Swedish, Finnish, Estonian and Latvian churches) mutual participation in episcopal consecrations. Because of the Soviet occupation of the Baltic States, however, it was only in 1989 and 1992 respectively that it was possible for an Anglican bishop to participate in a Latvian and an Estonian consecration for the first time.

The Porvoo Declaration commits the signatory churches 'to regard baptized members of all of our churches as members of our own'. It also means that clergy ordained by bishops of the signatory churches are placed in the same position with regard to ministry in the Church of England as those ordained by Anglican bishops overseas.

The text of the Porvoo Common Statement is available as CCU Occasional Paper No. 3 (£2.85 inc. p&p) and in *Together in Mission and Ministry. The Porvoo Common Statement with Essays on Church and Ministry in Northern Europe* (Church House Publishing, 1993), which also contains fuller information on the history of the churches and the earlier agreements. Further information can be found on The Porvoo Page: The Homepage of the Porvoo Communion: www.svkyrkan.porvoo.

The Porvoo Agreement Contact Group
Co-Chairmen
Rt Revd John Neill (*Bishop of Cashel and Ossory*);
Rt Revd Dr Erik Vikström (*Bishop of Porvoo*)

Co-Secretaries
Revd Dr Johan Dalman (Church of Sweden);
Revd Dr Charles Hill (Church of England Council for Christian Unity – *see* page 19)

KEY

⚲ Cathedral city
+ Suffragan see

The Diocese of Porvoo is a
non-geographical diocese, consisting
of the Swedish language parishes
in Finland.

Churches in the Porvoo Communion

NORDIC LUTHERAN CHURCHES

The Evangelical–Lutheran Church of Finland

The first bishop in the Finnish Church was St Henrik, the Apostle of Finland. According to tradition, St Henrik was an Englishman who accompanied the Swedish king on a military expedition to south-western Finland in 1155 and was martyred there the following year. From the middle of the thirteenth century until 1809 Finland was part of Sweden, and until the Reformation it formed a single diocese (Turku) in the Province of Uppsala.

In 1554 the Swedish king appointed the Finnish Lutheran Reformer Mikael Agricola (d. 1557) as Bishop of Turku, at the same time founding a second Finnish see, Viipuri (eventually transferred to Tampere). In addition to translating the New Testament and parts of the Old into Finnish, Mikael Agricola compiled the first hymnal, liturgy and ritual in Finnish. He is regarded as the father of Finnish as a written language.

A wave of revivals, beginning in the eighteenth century, gave rise in the nineteenth to four mass movements. These remained within the Church of Finland and are still influential on its life today.

In 1809 Finland was annexed by Russia. As a result, the Finnish Church became entirely independent of the Church of Sweden, and from 1817 the Bishop of Turku was styled Archbishop. Finland finally gained its independence in 1917.

Today, 86 per cent of Finns are members of the Church of Finland, while only 4 per cent are members of other churches. The Church of Finland is a 'folk church' (as is the Orthodox Church). The framework for its life is set by the Ecclesiastical Act. Amendments to this state law can only be proposed by the Synod, and Parliament can accept or reject but not amend such proposals. The Church is governed by the Synod, the Ecclesiastical Board and the Bishops' Conference. Although the archbishop is only *primus inter pares* of the Finnish bishops, he is the President of the Synod and chairs both the Bishops' Conference and the Ecclesiastical Board.

Porvoo Agreement Contact Revd Dr Juhani Forsberg, Department for International Relations, Satamakatu 11, Box 185, FIN-00161 Helsinki   *Tel*: 00 358–9 1802 290
Fax: 00 358–9 1802 230
email: juhani.forsberg@evl.fi

HELSINKI
Bishop Rt Revd Dr Eero Huovinen, Diocesan Chapter, PL 142, FIN-00121 Helsinki
Tel: 00 358–9 709 25 70
Fax: 00 358–9 709 25 88
email: eero.huovinen@evl.fi

KUOPIO
Bishop Rt Revd Dr Wille Riekkinen, Diocesan Chapter, PL 42, FIN-70101 Kuopio
Tel: 00 358–17 261 3801
Fax: 00 358–17 261 3836
email: wille.riekkinen@evl.fi

LAPUA
Bishop Rt Revd Dr Jorma Laulaja, Diocesan Chapter, PL 60, FIN-62101 Lapua
Tel: 00 358–6 438 8623
Fax: 00 358–6 437 4214
email: jorma.laulaja@evl.fi

MIKKELI
Bishop Rt Revd Dr Voitto Huotari, Diocesan Chapter, PL 122, FIN-50101 Mikkeli
Tel: 00 358–15 151 390
Fax: 00 358–15 151 003
email: voitto.huotari@evl.fi

OULU
Bishop Rt Revd Dr Olavi Rimpiläinen, Diocesan Chapter, PL 85, FIN-90101 Oulu
Tel: 00 358–8 311 4654
Fax: 00 358–8 311 0659
email:
olavi.rimpilainen@oulun-tuomiokapituli.inet.fi

PORVOO
[The Diocese of Porvoo (Borgå) is a non-geographical Swedish-language diocese.]
Bishop Rt Revd Dr Erik Vikström, Diocesan Chapter, PB 30, FIN-06101 Borgå
Tel: 00 358–19 527 716
Fax: 00 358–19 585 705
email: erik.vikstrom@evl.fi

TAMPERE
Bishop Rt Revd Dr Juha Pihkala, Diocesan Chapter, PL 53, FIN-33201 Tampere
Tel: 00 358–3 223 1960
Fax: 00 358–3 212 9493
email: juha.pihkala@evl.fi

ANGLICAN AND PORVOO COMMUNIONS

TURKU
Archbishop of Turku and Finland Vacancy, PL 60,
FIN-20501 Turku   *Tel*: 00 358–2 251 6500
                   Fax: 00 358–2 251 6541
                   email: Arkkipiispa@evl.fi

Bishop of Turku Rt Revd Dr Ilkka Kantola (*same address*)   *email*: Ilkka.Kantola@evl.

The Evangelical–Lutheran Church of Iceland

Christianity was adopted at Thingvellir by decree of the legislature in the year 1000. The ancient Icelandic sees of Skálholt and Hólar were founded in 1055 and 1106, respectively. Having previously been under the jurisdiction of Bremen and Lund, from 1153 Iceland belonged to the Province of Nidaros (Trondheim). Part of the Kingdom of Norway from 1262, Iceland eventually came under Danish rule. The Lutheran Reformation was introduced in 1541. From this time onwards until 1908 (with one exception in the late eighteenth century), Icelandic bishops were consecrated by the Bishops of Sealand (Copenhagen).

The two Icelandic sees were united in 1801, but in 1909 they were revived as suffragan sees. Iceland gained its independence from Denmark in 1918, becoming a republic in 1944.

A new church law came into effect on 1 January 1998, granting the Church considerable autonomy from the state. The Church Assembly is its highest organ of the Church. Today, around 90 per cent of the Icelandic population are members of the Church of Iceland.

Porvoo Agreement Contact Revd Baldu Kristjánsson, Háaleiti, 815 Thorlákshöfn
                   Tel: 00 354–483 377
                   Fax: 00 354–483 356
                   email: baldurkr@centrum.i

The Church of Iceland comprises a single diocese, with two suffragan bishops in the ancient sees of Hólar and Skálholt.

Bishop of Iceland Most Revd Karl Sigurbjörnsson Laugavegur 31, 150 Reykjavík
                   Tel: 00 354–535 1500
                   Fax: 00 354–551 328
                   email: biskup@kirkjan.i

Bishop of Skálholt Rt Revd Sigurdur Sigurdarson Skálholti biskupshúsi, 801 Selfoss
                   Tel: 00 354 486 8972
                   Fax: 00 354 486 897
                   email: srsig@eyjar.is

Bishop of Hólar Rt Revd Bolli Þorir Gústavsson Hólum, biskupssetri, 551 Sauðákrókur
                   Tel: 00 354 453 6593

The Church of Norway

From around AD 1000 Christianity was brought to Norway by missionaries both from the British Isles and from Germany. Central to the Christianizing of Norway was King Olav Haraldsson. After his death in 1030 he was venerated as St Olave, and his shrine in Nidaros Cathedral (Trondheim) was a centre of pilgrimage. Episcopal sees were established in Nidaros, Bergen, Oslo (by 1100), and in Stavanger (1125) and Hamar (1153). Part of the Province of Lund from 1103, Norway became a separate province when Nidaros was raised to an archiepiscopal see in 1153. In addition to the five Norwegian sees, the Province of Nidaros also included six further dioceses covering Iceland, the Faeroes, Greenland, the Shetland and Orkney Islands, the Hebrides and the Isle of Man. Under Olav IV (1380–87) Norway was united with Denmark.

The Norwegian Reformation of 1537 was imposed by the new King of Denmark, Christian III, with little evidence of popular enthusiasm. New bishops ('superintendents') were ordained to the sees of Nidaros, Bergen and Stavanger by Johannes Bugenhagen, the Superintendent of Wittenberg, in 1537, and Bugenhagen's Danish Church Order was extended to Norway in 1539. Of the pre-Reformation bishops, Bishop Hans Rev of Oslo alone accepted the Reformation, and returned to his see (to which that of Hamar had been united) as Superintendent in 1541. The diocesan structure had been retained, with four of the five historic sees, and the term 'bishop' soon replaced its Latin synonym 'superintendent', but until recent years neither Bishop Rev nor any other bishop consecrated in the historic succession of the laying on of hands participated in the consecration of future bishops. Nidaros ceased to be an archiepiscopal see, Oslo replacing it *de facto* as the senior Norwegian see.

In the eighteenth and nineteenth centuries, pietist movements became influential, but they remained within the Church of Norway, the membership of which still amounts to 88 per cent of the population. During the German occupation of 1940–45, the Church was a focus of resistance under the leadership of Bishop Eivind Berggrav of Oslo (1884–1959). In 1993 Rosemarie Köhn became the Church of Norway's first (and so far only) woman bishop, when the Norwegian government appointed her Bishop of Hamar.

The Church of Norway has an 86-member General Synod, consisting of the 77 members of the eleven diocesan councils (including the bishops), three members representing clergy, laity and lay employees, three non-voting representatives of the theological faculties and three Sami representatives. Its executive is the 15-member National Council, which has a lay chairman. Related central bodies include the Bishops' Conference, the Council on Foreign Relations, the Sami Church Council and a doctrinal commission. Church legislation still requires parliamentary approval. The King of Norway remains the Church's constitutional head, and the government retains powers over the Church, exercised through the Ministry of the Church, Education and Research.

Porvoo Agreement Contact Revd Dr Stephanie Dietrich, Council on Ecumenical and International Relations, PO Box 5816, Majorstua, N-0308 Oslo 3   *Tel*: 00 47–22 93 27 50
Fax: 00 47–22 93 28 28/29

AGDER
Bishop Rt Revd Olav Skjevesland, Diocesan Centre, Gyldenloves gate 9, N-4611 Kristiansand
Tel: 00 47–38 02 27 33
Fax: 00 47–38 02 92 50

BJØRGVIN
Bishop Rt Revd Ole Hagescœther, Diocesan Centre, Kalvedalsveien 45A, N-5018 Bergen
Tel: 00 47–55 30 64 70
Fax: 00 47–55 30 64 85
email: bjoergvin.biskop:kirken.no

BORG
Bishop Rt Revd Ole Chr. M. Kvarme, PO Box 403, N-1601 Fredrikstad   *Tel*: 00 47–69 30 79 00
Fax: 00 47–69 31 01 74
email: borg.bdr@kirken.no

HAMAR
Bishop Rt Revd Rosemarie Köhn, Folkestadgt 52, N-2300 Hamar   *Tel*: 00 47–62 53 01 11
Fax: 00 47–62 52 92 71
email: hamar.bdr@kirken.no

MØRE
Bishop Rt Revd Odd Bondevik (*Praeses of the Bishop's Conference*), Diocesan Centre, Julsundveien 30, N-6400 Molde
Tel: 00 47–71 25 06 70
Fax: 00 47–71 25 06 71
email: moere.bdr@kirken.no

NIDAROS
Bishop Rt Revd Finn Wagle, Archbishop's House, N-7013 Trondheim   *Tel*: 00 47–73 53 91 00
Fax: 00 47–73 53 91 11
email: nidaros.bdr@kirken.no

NORD-HÅLOGALAND
Bishop Rt Revd Ola Steinholt, PO Box 790, N-9001 Tromsø   *Tel*: 00 47–77 60 39 60/61
Fax: 00 47–77 68 00 87
email: nord-haalogaland.bdr@kirken.no

OSLO
Bishop Rt Revd Gunnar Staalsett, PO Box 9307, Gronland, N-0135 Oslo   *Tel*: 00 47–22 19 37 00
Fax: 00 47–22 68 28 92
email: oslo.biskop@kirken.no

SØR-HÅLOGALAND
Bishop Rt Revd Øystein Larsen, PO Box 374, N-8001 Bodø   *Tel*: 00 47–75 52 55 73
Fax: 00 47–75 52 39 33
email: soer-haalogaland.bdr@kirken.no

STAVANGER
Bishop Rt Revd Dr Ernst Oddvar Baasland, Diocesan Centre, Eiganesveien 113, N-4009 Stavanger   *Tel*: 00 47–51 84 62 70
Fax: 00 47–51 84 62 71
email: stavanger.biskop@kirken.no

TUNSBERG
Bishop Rt Revd Sigurd Osberg, PO Box 1253, Trudvang, N-3105 Tønsberg
Tel: 00 47–33 31 73 00
Fax: 00 47–33 31 40 11
email: tunsberg.bdr@kirken.no

The Church of Sweden

The first to preach the gospel in Sweden was St Ansgar (801–65), the first Archbishop of Hamburg-Bremen, but it was in the eleventh century that the systematic conversion of Sweden was begun, largely by missionaries from England. From 1104 the new Swedish dioceses formed part of the Nordic Province of Lund (which was Danish until 1658), but only until 1164, when Uppsala was raised to an archiepiscopal see. The most celebrated figure of the medieval Swedish Church was St Birgitta of Vadstena (1303–73), foundress of the Brigittine Order.

Under the Lutheran Reformers Olaus Petri (1493–1552) and his brother Laurentius (d. 1573), who became the first Lutheran archbishop in 1531, the Swedish Reformation was gradual, and moderate in character. The Augsburg Confession was adopted in 1593.

The eighteenth and nineteenth centuries saw both latitudinarian and pietist movements, and in the early twentieth century a strong high-church movement developed. Archbishop Nathan Söderblom (1866–1931), one of the leading figures of the Ecumenical Movement, used the concept of 'evangelical catholicity' to describe the Church of Sweden's position. In 1997 Christina Odenberg became the Church of Sweden's first woman bishop, when she was appointed Bishop of Lund.

The Church of Sweden is governed by a General Synod with 251 members and a 15-member Central Board (chaired by the Archbishop), together with the Bishops' Conference. The bishops attend the Synod, but are not members of it, although they have all the rights of members except the right to vote. They are *ex-officio* members of the Synod Committee on Church Doctrine. A separation of Church and State will be effected in the year 2000. Some 87 per cent of Swedish citizens are members of the Church of Sweden.

Porvoo Agreement Contact Revd Dr Johan Dalman, Church of Sweden, S-75170 Uppsala
Tel: 00 46–18 169 573
Fax: 00 46–18 169 538

GÖTEBORG
Bishop Rt Revd Dr Lars Eckerdal, Stiftskansliet, Box 11937, S-404 39 Göteborg
Tel: 00 46–31 771 30 30
Fax: 00 46–31 771 30 30

HÄRNÖSAND
Bishop Rt Revd Dr Karl-Johan Tyrberg, Stiftskansliet, Box 94, S-871 22 Härnösand
Tel: 00 46–611 254 00
Fax: 00 46–611 134 75

KARLSTAD
Bishop Rt Revd Dr Bengt Wadensjö, Stiftskansliet, Box 186, S-651 05 Karlstad
Tel: 00 46–54 17 24 00
Fax: 00 46–54 17 24 70

LINKÖPING
Bishop Rt Revd Dr Martin Lind, Stiftskansliet, Agatan 65, S-582 22 Linköping
Tel: 00 46–13 24 26 00
Fax: 00 46–13 14 90 95

LULEÅ
Bishop Rt Revd Rune Backlund, Stiftskansliet, Stationsgatan 40, S-972 32 Luleå
Tel: 00 46–920 26 4700
Fax: 00 46–920 26 47 27

LUND
Bishop Rt Revd Christina Odenberg Stiftskansliet, Box 32, S-221 00 Lund
Tel: 00 46–46 35 87 00
Fax: 00 46–46 18 49 48

SKARA
Bishop Rt Revd Lars-Göran Lönnermark Malmgatan 14, S-532 32 Skara
Tel: 00 46–511 262 00
Fax: 00 46–511 262 70

STOCKHOLM
Bishop Rt Revd Caroline Krook, Stiftskansliet, Box 2016, S-103 11 Stockholm
Tel: 00 46–8 508 940 00
Fax: 00 46–8 24 75 75

STRÄNGNÄS
Bishop Rt Revd Dr Jonas Jonson, Stiftskansliet, Box 84, S-645 22 Strängnäs
Tel: 00 46–152 234 00
Fax: 00 46–152 234 56

UPPSALA
Archbishop Most Revd Dr Karl Gustav Hammar, S-751 70 Uppsala
Tel: 00 46–18 16 95 00
Fax: 00 46–18 16 96 25

Bishop Rt Revd Dr Tord Harlin, Box 1314, S-751 43 Uppsala
Tel: 00 46–18 68 07 00
Fax: 00 46–18 12 45 25

VÄSTERÅS
Bishop Rt Revd Dr Claes-Bertil Ytterberg, Stiftskansliet, V Kyrkogatan 9, S-722 15 Västerås
Tel: 00 46–21 17 85 00
Fax: 00 46–21 12 93 10

VÄXJÖ
Bishop Rt Revd Anders Wejryd, Östrabo, S-352 39 Växjö
Tel: 00 46–470 77 38 00
Fax: 00 46–470 72 95 50

VISBY
Bishop Rt Revd Dr Biörn Fjärstedt, Stiftskansliet, Box 1334, S-621 24 Visby
Tel: 00 46–498 29 26 00
Fax: 00 46–498 21 01 03

Further information about the history of the Nordic Lutheran churches and of their relations with the Church of England can be found in Lars Österlin, *Churches of Northern Europe in Profile. A Thousand Years of Anglo-Nordic Relations* (Norwich, 1995).

BALTIC LUTHERAN CHURCHES

The Estonian Evangelical–Lutheran Church

The conversion of Estonia to Christianity began at the end of the tenth century, and the first known bishop was consecrated in 1165. The mission was prosecuted by the Brethren of the Sword, an order founded in 1202 which merged with the Teutonic Order in 1237. In 1219 the Danes conquered the northern area and founded the capital Reval (Tallinn), which became an episcopal see within the Province of Lund. Further sees were established at Dorpat (Tartu) in 1224 and Hapsal (Saare-Lääne) in 1227, within the Province of Riga, the capital of Livonia, which included the southern part of modern Estonia. In some areas secular authority was in the hands of the bishops, while in others the Teutonic Order held sway. The entire area was very much under German dominance.

The Lutheran movement reached Estonia in 1523, and as early as the following year an assembly in Reval decided to adhere to the Reformation. Later in the century, however, the twin provinces of Estonia and Livonia became divided between neighbouring powers. Most of Estonia placed itself under Swedish rule in 1561, but Denmark ruled the island of Oesel (Saarema) from 1560 to 1645 and Livonia was annexed by Poland from 1561 to 1621. In Swedish Estonia, the Church was governed by a bishop and consistory, but Danish ecclesiastical law was introduced in Oesel, while Livonia came under the influence of the Counter-Reformation. Superintendents, rather than bishops, were appointed for these areas after they came under Swedish rule (in 1621 and 1645).

In 1710 both provinces came under Russian rule. In Estonia the office of bishop was replaced with that of superintendent. The consistories were chaired by laymen. In 1832 the Lutheran churches of all three Baltic provinces were united with Russia's German-speaking Lutheran Church into a Russian Lutheran Church, with a General Consistory in St Petersburg. Each province (and – until 1890 – Reval, Oesel and Riga separately) had its own General superintendent and consistory. The University of Dorpat (Tartu), originally founded in 1632, was refounded in 1802. As the only Protestant theological faculty in the Russian Empire, it was of great importance.

Throughout the period up to 1918 the clergy were German, like the ruling elite. The Moravian Church, which was active in Estonia and Livonia from 1736, enjoyed considerable influence over the Estonian peasantry, and by 1854 there were 276 Moravian prayer halls. However, the Moravian authorities blocked the development of this movement into a separate Moravian Church, and the Moravians' adherents remained within the Lutheran Church.

In 1918 Estonia and the Estonian northern part of Livonia became an independent state. The Church too became independent. It remained united, having both German and Estonian clergy and members. The office of bishop was immediately restored, the first bishop being consecrated in 1921 by the Archbishop of Uppsala and a Finnish bishop.

Estonia's independent existence lasted little more than 20 years, however. In 1940 it was occupied by the Red Army. German occupation followed, but Soviet rule was restored in 1944. Archbishop Kópp, who had remained unconsecrated because the war prevented bishops from other countries travelling to Estonia, went into exile with 70 other clergy and members of congregations. Of the clergy who remained, one third were eventually deported to Siberia. Not until 1968 was it possible for an archbishop to be consecrated.

In 1988, Estonia began to move towards independence, which was achieved in 1991. This was accompanied by a remarkable blossoming of church life. The Theological Faculty at Tartu, which had been dissolved by the Soviet authorities, was reopened.

The Estonian Evangelical-Lutheran Church is governed by a General Synod, the executive organ of which is the six-member Consistory.

Porvoo Agreement Contact Dr Alar Laats, Consistory of the EELC, Kiriku plats 3, 10130 Tallinn

Tel: 00 372–6 27 73 66
Fax: 00 372–6 27 73 52

Archbishop of Estonia Most Revd Jaan Kiivit, Consistory of the EELC, Kirikuplats 3, EE-10130 Tallinn

Tel: 00 372–6 27 73 50
Fax: 00 372–6 27 73 52

The Evangelical–Lutheran Church of Lithuania

Not until 1387 was an episcopal see established in Vilnius, following the baptism the previous year of Grand Duke Jogaila (whose coronation as King of Poland inaugurated a union lasting until 1795), and it was 1418 before the inhabitants of German-dominated Samogitia (covering much of present-day Lithuania) were forced to accept baptism.

A Lutheran congregation was founded in Vilnius as early as 1521, but persecution forced the Lithuanian Reformer Martin Mazvydas to flee to Königsberg. In time the Lithuanian nobility established the Reformed faith on their estates, while the numerous German merchants and craftsmen established Lutheran congregations in the towns from the 1550s. Until the early nineteenth century, the Lutheran Church continued to be a German and urban minority church. Sigismund Vasa (1587–1632) successfully restored Roman Catholicism as the religion of the people, and subsequent anti-Protestant policies meant that by 1775, when religious freedom was granted, just 30 Reformed and five Lutheran congregations remained (except those in Prussian-ruled Tauragé/Tauroggen).

In 1795 most of Lithuania was ceded to Russia, and Lithuania's Lutheran congregations were placed under the Consistory of Courland (now southern Latvia). Immigration of Lutheran Letts, Germans and Lithuanians from East Prussia produced new Lutheran congregations, especially in the countryside. The pastors (only nine in 1918) were all Germans.

At independence in 1918, Lithuania's population included 75,000 Lutherans, of whom roughly 30,000 were Germans, 30,000 Lithuanians and 15,000 Letts. In 1920 separate synods had to be formed for the three linguistic groups, and for much of the inter-war period tension between them paralysed the Lutheran Church. By 1939, however, there were 55 congregations with 33 pastors. To these should be added the separate Lutheran Church of the Prussian *Memelgebiet*, which Lithuania annexed in 1923. By 1939 this had 135,000 members (the majority German) in 32 parishes, served by 39 pastors.

Lithuanian Lutheranism was soon to be decimated. In 1941, following the 1940 Soviet annexation of Lithuania, most of the German population, together with a large number of Lithuanian Lutherans, emigrated to Germany. In Memelland and the Vilnius area, both reintegrated into Lithuania and thus the Soviet Union in 1945, the picture was even more stark. All but 30,000 inhabitants fled, while the pastor of the historic Lutheran church in Vilnius emigrated with his entire congregation.

A provisional Lutheran Consistory found itself responsible for 20,000 Lithuanians and Letts in Lithuania proper, together with just 15,000 Lithuanians in Klaipéda (Memelland). There were no pastors in Klaipéda and only six in the rest of the country, three of whom were soon banished to Siberia. After Stalin's death in 1953 and a first post-war synod in 1955, the structures of church life were gradually restored, but several thousand more Protestants emigrated between 1957 and 1965. At a second synod in 1970, Jonas Kalvanas, the only pastor left who had studied theology at university (he was ordained in 1940), was elected to chair the Consistory. It was with his consecration as Bishop by the Archbishop of Estonia in 1976 that his church gained the historic episcopate. He was succeeded in 1995 by his son and namesake, in whose consecration the Bishop of Tonbridge shared.

In 1992 the Lutheran Church had 41 congregations, with about 15,000 communicant members and twelve clergy (including deacons).

Porvoo Agreement Contact Revd Darius Petkunas, Simonaitytes 18–21, LIT-5814 Klaipeda
Tel: 00 370–6 220 409
Fax: 00 370–6 258 270
email: petkunas@usa.net

Bishop of the Evangelical-Lutheran Church of Lithuania Rt Revd Jonas Kalvanas, Bretkuno 13, LIT-5900 Taurage   *Tel*: 00 370–46 53 451

NON-SIGNATORY CHURCHES

The Evangelical–Lutheran Church in Denmark

n August 1995 the bishops of the fifth Nordic Lutheran church, the Evangelical-Lutheran Church in Denmark, announced that they were not able to approve the Porvoo Declaration. Its provisions therefore do not apply to that church. At meetings held under the Porvoo Agreement, the Church of Denmark is represented by observers.

However, an agreement providing for mutual eucharistic hospitality between the Church of England and the Evangelical-Lutheran Church in Denmark (approved by the churches in 1954 and 1956 respectively) remains in force.

Observer at meetings of the Porvoo Agreement Contact Group Revd Ane Hjerrild, Council on Inter-national Relations, Vestergade 8, 1 DK-1456 Copenhagen K *Tel*: 00 45–33 114488
Fax: 00 45–33 119588
email: interchurch@folkekirken.dk

Bishop of Copenhagen Rt Revd Erik Norman Svendsen, Nørregade 11, DK-1165 Copenhagen
Tel: 00 45–33 13 35 08
Fax: 00 45–33 14 39 69

The Evangelical–Lutheran Church of Latvia

The Church of Latvia has not yet voted on the Porvoo Declaration.

Porvoo Agreement Contact The Archbishop

Archbishop of Riga and Latvia Most Revd Jānis Vanags, M. Pils iéla 4, LV-1050 Riga
Tel: 00 371–722 6057
Fax: 00 371–782 0041
email: vanags@lanet.lv

There are also Anglican chaplaincies in most of the countries covered by the Porvoo Agreement. These belong to the Archdeaconry of Scandinavia and Germany within the Diocese in Europe. A leaflet giving details is available from the Diocesan Office of the Diocese in Europe, *see below*.

The *Directory of English-speaking Churches Abroad* is available from Intercontinental Church Society, 1 Athena Drive, Tachbrook Park, Warwick CV34 6NL. *Tel*: (01926) 430347
Fax: (01926) 330238
email: enquiries@ics-uk.org

Continental Anglican churches are listed in the *Diocesan Directory* of the Diocese of Gibraltar in Europe, available from the Diocesan Office, 14 Tufton St, Westminster, London SW1P 3QZ *Tel*: 020–7976 8001
Fax: 020–7976 8002

Ecumenical | **PART 6**

PART 6 CONTENTS

ECUMENICAL

The Church of England is committed to the search for full, visible unity with other Christian churches, and to the bodies which promote this at the local, intermediate, national, European and world levels. The Council for Christian Unity acts, on behalf of the Bishops' Council, as the principal channel of communication between the General Synod and the national and international bodies.

ECUMENICAL CANONS

Canon B43 (Of Relations with Other Churches) and Canon B44 (Of Local Ecumenical Projects) encourage and make provision for sharing in worship with other churches. Full details are given in *The Ecumenical Relations Code of Practice* (Church House, 1989) and Supplement (CCU, 1997, 50p). The following churches in England have been designated by the Archbishops of Canterbury and York as churches to which the Church of England (Ecumenical Relations) Measure, and thus Canons B43 and B44, apply: The Baptist Union, The Methodist Church, The Moravian Church, The Roman Catholic Church in England and Wales, The United Reformed Church, The Congregational Federation, The International Ministerial Council of Great Britain, The Lutheran Council of Great Britain, The Greek Orthodox Archdiocese of Thyateira and Great Britain, The Council of African and Afro-Caribbean Churches, The Free Church of England, The Southam Road Evangelical Church Banbury, The Assemblies of God in Great Britain and Ireland, The New Testament Church of God, the Russian Orthodox Church, the Church of Scotland (presbyteries in England).

The Evangelical Church in Germany

The Evangelical Church in Germany (Evangelische Kirche in Deutschland – EKD) is a Communion of 25 member churches (mostly *Landeskirchen* or territorial churches). Of these, ten are Lutheran (eight of them forming the United Evangelical Lutheran Church – VELKD), one is purely Reformed, one is predominantly Reformed and twelve are United (seven forming the Evangelical Church of the Union – EKU, which is the twenty-fifth member church). In many of the United churches the Lutheran tradition predominates.

In November 1988 the General Synod welcomed the Meissen Common Statement, *On the Way to Visible Unity*, which called for a closer relationship between the Church of England and the German Evangelical Churches. The Meissen Declaration, which it recommended, was approved by the General Synod in July 1990 without dissent, and solemnly affirmed and proclaimed an Act of Synod on 29 January 1991. The Meissen Declaration makes provision for the Church of England and the Evangelical Church in Germany to live in closer fellowship with one another (though not yet with interchangeable ministries) and commits them to work towards the goal of full visible unity. The member churches of the EKD have been designated as churches to which the Ecumenical Canons apply (*see* **Ecumenical Canons**).

The Meissen Commission (the Sponsoring Body for the Church of England–EKD Relations) exists to oversee and encourage relationships (*see* Council for Christian Unity). Fuller information is contained in *The German Evangelical Churches* (CCU Occasional Paper No 1 – £2.95 + 35p p&p) and Anglo-German Ecumenical Links: An Information Pack (£1 inc. p&p). The text of the Meissen Agreement can be found in *The Meissen Agreement: Texts* (CCU Occasional Paper No 2 – £2.10 inc. p&p). These are all available from the Council for Christian Unity.

Chairman of the EKD Council Präses Manfred Kock (*Präses of the Evangelical Church in the Rhineland*)

German Co-Secretary of the Meissen Commission OKR Paul Oppenheim, EKD Kirchenamt, Postfach 21 02 20, D–30402 Hannover, Germany
Tel: (00 49) 511 2796 127
Fax: (00 49) 511 2796 725
email: ekd@ekd.de

Churches Together in England

Churches Together in England is in association with Churches Together in Britain and Ireland. Its basis is as follows:

Churches Together in England unites in pilgrimage those Churches in England which, acknowledging God's revelation in Christ, confess the Lord Jesus Christ as God and Saviour according to the Scriptures, and, in obedience to God's will and in the power of the Holy Spirit, commit themselves:

– to seek a deepening of their communion with Christ and with one another in the Church, which is his body; and
– to fulfil their mission to proclaim the Gospel by common witness and service in the world

to the glory of the one God, Father, Son and Holy Spirit.

The Presidents of Churches Together in England are: The Archbishop of Canterbury, the Cardinal Archbishop of Westminster, Revd Dr Kathleen Richardson, and Rowena Loverance, who meet together quarterly.

It has 23 Member Churches: Baptist Union of Great Britain, Cherubim and Seraphim Council of Churches, Church of England, Church of Scotland, Congregational Federation, Council of African and Afro-Caribbean Churches, Council of Oriental Orthodox Christian Churches, Free Churches' Federal Council, Greek Orthodox Church, Ichthus Christian Fellowship, Independent Methodist Churches, International Ministerial Council of Great Britain, Joint Council for Anglo-Caribbean Churches, Lutheran Council of Great Britain, Methodist Church, Moravian Church, New Testament Assembly, Religious Society of Friends, Roman Catholic Church, Russian Orthodox Church, Salvation Army, United Reformed Church, Wesleyan Holiness Church.

The Religious Society of Friends has membership under a clause designed for 'any Church or Association of Churches which on principle has no credal statements in its tradition'.

All substantive decisions are taken by these Member Churches.

The Seventh Day Adventist Church is an Observer.

Churches Together in England encourages its Member Churches to work together nationally, and provides various means for this purpose. There is an *Enabling Group*, which meets three times a year. There is a *Forum* of 300 members, which meets every other year. Its Moderator is Mrs Terry Garley and its Deputy Moderator Rt Revd David Hawtin (*Bishop of Repton*).

There are 16 *Co-ordinating Groups* (*see below*).

There are also a large number of informal or as yet not formally recognized groups and networks.

Churches Together in England encourages its Member Churches to work together locally. To enable this most counties and metropolitan areas have established ecumenical councils and officers, whose task is to foster and encourage all sorts of ecumenical work locally within their areas. The main task of the two Field Officers (*see below*) is to support those working in counties and metropolitan areas.

Churches Together in England publishes an ecumenical news bulletin, *Pilgrim Post*, six times a year.

General Secretary Revd Bill Snelson, Churches Together in England, 101 Queen Victoria St, London EC4V 4EN *Tel*: 020–7332 8230/1
Fax: 020–7332 8234

Executive and Communications Officer Mrs Judith Lampard (*same address*)

Field Officer South Revd Roger Nunn (*same address*)

Field Officer North & Midlands Mrs Jenny Carpenter, Churches Together in England, Crookesmoor Valley Methodist Church, Crookesmoor Road, Sheffield S6 3FQ
Tel: 0114–268 2151
Fax: 0114–266 8731

CO-ORDINATING GROUPS
GROUP FOR LOCAL UNITY
Secretary Mrs Jenny Carpenter (*address see above*)

GROUP FOR EVANGELIZATION
Secretary Revd Roger Whitehead, The Manse, 116 High St, Harrold, Beds MK43 7BJ
Tel: (01234) 721127

CHRISTIAN ADULT LEARNING MEETING
Secretary Tony McCaffry, St Mary's University College, Waldegrave Rd, Twickenham TW1 4SX
Tel: 020–8240 4196

CHURCHES JOINT EDUCATION POLICY COMMITTEE
Miss Gillian Wood, Free Churches' Council, 27 Tavistock Square, London WC1H 9HH
Tel: 020–7387 8413

CHURCHES COMMITTEE FOR HOSPITAL CHAPLAINCY
Secretary Revd Christine Pocock, Free Churches' Council, 27 Tavistock Square, London WC1H 9HH *Tel*: 020–7387 8413

CHURCHES COMMUNITY WORK ALLIANCE
Secretary Revd Brian Ruddock, 36 Sandygate, Wath-upon-Dearne, Rotherham S63 7LW
Tel and *Fax*: 01709 873254
email: ccwa@btinternet.com

ENGLISH CHURCHES YOUTH SERVICE
Secretary Peter Ball, Church House, Great Smith St, London SW1P 3NZ *Tel*: 020–7898 1506

THEOLOGY AND UNITY GROUP
Secretary Revd Bill Snelson (*address see above*)

CHURCHES RURAL GROUP
Secretary Revd Michael Cruchley, Arthur Rank Centre, The National Agricultural Centre, Stoneleigh Park, Warws CV8 2LZ

CHURCHES TOGETHER FOR FAMILIES
Secretary Pauline Butcher, FCC, 27 Tavistock Square, London WC1H 9HH   *Tel*: 020–7387 8413

CHURCHES MILLENNIUM GROUP
Executive Secretary Revd Stephen Lynas, Church House, Great Smith St, London SW1P 3NZ
Tel: 020–7898 1436

INDEM (Group for Mission in Industry and the Economy)
Paul Fuller, Pump Hill Cottage, Donington Rd, South Willingham, Lincs LN8 6NJ

SPIRITUALITY GROUP
Secretary Judith Lampard (*as above*)

WOMEN'S CO-ORDINATING GROUP
Secretary Vacancy

There are also five *Agencies*:

CHURCHES ADVISORY COUNCIL FOR LOCAL BROADCASTING
General Secretary Mr Jeff Bonser, PO Box 124, Westcliff on Sea, Essex SSO 0QU
Tel: (01702) 348369

CHRISTIAN ENQUIRY AGENCY
Secretary Phillip Clements-Jewery, Inter-Church House, 35–41 Lower Marsh, London SE1 7RL
Tel: 020–7620 4444

CHRISTIAN AID
Director Dr Daleep Mukarji, PO Box 100, London SE1 7RL   *Tel*: 020–7620 4444

CAFOD
Director Mr Julian Filochowski, 2 Romero Close, Stockwell Rd, London SW9 9TY
Tel: 020–7733 7900

OPPORTUNITIES FOR VOLUNTEERING
Secretary Mr Malcolm Smart, Inter-Church House, 35–41 Lower Marsh, London SE1 7RL
Tel: 020–7620 4444

The following are *Bodies in Association* with Churches Together in England: Afro-West Indian United Council of Churches, Association of Interchurch Families, Bible Society, Christians Aware, College of Preachers, Fellowship of Prayer for Unity, Focolare Movement, Iona Community, National Retreat Association, Student Christian Movement, Young Men's Christian Association, Young Women's Christian Association.
The address of the Focolare Movement is Mari Ponticaccia, 62 King's Ave, London SW4 8BH. For other addresses, *see* pages 421–3 (under CTBI) or the **List of Organizations** (pages 266–320).

Intermediate County Bodies and Area Ecumenical Councils

Avon (Area of Greater Bristol)
Churches Together in Greater Bristol
Executive Secretary
Revd Brian Scott
9 Lodway Close
Pill
Bristol BS20 0DE
Tel: 01275 373488
Fax: 01275 373488

Avon (South)
see **Somerset**

Bedfordshire
Churches Together in Bedfordshire
Ecumenical Officer
(also Hertfordshire)
Revd Dr David Butler
114 High St
Watton-at-Stone
Herts SG14 3RZ
Tel: 01920 426829

Berkshire
Churches Together in Berkshire
County Ecumenical Officer
Revd Phil Abrey
51 Galsworthy Drive
Caversham Park
Reading RG4 0PR
Tel: 0118 947 5152

Birmingham, Greater
Birmingham Churches Together
General Secretary
Revd Mark Fisher
Carrs Lane Church Centre
Birmingham B4 7SX
Tel: 0121–643 6603

Buckinghamshire
(except Milton Keynes)
Buckinghamshire Ecumenical Council
County Ecumenical Officer
Canon Derek Palmer
124 Bath Rd
Banbury
Oxon OX16 0TR
Tel: 01295 268201

Cambridgeshire
Cambridgeshire Ecumenical Council
County Ecumenical Officer
Revd Frank Fisher
Stapleford Vicarage
Cambridge CB2 5BG
Tel: 01223 842150

Cheshire
Churches Together in Cheshire
County Ecumenical Officer
Canon Michael Rees
5 Abbey Green
Chester CH1 2JH
Tel: 01244 347500

Cleveland (North)
see **Durham**

Cleveland (South)
see **Yorkshire (North)**

Cornwall
Churches Together in
  Cornwall
Secretary

Revd Ian Haile
186 Bodmin Road,
Truro TR1 1RB
Tel: 01872 223755

Cumbria
Churches Together in
  Cumbria
*County Ecumenical
  Officer*

Revd Andrew Dodd
Church House
West Walls
Carlisle CA3 8UE
Tel: 01228 22573

Derbyshire
Churches Together in
  Derbyshire
Secretary

Mr Colin Garley
64 Wyndale Drive
Ilkeston,
Derbyshire DE7 4JG
Tel: 0115 932 9402

*Counties Ecumenical
  Officer for Derbyshire
  and Nottinghamshire*

Mrs Terry Garley
64 Wyndale Drive
Ilkeston,
Derbyshire DE7 4JG
Tel: 0115 932 9402

Devon
Christians Together in
  Devon
*County Ecumenical
  Officer*

Revd John Bradley
Grenville House
Whites Lane
Torrington
Devon EX38 8DS
Tel: 01805 625059

Dorset
Churches Together in
  Dorset
*County Ecumenical
  Officer*

Mrs Val Potter
22 D'Urberville Close
Dorchester
Dorset DT1 2JT
Tel: 01305 264416

**Durham (and North
  Cleveland)**
Durham Church
  Relations Group
  (DCRG)
Secretary

Canon John Hancock
St Michael's Vicarage
Westoe Rd
South Shields
NE33 3PJ
Tel: 0191–425 2074

Essex
Essex Churches
  Consultative Council
*County Ecumenical
  Officer*
(also London, Barking
  Area Church Leaders'
  Group)

Revd David
  Hardiman
349 Westbourne
  Grove
Westcliff on Sea
Essex SSO 0PU
Tel and *Fax*: 01702
  342327

**Gloucestershire (and
  North Avon)**
Gloucestershire
  Churches Together
*County Ecumenical
  Officer*

Revd Dr David
  Calvert
151 Tuffley Ave
Gloucester GL1 5NP
Tel: 01452 301347

Guernsey
Guernsey Council of
  Churches

Gillian Lenfestey
Les Adams de haut
St Pierre du Bois
Guernsey GY7 9LJ
Tel: 01481 63181

**Hampshire (and Isle of
  Wight and Channel
  Islands)**
Churches Together in
  Hampshire and the
  Isle of Wight
Area Ecumenical Officer

Dr Paul Rolph
71 Andover Rd
Winchester SO22 6AU
Tel: 01962 862574

Herefordshire
Churches Together in
  Herefordshire
Secretary

Mrs Anne Double
Malvern View
Garway Hill, Orcop
Hereford HR2 8EZ
Tel: 01981 580495

Hertfordshire
Churches Together in
  Hertfordshire
Ecumenical Officer
(also Bedfordshire)

Revd Dr David Butler
114 High St
Watton-at-Stone
Herts SG14 3RZ
Tel: 01920 426829

Hull and East Yorkshire
Churches Together in
  Kingston-upon-Hull
  and East Yorkshire
  (KEY)
Secretary

Revd David Perry
Skirlaugh Vicarage
Hull HU11 5HE
Tel: 01964 562259

Isle of Man
Churches Together in
  Man
Secretary

Revd Stephen Caddy
The Manse
11 Bayr Grianagh
Castletown
Isle of Man IM9 1HN
Tel: 01624 822541

Jersey
Christians Together in
  Jersey

Sister Loretta
  Madigan
Catholic Pastoral
  Centre
St Mary and St Peter's
  Church
Wellington Rd
St Helier
Jersey JE2 4RJ
Tel: 01534 732583
Fax: 01534 618833

Kent
Churches Together in
  Kent
*County Ecumenical
  Officer*
(including London
  Boroughs of Bexley
  and Bromley)

Revd Michael Cooke
St Lawrence Vicarage
Stone St, Seal
Sevenoaks
Kent TN15 0LQ
Tel: 01732 761766

Lancashire
Churches Together in
  Lancashire
*County Ecumenical
  Officer*

Revd Donald Parsons
45 Alder Drive
Hoghton
Preston PR5 0AS
Tel: 01254 852860

Leicestershire
Churches Together in
  Leicester
Secretary

Revd Barbara Stanton
The Rectory
Honeypot Lane
Husbands Bosworth
Lutterworth LE17 6LY
Tel: 01858 880351

All Lincolnshire
Churches Together in
  All Lincolnshire
Ecumenical Officer

Revd John Cole
c/o YMCA
St Rumbold St
Lincoln
Tel: 01522 520984
Fax: 01652 657484

London
**Barking and
  Dagenham,
  Havering, Newham,
  Redbridge and
  Waltham Forest**
Barking Area Church
  Leaders' Group
Secretary
(also Essex Churches
Consultative Council)

Revd David
  Hardiman
349 Westbourne
  Grove
Westcliff on Sea
Essex SSO 0PU
Tel: 01702 342327

London
**Enfield, Haringey,
  Camden, East Barnet**
North London Church
  Leaders' Group
Secretary

Revd Dr Philip
  Morgan
1 Ellesmere Ave
Mill Hill
London NW7 3EX
Tel: 020–8959 7246

London
**Hackney, Islington,
  Tower Hamlets**
East London Church
  Leaders' Group
Secretary

Revd Pauline Barnett
The Manse
Bethnal Green
London E2 9JP
Tel: 020–8980 5278

London
**Brent, Ealing, Harrow,
  Hillingdon**
Churches Together in
  North West London
Convenor

Mr Bill Boyd
20 Radnor Ave
Harrow
Middx HA1 1SB
Tel and Fax: 020–8427
  3418

London
**Hammersmith, Fulham,
  Hampton, Hounslow,
  Kensington, Chelsea,
  Spelthorne,
  Richmond (north of
  the Thames)**
Churchlink West
Convenor

Mr Tom Flynn
30 Glencairn Drive
Ealing
London W5 1RT
Tel: 020–8248 9947

**London
(South of the Thames)
Croydon, Greenwich,
  Kingston, Lambeth,
  Lewisham, Merton,
  Richmond,
  Southwark, Sutton,
  Wandsworth**
Churches Together in
  South London
Secretary

Sister Liz Grant
Hawkstone Hall
1A Kennington Rd
London
Tel: 020–7928 5395
Fax: 020–7928 8222

Manchester (Greater)
Greater Manchester
  Churches Together
*County Ecumenical
  Officer*

Sister Maureen
  Farrell FCJ
St Peter's House
Oxford Rd
Manchester
M13 9GH
Tel: 0161–273 5508
Fax: 0161–272 7172

Merseyside
Merseyside and Region
  Churches' Ecumenical
  Assembly (MARCEA)
Ecumenical Officer

Revd Martyn
  Newman
Friends Meeting
  House
65 Paradise St
Liverpool L1 3BP
Tel: 0151–709 0125

Milton Keynes
Milton Keynes Christian
  Council
Ecumenical Moderator

Revd Murdoch
  Mackenzie
c/o Christian
  Foundation
The Square
Aylesbury St
Wolverton
Milton Keynes
MK12 5HX
Tel: 01908 311310

Norfolk
Norfolk and Waveney
  Churches Together
Executive Officer

Revd Robin
  Hewetson
The Rectory
Marsham
Norwich NR10 5PP
Tel: 01263 733249

Northamptonshire
Northamptonshire
  Ecumenical Council
Executive Secretary

Mrs Christine Nelson
4 The Slade
Daventry
Northants NN11 4HH
Tel: 01327 705803

**Northumberland (and
  Tyne & Wear north of
  the Tyne)**
Newcastle Church
  Relations Group
Secretary

Revd Gordon Shaw
Pinehurst
Wansbeck Rd
Ashington
Northumberland
NE63 8JE
Tel: 01670 812137

ECUMENICAL

Nottinghamshire
Churches Together in
  Nottinghamshire
Secretary

Mr Alan Langton
35 Aylesham Ave
Woodthorpe View
Arnold
Nottingham NG5 6PP
Tel: 0115 926 9090

*Counties Ecumenical
  Officer for Derbyshire
  and Nottinghamshire*

Mrs Terry Garley
64 Wyndale Drive
Ilkeston
Derbyshire DE7 4JG
Tel: 0115 932 9402

Oxfordshire
Oxfordshire Ecumenical
  Council
Executive Secretary

Revd Dr Graeme
  Smith
Westminster College
Oxford OX2 9AT
Tel: 01865 247644
Fax: 01865 251847

Peterborough
Greater Peterborough
  Ecumenical Council

Mr Frank Smith
61 Hall Lane
Werrington
Peterborough
PE4 6RA
Tel: 01733 321245
(Home)
01733 51915 (Office)

Shropshire (not Telford)
Churches Together in
  Shropshire
Secretary

Mr Ged Cliffe
Fern Villa
Four Crosses
Llanymynech
SY22 6PR
Tel: 01691 831374

Somerset
Somerset Churches
  Together
Ecumenical Officer

Mr Robin Dixon
12 Lawson Close
Saltford
Bristol BS18 3LB
Tel: 01225 872903

Staffordshire
Staffordshire Plus
  Ecumenical Council
Secretary

Mr Mike Topliss
18 Selman's Hill
Bloxwich
Walsall WS3 3RJ
Tel: 01922 475932

Suffolk
Suffolk Churches
  Together
Ecumenical Officer

Mrs Margaret
  Condick
34 Rectory Lane
Kirton
Ipswich IP10 0PY
Tel: 01394 448576

Surrey
Churches Together in
  Surrey
Ecumenical Co-ordinator

Mrs Rosemary
  Underwood
The Parish Centre
Station Approach
Stoneleigh, Epsom
Surrey KT19 0QZ
Tel and *Fax*: 020–8394
  0536

Sussex
Sussex Churches
Ecumenical Officer

Revd Terry Stratford
14 Ledgers Meadow
Cuckfield
W. Sussex RH17 5EB
Tel: 01444 456588

Swindon
Churches Together in
  Swindon
Secretary

Anne Doyle
16 Sherwood Ave
Melksham
Wilts SN12 7HJ
Tel: 01225 704748

Telford
Telford Christian
  Council
Development Officer

Revd David Lavender
Parkfield
Park Avenue
Madeley
Telford TF7 5AB
Tel: 01952 585731

Tyne & Wear (South)
see **Durham**

Tyne & Wear (North)
  see **Newcastle
  Church Relations
  Group**

Warwickshire
Coventry &
  Warwickshire
  Ecumenical Council
Ecumenical Officer

Revd David Rowland
59 Tiverton Drive
Nuneaton CV11 6YJ
Tel: 01203 352551

West Midlands
West Midlands Region
  Churches Forum
General Secretary

Revd Mark Fisher
Carrs Lane Church
  Centre
Birmingham B4 7SX
Tel: 0121–643 6603

Wiltshire
Wiltshire Churches
  Together
Secretary

Anne Doyle
16 Sherwood Avenue
Melksham
Wilts SN12 7HJ
Tel: 01225 704748

Worcester
Dudley and
  Worcestershire
  Ecumenical Council
  (OWEC)
Ecumenical Officer

Revd Clifford Owen
The Rectory
Clifton-upon-Teme
Worcester WR6 6DJ
Tel: 01886 812483

Yorkshire (North)
divided into three
  Regional
  Ecumenical Forums:
  North York Moors,
  Vale of York

North York Moors

Revd Harold Dixon
Skirrid
102 Outgang Rd
Pickering YO18 7EL
Tel: 01751 473488

South Teesside	Vacancy	**Yorkshire (West)**	Dr Stephanie Rybak

South Teesside   Vacancy

Vale of York   Jean Abbey
The Manor
Moss End Farm
Hawkhills
Easingwold
York YO6 3EW
Tel: 01347 838593

Yorkshire (South)   Revd Louise Dawson
Churches Together in   Crookes Valley
    South Yorkshire   Methodist Church
Ecumenical Development   Crookesmoor Rd
    Officer   Sheffield S6 3FQ
        Tel: 0114 266 6156

Yorkshire (West)   Dr Stephanie Rybak
West Yorkshire   WYEC
    Ecumenical Council   62 Headingley Lane
    (WYEC)   Leeds LS6 2BU
Ecumenical Officer   *Tel*: 0113 274 7912
        Fax: 0113 224 9998

Churches Together in Britain and Ireland

Office Inter-Church House, 35–41 Lower Marsh, London SE1 7RL
Tel: 020–7620 4444
Fax: 020–7928 0010
email: gensec@ctbi.org.uk
Web: www.ctbi.org.uk

Presidents
Rt Revd Mario Conti
Rt Revd Barry Rogerson
Revd Nezlin Sterling
Sister Eluned Williams
(One vacancy)

Hon Treasurer Dr Jeremy Gerhard

General Secretary Dr David Goodbourn

Churches Together in Britain and Ireland (CTBI) is a fellowship of churches in Britain and Ireland which 'confess the Lord Jesus Christ as God and Saviour according to the Scriptures and therefore seek to fulfil together their common calling to the glory of the one God, Father, Son and Holy Spirit'. Churches Together in Britain and Ireland was renamed in 1999; it was previously the Council of Churches for Britain and Ireland. CTBI co-ordinates the work of its 32 member churches and liaises with ecumenical bodies in Britain and Ireland as well as ecumenical organizations at European and international level. Its work includes Church life, Church and Society, Mission, International Affairs and Racial Justice. It provides a forum for joint decision-making and enables the Churches to take action together.

CTBI, which is an Associated Council of Churches of the World Council of Churches and the Conference of European Churches, co-ordinates the work of the member churches and bodies in association in Britain and Ireland which are themselves grouped together in Churches Together in England, CYTUN (Churches Together in Wales), ACTS (Action of Churches Together in Scotland) and Irish ecumenical bodies, particularly the Irish Council of Churches.

CTBI works through an Assembly meeting every two years and a Church Representatives' Meeting, meeting at least twice each year. The Church of England members of the CRM are the Rt Revd Barry Rogerson, Mr Philip Mawer, Mrs Margaret Swinson and the Revd Sam Philpott. Ultimately authority for the Council is rooted in the decision-making bodies of the participating churches and the different patterns of authority in the churches are reflected in the balance between the meetings of CTBI. These meetings of CTBI give direction to the Council and are the means by which the churches decide on work which can appropriately be done together and the priority to be placed on such work. CTBI is financed by the member churches and bodies in association and by other donations.

The Week of Prayer for Christian Unity is observed each year from 18 to 25 January. The leaflets are available from September each year from CTBI Publications. Other ecumenical publications and a catalogue may be obtained from CTBI Publications, Inter-Church House, 35–41 Lower Marsh, London SE1 7RL.

CTBI works in co-operation with agencies which undertake work entrusted to them by the churches. In particular there is a very close relationship with Christian Aid, CAFOD and SCIAF, three overseas agencies sponsored by the member churches of the Council. Other agencies are One World Week, Christians Abroad and the Churches Commission on Overseas Students.

There is a provision in CTBI's constitution for the emergence of Commissions through which the churches will co-operate on particular aspects of work which they have decided to undertake together. The first Commission was the Churches' Commission on Mission which grew out of the work of the Conference for World Mission. The further Commissions for Racial Justice and Inter-Faith Relations have also been established. The decisions about recognizing Commissions are taken by the Church Representatives'

Meeting, and the integration of their work into the wider work of the churches is partly the responsibility of the Co-ordinating Secretaries. Commissions, to qualify for establishment within CTBI, must be supported by the churches with appropriate financing, staffing and other resourcing.

The most common method of working is through Networks of formal and informal organizations and groupings that help to develop the witness of the churches and whose work and insights are made available to the churches together through CTBI's Co-ordinating Secretaries.

SCHEDULE OF REPRESENTATION

The schedule of representation in the Council is as follows:

Full Members Baptist Union of Great Britain, 12; Cherubim & Seraphim Council of Churches, 2; Church in Wales, 8; Church of England, 45; Church of Ireland, 12; Church of Scotland, 30; Congregational Federation, 2; Council of African & Afro-Caribbean Churches, 3; Council of Oriental Orthodox Christian Churches, 3; Free Churches' Council, 2; Greek Orthodox Church, 5; Independent Methodist Churches, 2; International Ministerial Council of Great Britain, 2; Joint Council for Anglo-Caribbean Churches, 2; Lutheran Council of Great Britain, 2; Methodist Church, 20; Methodist Church in Ireland, 3; Moravian Church, 2; New Testament Assembly, 2; Presbyterian Church of Wales, 6; Religious Society of Friends, 3; Roman Catholic Church in England and Wales, 40; Roman Catholic Church in Scotland, 20; Russian Orthodox Church, 2; Salvation Army (British Territory), 5; Scottish Episcopal Church, 3; Scottish Congregational Church, 3; Serbian Orthodox Church, 3; Undeb yr Annibynwyr Cymraeg (Union of Welsh Independents), 5; United Free Church of Scotland, 2; United Reformed Church, 12; Wesleyan Holiness Church, 2.

Bodies in Association Action of Christians Against Torture, 1; Afro-West Indian United Council of Churches, 1; Association of Centres of Adult Theological Education, 1; Associations of Interchurch Families in Britain and Ireland, 1; Centre for Black and White Christian Partnership, 1; Christian Council on Ageing, 1; Christian Education Movement, 1; Christianity and the Future of Europe, 1; Church Action on Poverty, 1; Churches Council for Health and Healing, 1; Churches' East West European Relations Network, 1; Ecumenical Council for Corporate Responsibility, 1; Feed the Minds, 1; Fellowship of Prayer for Unity, 1; Fellowship of St Alban and St Sergius, 1; Iona Community, 1; Irish School of Ecumenics, 1; Living Stones, 1; National Association of Christian Communities & Networks, 1; National Christian Education Council, 1; New Assembly of Churches, 1; YMCA, 1; YWCA, 1.

Associate Members Roman Catholic Church in Ireland, 2; Seventh Day Adventist Church, 2.

STAFF

General Secretary Dr David Goodbourn

Co-ordinating Secretaries
Revd Dr Colin Davey (*Church Life*);
Revd John Kennedy (*Public Affairs*)
Mr Paul Renshaw (*International Affairs*)

Associate Secretary Revd Jean Mayland (*Community of Women and Men*)

Churches' Commission on Mission Revd Donald Elliott (*Commission Secretary*); Mr Edmond Tang (*China*); Mr Simon Barrow (*Associate Commission Secretary*)

Churches' Commission for Racial Justice Revd Arlington Trotman (*Associate Secretary*); Apostle James Ozigi (*Projects Fund*)

Churches' Commission for Interfaith Relations Canon Michael Ipgrave, Church House, Great Smith St, London SW1P 3NZ   *Tel*: 020–7898 1477

BODIES IN ASSOCIATION

ACTION OF CHRISTIANS AGAINST TORTURE
Mr Ken Smith, 35 North Hill, Highgate, London N6 4BD

AFRO-WEST INDIAN UNITED COUNCIL OF CHURCHES
Revd Eric Brown, Arcadian Gardens, High Rd, Wood Green, London N22 5AA
Tel: 020–8888 9427

ASSOCIATION OF CENTRES OF ADULT THEOLOGICAL EDUCATION
Helen Stanton, The Old Deanery, Wells, Somerset BA5 2UG   *Tel*: 01749 670777

ASSOCIATIONS OF INTERCHURCH FAMILIES IN BRITAIN AND IRELAND
Ruth Reardon, Inter-Church House, 35–41 Lower Marsh, London SE1 7RL   *Tel*: 020–7620 4444

CENTRE FOR BLACK AND WHITE CHRISTIAN PARTNERSHIP
Rt Revd Joseph Aldrad, Centre for Black and White Christian Partnership, Selly Oak Colleges, Birmingham B29 6LQ   *Tel*: 0121–472 7952
Fax: 0121–472 2400

CHRISTIAN COUNCIL ON AGEING
Mrs Margaret Stevens, Epworth House, Stuart St, Derby DE1 2EQ   *Tel* and *Fax*: (01335) 390484

CHRISTIAN EDUCATION MOVEMENT
Revd Prof Stephen Orchard, Royal Buildings, Victoria Street, Derby DE1 1GW
Tel: (01332) 296655

CHRISTIANITY AND THE FUTURE OF EUROPE
Revd Prof Kenneth Medhurst, c/o Lincoln Theological Institute, 36 Wilkinson St, Sheffield S10 2LB *Tel*: 0114–276 3973

CHURCH ACTION ON POVERTY
The Co-ordinator, Central Buildings, Oldham Street, Manchester M1 1JT *Tel*: 0161–236 9321

CHURCHES COUNCIL FOR HEALTH AND HEALING
St Luke's Hospital for the Clergy, 14 Fitzroy Square, London W1P 6AH *Tel*: 020–7388 7903

CHURCHES' EAST WEST EUROPEAN RELATIONS NETWORK
Dr Philip Walters, 81 Thorney Leys, Witney, Oxon OX8 7AY *Tel*: 01993 77178

ECUMENICAL COUNCIL FOR CORPORATE RESPONSIBILITY
Revd Crispin White, PO Box 4317, Bishop's Stortford, Herts CM22 7EZ *Tel*: (01279) 718274

FEED THE MINDS
Dr Alwyn Marriage, Albany House, 67 Sydenham Rd, Guildford GU1 3RY *Tel*: (01483) 888580

FELLOWSHIP OF PRAYER FOR UNITY
Revd Paul Renyard, 29 Ramley Rd, Pennington, Lymington, Hants SO41 8LH *Tel*: (01590) 672646

FELLOWSHIP OF ST ALBAN AND ST SERGIUS
Revd Stephen Platt, 1 Canterbury Rd, Oxford OX2 6LU *Tel*: (01865) 52991

IONA COMMUNITY
Revd Norman Shanks, Pearce Institute, Govan, Glasgow G51 3UU *Tel*: 0141–445 4561
Fax: 0141–445 4295

IRISH SCHOOL OF ECUMENICS
Pamela Stotter, Milltown Park, Dublin 6, Ireland
Tel: 00–3531 2698607

LIVING STONES
Revd Dr Michael Prior, St Mary's College, Strawberry Hill, Twickenham TW1 4SX
Tel: 020–8892 0051

NATIONAL ASSOCIATION OF CHRISTIAN COMMUNITIES AND NETWORKS
Revd Stanley Baxter, Holyrood House with Thorpe House, 10 Sowerby Rd, Sowerby, Thirsk YO7 1HX *Tel*: (01845) 522580

NATIONAL CHRISTIAN EDUCATION COUNCIL
General Secretary, 1020 Bristol Rd, Selly Oak, Birmingham B29 6LB *Tel*: 0121–472 4242
Fax: 0121–472 7575

NEW ASSEMBLY OF CHURCHES
Revd Carmel Jones, 15 Oldridge Rd, London SW12 8PL *Tel*: 020–8673 0595

WILLIAM TEMPLE FOUNDATION
Revd Malcolm Brown, Manchester Business School, Manchester M15 6PB *Tel*: 0161–275 6534

YOUNG MEN'S CHRISTIAN ASSOCIATION
Mr Tony Malcolm, YMCA Christian and Spiritual Development Unit, Colman House, Station Rd, Knowle B93 0HL *Tel*: 01564 730229

YOUNG WOMEN'S CHRISTIAN ASSOCIATION
Ms Gill Tishler (*Gen Secretary*), YWCA Headquarters, Clarendon House, 52 Cornmarket St, Oxford OX1 3EJ *Tel*: 01865 304200
Fax: 01865 204805

For addresses of Full Members *see* pages 427–8.

The Churches' Commission on Mission

Moderator Revd Dr Janet Wootton

Deputy Moderator Mr John Clark

Secretaries
Revd Donald Elliott (*Commission Secretary*)
Mr Edmond Tang (*China*)
Mr Simon Barrow (*Associate Commission Secretary*)

Office Inter-Church House, 35–41 Lower Marsh, London SE1 7RL *Tel*: 020–7620 4444
Fax: 020–7928 0010

The Conference of Missionary Societies in Great Britain and Ireland was founded in 1912 as a result of the Edinburgh World Missionary Conference, and has been the centre of co-operative consultation, planning and common action among missionary agencies in Britain. In 1978 the Conference became a Division of the British Council of Churches, with the title of 'Conference for World Mission'.

With the termination of the British Council of Churches, much of the Conference's work has been taken up through the Churches' Commission on Mission of Churches Together in Britain and Ireland.

The Commission assists the churches and mission bodies to relate together to missionary and evangelistic work in all overseas areas, particularly through regional and national ecumenical councils, and to bring that work to bear on mission education and evangelism in Britain and Ireland. To that end, the Commission assists the churches in their organizing of ecumenical forums with a broad agenda on specific world regions and mission tasks, including health care overseas. It works closely with the churches' aid and development agencies and relates especially to the relevant units of the World Council of Churches. The Commission is financed according to negotiated formulae by the participating bodies and from some special sources. Its total budget for 1998 was £256,000. Some bodies additionally contribute through the Commission to specific joint projects (e.g. China work, ecumenical bursaries, research on missionary congregations).

The following organizations have been providing resource persons for particular forums of the Commission:

Board of Mission (C of E) – Mission Theology
Church of Scotland – Middle East
Methodist Church – Pacific, and India Relations
Medical Missionaries of Mary – Overseas Health Care
Presbyterian Church of Wales – Asia
South American Missionary Society – Caribbean and Latin America
Union of Welsh Independents – Europe
United Society for the Propagation of the Gospel – International Encounter

PARTICIPATING BODIES
Most Full Members of, and some Bodies in Association with, Churches Together in Britain and Ireland (*see* page 421).
(N.B. Missionary and evangelistic societies of the Church of England working through PWM participate through Church of England representation – *see* page 23.)

In addition:

BAPTIST MISSIONARY SOCIETY
PO Box 49, Didcot, Oxon OX11 8XA
Revd Dr Alistair Brown

CATHOLIC FUND FOR OVERSEAS DEVELOPMENT
2 Romero Close, Stockwell Rd, London SW9 9TY
Mr Julian Filochowski

CATHOLIC INSTITUTE FOR INTERNATIONAL RELATIONS
Unit 3, Canonbury Yard, 190A New North Rd, London NW1 7BJ
Mr Ian Linden

CENTRE FOR BLACK AND WHITE CHRISTIAN PARTNERSHIP
Selly Oak Colleges, Bristol Rd, Birmingham B29 6LQ
Bishop Joe Aldred

CHRISTIAN AID
35–41 Lower Marsh, London SE1 7RL
Dr Daleep Mukarji

CHRISTIANS ABROAD
1 Stockwell Green, London SW9 9HP
Mr Colin South

CHRISTIANS AWARE
Bishop's House, 38 Tooting Bec Gardens, London SW16 1QZ
Mrs Barbara Butler

CHRISTIAN EDUCATION MOVEMENT
Royal Buildings, Victoria St, Derby DE1 1GW
Revd Prof Stephen Orchard

CHURCHES' COMMISSION ON OVERSEAS STUDENTS
1 Stockwell Green, London SW9 9HP
Ms Gillian Court

FEED THE MINDS
Albany House, 67 Sydenham Rd, Guildford, Surrey GU1 3RY
Dr Alwyn Marriage

GRASSROOTS
Luton Industrial College, Chapel St, Luton LU1 2SL
Dr David Cowling

INTERSERVE (UK)
325 Kennington Rd, London SE11 4QH
Mr Richard Clark

IRISH MISSIONARY UNION
Orwell Park, Rathgar, Dublin 6, Ireland
Fr Tom Kiggins

LEPROSY MISSION INTERNATIONAL
80 Windmill Rd, Brentford, Middx TW8 0GA
Mr Trevor Durston

QUAKER PEACE AND SERVICE
Friends House, Euston Rd, London NW1 2BJ
Mr Andrew Clark

SCHOOL OF MISSION AND WORLD CHRISTIANITY
Selly Oak Colleges, Birmingham B29 6LE
Revd Dr Andrew Kirk

WORLD CONFERENCE (THE BOYS' BRIGADE ETC)
Church House, Belfast, Northern Ireland BT1 6DW
Mr Eric Woodburn

YMCA
Colman House, Station Rd, Knowle, Solihull B93 0HL
Mr Tony Malcolm

The Churches' Commission for Racial Justice

Moderator Rt Revd Roger Sainsbury (*Bishop of Barking*)

Deputy Moderators
Ms Maryanne Ure
Ms Pat White

Associate Secretary Revd Arlington Trotman

Executive Secretary for the Racial Justice Fund Senior Apostle James Ozigi

Office Inter-Church House, 35–41 Lower Marsh, London SE1 7RL   *Tel*: 020–7620 4444
Fax: 020–7928 0010
email: ccrj@ccbi.org.uk

The Churches' Commission for Racial Justice (CCRJ) is a Commission of Churches Together in Britain and Ireland, and reports annually to the CTBI. It has been formed by the churches themselves to monitor trends in race relations in British society, to encourage the exchange of information among the churches regarding these trends and, in conjunction with the churches' own committees responsible for race issues, to co-ordinate a response.

It manages the Ecumenical Racial Justice Fund, supported mainly by Christian Aid, the Church Urban Fund, the Catholic Association for Racial Justice and the Methodist Church which funds local and national groups, and organizations combating racism or overcoming racial discrimination. Its policy is decided by a Commission of 25 representatives from CTBI member churches, including those of African, African Caribbean and Asian origin.

Scotland, Wales and Ireland

ACTION OF CHURCHES TOGETHER IN SCOTLAND

Scottish Churches House, Dunblane, Perthshire FK15 0AJ   *Tel*: (01786) 823588
Fax: (01786) 825844
email: acts.ecum@dial.pipex.com

General Secretary Revd Dr Kevin Franz

Convenor of Central Council Sister Maire Gallagher

ACTS is ten Scottish churches working together in the cause of Christ's kingdom. It embraces what the Church and Christian people plan to do together in Scotland. It has a Central Council to enable this wider pilgrimage and action. It has three Commissions: Unity, Faith and Order; Mission, Evangelism and Education; Justice, Peace, Social and Moral Issues.

Member Churches Church of Scotland, Congregational Federation, Methodist Church, Religious Society of Friends, Roman Catholic Church, Salvation Army, Scottish Congregational Church, Scottish Episcopal Church, United Free Church, United Reformed Church.

Associate Members Christian Aid, Feed the Minds (Scotland), Iona Community, Lutheran Council of Great Britain, National Bible Society of Scotland, Orthodox Church, Scottish Catholic International Aid Fund, Student Christian Movement, World Day of Prayer, YMCA, YWCA.

Observer Unitarian Church

CYTUN: CHURCHES TOGETHER IN WALES
President Vacancy

General Secretary Revd Gethin Abraham Williams, 11 St Helen's Rd, Swansea SA1 4AL
Tel: (01792) 460876
Fax: (01792) 469391
email: gethin@cytun.freeserve.co.uk
Web: http://www.cytun.freeserve.co.uk

The objects of CYTUN are the advancement of the Christian religion and of any other purposes which are charitable according to the law of England and Wales.

CYTUN shall seek to further its objects by (1) gathering together the churches in Wales in all the richness of their present diversity so that they can learn from and value each other's traditions in a parity of esteem; (2) offering the churches the opportunity to enter into a new commitment to reflect together theologically on matters of faith, order and ethics; to pray together and to learn to appreciate each other's pattern of prayer; to work together, sharing resources and presenting the gospel in word and action; (3) seeking to help the churches to arrive at a common mind so that they might become more fully united in faith, communion, pastoral care and mission; (4) acting as a body which enables the churches themselves to reach their decisions in the context of common study, prayer and worship; (5) enabling the churches to do together whatever they can.

Member Churches The Salvation Army, The Presbyterian Church of Wales, Covenanted Baptist Churches in Wales, The United Reformed Church, The Methodist Church, The Roman Catholic Church, The Church in Wales, The

Congregational Federation, The Union of Welsh Independents, The Baptist Union of Wales, Religious Society of Friends.

Observers The Lutheran Council of Great Britain, The Orthodox Churches in Wales, The Seventh Day Adventist Church.

Bodies in Association Bible Society, Cardiff Centre for Christian Adult Education, Christian Education Movement, Enfys, Fellowship of Reconciliation, Free Church Council for Wales, Free Churches' Federal Council for England and Wales, Student Christian Movement, Sunday Schools Council for Wales, National Association of Christian Communities and Networks, National Retreat Association, Women's World Day of Prayer, YWCA.

Agencies Christian Aid, CAFOD, Christians against Torture, Churches' National Housing Coalition, Welsh Council on Alcohol and Drugs.

CYTUN also works in close collaboration with Enfys: The Commission of the Covenanted Churches in Wales.

CYTUN functions through the following structures:
(a) GYMANFA (The Assembly) meeting once every three/four years and as broadly representative as possible of the life of the churches in Wales at all levels.
(b) The Council meeting three times annually on which senior representatives of the churches will serve as well as those who are representative of the diversity of the life of the churches.

A recent review has led to the discontinuation of the three Commissions. Consultations are currently underway to explore other patterns of collaboration in specialist fields, through regular meetings of denominational officers and short-term working groups on specialist topics.

THE IRISH COUNCIL OF CHURCHES
Inter-Church Centre, 48 Elmwood Ave, Belfast
BT9 6AZ   *Tel*: 028–9066 3145
                                 Fax: 028–9038 1737
                         email: Icpep@unite.co.uk
            Web: www.unite.co.uk/customers/Icpep

President Revd Edmund Mawhinney

Vice-President Revd Dr Ian Ellis

Hon Treasurer Miss Hazel McMillan

General Secretary Dr David Stevens

Administrative Secretary Mrs Florence Pyper

From 1906 the Presbyterian and Methodist Churches had a joint committee for united efforts. In 1910 the General Assembly of the Presbyterian Church invited other evangelical churches to set up similar joint committees with it. The Church of Ireland accepted and by 1911 the joint committee of these two churches was in action. Following a recommendation of the 1920 Lambeth Conference, these joint committees developed in 1922 into the United Council of Christian Churches and Religious Communions in Ireland by the inclusion of most of its present constituents. In 1966 the United Council changed its name to the Irish Council of Churches. The Council employed its first full-time secretary in April 1972.

The Irish Council of Churches is constituted by Christian Communions in Ireland willing to join in united efforts to promote the spiritual, physical, moral and social welfare of the people and the extension of the rule of Christ among all nations and over every region of life.

Member Churches The Church of Ireland, The Coptic Orthodox Church, The Greek Orthodox Church, Lifelink Network of Churches, The Lutheran Church in Ireland, The Methodist Church in Ireland, The Irish District of the Moravian Church, The Non-Subscribing Presbyterian Church of Ireland, The Presbyterian Church in Ireland, The Salvation Army (Ireland Division), The Religious Society of Friends in Ireland.

The Council consists of 75 members appointed by the member churches, together with the Heads of the member churches and up to ten co-opted members, the General Secretary, Treasurer and immediate Past President of the Council. It meets twice a year. The member churches appoint an Executive Committee which is responsible for the day-to-day affairs of the Council.

The work of the Council is structured into two Boards: Inter-Church Affairs (including the Child in the Church group, ICC Women's Link, and local ecumenical activity) and Overseas Affairs (including World Mission and Christian Aid). Every member of the Council can be a member of a Board.

The Council puts considerable emphasis on peace and reconciliation work. A peace programme has been developed since July 1978 in conjunction with the Irish Commission for Justice and Peace, and materials for schools and adult Bible study guides have been produced.

More information about the Council's work can be obtained from the Annual Report (available free).

Churches in Britain and Ireland: Addresses

FULL MEMBERS OF CTBI

BAPTIST UNION OF GREAT BRITAIN
Revd David Coffey (*General Secretary*), Baptist House, 129 Broadway, Didcot, Oxon OX11 8RT
Tel: (01235) 512077
Fax: (01235) 811537

CHERUBIM AND SERAPHIM COUNCIL OF CHURCHES (UK)
Most Senior Apostle S. A. Abidoye, 175 Earlham Rd, London E7 9AP   *Tel*: 020–8244 7428

CHURCH IN WALES
Mr David McIntyre (*Secretary General*), 39 Cathedral Rd, Cardiff, S. Glam CF1 9XF
Tel: 029–2023 1638
Fax: 029–2038 7835

CHURCH OF ENGLAND
Mr Philip Mawer (*Secretary General of the General Synod*), Church House, Great Smith St, London SW1P 3NZ   *Tel*: 020–7898 1360
Fax: 020–7898 1369
email: philip.mawer@c-of-e.org.uk

CHURCH OF IRELAND
Mr David Meredith, The Chief Officer, Representative Body, Church of Ireland House, Upper Rathmines, Dublin 6, Eire   *Tel*: 0001–4978 422
Fax: 0001–4978 821

CHURCH OF SCOTLAND
Revd Dr F. A. J. Macdonald, 121 George St, Edinburgh EH2 4YN   *Tel*: 0131–225 5722
Fax: 0131–226 6121

CONGREGATIONAL FEDERATION
Pastor Graham Adams, 4 Castle Gate, Nottingham NG1 7AS   *Tel*: 0115–941 3801
Fax: 0115–948 0902

COUNCIL OF AFRICAN AND AFRO-CARIBBEAN CHURCHES
Most Revd Fr Olu Abiola, 31 Norton House, Sidney Rd, London SW9 0UJ   *Tel*: 020–7274 5589

COUNCIL OF THE ORIENTAL ORTHODOX CHRISTIAN CHURCHES
Rt Revd Yegishe Gizirian, The Armenian Vicarage, Iverna Gardens, London W8 6BR
Tel: 020–7937 0152

FREE CHURCHES' COUNCIL
Revd Geoffrey Roper (*Secretary*), 27 Tavistock Place, London WS1H 9HH   *Tel*: 020–7387 0150

GREEK ORTHODOX CHURCH
The Most Revd Archbishop Gregorios, 5 Craven Hill, London W2 3EN   *Tel*: 020–7723 4787
Fax: 020–7224 9301

INDEPENDENT METHODIST CHURCHES
Mr John M. Day (*General Secretary*), Old Police House, Croxton, Stafford ST1 6PE
Tel: (0163 082) 671

INTERNATIONAL MINISTERIAL COUNCIL OF GREAT BRITAIN
Revd Sheila Douglas, 55 Tudor Walk, Watford, Herts WD2 4NY   *Tel*: (01923) 239266

JOINT COUNCIL FOR ANGLO-CARIBBEAN CHURCHES
Revd Esme Beswick, 141 Railton Rd, London SE24 0LT   *Tel*: 020–7737 6542
Fax: 020–7733 2821

LUTHERAN COUNCIL OF GREAT BRITAIN
Revd Thomas Bruch, Lutheran Church House, 8 Collingham Gardens, London SW5
Tel and *Fax*: 020–8904 2849

METHODIST CHURCH
Revd Nigel Collinson (*Secretary of the Conference*), 25 Marylebone Rd, London NW1 5JR
Tel: 020–7486 5502
Fax: 020–7233 1295

METHODIST CHURCH IN IRELAND
Revd Dr Edmund Mawhinney (*Secretary of the Conference*), 3 Upper Malone Rd, Belfast BT9 6TD
Tel: 028–9032 4554
Fax: 028–9023 99467

MORAVIAN CHURCH
Mrs Jackie Morten (*Secretary Provincial Board*), 5 Muswell Hill, London N10 3TJ *Tel*: 020–8883 3409
Fax: 020–8442 0112

NEW TESTAMENT ASSEMBLY
Revd Nezlin Sterling, 5 Woodstock Ave, London W13 9VQ   *Tel*: 020–8579 3841

PRESBYTERIAN CHURCH OF WALES
Revd Gareth Edwards, Presbyterian Church of Wales, 53 Richmond Rd, Cardiff CF2 3UP
Tel: 029–2049 4913
Fax: 029–2046 4293

RELIGIOUS SOCIETY OF FRIENDS
Elsa Dicks (*Recording Clerk*), Friends House, Euston Rd, London NW1 2BJ *Tel*: 020–7387 3601
Fax: 020–7388 1977

ECUMENICAL

ROMAN CATHOLIC CHURCH IN ENGLAND AND
WALES
Rt Revd Mgr Arthur Roche, 39 Eccleston Square,
London SW1V 1PD   *Tel*: 020–7630 8220
                         Fax: 020–7630 5166

ROMAN CATHOLIC CHURCH IN SCOTLAND
Rt Revd Mgr Henry Docherty, 64 Aitken St,
Airdrie, Lanarkshire ML6 6LT
                         Tel: (01236) 764061
                         Fax: (01236) 762489

RUSSIAN ORTHODOX CHURCH
The Most Revd Metropolitan Anthony of
Sourozh, Cathedral of the Assumption and All
Saints, Ennismore Gardens, London SW7 1NH
                         Tel: 020–7584 0096

SALVATION ARMY (British Territory)
Commissioner Alex Hughes, 101 Newington
Causeway, London SE1 6BN   *Tel*: 020–7367 4000
                         Fax: 020–7236 6272

SCOTTISH CONGREGATIONAL CHURCH
Revd John Arthur (*Secretary*), PO Box 189, Glasgow G1 2BX   *Tel*: 0141–332 7667
                         Fax: 0141–332 8463

SCOTTISH EPISCOPAL CHURCH
Mr John Stuart (*Secretary*), 21 Grosvenor Cresc,
Edinburgh EH12 5EE   *Tel*: 0131–225 6357
                         Fax: 0131–346 7247

SERBIAN ORTHODOX CHURCH
Very Revd Milenko Zebic, 131 Cob Lane, Bournville, Birmingham B30 1QE   *Tel*: 0121–458 5273
                         Fax: 0121–458 4986

UNDEB YR ANNIBYNWYR CYMRAEG (UNION OF
WELSH INDEPENDENTS)
Revd Dewi Myrdlin Hughes (*Secretary*), 11 Heol
Sant Helen, Swansea SA1 4AL
                         Tel: (01792) 652542
                         Fax: (01792) 650647

UNITED FREE CHURCH OF SCOTLAND
Revd John Fulton (*Secretary*), 11 Newton Place,
Glasgow G3 7PR   *Tel*: 0141–332 3435

UNITED REFORMED CHURCH
Revd Anthony Burnham (*General Secretary*), 86
Tavistock Place, London WC1H 9RT
                         Tel: 020–7916 2020
                         Fax: 020–7916 2021

WESLEYAN HOLINESS CHURCH
Revd Kecious Gray, Holyhead Rd, Handsworth,
Birmingham B21 0LA   *Tel*: 0121–520 7849

ASSOCIATE MEMBERS
ROMAN CATHOLIC CHURCH IN IRELAND
Revd Aidan O'Boyle, Iona, 65 Newry Rd,
Dundalk, Co Louth   *Tel*: 00353 423 8087
                         Fax: 042–33575

SEVENTH DAY ADVENTIST CHURCH
Pastor Cecil Perry, Stanborough Park, Watford
WD2 6JP   *Tel*: 01923 672251
                         Fax: 01923 893212

Conference of European Churches

Moderator Metropolitan Jérémie Caligiorgis

Vice-Moderator Oberkirchenrätin Rut Rohrandt

Deputy Vice-Moderator Prof Dr Jean-Marc Prieur

General Secretary Revd Dr Keith Clements, PO
Box 2100, 150 Route de Ferney, 1211 Geneva 2,
Switzerland   *Tel*: 41 22 791 61 11
                         Fax: 41 22 791 62 27
                         email: reg@wcc-coe.org

Born in the era of the 'cold war' some 30 years
ago, the CEC emerged into a fragmented and divided continent. Thus it was that churches of Eastern and Western Europe felt one priority of their
work to be promoting international understanding – building bridges. This the CEC has consistently tried to do, always insisting that no 'iron
curtain' exists among the churches.

The supreme governing body of the Conference is the Assembly. Here all 123 member
churches are represented. The first Assembly was
in 1959 and further Assemblies were held in 1960,
1962, 1964, 1967, 1971, 1974, 1979, 1986, 1992 and
1997.

The CEC initiated the European Ecumenical
Assembly 'Peace with Justice' held in Basel in
May 1989, co-sponsored with the Council of
European Bishops' Conferences (Roman Cath-
olic). A second European Ecumenical Assembly
was held in Graz, Austria, in 1997 with the theme
'Reconciliation: Gift of God and Source of New
Life'.

The 40-member Central Committee oversees
the implementation of the decisions of the
Assembly. A Presidium, drawn from the Central
Committee, acts as the Executive Council of the
Conference.

Since 1 January 1999 the European Ecumenical
Commission on Church and Society (EECCS)
with officers in Brussels and Strasbourg integrated with CEC, and together with CEC's exist-

ing work, created the new Church and Society Commission of the CEC.

The Secretariats in Geneva, Brussels and Strasbourg ensure the continuity of the activities. There are approximately 14 staff: the General Secretary and Secretaries responsible for finance and administration, communications and information, Churches in Dialogue and Church and Society.

Publications include occasional papers, and *Monitor*, a quarterly news-sheet.

World Council of Churches

The Church of England has taken its full share in the international ecumenical movement since the Edinburgh Conference of 1910. In 1999 the General Synod made a grant of £120,900 to the General Budget of the World Council of Churches.

Presidium Dr Agnes Abuom, Revd Kathryn Bannister, Rt Revd Jabez Bryce, His Eminence Metropolitan Chrysostomos of Ephesus, His Holiness Ignatius Zakka Iwas, Dr Kang Moon-Kyu, Bishop Federico Pagura, Bishop Eberhardt Renz

Moderator of Central Committee His Holiness Aram I, Catholicos of Cilicia (Armenian Apostolic Church (Cilicia), Lebanon)

Vice-Moderators
Mrs Justice Sophia Adinyira (Church of the Province of West Africa, Ghana)
Dr Marion Best (United Church of Canada)

General Secretary Revd Dr Konrad Raiser (Evangelical Church in Germany)

Office 150 route de Ferney, 1211 Geneva 2, Switzerland   *Tel*: 00–41–22–791 61 11
Fax: 00–41–22 791 03 61
Cable: Oikoumene Geneva
email: info@wcc-coe.org

The World Council of Churches was brought into formal existence by a resolution of its first Assembly at Amsterdam in 1948.

Member churches agree to the following basis:

The World Council of Churches is a fellowship of churches which confess the Lord Jesus Christ as God and Saviour according to the Scriptures and therefore seek to fulfil together their common calling to the glory of the one God, Father, Son and Holy Spirit.

Extract from the Constitution
The primary purpose of the fellowship of churches in the WCC is to call one another to visible unity in one faith and in one eucharistic fellowship, expressed in worship and common life in Christ, through witness and service to the world, and to advance towards that unity in order that the world may believe.

In seeking *koinonia* in faith and life, witness and service, the churches through the Council will:

1. promote the prayerful search for forgiveness and reconciliation in a spirit of mutual accountability, the development of deeper relationships through theological dialogue, and the sharing of human, spiritual and material resources with one another;
2. facilitate common witness in each place and in all places, and support each other in their work for mission and evangelism;
3. express their commitment to *diakonia* in serving human need, breaking down barriers between people, promoting one human family in justice and peace, and upholding the integrity of creation, so that all may experience the fullness of life;
4. nurture the growth of an ecumenical consciousness through processes of education and a vision of life in community rooted in each particular cultural context;
5. assist each other in their relationships to and with people of other faith communities;
6. foster renewal and growth in unity, worship, mission and service.

In order to strengthen the one ecumenical movement, the Council will:

1. nurture relations with and among churches, especially within but also beyond its membership;
2. establish and maintain relations with national councils, regional conferences of churches, organizations of Christian World Communions and other ecumenical bodies;
3. support ecumenical initiatives at regional, national and local levels;
4. facilitate the creation of networks among ecumenical organizations;
5. work towards maintaining the coherence of the one ecumenical movement in its diverse manifestations.

The World Council shall offer counsel and provide opportunity for united action in matters of common interest.

It may take action on behalf of constituent churches only in such matters as one or more of them may commit to it and only on behalf of such churches.

The World Council shall not legislate for the

churches; nor shall it act for them in any manner except as indicated or as may hereafter be specified by the constituent churches.

The WCC is governed by an Assembly of Member Churches, a Central Committee, and by an Executive Committee and other subordinate bodies as may be established.. Assemblies are held every seven years and have been as follows:

1. AMSTERDAM, 1948 – theme: 'Man's Disorder and God's Design'
2. EVANSTON, 1954 – theme: 'Christ the Hope of the World'
3. NEW DELHI, 1961– theme: 'Jesus Christ, the Light of the World'
4. UPPSALA, 1968 – theme: 'Behold, I Make All Things New'
5. NAIROBI, 1975 – theme: 'Jesus Christ Frees and Unites'
6. VANCOUVER, 1983 – theme: 'Jesus Christ the Life of the World'
7. CANBERRA, 1991– theme: 'Come, Holy Spirit – Renew the Whole Creation'
8. HARARE 1998 – theme: 'Turn to God – Rejoice in Hope'

The Central Committee elected by the Eighth Assembly includes one member of the Church of England: Rt Revd Barry Rogerson (*Bishop of Bristol*).

The World Council has 336 member churches, including 32 which are associated. Almost every Church of the Anglican Communion is included, together with Orthodox churches and all the main Protestant traditions. The Roman Catholic Church is not in membership but has sent official observers to all main World Council meetings since 1960. It is a full member of the Faith and Order Commission of the World Council.

WCC MEMBER CHURCHES, ASSOCIATE MEMBER CHURCHES AND ASSOCIATE COUNCILS

* Associate member church.
** Associate council.
† Names and locations of churches are given according to information available to the WCC at the time of publication. The name of the country appears in square brackets where it is not obvious from the name of the church. Geographical references are provided only where they are necessary to identify the church or when they indicate the location of headquarters of churches with regional or world membership.
   The mention of a country in this list does not imply any political judgement on the part of the WCC.

AFRICA
African Christian Church and Schools [Kenya]
African Church of the Holy Spirit [Kenya]*
African Israel Church, Nineveh [Kenya]
African Protestant Church [Cameroon]*
Anglican Church of Kenya
Anglican Church of Tanzania
Botswana Christian Council**
Christian Council of Churches in Madagascar**
Christian Council of Ghana**
Christian Council of Tanzania**
Christian Council of Zambia**
Church of Christ in Congo
 – Anglican Community of Congo [DRC]
 – Baptist Community of Western Congo [DRC]
 – Community of Disciples of Christ [DRC]
 – Episcopal Baptist Community [DRC]
 – Evangelical Community [Rep. of Congo]
 – Mennonite Community [DRC]
 – Presbyterian Community [DRC]
 – Presbyterian Community of Kinshasa [DRC]
Church of Christ – Light of the Holy Spirit [DRC]
Church of Jesus Christ in Madagascar
Church of Jesus Christ on Earth by His Messenger Simon Kimbangu [DRC]
Church of the Brethren in Nigeria
Church of the Lord (Aladura) Worldwide [Nigeria]
Church of the Province of Burundi
Church of the Province of Central Africa [Botswana]
Church of the Province of Nigeria
Church of the Province of Rwanda
Church of the Province of Southern Africa [South Africa]
Church of the Province of the Indian Ocean [Seychelles]
Church of the Province of Uganda
Church of the Province of West Africa [Ghana]
Council of African Instituted Churches [South Africa]
Council of Christian Churches in Angola**
Council of Churches in Namibia**
Council of Churches in Sierra Leone**
Council of Swaziland Churches**
Ecumenical Council of Christian Churches of Congo**
Episcopal Church of the Sudan
Ethiopian Evangelical Church Mekane Yesus
Ethiopian Orthodox Tewahedo Church
Evangelical Church of Cameroon
Evangelical Church of Gabon
Evangelical Church of the Congo [Rep. of Congo]
Evangelical Congregational Church in Angola
Evangelical Lutheran Church in Southern Africa [South Africa]
Evangelical Lutheran Church in the Rep. of Namibia
Evangelical Lutheran Church in Tanzania
Evangelical Lutheran Church in Zimbabwe
Evangelical Pentecostal Mission of Angola
Evangelical Presbyterian Church, Ghana
Evangelical Presbyterian Church in South Africa
Evangelical Presbyterian Church of Togo
Evangelical Reformed Church of Angola

Gambia Christian Council**
Harrist Church [Ivory Coast]
Kenya Evangelical Lutheran Church*
Lesotho Evangelical Church
Liberian Council of Churches**
Lutheran Church in Liberia
Malagasy Lutheran Church [Madagascar]
Methodist Church, Ghana
Methodist Church in Kenya
Methodist Church in Togo
Methodist Church in Zimbabwe
Methodist Church, Nigeria
Methodist Church of Southern Africa [South
 Africa]
Methodist Church, Sierra Leone
Moravian Church in Southern Africa [South
 Africa]
Moravian Church in Tanzania
Native Baptist Church of Cameroon
Nigerian Baptist Convention
Presbyterian Church in Cameroon
Presbyterian Church of the Sudan
Presbyterian Church of Africa [South Africa]
Presbyterian Church of Cameroon
Presbyterian Church of East Africa [Kenya]
Presbyterian Church of Ghana
Presbyterian Church of Mozambique*
Presbyterian Church of Nigeria
Presbyterian Church of Rwanda
Presbyterian Church of Southern Africa [South
 Africa]
Presbyterian Community of Kinshasa [Congo]
Presbytery of Liberia*
Protestant Church of Algeria*
Protestant Methodist Church of Benin
Protestant Methodist Church, Ivory Coast
Reformed Church in Zambia
Reformed Church in Zimbabwe
Reformed Church of Christ in Nigeria
Reformed Presbyterian Church of Equatorial
 Guinea*
Reformed Presbyterian Church in Southern
 Africa [South Africa]
South African Council of Churches**
Sudan Council of Churches**
Uganda Joint Christian Council**
Union of Baptist Churches of Cameroon
United Church of Christ in Zimbabwe
United Church of Zambia
United Congregational Church of Southern
 Africa [South Africa]
United Evangelical Church 'Anglican Com-
 munion in Angola'*
Uniting Reformed Church in Southern Africa
Zimbabwe Council of Churches**

ASIA
Anglican Church in Aotearoa, New Zealand and
 Polynesia
Anglican Church of Australia
Anglican Communion in Japan
Associated Churches of Christ in New Zealand
Bangladesh Baptist Sangha

Baptist Union of New Zealand
Batak Christian Community Church [Indonesia]*
Batak Protestant Christian Church [Indonesia]
Bengal–Orissa–Bihar Baptist Convention [India]*
China Christian Council
Christian Church of Central Sulawesi [Indonesia]
Christian Church of Sumba
Christian Church of East Timor (GKTT)
Christian Evangelical Church in Minahasa
 [Indonesia]
Christian Evangelical Church in Sangihe Talaud
 [Indonesia]
Christian Protestant Angkola Church [Indonesia]
Christian Protestant Church in Indonesia
Church of Bangladesh*
Church of Ceylon [Sri Lanka]
Church of Christ in Thailand
Church of North India
Church of Pakistan
Church of South India
Church of the Province of Myanmar
Churches of Christ in Australia
Communion of Churches in Indonesia**
Conference of Churches in Aotearoa – New
 Zealand**
Council of Churches of Malaysia**
East Java Christian Church [Indonesia]
Episcopal Church in the Philippines
Evangelical Christian Church in Halmahera
 [Indonesia]
Evangelical Christian Church in Irian Jaya
 [Indonesia]
Evangelical Methodist Church in the Philippines
Hong Kong Christian Council**
Hong Kong Council of the Church of Christ in
 China
Indonesian Christian Church (GKI)
Indonesian Christian Church (HKI)
Javanese Christian Churches [Indonesia]
Kalimantan Evangelical Church [Indonesia]
Karo Batak Protestant Church [Indonesia]
Korean Christian Church in Japan*
Korean Methodist Church
Malankara Orthodox Syrian Church [India]
Maori Ecumenical Body in Aotearoa – New
 Zealand**
Mar Thoma Syrian Church of Malabar [India]
Methodist Church in India
Methodist Church in Malaysia
Methodist Church in Singapore*
Methodist Church of New Zealand
Methodist Church [Sri Lanka]
Methodist Church, Upper Burma [Myanmar]
Myanmar Baptist Convention
Myanmar Council of Churches**
National Christian Council in Japan**
National Christian Council of Sri Lanka**
National Council of Churches in Australia**
National Council of Churches in India**
National Council of Churches in Korea**
National Council of Churches in the
 Philippines**
National Council of Churches of Singapore**

Nias Protestant Christian Church [Indonesia]
Orthodox Church in Japan
Pasundan Christian Church [Indonesia]
Philippine Independent Church
Presbyterian Church in Taiwan
Presbyterian Church in the Republic of Korea
Presbyterian Church of Aotearoa New Zealand
Presbyterian Church of Korea
Presbyterian Church of Pakistan
Protestant Christian Church in Bali [Indonesia]*
Protestant Church in Indonesia
Protestant Church in Sabah [Malaysia]
Protestant Church in South-East Sulawesi
  [Indonesia]
Protestant Church in the Moluccas [Indonesia]
Protestant Church in Western Indonesia
Protestant Evangelical Church in Timor
  [Indonesia]
Samavesam of Telugu Baptist Churches [India]
Simalungun Protestant Christian Church
  [Indonesia]
Toraja Church [Indonesia]
United Church of Christ in Japan
United Church of Christ in the Philippines
United Evangelical Lutheran Church in India
Uniting Church in Australia

CARIBBEAN
Church in the Province of the West Indies
  [Antigua]
Council of Churches of Cuba**
Jamaica Baptist Union
Jamaica Council of Churches**
Methodist Church in Cuba*
Methodist Church in the Caribbean and the
  Americas [Antigua]
Moravian Church, Eastern West Indies Province
  [Antigua]
Moravian Church in Jamaica
Moravian Church in Surinam
Presbyterian Church in Trinidad and Tobago
Presbyterian Reformed Church in Cuba*
St Vincent and the Grenadines Christian
  Council**
United Church of Jamaica and the Cayman
  Islands
United Protestant Church [Netherlands
  Antilles]*

EUROPE
Action of Churches Together in Scotland**
Armenian Apostolic Church
Autocephalous Orthodox Church in Poland
Baptist Union of Denmark
Baptist Union of Great Britain
Baptist Union of Hungary
Catholic Diocese of the Old Catholics in
  Germany
Christian Council of Sweden**
Church in Wales
Church of England
Church of Greece
Church of Ireland

Church of Norway
Church of Scotland
Church of Sweden
Churches Together in Britain and Ireland**
Churches Together in England**
Council of Christian Churches in Germany**
Council of Churches in the Netherlands**
Cytun: Churches Together in Wales**
Czechoslovak Hussite Church
Ecumenical Council of Churches in Austria**
Ecumenical Council of Churches in the Czech
  Republic**
Ecumenical Council of Churches in Hungary**
Ecumenical Council of Churches in the Slovak
  Republic**
Ecumenical Council of Churches in Yugoslavia**
Ecumenical Council of Denmark**
Ecumenical Patriarchate of Constantinople
  [Turkey]
Estonian Evangelical Lutheran Church
European Continental Province of the Moravian
  Church [Netherlands]
Evangelical Baptist Union of Italy*
Evangelical Church in Germany –
  Church of Lippe
Evangelical Church in Baden
Evangelical Church in Berlin – Brandenburg
Evangelical Church in Hesse and Nassau
Evangelical Church in Württemberg
Evangelical Church of Anhalt
Evangelical Church of Bremen
Evangelical Church of Hesse Electorate –
  Waldeck
Evangelical Church of the Palatinate
Evangelical Church of the Province of Saxony
Evangelical Church of the Rhineland
Evangelical Church of the Silesian Oberlausitz
Evangelical Church of Westphalia
Evangelical Lutheran Church in Bavaria
Evangelical Lutheran Church in Brunswick
Evangelical Lutheran Church in Oldenburg
Evangelical Lutheran Church in Thuringia
Evangelical Lutheran Church of Hanover
Evangelical Lutheran Church of Mecklenburg
Evangelical Lutheran Church of Saxony
Evangelical Lutheran Church of Schaumburg –
  Lippe
Evangelical Reformed Church in Bavaria and
  Northwestern Germany
North Elbian Evangelical Lutheran Church
Pomeranian Evangelical Church
Evangelical Church of Czech Brethren [Czech
  Republic]
Evangelical Church of the Augsburg and Hel-
  vetic Confessions in Austria
Evangelical Church of the Augsburg Confession
  in Poland
Evangelical Church of the Augsburg Confession
  in Romania
Evangelical Church of the Augsburg Confession
  in the Slovak Republic
Evangelical Church of the Augsburg Confession
  of Alsace and Lorraine [France]

Evangelical Lutheran Church in Denmark
Evangelical Lutheran Church in the Kingdom of
  the Netherlands
Evangelical Lutheran Church of Finland
Evangelical Lutheran Church of France
Evangelical Lutheran Church of Iceland
Evangelical Lutheran Church of Latvia
Evangelical Methodist Church of Italy
Evangelical Presbyterian Church of Portugal*
Evangelical Synodal Presbyterial Church of the
  Augsburg Confession in Romania
Finnish Ecumenical Council**
Greek Evangelical Church
Latvian Evangelical Lutheran Church Abroad
  [Germany]
Lusitanian Catholic Apostolic Evangelical
  Church [Portugal]*
Lutheran Church in Hungary
Mennonite Church [Germany]
Mennonite Church in the Netherlands
Methodist Church [UK]
Methodist Church in Ireland
Mission Covenant Church of Sweden
Moravian Church in Great Britain and Ireland
Netherlands Reformed Church
Old Catholic Church of Austria
Old Catholic Church of Switzerland
Old Catholic Church of the Netherlands
Old Catholic Mariavite Church in Poland
Orthodox Autocephalous Church of Albania
Orthodox Church in the Czech Lands and
  Slovakia
Orthodox Church of Finland
Polish Catholic Church in Poland
Polish Ecumenical Council**
Presbyterian Church of Wales
Reformed Christian Church in Slovakia [Slovak
  Republic]
Reformed Christian Church in Yugoslavia
Reformed Church in Hungary
Reformed Church of Alsace and Lorraine
  [France]
Reformed Church of France
Reformed Church in Romania
Reformed Churches in the Netherlands
Remonstrant Brotherhood [Netherlands]
Romanian Orthodox Church
Russian Orthodox Church
Scottish Congregational Church
Scottish Episcopal Church
Serbian Orthodox Church [Federal Rep. of
  Yugoslavia]
Silesian Evangelical Church of the Augsburg
  Confession [Czech Republic]
Slovak Evangelical Church of the Augsburg Con-
  fession in Yugoslavia
Spanish Evangelical Church
Spanish Reformed Episcopal Church*
Swiss Protestant Church Federation
Union of Welsh Independents
United Free Church of Scotland
United Protestant Church of Belgium
United Reformed Church in the United Kingdom

Waldensian Church [Italy]

LATIN AMERICA
Anglican Church of the Southern Cone of
  America [Argentina]
Baptist Association of El Salvador*
Baptist Convention of Nicaragua
Bolivian Evangelical Lutheran Church*
Christian Biblical Church [Argentina]*
Christian Reformed Church of Brazil
Church of God [Argentina]*
Church of the Disciples of Christ [Argentina]*
Episcopal Anglican Church of Brazil
Evangelical Church of Lutheran Confession in
  Brazil
Evangelical Church of the River Plate [Argentina]
Evangelical Lutheran Church in Chile
Evangelical Methodist Church in Bolivia*
Evangelical Methodist Church in Uruguay*
Evangelical Methodist Church of Argentina
Evangelical Methodist Church of Costa Rica*
Free Pentecostal Mission Church of Chile
Methodist Church in Brazil
Methodist Church of Chile*
Methodist Church of Mexico
Methodist Church of Peru*
Moravian Church in Nicaragua
National Council of Christian Churches in
  Brazil**
Pentecostal Church of Chile
Pentecostal Mission Church [Chile]
Salvadorean Lutheran Synod*
United Evangelical Lutheran Church
  [Argentina]*
United Presbyterian Church of Brazil*

MIDDLE EAST
Armenian Apostolic Church [Lebanon]
Church of Cyprus
Coptic Orthodox Church [Egypt]
Episcopal Church in Jerusalem and the Middle
  East
Greek Orthodox Patriarchate of Alexandria and
  All Africa [Egypt]
Greek Orthodox Patriarchate of Antioch and All
  the East [Syria]
Greek Orthodox Patriarchate of Jerusalem
Holy Apostolic Catholic Assyrian Church of the
  East [Iraq]
National Evangelical Synod of Syria and Leba-
  non [Lebanon]
Syrian Orthodox Patriarchate of Antioch and All
  the East [Syria]
Synod of the Evangelical Church of Iran
Synod of the Nile of the Evangelical Church
  [Egypt]
Union of the Armenian Evangelical Churches in
  the Near East [Lebanon]

NORTH AMERICA
African Methodist Episcopal Church [USA]
African Methodist Episcopal Zion Church [USA]
American Baptist Churches in the USA

ECUMENICAL

Anglican Church of Canada
Canadian Council of Churches**
Canadian Yearly Meeting of the Religious Society
of Friends
Christian Church (Disciples of Christ) [Canada]
Christian Church (Disciples of Christ) [USA]
Christian Methodist Episcopal Church [USA]
Church of the Brethren [USA]
Episcopal Church [USA]
Estonian Evangelical Lutheran Church Abroad
[Canada]
Evangelical Lutheran Church in America
Evangelical Lutheran Church in Canada
Hungarian Reformed Church in America [USA]
International Council of Community Churches
[USA]
International Evangelical Church [USA]
Moravian Church in America (Northern
Province)
Moravian Church in America (Southern
Province)
National Baptist Convention of America
National Baptist Convention, USA, Inc.
National Council of the Churches of Christ in the
USA**
Orthodox Church in America
Polish National Catholic Church [USA]
Presbyterian Church in Canada
Presbyterian Church (USA)
Progressive National Baptist Convention, Inc.
[USA]
Reformed Church in America

Religious Society of Friends: Friends General
Conference and Friends United Meeting [USA]
United Church of Canada
United Church of Christ [USA]
United Methodist Church [USA]

PACIFIC
Church of the Province of Melanesia [Solomon
Islands]
Congregational Christian Church in American
Samoa
Congregational Christian Church in Samoa
Cook Islands Christian Church
Evangelical Church in New Caledonia and the
Loyalty Isles [New Caledonia]
Evangelical Church of French Polynesia
Evangelical Lutheran Church of Papua New
Guinea
Kiribati Protestant Church
Methodist Church in Fiji
Methodist Church in Samoa
Methodist Church in Tonga
National Council of Churches of American
Samoa**
Papua New Guinea Council of Churches**
Presbyterian Church of Vanuatu
Tonga National Council of Churches**
Tuvalu Christian Church
United Church in Papua New Guinea
United Church in the Solomon Islands
United Church of Christ – Congregational in the
Marshall Islands

Regional Conferences

ALL AFRICA CONFERENCE OF CHURCHES
General Secretary Revd José Belo Chipenda,
Waiyaki Way, PO Box 14205, Westlands, Nairobi,
Kenya

Founded 1963.

CHRISTIAN CONFERENCE OF ASIA
General Secretary Bishop John Victor Samuel
(Church of Pakistan)

Central Office Pak Tin Village, Mei Tin Rd, Shatin,
N.T., Hong Kong   *Fax*: 852 721 6007

Founded 1959.

CARIBBEAN CONFERENCE OF CHURCHES
General Secretary Mr Gerard Grenado, PO Box
616, Bridgetown, Barbados, WI *Fax*: 246 427–2681
            email: cccbdos@ndlc.com

Founded 1973.

CONFERENCE OF EUROPEAN CHURCHES
See page 428.

**LATIN AMERICAN COUNCIL OF
CHURCHES**
(Consejo Latinoamericano de Iglesias (CLAI))

President Dr Walter Altmann, Rua Martin Lutero

358, Sao Leopoldo/ R. S. B. R. 93030–120, Brasil
            Tel and *Fax*: 5551–5926835
            email: waltmann@plug-in.com.br

General Secretary Mr Israel Batista, Casilla 17–08
8522, Quito, Ecuador   *Fax*: 5932–553996
            email: israel@clai.ecuanex.net.ec

**MIDDLE EAST COUNCIL OF CHURCHES
(MECC)**
HQ Address PO Box 5376, Beirut, Lebanon
            Fax: 961 1 344 894
            email: mecc@cyberia.net.lb

Liaison Office PO Box 54259, 3722 Limassol,
Cyprus   *Fax*: 357–5–586 496
            email: mecccypr@spidernet.com.cy

General Secretary Revd Dr Riad Jarjour (*same
address*)   *email*: jarjour@spidernet.com.cy
Organized 1974. It comprises 26 member
churches from: Eastern Orthodox, Oriental
Orthodox, Catholic, and Evangelical (Protestant)
Churches.

PACIFIC CONFERENCE OF CHURCHES
Moderator Revd Reuben Magekon

Acting General Secretary Revd Valamotu Palu,
PCC Secretariat, 4 Thurston St, Suva, Fiji
            Fax: (679) 303205

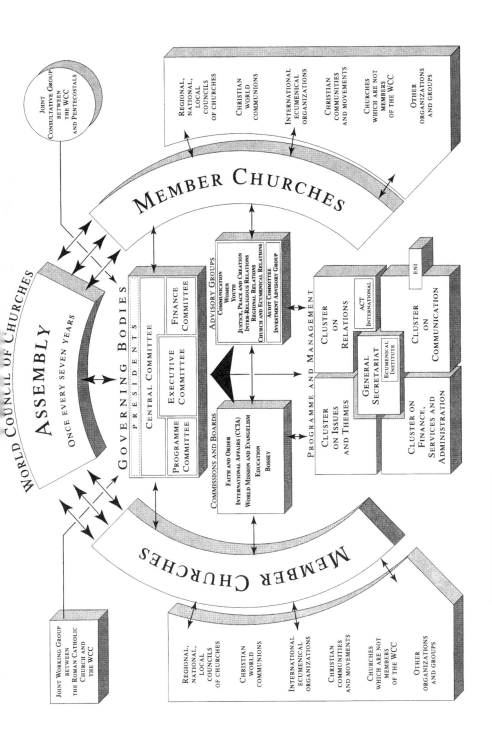

WORLD COUNCIL OF CHURCHES

ASSEMBLY
ONCE EVERY SEVEN YEARS

MEMBER CHURCHES

MEMBER CHURCHES

JOINT CONSULTATIVE GROUP BETWEEN THE WCC AND PENTECOSTALS

REGIONAL, NATIONAL, LOCAL COUNCILS OF CHURCHES

CHRISTIAN WORLD COMMUNIONS

INTERNATIONAL ECUMENICAL ORGANIZATIONS

CHRISTIAN COMMUNITIES AND MOVEMENTS

CHURCHES WHICH ARE NOT MEMBERS OF THE WCC

OTHER ORGANIZATIONS AND GROUPS

GOVERNING BODIES

PRESIDENTS

CENTRAL COMMITTEE

PROGRAMME COMMITTEE

EXECUTIVE COMMITTEE

FINANCE COMMITTEE

ADVISORY GROUPS
COMMUNICATION
WOMEN
YOUTH
JUSTICE, PEACE AND CREATION
INTER-RELIGIOUS RELATIONS
REGIONAL RELATIONS
CHURCH AND ECUMENICAL RELATIONS
AUDIT COMMITTEE
INVESTMENT ADVISORY GROUP

COMMISSIONS AND BOARDS
FAITH AND ORDER
INTERNATIONAL AFFAIRS (CCIA)
WORLD MISSION AND EVANGELISM
EDUCATION
BOSSEY

PROGRAMME AND MANAGEMENT

CLUSTER ON RELATIONS

ACT INTERNATIONAL

ENI

CLUSTER ON COMMUNICATION

GENERAL SECRETARIAT

ECUMENICAL INSTITUTE

CLUSTER ON ISSUES AND THEMES

CLUSTER ON FINANCE, SERVICES AND ADMINISTRATION

JOINT WORKING GROUP BETWEEN THE ROMAN CATHOLIC CHURCH AND THE WCC

REGIONAL, NATIONAL, LOCAL COUNCILS OF CHURCHES

CHRISTIAN WORLD COMMUNIONS

INTERNATIONAL ECUMENICAL ORGANIZATIONS

CHRISTIAN COMMUNITIES AND MOVEMENTS

CHURCHES WHICH ARE NOT MEMBERS OF THE WCC

OTHER ORGANIZATIONS AND GROUPS

ECUMENICAL

World Council of Churches   **435**

WCC Programme and Management

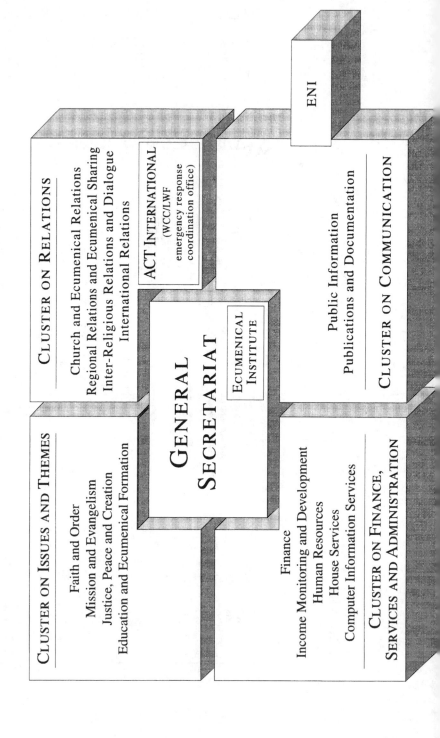

Cluster on Issues and Themes

Faith and Order
Mission and Evangelism
Justice, Peace and Creation
Education and Ecumenical Formation

Cluster on Relations

Church and Ecumenical Relations
Regional Relations and Ecumenical Sharing
Inter-Religious Relations and Dialogue
International Relations

ACT International
(WCC/LWF
emergency response
coordination office)

General Secretariat

Ecumenical Institute

ENI

Finance
Income Monitoring and Development
Human Resources
House Services
Computer Information Services

Cluster on Finance, Services and Administration

Public Information
Publications and Documentation

Cluster on Communication

Who's Who | **PART 7**

Abbreviations used in the biographies

pt .... part time
Aber .... Aberdeen
ABM .... Advisory Board of Ministry
Abth .... Aberystwyth
ACA .... Associate of the Institute of
Chartered Accountants
ACC .... Anglican Consultative Council
ACCM .... Advisory Council for the Church's
Ministry
ACIB .... Associate of the Chartered Institute
of Bankers
ACIS ..... Associate of the Institute of Chartered
Secretaries and Administrators
ACORA .... Archbishops' Commission on
Rural Areas
ACP ...... Associate of the College of Preceptors
ACS .... Additional Curates Society
ACU .... Actors Church Union
AD .... Area Dean
Adn .... Archdeacon
Adnry .... Archdeaconery
AHA .... Area Health Authority
AIA .... Associate of the Institute of Actuaries
Aid .... Aidan
AIMLS ......Associate of the Institute of Medical
Laboratory Sciences
AKC .... Associate of King's College, London
ALAM .... Associate of the London Academy
of Music
ALCD .... Associate of the London College
of Divinity
ALCM .... Associate of the London College
of Music
Ant .... Anthony
APF .... Anglican Pacifist Fellowship
APMI ... Associate of the Pensions Management
Institute
APR .... Association for Promoting Retreats
ARAM .... Associate of the Royal Academy
of Music
ARCIC . Anglican-Roman Catholic International
Commission
ARCM . Associate of the Royal College of Music
ARCO(CHM) ..Associate of the Royal College of
Organists with Diploma in Choir Training
ARICS .... Associate of the Royal Institute of
Chartered Surveyors
ASA .... Associate of the Society of Actuaries
ATII .... Associate Member of the Institute
of Taxation
AYPA .... Anglican Young People's Assembly
B & W .... Bath and Wells
BAGUPA ... Bishop's Advisory Group on UPA's
BCC .... British Council of Churches
BCL .... Bachelor of Civil Law
B COMM .... Bachelor of Commerce
BD .... Bachelor of Divinity
BDS .... Bachelor of Dental Surgery

BM .... Board of Mission
BMU .... Board for Mission and Unity
BNC .... Brasenose College
BRF .... Bible Reading Fellowship
BS .... Bachelor of Surgery / Science
BSR .... Board for Social Responsibility
Bt .... Baronet
C .... Curate
C and YP .... Children and Young People
C-in-c .... Curate-in-charge
CA .... Church Army
CA .... Member of the Institute of Chartered
Accountants of Scotland
CAB .... Citizens Advice Bureau
CAC .... Crown Appointments Commission
CACLB ... Churches Advisory Council for Local
Broadcasting
Carl .... Carlisle
CB .... Companion of the Order of the Bath
CBF .... Central Board of Finance
CCBI .... Council of Churches in Britain and
Ireland
CCC Cam ... Corpus Christi College Cambridge
CCC .... Council for the Care of Churches
C CHEM .... Certified Chemist
CCHH .... Churches Council for Health
and Healing
CCRJ .. Churches' Commission for Racial Justice
CCU .... Council for Church Unity
CD .... Conventional District
CEC .... Conference of European Churches
CECC .... Church of England Committee for
Communications
CEDR .... Centre for Dispute Resolution
CEIG .... Christian Ethical Investment Group
CEMS .... Church of England Men's Society
C ENG .... Chartered Engineer
CERC .... Church of England Record Centre
CERT SPECIAL EDUC MGT ...... Certificate in
Special Education Management
CERT TH .... Certificate in Theology
CF .... Chaplain to the Forces
CF(TA) Chaplain to the Forces (Territorial Army)
CFE .... College of Further Education
Ch .... Christ
CH B .... Bachelor of Surgery
Ch Ch .... Christ Church
Ch Hosp .... Christ's Hospital
Ch(s) .... Church(es)
Chan .... Chancellor
Chr .... Christian
CME .... Continuing Ministerial Education
CMEAC .... Committee for Minority Ethnic
Anglican Concerns
CMJ .... Church's Ministry Among the Jews
CMS .. Church Mission Society or Church Music
Society
CND .... Campaign for Nuclear Disarmament

C PHYS ..... Chartered Physicist of the Institute of Physics
CQSW ...... Certificate of Qualification in Social Work
CR .... Community of the Resurrection
CRAC Central Religious Advisory Committee of the BBC and ITA
CRC .... Central Readers Council
CSA .... Community of Saint Andrew
CSC ...... Community of Sisters of the Church
CSMV ..... Community of Saint Mary the Virgin
CSO .... Central Statistical Office
CSR .... Council for Social Responsibility
C STAT .... Chartered Statistician
CTE .... Churches Together in England
CU .... Church Union
CUF .... Church Urban Fund
CYFA ... Church Youth Fellowships Association
DA .... Diploma in Anaesthetics
DAA .... Diploma in Archive Administration
DAC .... Diocesan Advisory Committee
DACE .... Diaconal Association of the Church of England
DASS .... Diploma in Applied Social Studies
Dav .... David
DBF .... Diocesan Board of Finance
D CH .... Doctor of Surgery
DCH .... Diploma in Child Health
DCL .... Doctor of Civil Law
DCO .... Diocesan Communications Officer
DDO .... Diocesan Director of Ordinands
DDS .... Doctor of Dental Surgery
DFF .... Diocesan Finance Forum
DHA .... District Health Authority
DIC .... Diploma of Imperial College
DIP AD .... Diploma in Advertising
DIP AD ED ... Diploma in Advanced Education
DIP EE .... Diploma in Electrical Engineering
DIP HE .... Diploma in Higher Education
DIP L & A .... Diploma in Liturgy and Architecture
DIP LIB .... Diploma of Librarianship
DIP N .... Diploma in Nursing
DIP PE .... Diploma in Physical Education
DIP RJ .... Diploma in Retail Jewellery
DIP SOC STUDY ...... Diploma in Social Study
DIP SOC WORK .... Diploma in Social Work
DIP SP ED .... Diploma in Special Education
DIP TH .... Diploma in Theology
DIPTP .... Diploma in Town Planning
DL .... Deputy Lieutenant
D MIN .... Doctor of Ministry
Dn .... Deacon
DN .... Diploma in Nursing
Dny .... Deanery
Dny Syn .... Deanery Synod
D OBSTRCOG .... Diploma in Obstetrics, Royal College of Obstetricians and Gynaecologists
Doct .... Doctrine
DPA .... Diploma in Public Administration
DPS .... Diploma in Pastoral Studies
DRACSC ...... Deployment, Remuneration and Conditions of Service Committee

DRCOG .... Diploma of the Royal College of Obstetricians and Gynaecologist
Dss .... Deacones
DTM&H ..... Diploma in Tropical Medicine and Hygien
DTPH .... Diploma in Tropical Public Health
DTS .... Diploma in Theological Studie
E .... Eas
ECUSA .. Episcopal Church of the United State of America
Edm .... Edmund
EFAC ... Evangelical Fellowship in the Anglican Communion
EIG .... Ecclesiastical Insurance Group
EJM(RC) ..... Ecclesiastical Jurisdiction Measure (Revision Committee)
EKD .... Evangelische Kirche Deutschland
EUR ING .... European Engineer
Ev .... Evangelis
FAC .... Fabric Advisory Committee
FBIM ... Fellow British Institute of Management
FC INST M . Fellow of the Chartered Institute of Marketing
FCA .... Fellow of the Institute of Chartered Accountants
FCCA ... Fellow of the Chartered Association of Certified Accountants
FCII .... Fellow of the Chartered Insurance Institute
FCMA .... Fellow of the Institute of Cost and Management
FCO .... Foreign and Commonwealth Office
FCP .... Fellow of the College of Preceptors
FDSRCS .... Fellow in Dental Surgery of the Royal College of Surgeons of England
FHSM .... Fellow, Institute of Health Service Management
FIA .... Fellow of the Institute of Actuaries
FIAA ...... Fellow of the Institute of Actuaries of Australia
FIBMS . Fellow, Institute of Biomedical Sciences
FIED ...... Fellow of the Institute of Engineering Designers
FIHT Fellow of the Institution of Highways and Transportation
FIPD .... Fellow of the Institute of Personnel Directors
FIWSC .. Fellow of the Institute of Wood Science
FJM .... Faculty Jurisdiction Measure
FKC .... Fellow of King's College, London
FLAME .... Family Life and Marriage Education
FOAG .... Faith and Order Advisory Group
FPMI .... Fellow of the Pensions Management Institute
FRCA .... Fellow of the Royal College of Anaesthetists
FRCO . Fellow of the Royal College of Organists
FRCS ED .... Fellow of the Royal College of Surgeons of Edinburgh
FRCS ENG .... Fellow of the Royal College of Surgeons of England
FRGS . Fellow of the Royal Geographical Society
FRHIST S Fellow of the Royal Historical Society

FRICS Fellow of the Royal Institute of Chartered Surveyors

FRIPHH . Fellow of the Royal Institute of Public Health and Hygiene

FROCG .... Fellow of the Royal College of Obstetricians and Gynaecologists

FRS .... Fellow of the Royal Society

FRSA .... Fellow of the Royal Society of Arts

FRSC . Fellow of the Royal Society of Chemistry

FRSL .. Fellow of the Royal Society of Literature

FSA .... Fellow of the Society of Antiquaries

FSCA .. Fellow of the Royal Society of Company and Commercial Accountants

H .... Holy

HA .... Health Authority

HCC .... Hospital Chaplaincies Council

HMDC .... Her Majesty's Detention Centre

IBA .... Independent Broadcasting Authority

ICS .... Intercontinental Church Society

IDC .... Inter-Diocesan Certificate

IMEC .. Initial Ministerial Education Committee

in-c .... in-charge

IOM .... Isle of Man

IPR .... Institute of Public Relations

K .... King(s)

LDSRCS ..... Licentiate in Dental Surgery of the Royal College of Surgeons

LEP .... Local Ecumenical Project

LIC IPD ... Licentiate Member of the Institute of Personnel and Development

LIM .... Licentiate of the Institute of Metals

LLD .... Doctor of Laws

LLAM .... Licentiate of the London Academy of Music and Dramatic Art

Llan .... Llandaff

LLM .... Master of Laws

LRAM .... Licentiate of the Royal Academy of Music

LRCP .... Licentiate of the Royal College of Physicians

LTCL . Licentiate of the Trinity College of Music, London

L TH .... Licentiate in Theology

M .... Member

MAFF .... Ministry for Agriculture Fisheries and Food

MB .... Bachelor of Medicine

MBC .... Metropolitan Borough Council

MBCS . Member of the British Computer Society

MBIM .... Member of the British Institute of Management

MCAD .... Marriage in Church after Divorce

MCIM ..... Member of the Chartered Institute of Marketing

MCT ... Member of the Association of Corporate Treasurers

MICE .... Member of the Institution of Civil Engineers

MIEE .... Member of the Institution of Electrical Engineers

MIM .... Member of the Institute of Metals

MIMGT .... Member of the Institute of Management

M INST D . Member of the Institute of Directors

M INST P .... Member of the Institute of Physics

M INST R .... Member of the Institute of Refrigeration

MIPD Member of the Institute of Personnel and Development

MIPR .... Member of the Institute of Public Relations

MJI .... Member of the Institute of Journalists

Mod .... Moderator

MOW . Movement for the Ordination of Women

MRCGP .... Member of the Royal College of General Practitioners

MRCS Member of the Royal College of Surgeons

MRTPI .... Member of the Royal Town Planning Institute

MSF Manufacturing, Science and Finance Union

N .... North

NACRO . National Association for the Care and Rehabilitation of Offenders

NAHT ... National Association of Headteachers

NCA .... National Certificate in Agriculture

NCEC .... National Christian Education Council

NDA .... National Diploma in Agriculture

NDD .... National Diploma in Design

NFF .... National Froebel Foundation

NNEB .... Nursery Nurse Examination Board

NS .... National Service

NSM .... Non Stipendary Minister/Ministry

NT .... New Testament

NTMTC ..... North Thames Ministerial Training Course

OCF .... Officiating Chaplain to the Forces

OGS .... Order of the Good Shepherd

OHP .... Order of the Holy Paraclete

OM .... Order of Merit

OTC .... Open Theology College

OU .... Open University

PACTA .... Professional Associate of the Clinical Theology Association

Perm .... Permission

P-in-c .... Priest-in-charge

POT .... Post Ordination Training

PPS .... Personal Private Secretary

Prec .... Precentor

Pres .... President

PROs .... Public Relations Officers

PWM .... Partnership for World Mission

QHC .... Queen's Honorary Chaplain

R .... Rector or Royal

RAChD(TA) .... Royal Army Chaplains' Department (Territorial Army)

RCHME .... Royal Commission on Historical Monuments

RD .... Rural Dean

Red .... Redundant

RGN .... Registered General Nurse

RHM .... Rank Hovis McDougall

RIBA .... Royal Institute of British Architects

RICS .... Royal Institute of Chartered Surveyors

RM .... Registered Midwife

RMA .... Royal Military Academy

RMN .... Registered Mental Nurse

RN .... Royal Navy
RSCM .... Royal School of Church Music
S .... South
SAMS .... South American Mission Society
SBL .... Society of Biblical Literature
SC D .... Doctor of Science
SCM .... Student Christian Movement
SOAS ... School of Oriental and African Studies
SPI .... Society of Practitioners of Insolvency
SSC .... Society of the Holy Cross
SSF .... Society of Saint Francis
SST .... Society for the Study of Theology
St .... Saint
St As .... Saint Asaph
STB .... Bachelor of Theology
STETS Southern Theological Education Training
Scheme
STH .... Scholar in Theology
STL .... Reader of Sacred Theology
STM .... Master of Theology
Succ .... Succentor

Suff .... Suffragan
TD .... Territorial (Officers') Decoration
TEC .... Training and Enterprise Council
TETC .... Theological Education and Training
Committee
TM .... Team Ministry or Team Minister
TR .... Team Rector
TV .... Team Vicar
UA(IG) .... Under Authority Implementation
Group
UEA .... University of East Anglia
UPAs .... Urban Priority Areas
USCL .... United Society for Christian Literature
UWIST . University of Wales Institute of Science
and Technology
V .... Vicar
VRSC ..... Vocations, Recruitment and Selection
Committee
W .... West
w .... with
WWDP .... Women's World Day of Prayer

A Directory of General Synod members, together with those suffragan bishops, deans, provosts and archdeacons who are not members of General Synod, and principal staff members of the General Synod, Church Commissioners and Lambeth Palace, and Church Commissioners who are not members of General Synod. General Synod members are distinguished by the date of their membership, printed at the end of their entry, following the letters GS. Current membership of the General Synod is denoted by the lack of a closing date. All details are fully accurate at the time of going to press.

AAGAARD, Mr Robert
Manor House, High Birstwith, Harrogate, N Yorks HG3 2LG [RIPON] *b* 27 Jun 1932; *educ* Gresham's Sch Holt; Managing Dir Robert Aagaard Ltd Antiques 1960–80, Consultant 1980–95; Dir Aagaard-Hanley Ltd Fibrous Plasterers 1970–80, Consultant from 1980; Partner R & F C Aagaard Designers and Decorators of Historic House Interiors from 1980; Founder and Chmn Cathl Camps from 1980; Consultant Robert Aagaard & Co Period Chimneypieces and Marble Processing from 1995; M Cathls Fabric Commn for England; Chmn Ripon DAC; M Ripon Cathl Fabric Adv Ctee; M Bradf Cathl Fabric Adv Ctee; M Dioc Redundant Chs Uses Ctee; M Dioc Worship Ctee; M Dioc Rural Min Grp
GS 1995–   *Tel:* (01423) 770385
       Fax: (01423) 770714

ACWORTH, Ven Dick (Richard Foote)
Old Rectory, Croscombe, Wells, Som BA5 3QN [ARCHDEACON OF WELLS] *b* 19 Oct 1936; *educ* St Jo Sch Leatherhead; SS Coll Cam; Cuddesdon Th Coll; C St Etheldreda's Fulham 1963; All SS & Martyrs, Langley 1964–66; C St Mary Bridgwater 1966–69; V Yatton 1969–81; R Yatton Moor 1981; P-in-c St Jo Ev 1981–84; St Mary Magd Taunton 1981–85; V St Mary Magd Taunton 1985–93; Adn of Wells from 1993
GS 1980–95, 1998– *Tel:* (01749) 342242
       Fax: (01749) 330060

ADAMS, Mrs Marian, BA
Church Commissioners, 1 Millbank, London SW1P 3JZ [CHIEF ACCOUNTANT, CHURCH COMMISSIONERS] *b* 21 Oct 1957; *educ* Henry Box Sch Witney; Leeds Univ; On staff of Ch Commrs from 1979; Property Accountant Ch Commrs 1996–99; Chief Accountant from 1999 *Tel:* 020–7898 1677
       Fax: 020–7222 1653
  email: marian.adams@c-of-e.org.uk

ADAMS, Canon Ray (Raymond) Michael, BD, ALCD
Ipsley Rectory, Icknield St, Ipsley, Redditch, Worcs B98 0AN [WORCESTER] *b* 4 Dec 1941; *educ* Gravesend Tech Sch; Lon Univ; Lon Coll of Div; C Holy Trin Old Hill Worc 1967–73; TR Ipsley from 1973; Hon Can Worc Cathl from 1984; Grp Chmn Redditch Grp Min from 1985; M Gen Syn Revision Ctee The Service of the Word; M Calendar, Lectionary and Collects Revision Ctee; Appeal Panel Proctor under 1983 Pastl Measure; M Bp's Coun and Stg Ctee; M Dioc Liturg Ctee; Bp's Selector; ABM Selector; M Dioc Patronage Bd
GS 1990–   *Tel:* (01527) 523307

ADCOCK, Mr Roger Anthony, MA, PGCE, FBIM
The Barn, North Sidborough, Loxbeare, Tiverton, Devon EX16 8BY [EXETER] *b* 21 Mar 1927; *educ* Win Coll Quirister Sch; Ardingly Coll; St Cath's Coll Cam; St Edm Hall Ox; McGill Univ Montreal; Asst Master Southend High Sch 1952–55; Hd of History Marlborough Gr Sch 1955–59; Warden Comberton Village Coll 1959–64; Hdmaster Wells Blue Sch 1964–68; Hd of Educ Bede Coll Dur 1968–71; Prin Coll of St Matthias Bris 1971–78; Asst Co-ord Gov Tr Devon CC 1990–94; Sec Nat Govs Coun; M Dioc Syn; Rdr
GS 1985–   *Tel:* (01884) 881361
       Fax: (01884) 881534
  email: roger.adcock@ngc.org.uk

AINSWORTH, Revd Michael Ronald, LLM, MA
Rectory, Walkden Rd, Worsley, Manchester M28 2WH [MANCHESTER] *b* 18 Jun 1950; *educ* K Edw VII Gr Sch Sheff; K Coll Lon; Trin Hall Cam; Westcott Ho Th Coll; C St Paul Scotforth 1975–78; Chapl St Martin Coll Lanc 1978–82; Chapl and Tutor Nn Ord Course 1982–89; R St Chris Withington 1989–94; TR Worsley TM from 1994; Bps' Inspector of Th Colls and Courses; M CCC; Dioc Moderator of Rdr Tr; M Dioc Worship Ctee; M DAC; M Dioc Red Chs Uses Ctee
GS 1995–   *Tel and Fax:* 0161–790 2362

ALDERTON-FORD, Revd Jonathan Laurence, B TH
18 Heldhaw Rd, Bury St Edmunds, Suffolk IP32 7ER [ST EDMUNDSBURY AND IPSWICH] *b* 20 Oct 1957; *educ* Denes High Sch Lowestoft; Nottm Univ; St Jo Coll Nottm; C St Faith Gaywood Nor 1985–87; C St Andr Herne Bay 1987–90; V Ch Ch Moreton Hall from 1990; CME and POT Tutor; M Dioc Child Protection Ctee; Chmn Prayer for Revival; Convenor Dioc Renewal Fellowship; M Exec Ctee Chs Together for Bury St Edmunds; Trustee Bury Chr Youth
GS 1999–   *Tel:* (01284) 769956 (Home)
  Tel and Fax: (01284) 725391 (Office)
     email: ccmh@iname.com

ALLAN, Mrs Kate (Kathleen Mabel), T CERT
19 Beech Rd, Stockton Heath, Warrington WA4 6LT
[CHESTER] *b* 23 Mar 1935; *educ* Blackburn High Sch
for Girls; Cartrefle Teacher Coll, Wrexham; Open
Univ; Secondary School teacher 1955–88; Rtd;
Open Univ Student; M Bp's Coun; M Dioc CSR
GS 1990–   *Tel:* (01925) 266331
email: Kate.Allan@ukgateway.net

ALLEN, Ven Geoffrey Gordon
Ijsselsingel 86, 6991 ZT Rheden, Netherlands
[ARCHDEACON IN NORTH-WEST EUROPE] *b* 14 May
1939; *educ* Alton Co Sec Sch; K Coll Lon; Sarum
Th Coll; C St Mary Langley 1966–70; Miss to
Seamen Tilbury 1970–72; Schiedam 1972–74; Port
Chapl Antwerp and OCF 1974–78; Chapl Tildonk
1974–78; Chapl St Mary Rotterdam and Sen
Chapl Miss to Seamen 1978–82; Chapl Pernis
1982–83; Assoc Chapl The Hague, Voorschoten
and Leiden 1983–93; Warden to Rdrs dio of Eur
1983–95; Chapl E Netherlands from 1993; Adn in
NW Europe from 1993; Canon Brussels Pro Cathl
from 1993; Chmn Angl Netherlands Area Coun
1983–98; P-in-c Haarlem from 1995
                                    Tel: 00–31–26–4953800
                                    Fax: 00–31–26–4954922
email: 106362,1337@compuserve.com

ANDREWS, Canon Brian Keith, MA
Vicarage, High St, Abbots Langley, Herts WD5 0AS
[ST ALBANS] *b* 8 May 1939; *educ* Alleyns Sch; Keble
Coll Ox; Coll of Resurr Mirfield; C Isle of Dogs,
Poplar 1964–68; TV St Mary Hemel Hempstead
1968–79; RD Watford 1988–94; V Abbots Langley
from 1979; Hon Can St Alb Cathl from 1994; M
Gov Body St Alb and Ox Min Course from 1994;
Chmn Dioc Assisted Self Appraisal Scheme
1990–96; Chmn Dioc Ho of Clergy from 1993; M
Gov Body Ripon Coll Cuddesdon from 1996
GS 1995–   *Tel:* (01923) 263013
                                    Fax: (01923) 261795

APPELBEE, Mrs Elaine, BA, CQSW
168 Highfield Lane, Keighley, W Yorks BD21 2HU
[BRADFORD] *b* 9 Jun 1954; *educ* Lanc Girls' Gr Sch;
Bradf Univ; Social Worker Lynfield Mount Hos-
pital 1977–78; Community Worker Bradf Social
Services 1979–86; Senior Community Worker
Bradf dio 1987–91; Bp's Officer for Church in
Society Bradf dio from 1992; M BSR
GS 1990–   *Tel and Fax:* (01535) 671377
                                    email: appelbee@zetnet.co.uk

ARCHER, Mr Anthony William, LL B, ACA
*Manor End, Little Gaddesden, Berkhamsted, Herts
HP4 1PL* [ST ALBANS] *b* 17 Jan 1953; *educ* St Edw
Sch Ox; Birm Univ; Mgment Consultant Ray &
Berndtson from 1995; M ABM 1994–98; M Appts
Ctee from 1999; M Rev Ctee on Ch Representa-
tion Rules etc; M Recruitment Strategy Working

Party; Coun M Oak Hill Th Coll; M Gen Syn
Panel of Chmn from 1999; Regional Adv fo
Alpha Course
GS 1993–   *Tel:* (01442) 843249 (Home
                                    020–7233 8888 (Office
email: awarcher@compuserve.com

ARNOLD, Very Revd John Robert, MA, DD
The Deanery, Durham DH1 3EQ [DEAN OF DURHAM
b 1 Nov 1933; *educ* Ch Hosp; SS Coll Cam; West
cott Ho Th Coll; C H Trin Millhouses, Shef
1960–63; Sir Henry Stephenson Fell Sheff Univ
1962–63; Angl Chapl and Vis Lect Southn Univ
1963–72; Sec BMU 1972–78; Dean of Rocheste
1978–89; Dean of Durham from 1989; M Centra
Ctee Conf of Eur Chs from 1993, Pres and Chmr
1993–97; M CCU; Chmn Angl-Lutheran Soc from
1999
GS 1980–   *Tel:* 0191–384 7500
                                    Fax: 0191–386 4267
email: john.arnold@durhamcathedral.co.uk

ARRAND, Ven Geoffrey William, BD, AKC
*Glebe House, The Street, Ashfield cum Thorpe, Stow-
market, Suffolk IP14 6LX* [ARCHDEACON OF SUF-
FOLK] *b* 24 Jul 1944; *educ* Scunthorpe Gr Sch; K
Coll Lon; St Boniface Warminster; C Washington
1967–70; C S Ormsby Grp 1970–73; TV Gt Grimsby
TM 1973–79; TR Halesworth 1979–85; Dean of
Bocking 1985–94; R Hadleigh w Layham and
Shelley 1985–94; RD Hadleigh 1986–94; Hon Can
St Eds Cathl from 1991; Adn of Suffolk from 1994
                                    Tel: (01728) 685497
                                    Fax: (01728) 685969

ASHENDEN, Revd Dr Gavin Roy Pelham, LL B,
BA, M TH, D PHIL
42 New Rd, Shoreham by Sea BN43 6RA [UNI-
VERSITIES, SOUTH] *b* 3 Jun 1954; *educ* K Sch Cant;
Bris Univ; Heythrop Coll Lon; Oak Hill Th Coll;
Sussex Univ; C St Jas w Ch Ch Bermondsey
1980–83; TV All SS Sanderstead 1983–89; Dir Aid
to Russian Christians 1982–89; Coun M Keston
Inst from 1983, Vc-Chmn from 1992; Chapl and
Lect Sussex Univ from 1989; M CCU; Delegate to
WCC
GS 1995–   *Tel:* (01273) 606755 (Office)
                                    Fax: (01273) 453277
email: G.Ashenden@Sussex.ac.uk

ASHTON, Mr David
*2 Manor Drive, Battyeford, Mirfield, W Yorks WF14
0ER* [WAKEFIELD] *b* 2 Jul 1941; *educ* Warw Rd Jun-
ior Sch; Dewsbury and Batley Tech Sch; Kitson
Eng Coll; Br Telecom Grp Logistics Service
Centre Operations Mgr (NE and Midlands Zone);
M Bp's Coun; Chmn Ho of Laity Dioc Syn; Vc-
Pres Dioc Syn; M Dioc Pastl Ctee
GS 1972   *Tel:* (01924) 497996
                                    email: ashtond@boat.bt.com

SKEW, Prebendary Richard George, MA,
MP TH
he Abbey Rectory, Redwood House, Trossachs Drive,
athampton, Bath BA2 6RP [BATH AND WELLS] *b* 16
May 1935; *educ* Harrow; BNC Ox; Ridley Hall Th
Coll; C St Mary Chesham 1964–66; C St Matt and
t Jas Mossley Hill Liv 1966–67; Chapl Ox Pastor-
te 1967–72; Asst Chapl BNC Ox 1967–71; R St
Giles and St Geo Ashtead 1972–83; Dioc Adv on
Miss and Min Sarum 1983–90; Can Res and Treas
Sarum Cathl 1983–90; R Bath Abbey from 1990;
Preb Wells Cathl from 1992; M Bp's Coun
GS 1985–90, 1995–   *Tel:* (01225) 464930 (Home)
                               (01225) 422462 (Office)
                               Fax: (01225) 429990

ASTON, Bishop of [SUFFRAGAN, BIRMINGHAM]
Rt Revd John Michael Austin, BA
Strensham House, 8 Strensham Hill, Moseley, Bir-
mingham B13 8AG b 4 Mar 1939; *educ* Worksop
Coll; St Edm Hall Ox; St Steph Ho Ox; C St Jo E
Dulwich 1964–68; St Jas Cathl Chicago USA
1968–69; Warden Pemb Ho Miss Walworth
1969–76; Soc Resp Adv St Alb 1976–84; Dir Lon
Dioc BSR 1984–92; Bp of Aston from 1992
                               Tel: 0121–428 2228
                               Fax: 0121–428 1114

ATKIN, Dr Susan Anne Jennifer, BA, PH D
3 *St Bride Court, Colchester, Essex CO4 4PQ*
[CHELMSFORD] *b* 2 Aug 1948; *educ* Qu Eliz Girls'
Gr Sch Barnet; Reading Univ; Admin Trainee Min
of Defence 1973–75; Admin Asst City Univ
1975–78; Asst Registrar City Univ 1978–83; Dep
Registrar City Univ 1983–86; Dep Registrar York
Univ 1986–90; Planning Officer Essex Univ from
1990; M Dioc Syn from 1995; M Bp's Coun from
1998
GS 1995–   *Tel:* (01206) 854976 (Home)
                      (01206) 872422 (Office)
                      Fax: (01206) 873082 (Office)
                      email: saja@essex.ac.uk

ATKINSON, Ven David John, B SC, PH D, M LITT,
MA
3A Court Farm Rd, Mottingham, London SE9 4JH
[ARCHDEACON OF LEWISHAM] *b* 5 Sep 1943; *educ*
Maidstone Gr Sch; K Coll Lon; Bris Univ; Tyndale
Hall Th Coll; Tchr Maidstone Tech High Sch
1968–69; C St Pet Halliwell Bolton 1972–74; Sen C
St Jo Harborne Birm 1974–77; Libr Latimer Ho Ox
1977–80; Lect and Chapl CCC Ox 1980–93; Fell
CCC Ox 1984–93; External Examiner St Jo Coll
Nottm 1989–93; Can Res S'wark Cathl 1993–96;
Exam Chapl 1993–96; External Examiner and
ABM Moderator Trin Coll Bris 1994–98; Adn of
Lewisham from 1996; M Dioc Bd for Ch in
Society; M Dioc Syn; M Bp's Coun; M Soc of
Ordained Scientists   *Tel:* 020–8857 7982 (Home)
                               020–7403 8696 (Office)
                               Fax: 020–8249 0350 (Home)
                               020–7403 4770 (Office)
      email: david.atkinson@dswark.org.uk

ATKINSON, Mrs Janet Mary, MA
548 Yarm Rd, Eaglescliffe, Stockton-on-Tees, Cleve-
land TS16 0BX [DURHAM] *b* 4 Sep 1932; *educ*
Huyton Coll; St Anne's Coll Ox; Tchr St Leon Sch
St Andr 1954–55; Hartlepool Coll of Further Educ
(pt) 1979–84; pt Lect WEA from 1979; JP; M Dios
Commn; Ch Commr 1993–99; M CE Pensions Bd
1994–97; M Business Ctee from 1999; M Crown
Appts Commn Review Grp from 1999; M Bp's
Coun
GS 1985–   *Tel:* (01642) 782292

ATKINSON, Mr Roger Douglas, MA, LLM
115 Eastbrook Rd, Lincoln LN6 7EW [LINCOLN] *b* 24
Dec 1938; *educ* Haileybury Coll; Selw Coll Cam;
Solicitor from 1965; Partner Andrew & Co
Solicitors Linc from 1969; HM Coroner for Linc
from 1994
GS 1990–   *Tel:* (01522) 683209
                      Fax: (01522) 546713

ATKINSON, Canon Richard William Bryant,
MA
Rotherham Vicarage, 2 Heather Close, Rotherham S60
2TQ [SHEFFIELD] *b* 17 Dec 1958; *educ* St Paul's Sch
Lon; Magd Coll Cam; Ripon Coll Cuddesdon; C
Abingdon w Shippon 1984–87; TV Sheff Manor
Par 1987–91; Hon M of Staff Ripon Coll Cud-
desdon 1987–92; TR Sheff Manor Par 1991–96; V
All SS Rotherham from 1996; Dep Chair N Br
Housing Assn; Chair Open Syn Grp from 1997; M
CTE and CTBI; Hon Can Sheff Cathl from 1998;
M Central Ch Fund Ctee; M Business Ctee
GS 1991–   *Tel:* (01709) 364341 (Home)
                 Tel and Fax: (01709) 364737 (Office)

ATWELL, Very Revd James Edgar, MA, TH M, BD
The Provost's House, Bury St Edmunds, Suffolk IP33
1RS [PROVOST OF ST EDMUNDSBURY] *b* 3 Jun 1946;
educ Dauntsey's Sch; Ex Coll Ox; Harvard Univ;
Cuddesdon Th Coll; C St Jo E Dulwich 1970–74; C
Gt St Mary Cam 1974–77; Chapl Jes Coll Cam
1977–81; V Towcester w Easton Neston 1981–95;
RD Towcester 1983–91; Provost of St Eds from
1995   *Tel:* (01284) 754852 (Home)
                      (01284) 754933 (Office)
                      Fax: (01284) 768655

AVIS, Prebendary Paul David Loup, BD, PH D
Church House, Great Smith St, London SW1P 3NZ
[GENERAL SECRETARY, COUNCIL FOR CHRISTIAN
UNITY] *b* 21 Jul 1947; *educ* St Geo Monoux Gr Sch
Walthamstow; Lon Univ; Westcott Ho Th Coll; C
S Molton Grp 1975–80; V Stoke Canon, Poltimore
w Huxham, Rewe w Netherexe 1980–89; Sub
Dean Ex Cathl from 1997; Dir Centre for Study of
the Christian Church from 1997; Gen Sec CCU
from 1998; Vc-Chmn FOAG 1994–98; Chmn Ho
of Clergy Ex Dioc Syn 1996–98
GS 1990–95   *Tel:* 020–7898 1470
      email: paul.avis@ccu.c-of-e.org.uk

AXTELL, Mrs Jessie Mary, BA, PGCE
15 Berwick Ave, Heaton Mersey, Stockport SK4 3AA
[MANCHESTER] *b* 5 May 1934; *educ* Market Bos-
worth Dixie Gr Sch; Bedf Coll Lon; Inst of Educ
Lon; Classics Tchr Eothen Sch Caterham 1956–59;
Classics Tchr Prescot Girls' Gr Sch 1959–61; Miss
CMJ Iran 1962–78; Admin Sec Nn Ord Course
1979–98; M Dioc Children and Young People's
Ctee; M Dioc Liturg Ctee
GS 1995–   *Tel:* 0161–432 5943
                                Fax: 0161–283 2509
                email: ronaxtell@compuserve.com

AYERS, Revd Paul Nicholas, MA
Vicarage, Vicarage Drive, Pudsey LS28 7RL [BRAD-
FORD] *b* 26 Sep 1961; *educ* Bradf Gr Sch; St Pet Coll
Ox; Trin Coll Bris; C St Jo Bapt Clayton 1985–88;
C St Andr Keighley 1988–91; V St Cuth Wrose
1991–97; V St Lawr and St Paul Pudsey from 1997
GS 1995–   *Tel:* 0113–256 4197

BADDELEY, Ven Martin James, MA
*89 Nutfield Rd, South Merstham, Redhill, Surrey
RH1 3HD* [ARCHDEACON OF REIGATE] *b* 10 Nov
1936; *educ* St Pet Sch York; Keble Coll Ox; Makerere Univ Coll of E Africa; Linc Th Coll; C St
Matt Stretford 1962–65; M Staff Linc Th Coll
1965–69; Chapl Fitzw Coll Cam 1969–74; Fell
1972–74; Chapl New Hall Cam 1969–74; Res Can
Roch Cathl 1974–80; Prin S'wark Ord Course
1980–94; Jt Prin SE Inst for Th Educ 1994–96; Adn
of Reigate from 1996   *Tel:* (01737) 642375
                email: martin.baddeley@dswark.org.uk

BAINES, Revd Nicholas, BA
*Vicarage, 128 Hallfields Lane, Rothley, Leicester LE7
7NG* [LEICESTER] *b* 13 Nov 1957; *educ* Holt Comp
Sch Liv; Bradf Univ; Trin Coll Bris; C St Thos
Kendal 1987–91; C H Trin Leic 1991–92; V Roth-
ley from 1992; M PWM; M Dioc Syn; M Bd of
Patronage; M Vacancy in See Ctee; M Spiritual
Direction Working Grp; M Bp's Th Issues Grp;
RD Goscote; M Cathl Provisional Coun from1998;
M CAC Review Grp
GS 1995–   *Tel:* 0116–230 2241
                email: baines@leicester.anglican.org

BAKER, Canon Robert Mark, BA
Rectory, 73 The Street, Brundall, Norwich NR13 5LZ
[NORWICH] *b* 20 Jun 1950; *educ* Northgate Gr Sch
Ipswich; Bris Univ; St Jo Coll Nottm; C Ch Ch
Portswood 1976–80; R Brundall, Braydeston and
Postwick from 1980; Ch Commr from 1992, Bd of
Govs from 1995; Hon Can Nor Cathl from 1993;
Exam Chapl to Bp of Nor
GS 1985–   *Tel:* (01603) 715136

BAKER WILBRAHAM, Sir Richard, BT, DL
Rode Hall, Scholar Green, Cheshire ST7 3QP
[CHURCH COMMISSIONER] *b* 5 Feb 1934; *educ*
Harrow Sch; J. Henry Schroder Wagg & Co Ltd

1954–89; Chmn Bibby Line Grp Ltd 1992–97; De
Chmn Brixton Estate plc; Dep Chmn Grosvenc
Estate Holdings 1989–99; Dir Majedie Inves
ments plc; Ch Commr from 1994, Assets Cte
from 1994, Bd of Govs from 1995; Gov Man Me
ropolitan Univ from 1998   *Tel:* (01270) 88296

BAMPFYLDE, Mr Stephen John, MA
35 Old Queen St, London SW1H 9JA [APPOINTE
MEMBER, ARCHBISHOPS' COUNCIL] *b* 31 Mar 1952
educ Portsm Gr Sch; Jes Coll Cam; Civil Servan
1973–80; Managing Dir Saxon Bampfylde Heve
from 1986; Apptd M Abps' Coun from 1999
                                Tel: 020–7799 143
                                Fax: 020–7222 048

BANKS, Revd Norman, MA
*St Paul's Vicarage, 53 Grosvenor Drive, Whitley Bay
Tyne and Wear NE26 2JR* [NEWCASTLE] *b* 4 Ap
1954; *educ* Wallsend Gr Sch; Oriel Coll Ox; S
Steph Ho Th Coll; C Ch Ch w St Ann Newcastl
1982–84; C-in-c St Ann 1984–87; P-in-c Ch Ch w
St Ann 1987–90; V Tynemouth St Paul Cullercoat
from 1990
GS 1990–   *Tel:* 0191–252 4916

BANNER, Revd John William, BA
63 Claremont Rd, Tunbridge Wells, Kent TN1 1TE
[ROCHESTER] *b* 4 Jun 1936; *educ* Prenton Sch Birk-
enhead; Liv Coll of Building Tech; Tyndale Hal
Th Coll; C St Leon Bootle 1964–67; C St Jas Wigar
1967–70; Gen Sec Scripture Union 1970–72; V Ch
Ch Norris Green Liv 1972–82; V H Trin w Ch Ch
Tunbridge Wells from 1982; M Dioc Parsonages
Ctee; M Dioc Pastl Ctee; M DBF; M Dioc Syn
GS 1995–   *Tel and Fax:* (01892) 526644

**BANTING, Ven (Kenneth) Mervyn Lancelot
Hadfield,** MA
*5 The Boltons, Wootton Bridge, Ryde, Isle of Wight
PO33 4PB* [ARCHDEACON OF THE ISLE OF WIGHT]
b 8 Sep 1937; *educ* Tonbridge Sch; Pemb Coll Cam;
Cuddeson Th Coll; Asst Chapl Win Coll 1965–70;
C St Fran Leigh Park 1970–73; TV Highfield
Hemel Hempstead 1973–79; V Goldington
1979–88; RD Bedford 1984–87; V St Cuth Portsea
1988–96; RD Portsm 1994–96; Adn of the Isle of
Wight from 1996
GS 1998–   *Tel and Fax:* (01983) 884432

BARKER, Dr Keith, B SC, PH D, C ENG, MIM, FRSA
36 Tring Rd, Dunstable, Beds LU6 2PT [ST ALBANS]
b 10 Sep 1941; *educ* Scunthorpe Tech High Sch; N
Lindsey Tech Coll; Nottm Univ; Birm Univ; Tech
Asst Appleby-Frodingham Steel Co 1965–66;
Research Assoc Birm Univ 1966–69; Asst Tchr
Long Eaton Gr Sch 1969–73; Hd of Mathematics
Pingle Sch Swadlincote 1973–76; Dep Hdmaster
Greenhead Gr Sch Keighley 1977–84; Hdmaster
Queensbury Sch Dunstable 1985–93; Rtd
GS 1995–   *Tel:* (01582) 607163

BARKING, Bishop of [AREA BISHOP, CHELMSFORD] **Rt Revd Roger Frederick Sainsbury,** MA
Barking Lodge, 110 Capel Rd, Forest Gate, London E7 0JS b 2 Oct 1936; *educ* High Wycombe R Gr Sch; Jes Coll Cam; Clifton Th Coll; C Ch Ch Spitalfield 1960–63; Missr Shrewsbury Ho Liv 1963–74; P-in-c St Ambrose w St Tim Everton 1967–74; Warden Mayflower Family Centre Canning Town 1974–81; P-in-c St Luke Victoria Dock 1978–81; Alderman Lon Boro Newham 1976–78; V Walsall 1981–87; R Walsall TM 1987–88; Adn of W Ham 1988–91; Chmn Frontier Youth Trust Trustees 1987–92; Bp of Barking from 1991; Chmn Bps Urban Panel from 1996; M CTBI Balkans Working Grp from 1994; Vc-Chair Lon Chs Grp from 1998, Chair from 1999; Co-Chair BSR Community and Urban Affairs Ctee from 1998; Moderator CCRJ from 1999
GS 1985–88, 1996–
Tel and *Fax:* 020–8478 2456 (Home)
Tel: 020–8514 6044 (Office)
Fax: 020–8514 6049 (Office)
email: bishoproger@chelmsford.anglican.org

BARNES, Mr Barry Karl
30 Junction Rd, S Croydon, Surrey CR2 6RB [SOUTHWARK] *b* 11 May 1946; *educ* Selhurst Gr Sch; Solicitor; Chmn Croydon YMCA Housing Assoc from 1993; M Legal Aid Commn from 1996
GS 1995–
Tel: 020–8686 5179 (Home)
020–8681 6116 (Office)
Fax: 020–8686 9776 (Office)

BARTLES-SMITH, Ven Douglas Leslie, MA
1A Dog Kennel Hill, East Dulwich, London SE22 8AA [ARCHDEACON OF SOUTHWARK] *b* 3 Jun 1937; *educ* Shrewsbury Sch; St Edm Hall Ox; Wells Th Coll; C St Steph Rochester Row 1963–68; C-in-c St Mich w Em and All So Camberwell 1968–72; V 1972–75; V St Luke Battersea 1975–85; RD Battersea 1981–85; Adn of S'wark from 1985; Chapl to HM The Queen from 1996 *Tel:* 020–7274 6767
Fax: 020–7274 0899
email: douglas.bartles-smith@dswark.org.uk

BARTON, Ven (Charles) John Greenwood, ALCD
Birmingham Diocesan Office, 175 Harborne Park Rd, Birmingham B17 0BH [ARCHDEACON OF ASTON] *b* 5 Jun 1936; *educ* Battersea Gr Sch; Lon Coll of Div; Asst C St Mary Bredin, Cant 1963–66; V Whitfield w W Langdon 1966–75; V St Luke's Redcliffe Square, Lon and AD Chelsea 1975–83; Chief Broadcasting Offcr 1983–90; M Coun Corp of Ch Ho; Adn of Aston from 1990; Can Res Birm Cathl from 1990 *Tel:* 0121–454 5525 (Home)
0121–427 5141 (Office)
Fax: 0121–455 6085 (Home)
0121–428 1114 (Office)
0976 747535 (Mobile)
email: venjb@globalnet.co.uk

BARTON, Revd Dr (Margaret) Anne, MA, D PHIL
Rectory, Wolverton, Tadley, Hants RG26 5RU [WINCHESTER] *b* 22 Feb 1954; *educ* Nottm High Sch for Girls; St Anne's Coll Ox; Selw Coll Cam; Ridley Hall Th Coll; C Burley 1990–94; Chapl K Alfred's Coll Win from 1994; Sec Dioc Liturg Ctee
GS 1995–
Tel and *Fax:* (01635) 298008 (Home)
Tel: (01962) 827246 (Office)
email: anneba@patrol.i-way.co.uk (Home)
anne.barton@wkac.ac.uk (Office)

BASINGSTOKE, Bishop of [SUFFRAGAN, WINCHESTER] **Rt Revd (Douglas) Geoffrey Rowell,** MA, PH D, DD
Bishopswood End, Kingswood Rise, Four Marks, Alton, Hants GU34 5BD b 13 Feb 1943; *educ* Eggar's Gr Sch Alton; Win Coll; CCC Cam; Cuddesdon Th Coll; Asst Chapl and Hastings Rashdall Student New Coll Ox 1968–72; Hon C St Andr Headington 1968–72; Fell, Chapl and Tutor in Th Keble Coll Ox 1972–94, Emer Fell from 1994; Univ Lect in Th 1977–94; M Liturg Commn 1980–90; Gov Pusey Ho Ox from 1979, Pres from 1995; M Gov Body SPCK 1984–94 and from 1997; Hon Dir Abp's Exam in Th from 1986; Can and Preb Chich Cathl from 1981; M Angl-Oriental Orthodox Internat Forum from 1985, Angl Co-Chmn from 1996; Conservator Mirfield Cert in Pastl Th 1987–93; M Coun Management St Steph Ho Ox from 1988; M Doct Commn 1990–95, Consultant 1996–99, M from 1999; Bp of Basingstoke from 1994; CE Rep on CTBI from 1995; Vis Prof Chich Inst (Sch of Religion and Th) from 1996; Chmn Chs Grp on Funeral Services at Cemeteries and Crematoria from 1997 *Tel:* (01420) 562925
Fax: (01420) 561251
email: geoffrey.rowell@dial.pipex.com

BASSETT, Mrs Rosemary Louise
Hengistbury, Winterbourne Steepleton, Dorset DT2 9LQ [SALISBURY] *b* 11 Aug 1942; *educ* City of Lon Sch for Girls; Housewife; M Bp's Coun
GS 1990–
Tel: (01305) 889466

BASSHAM, Ms Sallie, B SC
Winshaw Barn, Chapel-le-Dale, Ingleton, Yorks, (via Carnforth LA6 3AT) [BRADFORD] *b* 19 Mar 1947; *educ* Qu Eliz Gr Sch Hexham; Salford Univ; Mathematics Lect Univ of Salford; M ABM from 1996; Chair Dioc Adv Coun for Min and Tr; Lay Chair Bowland Dny Syn GS 1995–

BATH AND WELLS, Bishop of, Rt Revd James Lawton Thompson, MA, FCA, DD
The Palace, Wells, Som BA5 2PD b 11 Aug 1936; *educ* Dean Close Sch Cheltenham; Em Coll Cam; Cuddesdon Th Coll; Hon Fell Qu Mary Coll Lon; Hon Fell Em Coll Cam; Hon D Litt E Lon Poly; Hon DD Ex; Hon D Litt Bath; 2nd Lt 3rd R Tank Regiment 1959–61; C E Ham 1966–68; Chapl Cuddesdon Th Coll 1968–71; R Thamesmead Dio S'wark 1971–78; Bp of Stepney 1978–91; Chmn

Urban Learning Foundation -1991; Jt Chmn Interfaith Network UK 1987–1992; Bp of B & W from 1991; Chmn Social Policy Ctee BSR 1990–96; Chmn Social, Economic and Industrial Ctee BSR 1996–97; Chmn Childrens Soc from 1997; Pres R Bath and W of England Soc 1997–98; Commis to Bp of Namibia
GS 1985–   *Tel:* (01749) 672341
           Fax: (01749) 679355
      email: bishop@bathwells.anglican.org

BAXTER, Canon Christina Ann, BA, PH D
St John's College, Chilwell Lane, Bramcote, Nottingham NG9 3DS [SOUTHWELL] *b* 8 Mar 1947; *educ* Walthamstow Hall Sevenoaks; Dur Univ; Bris Univ; Hd Relig Studies John Leggott Sixth Form Coll; Dur Research Student and pt staff M St Jo Coll Dur; Prin St Jo Coll Nottm; M Gen Syn Stg Ctee 1985–95; Vc-Chmn Ho of Laity 1990–95; Chmn Ho of Laity from 1995; M ACC from 1993; M Doct Commn; M Abps' Coun and Fin Ctee
GS 1985–   *Tel:* 0115–922 4087 (Home)
           0115–925 1114 (Office)
           Fax: 0115–943 6438
           07990 590231 (Mobile)
    email: principal@stjohns-nottm.ac.uk

BAXTER, Mrs Margaret Ann, BA
Diocesan Office, Cathedral Close, Blackburn, Lancs BB1 5AA [BLACKBURN] *b* 27 Jan 1942; *educ* Weston-super-Mare Gr Sch; Nottm Univ; Homerton Coll Cam; RE Tchr Chatteris Cambs 1964–65; Navrongo, Ghana 1965–70; pt Tutor Sierra Leone Th Hall 1977–83; Dir Rdr Tr Blackb dio 1990–93; Asst Dioc Dir of Tr from 1993; Author
GS 1990–   *Tel:* (01254) 54421
   email: margaret.baxter@blackburn.anglican.org

BEAL, Dr John Frank, PH D, BDS, LDSRCS
Oakroyd, 4 North Park Rd, Leeds LS8 1JD [RIPON] *b* 21 Jul 1942; *educ* Finchley Co Gr Sch; R Dental Hosp; Lon Univ; Birm Univ; Lect in Dental Health Birm Univ 1968–76; Sen Dental Officer Avon AHA (Teaching) 1977–79; Area Dental Officer Birm AHA 1979–83; Hon Lect in Community Dental Health Leeds Univ from 1983; Consultant in Dental Public Health Leeds HA from 1983; Regional Dental Adv N Yorks NHS Exec from 1991; JP; M HCC from 1996; M Dioc BMU 1990–93; M Bp's Coun from 1993
GS 1995–   *Tel:* 0113–294 8795
        Fax: 0113–295 2152 (Office)
   email: john@beal01.freeserve.co.uk

BEAVER, Revd Dr William Carpenter II, BA, D PHIL, ABC
Church House, Great Smith St, London SW1P 3NZ [DIRECTOR OF COMMUNICATIONS FOR THE CHURCH OF ENGLAND] *b* 17 Sep 1945; *educ* St Jo Military Sch Salina, Kansas; Colorado Coll; Wolfson Coll Ox; St Steph Ho Ox; Exec Dir Ox Development Records Project 1977–80; Sen Rep J Walter Thompson 1980–83; Dir of Publicity Barnardo's

1983–89; Grp Dir of Public Affairs Pergamon AGB Research Internat 1989–91; Grp Dir Corporate Affairs NatWest 1991–92; NSM St Jo the Divine Kennington 1980–95; Dir of Marketing The Industrial Soc 1992–97; NSM St Mary Redcliffe Bris from 1995; NSM St Andr Avonmouth 1995–97; Dir of Communications for C of E from 1997   *Tel:* 020–7898 1462
           Fax: 020–7898 1461
     email: bill.beaver@c-of-e.org.uk

BEDFORD, Bishop of [SUFFRAGAN, ST ALBANS]
Rt Revd John Henry Richardson, MA
168 Kimbolton Rd, Bedford MK41 8DN b 11 Jul 1937; *educ* Winchester Coll; Trin Hall Cam; Cuddesdon Th Coll; C Stevenage 1963–66; C St Mary Eastbourne 1966–68; V St Paul Chipperfield 1968–75; V St Mary Rickmansworth 1975–86; RD Rickmansworth 1977–86; V St Mich Bishop's Stortford 1986–94; Bp of Bedford from 1994
           Tel: (01234) 357551
           Fax: (01234) 218134

BEDI, Prof Raman, BDS, M SC, DDS, FDSRCS, DIP HE
Oak Cottage, 12 Manor Way, Potters Bar, Herts EN6 1EL [BIRMINGHAM] *b* 20 May 1953; *educ* Headlands Sch Swindon; Bris Univ; Trin Coll Bris; Dir WHO Collaborating Centre for disability, culture and oral health; Head Nat Centre for Transcultural Oral Health; M BSR; Co-Chair Community and Urban Affairs Ctee BSR
GS 1995–   *Tel:* 020–7915 2314
           Fax: 020–7915 1233
     email: R.Bedi@eastman.ucl.ac.uk

BEER, Ven John Stuart, MA
Rectory, Hemingford Abbots, Huntingdon PE18 9AN [ARCHDEACON OF HUNTINGDON] *b* 15 Mar 1944; *educ* Roundhay Sch Leeds; Pemb Coll Ox; Westcott Ho Th Coll; C St Jo Knaresborough 1971–74; Fell and Chapl Fitzw Coll and New Hall Cam 1974–80; R Toft w Caldecote and Childerley and Harwick 1980–87; V Grantchester 1987–97; DDO, Dir of POT and Rdr Tr 1987–97; Hon Can Ely Cathl from 1989; Chmn Cathl Pilgrims Assoc Conference 1986–96; M Ethics Ctee Dunn Nutrition Unit from 1985; Adn of Huntingdon from 1997; Co-DDO and Dir POT from 1997; M Bp's Coun; Dioc Pastl Ctee; Communications Ctee; Bd of Patronage; Houses Ctee; Dioc Bd of Educ; DAC   *Tel:* (01480) 469856
           Fax: (01480) 496073
   email: archdeacon.huntingdon@ely.anglican.org

BEHENNA, Mrs Margaret Rose, BA, M ED, PGCE
Windjammer, Holcombe Rd, Teignmouth, Devon TQ14 8UP [EXETER] *b* 10 Feb 1938; *educ* Heathfield Ho High Sch Cardiff; Bris Univ; Ex Univ; Dep Prin Teignmouth Community Coll 1979–88; Dioc Dir of Educ 1988–96
GS 1995–   *Tel* and *Fax:* (01626) 774124

BELL, Mr Stuart, MP

Church Commissioners, 1 Millbank, London SW1P 3JZ [SECOND CHURCH ESTATES COMMISSIONER] *b* 16 May 1938; *educ* Hookergate Gr Sch Durham; Gray's Inn Lon; Barrister-at-Law; MP for Middlesbrough from 1983; PPS to Rt Hon Roy Hattersley 1983–84; Front bench spokesperson N Ireland 1984–87; Vc-Chair Inter-Parliamentary Union Exec British Grp 1991–94; Vc-Chair British Irish Inter-Parliamentary Body 1990–92; Front bench spokesperson trade and industry 1992–97; Second Ch Estates Commr from 1997

GS 1997–　　　　　*Tel:* 020–7898 1000
　　　　　　　　　Fax: 020–7898 1131

BENTLEY, Ven Frank W. H., AKC

Archdeacon's House, 56 Battenhall Rd, Worcester WR5 2BQ [ARCHDEACON OF WORCESTER] *b* 4 Mar 1934; *educ* Yeovil Sch; K Coll Lon; C Shepton Mallet 1958–62; R Kingsdown Podymore Milton, C-in-c Yeovilton 1962–66; R Babcary 1964–66; V Wiveliscombe 1966–76; RD Tone 1973–76; V St Jo-in-Bedwardine Worc 1976–84; RD Martley and Worc W 1979–84; Hon Can Worc Cathl from1981; Adn of Worc and Can Res Worc Cathl from 1984; Chapl to HM The Queen from 1994

GS 1986–95　　　*Tel:* (01905) 764446 (Home)
　　　　　　　　　　(01905) 20537 (Office)
　　　　　　　　　　Fax: (01905) 612302

BERRY, Prof Anthony John, B SC, M PHIL, PH D, DIC

24 Leafield Rd, Disley, Stockport, Cheshire SK12 2JF [CHESTER] *b* 22 Aug 1939; *educ* Bath Univ; Imp Coll Lon; Seattle Univ; Man Univ; Aerodynamicist Br Aircraft Corp 1962; Aerodynamics Engineer The Boeing Co Seattle 1965–69; Rsch Fell 1971–73, Lect 1973–86, Sen Lect 1986–95 in Management Development Man Univ; Prof Sheff Hallam Univ from 1995; M Bp's Coun; M DBF; M Dioc Syn; Rdr

GS 1994–　　　　　　*Tel:* (01663) 762393
　　　　email: A.J.BERRY@shu.ac.uk/
　　　　　　tonyberry3@compuserve.com

BEVERLEY, Bishop of [PROVINCIAL EPISCOPAL VISITOR: YORK] **Rt Revd John Scott Gaisford,** BA, MA

3 North Lane, Roundhay, Leeds LS8 2QJ b 7 Oct 1934; *educ* Burnage Gr Sch Man; St Chad's Coll Dur; Asst C St Hilda Audenshaw 1960–62; Asst C Bramhall 1962–65; V St Andr Crewe 1965–86; Asst Warden of Rdrs for Dio 1967–81; RD Nantwich 1974–86; Hon Can Ches Cathl 1980–86; Chmn Ho of Clergy Dioc Syn 1983–85; Adn of Macclesfield 1986–94; Ch Commr 1986–94; Wrdn of Rdrs 1986–94; M CE Pensions Bd 1982–97; Vc-Chmn Housing and Resid Care Ctee; Trustee Churches Conservation Trust 1989–98; Bp of Beverley from 1994

GS 1975–94, 1994–95　　*Tel:* 0113–273 2003
　　　　　　　　　　0410 887756 (Mobile)
　　　　　　　　　　Fax: 0113–273 3002
email: 101740,2725@compuserve.com

BEVINGTON, Canon Colin Reginald, ALCD

44 Thorney Rd, Capel St Mary, Ipswich IP9 2LH [ST EDMUNDSBURY AND IPSWICH] *b* 1 Jan 1936; *educ* Monkton Combe Sch; Lon Coll of Div; C St Budeaux Devonport 1963–65; C Ch Ch Attenborough w Chilwell 1965–68; R Benhall w Sternfield 1968–74; P-in-c Snape 1973–74; V St Steph Selly Hill 1974–81; P-in-c St Wulstan Selly Oak 1980–81; V St Steph and St Wulstan Selly Park 1981–88; St Eds and Ips Dioc Ecum Officer 1988–99; Adv on Miss 1988–95; Co Ecum Officer 1990–99; Hon Can St Eds Cathl from 1993; Chapl to Bp of St Eds and Ips 1995–99; M Dioc Syn; R Holbrook from 1999; RD Samford from 1999

GS 1995–　　　*Tel:* (01473) 310069 (Home)
　　　　　　　　　　(01473) 252829 (Office)
　　　　　　　　　　Fax: (01473) 232552 (Office)

BIRCHALL, Mr Mark Dearman, MA

3 Melrose Rd, London SW18 1ND [SOUTHWARK] *b* 26 Jul 1933; *educ* Eton; Trin Coll Ox; Stockbroker 1956–82; Rtd; Coun Evang Alliance; Rdr; Trustee Ridley Hall and Wycliffe Hall

GS 1980–　　　　　*Tel:* 020–8265 9736
　　　　　　　email: mdbirchall@aol.com

BIRD, Revd David Ronald, BA, L TH

St Giles Vicarage, Spring Gardens, Northampton NN1 1LX [PETERBOROUGH] *b* 14 Aug 1955; *educ* K Edw VI Gr Sch Nuneaton; York Univ; Westhill Coll Birm; St Jo Coll Nottm; Youth Worker All So Clubhouse Lon 1977–80; Community Centre Warden Nottm City Coun 1980–83; C Kinson TM 1986–90; R Thrapston 1990–97; V St Giles Northn from 1997; M Bp's Coun from 1994; Chmn CPAS from 1996

GS 1995–　　　　　*Tel:* (01604) 634060
　　　　　　　email: drbird1408@aol.com

BIRD, Canon (Frederick) Hinton, MA, BD, M ED, PH D, PGCE

Rushen Vicarage, Port St Mary, Isle of Man IM9 5LP [SODOR AND MAN] *b* 30 Jun 1938; *educ* Pontywaun Gr Sch Risca; St Edm Hall Ox; St D Coll Lamp; C Mynyddislwyn Monmouth 1965–67; Min Can St Woolos Cathl Newport 1967–70; Chapl Anglo-American Coll Faringdon 1970–71; Head of RE Folkestone Tech High Sch 1972–75; Head of RE Caerleon Comp Sch 1975–82; V Rushen from 1982; Chmn Ho of Clergy Dioc Syn; Sec Manx Convocation; M DBF, Stg Ctee, Legisl Ctee, Vacancy in See Ctee

GS 1995–　　　　　　*Tel:* (01624) 832275

BIRKENHEAD, Bishop of [SUFFRAGAN, CHESTER]

[Not appointed at time of going to press.]

BIRMINGHAM, Bishop of, Rt Revd Mark Santer, MA, DD

Bishop's Croft, Old Church Rd, Harborne, Birmingham B17 0BG b 29 Dec 1936; *educ* Marlboro Coll; Qu Coll Cam; Westcott Ho Th Coll; Tutor

Cuddesdon Coll 1963–67; Asst C Cuddesdon 1963–67; Fell and Dean Clare Coll Cam 1967–72 (and Tutor 1968–72); Asst Lect in Div Univ of Cam 1968–72; Prin Westcott Ho Cam 1973–81; M Angl-Orthodox Jt Doctrinal Commn 1974–82; Area Bp of Kensington 1981–87; Bp of Birm from 1987; Co-Chmn ARCIC 1983–99; M Doct Commn from 1997; M Coun NACRO from 1984; Hon Fell Clare Coll Cam from 1987; Qu Coll Cam from 1991; Non Exec Dir Univ Hospital NHS Trust Birm from 1999; Hon DD Univ of Birm 1999; Lambeth DD 1999
GS 1985–   Tel: 0121–427 1163
                            Fax: 0121–426 1322

BISHOP, Ven (Anthony) Peter, L TH, M PHIL, FRSA
Ministry of Defence, RAF Innsworth, Gloucester GL3 1EZ [CHAPLAIN-IN-CHIEF, RAF] *b* 24 May 1946; *educ* Gravesend Gr Sch; Lon Coll of Div; St Jo Coll Nottm; C St Geo Beckenham 1971–75; Chapl RAF 1975–91; Asst Chapl-Chief 1991–98; Chapl-in-Chief from 1998; Hon Chapl to HM The Queen from 1996
GS 1998–   Tel: (01452) 712612 Ext 5030
                            Fax: (01452) 510828

BISSON, Ms Jane Victoria
Glenhaven, La Rocque, Grouville, Jersey JE3 9BB [WINCHESTER-CHANNEL ISLANDS] Bank Manager
GS 1995–

BLACK, Canon Neville, MBE, DMS, DASHE
445 Aigburth Rd, Liverpool L19 3PA [LIVERPOOL] *b* 25 Apr 1936; *educ* Bootle Gr Sch; Liv Poly; Oak Hill Th Coll; C St Ambrose w St Tim Everton 1964–69; P-on-c St Geo Everton 1969–71; V 1971–81; Project Officer Evang Urban Tr Project 1974–81; Dir Dioc Grp for Urban Min and Leadership 1984–95; TR St Luke in the City from 1981; M Bp's Coun 1984–89; Chmn Dioc Ho of Clergy 1991–98
GS 1995–   Tel: 0151–427 9803
                            01399–727640 (Pager)
                            Fax: 0151–494 0736

BLACKBURN, Bishop of, Rt Revd Alan David Chesters, BA, MA
Bishop's House, Ribchester Rd, Blackburn BB1 9EF *b* 26 Aug 1937; *educ* Elland Gr Sch; St Chad's Coll Dur; St Cath's Coll Ox; St Steph Ho Th Coll; C St Anne Wandsworth Lon 1962–66; Chapl Tiffin Sch Kingston-u-Thames 1966–72; Hon C St Richard's Ham 1967–72; R Brancepeth 1972–84; Dioc Dir Educ 1972–84; Adn of Halifax 1985–89; Bp of Blackb from 1989; Ch Commr 1983–99, Bd of Govs 1992–99; Pres Woodard Corp 1993–99; M Countryside Commn 1995–99; M Countryside Agency Bd from 1999; Chair Gen Syn Bd of Educ and Nat Soc from 1999
GS 1975–   Tel: (01254) 248234
                            Fax: (01254) 246668
            email: bishop.blackburn@ukonline.co.uk

BLACKBURN, Ven John , BA, DIP TH, DPS, ADV DIP ED, QHC
Ministry of Defence Chaplains (Army), Trenchard Lines, Upavon, Wilts SN9 6BE [DEPUTY CHAPLAIN GENERAL AND ARCHDEACON TO THE ARMY] *b* 3 Dec 1947; *educ* Hartridge High Sch; Cardiff Univ; St Mich Coll Llandaff; Open Univ; Dep Chapl Gen and Adn to the Army from 1999
GS 1999–   Tel: (01980) 615802 (Office)
                            (01980) 620436 (Home)
                            Fax: (01980) 615800

BLACKBURN, Ven Richard Finn, BA, MA
Home: 34 Wilson Rd, Sheffield S11 8RN, Office: Diocesan Church House, 95–99 Effingham St, Rotherham S65 1BL [ARCHDEACON OF SHEFFIELD] *b* 22 Jan 1952; *educ* Aysgarth Sch; Eastbourne Coll; St Jo Coll Dur; Hull Univ; Westcott Ho Th Coll; Natwest Bank 1976–81; C St Dunstan and All SS Stepney 1983–87; P-in-c St Jo Bapt Isleworth 1987–92; V St Mark Mosborough w Em Waterthorpe 1992–99; RD Attercliffe 1996–99; Hon Can Sheff Cathl 1998–99; Adn of Sheff and Can Res Sheff Cathl from 1999   Tel: 0114–266 6009 (Home)
                            (01709) 5112449 (Office)
                            Fax: 0114–267 9782 (Home)
                            (01709) 512550 (Office)
            email: sheffield.diocese@ukonline.co.uk

BLACKMORE, Dr David Richard, MA, D PHIL
Coniston, Newton Lane, Chester CH2 2HJ [CHESTER] *b* 16 Dec 1938; *educ* Whitgift Sch S Croydon; CCC Ox; UMIST; Rsch Associate UMIST 1962–64; Rsch Scientist Wood River (Illinois) Shell Development Co 1973–75; Sen Prin Scientist Shell Rsch Ltd, Thornton; Rtd 1997; Rdr; Lay Chmn Dioc Syn; Lay Chmn Ches Dny
GS 1980–   Tel: (01244) 323494
            email: blackmore@virtual-chester.com

BLADON, Mr Keith Victor, B COMM, FCA
11 Salisbury Ave, Tupsley, Hereford HR1 1QG [HEREFORD] *b* 29 Mar 1933; *educ* K Geo V Sch Southport; Liv Univ; Partner Thorne Widgery Chartered Accountants 1966–88, Man Partner 1985–88; Business Consultancy 1988–93; JP; Dep Chmn Herefs Bench from 1998; Chmn Herefs Youth Court Panel 1995–97; M Dioc Syn from 1986; Chmn Ho of Laity from 1995; M Bp's Coun; M DBF, Chmn 1990–95; M CBF and Exec Ctee 1995–99; Rdr
GS 1995–   Tel: (01432) 272402 (Home)
                            (01432) 355335 (Office)

BLAKE, Mrs Katy Vivian, LL B
106 Cooks Close, Bradley Stoke, Bristol BS32 0BB [BRISTOL] *b* 6 Jan 1960; *educ* Cheltenham Bournside Sch; Reading Univ; Bris Poly; Articled Clerk to Solicitor Woodspring Distr Coun 1982–84; Asst Solicitor Cheltenham Boro Coun 1984–88; OFSTED trained Lay Inspector of Schs and Nat Soc trained denominational inspector; M Bd of

Educ and Schs Ctee; M Dioc Fin Ctee; M Bp's Coun; M Dioc Bd of Educ
GS 1995– Tel: (01454) 617569
email: colin@ckdblake.freeserve.co.uk

BLAKEY, Revd Cedric Lambert, BA, MA, DPS
Derby Church House, Full St, Derby DE1 3DR [DERBY] *b* 16 Aug 1954; *educ* Worksop Coll; Fitzw Coll Cam; St Jo Coll Nottm; C Cotmanhay 1979–83; C-in-c St Andr Blagreaves CD 1983–89; P-in-c Sinfin Moor 1984–89; V Heanor 1989–97; RD Heanor 1994–97; Chapl to Bp of Derby from 1997
GS 1995– Tel: (01332) 382233
email: C.Blakey@btinternet.com

BOARDMAN, Revd Philippa Jane, MA
Vicarage, St Stephen's Rd, London E3 5JL [LONDON] *b* 24 Mar 1963; *educ* Haberdashers' Aske's Sch for Girls; Jes Coll Cam; Ridley Hall Th Coll; C St Mary and St Steph Walthamstow 1990–93; Asst Pr St Mary of Eton Hackney Wick 1993–96; Dean of Women's Min Stepney Area from 1994; P-in-c St Paul w St Mark Old Ford from 1996
GS 1994– *Tel and Fax:* 020–8980 9020

BOLTON, Bishop of [SUFFRAGAN, MANCHESTER]
Rt Revd David Keith Gillett, BA, M PHIL
Bishop's Lodge, Bolton Rd, Hawkshaw, Bury BL8 4JN b 25 Jan 1945; *educ* Wellingborough Gr Sch; Leeds Univ; Oak Hill Th Coll; C St Luke Watford 1968–71; Sec Pathfinders and CYFA N Area 1971–74; Tutor and Dir of Extension Studies St Jo Coll Nottm 1974–79; Chr Renewal Centre Rostrevor Nn Ireland 1979–82; V St Hugh Lewsey Luton 1982–88; Prin Trin Coll Bris 1988–99; Hon Can Bris Cathl 1991–99; Bp of Bolton from 1999; M BM 1991–96; M Inter Faith Consultancy Grp 1991–96; M ABM 1995–99; M CMEAC 1995–99; M CMEACC Vocations Ctee from 1997
GS 1985–88, 1990–99 Tel: (01204) 882955

BONE, Mr David Hugh, MA
3 Hardy Lane, Tockington, Bristol BS12 4LJ [BRISTOL] *b* 18 Jan 1939; *educ* Harrow Co Boys' Gr Sch; Worc Coll Ox; Univ of Aston; Asst Tutor Kingsgate Coll (YMCA) Broadstairs 1957–59; Assembly Hand Joseph Lucas 1963–64; Tchr RE Classics Kettering Boys' Gr Sch 1965–67; Hd of Divinity Crypt Boys' Gr Sch Gloucester 1967–72; Student Counsellor Plymouth Poly 1972–74; Careers Adv UWE (formerly Bristol Poly) from 1975; M Dioc Syn from 1994; M Vacancy-in-See Ctee; Rdr from 1996
GS 1997– Tel: (01454) 614601
Fax: 0117–976 3819 (Office)

BONHAM, Revd Valerie, ALA
12 Wakelins End, Cookham, Berks SL6 9TQ [OXFORD] *b* 26 Aug 1947; *educ* Wing Co Sec Sch; Coll of Librarianship Abth; St Alb and Ox Min Course; Bucks Co Library 1964–68 and 1970–72; Hillingdon Libraries 1972–75; E Berks AHA

1989–90; Par Dn St Mary Speen 1997–98; C H Trin Cookham-on-Thames from 1998; Hon Historian Community of St Jo B Clewer; M Lord's Prayer Revision Ctee 1998; M Berks Sub-ctee Ox Dioc Buildings Ctee; M Berks Chs Trust Exec Ctee
GS 1990–95, 1998– Tel: (01628) 531434

BONNEY, Revd Mark Philip John, MA, PGCE
Rectory, Berkhamsted, Herts HP4 2DH [ST ALBANS] *b* 2 Mar 1957; *educ* Northgate Gr Sch Ipswich; St Cath Coll Cam; St Steph Ho Ox; C St Pet Stockton-on-Tees 1985–88; Chapl St Alb Abbey 1988–90; Prec St Alb Abbey 1990–92; V Eaton Bray w Edlesborough 1992–96; R Gt Berkhamsted from 1996
GS 1995– Tel: (01442) 864194
email: m.bonney@c-of-e.freeserve.co.uk

BOOTH, Mr John David Sebastian, MA,
The Pest House, Watersfield, W Sussex RH20 1NG, and 4 Green St, Mayfair, London W14 3RG [CHICHESTER] *b* 25 Jul 1958; *educ* Huish's Gr Sch Taunton; Mert Coll Ox; Vc-Pres Merrill Lynch 1983–86; Sen Vc-Pres Prudential Bache 1988–93; Managing Dir Bankers Trust Internat 1993–96; Chmn Luther Pendragon Ltd from 1992; Maintel Holding Ltd from 1996; Gen Interest Ltd from 1997; Integrated Asset Management plc from 1998; Exec Vc-Chmn Link Asset and Securities Co; M Abps' Coun Fin Ctee; M DBF; M Dioc Syn; M Stg Ctee CU; Dir CE Newspaper
GS 1999– Tel: (01798) 831344
0467 474343 (Mobile)
Fax: 020–7495 3236

BOOTH, Miss Sue (Susan) Nancy
6 Fairoak Flats, Harrowby Drive, Newcastle, Staffs ST5 3JR [LICHFIELD] *b* 15 May 1931; *educ* Ipswich High Sch; Birm Univ; Secretarial posts 1952–55; BBC Studio Manager, External Services 1955; Asst Overseas Instructor BBC Staff Tr 1959–68; Programme Tr Officer Zambia Broadcasting Corp 1965; Producer BBC Radio Stoke-on-Trent 1968; Freelance Broadcaster and Lect in Communications from 1978; Chmn Ecum Ctee Dioc BMUW; M Black and White Together in Faith Ctee Lichf; Forum Elected M CTE Enabling Grp; Angl Rep Stg Ctee Staffs Plus Ecum Coun; M N Staffs Faiths in Friendship
GS 1997– Tel: (01782) 613855

BORDASS, Mrs (Elizabeth) Mary, T CERT
8 Bishop's Mead, Laverstock, Salisbury, Wilts SP1 1RU [SALISBURY] *b* 9 Jan 1943; *educ* Ilkeston Gr Sch; Glouc Tr Coll; Tchr Home Economics/Food Tech 1964–73 and 1979–95; Hd of Dept from 1966; Made Redundant 1995
GS 1995– Tel: (01722) 336698

BOSWELL, Revd Colin John Luke
Brandon Lodge, Croydon Vicarage, 22 Bramley Hill, Croydon CR0 5EG [SOUTHWARK] *b* 12 Jun 1947; *educ*

Elliot Sch Putney; Sarum and Wells Th Coll; C H Trin Upper Tooting 1974–78; C St Phil Sydenham 1978–79; P-in-c St Helier 1979–83; Chapl St Helier Hosp 1979–83; R Caterham 1983–95; R Chaldon 1985–95; V St Jo Croydon from 1995; Borough Dean Croydon
GS 1998–   *Tel:* 020–8688 1387 (Home)
                  020–8688 8104 (Office)
                  Fax: 020–8688 5877

BOWEN, Dr David Vaughan, MA, PH D, C CHEM, FRSC
30 Salisbury Rd, Canterbury, Kent CT2 7HH [CAN-TERBURY] *b* 15 Jul 1945; *educ* Phillips Academy, Mass, USA; St Jo Coll Cam; Lon Univ; Instructor Wayne State Sch of Medicine 1970–72; Asst Prof Rockefeller Univ 1972–77; Sen Scientist Union Carbide Corp 1977–80; Head of Spectroscopy Pfizer Central Research, Sandwich 1980–93; Info Techn Consultant Pfizer 1993–98; Mgr Dir SME 2000 Ltd and Audata Ltd from 1998
GS 1990–   *Tel:* (01227) 453026
                  Fax: (01227) 479808
                  email: bowenvt@surfaid.org

BOWEN, Mr John Ivor
Dept FGY, PO Box 99, Bracknell, Berks RG42 5NQ [OXFORD] *b* 29 Dec 1942; *educ* Melbourne CE Sch Australia; City of Lon Sch; MIT USA; Man Dir Elex Systems from 1971; Lay Chmn Bracknell Dny Syn 1984–94; M Dioc Syn from 1985; M Bp's Coun; M DBF
GS 1995–   *Tel:* (01344) 452929

BOWERING, Ven Michael Ernest
12 Rectory Park, Morpeth, Northumberland NE61 2SZ [ARCHDEACON OF LINDISFARNE] *b* 25 Jun 1935; *educ* Barnstaple Gr Sch; Kelham Th Coll; C St Oswald Middlesbrough 1959–62; C Huntington w New Earswick 1962–64; V Brayton w Barlow 1964–72; RD Selby 1971–72; V Saltburn by the Sea 1972–81; Res Can York Minster and Sec for Miss and Evang 1981–87; Adn of Lindisfarne from 1987
GS 1985–87, 1990–   *Tel:* (01670) 513207
                           Fax: (01670) 503837
                  email: m.bowering@newcastle.anglican.org

BOWLER, Prebendary Kenneth Neville
70 Fulham High St, London SW6 3LG [LONDON] *b* 14 Jan 1937; *educ* Ernest Bailey Gr Sch Matlock; K Coll Lon; St Boniface Th Coll Warminster; C Buxton 1961–67; R Sandiacre 1967–75; V Bedfont 1975–87; AD Hounslow 1982–87; Preb St Paul's Cathl from 1985; V All SS Fulham from 1987
GS 1995–   *Tel:* 020–7736 6301

BOWLER, Mr Stephen Raymond, MA
Fielden House, 13 Little College St, London SW1P 3SH [SUPPORT AND DEVELOPMENT OFFICER, COUNCIL FOR THE CARE OF CHURCHES] *b* 24 Feb 1964; *educ* Dulwich Coll; Qu Coll Ox; On staff of

Ch Commrs from 1987; Seconded to CCC as Support and Development Officer from 1999
                  Tel: 020–7898 1866
                  Fax: 020–7898 1881
          email: stephen.bowler@ccc.c-of-e.org.uk

BOYD-LEE, Mr Paul Winston Michael, BA, DIP TH
Manor Barn, Horsington, Templecombe, Som BA8 0ET [SALISBURY] *b* 3 May 1941; *educ* Brighton Coll; Open Univ; Ex Univ; Theatre Manager Rank Organisation 1963–66; Credit Controller Internat Factors Ltd 1966–72; Self-employed publisher from 1972
GS 1991–   *Tel:* (01963) 371137

BRACEGIRDLE, Canon (Cynthia) Wendy Mary, MA
Rectory, Parsonage Close, Salford M5 3GS [MAN-CHESTER] *b* 2 Mar 1952; *educ* Qu Sch Ches; LMH Ox; Nn Ord Course; Tutor Nn Ord Course 1976–85; Asst Chapl Cen Man Hosps 1985–88; Prin Man Ordained Local Min Scheme from 1989; Hon Can Man Cathl from 1998; M ABM Working Party on LNSM 1996–98; Exam Chapl to Bp of Man from 1999
GS 1998–   *Tel:* 0161–872 0800 (Home)
                  0161–832 5785 (Office)
                  Fax: 0161–832 1466
          email: ignatius@globalnet.co.uk

BRADFORD, Bishop of, Rt Revd David James Smith, AKC, FKC
Bishopscroft, Ashwell Rd, Heaton, Bradford, W Yorks BD9 4AU b 14 Jul 1935; *educ* Hertf Gr Sch; K Coll Lon; St Boniface Coll Warminster; C All SS Gosforth 1959–62; C St Fran High Heaton 1962–64; P-in-c St Mary Magd Long Benton 1964–68; V Longhirst w Hebron 1968–75; V St Mary Monk-seaton 1975–82; V Felton 1982–83; Adn of Lindis-farne 1981–87; Bp of Maidstone 1987–92; Bp to the Forces 1990–92; Bp of Bradf from 1992
GS 1973–80, 1983–87, 1992–   *Tel:* (01274) 545414
                           Fax: (01274) 544831
          email: bishbrad@nildram.co.uk

BRADLEY, Revd Peter David Douglas, B TH
Rectory, 1A College Rd, Up Holland, Skelmersdale WN8 0PY [LIVERPOOL] *b* 4 Jun 1949; *educ* Brook-field Comp Sch; Nottm Univ; Ian Ramsey Coll; Linc Th Coll; C Up Holland 1979–83; V H Spirit Dovecot 1983–94; Sec Dioc Bd of Min 1983–88; Sec Grp for Urban Min and Leadership 1984–88; Asst Dir In-Service Tr 1988–89; Dir CME from 1989; TR Up Holland from 1994; M BM Mission at Home Ctee; M Dioc Bd of Min
GS 1990–   *Tel and Fax:* (01695) 622936

BRADNUM, Canon (Ella) Margaret, MA, PGCE
13 Boothtown Rd, Halifax, W Yorks HX3 6EU [WAKEFIELD] *b* 5 Sep 1941; *educ* Abbey Sch Read-ing; St Hugh's Coll Ox; Lon Inst of Educ; Dss St Mary Illingworth 1969–72; Dss All SS Batley

1972–73; Lay Tr Officer 1977–82; Minl Tr Officer 1982–93; Warden of Rdrs from 1986; Co-ord Lay Tr from 1993; Prin Wakef Min Scheme from 1997
GS 1995–   *Tel:* (01422) 321740

BRADWELL, Bishop of [AREA BISHOP, CHELMSFORD] **Rt Revd Laurie (Laurence Alexander) Green,** BD, AKC, STM, D MIN
Bishop's House, Orsett Rd, Horndon-on-the-Hill, Essex SS17 8NS b 26 Dec 1945; *educ* East Ham Gr Sch; K Coll Lon; New York State Univ; New York Th Seminary; St Aug Coll Cant; C St Mark Kingstanding Birm 1970–73; V St Chad Erdington 1973–83; Prin Aston Tr Scheme 1983–89; Hon C H Trin Birchfield 1984–89; TR All SS Poplar Lon 1989–93; Bp of Bradwell from 1993
                             Tel: (01375) 673806
                             Fax: (01375) 674222
                email: lauriegr@globalnet.co.uk
                /b.bradwell@chelmsford.anglican.org

BRAMHALL, Revd Eric, MA
All Saints' Vicarage, Childwall Abbey Rd, Liverpool L16 0JU [LIVERPOOL] *b* 15 May 1939; *educ* Liv Inst High Sch for Boys; St Cath Coll Cam; Tyndale Hall Th Coll; C St Luke Eccleston St Helens 1963–66; C Em Bolton 1966–69; Hd of RE Wallasey Gr Sch 1969–74; V Ch Ch Aughton 1975–92; V All SS Childwall from 1992
GS 1995–   *Tel:* 0151–737 2169

BRANDON, Mrs Beatrice, DMS
Clopton Manor, Clopton, Kettering, Northants NN14 3DZ [PETERBOROUGH] *b* 28 May 1955; *educ* Design Consultant; M Follow-up Grp Abps' Commn on the Organisation of the C of E; M Abps' Millennium Adv Grp from 1996; M Ho of Bps' Working Grp on Healing Min from 1998; Lay Chmn Dioc Syn; M Dioc Pastl Ctee; M Vacancy-in-See Ctee; Lay Chmn Oundle Dny Syn 1994–98; M Bp's Coun and Stg Ctee; M Dioc Budget Review Grp; M Dioc Pastl Ctee; M Dioc Bd of Patronage; M Dioc Millennium Ctee
GS 1995–   *Tel:* (01832) 720346
                             Fax: (01832) 720446
           email: beatrice.brandon@btinternet.com

BRAY, Mr Peter, M INST R, MDT
4 Lupin Rd, Southampton SO16 3LB [WINCHESTER] *b* 12 Jan 1936; *educ* Truro Sch; Swansea Univ; Southn Univ; Chmn Southn Sail Tr Assn Comm 1976–86; Managing Dir Braeaire Ltd from 1980; Southn and Fareham Chamber of Trade and Ind, M Manufacturing Ctee and Educ and Tr Ctee from 1992
GS 1995–   *Tel:* 023–8055 6866 (Office)
                        023–8055 3070 (Home)
                          Fax: 023–8032 2581

BREEN, Revd Michael James, MA, L TH
Rectory, 18A Hallam Gate Rd, Sheffield S10 5BT [SHEFFIELD] *b* 13 Jun 1958; *educ* Oak Hill Th Coll; Cranmer Hall Dur; C St Martin Cam 1983–87; V

All SS Clapham Park 1987–92; USA 1992–94; TR St Thos Crookes Sheff from 1994
GS 1996–   *Tel:* 0114–268 6362

BREGAZZI, Dr Paul Kneen, MA, PH D, CERT ED
Ballachree, Ballaugh, Isle of Man IM7 5EB [SODOR AND MAN] *b* 18 Oct 1935; *educ* K William's Coll Isle of Man; Ch Coll Cam; Nottm Univ; Univ of Wales; Asst Master Cheltenham Coll 1962–66 and 1971–79; Marine Biologist British Antarctic Survey 1967–71; Prin K William's Coll Isle of Man 1979–89; Rtd
GS 1990–   *Tel:* (01624) 897715

BRENTFORD, Viscountess Gill (Gillian) Evelyn, OBE, FCA
Cousley Place, Wadhurst, E Sussex TN5 6HF [THIRD CHURCH ESTATES COMMISSIONER AND CHICHESTER] *b* 22 Nov 1942; *educ* West Heath Sch; Ch Commr from 1991; Bd of Govs from 1994; Lay Chmn Dioc Syn 1992–99; M Crown Appts Commn from 1995; Joint Chair Springboard from 1996; Pres CMS from 1998; Third Ch Estates Commr from 1999
GS 1990–   *Tel:*(01892) 783737
                             Fax: (01892) 784428
              email: 101563.2113@compuserve.com

BRETT, Canon Paul Gadsby, MA
Rectory, 41 Worrin Rd, Shenfield, Brentwood, Essex CM15 8DH [CHELMSFORD] *b* 19 Feb 1941; *educ* Monkton Combe Sch; Wycliffe Hall Th Coll; C St Pet Bury 1965–68; Asst Ind Missr Man 1968–72; Sen Ind Chapl Kidderminster 1972–76; Asst Sec (Ind and Economic Affairs) Gen Syn BSR 1976–84; Res Can Chelmsf Cathl and Dir Social Resp Chelmsf 1985–94; M BSR from 1994; R Shenfield from 1994; Res Can Emer Chelmsf Cathl from 1994; M BM Rural Affairs Ctee from 1994; Ctee M Open Syn Grp 1994–96; Ctee M CEIG from 1995
GS 1993–   *Tel:* (01277) 220360
                email: paul.brett@btinternet.com

BRIDGER, Revd Francis William, MA, PH D, DIP TH
Trinity College, Stoke Hill, Bristol BS9 1JP [SOUTHWELL] *b* 27 May 1951; *educ* Gravesend Sch for Boys; Pemb Coll Ox; Bris Univ; Trin Coll Bris; C St Jude Mildmay Grove and St Paul Canonbury 1978–82; Lect St Jo Coll Nottm 1982–90, Dir of Studies 1989–90, Assoc Lect 1990–96; V St Mark Woodthorpe 1990–99; Prin Trin Coll Bris from 1999
GS 1998–   *Tel:* 0117–968 2803
                             Fax: 0117–968 7470
                                       email:
        fbridger@yahoo.ie/principal@trinity.bris.ac.uk

BRIDGEWATER, Mr Allan, CBE, ACII, FIPD, CIMGT, FRSA
Linquenda, 447 Unthank Rd, Norwich NR4 7QN [EX-OFFICIO, CHAIRMAN, CHURCH OF ENGLAND PENSIONS BOARD] *b* 26 Aug 1936; Group Chief

Exec Nor Union 1989–97; main Bd Dir 1985–97; Chmn Swiss Re UK Ltd and Swiss Re Life & Health UK Ltd; Chmn Divisional Bd for Swiss Re Life & Health from 1998; Dir Riggs Bank Europe from 1991   *Tel and Fax:* (01603) 455120

BRISTOL, Bishop of, Rt Revd Barry Rogerson,
BA, LLD
Bishop's House, Clifton Hill, Bristol, Avon BS8 1BW
b 25 Jul 1936; *educ* Magnus Gr Sch Newark, Notts; Leeds Univ; Wells Th Coll; C St Hilda's S Shields 1962–65; C St Nic Bishopwearmouth Sunderland 1965–67; Lect Lich Th Coll 1967–71; Vc-Prin Lich Th Coll 1971–72; Lect Sarum-Wells Th Coll 1972–75; V St Thos Wednesfield Wolv 1975–78; TR Wednesfield 1979; Bp of Wolv 1979–85; Bp of Bris from 1985; M Faith & Order Commn WCC 1987–98; Chmn ACCM 1987–91; Chmn ABM 1991–93; M Cen Ctee WCC from 1991
GS 1982–   *Tel:* 0117–973 0222
          Fax: 0117–923 9670
          email: 106430.1040@compuserve.com

BRIXWORTH, Bishop of [SUFFRAGAN,
PETERBOROUGH**] Rt Revd Paul Everard Barber,** MA
4 The Avenue, Dallington, Northampton NN5 7AN
b 16 Sep 1935; *educ* Sherborne Sch; St Jo Coll Cam; Wells Th Coll; Asst C St Fran Westborough 1960–66; V St Mich Camberley w Yorktown 1966–73; V St Thos-on-the Bourne Farnham 1973–80; RD Farnham 1974–79; Hon Can Guildf 1980–89; Adn of Surrey 1980–89; Bp of Brixworth from 1989; Hon Can Pet Cathl from 1997; Abp's Adv to Hdmasters' and Headmistresses' Conf from 1993
GS 1979–85   *Tel:* (01604) 759423
          Fax: (01604) 750925

BROAD, Revd Hugh Duncan, NDA, CERT ED
St George's Vicarage, Grange Rd, Tuffley, Gloucester GL4 0PE [GLOUCESTER] *b* 28 Oct 1937; *educ* Bishop's Castle Co High Sch Shropshire; Shropshire Inst of Agric; Hereford Coll of Educ; Bernard Gilpin Soc; Lichf Th Coll; C H Trin Hereford 1967–72; Tchr Bp of Heref's Blue Coat Sch 1972–74; C SS Peter and Paul Fareham 1974–76; V All SS and St Barn Hereford 1976–90; R St Kath Matson 1990–97; V St Geo Glouc and St Marg Whaddon from 1997; M Dioc Coun of Par Resources; M Crown Appts Commn from 1997; Convenor Affirming Catholicism Grp in Gen Syn from 1997
GS 1995–   *Tel and Fax:* (01452) 520851
          0780 8458233 (Mobile)

BROADBENT, Ven Pete (Peter Alan), MA
247 Kenton Rd, Harrow, Middx HA3 0HQ [ARCH-DEACON OF NORTHOLT] *b* 31 Jul 1952; *educ* Merchant Taylors Sch Northwood; Jes Coll Cam; St Jo Coll Nottm; C St Nic Dur City 1977–80; C Em Holloway 1980–83; Chapl to N Lon Poly and Hon C St Mary Islington 1983–89; Bps Chapl for Miss in Stepney 1980–89; Councillor and Chair of

Planning Lon Boro of Islington 1982–89; M Dioc Commn 1989–92; M Panel of Chmn Gen Syn 1990–92; M CE Evang Coun 1984–95; Chair Vacancy-in-See Ctee Regulation Working Party 1991–93; M Gen Syn Stg Orders Ctee 1991–95; M Appointments Sub-Ctee 1992–95; V Trin St Mich Harrow 1989–95; AD Harrow 1994; Adn of Northolt from 1995; M CBF 1991–98; M Gen Syn Stg Ctee 1992–98; Chair Gen Syn Business Sub-Ctee 1996–98; Chair Elections Review Grp from 1996; Chair Lon Dioc Bd for Schs from 1996; M Spring Harvest Leadership Tm; M Abp's Coun from 1999; Chmn Business Ctee from 1999; M Cen Gov Body City Pastl Foundation from 1999
GS 1985–   *Tel:* 020–8907 5941 (Home)
          020–8907 5993 (Area Office)
          07957 1444 674 (Mobile)
          Fax: 020–8909 2368
          email: pete@arch-northolt.demon.co.uk

BROGGIO, Canon Bernice, BA, BD, DIP SOC
STUDY, CQSW
Holy Trinity Vicarage, 14 Upper Tooting Park, London SW17 7SW [SOUTHWARK] *b* 4 Dec 1935; *educ* High Wycombe High Sch; Bedford Coll Lon; K Coll Lon; Glasgow Univ; Geography Tchr 1957–59; Company of St Francis 1960–63; Accredited Lay Worker Killingworth Newcastle 1966–70; Psychiatric Social Worker Nuffield Child Psychiatry Unit Newc 1972–77; Deputy Head Benton Grange (RC Residential) School 1977–80; Tm Mgr C and YP Residential Services Avon Co Coun 1980–88; NSM St Thos Newc 1972–80; NSM St Paul Bris 1981–88; C St Luke w H Trin Charlton 1988–95; Hon Can S'wark Cathl from 1995; V H Trin Upper Tooting from 1995; RD Tooting from 1996; M Dioc Bd of Ch and Society; M Open Syn Grp; M Ctee CEIG
GS 1990–   *Tel:* 020–8672 4790

**BROTHERTON, Mrs Daphne Margaret
Yvonne,** MA
4 Canon Lane, Chichester, W Sussex PO19 1PX
[CHICHESTER] *b* 27 Oct 1936; *educ* St Leon Sch St Andr Fife; St Hugh's Coll Ox; Economic Research 1958–64; Statistician w CSO in Trinidad 1965–67; Dir Caribbean Market Research Trinidad 1967–75; Housewife; M DBF; Trustee Cleaver Trust; Chmn Regnum Crossroads Scheme from 1995; Lay Chmn Chich Dny Syn from 1997
GS 1993–   *Tel:* (01243) 779134
          Fax: (01243) 536452

BROTHERTON, Ven John Michael, MA
4 Canon Lane, Chichester, W Sussex PO19 1PX
[ARCHDEACON OF CHICHESTER] *b* 7 Dec 1935; *educ* Hipperholme Sch Yorks; St Jo Coll Cam; Cuddesdon Th Coll; C St Nic Chiswick 1961–64; Inst of Educ Univ of Lon; Chapl Trin Coll Port of Spain, Trinidad 1965–69; R St Mich Diego Martin Trinidad 1969–75; V St Mary and St Jo Ox 1976–81; Chapl St Hilda's Coll Ox 1976–81; RD Cowley 1978–81; V St Mary Portsea 1981–91; Hon

Can St Mich Cathl Kobe from 1986; Adn of Chich from 1991; Res Can Chich Cathl from 1991; Chmn Dioc Overseas Ctee from 1994; M Legal Adv Commn from 1996
GS 1995–   Tel: (01243) 779134
                            Fax: (01243) 536452

BROWN, Mr Andrew Charles, B SC, FRICS
Church Commissioners, 1 Millbank, London SW1P 3JZ [CHIEF SURVEYOR, CHURCH COMMISSIONERS] *b* 30 Oct 1957; *educ* Ashmole Comp Sch; S Bank Poly; Healey & Baker 1981–84; St Quintin 1984–94; Chief Surveyor Ch Commrs from 1994
                            Tel: 020–7898 1634
                            Fax: 020–7898 1132

BROWN, Mr Alan Scott, BA, M PHIL
Church House, Great Smith St, London SW1P 3NZ [RE SCHOOLS OFFICER, GENERAL SYNOD BOARD OF EDUCATION AND DIRECTOR NATIONAL SOCIETY'S RE CENTRE] *b* 27 Jun 1944; *educ* Newport High Sch Gwent; Leeds Univ; Tchr Northwich Girls Sch 1967–69; Temple Moor Sch 1969–71; Bishop Otter Coll Chich 1971–80; Schools (RE) Offcr Bd of Educ from 1980; Dir Nat Soc RE Centre from 1986; Pres InterEuropean Commn on Ch and Schs 1988–96; Dir The Chichester Project; Sec Shap Working Party on World Religions in Educ from 1996   Tel: 020–7898 1494

BROWN, Canon Christopher Francis
Rectory, Union St, Trowbridge, Wilts BA14 8RU [SALISBURY] *b* 23 Apr 1944; *educ* Bridgemary Sch Gosport; Bernard Gilpin Soc Dur; Sarum Th Coll; C High Wycombe 1971–74; C Sherborne 1974–77; R Yarnbury 1977–82; R Portland 1982–88; RD Weymouth 1985–88; R St Jas Trowbridge from 1988; RD Bradford from 1994; Non Res Can Sarum Cathl from 1998
GS 1993–
                            Tel: (01225) 755121

BROWN, Ven Gerald Arthur Charles, MA
Styrmansgatan 1, 11454, Stockholm, Sweden [ARCHDEACON OF SCANDINAVIA, DIOCESE IN EUROPE] *b* 24 Apr 1935; *educ* Alderman Newton's Sch Leic; CCC Cam; St Steph Ho Ox; C St Pet Wolverhampton 1960–66; V Trent Vale 1966–74; V St Andr Wolverhampton 1974–82; Chapl All SS Milan 1982–89; Chapl St Edmund Oslo and Adn of Scandinavia 1990–92; Chapl St Pet and St Sigrid Stockholm and Adn of Scandinavia from 1992; P-in-c Angl Chaplaincy Riga from 1994
                            Tel: 00–46–8663–82–48

BROWN, Mrs Margaret Mary
Luckhurst, Mayfield, E Sussex TN20 6TY [CHICHESTER] *b* 9 Nov 1934; *educ* Braemar Sch, Tunbridge Wells
GS 1985–   Tel: (01435) 873007

BROWN, Mrs (Mary) Patricia, NFF T DIP
30 Chirgwin Rd, Tregolls, Truro, Cornwall TR1 1TT [TRURO] *b* 31 Mar 1929; *educ* Truro Co Gr Sch;

Maria Grey Coll of Educ; Kindergarten Mistress Bath High Sch 1950–54; Hd of Infant Dept Cardinham Co Primary Sch 1967–77; Hdmistress Lanlivery Primary Sch 1977–84; Rtd; Housewife; M Bp's Coun, Vacancy in See Ctee from 1985; M Dioc Bd of Educ from 1990; M Cathls Commn Follow Up Grp 1994–98; Lay Can Emer Truro Cathl 1999; M Cathls Measure Steering Grp 1996–98
GS 1985–   Tel: (01872) 70350

BROWN, Canon Simon Nicolas Danton, MA
Rectory, The Precincts, Burnham, Slough, Berks SL1 7HU [OXFORD] *b* 23 Feb 1937; *educ* Merchant Taylors Sch Northwood; Clare Coll Cam; S'wark Ord Course; Linc Th Coll; NS 1956–58; Youth Leader Bede Ho Bermondsey 1961–63; C Lambeth 1964–66; Warden LMH Settlement 1966–72; TV Southn City Cen 1972–79; R Gt Brickhill w Bow Brickhill and Lt Brickhill 1979–84; TR Burnham TM Slough from 1984; RD Burnham from 1988; Dioc Consultant for Dny Development from 1997; M Bp's Coun
GS 1995–   Tel: (01628) 604173 (Home)
                         (01628) 664338 (Office)

BROWNE, Revd Dr Herman Beseah, BA, BD, AKC, D PHIL
Lambeth Palace, London SE1 7JU [ARCHBISHOP OF CANTERBURY'S ASSISTANT SECRETARY FOR ANGLICAN COMMUNION AND ECUMENICAL AFFAIRS] *b* 11 Mar 1965; *educ* St Patr Sch Monrovia; Cuttington Univ; K Coll Lon; Heythrop Coll; C N Lambeth 1990–91; Tutor Simon of Cyrene Th Inst 1990–96; Abp of Cant's Asst Sec for Angl Communion and Ecum Affairs from 1996   Tel: 020–7928 8282
                            Fax: 020–7401 9886
email: herman.browne@lampal.c-of-e.org.uk

BROWNSELL, Prebendary John Kenneth, MA
All Saints' Vicarage, Powis Gardens, London W11 1JG [LONDON] *b* 16 May 1948; *educ* Ashby de la Zouch Gr Sch; Hertf Coll Ox; Cuddesdon Th Coll; C All SS w St Columba Notting Hill 1973–74; C Notting Hill 1974–76; TV 1976–82; V from 1982; AD Kensington 1984–92; Preb St Paul's Cathl from 1992; Dir of Ords Kensington Area Lon dio; Commissary for Bp of Windward-Islands; M Initiation Services Revision Ctee; M Legal Aid Commn
GS 1995–   Tel: 020–7727 5919

BRUINVELS, Mr Peter Nigel Edward, LL B, FRSA, FCIM, MCIJ, MIPR
14 High Meadow Close, Dorking, Surrey RH4 2LG [GUILDFORD] *b* 30 Mar 1950; *educ* St Jo Sch Leatherhead; Lon Univ; Inns of Court Sch of Law; MP Leic E 1983–87; Party Candidate The Wrekin 1997; Prin – Peter Bruinvels Associates – Media Management and Public Affairs Consultants from 1986; M Dioc Syn and Dorking Dny Syn from 1974; Freeman of City of Lon 1980; M Dios Commn 1991–96; M Legislative Ctee 1991–96;

News Broadcaster, Political Commentator and Freelance Journalist; Ch Commr from 1992, Bd of Govs from 1998, Pastl Ctee from1993, Management Adv Ctee from 1999; S,23 OFSTED RE Schs Inspector from 1994; Managing Editor Bruinvels News & Media – Press and Broadcasting Agents from 1993; M Dioc Bd of Educ from 1994; M Gen Syn Bd of Educ from 1996; Co-opted M Surrey LEA from 1997; Gov Univ Coll of Ripon and York St Jo from 1999; Dir Ch Army from 1999; Independent Lay Chmn NHS Complaints Procedure from 1999
GS 1985–   Tel: (01306) 887082 (Home and Office)
0336 764440 (Pager)
07050 085 456 (Mobile)
Fax: 0870 458 6483
email: peterbruinvels@hotmail.com

BRYANT, Canon Mark Watts, BA
Stoke Rectory, 365A Walsgrave Rd, Coventry CV2 4BG [COVENTRY] *b* 8 Oct 1949; *educ* St Jo Sch Leatherhead; St Jo Coll Dur; Cuddesdon Th Coll; C Addlestone 1975–79; C St Jo Studley, Trowbridge 1979–83, V 1983–88; Chapl Trowbridge CFE 1979–83; DDO and Dir Vocations and Tr, Cov 1988–96; Hon Can Cov Cathl from 1993; TR Cov Caludon from 1996
GS 1998–   Tel and Fax: 024–7663 5731

BRYANT, Canon Richard Kirk, MA, DIP TH
2 Burlington Court, Hadrian Park, Wallsend NE28 9YH [NEWCASTLE] *b* 28 Apr 1947; *educ* Hillfoot Hey High Sch Liv; Ch Coll Cam; Nottm Univ; Cuddesdon Th Coll; C St Gabr Heaton 1972–75; C Morpeth 1975–78; P-in-c Ven Bede Benwell 1978–82; V Earsdon and Backworth 1982–93; V Wylam 1993–97; Dir Rdr Tr Course 1990–98; Dir of Tr for Local Min 1997–98; Prin Local Min Scheme and Rdr Tr Course from 1998; Hon Can Newc Cathl from 1997
GS 1995–   Tel: 0191–263 7922 (Home)
0191–281 9930 (Office)
email: richard@newcastle.anglican.org

BUCKINGHAM, Bishop of [AREA BISHOP, OXFORD] **Rt Revd Michael Arthur Hill**
Sheridan, Grimms Hill, Great Missenden, Bucks HP16 9BD b 17 Apr 1949; *educ* Wilmslow Gr Sch; NW Cheshire CFE; Man Coll of Commerce; Ridley Hall Cam; Fitzw Coll Cam; C St Mary Magd Addiscombe 1977–80; C St Paul Slough 1980–83; P-in-c St Leon Chesham Bois 1983–90; R 1990–92; RD Amersham 1989–92; Adn of Berks 1992–98; Bp of Buckingham from 1998
GS 1995–98   Tel: (01494) 862173
Fax: (01494) 890508
email: bishopbucks@oxford.anglican.org

BULL, Dr John, B SC, PH D, EUR ING, C ENG, FIHT, FIWSC, MICE
Gable Ends, 11 Glebe Mews, Bedlington, Northumberland NE22 6LJ [NEWCASTLE] *b* 13 Oct 1944; *educ* Farnborough Gr Sch; Ches Coll of Educ; Univ

Coll Cardiff; Tchr ILEA 1966–68; Engineer/Chartered Engineer Dur Co Coun 1974–79; Lect i~ Structural Engineering Newc Univ from 1979; M Dioc Syn from 1988; M Bp's Coun from 1988; V~ Pres Dioc Syn from 1994; Chmn Dioc Bd of Educ 1991–97; Lay Chmn Bedlington Dny Syn 1990–97
GS 1995–   Tel: 0191–222 7924 (Office)
Fax: 0191–261 605~
email: John.Bull@newcastle.ac.uk

BULLEN, Mr Colin Richard, MIDPM, MBCS
1 Millbank, London SW1P 3JZ [DEPUTY COMPUTER MANAGER, CHURCH COMMISSIONERS] *b* 8 Mar 1947, *educ* Bexley Gr Sch; W Kent Coll; Programs/Systems Development Ch Commrs from 1967; Dep Computer Mgr Ch Commrs from 1987
Tel: 020–7898 163~
email: colin.bullen@c-of-e.org.uk

BULLIMORE, His Honour Judge John Wallace MacGregor, LL B
Rectory, 14 Grange Drive, Emley, Huddersfield HD8 9SF [WAKEFIELD] *b* 4 Dec 1945; *educ* Qu Eliz Gr Sch Wakefield; Bris Univ; Circuit Judge from 1991; Chan Dio of Derby from 1980; Chan Dio of Blackb from 1990; Rdr from 1968; M Bp's Coun
GS 1970–   Tel: (01924) 849161

BUNKER, Very Revd Michael
The Deanery, Peterborough PE1 1XS [DEAN OF PETERBOROUGH] *b* 22 Jul 1937; *educ* Benjamin Adlard Sch Gainsborough; Acton and Brunel Colls Lon; Oak Hill Th Coll; C St Jas Alperton 1963–66; C St Helen St Helens 1966–70; V St Matt Muswell Hill 1970–78; V St Jas w St Matt Muswell Hill 1978–92; Preb St Paul's Cathl 1990–92; Dean of Petrb from 1992
Tel: (01733) 562780
Fax: (01733) 897874
email: deanbunker@aol.com

BURBRIDGE, Mrs Bernadette Celina Genevieve, BA
14 Clifton Dale, York YO3 6LJ [YORK] *b* 17 Sep 1954; *educ* Camborne Gr Sch; LMH Ox; Broadcast Journalist
GS 1990–   Tel: (01904) 658908

BURDETT, Revd Stephen Martin, AKC
144 Alexandra Rd, Southend on Sea, Essex SS1 1HB [SOUTHWARK] *b* 21 Dec 1949; *educ* Abp Tenison's Gr Sch; K Coll Lon; St Aug Coll Cant; C St Pet Walworth 1974–77; C All SS Benhilton 1977–80; P-in-c St John Earlsfield 1980–83; V 1983–89; V St Faith N Dulwich 1989–99; TR Southend from 1999; M Draft Churchwardens and Amending Canon 1995
GS 1990–   Tel: (01702) 342687
email: Burdetts1@compuserve.com

BURNHAM, Revd Andrew, MA, ARCO (CHM)
St Stephen's House, 16 Marston St, Oxford OX4 1JX [OXFORD] *b* 19 Mar 1948; *educ* S'well Minster Gr

Sch; New Coll Ox; St Steph Ho Ox; Schoolmaster 1972–78; Freelance Conductor and Music Tchr 1978–85; NSM Clifton TM Nottm 1983–85; C Beeston 1985–87; V St Jo Ev Carrington 1987–94; Vc Prin St Steph Ho from 1995; M Steering Ctee Eucharistic Prayers 1995; M Steering Ctee Calendar and Lectionary 1996; M Liturg Commn from 1996; Gen Syn Rep NTMTC Coun from 1996; M Steering Ctee Amending Canon 22 1998; M Steering Ctee Pastl Rites 1998
GS 1990– Tel: (01865) 247874
  Fax: (01865) 794338
email: aburnham@ststephenshouse.demon.co.uk

BURNLEY, Bishop of [SUFFRAGAN, BLACKBURN]
Rt Revd Martyn William Jarrett, BD, AKC, M PHIL
449 Padiham Rd, Burnley, Lancs BB12 6TE b 25 Oct 1944; *educ* Cotham Gr Sch Bris; K Coll Lon; St Boniface Th Coll Warminster; Hull Univ; C St Geo Bris 1968–70; C Swindon New Town 1970–74; P-in-c St Jos the Worker Northolt 1974–76; V 1976–81; V St Andr Uxbridge 1981–85; Selection Sec ACCM 1985–88; Sen Selection Sec ACCM 1989–91; V Our Lady and All SS Chesterfield 1991–94; Bp of Burnley from 1994
  Tel: (01282) 423564
  Fax: (01282) 835496

BURNLEY, Mrs Isobel Margaret, BA, DIP SP ED
41 Marsh Lane, Nantwich, Cheshire CW5 5HP [CHESTER] *b* 1 Apr 1938; *educ* Chelmsford Co High Sch; Tiffin Sch Kingston; Gipsy Hill Tr Coll; Crewe and Alsager Coll of HE; Open Univ; Tchr Special Educational Needs; M Bp's Coun; Rdr
GS 1995– Tel: (01270) 624521
  email: 100417.3613@compuserve.com

BURNS, Canon Edward Joseph, B SC, MA
Christ Church Vicarage, 19 Vicarage Close, Fulwood, Preston, Lancs PR2 8EG [BLACKBURN] *b* 16 May 1938; *educ* Baines Gr Sch Poulton-le-Fylde; Liv Univ; St Cath's Coll Ox; Wycliffe Hall Th Coll; C Leyland Parish Ch 1961–64; C Burnley Parish Ch 1964–67; V St Jas Chorley, 1967–75; RD Preston 1979–86; V Ch Ch Fulwood from 1975; Hon Can Blackb Cathl from 1986; Bp of Blackb's Adv for Hosp Chapl 1989–94; M Hosp Chapl Coun from 1991; M Dioc Pastl Ctee 1974–98; M Bp's Coun from 1979; M Dioc Bd of Patronage from 1987; M Dioc Syn from 1970; Vc-Pres Dioc Syn and Chmn Dioc Ho of Clergy from 1993
GS 1970– Tel: (01772) 719210

BURRIDGE, Revd Dr Richard Alan, MA, PH D, PGCE, DIP TH
King's College, Strand, London WC2R 2LS [UNIVERSITIES, LONDON] *b* 11 Jun 1955; *educ* Bris Cathl Sch; Univ Coll Ox; Nottm Univ; St Jo Coll Nottm; Classics Master and Ho Tutor Sevenoaks Sch 1978–82; C SS Pet and Paul Bromley 1985–87; Chapl and pt Lect in Depts of Th and Classics & Ancient History Univ of Ex 1987–94; Dean of K Coll Lon from 1994; M Coun of Management St Jo

Coll Nottm from 1986; M Coun of Reference Monarch Publications from 1992; M Bd of Studies N Thames Min Tr Course from 1994; Trustee Chr Evidence Soc from 1994; Chmn Eric Symes Abbott Memorial Fund from 1994; M Studiorum Novi Testamenti Societas from 1995; M SST from 1995; M SBL from 1995; ABM External Moderator to SW Min Tr Course from 1995; Chmn Min Div Educ Validatory Panel; M Min Div TETC; M CECC; Commis to Bp of High Veld from 1996; Gen Syn Rep PIM Consultation to Province of W Africa from 1997
GS 1994– Tel: 020–7873 2333
  Fax: 020–7873 2344
  email: richard.burridge@kcl.ac.uk

BURROWS, Mr Gerald David, B SC, M SC, T CERT
3 Hall Rd, Fulwood, Preston, Lancs PR2 4QD [BLACKBURN] *b* 26 Dec 1942; *educ* Wellington Gr Sch; Univ Coll of N Wales, Bangor; Scientific Officer Rutherford High Energy Laboratory 1967–69; Lect Grimsby Coll of Technology 1969–71; Sen Lect Blackb Coll from 1971
GS 1990– Tel: (01772) 719159

BURY, Very Revd Nicholas Ayles Stillingfleet, MA
The Deanery, Miller's Green, Gloucester GL1 2BP [DEAN OF GLOUCESTER] *b* 8 Jan 1943; *educ* K Sch Cant; Qu Coll Cam; Cuddesdon Th Coll; C Liv Par Ch 1968–71; Chapl Ch Ch Ox 1971–75; V St Mary Shephall Stevenage 1975–84; V St Pet-in-Thanet 1984–97; RD Thanet 1993–97; Dean of Gloucester from 1997
GS 1990–96 Tel: (01452) 524167
  Fax: (01452) 300469

BUTTERFIELD, Revd David John, B MUS, DIP TH
25 Church Rd, Lilleshall, Newport, Shropshire TF10 9HE [LICHFIELD] *b* 1 Jan 1952; *educ* Belle Vue Boys Gr Sch Bradf; R Holloway Coll Lon; St Jo Coll Nottm; C Ch Ch Southport 1977–81; Min St Thos CD Aldridge 1981–91; V St Mich Lilleshall w St Mary Sheriffhales from 1991; M BM 1995–96; RD Edgmond 1997–98; RD Edgmond and Shifnal from 1999
GS 1990– Tel and Fax: (01952) 604281
  email: davidb1152@aol.com

BUTTERY, Revd Graeme, BA, MA
St Lawrence House, 84 Centenary Ave, South Shields, Tyne and Wear NE34 6SF [DURHAM] *b* 24 Nov 1962; *educ* Dame Allan's Boys Sch Newc; York Univ; Newc Univ; St Steph Ho Th Coll; C Peterlee 1988–91; C Sunderland TM 1991–92; TV Sunderland TM 1992–94; V St Lawr the Martyr Horsley Hill from 1994; M Dioc Pastl Ctee; M Seahouses Hostel Management Ctee
GS 1995– Tel: 0191–456 1747

BYRNE, Canon John Victor, FCA, L TH
Vicarage, 7 Hereford Rd, Southsea, Hants PO5 2DH [PORTSMOUTH] *b* 14 Nov 1947; *educ* John Lyon Sch

Harrow; St Jo Coll Nottm; Chartered Accountant; C St Mark Gillingham 1973–76; C St Luke Cranham Park 1976–80; V St Mary Balderstone, Rochdale 1980–87; V St Jude Southsea from 1987; ABM Pastl Selector 1993–97; Dioc Adv for Renewal of Resources 1994–97; P-in-c St Pet Southsea from 1995; Bp's Exam Chapl; M Bp's Coun; M DBF; M Vacancy in See Ctee; Hon Can Portsm Cathl from 1997; Abps' Pastl Adv from 1999
GS 1995–　　　　　　Tel and Fax: 023–9282 1071
email: john@byrne07.freeserve.co.uk

CAMERON, The Worshipful Sheila Morag Clark, QC, MA
2 Harcourt Buildings, Temple, London EC4Y 9DB [EX-OFFICIO, VICAR-GENERAL OF THE PROVINCE OF CANTERBURY] *b* 22 Mar 1934; *educ* Commonweal Lodge Sch Purley; St Hugh's Coll Ox; Barrister-at-Law; Official Prin Adnry of Hampstead 1968–86; Chan Chelmsf Dio from 1969; Chan Lon Dio from 1992; Chmn Eccles Judges Assn from 1997; M Legal Adv Commn from 1975; M Marriage Commn 1975–78; Chmn Abps' Grp on the Episcopate 1986–90; Boundary Commr Commn for England 1989–96; Vic-Gen Province of Cant from 1983; Recorder of Crown Court 1985–99; M Coun on Tribunals 1986–90
GS 1983–　　　　　　Tel: 020–7353 8415
Fax: 020–7353 7622

CAMPBELL, Mrs Rosalind Irene, B SC
18 Eaglesfield, Hartford, Northwich, Cheshire CW8 1NQ [CHESTER] *b* 4 May 1942; *educ* K Edw VI High Sch for Girls Birm; Birm Univ; Chemistry Tchr Redditch Co High Sch 1963–66; Crewe Co Gr Sch for Girls 1966–68; Hd of Chemistry Northwich Girls Gr Sch 1968–75; Supply and pt Teaching from 1982
GS 1995–　　　　　　Tel: (01606) 75849
email: GCampb1066@aol.com

CANTERBURY, Archbishop of, Most Revd and Rt Hon George Leonard Carey, BD, ALCD, M TH, PH D
Lambeth Palace, London SE1 7JU and The Old Palace, Canterbury, Kent CT1 2EE b 13 Nov 1935; *educ* Bifrons Sec Mod Sch Barking; Lon Univ; Lon Coll of Div; C St Mary Islington 1962–66; Lect Oak Coll 1966–70; Lect St Jo Coll Nottm 1970–75; V St Nich Dur 1975–82; Prin Trin Th Coll Bris 1982–87; Bp of B & W 1987–91; Abp of Cant from 1991
GS 1985–　　　　　　Tel: 020–7928 8282
Fax: 020–7261 9836

CAPON, Dr Peter Charles, B SC, PH D, MBCS, C ENG
137 Birchfields Rd, Manchester M14 6PJ [MANCHESTER] *b* 19 Jan 1944; *educ* Kimbolton Sch; Southn Univ; Cam Univ; Man Univ; Sen Lect in Computer Science Man Univ from 1976
GS 1995–　　　　　　Tel: 0161–225 5970
email: pcc@cs.man.ac.uk

CARLISLE, Bishop of, Rt Revd Ian Harland
Rose Castle, Dalston, Carlisle CA5 7BZ b 19 Dec 1932; *educ* Dragon Sch Ox; Haileybury Coll, Peterho Cam; Wycliffe Hall Th Coll; C Melton Mowbray 1960–63; V Oughtibridge Sheff 1963–72; M Wortley Rural Distr Coun 1969–73; V St Cuthb's Fir Vale Sheff 1972–75; P-in-c All SS Brightside 1973–75; RD Ecclesfield 1973–75; V Rotherham 1975–79; RD Rotherham 1976–79; Adn of Doncaster 1979–85; Bp of Lanc 1985–89; Bp of Carl from 1989
GS 1975–85, 1989–　　　　Tel: (01697) 476274
Fax: (01697) 476550
email: bishcarl@carlisle-c-of-e.org

CARR, Very Revd (Arthur) Wesley, MA, PH D
The Deanery, Westminster Abbey, London SW1P 3PA [DEAN OF WESTMINSTER] *b* 26 Jul 1941; *educ* Dulwich Coll; Jes Coll Ox; Jes Coll Cam; Univ of Sheff; Ridley Hall Th Coll; C Luton 1967–71; Tutor Ridley Hall 1970–71; Chapl Ridley Hall 1971–72; Fell Univ of Sheff Biblical Studies 1972–74; Hon C Ranmoor 1972–74; Chapl Chelmsf Cathl 1974–78; Dep Dir Chelmsf Cathl Cen for Rsch and Tr 1974–82; Dir of Tr Dio of Chelmsf 1976–84; Select Prchr Ox Univ 1984–85; Can Res Chelmsf Cathl 1978–87; Hon Fell New Coll Edin 1986–94; Dean of Bris 1987–97; Dean of Westmr from 1997
GS 1980–87, 1989–　　　　Tel: 020–7222 2953
Fax: 020–7799 2464
email: Dean@westminster-abbey.org

CARR, Mrs Katherine Mary, BA, PGCE
22 Frenchgate, Richmond, N Yorks DL10 7AG [RIPON] *b* 7 Jun 1932; *educ* Richmond High Sch for Girls; Westf Coll Lon; Lon Univ Inst of Educ; Asst Mistress Burghley Primary Sch Lon 1953–55; Asst Mistress Parliament Hill Comp Sch 1955–59; Lect Darlington Coll of Educ 1959–60, 1969–72; Dep Hd Sedgefield Comp Sch 1972–80; Hd Woodham Comp Sch Newton Aycliffe 1980–90; Rtd; JP; M Dioc Syn; Lay Chmn Richmond Dny Syn; M Bp's Coun
GS 1995–　　　　　　Tel: (01748) 823253
(01748) 884216

CASSIDY, Revd Dr Joseph Patrick Michael Aidan, BA, MA, B TH, M DIV, STL, PH D, D TH, FRSA, FICPD
Dun Cow Cottage, Dun Cow Lane, Durham DH1 3ES [UNIVERSITIES, DURHAM AND NEWCASTLE] *b* 11 Aug 1954; *educ* St Thos Sch, Pointe Claire, Quebec; Concordia Univ Montreal; Detroit Univ; Regis Coll Toronto; Ottawa Univ; St Paul Univ Ottawa; Univ of Toronto; Assoc Jesuit Centre Toronto 1982–86; Retreat Dir Loyola Ho Guelph, Canada 1986–87; Assoc Dir Ignatian Centre Montreal 1987–88; Vis Prof Concordia Univ Montreal 1987–88; Bursar Jesuit Community Ottawa 1988–90; Editor Central America Update 1990–92;

Sen Lect LSU Coll 1992–97; Prin St Chad's Coll Dur from 1997
GS 1999–   *Tel:* 0191–374 3362/3367
                              Fax: 0191–386 3422
                email: j.p.cassidy@durham.ac.uk

CATTON, Canon (Cedric) Trevor, STH, DIP RJ, CERT M
Exning Vicarage, New River Green, Exning, Newmarket, Suffolk CB8 7HS [ST EDMUNDSBURY AND IPSWICH] *b* 23 Mar 1936; *educ* Ipswich Sch; Wells Th Coll; In Retail Management 1956–70; C Solihull 1972–74; R Hawstead and Nowton w Stanningfield etc 1974–79; R Cockfield 1979–83; Dioc Stewardship Adv 1977–83; V St Martin Exning w Landwade from 1983; Chapl Newmarket Hosp from 1985; Hon Can St Eds Cathl from 1990
GS 1995–   *Tel and Fax:* (01638) 577413
         email: moretee@vicar1.freeserve.co.uk

CATTY, Mr Michael Anthony, BA, M SC
78 Dryden Crescent, Stevenage, Herts SG2 0JH [ST ALBANS] *b* 7 Jan 1942; *educ* St Paul's Sch Lon; Trin Coll Dublin; Open Univ; Secondary School Tchr from 1972;M Dioc BSR Exec from 1995; M Dioc Bd of Educ from 1997
GS 1992–   *Tel:* (01438) 350033

CAWDRON, Mr Keith William
Baringo, 61 Burbo Bank Rd, Blundellsands, Liverpool L23 6TQ [LIVERPOOL] *b* 3 Jan 1956; *educ* Stockport Gr Sch; Dur Univ; Civil Servant DES 1977–85; Admin and Research Officer to Abp of Cant 1985–87; Dioc Sec from 1987; Sec Dioc Syn, Bp's Coun and DBF; Rdr; M Coun CPAS
GS 1995–   *Tel:* 0151–931 2098 (Home)
                       0151–709 9722 (Office)
                      Fax: 0151–709 2885

CHALMERS, Canon Brian, MA, D PHIL
Vicarage, Pett Lane, Charing, Kent TN27 0DL [CANTERBURY] *b* 18 Sep 1942; *educ* Mercers Sch Holborn; Mill Hill Sch Lon; Oriel Coll Ox; Wycliffe Hall Th Coll; C St Mary Luton 1972–76; Chapl Cranfield Inst of Tech 1976–81; Sen Chapl Univ of Kent 1981–89; Six Prchr Cant Cathl 1985–95; Hon Can Cant Cathl from 1997; V Charing w Charing Heath and Little Chart from 1989; Chmn Dioc Ho of Clergy from 1994; M Dioc Abp's Coun and Business Ctee; M Dioc Bd of Min and Tr; Chair Dioc Structures Review Grp
GS 1999–   *Tel and Fax:* (01233) 712598
         email: Brian.Chalmers@tesco.net

CHAMBERLAIN, Mr Michael Aubrey, LL D, FCA
1 Waterloo Way, Leicester LE1 6LP [APPOINTED MEMBER, ARCHBISHOPS' COUNCIL] *b* 14 Apr 1939; *educ* Repton Sch; KPMG Peat Marwick 1974–93; Pres Inst of Chartered Accountants in England and Wales 1993–94; M Coun Leic Univ from 1996,

Treas from 1999; Consultant KPMG; Lay Can Leic Cathl; Apptd M Abps' Coun from 1999
GS 1999–   *Tel:* 0116–256 6000
                      Fax: 0116–256 6050

CHANTRY, Revd Helen Fiona, B SC, BA
Rectory, Nantwich, Cheshire CW5 5RQ [CHESTER] *b* 16 Oct 1959; *educ* Arnold High Sch for Girls; Bradf Univ; Trin Coll Bris; Tchr Aylesbury Gr Sch; NSM Par Dn St Geo Hyde; Dioc Youth Offcr from 1992; NSM Assoc Priest St Bart Barrow from 1994
GS 1994–   *Tel:* (01270) 626737

CHAPMAN, Ven Michael Robin, BA
Westbrook, 11 The Drive, Northampton NN1 4RZ [ARCHDEACON OF NORTHAMPTON] *b* 29 Sep 1939; *educ* Ellesmere Coll; Leeds Univ; Coll of the Resurr Mirf; C St Columba Sunderland 1963–68; Chapl RN 1968–84; V Hale 1984–91; RD Farnham 1988–91; Adn of Northampton from 1991
GS 1995–   *Tel:* (01604) 714015
                      Fax: (01604) 792016
      email: MichaelRChapman@compuserve.com

CHAPMAN, Canon Rex Anthony, BA, MA, DPS
1 The Abbey, Carlisle, Cumbria CA3 8TZ [CARLISLE] *b* 2 Sep 1938; *educ* Leeds Gr Sch; Univ Coll Lon; St Edm Hall Ox; Birm Univ; Wells Th Coll; C St Thos Stourbridge 1965–68; Chapl Aber Univ 1968–78; Hon Can St Andr Cathl Aber 1976–78; Res Can and Dioc Dir Educ from 1978; M Gen Syn Bd of Educ and Chmn Schs Ctee 1990–96; M Nat Soc Stg Ctee 1983–97; ABM Sen Selector; Chmn Dioc Ho of Clergy from 1996; Chapl to HM The Queen from 1997
GS 1985–   *Tel:* (01228) 597614 (Home)
                 (01228) 538086 (Office)
              Fax: (01228) 815409 (Office)
        email: RexChapman@ukgateway.net

CHAPMAN, Revd Sally Anne, B SC, MA, PGCE
18 Heather Grove, Willenhall, West Midlands WV12 4BT [LICHFIELD] *b* 6 Jan 1955; *educ* Kingswood Gr Sch; Lanchester Poly; Swansea Univ; Wolv Univ; Qu Coll Birm; C Glascote and Stonydelph TM Tamworth 1990–93; TV Short Heath from 1993; M Dioc Bd of Min 1991–97; M Dioc Bd of Educ from 1997
GS 1998–   *Tel:* (01902) 631498
         email: r.chapman@connect-2.co.uk

CHATTERLEY, Mrs Dorothy, BA
Kalyan, The Banks, Seascale, Cumbria CA20 1QW [CARLISLE] *b* 21 Dec 1932; *educ* Darwen Gr Sch; Man Univ; Tchr w CJGS Newbury 1954–56; Tchr Cumbria Educ Auth 1966–86; Rdr; Lay Chmn Calder Dny Syn 1990–96; Area Sec RSCM Cumbria 1986–97; M Coun Guild of Ch Musicians; M Gen Syn Stg Ctee and Appts Sub-Ctee 1990–98; M Coun of Corp of Ch Ho from 1989; M CTBI and CTE from 1990; Lay Vc-Chmn Catholic Grp in Gen Syn 1990–94; CE Rep at Gen Assembly of Ch of Scotland 1993 and 1994; M

EKD Consultations Sept 1993; M In Tune w Heaven follow up grp 1993; Ch Commr from 1993; Gen Syn Rep on RSCM Coun; Elected Delegate to CEC Graz 1997 and WCC Harare 1998; M CU Coun
GS 1985–   Tel: (019467) 28379

CHEESEMAN, Mr James Reginald
25 Lambarde Drive, Sevenoaks, Kent TN13 3HX [ROCHESTER] *b* 2 Nov 1934; *educ* Sevenoaks Sch; Coll of St Mark and St Jo; Supply Staff Kent Educ Ctee 1954–55; Asst Tchr Midfield Prim Sch 1957–68; Dep Hdmaster Edgebury Prim Sch 1968–69; Chmn Ho of Laity Roch Dioc Syn 1976–79; M Gen Syn Bd of Educ 1981–91; Hdmaster Pet Hills' Sch Rotherhithe 1969–97; Rdr; Co-Chmn Sevenoaks Dny Syn 1976–96; Sec Sevenoaks Dny Syn; Trustee Guild of All So; Treas Qu Victoria Clergy Fund from 1991; Lay Chmn Forward In Faith Roch; Chmn Dioc Bd of Patronage
GS 1975–   Tel: (01732) 455718
      email: 106542.320@compuserve.com

CHEETHAM, Ven Richard Ian, MA, PGCE, CERT TH
6 Sopwell Lane, St Albans, Herts AL1 1RR [ARCH-DEACON OF ST ALBANS] *b* 18 Aug 1955; *educ* Kingston Gr Sch; CCC Ox; K Coll Lon; Ripon Coll Cuddesdon; C H Cross Fenham 1987–90; V St Aug of Cant Limbury, Luton 1990–99; RD Luton 1995–98; Adn of St Albs from 1999; M Bp's Coun; M Dioc Pastl Ctee; M DBF; M Dioc BMU; M DAC
                              Tel: (01727) 847212
                              Fax: (01727) 848311
      email: archdstalbans@stalbansdioc.org.uk

CHELMSFORD, Bishop of, Rt Revd John Freeman Perry, M PHIL, L TH
Bishopscourt, Margaretting, Ingatestone, Essex CM4 0HD b 15 Jun 1935; *educ* Mill Hill Sch; Lon Coll of Div; C Ch Ch Woking 1959–62; C Ch Ch Chorleywood 1962–63; V St Andr Chorleywood 1963–77; RD Rickmansworth 1972–77; Warden Lee Abbey 1977–89; RD Shirwell 1979–83; Bp of Southn 1989–96; Can Win Cathl from 1989; Bp of Chelmsf from 1996; M Min Div Bps Ctee for Min from 1991; Chmn Min Div Ctee for Min among Deaf People; Chmn Trustees of Burrswood; Chmn CCHH
GS 1995–   Tel: (01277) 352001
                              Fax: (01277) 355374
      email: bishopscourt@chelmsford.anglican.org

CHERRY, Revd Stephen Arthur, MA, B SC, PH D
Rectory, Steeple Rd, Loughborough LE11 1UX [LEICESTER] *b* 12 Jul 1958; *educ* Qu Eliz Sch Crediton; St Chad's Coll Dur; K Coll Lon; Westcott Ho Th Coll; C St Jo the Divine Manchester 1986–89; Chapl K Coll Cam 1989–94; R All SS w H Trin Loughborough from 1994; RD Akeley E 1996–99; Chmn Dioc Liturg Ctee
GS 1999–   *Tel* and *Fax:* (01509) 212780 (Home)
             Tel: (01509) 217029 (Office)

CHESTER, Bishop of, Rt Revd Peter Robert Forster, MA, BD, PH D
Bishop's House, Abbey Square, Chester CH1 2JD b 16 Mar 1950; *educ* Tudor Grange Gr Sch Solihull; Merton Coll Ox; Edin Univ; Edin Th Coll; C St Matt and St Jas Mossley Hill Liv 1980–82; Sen Tutor St Jo Coll Dur 1983–91; V Beverley Minster 1991–96; Bp of Ches from 1996
GS 1985–91, 1996–   Tel: (01244) 350864
                          Fax: (01244) 314187

CHETWOOD, Mr Nigel John, B SC
15 Tretawn Gardens, Tewkesbury, Glos GL20 8EF [GLOUCESTER] *b* 30 Jan 1939; *educ* Oswestry Gr Sch; Man Univ; M CPAS Coun; Purchasing Mgr Micro Circuit Engineering Ltd; Rdr
GS 1985–   Tel: (01684) 292473
      email: Nigel.Chetwood@ibm.net

CHICHESTER, Bishop of, Rt Revd Eric Waldram Kemp, DD, D LITT, D TH
The Palace, Chichester, W Sussex PO19 1PY b 27 Apr 1915; *educ* Brigg Gr Sch; Ex Coll Ox; St Steph Ho Th Coll; St Luke Southn 1939–41; Lib Pusey Ho Ox 1941–46; Fell, Chapl, Tutor, Lect, Ex Coll Ox 1946–69; Dean of Worc 1969–74; Bp of Chich from 1974
GS 1970–   Tel: (01243) 782161
                              Fax: (01243) 531332
      email: bishopchi@diochi.freeserve.co.uk

CHRISTIE, Canon Thomas Richard, MA
Prebendal House, The Precincts, Peterborough PE1 1XX [PETERBOROUGH] *b* 8 Aug 1931; *educ* Clifton Coll Bris; CCC Cam; Linc Th Coll; C St Mark Portsea 1957–60; C Cherry Hinton 1960–61; P-in-c St Jas Cherry Hinton CD 1961–66; V St Aug Wisbech 1966–73; V Whitstable 1973–80; Can Res Petrb Cathl from 1980; RD Petrb 1987–96; Chmn Ho of Clergy Dioc Syn; Vc-Pres SPCK; Warden Community of the Holy Cross; Prov En Div Woodard Corp from 1994
GS 1970–73, 1975–90, 1993–   Tel: (01733) 569441
                              Fax: (01733) 552465

CLARK, Mr John Guthrie
12 Ash Drive, Haughton, Stafford ST18 9EU [LICHFIELD] *b* 9 Jun 1938; *educ* Slough Gr Sch; Wrekin Coll; Ches Dio Tr Coll; Tchr Dawley Sec Mod Sch 1960–65; Phoenix Comp Sch 1965–67; Wobaston Sec Mod Sch 1967–68; Aelfgar Comp Sch 1968–86; Hd of Relig and Socl Educ Hagley Park Comp Sch Rugeley 1986–93; M Dioc Pastl Ctee, Bp's Coun and Bd of Educ; Local Min Consultant
GS 1970–   Tel: (01785) 780689

CLARK, Mr John Mullin, MA, PGCE
Partnership House, 157 Waterloo Rd, London SE1 8XA [PARTNERSHIP SECRETARY, BOARD OF MISSION] *b* 19 Apr 1946; *educ* St Paul's Sch; St Pet Coll Ox; Inst of Educ Lon; K Coll Lon; Publisher, Tehran, Iran 1967–80; CMS Regional Sec Middle

East and Pakistan 1980–86; Communications Sec CMS 1987–91; Sec PWM, BM from 1992; Chmn Feed the Minds and USCL; Sec Overseas Bishoprics Fund; Chmn Friends of Dio of Iran; MCE delegation to WCC Assembly 1998
Tel: 020–7928 8681
email: john.clark@pwm.c-of-e.org.uk

CLARKE, Canon (Hilary) James
Church House, Great Smith St, London SW1P 3NZ [SECRETARY, COMMITTEE FOR MINISTRY AMONG DEAF PEOPLE] *b* 9 Sep 1941; *educ* Sandbach Sch; St David's Coll Lampeter; St Steph Ho Th Coll; C Kibworth 1966–68; Chapl/Social Worker Leic and Co Miss for the Deaf 1968–71; Prin Officer, Chapl Ch Miss for Deaf Walsall and S Staffs 1971–73; Prin Officer, Chapl and Sec Leic Co Miss for the Deaf 1973–89; Sec Gen Syn Coun for the Deaf 1989–91; Ctee for Min among Deaf People from 1991
Tel: 020–7233 1153 (Office)
020–7898 1429 (text phone)
0850–144150 (Mobile)
email: 106575.2374@compuserve.com

CLARKE, Mrs (Margaret) Ann, T CERT, CERT SPECIAL EDUC MGT
St Saviour's and All Saints' Vicarage, 46 Manor Rd, Weston-super-Mare, Avon BS23 2SU [BATH AND WELLS] *b* 7 Jul 1937; *educ* Hastings High Sch for Girls; St Gabriel's Coll Camberwell; Tchr Hailsham Co Primary Sch 1957–58; Bexhill C E Junior Sch 1958–62; Ch Ch Primary Sch St Leonards on Sea 1962–67; Tchr/Hd of Dept Fairmead Special Sch Yeovil 1972–80; Dep Hd 1980–92; Housewife; M Forward in Faith Dioc Assembly; Delegate to Forward in Faith Nat Assembly
GS 1995–
Tel and *Fax:* (01934) 623230

CLARKE, Prof Michael Gilbert, BA, MA, FIPD, FRSA
Millington House, 15 Lansdowne Crescent, Worcester WR3 8JE [WORCESTER] *b* 21 May 1944; *educ* Qu Eliz Gr Sch Wakef; Sussex Univ; Lect in Politics Edin Univ 1969–75; Dep Dir Policy Planning Lothian Regional Coun 1975–81; Dir Local Government Tr Bd 1981–90; Chief Exec Local Government Management Bd 1990–93; Hd of Sch of Public Policy Birm Univ 1993–98; Pro-Vc-Chan Birm Univ from 1998; M Gen Syn Panel of Chairmen from 1996
GS 1990–93, 1995–
Tel: (01905) 617634
Fax: (01905) 29502

CLARKE, Revd Robert Sydney, MA, AKC
Fielden House, Little College St, London SW1P 3SH [SECRETARY AND DIRECTOR OF TRAINING, HOSPITAL CHAPLAINCIES COUNCIL] *b* 31 Oct 1935; *educ* St Dunstan's Coll; K Coll Lon; St Boniface Th Coll Warminster; C St Mary Hendon 1965–69; C Langley Marish 1969–70; Chapl New Cross Hosp Wolv 1970–74; Chapl Herrison Hosp Dorchester 1974–80; Sen Chapl Westmr Hosp Lon and

Westmr Medical Sch 1980–85; Chapl R Hants Co Hosp Win 1985–94; Sen Chapl Win HA 1988–94; Chapl to The Queen from 1987; Sec and Dir of Tr Hosp Chapl Coun from 1994
Tel: 020–7898 1892
Fax: 020–7891 1891

COCKE, Dr Thomas Hugh, MA, PH D, FSA
15 Lyndewode Rd, Cambridge CB1 2HL [SECRETARY, COUNCIL FOR THE CARE OF CHURCHES] *b* 19 Feb 1949; *educ* Marlboro Coll; Pemb Coll Cam; Courtauld Inst Lon; Lect in Art Hist Man Univ 1973–76; Investigator of hist buildings RCHME 1976–90; Sec Coun for Care of Chs from 1990
Tel: 020–7898 1882
Fax: 020–7898 1881

COLCHESTER, Bishop of [AREA BISHOP, CHELMSFORD] **Rt Revd Edward Holland,** AKC
1 Fitzwalter Rd, Lexden, Colchester, Essex CO3 3SS *b* 28 Jun 1936; *educ* New Coll Sch Ox; Dauntsey's Sch, W Lavington; K Coll Lon; C H Trin Dartford 1965–69; C Jo Keble Mill Hill 1969–72; Prec Gib Cathl and Seamen's Missr 1972–74; Chapl in Naples 1974–79; V St Mark Bromley 1979–86; Chapl Bromley Hosp 1979–86; Suff Bp in Eur 1986–95; Bp of Colchester from 1995
Tel: (01206) 576648
Fax: (01206) 763868
email: bishopedward@chelmsford.anglican.org

COLMER, Ven Malcolm John, M SC, BA, SO SC
59 Sutton Lane South, London W4 3JR [ARCHDEACON OF MIDDLESEX] *b* 15 Feb 1945; *educ* R Gr Sch Guildf; Sussex Univ; Nottm Univ; St Jo Coll Nottm; C St Jo Egham 1973–76; C Chadwell St Mary 1976–79; V S Malling, Lewes 1979–85; V St Mary w St Steph Hornsey Rise 1985–87; TR Hornsey Rise Whitehall Park Tm 1987–96; AD Islington 1990–95; Adn of Middx from 1996; M Dioc Liturg Grp
Tel: 020–8994 8148
email: archdeacon.middlesex@dlondon.org.uk

COMBES, Revd Roger Matthew, LL B
St Matthew's Rectory, St Matthew's Rd, St Leonards-on-Sea, E Sussex TN38 0TN [CHICHESTER] *b* 12 Jun 1947; *educ* Sherborne Sch; K Coll Lon; Ridley Hall Th Coll; C St Paul Onslow Sq Lon 1974–77; C H Trin Brompton Lon 1976–77; C H Sepulchre Cam 1977–86; R St Matt St Leonards-on-Sea from 1986; M Bp's Coun from 1998; RD Hastings from 1998
GS 1995–
Tel: (01424) 423790

CONINGSBY, Chancellor His Honour Judge Thomas Arthur Charles, QC, MA
Leyfields, Elmore Rd, Chipstead, Surrey CR3 3SG [VICAR-GENERAL OF YORK] *b* 21 Apr 1933; *educ* Epsom Coll; Qu Coll Cam; Barrister 1957–92; Circuit Judge from 1992; Designated Civil Judge (Croydon Grp) from 1999; Chmn Family Law Bar Assn 1988–90 (Sec 1986–88); M Gen Coun Bar 1988–90; M Supreme Court Procedure Ctee

1988–92; M Matrimonial Causes Rule Ctee 1985–89; Recorder from 1986; QC from 1986; Dep High Court Judge from 1988; M Legal Adv Commn from 1973; Chan York Dio from 1977; M Marriage Commn 1975; Lay Chmn Croydon Dny Syn 1979–80; Vic Gen of York from 1980; M Legal Offcrs Fees Adv Ctee 1982–93; Chan Petrb Dio from 1989; M Stg Ctee Ecclesiastical Judges Assn from 1989; M Gov Body SPCK 1990–92; M Ctee Eccles Law Soc from 1996
GS 1970–   *Tel:* (01737) 553304

CONNER, Rt Revd David John , MA
The Deanery, Windsor Castle, Berks SL4 1NJ [DEAN OF WINDSOR] *b* 6 Apr 1947; *educ* Ex Coll Ox; St Steph Ho Th Coll; Hon C Summertown Ox 1971–76; Asst Chapl St Edw Sch Ox 1971–73; Chapl 1973–80; TV Wolvercote w Summertown 1976–80; Chapl Win Coll 1980–87; V Gt St Mary w St Mich Cam 1987–94; RD Cam 1989–94; Bp of Lynn 1994–98; Dean of Windsor from 1998
                                  Tel: (01753) 865561

CONWAY, Revd Stephen David, MA, BA, PGCE
Auckland Castle, Bishop Auckland, Co Durham DL14 7NR [DURHAM] *b* 22 Dec 1957; *educ* Abp Tenison's Gr Sch Kennington; Keble Coll Ox; Selw Coll Cam; Westcott Ho Th Coll; C St Mary Heworth 1986–89; C St Mich w St Hilda Bishopwearmouth 1989–90; DDO 1989–94; Hon C St Marg Dur 1990–94; P-in-c St Mary Cockerton 1994–98, V from 1998; Sen Chapl and Press Officer to Bp of Dur and DCO from 1998
GS 1995–   *Tel:* (01388) 835842 (Home)
                             (01388) 602576 (Office)

COOK, Revd John Richard Millward, BA
Vicarage, 43 Park Walk, London SW10 0AU [LONDON] *b* 3 Mar 1961; *educ* Repton Sch; St Jo Coll Dur; Wycliffe Hall Th Coll; C St Thos Brampton 1985–89; C St Pet Farnboro 1989–92; C and Dir of Tr All So Langham Place Lon 1992–98; V St Jo w St Andr Chelsea from 1998; M Selection Tm for Ord Min Cen Lon; M CCU 1996–99; M VRSC from 1999
GS 1995–   *Tel and Fax:* 020–7352 1675

COOPER, Mr Alan, OBE, B ED
11 Ravensdale Gardens, Eccles, Manchester M30 9JD [MANCHESTER] *b* 11 Mar 1927; *educ* St Andr Sch Eccles; Didsbury Coll of Educ; Liv Univ; Hdmaster; Councillor Eccles Boro Coun 1958–73; Mayor of Eccles 1972–73; Councillor Salford 1975–79; Lay Chmn Eccles Dny Syn; Chmn DBF; M Bp's Coun; Dep Vc-Chmn Abps' Coun Finance Ctee; Ch Commr; JP
GS 1970–   *Tel:* 0161–789 1514

CORMACK, Sir Patrick Thomas, MP, BA, FSA
The Lyons, Enville, Staffs DY7 5LD [LICHFIELD] *b* 18 May 1939; *educ* St Jas Choir Sch Grimsby; Havelock Sch Grimsby; Hull Univ; Schmaster

1961–70; MP for S Staffs from 1970; M Ecclesiastical Ctee from 1970; Trustee Historic Chs Trust from 1972; Vis Lect Univ of Texas 1984; Vis Fell St Ant Coll Ox 1994–95; M Faculty Jurisdiction Commn; M R Commn on Hist Mss from 1980; M DBF
GS 1995–   *Tel:* 020–7219 5514

COSH, Mrs Margaret Allen
Church House, Aston Eyre, Bridgnorth, Shropshire WV16 6XD [HEREFORD] *b* 15 Aug 1935; *educ* Lowther Coll Abergele; Liv Univ; Dio of Yukon 1963–65; Social Worker Tr Shropshire Social Services 1984–94; Independent Practice Tchr from 1994; Lay Co-Chmn Bridgnorth Dny Syn 1987–93; M Dioc CSR; M Dioc Pastl Ctee
GS 1994–   *Tel and Fax:* (01746) 714248
                             email: astoneyre@aol.com

COULTON, Very Revd Nicholas Guy, BD
The Cathedral Vicarage, 26 Mitchell Ave, W Jesmond, Newcastle upon Tyne NE2 3LA [PROVOST OF NEWCASTLE] *b* 14 Jun 1940; *educ* Blundell's Sch Tiverton; Cuddesdon Th Coll; Lon Univ; C Pershore Abbey 1967–71; Chapl to Bp of St Alb 1971–75; V St Paul's Bedf 1975–90; pt Chapl Herts and Beds Ind Miss 1976–89; Hon Can St Alb Cathl 1989–90; V of Newc and Provost of St Nic's Cathl 1990; Chmn NE Coun of Christians and Jews from 1991; Co Chapl Order of St Jo from 1994; Dir EIG from 1997
GS 1985–90, 1998–   *Tel:* 0191–281 6554 (Home)
                             0191–232 1939 (Office)
                             Fax: 0191–230 0735
                             email: stnicholas@aol.com

COUSSMAKER, Canon (Colin Richard) Chad, OBE, MA, M SC
533 Route de Vallette Sud, 06140 Tourrettes-sur-Loup, France [EUROPE] *b* 13 Apr 1934; *educ* K Edw VI Sch Lich; W'hampton Gr Sch; Worc Coll Ox; Chich Th Coll; Asst C St Luke Newtown Southn 1960–64; Asst C Ch Ch Reading (in-c St Agnes Whitley) 1964–67; Chapl Ch Ch w St Helena Istanbul and All SS Moda and Apokrisarios of the Abp of Cant to the Oecumenical Patriarch of Constantinople 1967–72; Chapl H Trin Sliema Malta 1972–77; Chapl St Boniface Antwerp 1977–93; Chapl St Andr Moscow and Apokrisarios of the Abp of Cant to the Patriarch of Moscow, to the Patriarch-Catholicos of Georgia, and to the Catholicos-Patriarch of Armenia 1993–99; Asst Chapl H Trin Nive w St Hugh Vence from 1999; M CCU from 1992; M Dioc Syn from 1981
GS 1988–

COVENTRY, Bishop of, Rt Revd Colin James Bennetts, MA
Bishop's House, 23 Davenport Rd, Coventry CV5 6PW b 9 Sep 1940; *educ* Battersea Gr Sch; Jes Coll Cam; Ridley Hall Th Coll; C St Steph Tonbridge 1965–69; Chapl Ox Pastorate 1969–73; Chapl Jes Coll Ox 1973–79; V St Andr Ox 1979–90; Can Res

hes Cathl and DDO 1990–94; Bp of Buckm
)94–98; Bp of Cov from 1998
S 1998–   *Tel:* 024–7667 2244
                               Fax: 024–7671 3271
                        email: bishcov@clara.net

OX, Ven John Stuart, BA, MA
4 Southgate St, Bury St Edmunds, Suffolk IP33 2BJ
[ARCHDEACON OF SUDBURY] *b* 13 Sep 1940; *educ*
add Sch Tonbridge; Univ Coll of Rhodesia and
Nyasaland; Ox Univ; Birm Univ; Fitzw Ho Cam;
Wycliffe Hall Ox; C St Mary Prescot 1968–71; C St
Leo Birmingham 1971–73; R 1973–78; Selection
Sec ACCM 1978–83; DDO S'wark 1983–91; Can
Res and Treas S'wark Cathl 1983–91;V Roehamp-
on 1991–95; Can Emer 1991; Adn of Sudbury
rom 1995
GS 1990–95   *Tel:* (01284) 766796
                               Fax: (01284) 723163

CRAMERI, Revd Mary Barbara, BD, AKC, PGCE
Vicarage, Wilcot, Pewsey, Wilts SN9 5NS [SALIS-
BURY] *b* 27 May 1944; *educ* Brentwood Co High Sch
for Girls; K Coll Lon; Lon Univ Inst of Educ; Sn
Dios Min Tr Scheme; Various teaching posts
1965–88; C SS Phil and Jas Whitton 1988–91; pt Par
On Bemerton TM 1991–93; pt Core Staff M Sn Dios
Min Tr Scheme 1991–93; Vc-Prin Sn Tr Scheme for
Chr Min from 1993, Acting Prin 1996–97; Dep Dir
TETS and Minl Formation Officer 1997–98; TV
Pewsey and Swanborough from 1998
GS 1995–   *Tel* and *Fax:* (01672) 562282
      email: mary@mcrameri.freeserve.co.uk

CREDITON, Bishop of [SUFFRAGAN, EXETER] **Rt
Revd Richard Stephen Hawkins,** MA, B PHIL
10 The Close, Exeter, Devon EX1 1EZ b 2 Apr 1939;
educ Ex Coll Ox; Univ of Ex; St Steph Ho Th Coll;
Asst C St Thos Ex 1963–66; TV Clyst Valley TM
1966–78; TV Central Ex TM, Bp's Offcr for Min and
t Dir Exeter-Truro Min Tr Scheme 1978–81; DDO
1979–81; P-in-C Whitestone w Oldridge 1981–87;
Adn of Totnes 1981–88; Bp of Plymouth 1988–96;
Bp of Crediton from 1996   *Tel:* (01392) 273509
                               Fax: (01392) 431266

CROYDON, Bishop of [AREA BISHOP,
SOUTHWARK] **Rt Revd Wilfred Denniston Wood,**
DD
Home: 53 Stanhope Rd, Croydon, Surrey CR0 5NS,
*Office: St Matthew's House, 100 George St, Croydon
CR0 1PJ b* 15 Jun 1936; *educ* Combermere Sch Bar-
bados; Codrington Coll, Barbados; Provincial Th
Coll of the W Indies; C St Steph w St Thos Shep-
herds Bush 1962–66; Hon C 1966–74; Bp of Lon's
Offcr in Race Relations 1966–74; V St Laur Cat-
ford 1974–82; Hon Can of S'wark Cathl since
1977; RD E Lewisham 1977–82; Adn and Boro
Dean of S'wark 1982–85; Bp of Croydon from
1985; Area Bp from 1991
GS 1987–95   *Tel:* 020–8686 1822 (Home)
                    020–8681 5496 (Office)
                    Fax: 020–8686 2074
      email: bishop.wilfrid@dswark.org.uk

CULL, Dr Carole Anne, B SC, M SC, PH D, C STAT
*6 Forndon Close, Lower Earley, Reading, Berks RG6
3XR* [OXFORD] *b* 20 Oct 1947; *educ* Bexley Gr Sch;
Liv Univ; Sheffield Hallam Univ; Lucy Cavend-
ish Coll Cam; Medical Statistician Radcliffe
Infirmary Ox; Rdr; M CRC Exec 1989–94; Hon
Editor *The Reader* 1989–94; M ABM Ctee for
Min Development and Deployment 1991–96; M
Gov Body Sarum & Wells Th Coll 1992–94; M
Revision Ctee Tm and Grp Min Measure; Sec
Open Synod Grp from 1993; Chmn Reading
Dusseldorf Chs Interchange 1994–97; M Dioc
Coun for Min from 1994; M Revision Ctee Calen-
dar, Lectionary and Collects; M CCU from 1996;
M Liturg Commn from 1996; M Elections Review
Grp from 1996; M Steering Ctee Lord's Prayer; M
Steering Ctee The Service of The Word; M Stat-
istics Review Grp; M Baptist Union C of E
Informal Conversations from 1998
GS 1985–87, 1990–   *Tel:* 0118–961 7923
          (01865) 224080/248418 (Office)
                    Fax: (01865) 723884 (Office)
           email: carole@drl.ox.ac.uk /
                    ukpds@ermine.ox.ac.uk

**CUMMINGS, Very Revd William Alexander
Vickery,** MA
The Deanery, Battle, E Sussex TN33 0JY [DEAN OF
BATTLE] *b* 6 Apr 1938; *educ* K Coll Sch Wimbledon;
Ch Ch Ox; Wycliffe Hall Ox; C St John Leyton-
stone 1964–67; C Writtle 1967–71; R Stratton St
Mary w St Mich and Wacton 1971–91; RD Dep-
wade 1981–91; Hon Can Nor Cathl 1990; Can
Emer from 1991; Dean of Battle from 1991
                               Tel: (01424) 772693

CURRALL, Dr Arnold Edward, MA, D PHIL
*Kelsyke, Great Strickland, Penrith, Cumbria CA10
3DJ* [CARLISLE] *b* 1 Jul 1924; *educ* Warwick Sch;
Reading Univ; Keble Coll Ox; Geology Lect Sheff
Univ 1952–66; Warden Freemens Hall and
Admin Castle Leazes Hall Newc Univ 1966–82;
Rtd; M DBF; M DAC; M Bp's Coun; M Dioc Pastl
Ctee
GS 1995–   *Tel:* (01931) 712242
                               Fax: (01931) 712462

DA-COCODIA, Mrs Louise Adassa, BEM, MA
(HON)
9 Arliss Ave, Levenshulme, Manchester M19 2PD
[MANCHESTER] *b* 9 Nov 1934; *educ* Delrose High
Sch Kingston, Jamaica; Sen Nurse Manager
1977–88; Self Employed Project Consultant; M
Commn for Racial Justice; M Dioc Syn from 1989;
Chair Dioc Establishment Ctee; Chair Dioc
Community Relations Ctee; Man City Magis-
trates Bench (JP) from 1990; Bd M Cariocca
Enterprises Ltd; Chair Arawak Walton Housing
Assn; Chair Moss Side and Hulme Women's
Action Forum; Co-opted Gov Man Metropolitan
Univ; Lay M Court Man Univ
GS 1990–
                               Tel: 0161–224 0209

WHO'S WHO

DALBY, Ven (John) Mark Meredith, MA, PH D
21 Belmont Way, Rochdale OL12 6HR [ARCH-
DEACON OF ROCHDALE] *b* 3 Jan 1938; *educ* K Geo V
Sch Southport; Ex Coll Ox; Nottm Univ; Ripon
Hall Th Coll; C Hambleden 1963–68; C Fawley,
Fingest, Medmenham and Turville 1966–68; V St
Pet Spring Hill Birm 1968–75; RD Birm City
1973–75; Sec Ctee for Th Educ and Selection Sec
ACCM 1975–80; Hon C All Hallows Tottenham
1975–80; TR Worsley 1980–91; RD Eccles 1987–91;
Exam Chapl to Bp of Man from 1980; Hon Tutor
Dept of Th Studies Man Univ 1985–91; Adn of
Rochdale from 1991
GS 1985–95
Tel and *Fax:* (01706) 648640

DALES, Mr Martin Paul
Priory Cottage, Old Malton, N Yorks YO17 7HB
[YORK] *b* 27 Dec 1955; *educ* St Dunstan's Coll; Bret-
ton Hall; Open Univ; Dep Hd, Housemaster and
Dir of Music various schs 1976–94; Organist and
Choirmaster from 1976; Broadcaster from 1976;
Music Publisher from 1981; Media Relations,
Educ and Tr Officer RSCM NE Yorks Area from
1994; M Revision Ctee Draft Amending Canon
No 22; Coun Malton Town Coun 1989–99 (Mayor
1991–92, 1996–97); Sch Gov; M Dioc Coun for
Min and Tr
GS 1995–
Tel: (01653) 600990
Fax: (01653) 692746
email: martin.dales@virgin.net

DARLINGTON, Lt Col John
32 The Close, Salisbury, Wilts SP1 2EJ [SALISBURY]
b 24 Sep 1932; *educ* St Jo Sch Leatherhead; Royal
Tank Regiment 1950–86; Bursar Sarum and Wells
Th Coll 1986–94; Bursar Sarum College 1994–96;
M Dioc Bd of Min from 1991; Vocations Adv from
1992; Lay Can Sarum Cathl from 1997; M Close
Chapter from 1998
GS 1990–
Tel: (01722) 415622
Fax: (01722) 555116

DARLOW, Mr Stewart Francis, MA, PH D
6 Harboro Grove, Sale, Cheshire M33 5BA [CHESTER]
b 30 Apr 1934; *educ* Latymer Upper Sch Hammersmith; Jesus Coll Cam; Physics Dept UMIST
1959–89; Sen Lect 1973–89; Asst Dir of Laborator-
ies 1983–89; Rtd; M Inter-Dioc Finance Forum; M
Consultative Grp of Dioc Chmn and Secretaries;
Chmn DBF; Chmn Finance and Central Services
Ctee; Bp's Coun; Benefice Trustee; Rdr
GS 1990–
Tel: 0161–973 4697

DAVID, Mr Andrew Morgan
*1 Church House, Main St, Farnsfield, Newark, Notts
NG22 8EY* [SOUTHWELL] *b* 27 May 1954; *educ* K Sch
Roch; BBC Popular Music Lib Lon and Scotland
1972–75; Presenter/Producer BBC Radio Nottm
1975–87; Presenter/Reporter BBC TV Midlands
1987–91; Freelance Producer/Presenter/Dir
Corporate and Broadcast Video Films from 1991;

Conference MC and Concert Compere; BB
Radio Nottm Sunday Breakfast Show Present
from 1998; Organist and Dir of Music St Mic
Farnsfield; Chair S'well Dioc Communicatior
Ctee
GS 1995–
Tel and *Fax:* (01623) 8828:
0410 088353 (Mobil
01426 108410 (Page
email: a.m.david@btinternet.cor

DAVIDSON, Revd Donald Hugh, MA
43 Inverleith Gardens, Edinburgh EH3 5PR [ECL
MENICAL REPRESENTATIVE (CHURCH OF SCO
LAND)] *b* 6 Nov 1939; *educ* Peebles High Sch; Edi
Univ; Par Min St Mary's Biggar; Par Min Inve
leith from 1975
GS 1999–
Tel and *Fax:* 0131–552 387
email: hdavidson@freeuk.cor

DAVIDSON, Mr Keith Thomas, LL B
*The Poplars, Sandy Lane, Church Brampton, North
ampton NN6 8AX* [PETERBOROUGH] *b* 12 Sep 193:
educ Whitgift Sch; Solicitor; Rdr
GS 1970–
Tel: (01604) 233233 (Office
(01604) 845489 (Home

**DAVIES, Canon Jeremy (David Jeremy
Christopher),** MA
*Home: The Hungerford Chantry, 54 The Close
Salsbury SP1 2EL, Office: Ladywell, 33 The Close
Salsbury SP1 2EJ* [SALISBURY] *b* 7 Jan 1946; *edu*
Cathl Sch Llandaff; Hurstpierpoint Coll; CCC
Cam; Westcott Ho Th Coll; C St Dunstan Stepne
1971–74; Chapl Qu Mary Coll Lon 1974–78
Chapl Univ Coll Cardiff 1978–85; Prec and Car
Res Sarum Cathl from 1985
GS 1993–
Tel: (01722) 555179 (Home
(01722) 555128 (Office
Fax: (01722) 55511:
email: jeremy@mcenery.demon.co.uk

DAVIES, Ven Lorys Martin, JP, BA, ALCM
*45 Rudgwick Drive, Brandesholme, Bury, Lancs BLE
1YA* [ARCHDEACON OF BOLTON] *b* 14 Jun 1936; *educ*
Whitland Gr Sch; St David's Coll Lamp; Univ oI
Wales; Wells Th Coll; C St Mary Tenby 1959–61,
Asst Chapl Brentwood Sch 1962–66; Chapl and
Hd of Dept Solihull Sch 1966–68; V St Mary
Moseley 1968–81; Can Res Birm Cathl 1981–92
DDO 1982–90; Chmn Dioc Ho of Clergy 1991–92,
Adn of Bolton from 1992; Bp's Adv for Hosp
Chapls from 1992; Chmn Stewardship Ctee from
1992; Wrdn of Rdrs from 1994; Proctor in Conv
from 1998
GS 1998–
Tel and *Fax:* 0161–761 6117

DAVIES, Ven Tony (Vincent Anthony)
*246 Pampisford Rd, S Croydon CR2 6DD, Office: St
Matthew's House, 100 George St, Croydon CR0 1PE*
[ARCHDEACON OF CROYDON] *b* 15 Sep 1946; *educ*
Green Lane Sec Mod Sch Leic; Brasted Th Coll; St
Mich Coll Llan; C St Jas Owton Manor Hartlepool
1973–76; C St Faith Wandsw 1976–78; V 1978–81;

St Jo Walworth 1981–93; RD S'wark and New-ington 1988–93; Adn of Croydon from 1994
Tel: 020–8688 2943 (Home)
020–8681 5496 (Office)
Fax: 020–8686 2074
email: tony.davies@dswark.org.uk

DAVIS, Ven Alan Norman, BA
10 Stainburn Rd, Workington, Cumbria CA14 1SN [ARCHDEACON OF WEST CUMBERLAND] *b* 27 Jul 1938; *educ* K Edw Sch Birm; Dur Univ; Lich Th Coll; C St Luke Kingstanding 1965–68; P-in-c St Paul Ecclesfield CD 1968–73; V St Paul Wordsworth Ave 1973–75; V St Jas and St Chris Shiregreen 1975–80; V Maltby 1980–81; TR Malt-by TM 1981–89; Abp's Officer for UPAs 1990–92; P-in-c St Cuth w St Mary Carlisle and DCO 1992–96; Adn of W Cumberland from 1996; Chmn Dioc BSR
Tel: (01900) 66190
Fax: (01900) 873021

DAWS, Mr Christopher William, MA, FCA, ATII, ACT
Church Commissioners, 1 Millbank, London SW1P 3JZ [FINANCIAL AND DEPUTY SECRETARY , CHURCH COMMISSIONERS] *b* 31 Aug 1947; *educ* Win Coll; Trin Coll Cam; Coopers & Lybrand 1969–79; Cadbury Schweppes 1979–87; Dowty Grp 1987–92; Sycamore Holdings 1993; Dep Sec Finance and Investment) Ch Commrs from 1994
Tel: 020–7898 1786
email: christopher.daws@c-of-e.org.uk

DELANEY, Ven Peter Anthony, AKC
Parish House, 43 Trinity Square, London EC3N 4DJ [ARCHDEACON OF LONDON] *b* 20 Jun 1939; *educ* Hendon Gr Sch; Hornsey Coll of Art; K Coll Lon; St Boniface Coll Warminster; C St Marylebone 1966–70; Chapl Univ Ch of Ch the K 1970–73; Res Can and Prec S'wark Cathl 1973–77; V All Hal-lows by the Tower from 1977; Guild V St Katharine Cree from 1997; Adn of Lon from 1999; M DAC from 1980; M Dioc Communications Ctee from 1994; M Dioc Syn from 1995
GS 1985–90
Tel: 020–7488 2335
Fax: 020–7488 2648
email: archdeacon.london@dlondon.org.uk

DE LANGE, Mrs Anna Margaret, BA, MA
20 Aykley Vale, Durham DH1 5WA [ST ALBANS] *b* 26 Jun 1950; *educ* Newbury Girls Gr Sch; Ex Univ; Sheff Univ; Hants Co Lib Service 1973–77; Staff M Administry 1987–92; Mother; Rdr and M Staff Tm St Andr Woodside 1993–99; M Liturg Commn from 1996; M Coun St Jo Coll Nottm from 1996
GS 1995–
Tel: 0191–383 2704

DENNEN, Ven Lyle, LLB, MA
St Andrew's Vicarage, 5 St Andrew's St, London EC4A 3AB [ARCHDEACON OF HACKNEY] *b* 8 Jan 1942; *educ* Harvard Univ; Trin Coll Cam; Cud-desdon Th Coll; C St Ann S Lambeth 1972–75; C St Mary Richmond 1975–78; P-in-c St Jo Ken-nington 1978–79; V 1979–99; RD Brixton 1990–99; Hon Can S'wark Cathl 1999; Adn of Hackney from 1999; V St Andr Holborn from 1999
Tel: 020–7353 3544

DERBY, Bishop of, Rt Revd Jonathan Sansbury Bailey, MA
Office: Derby Church House, Full St, Derby DE1 3DR, Home: Bishop's House, 6 King St, Duffield, Belper, Derby DE56 4EU b 24 Feb 1940; *educ* Quarry Bank High Sch Liv; Trin Coll Cam; Ridley Hall Th Coll; C Sutton St Helens 1965–68; C St Paul War-rington 1968–71; Warden, Marrick Priory 1971–76; V Wetherby 1976–82; Adn of Southend 1982–92; Bp of Dunwich 1992–95; Bp of Derby from 1995; Clerk of the Closet to HM The Queen from 1996
GS 1988–92, 1995–
Tel: (01332) 346744 (Office)
(01332) 840132 (Home)
Fax: (01332) 295810 (Office)
(01332) 842743 (Home)
email: bishopderby@clara.net

DEUCHAR, Canon Andrew Gilchrist, B TH
Lambeth Palace, London SE1 7JU [SECRETARY FOR ANGLICAN COMMUNION AFFAIRS] *b* 3 Jun 1955; *educ* R Hosp Sch Ipswich; Southn Univ; Sarum and Wells Th Coll; HM Diplomatic Service 1974–81; C SS Mich and Paul Alnwick 1984–88; TV S Wye Hereford 1988–90; Adv Cant and Roch Joint Dioc Coun for Social Responsibility 1990–94; Abp of Cant's Sec for Anglican Com-munion Affairs from 1994; Non Res Can Cant Cathl from 1995
Tel: 020–7928 8282
Fax: 020–7401 9886
email: andrew.deuchar@lampal.c-of-e.org.uk

DEXTER, Canon Frank Robert
Vicarage, St George's Close, Newcastle upon Tyne NE2 2TF [NEWCASTLE] *b* 2 Aug 1940; *educ* Isle-worth Gr Sch; Cuddesdon Th Coll; C H Cross Fenham Newc 1968–71; C Whorlton 1971–73; V Ch Carpenter Pet 1973–80; V St Phil High Els-wick 1980–85; P-in-c St Aug Newc 1985; RD Newc W 1981–85; RD Newc Cen 1985–86; V St Geo Jesmond from 1985; P-in-c St Hilda Jes-mond 1995–98; M Bp's Coun; Chmn Ho of Clergy Dioc Syn from 1993; RD Newc Cen 1994–95
GS 1992–
Tel: 0191–281 1628 (Home)
0191–281 1659 (Office)
Fax: 0191–281 1628

DIBDIN, Mrs Jane Penelope
Hill Top, Park Rd, Bridport, Dorset DT6 5DA [SALISBURY] *b* 25 Feb 1937; *educ* St Mich Sch Limpsfield; Froebel Educl Inst Roehampton; Tchr St Mary's Primary Sch Bridport 1958–60; JP 1973–98; Trustee Pilsdon Community from 1996; M Sarum Dioc Bd for Ch and Society from 1997
GS 1990–
Tel: (01308) 422980

DICKINSON, Ms Jill Susan, BA
34 Chesterfield Rd, St Andrew's, Bristol BS6 5DL
[BRISTOL] *b* 19 Jan 1958; *educ* Plymouth High Sch
for Girls; Bris Univ; Tchr of RE
GS 1990–   *Tel:* 0117–942 9378

DONCASTER, Bishop of [SUFFRAGAN,
SHEFFIELD] **Rt Revd Cyril Guy Ashton,** MA
3 Farrington Court, Wickersley, Rotherham b 6 Apr
1942; *educ* Lanc Univ; Oak Hill Th Coll; C St Thos
Blackpool 1967–70; Voc Sec CPAS 1970–74; V
St Thos Lanc 1974–91; Dioc Dir of Tr Blackb
1991–99; Hon Can Blackb Cathl from 1991; Bp of
Doncaster from 1999   *Tel:* (01709) 512449
                                            Fax:(01709) 512550

DORCHESTER, Bishop of [AREA BISHOP,
OXFORD] Rt Revd Anthony Russell, D PHIL
*Holmby House, Sibford Ferris, Banbury, Oxon OX15
5RG b* 25 Jan 1943; *educ* Uppingham Sch; St Chad's
Coll Dur; Trin Coll Ox; Cuddesdon Th Coll; C
Hilborough Grp of Parishes 1970–73; V of
Preston-on-Stour,   Atherstone-on-Stour   and
Whitchurch 1973–88; Chapl Arthur Rank Centre
(Nat Agric Centre) 1973–82; Dir Arthur Rank Cen
1983–88; Can Th Cov Cathl 1977–88; Chapl to
HM Queen 1983–88; Exam Chapl to Bp of Here-
ford 1983–88; M BMU 1986–88; Bp of Dorchester
from 1988; Vc-Pres R Agric Soc of England from
1991; Commr Rural Development Commn from
1991
GS 1980–88   *Tel:* (01295) 780589/3
                                         Fax: (01295) 788686
     email: bishopdorchester@oxford.anglican.org

DORKING, Bishop of [SUFFRAGAN, GUILDFORD]
Rt Revd Ian James Brackley, MA
*Dayspring, 13 Pilgrims Way, Guildford, Surrey GU4
8AD b* 13 Dec 1947; *educ* Westcliff High Sch; Keble
Coll Ox; Cuddesdon Th Coll; C St Mary Magd w
St Fran Lockleaze Bris 1971–74; Asst Chapl Bry-
anston Sch 1974–77; Chapl 1977–80; V St Mary E
Preston Chich 1980–88; RD Arundel and Bognor
1982–87; TR St Wilfrid Haywards Heath 1988–96;
RD Cuckfield 1989–95; Bp of Dorking from 1996
GS 1990–95   *Tel:* (01483) 570829
                                         Fax: (01483) 567268
     email: bishop.ian@cofeguildford.org.uk

DOVER, Bishop of [SUFFRAGAN, CANTERBURY] Rt
Revd Stephen Squires Venner, BA, MA
*Upway, St Martin's Hill, Canterbury, Kent CT1 1PR
b* 19 Jun 1944; *educ* Hardye's Sch Dorchester; Birm
Univ; Linacre Coll Ox; Lon Inst of Educ; St Steph
Ho Th Coll; C St Pet Streatham 1968–71; Hon C St
Marg Streatham Hill 1971–72; Hon C Ascen Bal-
ham 1972–74; V St Pet Clapham and Bp's Chapl
to Overseas Students 1974–76; V St Jo Trowbridge
1976–82; V H Trin Weymouth 1982–94; M Dorset
LEA 1982–94; Chmn Dioc Bd of Educ Sarum
1989–94; RD Weymouth 1988–94; Non-Res Can

Sarum Cathl 1989–94; Chmn Ho of Clergy Dio
Syn 1993–94; M Gen Syn Bd of Educ from 198?
Chmn VCE Ctee from 1997; Bp of Middleto⬛
1994–99; Chmn Dioc Bd of Educ 1994–99; Bp ⬛
Dover from 1999; Co-Chmn CE/Moravian Co⬛
tact Grp 1994–99; Pres Woodard Corp from 199⬛
GS 1985–94   *Tel:* (01227) 459382 (Office⬛
            Tel and Fax: (01227) 464537 (Hom⬛
                         Fax (01227) 784985 (Offic⬛
     email: Stephen.Venner@btinternet.co⬛

DOW, Mrs Molly Patricia, MA, DIP TH
*173 Willesden Lane, Brondesbury, London NW6 7Y⬛
[LONDON] *b* 23 Sep 1942; *educ* N Lon Collegiat⬛
Sch; St Hilda's Coll Ox; pt Tchr Portway Com⬛
Sch Bris 1966–67; pt Tchr Tonbridge Tech Hig⬛
Sch 1967–68; Rdr from 1970; Supply Tchr Math⬛
ematics Cov 1981–90; M Liturg Commn 1987–9⬛
GS 1985–92, 1995–   *Tel:* 020–8451 124⬛
                                             020–8451 018⬛
                                       Fax: 020–8451 460⬛
     email: molly.dow@btinternet.co⬛

DOWLING, Mr Jeremy Nicholas, DIP ED
*Rosecare Villa Farm, St Gennys, Bude, Cornwa⬛
EX23 0BG* [TRURO] *b* 6 Jul 1938; *educ* Clayesmor⬛
Sch Dorset; Ox Inst of Educ; DCO; Lay Can Trur⬛
Cathl; Smallholder; Radio and TV Interviewer⬛
Commentator/Producer; Rdr
GS 1978–   *Tel:* (01840) 23032⬛
                                       Fax: (01288) 35278⬛

DRAPER, Ven Martin Paul, BA, B TH
*7 rue Auguste-Vacquerie, 75116 Paris, Franc⬛
[ARCHDEACON OF FRANCE] *b* 22 Apr 1950; *edu⬛
Arnold Co High Sch Nottm; Birm Univ; Southr⬛
Univ; Chich Th Coll; C St Mary Primrose Hil⬛
1975–78; C St Matt Westmr 1979–84; Chapl St Ge⬛
Paris from 1984; Adn of France from 1994; Co-
Chmn French ARC from 1984; M Abp of Cant's⬛
Ecum Adv Ctee from 1990; M Conversations
between CE and French Lutheran and Reformed
Chs from 1993   *Tel:* 00–33–1–4720–22–51

DRIVER, Canon Penny (Penelope May)
7 Loxley Grove, Wetherby, W Yorks LS22 7YG
[RIPON] *b* 20 Feb 1952; *educ* Nn Ord Course; Dioc
Youth Adv Newc 1986–88; C St Geo Cullercoats
1987–88; Dioc Youth Chapl Ripon from 1988
GS 1995–   *Tel:* (01937) 585440

DRURY, Very Revd John Henry, BA, MA
The Deanery, Christ Church, Oxford OX1 1DP
[DEAN OF CHRIST CHURCH, OXFORD] *b* 23 May 1936;
educ Trin Hall Cam; Westcott Ho Th Coll; C St
John's Wood Lon 1963–66; Chapl Down Coll Cam
1966–69; Chapl Ex Coll Ox 1969–73; Can Res Nor
Cathl 1973–79; Vc-Dean Nor Cathl 1978–79; Lect
Sussex Univ 1979–81; Dean K Coll Cam 1981–91;
Dean Ch Ch Ox from 1991
                          Tel: (01865) 276162 (Home)
                                   (01865) 276161 (Office)
     email: jan.bolongaro@christ-church.ox.ac.uk

UCKER, Mrs Deirdre Ann Josephine, NDD
The Common, Broughton Gifford, Melksham, Wilts SN12 8ND [SALISBURY] *b* 8 Jul 1935; *educ* Abbotts Hill Sch Hemel Hempstead; Chelsea Sch of Art, Lon Univ; Farel House, L'Abri Fellowship Switzerland; Graphic Artist; Fine Artist; Theatre Designer; M Sarum dio Communications Tm; M Sarum Bd for Ch and Society; Bradf Dny Communications Offcr
GS 1990–   *Tel and Fax:* (01225) 783330
                       email: dducker@dircon.co.uk

DUDLEY, Bishop of [AREA BISHOP, WORCESTER]
Not appointed at time of going to press.]

DUNCAN, Ven John Finch, MBE, MA
22 Westfield Rd, Edgbaston, Birmingham B15 3JQ [ARCHDEACON OF BIRMINGHAM] *b* 9 Sep 1933; *educ* Qu Eliz Gr Sch Wakefield; Univ Coll Ox; Cuddesdon Th Coll; C S Bank Middlesbrough 1959–61; Novice SSF 1961–62; C St Pet Birm 1962–65; Chapl Birm Univ 1965–76; V K Heath Birm 1976–85; Adn of Birm from 1985; M CBF
GS 1990–   *Tel:* 0121–454 3402
                       Fax: 0121–455 6178

DUNNETT, Mrs Ruth Elizabeth, B ED
Shepherd's Fold, Beech Hill, Wadhurst, E Sussex TN5 6JR [CHICHESTER] *b* 12 Feb 1955; *educ* Bromley Gr Sch for Girls; Sussex Univ; OTC; Special Educ and Remedial Supply Tchr Montreal 1977–78; Adult Educ Tutor Montreal 1978–86; Admin 'The Ford' retreat facility for full-time clergy from 1986; Knowle Court Sch Tunbridge Wells 1991; pt and Supply Tchr Bennett Mem Sch Tunbridge Wells from 1995; Student with OTC from 1995; Community Tchr from 1999; M Bp's Coun; M Dioc Ctee for Educ and Tr of Adults
GS 1999–   *Tel:* (01892) 784117
                       Fax: (01892) 784696
              email: 113166.1265@compuserve.com

DUNWICH, Bishop of [SUFFRAGAN, ST EDMUNDSBURY AND IPSWICH] **Rt Revd Clive Young,** BA
28 Westerfield Rd, Ipswich, Suffolk IP4 2UJ b 31 May 1948; *educ* K Edw VI Gr Sch Chelmsf; Dur Univ; Ridley Hall Cam; C Neasden cum Kingsbury 1972–75; C St Paul Hammersmith 1975–79; P-in-c St Paul w St Steph Old Ford 1979–82; V 1982–92; AD Tower Hamlets 1988–92; Adn of Hackney 1992–99; V St Andr Holborn 1992–99; Bp of Dunwich from 1999   *Tel:* (01473) 222276
                       Fax: (01473) 210303

DURHAM, Bishop of, Rt Revd Michael Turnbull, MA, HON D LITT
Auckland Castle, Bishop Auckland, Co Durham DL14 7NR b 27 Dec 1935; *educ* Ilkley Gr Sch; Keble Coll Ox; Cranmer Hall Dur; C Middleton 1960–61; C and Lect Luton Par Ch 1961–65; Dom Chapl to Abp of York and DDO 1965–69; R Heslington and Chapl Univ of York 1969–76; M BMU 1975–85; Chief Sec CA 1976–84; Adn of Roch and Can Res Roch Cathl 1984–88; Bp of Roch 1988–94; Chmn Abps Commn on Organisation of CE; M Cathls Commn 1992–94; Bp of Dur from 1994; M Abps' Coun and Chmn Min Div from 1999; M Legislative Ctee; Select Preacher Univ of Ox 1996
GS 1970–75, 1987–   *Tel:* (01388) 602576
                       Fax: (01388) 605264
                 email: bishdur@btinternet.com

EATON, Revd Julie Elizabeth, DIP HE, SEN (G), SEN (M)
Vange Rectory, 782 Clay Hill Rd, Vange, Basildon, Essex SS16 4NG [CHELMSFORD] *b* 22 Jun 1957; *educ* Beyton Sch Suffolk; Trin Coll Bris; C St Andr Gt Ilford 1989–92; C (NSM) Billericay and Little Burstead TM and pt Hosp Chapl 1992–95; Stipend full time from 1995, V from 1996; Bp of Bradwell's Dny Voc Adv
GS 1995–   *Tel:* (01268) 557332
                       Fax: (01268) 581574

EBBSFLEET, Bishop of [PROVINCIAL EPISCOPAL VISITOR, CANTERBURY] **Rt Revd Michael Alan Houghton,** BA, B TH, PGCE
8 Goldney Ave, Clifton, Bristol BS8 4RA b 14 Jun 1949; *educ* Harold Hill Gr Sch; Lanc Univ; Dur Univ; Chich Th Coll; C All Hallows Wellingborough 1980–84; V Jamestown St Helena 1984–89; Hon Can St Paul's Cathl St Helena from 1994; Tutor Coll of Ascension Selly Oak 1990; V St Pet Folkestone 1990–98; Bp of Ebsfleet from 1998
                       Tel: 0117–973 1752
                       Fax: 0117–973 1762
                email: flybishop@hotmail.com

EDEBOHLS, Ven William Ernest
c/o All Saints' Church, Via Solferino 17, 20121 Milan, Italy [ARCHDEACON OF ITALY AND MALTA] *b* 18 Jun 1954; *educ* Traralgon High Sch; Trin Coll Th Sch Victoria Australia; C S Ballarat 1978; C St Pet Ballarat 1979; V St Jude Timboon 1980–87; Prec Ch the King Cathl Ballarat 1987; Dean of Ballarat 1987–98; Adn of Italy and Malta and Chapl All SS Milan from 1998; M Bp's Coun
                       Tel: 00–39–02–655–2258
                       Fax: 00–39–02–655–2258
                   email: allsaint@tin.it

EDMONTON, Bishop of [AREA BISHOP, LONDON] **Rt Revd Peter William Wheatley,** MA
27 Thurlow Rd, London NW3 5PP b 7 Sep 1947; *educ* Ipswich Sch; Qu Coll Ox; Pemb Coll Cam; Coll of the Resurr Mirf; Ripon Hall Th Coll; C All SS Fulham 1973–78; V H Cross, Cromer St, St Pancras 1978–82; V St Jas W Hampstead, P-in-c St Mary w All So Kilburn 1982–95; Chmn Chr Concern for S Africa 1992–95; Dir POT Edmonton Area 1985–95; M BSR Internat Affairs Ctee 1981–96; Adn of Hampstead 1995–99; Bp of Edmonton from 1999
GS 1975–95   *Tel:* 020–7435 5890
                       Fax: 020–7435 6049
          email: bishop.edmonton@dlondon.org.uk

EDSON, Ven Michael, B SC, BA
13 Stoneygate Ave, Leicester LE2 3HE [ARCH-
DEACON OF LEICESTER] *b* 2 Sep 1942; *educ* Mansfield Tech Sch; Birm Univ; Leeds Univ; Coll of the
Resurr Mirfield; C St Pet w H Trin Barnstaple
1972–77; TV Barnstaple Central 1977–82; V St
Andr Roxbourne 1982–89; P-in-c St Paul Harrow
1987–89; AD Harrow 1985–89; Warden Lee
Abbey 1989–94; Adn of Leic from 1994; Dioc
Missr from 1996   *Tel:* 0116–270 4441
                         Fax: 0116–270 1091
email: medson@leicester.anglican.org

EGAR, J A Judith Anne, MA
1 Millbank, London SW1P 3JZ [ASSISTANT SOLICI-
TOR TO THE GENERAL SYNOD] *b* 7 Feb 1957; *educ*
The Abbey Sch Reading; Somerville Coll Ox;
Solicitor in private practice 1983–85; Ch Commrs
Legal Dept from 1985; Asst Solicitor to the Gen
Syn from 1998; Rdr from 1996 *Tel:* 020–7898 1722
email: judith.egar@c-of-e.org.uk

ELENGORN, Mr Martin David, MA
1 Millbank, London SW1P 3JZ [PASTORAL AND
REDUNDANT CHURCHES SECRETARY, CHURCH
COMMISSIONERS] *b* 17 Sep 1944; *educ* Enfield Gr
Sch; G & C Coll Cam; On staff of Ch Commrs
from 1966; Pastl and Red Chs Sec from 1993
                         Tel: 020–7898 1741
email: martin.elengorn@c-of-e.org.uk

ELLIOTT, Ven Peter, MA
*80 Moorside North, Fenham, Newcastle upon Tyne
NE4 9DU* [ARCHDEACON OF NORTHUMBERLAND]
b 14 Jun 1941; *educ* Qu Eliz Gr Sch Horncastle;
Hertf Coll Ox; Linc Th Coll; C All SS Gosforth
1965–68; C St Pet Balkwell 1968–72; V St Phil
High Elswick 1972–80; V N Gosforth 1980–87; V
Embleton w Rennington and Rock 1987–93; RD
Alnwick 1989–93; Adn of Northumberland from
1993; M Eng Heritage Cathls and Chs Adv Ctee
from 1998; M Heritage Forum from 1998
                         Tel: 0191–273 8245
                         Fax: 0191–226 0286

ELLIS, Mrs Anne
33 Leat Walk, Roborough, Plymouth, Devon PL6 7AT
[EXETER] *b* 27 Aug 1936; *educ* Eccles Gr Sch;
Alsager Tr Coll; Dartington Coll of Arts; Asst
Tchr and Head of Music in primary and second-
ary schools Lancs 1956–64; Notts 1964–67; Cambs
1967–82; Deputy Head Walkhampton C E Pri-
mary School Devon 1984–89; Housewife and
Musician from 1990; M Nat Coun Forward in
Faith
GS 1990–   *Tel:* (01752) 793397
                      Fax: (01752) 774618

ELLIS, Revd Robert Albert, BD, AKC, DIP ED
*The Pump House, Jacks Lane, Marchington,
Uttoxeter, Staffs ST14 8LW* [LICHFIELD] *b* 8 Jul 1948;
educ K Coll Lon; St Aug Coll Cant; Ch Ch Coll
Cant; C Our Lady and St Nic w St Anne Liv

1972–76; P-in-c Meerbrook 1976–80; Produc▪
Relig Progr BBC 1976–80; V All SS Highgate L▪
1980–81; P-in-c Longdon 1981–87; DCO fro▪
1981; M CECC from 1995
GS 1995–   *Tel:* (01283) 820732 (Hom▪
                      (01543) 306030 (Offic▪
                      Fax: (01543) 3060▪
email: info@lichfield.anglican.o▪

ELLIS, Ven Robin Gareth, BCL, MA
33 Leat Walk, Roborough, Plymouth, Devon PL6 7A
[ARCHDEACON OF PLYMOUTH] *b* 8 Dec 1935; *ed▪*
Worksop Coll; Pemb Coll Ox; Chich Th Coll; As▪
C St Pet Swinton 1960–63; Asst Chapl Workso▪
Coll 1963–66; V of Swaffham Prior w Reach, an▪
Asst Dir of Educ Ely dio 1966–74; V St Aug Wi▪
bech 1974–82; V St Paul Yelverton 1982–86; Ad▪
of Plymouth from 1982; M Gen Syn Workin▪
Party on Clerical Discipline from 1995, Impl▪
mentation Grp from 1997; Chmn Catholic Grp i▪
Syn 1995–98; M Appts Ctee from 1998
GS 1980–82, 1994–   *Tel:* (01752) 7933▪
                        Fax: (01752) 77461

ELLOY, Mr Jeremy Andrew
Church House, Great Smith St, London SW1P 3N▪
[HEAD OF FINANCIAL PLANNING AND BUDGET▪
ARCHBISHOPS' COUNCIL] *b* 2 Nov 1951; *educ* Hov▪
Gr Sch; Selw Coll Cam; On staff of Ch Comm▪
1975–94; Seconded to CBF from 1994; Budgetin▪
Officer/Administrative Sec CBF 1994–96; De▪
Sec/Budgeting Officer 1996–98; Hd of Financia▪
Planning and Budgets Abps' Coun from 1999
                        Tel: 020–7898 156▪
email: jerry.elloy@c-of-e.org.u▪

ELY, Bishop of
[Not appointed at time of going to press.]

EMMASON, Mr Stuart Geoffrey
5 Regan St, Halliwell, Bolton BL1 8AR [MANCHE▪
TER] *b* 21 Dec 1973; Fin Dept CMP Batteries Lt▪
from 1990; M Bp's Coun from 1997; M Dioc B▪
of Educ and Children and Youth Ctee from 1994▪
M Dioc Vacancy-in-See Ctee from 1998
GS 1999–   *Tel:* (01204) 493397 (Home▪
                      (01204) 661355 (Office▪
                      Fax: (01204) 658284 (Office▪
email: emmasons@exideuk.co.uk

EPTON, Mrs Joy, MBE, CERT ED
Northolme Hall, Wainfleet PE24 4AE [LINCOLN▪
educ King's Lynn High Sch for Girls; Hockeril▪
Tchr Tr Coll; Cen Pres Girls' Friendly So▪
1990–96; World Chmn Girls' Friendly So▪
1993–96; JP; Angl Rep WWDP Ctee; Chmn Angl▪
Voluntary Socs Forum 1933–95; Rdr from 1999▪
Local Min Wainfleet Grp of Parishes; Dny La▪
Chmn Calcethwaith and Candleshoe 1982–92▪
Vc-Chmn Gov Bp Grosseteste Coll; M Dioc Past▪
Ctee
GS 1995–

JROPE, Bishop of Gibraltar in, Rt Revd John
illiam Hind, BA

shop's Lodge, Church Rd, Worth, Crawley, W Sus-
x RH10 7RT b 19 Jun 1945; *educ* Watford Gr Sch;
eds Univ; Cuddesdon Th Coll; Asst Master
eds Modern Sch 1966–69; Asst Lect K Alfred's
oll Win 1969–70; C Catford, Southend and
ownham 1972–76; V Ch Ch Forest Hill 1976–82;
in-c St Paul Forest Hill 1981–82; Prin Chich Th
oll 1982–91; Bursalis Preb Chich Cathl 1982–91;
o of Horsham 1991–93; Chmn FOAG from 1991;
o of Gibraltar in Europe from 1993; Consultant
CCU; M Ho of Bps Th Grp; M Faith and Order
ommn of WCC
S 1993–   *Tel:* (01293) 883051
                                             Fax: (01293) 884479
                        email: bishop@eurobish.clara.co.uk

JROPE, Suffragan Bishop in, Rt
evd Henry William Scriven, BA, DPS

iocese in Europe, 14 Tufton St, London SW1P 3QZ
30 Aug 1951; *educ* Repton Sch; Sheff Univ; St Jo
oll Nottm; C H Trin Wealdstone 1975–79; SAMS
rgentina 1979–82; Assoc R Ch Ch Little Rock
rkansas 1982–83; SAMS w Spanish Episc
eformed Ch Salamanca Spain 1984–88, Madrid
988–90; Chapl Br Embassy Ch St Geo
ladrid 1990–95; Suff Bp in Europe from 1995
                                             Tel: 020–7976 8001
                                             Fax: 020–7976 8002
                        email: henry@dioeurope.clara.net

VANS, Rt Revd David Richard John, MA

2 Fox Hill, Birmingham B29 4AG [GENERAL SEC-
ETARY, SAMS] *b* 5 Jun 1938; *educ* Ch Hosp; Cam
Jniv; Clifton Th Coll; C Ch Ch Cockfosters
965–68; Asst Pr H Trin Lomas de Zamora
uenos Aires 1969–77; Gen Sec Asociacion Biblic
rgentina Univ 1971–76; Pr Lima Peru 1977–78;
hapl Gd Shep Lima 1977–83; Bp of Peru
978–88, and Bolivia 1982–88; Asst Bp Bradf
988–93; Gen Sec SAMS from 1993; Internat Co-
rdinator EFAC from 1989; Asst Bp Chich from
994–97; Asst Bp Roch 1994–97; Asst Bp Birm
rom 1997; Focal Person of Latin American
orum CCOM 1993–97; Co-ordinator S American
Network PWM from 1995; M BM from 1995; Lic
o officiate in Provinces of Cant and York
                                    Tel: 0121–472 2616 (Office)
                        Tel and *Fax:* 0121–472 5731 (Home)
                                    Fax: 0121–472 7977 (Office)
                        email: SAMSGB@compuserve.com

EVANS, Ven Patrick Alexander Sidney

The Old Rectory, The Street, Pluckley, Kent TN27
)QT [ARCHDEACON OF MAIDSTONE] *b* 28 Jan 1943;
educ Clifton Coll; Linc Th Coll; C Lyonsdown
1973–76; C Royston 1976–78; V Gt Gaddesden
and Dioc Stewardship Adv 1978–82; V Tenterden
w Smallhythe 1982–89; RD W Charing 1988–89;
DDO 1989–94; Adn of Maidstone from 1989;
Chmn Dioc Bd of Miss 1994–96; Chmn Dioc Pastl

Ctee from 1994; Chmn Cant and Roch CSR from
1996
GS 1996–99   *Tel:* (01233) 840291
                                             Fax: (01233) 840759

EVENS, Ven Bob (Robert John Scott), DIP TH,
ACIB

56 Grange Rd, Saltford, Bristol BS31 3AG [ARCH-
DEACON OF BATH] *b* 29 May 1947; *educ* Maidstone
Gr Sch; Trin Coll Bris; C St Simon Southsea
1977–79; C St Mary Portchester 1979–83; V St Jo B
Locks Heath 1983–95; RD Fareham 1993–95; Adn
of Bath from 1995; Chmn Somerset Chs Together
from 1996; Chmn Dioc Coun for Miss from 1999
GS 1994–95   *Tel:* (01225) 873609
                                             Fax: (01225) 874110
                        email: 113145.1175@compuserve.com

EXETER, Bishop of, Rt Revd Michael Laurence
Langrish, B SOC SC, BA, MA

The Palace, Exeter, Devon EX1 1HY b 1 Jul 1946;
educ K Edward Sch Southn; Birm Univ; Fitzw
Coll Cam; Ridley Hall Th Coll; C Stratford-upon-
Avon 1973–76; Chapl Rugby Sch 1976–81; V Off-
church and DDO 1981–87; Exam Chapl to Bp of
Cov 1982–89; Chmn ACCM Vocations Ctee
1984–91; TR Rugby 1987–93; Chmn Ho of Clergy
Dioc Syn 1988–93; Hon Can Cov Cathl 1990–93;
Bp of Birkenhead 1993–2000; M BAGUPA
1996–98; M Urban Bps' Panel from 1996; M BSR
Community and Urban Affairs Ctee from 1998;
Bp of Ex from 2000
GS 1985–93, 1999–

                                             Tel: (01392) 272362
                                             Fax: (01392) 430923

FARRELL, Mr (Michael Geoffrey) Shaun, LIC
IPD

Church House, Great Smith St, London SW1P 3NZ
[FINANCIAL SECRETARY, ARCHBISHOPS' COUNCIL]
b 27 Apr 1950; *educ* Gillingham Gr Sch; On staff of
Ch Commrs from 1969; Stipends and Allocations
Sec 1994–98; Fin Sec Abps' Coun from 1999
                                             Tel: 020–7898 1795
                        email: shaun.farrell@c-of-e.org.uk

FARRINGTON, Canon Christine Marion, BA,
MA, DASS

St Mark's Vicarage, Barton Rd, Cambridge CB3 9JZ
[ELY] *b* 11 Jun 1942; *educ* Cheshunt Gr Sch; Lon
Univ; Nottm Univ; Middx Poly; St Alb Minl Tr
Scheme; Asst Libr 1960–62; Primary Sch Tchr
1962–65; Probation Officer 1967–71; Social Work
Lect 1971–79; Sen Probation Officer 1979–86; Asst
Prison Chapl and Asst Dir of Pastl Studies Linc
Th Coll 1986–87; Dn Sarum Cathl and Dir Sarum
Chr Centre 1987–93; Co-DDO and Dir of
Women's Min from 1993; V St Mark Cam from
1996; Chapl to HM The Queen from 1998; M Bp's
Coun; M Bp's Tm
GS 1985–93, 1995–   *Tel:* (01223) 363339

FELL, Canon Alan William, BA, MA, DIP TH
Vicarage, Loftus Hill, Sedbergh, Cumbria LA10 5SQ
[BRADFORD] *b* 27 Oct 1946; *educ* Man Gr Sch; Ball Coll Ox; Leeds Univ; Coll of the Resurr Mirfield; C Woodchurch Birkenhead 1971–74; C St Cross Clayton Man 1974–75; C St Marg Prestwich 1975–77; V St Thos Hyde 1977–80; R Tattenhall and Handley 1980–86; V Sedbergh, Cautley and Garsdale from 1986; M Bp's Coun; M Synodical Agenda Grp; M Dioc Adv Coun for Min and Tr; M DAC; Hon Can Bradf Cathl from 1996; Chmn Vacancy-in-See Ctee
GS 1994– 　　　　　　　　*Tel:* (01539) 620283

FENWICK, Revd Dr John Robert Kipling, B SC,
BA, M TH, PH D, S TH
Rectory, Rectory Close, Chorley, Lancs PR7 1QW
[BLACKBURN] *b* 17 Apr 1951; *educ* Nelson Thomlinson Gr Sch Wigton; Dur Univ; Nottm Univ; K Coll Lon; St Jo Coll Nottm; C Dalton-in-Furness 1977–80; Lect in Chr Worship Trin Coll Bris 1980–88; Abp of Cant's Asst Sec for Ecum Affairs 1988–92; R Chorley from 1992; M Revision Ctee Clergy Representation Rules (Amendment); Chmn Dioc Chr Unity Ctee; Moderator Chs Together in Chorley 1997–2000
GS 1998– 　　　　*Tel:* (01257) 263114 (Home)
　　　　　　　　　　(01257) 231360 (Office)
　　　　　　　　　　Fax: (01257) 231374

FERGUSON, Mr John William
1 Millbank, London SW1P 3JZ [HEAD OF INFORMATION TECHNOLOGY AND OFFICE SERVICES, ARCHBISHOPS' COUNCIL] *b* 23 Dec 1947; *educ* Jo Watson's Sch Edin; Computer Services Manager Matthew Hall Grp 1981; Computer Services Manager Ch Commrs from 1981; Computer and Office Services Manager from 1994; Hd of Information Technology and Office Services Abps' Coun from 1998 　　　　　　　　*Tel:* 020–7898 1640
　　　email: john.ferguson@c-of-e.org.uk

FIFE, Revd Janet Heather, BA, CERT TH, M PHIL
2 Hilton Drive, Prestwich, Manchester M25 9NN
[MANCHESTER] *b* 19 Oct 1953; *educ* Washington Elementary Sch, Illinois; Herrick Jun High Sch; NE Jun High Sch Gainsville, Florida; Univ of California; Sussex Univ; Man Univ; Wycliffe Hall Th Coll; Editorial Asst Kingsway Publications 1977–80; Eastbourne Bible Centre 1980–84; Chapl Bradf Cathl 1987–89; Par Dn St Mich-le-Belfrey 1989–92; Chapl Salford Univ from 1992; Sec Bradf Dioc Ctee for Career Structure of Women Clergy 1987; M Nat Stg Ctee Chapls in HE 1992–95; M Dioc Liturg Ctee 1994–99; Trustee Direction Mime Trust from 1991
GS 1999– 　　　*Tel:* 0161–773 9408 (Home)
　　　　　　　　　0161–295 4660 (Office)
　　　　　　　email: jfife@nildram.co.uk

FILBY, Ven William Charles Leonard
The Archdeaconry, Itchingfield, W Sussex RH13 7NX
[ARCHDEACON OF HORSHAM] *b* 21 Jan 1933; *educ*

Ashford Co Gr Sch; Lon Univ; Oak Hill Th Co V H Trin Richmond 1965–71; V Bp Hanningte Mem Ch Hove 1971–79; R Broadwater 1979–8 RD Worthing 1980–83; Hon Can of Chich Cat 1981–83; Pres Chic Dio Ev Union 1978–84; Chn Redcliffe Missry Tr Coll 1970–92; M Keswi Convention Coun 1973–90; Chmn Trustees Di ine Healing Miss Crowhurst 1987–91; Adn Horsham from 1983; Chmn Dioc Ctee for Mi and Renewal 1987–92; Chmn Sussex Chs Broa casting Ctee 1984–95; Bp's Adv for Hosp Chap 1986–97; Govnr St Mary's Hall, Brighton fro 1984; Gov Univ Coll Chich (formerly W Susse Inst of HE) from 1985; Chmn Dioc Ind Miss Ac Panel from 1989; Chmn Dioc ACORA Grp fro 1997
GS 1975–90 　　　　　*Tel:* (01403) 7903٭
　　　　　　　　　　Fax: (01403) 7911٤

FISHER, Mrs Nicolete Anne, BA
7 Northorpe Lane, Thurlby, Bourne, Lincs PE10 0H [LINCOLN] *b* 10 Dec 1948; *educ* Croydon High Sc for Girls; Kent Univ; Research Asst St Thos Hos Lon 1970–73; Personnel/Ind Relations Office Perkins Engines 1973–80; pt Personnel Consul ant RDA Consultancy 1988–90; pt Personne Manager British Sugar 1990–91; pt Personnel Prc jects Manager Berisford from 1991; M Bp's Cou
GS 1995– 　　　　　　　*Tel:* (01778) 42395

FISHER, Mrs (Rita) Elizabeth, BA, M ED, PGCE
71 Farquhar Rd, Edgbaston, Birmingham B15 2Q [BIRMINGHAM] *b* 16 Nov 1946; *educ* Wolsinghar Sch; Dur Univ; Ox Univ; Hull Univ; Tchr New bury Girls' Gr Sch 1969–70; Tchr Pilgrim Sch Bed 1970–72; Adult Educ Officer Linc Dio 1980–84 Asst Dir/Project Officer N England Inst for Ch Educ 1984–91; Dir of Studies NE Ord Cours 1989–91; M Panel of Chairmen 1989–91; M ABM 1986–96; M Heref Commn from 1993; IMEC 1994–98; M CCU from 1996; Vc-Chair CCU; Hor Moderator Abps' Diploma for Rdrs 1994–98 Chair Birm Dioc Bd of Educ; M Bp's Coun; p Lect
GS 1985– 　　　*Tel* and *Fax:* 0121–452 261٤

FLEMING, Ven David
'Fair Haven', 123 Wisbech Rd, Littleport, Cambs CB٭ 1JJ [CHAPLAIN GENERAL OF PRISONS AND ARCH DEACON] *b* 8 Jun 1937; *educ* K Edw VII Gr Sch King's Lynn; Kelham Th Coll; Asst C St Marg Walton-on-Hill Liv 1963–67; Attached Sandring ham Grp of Chs 1967–68; V Gt Staughton and Chapl Gaynes Hall Borstal 1968–76; RD St Neots 1972–76; V Whittlesey 1976–85; P-in-c Ponders bridge 1983–85; Chmn Ho of Clergy Dioc Syn 1982–85; RD March 1977–82; V Wisbech St Mary 1985–88; Hon Can Ely Cathl from 1982; Adn of Wisbech 1985–93; Chapl Gen of HM Prisons and Adn of Prisons from 1993; Chapl to HM The Queen from 1995
GS 1990– 　　　*Tel:* (01353) 862498 (Home)
　　　　　　　　　020–7217 5683 (Office)
　　　　　　　Fax: 020–7217 5090 (Office)

FLETCHER, Canon Colin William, MA
7 The Cottages, Lambeth Palace, London SE1 7JU
[DOMESTIC CHAPLAIN TO THE ARCHBISHOP OF
CANTERBURY] *b* 17 Nov 1950; *educ* Marlborough
Coll; Trin Coll Ox; Wycliffe Hall Th Coll; C St Pet
Shipley 1975–79; Tutor Wycliffe Hall and C St
Andr Ox 1979–84; V H Trin Margate 1984–93; RD
Thanet 1988–93; Dom Chapl to Abp of Cant from
1993   *Tel:* 020–7928 8282
                                            Fax: 020–7261 9836

FLETCHER, Revd Jeremy James, BA, MA, DIP TH
Vicarage, Mansfield Rd, Skegby, Notts NG17 3ED
[SOUTHWELL] *b* 31 Jul 1960; *educ* Woodhouse
Grove Sch Bradf; Univ Coll Dur; St Jo Coll Nottm;
Eng Tchr Belper High Sch 1982–85; C All SS
Stranton, Hartlepool 1988–91; Assoc Min St Nic
Nottm 1991–94; P-in-c Skegby from 1994 and P-
in-c Teversal from 1996; Chair Dioc Liturg Ctee;
M Coun St Jo Coll Nottm; M Liturg Commn from
1998
GS 1995–   *Tel* and *Fax:* (01623) 558800
                            email: RevJFletch@aol.com

FLETCHER, Mrs Sheila Evelyn, BA, DIP TH, CERT
ED
*11 Troarn Way, Chudleigh, Newton Abbot, Devon
TQ13 0PP* [EXETER] *b* 22 Oct 1946; *educ* Warling-
ham Sch; Leeds Univ; Nottm Univ; Ex Dioc
FLAME Adv from 1989; Rdr from 1994; M Bp's
Coun and Stg Ctee; M Dioc Syn; M FLAME Ctee
GS 1995–   *Tel* and *Fax:* (01626) 853998

FORD, Canon John Frank
*27 Gatesmead, Haywards Heath, W Sussex RH16
1SN* [CHICHESTER] *b* 14 Jan 1952; *educ* Chich Th
Coll; C Ch Ch Forest Hill 1979–82; V St Aug Lee
1982–91; V Lower Beeding 1991–94; Dom Chapl
to Bp of Horsham 1991–94; Dioc Missr from 1994;
Can and Preb Chich Cathl from 1997
GS 1999–   *Tel* and *Fax:* (01444) 414658

FOREMAN, Mrs Anne (Antoinette Joan), CYCW
*Aldersley Place, 48 London Rd, Guildford, Surrey
GU1 2AL* [GUILDFORD] *b* 8 Jun 1943; *educ* Teign-
mouth Gr Sch; Bradf and Ilkley Community Coll;
Youth Worker Sutton and Kingston 1983–88;
Asst Prin Youth and Community Officer Lon
Boro of Sutton 1988–90; Nat Youth Officer Gen
Syn Bd of Educ 1991–94; M Adv Coun Com-
munity and Youth Work Course Goldsmiths Coll
1989–91; External Examiner B Ed Fieldwork St
Martin's Coll Lancaster 1991–93; M Dioc Syn
from 1997; M Dioc Bd of Educ from 1997; M Bp's
Coun from 1997
GS 1999–   *Tel:* (01483) 576855

FORRESTER, Revd James Oliphant, MA
*Vicarage, 230 The Wheel, Ecclesfield, Sheffield S35
9ZB* [SHEFFIELD] *b* 8 Oct 1950; *educ* Bradfield Coll;
SS Coll Cam; Wycliffe Hall Th Coll; C St Jo New-
land Hull 1976–80; C Fulwood Sheff 1980–87; V St
Luke Lodge Moor 1987–90; V St Mary Ecclesfield

from 1990; AD Ecclesfield from 1999; M Dioc
Pastl Ctee
GS 1995–   *Tel:* 0114–257 0002

FOSTER, Revd Stephen Arthur
*St Matthew's Vicarage, 99 Chatham St, Stockport
SK3 9EG* [CHESTER] *b* 7 Mar 1954; *educ* Coll of Res-
urr Mirfield; C H Trin Ches 1978–82; C St Paul w
St Luke Tranmere 1982–83; V St Andr Grange
1983–88; V All SS Cheadle Hulme 1988–94; P-in-c
St Matt Stockport from 1994; Asst DDO from
1996
GS 1998–   *Tel:* 0161–480 5515

FOWELL, Revd Graham Charles, B TH
*Vicarage, Lymer Rd, Oxley, Wolverhampton WV10
6AA* [LICHFIELD] *b* 17 Dec 1948; *educ* Southn Univ;
Chich Th Coll; C Clayton 1982–86; C Uttoxeter w
Bramshall 1986–70; V Oxley from 1990
GS 1995–   *Tel:* (01902) 783342

FOX, Ven Michael John, B SC
86 Aldersbrook Rd, Manor Park, London E12 5DH
[ARCHDEACON OF WEST HAM] *b* 28 Apr 1942; *educ*
Barking Abbey Gr Sch; Hull Univ; Mirfield Th
Coll; C St Eliz Becontree 1966–70; C H Trin S
Woodford 1970–72; V Ascen Victoria Docks
1972–76; V All SS Chelmsf 1976–88; P-in-c Ascen
Chelmsf 1985–88; RD Chelmsf 1986–88; R St Jas
Colchester 1988–93; Adn of Harlow 1993–96; Adn
of W Ham from 1996   *Tel:* 020–8989 8557
                                    Fax: 020–8530 1311
email: a.westham@chelmsford.anglican.org

FRAYNE, Very Revd David, MA, DIP TH
*The Provost's House, Preston New Rd, Blackburn
BB2 6PS* [PROVOST OF BLACKBURN] *b* 19 Oct 1934;
educ Reigate Gr Sch; St Edm Hall Ox; Qu Coll
Birm; C E Wickham 1960–63; P-in-c St Barn
Downham 1963–67; V N Sheen 1967–73; R Cater-
ham 1973–83; RD Caterham 1981–83; Hon Can
S'wark Cathl 1982–83; Can Emer from 1983; V St
Mary Redcliffe w Temple Bris and St Jo B Bed-
minster 1983–92; RD Bedminster 1986–92; Hon
Can Bris Cathl from 1991; Prov of Blackb from
1992; Ch Commr 1994–98; M Red Chs Ctee from
1999
GS 1987–90   *Tel:* (01254) 52502 (Home)
                                    (01254) 51491 (Office)
                                    Fax: (01254) 689666
email: provost@blackburn.anglican.org

FREEMAN, Mrs Jenifer Jane, SRN, SCM
*Lavender Cottage, Harkstead, Ipswich, Suffolk IP9
1BN* [ST EDMUNDSBURY AND IPSWICH] *b* 12 Dec
1937; *educ* St Brandon's Sch Clevedon; Staff
Midwife Gosport 1961–62; Nat Childbirth Trust
Tchr 1964–89; Lay Chmn Samford Dny Syn
1979–88; Wife and Mother; M Bp's Coun from
1983; M Dioc Patronage Ctee; Bp's Visitor; M
Transitional Cathl Coun
GS 1985–   *Tel:* (01473) 328381

FROST, Ven George, MA
24 The Close, Lichfield, Staffs WS13 7LD [ARCH-
DEACON OF LICHFIELD] *b* 4 Apr 1935; *educ* Westcliff
High Sch; Hatf Coll Dur; Linc Th Coll; C Barking
1960–64; C-in-c Marks Gate CD 1964–70; V Tipton
1970–77; V Penn 1977–87; RD Trysull 1984–87;
Preb Lich Cathl 1985–87; Adn of Salop and V
Tong 1987–98; Adn of Lichf from 1998
GS 1988–99 *Tel:* (01543) 306145/6
Fax: (01543) 306147

FRY, Revd Barry James, ACIB
*St Barnabas' Vicarage, 12 Rose Rd, Southampton,
Hants SO14 6TE* [WINCHESTER] *b* 8 May 1949; *educ*
Ripon Coll Cuddesdon; C Highcliffe w Hinton
Admiral 1983–87; V St Barn Southn from 1987;
Regional Dean Forward in Faith E Wessex
GS 1990– *Tel and Fax:* 023–8022 3107

FRY, Ms Christine Ann, BA, DIP SOC WORK
7 Merryfield, Chineham, Basingstoke RG24 8XW
[WINCHESTER] *b* 12 Jul 1964; *educ* Arden Sch
Knowle; Solihull Sixth Form Coll; Southn Univ;
Middx Poly; Family Court Welfare Officer from
1995
GS 1995– *Tel:* (01256) 474466

FULHAM, Bishop of [SUFFRAGAN, LONDON] **Rt
Revd John Charles Broadhurst,** STH, AKC
26 Canonbury Park South, London N1 2FN b 20
Jul 1942; *educ* Owen's Sch Lon; K Coll Lon; St
Boniface Th Coll Warminster; C St Michael-at-
Bowes 1966–70; P-in-c St Aug Wembley Pk
1970–75; V 1975–85; M Stg Ctee Ho of Clergy
1981–88; AD Brent 1982–85; AD Haringey E
1986–92; M Panel of Chairmen 1981–84; M Coun
Corp of Ch Ho 1980–90; TR Wood Green 1985–96;
Bp of Fulham from 1996; M Gen Syn Stg Ctee
1988–96; Pro-Prolocutor Conv of Cant 1990–96;
Chmn Dioc Ho of Clergy 1986–96; M Legal Aid
Commn 1991–96; M Fees Adv Commn 1991–96;
Delegate WCC Canberra 1991; M ACC from 1991;
M CTE; Delegate CEC Prague 1992; Nat Chmn
Forward in Faith
GS 1973–96 *Tel:* 020–7354 2334
Fax: 020–7354 2335
email: bpfulham@compuserve.com

FULLARTON, Mr Derek, FRSA
Lambeth Palace, London SE1 7JU [ADMINISTRATIVE
SECRETARY TO THE ARCHBISHOP OF CANTERBURY]
b 3 Apr 1952 *Tel:* 020–7898 1200
Fax: 020–7261 9836
email: derek.fullarton@lampal.c-of-e.org.uk

FURNELL, Very Revd Raymond
The Deanery, York YO1 2JQ [DEAN OF YORK] *b* 18
May 1935; *educ* Hinchley Wood Sch; Brasted
Place and Linc Th Coll; C St Luke's Cannock
1965–69; V St Jas Clayton 1969–75; R Hanley TM
and RD N Stoke 1975–1981; Prov of St Eds

1981–94; Dean of York from 1994; Chmn Assn o<
English Cathls; Chmn CCC
GS 1989– *Tel:* (01904) 62360<
email: R.Furnell@btinternet.com

GARBETT, Mr (George) James, MA, MA (ED),
PGCE
Annandale, 72 Scotforth Rd, Lancaster LA1 4S<
[BLACKBURN] *b* 20 Feb 1931; *educ* Blackpool Gr Sch;
St Jo Coll Cam; Ball Coll Ox; Leeds Univ; English
Master Bolton Sch 1958–67, Sen English Master
1964–67; Dean of Initial Tchr Educ St Martin's
Coll Lancaster 1975–89, Asst Prin (Academic)
1989–93; Rdr from 1990; Rtd; M Dioc Syn; M Dioc
Bd of Educ, Chmn Schs Ctee; Lay Chair Lancaster
Dny Syn
GS 1995– *Tel:* (01524) 65746
email: jim@annandale72.freeserve.co.uk

GARDEN, Mr Ian Harrison, LL B
*Old Church Cottage, 29 Church Rd, Rufford,
Ormskirk, Lancs L40 1TA* [BLACKBURN] *b* 18 Jun
1961; *educ* Sedbergh Sch; Univ Coll of Wales Abth;
Barrister from 1989; M Bp's Coun from 1996;
M Legislative Ctee from 1996; M Initiation Ser-
vices Revision Ctee; M Appeals Tribunal Panel
Pastl Measure 1983 and Incumbents (Vacation of
Benefices) Measure 1977; M Appeals Tribunal
Panel Ord of Women (Financial Provisions)
Measure 1993; Guardian, Nat Shrine of Our Lady
Walsingham from 1996; M Crown Appts Commn
from 1997
GS 1995– *Tel:* 0151–709 4222 (Office)
(01704) 821303 (Home)
Fax: 0151–708 6311

**GARLICK, Prebendary Kay (Kathleen
Beatrice),** BA, CERT ED
Birch Lodge, Much Birch, Hereford HR2 8HT [HERE-
FORD] *b* 26 Feb 1949; *educ* Prendergast Gr Sch Cat-
ford; Leeds Univ; Birm Univ; Glouc Sch of Min;
Hon C Much Birch w Lt Birch, Much Dewchurch
etc from 1990; Ecum Chapl Heref Sixth Form Coll
from 1996
GS 1995– *Tel:* (01981) 540666

GARNETT, Ven David Christopher, BA, MA
Vicarage, Baslow, Bakewell, Derbys DE45 1RY
[ARCHDEACON OF CHESTERFIELD] *b* 26 Sep 1945;
educ Giggleswick Sch; Nottm Univ; Fitzw Coll
Cam; Westcott Ho Th Coll; C Cottingham
1969–72; Chapl and Fell Selw Coll Cam 1972–77;
Pastl Adv Newnham Coll Cam 1972–77; R Pat-
terdale 1977–80; DDO Carlisle 1977–80; V Heald
Green 1980–87; Chapl St Ann's Hospice
1980–87; R Christleton 1987–92; TR Ellesmere Port
1992–96; Adn of Chesterfield from 1996; Chmn
Bp's Th Adv Grp 1987–93; Chmn Assn of Ch Fel-
lowships from 1987–92
GS 1990–96 *Tel:* (01246) 583928
Fax: (01246) 583949

GATFORD, Ven Ian, AKC
72 Pastures Hill, Littleover, Derby DE23 7BB

ARCHDEACON OF DERBY] *b* 15 Jun 1940; *educ* Dray-on Manor Gr Sch Hanwell; K Coll Lon; St Boniface Coll Warminster; C St Mary Clifton Nottm 1967–71; TV H Trin Clifton 1971–75; V St Martin Sherwood 1975–84; Can Res Derby Cathl from 1984; Sub Provost Derby Cathl 1990–93; Adn of Derby from 1993

GS 1995–   *Tel:* (01332) 382233 (Office)
(01332) 512700 (Home)
Fax: (01332) 292969 (Office)
(01332) 523332 (Home)

GATHERCOLE, Ven John Robert, MA
5 Worcester Rd, Droitwich, Worcs WR9 8AA [ARCHDEACON OF DUDLEY] *b* 23 Apr 1937; *educ* Judd Sch Tonbridge; Fitzw Coll Cam; Ridley Hall Th Coll; C St Nic Dur 1962–66; C St Bart Croxdale 1966–70; Soc and Ind Adv to Bp of Dur 1967–70; Ind Chapl Worc 1970–87; RD Bromsgrove 1978–85; Tm Ldr Worc Ind Miss 1985–91; Hon Can Worc Cathl from 1980; Adn of Dudley from 1987; Chmn Dioc Ho of Clergy 1991–98; M Elections Review Grp from 1997; M CCC from 1998

GS 1995–   *Tel* and *Fax:* (01905) 773301

GAWEDA, Mr Ian, AMCA, AMCT
12 Hartslade, Lichfield, Staffs   WS14 9RH [LICHFIELD] *b* 1 Oct 1951; *educ* W Bromwich Gr Sch; William Booth Memorial Coll; Salvation Army Officer 1981–84; Asst Dioc Sec (Finance) from 1991

GS 1998–

GEM, Dr Richard David Harvey, MA, PH D, FSA, MIFA
Fielden House, 13 Little College St, London SW1P 3SH [SECRETARY, CATHEDRALS FABRIC COMMISSION] *b* 10 Jan 1945; *educ* Eastbourne Coll; Peterho Cam; Inspector of Ancient Monumentss and Historic Buildings Dept of Environment 1970–80; Research Officer CCC and Cathls Adv Commn 1981–88; Sec Cathls Adv Commn 1988–91; Sec Cathls Fabric Commn from 1991

Tel: 020–7898 1887
Fax: 020–7898 1881
email: richard.gem@c-of-e.org.uk

GERRARD, Ven David Keith Robin, BA
Home: 68 North Side, Wandsworth Common, London SW18 2QX; Office: Whitelands Coll, West Hill, London SW15 3SN [ARCHDEACON OF WANDSWORTH] *b* 15 Jun 1939; *educ* Guildf R Gr Sch; St Edm Hall Ox; Linc Th Coll; C St Olave Woodberry Down 1963–66; C St Mary Primrose Hill 1966–69; V St Paul Newington 1969–79; V St Mark Surbiton 1979–89; Adn of Wandsworth from 1989; Ch Commr from 1995, M Pastl Ctee from 1996

GS 1993–   *Tel* and *Fax:* 020–8874 5766 (Home)
Tel: 020–8392 3742 (Office)
Fax: 020–8392 3743 (Office)
email: david.gerrard@dswark.org.uk

GIBSON, Ven (George) Granville
2 Etherley Lane, Bishop Auckland, Co Durham DL14 7QR [ARCHDEACON OF AUCKLAND] *b* 28 May 1936; *educ* Qu Eliz Gr Sch Wakef; Barnsley Coll of Techn; Cuddesdon Th Coll; C St Paul Cullercoats 1971–73; TV Cramlington 1973–77; V St Clare Newton Aycliffe 1977–85; M Broadcasting Panel of CECC 1981–85; R St Mich w St Hilda Bishopwearmouth 1985–90; M Panel of Assessors York Conv 1980–90; M BSR 1987–90; Chmn Dioc Ho of Clergy 1985–91; RD Wearmouth 1985–93; R Sunderland TM 1990–93; M Communications Ctee 1991–93; M Bp's Coun; Hon Can Dur Cathl from 1988; Ch Commr from 1991, Bd of Govs from 1993, M Gen Purposes Ctee from 1993; Trustee Ch Urban Fund from 1991; Adn of Auckland from 1993; Chmn Dioc Pastl Ctee from 1993; Chmn DBF from 1995; M Conditions of Service Working Party 1992–95; M Panel of Assessors York Conv from 1995; Chmn CUF Grants Ctee from 1997; Stavrofor in Romanian Orthodox Ch from 1997

GS 1980–   *Tel:* (01388) 451635
Fax: (01388) 607502
email:
Archdeacon.of.Auckland@durham.anglican.org

GIBSON, Ven Terence Allen, MA
99 Valley Rd, Ipswich, Suffolk IP1 4NF [ARCHDEACON OF IPSWICH] *b* 23 Oct 1937; *educ* Boston Gr Sch; Jes Coll Cam; Cuddesdon Th Coll; C St Chad, Kirkby, Liv 1963–66; Wrdn Cen 63 Kirkby 1966–75; Area Yth Chapl 1966–72; TV for Yth Work Kirkby 1972–75; R Kirkby 1975–84; RD Walton 1979–84; Adn of Suffolk 1984–87; Adn of Ipswich from 1987

GS 1990–   *Tel:* (01473) 250333
Fax: (01473) 286877

GIDDINGS, Dr Philip James, MA, D PHIL
5 Clifton Park Rd, Caversham, Reading, Berks RG4 7PD [OXFORD] *b* 5 Apr 1946; *educ* Sir Thomas Rich's Sch Glouc; Worc and Nuff Colls Ox; Lect in Public Admin Ex Univ 1970–72; Sen Lect in Politics Reading Univ; Rdr; M Dioc Syn from 1974; M Bp's Coun from 1979; Lay Vc-Pres Dioc Syn from 1989; M BSR 1991–96, Exec Ctee 1992–96; M Crown Appts Commn 1992–97; M Gen Syn Panel of Chairmen 1995–96; Vc-Chmn Dioc Ho of Laity from 1995; M Abps' Coun from 1999; Chair Ch and World Division Abps' Coun from 1999; M Crown Appts Commn Review Grp from 1999

GS 1985–   *Tel:* 0118–954 3892 (Home)
0118–931 8207 (Office)
Fax: 0118–975 3833
email: P.J.Giddings@reading.ac.uk

GILBERT, Mr Tom
104 Church Rd, Gorleston, Great Yarmouth NR31 6LS [NORWICH] *b* 25 Apr 1934; *educ* Ruskin Coll Ox; Newc Univ; Social Responsibility Officer Nor BSR from 1981

GS 1998–   *Tel:* (01493) 604220

GILLINGHAM, Mr (George) Michael, B SC, AKC, PGCE
5 Feversham Way, Taunton, Som TA2 8SD [BATH AND WELLS] *b* 15 Oct 1949; *educ* Weston-super-Mare Gr Sch; K Coll Lon; Tchr Bp Fox's Community Sch from 1971; M Bp's Coun; M Dioc Coun for Min
GS 1990–   *Tel:* (01823) 270044
             email: mike@ggillingham.freeserve.co.uk

GILLINGS, Ven Richard John, BA
Vicarage, Robins Lane, Bramhall, Stockport SK7 2PE [ARCHDEACON OF MACCLESFIELD] *b* 17 Sep 1945; *educ* Sale Co Gr Sch; St Chad's Coll Dur; Linc Th Coll; C St Geo Altrincham 1970–75; P-in-c St Thos Stockport 1975–77; R St Thos Stockport 1977–83 and P-in-c St Pet's Stockport 1978–83; R Priory Tm Par Birkenhead 1983–93; RD Birkenhead 1985–93; Hon Can Ches Cathl 1992–94; V St Mich Bramhall from 1993; Adn of Macclesfield from 1994
GS 1980–   *Tel:* 0161–439 2254
                                         Fax: 0161–439 0878

GILPIN, Ven Richard Thomas
Blue Hills, Bradley Rd, Bovey Tracey, Newton Abbot TQ13 9EU [ARCHDEACON OF TOTNES] *b* 25 Jul 1939; *educ* Ashburton Coll; Lich Th Coll; C Whipton 1963–66; C Tavistock and Gulworthy 1966–69; V 1973–91; V Swimbridge 1969–73; Preb Ex Cathl from 1982; Sub-Dean Ex Cathl from 1992; RD Tavistock 1987–90; DDO 1990–91; Adv for Voc and DDO 1991–96; Sub-Dean Ex Cathl 1992–96; Adn of Totnes from 1996
GS 1995–   *Tel:* (01626) 832064
                                         Fax: (01626) 834947

GLOUCESTER, Bishop of, Rt Revd David Edward Bentley, BA
Bishopscourt, Pitt St, Gloucester GL1 2BQ b 7 Aug 1935; *educ* Gt Yarmouth Gr Sch; Leeds Univ; Westcott Ho Th Coll; C St Ambrose Bris 1960–62; C H Trin w St Mary Guildf 1962–66; R Headley, Bordon 1966–73; R Esher 1973–86; RD Emly 1977–82; Hon Can Guildf Cathl 1980–86; Chmn Guildf Dioc CSR 1980–86; Chmn Guildf Dioc Ho of Clergy 1977–86; Bp of Lynn 1986–93; Chmn ACCM Candidates Ctee 1987–93; M ABM and Bp's Ctee for Min from 1987; Bp of Glouc from 1993; Chmn ABM Min Development and Deployment Ctee 1995–98; Vc-Chmn ABM 1995–98; Chmn DRACSC from 1999
GS 1993–   *Tel:* (01452) 524598
                                         Fax: (01452) 310025
                             email: bshpglos@star.co.uk

GNANADOSS, Miss Vasantha Berla Kirubaibai, B SC
242 Links Rd, London SW17 9ER [SOUTHWARK] *b* 25 Jun 1951; *educ* Portsm S Gr Sch; Birkbeck Coll Lon; Strategic Co-ordination Grp of Metropolitan Police Service
GS 1990–   *Tel:* 020–8769 3515

GODFREY, Mr Paul Alexander, MA, PGCE
15 Irwin Rd, Bedford MK40 3UL [ST ALBANS] *b* May 1957; *educ* K Edw VI Sch Southn; St Edm Hall Ox; Scripture Union Evang from 1991
GS 1995–   *Tel:* (01234) 34286.
             email: paulg@scriptureunion.org.uk

GOLDIE, Ven David, MA
60 Wendover Rd, Aylesbury HP21 9LW [ARCH DEACON OF BUCKINGHAM] *b* 20 Dec 1946; *educ* Glas Academy; Glas Univ; Fitzw Coll Cam; Westcott Ho Th Coll; C Ch Ch Swindon 1970–73; C Troor 1973–75; Mission Priest Irvine New Town and I Ardrossan 1975–82; Priest Missr Milton Keynes 1982–86; RD Milton Keynes 1986–90; V Ch the Cornerstone Milton Keynes 1986–98; Borough Dean Milton Keynes 1990–98; Chmn Ho of Clergy Dioc Syn 1991–98; M Local Unity Ctee from 1993; M CTE and CTBI from 1996; Adn of Buckingham from 1998
GS 1990–   *Tel:* (01296) 423269
                                         Fax: (01296) 397324
             email: archdbuc@oxford.anglican.org

GOLDING, Ven Simon Jefferies, QHC
Room 201, Victory Building, HM Naval Base, Portsmouth PO1 3LS [ARCHDEACON FOR THE ROYAL NAVY] *b* 30 Mar 1946; *educ* Bp's Sch Poona; HMS Conway; Brasted Place Th Coll; Linc Th Coll; C Wilton 1974–77; Chapl RN from 1977; Chapl of the Fleet and Adn for the Royal Navy 1997–98; Adn for the Royal Navy from 1998
GS 1997–   *Tel:* 023–9272 7904
                                         Fax: 023–9272 7112

GOOD, Ven Kenneth Roy, BD, AKC
62 Palace Rd, Ripon, N Yorks HG4 1HA [ARCHDEACON OF RICHMOND] *b* 28 Sep 1941; *educ* Stamford Sch; K Coll Lon; St Boniface Coll Warminster; C St Pet Stockton on Tees 1967–70; Miss to Seamen Chapl Antwerp 1970–74; Kobe 1974–79; Asst Gen Sec Miss to Seamen 1979–85; Hon Can Kobe from 1985; V Nunthorpe 1985–93; RD Stokesley 1989–93; Adn of Richmond from 1993   *Tel* and *Fax:* (01765) 604342

GORE, Mr Philip, BA, M I MGT
12 Ellesmere Rd, Morris Green, Bolton BL3 3JT [MANCHESTER] *b* 15 Nov 1957; *educ* Smithills Gr Sch Bolton; Hull Univ; Chmn Philip Gore (Bolton) Ltd from 1981; Dir Silverwood Forestry Ltd from 1991; pt Tutor and Lect; M Bp's Coun; DBF, Trust and Fin Ctee; M Dioc Bd of Min; M Dioc Bd of Patronage; M Ch Soc Trust from 1988; Lay Chmn Deane Dny Syn from 1990; Chmn Makerfield Conservative Assn from 1992; M Dios Commn 1991–95; M Coun Ch Soc; M BSR Exec from 1996; JP
GS 1985–   *Tel:* (01204) 63798 (Home)
                     (01204) 363000 and 524262 (Office)
                                         Fax: (01204) 659750
             email: 106071.2156@compuserve.com

GRANGER, Mrs Penelope Ruth, BA, CERT ED
3 Chesterton Towers, Cambridge CB4 1DZ [ELY] *b* 14
Jul 1947; *educ* Nor High Sch for Girls; Univ of
Sheff; UEA; Lucy Cavendish Coll Cam; Post-
graduate Student; M Gen Syn Stg Ctee 1985–90
and 1991–95; Ch Commr 1983–98; M Ord of
Women Steering Ctee 1987–94; M CTBI
Assembly; M CTE Forum; M Coun Westcott Ho;
Lay Vc-Pres Dioc Syn 1988–97; M Dioc Liturg
Ctee
GS 1980–   *Tel:* (01223) 354961
            email: p.r.granger@dial.pipex.com

GRANTHAM, Bishop of [SUFFRAGAN, LINCOLN]
Rt Revd Alastair Llewellyn John Redfern, MA
Fairacre, 243 Barrowby Rd, Grantham, Lincs NG31
8NP b 1 Sep 1948; *educ* Bicester Sch; Ch Ch Ox;
Trin Coll Cam; Westcott Ho Th Coll; C Tettenhall
1976–79; Lect in Ch Hist, Dir of Pastl Studies and
Vc-Prin Ripon Coll Cuddesdon 1979–87; C All SS
Cuddesdon 1983–87; Can Res Bris Cathl 1987–97;
Can Theologian and Dir of Tr 1987–97; Moder-
ator of Par Resource Tm 1995–97; Moderator
Abps Dip for Rdrs; Bp of Grantham from 1997;
Dean of Stamford from 1998
                                Tel: (01476) 564722
                                Fax: (01476) 592468

GRAY, Ven Martin Clifford, DIP CHEM ENG
Holly Tree House, Whitwell Rd, Sparham, Norfolk
NR9 5PW [ARCHDEACON OF LYNN] *b* 19 Jan 1944;
educ Trin Gr Sch Wood Green; W Ham Coll of
Tech; Westcott Ho Th Coll; C St Faith Kings Lynn
1980–84; V Sheringham 1984–94; TR St Marg
Lowestoft 1994–99; Adn of Lynn from 1999
                        Tel and *Fax:* (01362) 688032
    email: Martin.Gray@lynnarch.freeserve.co.uk

GREENWOOD, Mr Nigel Desmond, M PHIL, M
ED, C CHEM, FRSC, FIBMS, FRIPHH
47 Broomfield, Adel, Leeds LS16 7AD [RIPON] *b* 18
Oct 1944; *educ* Leeds Gr Sch; Leeds Univ; Leic
Univ; Posts in Public Health Services and Further
Educ – Leeds Public Health Dept 1962–68;
Tobacco Research Coun 1968–69; United Leeds
Hosps 1969–74; Wigston CFE 1974–77; Keighley
Tech Coll 1978–80; Airedale and Wharfedale
Coll 1981–95; Educ and Tr Consultant from 1995;
M Gen Syn Bd of Educ and F and HE Ctee; Sch
Gov; M Dioc Bd of Educ and F and HE Ctee; M
Nn Ord Course Gov Coun
GS 1990–   *Tel:* 0113–261 1438

GRIEVE, Dr (Annie) Sheila, MB, CH B
14 Moseley Rd, Cheadle Hulme, Cheshire SK8 5HJ
[CHESTER] *b* 27 Mar 1937; *educ* Blackpool Collegi-
ate Sch for Girls; Man Univ; General Practitioner
(Man Family Practitioner Ctee)
GS 1985–   *Tel:* 0161–485 2096

GRIMLEY, Very Revd Robert William, MA
The Deanery, 20 Charlotte St, Bristol BS1 5PZ [DEAN
OF BRISTOL] *b* 26 Sep 1943; *educ* Derby Sch; Ch Coll
Cam; Wadham Coll Ox; Ripon Hall Th Coll; C

Radlett 1968–72; Chapl K Edw Sch Birm 1972–84;
V St Geo Edgbaston 1984–97; Exam Chapl to Bp
of Birm 1988–97; Vc-Chmn Dioc Pastl Ctee
1996–97; Dean of Bris from 1997; Bps' Inspector of
Th Colls from 1998   *Tel:* 0117–926 2443 (Home)
                                0117–926 4879 (Office)
                                Fax: 0117–925 3678
            email: dean@bristol.anglican.org

GRIMSBY, Bishop of [SUFFRAGAN, LINCOLN] **Rt**
Revd David Tustin, MA, DD
Bishop's House, Church Lane, Irby-on-Humber,
Grimsby, N E Lincs DN37 7JR b 12 Jan 1935; *educ*
Solihull Sch; Magd Coll Cam; Cuddesdon Th
Coll; C Stafford 1960–63; Asst Gen Sec CE Coun
on Foreign Relns and C St Dunstan-in-the-W Lon
1963–67; V St Paul Wednesbury 1967–71; V Tet-
tenhall Regis 1971–79; RD of Trysull 1976–79; Bp
of Grimsby from 1979; Can and Preb of Brampton
in Linc Cathl from 1979; Chmn Angl/Lutheran
Internat Commn 1986–2000; Pres Angl-Lutheran
Society 1986–99; Chmn Conversations with German Evangelical Ch 1987–88; Chmn Conversations with Nordic/Baltic Lutheran Chs 1989–92;
Chmn Porvoo Chs Contact Grp 1992–98; M CCU
1991–98; Chmn CCU 1992–98; Acting Chmn
Philip Usher Memorial Fund from 1986
GS 1990–   *Tel:* (01472) 371715
                                Fax: (01472) 371716

GRUNDY, Ven Malcolm Leslie, BA, AKC
Vicarage, Gisburn, Clitheroe, Lancs BB7 4HR
[ARCHDEACON OF CRAVEN] *b* 22 Mar 1944; *educ*
Sandye Place Sch; Mander Coll Bedf; K Coll Lon;
Open Univ; St Boniface Th Coll Warminster; C St
Geo Doncaster 1969–72; Chapl Sheff Ind Miss
1972–74; Sen Chapl 1974–80; Dioc Dir of Educ
and Community Lon 1980–86; TR Huntingdon
1986–91; Hon Can Ely Cathl 1987–94; Dir
AVEC 1991–94; Adn of Craven from 1994; Com-
mis Owo, Nigeria from 1994
GS 1998–   *Tel:* (01200) 445214
                                Fax: (01200) 445816
        email: adcraven@gisburn.u-net.com

GUILDFORD, Bishop of, Rt Revd John Warren
Gladwin, MA, DIP TH
Willow Grange, Woking Rd, Guildford GU4 7QS b 30
May 1942; *educ* Hertford Gr Sch; Chu Coll Cam;
St Jo Coll Dur; C St Jo the B Kirkheaton 1967–71;
Tutor St Jo Coll Dur 1971–77; Dir of Shaftesbury
Project 1977–82; Sec to Gen Syn BSR 1982–88;
Preb of St Paul's Cathl 1984–88; Provost of Sheff
1988–94; Bp of Guildf from 1994
GS 1990–   *Tel:* (01483) 590500
                                Fax: (01483) 590501
    email: bishop.john@cofeguildford.org.uk

GUILLE, Ven John Arthur, B TH, CERT ED
6 The Close, Winchester, Hants SO23 9LS [ARCH-
DEACON OF BASINGSTOKE] *b* 21 May 1949; *educ*
Guernsey Gr Sch; Ch Ch Coll Cant; Southn Univ;
Sarum and Wells Th Coll; C Chandlers Ford
1976–80; P-in-c St John Bournemouth 1980–83;

P-in-c St Mich Bournemouth 1983–84; V St John
w St Mich Bournemouth 1984–89; R St Andre de
la Pommeraye Guernsey 1989–99; Vc-Dean of
Guersey 1996–99; Adn of Basingstoke from 1999;
Can Res Win Cathl from 1999; M Dioc Syn from
1977; M Guernsey LEA 1990–98; Chmn N Area
Pastl Ctee from 1999; Dir and Trustee Old Alresford Place Retreat and Conf Centre from 1999;
Vc-Chair Dioc Bd of Educ from 1999
GS 1990–　　　*Tel:* (01962) 844644 Ext. 271 (Office)
　　　　　　　　(01962) 863603 (Home)
　　　　　　　　　　　Fax: (01962) 857242
email: john.guille@winchester-cathedral.org.uk

HALL, Revd (Alfred) Christopher, MA
*The Knowle, Philcote St, Deddington, Banbury OX15
0TB* [OXFORD] *b* 10 Dec 1935; *educ* Bromsgrove Sch;
Trin Coll Ox; Westcott Ho Th Coll; C St Cyprian
Frecheville 1961–64; C St Jo Dronfield 1964–67; V
St Matt Smethwick 1967–75; Can Res Man and
Adult Educ Offcr 1975–83; World Development
Offcr 1976–89; V St Pet Bolton 1983–90; Co-
ordinator Chr Concern for One World from 1990;
M BM from 1996; Sec Li Tim Oi Foundation; Sec
Dioc World Development Advs Core Grp; Editor
SYNEWS; M Dioc BSR and PWM; M Co Ecum
Coun; Adv Christian Aid SE Asia; M Nat Coun
World Development Movement
GS 1972–85, 1994–　　　　*Tel:* (01869) 338225
　　　　　　　　　　　　　Fax: (01869) 337766
　　　　email: achall@mail.globalnet.co.uk

HALL, Ven John Barrie
Tong Vicarage, Shifnal, Shropshire TF11 8PW
[ARCHDEACON OF SALOP] *b* 27 May 1941; *educ*
Sarum and Wells Th Coll; C St Edw Cheddleton
1984–88; V Rocester 1988–94; V Rocester and
Croxden w Hollington 1994–98; RD Uttoxeter
1991–98; Adn of Salop and V Tong from 1998;
Hon Can Lichf Cathl; P-in-c Donington from
1999; M DBF; M DAC; M Dioc Pastl Ctee
　　　　　　　　　　　　　Tel: (01902) 372622
　　　　　　　　　　　　　Fax: (01902) 374021

HALL, Canon John Robert, BA
*Church House, Great Smith Street, London SW1P
3NZ* [GENERAL SECRETARY, BOARD OF EDUCATION
AND NATIONAL SOCIETY] *b* 13 Mar 1949; *educ* St
Dunstan's Coll Catford; St Chad's Coll Dur;
Cuddesdon Th Coll; Head of RE Malet Lambert
High Sch Hull 1971–73; C St Jo the Divine Ken-
nington 1975–78; P-in-c All SS S Wimbledon
1978–84; V St Pet Streatham 1984–92; Exam Chapl
to Bp of S'wark 1988–92; M Gen Syn Bd of Educ
1991–92; Chmn FCP 1990–93; Dioc Dir of Educ
Blackb 1992–98; Hon Can Blackb Cathl 1992–94
and from 1998; Res Can Blackb Cathl 1994–98; M
Nat Soc Coun 1997–98; Gen Sec Bd of Educ and
Nat Soc from 1998
GS 1984–92　　　　　　　*Tel:* 020–7340 0283
　　　　　　　　　　　　Fax: 020–7233 1094
　　　　　email: john.hall@c-of-e.org.uk

HALL, Mrs Viviane Maria, BA
The Knowle, Philcote St, Deddington, Banbury, Oxo
OX15 0TB [OXFORD] *b* 20 Jun 1937; *educ* Surbito
High Sch; Southn Univ; Housewife; CA
Adviser; M Dioc Buildings Ctee; Bp's Visitor
GS 1994–　　　　　　　　*Tel:* (01869) 33822
　　　　　　　　　　　　Fax: (01869) 33776
　　　email: achall@mail.globalnet.co.u

**HALSTEAD, Mrs Joy (Josephine Elizabeth
Grace)**
23 Heath Drive, Chelmsford, Essex CM2 9H
[CHELMSFORD] *b* 28 Sep 1940; *educ* Holy Cros
Convent, George, S Africa; Trustee Visitor Joh
Henry Keene Memorial Homes from 1985; La
Chmn Chelmsf N Dny; M Dioc Conf Manage
ment Ctee from 1989; M Bp's Coun from 1991; M
Dioc Pastl Ctee from 1991; M Dioc Vacancy-in
See Ctee from 1991
GS 1995–　　　　　　　　*Tel:* (01245) 35492

HANCOCK, Ven Peter, MA, BA
Victoria Lodge, 36 Osborn Rd, Fareham, Hants PO1
7DS [ARCHDEACON OF THE MEON] *b* 26 Jul 1955
educ Price's Sch Fareham; Selw Coll Cam; Oak
Hill Th Coll; C Radipole and Melcombe Regis TM
1983–87; V St Wilf Cowplain 1987–99; RD Havan
1993–98; Adn of The Meon from 1999; M Bp's
Coun; M Dioc Ctee for Social Responsibility; M
Dioc Bd of Min; M DAC; M Dioc Patronage and
Property Ctee; M Dioc Ctee for Miss and Unity
　　　　　　　　　　　　Tel: (01329) 280101
　　　　　　　　　　　　Fax: (01329)281603

HANDLEY, Ven (Anthony) Michael
40 Heigham Rd, Norwich NR2 3AU [ARCHDEACON
OF NORFOLK] *b* 3 Jun 1936; *educ* Spalding Gr Sch;
Selw Coll Cam; Chich Th Coll; Asst C Thorpe
Episcopi 1962–66; P-in-c Fairstead Estate, King's
Lynn 1966–72; V Hellesdon 1972–81; RD Nor N
1979–81; Adn of Nor 1981–93; Adn of Norfolk
from 1993
GS 1980–85, 1990–95　　　*Tel:* (01603) 611808
　　　　　　　　　　　　Fax: (01603) 618954

HANFORD, Revd (William) Richard, MA, BD,
LLM
*Ewell Vicarage, Church St, Ewell, Epsom, Surrey
KT17 2AQ* [GUILDFORD] *b* 19 Nov 1938; *educ* Dyf-
fryn Gr Sch Port Talbot; Keble Coll Ox; St Steph
Ho Ox; C St Martin Roath 1963–66; C Llantwit
Major 1967–68; Succ Llan Cathl 1968–72; Chapl
Llan Coll of Educ 1969–72; Chapl RN 1972–76;
Hon Chapl Gibraltar Cathl 1974–76; C St Pet
Brighton 1977–78; Can Res and Prec Guildf Cathl
1978–83; Tutor and Lect in Liturgy Chich Th Coll
1980–86; V Ewell from 1983; M Cathls Fabric
Commn for England from 1991; M Coun SE Inst
for Th Educ from 1994; M Gen Syn Business Ctee
from 1999
GS 1990–　　　　　　　　*Tel:* 020–8393 2643

HANSON, Mr Brian John Taylor, CBE, LLM, FRSA
Church House, Great Smith St, London SW1P 3NZ
[REGISTRAR AND LEGAL ADVISER TO THE GENERAL
SYNOD, JOINT REGISTRAR OF THE PROVINCES OF
CANTERBURY AND YORK, AND DIRECTOR OF LEGAL
SERVICES TO THE ARCHBISHOPS' COUNCIL] *b* 23 Jan
1939; *educ* Hounslow Coll; Law Society's Coll of
Law; Univ of Wales; Solicitor (admitted 1963) and
Ecclesiastical Notary; In private practice 1963–65;
Solicitor w Ch Commrs from 1965; Asst Legal
Adv Gen Syn 1970–75; Solicitor to Gen Syn
1975–77; Legal Adv to Gen Syn from 1977; Joint
Registrar of the two Provinces from 1980; Regis-
trar of the Conv of Cant from 1982; Dir of Legal
Services to the Abps' Coun from 1998; M Legal
Adv Commn from 1980 (Sec 1970–86); Guardian,
Nat Shrine of Our Lady of Walsingham from
1984; M Coun of St Luke's Hosp for Clergy from
1985; Fell Woodard Corp and Sch Govnr from
1987; M Coun of Ecclesiastical Law Soc from
1987; Gov Pusey Ho from 1993; Abp's Nominee
on St Luke's Research Foundn from 1998; Chmn
Chich Dioc Bd of Patronage from 1998; Professional Assoc M Centre for Law and Religion Cardiff Law Sch from 1998; Pres Soc for Maintenance
of the Faith from 1999
Tel: 020–7898 1366 (Office)
(01444) 881890 (Home)

HANSON, Mrs (Margaret) Faith, T CERT
Ivy House, Gressenhall, Dereham, Norfolk NR20 4EU
[NORWICH] *b* 18 Apr 1945; *educ* Derby High Sch;
Whitelands Coll Lon; Rdr from 1992; Housewife
GS 1995– *Tel:* (01362) 860339

HARBIDGE, Ven Adrian Guy, BA
*Glebe House, 22 Bellflower Way, Chandler's Ford,
Hants SO53 4HN* [ARCHDEACON OF WINCHESTER]
b 10 Nov 1948; *educ* Marling Sch Stroud; St Jo Coll
Dur; Cuddesdon Th Coll; C Romsey 1975–80; V
St Andr Bournemouth 1980–86; V Chandler's
Ford 1986–99; RD Eastleigh 1993–98; Adn of Win
from 1999 *Tel and Fax:* 023–8026 0955
email: adrian.harbidge@dial.pipex.com

HARDMAN, Revd Christine Elizabeth, B SC,
M TH
Vicarage, Letchmore Rd, Stevenage, Herts SG1 3JD
[ST ALBANS] *b* 27 Aug 1951; *educ* Qu Eliz Girls' Gr
Sch Barnet; City of Lon Poly; Westmr Coll Ox; St
Alb Dio Minl Tr Scheme; Dss St Jo B Markyate
1984–87; C 1987–88; Course Dir St Alb Minl Tr
Scheme 1988–96; V H Trin Stevenage from 1996;
RD Stevenage from 1999; M Dioc Syn; M Bp's
Coun
GS 1998– *Tel:* (01438) 353229
Fax: (01438) 314127
email: chris@hardman.demon.co.uk

HARDY, Mr Antony Scott
1 Millbank, London SW1P 3JZ [STOCK EXCHANGE
INVESTMENTS MANAGER, CHURCH COMMIS-
SIONERS] *b* 10 Feb 1940; On staff of Ch Commrs

from 1988; Stock Exchange Investments Manager
from 1992; Sec to Ethical Investment Working
Group *Tel:* 020–7898 1122

HARDY, Mr Brian James, B SC, FCA
1 Millbank, London SW1P 3JZ [MANAGEMENT
ACCOUNTANT, CHURCH COMMISSIONERS] *b* 27 Nov
1952; *educ* Jarrow Gr Sch; Hull Univ; On staff of
Ch Commrs since 1988 *Tel:* 020–7898 1667
email: brian.hardy@c-of-e.org.uk

HARPER, Prebendary Horace Frederic
*Dresden Vicarage, 22 Red Bank, Longton, Stoke-on-
Trent, Staffs ST3 4EY* [LICHFIELD] *b* 25 Jan 1937;
educ Wolv Gr Sch; Keele Univ; Lichf Th Coll; C
Stoke-upon-Trent 1960–63; C Fenton 1963–66; V
Ch Ch Coseley 1966–75; V Trent Vale 1975–88; V
Dresden from 1988; P-in-c Normacot from 1994;
Preb Lichf Cathl from 1996; M Dioc Syn; M Dioc
Bd of Min; M Vacancy-in-See Ctee; Dny Vocations
Adv; Sch Gov various schs from 1966
GS 1995– *Tel:* (01782) 321257

HARRIS, Mr Jeremy Michael, BA, PGCE
Lambeth Palace, London SW1P 7JU [ARCHBISHOP OF
CANTERBURY'S SECRETARY FOR PUBLIC AFFAIRS]
b 31 Oct 1950; *educ* Sevenoaks Sch; Clare Coll
Cam; Nottm Univ; Journalist and Broadcaster
1974–98; BBC Madrid Correspondent 1982–86;
BBC Moscow Correspondent 1986–89; BBC
Washington Correspondent 1990–95; Radio Pre-
senter Radio 4 1995–98; Abp of Cant's Sec for
Public Affairs from 1998 *Tel:* 020–7898 1200
Fax: 020–7261 9836
email: jeremy.harris@lampal.c-of-e.org.uk

HARRIS, Mrs Pat (Patricia Ann), T DIP
Vicarage, Elm Rd, Stonehouse, Glos GL10 2NP
[GLOUCESTER] *b* 29 May 1939; *educ* St Julian's High
Sch Newport; Trin Coll Carmarthen; Tchr; Dioc
Pres MU 1980–85; Pres World Wide MU (Cen
Pres) 1989–94; M Bp's Coun from 1985; MU Rep
on Womens Nat Commn from 1994; Hon Fell Trin
Coll Carmarthen from 1995; Awarded Cross of St
Aug 1995; Vc-Chmn BM from 1996; M PWM
Ctee; M CMEAC 1994–96; M Abps Bd of Examin-
ers 1996–99; M Coun BRF and Publications Ctee
from 1997; Chmn Carl Dioc Infrastructure
Review Grp 1997–98
GS 1985– *Tel and Fax:* (01453) 822332

HARRISON , Ven Peter Reginald Wallace, BA
*Brimley Lodge, 27 Moulscroft Rd, Beverley HU17
7DX* [ARCHDEACON OF EAST RIDING] *b* 22 Jun 1939;
educ Charterhouse; Selw Coll Cam; Ridley Hall
Th Coll; C St Luke Barton Hill Bris 1964–69; Chapl
Greenhouse Trust 1969–77; Dir Northorpe Hall
Trust 1977–84; TR Drypool 1984–98; AD E Hull
1988–98; Hon Can York Minster from 1994; Adn
of E Riding from 1998 *Tel:* (01482) 881659
email: PeterRWHarrison@breathemail.net

HARRISON, Dr Jamie (James Herbert), MB, BS, MRCGP, MA
5 Dunelm Court, South St, Durham DH1 4QX [DURHAM] *b* 17 Sep 1953; *educ* Stockport Gr Sch; Magd Coll Ox; K Coll Hosp Medical Sch Lon; General Medical Practitioner Durham City from 1990; M Coun St Jo Coll Dur; Rdr
GS 1995–   *Tel:* 0191–384 8643 (Home)
        0191–386 4285 (Office)
        Fax: 0191–386 5934 (Office)

HARRISON, Mrs Rachel Elizabeth, NNEB
St Margaret's Rectory, 9 Crispin Court, Brotton, Saltburn-by-the-Sea TS21 2XL [YORK] *b* 18 Feb 1953; *educ* Northn Sch for Girls; Northn CFE; NVQ Childcare Assessor; M Dioc Syn; Hon Sec Chs Together in N York Moors
GS 1995–   *Tel:* (01287) 676275

HASELOCK, Canon Jeremy Matthew, BA, B PHIL, MA
34 The Close, Norwich NR1 4DZ [CHICHESTER] *b* 20 Sep 1951; *educ* St Nic Gr Sch Northwood; York Univ; York Cen for Medieval Studies; St Steph Ho Ox; C St Gabr Pimlico 1983–86; C St Jas Paddington 1986–88; Dom Chapl to Bp of Chich 1988–91; V Boxgrove 1991–98; Dioc Liturg Adv Chich 1991–98; Preb of Fittleworth and Canon Chich Cathl from 1994; Can Res and Prec Nor Cathl from 1998; M Liturg Commn from 1996; M Initiation Rites Revision Ctee; M Wholeness and Healing Revision Ctee; M Steering Ctee Eucharistic Rites Revision; M Steering Ctee Eucharistic Prayers Revision; Chmn Steering Ctee Extended Communion
GS 1995–   *Tel and Fax:* (01603) 619169 (Home)
        Fax: (01603) 218314 (Office)
        email: jeremy@jhaselock.force9.co.uk

HAWES, Ven Arthur John, BA, DPS, DIP L&A
Archdeacon's House, Northfield Rd, Quarrington, Lincs NG34 8RT [ARCHDEACON OF LINCOLN] *b* 31 Aug 1943; *educ* City of Ox High Sch for Boys; Birm Univ; UEA; Chich Th Coll; C St Jo Kidderminster 1968–72; P-in-c St Richard Droitwich 1972–76; R Alderford w Attlebridge and Swannington 1976–92; Chapl Hellesdon & Dav Rice Hosps and Yare Clinic 1976–92; RD Sparham 1981–91; Mental Health Act Commr for Eng and Wales 1986–94; Hon Can Nor Cathl 1988–95; R St Faith King's Lynn 1992–95; Chmn Dioc BSR 1990–95; Adn of Linc from 1995; Can and Preb Linc Cathl from 1995; Adv on Mental Health Matters to BSR Social Policy Ctee from 1989; Patron Mind from 1996; Pres Lincs Rural Housing Assn from 1998   *Tel:* (01529) 304348
        Fax: (01529) 304354

HAWES, Revd Andrew Thomas, BA, MA
Vicarage, Church Lane, Edenham, Bourne, Lincs PE10 0LS [LINCOLN] *b* 18 Dec 1954; *educ* De Aston Sch Market Rasen; Sheff Univ; Em Coll Cam; Westcott Ho Th Coll; C Gt Grimsby TM 1980–84;

V Lutton w Gedney Drove End 1984–89; V Edenham w Witham-on-the-Hill from 1989; RD Beltisloe from 1997; Warden Edenham Regional Ho
GS 1995–   *Tel:* (01778) 59135∎
        email: EdenhamRH@aol.com

HAWKER, Ven Alan Fort, BA, DIP TH, PACTA
The Paddock, Church Lane, Kington Langley, Chippenham, Wilts SN15 5NR [ARCHDEACON OF MALMESBURY] *b* 23 Mar 1944; *educ* Buckhurst Hill C∎ High Sch; Hull Univ; Clifton Th Coll; C St Leon Bootle 1968–71; C-in-c Em Fazakerley 1971–73; ∖ St Paul Goose Green 1973–81; TR S Crawley TM 1981–98; Preb of Bury and Can Chich Cath 1991–98; RD E Grinstead 1994–98; M CBF; Adn o∎ Swindon 1998–99; Adn of Malmesbury from 1999; Chmn Working Grp on Clergy Discipline and Reform of Ecclesiastical Courts from 1994; M Gen Syn Stg Ctee 1995–98; M Gen Syn Policy Ctee 1995–98; M CBF Budget Ctee 1995–98; M DBF; M Bp's Coun
GS 1990–   *Tel:* (01249) 75008∎
        Fax: (01249) 75008∎

HAWKER, Ven Peter John
St Andrew's, Promenadengasse 9, 8001 Zurich, Switzerland [ARCHDEACON IN SWITZERLAND, DIOCESE IN EUROPE] *b* 10 Jun 1937; *educ* Yeovil Gr Sch; E∎ Univ; Wycliffe Hall Th Coll; Asst Chapl St Ursula Berne 1970–76; Chapl 1976–89; Lect Berne Univ 1976–89; Adn in Switzerland from 1986; Chapl St Andr Zurich from 1989   *Tel:* 00–41–1–261–22–41
        Fax: 00–41–1–252–60–42

HAWLEY, Canon John Andrew, BD, AKC,CERT TH
Rectory, 16A Oxford Rd, Dewsbury, W Yorks WF13 4JT [WAKEFIELD] *b* 27 Apr 1950; *educ* Ecclesfield Gr Sch; K Coll Lon; Wycliffe Hall Th Coll; C H Trin Hull 1974–77; C Bradf Cathl 1977–80; V All SS Woodlands, Doncaster 1980–91; TR Dewsbury from 1991; Vc-Chmn Dioc BMU 1991–96; Chmn Dioc Communications Grp from 1996;
GS 1996–   *Tel:* (01924) 465491
        (01924) 457057
        Fax: (01924) 458124

HAWTHORN, Ven Christopher John, MA
Park House, Rosehill, Great Ayton, Middlesbrough TS9 6BH [ARCHDEACON OF CLEVELAND] *b* 29 Apr 1936; *educ* Marlboro Coll; Qu Coll Cam; Ripon Hall Ox; C St Jas Sutton, York 1962–66; V St Nic Kingston-upon-Hull 1966–72; V Coatham 1972–79; V St Martin Scarborough 1979–91; RD Scarborough 1982–91; Can and Preb York Minster from 1987; Chmn NE Ord Course Coun from 1994; Adn of Cleveland from 1991; M CE Pensions Bd from 1998
GS 1987–90, 1995–   *Tel:* (01642) 723221
        Fax: (01642) 724137

HEBBLETHWAITE, Mr (John) David, BA
Church House, Great Smith St, London SW1P 3NZ [ADMINISTRATIVE SECRETARY, CENTRAL SECRE-

TARIAT] *b* 16 Aug 1944; *educ* Bradf Gr Sch; Nottm Univ; Birm Univ; On staff of Ch Commrs 1966–84 (seconded to Gen Syn 1977–79); Seconded to Gen Syn from 1984; Sec Liturg Commn; Sec Dios Commn; Sec Ho of Clergy   *Tel:* 020–7898 1364

HEDGES, Mr Christopher, B SC
51 High St, Old Portsmouth, Hants PO1 2LU [PORTSMOUTH] *b* 30 Sep 1958; *educ* Hreod Burna Sen High Sch, Swindon; Nottm Univ; Production Engineer 1980–84; Product Manager 1984–88; Tr Manager 1988–91; Househusband 1991–97; Civil Servant from 1997; M Bp's Coun
GS 1990–   *Tel:* 023–9273 1282
                                   Fax: 023–9236 6928
                          email: hedges@newnet.co.uk

HENDERSON, Mr Ian James, ACP, RD
14 Monks Park, Malmesbury, Wilts SN16 9JF [BRISTOL] *b* 22 Jul 1942; *educ* K Sch Roch; Culham Coll of Educ; Rtd Hdmaster; M Bp's Coun; M Dioc Housing and Glebe Ctee; M Dioc Vacancy in See Ctee; Treas Malmesbury Dny Syn
                          Tel and Fax: (01666) 826051

HENDERSON, Mr (Robin Alan) Louis, BA
Lambeth Palace, London SE1 7JU [PUBLIC AFFAIRS OFFICER TO THE ARCHBISHOP OF CANTERBURY] *b* 12 Nov 1949; *educ* Univ Coll Sch Hampstead; Merton Coll Ox; On staff of Ch Commrs from 1975; Seconded to ABM/Ho of Bps 1991–95; Sec to Bps' Inspectorate of Th Colls and Courses 1995–96; Seconded to Lambeth Palace 1995; Public Affairs Officer from 1995   *Tel:* 020–7898 1200
                                   Fax: 020–7261 9836

HEREFORD, Bishop of, Rt Revd John Keith Oliver
The Bishop's House, The Palace, Hereford HR4 9BN b 14 Apr 1935; *educ* Collyer's Sch Horsham; Westmr Sch; G & C Coll Cam; Westcott Ho Th Coll; C Hilborough Grp 1964–68; Chapl Eton Coll 1968–72; TR S Molton Grp 1973–82; TR Cen Ex 1982–85; Adn of Sherborne and P-in-c W Stafford w Frome Billett 1985–90; Bp of Heref from 1990; Chmn ABM 1993–98
GS 1980–85, 1990–   *Tel:* (01432) 271355
                                   Fax: (01432) 343047

HERTFORD, Bishop of [SUFFRAGAN, ST ALBANS] **Rt Revd Robin Jonathan Norman Smith,** MA
Hertford House, Abbey Mill Lane, St Albans, Herts AL3 4HE b 14 Aug 1936; *educ* Bedf Sch; Worc Coll Ox; Ridley Hall Th Coll; C St Marg Barking 1962–67; Chapl Lee Abbey 1967–72; V St Mary Chesham 1972–80; RD Amersham 1970–82; R Gt Chesham 1980–90; Bp of Hertford from 1990
                                   Tel: (01727) 866420
                                   Fax: (01727) 811426

HESSELWOOD, Mr Anthony Peter, FCA
38 Bromley Rd, Shipley, W Yorks BD18 4DT [BRADFORD] *b* 16 Nov 1949; *educ* Belle Vue Boys Sch

Bradf; Partner Firth Parish Chartered Accountants from 1979; Chmn DBF from 1982; Hon Lay Can Bradf Cathl 1994–98; M Bp's Coun; Treas Scargill Ho
GS 1995–   *Tel:* (01274) 586613 (Home)
                                   (01484) 422560 (Office)
                              Fax: (01484) 513523 (Office)

HEWETSON, Ven Christopher, MA
8 Queen's Park Rd, Chester CH4 7AD [ARCHDEACON OF CHESTER] *b* 1 Jun 1937; *educ* Shrewsbury Sch; Trin Coll Ox; Chich Th Coll; V St Pet Didcot 1973–82; R Ascot Heath 1982–90; Chapl St Geo Sch Ascot 1985–88; RD Bracknell 1986–90; P-in-c H Trin Headington Quarry 1990–94; RD Cowley 1994; Adn of Chester from 1994
                                   Tel: (01244) 675417
                                   Fax: (01244) 681959

HIGGINBOTHAM, Mr John Eagle, MA
16 Holmfield Ave, Stoneygate, Leicester LE2 2BF [LEICESTER] *b* 28 Feb 1933; *educ* Bradf Gr Sch; Trin Hall Cam; Leic Univ; Housemaster and Hd of Classics Lancing Coll 1957–80; Hdmaster Leic Gr Sch 1980–89; Lect (TESOL) Leic Univ 1990–92; Freelance Lect, Writer and Course Dir from 1992; M Dioc Bd of Educ 1982–89; Bp's Nominee on Dioc Syn from 1985; M Ecum Ctee Bp's Coun from 1989; Frank Fisher Fell for study of Angl-RC Relations 1989–90; M Friends of Ang Centre in Rome from 1990; Vc-Chmn Leic Dioc Prayer Book Soc from 1992; Chmn Leic Dioc Forward in Faith from 1993; M Coun Friends of the Diocese of Uruguay; Fell Woodard Corp from 1996; Dioc Rep Qu Victoria Clergy Fund from 1996; Dioc Rep CBF from 1997; M Friends of Dio of Gibraltar in Eur from 1997; M Dioc Pastl Ctee from 1999; Dioc Rep Chs Forum for E Midlands and the Regional Development Agency from 1999
GS 1995–   *Tel:* 0116–270 9462

HIGGINS, Very Revd Michael John, LL B, PH D
The Deanery, The College, Ely, Cambs CB7 4DN [DEAN OF ELY] *b* 31 Dec 1935; *educ* Whitchurch Gr Sch Cardiff; Birm Univ; Cam Univ; Harvard Univ; Ridley Hall Th Coll; C Ormskirk 1965–68; Selection Sec ACCM 1968–74; V Frome 1974–80; R Preston 1980–91; Dean of Ely from 1991
GS 1994–   *Tel:* (01353) 667735
                                   Fax: (01353) 665658

HILARY, Sister , CSMV, B MUS, DIP TH, DIP ED
Chapter Office, 20 Dean's Yard, London SW1P 3PA [RELIGIOUS COMMUNITIES, SOUTH, LAY] *b* 11 Mar 1925; *educ* Barnsley High Sch; Birm Univ; St Anne's Coll Ox; Tchr UK 1947–49, 1952–56, 1963–69; S Africa 1958–63; Pastl Tm St Paul's Cathl from 1985; Pastl Asst Westmr Abbey from 1988
GS 1995–   *Tel:* 020–7222 5152 (Office)
                                   020–7928 4844
                              Fax: 020–7233 2072

HILL, Revd Peter, B SC, M TH
Vicarage, 18 Crookdole Lane, Calverton, Nottingham NG14 6GF [SOUTHWELL] *b* 4 Feb 1950; *educ* Bp Gore Gr Sch Swansea; Man Univ; Nottm Univ; Wycliffe Hall Ox; Sheetmetal worker 1971–72; Schoolteacher 1972–78; Dep Hd Beaches Primary Sch Sale 1978–81; C Porchester 1983–86; V Huthwaite 1986–95; P-in-c Calverton from 1995; RD S'well from 1997; Chair Dioc Ho of Clergy from 1997; M Bp's Coun; M Dioc Fin Ctee
GS 1993–   *Tel:* 0115–965 2552
             email: Peter@stwilfrids.freeserve.co.uk

HIND, Mr Timothy Charles, MA, FCII
Plowman's Corner, The Square, Westbury-sub-Mendip, Wells, Som BA5 1HJ [BATH AND WELLS] *b* 10 Aug 1950; *educ* Watford Boys Gr Sch; St Jo Coll Cam; Various posts at AXA Sun Life Services from 1972; M Bp's Coun; Chmn Dioc Vacancy-in-See Ctee 1996–98; M Dioc Bd of Educ 1995–97; M Board of Educ (Schs and Colls) 1995–97; M CE Pensions Bd; M CE Pensions Bd Investment and Finance Ctee 1996–97; M ABM 1998; M DRACSC from 1999; Lay Vc-Chair Dioc Syn from 1999; Lay Chmn Axbridge Dny Syn 1984–91; M Dioc Bd of Patronage 1986–94; Vc-Chair Bd of Govs Kings of Wessex Community Sch 1996–99
GS 1995–   *Tel:* (01749) 870356 (Home)
                          0117–989 9000 Ext 3631 (Office)
             email: Tim.Hind@axa-sunlife.co.uk

HOARE, Rt Revd Rupert William Noel , MA, PH D
The Cathedral, St James' Mount, Liverpool L1 &AZ [DEAN OF LIVERPOOL] *b* 3 Mar 1940; *educ* Rugby Sch; Trin Coll Ox; Fitzw Ho Cam; Berlin Univ; Birm Univ; Westcott Ho Th Coll; C St Mary Oldham 1964–68; Lect Qu Coll Birm 1968–72; Can Th Cov Cathl 1970–75; R Resurr Man 1972–78; Can Res Birm Cathl 1978–81; Prin Westcott Ho Cam 1981–93; Bp of Dudley 1993–99; Dean of Liv from 1999
GS 1995–99   *Tel:* 0151–709 6271

HOARE, Sir Timothy Edward Charles Bt, OBE, MA
10 Belitha Villas, London N1 1PD [LONDON] *b* 11 Nov 1934; *educ* Radley Coll; Worc Coll Ox; Birkbeck Coll Lon; Army NS; Staff M Pathfinders and CYFA 1958–64; Staff M St Helen's Bishopsgate 1964–69; M Ch Assembly 1960–70; M ACCM 1971–86; M Chadwick Commn on Ch and State; Chmn, Law of Marriage Grp; M Crown Appts Commn 1987–92; CE Delegate to WCC Canberra 1991; Personnel Consultant from 1970, Dir Career Plan Ltd; Dir New Metals and Chemicals Ltd; M Stg Ctee 1981–98; M Sen Ch Appts Review Grp; Chmn Appts Sub-Ctee 1988–98; Chmn Steering Grp on Clergy Conditions of Service 1992–98; Treas Lon Dioc Fund; Chmn Dioc Ho of Laity; M Coun St Jo Coll Dur and Oak Hill Coll
GS 1970–   *Tel:* 020–7607 7359 (Home)
                       020 7242 5775 (Office)
             email: techoare@msn.com

HODGE, Canon Michael Robert
Braxton Cottage, Halletts Shute, Norton, Yarmouth, Isle of Wight PO41 0RH [SYNODICAL SECRETARY, CONVOCATION OF CANTERBURY] *b* 24 Apr 1934; *educ* Rugby Sch; Pemb Coll Cam; Ridley Hall Th Coll; Asst C Ch Ch Harpurhey Man 1959; Asst C St Mark Layton Blackpool 1959–62; V Old St Geo Stalybridge 1962–67; V Cobham w Luddesdowne and Dode 1967–81; R Bidborough 1981–99; Chmn Dioc Ho of Clergy 1985–94; Chmn Dioc Bd of Patronage 1989–99; Chmn DAC 1991–99; Synodical Sec, Conv of Cant from 1995
GS 1970–95   *Tel* and *Fax:* (01983) 761121
             email: michael@braxton.ndo.co.uk

HOLDAWAY, Revd Stephen Douglas, BA
Rectory, Westgate, Louth, Lincs LN11 9YE [LINCOLN] *b* 3 Oct 1945; *educ* Hornchurch Gr Sch; Hull Univ; Ridley Hall Th Coll; C St Chris Thornhill Southn 1970–73; Ind Chapl Redditch and P-in-c St Phil Webheath 1973–78; Ind Chapl Linc 1978–93; Co-ordinator Linc City Centre Grp Min 1981–93; TR Louth from 1993; RD Louthesk from 1995
GS 1988–   *Tel:* (01507) 603213
             email: Stephen.Holdaway@btinternet.com

HOLDEN, Dr John Thomas, B SC, PH D
199 Musters Rd, West Bridgford, Nottingham NG2 7DQ [SOUTHWELL] *b* 8 Sep 1938; *educ* Chiswick Co Gr Sch; Man Univ; Dur Univ; Research Fell Johns Hopkins Univ 1963–64; Lect Univ of Nottm 1964–91; Vis Prof Northwestern Univ 1979; Sen Lect Univ of Nottm 1991–97; Rtd; M Dios Commn; M Bp's Coun
GS 1985–

                                    Tel: 0115–981 2043
             email: j-h@holden199.swinternet.co.uk

HOLDRIDGE, Ven Bernard Lee
Fairview House, 14 Armthorpe Lane, Doncaster DN2 5LZ [ARCHDEACON OF DONCASTER] *b* 24 Jul 1935; *educ* Thorne Gr Sch; Lich Th Coll; C Swinton 1967–71; V St Jude Doncaster 1971–81; R Rawmarsh w Parkgate 1981–88; RD Rotherham 1986–88; V Worksop Priory 1988–94; Adn of Doncaster from 1994; Guardian Shrine of Our Lady of Walsingham from 1997
GS 1999–   *Tel:* (01302) 325787
                                   Fax: (01302) 760493

HOLMES, Mr Nigel Craven, BA, PGCE
Woodside, Great Corby, Carlisle CA4 8LL [CARLISLE] *b* 25 Jan 1945; *educ* Rossall Sch Fleetwood; Dur Univ; Joined BBC Radio 1968; BBC Radio Producer 1970–97; M CECC 1986–95; M CACLB from 1993; M BM from 1996; Rdr; Chmn Editorial Ctee CRC from 1997; Chmn Ho of Laity Dioc Syn from 1997
GS 1985–   *Tel:* (01228) 560617
                                   Fax: (01228) 562372
             email: nigel@gt corby demon.co.uk

HOOPER, Ven Michael Wrenford, BA

The Archdeacon's House, The Close, Hereford HR1 2NG [ARCHDEACON OF HEREFORD] *b* 2 May 1941; *educ* Crypt Sch Glouc; St D Coll Lampeter; St Steph Ho Th Coll; C St Mary Bridgnorth 1966–70; V Minsterley and R Habberley 1970–81; R Leominster 1981–85; TR Leominster 1985–97; RD Leominster 1981–97; Adn of Heref from 1997; Can Res Heref Cathl from 1997
GS 1993– *Tel:* (01432) 272873
email:
    archdeacon@theclosehereford.freeserve.co.uk

HOPGOOD, Mr Richard Simon, BA

Church House, Great Smith St, London SW1P 3NZ [DIRECTOR OF POLICY AND DEPUTY SECRETARY GENERAL, ARCHBISHOPS' COUNCIL] *b* 7 Oct 1952; *educ* Ch Hosp; Wadh Coll Ox; On staff of CH Commrs from 1977; Dep Sec (Policy and Planning) 1994–98; Dir of Policy and Dep Sec Gen Abps' Coun from 1999 *Tel:* 020–7898 1530
    email: richard.hopgood@c-of-e.org.uk

HOPKINSON, Revd Benjamin Alaric, MA

Vicarage, 21 Thornton Rd, Stainton, Middlesbrough TS8 9BS [YORK] *b* 24 Feb 1936; *educ* Marlboro Coll; Trin Coll Ox; Chich Th Coll; C St Luke Pallion, Sunderland 1961–66; C Ascen Bulawayo 1966–67; P-in-c St Pet Mmadinare, Botswana 1967–70; Urban and Ind Missr Selebi-Pikwe, Botswana 1970–73; Pr Missr Sherwood and Carrington 1974–77; V Lowdham w Gunthorpe and Caythorpe 1977–85; R Whitby 1985–95; V Stainton-in-Cleveland and Hilton-in-Cleveland from 1995; Chapl to Cleveland Police; Chair Dioc CSR; M Dioc CMEAC
GS 1980–85, 1995– *Tel* and *Fax:* (01642) 590423
    email: dumela@dial.pipex.com

HOPKINSON, Ven Barney (Barnabas John), MA

Sarum House, High St, Urchfont, Devizes, Wilts SN10 4QH [ARCHDEACON OF WILTS] *b* 11 May 1939; *educ* Em Sch; Trin Coll Cam; Linc Th Coll; C All SS and Martyrs Langley 1965–67; C Gt St Mary Cam 1967–70; Asst Chapl Charterhouse 1970–75; TV Preshute 1975–81; RD Marlborough 1977–81; TR Wimborne Minster and Holt 1981–86; RD Wimborne 1985–86; Adn of Sarum from 1986; P-in-c Stratford-sub-Castle 1987–98; Adn of Wilts from 1998
GS 1995– *Tel:* (01380) 840373
    Fax: (01380) 848247
    email: adsarum@compuserve.com

HOPKINSON, Revd William Humphrey, B SC, MA, M SC, M PHIL

Diocesan House, Lady Woottons Green, Canterbury, Kent CT1 1NQ [CANTERBURY] *b* 4 Jun 1948; *educ* Herbert Strutt Gr Sch Belper; Univ Coll Lon; Dur Univ; Nottm Univ; Man Poly; Cranmer Hall Th Coll; C Normanton 1977–80; C Sawley 1980–82; pt Tutor St Jo Coll Nottm 1981–82; V Birtles 1982–87; Dir Pastl Studies N Ord Course 1982–94;

Dir of Course Development 1990–94; CME Officer and Dir POT Chester 1987–94; V St Mich Tenterden 1994–96; Dir Min and Tr from 1994
GS 1990–94, 1997– *Tel:* 0410 033575 (Mobile)
    Fax: (01227) 450964
    email: hpknsn@surfaid.org

HORSFIELD, Prebendary Robert Alan, BA, MA

Vicarage, The Hurst, Cleobury Mortimer, Kidderminster, Worcs DY14 8EG [HEREFORD] *b* 5 Sep 1938; *educ* Batley Gr Sch; Leeds Univ; Inst of Historical Research Lon; Coll of the Resurr Mirfield; C St Jas Lower Gornal 1963–66; C H Trin Bridlington Quay and Sewerby w Marton; P-in-c St Matt Fairfield 1968–73; R Scartho 1973–79; V Cleobury Mortimer w Hopton Wafers from 1979, now R United Benefice; RD Ludlow 1989–96; Preb Heref Cathl from 1992; M Bp's Coun from 1989; M DBF and Exec Ctee 1989–98; M BM from 1997
GS 1994– *Tel* and *Fax:* (01299) 270264

HORSHAM, Bishop of [AREA BISHOP, CHICHESTER] **Rt Revd Lindsay Goodall Urwin,** OGS

21 Guildford Rd, Horsham RH12 1LU b 13 Mar 1956; *educ* Camberwell Gr Sch Victoria, Australia; Ripon Coll Cuddesdon; C St Pet Walworth 1980–83; V St Faith Red Post Hill 1983–88; Dioc Missr Chich 1988–93; OGS from 1990; Bp of Horsham from 1993; M Springboard Exec from 1995; Nat Chmn CU 1995–99; UK Provincial OGS from 1996 *Tel:* (01403) 211139
    Fax: (01403) 217349
    email: bishhorsham@clara.net

HOULDING, Revd David Nigel Christopher, AKC

All Hallows' House, 52 Courthope Rd, London NW3 2LD [LONDON] *b* 25 Jul 1953; *educ* K Sch Cant; K Coll Lon; St Aug Coll Cant; Lay Chapl Chr Medical Coll Vellore, S India 1976–77; C All SS Hillingdon 1977–81; C St Alb Holborn w St Pet Saffron Hill 1981–85; V St Steph w All Hallows Hampstead from 1985; M Dioc Bishops Coun from 1997), Dioc Liturg Grp; M Coun ACS; Adv Panel for Vocations; Master SSC from 1997; ProProlocutor Conv of Cant from 1998
GS 1995– *Tel:* 020–7267 7833
    020–7267 6317

HOWDEN, Canon John Travis, RIBA

Vicarage, The Street, Pleshey, Chelmsford, Essex CM3 1HA [CHELMSFORD] *b* 12 Oct 1940; *educ* Sevenoaks Sch; Beckenham Gr Sch; Regent St Poly Sch of Architecture; Sarum Th Coll; C St Matt Gillingham 1969–72; TV Banbury 1972–73; Producer BBC Radio 1973–81; Sen Tr Officer BBC Radio 1981–86; R Doddinghurst and V Mountnessing 1986–91; Warden Pleshey (Chelmsf Dioc Ho of Retreat) and P-in-c Pleshey from 1991; M Dioc

Millennium Grp; M DAC; Dir Pleshey Course for Spiritual Dirs
GS 1997–
Tel: (01245) 237251
(01245) 237236
Fax: (01245) 237594

HOWE, Ven George Alexander, BA
Vicarage, Windermere Rd, Lindale, Grange-over-Sands, Cumbria LA11 6LB [ARCHDEACON OF WESTMORLAND AND FURNESS] *b* 22 Jan 1952; *educ* Liv Inst High Sch; St Jo Coll Dur; Westcott Ho Th Coll; C St Cuth Peterlee 1975-79; C St Mary Norton-on-Tees 1979–81; V Hart w Elwick Hall 1981–85; R Sedgefield 1985–91; RD Sedgefield 1988–91; V H Trin Kendal 1991–2000; RD Kendal 1994–99; Adn of Westmorland and Furness from 2000; Vc-Chair DAC; M Dioc Bd for Min and Tr
Tel: (015395) 34717

HUDSON, Mr John, BA, M ED, PGCE
4 The Brambles, Barrow, Clitheroe, Lancs BB7 9BF [BLACKBURN] *b* 27 Jan 1935; *educ* Percy Jackson Gr Sch Adwick-le-Street; Sheff Univ; Univ of Alberta Canada; Sch Tchr 1958–65; Educational Administration 1965–92; Rtd
GS 1990–
Tel: (01254) 824481

HUDSON, Miss Julia
Lambeth Palace, London SE1 7JU [ADMINISTRATIVE SECETARY, LAMBETH PALACE] *educ* On staff of Ch Commrs from 1977; Seconded as Asst Sec CUF 1988–91; Head of Personnel 1994–96; Admin Sec Lambeth Palace from 1996   *Tel:* 020–7928 8282

HUDSON, Canon (John) Leonard, AKC
The Clergy House, Church St, Royston, Barnsley, S Yorks S71 4QZ [WAKEFIELD] *b* 10 Feb 1944; *educ* The Crossley and Porter Gr Sch Halifax; K Coll Lon; St Boniface Th Coll Warminster; C St Jo Bapt Dodworth 1967–70; Prec Wakef Cathl 1970–73; V St Sav Ravensthorpe 1973–80; V St Jo Bapt Royston from 1980; RD Barnsley from 1993; P-in-c St Jo Ev Carlton from 1990; Chmn DAC; Chmn Wakef Cathl FAC; Chmn Wakef Dioc Forward in Faith; Hon Can Wakef Cathl from 1997
GS 1995–
Tel: (01226) 722410

HUGHES, Mr Howell Harris, MA, MSI (DIP)
Church Commissioners, 1 Millbank, London SW1P 3JZ [SECRETARY, CHURCH COMMISSIONERS] Sec to Ch Commrs from 1998   *Tel:* 020–7898 1785

HULL, Bishop of [SUFFRAGAN, YORK] **Rt Revd Richard Michael Cokayne Frith,** MA
Hullen House, Woodfield Lane, Hessle HU13 0ES b 8 Apr 1949; *educ* Marlboro Coll; Fitzw Coll Cam; St Jo Coll Nottm; C Mortlake w E Sheen 1974–78; TV Thamesmead 1978–83; TR Keynsham 1983–92; Adn of Taunton 1992–98; Bp of Hull from 1998
GS 1995–98
Tel: (01482) 649019
Fax: (01482) 647449

HULME, Bishop of [SUFFRAGAN, MANCHESTER] **Rt Revd Stephen Richard Lowe,** B SC
14 Moorgate Ave, Withington, Manchester M20 1HE b 3 Mar 1944; *educ* Leeds Gr Sch; Reading Sch; Lon Univ; Ripon Hall Th Coll; C St Mich Angl/Methodist Ch Gospel Lane Birm 1968–72; P-in-c Woodgate Valley CD 1972–75; TR E Ham 1975–88; Chelmsf Dioc Urban Officer 1986–88; Hon Can Chelmsf Cathl from 1985; Adn of Sheff 1988–99; Bp of Hulme from 1999; Ch Commr from 1992, M Bishoprics Ctee from 1991, M Bd of Govs from 1994; Trustee Ch Urban Fund 1991–97, Chmn Grants Ctee from 1993; M BAGUPA 1993–96; M CTBI 1991–96; M CBF Exec 1993–96; M Gen Syn Staff Ctee 1991–96; M Abps' Commn on Organisation of CE 1994–95; Chair Dioc Social Resp Ctee 1995–99; Chair Dioc Faith in the City Ctee; Chair Yorkshire/Humberside Regions Adv Coun for BBC 1992–96; M English Nat Forum of BBC 1994–96
GS 1990–99
Tel: 0161–445 5922
Fax: 0161–448 9687
email: 100737.634@compuserve.com

HUMPHERY, Mr James Hambrook
Pound Cottage, Middle Woodford, Salisbury, Wilts SP4 6NR [SALISBURY] *b* 13 Dec 1954; *Mgr* The Hill Drug Scheme Britain–Nepal Medical Trust 1973–75; M DBF from 1991; Lawyer from 1981; CEDR accredited mediator
GS 1993–
Tel: (01703) 321000
email: james.humphery@treth.co.uk

HUNTINGDON, Bishop of [SUFFRAGAN, ELY] **Rt Revd John Robert Flack,** BA
14 Lynn Rd, Ely, Cambs CB6 1DA b 30 May 1942; *educ* Hertf Gr Sch; Leeds Univ; Coll of Resurr Mirf; C St Bart Armley 1966–69; C St Mary Northn 1969–72; V Chapelthorpe 1972–81; V Ripponden 1981–85; V Brighouse 1985–92; TR 1988–92; RD Brighouse and Elland 1986–92; Hon Can Wakef Cathl 1989–97; Chmn Dioc Ho of Clergy 1988–92; Adn of Pontefract 1992–97; Bp of Huntingdon from 1997
GS 1994–97
Tel: (01353) 662137
Fax: (01353) 669357
email: suffragan@ely.anglican.org

INGRAM, Mrs Joanna Mary
25 The Woodlands, Melbourne, Derbys DE73 1DP [DERBY] *b* 9 Sep 1950; *educ* Broxbourne Gr Sch; M CCC 1986–96; M CBF from 1990; M CBF Publishing Ctee; M Gen Syn Stg Orders Ctee from 1996; M Faculty Rules Ctee; M DBF; M DAC; Sec Dioc Coun for Min; M Dioc Bd of Patronage
GS 1980–
Tel: (01332) 862548

INWOOD, Ven Richard Neil, MA, B SC, BA
2 Vicarage Gardens, Rastrick, Brighouse, W Yorks HD6 3HD [ARCHDEACON OF HALIFAX] *b* 4 Mar 1946; *educ* Burton-on-Trent Gr Sch; Univ Coll Ox; St Jo Coll Nottm; C Ch Ch Fulwood Sheff 1974–78; C (Dir of Pastoring) All So Langham Place 1978–81; V St Luke Bath 1981–89; R Yeovil w

Kingston Pitney 1989–95; Preb Wells Cathl 1990–95; Ch Commr 1991–95; Hon Treas Simeon's Trustees/Hyndman Trust; Adn of Halifax from 1995; Chmn Coun St Jo Coll Nottm from 1998
GS 1985–95, 1997– *Tel:* (01484) 714553
  Fax: (01484) 711897
  email: richard@inwood53.freeserve.co.uk

ISAAC, Canon David Thomas, BA
Education Office, Cathedral House, St Thomas St, Portsmouth, Hants PO1 2HA [PORTSMOUTH] *b* 20 Sep 1943; *educ* Rhondda Gr Sch; Univ Coll of Wales, Abth; Cuddesdon Th Coll; C Llandaff Cathl 1967–71; C St Mary Swansea 1971–73; Prov Youth Chapl Ch in Wales 1973–77; V Pontardawe 1977–79; Ripon Dioc Youth Officer 1979–83; Nat Youth Officer Gen Syn Bd of Educ 1983–90; Res Can and Dir of Educ Portsm from 1990; Chmn St Chris Educnl Trust from 1998
GS 1995– *Tel:* 023–9282 2053
  Fax: 023–9229 5081

ISON, Revd Hilary Margaret, BA, DIP TH, DPS
12 The Close, Exeter EX1 1EZ [EXETER] *b* 4 Mar 1955; *educ* Bilston Girls High Sch; Leic Univ; St Jo Coll Nottm; Par Worker NSM SS Nic and Luke Deptford 1980–87; Dn NSM 1987–88; C NSM St Phil Cov 1988–90; Par Dn Rugby TM 1990–93; Chapl Ex and Distr Hospice from 1993; Chair Assoc of Hospice Chapls from 1997
GS 1995– *Tel:* (01392) 275745

JACKSON, Monsignor Michael Joseph, STL
c/o Notre Dame Convent, Burwood House, Cobham, Surrey KT11 1HA [ECUMENICAL REPRESENTATIVE (ROMAN CATHOLIC CHURCH)] *b* 13 Apr 1951; *educ* St Pet Sch Guildf; St Edm Coll Cam; Ven English Coll Rome; Asst Pr St Mary Worthing 1977–79; Lect in Th St Jo Seminary Wonersh 1979–85; Doctoral Student St Edm Coll Cam 1985–87; Sec Ctee for Chr Unity Catholic Bps' Conf of England and Wales 1988–96; RC Co-Sec English ARC 1988–92; Chmn Commissioning Ctee CTE 1989–90; Chair Enabling Grp CTE 1993–95; Par Pr Chichester 1996–99; Sabbatical 2000
GS 1998– *Tel:* 07931 809721 (Mobile)

JACKSON, Mrs Shirley Angela
Batemans, Much Hadham, Herts SG10 6DA [ST ALBANS] *b* 23 Aug 1933; *educ* Herts and Essex High Sch for Girls; Insolvency Practitioner; Chair Bishop's Stortford Dny Pastl Ctee from 1983; M DBF from 1986; M Bp's Coun from 1986; M Property Ctee from 1989; M Glebe Ctee from 1989; Pres Trad Anglicans St Albs dio 1985–92; M CBF from 1988; Gov Whitelands Coll from 1989; M Educ Working Party from 1992; Gen Syn M MU Cen Coun 1990–95; M Coun and Publications and Publishing Ctee Soc of Practitioners of Insolvency; Fell SPI from 1994; M Environment Agency Adv Panel 1994–95; Chair SPI Smaller Practices Ctee from 1997; M Pensions Regulations Steering Ctee
GS 1985– *Tel:* 020–7430 2321
  email: sjackson@begbenor.co.uk

JACOB, Ven William Mungo, LL B, MA, PH D
4 Cambridge Place, London W8 5PB (Home), The Old Deanery, Dean's Court, London EC4V 5AA (Office) [ARCHDEACON OF CHARING CROSS AND ARCHDEACON AT LONDON HOUSE] *b* 15 Nov 1944; *educ* K Edw VII Sch King's Lynn; Hull Univ; Linacre Coll Ox; Edin Univ; Ex Univ; St Steph Ho Th Coll; C Wymondham 1970–73; Asst Chapl Ex Univ 1973–75; Dir of Pastl Studies Sarum and Wells Th Coll 1975–80; Vc-Prin 1977–80; Sec Ctee for Th Educ ACCM 1980–86; Warden Linc Th Coll 1986–96; Adn of Charing Cross and Adn at The Old Deanery from 1996
GS 1999– *Tel:* 020–7937 2560 (Home)
  020–7248 6233 (Office)
  email: archdeacon.charingcross@dlondon.org.uk

JÄGERS, Mrs Maryon Patricia, SRN, SCM
Hoefbladhof 61, 3991 GG Houten, The Netherlands [EUROPE] *b* 22 Jan 1942; *educ* St Chris Sch; The Hall, Beckenham, Kent; Dioc Elector for Utrecht 1980–90; M Bp's Coun 1980–85; M Dioc Syn for Europe from 1985; M BM 1985–90; M and Vc-Chmn CCU and Exec Ctee from 1990; Lay Chmn Adnry NW Europe from 1989; M Conversations w German Evan Chs 1987–88; M Conversations w Nordic and Baltic Lutheran Chs 1989–92; Gen Syn Delegate to WCC Canberra 1991; M Cen Ctee WCC from 1991; M Gen Syn Panel of Chmn 1991; Lay Vc-Pres Dioc Syn; M Dioc Vacancy-in-See Ctee from 1993; Lay Chmn Dioc Ho of Laity, M Stg Ctee; M Bp's Coun from 1995; M Gen Syn Stg Ctee from 1996; M Gen Syn Business Sub Ctee from 1996; Commiss to Bp of Ballarat Australia from 1996; Gen Syn Delegate to WCCAssembly Harare 1998 and Decade in Solidarity of Women Harare 1998
GS 1985– *Tel:* 0031–30 6371780
  Fax: 0031–30 6351034
  0655 858337 (Mobile)

JAGO, Mr Derek
21 Clarence Gardens, Bishop Auckland DL14 4QX [DURHAM]
GS 1998–

JAMES, Dr Richard Hugh, M SC, MB, BS, FRCA, DTM&H, D OBSTRCOG, DA, AKC
36 Ridgeway, Oadby, Leicester LE2 5TN [LEICESTER] *b* 21 Dec 1945; *educ* St Lawr Coll Ramsgate; K Coll Lon; K Coll Hosp; Medical Missry Burundi 1971–74; Tr Posts in Anaesthesia K Coll Hosp 1974–80; Consultant Anaesthetist Leic R Infirmary from 1980; M Dioc Syn from 1985
GS 1995– *Tel:* 0116–271 4596

JAMES, Mrs Sarah Alison Livingston
Canton House, New St, Painswick, Glos GL6 6XH [GLOUCESTER] *b* 4 Aug 1938; *educ* St Leon Sch St Andrews Fife; Chmn *Home & Family* Editorial Ctee 1982–86; MU Dioc Pres (Roch) 1980–85; MU Cen Vc-Pres 1986–91, MU Trustee 1995–97; Chmn Dioc MU Money Advice Service from 1998; Dir Highway Journeys from 1998; Lay Chmn Brom-

ley Dny Syn 1984–90; Rdr; Wrdn Rdrs Roch Dio 1989–95; Vc-Chair CRC from 1995; M DRACSC; Ctee for Min Among Deaf People
GS 1985– *Tel* and *Fax:* (01452) 812419

JARROW, Bishop of [SUFFRAGAN, DURHAM] **Rt Revd Alan Smithson,** MA
The Old Vicarage, Hallgarth, Pittington, Durham DH6 1AB b 1 Dec 1936; *educ* Bradf Gr Sch; Qu Coll Ox; Qu Coll Birm; C Ch Ch Skipton 1964–68; C St Mary V w St Cross and St Pet Ox 1968–72; Chapl Qu Coll Ox 1969–72; Chapl Reading Univ 1972–77; V Bracknell 1977–84; Dir of Tr Inst Carl 1984–90; Can Res Carl Cathl 1984–90; Bp of Jarrow from 1990 *Tel:* 0191–372 0225
Fax: 0191–372 2326
email: 114216.1633@compuserve.com

JEFFERSON, Mr Timothy Paul, NCA
26 Allergate, Durham DH1 4ET [DURHAM] *b* 14 Aug 1944; *educ* K Edw VII Sch Lytham; Lanc Coll of Agriculture; Dairy Farmer New Zealand 1979; Farm Manager Dur Coll of Agriculture 1980–89; Regional Manager (Internat Division) Milk Marketing Bd 1989–93; Manager (Internat Division) Pig Improvement Co 1993–94; Exec Officer Dur—Lesotho Link from 1994; M Dioc BMU; Ctee M Lesotho Dioc Assn
GS 1998– *Tel:* 0191–384 8385
Fax: 0191–386 2863
email: TPJ@BTInternet.com

JEFFERY, Mr Harry Ernest, B SC, FCA, FIIA
Stonetiles, Teddington, Tewkesbury, Glos GL20 8JA [WORCESTER] *b* 1 Aug 1947; *educ* Cheltenham Gr Sch; N Glos Tech Coll; Reading Univ; Price Waterhouse & Co 1969–76; Lucas Industries plc 1976–87; Renishaw plc 1987–91; pt Longborough Holdings Ltd 1992–95; Chartered Accountant in Private Practice since 1991
GS 1994– *Tel:* (01242) 620515
Fax: (01242) 620901

JEFFERY, Ms Margaret, B SC
Church House, Great Smith St, London SW1P 3NZ [SECRETARY, DEPLOYMENT, REMUNERATION AND CONDITIONS OF SERVICE COMMITTEE, MINISTRY DIVISION] *b* 6 May 1945; *educ* Sittingbourne Girls' Gr Sch; Leic Univ; Southn Univ; Sec DRACS Ctee Min Div from 1998 *Tel:* 020–7898 1411
email: margaret.jeffery@mindiv.c-of-e.org.uk

JENKINS, Ven David Thomas Ivor
Irvings House, Sleagill, Penrith, Cumbria CA10 3HD [SYNODAL SECRETARY AND TREASURER YORK CONVOCATION] *b* 3 Jun 1929; *educ* Maesteg Gr Sch; K Coll Lon; Asst C St Mark's Bilton, Rugby 1953–56; V St Marg Wolston, Cov 1956–61; Asst Dir of Relig Educ Dio Carl 1961–63; V St Barn Carl 1963–72; V St Cuth w St Mary Carl 1972–91; Hon Can of Carl 1975–91; Can Res Carl Cathl 1991–95; Sec Carl Dioc Syn and Bp's Coun 1972–95; Dioc Sec 1984–95; Sec DBF 1990–95; Sec

and Treas Conv of York from 1986; Adn of Westmor and Furness 1995–99; Hon Can Carl Cathl from 1995
GS 1978–85 *Tel:* (01931) 714400

JENKINS, Mr Steve (Stephen) Lewis, B SC
Church House, Great Smith St, London SW1P 3NZ [HEAD OF MEDIA RELATIONS, ARCHBISHOPS' COUNCIL] *b* 1 Dec 1955; *educ* Reading Sch; Univ Coll of N Wales, Bangor; Agricultural Journalist/Dep Editor from 1972; Press Officer The Childrens' Soc 1987–90; Press Officer Gen Syn 1991–98; Head of Media Relations Abps' Coun from 1999 *Tel:* 020–7898 1326
Fax: 020–7222 6672
email: steve.jenkins@c-of-e.org.uk

JENNINGS, Ven David Willfred Michael, AKC
136 Broomfield Rd, Chelmsford CM1 1RN [ARCHDEACON OF SOUTHEND] *b* 13 Jul 1944; *educ* Radley Coll; K Coll Lon; St Boniface Coll Warminster; C Walton Liv 1967–69; C Ch Ch Win 1969–73; V Hythe 1973–80; V St Edw Romford 1980–92; RD Havering 1985–92; Hon Can Chelmsf Cathl 1987–92; Adn of Southend from 1992
GS 1997– *Tel:* (01245) 258257
Fax: (01245) 250845
email: a.southend@chelmsford.anglican.org

JENNINGS, Dr Helen Marina, BA, PH D
14 Glenfield Rd, Banstead, Surrey SM7 2DG [ROCHESTER] *b* 4 Jul 1973; *educ* Chatham Gr Sch; Univ of Kent; Civil Servant; M Dioc Syn from 1995; M Bp's Coun and Stg Ctee 1995–98; M CTE Forum from 1996; M CCU Local Unity Ctee 1996–99; M Dioc Ecum Ctee 1997–99; Delegate to WCC Forum 1998
GS 1995– *email:* DrHelenJ@aol.com

JOHN, Canon Jeffrey Philip Hywel, MA, D PHIL
2 Harmsworth Mews, West Square, London SE11 4SQ [SOUTHWARK] *b* 10 Feb 1953; *educ* Tonyrefail Gr Sch Rhondda; Hertf Coll Ox; BNC Ox; Magd Coll Ox; St Steph Ho Th Coll; C St Aug Penarth 1978–80; Asst Chapl Magd Coll Ox 1980–82; Chapl and Lect BNC Ox 1982–84; Fell and Dean of Div Magd Coll Ox 1984–91; V H Trin Eltham 1991–97; M Gen Syn Stg Ctee and Appts Sub Ctee from 1995; M Exec Affirming Catholicism Grp in Gen Syn from 1995; Can Chan and Can Th S'wark Cathl and Bp's Adv for Min from 1997; M Dioc Syn; M Dioc Min Policy Ctee; Exam Chapl to Bp of Worc; M TETC; M Bp's Coun
GS 1995– *Tel:* 020–7403 8686 (Office)
Fax: 020–7403 4770
email: jeffrey.john@dswark.org.uk

JOHNS, Mrs Sue (Susan Margaret), HNC, M PHIL
103 Greenways, Eaton, Norwich NR4 6PD [NORWICH] *b* 20 Mar 1955; *educ* Thorpe Gr Sch; Nor City Coll; Leeds Univ; Analytical Chemist and Public Analyst 1973–80; Housewife and Mother; Food Scientist MAFF CSL Food Science Lab Nor

1991–98; Higher Scientific Officer Jt Food Standards and Safety Grp
GS 1990– Tel: (01603) 455029 (Home)
020–7238 6772 (Office)
email: s.johns@jfssg.maff.gov.uk

JOHNSON, Revd Malcolm Arthur, MA
St Martin in the Fields, Trafalgar Square, London WC2N 4JJ [LONDON] *b* 8 Sep 1936; *educ* Framlingham Coll; Dur Univ; Cuddesdon Th Coll; C St Mark Portsea 1962–67; Chapl Qu Mary Coll Lon 1967–74; AD City of Lon 1985–90; R St Botolph Aldgate 1974–92; Master R Found of St Katharine 1993–97; Master Emer 1997; Bp of Lon's Adv on Past Care and Counselling from 1997
GS 1985– Tel: 020–7930 0089
Fax: 020–7839 5163

JOHNSON, Mr Nigel Ian, B SC
Church Commissioners, 1 Millbank, London SW1P 3JZ [OFFICIAL SOLICITOR, CHURCH COMMISSIONERS] *b* 23 Sep 1954; *educ* Oundle Sch; Univ of Wales; Coll of Law; Solicitor in private practice 1980–84; Solicitor Cheltenham & Gloucester Building Soc 1984–95, Chief Solicitor 1987–95; Chief Solicitor Cheltenham & Gloucester plc 1995–97; Official Solicitor Ch Commrs from 1997
Tel: 020–7898 1712
Fax: 020–7898 1798
email: nigel.johnson@c-of-e.org.uk

JOHNSTON, Mrs Mary Geraldine, BA, AKC, MIPD
56 Fairlawn Grove, Chiswick, London W4 5EH [LONDON] *b* 8 Jan 1939; *educ* Barking Abbey Sch; K Coll Lon; Personnel Dept ICI 1961–66; Personnel Admin and Employee Relations Singer Co New York 1966–68; American Express New York 1968–70; Asst Personnel Manager and Staff Dev Manager Guinness Overseas 1970–80; Housewife from 1980; M Dioc Vacancy-in-See Ctee; M Eccles Jurisdiction Panel of Assessors; M Coun Corp of Ch Ho
GS 1995– Tel: 020–8995 6427

JONES, Mr David Arthur
St Chad's Vicarage, Hillmorton Rd, Wood End, Coventry CV2 1FY [COVENTRY] *b* 3 Aug 1936; *educ* Abingdon Sch; RMA Sandhurst; RAF Staff Coll Bracknell; Army Officer 1957–85 (Colonel); Assoc Dir Oxfam 1985–93; Assoc Dir Internat Alert 1995–97; Dioc Adv CUF and Dioc Development Fund; M Bp's Coun; M DBF
GS 1995– Tel: 024–7661 2909
Fax: 024–7662 2834

JONES, Mr (James) Allan
30 Pimbo Rd, Kings Moss, St Helens, Merseyside WA11 8RD [LIVERPOOL] *b* 21 Jan 1950; *educ* Central Secondary Boys' Sch St Helens; St Helens Coll of Tech; Production Control Clerk 1966–84; Navigator for Emergency Doctor Service 1987–98; M Liv Dioc Bd of Educ 1991–94; Vc-Chmn Liv Branch

Prayer Book Soc 1991–95; Dioc Lay Co-ordinator Forward in Faith from 1993; M Dioc BSR and Exec Ctee from 1998; M Dioc Regional Issues Sector Ctee from 1998
GS 1990– Tel: (01744) 893367

JONES, Very Revd Keith Brynmor, MA
The Deanery, Exeter EX1 1HT [DEAN OF EXETER] *b* 27 Jun 1944; *educ* Ludlow Gr Sch; Selw Coll Cam; Cuddesdon Th Coll; C Limpsfield w Titsey 1969–72; Dean's V St Alb Abbey 1972–76; P-in-c St Mich Borehamwood 1976–79; TV 1979–82; V St Mary le Tower Ipswich 1982–96; RD Ipswich 1993–95; Dean of Ex from 1996
GS 1999– Tel: (01392) 252891 (Office)
(01392) 272697 (Home)
Fax: (01392) 433598
email: dean@exeter-cathedral.org.uk

JONES, Revd Robert George, BA, MA
St Barnabas Rectory, Church Rd, Worcester WR3 8NX [WORCESTER] *b* 30 Oct 1955; *educ* K Edw Sch Birm; Hatf Coll Dur Univ; Ripon Coll Cuddesdon; Ecum Inst Bossey; C H Innocents Kidderminster 1980–84; V St Fran 1984–92; TR St Barn w Ch Ch Worc from 1992; M Dioc BM; DAC Adv; M Magdesburg Partnership Grp
GS 1995– Tel and Fax: (01905) 23785

JONES, Miss Susan Margaret Shirley, LL B
Church Commissioners, 1 Millbank, London SW1P 3JZ [DEPUTY OFFICIAL SOLICITOR, CHURCH COMMISSIONERS] *educ* Alice Ottley Sch Worc; Bris Univ; Official Deputy Solicitor Ch Commrs from 1993
Tel: 020–7898 1704
Fax: 020–7976 8473
email: sue.jones@c-of-e.org.uk

JONES, Ven Trevor Pryce, B ED, B TH
St Mary's House, Church Lane, Stapleford, Hertford SG14 3NB [ARCHDEACON OF HERTFORD] *b* 24 Apr 1948; *educ* Dial Stone Sch Stockport; St Luke's Coll Ex; Southn Univ; Sarum and Wells Th Coll; C St Geo Glouc 1976–79; Warden Bp Mascall Centre Ludlow and M Heref Dioc Educ Tm 1979–84; DCO 1981–96; Sec Heref-Nurnberg European Ecum Partnership 1982–87; M Bp's Coun 1987–87; M Dioc Ecum Ctee 1985–87, Chmn 1996–97; TR Heref S Wye TM 1984–97; OCF 1985–97; M Dioc Pastl/Minl Ctee 1996–97; Adn of Hertford from 1997; Chmn St Alb and Ox Min Course from 1998 Tel: (01992) 581629
Fax: (01992) 558745
email: archdhert@stalbansdioc.org.uk

JUDD, Very Revd Peter Somerset Margesson, MA
Provost's House, 3 Harlings Grove, Waterloo Lane, Chelmsford CM1 1YQ [PROVOST OF CHELMSFORD] *b* 20 Feb 1949; *educ* Charterhouse Sch; Trin Hall Cam; Cuddesdon Th Coll; C St Phil w St Steph Salford 1974–76; Chapl Clare Coll Cam 1976–81; Acting Dean Clare Coll 1980–81; TV Burnham w

Dropmore, Hitcham and Taplow 1981–88; V St Mary V Iffley 1988–97; RD Cowley 1995–97; R and Prov of Chelms from 1997
Tel: (01245) 354318 (Home)
(01245) 294492 (Office)
Fax: (01245) 294499
email: provost@chelmsford.anglican.org

JUDKINS, Mrs Mary, BA, PGCE, MA
Old Vicarage, 3 Church Lane, East Ardsley, Wakefield WF3 2LJ [WAKEFIELD] b 29 Mar 1951; educ Leominster Gr Sch; Bris Univ; St Mary's Coll Cheltenham; Open Univ; Tchr in Bris and E Grinstead 1984–94; Supply Tchr; Homemaker/Mother; Lay Chmn Dioc Syn; Gen Syn Rep SAMS
GS 1995–   Tel: (01924) 826802
email: elephantmj@aol.com

KAVANAGH, Revd Michael Lowther,
CPSYCHOL, BA, M SC
Bishopthorpe Palace, Bishopthorpe, York YO2 1QE [DOMESTIC CHAPLAIN TO THE ARCHBISHOP OF YORK] b 24 Sep 1958; educ Beverley Gr Sch; York Univ; Newc Univ; Leeds Univ; Coll of Resurr Mirfield; C Boston Spa 1987–91; V St Nic Beverley 1991–97; RD Beverley 1995–97; Dom Chapl to Abp of York and DDO from 1997; Sec York Ord Candidates Coun; M Dioc Syn Tel: (01904) 707021
Fax: (01904) 709204
email: office@bishopthorpe.u-net.com

KEATING, Mr Colin Henderson
Whitridge House, Kirkwhelpington, Newcastle upon Tyne NE19 2SA [NEWCASTLE] b 24 Dec 1930; educ Leamington Gr Sch; Managing Dir Family Engineering Business 1960–87; M Bp's Coun; Dioc Funding Adv 1987–97; M Dioc Syn from 1987; M DBF from 1987; M Dioc Deployment Grp from 1993
GS 1990–   Tel: (01830) 540363

KEENS, Mrs Penny (Penelope Jane)
9 St Paul's Court, Stony Stratford, Milton Keynes MK11 1LJ [OXFORD] b 22 Mar 1941; educ Felixstowe Coll; Hon Sec Bucks Historic Chs Trust from 1996; Lay Chmn Milton Keynes Dny Syn 1979–90 and from 1993; M Bp's Coun; M Dioc Pastl, Buildings, and Communications Ctees; M Chr Giving Grp; M Bd of Patronage
GS 1998–   Tel and Fax: (01908) 571232

KENSINGTON, Bishop of [AREA BISHOP, LONDON] **Rt Revd Michael John Colclough,** BA
19 Campden Hill Square, London W8 8JY b 29 Dec 1944; educ Stanfield Tech High Sch; Leeds Univ; Cuddesdon Th Coll; C St Werburgh Burslem 1971–75; C St Mary S Ruislip 1975–79; V St Anselm Hayes 1979–86; AD Hillingdon 1985–92; P-in-c St Marg Uxbridge 1986–88; P-in-c St Andr w St Jo Uxbridge 1986–88; TR Uxbridge 1988–92; Adn of Northolt 1992–94; PA to Bp of Lon 1994–96; Dep Priest-in-Ordinary to HM The Queen 1995–96; Bp of Kensington from 1996;

Chmn Lon and S'wark Dios Prisons and Penal Concerns Grp; Vc-Pres Chr Children's Fund of GB from 1998; Chmn BM Miss, Evang and Renewal Ctee from 1999   Tel: 020–7727 9818
Fax: 020–7229 3651
email: bishop.kensington@dlondon.org.uk

KEY, Revd Robert Frederick, BA, DPS
St Andrew's Vicarage, 46 Charlbury Rd, Oxford OX2 6UX [OXFORD] b 29 Aug 1952; educ Alleyn's Sch Dulwich; Bris Univ; Oak Hill Th Coll; C St Ebbe Ox 1976–80; Min St Patr Wallington 1980–85; V Eynsham and Cassington 1985–91; V St Andr Ox from 1991; M Coun Wycliffe Hall from 1985
GS 1995–   Tel: (01865) 311212 (Office)
(01865) 311695 (Home)
Fax: (01865) 311320

KILLWICK, Revd Simon David Andrew, BD, AKC, CERT TH
Christ Church Rectory, Monton St, Moss Side, Manchester M14 4GP [MANCHESTER] b 14 Nov 1956; educ Westmr Sch; K Coll Lon; St Steph Ho Th Coll; C St Mark Worsley 1981–84; TV St Mary Ellenbrook 1984–97; P-in-c Ch Ch Moss Side from 1997
GS 1999–   Tel and Fax: 0161–226 2476

KILNER, Canon Fred (Frederick James), MA
St Mary's Vicarage, St Mary's St, Ely, Cambs CB7 4ER [ELY] b 20 Jan 1943; educ Millfield Sch; Qu Coll Cam; Ridley Hall Th Coll; C St Paul Harlow 1970–74; P-in-c St Steph Cam 1974–79; R Milton 1979–94; Hon Can Ely Cathl from 1988; TR Ely TM 1994–96, TR from 1996; Sec Ridley Hall Coun; M Bp's Coun; M Dioc Fin Ctee
GS 1995–   Tel: (01353) 662308

KING, Mr Alan Edwin
97 St Ladoc Rd, Keynsham, Bristol BS31 2EN [BATH AND WELLS] b 27 Jun 1938; educ K Sch Peterb; Journalist Peterb Evening Telegraph 1954–65; Assoc Ed Nassau Tribune, Bahamas 1965–70; Sports Ed, Features Ed, Dep Ed, Acting Ed Bristol Evening Post 1970–90, Man Ed 1990–98; Journalist and Communications Consultant; Chmn DBF; Vc-Chair DRACS Ctee, Min Div Abps' Coun; M Fin Ctee Abps' Coun; Chmn Consultative Grp of Dioc Chmn and Secs
GS 1999–   Tel: 0117–986 3053
Fax: 0117–914 9521
email: alank@bathwells.anglican.org

KING, Canon Malcolm Stewart
St Martin's Vicarage, Westcott Rd, Dorking, Surrey RH4 3DP [GUILDFORD] b 9 Mar 1956; educ Kingston Gr Sch; Sarum and Wells Th Coll; C Farnham 1980–83; C Chertsey 1983–86; Chapl St Pet Hosp Chertsey 1983–86; V St Paul Egham Hythe 1986–91; TR Cove 1991–98; RD Aldershot 1993–98; V St Martin Dorking w Ranmore from 1998; Chmn Dioc Ho of Clergy from 1997; M Iona Community; M Bp's Coun from 1985; M Dioc Bd

of Educ from 1986; Assessor under Ecclesiastical Jurisdiction Measure; M Dioc Pastl Ctee; M Dioc Bd of Patronage; Hon Can Guildf Cathl from 1999
GS 1990–　　　　Tel: (01306) 882875 (Home)
　　　　　　　　　(01306) 886830 (Office)

KING, Canon Philip David, MA
Church House, Great Smith St, London SW1P 3NZ [SECRETARY, GENERAL SYNOD BOARD OF MISSION] *b* 6 May 1935; *educ* Ch Hosp; Keble Coll Ox; Tyndale Hall Th Coll; C H Trin Redhill 1960–63; C-in-c St Pat Wallington 1963–68; V Ch Ch Fulham 1968–74; Gen Sec SAMS 1974–86; NSM H Trin Wallington 1974–86; M BMU 1982–86; M ACC Miss Issues and Strategy Adv Grp 1982–86; Chair BMU Miss Th Adv Grp 1985–89; V Ch Ch Roxeth and St Pet Harrow 1986–89; Sec BMU 1989–91; NSM Em Northwood 1989–97; Sec BM from 1991
　　　　　　　　　　　　Tel: 020–7898 1468
　　　　　　　　　　　　Fax: 020–7898 1431
　　　　　email: philip.king@c-of-e.org.uk

KING, Major Patrick Whittenham
10 Bridewell St, Walsingham, Norfolk NR22 6BJ [NORWICH] *b* 21 Aug 1937; *educ* Marlborough Coll; RMA Sandhurst; Rtd Army Officer; M Dioc Liturg Ctee from 1987; Guardian Shrine of Our Lady of Walsingham from 1991; Lay Vc-Chmn Burnham and Walsingham Dny Syn from 1995; Bp's Furnishings Officer from 1995; M Steering Ctee Chr Initiation Gen Syn Liturg Commn; Trustee Ox Movement Anniversary Appeal from 1996; M DAC from 1996; M Dioc Red Chs Ctee from 1996; M Dioc Ctee for the Deaf from 1998; M Fin and Gen Purposes Ctee and M Coun St Steph Ho Ox from 1997
GS 1990–　　　　　　　Tel: (01328) 820709
　　　　　　　　　　　　Fax: (01328) 820098

KINGSTON, Bishop of [AREA BISHOP, SOUTHWARK] **Rt Revd Peter Bryan Price,** CERT ED, DPS
24 Albert Drive, London SW19 6LS b 17 May 1944; *educ* Glastonbury Sch Morden; Redland Coll of Educ Bris; Oak Hill Th Coll; Heythrop Coll Lon; Asst Tchr Ashton Park Sch Bris 1966–70; Sen Tutor Lindley Lodge Young People's Centre 1970; Head of RE Cordeaux High Sch Louth 1970–72; Community Chapl and C Ch Ch Portsdown 1974–78; Chapl Scargill Ho 1978–80; V St Mary Magd Addiscombe 1980–88; Can Chan S'wark Cathl 1988–91; Gen Sec USPG 1992–97; M Miss Agencies Working Grp 1992–93; M Angl Commn on Miss 1993–96; Bp of Kingston from 1997; M BM; M PWM; M Ch Commn on Miss; M Miss Th Adv Grp; M Gov Body SPCK; Chmn The Manna Soc　　　　　　　　Tel: 020–8392 3742
　　　　　　　　　　　　Fax: 020–8392 3743
　　　　　email: bishop.peter@dswark.org.uk

KINSON, Mrs Wendy Elizabeth, BA
The Old Laundry, Maer, Newcastle, Staffs ST5 5EF [LICHFIELD] *b* 24 Feb 1953; *educ* Bp Blackhall Sch

Ex; Sussex Univ; Citizens Advice Bureau Adv from 1993; M Bp's Coun
GS 1995–　　　　　　　Tel: (01782) 680613

KIRK, Revd Geoffrey, BA
St Stephen's Vicarage, Cressingham Rd, London SE13 5AG [SOUTHWARK] *b* 10 Dec 1945; *educ* Coll of Resurr Mirfield; C St Aid Leeds 1972–74; C St Mark w St Luke Marylebone 1974–76; C St Jo Kennington 1977–79; C St Jo w St Jas Kennington 1979–81; P-in-c St Steph and St Mark Lewisham 1981–87; V from 1987
GS 1996–　　　　　　　Tel: 020–8318 1295

KNAGGS, Mr Frank Aylesbury
52 Huntcliffe Gardens, North Heaton, Newcastle upon Tyne NE6 5UD [NEWCASTLE] *b* 2 Oct 1937; *educ* Felsted Sch; Rutherford Coll of Tech; Production and Commercial Engineer and Mgr in power generation and aerospace industries 1956–93; Exec Officer CEEC from 1997; M CCU and Exec Ctee; M Bp's Coun; M DBF; M Dioc Bd of Miss and Social Responsibilty; Chmn Cruddas Youth Worker Project; Elder Bethel Chr Fell Newc
GS 1985–　　　Tel: 0191–265 9603 (Home)
　　　Tel and Fax: 0191–240 2084 (Office)
　　　　　email: CEEC@cableinet.co.uk

KNARESBOROUGH, Bishop of [SUFFRAGAN, RIPON] **Rt Revd Frank Valentine Weston,** MA
16 Shaftesbury Ave, Roundhay, Leeds LS8 1DT b 16 Sep 1935; *educ* Ch Hospital; Qu Coll Ox; Lich Th Coll; C St Jo B Atherton 1961–65; Chapl Coll of the Ascen Selly Oak 1965–69, Prin 1969–76; Prin Edin Th Coll 1976–82; Adn of Ox and Can of Ch Ch 1982–97; Bp of Knaresborough from 1997
GS 1985–95　　　　　Tel: 0113–266 4800
　　　　　　　　　　　　Fax: 0113–266 5649
　　　　　email: Knaresborough@btinternet.com

KNIGHT, Very Revd Alec (Alexander Francis), MA
The Deanery, 12 Eastgate, Lincoln LN2 1QG [DEAN OF LINCOLN] *b* 24 Jul 1939; *educ* Taunton Sch; St Cath Coll Cam; Wells Th Coll; C Hemel Hempstead 1963–68; Chapl Taunton Sch 1968–74; Dir Bloxham Project 1975–81; Dir of Studies Aston Tr Scheme 1981–83; P-in-c Easton and Martyr Worthy 1983–91; Adn of Basingstoke 1990–98; Can Res Win Cathl 1991–98; Dean of Linc from 1998
GS 1995–98　　　　　Tel: (01522) 523608
　　　　　　　　　　　　Fax: (01522) 511307

KNOWLES, Very Revd Graeme Paul, AKC
The Deanery, Carlisle, Cumbria CA3 8TZ [DEAN OF CARLISLE] *b* 25 Sep 1951; *educ* Dunstable Gr Sch; K Coll Lon; St Aug Coll Cant; C St Peter-in-Thanet 1974–79; C and Prec Leeds Par Ch 1979–81; Chapl Prec Portsm Cathl 1981–87; V Leigh Park 1987–93; RD Havant 1990–93; Adn of Portsm 1993–98; Dean of Carl from 1998; M CCC, Vc-Chmn from 1996
GS 1995–98　　　　　Tel: (01228) 523335

KNOWLES, Revd (Melvin) Clay, MA, DIP THEOL
*St John's Rectory, Park Rd, Burgess Hill, W Sussex
RH15 8HG* [CHICHESTER] *b* 4 Dec 1943; *educ* RE Lee
High Sch; Stetson Univ, USA; Ex Univ; Ripon
Coll Cuddesdon; C Minchinhampton 1977–80; V
Cathl Par St Helena 1980–82; TV Gd Shep Hay-
wards Heath 1982–89; Adult Educ Adv Chich
1989–94; R St Jo w St Edw Burgess Hill from 1994
GS 1991– *Tel:* (01444) 232582

KOVOOR, Revd George Iype, BA, BD, MA
*Crowther Hall, Weoley Park Rd, Selly Oak, Birming-
ham B29 6QT* [BIRMINGHAM] *b* 6 Jun 1957; *educ*
Airforce Public Sch; St Steph Coll Delhi Univ;
Hindu Coll Delhi Univ; Serampore Univ; Nottm
Univ; Union Bibl Sem Yavatmal; C Shanti Niwas
Ch Faridabad 1980–82; Presbyter Santokh Majra
Par Ch 1982–83; Hon Chapl to Indian Army and
Airforce 1984–88; Presbyter St Paul Cathl Ambala
1984–88; Nat Youth Dir Ch of N India 1987–90;
Chapl St Steph Hosp Delhi 1988–90; Min Derby
Asian Chr Min Project 1990–94; Tutor Bibl Stud-
ies and Miss Crowther Hall 1994–97; Prin
Crowther Hall and Miss Educ Dir CMS from
1997; M Dioc Syn from 1994
GS 1995– *Tel:* 0121–472 4228 (Office)
Tel and Fax: 0121–415 5738 (Home)

KUHRT, Ven Gordon Wilfred, BD
*Church House, Great Smith St, London SW1P 3NZ,
London SW1P 3NZ* [DIRECTOR OF MINISTRY,
ARCHBISHOPS' COUNCIL] *b* 15 Feb 1941; *educ*
Colfe's Gr Sch; Lon Univ; Oak Hill Th Coll; RE
Tchr 1963–65; C Illogan 1967–70; C Wallington
1970–73; V Shenstone 1973–79; V Em S Croydon
1979–89; RD Croydon Central 1981–86; Hon Can
S'wark Cathl 1987–89; Th Lect Lon Univ Extra
Mural Dept 1984–89; Adn of Lewisham 1989–96;
M Ord of Women Steering Ctee 1987–93; M ABM
1990–96; M CTBI 1990–95; Sen Inspector of Th
Colls and Courses 1988–96; Chief Sec ABM
1996–98; Dir of Min Abps' Coun from 1998; M
CTE; Fell and M Coun Coll of Preachers; M
Trustees *Anvil* Th Journal
GS 1986–96 *Tel:* 020–7898 1390
Fax: 020–7898 1419
email: gordon.kuhrt@mindiv.c-of-e.org.uk

LADDS, Mrs Roberta Harriet
60 West Green, Stokesley, Middlesbrough TS9 5BD
[BLACKBURN] *b* 3 Jul 1942; *educ* Medway Tech High
Sch; Medway Coll of Tech; Industrial Chemist
Reed Internat 1959–65; Chmn Blackb MU Social
Concern Dept 1988–91; M Dioc BSR; M Liturg
Ctee; M Communications Ctee; CE Rep CTE from
1990; Housewife; Clergy wife
GS 1990–

LAMBERT, Mr (Joseph) David, FIM, MCIPS
48 Broomleaf Rd, Farnham, Surrey GU9 8DQ
[GUILDFORD] *b* 29 Apr 1935; *educ* Shoreham Gr
Sch; Worc Coll Ox; Overseas Service 'A' Course;
Distr Offcr/Distr Commr Kenya 1955–63; Production and Supplies Management posts in Elec-
tronics and Motor Industries 1963–71; Manag-
ment Services Dir Crosby Grp Ltd 1971–80; Head
of Information Systems Meyer Internat plc
1980–94; Rtd; Treas Nat Soc from 1991; Vol Adv
Citizens Advice Bureau; M CBF 1994–95; M Ch
Ho Publishing Ctee 1993–98; M DBF from 1994;
DBF Exec Ctee from 1997;
GS 1994– *Tel and Fax:* (01252) 722161
email: pandalambert@ukgateway.net

LAMMY, Mr David Lindon, LL B, LL M
43 Fetter Lane, London EC4A 1JU [APPOINTED
MEMBER, ARCHBISHOPS' COUNCIL] *b* 19 Jul 1972;
educ K Sch Peterb; SOAS Lon Univ; Harvard Law
Sch; Barrister-at-Law, Lincoln's Inn; Called to the
Bar 1995; Apptd M Abp's Coun from 1999
GS 1999– *Tel:* 020–7284 0001

LANCASTER, Bishop of [SUFFRAGAN,
BLACKBURN] **Rt Revd (Geoffrey) Stephen
Pedley,** MA
Vicarage, Shireshead, Forton, Preston PR3 0AE b 13
Sep 1940; *educ* Marlborough Coll; Qu Coll Cam;
Cuddesdon Th Coll; C Our Lady and St Nic Liv
1966–69; C H Trin Cov 1969–71; P-in-c Kitwe, N
Zambia 1971–77; V St Pet Stockton-on-Tees
1977–88; R Whickham 1988–93; Can Res Dur
Cathl 1993–98; Bp of Lanc from 1998; Chair Dioc
BMU; Chair Dioc Liturg Coun
GS 1985–90 *Tel:* (01524) 799900
Fax: (01524) 799901
email: bishop.lancaster@ukonline.co.uk

LANCASTER, Miss Patricia Margaret, DIP ED, BA
8 Vectis Rd, Alverstoke, Gosport, Hants PO12 2QF
[CHURCH COMMISSIONER] *b* 22 Feb 1929; *educ*
Southn Univ; Lon Univ; Hdmistress St Mich Sch
Burton Park 1962–73; Hdmistress Wycombe
Abbey Sch 1973–89; Ch Commr, M Houses Ctee
1989–95, M Bishoprics Ctee from 1995, M Red
Chs Ctee 1991–96; Co-opted Bd of Govs from
1995; Sch Gov *Tel:* 023–9258 3189

LANDSBERT, Mr Terry (Terence) Carl, FCA
*West Manor, Church St, Upwey, Weymouth DT3
5QB* [OXFORD] *b* 21 Dec 1936; *educ* St Albans Sch;
Rank Xerox 1972–74; Finance Dir Lake & Elliot
Ltd 1974–76; PA Internat Management Consult-
ants 1976–82; Sec Ox DBF 1982–98; M CBF
1985–98; M Cen Ch Fund from 1986
GS 1985–

LANGLEY, Canon Myrtle Sarah, MA, BD, PH D, H
DIP ED, FRAI, IDC
*Rectory, Long Marton, Appleby-in-Westmorland,
Cumbria CA16 6BN* [CARLISLE] *b* 24 Oct 1939; *educ*
Colaiste Moibhi Shankill, Co Dublin; C of I Tr
Coll/Dubin Univ; Bris Univ; Dalton Ho Bris;
Teaching Ireland 1959–64; Teaching Kenya
1966–73; Tutor and Course Leader Trin Coll Bris
1974–82; Dioc Missr and Asst Padgate TM Liv
1982–87; Dioc Dir of Chr Development for Miss

and Co-ord of Tr Liv 1987–89; Hon Lect Faculty of Th Man Univ; Prin Carl and Blackb Dioc Tr Inst 1990–98; P-in-c Long Marton w Dufton and Milburn from 1998; M Dioc Syn; M Vacancy in See Ctee
GS 1998–   *Tel:* (01768) 361269

LANGSTAFF, Ms Bridget Jane, RGN, RM, DN, B SC
East Wing, Bishop's Croft, Old Church Rd, Harborne, Birmingham B17 0BE [BIRMINGHAM] *b* 18 Jul 1954; *educ* Thorpe Ho Sch Norwich; Norwich High Sch; Middx Hosp Lon; John Radcliffe Hosp Ox; Birm Poly; Distr Nurse S Birm Health Authority 1986–94; Nurse Practitioner for the Homeless from 1994
GS 1990–   *Tel:* 0121–427 2295

LANKSHEAR, Mr David William, M PHIL, FCP, T CERT
Church House, Great Smith St, London SW1P 3NZ [SCHOOLS OFFICER, BOARD OF EDUCATION AND DEPUTY GENERAL SECRETARY, NATIONAL SOCIETY] *b* 30 Jun 1943; *educ* Highgate Sch; Bp Otter Coll; Univ of Wales; Teaching 1965–69; Warden Haringey Tchrs Centre 1970–75; Hdtchr St Katherine's VA Prim Sch 1975–80; Dioc Educ Adv Chelmsf 1981–88; Dioc Dir of Educ 1988–90; Schs Officer Bd of Educ and Dep Gen Sec Nat Soc from 1991
                                            Tel: 020–7898 1490
                                            Fax: 020–7898 1493
email: david.lankshear@natsoc.c-of-e.org.uk

LARKIN, Canon Peter John, ALCD
Rectory, 9 Seymour Drive, Mannamead, Plymouth, Devon PL3 5BG [EXETER] *b* 29 Apr 1939; *educ* Qu Eliz Sch Crediton; Leic Coll of Art and Tech (Sch of Textiles); Lon Coll of Div; C Liskeard 1962–64; C St Andr Rugby 1964–67; Organising Sec Bp of Cov's Call to Mission 1967–68; V Kea Truro 1968–78; Sec Dioc Coun for Miss and Unity 1968–78; P-in-c St Jo Bromsgrove 1978–81; R St Matthias Torquay 1981–97; Can Sokoto dio Nigeria 1991–98; R N Sutton TM Plymouth from 1997; Can Kaduna Nigeria from 1998
GS 1993–   *Tel* and *Fax:* (01752) 663321

LASH, Very Revd Archimandrite Ephrem
Monastery of SS Peter and Paul, Normanby, Whitby, N Yorks YO22 4PS [ECUMENICAL REPRESENTATIVE (ORTHODOX CHURCH)]
GS 1995–

LAW, Canon Robert Frederick, HNC, DIP TH
Rectory, St Columb Major, Cornwall TR9 6AE [TRURO] *b* 12 Jan 1943; *educ* St Aid Birkenhead; C Bengeo 1969–72; C Sandy 1972–76; P-in-c St Ippolyts and Chapl Lister Hosp Stevenage 1976–81; Chapl Jersey Grp of Hosps 1981–84; V Crowan w Godolphin 1984–92; RD Kerrier 1990–92; R St Columb Major w St Wenn from 1992; RD Pydar from 1996; Hon Can Truro Cathl from 1999
GS 1995–   *Tel:* (01637) 880252
                                            0468 820310 (Mobile)
                                            Fax: (01637) 820310

LAWSON, Ven Michael Charles, BA
The Archdeacon of Hampstead's Office, The Basement, 44 King Henry's Rd, London NW3 3RP [ARCHDEACON OF HAMPSTEAD] *b* 23 May 1952; *educ* Hove Gr Sch; Guildhall Sch of Music; Sussex Univ; Ecoles d'Art Americaines, Conservatoire de Musique Fontainebleau, France; Trin Coll Bris; C St Mary Horsham 1978–81; Dir of Pastoring All So Langham Place 1981–86; V Ch Ch Bromley 1987–99; Adn of Hampstead from 1999; Dir and Trustee Langham Arts Trust from 1987; Coun and Exec M CEEC from 1996   *Tel:* 020–7586 3224
                                            Fax: 020–7586 9976
email: archdeacon.hampstead@dlondon.org.uk

LAYTON, Mr John Keith, LIM, MIM
50 Wall Well, Hasbury, Halesowen, W Midlands B63 4SJ [WORCESTER] *b* 7 Aug 1944; *educ* Grp Quality/Techical Manager Folkes Forgings Ltd; M Bp's Coun and Stg Ctee; M Vacancy in See Ctee; Jt Lay Chmn Dudley Dny Syn from 1986
GS 1995–   *Tel:* 0121–550 2362

LEACH, Mr Robert, FCCA, FIPPM
19 Chestnut Ave, Stoneleigh, Epsom, Surrey KT19 0SY [GUILDFORD] *b* 19 Nov 1949; *educ* Glyn Gr Sch Ewell; Financial Author from 1986; M CBF from 1996; M CE Pensions Bd 1996–97; M Dioc Syn from 1990; Lay Chmn Epsom Dny Syn from 1996; Dir and Trustee *CE Newspaper* from 1992, Chmn from 1997
GS 1995–   *Tel:* 020–8224 5695/6
                                            Fax: 020–8393 6413
email: 106234.3636@compuserve.com

LEANING, Very Revd David
The Residence, Southwell, Notts NG25 0HP [PROVOST OF SOUTHWELL] *b* 18 Aug 1936; *educ* Brigg Gr Sch Lincs; Keble Coll Ox; Lich Th Coll; Asst C Gainsborough, Lincs 1960–65; (P-in-c Morton and East Stockwith 1963–65); R Warsop w Sookholme 1965–76; V Kington w Huntington 1976–80; RD Kington Weobley 1976–80; Adn of Newark 1980–91; Prov of Southwell from 1991; Warden Community of St Laur, Belper 1984–96; Chmn ABM Selection Confs 1988–96
GS 1984–91   *Tel:* (01636) 812593 (Home)
                         (01636) 812649 (Office)
                Fax: (01636) 812782 (Home)
                         (01636) 815904 (Office)

LEE, Revd John, B SC, M SC, M INST GA
Fielden House, Little College St, London SW1P 3SH [CLERGY APPOINTMENTS ADVISER] *b* 21 Oct 1947; *educ* St Dunstan's Coll Catford; Univ Coll Swansea; Inst of Grp Analysis Lon; Ripon Hall Th Coll; Research Scientist R Australian Navy Research Laboratory Sydney 1971–73; pt Nursing Auxiliary Chu Hosp Ox 1973–75; C Cockett 1975–78; P-in-c St Teilo Cockett 1976–78; Pr/Counsellor St Botoloph Aldgate 1978–84; Hon Psychotherapist Dept of Psychological Medicine St Bart's Hosp Lon 1980–86; Course Consultant St Albs Minl Tr

Scheme 1980–85; P-in-c Chiddingstone w Chiddingstone Causeway 1984–89; R 1989–98; Tutor in Individual and Grp Psychotherapy Dept of Psychological Medicine St Bart's Medical Sch 1987–92; Staff Consultant Richmond Fellowship 1989–98; Psychotherapist and Grp Analyst in private practice 1987–98; Clergy Appointments Adv from 1999   *Tel:* 020–7898 1897/8
Fax: 020–7898 1899
email: sue.manners@caa.c-of-e.org.uk

LEICESTER, Bishop of, Rt Revd Timothy John Stevens, MA
Bishop's Lodge, 10 Springfield Rd, Leicester LE2 3BD b 31 Dec 1946; *educ* Chigwell Sch; Selw Coll Cam; Ripon Hall Th Coll; C E Ham TM 1976–79; TV St Alban Upton Park 1979–80; TR Canvey Island 1980–88; Bp of Chelmsf's Urban Offcr 1988–91; Adn of West Ham 1991–95; Bp of Dunwich 1995–99; Bp of Leic from 1999
GS 1987–95, 1999–   *Tel:* 0116–270 8985
Fax: 0116–270 3288
email: bptim@leicester.anglican.org

LEIGH, Mr John Roland, MA, ATII
Robin Hood Cottage, Blue Stone Lane, Mawdesley, Ormskirk, Lancs L40 2RG [BLACKBURN] b 11 Mar 1933; *educ* Winchester Coll; K Coll Cam; Partner/Dir Rathbone Bros plc 1963–93; Dir The Greenbank Trust Ltd 1969–81; Dir Albany Investment Trust plc 1979–95; Rtd; M CBF 1995–98; M CBF Investment Ctee 1996–99; M Nat Soc Investment Ctee; Dir Nat Soc Enterprises Ltd; Chmn The Hulme Trust
GS 1995–   *Tel:* (01704) 822641
Fax: (01704) 822691

LENNOX, Mr Lionel Patrick Madill, LL B
Provincial and Diocesan Registry, Stamford House, Piccadilly, York YO1 9PP [REGISTRAR, PROVINCE OF YORK] *educ* St Jo Sch Leatherhead; Birm Univ; Solicitor from 1973; In private practice 1973–80; Asst Legal Adv Gen Syn 1981–87; Sec Abp of Cant's Grp on Affinity 1982–84; Sec Bp of Lon's Grp on Blasphemy 1981–87; Sec Legal Adv Commn 1986–89; Registrar Province and Dio York and Registrar York Conv from 1987 and Solicitor in private practice; M Legal Adv Commn from 1987; Notary Public from 1992; M Ecclesiastical Rule Ctee from 1992; Trustee Yorks Hist Chs Trust   *Tel:* (01904) 623487
Fax: (01904) 611458
email: denison.till@dial.pipex.com

LEROY, Mr Peter John, MA, CERT ED
8 Brook Cottage, Lower Barton, Corston, Bath BA2 9BA [BATH AND WELLS] b 17 Jun 1944; *educ* Monkton Combe Sch; Qu Coll Cam; Asst Master, Head of History and Housemaster Radley Coll 1967–84; Hdmaster Monkton Combe Jun Sch 1984–94; Vc-Chmn Incorp Assn of Prep Schs 1993–94; Sec Studylink EFAC Internat Tr Partnership from 1995; Area Rep for Jt Educl Trust from

1994; M Bd of Educ and Schs Ctee; M Dioc Bd of Educ from 1997; M Scripture Union Coun; Rd from 1997
GS 1975–85, 1995–   *Tel:* (01225) 873023
Fax: (01225) 873871
email: a.leroy@clara.net

LESITER, Ven Malcolm Leslie, MA
17 Lansdowne Rd, Luton LU3 1EE [ARCHDEACON OF BEDFORD] b 31 Jan 1937; *educ* Cranleigh Sch; Selw Coll Cam; Cuddesdon Th Coll; C St Marg Eastney Portsm 1963–66; TV St Paul Highfield Hemel Hempstead 1966–73; V Leavesden 1973–88; RD Watford 1981–88; Chmn St Alb Dioc Minl Tr Scheme 1980–83; V Radlett 1988–93; Adn of Bedf from 1993; M Clergy Conditions of Service Steering Grp; M Ch Grp on Funeral Services at Cemeteries and Crematoria
GS 1985–   *Tel:* (01582) 730722
Fax: (01582) 877354

LEWES, Bishop of [AREA BISHOP, CHICHESTER] **Rt Revd Wallace Parke Benn,** BA, DIP TH
Bishop's Lodge, 16A Prideaux Rd, Eastbourne BN21 2NB b 6 Aug 1947; *educ* St Andr Coll Dublin; Univ Coll Dublin; Univ of Lon; Trin Coll Bris; C St Mark New Ferry, Wirral 1972–76; C St Mary Cheadle 1976–82; V St Jas the Great Audley 1982–87; V St Pet Harold Wood 1987–97; pt Chapl Harold Wood Hosp 1987–96; Bp of Lewes from 1997; M Dioc Syn; M Dioc Staff Tm; Bp's Coun; M DBF; Bp w oversight for Youth and Children's Work   *Tel:* (01323) 648462
Fax: (01323) 641514
email: lewes@clara.net

LEWIS, Very Revd Christopher Andrew, BA, PH D
The Deanery, St Albans, Herts AL1 1BY [DEAN OF ST ALBANS] b 4 Feb 1944; *educ* Marlboro Coll; Bris Univ; CCC Cam; Westcott Ho Th Coll; Episc Th Sch Cam Mass; C Barnard Castle 1973–76; Tutor Ripon Coll Cuddesdon 1976–81; Dir Ox Inst for Ch and Soc 1976–79; P-in-c Aston Rowant and Crowell 1978–81; Vc Prin 1981–82; V Spalding 1982–87; Can Res Cant Cathl 1987–94; Dir Minl Tr Cant dio 1989–94; Dean of St Alb from 1994; Chmn Inspections Working Party Ho of Bps Ctee for Min
GS 1985–88, 1995–   *Tel:* (01727) 852120
Fax: (01727) 850944
email: cathedra@alban.u-net.com

LEWIS, Very Revd Richard, MA
The Dean's Lodging, 25 The Liberty, Wells, Som BA5 2SZ [DEAN OF WELLS] b 24 Dec 1935; *educ* R Masonic Sch; Fitzw Coll Cam; Ripon Hall Ox; C Hinckley 1960–63; C Sanderstead (in-c St Edm) 1963–66; V All SS S Merstham 1967–72; V H Trin S Wimbledon 1972–79; V St Barn Dulwich and Fndtn Chapl Alleyn's Coll 1979–90; Exam Chapl

to Bp of S'wark; Dean of Wells from 1990
GS 1984–

Tel: (01749) 670278
Fax: (01749) 679184
email: deanofwells@barclays.net

LEYTON, Mr Richard Charles, MBCS
Dormer Cottage, 49 Chilbolton Ave, Winchester, Hants SO22 5HJ [WINCHESTER] *b* 7 Nov 1944; *educ* Pet Symonds Sch Win; IS Management Consultant Digital Equipment Co from 1987; M CBF from 1995; Gen Syn Rep Ch Army Bd; M DBF, M Bp's Coun; Rdr; Lay Chmn Winchester Dny Syn
GS 1995–

Tel: (01962) 863046
Fax: (01962) 841471
email: leyton@mail.dec.com

LICHFIELD, Bishop of, Rt Revd Keith Norman Sutton, MA, D UNIV, D LITT
Bishop's House, 22 The Close, Lichfield, Staffs WS13 7LG b 23 Jun 1934; *educ* Woking and Battersea Gr Schs; Jes and St Jo Colls Cam; Ridley Hall Th Coll; C St Andr Plymouth 1959–62; Chapl St Jo Coll Cam 1962–68; Tutor and Chapl of Bp Tucker Th Coll Uganda 1968–73; Prin Ridley Hall Th Coll 1973–78; Bp of Kingston-upon-Thames 1978–84; Bp of Lich from 1984; Chmn BMU 1989–91; Chmn BM 1991–94; Pres Qu Coll Birm 1986–94; Visitor Simon of Cyrene Th Inst from 1992; Vc Pres CMS from 1995
GS 1984–

Tel: (01543) 306000
Fax: (01543) 306009

LICKESS, Canon David Frederick, BA
Vicarage, Hutton Rudby, Yarm, N Yorks TS15 0HY [YORK] *b* 3 Oct 1937; *educ* Scarborough High Sch; Dur Univ; St Chad's Coll Dur; C Howden Minster 1965–70; V Rudby-in-Cleveland w Middleton from 1970; Non-res Can York Minster from 1990; M CCU from 1991; M CTBI & CTE 1990–94; CE Rep to Methodist Conf 1993 and 1994; RD Stokesley from 1993; M CCBI Ch Representatives Meeting 1996; M CTE Enabling Grp 1996–97
GS 1985–

Tel: (01642) 700223

LILLEY, Revd Christopher Howard, DIP CM, FCA, FTII
Vicarage, North St, Middle Rasen, Market Rasen, Lincs LN8 3TS [LINCOLN] *b* 11 Oct 1951; *educ* K Sch Grantham; St Jo Coll Nottm; Hon C Skegness and Winthorpe 1985–93; C Gt Limber w Brocklesby 1993–96; P-in-c Middle Rasen Grp 1996–97; R Middle Rasen Grp from 1997; M DBF; Ch Commr 1997–98; M Abps' Coun Finance Ctee from 1999; M Ch Commrs Bishoprics and Cathls Ctee from 1999
GS 1996–

Tel: (01673) 842249

LINCOLN, Bishop of, Rt Revd Robert Maynard Hardy, MA, DD
Bishop's House, Eastgate, Lincoln LN2 1QQ b 5 Oct 1936; *educ* Qu Eliz Gr Sch Wakef; Clare Coll Cam; Cuddesdon Th Coll; Asst C All SS & Martyrs

Langley 1962–65; Fell and Chapl Selw Coll Cam 1965–72; V All SS Borehamwood 1972–75; P-in-c Aspley Guise and Dir of St Alb's Dio Minl Tr Scheme 1975–80; R Aspley Guise w Husborne Crawley and Ridgmont 1980; Bp of Maidstone 1980–87; Bp to HM Prisons from 1985; Bp of Linc from 1987
GS 1987–

Tel: (01522) 534701
Fax: (01522) 511095
email: bishlincoln@claranet.co.uk

LITTEN, Mr Julian William Sebastian, FSA
Vicarage, St Barnabas Rd, Walthamstow, London E17 8JZ, and 11 Hampton Court, Nelson St, King's Lynn PE30 5DX [CHELMSFORD] *b* 6 Nov 1947; *educ* St Pet Collegiate Sch, Wolverhampton; NE Lon Poly; Cardiff Univ; Victoria and Albert Museum Lon 1966–99; Court of Fells, Soc of the Faith from 1984; Chmn Portsm Cathl FAC from 1988; M Cathl Fabric Commn from 1991; M Westmr Abbey Architectural Adv Panel from 1993; Trustee Buildings Crafts and Conservation Trust from 1993; Chmn Ch Maintenance Trust from 1997; Trustee Mausolea and Monuments Trust from 1997; Trustee Traditional Buildings Trust from 1998
GS 1985–

Tel: 020–8521 5523
(01553) 766643

LIVERPOOL, Bishop of, Rt Revd James Stuart Jones, BA, PGCE, DD
Bishop's Lodge, Woolton Park, Liverpool L25 6DT b 18 Aug 1948; *educ* Duke of York's Military Sch Dover; Ex Univ; Wycliffe Hall Th Coll; C Ch Ch Clifton 1982–90; V Em S Croydon 1990–94; Bp of Hull 1994–98; Bp of Liv from 1998
GS 1995–

Tel: 0151–421 0831
Fax: 0151–428 3055
email: Bishop@Bishopslodge.freeserve.co.uk

LLEWELLIN, Rt Revd (John) Richard Allan, MA
Lambeth Palace, London SE1 7JU [BISHOP AT LAMBETH (HEAD OF STAFF)] *b* 30 Sep 1938; *educ* Clifton Coll; Law Soc Sch of Law; Fitzwm Coll Cam; Westcott Ho Th Coll; C Radlett 1964–68; C Johannesburg Cathl 1968–71; V Waltham Cross 1971–79; R Harpenden 1979–85; Bp of St Germans 1985–92; Bp of Dover 1992–99; Bp at Lambeth (Head of Staff) from 1999
GS 1992–95

Tel: 020–7898 1200
Fax: 020–7261 9836
email: richard.llewellin@lampal.c-of-e.org.uk

LLOYD, Ven (Bertram) Trevor, MA
Stage Cross, Whitemoor Hill, Bishop's Tawton, Barnstaple, N Devon EX32 0BE [ARCHDEACON OF BARNSTAPLE] *b* 15 Feb 1938; *educ* Highgate Sch; Hertf Coll Ox; Clifton Th Coll; C Ch Ch Barnet 1964–69; V H Trin Wealdstone 1970–84; P-in-c St Mich Harrow Weald 1980–84; V Trin St Mich Harrow 1984–89; AD Harrow 1977–82; Adn of Barnstaple from 1989; M Liturg Commn from 1981; M CBF from 1991; M CBF Publishing Ctee 1991–98; M

CCC from 1992; Preb of Ex Cathl from 1991; M Liturg Publishing Grp from 1995; M Gen Syn Stg Ctee 1996–98; M Policy Ctee 1996–98; M Chs Main Ctee from 1996; Chapl to Syn; Chmn SW Children's Hospice; Chmn Dioc Adult Tr Ctee; Chmn Dioc Liturg Ctee
GS 1991–   *Tel:* (01271) 375475
  Fax: (01271) 377934

LOCK, Canon Peter Harcourt D'Arcy, AKC
Vicarage, 9 St Paul's Square, Bromley, Kent BR2 0XH [ROCHESTER] *b* 2 Aug 1944; *educ* Kingston Gr Sch; K Coll Lon; St Boniface Warminster; C St Jo B Meopham1968–72; C St Matt Wigmore w All SS Hempstead 1972–73; C Parish of S Gillingham 1973–77; R All SS Hartley 1977–83; R Fawkham and Hartley 1983–84; V H Trin Dartford 1984–93; Hon Can Roch Cathl from 1990; V St Pet & St Paul Bromley from 1993; RD Bromley from 1996; M Bp's Coun from 1994; Chmn Dioc Ho of Clergy from 1996; M Revision Ctee Eucharistic Prayers
GS 1980–   *Tel:* 020–8460 6275 (Home)
  020–8464 5244 (Office)
  Fax: 020–8460 3732 (Office)

LOCKE, Mr Geoff
Narnia II, 88 Ravenscliffe Rd, Kidsgrove, Stoke-on-Trent ST7 4HX [LICHFIELD] *b* 17 Feb 1943; *educ* Woodhouse Gr Sch Finchley; Lon Univ; Derby Univ; Telecommunications Traffic Superintendent Post Office 1963–68; Asst Prin Min to Tech 1968–69; Teaching 1969–71; Tutor Stoke-on-Trent Sixth Form Coll 1971–76; St Jo Coll Nottm 1977; CPAS NW Eng Youth Work Co-ord 1978–80; Educationist; M W Midl Min Tr Course Ctee 1986–90; M Revision Ctee Dioc Bds of Educ Measure 1987–90; Rdr; M CEEC Exec; Vc-Chmn Dioc Bd of Educ; Lay Chmn Dioc Syn; M Bd of Educ and Further and Higher Educ Ctee; M CMEAC; Chmn Evang Grp in Gen Syn; Lecturer
GS 1985–90, 1995–   *Tel:* (01782) 785544
  Fax: (01782) 785588

LOMAX, Canon Barry Walter John, STH
Rectory, 2 Portman Place, Deer Park, Blandford Forum, Dorset DT11 7DG [SALISBURY] *b* 26 Dec 1939; *educ* W Taring High Sch Worthing; Worthing CFE; Lon Coll of Div; C St Nic Sevenoaks 1966–71; C Ch Ch Southport 1971–73; V St Matt Bootle 1973–78; P-in-c St Andr Litherland 1976–78; V St Jo New Boro and Leigh 1978–94; Hon Can and Preb Sarum Cathl from 1991; R Blandford Forum and Langton Long from 1994
GS 1994–   *Tel:* (01258) 480092

LONDON, Bishop of, Rt Revd and Rt Hon Richard John Carew Chartres, MA, BD, DD, D LITT, FSA
The Old Deanery, Dean's Court, London EC4V 5AA b 11 Jul 1947; *educ* Hertf Gr Sch; Trin Coll Cam; Cuddesdon Th Coll; Linc Th Coll; C St Andr Bedford 1973–75; Bp's Dom Chapl 1975–80; Chapl to Abp of Cant 1980–84; P-in-c St Steph w St Jo

Westmr 1984–85; V 1986–92; DDO 1985–92; Prof Div Gresham Coll 1986–92; Six Preacher Cant Cathl 1991–96; Bp of Stepney 1992–95; Bp of London from 1995; Chmn Chs Main Ctee; Chmn Ch Heritage Forum
GS 1995–   *Tel:* 020–7248 6233
  email: bishop@londin.clara.co.uk

LONG, Mr David John Baverstock
Epwell Mill, Banbury, Oxon OX15 6HG [ADMINISTRATIVE SECRETARY TO THE REVIEW GROUP ON ROYAL PECULIARS] *b* 15 May 1949; *educ* Uppingham Sch; St Jo Coll Dur; Ripon Coll Cuddesdon; On staff of Ch Commrs from 1973; Seconded as Admin Sec to Review Group on Royal Peculiars from 1999
  Tel and *Fax:* (01295) 788242

LOVEGROVE, Mr Canon Philip Albert, LL B, LLM
159 Baldwins Lane, Croxley Green, Herts WD3 3LL [ST ALBANS] *b* 15 Aug 1937; *educ* Pet Symonds' Win; K Coll Lon; Investment Banker and Financial Consultant from 1962; Ch Commr 1983–98; Chmn St Alb DBF from 1970; M Bp's Coun from 1970; M Gen Syn Stg Ctee 1980–85 and 1990–98; Lay Can St Albs Cathl from 1998
GS 1977–   *Tel:* (01923) 232387 (Home)
  020–7600 4800 (Office)
  Fax: 020–7600 4622 (Office)

LOVELESS, Mrs Jill (Gillian Margaret), BA, DL
Springfield House, Dyers Lane, Slindon, Arundel, W Sussex BN18 0RE [CHICHESTER] *b* 1 Dec 1932; *educ* Hawnes Sch Beds; Westf Coll Lon; Birm Univ; Child Care Officer Middx Co Coun 1957–60; Adoption Social Worker; Dioc Assn for Family Social Work 1976–81; JP 1974–98; Chmn Arundel Bench 1990–95; Lay Chmn Arundel & Bognor Dny Syn 1993–96; M Bp's Coun
GS 1990–   *Tel:* (01243) 814356

LOWATER, Mr Peter Alexander, MA
Lower Gubbles, Hook Lane, Warsash, Southampton SO31 9HH [PORTSMOUTH] *b* 30 Nov 1935; *educ* R Masonic Sch; Lay Can Portsm Cathl from 1984; Chmn DBF from 1991; Nurseryman; Chmn Mutual Support Grp; Chmn Allocations and Apportionment Review Grp
GS 1994–   *Tel:* (01489) 572156

LOWMAN, Canon David Walter, BD, AKC
25 Roxwell Rd, Chelmsford, Essex CM1 2LY [CHELMSFORD] *b* 27 Nov 1948; *educ* Crewkerne Gr Sch; K Coll Lon; St Aug Coll Cant; Civil Servant 1966–70; C Notting Hill TM 1975–78; C St Aug w St Jo Kilburn 1978–81; Selection Sec and Voc Adv ACCM 1981–86; TR Wickford and Runwell 1986–93; DDO, Lay Min Adv and NSM Officer from 1993; Hon Can Chelmsf Cathl from 1993; M ABM Min Development and Deployment Ctee 1990–98; M VRSC from 1999; M CMEAC Vocations Sub-Ctee from 1998; M Dioc Syn from 1986;

Chmn Dioc Ord Adv Ctee; Coun M N Thames Min Tr Course; E Anglian Min Course; SE Inst for Th Educ; Coun M Oak Hill Th Coll
GS 1995–   Tel: (01245) 264187
                            Fax: (01245) 348789
        email: ddo@chelmsford.anglican.org

LOWSON, Ven Christopher, M TH, STM, AKC
5 Brading Ave, Southsea, Hants PO4 9QJ [ARCH-DEACON OF PORTSDOWN] *b* 3 Feb 1953; *educ* Newc Cathl Sch; Consett Gr Sch; K Coll Lon; St Aug Coll Cant; Pacific Sch of Religion Berkeley California; Heythrop Coll Lon; C St Mary Richmond 1977–82; P-in-c H Trin Eltham 1982–83, V 1983–91; Chapl Avery Hill Coll 1982–85; Chapl Thames Poly 1985–91; V Petersfield and R Buriton 1991–99; RD Petersfield 1995–99; Vis Lect Portsm Univ from 1998; Adn of Portsdown from 1999   email: lowson@surfaid.org

LUDLOW, Bishop of [SUFFRAGAN, HEREFORD] **Rt Revd John Charles Saxbee,** BA, PH D
The Bishop's House, Corvedale Rd, Craven Arms, Shropshire SY7 9BT b 7 Jan 1946; *educ* Cotham Gr Sch Bris; Bris Univ; Dur Univ; Cranmer Hall Dur; C Em w St Paul Plymouth 1972–76; V St Phil Weston Mill 1976–81; TV Cen Ex 1981–87; Dir SW Minl Tr Course 1981–92; Preb of Ex Cathl 1988–92; Adn of Ludlow from 1992; Bp of Ludlow from 1994; M Springboard Exec from 1996; Pres Modern Churchpeople's Union from 1997; Religious Adv to Central TV from 1997
GS 1985–94   Tel: (01588) 673571
                            Fax: (01588) 673585

LYNN, Bishop of [SUFFRAGAN, NORWICH] **Rt Revd Anthony Charles Foottit,** MA
The Old Vicarage, Castle Acre, King's Lynn, Norfolk PE32 2AA b 28 Jun 1935; *educ* Lancing Coll; K Coll Cam; Cuddesdon Th Coll; C Wymondham 1961–64; TV Blakeney Grp 1964–71; TR Camelot Grp 1971–81; RD Cary 1979–81; St Hugh's Missr Lincs 1981–87; Hon Can Linc Cathl 1986–87; Adn of Lynn 1987–99; Bp of Lynn from 1999
GS 1995–99   Tel: (01760) 755553
                            Fax: (01760) 755085

MACKENZIE, Revd Murdoch, MA, BD
c/o Christian Foundation, The Square, Aylesbury St, Wolverton, Milton Keynes MK12 5HX [ECUMENICAL REPRESENTATIVE, UNITED REFORMED CHURCH] *b* 23 Feb 1938; *educ* Birkenhead Sch; Hertf Coll Ox; New Coll Edin; Presbyter Madras, Ch of S India 1966–78; Ch of Scotland 1978–81; Hallwood Par LEP Runcorn 1981–88; Carrs Lane Church Centre URC Birm 1988–96; Ecum Moderator Milton Keynes Chr Coun from 1996
GS 1998–

MacLEAY, Revd Angus Murdo, BA, MA, M PHIL
Vicarage, Houghton, Carlisle, Cumbria CA6 4HZ [CARLISLE] *b* 10 Jun 1959; *educ* Vyne Sch Basingstoke; Qu Mary's 6th Form Coll Basingstoke;

Univ Coll Ox; Wycliffe Hall Th Coll; Solicitor 1982–85; C H Trin Platt 1988–92; V Houghton w Kingmoor from 1992
GS 1995–   Tel: (01228) 810076
        email: angus@hkchurch.freeserve.co.uk

MAGOWAN, Revd Alistair James, B SC, DIP HE
Vicarage, Vicarage Rd, Egham, Surrey TW20 9JN [GUILDFORD] *b* 10 Feb 1955; *educ* K Sch Worc; Leeds Univ; Trin Coll Bris; C St Jo Bapt Owlerton 1981–84; C St Nic Dur 1984–89; Chapl St Aid Coll Dur 1984–89; V St Jo Bapt Egham from 1989; RD Runnymede from 1993; Chmn Dioc Bd of Educ from 1996
GS 1995–   Tel: (01784) 432066

MAIDSTONE, Bishop of [SUFFRAGAN, CANTERBURY] **Rt Revd Gavin Hunter Reid,** BA
Bishop's House, Pett Lane, Charing, Ashford, Kent TN27 0DL b 24 May 1934; *educ* Roan Sch for Boys Greenwich; K Coll Lon; Oak Hill Th Coll; C St Paul E Ham 1960–63; C Rainham (P-in-c St Jo and St Matt S Hornchurch) 1963–66; Publications Sec CPAS 1966–71; NSM St Barn Cray 1967–71; Editorial Sec USCL 1971–74; M CRAC 1979–84; Dir of Evang CPAS 1974–90; Seconded Nat Dir Miss England 1982–85; Seconded Project Dir Miss 89 1988–89; M BMU 1986–90; Consultant Missr CPAS 1990–92; M BM 1991–92; Stg Ctee 1989–92; NSM St Jo Woking 1972–92; BM Decade of Evang Adv 1990–92; Bp of Maidstone from 1992; Chmn Abps' Adv Grp for the Millenium from 1995; Consultant to BM from 1997
GS 1985–92, 1995–   Tel: (01233) 712950
                            Fax: (01233) 713543

MANCHESTER, Bishop of, Rt Revd Christopher John Mayfield, BA, MA, DIP TH, M SC
Bishopscourt, Bury New Rd, Manchester M7 4LE b 18 Dec 1935; *educ* Sedbergh Sch; G and C Coll Cam; Linacre Ho Ox; Wycliffe Hall Th Coll; Cranfield Inst of Techn; C St Martin-in-the-Bullring Birm 1963–67; Lect St Martin-in-the-Bullring Birm 1967–71; V St Mary's Luton 1971–80; RD Luton 1974–79; Adn of Bedford 1979–85; Bp of Wolverhampton 1985–93; Chmn Inter-Faith Consultative Grp 1988–95; Bp of Man from 1993; Chmn CRC from 1995
GS 1981–85, 1992–   Tel: 0161–792 2096 (Office)
                            Fax: 0161–792 6826
email:
        +Chris@bishopscourtman.free-online.co.uk

MANN, Mr Ernie (Ernest George), DIP EE, C ENG, MIEE
39 Windyridge, Gillingham, Kent ME7 3BB [ROCHESTER] *b* 18 Nov 1936; *educ* Sheerness Tech Sch; Medway Coll of Tech; City Univ; Chartered Elect Eng and Mgr SEEBoard 1960–93; Inter Soc Administrator Abbeyfield Soc Ltd from 1993; M Dioc Syn from 1990; M Bp's Coun from 1994; M Dioc Pastl Ctee; M Dioc Bd of Patronage; Lay Vc-Pres Dioc Syn from 1999
GS 1995–   Tel: (01634) 304893

MANSELL, Revd Clive Neville Ross, LL B, DIP HE
Rectory, Kirklington, Bedale, N Yorks DL8 2NJ
[RIPON] *b* 20 Apr 1953; *educ* City of Lon Sch; Leic Univ; Coll of Law; Trin Coll Bris; Solicitor (no longer practising); C Gt Malvern Priory 1982–85; Min Can Ripon Cathl 1985–89; R Kirklington w Burneston, Wath and Pickhill from 1989; AD Wensley from 1998; M Revision Ctee on the Draft Churchwardens Measure from 1996; M Legal Aid Commn from 1996; Ch Commr from 1997; M Revision Ctee on Draft Amending Canon No 22; M Revision Ctee on Draft Church of England (Misc Provisions) Measure and Draft Amending Canon No 23; M Dioc Bd of Educ; M Dioc Bd of Patronage; M Dioc Rural Min Grp; M Ecclesiastical Law Soc
GS 1995– *Tel:* (01845) 567429

MARGARET SHIRLEY, Sister, OHP
St Oswald's Pastoral Centre, Woodlands Drive, Sleights, Whitby, N Yorks YO21 1RY [RELIGIOUS COMMUNITIES NORTH, LAY] *b* 10 Jul 1934; *educ* Herts and Essex High Sch; Bp Otter Coll Chichester; Teaching in UK 1955–58, 1960–66; Teaching in Swaziland and Zimbabwe 1966–82; Lay tr and par work in Zimbabwe 1982–89; Par Worker Ch Ch Lancaster 1991–93; Asst Warden of Retreat House from 1995
GS 1990– *Tel:* (01947) 810496
Fax: (01947) 810750
email: ohpstos@globalnet.co.uk

MARSH, Ven (Francis) John, BA, D PHIL, CERT TH, ARCO, ARCM, ATCL
19 Clarence Park, Blackburn BB2 7FA [ARCHDEACON OF BLACKBURN] *b* 3 Jul 1947; *educ* Beckenham and Penge Gr Sch; York Univ; Oak Hill Th Coll; Selw Coll Cam; C St Matt Cambridge 1975–78; C Ch Ch Pitsmoor Sheff 1979–81; C St Thos Crookes 1981–85; V Ch Ch S Ossett 1985–96; RD Dewsbury 1993–96; Adn of Blackb from 1996; M Coun RSCM; Chmn Trustees Angl Renewal Ministries
GS 1990–96, 1997– *Tel:* (01254) 262571
Fax: (01254) 263394
email: vendocjon@aol.com

MARSH, Mr Harry (Henry Arthur)
5 Vicarage Lane, Great Baddow, Chelmsford CM2 8HY [CHELMSFORD] *b* 18 Feb 1943; *educ* Wirral Gr Sch; Inspector of Taxes from 1961; M Bp's Coun; M DBF; M Dioc Pastl Ctee; M CPAS Coun
GS 1994– *Tel:* (01245) 478038

MARSH, Canon Richard St John Jeremy, MA, PH D
Lambeth Palace, London SE1 7JU [SECRETARY FOR ECUMENICAL AFFAIRS TO THE ARCHBISHOP OF CANTERBURY] *b* 23 Apr 1960; *educ* Trin Sch of John Whitgift; Keble Coll Ox; Dur Univ; Mirfield Th Coll; C Grange St Andr Runcorn 1985–87; Chapl and Solway Fell Univ Coll Dur; Asst Sec for Ecum Affairs to the Abp of Cant 1992–95; Sec

from 1995; Can Dio of Gibraltar in Eur from 1995. Non Res Can Cant Cathl from 1998
Tel: 020–7898 1232
Fax: 020–7401 9886
email: richard.marsh@lampal.c-of-e.org.uk

MARSHALL, Canon Geoffrey Osborne, BA
24 Kedleston Rd, Derby DE22 1GU [DERBY] *b* 5 Jan 1948; *educ* Repton Sch; Dur Univ; Mirf Th Coll; C Waltham Cross 1973–76; C Digswell 1976–78; P-in-c Ch Ch Belper and Milford 1978–86; V Spondon 1986–93; RD Derby N 1990–95; Res Can and Sub Provost Derby Cathl from 1993; DDO from 1995; Chair E Midlands Min Tr Course from 1998; M Dioc Bd of Min
GS 1995– *Tel:* (01332) 343144 (Home)
(01332) 341201 (Office)
Fax: (01332) 203991 (Office)
email: Geoffrey@canonry.demon.co.uk

MARSHALL, Very Revd Peter Jerome
The Deanery, 10 College Green, Worcester WR1 2LH [DEAN OF WORCESTER] *b* 10 May 1940; *educ* McGill Univ Montreal; Westcott Ho Th Coll; C St Mary E Ham 1963–66; C St Mary Woodford 1966–71; C-in-c S Woodford 1966–71; V St Pet Walthamstow 1971–81; Dep Dir of Tr Chelmsf dio 1981–84; Can Res Chelmsf Cathl 1981–85; Dioc Dir of Tr Ripon dio 1985–97; Can Res Ripon Cathl 1985–97; Dean of Worc from 1997; Chmn Dioc Pastl Ctee from 1998; M Ch Commrs Bishoprics and Cathls Ctee from 1999 *Tel:* (01905) 27821 (Home)
(01905) 28854 (Office)
Fax: (01905) 61139
email: WorcesterDeanPJM@compuserve.com

MARSHALL, Mrs Sonia Margaret Cecilia, BA
135c Eastgate, Deeping St James, Peterborough PE6 8RB [LINCOLN] *b* 26 Mar 1949; *educ* Nuneaton High Sch for Girls; Westf Coll Lon; Various posts in personal taxation – Inland Revenue 1971–73; Barclays Bank Trust Co 1973–76; Thornton Baker Chartered Accountants 1976–79; Rdr from 1991; Tutor Dioc Rdrs Tr Course from 1995; M Dioc Liturg Ctee from 1996; Mod Linc Dioc from 1999
GS 1995– *Tel: and Fax* (01778) 346420
email: smcmarshall@deeping77.freeserve.co.uk

MARTIN, Revd Penny (Penelope Elizabeth), MA
St Mary's Vicarage, 89 Front St, Sherburn Village, Durham DH6 1HD [DURHAM] *b* 23 Oct 1944; *educ* Croydon High Sch; Cranmer Hall Dur; St Jo Coll Dur; Dss Seaham w Seaham Harbour 1986–87; Par Dn 1987–89; Par Dn Cassop cum Quarrington 1989–93; C Sherburn w Pittington in plurality w Shadforth 1993–95; V from 1995
GS 1992– *Tel:* 0191–372 0374

MARTINEAU, Revd Jeremy Fletcher, BD, AKC
Arthur Rank Centre, National Agricultural Centre, Stoneleigh Park, Warws CV8 2LZ [NATIONAL RURAL

FFICER] *b* 18 Mar 1940; *educ* Linc Gr Sch; Nottm
niv; K Coll Lon; C St Paul Jarrow 1966–73; Bp's
d Adv 1966–73; P-in-c Raughton Head 1973–80;
hapl to Agric Carl 1973–80; Social and Ind Adv
ris 1980–90; Joint Sec ACORA 1987–90; Abps'
ural Officer from 1990–93; Nat Rural Officer
om 1994   *Tel:* 024–7669 6460 (Office)
                                    (01926) 812130 (Home)
                                  Fax: 024–7669 6460
             email: J.Martineau@ruralnet.org.uk

MASTERS, Mr Keith William, MB, CH B, FRCOG
78 Birmingham Rd, Walsall, W Midlands WS5 3NX
LICHFIELD] *b* 5 Apr 1938; *educ* K Edw Sch Birm;
irm Univ Medical Sch; GP Prin Minehead
963–65; Medical Offcr (Obstetrics) Uganda
965–72; Consultant Obstetrician Br Birth Survey
973–75; Consultant Adv on Maternity Care in
he World 1973–85; Consultant Adv to World
Bank on Maternal/Child Health/Family Plan-
ing 1975–86; Consultant Obstetrician and
Gynaecologist Walsall Hosp NHS Trust 1973–99;
Rtd; Rdr; ABM Pastl Selector from 1987
GS 1994–   *Tel:* (01922) 23828
                                  Fax: (01922) 649075
             email: K.M.Masters@btinternet.com

MAWER, Mr Philip John Courtney, MA, DPA,
FRSA
Church House, Great Smith St, London SW1P 3NZ
SECRETARY GENERAL OF THE GENERAL SYNOD AND
THE ARCHBISHOPS' COUNCIL] *b* 30 Jul 1947; *educ*
Hull Gr Sch; Edin Univ; Home Office 1971–89;
Prin Private Sec to Home Sec 1987–89; Under Sec
Cabinet Office 1989–90; Lay Chmn Reading Dny
Syn and M Ox Dioc Syn 1984–86; Sec Gen of the
Gen Syn from 1990; Sec Gen of Abps' Coun from
1998; M Steering Ctee CTBI and of the Enabling
Grp CTE; M Gov Body SPCK; Non-Exec Dir EIG;
Patron Ch Housing Trust   *Tel:* 020–7898 1360
             email: philip.mawer@c-of-e.org.uk

MAY, Dr Peter George Robin, MRCS, LRCP,
MRCGP
41 Westridge Rd, Southampton, Hants SO17 2HP
[WINCHESTER] *b* 29 Oct 1945; *educ* R Free Hosp
Medical Sch; Ho Officer Northallerton Hosp
1973–74; Travelling Sec UCCF 1974–77; Senior Ho
Officer Southn Gen Hosp 1977–79; GP Shirley
Health Centre Southn from 1980; M BM from
1991
GS 1985–   *Tel:* 023–8055 8931

MAYOSS, Father Aidan (Anthony), CR, BA
*St Michael's Priory, 14 Burleigh St, London WC2E
7PX* [RELIGIOUS COMMUNITIES IN CONVOCATION,
NORTH] *b* 5 Mar 1931; *educ* Haberdashers' Askes
Sch; Leeds Univ; Coll of the Resurr Mirfield; C
Meir Stoke-on-Trent 1957–62; CR from 1964; Angl
Chapl Univ of Stellenbosch 1973–76; Chapl Lon
Univ 1976–78; Bursar CR 1983–90; Dir Fraternity

of the Resurr from 1990; M Min Div VRSC Pre-
Theol Educ Panel
GS 1993–   *Tel:* 020–7379 6669
                                  Fax: 020–7240 5294
             email: amayoss@mirfield.org.uk

McCLEAN, Prof (John) David, CBE, QC, DCL
6 Burnt Stones Close, Sheffield, S Yorks S10 5TS
[SHEFFIELD] *b* 4 Jul 1939; *educ* Qu Eliz Gr Sch
Blackb; Magd Coll Ox; Prof of Law Univ of Sheff
from 1973; Vc-Chmn Ho of Laity 1979–85; Chmn
1985–95; Chmn Legal Adv Commn; Rdr; Chan
Sheff dio from 1992; Chan Newc dio from 1998
GS 1970–   *Tel:* 0114–230 5794
             email: j.d.McClean@Sheffield.ac.uk

McCLURE, Ven Tim (Timothy Elston), BA
*10 Great Brockeridge, Westbury-on-Trym, Bristol
BS9 3TY* [ARCHDEACON OF BRISTOL] *b* 20 Oct 1946;
educ Kingston Gr Sch; St Jo Coll Dur; Ridley Hall
Th Coll; C Kirkheaton 1970–73; Marketing Mgr
Agrofax L.I.P. Ltd 1973–74; C St Ambrose
Chorlton-on-Medlock 1974–79; Chapl Man Poly
1974–82; TR Withington Man and Presiding
Chapl 1979–82; Gen Sec SCM 1982–92; Dir Chs
Coun for Industry and Social Responsibility
1992–99; Lord Mayor's Chapl Bris 1996–99; Hon
Can Bris Cathl from 1992; Adn of Bris from 1999;
Chair Traidcraft plc 1990–97; Chair Chr Conf
Trust from 1998   *Tel:* 0117–962 2438 (Home)
                          0117–921 4411 (Office)
                                  Fax: 0117–925 0460

McHENRY, Mr Brian Edward, MA
216 Friern Rd, E Dulwich, London SE22 0BB
[SOUTHWARK] *b* 12 Dec 1950; *educ* Dulwich Coll;
New Coll Ox; Barrister; Government Legal Ser-
vice from 1978; Sen Civil Service Lawyer from
1996; Rdr; Lay Chmn Dulwich Dny Syn 1987–91;
Lay Chmn Dioc Syn 1988–96 and 1997–99; M Gen
Syn Stg Ctee 1990–95; M Stg Orders Ctee 1988–90;
Chmn Stg Orders Ctee 1991–99; M Legislative
Ctee 1981–85 and 1991–95; M Panel of Chairmen
1990 and 1996–98; M Crown Appts Commn from
1997; M Abps' Coun from 1999; CE Delegate
Porvoo Leaders Consultation 1998
GS 1980–85, 1987–   *Tel:* 020–8693 1226 (Home)
                                  Fax: 020–8516 6305 (Home)
             email: brian@mchenry.co.uk

McMULLEN, Mrs Christine Elizabeth, BA,
DIP AD ED, MA
114 Brown Edge Rd, Buxton, Derbys SK17 7AB
[DERBY] *b* 9 Mar 1943; *educ* St Helena Sch Chester-
field; Homelands Sch Derby; R Holloway Coll
Lon; Rdr from 1986; M Coun Trin Coll Bris from
1991; M Womens Inter Ch Coun from 1991; Nat
Co-ordinator FLAME 1992–96; Tutor and Dir of
Pastl Studies Nn Ord Course from 1994; M BM
from 1993, M BM Exec from 1996; Sec Broken
Rites; M CMEAC from 1996; M MCAD Working

Party; M FJM Rule Ctee; M EJM(RC) and UAA(IG)
GS 1990–   *Tel:* (01298) 73997
                           Fax: (01298) 72448
                   email: christin@noc6.u-net.com

MELLOR, Canon (Kenneth) Paul, BA, MA
Lemon Lodge, Lemon St, Truro, Cornwall TR1 2PE [TRURO] *b* 11 Aug 1949; *educ* Ashfield Sch; Southn Univ; Leeds Univ; Cuddesdon Th Coll; C St Mary V Cottingham 1973–76; C All SS Ascot 1976–80; V St Mary Magd Tilehurst 1980–85; V Menheniot 1985–94; RD E Wivelshire 1990–94; Hon Can Truro Cathl 1990–94; Can Treas Truro Cathl from 1994; M CFCE; M DBF
GS 1994–   *Tel:* (01872) 276782 (Office)
                           (01872) 272094 (Home)
                     Fax: (01872) 277788
                  email: KPMellor@aol.com

MENON, Mr Vijay
97 Marlborough Gdns, Upminster, Essex RM14 1SR [CHELMSFORD] *b* 21 Aug 1930; *educ* St Thos Sch Kerala State, India; St Thos Coll Madras Univ India; Poplar Tech Coll Lon; S Shields Marine Coll Co Dur; Jnr Eng Mogul Lines 1952–55; Fourth Eng to Chief Eng Officer Admiralty 1956–60; Chief Eng Officer Stephenson Clarks Newc 1961; Senr Eng Surveyor, Lloyds Register Lon from 1961; Former M Stg Ctee and Miss Op Ctee CMS; M Coun Crosslinks; M Coun CPAS; M CEEC; M Coun Ch Soc; Rtd for full-time Chr Preaching/Teaching; On staff St Helens Bishopsgate Lon from 1988; M Br Nuclear Soc; Fell Inst Marine Engs
GS 1970–   *Tel:* (01708) 501592

MENZIES, Mr Colin Douglas Livingstone, MA, FRSA
Church House, Great Smith St, London SW1P 3NZ [SECRETARY, CORPORATION OF THE CHURCH HOUSE] *b* 8 Apr 1944; *educ* Glenalmond Coll; Keble Coll Ox; Christian Salvesen plc Edin 1971–84; RICS Edin 1984–86; City admin and recruitment 1986–90; Sec to Corp of Ch Ho from 1990
                           Tel: 020–7898 1310
                  email: colin.menzies@c-of-e.org.uk

METCALF, Ven Robert Laurence, BA, DIP TH
38 Menlove Ave, Allerton, Liverpool L18 2EF [ARCHDEACON OF LIVERPOOL] *b* 18 Nov 1935; *educ* Oldershaw Gr Sch Wallasey; St Jo Coll Dur; Cranmer Hall Dur; C Ch Ch Bootle 1962–65; C St Luke Farnworth in-c St Jo 1965–67; V St Cath Wigan 1967–75; R H Trin Wavertree 1975–94; Chapl Liv Blue Coat Sch 1975–94; Chapl R Sch for Visually Handicapped 1975–94; DDO 1982–94; Hon Can Liv Cathl from 1988; Adn of Liv from 1994   *Tel:* 0151–724 3956
                           01426 187327 (Pager)
                     Fax: 0151–729 0587

METCALFE, Mrs Elizabeth Mavis Dorothy, BA, AKC
11 Lismore St, Carlisle, Cumbria CA1 2AH [CARLISLE] *b* 5 Mar 1935; *educ* Hemel Hempstead C Sch; K Coll Lon; Tchr Sydenham Girls' High Sc 1957–60; Carlisle and Co High Sch for Gir 1960–65; Trin Sch Carlisle 1972–94; Rtd; M Dic Syn from 1981; M Bp's Coun from 1988; M Dic Bd of Educ 1981–93; M Dioc Coun for Min wit Deaf and Hard-of-Hearing People from 1991; N Dioc Bd for Min and Tr from 1995; M ABM Cte for Min among Deaf People from 1997; La Chmn Carl Dny Syn from 1999
GS 1987–   *Tel:* (01228) 2297

METHUEN, Very Revd John Alan Robert, MA
The Minster House, Ripon, N Yorks HG4 1PE [DEA* OF RIPON] *b* 14 Aug 1947; *educ* Eton Coll Choir Sch St Jo Sch Leatherhead; BNC Ox; Cuddesdon Th Coll; C Fenny Stratford and Water Eaton TM Mil ton Keynes 1971–74; Asst Chapl Eton Co 1974–77; P-in-c St Jas Dorney 1974–77; Warde Dorney Parish–Eton Coll Project Conf Centr 1974–77; V St Mark Reading 1977–83; R Th Ascension Hulme 1983–95; Dean of Ripon from 1995; Chair Dioc BSR; Chair Dioc Music Ctee Chair Dioc Worship Ctee; M Cathls Liturgy Grp Ch Commr; Lect Swan Hellenic Tours; Writer and Dir Chr Educ Videos   *Tel:* (01765) 60361!
                           Fax: (01765) 69053(
           email: postmaster@riponcathedral.org.uk

MICHELL, Mrs Lesley Violet, MA
Vicarage, Church Rd, Rainford, St Helens, Mersey side WA11 8H [LIVERPOOL] *b* 3 Sep 1943; *edu* Talbot Heath Sch Bournemouth; Girton Col' Cam; Tchr Lawrence Weston Comp Sch Bris 1965–66; pt Lect Prescot CFE 1980–85; Dioc Pres MU 1989–94; Rdr from 1995; Home Tutor for children w special needs from 1996; N Area Co-ord BRF Reps from 1997
GS 1990–   *Tel:* (01744)88220C

MIDDLEMISS, Mr Peter James, BA (THEOL)
Vine Cottage, Kennel Bank, Cropthorne, Pershore, Worcs WR10 3NB [WORCESTER] *b* 25 Jul 1943; *educ* Carlton le Willows Sch Notts; Man Univ; Birm Univ; Chapl to Overseas Students Man Univ 1967–76; Par Educ Adv St Bart and St Chris Haslemere 1976–77; Warden Morley Retreat and Conference Centre Derby and S'well 1977–83; Warden Holland House Retreat, Conference and Laity Centre Worc dio from 1983; Trustee Saltley Trust; M Exec APR; M Exec Ecum Assn of Academies and Laity Centres in Europe; M Bd of Educ and Vol and Continuing Educ Ctee
GS 1990–   *Tel:* (01386) 860330
                           Fax: (01386) 861208
            email: peter@laycentre.surfaid.org

MIDDLETON, Bishop of [SUFFRAGAN, MANCHESTER] **Rt Revd Michael Augustine Owen Lewis** MA
The Hollies, Manchester Rd, Rochdale, Lancs OL11

QY *b* 8 Jun 1953; *educ* K Edw VI Sch Soton; Mer-ın Coll Ox; Cuddesdon Th Coll; C Ch the K Sal-ırds 1978–80; Chapl Thames Poly 1980–84; V St ıary V Welling 1984–91; TR Worcester SE 1991–9; RD Worcester E 1993–99; Chmn DAC 1998–99; hmn Ho of Clergy Dioc Syn 1997–99; Bp of ıiddleton from 1999 *Tel:* (01706) 358550
Fax: (01706) 354851

ıILFORD, Revd Catherine Helena, MA, DIP TH
icarage, Barnham Broom, Norwich NR9 4DB ʌORWICH] *b* 17 Oct 1939; *educ* Headington Sch ʌx; LMH Ox; Gilmore Course; Dss St Barn Hea-ın 1982–87; Par Dn 1987–88; Adult Educ Adv ʌin 1988–96; Moderator MOW 1988–94; TR arnham Broom and Upper Yare Grp from 1996; ps' Selector Min Div; M Bp's Coun; M Dioc ʌorld Miss Ctee
ʒS 1999– *Tel:* (01603) 759204

ıILLS, Mr David John
1 Greenways, Over Kellet, Carnforth, Lancs LA6 DE [CARLISLE] *b* 19 Feb 1937; *educ* Civil Servant 968; Probation Service from 1968; Senior Proba-ıon Officer; Rdr; Bp's Selector Bd of Min; M Dioc ʒd of Educ and Youth Ctee; Child Protection Adv ʒ Bp of Carl
ʒS 1985– *Tel:* (01524) 732194

ıITCHELL, Mr Alan Bryce, BA, MA, M SC
church House, Great Smith Street, London SW1P ʒNZ [PUBLISHING MANAGER, CHURCH HOUSE PUB-ışHING AND NATIONAL SOCIETY] *b* 30 Sep 1957; *ʾduc* Man Gr Sch; St Andr Univ; Leic Poly; Nottm ʊniv; Loughb Univ; Editor Macmillan Press ı987–88; Commissioning Editor HarperCollins ı988–91; Editor Nat Society 1991–94; Publishing ʌgr Church House Publishing and National ʒociety from 1994 *Tel:* 020–7898 1450
Fax: 020–7898 1449
email: alan.mitchell@c-of-e.org.uk

ıITCHELL, Canon (David) George, BA
Vicarage, Church Ave, Warmley, Bristol BS30 5JJ ʒRISTOL] *b* 5 Jul 1935; *educ* Methodist Coll Belfast; ʒu Univ Belfast; Sarum Th Coll; C Westbury-on-Trym 1961–64; C Cricklade w Latton 1964–68; V ʒt Jo Fishponds 1968–77; TR E Bris 1977–87; V Warmley, Syston and Bitton from 1987; Chmn Ho ʼof Clergy Dioc Syn; M Bp's Coun; M Bd of Dirs DBF
ʒGS 1995– *Tel:* 0117–967 3965

MONBERG, Revd Ulla Stefan, BA
11 Ormonde Mansions, 106 Southampton Row, London WC1B 4BP [LONDON] *b* 16 Jul 1952; *educ* Ore-gaard Sch Copenhagen; Copenhagen Univ; Oregon Univ; Westcott Ho Th Coll; C St Jas Pic-cadilly 1990–94; Area Dir of Ords and Dean of Women's Min and Sec Board for Women Candi-dates in Lon dio from 1994; Assoc V St Jo Hyde Park from 1995
GS 1995– *Tel:* 020–7242 7533

MONCKTON, Mrs Joanna Mary
Stretton Hall, Stafford ST19 9LQ [LICHFIELD] *b* 31 May 1941; *educ* Oxton Ho Sch Kenton Exeter; High Sheriff of Staffordshire 1995–96; Dir Penk Ltd; Housewife; M Bp's Coun; Chmn Lichf Branch Prayer Book Soc
GS 1990– *Tel:* (01902) 850288
Fax: (01902) 850354

MOORE, Canon John Richard
14 Grange Mews, Beverley Rd, Leamington Spa CV32 6PX [COVENTRY] *b* 15 Feb 1935; *educ* Wor-thing High Sch for Boys; Lon Coll of Div; C Em Northwood 1959–63; V Burton Dassett 1963–67; Youth Chapl Cov dio 1967–71; Dir Lindley Educ Trust 1971–82; TR Kinson 1982–88; Gen Dir CPAS 1988–96; Dir Intercontinental Ch Soc from 1996; M BM
GS 1970–75, 1985–88, 1995–
Tel: (01926) 470636 (Home)
(01926) 430347 (Office)
Fax: (01926) 330238
email: jrmoore@ics-uk.org

MORFEY, Dr Kathryn Margaret Victoria, LL B, MA, PH D
2 Royston Close, Southampton SO17 1TB [WIN-CHESTER] *b* 26 May 1942; *educ* Stourbridge Co High Sch; Cam Univ; Southn Univ; Lect in Eco-nomics Bris Univ 1963–64; Southn Univ 1967–69; Qualified as Solicitor 1980; Solicitor in Private Practice from 1980; Partner 1985–91; M Legal Adv Commn 1991–93; M Cathl Fabric Commn 1991–96; Gov K Alfred's Coll of HE 1992–99; M Cathl Statutes Commn from 1996; M Pastl Meas-ure 1983 Appeals Panel from 1996; M Ord of Women (Financial Provisions) Measure 1993 Appeals Panel from 1996; Chair Ho of Laity Dioc Syn from 1997
GS 1990– *Tel:* 023–8055 4396

MORGAN, Mr David Geoffrey Llewelyn
25 Newbiggen St, Thaxted, Great Dunmow, Essex CM6 2QS [CHELMSFORD] *b* 1 Mar 1935; *educ* St Jo Sch Leatherhead; Sen Partner Duffields Solicitors Chelmsford from 1962; Company Dir; Vc-Chmn Dioc Bd of Patronage; M Dioc Fin Ctee from 1988; Trustee Victoria Clergy Fund from 1989; Chmn Nat CU Coun from 1998
GS 1990– *Tel:* (01371) 830132
Fax: (01371) 831430

MORGAN, Mrs Heather Margaret, BA
40 Countess Wear Rd, Exeter EX2 6LR [EXETER] *b* 15 Jul 1953; *educ* Arnold High Sch for Girls Black-pool; Ex Univ; Solicitor; Pres Mental Health Review Tribunals; Section 13 Insp Ch Schs; M Ex Cathl Community Ctee and M Liturgy Working Party; M Bp's Coun; M Dioc Bd of Educ; M Dioc Communications Ctee; Lay Chmn Christianity Dny Syn
GS 1995– *Tel:* (01392) 877623
Fax: (01392) 876344

MORGAN, Mrs Susan Deirdre, BA, FIPD, MHSM
Church House, Great Smith St, London SW1P 3NZ
[DIRECTOR OF HUMAN RESOURCES, ARCHBISHOPS'
COUNCIL] *b* 7 Apr 1956; *educ* Dame Alice Harpur
Sch Bedford; N Lon Poly; Asst Personnel Officer
NW Thames Regional Health Authority 1978–80;
Personnel Officer Charing Cross Hosp 1980–83;
Sen Personnel Officer W Essex Health Authority
1983–85, Dep Dir of Personnel 1985–91; Dir of
Personnel Essex and Herts Health Services
1991–94; Dir Human Resources and Commercial
Services Princess Alexandra Hosp NHS Trust
Harlow 1994–97; Employers' rep on the
Employment Tribunals for Eng and Wales from
1992; Personnel Dir CBF 1997–98; Dir of Human
Resources to Abps' Coun from 1998
Tel: 020–7898 1565
email: su.morgan@c-of-e.org.uk

MORIARTY, Mrs Rachel Milward, MA, M TH
22 Westgate, Chichester, W Sussex PO19 3EU
[CHICHESTER] *b* 22 Mar 1935; *educ* Bedf High Sch;
St Hugh's Coll Ox; K Coll Lon; Sen Classics Tchr
in Lon schs; M Lon Dioc Syn and Ctees; Tutor in
Ch Hist Chich Th Coll 1990–94; Lect Univ Southn
Sch of Th and Relig from 1994; Research Fell/
Lect in Th K Alfred's Coll Win and Tutor Southn
Univ ACE; Chair of Govs Bp Luffa CE School
(Tech Coll) Chich; M Chich Dioc Syn from 1991;
M Dioc European Ecum Ctee from 1992; Adult
Ed Bd of Studies; Lay Chmn Chich Dny Syn
1992–97; M CCU from 1996; Moderator Guildf
LNSM Scheme
GS 1995– *Tel and Fax:* (01243) 789985
email: moriartyrm@aol.com

MORRIS, Mr David Douglas, FCMA
Church House, Great Smith St, London SW1P 3NZ
[FINANCE AND ADMINISTRATIVE SECRETARY, MIN-
ISTRY DIVISION] *b* 11 Dec 1944; *educ* Perth Acad-
emy; Government Official various posts 1964–91;
Dir of Finance Inst of Child Health Lon 1991–96;
Fin and Admin Sec Min Division from 1995
Tel: 020–7898 1392
email: david.morris@c-of-e.org,uk

MORRISON, Ven John Anthony, BA, MA
*Archdeacon's Lodging, Christ Church, Oxford OX1
1DP* [ARCHDEACON OF OXFORD] *b* 11 Mar 1938;
educ Haileybury Coll; Jes Coll Cam; Chich Th
Coll; C St Pet Birm 1964–68; St Mich Ox 1968–74;
Chapl Linc Coll Ox 1968–74; V Basildon 1974–82;
RD Bradfield 1978–82; V Aylesbury 1982–89; RD
Aylesbury 1985–89; TR Aylesbury 1989–90; Adn
of Buckingham 1990–98; P-in-c Princes Risbor-
ough w Ilmer 1996–97; Adn of Ox and Res Canon
Ch Ch from 1998
GS 1980–90, 1998– *Tel:* (01865) 204440
Fax: (01865) 204465
email: archdoxf@oxford.anglican.org

MOSES, Very Revd John Henry, BA, PH D
The Deanery, 9 Amen Court, London EC4M 7BU
[DEAN OF ST PAUL'S] *b* 12 Jan 1938; *educ* Ealing Gr

Sch; Univ of Nottm; Trin Hall Cam; Linc Th Co
Visiting Fell Wolfs Coll Cam 1987; Asst C St Anc
Bedf 1964–70; R Cov East TM 1970–77; Exar
Chapl to Bp of Cov 1972–77; RD Cov Ea
1973–77; Adn of Southend 1977–82; Prov ᴇ
Chelmsf 1982–96; Dean of St Paul's from 1996; C
Commr from 1988; M ACC from 1998
GS 1985– *Tel:* 020–7236 282
Fax: 020–7332 02ᴈ

MOXON, Very Revd Michael Anthony, LVO, BE
MA
The Deanery, Lemon St, Truro, Cornwall TR1 2P
[DEAN OF TRURO] *b* 23 Jan 1942; *educ* Merchar
Taylors' Sch; Heythrop Coll Lon; Sarum Th Col
C Kirkley St Pet Lowestoft 1970–74; Min Can S
Paul's Cathl 1974–81; Sacrist 1977–81; Warden c
Coll of Min Canons 1979–81; V Tewkesbury v
Walton Cardiff 1981–90; Can of Windsor anᴇ
Chapl in the Great Park 1990–98; Chapl to HN
The Queen 1986–98; M CCC 1985–90; Dean c
Truro and R St Mary Truro from 1998; Chaᴘ
Cornwall Co Fire Brigade from 1998
GS 1985–90 *Tel:* (01872) 272661 (Home
(01872) 276782 (Office
Fax: (01872) 277883 (Office

MULLINS, Revd Peter Matthew, MA, M PHIL
26 Meadowbank, Great Coates, Grimsby DN37 9Pᴄ
[LINCOLN] *b* 12 May 1960; *educ* Berkhamsted Sch
Ch Ch Ox; Irish Sch of Ecumenics; Qu Coll Birm
C Caversham and Mapledurham 1984–88; TV Olᴄ
Brumby Linc 1989–94; Clergy Tr Adv Linc from
1994
GS 1995– *Tel:* (01472) 32954ᴈ
email: peter.mullins@virgin.ne

MUNRO, Ms Josile Wenus, B SC, DTS
89 Brougham Rd, London E8 4PD [LONDON] *b* 2ᴇ
Apr 1963; *educ* Haggerston Girls Sch; Kingsway
Princeton Coll; S Bank Poly; Prin Trading Stand-
ards Officer from 1994; M Bp's Coun; Trustee Lor
Dioc Fund; Coun M N Thames Min Tr Course,
Bp's Selector; Lay Chair Hackney Dny Syn; Vc-
Chair Area Bp's Coun
GS 1994–95, 1997– *Tel:* 020–7254 5577

MURSELL, Very Revd (Alfred) Gordon, MA, BD,
ARCM
13 Pebble Mill Rd, Birmingham B5 7SA [PROVOST OF
BIRMINGHAM] *b* 4 May 1949; *educ* Ardingly Coll;
Pontifical Inst of Sacred Music Rome; BNC Ox;
Cuddesdon Th Coll; C St Mary Walton Liv
1973–77; V St Jo E Dulwich 1977–87; Tutor in Spir-
ituality Sarum and Wells Th Coll 1987–91; TR
Stafford 1991–99; Provost of Birm from 1999
Tel: 0121–472 0709
0121–236 4333
Fax: 0121–212 0868

MUSSON, Mr Terence Robert, HND
*Worthen Farm, Pyworthy, Holsworthy, Devon EX22
6LQ* [TRURO] *b* 10 Jul 1940; *educ* Grantham Boys
Central Sch; Caythorpe Coll; Self Employed

rmer from 1962; Company Chairman 1981–90
S 1995–   Tel: (01288) 381464
                                   Fax: (01288) 381575
              email: TMUSSON@AOL.COM

IYERS, Mr Ian, BA, PGCE
41 St John's Rd, Tunbridge Wells, Kent TN4 9UG
[ROCHESTER] *b* 12 Sep 1939; *educ* The Skinners'
ch Tunbridge Wells; St David's Coll Lamp; Univ
f Lon Inst of Educ; Asst Teacher Highbury Sch
on 1962–67; Hd of Classics Dept Stratford Gr
ch Lon 1967–72; Dir of Studies Brampton Manor
ch Lon 1972, Dep Hd Teacher 1977–96; pt Teach-
r of Classical Greek Rose Hill Sch Tunbridge
Vells from 1998; Lay Chmn Tunbridge Wells Dny
yn; M Dioc Syn; M Bp's Coun; M Dioc Adv Ctee
or Min and Tr
S 1999–   Tel: (01892) 531453

IAGEL, Mrs Mary Philippa, B ED
Idwick Vicarage, 25 Gossamer Lane, Bognor Regis,
V Sussex PO21 3AT [CHICHESTER] *b* 8 Mar 1954;
luc Worthing High Sch; Lon Univ; Section 23
nspector of Schs
S 1990–   Tel and Fax: (01243) 262049
                         email: lnagel@netcomuk.co.uk

NAIRN-BRIGGS, Very Revd George Peter, AKC
Cathedral Close, Margaret St, Wakefield WF1 2DP
[PROVOST OF WAKEFIELD] *b* 5 Jul 1945; *educ* Slough
Tech High Sch; K Coll Lon; St Aug Coll Cant; C St
Laur Catford 1970–73; C St Sav Raynes Park
1973–75; V Ch the King Salfords 1975–81; V St Pet
St Helier 1981–87; Bp's Adv for Soc Resp Wakef
1987–97; Can Res Wakef Cathl 1992–97; Provost
of Wakef from 1997; M Bp's Senior Staff Meeting;
M Gen Syn Panel of Chmn from 1997; M BSR; M
BSR Exec Ctee; Dep Prolocutor York Conv; M
BSR Working Party on the Family 1992–95; M
Bps' Adv Grp on UPAs; M Gen Syn Stg Orders
Ctee 1993–95; Assessor York Conv; M Third
National Consultation Planning Grp 1993–95
GS 1980–87, 1990–   Tel: (01924) 210005 (Home)
                          (01924) 373923 (Office)
                     Fax: (01924) 210009 (Home)
   email: provost@nairn-briggs.freeserve.co.uk

NAPPIN, Miss Patricia, MA
7 Mavis Walk, Tollgate Rd, Mid Beckton, London E6
5TL [CHELMSFORD] *b* 17 Dec 1934; *educ* City of
Bath Girls' Sch; Whitelands Coll Putney; Bris
Univ; Open Univ; Tchr Lozells JM & I Sch Birm
1958–59; Tchr Southdown Inf Sch Bath 1959–70;
Exch Tchr USA 1965–66; CE Prim Sch Barking,
Hd Infs' Dept 1970–73; Hd Tchr Henry Green
Infs' Sch Dagenham 1973–80; Hd Wm Bellamy
Infs' Sch Dagenham 1980–Dec 87; Co Commr in
Guiding for the London-over-the-Border Co
1978–87; Hd Becontree Prim Sch Dagenham
1988–97; Rdr; Chmn Ho of Laity Dioc Syn
1988–97; Dep Hon Sec CRC 1997–99; Hon Sec
from 1999
GS 1975–   Tel: 020–7474 0222
                   email: patnappin@aol.com

NEAL, Canon Anthony Terrence, BA, CERT ED
Rectory, Forth-an-Tewennow, Phillack, Hayle, Corn-
wall TR27 4QE [TRURO] *b* 11 Jan 1942; *educ* Ger-
mains Co Sec Sch Chesham; Open Univ; Leeds
Univ; Bernard Gilpin Soc Dur; Chich Th Coll; C St
Hilda Leeds 1968–73; Chapl and Head of RE
Abbey Grange CE High Sch Leeds 1973–81; Dioc
RE Adv Truro and P-in-c St Erth 1981–84;
Children's Officer 1985–87; Stewardship Adv
1987–88; V St Erth from 1984; Hon Can Truro
Cathl from 1994; P-in-c Phillack w Gwithian,
Gwinear and St Elwyn Hayle 1994–96; TR
Godrevy TM from 1996
GS 1990–   Tel: (01736) 753541 (Home)
                             (01736) 754866 (Office)

NEED, Very Revd Philip, AKC
The Deanery, Bocking, Braintree, Essex CM7 5SR
[DEAN OF BOCKING] *b* 28 Apr 1954; *educ* Carlton-le-
Willows Gr Sch; K Coll Lon; Chich Th Coll; C Ch
Ch and St Jo Clapham 1977–80; C All SS Luton w
St Pet 1980–83; V St Mary Magd Harlow 1983–89;
P-in-c St Phil Chaddesden 1989–91; Dom Chapl
to Bp of Chelmsf 1991–96; Dean and R St Mary
Bocking from 1996   Tel: (01376) 324887
                             (01376) 553092
      email: philip.need@bocking81.freeserve.co.uk

NEIL-SMITH, Mr (Noel) Jonathan, MA
Church House, Great Smith St, London SW1P 3NZ
[ADMINISTRATIVE SECRETARY, CENTRAL SECRE-
TARIAT] *b* 5 Oct 1959; *educ* Marlboro Coll; St Jo Coll
Cam; On staff of Ch Commrs from 1981; Bishop-
rics Offcr 1994–96; Seconded to Gen Syn from
1997; Asst Sec Ho of Bps 1997–98; Acting Sec Ho
of Bps from 1998   Tel: 020–7898 1373
                            Fax: 020–7898 1369
       email: jonathan.neil.smith@c-of-e.org.uk

NENER, Canon (Thomas) Paul Edgar, MB, CH B,
FRCS ED, FRCS
St John's Vicarage, 2 Green Lane, Tuebrook, Liverpool
L13 7EA [LIVERPOOL] *b* 11 Sep 1942; *educ* Liverpool
Inst High Sch; Liv Univ Medical Sch; Coll of
Resurr Mirfield; C Warrington 1980–83; V St Jas
the Great Haydock 1983–95; V St Jo Tuebrook, Liv
from 1995; Hon Can Liv Cathl from 1995; Chmn
Dioc Healing Panel; ABM Selector; Subwarden-
Guild of St Raphael
GS 1990–   Tel: 0151–228 2023

NEWCASTLE, Bishop of, Rt Revd (John)
Martin Wharton, MA
Bishop's House, 29 Moor Rd South, Gosforth, New-
castle upon Tyne NE3 1PA b 6 Aug 1944; *educ* Ulver-
ston Gr Sch; Dur Univ; Linacre Coll Ox; Ripon
Hall Ox; C St Pet Birm 1972–75; C St Jo B Croydon
1975–77; Dir of Pastl Studies Ripon Coll Cud-
desdon 1977–83; Exec Sec Bd of Min and Tr Bradf
dio 1983–91; Can Res Bradf Cathl and Bp's
Officer for Min and Tr 1992; Bp of Kingston-upon-
Thames 1992–97; Bp of Newc from 1997
GS 1998–   Tel: 0191–285 2220
                              Fax: 0191–284 6933
      email: Bishop@newcastle.anglican.org

NEWLANDS, Revd Christopher William, BA
All Saints Vicarage, 270 Shrub End Rd, Colchester, Essex CO3 4RL [CHELMSFORD] *b* 8 Feb 1957; *educ* K Sch Pontefract; Bris Univ; Westcott Ho Th Coll; C Bishop's Waltham 1984–87; Prec, Sacr and Min Can Dur Cathl 1987–92; Chapl Bucharest w Sofia and Apokrisarios of Abp of Cant to the Patriarch of Romania and to the Patriarch of Bulgaria 1992–95; V Shrub End Colchester from 1996; Hon Chapl to Mercury Theatre Colchester from 1999; M Dioc Resource Coun from 1997; M Dioc Eur Group from 1998; M Dioc Ecum Group from 1998; M Dioc Internat Group from 1999
GS 1999–   *Tel:* (01206) 503131
     0802 733254 (Mobile)
     Fax: (01206) 503125
     email: ChrisTheVic@compuserve.com

NEWMAN, Revd David
28 Fairfield Square, Droylsden, Manchester M43 6AE [ECUMENICAL REPRESENTATIVE (MORAVIAN CHURCH)]
GS 1998–

NEWSUM, Mr Jeremy Henry Moore, B SC, ARICS
Priory House, Swavesey, Cambs CB4 5QJ [CHURCH COMMISSIONER] *b* 4 Apr 1955; *educ* Rugby Sch; Reading Univ; Chief Exec Grosvenor Estate Holdings; Ch Commr from 1993, Assets Ctee from 1993   *Tel:* (01954) 232084

NIXSON, Revd Rosie (Rosemary Clare), BA, MA, M PHIL
15 Glendale, Bromley Heath, Bristol BS16 6EQ [BRISTOL] *b* 4 Jul 1957; *educ* Headington Sch Ox; Westf Coll Lon; Liv Univ; Aston Tr Scheme; Trin Coll Bris; C E Bris 1994; C St Andr Hartcliffe 1994–98; C Downend from 1998 M Dioc Par Resources Ctee; M Gov Body Coll of Evangelists
GS 1999–   *Tel:* 0117–956 8109
     email: RC@nixsonr.freeserve.co.uk

NOEL, Mr Marcel Paul, MA
7 Canterbury Rd, Wolverhampton, W Midlands WV4 4EQ [LICHFIELD] *b* 19 Mar 1920; *educ* Em Sch Lon; St Cath Coll Ox; RAF (Flt-Lt) 1941–46; Schmaster Wolverhampton Gr Sch Head of Maths for Science 1948–81; Rdr from 1984; Examiner in Maths GCSE 1981–93
GS 1985–90, 1991–   *Tel:* (01902) 335238

NORMAN, Ven Garth, BA, DIP TH, MA, M ED, PGCE
6 Horton Way, Farningham, Kent DA4 0DQ [ARCH-DEACON OF BROMLEY] *b* 26 Nov 1938; *educ* Henry Mellish Gr Sch Nottm; St Chad's Coll Dur; UEA; C St Anne Wandsw 1963–66; TV Trunch 1966–71; TR Trunch 1971–83; RD Repps 1975–83; Prin Chiltern Chr Tr Scheme 1983–87; Dioc Dir of Tr Roch 1988–94; Adn of Bromley from 1994
GS 1995–   *Tel:* (01322) 864522

NORMAN, Revd Michael John, LL B
St Saviour's Rectory, Claremont Rd, Bath, Somerset

BA1 6LX [BATH AND WELLS] *b* 17 Aug 1959; *educ* I Challoner's Gr Sch; Southn Univ; Wycliffe Ha Th Coll; C St Jo Woodley 1985–89; C Uph 1989–92; TV St Barn Uphill 1992–98; R St Sav Ba w Swainswick and Wooley from 1998; M DBF; I Dioc Renewal Grp
GS 1995–   *Tel:* (01225) 3116?

NORWICH, Bishop of, Rt Revd Graham Richard James, BA
Bishop's House, Norwich, Norfolk NR3 1SB b 19 Ja 1951; *educ* Northampton Gr Sch; Lanc Univ Cuddesdon Th Coll; C Christ Carpenter Petr 1975–78; C Digswell 1978–82; TV Digswe 1982–83; Selection Sec and Sec for CME ACC? 1983–85; Sen Selection Sec 1985–87; Chapl to Ab of Cant 1987–93; Bp of St Germans 1993–99; Bp o Nor from 1999; Chmn Communications Offcr Panel; Vc-Moderator Chs Commn for Inter-Fait Relations
GS 1995–   *Tel:* (01603) 62900
     Fax: (01603) 76161

NUGEE, Mr Edward George, MA, TD, QC
Wilberforce Chambers, 8 New Square, Lincoln's Inr London WC2A 3QP [CHURCH COMMISSIONER] *b* Aug 1928; *educ* Radley Coll; Worc Coll Ox Barrister-at-Law 1955; QC 1977; Ch Commr from 1989, Bd of Govs from 1993   *Tel:* 020–7306 010?
     Fax: 020–7306 009?
     email: enugee@wilberforce.co.u

O'BRIEN, Mr Gerald Michael, B SC, DMS
Chestnuts, 14 Oakhill Rd, Sevenoaks, Kent TN1? 1NP [ROCHESTER] *b* 4 Nov 1948; *educ* Dulwich Coll; Bris Univ; Dir of Communications Crosslinks; M CEEC 1988–92, 1996–
GS 1980–85, 1987–   *Tel:* (01732) 45389?
     email: gerry@crosslinks.org

OFFER, Ven Clifford Jocelyn, BA, FRSA
26 The Close, Norwich, Norfolk NR1 4DZ [ARCH-DEACON OF NORWICH] *b* 10 Aug 1943; *educ* K Sch Cant; Ex Univ; Westcott Ho Th Coll; C Bromley 1969–74; TV Southn City Cen 1974–83; TR Hitch-in 1983–94; Chmn Nor Dioc Bd of Min 1994–98; Adn of Nor, Can Res and Libr Nor Cathl from 1994; Warden of Rdrs from 1994; Chmn Nor Course Management Ctee from 1998
GS 1999–   *Tel:* (01603) 630525
     Fax: (01603) 661104

OGILVIE, Ven Gordon, MA, BD, ALCD
2B Spencer Ave, Mapperley, Nottingham NG3 5SP [ARCHDEACON OF NOTTINGHAM] *b* 22 Aug 1942; *educ* Hillhead High Sch Glasgow; Glasgow Univ; Lon Univ; Lon Coll of Div; C Ashtead 1967–72; V St Jas New Barnet 1972–80; Dir Pastl Studies Wycliffe Hall Ox 1980–87; TR St Paul Harlow Town Centre w St Mary Little Parndon 1987–96; Chapl Princess Alexandra Hosp Harlow 1988–96; Chmn Harlow Grp Min 1989–96; Chmn Dioc Ho of Clergy 1994–96; Adn of Nottm from 1996;

mn Grove Books Ltd; M Simeon's Trustees; M
EC from 1974; Chmn Dioc Miss Grp
S 1990–96, 1999–   *Tel:* 0115–967 0875 (Home)
                         (01636) 814490 (Office)
                     Fax: 0115–967 1014 (Home)
                         (01636) 815882 (Office)

GLESBY, Canon Leslie Ellis, MA, M PHIL
*erwent House, 21 West Hill, Hitchin, Herts SG5
HZ* [ST ALBANS] *b* 24 Sep 1946; *educ* K Sch Ponte-
act; Univ Coll Ox; City Univ Lon; Wesley Ho
am; Fitzw Coll Cam; Ripon Coll Cuddeson; C St
Mary Shephall Stevenage 1978–80; V Markyate
reet 1980–87; Dir St Alb Minl Tr Scheme
980–87; Dir Continuing Minl Educ 1987–94; Hon
an St Alb Cathl from 1993; TR Hitchin TM and
St Mary from 1994; Inspector Ho of Bps Panel
f Inspectors of Colls and Courses; Gen Syn Rep
SPG Coun; M Bp's Coun; M Dioc Syn; Chmn
erulam Ho Fund Trust; Trustee Grassroots Pro-
ramme Luton
S 1995–   *Tel:* (01462) 434017

OLDHAM, Mr Gavin David Redvers, MA
ashfield House, St Leonards, Tring, Herts HP23 6NP
OXFORD] *b* 5 May 1949; *educ* Eton; Trin Coll Cam;
Wedd Durlacher Mordaunt 1975–86, Partner
984–86; Secretariat Barclays De Zoete Wedd
BZW) 1984–88; Chief Exec Barclayshare Ltd
986–89, Chmn 1989–90; Chmn/Chief Exec The
hare Centre Ltd from 1990; Ch Commr from
999
S 1995–   *Tel:* (01442) 829100 (Office)
                     (01494) 758348 (Home)
                     Fax: (01442) 891191
                 email: gavin@share.co.uk

OLIVER, Ven John Michael, BA
*Archdeacon's Lodge, 3 West Park Grove, Leeds LS8
2HQ* [ARCHDEACON OF LEEDS] *b* 7 Sep 1939; *educ*
Ripon Coll St David Coll Lamp; Ripon Hall
Ox; C St Pet Harrogate 1964–67; C St Pet Bramley
Leeds 1967–72; V St Mary Harrogate 1972–78; V
Beeston 1978–92; Ecum Officer Leeds 1981–86;
Hon Can Ripon Cathl 1986–92; RD Armley
1986–92; Adn of Leeds from 1992
GS 1992–   *Tel* and *Fax:* 0113–269 0594
                         email:
john.anne@archdeaconleeds.freeserve.co.uk

OLIVER, Canon Thomas Gordon, L TH, B TH, DIP
AD ED
18 Kings Ave, Rochester, Kent ME1 3DS [ROCHES-
TER] *b* 25 May 1948; *educ* Whinney Hill Sec Mod
Sch Dur; Dur Johnson Gr Tech Sch; Lon Coll of
Div; St Jo Coll Nottm; C St Jo the Divine Thorpe
Edge 1972–76; C St Mark Woodthorpe 1976–80; V
All SS Huthwaite 1980–85; Dir Past Studies St Jo
Coll Nottm 1985–94; Dioc Dir of Tr from 1994
GS 1995–   *Tel:* (01634) 830333 (Office)
                     (01634) 841232 (Home)
                 email: gordon.oliver@rochdiooff.co.uk

OSBORNE, Revd Hayward John, MA, PGCE
*St Mary's Vicarage, 18 Oxford Rd, Moseley, Bir-
mingham B13 9EH* [BIRMINGHAM] *b* 16 Sep 1948;
educ Sevenoaks Sch; New Coll Ox; Westcott Ho
Th Coll; C St Pet and St Paul Bromley 1973–77; TV
Halesowen 1977–83; TR St Barnabas Worc
1983–88; V St Mary Moseley from 1988; AD
Moseley from 1994
GS 1998–   *Tel:* 0121–449 1459

**OWEN, The Hon and Rt Worshipful Sir John
Arthur Dalziel,** DCL, MA, BCL, LLM
*Bickerstaff Farmhouse, Idlicote, Shipston-on-Stour,
Warws CV36 5DT* [DEAN OF THE ARCHES AND
AUDITOR OF THE CHANCERY COURT OF YORK] *b* 22
Nov 1925; *educ* Solihull Sch; BNC Ox; Univ of
Wales; High Court Judge; Dean of the Arches and
Auditor of Chancery Court of York from 1980
GS 1970–

OWEN, Dr Peter Russell, B SC, D PHIL, C PHYS,
EUR PHYS, M INST P, FRAS
*11 The Downs, Blundellsands Rd West, Liverpool L23
6XS* [LIVERPOOL] *b* 29 Mar 1947; *educ* Southend
High Sch for Boys; Birm Univ; Sussex Univ;
Lect/Sen Lect R Military Coll of Science 1970–84;
Sen Lect Liv John Moores Univ from 1985; Lay
Chmn Sefton Dny Syn
GS 1995–   *Tel:* 0151–931 2251
                 email: peter.owen@physics.org

**OXFORD, Bishop of, Rt Revd Richard Douglas
Harries,** DD, FKC, FRSL
*Diocesan Church House, North Hinksey, Oxford OX2
0NB b* 2 Jun 1936; *educ* Wellington Coll; Selw Coll
Cam; Cuddesdon Th Coll; C St Jo Hampstead
1963–69; Chapl Westf Coll Lon 1967–69; Tutor
Wells Th Coll 1969–71; Warden, Wells, Sarum and
Wells Th Coll 1971–72; V All SS Fulham 1972–81;
Dean K Coll Lon 1981–87; Bp of Ox from 1987; M
ACC; M Bd Christian Aid; Chmn Coun of Chris-
tians and Jews; Chair BSR from 1996
GS 1987–   *Tel:* (01865) 208222
                     Fax: (01865) 790470
         email: bishopoxon@oxford.anglican.org

OZANNE, Ms Jayne Margaret, MA
21 Rockley Rd, London W14 0BT [APPOINTED MEM-
BER, ARCHBISHOPS' COUNCIL] *b* 13 Nov 1968; *educ*
The Ladies' Coll Guernsey; St Jo Coll Cam; Brand
Management Procter & Gamble 1990–93; Kim-
berley Clark 1993–96; BBC Broadcast 1996–97;
Freelance Strategic Consultant from 1998; Apptd
M Abps' Coun from 1999; M Appts Ctee from
1999
GS 1999–   *Tel:* 020–7602 2787
                     Fax: 020–7603 2924
                 email: jayneozanne@freenet.co.uk

PAGE, Canon Michael John, BD, AKC
*Vicarage, Langley Rd, Winchcombe, Cheltenham
GL54 5QP* [GLOUCESTER] *b* 11 Oct 1942; *educ* High
Wycombe Tech High Sch; K Coll Lon; St Boniface

Th Coll Warminster; C Rawmarsh w Parkgate 1967–72; P-in-c Holy Cross Gleadless Valley 1972–74, TR 1974–77; V Lechlade 1977–86; RD Fairford 1981–86; Hon Can Glouc Cathl from 1991; V Winchcombe from 1986; RD Winchcombe 1994–99
GS 1998– Tel: (01242) 602368
Fax: (01242) 602067
email: pagem@winchco9.freeserve.co.uk

PAGE, Mrs Sue (Susan Margaret Brinley)
The Greyhound, Back St, Reepham, Norfolk NR10 4SJ [NORWICH] *b* 4 May 1941; *educ* St Paul's Girls Sch; Rose Bruford Coll of Speech and Drama; Actress; M Bp of Willesden's Commn 1968–72; M Abp's Commn on Ch Music 1989–92; M Ctee for Communications 1991–98; M TETC Min Div Abps' Coun from 1999; Tchr of Drama; Voice Tutor; Lect in Communication Skills; Speaker at Confs and Retreats; Rdr
GS 1984– Tel: (01603) 870886

PAGET-WILKES, Ven Michael Jocelyn James,
ALCD, NDA
10 Northumberland Rd, Leamington Spa, Warws CV32 6HA [ARCHDEACON OF WARWICK] *b* 11 Dec 1941; *educ* Dean Close Sch Cheltenham; Harper Adams Agric Coll; Lon Coll of Div; C All SS Wandsworth 1969–74; V St Jas Hatcham 1974–82; V St Matt Rugby 1982–90; Adn of Warwick from 1990 Tel: (01926) 313337 (Home)
024–7667 4328 (Office)

PAINTER, Ven David Scott, MA, LTCL, CERT ED
7 Minster Precincts, Peterborough, Cambs PE1 1XX [ARCHDEACON OF OAKHAM] *b* 3 Oct 1944; *educ* Qu Eliz Sch Crediton; Trin Coll of Music; Worc Coll Ox; Cuddesdon Th Coll; C St Andr Plymouth 1970–73; C All SS Marg St 1973–76; Dom Chapl to Abp of Cant and DDO 1976–80; V Roehampton 1980–91; RD Wandsworth 1985–90; Can Res and Treas S'wark Cathl and DDO 1991–2000; Adn of Oakham and Can Res Peterb Cathl from 2000; M Panel of Bps' Selectors from 1997

PAKENHAM-WALSH, Mr John, CB, QC, MA
Crinken, Weydown Rd, Haslemere, Surrey GU27 1DS [STANDING COUNSEL TO THE GENERAL SYNOD] *b* 7 Aug 1928; *educ* Bradfield Coll; Univ Coll Ox; Crown Counsel Hong Kong 1953–57; Parl Counsel Federation of Nigeria 1958–61; Home Office 1961–87; Stg Counsel to Gen Syn from 1988
Tel: (01428) 642033
email: john.pw@lineone.net

PARKER, Miss Diane Elizabeth Alice, DASS, CQSW
246 Bloomfield Rd, Blackpool, Lancs FY1 6QG [BLACKBURN] *b* 4 Aug 1936; *educ* Wyggeston Sch Leic; Liv Univ; Asst Chief Probation Offcr Lancs 1979–94; Rtd; Vc-Chair Dioc Ho of Laity from 1991; Rdr from 1991; Chmn Bay Housing Assn from 1995; M Gov Body APF from 1995; M

Vacancy-in-See Legislation Working Party; Churchwardens Measure Steering and Revisic Ctee; M Panel of Chairmen 1996–97; Bp's Adv fe Child Protection from 1996; Lay Chmn Blackpo Deanery Syn from 1997
GS 1985– Tel and Fax: (01253) 7660:

PARRY, Mrs Elisabeth Anne
The Cottage, 13 Holton Heath, Poole, Dorset BH1 6JT [SALISBURY] *b* 28 Feb 1933; *educ* Queensmou Sch Bournemouth; Sch Gov; Lay Co-Chmn Pu beck Dny Syn; Sec to Bp of Sherborne from 198 M Exec Wessex Autistic Soc
GS 1992– Tel: (01202) 625383 (Home
(01258) 857659 (Office

PARTINGTON, Ven Brian Harold
St George's Vicarage, 16 Devonshire Rd, Douglas, Is. of Man IM2 3RB [ARCHDEACON OF THE ISLE C MAN] *b* 31 Dec 1936; *educ* St Aidan's Coll Birker head; C Barlow Moor 1963–66; C Deane 1966–6£ V Patrick IOM 1968–96; Bp's Youth Char 1968–77; RD Peel 1976–96; P-in-c St Jo Germa 1977–78, V 1978–96; P-in-c Foxdale 1977–78, 1978 -96; Can St German's Cathl 1985–96; Adn o the Isle of Man from 1996; V St Geo and St Bar Douglas from 1996; Chmn DAC; M Isle of Ma Ch Commrs; M DBF, Stg Ctee, Legislative Ctee Vacancy in See Ctee and Communications Ctee Exec Chmn Isle of Man Sports Coun
GS 1996– Tel: (01624) 67543
Fax: (01624) 61613
email: arch-sodor@mcb.ne

PAVER, Mrs Elizabeth Caroline, ACP, CERT ED, FRSA
113 Warning Tongue Lane, Bessacar, Doncaster DN4 6TB [SHEFFIELD AND APPOINTED MEMBER, ARCH BISHOPS' COUNCIL] *b* 26 Nov 1944; *educ* Doncaste Girls High Sch; St Mary's Coll Cheltenham; Ir Primary Educ 28 years; Headtchr Crags Rc Nurs/Inf Sch 1976–80; Hdtchr Askern Nurs/In: Sch Littlemoor 1980–86; Hdtchr Intake Nursery and First Sch Doncaster from 1986; M Nat Coun NAHT from 1991; M Panel of Chmn Gen Syn, Lay Chmn Dioc Syn; M Bp's Coun; M Dioc Bd o: Educ Tr Ctee; Apptd M Abps' Coun from 1999
GS 1991– Tel: (01302) 530706
Fax: (01302) 360811

PEACOCK, Mr Edward Graham, MA
Church Commissioners, 1 Millbank, London SW1P 3JZ [BISHOPRICS AND CATHEDRALS SECRETARY, CHURCH COMMISSIONERS] *educ* K Sch Worc; St Jo Coll Ox; On staff of Ch Commrs from 1971; Abp of Cant's Admin Sec 1987–97; Bishoprics Sec 1997–99; Bishoprics and Cathls Sec from 1999
Tel: 020–7898 1062
Fax: 020–7898 1061
email: ed.peacock@c-of-e.org.uk

PEAKE, Ven (Simon) Jeremy Brinsley, MA
Thugutstrasse 2/12, A 1020 Vienna, Austria [ARCH-

EACON OF THE AEGEAN AND DANUBE] *b* 21 Oct
930; *educ* Eton Coll; Worc Coll Ox; St Steph Ho
)x; C St Andr Eastbourne 1957–60; C Ch the King
:laremont Cape, S Africa 1960–61; R All SS Wood-
tock Cape S Africa 1961–65; R Gd Shep Maitland
:ape S Africa 1965–69; R Kalulushi Zambia 1969–
1; Chapl Mindolo Ecum Foundn Kitwe Zambia
971–77; Chapl Athens 1977–87; Chapl Vienna
rom 1987; Adn of the Aegean and Danube from
995   *Tel:* 00–43–1–663–920–9264 (Office)
Tel: and *Fax:* 00–43–1–720–7973 (Home)

PENRITH, Bishop of [SUFFRAGAN, CARLISLE] **Rt
Revd Richard Garrard,** BD, AKC, M I MGT
Holm Croft, Castle Rd, Kendal, Cumbria LA9 7AU
) 24 May 1937; *educ* Northn Gr Sch; K Coll Lon; St
3oniface Warminster; C Woolwich Par Ch
1961–66; C Gt St Mary Cam 1966–68; Chapl/Lect
<eswick Hall Coll of Educ Nor 1968–74; Prin Ch
Army Tr Coll 1974–79; Can Chan S'wark Cathl
and Dir of Clergy In-Service Tr 1979–87; Can St
Eds and Adv for Clergy Tr 1987–91; Adn of Sud-
oury 1991–94; Bp of Penrith from 1994; M BM and
Miss Th Adv Grp from 1996; Chmn Coun Carl
and Blackb Dioc Tr Inst from 1997; M Bp's Coun;
M Dioc Syn; Chair Dioc Bd for Min and Tr; M
DBF; Chair Bd for Par Miss and Development
GS 1995–   *Tel:* (01539) 727836
Fax: (01539) 734380

PERHAM, Very Revd Michael Francis, MA
*The Provost's House, 9 Highfield Rd, Derby DE22
1GX* [PROVOST OF DERBY] *b* 8 Nov 1947; *educ*
Hardye's Sch Dorchester; Keble Coll Ox; Cud-
desdon Th Coll; C St Mary Addington 1976–81;
Chapl to Bp of Win 1981–84; TR Oakdale, Poole
1984–92; Can Res and Prec Nor Cathl 1992–98;
Vc-Dean 1995–98; Prov of Derby from 1998; M
Liturg Commn from 1986; M Cathls Fabric
Commn from 1996; M Abps' Coun from 1999; M
Ch Heritage Forum from 1999; Author; Chmn
Cathls Liturg Grp
GS 1989–92, 1993–
Tel and *Fax:* (01332) 342971 (Home)
Tel: (01332) 341201 (Office)
Fax: (01332) 203991 (Office)
email: Derby.Cathedral@btinternet.com

PERRY, Revd Lesley
Lambeth Palace, London SE1 7JU [SECRETARY FOR
BROADCASTING, PRESS AND COMMUNICATIONS TO
THE ARCHBISHOP OF CANTERBURY] *b* 1 Apr 1952;
educ Scarborough Girls High Sch; K Coll Lon; SE
Inst for Th Educ; Br Coun Offcr 1975–87; Head of
Public Affairs, R Inst of Internat Affairs 1987–91;
Sec for Broadcasting, Press and Communications
to the Abp of Cant from 1991
Tel: 020–7928 8282 (Office)
020–7373 3085 (Home)

**PETERBOROUGH, Bishop of, Rt Revd Ian
Patrick Martyn Cundy,** MA
Bishop's Lodgings, The Palace, Peterborough, Cambs

PE1 1YA b 23 Apr 1945; *educ* Monkton Combe Sch;
Trin Coll Cam; Tyndale Hall Th Coll; C Ch Ch
New Malden 1969–73; Tutor Oak Hill Th Coll
1973–77; TR Mortlake w E Sheen 1978–83; War-
den Cranmer Hall St Jo Coll Dur 1983–92; Bp of
Lewes 1992–96; Bp of Petrb from 1996; Chmn
CCU from1998; Pres St Jo Coll Dur from 1999
GS 1996–   *Tel:* (01733) 562492
Fax: (01733) 890077
email: bishop@peterborough-diocese.org.uk

PETERSON, Canon John Louis, BA, TH D, DD,
DCL
*Anglican Consultative Council, Partnership House,
157 Waterloo Rd, London SE1 8UT* [SECRETARY
GENERAL, ANGLICAN CONSULTATIVE COUNCIL] *b* 17
Dec 1942; *educ* Concordia Univ; Harvard Univ;
Chich Inst Advanced Th Studies; Instructor Sea-
bury Western Th Seminary 1972–73; Adjunct Prof
1973–75; Assoc St Aug Wilmette 1976; Can Th
Christ the King Cathl Kalamazoo; Hon Can Cathl
Ch of Ch the King Kalamazoo from 1982; V St
Steph Plainwell 1976–82; Angl Centre in Rome
1988–91; Consultant Ibru Centre Nigeria from
1990; Dean St Geo Coll Jerusalem 1983–94; Hon
Can St Geo Cathl Jerusalem from 1994; Sec Gen
ACC from 1995; Hon Can Cant Cathl from 1995;
M Gov Body Angl Centre in Rome from 1995;
Hon Can St Mich Cathl Kaduna from 1999
Tel: 020–7620 1110
Fax: 020–7620 1070
email: john.l.peterson@anglicancommunion.org

PETTY, Very Revd John Fitzmaurice, MA, HON D
LITT
7 Priory Row, Coventry CV1 5ES [PROVOST OF COV-
ENTRY] *b* 9 Mar 1935; *educ* K Sch Bruton; RMA
Sandhurst; Trin Hall Cam; Cuddesdon Th Coll; C
St Cuth Fir Vale Sheff 1966–69; P-in-c Bp
Andrewes' Ch St Helier Estate 1969–75; V St Jo
Hurst Ashton-under-Lyne 1975–88; AD Ashton-
under-Lyne 1983–87; Hon Can Man Cathl
1986–88; Provost of Cov Cathl from 1988
Tel: 024–7622 7597
Fax: 024–7663 1448
email: provost@coventrycathedral.org

PEYTON, Ven Nigel, MA, BD, STM
4 The Woodwards, Newark NG24 3GG [ARCH-
DEACON OF NEWARK] *b* 5 Feb 1951; *educ* Latymer
Sch Lon; Edin Univ; Union Th Seminary New
York; Edin Th Coll; Chapl St Paul Cathl Dundee
1976–82; P-in-c All So Invergowrie 1979–85; V
All SS Nottm 1985–91; P-in-c H Trin Lambley
1991–99; Dioc Min Development Adv 1991–99;
Adn of Newark from 1999; Bps' Educ Selector;
JP
GS 1995–   *Tel:* (01636) 612249 (Home)
(01636) 814490 (Office)
Fax: (01636) 611952 (Home)
(01636) 815882 (Office)
email: archdeacon-newark@southwell-
sdbf.prestel.co.uk

PHILPOTT, Prebendary Samuel
St Peter's Vicarage, Wyndham Square, Plymouth, Devon PL1 5EG [EXETER] *b* 6 Feb 1941; *educ* R Naval Hosp Sch Holbrook; Kelham Th Coll; C St Mark Swindon 1965–70; C St Martin Torquay 1970–73; TV All SS Exmouth 1973–76; V Shaldon 1976–78; V St Pet Plymouth from 1978; RD Plymouth Devonport 1985–91 and from 1995; Preb of Ex Cathl from 1991; M DBF; M Dioc Bd of Educ; M Dioc Pastl Ctee; M Dioc Vacancy-in-See Ctee; M Bp's Coun; M Dioc Children and Young People's Ctee; Chair Icthus Community Projects; Chair Ship Hostel Plymouth; M Nat Coun Forward in Faith; M CTBI and CTE Enabling Grp
GS 1990–   *Tel:* (01752) 222007
                            Fax: (01752) 257973

PHYTHIAN, Mr George, B SC (AGRIC), DIP ED, T CERT
2 Shaftesbury Place, Scotforth, Lancaster LA1 4PZ [BLACKBURN] *b* 17 Jul 1927; *educ* Upholland Gr Sch; Reading Univ; Asst Master Soham Gr Sch 1952–55; Head of Agric/Horticulture Worthing Tech High Sch 1955–60; Sen Master Pershore High Sch 1960–66; Hdmaster Ripley St Thos High Sch Lancaster 1966–91; Rtd; Rdr from 1954; M Dioc Syn; M Dioc Pastl Ctee; Sch Gov
GS 1991–   *Tel:* (01524) 65460

PICKFORD, Mr Christopher John, BA, DAA, FSA
Church of England Record Centre, 15 Galleywall Rd, South Bermondsey, London SE16 3PB [DIRECTOR, CHURCH OF ENGLAND RECORD CENTRE] *b* 2 Jun 1952; *educ* K Sch Worc; Leic Univ; Univ Coll Lon; Trainee Archivist Leics 1973–74; Asst Archivist Heref and Worc CC 1975–77; Asst Archivist Beds CC 1978–86; County Archivist Beds 1986–98; Dir CE Record Centre from 1998; M St Albs DAC 1986–91; M CCC Bells Sub-Ctee 1985–90; Bells Adv Birm DAC 1992–98   *Tel:* 020–7898 1034
                            Fax: 020–7394 7018
        email: chris.pickford@c-of-e.org.uk

PITHERS, Canon Brian Hoyle
Vicarage, 63 Michaelson Ave, Torrisholme, Morecambe LA4 6SF [BLACKBURN] *b* 6 Jun 1934; *educ* Rochdale High Sch; Chich Th Coll; C SS Pet and Paul Wisbech 1966–70; V Fenstanton 1970–75; V Hilton 1970–75; V St Matt Havergham Eaves 1975–85; P-in-c H Trin Habergham Eaves 1978–85; V St Matt w H Trin Habergham Eaves 1985–86; TR Ribbleton from 1986; V Ascen and St Martin Torrisholme from 1992; M BM 1990–97; M CBF 1990–95; M Cen Stewardship Ctee 1990–95; M Chs Commn on Miss 1994–95; M Gov Body Carl Dioc Tr Inst from 1993; Hon Can Blackb Cathl from 1997
GS 1989–   *Tel:* (01524) 413144
          email: canonbrian@msn.com

PITTS, Revd Eve (Evadne Ione)
19 Elmcroft Ave, Bartley Green, Birmingham B32

4LZ [BIRMINGHAM] *b* 23 Dec 1950; *educ* Coltesmore Sec Sch; Qu Coll Birm; C St Mich Bartle Green from 1989
GS 1990–   *Tel:* 0121–422 143●

PLATTEN, Very Revd Stephen George, B ED, DI THEOL
The Deanery, The Close, Norwich, Norfolk NR1 4EC [DEAN OF NORWICH] *b* 17 May 1947; *educ* Stationers' Company's Sch; Lon Univ Inst of Educ; Trin Coll Ox; Cuddesdon Th Coll; C Headington 1975–78; Chapl and Tutor Linc Th Coll 1978–82; DDO and Minl Tr and Can Res Portsm Cath 1982–89; Sec for Ecum Affairs to Abp of Can 1990–95; Dean of Nor from 1995
GS 1997–   *Fax:* (01603) 76603⎯
         email: dean@cathedral.org.u●

PLYMOUTH, Bishop of [SUFFRAGAN, EXETER] **Rt Revd John Henry Garton,** MA
31 Riverside Walk, Tamerton Foliot, Plymouth PL5 4AQ *b* 3 Oct 1941; *educ* Tudor Grange Gr Sch Solihull; RMA Sandhurst; Worc Coll Ox; Cuddesdon Th Coll; Commissioned in R Tank Regiment 1962; CF Guards Depot Pirbright 1969–70, RMA Sandhurst 1970–72; N Ireland 1972–73; Lect Linc Th Coll 1973–78; TR Cov E 1978–86; Prin Ripon Coll Cuddesdon 1986–96; V Cuddesdon 1986–96; Hon Can Worc Cathl 1987–96; Bp of Plymouth from 1996   *Tel:* (01752) 769836
                            Fax: (01752) 769818●

POLKINGHORNE, Canon John Charlton, KBE, MA, PH D, SC D, FRS, DD
74 Hurst Park Ave, Cambridge CB4 2AF [UNIVERSITIES, CAMBRIDGE] *b* 16 Oct 1930; *educ* Perse Sch Cam; Trin Coll Cam; Westcott Ho Th Coll; Prof of Mathematical Physics Cam Univ 1968–79; V Blean 1984–86; Dean Trin Hall Cam 1986–89; Pres Qu Coll Cam 1989–96; Fell Qu Coll Cam from 1996; Can Th Liv from 1994; M BSR from 1990
GS 1990–   *Tel and Fax:* (01223) 360743

POLLARD, Prof Arthur, BA, B TH, BD, B LITT, D LITT
Sand Hall, North Cave, Brough, E Yorks HU15 2LA [YORK] *b* 22 Dec 1922; *educ* Clitheroe R Gr Sch; Leeds Univ; Linc Coll Ox; Lect and Sen Lect Man Univ 1949–67; Prof of English Hull Univ 1967–84, Dean of Faculty of Arts 1976–78; Consultant Prof of English, Univ of Buckm 1983–89; Councillor, Alderman, Leader Congleton Boro Coun 1952–67; Co Councillor Humberside Co Coun (Educ Spokesman Conservative Grp) 1979–96; M E Riding Coun and Educ Spokesman from 1995; M Funding Agency for Schs 1996–98; M Gen Syn Bd of Educ and Schs Ctee from 1991, Chmn from 1996; M Abp's Coun 1991–97; M Dioc Bd of Educ 1990–93; Rdr from 1951
GS 1990–   *Tel:* (01430) 422202 (Home)
                         (01482) 885011 (Office)
                            Fax: (01430) 424890

PONTEFRACT, Bishop of [SUFFRAGAN, WAKEFIELD] **Rt Revd David Charles James,** B SC, A, PH D
Pontefract House, 181A Manygates Lane, Wakefield WF2 7DR b 6 Mar 1945; *educ* Nottm High Sch; Ex Univ; Nottm Univ; St Jo Coll Nottm; C Ch Ch Portswood 1973–76; C Goring-by-Sea 1976–78; Chapl UEA Nor 1978–82; V Ecclesfield 1982–90; RD Ecclesfield 1987–90; V Ch Ch Portswood 1990–98; Hon Can Win Cathl 1998; Bp of Pontefract from 1998
GS 1985–90   *Tel:* (01924) 250781
                              Fax: (01924) 240490
email:
davidjames@bishopofpontefract.freeserve.co.uk

POPE, Mr John Henry William
5 Hawthylands Rd, Hailsham, E Sussex BN27 1EU [CHICHESTER] *b* 8 Aug 1945; *educ* Roan Sch for Boys; Woolwich Poly; Rtd
GS 1997–   *Tel:* (01323) 841613

PORTER, Mr John Albert
165 Newland Park, Hull HU5 2DX [YORK] *b* 10 Oct 1941; *educ* Scarborough Boys High Sch; RAF Coll Cranwell; Computer Consultant; M Abp's Coun; Lay Chmn Hull Dny Syn; M DBF
GS 1995–   *Tel* and *Fax:* (01482) 346284
        email: John_Porter@japorter.karoo.co.uk

PORTSMOUTH, Bishop of, Rt Revd Kenneth William Stevenson, MA, PH D, DD, FR HIST S
Bishopsgrove, 26 Osborn Rd, Fareham, Hants PO16 7DQ b 9 Nov 1949; *educ* Edin Academy; Edin Univ; Southn Univ; Man Univ; Sarum and Wells Th Coll; C Grantham 1973–76; Lect Boston Par Ch 1976–80; pt Lect Linc Th Coll 1975–80; Chapl and Lect Man Univ 1980–86; TV Whitworth Man 1980–82; TR 1982–86; Vis Prof Univ of Notre Dame Indiana 1983; ABM Selector 1982–92; R H Trin w St Mary Guildf 1986–95; Chmn Anglo-Nordic-Baltic Th Conf from 1997; M Doct Commn from 1996; Bp of Portsm from 1995
GS 1995–   *Tel:* (01329) 280247
                              Fax: (01329) 231538

PRITCHARD, Ven John Lawrence, MA, M LITT
29 The Precincts, Canterbury, Kent CT1 2EP [ARCH-DEACON OF CANTERBURY] *b* 22 Apr 1948; *educ* Arnold Sch Blackpool; St Pet Coll Ox; Ridley Hall Th Coll; St Jo Coll Dur; C St Martins-in-the-Bull Ring Birm 1972–76; Dioc Youth Officer B & W 1976–79; V St Geo Wilton 1980–88; Dir Pastl Studies Cranmer Hall and St Jo Coll Dur 1989–93; Warden Cranmer Hall 1993–96; Adn of Cant and Can Res Cant Cathl from 1996
GS 1999–   *Tel:* (01227) 463036
                              Fax: (01227) 785209

PURCHAS, Canon (Catherine) Patience Ann, BA
Rectory, Church St, Wheathampstead, St Albans, Herts AL4 8AD [ST ALBANS] *b* 23 Mar 1939; *educ* St Alb Girls Gr Sch; St Mary's Coll Dur; St Alb Minl Tr Scheme; Relig Educ Resource Centre 1980–81;

Relig Broadcasting Chiltern Radio 1981–87; Hon Dss Wheathampstead 1980–87; Hon Par Dn Wheathampstead 1987–93; Sec to Dioc Bd of Min 1987–93; Bp's Officer for Women's and NSM from 1993; Pro-Prolocutor Lower Ho Conv of Cant 1994–98; M Gen Syn Stg Ctee 1996–98; Author; Broadcaster
GS 1990–   *Tel:* (01582) 833144 (Home)
        Tel and *Fax:* (01582) 834285 (Office)

PYBUS, Mr Roy
22 Beaclair Rd, Wavertree, Liverpool L15 6XG [LIVERPOOL] *b* 3 Nov 1941; *educ* Liv Inst High Sch; Univ Coll Lon; Solicitor admitted 1966
GS 1995–   *Tel* and *Fax:* 0151–722 9792

PYE, Mr Christopher Charles, BA, M SC
140 Hinckley Rd, St Helens, Merseyside WA11 9JY [LIVERPOOL] *b* 21 Apr 1946; *educ* Grange Park Sch St Helens; Open Univ; Technologist in Glass Industry from 1963; Occupational Hygienist; Lay Chmn St Helens Dny Syn from 1986; Lay Chmn Dioc Syn from 1991
GS 1985–90, 1992–   *Tel:* (01744) 609506

RADFORD, Mrs Jennifer, MA
Poplar Farm, Hognaston, Ashbourne, Derbys DE6 1PR [DERBY] *b* 30 Oct 1937; *educ* Arnold High Sch Blackpool; Girton Coll Cam; Head of English Bemrose Sch Derby 1974–77; Head of English Zahra Sch Muscat, Oman 1981–83; Co Councillor Derbys 1989–97; M Derbys Dales Distr Coun from 1995; Educ Consultant in Eng and RE and Insp of Schs
GS 1990–   *Tel* and *Fax:* (01335) 370143

RADFORD, Mr Roger George, AIA
7 Little College St, London SW1P 3SF [SECRETARY AND TREASURER TO THE CHURCH OF ENGLAND PENSIONS BOARD] *b* 17 Mar 1944; *educ* City of Lon Sch; Clerical, Medcl and Gen Life Assur Soc to May 1984; Dep Sec to Pensions Bd May–Sept 1984; Sec and Treas from Oct 1984   *Tel:* 020–7898 1800
                              Fax: 020–7898 1801

RAMSBURY, Bishop of [AREA BISHOP, SALISBURY] **Rt Revd Peter Fearnley Hullah,** BD, AKC, FRSA
Office: Ramsbury Area Office, Sarum House, High St, Urchfont, Devizes, Wilts SN10 4QH, Home: Bishop's Croft, Winterbourne Earls, Salisbury, Wilts SP4 6HJ b 7 May 1949; *educ* Bradf Gr Sch; K Coll Lon; Makerere Univ Kampala; Cuddesdon Th Coll; Asst Chapl St Edw Sch Ox 1974–77; Chapl Sevenoaks Sch 1977–82; Housemaster Internat Centre Sevenoaks 1982–87; Sen Chapl K Sch Cant 1987–92; Dir Cant K's Week Art Festival 1989–92; Hdmaster Chetham's Sch of Music 1992–99; Bp of Ramsbury from 1999   *Tel:* (01380) 840373 (Office)
                      (01980) 619126 (Home)
                Fax: (01380) 848247 (Office)
                      (01980) 619128 (Home)
        email: adsarum@compuserve.com

RATCLIFF, Ven David William, DIP AD ED
Styrmansgatan 1, S-114 54 Stockholm, Sweden
[ARCHDEACON OF SCANDINAVIA AND GERMANY] *b* 3
Nov 1937; *educ* Cant Cathl Choir Sch; St Mich Sch
Ingoldisthorpe; K Coll Lon; Lon Univ Extra-
Mural Dept; Edin Th Coll; C St Aug S Croydon
1962–65; P-in-c St Fran Selsdon 1965–69; V St
Mary Milton Regis 1969–75; Adult Educ and Lay
Tr Adv Cant dio 1975–91; Hon Min Can Cant
Cathl 1975–91; Hon Pres Ecum Assoc Adult Educ
in Eur 1982–88; M Internat Ctee German Evang
Kirchentag 1983–98; R American Episc Par Ch the
King Frankfurt 1991–98; Adn of Scandinavia and
Germany from 1996; Hon Can Gibraltar Cathl
from 1996; Representative at Gen Convention of
ECUSA 1994 and 1997; Chapl Stockholm from
1998   *Tel:* 00–46–8663–8248
                        Fax: 00–46–8663–8911
                email: anglican.church@telia.com

RAWES, Dr James Charteris Lea, MA, MB, B CHIR,
D OBST RCOG, D CH
Falcons, Little Easton, Dunmow, Essex CM6 2JH
[CHELMSFORD] *b* 16 Nov 1929; *educ* Marlboro Coll;
Jes Coll Cam; St Thos Hosp Lon; USPG Miss List
(Central and S Africa) 1960–66; GP 1966–90; pt
GP and Nursing Homes Adv N Essex HA
1991–95; Gov Helena Romanes Sch Dunmow
1971–94, Chmn 1988–94; Rtd 1990; USPG Gen
Ctee and Health Adv Grp 1969–82 and 1993–98
GS 1995–   *Tel:* (01371) 872640

RAYNER, Revd David
The Inner Cities Religious Council, Floor 4/K10,
Eland House, Bressenden Place, London SW1E 5DU
[SECRETARY, INNER CITIES RELIGIOUS COUNCIL] *b*
14 Dec 1949; *educ* Boteler Gr Sch Warrington; Trin
Hall Cam; Westcott Ho Th Coll; C St Clem Chorl-
ton 1978–81; C St Mary the Gt Cam 1981–84; V St
Geo Camberwell and Warden Trin Coll Centre
1984–88; Warden Bp Mascall Centre Heref
1989–90; V H Trin w St Alb Smethwick 1990–92;
P-in-c St Paul W Smethwick 1990–92; V Resurr
Smethwick 1992–99; RD Warley 1993–97; Sec
Inner Cities Relig Coun from 1999
                Tel: 020–7890 3704 (Office)
                        Fax: 020–7890 3709
            email: David_Rayner@detri.gsi.gov.uk

RAZZALL, Canon Charles Humphrey, MA, BA
Holy Trinity Vicarage, 46 Godson St, Oldham OL1
2DB [MANCHESTER] *b* 7 May 1955; *educ* St Paul's
Sch Lon; Worc Coll Ox; Qu Coll Cam; Westcott
Ho Th Coll; C Catford and Downham TM
1979–83; V St Hilda w St Cyprian Crofton Park
1983–87; Dioc UPA Officer Man 1987–92; TV
Oldham and AD Oldham from 1992; M BSR
Community and Urban Affairs Ctee
GS 1995–   *Tel:* 0161–627 1640

READE, Ven Nicholas Stewart, BA, DIP TH
27 The Avenue, Lewes BN7 1QT [ARCHDEACON OF
LEWES AND HASTINGS] *b* 9 Dec 1946; *educ* Eliz Coll

Guernsey; Leeds Univ; Coll of the Resurr Mir
field; C St Chad Coseley 1973–75; C-in-c H Cros
Bilbrook and C Codsall 1975–78; V St Pet Uppe
Gornal and Chapl Burton Rd Hosp Dudle
1978–82; V Mayfield 1982–88; RD Dallingto
1982–88; V and RD Eastbourne 1988–97; Chm
Dioc Liturg Ctee 1989–97; Can and Preb Chic
Cathl from 1990; Adn of Lewes and Hasting
from 1997; M Bp's Coun from 1989; Chmn Dio
Bd of Patronage 1992–97; Vc-Pres Dioc Syn an
Chmn Ho of Clergy from 1997
GS 1995–   *Tel:* (01273) 47953
                        Fax: (01273) 47652

READING, Bishop of [AREA BISHOP, OXFORD] **Rt**
Revd Dominic (Edward William Murray)
Walker, OGS, AKC, MA, D LITT
Bishop's House, Tidmarsh Lane, Tidmarsh, Reading
RG8 8HA b 28 Jun 1948; *educ* Plymouth Coll; K
Coll Lon; Heythrop Coll Lon; C St Faith Wands-
worth 1972–73; Dom Chapl to Bp of S'wark
1973–76; R Newington 1976–85; RD S'wark and
Newington 1980–85; V Brighton 1985–97; RD
Brighton 1985–97; Can and Preb Chich Cathl
1985–97; Superior OGS 1990–96; Bp of Reading
from 1997   *Tel:* 0118–984 1216
                        Fax: 0118–984 1218
        email: bishopreading@oxford.anglican.org

REDDEN, Mr Jonathan Francis, MB, BS, FRCS
ENG, FRCS ED (ORTH)
Tofield House, Carr Lane, Wadworth, Doncaster
DN11 9AR [SHEFFIELD] *b* 21 Feb 1947; *educ* Loughb
Gr Sch; St Bart Hosp Medical Coll Lon Univ;
Senior Registrar Edin 1977–81; Lect Orthopaedic
Surgery Wellington Medical Sch New Zealand;
Consultant Orthopaedic Surgeon Doncaster R
Infirmary from 1981
GS 1989–   *Tel:* (01302) 853829

REDMAN, Mr Anthony James, B SC, FRICS
The Cottage, Great Livermere, Bury St Edmunds, Suf-
folk IP31 1JG [ST EDMUNDSBURY AND IPSWICH] *b* 1
May 1951; *educ* Walton on Thames Sec Mod Sch;
Surbiton Gr Sch; Reading Univ; Chartered Build-
ing Surveyor; Conservation accredited; Rdr from
1976; M Dioc Property Ctee 1983–97; M Ecclesi-
astical Architects and Surveyors Assn Exec
1988–98; Pres 1993–94; M CCC from 1991, Jt Vc-
Chair (Conservation) from 1996; M CCC Publica-
tions Sub-Ctee 1991–95; Surveyor of Fabric St
Edm Cathl from 1992; M Exec Ctee Suffolk Hist
Chs Trust 1993–97; Chmn RICS Conservation
Skills Panel from 1998; M St Albs DAC from 1998;
M Westmr Abbey Fabric Adv Commn from 1998;
M Baptist Union Listed Building Adv Panel from
1998; M Ch and Community Trust Millennium
Design Panel 1998–99
GS 1989–   *Tel:* (01359) 269335
                        (01284) 760421
                        Fax: (01284) 704734
email:
    whitcp@globalnet.co.uk/tred@globalnet.co.uk

EED, Revd Keith Andrew, BA
5 *Marylebone Rd, London NW1 5JR* [ECUMENICAL
EPRESENTATIVE (METHODIST CHURCH)] *b* 26 Jul
939; *educ* Bradf Gr Sch; Bris Univ; Didsbury Th
Coll Bris; M Dursley and Stonehouse 1963–65;
Juddersfield (West) 1965–71; Leeds (Heading-
ey) 1971–80; York (North) 1980–95; Asst Sec of
Conf from 1995
GS 1995–   *Tel:* 020–7486 5502
         Fax: 020–7224 1510

REES, Mrs Christina (Henking Muller), MA
*Churchfield, Pudding Lane, Barley, Royston, Herts
SG8 8JX* [ST ALBANS] *b* 6 Jul 1953; *educ* Hampton
Day Sch; Pomona Coll; Wheaton Graduate Sch; K
Coll Lon; Researcher IBA 1980; Asst Public
Relations Offcr The Childrens Society 1985–87;
Writer from 1980; Broadcaster from 1990; M
Crown Appts Commn 1995; M Steering Ctee and
nitiation Services Revision Ctee from 1996; M
CECC from 1996; M ABM from 1996; Chair
WATCH (Women and the Church); M Dioc Bd for
Chr Development; Elected M Abps' Coun from
1999
GS 1990–   *Tel:* (01763) 848822
         (01763) 848472
         Fax:(01763) 848774
         email: chrisrees@xc.org

REES, Revd (Vivian) John (Howard), MA, LL B,
M PHIL
36 *Cumnor Hill, Oxford OX2 9HB* [OXFORD] *b* 21
Apr 1951; *educ* Skinners' Sch Tunbridge Wells;
Southn Univ; Ox Univ; Leeds Univ; Wycliffe Hall
Ox; Solicitor (Admitted 1975); C Moor Allerton
TM 1979–82; Chapl and Tutor Sierra Leone Th
Hall, Freetown 1983–86; Ptnr Winckworth Sher-
wood Solicitors from 1986; Sec Oxf Dny Syn
1993–98; Treas Eccles Law Soc from 1995; Joint
Registrar Ox Dio from 1998; Dep Registrar Prov
of Cant from 1998; Legal Adv ACC from 1998
GS 1995–   *Tel:* (01865) 865875
         Fax: (01865) 726274
         email: oxford@winckworths.co.uk

REESE, Prebendary John David, CERT ED
Tupsley Vicarage, 107 Church Rd, Hereford HR1 1RT
[HEREFORD] *b* 29 Apr 1949; *educ* Handsworth Gr
Sch; Coll of St Mark and St Jo; Ripon Coll Cud-
desdon; C St Mary and All SS Kidderminster
1976–81; V S Johor Malaysia 1982–85; V Bp's
Castle w Mainstone 1985–91; RD Clun Forest
1987–91; V Tupsley w Hampton Bp from 1991;
RD Heref City from 1996; M Dioc Bd of Educ; M
Dioc Pastl and Minl Ctee
GS 1997–   *Tel:* (01432) 274490

REID, Very Revd (William) Gordon, MA
The Deanery, Bomb House Lane, Gibraltar [ARCH-
DEACON IN EUROPE] *b* 28 Jan 1943; *educ* Galashiels
Academy; Edin Univ; Keble Coll Ox; Cuddesdon
Th Coll; C St Salvador Edin 1967–69; Chapl
Sarum Th Coll 1969–72; R St Mich and All SS

Edin 1972–84; Provost Inverness Cathl 1984–87;
Chapl St Nic Ankara, Turkey 1987–89; Chap St
Pet and St Seigfrid Stockholm 1989–92;V Gen Dio
in Eur 1992–98; Adn in Eur 1996–98; Dean of
Gibraltar from 1998   *Tel:* 00–350–78377(Home)
        00–350–75745 (Office)
        Fax: 00–350–78463

REISS, Ven Robert Paul, MA
*Archdeacon's House, New Rd, Wormley, Godalming,
Surrey GU8 5SU* [ARCHDEACON OF SURREY] *b* 20
Jan 1943; *educ* Haberdashers' Aske's Sch Hamp-
stead; Trin Coll Cam; Westcott Ho Th Coll; C St
John's Wood 1969–73; Asst Missr Rajshahi Miss
Dacca Bangladesh 1973; Chapl Trin Coll Cam
1973–78; Selection Sec ACCM 1978–85; Sen Selec-
tion Sec 1983–85; TR Grantham 1986–96; RD
Grantham 1991–96; Adn of Surrey from 1996;
Chmn ABM Wrkg Party on Minl Review; M
PWM 1993–96; M Bd of Educ from 1994; Chmn
Bd of Educ F and HE Ctee from 1995
GS 1990–   *Tel:* (01428) 682563
         Fax: (01428) 682993
         email: bob.reiss@cofeguildford.org.uk

REPTON, Bishop of [SUFFRAGAN, DERBY] Rt
Revd David Christopher Hawtin, MA
Repton House, Lea, Matlock DE4 5JP b 7 Jun 1943;
educ K Edw VII Sch Lytham St Annes; Keble Coll
Ox; Wm Temple Th Coll, Rugby; Cuddesdon Th
Coll; C St Thos Pennywell, Sunderland 1967–71;
C St Pet's Stockton 1971–74; P-in-c CD St Andr
Leam Lane, Gateshead 1974–79; R Washington
Grp Min and LEP 1979–88; ACCM Selector
1987–92; Dioc Ecum Officer Dur 1988–92; M BMU
1986–90; M BCC 1985–90; M CTE from 1990; M
CTE Enabling Grp 1991–99; Dep Moderator CTE
Forum 1995–99; M CTBI from 1990; Consultant to
CCU 1991–96, M Local Unity Ctee 1997–99;
Chmn Dioc Bd of Educ 1993–99; Chmn E Mid-
lands Consortium for Tr and Educ for Min from
1996; Gen Syn Rep on Gov Body E Midlands Minl
Tr Course 1997–99; Adn of Newark 1992–99; Bp
of Repton from 1999; Chmn Dioc Pastl Ctee from
1999; Chmn Dioc Pastl Ctee from 1999; Chmn
Dioc Coun for Miss and Unity from 1999
GS 1983–99   *Tel:* (01629) 534644
       Fax: (01629) 534003

RHODES, Revd David Grant, BA, CERT TH, DIP
AD ED
111 Potternewton Lane, Leeds LS7 3LW [RIPON] *b* 4
Apr 1943; *educ* Huddersfield New Coll; Ex Univ;
Sarum Th Coll; Journalist 1960–69; C Mirfield
1972–75; V St Thos Batley 1975–80; Adult Educ
Officer Wakef 1976–79; Journalist and NSM St Jo
Huddersfield 1982–86; Dir BRF 1986–87; V Robert-
town 1987–94; Originator of Prayer Lights Min
from 1989; NSM St Martin Potternewton from
1995; pt Project Worker w Faith in Leeds One City
Project from 1994
GS 1995–   *Tel:* 0113–274 2021
     Tel and *Fax:* 0113–262 7247

RICHARDSON, Mr Colin
379 Chester Rd, Hartford, Northwich, Cheshire CW8 1QR [CHESTER] Dep Headteacher
GS 1995–

RICHARDSON, Very Revd John Stephen, BA, M INST D
The Provost's House, 1 Cathedral Close, Bradford, W Yorks BD1 4EG [PROVOST OF BRADFORD] *b* 2 Apr 1950; *educ* Haslingden Gr Sch; Southn Univ; St Jo Coll Nottm; C Bramcote 1974–78; C Radipole and Melcombe Regis 1977–80; P-in-c Stinsford, Winterborne Came w Whitcombe 1980–83; Asst Dioc Missr Sarum 1980–83; V Ch Ch Nailsea 1983–90; Dioc Adv on Evang B & W 1986–90; M Coun St Jo Coll Nottm 1988–94; V and Provost Bradf Cathl from 1990; Trustee and Vc-Chmn Acorn Chr Healing Trust from 1990; Trustee Spennithorne Home of Healing and Holy Rood Ho from 1991; Bp's Selector ABM 1992–96; M BM from 1996; M Evang Alliance Exec from 1994; M Spring Harvest Coun from 1998
GS 1993–   *Tel:* (01274) 777722
                                                  (01274) 777727
                                       Fax: (01274) 777730

RICHBOROUGH, Bishop of [PROVINCIAL EPISCOPAL VISITOR, CANTERBURY] **Rt Revd Edwin Barnes,** MA
14 Hall Place Gardens, St Albans, Herts AL1 3SP b 6 Feb 1935; *educ* Plymouth Coll; Ox Univ; Cuddesdon Th Coll; C St Mark North End Portsm 1960–64; C All SS Woodham Guildf 1964–67; R Farncombe 1967–78; V All SS Hessle 1978–87; Prin St Steph Ho 1987–95; M Gen Syn Stg Ctee 1993–95; M ABM 1990–95; Hon Can Ch Ch Ox 1994–95; CTBI Rep and CTE Enabling Grp 1994–95; Bp of Richborough from 1995; Pres Guild of All So from 1996; Asst Bp and Hon Can St Albs from 1997
GS 1975–78, 1985–87, 1990–95 *Tel:* (01727) 857764
                                       Fax: (01727) 763025

RIDER, Mr Stephen Channing, BA, FCIS, FCMA
Church House, Great Smith St, London SW1P 3NZ [CHIEF ACCOUNTANT, ARCHBISHOPS' COUNCIL] *b* 12 Mar 1961; *educ* Fearnhill Comp Sch Letchworth; Univ of Kent; Fin Services Manager USPG 1988–94; Fin Sec St Alb 1994–99; Chief Accountant Abps' Coun from 1999
                                           Tel: 020–7898 1568
                           email: stephen.rider@c-of-e.org.uk

RIDING, Dr Irene Lilian, B SC, ARCS, DIC, PH D, T DIP
16 Upper Breach, South Harrington, Wells, Som BA5 3QG [BATH AND WELLS] *b* 30 Mar 1936; *educ* Park Sch Preston; Whitelands Coll Lon; Imp Coll Lon; Science Tchr Sleaford High Sch 1956–59; Garratt Green Comp Sch 1959–64; Asst Lect and Research Asst Imp Coll Lon 1967–72; Hdmistress St Geo Sch Ascot 1974–82; Rtd
GS 1999–   *Tel and Fax:* (01749) 679998

RILEY, Very Revd Ken (Kenneth Joseph), BA, M
1 Booth Clibborn Court, Park Lane, Manchester M 4PJ [DEAN OF MANCHESTER] *b* 25 Jun 1940; *edu* Holywell Gr Sch; Univ Coll of Wales Aberyswyth; Linacre Coll Ox; Wycliffe Hall Th Coll; Em Fazakerley 1964–66; Chapl Brasted Place Co 1966–69; Chapl Oundle Sch 1969–74; Chapl Li Univ 1974–83; V Mossley Hill 1975–83; RI Childwall 1982–83; Dioc Warden of Rdrs 1980–8; Can Res Liv Cathl 1983–93 (Treas 1983–87; Pre 1987–93); Dean of Man from 1993
GS 1995–   *Tel:* 0161–833 222
                                       Fax: 0161–839 622

RINGROSE, Ven Hedley Sidney, BA
The Sanderlings, Thorncliffe Drive, Cheltenhar GL51 6PY [ARCHDEACON OF CHELTENHAM] *b* 2 Jun 1942; *educ* W Oxfordshire Coll; Open Univ Sarum Th Coll; C Bishopston 1968–71; C East hampstead 1971–75; V St Geo Gloucester v Whaddon 1975–88; RD Gloucester City 1983–88 V Cirencester w Watermoor 1988–98; RI Cirencester 1989–97; Hon Can Glouc Cath 1986–98; Chmn Dioc Bd of Patronage 1990–98 Chmn Dioc Ho of Clergy 1994–98; Adn of Chel tenham from 1998; Reserved Can Glouc Cath from 1998; Chmn Dioc Bd of Educ from 1998 Trustee Glenfall Ho from 1998; Trustee S Matthias Trust from 1998
GS 1990–   *Tel:* (01242) 52292;
                                       Fax: (01242) 23592;
                           email: archdchelt@star.co.uk

RIPON, Bishop of
[Not appointed at time of going to press.]

RIPPETH, Mrs Ione
11 The Ridge, Ryton, Tyne and Wear NE40 3LN [DURHAM] *b* 1940; Lect and Counsellor
GS 1995–   *Tel:* 0191–413 3920

RISDON, Revd John Alexander, DIP TH
Stapleton Rectory, 21 Park Rd, Stapleton, Bristol BS16 1AZ [BRISTOL] *b* 5 Jul 1942; *educ* Churcher's Coll Petersfield; Lon Bible Coll; Clifton Th Coll; C St Jo W Ealing 1968–72; C St Pet Heref 1972–74; Hon C Ch Ch Bromley 1974–77; Ord Candidates Sec CPAS 1974–77; TV H Trin Cheltenham 1977–86; R H Trin Stapleton from 1986; M Bp's Coun; Dir DBF; M Coun Trin Coll Bris; M Dioc Pastl Ctee
GS 1995–   *Tel:* 0117–958 3858

ROBILLIARD, Mr David John
Le Petit Gree, Torteval, Guernsey GY8 0RD [WINCHESTER-CHANNEL ISLANDS] *b* 22 Nov 1952; *educ* Guernsey Gr Sch for Boys; Clearing and Internat Banking 1969–82; Her Majesty's Dep Greffier 1982–87; Prin Asst Chief Exec Guernsey Civil Service 1987–94; Hd of External and Constitutional Affairs States of Guernsey from 1994, M Dioc Vacancy in See Ctee; Sec Guernsey Dny
GS 1998–   *Tel:* (01481) 264344

ROBINSON, Ven Anthony William, CERT ED

0 Arden Court, Horbury, Wakefield WF4 5AH
[ARCHDEACON OF PONTEFRACT] *b* 25 Apr 1956; *educ*
Bedf Modern Sch; Bedf Coll of HE; Sarum and
Wells Th Coll; C St Paul Tottenham 1982–85; TV
Resurr Leic 1985–89, TR 1989–97; RD Christianity
N 1992–97; Hon Can Leic Cathl from 1994; M CBF
1995–97; M CMEAC 1996–97; Adn of Pontefract
from 1997

GS 1995–97   *Tel:* (01924) 276797
                  Fax: (01924) 261095
email: tonyrobinson@ardencourt.freeserve.co.uk

ROBINSON, Ven (John) Kenneth, BD, AKC

Rua João de Deus, Lote 5, Alcoitão, 2645–128 Alcabi-
deche, Portugal [ARCHDEACON OF GIBRALTAR] *b* 17
Dec 1936; *educ* Balshaw's Gr Sch Leyland; K Coll
Lon; St Boniface Th Coll Warminster; C Poulton-
e-Fylde 1962–65; C Lanc Priory 1965–66; Chapl
St Jo Sch Singapore 1966–68; V H Trin Colne
1968–70; Dir of Educ Windward Islands 1970–74;
V St Luke Skerton 1974–81; Area Sec (E Anglia)
USPG 1981–91; Min Can St Eds Cathl 1982–91;
Chapl Gtr Lisbon from 1991; Adn of Gibraltar
from 1994   *Tel* and *Fax:* 00–3511–469–2303

ROBOTTOM, Mr Peter Gordon, MA, DIPTP,
MRTPI, MIMGT

38B Whittingehame Gardens, Brighton, E Sussex
BN1 6PU [CHICHESTER] *b* 6 Feb 1946; *educ* Solihull
Sch; Jes Coll Ox; Birm Poly; Planning Asst Staffs
Co Coun 1967–70; Asst Planner/Prin Asst Plan-
ner Ox City Coun 1970–73; Dep City Planning
Officer Ox City Coun 1973–83; Boro Planning
Officer Brighton Boro Coun 1983–91; Sen Hous-
ing and Planning Inspector The Planning
Inspectorate from 1991; Sen Inspector Supervisor
from 1998; M Coun Corp of Ch Ho 1989–99; Lay
Chmn Brighton Dny Syn from 1990; M Bp's Coun
from 1991; M Dios Commn from 1991

GS 1985–   *Tel:* (01273) 559172 (Home)
                (01273) 557537 (Office)
email: peter@robottom.softnet.co.uk

ROBSON, Dr Frank Elms, OBE, DCL

16 Beaumont St, Oxford OX1 2LZ and 2 Simms
Close, Stanton St John, Oxford OX9 1HB [JOINT
REGISTRAR OF THE PROVINCE OF CANTERBURY] *b* 14
Dec 1931; *educ* K Edw VI Gr Sch Morpeth; Selw
Coll Cam; Solicitor; Registrar Ox Dio; Joint Regis-
trar, Province of Cant from 1982; Vc-Chmn Legal
Adv Commn; Chmn Ecclesiastical Law Soc
                  Tel: (01865) 241974

**ROCHESTER, Bishop of, Rt Revd Michael
James Nazir-Ali,** BA, B LITT, M LITT, PH D

Bishopscourt, Rochester, Kent ME1 1TS b 19 Aug
1949; *educ* St Paul's Sch Karachi; St Patr Coll
Karachi; Karachi Univ; Fitzw Coll Cam; St Edm
Hall Ox; Univ of N S Wales; Ridley Hall Th Coll;
Tutorial Supervisor Th Cam Univ 1974–76; C H
Sepulchre and All SS Cam 1974–76; Sen Tutor
Karachi Th Coll 1976–81; Provost of Lahore Cathl
1981–84; Bp of Raiwind 1984–86; Asst to Abp of

Cant and Dir in Residence Ox Cen for Miss
Studies 1986–89; Co-ord of Studies and Ed Lam-
beth Conf 1988; Hon C St Giles and SS Phil and
Jas w St Marg Ox 1986–89; Gen Sec CMS 1989–94;
Asst Bp S'wark 1989–94; Can Th Leic 1992–94;
Sec Abp's Commn on Communion and Women
in the Episcopate from 1988; M Bd Chr Aid
1988–97; M CCBI 1991–95; M ARCIC II from
1991; M BM from 1991, Chmn Miss Th Adv Grp
from 1992; Bp of Roch from 1994; M Ho of Bps'
Theol Grp from 1996; M Urban Bps' Panel from
1996; Vis Prof of Th and Rel Studies Univ of
Greenwich from 1996; M HFEA and Chmn Ethics
Ctee from 1998; Chmn Trin Coll Bris Coun; Fell St
Edm Hall Ox; Select Pchr Cam Univ and Ox
Univ; Qu Lect Belfast Univ; Selw Lect St Jo Coll
Auckland

GS 1994–   *Tel:* (01634) 842721
                Fax: (01634) 831136

RONAYNE, Revd Peter Henry

54 Maywater Close, South Croydon CR2 0LS
[SOUTHWARK] *b* 8 Jul 1934; *educ* Oak Hill Th Coll; C
St Mary Chesham 1966–69; C H Trin Worthing
1969–74; V St Leon w St Mich Shoreditch 1974–82;
P-in-c Norwood 1982–85; V from 1985; RD
Streatham 1987–91

GS 1995–   *Tel:* 020–8651 9743

RONE, Ven Jim (James), FSCA

Archdeacon's House, 24 Cromwell Rd, Ely, Cambs
CB6 1AS [ARCHDEACON OF WISBECH] *b* 28 Aug
1935; *educ* Skerry's Coll Liv; St Steph Ho Ox; Fin
Officer Ox dio 1973–79; C Stony Stratford
1980–82; V St Pet and St Mary Magd Fordham
1982–89; R St Nic Kennett 1982–89; Res Can Ely
Cathl 1989–95, Can Treas 1992–95; Adn of Wis-
bech from 1995; M CBF; M Corp of Ch Ho; M Bp's
Coun; DBF; Pastl Ctee; Houses Ctee; Investments
Ctee; Bd of Educ; DAC; Bp's Adv on Hosp Chap-
laincies; Chmn Dioc Rural Min Grp; Chmn Schs
Exec Bd of Educ

GS 1995–   *Tel:* (01353) 662909
                Fax: (01353) 662056
      email: archdeacon.wisbech@ely.anglican.org

ROSE, Ven (Kathleen) Judith, BD, DIP TH, IDC,
NDD

3 The Ridings, Tunbridge Wells, Kent TN2 4RU
[ARCHDEACON OF TONBRIDGE] *b* 14 Jun 1937; *educ*
Sexey's Gr Sch Blackford Som; Seale Hayne Agric
Coll; St Mich Ho Ox; Lon Bible Coll; Par Wrkr
Rodbourne Cheney Swindon 1966–71; Dss St Geo
Leeds 1973–81; Chapl Bradf Cathl 1981–85; Min
resp St Paul Parkwood S Gillingham 1986–90; RD
Gillingham 1988–90; Personal Chapl to Bp of
Roch, Bp's Offcr for Ordained Women and Assoc
Dir of Ords 1990–95; Acting Adn of Tonbridge
and Assoc DDO 1995–96; Adn of Tonbridge from
1996; M Crown Appts Commn; M Bp's Coun; M
Dioc Pastl Ctee; M DAC; Simeon Trustee

GS 1975–80, 1980–81, 1987–
          Tel and *Fax:* (01892) 520660
email:
    archdeacon.tonbridge@rochester.anglican.org

ROYLE, Mr Timothy Lancelot Fanshawe, FC
INST M
*Icomb Place, Nr Stow-on-the-Wold, Cheltenham, Glos
GL54 1JD* [GLOUCESTER] *b* 24 Apr 1931; *educ* Harrow; Rdr from 1959; Ch Commr 1967–82; MD
Hogg Robinson Grp 1953–82; Chmn Control
Risks Grp 1974–91; Chmn Berry Palmer Lyle
1983–91; Chmn Lindley Educl Trust 1970–98;
Chmn Chr Weekly Newspapers 1976–98; Dir
Well Marine Reinsurance Brokers from 1976;
Trustee ICS, Wycliffe Hall Ox, Ridley Hall Cam;
M Abp's Legal Commn 1966; M DBF; M Bp's
Coun; M Revision Ctee Draft Incumbents (Vacation of Benefices) (Amendment) Measure; Trustee Charinco; Charishare; Dir Imperio Grp UK
1993–98
GS 1985–   *Tel:* (01451) 830231
                              020–7373 3092
                         Fax: (01451) 832450
                      email: troyle@aol.com

RUDDOCK, Ms Beverley Elaine, M SC, BA, PGCE,
RGN, SCM
*Joydene, Murrell Hill Lane, Binfield, Berks RG42
4DA* [OXFORD] *b* 14 Jan 1947; *educ* Ardenne High
Sch Jamaica; Reading Univ; Univ Coll Lon; Midwifery Sister until 1982; pt FE Coll Tchr 1985–87;
Primary Tchr 1988–90; Educ Psychologist
from 1991; Sen Educ Psychologist from 1998
GS 1995–

RUOFF, Mrs Alison Laura, SRN, SCM, DN
*The White House, 75 Crossbrook St, Cheshunt, Herts
EN8 8LU* [LONDON] *b* 1 Nov 1942; *educ* Sutton
Coldfield Girls High Sch; Nightingale Sch of
Nursing, St Thos Hosp; Br Hosp for Mothers and
Babies; Nursing Inst Worc; VSO India 1961–62;
Asst Dir of Nursing Internat Grenfell Assn Newfoundland 1968–70; Admin Sister St Thos Hosp
Grp 1970–72; Nursing Officer/Sen Nursing
Officer Univ Coll Hosp 1972–74; Housewife; JP
from 1979 Cheshunt and E Herts Bench, M Family Panel; Vc-Chmn Herts Magistrates' Assn; M
Coun Nat Magistrates' Assn; M Bp's Coun; M
CEEC; M HCC; M Ch Soc Coun; regular contributor to Premier Radio
GS 1995–   *Tel:* (01992) 623113
           email: Alison.Ruoff@dlondon.org.uk

RUSSELL, Ven (Harold) Ian Lyle, BD, ALCD
9 Armorial Rd, Coventry CV3 6GH [ARCHDEACON
OF COVENTRY] *b* 17 Oct 1934; *educ* Epsom Coll;
Lon Univ; Lon Coll of Div; C Iver 1960–63; C-in-c
St Luke Lodge Moor Fulwood 1963–67; V
Chapeltown Sheff 1967–75; RD Tankersley
1973–75; V St Jude Mapperley 1975–89; AD
Nottm Cen 1986–89; Hon Can S'well Cathl
1988–89; M Hosp Chapl Coun 1986–96; Adn of
Cov from 1989; M CE Pensions Bd from 1991, Vc-
Chmn from 1998; Chmn Dioc Ho of Clergy from
1991; M Ethical Investment Working Grp from

1996; Chaplain to HM The Queen from 1997; M
FJM Rule Ctee from 1996
GS 1970–75, 1985–   *Tel:* 024–7641 7750 (Home
                              024–7667 4328 (Office
                         Fax: 024–7641 4640 (Home
                              024–7669 1760 (Office

RUSSELL, Ven Norman Atkinson, MA, BD
*Foxglove House, Love Lane, Donnington, Newbury
Berks RG14 2JG* [ARCHDEACON OF BERKSHIRE] *b* ?
Aug 1943; *educ* R Belfast Academical Inst; Chu
Coll Cam; Lon Coll of Div; C Ch Ch w Em Cliftor
1970–74; C Ch Ch Trent Park Enfield 1974–77; F
Harwell w Chilton 1977–84; P-in-c Gerrards
Cross 1984–88; P-in-c Fulmer 1985–88; R Gerrards
Cross and Fulmer 1988–98; Hon Can Ch Ch Ox
1995–98; RD Amersham 1996–98; Adn of Berks
from 1998; M Dioc BSR; M Dioc Ctee for Racial
Justice   *Tel:* (01635) 55282C
                         Fax: (01635) 522165
         email: archdber@oxford.anglican.org

SADGROVE, Very Revd Michael, MA
The Cathedral, Sheffield S1 1HA [PROVOST OF
SHEFFIELD] *b* 13 Apr 1950; *educ* Univ Coll Sch
Lon; Ball Coll Ox; Trin Coll Bris; Lic to Offic Ox
dio 1975–76; Lect OT Sarum & Wells Th Coll
1977–82; Vc-Prin 1980–82; V Alnwick 1982–87;
Can Res, Prec and Vc-Provost Cov Cathl 1987–95;
Provost of Sheff from 1995; Bps' Sen Inspector of
Th Colls and Courses; M Cathls Fabric Commn
for Eng
                              Tel: 0114–275 3434
                         Fax: 0114–278 0244
                   email: msadgrove@aol.com

SADLER, Ven Anthony Graham, MA
*The Archdeacon's House, 10 Paradise Lane, Pelsall,
Walsall, W Midlands WS3 4NH* [ARCHDEACON OF
WALSALL] *b* 1 Apr 1936; *educ* Bp Vesey's Gr Sch
Sutton Coldfield; Qu Coll Ox; Lichf Th Coll; C St
Chad Burton-upon-Trent 1962–65; V Rangemore
and Dunstall 1965–72; V Abbots Bromley
1972–79; V Pelsall 1979–90; RD Walsall 1982–90;
P-in-c Uttoxeter, Bramshall, Gratwich, Marchington, Marchington Woodlands, Kingstone, Checkley, Stramshall and Leigh 1990–97; R Uttoxeter
1997; Preb of Lichf Cathl 1987–97; Hon Can Lichf
Cathl from 1997; Adn of Walsall from 1997
                              Tel: (01922) 445353
                         Fax: (01922) 445354

SADLER, Mr Anthony John, MA, CIPD
Fielden House, Little College St, London SW1P 3SH
[ARCHBISHOPS' APPOINTMENTS SECRETARY] *b* 2 Oct
1938; *educ* Bedf Sch; Magd Coll Cam; Personnel
Mgr Hawker Siddeley Aviation 1964–68; Personnel Mgr Rank Audio Visual Ltd 1968–72; Personnel Dir RHM General Products Ltd 1972–75; Asst
Personnel Controller Rank Org 1975–78;
Employee Relations Mgr Lloyds Bank Internat
1978–83; Chmn S Lon Ind Miss 1980–82; Dir, Grp
Human Resources, Minet plc 1983–92; Chmn

S'wark Welcare Centenary Appeal Ctee 1993–95; Abps' Appointments Sec from 1996

Tel: 020–7898 1876
020 7233 0393
Fax: 020–7898 1867
email: anthony.sadler@c-of-e.org.uk

SALISBURY, Bishop of, Rt Revd David Staffurth Stancliffe, MA, D LITT
South Canonry, 71 The Close, Salisbury, Wilts SP1 2ER b 1 Oct 1942; *educ* Westmr Sch; Trin Coll Ox; Cuddesdon Th Coll; C St Bart's Armley, Leeds 1967–70; Chapl Clifton Coll Bris 1970–77; Can Res of Portsm, DDO and Dioc Lay Min Adv 1977–82; Prov of Portsm 1982–93; Bp of Sarum from 1993; M Liturg Commn from 1986, Chmn from 1993; M Cathls Fabric Commn from 1991
GS 1985–
Tel: (01722) 334031
Fax: (01722) 413112
email: dsarum@eluk.co.uk

SANDERS, Mr William Ashton, MA
Nine Chimney House, Balsham, Cambridge CB1 6ES [ELY] *b* 20 Nov 1934; *educ* Kingswood Sch; Ex Coll Ox; Public Relations Officer The Stock Exchange 1965–75; Sec Zululand Swaziland Assn 1977–96; Appeal Dir Angl Cen in Rome from 1996; M CCC from 1996; M Dioc Syn; M Dioc Coun for Miss and Unity; M DAC; Asst Sec Bp's Coun; Sec Dioc Bd of Patronage; M Cambs Ecum Coun
GS 1995–
Tel: (01233) 893063
Fax: (01223) 890846

SANDFORD, Mr Bryan Moile, CBE, M SC, MIEE
Lanterns, 54 Thames Ave, Guisborough, Cleveland TS14 8AF [YORK] *b* 3 Jun 1934; *educ* Man Gr Sch; Man Univ; Loughb Univ; Chartered Eng; Registered Safety Practitioner; Managing Dir Lantern Safety Services from 1989; M Abps Commn on the Organisation of the CE; M Abps' Coun Fin Ctee; M DRACSC; Chmn Dioc Commn; Chmn Qu Victoria Clergy Fund; Chmn Consultative Grp of DBF Chmn and Secs; Rdr
GS 1970–
Tel and *Fax:* (01287) 632442

SASSER, Revd Howard Crawford, BA, MA
Rua do Campo Alefre 640–5D, 4150 Porto, Portugal [EUROPE] *b* 25 Jul 1937; *educ* High Sch Florida USA; Maryland Univ; Geo Mason Univ Virginia; Westmr Coll Ox Washington Dioc Course Asst Chapl US Forces Germany 1977–80; Chapl Ch Ch Mogadishu Somalia 1981–83; Asst to Provost St Paul Cathl Nicosia 1984–87; Asst Chapl St Paul Athens 1989–92; Chapl St Jo Montreux 1992–97; Chapl St Jas Porto from 1997
GS 1998–
Tel and *Fax:* 00351–2–6091006

SAUNDERS, Mrs Sheila Constance
4 Edmonds Drive, Ketton, Stamford, Lincs PE9 3TH [PETERBOROUGH] *b* 25 Apr 1935; *educ* Rye Gr Sch; Leic Domestic Science Tchr Tr Coll; Sec Dioc Miss Coun 1986–92; Chmn MU Dioc Educ Dept

1980–86; Vc Pres Dioc MU from 1992; M Dioc Bd on Min from 1993
GS 1995–
Tel and *Fax:* (01780) 720228

SCHOFIELD, Prebendary Rodney, MA
West Monkton Rectory, Taunton, Som TA2 8QT [BATH AND WELLS] *b* 21 Mar 1944; *educ* St Albs Sch; St Jo Coll Cam; Bris Univ; St Pet Coll Ox; St Steph Ho Ox; C St Mary Northn 1971–76; V Irchester 1976–84; Warden Lelapa La Jesu Sem Lesotho and Dir of POT Lesotho dio 1984–86; R W Monkton from 1986; DDO from 1989; M Dioc Coun for Min; M Bp's Coun; M Board of Studies SW Minl Tr Scheme; M Bd of Govs STETS
GS 1990–
Tel and *Fax:* (01823) 412226

SCLATER, Mr John Richard, CVO, MA, MBA
Office: 117 Eaton Square, London SW1W 9AA, Home: Sutton Hall, Barcombe, Lewes, E Sussex BN8 5EB [FIRST CHURCH ESTATES COMMISSIONER] *b* 14 Jul 1940; *educ* Charterhouse; Trin Coll Cam; Yale Univ; Harvard Business Sch; Trainee Dir Glyn, Mills & Co 1964–67 and 1968–70; Dir Williams, Glyn & Co 1970–71; Dep Dir Williams & Glyn's Bank, Chmn Williams and Glyn's Leasing Co and Railway Fin Ltd 1971–73; Dep Dir Internat Division Williams & Glyn's 1973–76; Appointed Trustee Grosvenor Estate 1973; M City Taxation Ctee 1973–76; Man Dir Nordic Bank 1976–82; Chmn Assoc of Consortium Banks 1980–82; Chmn Nordic Bank 1985; Dir Guiness Peat Grp plc and Dep Chmn Guiness Mahon & Co Ltd 1985–87; Chmn Foreign & Colonial Investment Trust plc 1985; Chmn Guiness Mahon & Co Ltd 1987; M Coun Duchy of Lancaster from 1987; Dep Chmn Yamaichi Internat (Eur) Ltd 1987–97; Chmn Hafnia Grp 1989–93; Chairman Berisford plc from 1990; Vc-Chmn Hill Samuel Bank Ltd 1990–92, Chmn 1992–96; Freeman City of Lon from 1993; Liveryman Goldsmiths' Co from 1993; Pres Equitable Life Assurance Soc from 1994; Trustee Coll of Arms Trust from 1994; Dep Chmn Millennium and Copthorne Hotels plc from 1996; Consultant RP&C Internat from 1997; Chmn Argent Grp Eur Ltd from 1998; Dir Wates Grp from 1999; First Ch Estates Commr from 1999;
GS 1999–
Tel: 020–7235 2223 (Office)
020–7235 0446 (Home, weekdays)
Fax: 020–7235 1228 (Office)
(01273) 401086 (Home, weekends)
(01273) 400450 (Home, weekends)
email: john.sclater@talk21.com

SCREECH, Revd Royden, BD, AKC
Church House, Great Smith St, London SW1P 3NZ [SENIOR SELECTION SECRETARY, MINISTRY DIVISION] *b* 15 May 1953; *educ* Cotham Gr Sch Bris; K Coll Lon; St Aug Coll Cant; C St Cath Hatcham 1976–80; V St Ant Nunhead 1980–87; P-in-c St Silas Nunhead 1983–87; RD Camberwell 1983–87; V St Edw New Addington 1987–94; ABM Selection Sec and LNSM Co-ordinator 1994–96;

Sen Selection Sec ABM 1997–98; Sen Selection Sec Min Division from 1999; Staff M Min Division; Sec to Vocation, Recruitment and Selection Ctee

Tel: 020–7898 1402
Fax: 020–7898 1419
email: roy.screech@c-of-e.org.uk

SEAFORD, Very Revd John Nicholas, BA
The Deanery, David Place, St Helier, Jersey, Channel Islands JE2 4TE [DEAN OF JERSEY] *b* 12 Sep 1939; *educ* Radley Coll; Dur Univ; St Chad's Coll Dur; C Bush Hill Park 1968–71; C Stanmore Win 1971–73; V Chilworth w N Baddesley 1973–78; V Highcliffe w Hinton Admiral 1978–93; RD Christchurch 1990–93; Hon Can Win Cathl from 1993; Dean of Jersey and R St Helier from 1993; M States of Jersey from 1993
GS 1993–95
Tel: (01534) 720001
Fax: (01534) 617488
email: deanofjersey@anergy.co.uk

SEDGWICK, Mrs Margaret Anne
187 Rugby Road, Binley Woods, Coventry CV3 2AY [COVENTRY] *b* 7 Jul 1937; *educ* Chislehurst & Sidcup Tech High Sch; Rolle Coll; Leeds Univ; Asst Mistress Chislehurst & Sidcup Tech High Sch 1959–66; Hd of RE Basingstoke High Sch for Girls 1966–72; Hd of Relig Studies Qu Mary Sixth Form Coll Basingstoke 1972–74; Sen Tchr Coundon Court Sch Cov 1974–77; Dep Hdteacher Cov Blue Coat CE Sch 1977–92; Asst Dioc Educ Offcr (Vol) 1993–98; Rdr; M Gen Syn Bd of Educ 1994–96; M Dioc Bd of Educ; M Dioc Syn; M Dioc Rdrs Course Ctee; M Bd of Management NCEC
GS 1992–
Tel: 024–7654 2805

SEED, Ven Richard Murray Crosland, MA
Vicarage, Boston Spa, Wetherby, W Yorks LS23 6EA [ARCHDEACON OF YORK] *b* 9 May 1949; *educ* St Philip's Sch Burley-in-Wharfedale; Leeds Univ; Edin Th Coll; C Ch Ch Skipton 1972–75; C Baildon 1975–77; TV Kidlington Ox 1977–80; V Boston Spa 1980–99; Adn of York from 1999
Tel: (01937) 842454

SELBY, Bishop of [SUFFRAGAN, YORK] **Rt Revd Humphrey Vincent Taylor, MA**
10 Precentor's Court, York YO1 7EJ b 5 Mar 1938; *educ* Harrow; Cam Univ; Lon Univ; Coll of Resurr Mirfield; C St Kath N Hammersmith 1963–64; C St Mark Notting Hill 1964–66; R St Pet Lilongwe, Malawi 1967–71; Chapl Bp Grosseteste Coll Linc 1972–74; Sec for Chaplaincies in Higher Educ Gen Syn Bd of Educ 1974–80; Sec Miss Programmes USPG 1980–84; Sec USPG 1984–91; Bp of Selby from 1991; M BSR from 1996 and Chmn Internat and Development Affairs Ctee from 1996; Chmn NHS Exec N and Yorks Adv Ctee on Spiritual Care and Chaplaincy from 1997
GS 1999–
Tel: (01904) 656492
Fax: (01904) 655671
email: bishselby@clara.net

SHAW, Mr (Robert) Martin
Windmill Farm, Willingale, Ongar, Essex CM5 0SS [CHURCH COMMISSIONER] *b* 17 Jan 1941; *educ* Shrewsb Sch; Ox Univ; Managing Dir Baring Asset Management Ltd; Ch Commr from 1994, M Assets Ctee

SHEFFIELD, Bishop of, Rt Revd Jack (John) Nicholls
Bishopscroft, Snaithing Lane, Sheffield S10 3LG b 16 Jul 1943; *educ* Bacup and Rawtenstall Gr Sch; K Coll Lon; Warminster Th Coll; C St Clemw St Cyprian Ordsall 1967–69; C All SS and Martyrs Langley 1969–72; V 1972–78; Dir of Pastl Studies Coll of Resurr Mir 1978–83; Can Res Man Cathl 1983–90; Bp of Lanc 1990–97; Bp of Sheff from 1997
GS 1997–
Tel: 0114–230 2170
Fax: 0114–263 0110

SHERBORNE, Bishop of [AREA BISHOP, SALISBURY] **Rt Revd John Dudley Galtrey Kirkham**
Little Bailie, Dullar Lane, Sturminster Marshall, Wimborne, Dorset BH21 4AD b 20 Sep 1935; *educ* Lancing Coll; Trin Coll Cam; Westcott Ho Th Coll; C St Mary le Tower Ipsw 1962–65; Chapl to Bp of Nor 1965–69; Chapl to Bp of New Guinea 1969–70; C Martin-in-the-Fields Lon and St Marg's Westmr 1970–72; Dom Chapl to Abp of Cant 1972–76; Bp of Sherborne from 1976; Abp's Adv to Headmasters' Conference 1990–93; Bp to the Forces from 1992
GS 1980–85
Tel: (01258) 857659
Fax: (01258) 857961

SHERWOOD, Bishop of [SUFFRAGAN, SOUTHWELL] **Rt Revd Alan Wyndham Morgan**
Sherwood House, High Oakham Rd, Mansfield, Notts NG18 5AJ b 22 Jun 1940; *educ* Boys Gr Sch Gowerton; St D Coll Lamp; St Mich Coll Llan; Asst C Llangyfelach w Morriston 1964–69; Asst C Cockett 1969–72; V St Barnabas, Cov E 1972–77; Bp's Offcr for Social Resp Cov Dioc 1978–83; Adn of Cov 1983–89; Bp of Sherwood from 1989
GS 1980–89
Tel: (01623) 657491
Fax: (01623) 662526
email: bishop@bishopsherwood.prestel.co.uk

SHORT, Revd Martin Peter, MA
Church House, Great Smith St, London SW1P 3NZ [HEAD OF MEDIA TRAINING, ARCHBISHOPS' COUNCIL] *b* 25 Sep 1954; *educ* Warw Sch; Peterho Cam; Wycliffe Hall Th Coll; C St Pet Shipley 1979–82; C St Mary Becontree 1982–86; V St Jas Bolton, Bradf 1986–92; C All SS Otley and DCO Bradf 1992–98; Hon Chapl Bradf Cathl from 1998; Head of Media Training Abps' Coun from 1998
Tel: 020–7898 1458
Fax: 020–7222 6672
email: martin.short@c-of-e.org.uk

SHOTTER, Very Revd Edward Frank, BA
The Deanery, Rochester, Kent ME1 1TG [DEAN OF

ROCHESTER] *b* 29 Jun 1933; *educ* Humberstone Foundation Sch Clee; Univ of Wales, Lampeter; St Steph Ho Ox; C St Pet Plymouth 1960–62; SCM Intercollegiate Sec Lon 1962–66; Chapl Univ of Lon 1969–89; Dir Studies Lon Medical Grp 1966–89; Dir Inst of Medical Ethics 1974–89; M Editorial Bd Journal of Medical Ethics from 1975; Preb St Paul's Cathl 1977–89; Dean of Roch from 1989; Chmn Medway Enterprise Agency 1993–98; Chmn and Force Chapl Kent Police Chaplaincy from 1993; Sec Assn of Eng Cathls from 1994; Chmn Greenwich Univ Research Ethics Ctee from 1995; M Ch Heritage Forum from 1999
GS 1994–   *Tel:* (01634) 844023
                            Fax: (01634) 401410

SHREWSBURY, Bishop of [AREA BISHOP, LICHFIELD] **Rt Revd David Marrison Hallatt,** BA, MA
68 London Rd, Shrewsbury, Shropshire SY2 6PG b 15 Jul 1937; *educ* Birkenhead Sch; Southn Univ; St Cath Coll Ox; Wycliffe Hall Th Coll; C St Andr Maghull 1963–67; V All SS Totley 1967–75; TR St Jas and Em Didsbury 1975–89; Adn of Halifax 1989–94; Bp of Shrewsbury from 1994
GS 1990–94   *Tel:* (01743) 235867
                            Fax: (01743) 243296
email: bishop.shrewsbury@lichfield.anglican.org

SIDAWAY, Canon Geoffrey Harold
Vicarage, Church Lane, Bearsted, Maidstone, Kent ME14 4EF [CANTERBURY] *b* 28 Oct 1942; *educ* Kelham Th Coll; C Beighton 1966–70; C All SS Chesterfield 1970–72; V St Bart Derby 1972–77; V St Martin Maidstone 1977–86; V Bearsted and Thurnham from 1986; RD Sutton from 1992; Hon Can Cant Cathl from 1994; Commis for Bp of Kinkizzi Uganda from 1995; M Dioc Syn; M Abp's Coun
GS 1995–   *Tel* and *Fax:* (01622) 737135

SIMMONS, Mrs Hazel
16 Coanwood Drive, Cramlington, Northumberland NE23 6TL [NEWCASTLE] Rtd Medical Laboratory Scientific Officer; M CMEAC; M Dioc Ctee for Interfaith and Ethnic Relations; Rdr
GS 1995–   *Tel:* (01670) 739270
                            (01670) 730136

SIMMONS, Mr Richard
30 Laburnum Way, Nayland, Colchester CO6 4LG [ST EDMUNDSBURY AND IPSWICH] Senior Manager
GS 1995–

SIMPSON, Very Revd John Arthur
The Deanery, Canterbury, Kent CT1 2EP [DEAN OF CANTERBURY] *b* 7 Jun 1933; *educ* Cathays High Sch Cardiff; Keble Coll Ox; Clifton Th Coll; C Leyton 1958–59; C Ch Ch Orpington 1959–62; Tutor Oak Hill Coll 1962–72; V Ridge 1972–79; DDO and Dir POT St Alb 1975–81; Hon Can St Alb Cathl 1977–79; Can Res of St Alb Cathl and P-in-c Ridge

1979–81; Adn of Cant and Can Res of Cant Cathl 1981–86; Dean of Cant from 1986
GS 1981–86   *Tel:* (01227) 765983 (Home)
                         (01227) 762862 (Office)

SIMPSON, Mrs Marion Elizabeth, B ED
West Little Place, Godstone, Surrey RH9 8LT [SOUTHWARK] *b* 20 Dec 1933; *educ* Woodhouse Gr Sch Finchley; Lon Univ; Dispenser Boots the Chemists 1949–59; Mother at home 1959–70; Tchr Tr 1970–75; Sec Sch Teacher (Science and Maths) 1975–90; Supply Teacher 1990–94; Rtd; Rdr from 1981; Adnry Vocations Adv 1991–98; M Dios Commn from 1996; Unit Co-ord Prayer and Spirituality S'wark MU and Mary Sumner Ho; Hon Treas WATCH from 1996
GS 1990–   *Tel:* (01883) 742724

SINCLAIR, Canon Jane Elizabeth Margaret, MA, BA
The Cathedral Church of St Peter and St Paul, Church St, Sheffield S1 1HA [SHEFFIELD] *b* 1 Mar 1956; *educ* Westonbirt Sch Tetbury; St Hugh's Coll Ox; Nottm Univ; St Jo Coll Nottm; Dss St Paul w St Jo Herne Hill and St Sav Ruskin Park 1983–86; Lect in Liturg and Chapl St Jo Coll Nottm 1986–93; Can Res and Prec Sheff Cathl from 1993; M Liturg Commn from 1986
GS 1995–   *Tel:* 0114–275 3434 (Cathedral)
                         0114–255 7782 (Home)
                         Fax: 0114–278 0244
                         email: Shefflit@aol.com

SKIDMORE, Mr David Paul, BA, MA
Church House, Great Smith St, London SW1P 3NZ [SECRETARY, GENERAL SYNOD BOARD FOR SOCIAL RESPONSIBILITY] *b* 11 Mar 1943; *educ* Ampleforth Coll; Nottm Univ; Univ of Pennsylvania; LSE; Lect Univ of York 1971–85; Social Resp Adv St Alb dio 1985–89; Sec Gen Syn BSR from 1989
                    Tel: 020–7898 1521 (Office)
                         (01727) 868209 (Home)
                 email: david.skidmore@c-of-e.org.uk

SLATER, Mr Colin Stuart, FIPR
11 Muriel Rd, Beeston, Nottingham NG9 2HH [SOUTHWELL] *b* 28 Feb 1934; *educ* Belle Vue Gr Sch Bradford; Chief Public Relations Officer Notts Co Coun 1969–87, Severn Trent Water 1987–89, Notts Co Cricket Club 1989–95; Chmn BBC Radio Nottm Adv Coun 1975–79; former Chmn Soc of Co PROs and IPR Local Gvt Grp; M Coun Inst of PR 1986–90; JP from 1977; Public Relations Consultant and freelance broadcaster from 1994; M Bp's Coun, F & GP grp, Parish Giving Ctee
GS 1990–   *Tel* and *Fax:* 0115–925 7532

SLATER, Mr Timothy George
17 Wentworth St, Huddersfield HD1 5PX [WAKEFIELD] *b* 1 Jan 1954; *educ* K James' Gr Sch Huddersfield; Cam Coll of Arts and Tech; Bretton Hall Coll; Head of Music All SS High Sch Huddersfield from 1979; M Bp's Coun; M Dioc Pastl

Ctee; Lay Chair Huddersfield Dny Syn; M Liturg Commn from 1996
GS 1990–   *Tel:* (01484) 518504

SLAUGHTER, Miss Ingrid Elizabeth, LL B
Church House, Great Smith St, London SW1P 3NZ [ASSISTANT LEGAL ADVISER, GENERAL SYNOD] *b* 3 Mar 1947; *educ* Ursuline High Sch Brentwood; K Coll Lon; Barrister; In practice at Chancery Bar 1970–74; Legal Dept Nat Coal Bd 1974–83; Official Solicitor's Dept Ch Commrs from 1983; Asst Legal Adv Gen Syn from 1987; Rdr
                              Tel: 020–7898 1368
           email: ingrid.slaughter@c-of-e.org.uk

SLEE, Very Revd Colin Bruce, BD, AKC
Provost's Lodging, 51 Bankside, London SE1 9JE [PROVOST OF SOUTHWARK] *b* 10 Nov 1945; *educ* Ealing Gr Sch; K Coll Lon; St Aug Coll Cant; C St Fran Heartsease Nor 1970–73; C Gt St Mary Cam 1973–76; Chapl Girton Coll Cam 1973–76; Chapl and Tutor K Coll Lon 1976–82; Sub Dean and Can Res St Alb 1982–94; Provost of S'wark from 1994
GS 1995–   *Tel* and *Fax:* 020–7928 6414 (Home)
                   Tel: 020–7407 3708 (Office)
                  Fax: 020–7357 7389 (Office)
    email: cathedra@dswark.org.uk/SleeBanks
                              @aol.com (Home)

SMALLEY, Very Revd Dr Stephen Stewart, BD, MA, PH D
The Deanery, 7 Abbey St, Chester CH1 2JF [DEAN OF CHESTER] *b* 11 May 1931; *educ* Battersea Gr Sch; Jes Coll Cam; Ridley Hall Th Coll; Eden Th Sem USA; C St Paul Portman Sq Lon 1958–60; Chapl Peterho Cam 1960–63 (Acting Dean 1962–63); Select Prchr Univ of Cam 1963–64; Lect and Sen Lect Ibadan Univ, Nigeria 1963–69; Lect and Sen Lect Man Univ 1970–77; Wrdn St Anselm Hall 1972–77; Can Res and Prec Cov Cathl 1977–86; Vc-Prov 1986; M Abps' Doct Commn 1981–86; Dean of Ches from 1987; Author
                   Tel: (01244) 351380 (Home)
                        (01244) 324756 (Office)
                   Fax: (01244) 341110
    email: dean@chestercathedral.org.uk

SMALLWOOD, Mr John Frank Monton, CBE, MA
The Willows, Parkgate Rd, Newdigate, Dorking, Surrey RH5 5AH [SOUTHWARK] *b* 12 Apr 1926; *educ* City of Lon Sch; RAF 1944–48; Peterho Cam; Ch Assembly 1965–70; Bank of England 1951–79; Dep Chief Accntnt 1974–79; ACC 1975–87; BCC 1987–90; M numerous Ctees and Commns 1971–95; CBF 1965–99 (Dep Vc-Chmn 1972–82); Ch Commr 1966–99 (Bd of Gvnrs and M Gen Purposes Ctee); City Parchl Fdn 1969–99 (Chmn 1981–92); Lambeth Palace Lib 1977–99; Overseas Bishoprics Fund 1978–99 (Chmn 1992–99); Stg Ctee 1971–95; Pensions Bd 1985–95; Chs Main Ctee 1987–95; Coun Corp of Ch Ho 1987–95;

S'wark DBF 1962–2000 (Chmn 1975–2000); S'wark Ord Course Coun 1960–94 (Vc-Chmn 1980–94); Rdr from 1983
GS 1970–   *Tel:* (01306) 631457

SMITH, Ven Alan Gregory Clayton, BA, MA
Archdeacon's House, 39 The Brackens, Clayton, Newcastle-under-Lyme ST5 4JL [ARCHDEACON OF STOKE-UPON-TRENT] *b* 14 Feb 1957; *educ* Trowbridge High Sch for Boys; Birm Univ; Wycliffe Hall Th Coll; C St Lawr Pudsey 1981–82, w St Paul 82–84; Chapl Lee Abbey 1984–90; Dioc Missr and Exec Sec Lichf Dioc BMU 1990–97; TV St Matt Walsall 1990–97; Adn of Stoke-upon-Trent from 1997; Chmn Bd of Lee Abbey Household Communities
GS 1999–   *Tel:* (01782) 663066
                                 Fax: (01782) 711165

SMITH, Mrs Carol Alice, RGN, RMN, SCM
11 School Lane, Fulford, York YO10 4LU [YORK] *b* 2 Jan 1949; *educ* Elmslie Girls' Sch Blackpool; Middx Hosp; Derby City Hosp; Staff Nurse Middx Hosp 1971–72; Community Psychiatric Nurse Lon 1973; District Midwife Cheltenham 1977–79; Housewife and Mother 1980–93; Practice Nurse Stockton Hall Psychiatric Hosp York from 1993; Bank Psychiatric Nurse Bootham Hosp York from 1993
GS 1994–   *Tel:* (01904) 643646
            email: IanRSmith@compuserve.com

SMITH, Mr Christopher John Addison, BA, FCA
60 Roseneath Rd, London SW11 6AQ [LONDON] *b* 30 Mar 1949; *educ* St Pet Sch York; UEA; Price Waterhouse 1970–93, various trainee and management posts 1970–89; Human Resources Partner 1989–93; Gen Sec Lon dio from 1993; M CBF; M CBF Exec; M CBF Staff Ctee
GS 1995–   *Tel:* 020–7932 1221 (Office)
                          Fax: 020–7932 1114

SMITH, Mr Ian Rodney, B ED, FCII, MIMGT
11 School Lane, Fulford, York YO10 4LU [YORK] *b* 6 Mar 1948; *educ* Hyde Co Gr Sch Ches; Dur Univ; Tchr Fitzharry's Sch Abingdon 1970–71; Tchr Convent High Sch Stockport 1971–74; Personnel Management Eagle Star Insurance Co 1974–82; Personnel Management NEM Insurance Co 1982–84; CMS Area Co-ord Ripon and York dios from 1984 and CMS N Co-ord from 1998; Rdr; Hon Dioc Adviser in Evang from 1990; M BM from 1990; M PWM Ctee from 1996; M CECC 1996–98
GS 1990–   *Tel:* (01904) 659792
            email: ian.smith@cms-uk.org

SMITH, Revd Martin David, LTCL, BA, CERT TH
Rectory, 10 Stepping Lane, Rouen Rd, Norwich NR1 1PE [NORWICH] *b* 10 Sep 1952; *educ* Selhurst Gr Sch; Trin Coll of Music Lon; Hull Univ; Cuddesdon Th Coll; C St Thos Brentwood 1978–80; C St Giles Reading 1980–91; R Colkirk w Oxwick w

Pattesley, Whissonsett etc 1991–95; P-in-c St Pet Parmentergate w St Jo Nor from 1995
GS 1995– *Tel:* (01603) 622509
email: frmartinsmith@clara.net

SMITH, Mr Peter Reg, FRICS
Lusaka House, Great Glemham, Saxmundham, Suffolk IP17 2DH [ST EDMUNDSBURY AND IPSWICH] *b* 17 Apr 1946; *educ* K Edw VI Sch Southn; Coll of Estate Management; M Coun USPG from 1991; Chmn Dioc Overseas Miss Grp; Chmn Dioc Ho of Laity; Chmn Dioc Vacancy-in-See Ctee
GS 1993– *Tel* and *Fax:* (01728) 663466
email: happyhackers@usa.net(Peter and GeraldineSmith)

SMITH, Revd William Melvyn, BD, AKC, PGCE
330 Hagley Rd, Pedmore, Stourbridge, W Midlands DY9 0RD [WORCESTER] *b* 22 Feb 1947; *educ* Newc under Lyme High Sch; K Coll Lon; St Aug Coll Cant; C H Trin Wordsley 1971–73; Hon C Ch Ch Coseley 1973–74; C St Paul Wood Green Wednesbury, in-c St Luke Mesty Croft 1974–78; V St Chad Coseley 1978–91; RD Himley 1983–96; TR Wordsley 1991–96; Dioc Stewardship and Resources Officer from 1996
GS 1995– *Tel:* (01562) 720414 (Home)
(01562) 20537 (Office)

SODOR AND MAN, Bishop of, Rt Revd Noël Debroy Jones, CB, BA
Bishop's House, Quarterbridge Rd, Douglas, Isle of Man IM2 3RF b 25 Dec 1932; *educ* W Monmouth Gr Sch; St D Coll Lamp; Wells Th Coll; C St Jas Tredegar 1955–57; C St Mark Newport 1957–60; V Kano Nigeria 1960–62; Chapl RN 1962–84; Chapl of the Fleet 1984–89; CB 1986; OStJ 1996 Bp of Sodor and Man from 1989
GS 1984– *Tel:* (01624) 622108
Fax: (01624) 672890

SOUTHAMPTON, Bishop of [SUFFRAGAN, WINCHESTER] **Rt Revd Jonathan Michael Gledhill,** BA, MA, BCTS
Ham House, The Crescent, Romsey, Hants SO51 7NG b 15 Feb 1949; *educ* Strode's Sch Egham; Keele Univ; Bris Univ; Trin Coll Bris; C All SS Marple 1975–78; P-in-c St Geo Folkestone 1978–83; V St Mary Bredin Cant 1983–96; Tutor-/Lect Cant Sch of Min 1983–94; Tutor/Lect SE Inst for Th Educ 1994–96; RD Cant 1988–94; Hon Can Cant Cathl 1992–96; Bp of Southn from 1996; M Meissen Commn 1993–96; Chmn Angl Old Catholic Internat Consultative Coun from 1998; Chmn Nat Coll of Evangelists from 1998
GS 1995–96 *Tel:* (01794) 516005
Fax: (01794) 830242
email: jonathan.gledhill@dial.pipex.com

SOUTHERN, Mrs Angela Helen
Greystone House, Brackley Ave, Hartley Wintney, Hook, Hants RG27 8QX [WINCHESTER] *b* 5 May 1944; *educ* St Helen and St Kath Sch Abingdon; K

Coll Hosp Lon; Radiographer (not practising); M Canon B17 Revision Ctee
GS 1990– *Tel:* (01252) 842274

SOUTHWARK, Bishop of, Rt Revd Thomas Frederick Butler, M SC, PH D, LLD, D SC
Bishop's House, 38 Tooting Bec Gardens, London SW16 1QZ b 5 Mar 1940; *educ* K Edw's Sch Five Ways Birm; Univ Leeds; Coll of the Resurr Mirf; Asst C St Aug Wisbech 1964–66; Asst C St Sav Folkestone 1966–67; Lect and Chapl Univ Zambia 1967–73; Chapl Univ Kent 1973–80; Six Preacher Cant Cathl 1980–84; Adn of Northolt 1980–85; Bp of Willesden 1985–91; Bp of Leic 1991–98; Bp of S'wark from 1998; Chmn BM from 1995
GS 1991– *Tel:* 020–8769 3256
Fax: 020–8769 4126
email: bishops.house@dswark.org.uk

SOUTHWELL, Bishop of, Rt Revd George Henry Cassidy, B SC, M PHIL
Bishop's Manor, Southwell, Notts NG25 0JR b 17 Oct 1942; *educ* Belfast High Sch; Qu Univ Belfast; Univ Coll Lon; Oak Hill Th Coll; C Ch Ch Clifton Bris 1972–75; V St Edyth Sea Mills Bris 1975–82; V St Paul Portman Sq Lon 1982–87; Adn of Lon and Can Res St Paul's Cathl 1987–99; Bp of S'well from 1999
GS 1995– *Tel:* (01636) 812112
Fax: (01636) 815401
email: bishop@bishop-southwell.prestel.co.uk

SPENCER, Mrs Caroline Sarah, BA, PGCE
Little Eggarton, Godmersham, Canterbury, Kent CT4 7DY [CANTERBURY] *b* 9 Sep 1953; *educ* Wycombe Abbey Sch; St Hilda's Coll Ox; Lon Univ Inst of Educ; Asst Tchr Hist Sydenham High Sch 1976–80; pt Tutor Westmr Tutors Ltd 1981–84; Mother and Vol Worker for Ch and Community from 1980; M Abp's Coun; M Chs Together in Kent; Gov Ch Ch Coll Cant from 1997
GS 1995– *Tel* and *Fax:* (01227) 731170

ST ALBANS, Bishop of, Rt Revd Christopher William Herbert, BA
Abbey Gate House, Abbey Mill Lane, St Albans, Herts AL3 4HD b 7 Jan 1944; *educ* Monmouth Sch; St D Univ Coll Lamp; Wells Th Coll; C Tupsley and Schoolmaster Bp's Sch Heref 1967–71; Adv in Relig Educ Heref 1971–76; Dir of Educ Heref 1976–81; V Bourne 1981–90; Dir of POT Guildf 1983–90; Adn of Dorking 1990–95; Bp of St Alb from 1995
GS 1995– *Tel:* (01727) 853305
Fax: (01727) 846715

ST EDMUNDSBURY AND IPSWICH, Bishop of, Rt Revd (John Hubert) Richard Lewis, AKC
Bishop's House, 4 Park Rd, Ipswich, Suffolk IP1 3ST b 10 Dec 1943; *educ* Radley; K Coll Lon; St Boniface Coll Warminster; C Hexham 1967–70; Ind Chapl Newc 1970–77; DCO Dur 1977–82; Agric Chapl Heref 1982–87; Adn of Ludlow 1987–92;

Bp of Taunton 1992–97; Chmn ABM Recruitment and Selection Ctee 1993–96; Bp of St Eds & Ips from 1997; Chmn BSR Social, Economic and Indust Affairs Ctee from 1998

GS 1987–92, 1997–ㅤㅤㅤㅤ*Tel:* (01473) 252829
ㅤㅤㅤㅤㅤㅤㅤㅤㅤ*Fax:* (01473) 232552
email:
ㅤbishop.richard@stedmundsbury.anglican.org

ST GERMANS, Bishop of [SUFFRAGAN, TRURO]
[Not appointed at time of going to press.]

STAFFORD, Bishop of [AREA BISHOP, LICHFIELD]
Rt Revd Christopher John Hill, BD, AKC, M TH
Ash Garth, 6 Broughton Crescent, Barlaston, Stoke-on-Trent, Staffs ST12 9DD b 10 Oct 1945; *educ* Sebright Sch Worcs; K Coll Lon; C Tividale Lich 1969–73; C Codsall 1973–74; Abp's Asst Chapl on Foreign Relations 1974–81; Abp's Sec for Ecum Affairs 1981–89; Angl Sec ARCIC I and II 1974–91; Hon Can Cant Cathl 1982–89; Chapl to HM The Queen 1987–96; Can Res and Prec St Paul's Cathl 1989–96; M CE-German Chs Conversations 1987–89; CE Nordic-Baltic Conversations 1989–93; Vc-Chair Ecclesiastical Law Soc from 1993; Chair Cathl Precs Conf 1994–96; Co-Chmn CE-French Protestant Conversations from 1993; M Legal Adv Ctee from 1991; Co-Chair Lon Soc Jews and Chrs 1991–96; M CCU 1991–96; Bp of Stafford from 1996; M FOAG 1997–98, Vc-Chair from 1998; Co-Chair Meissen Th Conversations from 1998ㅤㅤㅤㅤㅤ*Tel:* (01782) 373308
ㅤㅤㅤㅤㅤㅤㅤㅤㅤ*Fax:* (01782) 373705

STALEY, Revd (John) Colin George, MA
Greenhills, Swanscoe, Rainow, Macclesfield SK10 5SZ [CHESTER] *b* 18 Jun 1944; *educ* Nottm High Sch; Southn Univ Sch of Navigation; Hull Univ; Wycliffe Hall Th Coll; C Tinsley 1971–73; C Slaithwaite 1973–75; V St Andr and St Mary Wakef 1975–80; Warden Scargill Ho 1980–82; TV Macclesfield from 1982; Sen Ind Chapl from 1987; M Bp's Dioc Miss Grp

GS 1996–ㅤㅤㅤㅤㅤㅤ*Tel:* (01625) 421296
ㅤㅤㅤㅤㅤㅤㅤ(01625) 517681 (Office)
ㅤㅤㅤㅤㅤㅤㅤㅤㅤ*Fax:* (01625) 517824

STANES, Ven Ian Thomas, B SC, MA
The Archdeaconry, 21 Church Rd, Glenfield, Leicester LE3 8DP [ARCHDEACON OF LOUGHBOROUGH] *b* 29 Jan 1939; *educ* City of Bath Boys Sch; Sheff Univ; Linacre Coll Ox; Wycliffe Hall Th Coll; C H Apostles Leic 1965–69; V St David Broom Leys 1969–76; Warden Marrick Priory 1976–82; Officer for Miss, Min and Evang Willesden Area Lon 1982–92; CME Officer Willesden Area Lon 1984–92; Preb St Paul's Cathl 1989–92; Adn of Loughb from 1992

GS 1994–ㅤㅤㅤㅤㅤㅤ*Tel:* 0116–231 1632
ㅤㅤㅤㅤㅤㅤㅤㅤㅤ*Fax:* 0116–232 1593

STANIFORD, Revd Doris Gwendoline, SRN
St Alban's Vicarage, Gossops Green, Crawley RH11

8LD [CHICHESTER] *b* 29 Dec 1943; *educ* Gilmore Course; Par Worker 1978–80; Dss Hangleton Hove 1980–82; Dss Durrington 1982–87; Hd Dss and Dioc Local Min Adv 1980–87; Par Dn 1987–89; M Staff Chich Th Coll 1983–89; Dioc Vocations Adv 1987–97; Par Dn Crawley TM 1989–97; Chapl Crawley Gen Hosp 1989–97; Chapl St Cath Hospice 1992–97; Asst DDO and Adv on Womens Min from 1997; C-in-c All So Southwick 1997–99; V St Alb Gossops Green from 1999

GS 1995–ㅤㅤㅤㅤㅤㅤ*Tel:* (01293) 529848

STANLEY, Canon John, OBE
Vicarage, Bluebell Lane, Huyton, Merseyside L36 7SA [LIVERPOOL] *b* 20 May 1931; *educ* Birkenhead Sch; Tyndale Hall Th Coll; C All SS Preston 1956–60; C St Mark's St Helens 1960–63; V St Cuthb's Everton 1963–70; P-in-c St Sav 1969–70; V St Sav w St Cuthb's 1970–74; Chmn Dioc Ho of Clergy 1979–85; M BCC 1984–87; V Huyton from 1974; AD Huyton from 1989; Ch Commr 1983–98; Bd of Govs 1989–98; Hon Can Liv Cathl from 1987; Trustee Ch Urban Fund from 1987; Prolocutor York Conv from 1990; Chapl to H M The Queen from 1993; M Abps' Coun from 1999; Chmn Abps' Coun Appts Ctee from 1999

GS 1973–ㅤㅤㅤㅤㅤㅤ*Tel:* 0151–449 3900
ㅤㅤㅤㅤㅤㅤㅤㅤ0385 564519 (Mobile)
ㅤㅤㅤㅤㅤㅤㅤㅤㅤ*Fax:* 0151–480 6002
ㅤㅤ*email:* John.Stanley@btinternet.com

STANLEY, Revd Simon Richard
St Barnabas' Vicarage, Jubilee Terrace, Leeman Rd, York YO26 4YZ [YORK] *b* 20 May 1944; *educ* Central Gr Sch Birm; Wells Th Coll; C St Lawr Cov 1969–71; C All SS Hessle 1971–75; P-in-c Flamborough 1975–80; R Dunnington 1980–92; P-in-c St Barnabas York and Producer/Presenter BBC Radio York from 1992

GS 1998–ㅤㅤㅤㅤㅤㅤ*Tel:* (01904) 654214
ㅤㅤㅤㅤㅤㅤㅤㅤㅤ*Fax:* (01904) 670519

STAPLE, Revd David, OBE, MA, BD, FRSA
1 Althorp Rd, St Albans, Herts AL1 3PH [ECUMENICAL REPRESENTATIVE (BAPTIST UNION)] *b* 30 Mar 1930; *educ* Watford Gr Sch; Ch Coll Cam; Wadham Coll Ox; Regent's Park Coll Ox; Assoc Min W Ham Cen Miss 1955–58; Min Llanishen Bapt Ch Cardiff 1958–74; Min Harrow Bapt Ch 1974–86; Gen Sec Free Ch Federal Coun 1986–96; Gen Sec Emer Free Chs Coun from 1996; M CTE Enabling Grp 1990–96; M CCBI Steering Ctee 1990–96; M CCBI Ch Representatives Meeting 1990–99; President CCBI 1995–99

GS 1995–ㅤㅤㅤㅤㅤㅤ*Tel:* (01727) 810009
ㅤㅤㅤㅤㅤㅤㅤㅤㅤ*Fax:* (01727) 867888
ㅤㅤ*email:* dstaple@compuserve.com

STEPNEY, Bishop of [AREA BISHOP, LONDON] **Rt Revd John Mugabi Sentamu,** BA, LL B, MA, PH D
63 Coborn Rd, Bow, London E3 2DB b 10 Jun 1949; *educ* Masooli, Kyambogo and Kitante Hill and

Old Kampala Sch Uganda; Makerere Univ; Law Development Cen, Inns of Court, Uganda; Cam Univ; Ridley Hall Th Coll; Barrister-at-Law; Chief Magistrate 1971–72; Judge High Court of Uganda 1972–74; Asst Chapl Selw Coll Cam 1979; Chapl HM Remand Cen Latchmere Ho 1979–82; C St Andr Ham 1979–82; C St Paul Herne Hill 1982–83; P-in-c H Trin Tulse Hill; Par Priest St Matthias 1983–84; V H Trin Tulse Hill and St Matthias 1984–96; P-in-c St Sav Brixton 1987–89; Bp of Stepney from 1996; M NACRO Coun from 1986; M Abp's Adv Grp on UPAs from 1985; Pro-Prolocutor Conv of Cant 1990–94; Chmn CMEAC from 1990; Prolocutor Conv of Cant 1994–96; M Police Liaison Grp Lambeth 1986–96; Coun M Fam Welfare Assn from 1989; M Health Adv Ctee HM Prisons; M CTE Forum; Adv M The Stephen Lawrence Judicial Inquiry 1997
GS 1985–96   *Tel:* 020–8981 2323
                               Fax: 020–8981 8015
        email: bishop.stepney@dlondon.org.uk

STERLING, Revd Nezlin Jemima, BA, CERT TH, SRN, RMN
5 Woodstock Ave, Ealing, London W13 9UR [ECU-MENICAL REPRESENTATIVE (BLACK MAJORITY CHURCHES, UK)] *b* 22 Feb 1942; *educ* Secondary Schs in Jamaica; Westmr Univ; Univ of Wales Lamp; Dir of Nursing Mental Health 1989–95; Internat Exec Sec NT Assembly from 1995, Gen Sec from 1998; Exec and Coun M African Caribbean Evang Alliance (Vs-Pres elect); Pres CTBI from 1999; M CTBI Steering Ctee from 1999; pt Management Consultant; pt Lect Univ of Wales
GS 1999–   *Tel:* 020–8579 3841
                               Fax: 020–8537 9253
        email: NJSterlNTA@aol.com

STEVENS, Mr Robin Michael, B SC
Church House, Great Smith St, London SW1P 3NZ [NATIONAL STEWARDSHIP OFFICER, ARCHBISHOPS' COUNCIL] *b* 30 Jun 1945; *educ* Chigwell Sch; Birm Univ; Marconi Communication Systems Ltd 1967–79; Engineering Project Supervisor Thames TV 1979–91; Chartered Engineer from 1978; Hon Stewardship Adv Chelmsf dio from 1982; Rdr from 1990; Cen Stewardship Offcr CBF 1992–98; Dep Sec 1996–98; Nat Stewardship Offcr Abps' Coun from 1999   *Tel:* 020–7898 1540
        email: robin.stevens@c-of-e.org.uk

STEVENSON, Mr Trevor John Philip, AIA, APMI
33 Saxonbury Close, Crowborough, E Sussex TN6 1EA [CHICHESTER] *b* 16 Aug 1931; *educ* Wyggeston Sch Leic; Royal Insurance Co 1949–59; Nat Provident Institution 1959–78; Asst Sec Life Offces Assn 1979–85; Asst Life Mgr Assoc of Br Insurers 1986–90; Exec Officer CEEC 1993–97; M Gen Syn Stg Orders Ctee; M Ch Commrs Gen Purposes and Audit Ctee; M CE Pensions Bd and Audit Ctee; Coun M CPAS, Ch Soc and Latimer Ho; M

Dioc Bd of Patronage; M DBF Finance Ctee; Vc Chmn Dioc Parsonages Ctee; M Dioc Stipends Ctee
GS 1985–   *Tel and Fax:* (01892) 655951

STEWART, Ms Dorothy Elaine, MA, BA, SRN, SCM, CERT ED
4 Cottingley Drive, Leeds LS11 0JG [RIPON] *b* 30 May 1951; *educ* Man Metropolitan Univ; Bradf Univ; Midwife Tchr Man Victoria Univ; M CMEAC; M Dioc BMU; Trustee CUF
GS 1997–   *Tel:* 0113–226 2392 (Home)
                        0161–237 2821 (Office)

STOCKPORT, Bishop of [SUFFRAGAN, CHESTER]
Rt Revd Geoffrey Martin Turner
Bishop's Lodge, Back Lane, Dunham Town, Altrincham WA14 4SG b 16 Mar 1934; *educ* Bideford Gr Sch; Sandhurst; Oak Hill Th Coll; C St Steph Tonbridge 1963–66; C St Jo Parkstone 1966–69; V St Pet Derby 1969–73; V Ch Ch Chadderton 1973–79; R St Andr Bebington 1979–93; Hon Can Ches Cathl 1989–93; RD North Wirral 1990–93; Adn of Chester 1993–94; Bp of Stockport from 1994
GS 1988–94   *Tel:* 0161–928 5611
                              Fax: 0161–929 0692
        email: bishop.stockport@cwcom.net

STONE, Revd Dr David Adrian, MA, BM, B CH
20 Collingham Rd, London SW5 0LX [LONDON] *b* 18 Sep 1956; *educ* Raynes Park Gr Sch; Oriel Coll Ox; Wycliffe Hall Th Coll; C St Geo the Martyr Holborn 1988–91; C-in-c St Jude S Kensington 1991–93; V from 1993; Area Adv for Evang 1992–97; M Bp's Coun; M Dioc BSR 1993–95; M Lee Abbey Coun from 1995; Chmn Lon Dioc Evang Coun from 1997; AD Chelsea from 1996; Bp of Kensington's Adv for Healing Min from 1998
GS 1995–   *Tel and Fax:* 020–7373 1693
        email: david.stone@dlondon.org.uk

STORKEY, Dr Elaine
3A Farm Lane, Southgate, London N14 4PP [LONDON] *educ* Ossett Gr Sch; Univ Coll of Wales Abth; McMaster Univ Ontario; York Univ; Tutor in Philosophy Man Coll Ox 1967–68; Rsch Fell in Sociology Stirling Univ 1968–69; Tutor Open Univ 1976–80; Visiting Lect Calvin Coll USA 1980–81; Covenant Coll USA 1981–82; Lect in Philosophy Oak Hill Th Coll 1982–87; Assoc Ed *Third Way* from 1984; Lect in Faculty of Social Science Open Univ 1987–91; Dir Inst for Contemporary Christianity 1992–98; Scriptwriter for BBC OU; M ACORA 1988–90; M Crown Appointments Commn 1990; Broadcaster BBC from 1987; Vc-Pres UCCF 1987–93; M Abps' Commn on Cathl 1992–94; M Lausanne Working Party on Th 1992–97; M CRAC 1993–98; Examiner Sociology of Religion Lon Univ from 1993; Trustee C of E Newspaper from 1994; Vc-Pres Cheltenham and Glouc Coll of HE from 1994; M

Forum for the Future 1995–98; Vis Lect in Th K Coll Lon 1996–99; M Orthodox-Evang Dialogue WCC from 1996; New Coll Scholar Univ of New S Wales Sydney 1997; Pres Tear Fund from 1997; M Working Party on Christian-Jewish Relations from 1998; Lambeth DD 1998
GS 1987–ㅤㅤㅤㅤ*Tel:* 020–8449 3034 (Home)
ㅤㅤㅤㅤㅤㅤㅤ020–8449 0467 (Office)
ㅤㅤㅤㅤ*email:* AlanS@oakhill.ac.uk

STRANACK, Very Revd David Arthur Claude
The Deanery, Hadleigh, Ipswich IP7 5DT [DEAN OF BOCKING] *b* 15 Aug 1943; *educ* Brighton Coll; Chich Th Coll; C St Edm Forest Gate 1968–69; C St Jas, St Nic and St Runwald Colchester 1969–74; V St Geo Brentwood 1974–82; V St Jas Nayland w St Mary Wiston 1982–99; Hon Can St E Cathl from 1994; Dean of Bocking, R Hadleigh w Layham and Shelley and Hintlesham w Chattisham from 1999; RD Hadleigh from 1999; M Adnry Pastl Cteeㅤㅤㅤㅤㅤㅤ*Tel:* (01473) 822218

SUTCLIFFE, Mr Tom (James Thomas), MA
12 Polworth Rd, Streatham, London SW16 2EU [SOUTHWARK] *b* 4 Jun 1943; *educ* Prebendal Sch Chich; Hurstpierpoint Coll; Magd Coll Ox; English teacher Purcell Sch 1964–65; Countertenor lay-clerk Westmr Cathl 1966–70; Advertisement Manager and Editor *Music and Musicians* magazine 1968–73; Sub-editor, opera critic, feature writer *The Guardian* 1973–96; Opera Critic *The Evening Standard* from 1996; Chmn Music Section of Critics' Circle
GS 1990–ㅤ*Tel:* 020–8677 5849 and 020–8677 7939
ㅤㅤㅤㅤ*email:* tomsutcliffe@email.msn.com

SUTTON, Revd John, BA
Timperley Vicarage, 12 Thorley Lane, Timperley, Cheshire WA15 7AZ [CHESTER] *b* 22 Feb 1947; *educ* Man Gr Sch; St Jo Coll Dur; Ridley Hall Th Coll; C St Lawr Denton Man 1972–74; C-in-c 1974–76; R 1976–82; V St Thos High Lane 1982–88; V St Anne w St Fran Sale 1988–96; V Timperley from 1996; Vc-Chair Dioc CSR from 1996
GS 1994–ㅤㅤㅤㅤㅤㅤ*Tel:* 0161–980 4330

SWAN, Prebendary Ronald Frederick, MA
Royal Foundation of St Katharine, 2 Butcher Row, London E14 8DS [LONDON] *b* 30 Jun 1935; *educ* St Cath Coll Cam; Coll of Resurr Mirfield; C Staveley 1961–66; Chapl Lon Univ 1966–72; C St Martin-in-the-Fields Lon 1972–77; V St Barn Ealing 1977–88; V St Steph Castle Hill Ealing 1981–88; AD Ealing E 1884–87; V St Mary Harrow 1988–97; AD Harrow 1989–94; Preb St Paul's Cathl from 1991; Master R Foundation of St Katharine from 1997
GS 1997–ㅤㅤㅤㅤㅤㅤ*Tel:* 020–7790 3540
ㅤㅤㅤㅤㅤㅤㅤㅤ*Fax:* 020–7702 7603

SWINDON, Bishop of [SUFFRAGAN, BRISTOL] **Rt Revd Michael David Doe,** BA
Mark House, Field Rise, Swindon SN1 4HP b 24 Dec

1947; *educ* Brockenhurst Gr Sch; Dur Univ; Ripon Hall Th Coll; C St Pet St Helier 1972–76; Hon C 1976–81; Youth Sec BCC 1976–81; Priest Missr Blackbird Leys LEP Oxford 1981–88; V 1988–89; RD Cowley 1987–89; Soc Resp Adv Portsm 1989–94; Can Res Portsm Cathl 1989–94; Bp of Swindon from 1994; M CTBI Assembly and CTE Enabling Grp/Forum from 1991; Episcopal Visitor to Dioc World Development Advisers from 1994; Chmn CCU Local Unity Ctee from 1995
GS 1990–94ㅤㅤ*Tel* and *Fax:* (01793) 538654
ㅤㅤㅤㅤ*email:* 106064.431@compuserve.com

SWINSON, Mrs Margaret Anne, BA, ACA, ATII
46 Glenmore Ave, Liverpool L18 4QF [LIVERPOOL] *b* 16 Dec 1957; *educ* Alice Ottley Sch Worc; Liv Univ; Accountant (Tax Specialist); Gen Syn Stg Ctee 1991–98; M BSR 1990–95; Chair Race and Community Relations Ctee 1990–95; Trustee Ch Urban Fund 1987–97; M CTBI; CE Delegate to WCC Canberra 1991; M CBF 1996–98
GS 1985–ㅤㅤㅤㅤㅤㅤ*Tel:* 0151–724 3533
ㅤㅤㅤ*email:* Maggie@Swinson.surfaid.org

SYKES, Rt Revd Stephen Whitefield, MA
St John's College, Durham DH1 3RJ [CHAIRMAN, DOCTRINE COMMISSION] *b* 1 Aug 1939; *educ* Bris Gr Sch; Monkton Combe Sch; St Jo Coll Cam; Harvard Univ; Ripon Hall Th Coll; Asst Lect Div Cam Univ 1964–68; Fell and Dean St Jo Coll Cam 1964–74; Lect 1968–74; Van Mildert Prof Dur Univ 1974–85; Can Res Dur Cathl 1974–85; Regius Prof Div Cam Univ 1985–90; Bp of Ely 1990–99; Prin St Jo Coll Dur from 1999; Chmn Doct Commn from 1997
GS 1990–99ㅤㅤㅤㅤㅤㅤ*Tel:* 0191–374 3579

TATTERSALL, Mr Geoffrey Frank, MA, QC
2 The Woodlands, Lostock, Bolton BL6 4JD [MANCHESTER] *b* 22 Sep 1947; *educ* Man Gr Sch; Ch Ch Ox; Barrister; Called to Bar Lincoln's Inn 1970; Bencher 1997; In practice Nn Circuit from 1970; Recorder Crown Court from 1989; QC from 1992; Called to Bar New South Wales 1992; SC from 1995; Judge of Appeal Isle of Man from 1997; Lay Chmn Bolton Dny Syn from 1993; Chmn Ho of Laity Dioc Syn from 1994; M Bp's Coun; M DBF and Trust and Fin Ctee; Chmn Stg Orders Ctee Gen Syn from 1999
GS 1995–ㅤㅤㅤㅤㅤㅤ*Tel:* (01204) 846265
ㅤㅤㅤㅤㅤㅤㅤㅤ*Fax:* (01204) 849863

TAUNTON, Bishop of [SUFFRAGAN, BATH AND WELLS] **Rt Revd Andrew John Radford**
Bishop's Lodge, Monkton Heights, West Monkton, Taunton, Som TA2 8LU b 26 Jan 1944; *educ* Kingswood Gr Sch Bris; Trin Coll Bris; C St Mary Shirehampton, Bris 1974–78; C St Pet Henleaze, Bris 1978–80; Producer Religious Programmes BBC Radio Bristol 1974–80; V St Barn w Englishcombe, Bath 1980–85; DCO Glouc 1985–93; Producer Religious Programmes Severn Sound Radio 1985–93; Hon Can Glouc Cathl from 1991;

Development and Tr Officer Communications Unit Church House 1993–98; Abps' Adv for Bps' Min 1998; Bp of Taunton from 1998

Tel: (01823) 413526
Fax: (01823) 412805
email: BishopTaunton@compuserve.com

TAYLOR, Mrs Diana Mary
Volis Farm, Hestercombe, Kingston St Mary, Taunton, Som TA2 8HS [BATH AND WELLS] *b* 24 Mar 1945; *educ* Scunthorpe Gr Sch; Harper Adams Agric Coll; Farmer; M BM Rural Affairs Ctee from 1993, Vc-Chmn from 1998; Bp's Visitor; M Dioc CSR; M Gov Body SW Min Tr Course from 1996; Chmn Dioc Ho of Laity; M Bp's Coun; M Dioc Rural Grp
GS 1993–
Tel: (01823) 451545
Fax: (01823) 451701

TAYLOR, Mr John Anthony, RIBA
Church Commissioners, 1 Millbank, London SW1P 3JZ [SENIOR ARCHITECT, CHURCH COMMISSIONERS] Sen Architect Ch Commrs from 1978
Tel: 020–7898 1026
Fax: 020–7898 1011

TAYLOR, Ven Peter Flint, MA, BD
Glebe House, Church Lane, Sheering, Bishop's Stortford CM22 7NR [ARCHDEACON OF HARLOW] *b* 7 Mar 1944; *educ* Clifton Coll Bris; Qu Coll Cam; Lon Univ; Lon Coll of Div; C St Aug Highbury New Park 1970–73; C St Andr Plymouth 1973–77; V Ironville, Derby 1977–83; P-in-c Riddings 1982–83; R Rayleigh 1983–96; pt Chapl HM Young Offenders Inst and Prison Bullwood Hall 1985–90; RD Rochford 1989–96; Adn of Harlow from 1996; M Dioc Syn; M DBF; M Coun for Min; M Family Purse Revision Ctee and Sub-ctee; Chmn Dioc Resource Coun
Tel: (01279) 734524
Fax: (01279) 734426
email: A.Harlow@chelmsford.anglican.org

TAYLOR, Mr Bill (William) Henry, ACII, CIP
8 Poplar Gardens, New Malden, Surrey KT3 3DW [SOUTHWARK] *b* 13 Oct 1932; *educ* Beverley Sch New Malden; Kingston Jun Tech Coll; 40 years in Insurance Industry, Yorks Ins Co Motor Underwriting, E W Payne/Sedgwick Insurance Brokers, UK and USA Reinsurance, Grp Tr Manager; Rtd/Tr Consultant; Rdr; M Dioc Pastl Ctee; Wandsworth Adny Pastl Ctee; M Dioc Ruri-decanal Conf then Lay Chair Kingston Dny Syn
GS 1996–
Tel: 020–8942 3596

TERESA, Revd Sister (Teresa Joan White), CSA, BA, STB, PGCE, DD
St Andrew's House, 2 Tavistock Rd, Westbourne Park, London W11 1BA [RELIGIOUS COMMUNITIES IN CONVOCATION, SOUTH] *b* 24 Apr 1936; *educ* Wellesley Coll; Harvard Univ; Ch Ch Coll Cant; California Sch for Deacons; Religious Sister from 1970; Tchr Burlington Danes Sch Lon 1974–76; Gen Sec World Congress of Faiths 1977–81; Asst

to Abp's Sec for Ecum Affairs 1981–82; NT Lect S'wark Dioc Rdrs Course 1981–89; Ed and Admin Distinctive Diaconate from 1981; Ed *DIAKONIA News* from 1987; Ed *Distinctive News of Women in Min* from 1994; Chair Soc for Min of Women in the Church from 1994; Consultant at DIAKONIA Fifth Faith and Order World Conf Santiago 1993; CE delegate to Anglo-Lutheran Internat Conversations special consultation on the diaconate 1995; M Calendar, Lectionary and Collects Revision Ctee 1996; M CTBI from 1996; M Extended Communion Revision Ctee 1998
GS 1995–
Tel: 020–7229 2662 Ext 24
Fax: 020–7792 5993
email: Sister.Teresa@dlondon.org.uk

TETLEY, Ven Joy Dawn, BA, CERT ED, MA, PH D
Archdeacon's House, 56 Battenhall Rd, Worcester WR5 2BQ [ARCHDEACON OF WORCESTER] *b* 9 Nov 1946; *educ* St Mary's Coll Dur; Leeds Univ; St Hugh's Coll Ox; Dur Univ; NW Ord Course; Dss Bentley Sheff 1977–79; Dss St Aid Buttershaw 1979–80; Chapl Dur Cathl 1980–83; Lect Trin Coll Bris 1983–86; Dss Chipping Sodbury and Old Sodbury 1983–86; Dn Roch Cathl 1987–89; Hon Can Roch Cathl 1990–93; Assoc Dir POT 1987–88; Dir POT 1988–93; Hon Par Dn H Family Gravesend w Ifield 1989–93; Prin E Anglian Minl Tr Course 1993–99; Adn of Worc from 1999
Tel: (01905) 764446 (Home)
(01905) 20537 (Office)
Fax: (01905) 612302 (Office)

TEWKESBURY, Bishop of [SUFFRAGAN, GLOUCESTER] **Rt Rev John Stewart Went,** MA
Green Acre, 166 Hempsted Lane, Gloucester GL2 5LG b 11 Mar 1944; *educ* Colchester R Gr Sch; Cam Univ; Oak Hill Th Coll; C Em Northwood 1969–75; V H Trin Margate 1975–83; Vc-Prin Wycliffe Hall Ox 1983–89; Adn of Surrey 1989–96; Bp of Tewkesbury from 1996
GS 1990–95
Tel: (01452) 521824
Fax: (01452) 505554
email: bshptewk@star.co.uk

THAKE, Prebendary Terry (Terence), ALCD
Vicarage, Main Rd, Little Haywood, Stafford ST18 0TS [LICHFIELD] *b* 10 Dec 1941; *educ* Hertf Gr Sch; Lon Coll of Div; Circulation Mgr CE Newspaper 1960–62; C Faringdon w Little Coxwell 1966–70; C Aldridge 1970–73; V Werrington and Chapl HMDC Werrington Ho 1973–82; TR Chell and Chapl Westcliffe Hosp 1982–94; RD Stoke North 1991–94; Jt Sec Dioc Syn 1988–95; V Colwich w Gt Haywood from 1994; Preb Lich Cathl from 1994; P-in-c Colton from 1995; Chmn Dioc Ho of Clergy from 1995; RD Rugeley from 1998
GS 1989–
Tel and Fax: (01889) 881624
email: Terry.Thake@btinternet.com

THETFORD, Bishop of [SUFFRAGAN, NORWICH]
Rt Revd Hugo Ferdinand de Waal, BA, MA
Rectory Meadow, Bramerton, Norwich NR14 7DW

b 16 Mar 1935; *educ* Tonbridge Sch; Pemb Coll Cam; Ridley Hall Cam; Munster Univ; C St Martin Birm 1960–64; P-in-c Dry Drayton 1964–68; R 1968–74; Chapl Pemb Coll Cam 1964–68; V St Jo Ev Blackpool 1974–78; Prin Ridley Hall Cam 1978–92; Bp of Thetford from 1992
Tel and *Fax:* (01508) 538251

THISELTON, Canon Prof Anthony Charles, BD, M TH, PH D, DD
South View Lodge, 390 High Rd, Chilwell, Nottingham NG9 5EG [UNIVERSITIES, NORTH] *b* 13 Jul 1937; *educ* City of Lon Sch; K Coll Lon; Sheff Univ; Oak Hill Th Coll; C H Trin Sydenham 1960–63; Tutor Tyndale Hall Bris 1963–67; Sen Tutor 1967–70; Lect Bibl Studies Sheff Univ 1970–79; Sen Lect 1979–85; Prof Calvin Coll Grand Rapids 1982–83; Prin St Jo Coll Nottm 1985–88; Special Lect Th Nottm Univ 1986–88; Prin St Jo Coll and Cranmer Hall Dur 1988–92; Hon Prof Th Dur Univ 1992; Prof Chr Th Nottm Univ from 1992 and Hd of Th Dept from 1992; Can Th Leic Cathl from 1994; Edit Bd Bib Int (Leiden) from 1992; HFEA 1995–98; M Doct Commn from 1996; Pres Soc for Study of Th 1998–2000; M Th Educ Tr Ctee from 1999
GS 1995– *Tel* and *Fax:* 0115–917 6392 (Home)
Tel: 0115–951 5852 (Office)
Fax: 0115–951 5887 (Office)
email: mary.elmer@nottingham.ac.uk

THOMAS, Mrs Anahid Heleni
Bowery Cottage, 188 Castle St, Portchester, Fareham, Hants PO16 9QH [PORTSMOUTH] *educ* Schnidts Girls Coll Jerusalem; Miniaturist; Designer in Silver and Gold; M Dioc Syn; M Bp's Coun; M Dioc Coun for Miss and Unity; M DBF; M Vacancy-in-See Ctee; M Dny Syn
GS 1995– *Tel* and *Fax:* 023–9242 0416

THOMAS, Revd Jennifer Monica, IDC, DCM
Christ Church Vicarage, 20 Gaynesford Rd, Forest Hill, London SE23 2HQ [SOUTHWARK] *b* 26 Aug 1958; *educ* Burlington High Sch Jamaica; St Cath's Convent High Sch Jamaica; Woolwich Coll; Wilson Carlile Coll of Evang; SE Surrey Coll; CA Tr Coll; Sarum and Wells Th Coll; Par Ev St Ann's Bay Jamaica 1982; Par Ev Herne Hill 1988; C St Paul Wimbledon Park 1993–97; V Forest Hill from 1997
GS 1998– *Tel:* 020–8291 2382

THOMAS, Revd Dr Philip Harold Emlyn, MA, BD, PH D
Vicarage, Heighington, Co Durham DL5 6PP [DURHAM] *b* 23 Apr 1941; *educ* Univ of Cant NZ; Melbourne Coll of Divinity; Dur Univ; C H Trin Adelaide 1967–70; Warden Latimer Ho Christchurch NZ 1971–77; Chapl and Solway Fell Univ Coll Dur 1978–82; V Ngaio Wellington NZ 1982–84; V Heighington from 1984; RD Darlington from 1993; Bp's Inspector of Th Colls and Courses
GS 1997– *Tel* and *Fax:* (01325) 312134

THOMAS-BETTS, Dr Anna, MA, PH D
68 Halkingcroft, Langley, Slough, Berks SL3 7AY [OXFORD] *b* 1 Feb 1941; *educ* Christava Mahilalayam, Alwaye, S India; Madras Chr Coll, Madras Univ; Keele Univ; Lect in Physics Madras Chr Coll 1960–62; Post-Doctoral Rsch Asst Imp Coll Lon 1966–74; Lect in Geophysics Imp Coll Lon 1974–92; Sen Lect from 1992; M Bps' Inspectorate of Th Colls and Courses from 1995; M CCU 1991–96; M CBF 1996–99
GS 1990– *Tel:* (01753) 822013 (Home)
020–7594 6430 (Office)
email: a.thomas-bts@ic.ac.uk

TICEHURST, Mrs Carol Ann
57 Silver St, Coningsby, Lincoln LN4 4SG [LINCOLN] *b* 29 Dec 1938
GS 1995– *Tel:* (01526) 342076

TILL, Very Revd Michael Stanley, MA
The Deanery, The Close, Winchester, Hants SO23 9LS [DEAN OF WINCHESTER] *b* 19 Nov 1935; *educ* Brighton, Hove and Sussex Gr Sch; Linc Coll Ox; Westcott Ho Th Coll; C St Jo St Jo Wood Lon 1964–67; Chapl K Coll Cam 1967–70; Dean and Fell 1970–81; V All SS Fulham 1981–86; RD Hammersmith 1982–86; Adn of Cant 1986–96; Dean of Win from 1996
GS 1986–96 *Tel* and *Fax:*(01962) 853738
email: dean.of.winchester@dial.pipex.com

TOMLINSON, Mr Arthur, B SC, M SC
4 Orchard Way, Congleton, Cheshire CW12 4PW [CHESTER] *b* 25 May 1930; *educ* Hutton Gr Sch Preston; Lon Univ; Graduate Apprentice Engl Electric 1952–54; Aerodynamicist Engl Electric Aviation 1952–58; Computer Programmer Engl Electric Aviation 1958–61; Computer Programming Instructor Engl Electric Computers 1961–68; Tr Officer Baric Computing Services 1968–70; Sen Lect Sch of Computing Staffordshire Univ 1970–95; pt Tutor Open Univ 1972–97; Rtd; M Arcidiaconal Pastl Ctee from 1994; M Bp's Coun from 1994; M Dioc CSR from 1998
GS 1990– *Tel:* (01260) 272618
email: atom@surfaid.org

TONBRIDGE, Bishop of [SUFFRAGAN, ROCHESTER] **Rt Revd Brian Arthur Smith,** BA, MA, M LITT
Bishop's Lodge, 48 St Botolph's Rd, Sevenoaks, Kent TN13 3AG b 15 Aug 1943; *educ* Geo Heriot Sch Edin; Edin Univ; Fitzw Coll Cam; Jes Coll Cam; Westcott Ho Th Coll; C Cuddesdon 1972–79; Tutor and Lib Cuddesdon Coll 1972–75; Dir of Studies 1975–78; Sen Tutor Ripon Coll Cuddesdon 1978–79; P-in-c Cragg Vale Wakef 1979–85; Dir In-Service Tr 1979–81; Dir POT 1980–81; Dir Minl Tr Wakef 1981–87; Wrdn of Rdrs 1982–87; Hon Can Wakef Cathl 1981–87; Exam Chapl to Bp of Wakef 1983–93; Adn of Craven, dio of Bradf 1987–93; Bp of Tonbridge

...rom 1993; Chmn Chs Together in Kent from .999

GS 1985–86, 1990–93   *Tel:* (01732) 456070
Fax: (01732) 741449
email: sevenoaks@clara.net

TOOKE, Mr Stephen Edgar
Rectory, Church Rd, Christchurch, Cambs PE14 9PQ [ELY] *b* 21 Dec 1946; *educ* Qu Sch Wisbech; Isle of Ely Coll; Rtd Police Superintendent; Area Fund-raising Mgr The Children's Soc; Lay Chair Dioc Syn; M Dioc Stewardship Ctee

GS 1995–   *Tel:* (01354) 638379
Fax: (01354) 638418

TOOP, Mrs Mary Lou (Mary Louise)
Vicarage, Clun Rd, Craven Arms, Shropshire SY7 9QW [HEREFORD] *b* 16 Feb 1955; *educ* Broxbourne Sch; W of England Min Tr Course; Accredited Lay Min Church Stretton 1993–94; Accredited Lay Min Stokesay, Sibdon Carwood and Halford from 1994; Dioc Vocations Adv from 1994; M Dioc Bd of Educ; Tutor W of England Minl Tr Course

GS 1995–   *Tel:* (01588) 672797

TOVEY, Revd Phillip, BA, M PHIL, MSLS, S TH
41 Mitchell Way, Woodley, Reading RG5 4NQ [OXFORD] *b* 4 Jul 1956; *educ* Oxf Sch; Lon Univ; Nottm Univ; Trin Coll Bris; Lon Bible Coll; St Jo Coll Nottm; C Beaconsfield 1987–90; C Banbury 1990–91, TV 1991–95; P-in-c Holton and Water-perry w Albury and Waterstock 1995–97; TV Wheatley 1997–98; Portfolio Co-ord and OLM Local Tr Officer Berks Archdny from 1998

GS 1998–   *Tel:* 0118–927 2568

TOWNSEND, Mrs Margot (Elizabeth Margaret Wynne)
The Cottage, Abbotts Ann, Andover, Hants SP11 7BG [WINCHESTER] *b* 6 Aug 1932; *educ* St Brandon's CDS; Qu Coll Harley St; Nor High Sch; Rdr; M DBF from 1990, Exec 1991–95; Budget 1995–97; Dioc Appts and Stg Ctees from 1995; Electoral Appeal Panel from 1996; Pastl Ctee from 1998; Chmn Andover Dny Fin Ctee from 1990; Test Valley Boro Councillor from 1999

GS 1998–   *Tel:* (01264) 710376

TOYNE, Professor Peter, BA, HON D ED, FRSA, CIMGT, FICPD, DL
Cloudeslee, Croft Drive, Caldy, Merseyside CH48 2JW [APPOINTED MEMBER, ARCHBISHOPS' COUNCIL] *b* 3 Dec 1939; *educ* Ripon Gr Sch; Bris Univ; The Sorbonne; Lect in Geography Ex Univ 1965–75, Sen Lect 1975–77; Dir Educational Credit Transfer Project DES 1977–80; Head of Bp Otter Coll Chich 1980–83; Dep Rector NE Lon Poly 1983–86; Vc Chan and Chief Exec Liv John Moores Univ from 1986; Apptd M Abps' Coun from 1999; Sen Inspector Bps' Inspections of Th Colls and Courses

GS 1999–   *Tel:* 0151–709 3676
Fax: 0151–709 9864

TREADGOLD, Very Revd John David, LVO, BA, FRSA
The Deanery, Chichester, W Sussex PO19 1PX [DEAN OF CHICHESTER] *b* 30 Dec 1931; *educ* West Bridgford Gr Sch; Nottm Univ; Wells Th Coll; V Choral Southwell Minster 1959–64; R Wollaton Nottm 1964–74; CF (TA) 1967–72, 74–78; V Darlington 1974–81; Chmn Dur DAC 1978–81; Can Windsor, Chapl R Chapel Windsor Gt Park 1981–89; Chapl to The Queen 1982–89; Dean of Chich from 1989; Chmn Chich DAC 1990–99; Chmn of Govs The Prebendal Sch Chich from 1989; Gov Wycombe Abbey Sch from 1995

    Tel: (01243) 787337 (Office)
(01243) 783286 (Home)

TREMLETT, Ven Tony (Anthony Frank)
St Matthew's House, 45 Spicer Rd, Exeter, Devon EX1 1TA [ARCHDEACON OF EXETER] *b* 25 Aug 1937; *educ* Plymouth Coll; S W Minl Tr Course; Asst C Plymouth Southway 1981–82; P-in-c 1982–84; V 1984–88; RD Plymouth Moorside 1986–88; Adn of Totnes 1988–94; Adn of Exeter from 1994

    Tel: (01392) 425432
Fax: (01392) 425783
email: TremlettAF@aol.com

TRICKEY, Very Revd (Frederick) Marc, BA, DIP TH
St Martin's Rectory, Guernsey GY4 6RR [DEAN OF GUERNSEY] *b* 16 Aug 1935; *educ* Bris Gr Sch; St Jo Coll Dur; Cranmer Hall Th Coll; Commercial Trainee Nat Smelting Co Avonmouth 1954–59; C St Lawr Alton 1964–68; R St Jo Bapt Win cum Winnall 1968–77; R St Martin Guernsey from 1977; M States of Guernsey Bd of Employment, Industry and Commerce 1982–95; Dean of Guernsey from 1995; Bp's Rep on Coun USPG; M States of Guernsey Broadcasting Ctee from 1979; Angl Religious Adv Channel TV from 1988; Hon Can Win Cathl from 1995; M Dioc Stg Ctee from 1995; Pres States of Guernsey Ecclesiastical Ctee from 1995; P-in-c Sark from 1996

GS 1995–   *Tel:* (01481) 38303
Fax: (01481) 37710

TRISTAM, Brother (Tristam Keith Holland), SSF, MA
Hilfield Friary, Dorchester, Dorset DT2 7BE [RELIGIOUS COMMUNITIES, SOUTH (LAY)] *b* 20 Mar 1946; *educ* Eastwood Hall Park Sch; Trin Coll Cam; M SSF from 1967; Guardian Fiwila Friary Zambia 1973–76; Provincial Sec UK 1976–83 and 1994–96; SSF Sec for Liturgy from 1976; Gen Sec 1983–97; Guardian Alnmouth Friary 1988–91; Consultant to Liturg Commn 1992–95; M from 1995

GS 1994–   *Tel:* (01300) 341346 (Friary)
(01300) 341160 (Direct Line)
Fax: (01300) 341293
email:
Tristam@franciscanmagazine.freeserve.co.uk

TROTT, Revd Stephen, BA, MA, FRSA
Rectory, 41 Humfrey Lane, Boughton, Northampton NN2 8RQ [PETERBOROUGH] *b* 28 May 1957; *educ* Bp Vesey's Gr Sch Sutton Coldfield; Birm Poly; Hull Univ; Fitzw Coll Cam; Leeds Univ; Westcott Ho Th Coll; C Hessle 1984–87; C St Alb Hull 1987–88; R Pitsford w Boughton from 1988; Sec CME 1988–93; M Dioc Syn from 1990; M Exec Coun Prayer Book Soc from 1994; M Revision Ctee on Calendar, Lectionary and Collects 2000; M Legislative Ctee from 1995; M Legal Adv Commn from 1996; M CCBI and CTE 1996–99; Ch Commr and M Pastl Ctee from 1997, Bd of Govs and Red Chs Ctee from 1999; M CE Pensions Bd from 1998
GS 1995–   *Tel:* (01604) 845655
                      Fax: (01604) 842026
      email: stephentrott@cw.com.net

TRURO, Bishop of, Rt Revd William Ind, BA
Lis Escop, Truro, Cornwall TR3 6QQ b 26 Mar 1942; *educ* Duke of York's Sch Dover; Leeds Univ; Coll of Resurr Mirf; C St Dunstan w St Cath Feltham 1966–70; P-in-c St Joseph the Worker Northolt 1970–73; TV Basingstoke TM 1973–87; Exam Chapl to Bp of Win 1976–82; pt Vc-Prin Aston Tr Scheme 1977–82; M Doct Commn 1980–86; DDO Win 1982–87; Hon Can Win Cathl 1985–87; Bp of Grantham 1987–97; Can and Preb of Thorngate in Linc Cathl 1987–97; Dean of Stamford 1988–97; Bp of Truro from 1997; Co-Chmn English ARC from 1993
GS 1997–   *Tel:* (01872) 862657
                      Fax: (01872) 862037
      email: bishop@truro.anglican.org

TURNBULL, Ven David Charles, BA, M ED
2 The Abbey, Carlisle, Cumbria CA3 8TZ [ARCHDEACON OF CARLISLE] *b* 16 Mar 1944; *educ* K James I Gr Sch Bp Auckland; Leeds Univ; Sheff Univ; Chich Th Coll; C Jarrow 1969–74; V Carlinghow 1974–83; V Penistone 1983–86; P-in-c Thurlstone 1985–86; TR Penistone and Thurlstone 1986–93; RD Barnsley 1988–93; Hon Can Wakef Cathl 1993; Adn of Carl and Can Res Carl Cathl from 1993; Chmn Dioc Coun for the Deaf and Hard of Hearing
GS 1996–   *Tel:* (01228) 23026
                      Fax: (01228) 594899
      email: adcncarl@carlisle-c-of-e.org

TURNBULL, Revd Dr Richard Duncan, BA, PH D, CA
1 Hartswood, Chineham, Basingstoke, Hants RG24 8SJ [WINCHESTER] *b* 17 Oct 1960; *educ* Moseley Gr Sch; Normanton High Sch; Reading Univ; Dur Univ; Cranmer Hall Th Coll; Ernst and Young Chartered Accountants 1982–90; C Highfield Southn 1994–98; V Chineham Basingstoke from 1998; M CBF 1997–98; M Abps' Coun Fin Ctee from 1999; M CBF Investment Ctee from 1997; M Clergy Stipends Review Group; M Dioc Pastl Ctee; M Dioc Fin Ctee; M Dioc Budget Ctee; M Steering Grp Evang Alliance Commn on Unity

and Truth among Evangelicals; M CEEC; Coun M Chs Together in Hampshire and the Island; Chmr Chs Together in Basingstoke
GS 1995–   *Tel:* (01256) 474285
                      Fax: (01256) 328912
      email: RDTurnbull@aol.com

TYLER, Mr (John) Malcolm, FRCO, ARAM, LRAM
34 Church Way, Weston Favell, Northampton NN3 3BT [PETERBOROUGH] *b* 31 Oct 1929; *educ* K Sch Pet; R Academy of Music Lon; Asst Organist Pet Cathl 1950–53; Asst Organist Cant Cathl 1953–56; Dir of Music K Coll Taunton 1957–62; Dir of Music St Jo Coll Johannesburg 1962–64; Co Music Adv Banffshire 1964–67; Dir of Music Northants Co Coun and Dir Co Music Sch 1967–92; Rtd; M Dioc Bd of Educ from 1990; M Bp's Coun from 1995
GS 1990–   *Tel:* (01604) 402589

TYRRELL, Mr Mike (Deryck Michael), BD, MA, PH D, ACIS, ACA
32 Warwick New Rd, Leamington Spa, Warws CV32 5JJ [COVENTRY] *b* 23 Jun 1948; *educ* High Storrs Gr Sch Sheff; SS Coll Cam; Aston Univ; Tr Adv Local Government Tr Bd 1975–77; Tr Services Mgr Inst of Chartered Accountants in England and Wales 1977–80; Mgr Price Waterhouse, Chartered Accountants 1980–89; Grp Development Mgr, Rugby Grp plc; Rdr; M CBF 1986–1998; Chr Stewardship Ctee 1986–95; M Bp's Coun from 1989; Chmn Dioc Stewardship Adv Ctee from 1990; Chmn Dioc Ho of Laity 1991–97; Chmn CEIG from 1993; M Gen Syn Stg Ctee 1996–98; M Business Ctee from 1999; M Abps' Coun Audit Ctee from 1999
GS 1985–   *Tel:* (01926) 429826
              07836 377673 (Mobile)
                      Fax: (01926) 744629
      email: tyrrellm@rugbygroup.co.uk

VOUT, Mrs Janet Mary, BA, IDC
87 Spinneyfield, Rotherham, S Yorks S60 3LZ [SHEFFIELD] *b* 9 Feb 1944; *educ* Gainsborough High Sch; Newc Univ; Gilmore Ho Lon; Par Worker Clifton, Rotherham 1968–70; Student Nurse Middlewood Hosp Sheff 1972–73; Licensed Worker NSM Clifton, Rotherham 1985–90; Hosp Chapl Asst Rotherham Hosps from 1991
GS 1990–   *Tel:* (01709) 839258 (Home)
              (01709) 820000 Ext 5578 (Office)

WAGSTAFF, Ven Christopher (John Harold), BA
Glebe House, Church Lane, Maisemore, Gloucester GL2 8EY [ARCHDEACON OF GLOUCESTER] *b* 25 Jun 1936; *educ* Bishop's Stortford Coll; St D Coll, Lampeter; C All SS Queensbury 1962–68; V St Mich Tokyngton Wembley 1968–73; RD S Forest 1975–82; V Coleford w Staunton 1973–83; Adn of Gloucester from 1982; Res Can Glouc Cathl from 1982; Chmn Glouc Dioc Trust; ABM Selector;

Hon Can Njombe Cathl dio SW Tanganyika from 1993; Chmn Dioc Coun for Min
GS 1988–98   *Tel:* (01452) 528500
                              Fax: (01452) 381528

WAKEFIELD, Bishop of, Rt Revd Nigel Simeon McCulloch, MA
Bishop's Lodge, Woodthorpe Lane, Wakefield WF2 6JL *b* 17 Jan 1942; *educ* Liv Coll; Selw Coll Cam; Cuddesdon Th Coll; C Ellesmere Port 1966–70; Chapl Ch Coll Cam 1970–73; Perm to Off Dio Liv 1970–73; Dir of Th Studies Ch Coll Cam 1970–75; Dioc Missr Nor Dioc 1973–78; R SS Thos & Edm Sarum 1978–86; Adn of Sarum 1979–86; Chmn ABM Finance Ctee 1987–92; Bp of Taunton 1986–92; Bp of Wakef from 1992; Chmn Communications Ctee 1993–98; Chmn BM Miss, Evang and Renewal Ctee 1989–99; Lord High Almoner from 1997
GS 1990–   *Tel:* (01924) 255349
                              Fax: (01924) 250202
              email: 100612.1514@compuserve.com

WALKER, Revd David
Priory Rectory, 29 Park Rd West, Birkenhead, Merseyside CH43 1UR [CHESTER] *b* 6 Aug 1948; *educ* Linc Th Coll; C Arnold 1974–77; C Crosby 1977–79; V Scrooby 1979–86; P-in-c St Mary Sutton in Ashfield 1986–94; P-in-c St Mich Sutton in Ashfield 1989–94; TR Birkenhead Priory from 1994
GS 1998–   *Tel:* 0151–652 1309
              email: david@park96.freeserve.co.uk

WALKER, Revd Peter Stanley, B COMB STUDS, SRN, RMN
Rectory, 76 East Hill, Colchester, Essex CO1 2QW [CHELMSFORD] *b* 20 Nov 1956; *educ* Laindon Sch; Princess Alexandra Coll of Nursing (R Lon Hosp); Nottm Univ; Linc Th Coll; C St Barn Woodford 1983–86; C St Thos Brentwood 1986–88; V St Barn Colchester 1988–94; P-in-c St Jas Colchester from 1994; P-in-c St Paul Colchester from 1995; R Colchester St Jas and St Paul w All SS, St Nic and St Runwald from 1996; M Dioc Coun for Miss and Unity 1989–92; Dioc Stewardship Support Grp 1992–94; Chapl Colchester Maternity Hosp 1993–95; Adv to DDO from 1994; M Exec CU 1992–95
GS 1995–   *Tel:* (01206) 866802

WALKER, Mr William Hugh Colquhoun, MA, FCA, AIIMR
Crown Piece, Church Rd, Wormingford, Colchester, Essex CO6 3AD [CHELMSFORD] *b* 30 Jul 1932; *educ* Wellington Coll; Selw Coll Cam; Rtd
GS 1995–   *Tel:* (01787) 227337
                              Fax: (01787) 228413

WALLACE, Ven Martin William, BD, AKC
63 Powers Hall End, Witham, Essex CM8 1NH [ARCHDEACON OF COLCHESTER] *b* 16 Nov 1948; *educ* Varndean Gr Sch for Boys Brighton; Tauntons Sch Southn; K Coll Lon; St Aug Coll Cant; C

Attercliffe Sheff 1971–74; C New Malden 1974–77; V St Mark Forest Gate 1977–93; Chapl Forest Gate Hosp 1977–80; RD Newham 1982–91; P-in-c Em Forest Gate 1985–89; P-in-c All SS Forest Gate 1991–93; Dioc Urban Officer 1991–93; Hon Can Chelmsf Cathl 1989–97; P-in-c St Lawr Bradwell and St Thos Bradwell 1993–97; Ind Chapl Maldon and Dengie 1993–97; Adn of Colchester from 1997   *Tel:* (01376) 513130
                              Fax: (01376) 500789
     email: a.colchester@chelmsford.anglican.org

WALTERS, Canon Michael William, B SC
Rectory, 14 Chapel St, Congleton, Cheshire CW12 4AB [CHESTER] *b* 26 Nov 1939; *educ* Derby Sch; K Coll Newc; Dur Univ; Clifton Th Coll; C H Trin Aldershot 1963–66; C Ch Ch Upper Armley 1966–69; NE Area Sec CPAS 1969–75; V St Geo Hyde 1975–82; V St Jo Knutsford and Toft 1982–97; Hon Can Ches Cathl from 1994; P-in-c St Pet and St Steph Congleton and TR Designate of Congleton 1997–98; TR Congleton from 1998; M Bp's Coun; Chmn Dioc Ho of Clergy; Chmn Dioc Bd of Patronage
GS 1980–90, 1995–   *Tel:* (01260) 273212
                              (01260) 290261

WALTON, Ven Geoffrey Elmer, BA, DIP TH
Vicarage, Witchampton, Wimborne, Dorset BH21 5AP [ARCHDEACON OF DORSET] *b* 19 Feb 1934; *educ* W Bridgford Gr Sch; St Jo Coll Dur; Qu Th Coll, Birm; C Warsop w Sookholme 1961–65; V Norwell and Dioc Youth Chapl (Southwell) 1965–69; Recruitment and Selection Sec ACCM 1969–75; V H Trin Weymouth 1975–82; Hon Can Sarum 1981; RD Weymouth 1980–82; Adn of Dorset from 1982; P-in-c Witchampton and Hinton Parva, Long Crichel w More Crichel from 1982
GS 1990–95   *Tel:* (01258) 840422
                              Fax: (01258) 840786

WARD, Mrs Elizabeth Joyce
The Gate House, Edge, Stroud, Glos GL6 6PE [GLOUCESTER] *b* 1 Dec 1942; *educ* Brierley Hill Gr Sch; Coll of Advanced Tech Birm; Dioc Stewardship Adv
GS 1995–   *Tel:* (01452) 812188 (Home)
                              (01452) 410022 (Office)
                              Fax: (01452) 308324

WARNER, Mr David Hugh, DIP ED
41 Ox Lane, Harpenden, Herts AL5 4HF [ST ALBANS] *b* 21 Feb 1932; *educ* St Jo Sch Leatherhead; St Mark and St Jo Coll Chelsea; St Alb Min Tr Scheme; Dep Head St Nic CE JMI Sch 1964–71; Head Wigginton CE JMI Sch 1972–73; Head Wheathampstead CE JMI Sch 1974–93; Rtd; M Dioc Bd of Educ; Sec Wheathampstead Dny Syn; M Bp's Coun
GS 1995–   *Tel* and *Fax:* (01582) 762379
              email: David@jdwarner.easynet.co.uk

WARREN, Mrs Ann, MA
Karibu, Fernhill Lane, Woking, Surrey GU22 0DR
[GUILDFORD] *b* 13 Jan 1936; *educ* Oakdene Sch
Beaconsfield; St Andr Univ; BBC Radio 1958–63;
Studio Manager, Scriptwriter, Producer *Children's
Hour*; Editorial Bd *CE Newspaper* 1975–85; Editor
company in-house magazine 1979–82; TVS *Company* 1983–85; Freelance Writer; Author; Pastl
Counsellor
GS 1980–85, 1990–95, 1997–   *Tel:* (01483) 767455

WARREN, Mr (Edward) Fiske
Church House, Great Smith St, London SW1P 3NZ
[HUMAN RESOURCES PROJECTS MANANGER, ARCH-
BISHOPS' COUNCIL] *b* 31 Dec 1950; *educ* Tonbridge
Sch; On staff of Ch Commrs from 1969; Personnel
Mgr 1996–98; Seconded to Abps' Coun from 1999
as Human Resources Projects Mgr
Tel: 020–7898 1561
email: fiske.warren@c-of-e.org.uk

WARREN, Ven Norman Leonard, MA
The Archdeaconry, Rochester, Kent ME1 1SX
[ARCHDEACON OF ROCHESTER] *b* 19 Jul 1934; *educ*
Dulwich Coll; CCC Cam; Ridley Hall Th Coll; C
Bedworth 1960–63; V St Paul Leamington Spa
1963–77; R Morden 1977–89; RD Merton 1987–89;
Adn of Rochester from 1989; RSCM Coun from
1989; Chmn Music in Worship Trust from 1989
GS 1974–77, 1990–95   *Tel:* (01634) 842527

WARREN, Canon Paul Kenneth, MA
*Rectory, 13 Rectory Lane, Standish, Wigan, Lancs
WN6 0XA* [BLACKBURN] *b* 3 May 1941; *educ* Rossall
Sch; Selw Coll Cam; Cuddesdon Th Coll; C Lanc
Priory 1967–70; Angl Chapl Univ of Lanc
1970–78; Prin Grizedale Coll, Univ of Lanc
1975–78; V St Leon Langho 1978–83; Chapl to
Brockhall Mental Hosp 1978–83; Dom Chapl to
Bp of Blackburn and Chapl Whalley Abbey
1983–88; R St Wilfrid Standish from 1988; Hon
Can Blackb Cathl from 1991; RD Chorley
1992–98; Chmn Dioc Liturg Ctee 1989–98
GS 1980–   *Tel:* (01257) 421396

WARRINGTON, Bishop of [SUFFRAGAN,
LIVERPOOL] **Rt Revd John Richard Packer,** MA
*34 Central Ave, Eccleston Park, Prescot, Merseyside
L34 2QP b* 10 Oct 1946; *educ* Man Gr Sch; Keble
Coll Ox; Ripon Hall Th Coll; C St Pet St Helier
1970–73; Dir Pastl Studies Ripon Hall 1973–75
and Ripon Coll Cuddesdon 1975–77; Chapl St
Nic Abingdon 1973–77; V Wath upon Dearne w
Adwick upon Dearne 1977–86; RD Wath 1983–86;
R Sheffield Manor 1986–91; RD Attercliffe
1990–91; Adn of W Cumberland 1991–96; P-in-c
Bridekirk 1995–96; Bp of Warrington from 1996
GS 1985–91, 1992–96 *Tel:* 0151–426 1897 (Home)
0151–708 9480 (Office)
Fax: 0151–493 2479 (Home)
0151–709 2885 (Office)

WARWICK, Bishop of [SUFFRAGAN, COVENTRY]
Rt Revd Anthony Martin Priddis, MA, DIP TH
*Warwick House, 139 Kenilworth Rd, Coventry CV4
7AP b* 15 Mar 1948; *educ* Watford Gr Sch; CCC
Cam; New Coll Ox; Cuddesdon Th Coll; C New
Addington 1972–75; Chapl Ch Ch Ox 1975–80;
TV St Jo High Wycombe 1980–86; P-in-c Amer-
sham 1986–90, R 1990–96; RD Amersham
1992–96; Hon Can Ch Ch Ox from 1995; Bp of
Warwick from 1996   *Tel:* 024–7641 6200
Fax: 024–7641 5254
email: bishwarwick@clara.net

WATKINS, Revd Peter, BA
*Vicarage, 136 Green Lane, Finham, Coventry CV3
6EA* [COVENTRY] *b* 24 May 1951; *educ* Monkton
Combe Sch; Oak Hill Th Coll; C St Marg Whit-
nash Leamington Spa 1982–85; V St Marg Wolston Cov w St Pet Church Lawford Rugby from
1985; RD Rugby 1994–99; V Finham from 1999
GS 1993–95, 1997–   *Tel and Fax:* 024–7641 8330

WATSON, Very Revd Derek Richard, MA
The Deanery, 7 The Close, Salisbury, Wilts SP1 2EF
[DEAN OF SARUM] *b* 18 Feb 1938; *educ* Uppingham
Sch; Selw Coll Cam; Cuddesdon Th Coll; C All SS
New Eltham 1964–66; Chapl Ch Coll Cam
1966–70; Dom Chapl to Bp of S'wark 1970–73; V
St Andr and St Mark Surbiton 1973–78; Can Treas
S'wark Cathl, DDO and POT 1978–82; R St Luke
w Ch Ch Chelsea 1982–96; Dean of Sarum from
1996   *Tel:* (01722) 555110

WATSON, Ven Jeffrey John Seagrief, MA
1A Summerfield, Cambridge CB3 9HE [ARCH-
DEACON OF ELY] *b* 29 Apr 1939; *educ* Univ Coll Sch
Hampstead; Em Coll Cam; Clifton Th Coll; C Ch
Ch Beckenham 1965–69; C St Jude Southsea
1969–71; V Ch Ch Win 1971–81; Exam Chapl to
Bp of Win 1976–93; V Bitterne 1981–93; RD
Southn 1983–93; Hon Can Win Cathl 1991–93;
Adn of Ely from 1993; Hon Can Ely Cathl from
1993; Chmn ABM Vocations Adv Sub-Ctee
1991–99; M ABM Recruitment and Selection Ctee
1991–99; M VRCS from 1999; Chmn Candidates
Casework Panel from 1999
GS 1985–93, 1993–95   *Tel:* (01223) 515725
Fax: (01223) 571322
email: archdeacon.ely@ely.anglican.org

WAUDE, Mr Andrew Leslie
*10 Huntwick Rd, Featherstone, Pontefract WF7 5JD ,
and The College of the Resurrection, Stocksbank Rd,
Mirfield WF14 0BW* [WAKEFIELD] *b* 13 Sep 1974;
educ St Wilfrid's RC High Sch Featherstone;
Clerical Officer Wakef HA 1995–96; Data Prepar-
ation Asst W Yorks Central Services Agency
(NHS) Leeds 1996–98; Par Asst Par of the Resurr
Leic 1998–99; M Dioc Syn from 1994; Sec Wakef
Dioc CU Ctee 1996–98; Student Coll of the Resurr
Mirf from 1999
GS 1997–   *Tel:* (01977) 797059 (Featherstone)
07958 642991 (Mobile)
email: andrew.waude@talk21.com

WEBSTER, Mr David Ernest Spencer
5 *Rosehill Walk, Tunbridge Wells, Kent TN1 1HL*
[ROCHESTER] *b* 21 Sep 1930; *educ* Dulwich Coll;
Financial Journalist; Rtd; Ch Commr, M Bd of
Govs, M Bishoprics and Cathls Ctee, M Man-
agement Adv Ctee; Vc-Pres Corp of Ch Ho, M
Coun and Home and Accts Ctee; M Invest Ctee
Nat Soc; M CCBI; M CTE; M Coun Chs Together
in Kent; Co-Chmn Tun Wells Dny Syn 1979–95;
Lay Chmn Dioc Syn 1979–82, 1995–99; M Bp's
Coun; Chmn Adv Coun for Communications and
Ed Consultant Roch LINK; M Coun SAMS; Talk-
ing Newspaper Editor; Chmn Tunbridge Wells
Blind Club; Rdr
GS 1975–   *Tel:* (01892) 526055

WEBSTER, Mrs Diana Theresa Muriel, MBE, MA
Kilpikuja 3, 02610 Espoo, Finland [EUROPE] *b* 9 Jan
1930; *educ* Lady Eleanor Holles Sch Hampton; St
Hugh's Coll Ox; Lect in Eng Lang Univ of
Helsinki 1953–93; Writer; Broadcaster; Radio
Dramatist
GS 1995–   *Tel:* 00–3589–520446
                                          Fax: 00–3589–520002
                          email: 75337.2763@compuserve.com

WEBSTER, Canon Glyn Hamilton, SRN
4 Minster Yard, York YO1 7JD [YORK] *b* 3 Jun 1951;
educ Darwen Sec Tech (Gr) Sch; Cranmer Hall, St
Jo Coll Dur; C All SS Huntington York 1977–81; V
St Luke Ev York and Sen Chapl York District
Hosp 1981–92; Sen Chapl York Health Services
NHS Trust 1992–99; Hon Can York Minster
1994–99; RD York from 1997; Can Res and Treas
York Minster from 1999
GS 1995–   *Tel:* (01904) 620877 (Home)
                            (01904) 557202 (Office)

**WEDDERSPOON, Very Revd Alexander
Gillan,** MA, BD
*The Deanery, 1 Cathedral Close, Guildford, Surrey
GU2 5TL* [DEAN OF GUILDFORD] *b* 3 Apr 1931; *educ*
Westmr Sch; Jes Coll Ox; Cuddesdon Th Coll; C
Kingston Par Ch 1961–63; Lect in RE Lon Univ
1963–66; Educ Adv CE Schs Coun 1966–69; P-in-c
St Marg Westmr 1969–70; Can Res Win Cathl
1970–87; Dean of Guildf from 1987
                        Tel: (01483) 560328 (Home)
                              (01483) 565287 (Office)
                              Fax: (01483) 303350

WEETMAN, Revd John Charles, MA, BA
*Vicarage, Church Drive, Boosbeck, East Cleveland
TS12 3AY* [YORK] *b* 11 Apr 1966; *educ* Rye Hills
Comp Sch Redcar; Sir William Turner Sixth Form
Coll Redcar; Qu Coll Ox; Trin Coll Bris; C St Jo
Newland Hull 1991–95; V Boosbeck w Moor-
sholm from 1995; RD Guisborough from 1999
GS 1998–   *Tel:* (01287) 651728

WELLINGTON, Canon James Frederick, LL B,
BA, M PHIL
*Rectory, 1 Upper Church St, Syston, Leicester LE7
1HR* [LEICESTER] *b* 11 Feb 1951; *educ* Wimborne Gr

Sch; Leic Univ; Fitzw Coll Cam; Ridley Hall Th
Coll; Nottm Univ; C John Keble Mill Hill
1977–80; C Wood Green TM and Asst Chapl
Middx Poly 1980–83; V St Luke Stocking Farm
1983–90; V Glen Magna cum Stretton Magna and
Wiston cum Newton Harcourt 1990–98; Warden
of Rdrs 1991–97; Hon Can Leic Cathl from 1994;
RD Gartree II 1996–98; TR Syston from 1998;
Chmn Ho of Clergy Dioc Syn
GS 1998–   *Tel:* 0116– 260 8276
                  email: j&hwelli@leicester.anglican.org

WELLS, Ven Roderick John, BA, MA
New Vicarage, Hackthorn, Lincoln LN2 3PF [ARCH-
DEACON OF STOW] *b* 17 Nov 1936; *educ* Haberdashers' Aske's Sch; Dur Univ; Hull Univ; Cuddesdon
Th Coll; C St Mary at Lambeth 1965–68; P-in-c
1968–71; R Skegness 1971–78; P-in-c Winthorpe
1977–78; TR Gt and Little Coates w Bradley
1978–89; RD Grimsby and Cleethorpes 1983–89;
Hon Can Linc Cathl from 1986; Adn of Stow from
1989; Adn in Lindsey from 1994; Chmn Dioc Bd
of Educ
GS 1995–   *Tel:* (01673) 860382

WEST, Preb Penny (Penelope) Anne Margaret,
CERT ED
*Vicarage, 35 Kewstoke Rd, Kewstoke, Weston-super-
Mare BS22 9YE* [BATH AND WELLS] *b* 14 Jun 1944;
educ Maynard Sch Ex; City of Birm Coll of Educ;
Glouc Sch for Min; Ridley Hall Th Coll; Tchr
North Cerney Primary Sch 1968–85; C Portishead
1986–92; Sen C Bath Abbey 1992–95; Chapl R Nat
Hosp for Rheumatic Diseases 1992–95; M Dioc
Coun for Min 1991–97; V Kewstoke w Wick St
Lawr from 1995; Chmn Dioc Ho of Clergy from
1994; M Bp's Coun and Joint Budget Ctee from
1994; Bp's Selector for ABM from 1993; Preb
Wells Cathl from 1996; M ABM 1997–98
GS 1995–   *Tel:* (01934) 416162

WESTON, Mrs Mary Louise
*Carpenters House, Tur Langton, Kibworth, Leicester
LE8 0PJ* [LEICESTER] *b* 4 Jul 1947; *educ* Portland Ho
Sch Leic; Wroxall Abbey Sch Warwick; Nottm
Univ; Co-ordinator of Organic Livestock Market-
ing Grp for farmers from 1996; pt Organic Farmer
from 1981; Sub Postmistress 1985–98; M Gen Syn
Rural Affairs Ctee from 1996; M Dioc Schs Prem-
ises and Trusts Ctee from 1997
GS 1995–   *Tel:* (01858) 545564

WHEATLEY, Ven Paul Charles, BA
West Stafford Rectory, Dorchester, Dorset DT2 8AB
[ARCHDEACON OF SHERBORNE] *b* 27 May 1938; *educ*
Wycliffe Coll, Stonehouse, Glos; St Jo Coll Dur;
Linc Th Coll; C St Mich Bishopston Bris 1963–68;
Dioc Youth Chapl Bris 1968–74; TR Dorcan Tm
Min Swindon 1974–79; R Ross Team Min Heref
1979–91; RD Ross and Archenfield 1979–91; Dioc
Ecum Officer Heref 1987–91; Adn of Sherborne
from 1991   *Tel:* (01305) 264637
                                          Fax: (01305) 260640
                  email: 101543.3471@compuserve.com

WHITBY, Bishop of [SUFFRAGAN, YORK] **Rt Revd Robert Sidney Ladds,** SSC, B ED, LRSC, FCS
60 West Green, Stokesley, Middlesbrough TS9 5BD
b 15 Nov 1941; *educ* Swanley Sch; NW Kent Coll; Ch Ch Coll Lon Univ; Cant Sch of Min; C St Leon Hythe 1980–83; R St Jo B Bretherton 1983–91; Chapl Bp Rawstorne Sch 1983–86; Bp's Chapl for Min 1986–90; Bp of Blackb Audit Officer 1990–91; R Preston 1991–97; Adn of Lanc 1997–99; Bp of Whitby from 1999

WHITE, Ven Frank (Francis), B SC, DIP TH
Greenriggs, Dipe Lane, East Boldon NE36 0PH [ARCHDEACON OF SUNDERLAND] *b* 26 May 1949; *educ* St Cuth Gr Sch Newc; Consett Tech Coll; UWIST Cardiff; Univ Coll Cardiff; St Jo Coll Nottm; Dir Youth Action York 1971–73; Detached Youth Worker Man Catacombs Trust 1973–77; C St Nic Dur 1980–84; C St Mary and St Cuth Chester-le-Street 1984–87; Chapl to Dur Health Auth Hosps 1987–89; V St Jo Ev Birtley 1989–97; RD Chester-le-Street 1993–97; Hon Can Dur Cathl from 1997; Adn of Sunderland from 1997
GS 1987–   *Tel:* 0191–536 2300
                            Fax: 0191–519 3369
                    email: F2awhite@aol.com

WHITE, Canon Robert Charles, MA, CERT TH
St Francis House, Riders Lane, Leigh Park, Havant, Hants PO9 4QT [PORTSMOUTH] *b* 30 Jan 1961; *educ* Portsm Gr Sch; Mansf Coll Ox; St Steph Ho Th Coll; C Forton 1985–88; C St Mark N End Portsea 1988–92; V St Clare Warren Park from 1992; P-in-c Leigh Park 1994–96; V from 1996; Hon Can Portsm Cathl from 1997; RD Havant from 1998; Vc-Chair DBF; M Bp's Coun; M Dioc Bd of Educ; Chair Community Educ Ctee
GS 1995–   *Tel:* 023–9247 5276
                            Fax: 023–9248 1228
                    email: RevPCWhite@aol.com

WHITEMAN, Ven Rodney David Carter
c/o Diocesan House, Kenwyn, Truro, Cornwall TR1 1JQ [ARCHDEACON OF CORNWALL] *b* 6 Oct 1940; *educ* St Austell Gr Sch; Ely Th Coll; C All SS Kingsheath Birm 1964–70; V St Steph Rednal Birm 1970–79; V St Barn Erdington 1979–89; RD Aston 1981–89; Hon Can Birm Cathl 1984–89; P-in-c Cardynham 1989–94; Hon Can Truro Cathl from 1989; Adn of Bodmin 1989–2000; DDO from 1999; Adn of Cornwall from 2000
GS 1994–   *Tel:* (01872) 274351
                            Fax: (01872) 222510

WHITWORTH, Mrs Ruth
Green End, Melmerby, Ripon HG4 5HL [ELY] *b* 1 Oct 1952; *educ* Ch High Sch Newc; Bank Clerk from 1974
GS 1990–   *Tel:* (01765) 640922

WIGLEY, Canon Max (Harry Maxwell), HNC
St John's Vicarage, Barcroft Grove, Yeadon, W Yorks LS19 7SE [BRADFORD] *b* 31 Jul 1938; *educ* K Jas Gr

Sch Knaresborough; Leeds Tech Coll; Oak Hill Th Coll; C St Mary Upton, Wirral 1964–67; C Ch Ch Chadderton 1967; C St Steph Gateacre Liv 1967–69; V St Jo Ev Gt Horton Bradf 1969–88; V St Lawr and St Paul Pudsey 1988–96; V St Jo Ev Yeadon from 1996; Hon Can Bradf Cathl from 1985; Chmn Dioc Ho of Clergy; M Bp's Coun; M Dioc Evang Grp
GS 1990–   *Tel:* 0113–250 2272

WILCOX, Canon Hugh Edwin, MA
St Mary's Vicarage, 31 Thundercourt, Milton Rd, Ware, Herts SG12 0PT [ST ALBANS] *b* 11 Dec 1937; *educ* Colchester R Gr Sch; St Edm Hall Ox; St Steph Ho Th Coll; C St Jas Colchester 1964–66; Hon C St Paul Clifton and SCM Sec S England 1966–68; Exec Sec Internat Affairs Dept BCC and CBMS 1968–76; Asst Gen Sec BCC 1974–76; V St Mary Ware from 1976; M DBF 1985–95; M Bp's Coun from 1991; Bp's Coun Agenda Grp Chmn from 1994; Ch Commr 1993–98, Bd of Govs 1996–98; M Redundant Chs Ctee 1993–94, Assets Ctee 1994–98; M Assets Ctee Ethical Investments Grp from 1995; M Liturg Publishing in 2000 Grp from 1995; Convenor Affirming Catholicism Grp in Gen Syn 1991–97; Hon Can St Alban's Cathl from 1996; Prolocutor Convocation of Cant from 1996; M Gen Syn Stg Ctee 1996–98; M Abps Adv Grp 1997–98; M Abps' Coun from 1999; M CMEAC from 1999; M Business Ctee from 1999
GS 1989–   *Tel:* (01920) 464817
        email: hwilcox@ware-vicarage.freeserve.co.uk

WILKINSON, Mr David Blair, MA
45 Burton Rd, Repton, Derby DE65 6FN [DERBY] *b* 16 Oct 1932; *educ* Repton Sch; Trin Coll Ox; Asst Master Repton Sch 1957–93 (Housemaster 1971–86); Chmn Bd of Visitors HM Prison Sudbury 1975–77; Rtd
GS 1995–   *Tel:* (01283) 702339

WILKINSON, Ven Guy Alexander, MA
c/o Diocesan Office, Cathedral Hall, Stott Hill, Bradford BD1 4ET [ARCHDEACON OF BRADFORD] *b* 13 Jan 1948; *educ* St Pet Coll Radley; Magd Coll Cam; Ripon Coll Cuddesdon; Prin Administrator Commn of European Communities 1973–80; Trade Relations Dir Express Goods Grp 1980–87; C Caludon Tm Cov 1987–90; Chapl to Bp of Guildf and R All SS Ockham 1990–94; V All SS Small Heath 1994–99; Adn of Bradf from 1999; M Dioc Syn; M Bp's Coun   *Tel:* (01274) 777722
                            Fax: (01274) 777730

WILLESDEN, Bishop of [AREA BISHOP, LONDON] **Rt Revd (Geoffrey) Graham Dow,** MA, M SC, M PHIL, DPS
173 Willesden Lane, London NW6 7YN *b* 4 Jul 1942; *educ* St Geo Sch Harpenden; St Alb Sch; Qu Coll Ox; Nottm Univ; Birm Univ; Clifton Th Coll; C St Pet and St Paul Tonbridge 1967–72; Chapl St Jo Coll Ox 1972–75; Lect in Chr Doct St Jo Coll

Nottm 1975–81; V H Trin Cov 1981–92; Can Th Cov Cathl 1988–92; Bp of Willesden from 1992
Tel: 020–8451 0189
Fax: 020–8451 4606
email: bishop.willesden@btinternet.com

WILLIAMS, Ms Anne
30 Blackhills Terrace, Horden, Peterlee, Co Durham SR8 4LJ [DURHAM] *b* 16 Jan 1946; *educ* A J Dawson Gr Sch Wellfield; Purchase Ledger Controller 1989–93; Communications/PR Support for Third World charity 1993–96; Asst Bursar from 1996
GS 1990– *Tel:* 0191–586 7238 (Home)

WILLIAMS, Ven Colin Henry, BA, MA
St Michael's House, Hall Lane, St Michael's-on-Wyre, Preston PR3 0TQ [ARCHDEACON OF LANCASTER] *b* 12 Aug 1952; *educ* K Geo V Gr Sch Southport; Pemb Coll Ox; St Steph Ho Th Coll; Solicitor; C St Paul Stoneycroft Liv 1981–84; TV St Aidan Walton 1984–89; Chapl Walton Hosp 1986–89; Dom Chapl to Bp of Blackb 1989–94; Chapl Whalley Abbey Retreat Ho and Conf Cen 1989–94; V St Chad Poulton-le-Fylde 1994–99; Adn of Lanc from 1999; M Dioc Syn; M Meissen Commn
GS 1995– *Tel:* (01995) 679242
Fax: (01995) 679747
email: archdeacon.lancaster@ukonline.co.uk

WILLIAMS, Canon David Gordon, MA
St Mark's Rectory, Fairmount Rd, Cheltenham, Glos GL51 7AQ [GLOUCESTER] *b* 13 Aug 1943; *educ* Cray Valley Sch Orpington; Selw Coll Cam; Oak Hill Th Coll; C St Luke Maidstone 1968–71; C St Matt Rugby 1971–73; P-in-c Budbroke 1973–74; V 1974–81; V H Trin and The Priory Lenton 1981–87; TR St Mark Cheltenham from 1987; M CBF 1991–99, DFF from 1999; Ch Commr from 1994, Bd of Govs from 1997; M Central Stewardship Ctee from 1994; M CE Pensions Bd from 1996; M Bp's Coun; M DBF
GS 1990– *Tel:* (01242) 255110

WILLIAMS, Mr David Michael, MA, DIP LIB, FSA, FRSA
Church House, Great Smith St, London SW1P 3NZ [DIRECTOR OF CENTRAL SERVICES, ARCHBISHOPS' COUNCIL] *b* 6 Apr 1950; *educ* Glyn Gr Sch Ewell; Ex Univ; Lon Univ; Employed at CCC 1972–73 and 1974–87; Dep Sec CCC 1982–87; Employed by CBF from 1987; Dep Sec CBF 1991–94; Sec CBF 1994–98; Dir Central Services, Abps' Coun and Clerk to Gen Syn from 1999; JP
Tel: 020–7898 1559

WILLIAMS, Mr Frank John
31 Manor Park Crescent, Edgware, Middx HA8 7NE [LONDON] *b* 2 Jul 1931; *educ* Ardingly Coll; Hendon Co Sch; Actor; Playwright; M Crown Appts Commn 1992–97; Lay Vc-Chmn Edmonton Area Coun
GS 1985– *Tel:* 020–8952 4871

WILLIAMS, Mr Paul Lloyd, BA, DIP TH, FRMS
21 Roseway, Rosemary Lane, Burton, Rossett, Chester LL12 0LF [CHESTER] *b* 5 Sep 1952; *educ* Ruthin Sch; Wolsey Hall Ox; Univ Coll Lon; Man Univ; Dur Univ; Proofreader/Analyst Derwent Publications Biotechnological Dept 1981–88; Clerk Intrada Shipping Co 1988; Independent Research Student Th from 1993; M Stipends Ctee from 1991; M Dioc Syn from 1991; M DBF from 1991; M Dioc BSR 1991–95; Ches Dyn Syn and Finance Link Co-ordinator from 1990; M Bp's Coun from 1998
GS 1995– *Tel:* (01244) 570134

WILLIAMS, Mrs Shirley-Ann, LRAM, LLAM, CERT TH
Miller's Farm, Talaton, Exeter, Devon EX5 2RE [EXETER] *educ* Barr's Hill Sch Cov; Leeds Univ; Ex Univ; Freelance Tutor in Speech and Drama, Public Speaking and Communication Skills; Broadcaster; M Gen Syn Appts Ctee; M Dioc Pastl Ctee; M Bp's Coun and Stg Ctee; Chair Dioc Bd of Patronage; M Dioc Children and Young People's Ctee; M Dioc Adult Tr Ctee; Vc-Pres and Chair Dioc Ho of Laity; Dir Rural Community Coun of Devon; Lay Chair Ottery Dny Syn; Chair Nat Working Party Ecum Decade of Chs in Solidarity with Women and Chair Follow-up Grp; M CTE and CTBI; Editor Open Syn Grp magazine; M Dioc Liturg Ctee; M Dioc Communications Ctee; M Devon and Ex Racial Equality Coun
GS 1985– *Tel and Fax:* (01404) 822469
email: shanwill@tinyonline.co.uk

WILLIAMS, Canon Trevor Stanley Morlais, MA
Trinity College, Oxford OX1 3BH [UNIVERSITIES, OXFORD] *b* 10 Jul 1938; *educ* Marlborough Coll; Jes Coll Ox; Univ of E Africa; Westcott Ho Th Coll; C St Paul Clifton Bris 1967–70; Asst Chapl Bris Univ 1967–70; Chapl and Fell Trin Coll Ox from 1970
GS 1990– *Tel:* (01865) 279886 (Office)
(01865) 553975 (Home)
Fax: (01865) 279911
email: trevor.williams@trinity.ox.ac.uk

WILLIS, Very Revd Robert Andrew, BA
The Deanery, The Cloisters, Hereford HR1 2NG [DEAN OF HEREFORD] *b* 17 May 1947; *educ* Kingswood Gr Sch; Warw Univ; Worc Coll Ox; Cuddesdon Th Coll; C St Chad Shrewsbury 1972–75; V Choral Sarum Cathl 1975–78; TR Tisbury and RD Chalke 1978–89; V Sherborne 1987–92; RD Sherborne 1991–92; Dean of Heref from 1992; M PWM Ctee from 1990; M Cathls Fabric Commn from 1993; M Liturg Commn from 1994
GS 1985–92, 1994– *Tel:* (01432) 359880
Fax: (01432) 355929

WILLMOTT, Ven Trevor, MA, DIP THEOL
15 The College, Durham DH1 3EQ [ARCHDEACON OF DURHAM] *b* 29 Mar 1950; *educ* Plymouth Coll; St Pet Coll Ox; Fitzw Coll Cam; Westcott Ho Th Coll; C St Geo Norton 1974–77; Asst Chapl Oslo

w Trondheim 1978–79; Chapl Naples w Capri, Bari and Sorrento 1979–83; R Ecton and Warden Peterb Dioc Retreat Ho 1983–89; DDO and Dir of POT 1986–97; Can Res and Prec Peterb Cathl 1989–97; Adn of Dur and Can Res Dur Cathl from 1997
Tel: 0191–384 7534
Fax: 0191–386 6915
email:
Archdeacon.of.Durham@durham.anglican.org

WILSON, Ven Mark John Crichton, MA, CERT TH
Littlecroft, Heathside Rd, Woking, Surrey GU22 7EZ [ARCHDEACON OF DORKING] *b* 14 Jan 1946; *educ* St Jo Sch Leatherhead; Clare Coll Cam; Ridley Hall Th Coll; C St Mary Luton w E Hyde 1969–72; C Ashtead 1972–77; Chapl Epsom Coll 1977–81; RD Epsom 1987–92; V Ch Ch Epsom Common 1981–96; Adn of Dorking from 1996; M Cathls Commn Follow Up Grp from 1995
GS 1992–
Tel: (01483) 772713
Fax: (01483) 757353
email: mark.wilson@cofeguildford.org.uk

WILSON-RUDD, Miss Fay (Felicity)
c/o The Old Deanery, Wells, Som BA5 2UG [BATH AND WELLS] *b* 15 Aug 1941; *educ* Filton High Sch; Asst Stewardship Adv St Alb dio 1981–84; Resources Adv B & W from 1984
GS 1993–
Tel: (01749) 670777 (Office)
(01749) 677286 (Home)
Fax: (01749) 677202 (Home)
email: faywilsonrudd@email.msn.com

WINCHESTER, Bishop of, Rt Revd Michael Charles Scott-Joynt, MA
Wolvesey, Winchester, Hants SO23 9ND b 15 Mar 1943; *educ* Bradfield Coll; K Coll Cam; Cuddesdon Th Coll; C Cuddesdon 1967–70; Tutor Cuddesdon Th Coll 1967–72; TV Newbury 1972–75; R Bicester 1975–81; Can Res St Alb Cathl, DDO and POT 1982–87; Bp of Stafford 1987–95; Bp of Win from 1995
GS 1993–
Tel: (01962) 854050
Tel and Fax: (01962) 842376
email: michael.scott-joynt@dial.pipex.com

WINTERBOTTOM, Mr Michael John
15 Harper Place, Ashton-under-Lyne, Lancs OL6 6LR [MANCHESTER] *b* 15 Jun 1959; *educ* Ashton-under-Lyne Gr Sch; Dioc Lay Chmn Forward in Faith; M Ctee Soc of Mary; M Ctee Man Branch Prayer Book Soc; Chmn Ashton-under-Lyne Conservative Assoc from 1993; Coun Tameside MBC 1991–95; JP from 1996
GS 1995–
Tel: 0161–330 9083 (Home)
0161–253 8381 (Office)
0831 899656 (Mobile)

WOLSTENCROFT, Ven Alan
2 The Walled Garden, Swinton, Manchester M27 0FR [ARCHDEACON OF MANCHESTER] *b* 16 Jul 1937; *educ* Wellington Tech Sch Altrincham; St Jo CFE Man; Cuddesdon Th Coll; C St Thos Halliwell 1969–71;

C All SS Stand 1971–73; V St Martin Wythenshawe 1973–80; Chapl then Asst Chapl Wythenshawe Hosp 1973–91; AD Withington 1978–91; V St Jo the Divine Brooklands, Sale 1980–91; V St Pe Bolton w H Trin Bolton-le-Moors 1991–98; Ho Can Man Cathl 1986–98; Adn of Man, Res Car Man Cathl and Fell of the Coll from 1998; M Dio Syn; M Bp's Coun; M DBF, Trust and Fin Ctee
Tel: 0161–794 240
Fax: 0161–794 241

WOLVERHAMPTON, Bishop of [AREA BISHOP, LICHFIELD] **Rt Revd Michael Gay Bourke,** MA
61 Richmond Rd, Wolverhampton WV3 9JH b 28 Nov 1941; *educ* Hamond's Gr Sch Swaffham; Cam Univ; Tübingen Univ; Cuddesdon Th Coll; C St Jas Grimsby 1967–71; P-in-c Panshanger CD Welwyn Garden City 1971–78; V Southill 1978–86; Course Dir St Alb Minl Tr Scheme 1975–87; Adn of Bedf 1986–93; Bp of Wolverhampton from 1993
GS 1975–80, 1987–93
Tel: (01902) 824503
Fax: (01902) 824504

WOODHOUSE, Ven (Charles) David Stewart, MA
22 Rob Lane, Newton le Willows, Merseyside WA12 0DR [ARCHDEACON OF WARRINGTON] *b* 23 Dec 1934; *educ* Silcoates Sch Wakef; Kelham Th Coll; C St Wilfrid's Halton 1959–63; Yth Chapl Kirkby TM 1963–66; C St Jo Pemb Bermuda 1966–69; Asst Gen Sec CEMS 1969–70; Gen Sec 1970–76; R Ideford, Luton and Ashcombe 1976–81; Dom Chapl to Bp of Ex 1976–81; V St Pet's Hindley 1981–92; Adn of Warrington from 1981; Hon Can Liv Cathl from 1983; M CBF from 1991; M Cen Ch Fund Ctee from 1992; ABM Selector from 1993; Chair Dioc Bd of Min; Gen Syn Stg Ctee Rep Chs Commn on Overseas Miss
GS 1990–
Tel: (01925) 229247
Fax: (01925) 220423

WOOLWICH, Bishop of [AREA BISHOP, SOUTHWARK] **Rt Revd Colin Ogilvie Buchanan,** MA, DD
37 South Rd, Forest Hill, London SE23 2UJ b 9 Aug 1934; *educ* Whitgift Sch Croydon; Linc Coll Ox; Tyndale Hall Bristol; Tutor St Jo Coll Nottm 1964–85; Prin 1979–85; Bp of Aston 1985–89; Hon Asst Bp Roch dio 1989–96; V St Mark Gillingham 1991–96; Bp of Woolwich from 1996; M CCU; M CTBI Assembly; M CMEAC
GS 1970–85, 1990–
Tel: 020–8699 7771
Fax: 020–8699 7949
email: bishop.colin@dswark.org.uk

WORCESTER, Bishop of, Rt Revd Peter Stephen Maurice Selby, MA, BD, PH D
Bishop's House, Hartlebury Castle, Kidderminster, Worcs DY11 7XX b 7 Dec 1941; *educ* Merchant Taylors Sch; St Jo Coll Ox; Episc Div Sch Cam, Mass; Bishops' Coll Cheshunt; K Coll Lon; Asst C Queensbury 1966–69; Assoc Dir of Tr S'wark

969–73; Asst C Limpsfield w Titsey 1969–77; Vc-
'rin S'wark Ord Course 1970–72; Asst Missr
'wark 1973–77; Can Missr Newc Dio 1977–84;
*p of Kingston-upon-Thames 1984–92; William
Leech Professorial Fellow in Applied Chr Th Dur
Jniv 1992–97; Hon Asst Bp Dur and Newc dios
992–97; Bp of Worc from 1997; M Doct Commn
rom 1991; Pres Modern Churchpeople's Union
990–96; Vis Gen CSC from 1991
;S 1997–   *Tel:* (01299) 250214
                                    Fax: (01299) 250027
      email: bishop.peter@CofE-worcester.org.uk

VRIGHT, Mr David John Vernon, MA
1 Davenant Rd, Oxford OX2 8BT [OXFORD] *b* 21
Mar 1932; *educ* Cheltenham Coll; St Edm Hall Ox;
Solicitor from 1958; M CE Pensions Bd from 1994;
M Bp's Coun; Rdr
;S 1985–   *Tel:* (01865) 556034
               email: DJVWright@ukgateway.net

YATES, Canon Timothy Edward, MA, D TH
*Vicarage, Great Longstone, Bakewell, Derbys DE45
1TB* [DERBY] *b* 1 May 1935; *educ* Eton; Magd Coll
Cam; Ridley Hall Th Coll; C SS Pet and Paul Ton-
bridge 1960–63; Tutor St Jo Coll Dur and Cranmer
Hall 1963–70; Warden Cranmer Hall 1970–79; R
St Helen Darley 1979–90; DDO 1985–95; Hon Can
Derby Cathl from 1988; Hon C Ashford w Shel-
don and Longstone from 1990; M Dioc Syn
;S 1995–   *Tel:* (01629) 640257

**YORK, Archbishop of, Most Revd and Rt Hon
David Michael Hope,** KCVO, BA, D PHIL, DD,
LLD (HON)
Bishopthorpe Palace, Bishopthorpe, York YO23 2GE
b 14 Apr 1940; *educ* Qu Eliz Gr Sch Wakef; Nottm
Univ; St Steph Ho Th Coll; C St Jo Tue Brook Liv
1965–70; Chapl Ch of the Resurr Bucharest
1967–68; V St Andr Orford 1970–74; Prin St Steph
Ho Ox 1974–82; V All SS Marg St Lon 1982–85;
Master Guardians Shrine of Our Lady Walsing-
ham 1982–93; Bp of Wakef 1985–91; Bp of Lon
1991–95; Dean of HM Chapels R and Prelate of
OBE 1991–95; Abp of York from 1995
GS 1985–   *Tel:* (01904) 707021
                                    Fax: (01904) 709204
      email: office@bishopthorpe.u-net.com

YORKE, Very Revd Michael Leslie, MA
The Deanery, The Close, Lichfield, Staffs WS13 7LD
[DEAN OF LICHFIELD] *b* 25 Mar 1939; *educ* Brighton
Coll; Magd Coll Cam; Cuddesdon Th Coll; C
Croydon 1964–67; Prec Chelmsf Cathl 1968–74; R
Ashdon w Hadstock 1974–78; Can Res Chelmsf
Cathl 1978–88; Vc Provost 1984–88; P-in-c St
Marg Kings Lynn 1988–94; Hon Can Nor Cathl
1993–94; Provost of Portsm 1994–99; Dean of Lich
from 1999; Chmn English Cathls Music Working
Party   *Tel:* (01543) 306250 (Home)
                               (01543) 306100 (Office)
                        Fax: (01543) 306255 (Home)
                               (01543) 306109 (Office)

YOUNG, Canon John David, BD, MA, DIP ED
73 Middlethorpe Grove, York YO2 2JX [YORK] *b* 20
Feb 1937; *educ* Spring Grove Gr Sch Isleworth;
Loughb Univ; Lon Univ; Sussex Univ; Clifton Th
Coll; C St Jude Plymouth 1965–68; Hd of RE
Northgate Gr Sch Ipswich 1968–71; Chapl and
Sen Lect Bp Otter Coll Chich 1971–81; Chapl and
Sen Lect Univ Coll of Ripon & York St John
1981–87; Dioc Ev from 1988
GS 1992–   *Tel:* (01904) 658820 (Office)
          Tel and Fax: (01904) 704195 (Home)
                     Fax: (01904) 671694 (Office)

YOUNG, Revd Jonathan Priestland, AKC,
CERT ED
*Ascension Rectory, Richmond Rd, Cambridge CB4
3PS* [ELY] *b* 12 Feb 1944; *educ* Nor Sch; K Coll Lon;
St Boniface Th Coll; Whitelands Coll Lon; C
Clapham 1969–73; C St Mark Mitcham 1973–74; V
Godmanchester 1974–82; Chapl St Jo Coll Sch
1987–93; R Ascen Cam, TM (St Giles w St Pet, St
Luke w St Aug, All Souls) from 1982; M Liturg
Canons Revision Ctee, Service of the Word and
Affirmations of Faith Revision Ctee; M Elections
Review Grp; M Legislative Ctee; M Bp's Coun;
DAC; Dioc Pastl Ctee; Dioc Bd of Educ; Dioc Bd
of Patronage; Dioc Coun for Miss and Unity; Dioc
Red Chs Uses Ctee; Hon Sec Dioc Liturg Ctee;
M Ctee Open Syn Grp; M Bach Choir; Vc Pres
Huntingdonshire Philharmonic; Chair E Anglian
Praxis Ctee
GS 1982–   *Tel:* (01223) 361919
                                    Fax: (01223) 322710

INDEX

GENERAL INDEX

Matron Ann Hales

Our Gift of Healing

Free medical treatment for the Clergy

St Luke's Hospital for the Clergy is the laity's gift to its priesthood. Founded in 1893, the Hospital exists to provide free treatment to active and retired Church of England clergy and their dependants, as

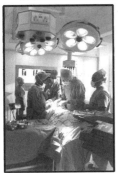

well as Ordinands, members of Anglican religious orders, Church Army officers, overseas missionaries, and priests from Anglican Churches abroad. Our object is to treat them at times convenient to them (and to their congregations) and get them back to their ministries as soon as we can.

St Luke's is a small acute hospital, with a very warm family atmosphere, and a very well-equipped operating theatre. And, in a moving example of Christian giving, 150 of the country's top Consultants give their services to St Luke's in their free time, entirely without charge.

Treatment for the laity

Through WPA, the Hospital also provides health insurance through the St Luke's Healthcare Scheme to lay church members, and it is doing important and pioneering work on stress control, both among clergy and in the community at large. (Please tell us if you would like to know more about this work).

Please help – or come and see us

Inevitably there is always a need for money, for the Hospital costs £4,000 a day to run, and we rely entirely on voluntary contributions. Please help if you can, with a gift or a fund-raising event. And if you would like someone to come and share your worship and talk to you about St Luke's, or if a party from your parish would like to visit the Hospital, please get in touch with Canon Paul Thomas, General Secretary and Hospital Administrator.

St Luke's
HOSPITAL FOR THE CLERGY
Caring for those who care for others

14 Fitzroy Square, London W1P 6AH
Tel. 020 7388 4954. Fax. 020 7383 4812

Registered Charity 209236

553

OUR WORK IS CARING . . .

The Church of England Pensions Board offers support to retired clergy and their spouses, the widows or widowers of clergy, and church workers retired from full time ministry.

Our greatest concern is for the welfare of our older pensioners, who because of age or infirmity need sheltered accommodation and some special care. The Pensions Board runs nine residential and nursing homes offering security and peace of mind to those who have given their lives towards helping others in the name of Christ. Assistance can also be given towards the fees payable for accommodation in homes run by other organisations.

The Board receives no help from central Church funds towards the cost of its residential and nursing care, and must rely on support from donations, deeds of covenant, and legacies in order to continue this much needed work. Please help us in any way you can.

For further information about ways to help, a form of words for inclusion in a Will, or more details about our work, please write to:

**The Secretary, Freepost CD,
The Church of England Pensions Board
7 LITTLE COLLEGE STREET
WESTMINSTER, LONDON SW1P 3SF**

Reg. Charity No. 236627

557

558

Clergy
Cassocks

This double breasted cassock is one of a variety of styles available from any of the addresses below. Enquiries or personal calls are always welcome.

Wippell's also stock a wide range of clerical and academic wear, including:-

Surplices
for clergy, choir and organists

albs and Tunics
for choir and servers

Cloaks
for clergy winter wear

Choir Robes
Readers' Robes
Preaching Gowns

also

Church Furnishings ∗ Stained Glass ∗ Altar Wines ∗ Textiles ∗ Metalwork ∗ Church Furniture

For further information on any of the above, please write or call

WIPPELL'S

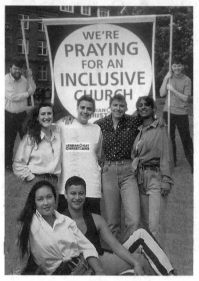

"I came that they might have life and have it abundantly"

John 10:10

As a Voluntary Society of The Church of England and the Church in Wales, The Children's Society reaches out unconditionally to children when they are at their most vulnerable.

Caring for children in the name of The Church of England and the Church in Wales since 1881

The Children's Society, Edward Rudolf House, Margery Street, London WC1X 0JL.
Tel: 020 7841 4400 Fax: 020 7841 4500
www.the-childrens-society.org.uk
Charity Registration No: 221124

The Children's Society

A Voluntary Society of The Church of England and The Church in Wales

564

Sunday Services

0800   **Holy Communion**

1015   **Sung Mattins**

1130   **Sung Eucharist**

1515   **Sung Evensong**

1800   **Evening Service**

*Evensong is usually sung at 1700hrs
every day (except Sunday)*

*For the latest information on services, please visit
our web site http://stpauls.london.anglican.org*
or telephone 020 7236 4128

St Paul's Cathedral

On Feast Days and at other times, service times may be subject to change.

566

Some People sail around the world for £30 or less

Pitiful wages are just the start of a seafarer's problems. Although most ships are perfectly well run, too many seafarers are trapped in a world of exploitation and abuse. Our chaplains in ports look after the physical and spiritual welfare of seafarers worldwide. Please help.

To Kathy Baldwin, The Missions to Seamen, St Michael Paternoster Royal, College Hill, London EC4R 2RL.

I enclose a donation of £10☐ £25☐ £50☐ £ _____

Name _____

Address _____

_____

The Missions to Seamen

CHARITY NO. 212432

CHURCH MISSION SOCIETY

**Linking the Church of England in
a global partnership for**

**Evangelism
Renewal
Justice**

Partnership House, 157 Waterloo Road, London SE1 8UU
Tel. 020 7928 8681 Fax. 020 7401 3215
www.cms-uk.org
Registered Charity No. 220297

The Church Lads' and Church Girls' Brigade
Registered Charity No. 276821

A nation-wide Anglican voluntary youth organisation offering fun and friendship
and handholds to life.

Parish-based, it brings the Gospel Message to youngsters.

For further details contact:

**The Church Lads' and Church Girls' Brigade
2 Barnsley Road, Wath-upon-Dearne, Rotherham S63 6PY**
Telephone: Rotherham (01709) 876535   Fax: (01709) 878089
e-mail: general-secretary@churchbrigade.syol.com

THE COLLEGE OF ST. BARNABAS
Retirement Accommodation for the Clergy,
Church Workers, and Readers
offering two-roomed flats, Chapels with daily services, libraries, full catering,
Nursing and Residential Care

Enquiries to:
**The Warden, The College of St. Barnabas
Lingfield, Surrey RH7 6NJ**
(Next to Dormans Station – Victoria 53 minutes)
Telephone: (01342) 870366/870260   Registered Charity No. 205220

Hart Advertising

Hart Advertising is the Agency which specialises in handling Religious and Charity clients who, within limited budgets, need to advertise in order to increase awareness and generate legacy income.

Our Services:

- Planning Legacy, Fundraising and Awareness advertising campaigns
- Local and National media buying
- Copywriting and design
- Brochures, leaflets, posters
- Business cards, annual reports, newsletters

Our Clients:

Aid for the Aged in Distress	National Animal Welfare Trust
Apostleship of the Sea	Open Spaces Society
Bield Housing Trust	Police Dependants' Trust
Camphill Village Trust	Queen Alexandra Hospital Home
Canterbury Press Norwich	Racing Welfare
Central Church Fund	Ramblers' Association
Church Times	Religious and Moral Education Press
Corporation of the Sons of the Clergy	Royal Alfred Seafarers' Society
Dogs for the Disabled	Scout Association
Friends of the Clergy Corporation	St Luke's Hospital for the Clergy
Greensleeves Homes Trust	St Paul's Cathedral
Grace and Compassion Benedictines	St Paul's Cathedral School
Historic Churches Preservation Trust	Sustrans
Kingwood Trust	Whitechapel Bell Foundry
Metropolitan Society for the Blind	J. Wippell & Co Ltd
Myasthenia Gravis Association	

If you would like to know more about us, call Agency Manager, Sandra Stevens

Bridge House, 181 Queen Victoria Street, London EC4V 4DZ
Telephone 020–7248 4759   *Facsimile* 020–7329 0575
E-mail: hartadvert@hotmail.com

Part of G J Palmer & Sons Ltd., Registered Company No. 291335, which is a subsidiary of Hymns Ancient & Modern, Registered Charity No. 270060